Street by Street

C000294684

KENT

Enlarged areas ASHFORD, CANTERBURY, CHATHAM, DOVER, FOLKESTONE, GILLINGHAM, MAIDSTONE, MARGATE, RAMSGATE, ROCHESTER, ROYAL TUNBRIDGE WELLS, SEVENOAKS
Plus Broadstairs, Bromley, Dartford, Gravesend, Herne Bay, Orpington, Tilbury, Tonbridge, Whitstable, Woolwich

2nd edition May 2005
© Automobile Association Developments Limited 2005

Original edition printed May 2001

Ordnance Survey This product includes map data licensed from Ordnance Survey® with the permission of the Controller of Her Majesty's Stationery Office. © Crown copyright 2005. All rights reserved. Licence number 399221.

Published by AA Publishing (a trading name of Automobile Association Developments Limited, whose registered office is Southwood East, Apollo Rise, Farnborough, Hampshire, GU14 0JW. Registered number 1878835).

Mapping produced by the Cartography Department of The Automobile Association. (A02421)

A CIP Catalogue record for this book is available from the British Library.

Printed and bound by Leo, China

The contents of this atlas are believed to be correct at the time of the latest revision. However, the publishers cannot be held responsible or liable for any loss or damage occasioned to any person acting or refraining from action as a result of any use or reliance on any material in this atlas, nor for any errors, omissions or changes in such material. This does not affect your statutory rights. The publishers would welcome information to correct any errors or omissions and to keep this atlas up to date. Please write to Publishing, The Automobile Association, Fanum House (FH17), Basing View, Basingstoke, Hampshire, RG21 4EA.

Ref: MX100z

Key to map pages	ii–iii
Key to map symbols	iv–1
Map pages - 1:10,000	2-23
Map pages - 1:17,500	24-225
Map pages - 1:25,000	226–335
Index – towns & villages	336-338
Index – streets	339-386
Index – featured places	386-395
Acknowledgements	395

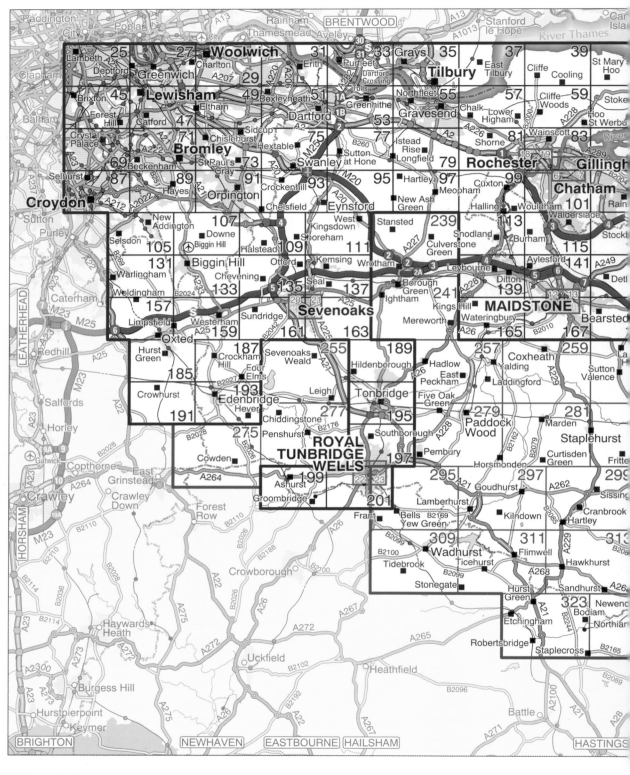

Scale of enlarged map pages 1:10,000 6.3 inches to 1 mile

| 0 | | 1/4 | miles | 1/2 | | 3/4 | |
| 0 | 1/4 | | 1/2 | kilometres | 3/4 | 1 | 1 1/4 |

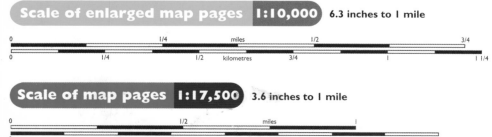

Scale of map pages 1:17,500 3.6 inches to 1 mile

| 0 | | 1/2 | miles | | 1 |
| 0 | 1/2 | | 1 | kilometres | 1 1/2 | 2 |

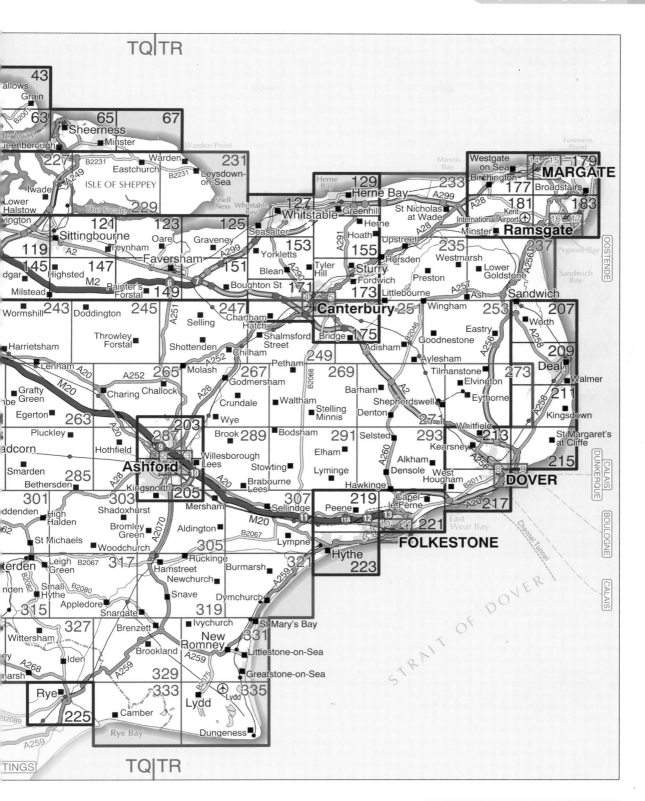

TQ|TR

43
allows
Grain
63
ledway
eenborough
227
Iwade
Lower
Halstow
vington
119
dgar
145
Milstead
243
Wormshill
Harrietsham
Lenham
Grafty
Green
Egerton
Pluckley
adcorn
Smarden
Bethersden
301
ddenden
62
terden
nden
315
Wittersham
ey
marsh
TINGS

65
Sheerness
Minster
B2231
Eastchurch
ISLE OF SHEPPEY
The Swale
229
121
Sittingbourne
A2
147
Highsted
M2
149
245
Doddington
Throwley
Forstal
A252
263
A20
285
303
Shadoxhurst
317
327

67
Warden
Warden Point
231
Leysdown-
on-Sea
Shell Ness
Whitstable
Bay
125
Seasalter
Oare
Graveney
A299
Teynham
151
Boughton St
Painter's
Forstal
A251
247
Selling
Chartham
Hatch
Shottenden
Chilham
265
Molash
267
Godmersham
Crundale
Charing
Challock
Wye
203
287
9
2
3
Ashford
10
205
A20
Kingsnorth
Aldington
305
Ruckinge
B2067
Hamstreet
Newchurch
Snave
319
Ivychurch
New
Romney
A259
329
333
Camber
Rye Bay

Herne
Bay
129
Herne Bay
127
Whitstable
Greenhill
Herne
153
Yorkletts
Hoath
155
Blean
Tyler
Hill
Sturry
Fordwich
171
173
Canterbury
Bridge
175
249
Petham
269
Waltham
Stelling
Minnis
Barham
Denton
291
Bodsham
289
Brook
Elham
Lyminge
307
Hawkinge
Sellindge
11
219
Peene
11A
Hythe
223
Dymchurch
St Mary's Bay
Littlestone-on-Sea
Greatstone-on-Sea
335
Lydd
Dungeness

Minnis
Bay
233
St Nicholas
at Wade
A299
A28
Upstreet
235
Westmarsh
Preston
Littlebourne
251
Wingham
Goodnestone
Adisham
Aylesham
Barham
Shepherdswell
271
293
Selsted
Alkham
Densole
West
Hougham
221
Capel-
le-Ferne
East
Wear Bay
FOLKESTONE

Westgate
on Sea
Birchington
International
Airport
Minster
Ramsgate
237
253
Eastry
Tilmanstone
Elvington
Eythorne
Whitfield
213
Kearsney
217
DOVER

14 15
177
181
16 17
MARGATE
Broadstairs
183
Kent
Ramsgate
OOSTENDE
Pegwell Bay
Sandwich
Bay
207
Worth
A258
209
Deal
Walmer
211
Kingsdown
273
St Margaret's
at Cliffe
215
CALAIS
DUNKERQUE
BOULOGNE
CALAIS

STRAIT OF DOVER
Channel Tunnel

National Grid references are shown on the map frame of each page.
Red figures denote the 100 km square and the blue figures the 1km square.

Example, page 205 : William Harvey Hospital 604 142

The reference can also be written using the National Grid two-letter prefix
shown on this page, where 6 and 1 are replaced by TR to give TR0442

2.5 inches to 1 mile **Scale of map pages 1:25,000**

0   1/2   miles   1   1 1/2
0   1/2   kilometres   1 1/2   2

Junction 9	Motorway & junction
Services	Motorway service area
	Primary road single/dual carriageway
Services	Primary road service area
	A road single/dual carriageway
	B road single/dual carriageway
	Other road single/dual carriageway
	Minor/private road, access may be restricted
← ←	One-way street
	Pedestrian area
=================	Track or footpath
	Road under construction
	Road tunnel
P	Parking
P+	Park & Ride
	Bus/coach station
	Railway & main railway station
	Railway & minor railway station
⊖	Underground station

⊖	Light railway & station
+++++++++++	Preserved private railway
LC	Level crossing
•—•—•—•—	Tramway
- - - - - - -	Ferry route
··············	Airport runway
—·—··—··—	County, administrative boundary
261	Page continuation 1:25,000
93	Page continuation 1:17,500
7	Page continuation to enlarged scale 1:10,000
	River/canal, lake
	Aqueduct, lock, weir
465 Winter Hill	Peak (with height in metres)
	Beach
	Woodland
	Park
	Cemetery
	Built-up area
	Featured building
⊓⊔⊓⊔⊓⊔⊓	City wall

A&E	Hospital with 24-hour A&E department	✗	Castle
PO	Post Office	🏛	Historic house or building
📖	Public library	Wakehurst Place NT	National Trust property
ℹ	Tourist Information Centre	Ⓜ	Museum or art gallery
ℹ	Seasonal Tourist Information Centre	🦅	Roman antiquity
⛽ ⛽	Petrol station, 24 hour Major suppliers only	⚱	Ancient site, battlefield or monument
†	Church/chapel	⚒	Industrial interest
🚻	Public toilets	✳	Garden
♿	Toilet with disabled facilities	◉	Garden Centre Garden Centre Association Member
PH	Public house AA recommended	🌼	Garden Centre Wyevale Garden Centre
🍽	Restaurant AA inspected	🌳	Arboretum
Madeira Hotel	Hotel AA inspected	🛒	Farm or animal centre
🎭	Theatre or performing arts centre	🦌	Zoological or wildlife collection
🎥	Cinema	🦜	Bird collection
⚑	Golf course	🦆	Nature reserve
▲	Camping AA inspected	🐟	Aquarium
🚐	Caravan site AA inspected	**V**	Visitor or heritage centre
▲🚐	Camping & caravan site AA inspected	♔	Country park
⚙	Theme park	⌒	Cave
🏠	Abbey, cathedral or priory	✗	Windmill
		🛢	Distillery, brewery or vineyard

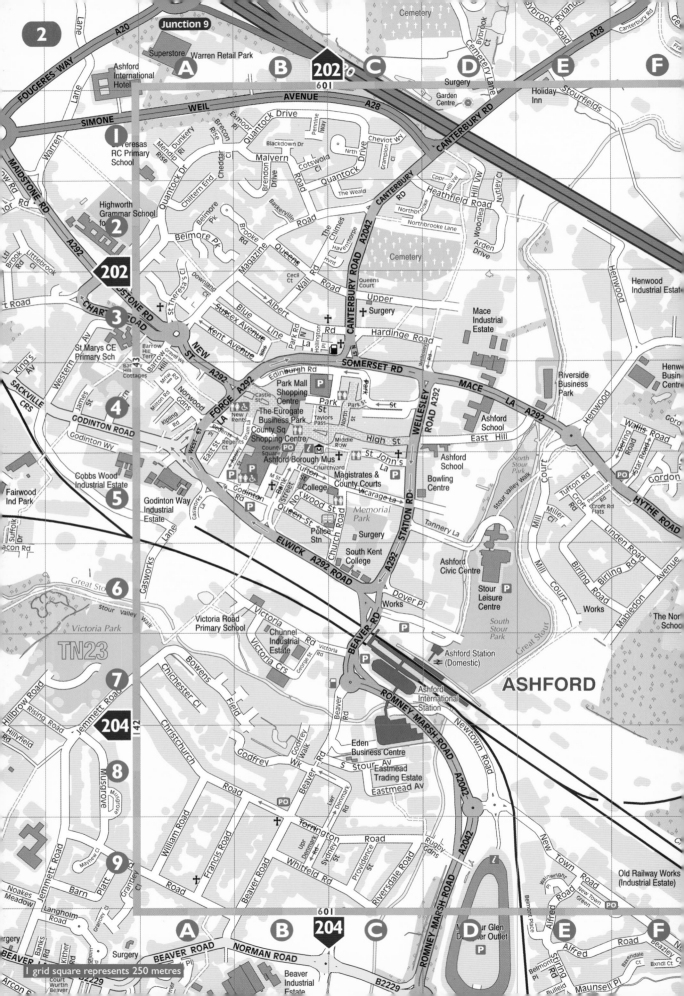

G H J K 203 L M

03

I

2

203

3

4

5

6

7

205

8

9

The Julie Rose Stadium

Conningbrook Manor

Factory

Willesborough Road

A2070

M20

TN24

Great Stour

Works

Great Stour

43

Blackwall Road

Stour Valley Walk

Blackwall Road North

Stour Va Walk

Kings Chase

Willesborough Lees

The Norton Knatchbull School

A292

Cradle Br Dr

Cradle Br Dr

Sandilands

As

Holmlea Ct

Foxglove Rd

Foxglove Rd

Birch Dr

Woodlands Rd

House Field

House Fld

Harvey Road

Hewitts Place Surgery

Willow Tree Close

Sprotlands Avenue

Clive Dennis Ct

Earls Avenue

Taywood

Fld End

Oast Meadow

Windmill Close

Harvey Rd

Abbey

Romsey

Thornton

Way

Fountains Cl

Silver Hill

Willesborough Ct

Blackwall Rd South

Kennington

Road

Redyear Court

Wilson Cl

Willesborough Industrial Pk

Silver Hill Gdns

Lees Road

Longbridge

Sandy Lane

A2070

142

205

Romney Road

Glover Road

Hunter Road

Albemarle Road

A292

PO

Camden Terrace

Osborne Road

Avenue

Orion Way

Orion Way

Orion Way

Hunter Cl

Wharton Gdns

Breadlands Close

Willesborough

Western Gdns

Eastern Gdns

Summer Leeze

Leeze Gdns

Summer Cl

Breadlands Road

Mill Vw Road

Osborne Rd

Mill Road

Twelve Acres

Blake Court

Sevington

03

Cemetery

Trenchard Cl

St Marys Mews Park Place

PO

Church Road

Elf Ct

Waterside

Waterside

HYTHE ROAD

Mill Lane

The Wyvern School

Willesborough Primary School

Lees Road

7 Cl

Cornes Close

A292

M20

HYTHE ROAD

Wickenden Crs

Charlton Close

Ripley Road

Hayward Close

Lacton Road

Highfield Road

Collard

Evans Rd

Cowdrey Cl

Jellicoe Cl

Foley Cl

Troubridge Cl

Drake Road

Raleigh Cl

Shb Dr

Nelson Cl

A292

Kennington Rd

A2070

Hythe Road

P

The

e St

205 Willesb'h lth Ce

G H J Bentley Road K L M

Bentley Road

Boys Hall Rd

Ash Mdw

Aylesford Road

Alsop Rd

Sotherton

Crowbridge Road

Albion

Rail line

A270

Road

A292

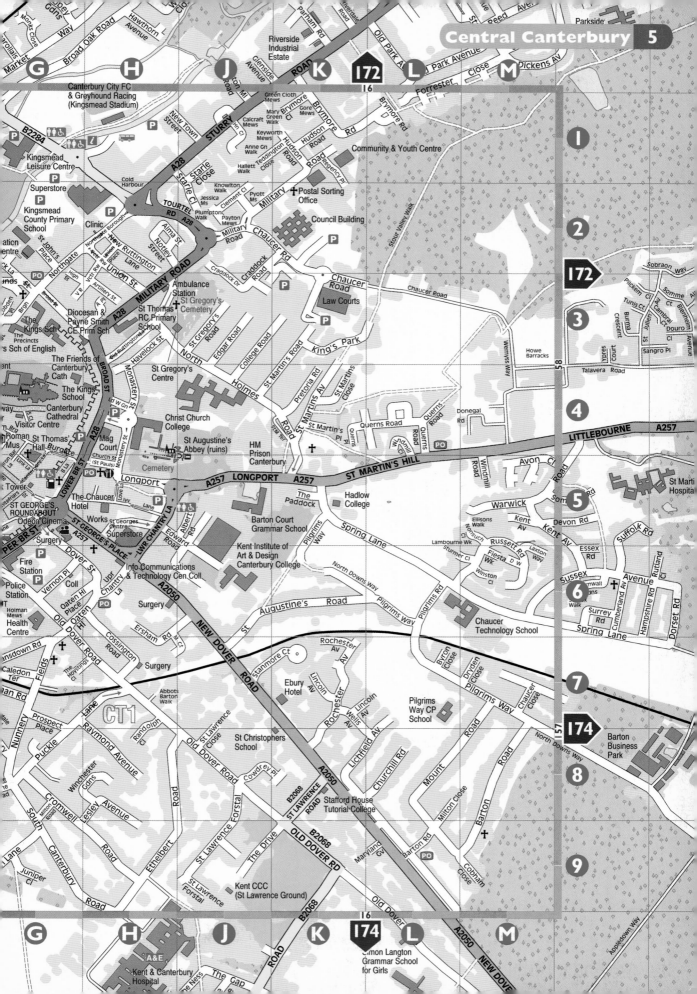

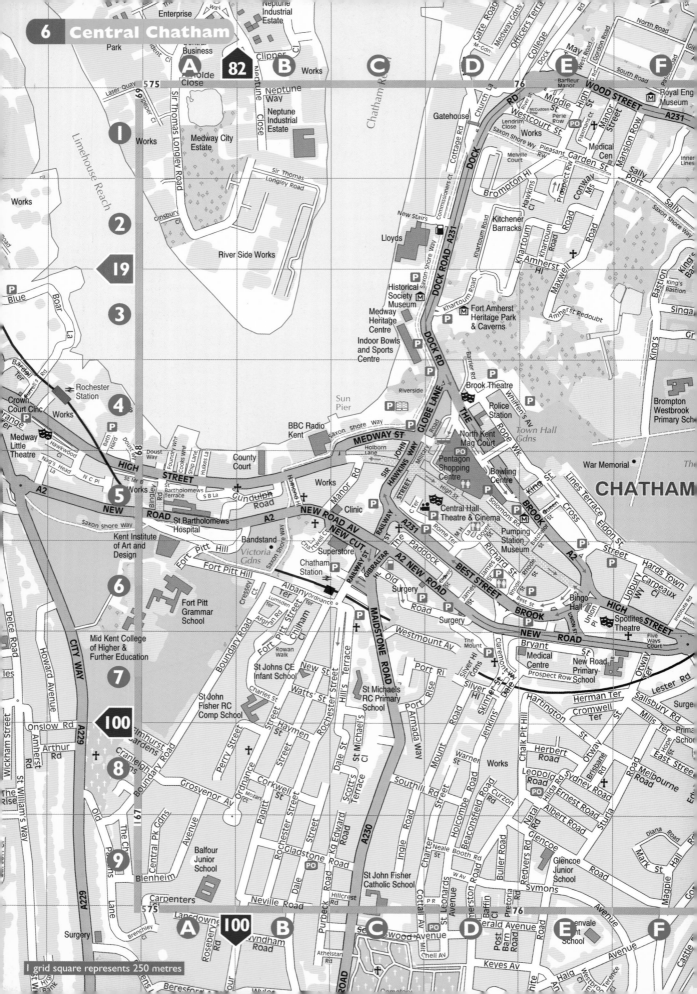

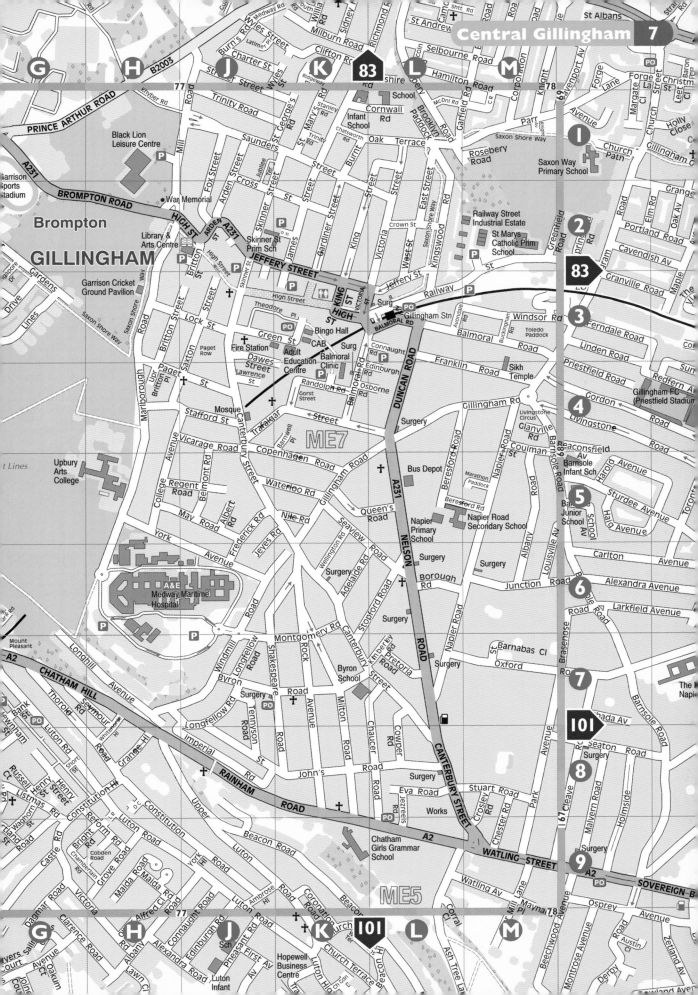

G   H   J   K   214   L   M

33   34

I

Saxon Shore

Langdon Cliffs
Visitor Centre
& Viewpoint (NT)
V P

Saxon Shore Way

Lang
Ba

2

Back   Road   (East)

The   Fan

Camber Way

42

Upper Road

Upper Road

JUBILEE WAY A2

JUBILEE

JUBILEE WAY
(ELEVATED ROAD)

inburgh Hill

Bleriot
Memorial

oad

3

East Ramp

Road

East Exit Road

P

P

P

Cargo Terminal

Keep

Godwin   Road

St Mary's
Church

Mortimer
Road

Pharos

East   Roman   Ditch

Dover Castle &
Secret Wartime
Tunnels

Queen   Elizabeth   Road

Saxon Shore Way

A2

Police Station

Dock

Atholl Ter

Cliff

P

P

Dock Exit Road

P

Travel
Centre

Freight
Services
Centre

Passenger Terminal
Building

4

East   Marine Pde

A2

A20

EASTERN DOCKS
ROUNDABOUT

5

tre

Eastern Docks

CALAIS

6

141

7

8

Breakwater

9

G   H   33   J   K   L   M   34

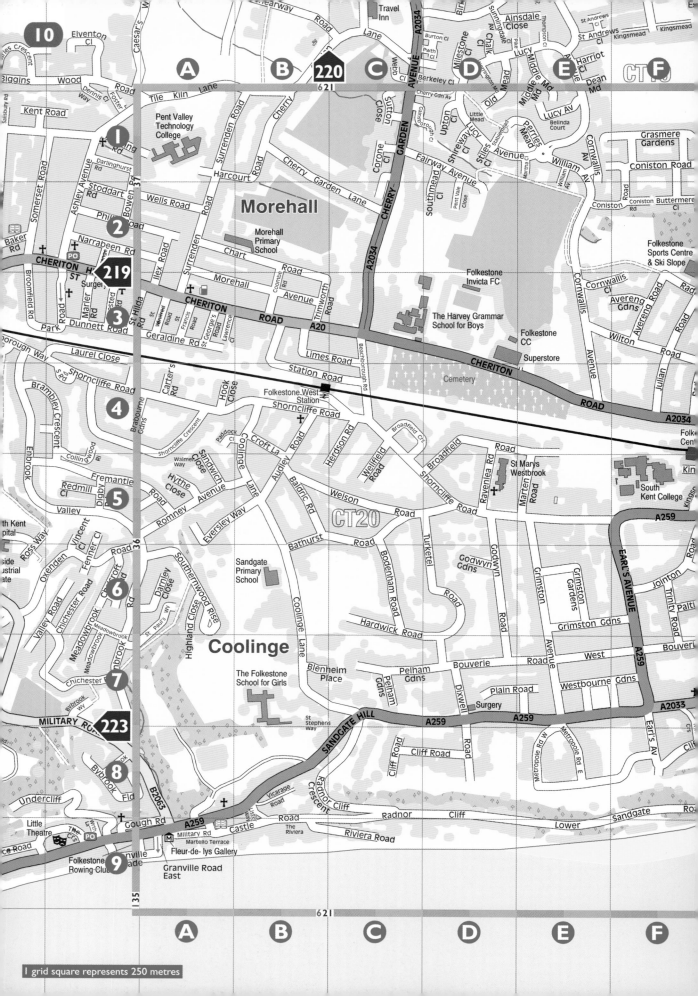

FOLKESTONE

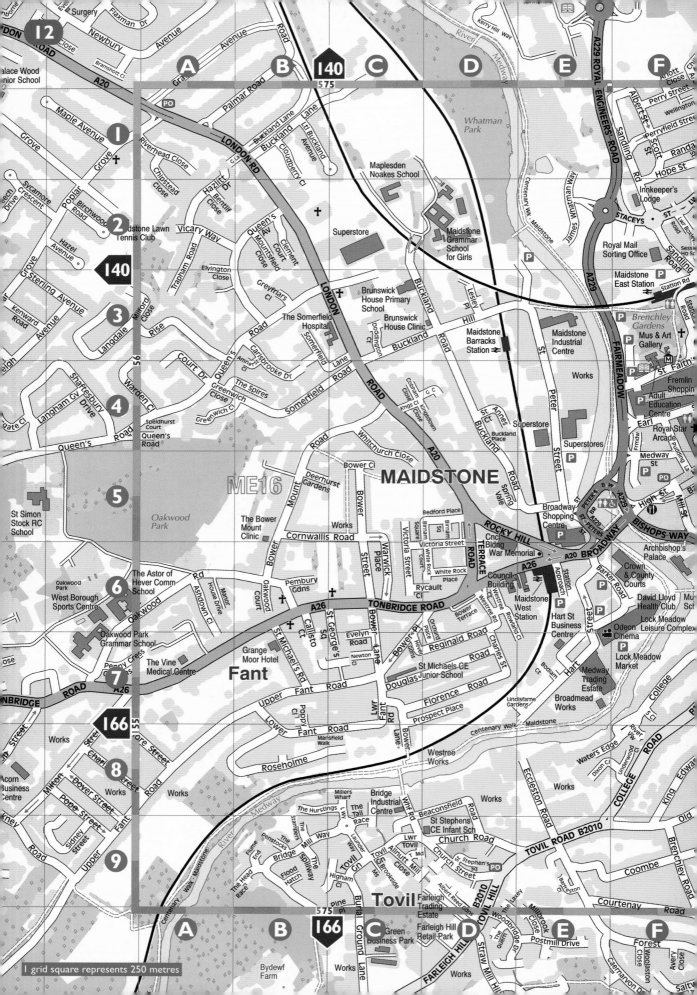

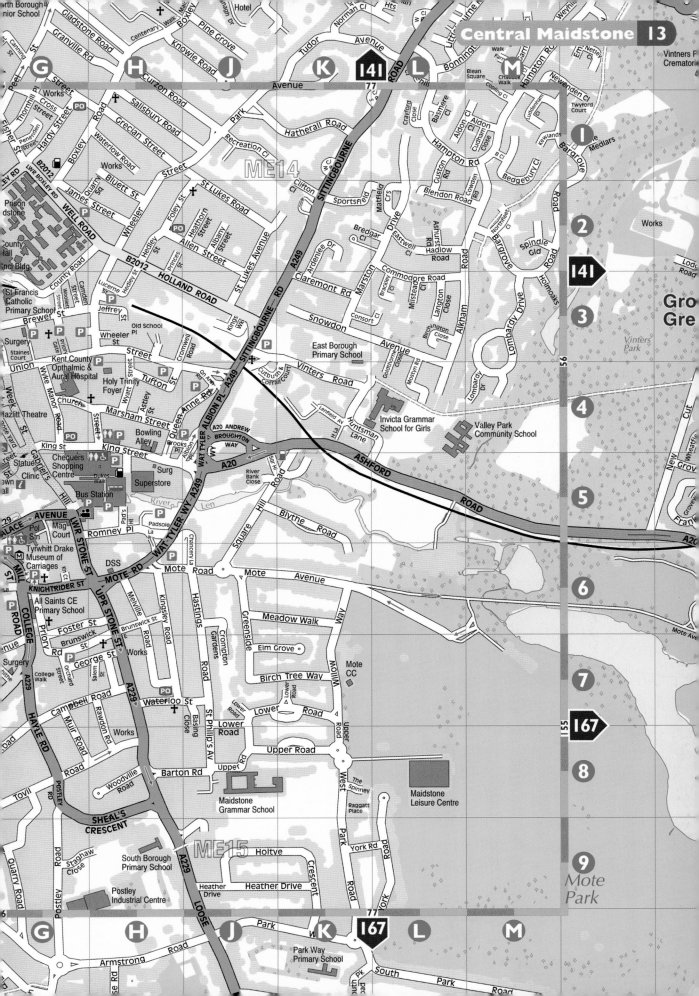

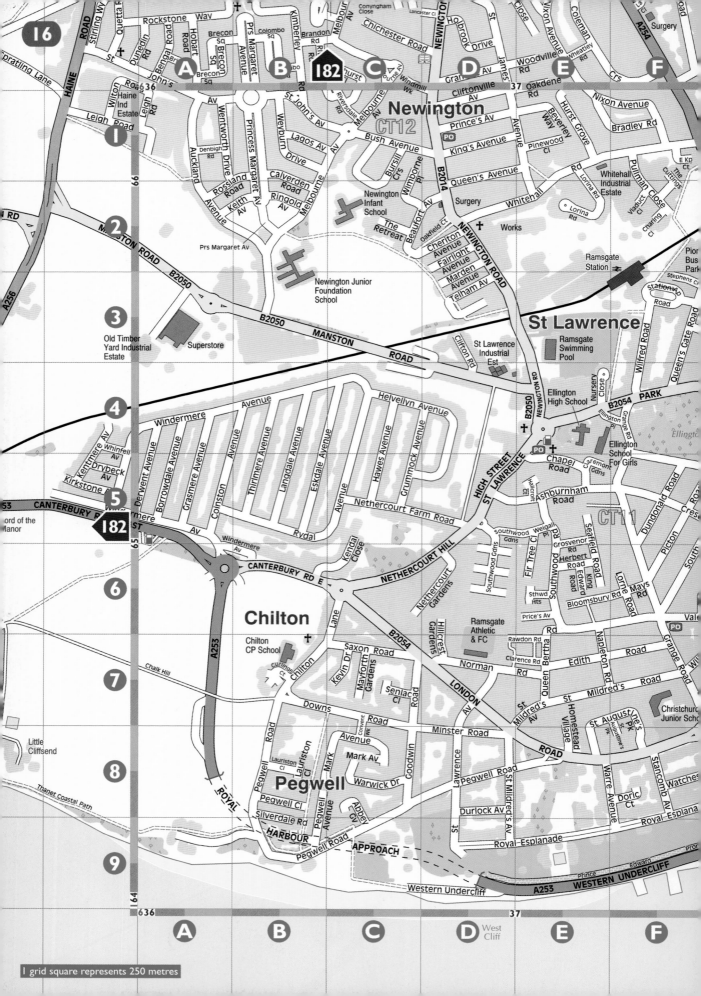

RAMSGATE

Council Building
James's
St J**G**n's
H
J
K
136
L
M

Sackville Cl
St Ge
St John's Road
Golding
Davis Cl
Road
Road
Westfield
Swaffield Road
Road
Little Wo
Hillingdon
The Green
Hillingdon Rise
Wickenden
53
Road
54
Garden
Road
Road

St Hilarys School
Sevenoaks Primary School
Camden
Amherst Rd
Morel Ct
St John's Hl
Nursery Cl
Allotment La
Quaker's
Road
Kennedy Gardens
Serpentine Ct
Lansdowne Rd
Hillborough Avenue
Quarry Hill
Road
Blackhall Lane
56
Woodland Rise

I

Linden Chase Road
Bradbourne Road
Pineneedle La
Mount
Birch Cl
Harry
Pendennis Rd
Road
Cobden Road
Prospect Road
Bethel Road
Hall
Hartsland
Road
Bayham
Sandy La
Holmesdale Rd
Knole Road
Serpentine
Road
Hillside Road
Quaker Cl
Quaker Cl

2

Woodside
The
a Glade
Road
Blair Cl
Dr
Woodside Rd
Carrick Dr
Hitchen Hatch Lane
Egdean Wk
Thicketts
Center Ter Rd
Road
DARTFORD
Road
Vine
Court
Bush
Road
Lane
Holmesdale Rd
The Paddocks
3

Merlewood Road
Winchester Grove
Oakwood Dr
Lane
White Ldg Cl
Ashley Cl
Pound
Avenue
Road
Road
Avenue Road
Hollybush Close
Hollybush Cl
HOLLOW
ROAD
SEAL
HOLLOW
4
Blackhall

Chestnut La
St
Ashley Rd
St Botolph's
Road
Park Lane
The Vine
Vine Cricket Ground
B2019
SEAL
Knole Park Golf Club

HILL
Emily Jackson Cl
A224
The Works
The Drive
Sevenoaks CC
Chartway
Plymouth
Plymouth Pk
5
162

Eardley Road
LONDON
Zobel College
Warren Ct
Plymouth Dr
Sevenoaks RFC
TN15
6

Council Building
Gordon Road
Pembroke Road
Suffolk
Knole Way
Lady Boswells CE Primary Sch

Argyle Road
Victoria Rd
Beech Road
Lime Tree Wk
ROAD
HIGH STREET
Bligh's Rd
Blighs Wk
Superstore
Way
Bligh's Court
B La
Blacks Yard
Surgery
Library & Museum
Sevenoaks Swimming Centre
7
Knole Park

South Park
St Thomas Primary School
South
Park
Surgery
Spielplatz
Medical Centre
Bank St
St Botolph's
Bucknurst Lane
Akehurst Lane
The Shambles
Bucknurst
SEVENOAKS
Greensand Way

Crow
Valley Dr
Rockdale
Road
Stag Theatre
PO
Superstore
Webbs Meadow
Akehurst La
Greensand
Way
Duchess Wk
8

Hill
Road
The Dene
Bourchier Close
Nicholas Dr
Six Bells La
St
Rectory La
HIGH ST
A225
Greensand Way
Knole
Lane
Knole
Lane
Knole (NT)
9

Oak Lane
Glebe Dr
Oakfields
Cemetery
PO
Sevenoaks School
A225
Greensand Way
154

Sevenoaks School Track

G
H
J
K
162
L
M
53
54

Soleoak Dr
TONBRIDGE

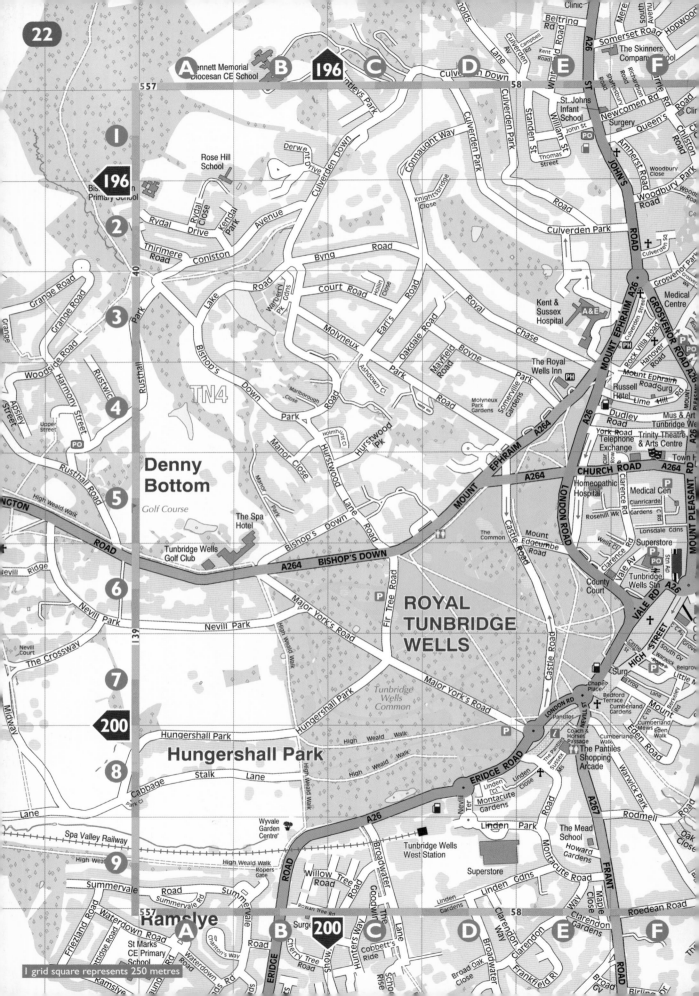

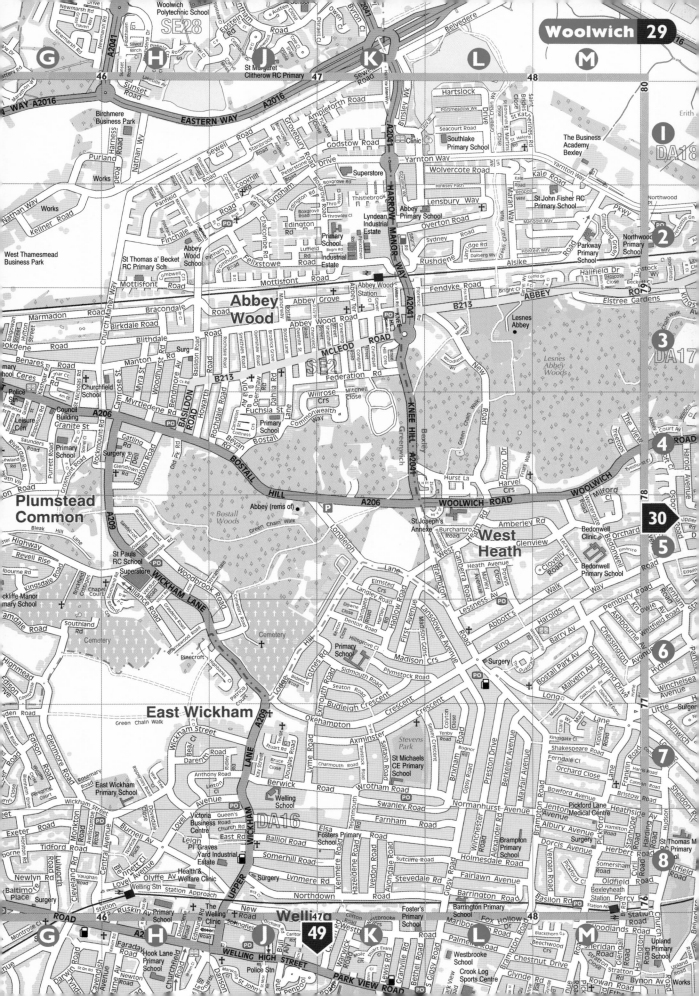

32

A1306 • London Rd • Juliette Wy • Kerry Avenue • Juliette Way • Juliette Way • Purfleet Ind Park • Channel Tunnel Rail Link under construction

Aveley Marshes

Fanns Farm

LC

LONDON ROAD

A1306

Milehams Industrial Estate

Water Surgery Lane • Marlow Av • Fanns Rise • Thamley • British Quarry Ms • Centurion Way • Crusader Close • Long Av • Saladin Ms • Hallron Cl

Council Building

Marine Court

Centurion Way • Cheftan Drive • Mulberry • PO • The Limes

A1090

TANK HILL RD

Purfleet Primary School

Travel Inn • HIGH ST • Church Lane • Works • Harrisons Wharf

Tank Lane

Beacon Hill Industrial Estate

Purfleet

River

Thames

Botany Way • Beacon Hill Industrial Estate • Wingrove Drive • Beacon Hill • Oakhill Rd • Way • Linnet

Purfleet Station • LC • A1090 • LONDON • ROAD

Mill Road • LC

Toplands • Manor Close • ge Road • Elm Rd • Chester • Stanford Gdns • Stifford Road • Lane

Blenheim Gdns • Lowlands Road • Purfleet • High • Dacre Avenue • Crescent Wy • Works • Aveley School (School House) • Surgery • Aveley Ct • Aveley Primary School

Arnhem Avenue • Hall Avenue • PO • Leonard St

Myrtle Grove • Gro • Beech • Eastern Av • Church View • Health Centre • A13

Love Lane • Central Av • Kent View • Hall • Crs • Crescent Walk • Hall Road • Ter • Hall Road

Mar Dyke

The Caravan Site • Causeway Bridge • South Wy • Back La

RM19

A1306 • **ARTERIAL ROAD PURFLEET** • A1306 • **Junction 31** • Premier Lodge

Wood Av • North Road • Fondu Sports Club • Cartel Cl • Baron Cl • Brimfield Rd • Gabion • Vel Cl • Talus • Rd Cl • Armor Road • Dolphin Wy

Channel Tunnel Rail Link under construction • Purfleet By-Pass

Works • Joslin Rd • Linden • Locker • Ct • Way

31 • LONDON • ROAD • **PURFLEET** • A1090 • STONEHOUSE LANE • London Rd • W Thurrock

LC • LC

Long Reach

Dartford Marshes

Works

Works • Works • A282 • CANTERBURY WAY

Works

Marsh Street

Dartford Tunnel

Queen Elizabeth II Bridge

A282

52 • Idlebrook Business Centre

Marsh Lane

Grove West • Salmon Rd • Cornwall Rd

G   H   J   K   L   M

70   71   72   80

I

2

3

79

4

78

38

5

Lower
Hope Point

Mead Wall

Nature Reserve

6

77

Saxon Shore Way

7

Thurrock
Medway Towns

Thurrock
Medway Towns
Kent County

8

176

A 573 B C 74 D E 75 F

80

I

2
79
3
4
78
37
5

Boatrick
House

6
77

Cliffe Marshes

Cliffe Fleet

Ryestreet Common

7

Mead Wall

Pickle's
Way

Hill Road
Church
Close

North
Road

Marsh
Lane

Wharf

Reed Street

Rookery Crescent

Common Lane

Saxon Shore Way

Buttway Lane

**West
Street**

Elford Rd

St Helens Rd

Quickrells

Swingate
Avenue

Cliffe

Rye Street
Farm

Wadlands
Road

Chancery Rd

Thatcher's Lane

Saxon Shore Way

Manor
Farm

CHURCH STREET

St Helens
CE Primary
School

8
176

Turner Street

Millcroft
Road

Saxon Shore Way

A 573 B C 74 **58** D E 75 F

B2000

Norwood
Close

Cooling Road

Restmore Cl
Higham Road

Road

Blythe
Sands

1

2

79

3

Salt Fleet

Hope Fleet

Halstow
Marshes

4

78

Decoy Fleet

40

5

Cooling
Marshes

Swig

Buckland Fleet

6

77

Decoy
Farm

Whalebone
Marshes

7

Saxon Shore Way

Nature Reserve

Bromhey
Farm

8

176

Cooling

Cooling Road

Saxon Shore Way

Marsh Crescent

Buckhole
Farm

Upwell Hill

Harrison Drive

Willowbank Drive

Longfield Avenue

Thames AV

P

River Thames

Allhall
on-Sea

The Brimp

Avery Way

Queensway
Surgery

PO

Avery
Close

Allhallows
Primary
School

Homewards Road

Dagnam
Farm

St. Luke's Way

Avery Way

St. David's Rd

St Matthews Wy

Binney Road

Jutland Close

Allhallows

Shakespeare Farm Road

Cuckolds Gn Rd

Brick
House
Farm

Stoke Road

Newhall
Farm

Farm Lane

New Hall

Hoopers Lane

Cuckold's
Green

Cuckolds

Green Road

Stoke Road

Marshland View

Stoke
Community
School

Button Drive

**Lower
Stoke**

Stoke Marshes

Malla
Mallard V

Chapel Row
Shepher

61

Little Oakham
Court

Mackay's

A228

A B C D E F

585 86 87

**Allhallows-
on-Sea**

Avery Close

North Level

Lees Ma

Yantlet Creek

Allhallows
Marshes

Grain
Marsh

Binney
Farm

Peat Way

Isle of Grain

585 86 87

A B C 62 D E F

W

1 grid square represents 500 metres

LC

Kent Oil Refinery

GRAIN ROAD

G H J K L M

88 89 90

I
2
3
4
5
6
7
8

80
79
78
77
176

Works

Peat Way

West Lane

Rose
Court Farm

Perry's
Farm

Pannell Road

HIGH STREET

Green Lane

St James CE
Primary School

Grain

B2001

Chapel

Road

Edinburgh Road

Coronation Road

St James
Road

Surgery

PO

Port

Grayne
Avenue

Ladwell Road

Rivendell
Close

Chapel Road

Victoria Road

Seaview

Smithfield Road

Medway Towns
Kent

GRAIN ROAD

G H J **63** K L M

88 89 90

Garris

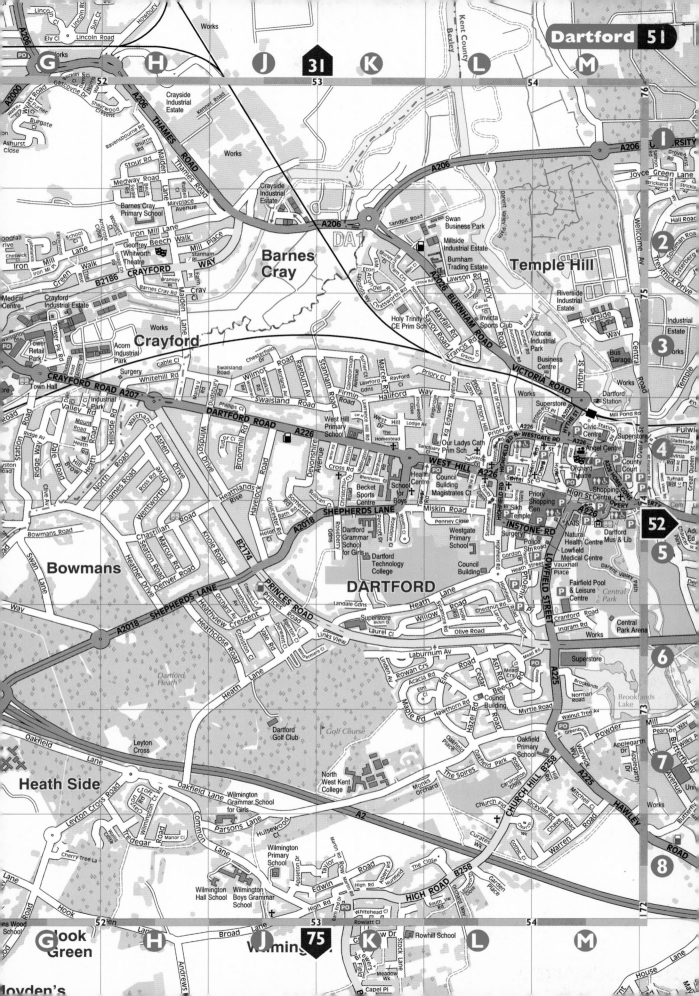

56

A B C **36** D E F
567 68 69 Coalhouse Point
76

1

75

2

3

Saxon Shore Way

4 Works Works LC

74

55

5 Denton Shamrock Rd Thistle Rd Farley Medbury Rd

Dickens Rd Ingoldsby Road Dering Way Damigos Rd Marsh Copperfield Close

North West Kent College

Chalk

Lower Higham Road Darenth Drive

6 Rose Nickleby Rd Ohlick Road Brooke Drive Castle Lane

Lower Higham Road PO Havisham Rd Lisle Cl Villa Romana

73 Forge Lane Miller Road Vicarage Lane Chalk Road

B261 Crescent Barr Road East Court Manor Lower Road

7 Westcourt Primary School Bourne Road Cruden Road Thong Lane A226 ROCHESTER ROAD

St Gregory's Medhurst Crs Medhurst Gdns Church La

Freeman Hibernia Dr Cervia Way ROCHESTER ROAD

8 St Chad's Raynehurst Junior School Thong Lane Church Lane Queen's Farm Road Green Farm Lane

Margaret Crs Thamesview School

72

80 GRAVESEND ROAD

A B C D E F
567 Cascades Leisure Centre Golf Course 68 69

Southern Valley Golf Club

1 grid square represents 500 metres

Riverview

Nature Reserve

Cooling

G Cooling Road **H** 76 **J** **39** 77 **K** **L** 78 **M** 76

Bromhey Farm

Buckhole Farm

Lipwell Hill

Buckhole Farm Road

Dalham Farm

Cooling Road

High Halstow Primary School

Wybournes Lane

LC

Wybournes Farm

Northwood Avenue
Marsh Crescent
Thames Av
P
Harrison Drive
Longfield Avenue
Medway
Street
Willowbank Drive
Eden Rd
The
Cobtree
Coolwood
Topley Drive
Holmes
Leaman Close
Britannia
Ruggles
Topley Drive
Mac...
Merton Cl
Cardigan

High Halstow

Forge Lane
The
Christmas Lane
PO
Gypsy Wrytch

I
2
75

Ducks Court

Dux Court Road

Solomons Farm

3

New Barn Farm

4

74

Deangate Ridge Athletics Stadium

Deangate

60
5

Depot

Dux Court Road

RATCLIFFE HIGHWAY

Tile Barn Farm

6

73

Deangate Ridge Golf Club

Golf Course

A228

Blackman Close

Bell's Lane

Wall Cl
Fourwents Road
Webb Close
Kingshill Drive
Rochester Crescent
Kingshill Drive
Grandsire Gardens
St Werburgh Medical Centre

7

Chattenden Farm

Stonebridge

RATCLIFFE HIGHWAY

Pankhurst Road
Linton Dann Close
Marley Rd
Walters Road
Bell's Lane

Central Ter

Hill Lane

Lodge H
Elmwood
Swinton Av

...nden
Road

Chattenden Lane

Chillwack Road

Hoo St Werburgh

Videgeon Av
Knights
Robson Drive
Wylie Road
Av???
Close
Wylie Road
Wylie Rd
John St
Knight Close
Miskin Road
Trubridge Road
Peal Cl
Peal Cl
Stoke Road

8

72

St Werburgh CP Junior School

Hundred of Hoo School

Pottery Road
Herdsdown
St Werburgh Crescent
Killick Rd
Gordon Road
Hoo St Werburgh Primary School
Newitt Road
Main Road
Coombe Road
Flack Gdns
The Elms Medical Centre
Brookside
PO
Church Street
Everest Ms
Armytage Close
Vicarage La
Church Farm
Abbots

G 76 **H** **J** **83** 77 **K** **L** 78 **M**

MAIN ROAD
A228
Kitch...
Road
Tudor
Hoo Common Rd
Broadwood Rd
Elm Avenue
Hill Lane
Main Road
Saxon Shore Way

Broad Street

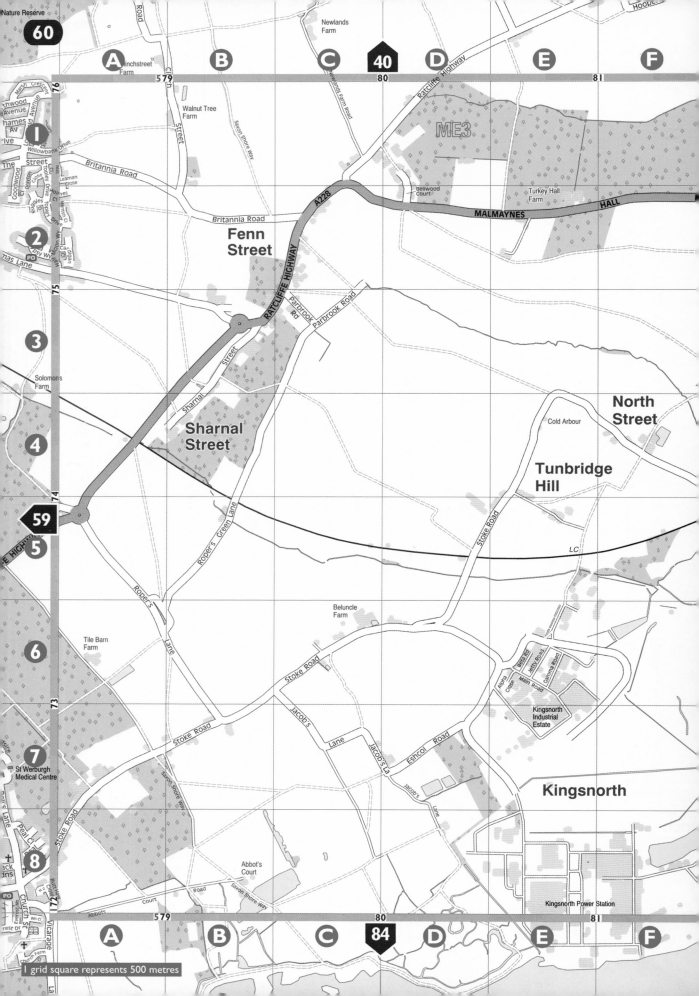

G H J **41** K L M

82 83 84 76

Cuckolds
Green

Stoke Community School

Allhallows Road

Button Drive

Lower Stoke

Mallard Way
Heron Way
Grn Cl
Grain Rd
PO
D Mll
Shepherds Way

Little Oakham Court

Mallard Way
Chapel Row

Mackay's
Court Farm

Middle Stoke

GRAIN ROAD

A228

GRAIN RO

LC

I

Malmaynes
Hall Farm

A228

Stoke

Burrows Lane

2

Vicarage Close

75

Dickensian Cl

3

LC

Tudor
Farm

LC

4

Stoke Saltings

74

62

Stoke Ooze

5

6

East Hoo Creek

73

Damhead Creek

Bee Ness Jetty

7

Oakham Ness Jetty

Oakham
Marsh

8

Slede Ooze

172

82 83 **85** 84

G H J K L M

Oakh
Ness

Ketthole Reach

dway

A B C 42 D E F

585 86 87

76

I

LC

LC

GRAIN ROAD A228

2

75

Works

Kent Oil Refinery

B2001

LC

GRAIN ROAD

3

74

Colemouth Creek

Works

4

61

Elphinstone Point

Works

5

6

73

Medway Towns
Kent

River Medway

7

Sharp Ness

Stangate Spit

8

172

Burntwick Island

Stangate Creek

585 86 87

A B C 226 D E F

I grid square represents 500 metres

G GRAIN ROAD H 88 J 43 89 K L 90 M 76

1 Garrison Point

2 75

3

Port Victoria Road

Grain Power Station

4 74

River Medway

64 West Minster 5

6 Newlar Road

Saltpan Reach

73 B2007

7 Works WHITEWAY ROAD

Queenborough Spit

Deadmans Island

West Swale

8 Queenborough Yacht Club

West Point Long Reach

172

G 88 H J 227 89 K L 90 M

A B C D E F

597 98 99
76

1

2
75

3

74
65
5

Royal
Oak Point

Bugsby's
Hole

East
End
Lane

Mill
Hill Windmill Rise
Oak Avenue
CHEQU OAD
Danedale Avenue
Pigtail
Corner
Bell Farm Lane
Farm Lane
Punnetts
Farm
Old Billet Lane
Connetts

Elm Lane
Plough Road
Cripps
Farm
Plough Road
Trouts

Tadwell
Farm
EASTCHURCH ROAD
Hustlings
Dr
Garretts
Plough Road
FIRST

8

The
Mount
B2008
Kingsborough
Farm
Coultrip Cl
Court Tree
Drive
Leet Close

72

597 98 99

Brambledown
A B
Norwood
Manor
C
229
EASTCHURCH RO
D E
Warden Road
F

I grid square represents 500 metres

Warden

I grid square represents 500 metres

North Cray

Sports Ground

Wicksteed

Bexley
Kent County

A · Bunkers Hill · B · Cocksure Lane · C · **50** · D · E · F

549

51

Joydens Wood
Junior School

PO

I
The Grove
James Way
A223

Cattons Wy
Cemetery

Joyden's
Wood

Woodlands Park

Eden Road

Summerhouse Drive
Norfield Road

Birchwood Road

Puddledock Lane

2
NORTH CRAY ROAD
PO

Manor Farm

Parsonage Lane

Greenfield Rd

3
Rux
Golf Course

Chalk Wood

Stonehill
Green

Puddledock

Stanhill Farm

Bexley Kent County

Birchwood Park
Golf Club

4
Garden Centre
Bexley Bromley
MAIDSTONE ROAD
Old Maidstone Road
B2173

Birchwood Road

Claremont Rd

Dawson Dr

73

5
Golf Course
Cookham Road
Upper Hockenden
A20 B2173
B2173
MAIDSTONE ROAD
B2173
Works

Works

Leydenhatch Lane

New

SWANLEY

Harris Way
Selan Dr

Birchwood Primary School

6
Chapman's Lane
Hockenden Lane
Bromley

Cedar Close
Heathwood Gdns

LONDON ROAD

Alder Way

White Oak Primary Sch

7
Star Lane
Hockenden
Farm Avenue
Lynden
Laburnum Av

The Croft
Sermon Drive
Dale Road
Brook

Lesley Close
Oliver Reeves Cresent
Lime Road

Swanley School

Police Station

Primary School

BARTHOLOMEW

Superstore
Surgery
Council Building
St Marys CE Primary School

8
Sheepcote Lane
Bourne Wood

Cherry Avenue
Hewett Place

Swanley Station
Station Approach

GOLDSEL ROAD

B258

BR

Sheepcote Farm

549

A · B · Bromley Kent County · C · **92** · D · Furness · Swanley FC · E · F

50

51

G H J **57** K L M **I**

70 71 72

A226

Hill Farm

Higham Primary School

School Lane

White House Farm

Hillyfield

Hermitage Road

Walmers Avenue

Evergreen Close

Briar Dale

Norah Lane

Holytree Drive

Carton Road

Chilton Drive

Villa

Darby Gardens

Brice Rd

Peggoty Cl

Irvine Lane

Oak Drive

Beech Grove

Ash Crs

Dombey Close

Forge Lane

Hayes Lane

Telegraph Hill

Crutches Lane

Peartree Lane

School Lane

High View

Mountbatten Av

St John's Rd

St John's Cl

Taylor's Ln

PO

The Braes

Elm Close

Telegraph Hill

Higham

The Knowle

Hermitage Road

Surgery

Kent County Medway Towns

2

HASTE

3

Dillywood Lane

Little Hermitage

A226

GRAVESEND ROAD

82

4

B2108

Westerga

Harlech Close

A226 GRAVES

Gadshill

Gads Hill School

Charles Dickens Avenue

Copperfield Crescent

Chapter Farm

Fountain Rd

Beaufort

Carisbr

B2108

Abbey Court School

18

REDE COURT ROAD

Romsey Close

Clayton

Cobb

Duchess Cl

Crispin

Russet

Bramley Rise

Worcester Close

Chapter Road

Allington Drive

5

Great Crabbles Wood

Bowesden Lane

Bowesden Lane

Pale Park

Crutches Lane

Colewood Drive

Old Watling Street

Junction 1

WATLING STREET A2

Millfordhope Rd

Parkfields

Chetney Cl

Yantlet Drive

Copperhouse Rd

The Shades

Squires Cl

Sharfleet Dr

Stangate Rd

Swale Road

Chapter School

Thurston Drive

Carnation Road

Linwood Av

Cadnam Cl

WATLING STREET

Columbine Rd

Daffodil Rd

Columbine Road

Lancelot Avenue

Elaine

Elaine Av

River Dr

Dean

Cobham

Stoke Close

Elaine Primary School

Clifton Cl

Tamar Dr

Darnley

Strood

6

Knights Place

M2

Kent County Medway Towns

Great Wood

Albatross Av

Pelican Close

Orchid Rd

PO

Tern Rd

Curlew Crs

Bligh

Scholars Rise

Widgeon Rd

Seagull

Portsmouth Road

Southwark Rd

Southwell

Chelmsford Rd

Chester Rd

St Albans Rd

Winston Rd

Bristol Cl

Wells Rd

Marlowe Park Medical Cen

Merrals Wood Rd

Ranscombe Cl

Rushdean Road

Bootham Rd

Hyacinth Road

Hawthorn

Child Health Cen

Lilac Crs

Lilac Road

Holly Road

Darnley Road

Laburnum Road

Poplar Road

Sycamore Road

Oak

Cedar

Beech Rd

Willow

Chestnut Rd

Sherwin Knight Primary School

Hever Cl

7

8

Ballard Business Park

B168

CUXTON ROAD

Diggerland

G H J **99** K L M

70 71 72

ME2

Junction 2

Ranscombe

North Downs Way

ESTER RD

Merrals Shaw

Oakham
Ness

Kethole Reach

G 82

H Slede Ooze

J 61 83

K

L 84

M 72

I

Medway

Long Reach

River

Bishop Spit

2

71

3 am O

Bishop Ooze

Medway Towns
Kent

Half Acre

4

70

226

5

Bartlett Creek

6

Bayford

Poot Lane

Saxon Shore

69

7 Har
Gre

Rainham Creek

RSPB
Reserve
Motney
Hill

Works

Ottetham Creek

Horsham
Marsh

8 Wetha
Green

68

G 82

H

Road

J 103 83

K

L 84

M Shore Way

Bloors
Wharf

Motney
Hill Road

The
Pole

Street

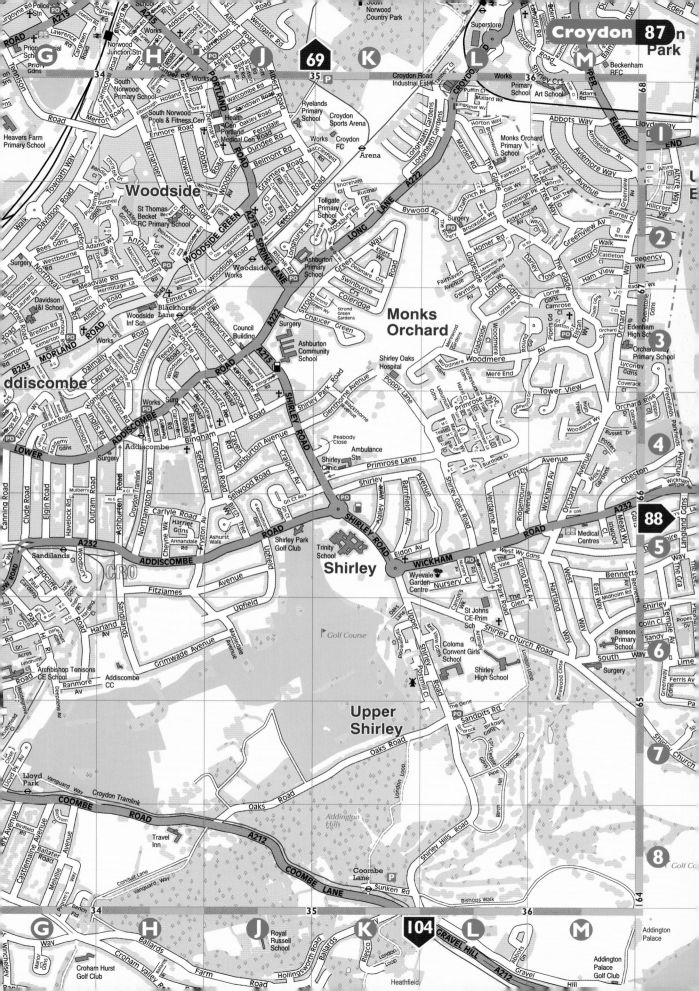

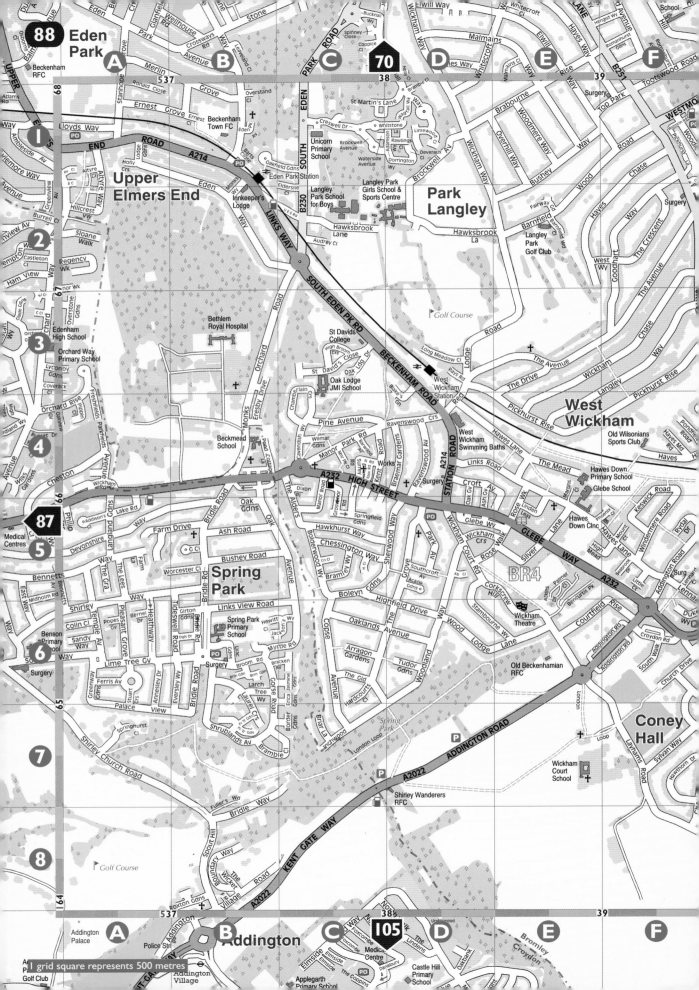

G H J 75 K L M

52 53 54

I

High Firs Primary School

St Georges Road
West Vi
Lower
B2173
Manse Way
Beechen
Farningham Woods (Nature Reserve)

Salisbury Avenue
Mayesbury Way
Wansbury Way
Abbots Close
LONDON ROAD
Moreton Industrial Estate

2

A20
Glendale
St George's Road

Pedham Place Industrial Estate

Teardrop Industrial Park

Hill Farm

Farningham Hill Rd

LONDON ROAD A20   MAIN ROAD

Petham Court

Junction 3/1

PO   Dartford Road

High

Works
The Mill House

3

sted

Wested Lane

River Darent

Sparepenny Lane

Oliver Crescent

Crockenhill Lane

4

A225

ANSFORD RD

Priory Lane

Old Mill

Mill Lane

Anthony Roper Primary School

HIGH STREET

Tower Croft

Priory

94

Hulberry

Eynsford Castle

Eynsford CC

5

EYNSFORD

Darent Valley Path

Riverside

Home Farm

PO

Lullingstone Lane

Saddlers Park

PH

Pollyhaugh

Bower Lane

Pollyhaugh Farm

6

Lullingstone Roman Villa

Darent Valley Path

STATION ROAD

St Martins Drive

Birch Close

Eynsford Rise

Upper

A225

Chalkhurst

7

Lullingstone Park Farm

Eynsford Station

Austin

Lullingstone Park

Lullingstone Castle

Darent Valley Path

Road

Lodge

8

Beechen Wood

Cash

Austin

Road

Lower Austin Lodge

164

52 53 54

G H J **110** K L M

G   H   J   **77**   K   L   M

58   59   60

Beeches Farm

Castle   Hill   Castle   Hill   Old Downs

Larks

Gresham Avenue

Church

Canada Farm Road

Scudders Hill

Dickens Close

Ash Road

Green Way

Stack Lane

Carmelite Way

Our Lady RC Prim

Cher Tree

Hartley Green

Broomfields

PO

Culvey Cl

Round Ash Way

Oast Way

Conifer Av

Ash Road

The Warrens

St John

Hartley Primary School

Fairby Lane

Chantry Avenue

Tates Orchard

Corinthian Sports Club

School Lane

Court Lodge

Manor Lane

DA3

Horton Wood

Three Gates Rd

Grove Farm

Valley Road

Fawkham CE Primary School

Fawkham Manor

Fawkham Manor Hospital

Milestone ool

Farm Holt

Speed Gate

Speedgate Hill

Michaels   Lane

Butchers   Lane

Chapel Wood Road

Chapel Wood

Millfield La

96

New Ash Primary

Surg

Ayelands Lane

Millfield

(East)

Sun   Hill

Valley Rd

PH

Small Grains

Fawkham Green

The Mead

Ayelands Lane

Turner's Oak Shaw

Coltstead

Centre Rd

PO

Colin Chapman Way

Fawkham   Green   Road

Brands Hatch Road

West Yoke

Beechcroft Farm Industrial Estate

Ash   Road

Punch Croft

Punch Croft

Knights Croft

Hatch Racing Circuit

Fawkham   Road

Brandshatch Place Hotel

Rogers   Wood   Lane

Billet   Hill

Ash   Road

Redhill Road

Crowhurst Lane

The   **Ash**

The Street

Pease

G   H   J   **238**   K   L   M

58   59   60

1

2

3

4

5

6

7

8

66

67

64

65

68

69

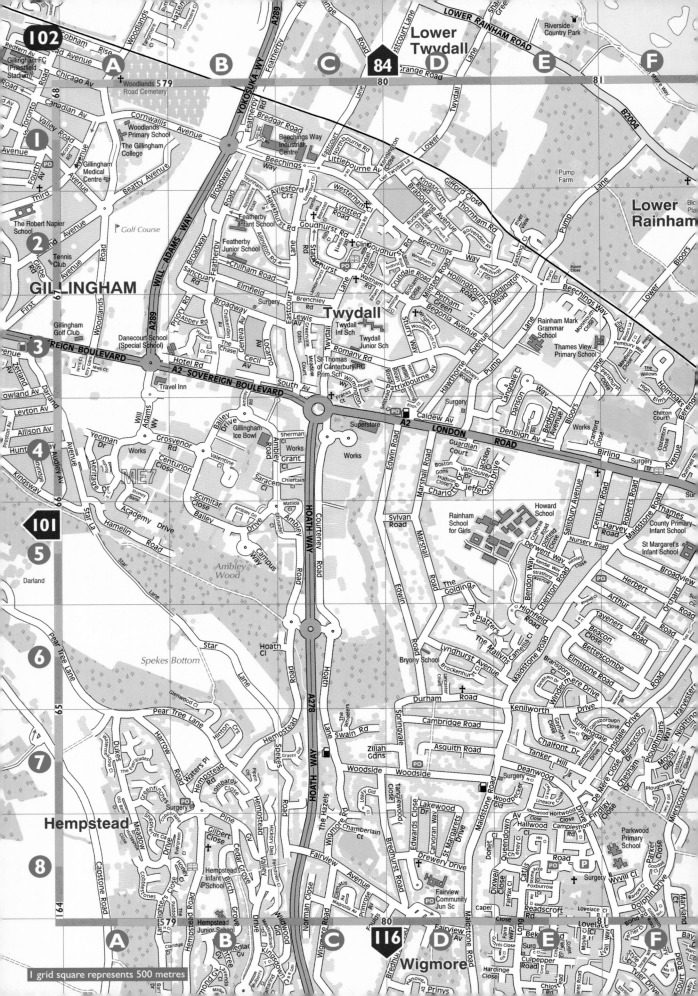

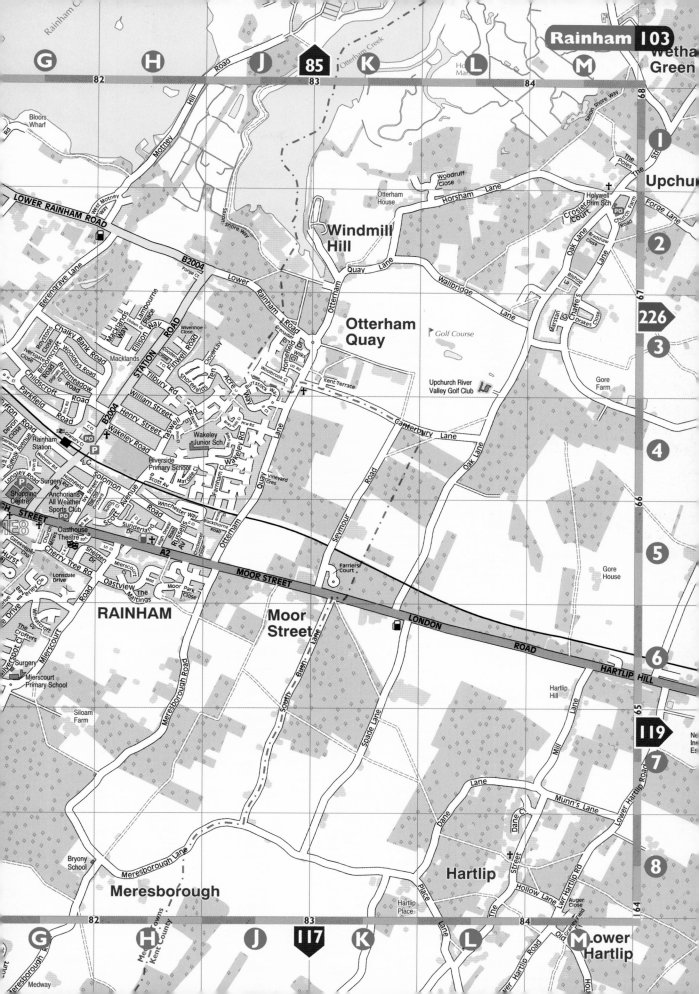

RAINHAM

Meresborough

Hartlip

Moor Street

Windmill Hill

Otterham Quay

G H J K L M

88

N 1

2

3

4

106

5

6

7

8

G H J K L M

131

New Addington

Fickleshole

Court

G Well Hill
H
J 92
K
L
M

Firmingers Road

Well Hill Road
Rock Hill
Well Hill Lane

Great Cockerhurst
Ridge Farm
Redmans Lane

Dalhanna

M25

Junction 4

Cockerhurst Road

Castle Farm Road

Darent Valley Path

Castle Farm
Preston

Hollows Wood

Chelsfield Lane

Darenthdale

Badgers Mount

Johnsons Avenue
Badgers Road
Badgers Road

Shacklands Road

Milton Avenue

Highland Road
Charles Road

BY-PASS

Shacklands Road

Timberden Bottom

Shacklands Road

Mill Lane

Crown Road

High Street

Shoreham
PO
Forge Way
Boakes Meadow

Garden Centre

A224

M25

Mildmay Place
Church Street
Bowers Road
Mesne Way

Shoreham County Primary School

Darenth Way

Station Road

Shoreham Station

Darent Valley Golf Club

Darent Valley Path

Shoreham Place

110

225

LONDON ROAD A224

Water Lane

Filston Lane

Filston Farm

Filston Hall

Golf Course

Darent Valley Path

Sepham Farm

Lower Barn

Darent

G
Beckman Cl
Crow
H
POT HILL
J
135
K
L
M

Fort Rd
Fort
Armstrong

50
51
52

64
I
63
2
3
62
4
5
61
6
7
60
8

G · H · J · **94** · K · L · M

I

2

3

4

238

5

6

7

8

Hog Wood

High Castle Wood

East Hill

Ashen Grove Road

Cherry Tree Grove

Botsom Lane

Knatts Valley Road

Blue Chalet Ind Park

Millfield Road

The Briars

Phelps Cl

St Cl

Gillies Road

Symonds Road

Oad

Viking Way

Hever Rd

Multon

Hever Road

Astor Rd

Wntgt Av

Hwlls Cl

PO

Mitchem Cl

W V Cl

Hever Wood Road

Sherbourne Close

Brakes Place

Oaklands Cl

Regency Close

Penthurst Close

Avenue

Clearways Industrial Estate

Works

Church Road

Chapel Close

Rushetts Road

Kingsingfield Road

WEST KINGSDOWN

Kingsdown House

Crowhurst

Southfields Road

Ash Tree Drive

Warland Road

Vernon Close

The Grange

PO

Hazelden Close

Forge Lane

A20 LONDON ROAD

West Kingsdown Industrial Estate

West Kingsdown Medical Centre

Knatts Valley

The Grove

Hollywood Lane

Pells Farm

Hollywood Manor

Pells Lane

School Lane

Manor Road

Knatts Lane

St

Clere Hill Road

Knockmill

East Hill Road

Hills Lane

Goodbury Road

Golf Course

Tinker Pot Lane

Tinker Pot Lane

Woodlands

Tinkerpot Rise

en Road

Fernbank Farm

Woodlands Manor Golf Club

Drane Farm

North Downs Way

Knock Mill Road

Lodge Road

Terry's

Kester

Cotman's

Ash

LONDON ROAD

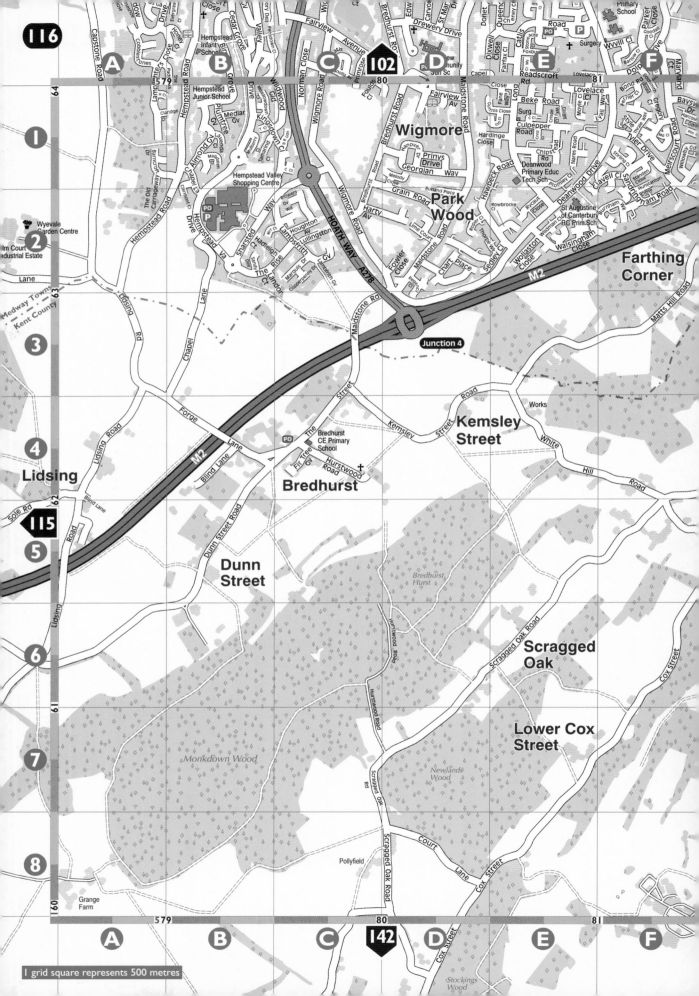

G H Mer**H**borough J 103 K Hartlip L M

Bryony School
Meresborough Lane
Meresborough

Hartlip Place

82 83 84

Medway Towns Kent County

Lower Hartlip

Medway
Medway Service Area
Medway Service Area
Travelodge

M2

Sweepstakes Farm

House Rd

Matts Hill Farm

Magpie Lane

Queen Down Warren

Yaugher Lane

Warren Lane

Mount Lane

Cowstead Road

Cowstead

Bull Lane

Green

Cox Street

Yelsted

Yelsted Road

Yelsted Lane

Magpie Lane

Cradles Road

Hill Green

Hill Green Road

The street

Bull Lane

Church Lane

Stockbury

PO

Plum Tree Farm

Plum Tree Lane

West Wood

Road

Parsonage Farm

Harrow

Cockhill Farm

South Street

South Street Road

Steps Hill Road

Church Hill

Beaux Aires Farm

Chalky Road

Binbury Lane

A249

Rumstead Lane

Rumstead Lane

Hayes Lane

Squirrel

G H J 143 K L M

82 83 84

Binbury Lane
A249
Rumsted Court

I 2 3 4 5 6 7 8

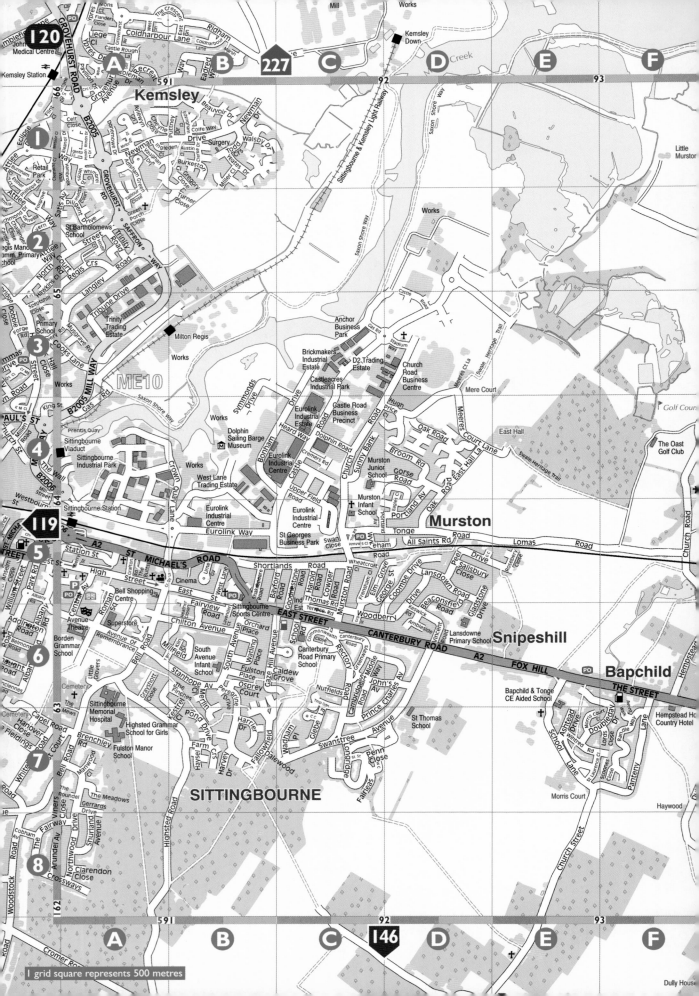

G   H   J   228   K   L   M

94   95   96   66

I

Saxon Shore Way

Tonge Corner

Church Road

Blacketts Rd

Swale Heritage Trail

Conyer Creek

2

Blacketts

Cheke's Court

Conyer

3

Church Road

Blacketts Road

Saxon Shore Way

Conyer Road

The Moorings

Brunswick Field

4

Binny Cotts

Conyer Road

122

Teynh

Teynham Court

5

Bax

LC

Teynham

Lower Road

LC

6

Lower Road

Teynham Station

Barrow Green

Osiers Farm

Osier Road

Conyer Road

A2

Works

Orchard WK

Harrys Rd

Baker Cl

Roper Road

The Crescent

Broadacre

LONDON   **ROAD**

Honeyball WK

Rivers Road

Roundel Close

Amber

7

Radfield

Frognal Lane

Frognal Close

Teynham Parochial CE Primary School

Belle Friday Cl

Station

Amber

Bradfield Avenue

Nutberry Close

Teynham Medical Centre

Nobel Close

Lower

Claxfield Road

Frognal Gdns

Donald Moor AV

Cherry Gdns

New Gardens Rd

PO

Surgery

Little Dully

Cellarhill

Lynsted Lane

Cellar Hill

A2

LONDON   **ROAD**

8

62

G   H   J   147   K   L   M

Upper Newlan

94   95   96

Wood   street

Batteries Close

A B C **229** D E F

597 98 99

1 Fowley Island
South Deep

2

Conver

3 Teynham Level

The Moorings
Brunswick Field

4 Conver Road

121

Teynham St
Teynham Street
Marsh La
Conver Road
Marsh Lane

5

6 Marsh Lane
Swale Heritage Trail

Luddenham Marshes

Poplar Hi

Howle

Luddenham Court

7 Deerton Street
Swale Heritage Trail
Deerton Street
Elverton
Swale Heritage Trail

Lower Road
Deerton Street

The Old Farmhouse

8 Lower Newlands
Norton Lane
LC
Mockbeggar
LC
Stone Farm

Four Oaks
Luddenham Primary School

ROAD
597 98 99

A **Nort B Ash** C **148** D Lower Road E F
Bysing

G H J K L M

230

Sayes Court

The Ferry Inn

1

2

3

Nature Reserve

Nagden Marshes

4

124

5

Uplees

Uplees Road

Court Lodge

PH

Saxon Shore Way

6

Ham Marshes

Uplees Road

Swale Heritage Trail

Works

Russell Pl

Church Road

PO

Colegates

Oare

The Street

Works

Works

Ham Marshes

Ham Farm

7

Nash's Farm

Colegates Road

Works

Works

John Hall Cl

Windmill La

Ham Road

The Brents

8

Bysing Wood Road

B2045

WESTERN LINK

Colegates Road

Seagar Rd

Oare Road

Works

Upper Brents Industrial Estate

Springhead Road

Larksfield Road

Saxon Shore Way

Waterside

149

Davington

Bysing Wood CP

Churchill Way

Bysing Wood

Wells Way

Priory Row

Brent Hill

Davington Hill

FAVERSHAM

Belvedere Road

Abbey Road

Abbey Street

Queen Elizabeths Grammar School

G H J K L M

06 07 08 66

1

2

Preston
Bowker
St
Mary's
Hook
Allan Road
Road
65
seas
Lucerne Drive
oss

3

Seasalter
Sailing Club

Faversham Road
PH

Bridge
Country
Leisure Club

Graveney
Marshes

Seasalter
Level

4

64

152

5

6

A296

THANET 63 WAY

Yo

Monkshill Farm

Waterham

Industrial
Estate

Travelodge

Da

7

Monkshill Road
Highstreet Road

Thanet
Way
Highstreet
Rd

Highstr

Lane

8

umpudding

62

06 07 A299 08

G H J **151** K L M

THANET

Wey Street
Farm

Dargate
House

Dargate

I

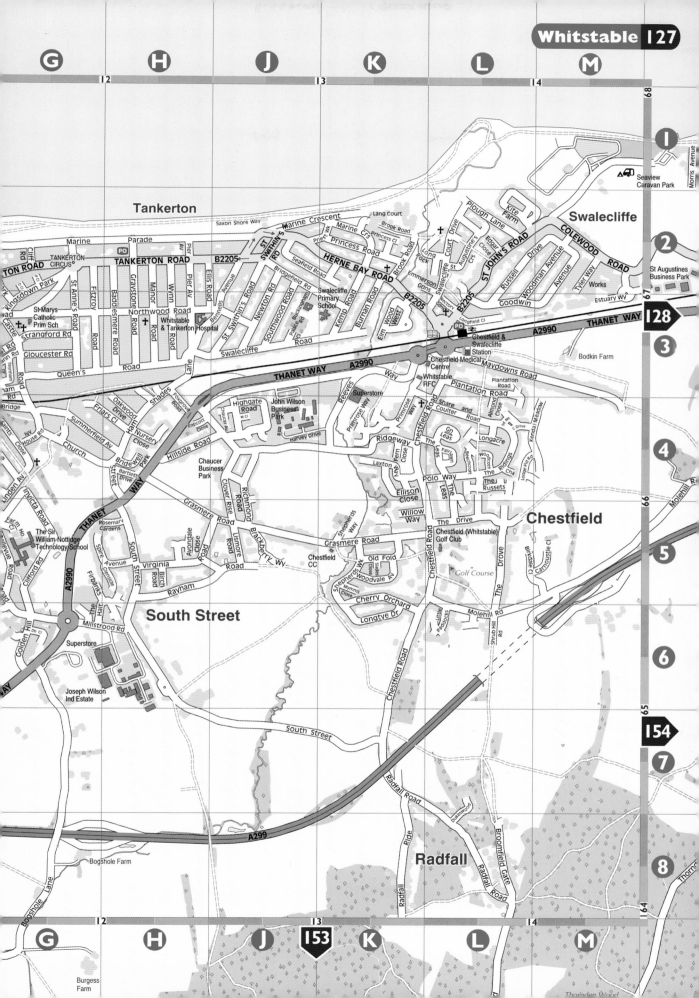

104

Farleigh

Farleigh Court Road

Farleig

Hamsey Green

West Parkside

Cemetery

Warlingham School

Hamsey Green Junior School

Hamsey Green Infant School

Batts Farm

Warlingham RFC & John Fisher Sports Club

Crewes House

Harrow Gdns

Farleigh Rovers FC

Parsonage Close

Warlingham Park School

Ledgers Road

Trenham Drive

Verdayne Gdns

Crewe's Avenue

Crewe's Lane

Warlingham Sports Club

Farleigh Primary School

Chelsham

Greenhill Lane

Chesham

The Maw

Farleigh Rd

Cranmer Gdns

Alexandra Rd

Sunny Bank

PH

Mint Walk

Farleigh Rd

Eglise Road

PO

Warren Pk

Chelsham Place Farm

Rogers Lane

Warlingham

Redvers Rd

Leas

Leas La

Mayes Rd

Birch Way

The Ct

Farm Road

Gresham Av

Eden Wy

LIMPSFIELD

High La

Hillbury Close

Hilbury Gdns

Bayards

Coneybury Cl

Paddock Walk

Westhall Road

Tandridge Road

Beechwood Lane

Plantation

Lane

Slines Oak

Slines Oak Road

West View Road

Narrow La

Westhall Pk

Broadlands Dr

High Pines

Huntsman's Cl

Overhill

Bug Hill

Golf Course

Slines New Road

Butlers Dene Road

Landscape Rd

Kooringa

Southview Rd

Southview Rd

Succombs Hill

Badgers La

Ashwood

Butterfly Wk

Woldingham Golf Club

Slines New Road

Dukes Hill

Beulah Wk

Woldingham Garden Village

Lunghurst Road

A22

Stuart Road

Woldingham Road

Beulah Walk

Hilltop Walk

Camp Rd

Marden Lodge Primary School

PO

Woldingham Road

Garden Centre

Birchwood House

Long Hill

Station Road

Long Hill

Park View Road

High Drive

The Wold

Tillingdown Hill

Waltham Road

Highfield Rd

Beechwood

Woldingham Station

Church Road

Park View Road

Southdown Rd

Woodlea Primary School

Station Road

Croft Rd

CATERHAM-BY-PASS

A22

156

Marden Park Farm

Woldin

Park

Cou **G** P

H

J

105

K

L

M

I

Skid Hill
Farm

Farleigh Ct

Scotshall Lane

38

39

40

60

Fairchildes Road

Skid Hill Lane

2

59

Holt Wood

Church Lane

✝

Heslers Road

BIGG HILL

3

Ledgers Farm

Heslers Hill

Court Road

Beddlestead Lane

Northeads Lane

4

ard Way

Lane

Washpond

Chelsham

Chelsham Court Farm

58

132

dingto
ose

5

Ledgers Road

Worms Heath

Broom Bank

Beech Farm Road

Beddlestead Farm

ROAD

Barnard Road

Vanguard Way

B269

6

57

Beech Farm

Beddlestead Lane

7

Vanguard Way

Cheverells Farm

8

CROYDON ROAD

156

G 38

H

J

157

39

K 69

L

M

Approach Road

Clarks

am

CLARKS

B2024

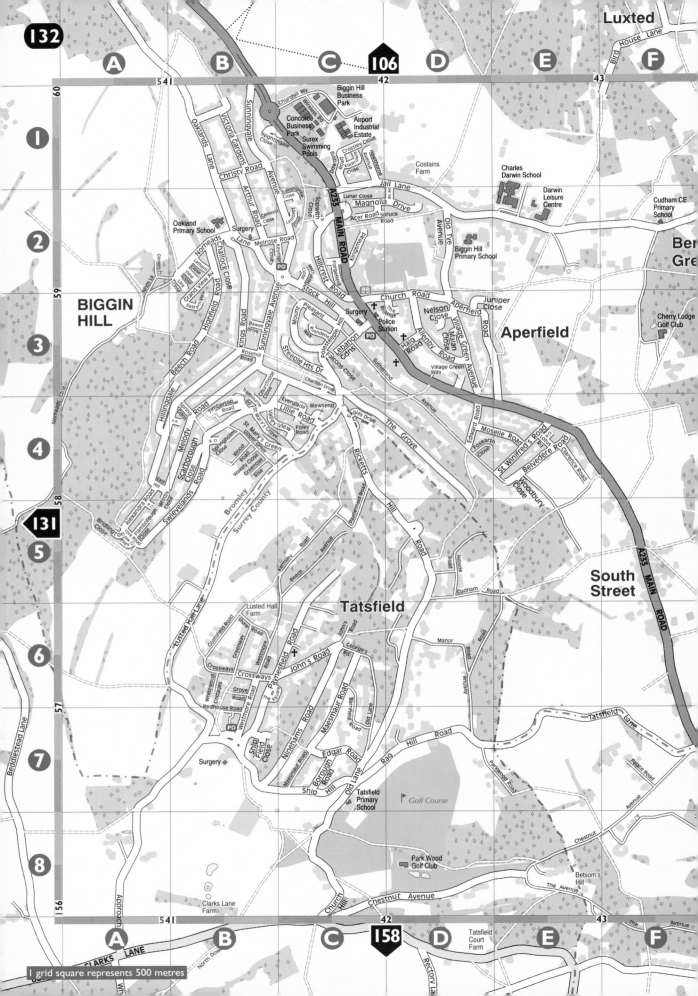

G H J III K L M

I

56 57 58 60

Fernbank Farm

Drane Farm

North Downs Way

Terry's Lodge Road

Old

2

Kester

Ash Lane

Cotman's Lane

Orford Manor

Pilgrim's Way

Pilgrims Way

St Clere

Crowdleham

Kemsing Primary School

238

Kemsi

Manor

3

Church Lane

Council ding

Heaverham Road

Heaverham

Lower St Clere

h Street

Broughton

red wy

59

58

M26

4

Ark

Chaucer Business Park

5

Honeypot Lane

Kemsing Station

Lane

6

Tanners Cross

Watery Lane

Stonepitts

Manor Farm

57

Fullers Hill

Broomsleigh

240

Styants Bottom

7 Old

Oldbury

Saxbys Road

MAIDSTONE

ROAD

Pillar Box Road

Styants Bottom Road

Spring Lane

Common

8

The Grove

A25

56

56 57 58

G H J **163** K L M

SEVENOAKS

Hall

Seal Chart

Frankfield

P

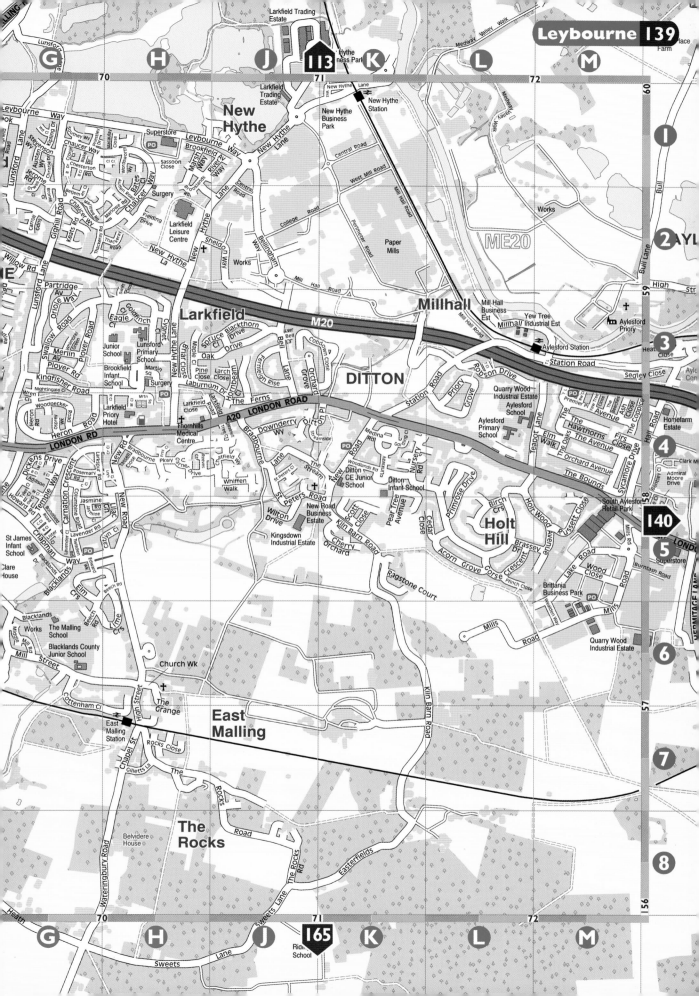

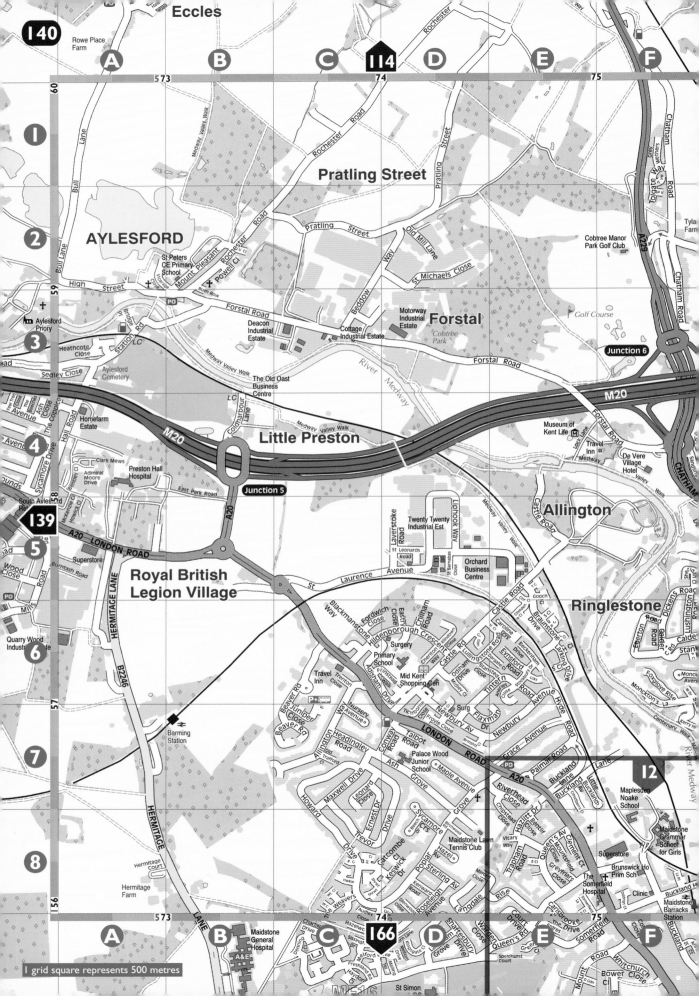

A · 579 · B · C **116** · 80 · D · Cox Street · E · 81 · F

60

Grange
Farm

1

's Way

Pilgrims Way 59

2

Mount
House

Hermitage Lane

Pollyfield

Cragged Oak

Court

Cox Lane

Stockings
Wood

3

ME14

North Downs Way

Broader Lane

Scragged Oak Road

Kent County
Showground

A249

Castle Hill

DETLING HILL

Pilgrims Wy

East Court

4

Harpole

Harple Lane

SITTINGBOURNE ROAD A249

The Street

Detling
CE Primary
School

PO

Queens Wy

Princes Wy

Pilgrims   Way

Detling

North Downs Wy

Castle Hill

58

St Martin's Cl

Works

Orchard
View

5

Horish
Wood

Hockers
Close

Thurnham

Aldington Lane

M20

Pilgrims

6

Works

Hockers Lane

Honeyhills Wood

Court
Farm

Thurnham Keep
Farm

57

7

Bea

Road

Shepherds Gate Dr

Harrow Way

Exton Gdns

Weavering Street

Wents Wd

Saddlers

Greenways

Birling House

Chapel Lane

Golf Course

Ware
Street

Bearsted
Golf Club

Water Lane

Longham
Wood

M20

8

Superstore

PO

The Hedges

Grove Gn Rd

Fitzwilliam Rd

Fulbert Rd

Peverel Drive

Ware Street

Bell Lane

Hill Brow

Mount Pleasant Drive

Ware Street

Hog Hill

Sandy Lane

Sandy Mt

Bearsted Station

Bearsted Green
Business Centre

PO

Works

56

Grove Gn La

Sparrow Rd

Weavering

St

Birling

Myrtle Cr

Fuller Close

Windmill Hts

Blakeney Close

Lane

The Elms

The Pilgrims

Roseacre

Roseacre
Junior School

Fremlins Rd

Mallings

A · B · C **168** · 80 · D · E · F

G H J **117** K L M

82 83 84 60

I

Binbury Lane

A249

Longton
Wood

Rumsted Lane

Squirrel
Wood

Rumstead Road

Rumsted
Court

Hayes Lane

Old Forge Lane

2

Farm

59

144

3

Pond
Farm

Little Budds
Farm

Rumstead Lane

Pond Farm Rd

Hucking

Friningham

Coldblow Lane

Lane

Coldharbour

Church Road

4

58

Coldblow

Oak

Road

Scragged

Coldharbour

Hucking Hill
House

Smokes
Wood

5

North Downs Way

North Downs Way

Broad Street Hill

Cobham
Manor
Farm

6

57

Whitehall

North Downs Way

242

7

Whitehall

Road

Pilgrims Way

Broad Street

156

8

Allington
Farm

Pilgrims Way

Lane

82 83 84

Snarkhurst

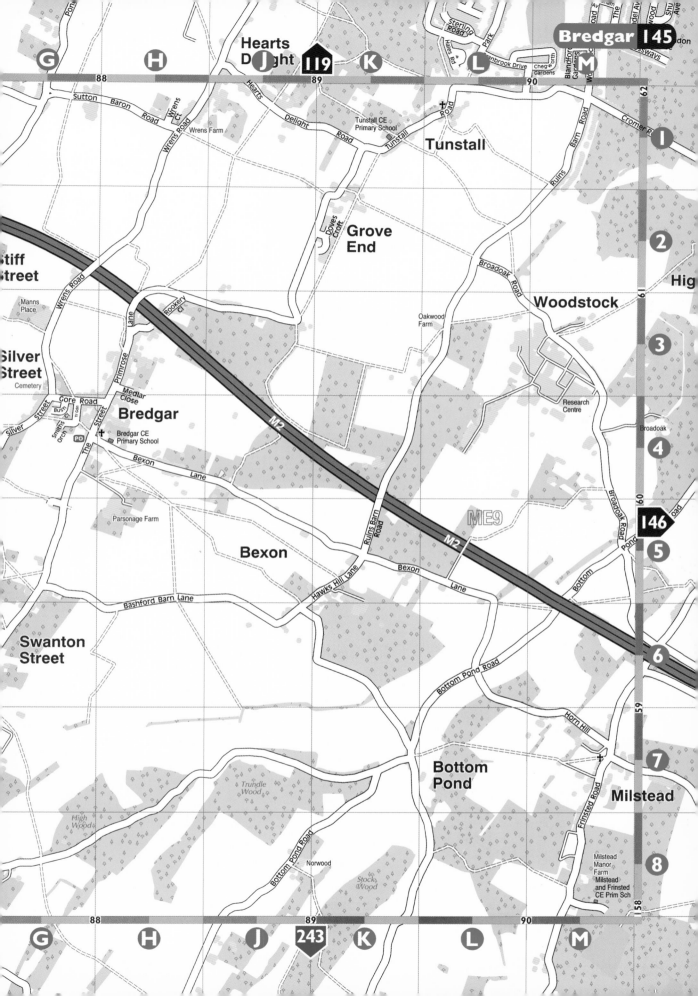

G   88   H   Hearts D**J**ght   **119**   K   89   L   90   M   62

Sterling Road

Park

Hates Rd

Penbrook Drive

Cheq worth

Blandford Gardens

Cromer R

I

Sutton Baron Road

Wrens Ct

Wrens Road

Wrens Farm

Hearts

Delight

Road

Tunstall

Road

Tunstall CE Primary School

Tunstall

Barn Road

Ruins

2

Hig

Stiff Street

Doves Croft

Grove End

Broadoak Road

Woodstock

19

3

Manns Place

Wrens Road

Lane

Rookery Cl

Oakwood Farm

Research Centre

Broadoak

4

Silver Street

Cemetery

Primrose

Medlar Close

Bredgar

Silver Street

Gore Road

Bus'h

SH'RTS Orch

PO

The Street

Bredgar CE Primary School

Parsonage Farm

Bexon

Bexon Lane

Ruins Barn Road

M2

ME9

M2

146

60

5

Broadoak Road

Pond

Bottom

Swanton Street

Bashford Barn Lane

Hawks Hill Lane

Bexon

Lane

6

59

Bottom Pond Road

Horn Hill

Frinsted Road

7

Milstead

Trundle Wood

High Wood

Norwood

Bottom Pond

Stock Wood

Bottom Pond Road

Milstead Manor Farm Milstead and Frinsted CE Prim Sch

8

58

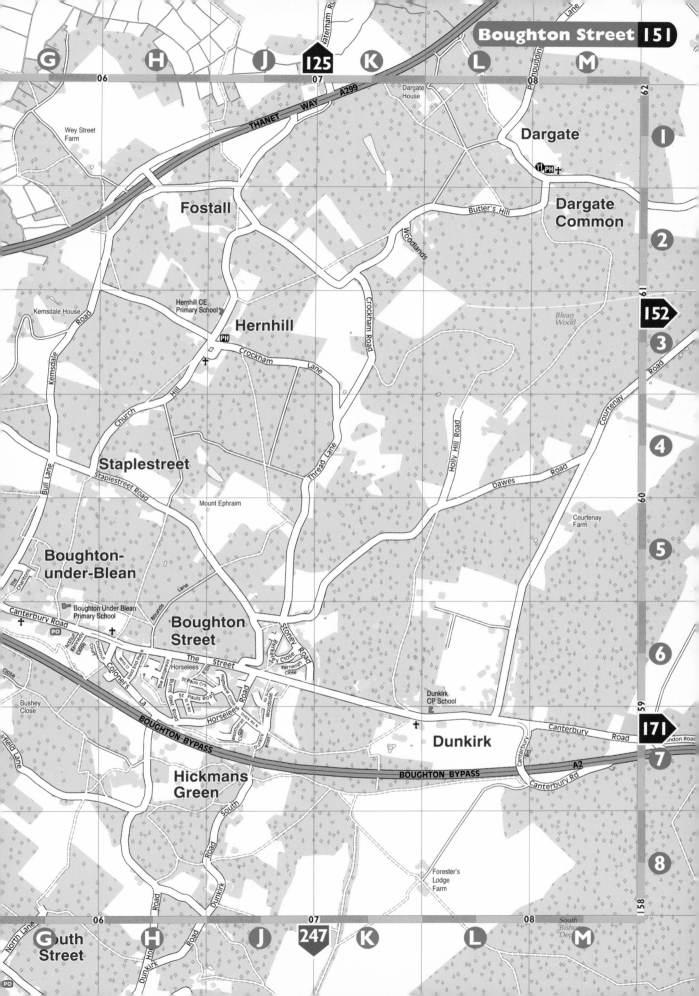

152

A B C 126 D Clapham E F

Willow Road
Royal AV
Willow Road
Wellington Street
Marlborough Road

I

609
Seasalter Lane
Harriet's Corner
Ladysm
10
CLAPHAM HILL
A290
Bogshole Lane
Court Lees

2

Thanet Way
Pilgrims Lane
Wralk Hill
Fox's Cross
Fox's Cross Hill
Fox's Cross Road
Pye Alley Lane
Pean Court Rd
PEAN HILL

A299
WAY
Barn Close
Yorkletts
Ellenden Farm
Carlton Road

125

Dargate Road

3

Highstreet Rd
Way
Highstreet
Pean Hill

4

Lamberhurst Farm
Works

5

Denstroude Lane
Denstroude Lane
Denstroude

Honey Hi

6

Dargate Road
Parsonage Farm

Denstroude Farm

151

7

Acorn Cott
Road

Courtenay

8

North Bishopden Wood

609
10
170
A B C D E F

Courtenay

I grid square represents 500 metres

154

A **B** A299 **C** 128 **D** Owl's Hatch Road **E** **F** Strode Farm
Molent 515 Owl's Hatch Road 16 Owl's Hatch Road 17
Lower Herne Road

1

West End

Bullockstone

2
Frogs
Island Farm
Lodge Field Road

127

3
Bleangate
Braggs Lane

P

4
West Blean
Wood

West Blean
House

5
New Road
Wildwood Wildlife
Park

New Road

6
Blaxland Farm

153

7
Calcott
Brambles
Farm

8
Vale Farm

162 515 16 17
A **B** Mayton Farm **C** 172 **D** **E** **F**
Mayton Lane Mayton Lane HERNE BAY ROAD A291

1 grid square represents 500 metres

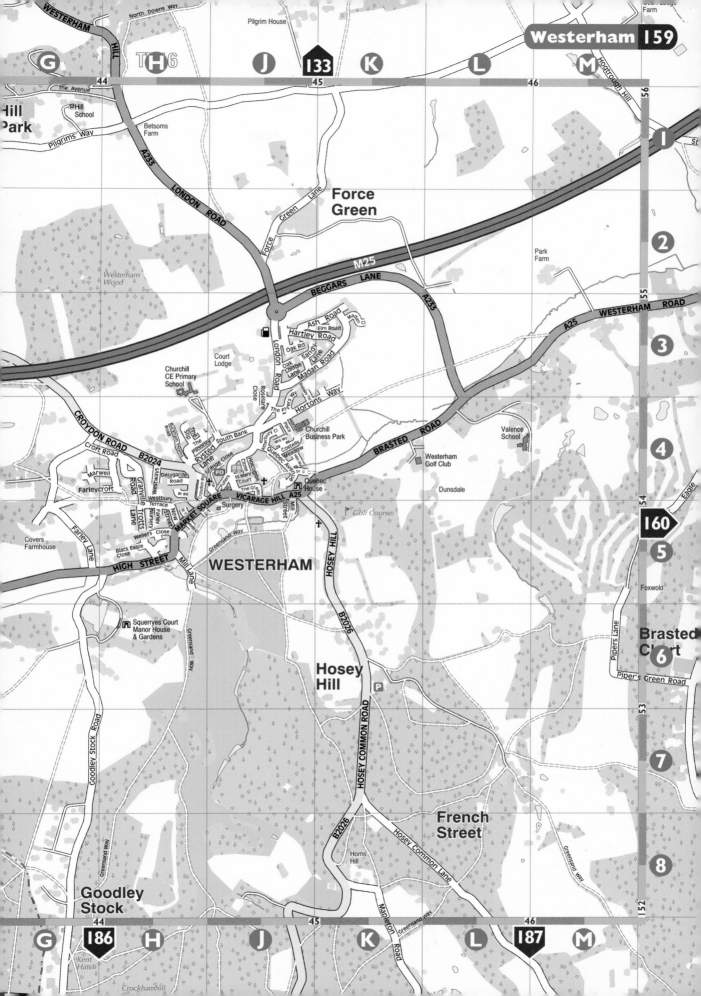

WESTERHAM HILL

G H 6 J 133 K L M

44 45 46 56

The Avenue

1

Hill Park

Hill School

Pilgrims Way

Betsoms Farm

North Downs Way

Pilgrim House

Hoatrough Hill

St

I

A233 LONDON ROAD

Force Green Lane

Force Green

2

M25

Park Farm

Westerham Wood

BEGGARS LANE

A235

55

WESTERHAM ROAD

A25

3

Ash Road

Elm Road

Madan Cl

Hartley Road

Court Lodge

London Road

Oak Rd

Sandy Lane

Madan Road

Churchill CE Primary School

Roselane Close

Oak Lodge Lane

The Flyers Wy

Hortons Way

Valence School

4

CROYDON ROAD

B2024

Croft Road

Marwell

Farleycroft

Granville Road

Trotts Lane

M&M&Wm

Delagarde Road

The Parade

The Ship

South Bank

Rysted Lane

Grange Close

Drury Cl

Wk Wy

Close

Costells Meadow

Quebec Avenue

BRASTED ROAD

Churchill Business Park

Westerham Golf Club

Dunsdale

54

5

Covers Farmhouse

Farley Lane

Westbury Terrace

New Street

Farley Nursery

Wellers Close

Black Eagle Close

Mill Street

PO

Croydon Wy

Br Rd

MARKET SQUARE

St Mary 'Court

The Green

VICARAGE HILL A25

Surgery

Greensand Way

Quebec House

Golf Course

160

Foxwold

HIGH STREET

Mill Lane

WESTERHAM

HOSEY HILL

Brasted Chart

6

Squerryes Court Manor House & Gardens

Greensand Way

Hosey Hill

B2026

Pipers Lane

Eagle

Piper's Green Road

53

7

HOSEY COMMON ROAD

P

French Street

8

B2026

Horns Hill

Hosey Common Lane

Greensand Way

Mapleton Road

52

Goodley Stock

Goodley Stock Road

Greensand Way

Kent Hatch

Crockhamhill

G 186 H J K L 187 M

44 45 46

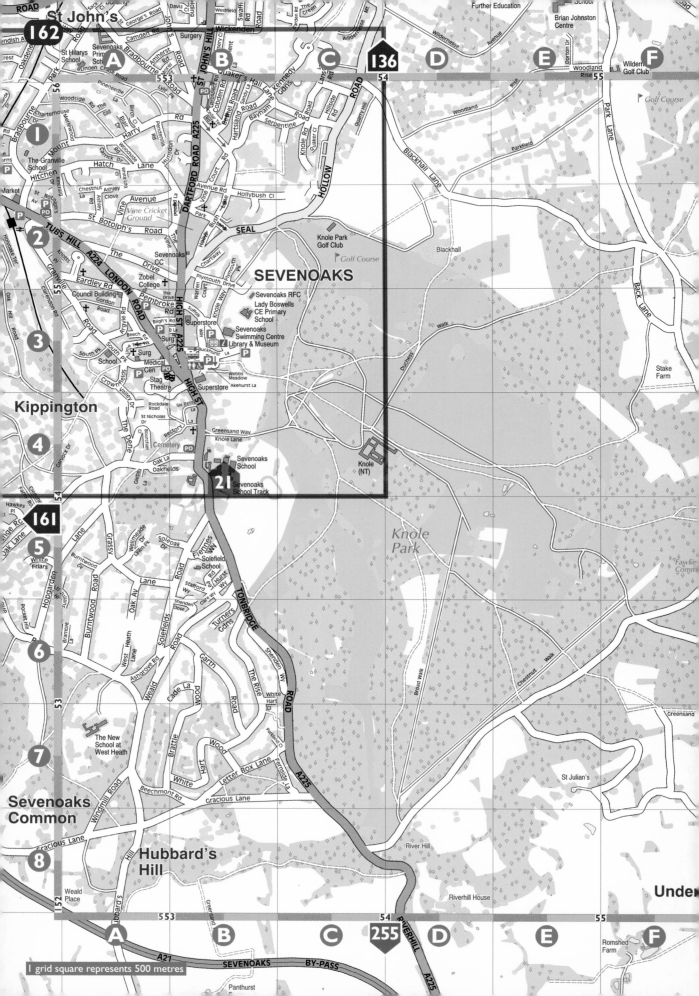

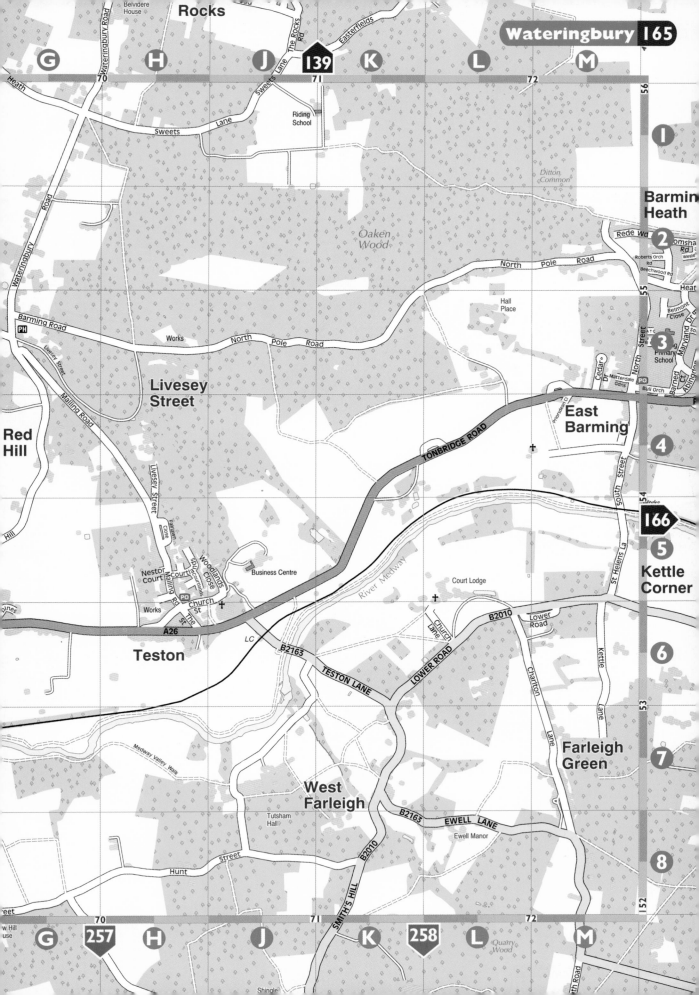

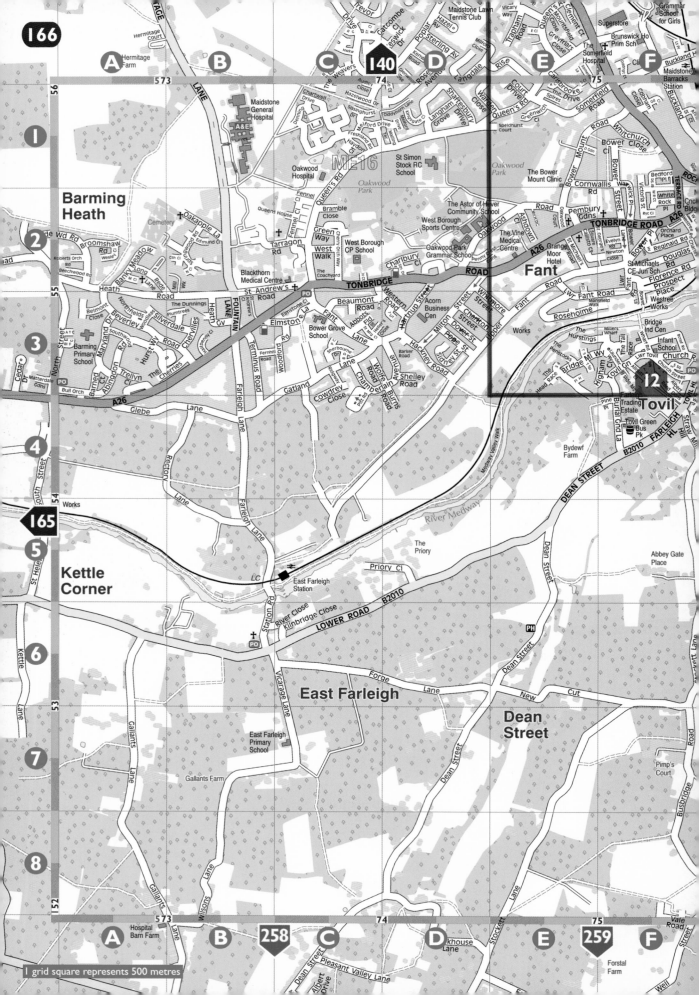

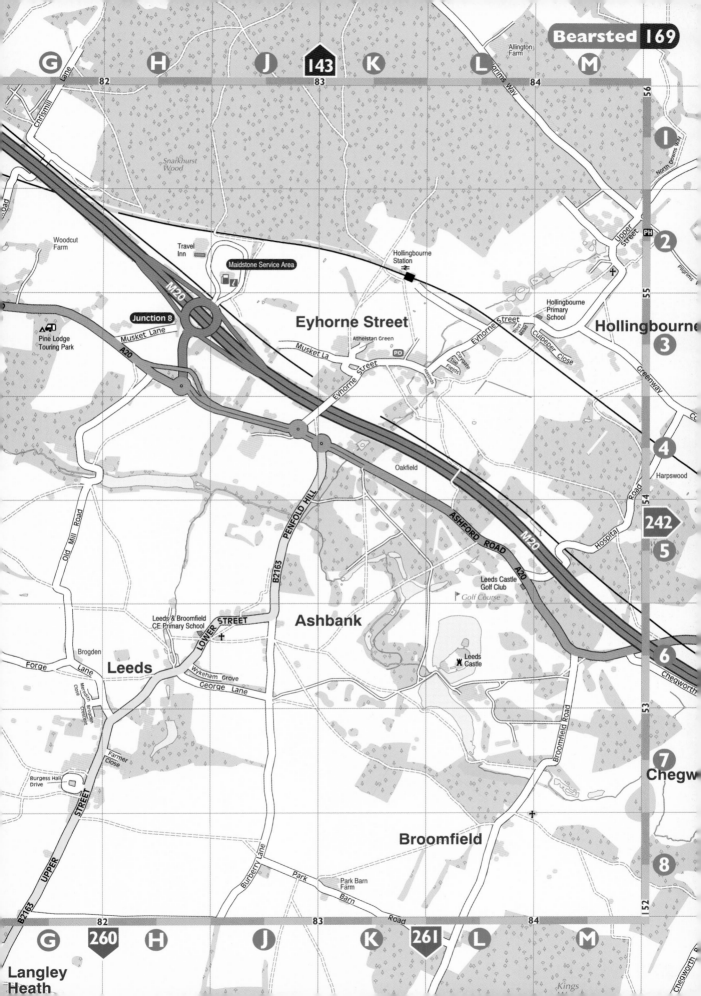

G H J 143 K L M

Allington
Farm

82 83 84 56

Chrismill
Lane

I

Snarkhurst
Wood

2 PH

Woodcut
Farm

Travel
Inn

Maidstone Service Area

Hollingbourne
Station

Upper Street

Pilgrims Way

Hollingbourne
Primary
School

Hollingbourne

55

Pine Lodge
Touring Park

M20

Junction 8

Musket Lane

A20

Eyhorne Street

Musket La

PO

Atheistan Green

Eyhorne Street

Mersham

Eyhorne Street

Hassells

Close
Mill
Fields

Culpeper Close

Greenway

3

Penfold Hill

Oakfield

ASHFORD ROAD

M20

A20

Harpswood

4

242

54

5

Old Mill Road

B2163

Leeds Castle
Golf Club

Golf Course

Hospital Road

B2163

Leeds & Broomfield
CE Primary School

LOWER STREET

Ashbank

Leeds Castle

Broomfield Road

Chegworth

6

Brogden

Forge Lane

Leeds

Wykeham Grove

George Lane

Leeds
Castle

53

Meredith
Brogden
Crescent

Farmer
Close

7

Chegw

Burgess Hall
Drive

UPPER STREET

Broomfield

B2163

Burnerry Lane

Park

Park Barn
Farm

8

152

Barn

Road

82 83 84

G 260 H J K 261 L M

Langley
Heath

Kings

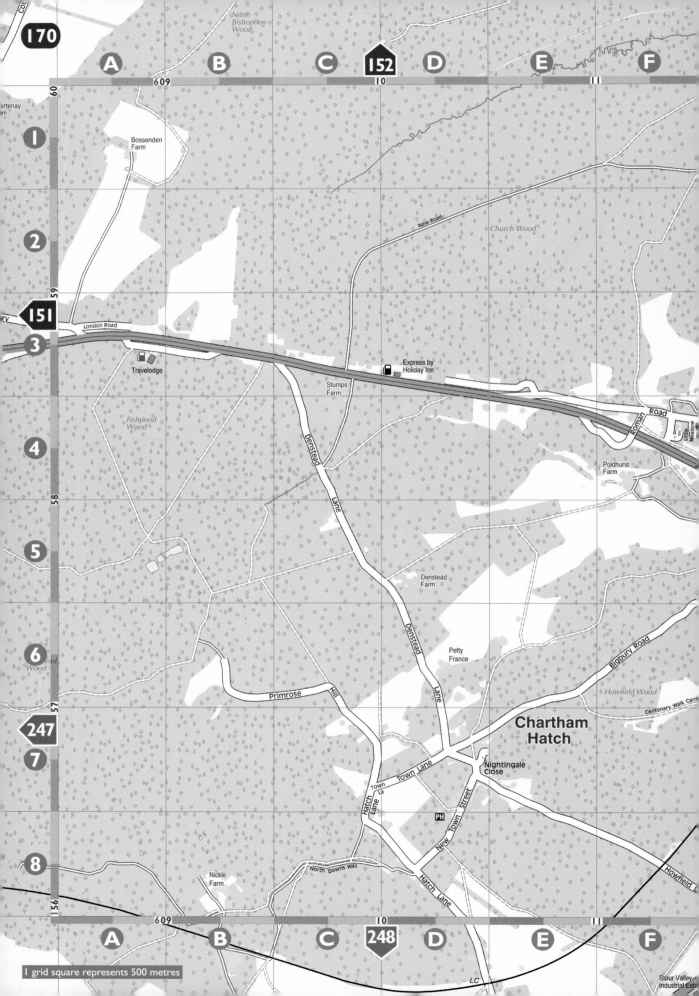

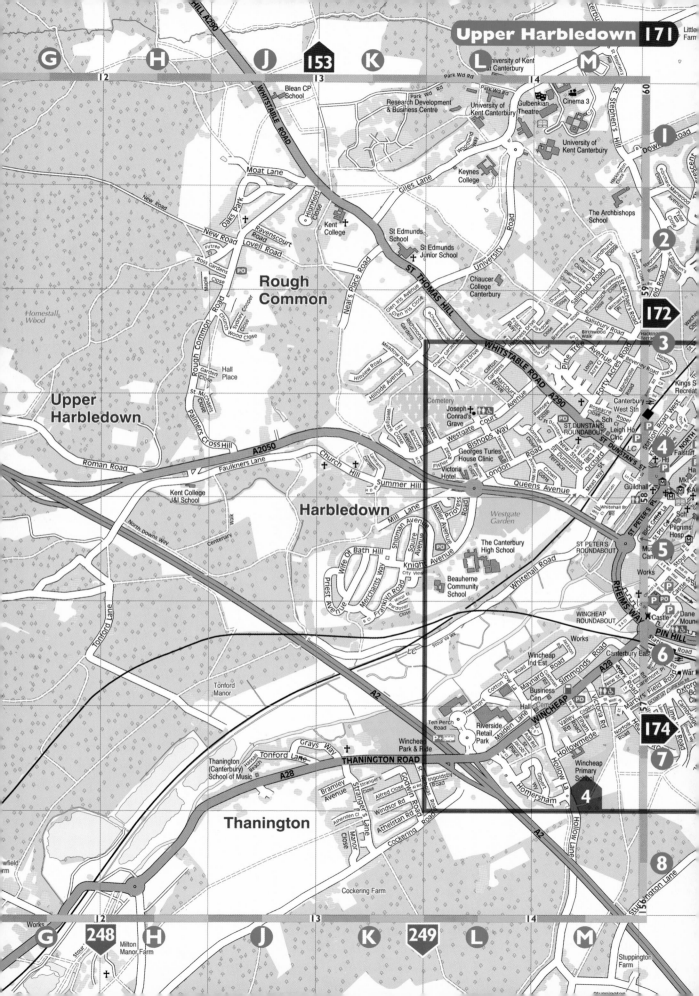

G H J **153** K L M

12 13 14 **60**

I

Little
Farm

University of Kent
at Canterbury

Park Wd Rd

Park Wd Rd

Research Development
& Business Centre

University of
Kent Canterbury

Gulbenkian
Theatre

Cinema 3

St Stephen's Hill

2

Moat Lane

Giles Lane

Keynes
College

University of
Kent Canterbury

The Archbishops
School

Tyler
Close

Oaks Park

Highfield Close

Kent
College

St Edmunds
School

St Edmunds
Junior School

Woodland Way

Downs Road

172

New Road

Ravenscourt
Road

Lovell Road

Chaucer
College
Canterbury

Lyndhurst
Close

Cadnam
Close

Amberham
Close

Ringwood
Close

St Michael's Road

59

58

3

New Road

Firtree

Ross Gardens

PO

**Rough
Common**

Glen Iris Avenue

Glen Iris Close

Richmond
Gardens

Cherry Avenue

Cherry Close

Cherry Garden Rd

Cherry Drive

Clifton
Gardens

Salisbury Road

Birchwood
Walk

Hacking Terrace

Kings S
Recreat

**Upper
Harbledown**

Rough Common Road

Church Wood Close

Sydney Cooper
Close

Garden Close

Hall
Place

St Michaels Close

Palmers Cross Hill

Hillview Road

Meadow Road

Hillside Avenue

Westgate Close

St Thomas Hill

Harcourt
Drive

Ramsey
Close

Rosemary
Close

Canterbury
West Stn

Roper
Rd

Leigh Ho
Clinic

**ST DUNSTAN'S
ROUNDABOUT**

A290

Whitstable Road

Homestall
Wood

Cemetery

Joseph
Conrad's
Grave

ST DUNSTAN'S

Station Road West

Falstaf

4

Roman Road

A2050

Faulkners Lane

Church Hill

Summer Hill

Westgate
Court

Bishops
Way

Georges Turles
House Clinic

Victoria
Hotel

London Road

New Street

St Dunstan's Terrace

Crown
Gdns

Orchard

Guildhall

Mkt

Sch

Pilgrims
Hosp

North Downs Way

Kent College
J&I School

Walk

Centenary

Church Hill

Mill Lane

Shipman Avenue

Squire Avenue

Priory Road

Millers Road

PO

Harbledown

Queens Avenue

**Westgate
Garden**

Westgate Br

Whitewall Br

**ST PETER'S
ROUNDABOUT**

St Peter's Pl

Works

5

Tonford Lane

Wife of Bath Hill

Merchants Way

Knight Avenue

City View

Franklyn Road

Minor Cl

Pardoner
Close

Priest Avenue

**The Canterbury
High School**

Beauherne
Community
School

Whitehall Road

Rheims Way

**WINCHEAP
ROUNDABOUT**

Castle

Dane
Moun

PIN HILL

Castle

6

Stour Va Wk

LC

Wincheap
Ind Est

Works

Simmonds Road

WINCHEAP

A28

Maynard Rd

Business
Cen

New St

Jackson
Road

Claremont Pl

Canterbury East

Road

Martyrs Field Road

Oxford

Camb

War

Tonford
Manor

A2

Ten Perch
Road

Riverside
Retail Park

Hall Rd

Malden Ave

Victoria Rd

Norfolk
Rd

Valley
Road

Coates
Rd

Cotton Rd

Hollowmede

Hollow La

Homersham

Hollow Lane

Limp
Road

174

7

Grays Way

Tonford Lane

THANINGTON ROAD

Wincheap
Park & Ride

P

Godwin Road

Ingoldsby Road

Manor Road

Wincheap
Primary
School

4

Thanington
(Canterbury)
School of Music

Hascall
Reach

Bramley
Avenue

Stranger's
Close

A28

Strangers Lane

Alfred Close

Windsor Rd

Athelstan Rd

Ashenden Cl

Manor
Close

Godwin Road

Cockering Road

A2

Stuppington Lane

Thanington

8

Cockering Farm

wfield
rm

Works

Milton Manor
Farm

Stuppington
Farm

G **248** H J K **249** L M

12 13 14

G H J **173** K L M

18 19 20 58

Canterbury
Christ Church
College

Polo Farm
Sports Club

JRNE ROAD CANTERBURY ROAD

A257 CANTERBURY ROAD THE HILL HIGH

St Vincent's
Close The Edge
Court Me
Lit
Pr

I

Rose Acre Road
Ewing Road
Evenhill Road
nn Rd

Littlebourne

The Hoath
Farm

2

57

Woolton Farm

3

Howletts
Wild Animal
Park

**Bekesbourne
Hill**

Bekesbourne Lane

4

Oakleigh Lane

Bekesbourne

Hode
Farm

North Downs Way

Bekesbourne Station

School Lane

56

Cranmer
Close
Birrons
Road
Station Road

251

5

School Lane

Bekesbourne

Patrixbourne

Birrons Hill

The Street

St Mary's Road

Chalkpit Hill

Aerodrome Rd
De
Havillands

6

Hop
Farm

Adisham Rd

Adisham Road

Bekesbourne
Road

55

Elham Valley Way

Patrixbourne Road

Keeper's Hill

7

Bridge &
Patrixbourne
CE Prim Sch

Corynoham Lane

Station Road

High Street

Pett Hill

Dering
Close
Filmer
Road

PO

Bridge

Churchill
Close

Union Road

Western
Avenue

Mill Lane

Brewery
Lane

Meadow Close

North Downs Way

Shepard's
Close

Shepherd's Close

8

154

Bridge Place
Country

Bridge Hill

Beech Hill

Bridge Down

Higham Lane

Elham Valley Way

G H J **250** K L M

18 19 20

G H J K L M

I
2
3
4
5
6
7
8

Palm Bay

Foreness Point

Botany Bay

Kingsgate Bay

NORTH FORELAND

...AY AVENUE

Palm Bay County Primary School

Springfield Road

Knockholt Road

Ridings

Marine Drive

The Fayreness Hotel

Staplehurst Gdns

Summerfield Road

Magnolia Avenue

Saltwood Gardens

Botany Road

Second Av

Avenue

Avenue

Kingsgate

Northdown

Regent Fitzroy

Percy Avenue

First Avenue

Fitzroy Avenue

Capel Cl

WHITENESS ROAD

Oakridge

KINGSGATE BAY ROAD

JOSS GAP ROAD

Thanet Coastal Path

GEORGE HILL ROAD

B2052

Whiteness Green

Convent

Golf Course

MILLMEAD ROAD

GREEN LANE

NORTHDOWN PK RD

St Michael Av

George Hill Road

Rosetower Court

North Foreland Golf Club

Avenue

North Foreland Road

Crescent Rd

B2053

Reading Street Road

Grafton Road

Lerryn Gdns

Convent

Reading Street

Elmwood Avenue

NORTH FORELAND ROAD

Victoria Avenue

Albert Road

Camden Road

Astor Road

Reading St

Elmwood Close

Cliff Road

Whitfield Avenue

PO

Balliol Road

Churchfields

Trinity Sq

PO

The Paddocks

B2052

Foster's Av

Linley Road

Coronation Close

Cedar Close

The Oaks

Fig Tree Road

Laking Avenue

Guy Close

Francis Road

Stone House

Dane Valley Road

NORTHDOWN HILL

Hugin Avenue

Westover Gdns

Callis Grange Nurs & Infant Sch

St. Peters CE Junior School

Grange Road

Lanthorne Road

The Foreland School

Bishop's Av

Castle Avenue

Park Road

Stone Bay School

Oakwood Trading Estate

WESTOVER ROAD

Cecilia Grove

Norman Road

Thanet Wanderers RUFC

Surgery

Rhodes Gardens

Stanley

Sea View Road

Queen's Avenue

King's Avenue

Knight's Av

CT10

CHURCH ST

ALBION ROAD

Works

Bairdsley Close

Hiller Close

Lindenthorpe Road

Maxton

Castle Eastern

Thanet Coastal Path

St Peters

Church Street

Victoria Road

High St

St Josephs School

St Peter's Court

Mill Field

Kendal Rise

Lauriston Mount

Bradstow Way

Cumberland Av

Dickens Road

Rectory Rd

Esplanade

ROAD

A256

A255

Green Lane

Wayne Close

Sowell St

Ethel Road

Walmsley Road

Selwyn

Upton Road

Percy Road

St. Peter's Pk RD

BROADSTAIRS

Broadstairs Station

Carlton

Nelson Pl

Broadstairs Youth & Leisure Centre

Royal Albion Hotel

Dickens House Mus

Bleak House Dickens Maritime Smuggling Muse

BROADSTAIRS ROAD

THE B39

Health Cen

HIGH STREET

G H J **183** K L M

Dane Court Grammar School

The Charles Dickens High School

Upt...

Upton Junior School

St. Mildreds Infant

Royal Close

Lnatt Close

Vale Road

Surgery

Edge End Road

Pierremont Avenue

Stephen Close

Surgery

High Street

Thanet Road

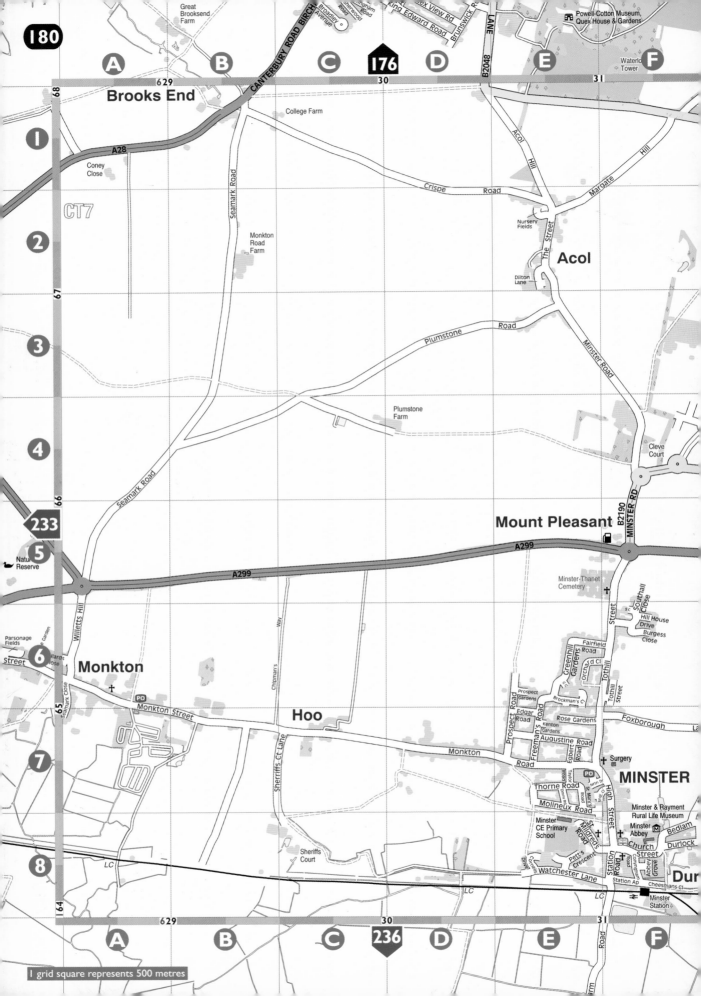

G
Two Chimneys
Caravan Park
Two Chimneys
Shottendane
32
H
J
177
K
L
M
68

Woodchurch Road
Park Road
Woodchurch
Flete Road

Westgate Avenue

I
Vincent Farm
Vincent
Flete
Farm

Queendown Road
Castle Mayne
Avenue
Trafalgar
Road
St Margarets
Road

B2050

2
67

Manston Road

Cheeseman's
Farm
MANSTON ROAD

3
Manston Caravan
& Camping Park

Works
Avenue
Grange Lane

Alland
Grange
Esmonde Dr
Beaumont Cl
RAF Manston
History Museum
B2050

Alland

Bell-Davies
Drive

4
Work

B2190

Manston
Street
Manston Court Road
Kent
International
Airport

66
182
Farm
5

A299

A299

Wayborough Road
Laundry Road
CT12
Way
Ivy Cottage Hill
Way Hill
Way Hill
Thorne Hill

6
King A
Road
Arundel
Road
A299
65
Cliff View Road
Cliff
Road
Foads Hill
Sea View Road

The Lanes
Grinsell Hill
Thorne
Farm

7
LC

Cli
End

Sevenscore
Cottington
St Augustine's
Golf Club
Lavender La
Cottington Road
Earlsmead
Crescent
Old Hall
Beech Grove
Nicholas
Drive

8
PO
Foads

ck
LC
LC
St Augustines
Cross
Oakland
Court
Oakland
Gardens
Cliffs End Grove

G
236
H
J
K
237
L
M
32
33
34
Golf Course

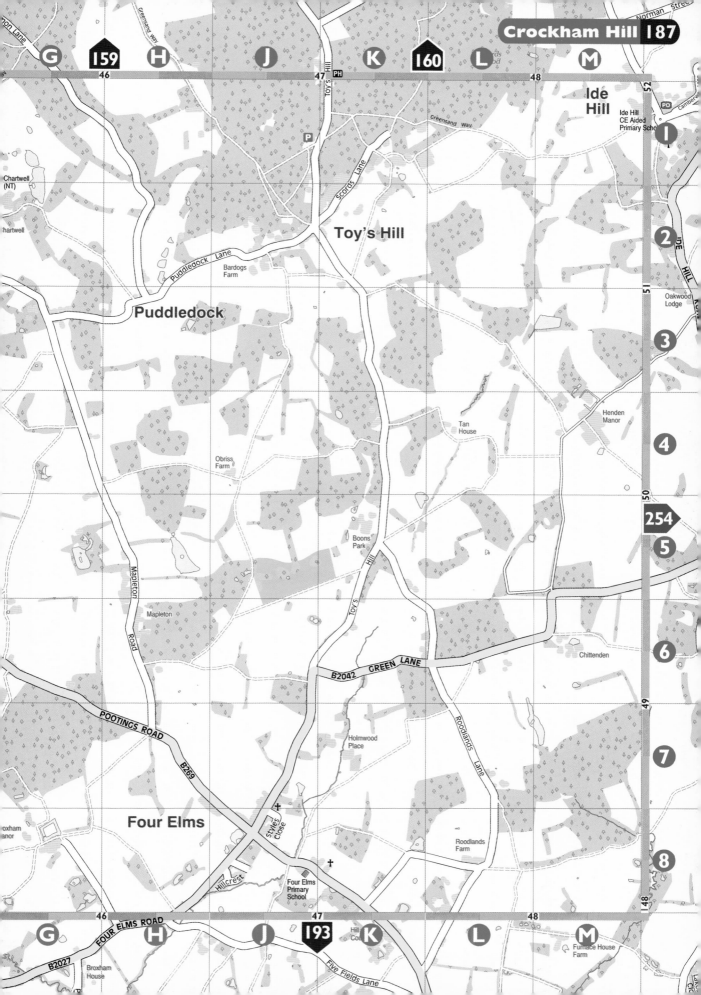

G **159** H J K **160** L M

46 47 PH 48 52

Ide Hill

I

Ide Hill
CE Aided
Primary Scho

Chartwell
(NT)

hartwell

51

Oakwood
Lodge

2

3

Puddledock Lane

Bardogs
Farm

Toy's Hill

Greensand Way

Scords Lane

Henden
Manor

4

Puddledock

Tan
House

50

254

Obriss
Farm

Boons
Park

5

Mapleton Road

Mapleton

Toy's Hill

Chittenden

6

B2042 GREEN LANE

Roodlands Lane

49

POOTINGS ROAD

Holmwood
Place

7

B269

Four Elms

Styles Close

Roodlands
Farm

oxham
anor

Hillcrest

Four Elms Primary
School

8

148

G H J **193** K L M

46 47 48

FOUR ELMS ROAD

B2027

Broxham
House

ve Fields Lane

Furnace House
Farm

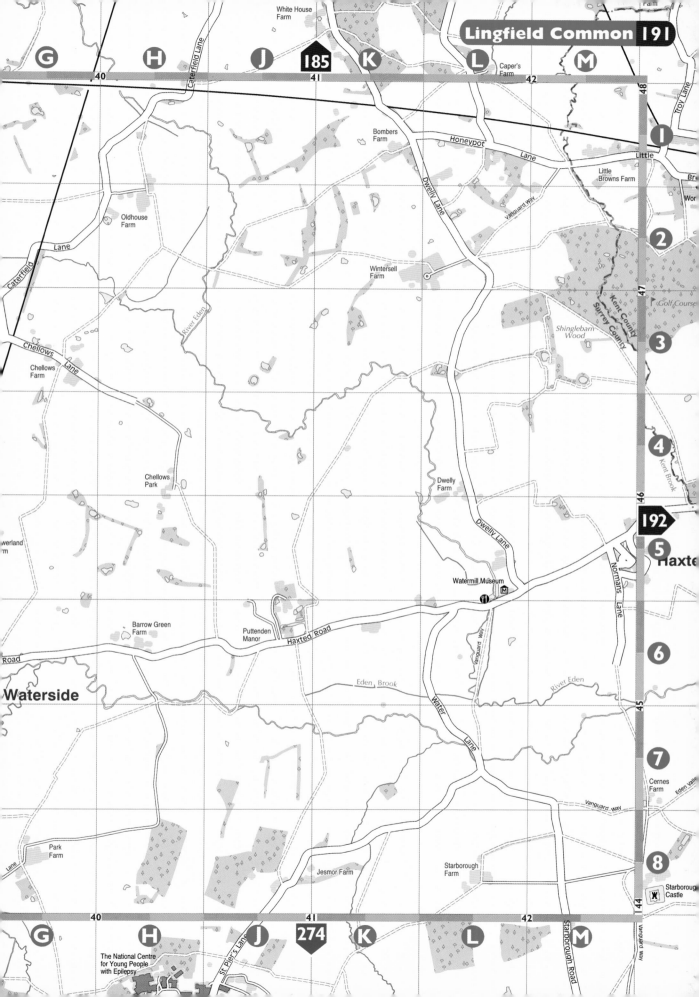

G H J K L M

185

White House Farm

Bombers Farm

Honeypot Lane

Caper's Farm

Little

Little Browns Farm

Bre

Wor

I

2

Caterfield Lane

Oldhouse Farm

Dwelly Lane

Vanguard Way

Kent County Surrey County

Golf Course

3

Caterfield Lane

Lane

River Eden

Wintersell Farm

Shinglebarn Wood

4

Chellows Lane

Chellows Farm

Dwelly Farm

Kent Brook

192

5 Haxte

Chellows Park

Dwelly Lane

Normans Lane

werland m

Watermill Museum

6

Barrow Green Farm

Puttenden Manor

Haxted Road

Vanguard Way

River Eden

Road

Eden Brook

Water

Waterside

Lane

7

Cernes Farm

Vanguard Way

Eden valle

Park Farm

8

Lane

Jesmor Farm

Starborough Farm

Starborough Castle

144

G H J K L M

274

The National Centre for Young People with Epilepsy

St Piers Lane

Starborough Road

Vanguard Way

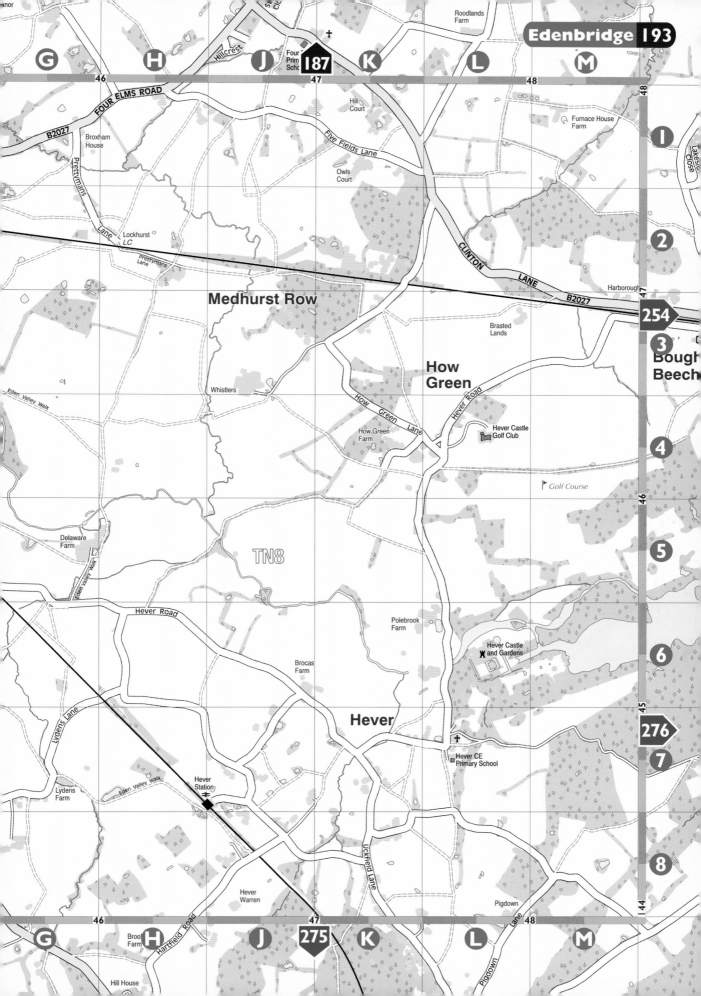

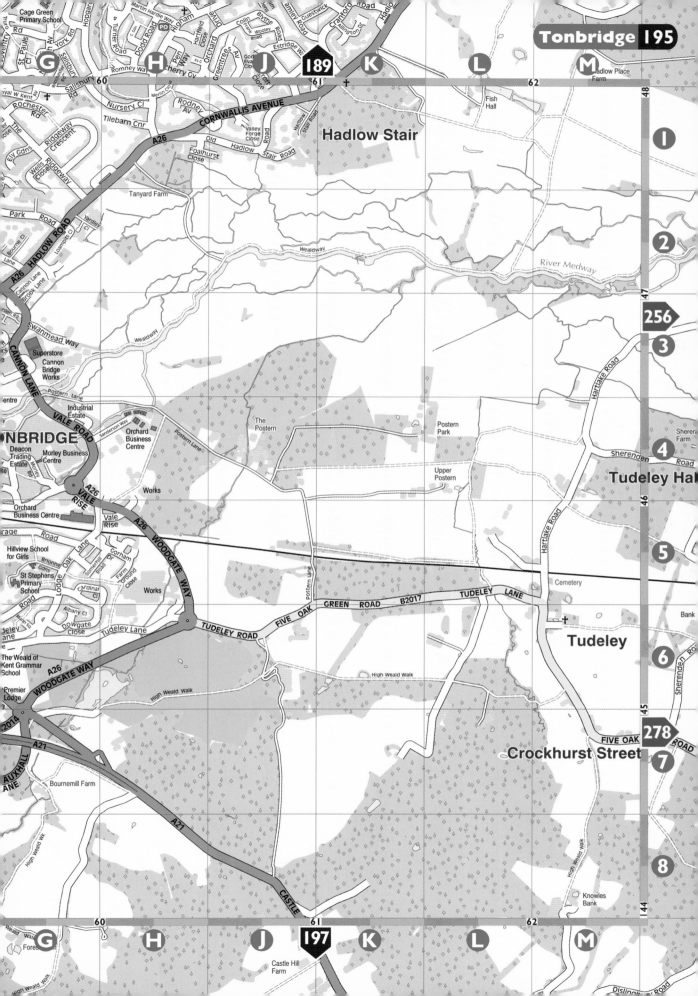

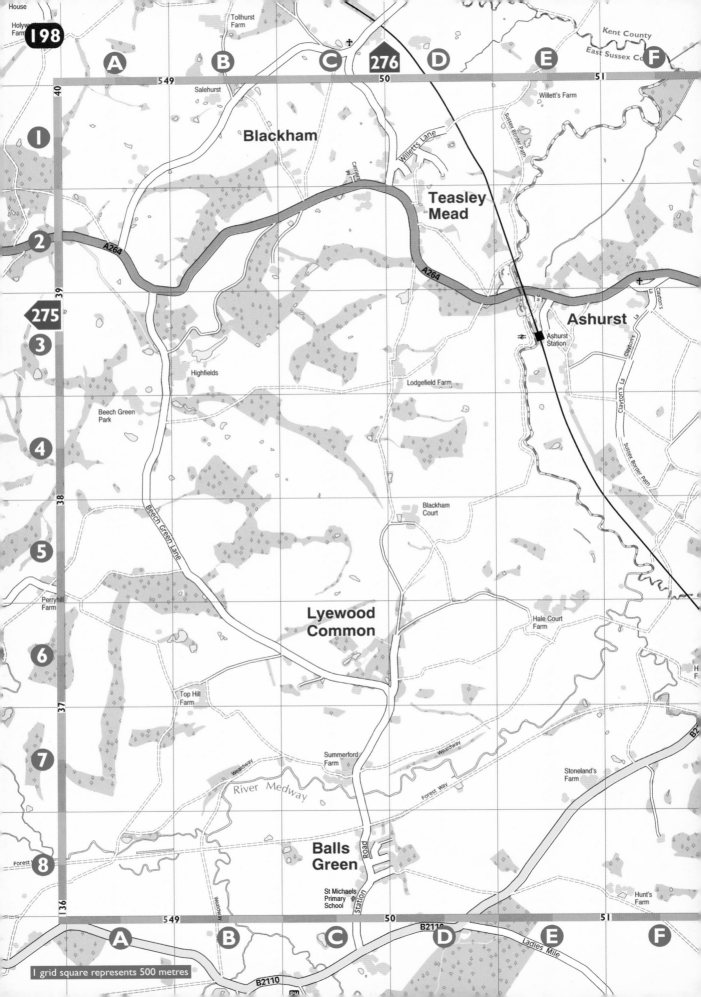

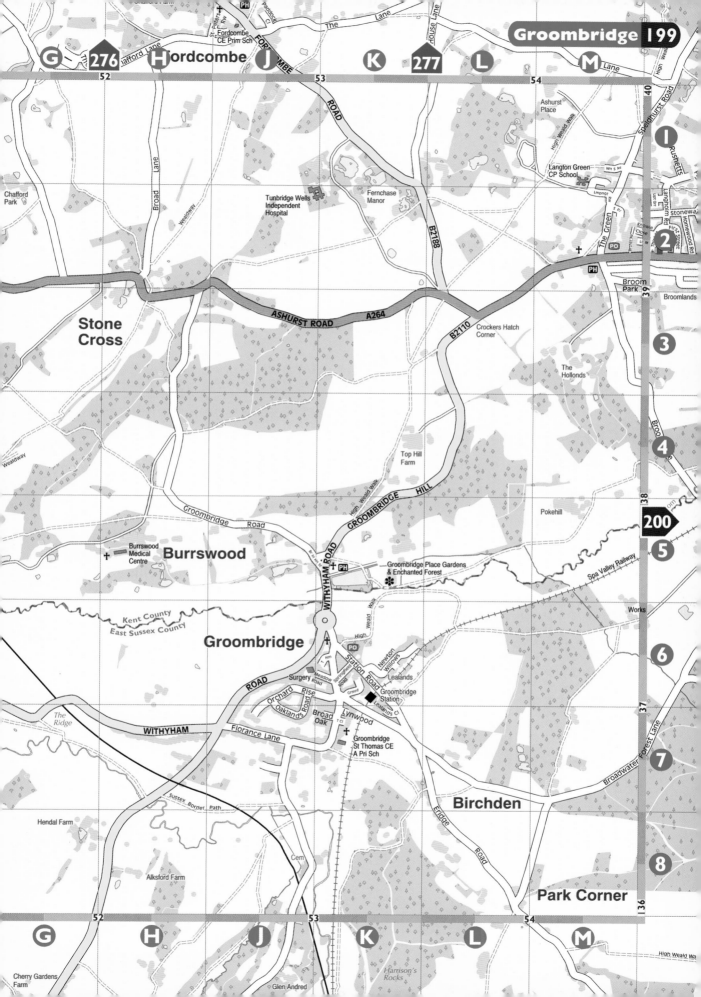

A   B   277   C   D   E   196   F

Green

Bishops Down Primary School

Rose Hill School

Langton Green

Cemetery

Southwood Road

Westwood Road

Tuxford Road

Shirley Gdns

Langton Green

Rusthall Medical Centre

St Pauls CE Infant School

Junior School

Rusthall

Denny Bottom

Golf Course

The Spa Hotel

Tunbridge Wells Golf Club

A264 LANGTON ROAD

BISHOP'S D

Broom Park

Broomlands

LANGTON ROAD A264

Holmewood Ridge

Barrow Lane

Hither Chantlers

Rusthall Home

Rusthall Farm

Nevill Ridge

Nevill Court

Nevill Park

The Crossway

Hunge

Hungershall

Cabbage Stalk Lane

Holmewood House School

High Rocks Lane

Park Close

Wyevale Garden Centre

High Weald Walk

Broom Lane

High Rocks Station

High Rocks

Kent County
East Sussex County

Summervale Road

Ropers Gate

Ramslye

Surgery

199

River Grom

Spa Valley Railway

Friezland Rd

Waterdown Road

St Marks CE Primary School

Saunders Road

Eastlands Rd

Ramslye

Lodge Lane

Broadwater Forest

Strawberry Hill

Kentish Gardens

Broadwater

Strawberry Close

Works

Broadwater Forest Lane

Broadwater Forest Lane

Spratsbrook Farm

Hargate Forest

Broadwater Forest Lane

The Warren

A26

Bunny

A   B   C   D   E   F

Warren Farm

High Weald Walk

Warren Farm

Eridge Park

1 grid square represents 500 metres

I grid square represents 500 metres

Sandwich Bay

G H J 237 K L M

36 37 38

1
2
3
4
5
6
7
8

58
57
56
55
154

Sandwich Bay Estate

Guilford Road
King's Avenue
North Road
Princes Drive
Av
Waldershare
Shawdon Avenue
Francis Avenue
Cambridge Avenue

White Cliffs Country Trail

Cliffs Country Trail

Mary Bax's Stone

PH

Golf Course

Sandhills

Redhouse

Wall

Royal Cinque Ports Golf Club

Golf Road

Canute Rd

S Cl

Ethelbert Road

Godwyn

The Sandown

Deal Squash Racket Club

Harold Rd

College Road

The Marina Road

G H J 209 K L M

36 37 38

Westernhout Close
Becket Cl
Courtenay Rd
Pavilion
Lanfranc Rd
Lnks Rd
Sydcot
King Edward
Bethany
College
Rackeb
Cliff

A **West B**
Street

Finglesham

C 206 D E F

Foulmead
Farm

54 53 34 A258 35

The
Street

Burgess
Green
Bridge Hl

I

Marley
Lane

Marley

LONDON ROAD

Cottington Court
Farm

2

North
Way

Broad Lane

North Circular Rd

Betteshanger
Colliery

253

3

Sholden
Downs

White Cliffs Country Trail

Northbourne
Court

Deal Road

Northbourne CE
Primary School

4

The
Grove

The Street

Coldharbour

5

Northbourne Northbourne Road

CT14

Mill Lane

Crixson Grove

Sholden
Bank

Minters
Industrial
Est

Mongeham
Church Close

Ashton
Close

Cherry Lane

6

White Cliffs Country Trail

Willow Road

**Great
Mongeham**

Pixwell La

273

7

Little Mongeham

Stoneheap
Farm

Mongeham Road

Manties Hill

Church Lane

8

Stoneheap Road

Northbourne Road

633 34 35

A B C 210 D Sutton Lane E F

White Cliffs Country Trail

The Ripple
School

Sunnyside Close

Ripple

Ripple Vale
School

Sutton Vale
House

A   B   C   **272**   D   E   F

627   28   29

Coldred Hill

A2

Singledge Lane

Singledge

I
Church Lane
✝ Lydden
Stonehall Broadacre
Lydden CP School
The Close
Stonehall Road
Stonehall
Temple Farm

anterbury Road
Road

Bosney Banks

London Road

Singledge Lane

Green La

2
45

3
Little Watersend
Woodville
Works
Side Temple Close
Temple Lane
The Green

4
44
Lord's Wood
Great Watersend
London Road
Riverside
Watersend
Brookside
PO
Temperly Road
M1 St
Temple Ewell CE Primary School
Temple Side
Target Firs
Wellington Rd
Temple Lane
Lower Ewell Road
The Avenue
Park Rd
Temple Ewell
Malvern Meadow
Malvern Close
Egerton Road
Woodside Close
Laburnum

5
The Minnis
Kearsney
Bushy Ruff House
Kearsney Station
Kearsney Abbey
Alkham Road
Abbey Road
Pavilion Meadow
Chisnall Road
Surgery
London Road
Surgery

6
43
Alkham Road
Chilton Avenue
Alkham Valley Road
Chilton Farm
Coxhill Crescent
Sanctuary Close
Lower Road
River Street
Chilton Way
Coxhill Gardens
River CP School
PO
Minnis Lane
Meadway
Dove Lea Gardens
Common Lane
Valley Road
Berea
Lewisham
Luckhurst
River

7
Wolverton
Badgers Rise
Cowper Road
Hazeldown Close
Westtoan Close
Wingrove Hill
Orchard Drive
The Ridgeway
Woodland Close
Crabble
Deanwood Road
Crabble

8
42
Minnis Lane
Abbey Road
Abbey Road
Homestone Road
Holm
ombe

627   28   29

A   B   C   **216**   D   E   F

St Radigund's Abbey

Mount Ararat

1 grid square represents 500 metres

East
Langdon

Martin
Mill

210

A B C D E F

1

2

3

4

213

5

6

7

8

9

Hawthorn Farm
Caravan Park

Solton Manor
Farm

West
Cliffe

Wallett's
Court
Wallett's Court Country
House Hotel

St M
at Cl

Dover Road

Pond Lane

Dover Road

Station Road

Nelson Park Ro

Hardy

Langdon Road

East Langdon Road

The Street

Bambye Close

The Lane

Chance Meadow

Prescott Close

Hangman's Lane

A258

PH

Bere Farm

Wanstor
Farm

Upper Road

Duke of York
School

A2

PO

Travel
Inn

Burgoyne Heights

Gibraltar
Square

Tana
Close

Dunkirk
Square

Lucknow
Close

Namur
Place

Anzio
Crs

Alamein
Close

Cassino
Square

Kohima
Place

Old Park
Barracks
(MOD)

Fort Burgoyne Road

A258

JUBILEE WAY

Saxon Shore Way

Fan
Bay

9

Edinburgh Hill

Langdon Cliffs
Visitor Centre
& Viewpoint (NT)

Saxon Shore Way

Langdon
Bay

Upper Road

HILL ROAD

Upper Road

Bleriot
Memorial

Constable
Road

A2

A258

Keep

St M
Church

Pharos

The Fan

Back Road (East)

Camber Way

Dane
Exit

Passenger Terminal
Building

Victoria Park

Western Heights
Tunnels

Old St James

Elizabeth Rd

Secret Wartime
Tunnels

1 grid square represents 500 metres

A B C D E F

G H J **211** K L M

36 37 38

46

1

45

2

3

44

4

5

43

6

42

7

8

G H J K L M

36 37 38

Seymour
Road

East Valley
Farm

Collingwood Road

Nelson Park Rd

Boyle's Rd

Collingwood Road

Fleet Road

Norway Road

Drove

Hog's
Bush

Bockhill
Farm

The Droveway

Kingsdown Road

The Freedown

The Avenue

Townsend Farm Road

Chapel Lane

PO

PH

High St

Minfield

St Margaret's
Ce

Well La

Vicarage
Road

St georges
Place

Glebe
C

Langdon C

Reach
Close

Roman
Way

Reach Close

Reach Close

Sea Street

Royston
Gardens

Townside

St Margarets at
Cliffe Prim Sch

Portal House
School

Medical Cen

Churchill
Close

Convent
Close

Kenilworth
Close

Norman
Road

The Rise

The Droveway

Salisbury
Road

Granville Road

Cheriton Road

Victoria Avenue

Chesham Road

Hotel Road

Granville Road

Saxon Shore Way

St Margaret's
Bay

Bay Hill

St Margaret's Road

Foreland Road

The Crescent

Beach Road

The Pines
Garden

The Bay
Museum

Reach Court
Farm

Lighthouse Road

Goodwin Road

Sea View Road

The Front

Shore Way

Saxon

South Foreland
Lighthouse (NT)

South
Foreland

Saxon Shore Way

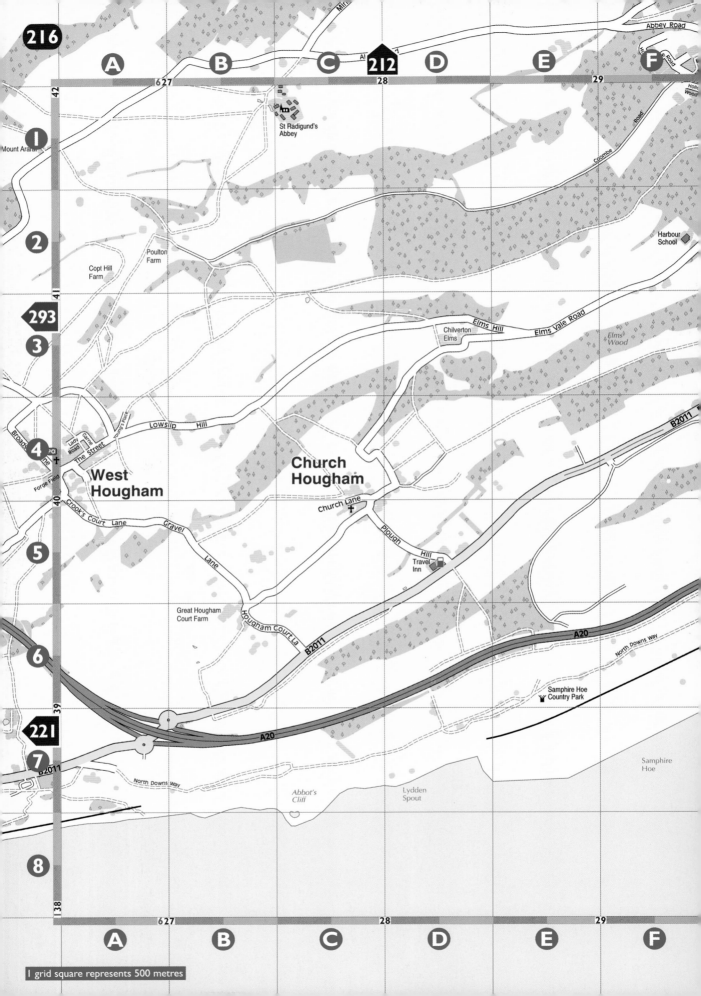

A   B   C   212   D   E   F

627   28   29

Abbey Road

Holl— Wood

Coombe Road

B2011

1

Mount Ararat

St Radigund's Abbey

Harbour School

2

Poulton Farm

Copt Hill Farm

293

3

Chilverton Elms

Elms Hill Elms Vale Road

Elms Wood

Lowslip Hill

Broads

Young's Place

The Street

Lady Road

Game

4

Forge Field

West Hougham

Church Hougham

Church Lane

Crook's Court Lane

Gravel

Plough

5

Lane

Hill Travel Inn

Great Hougham Court Farm

Hougham Court La

B2011

6

A20

North Downs Way

Samphire Hoe Country Park

221

A20

7

B2011

North Downs Way

Samphire Hoe

Abbot's Cliff

Lydden Spout

8

627   28   29

A   B   C   D   E   F

I grid square represents 500 metres

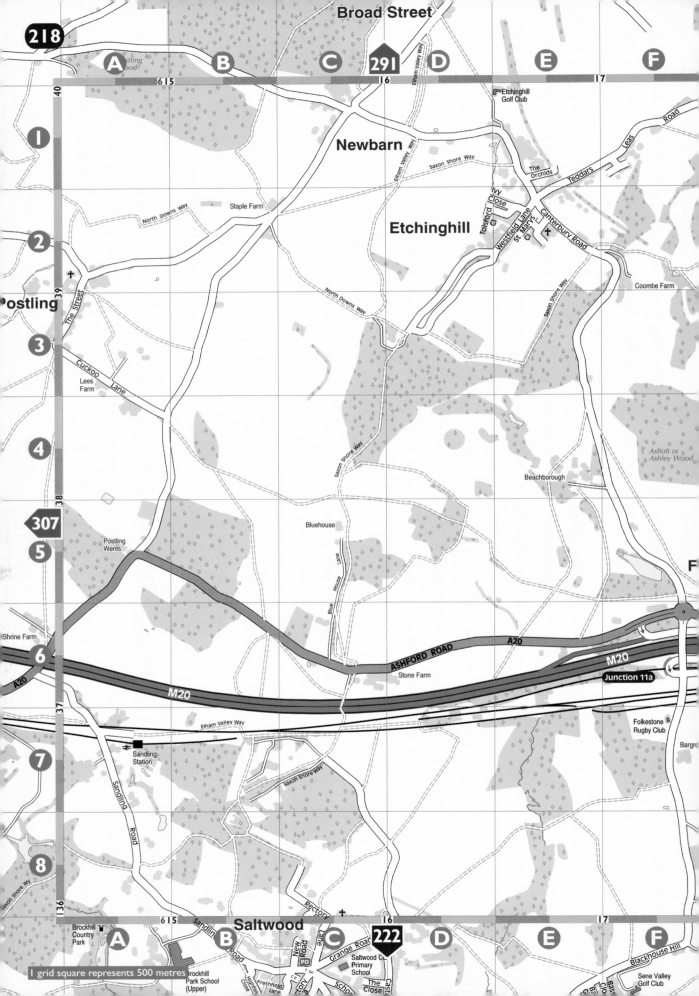

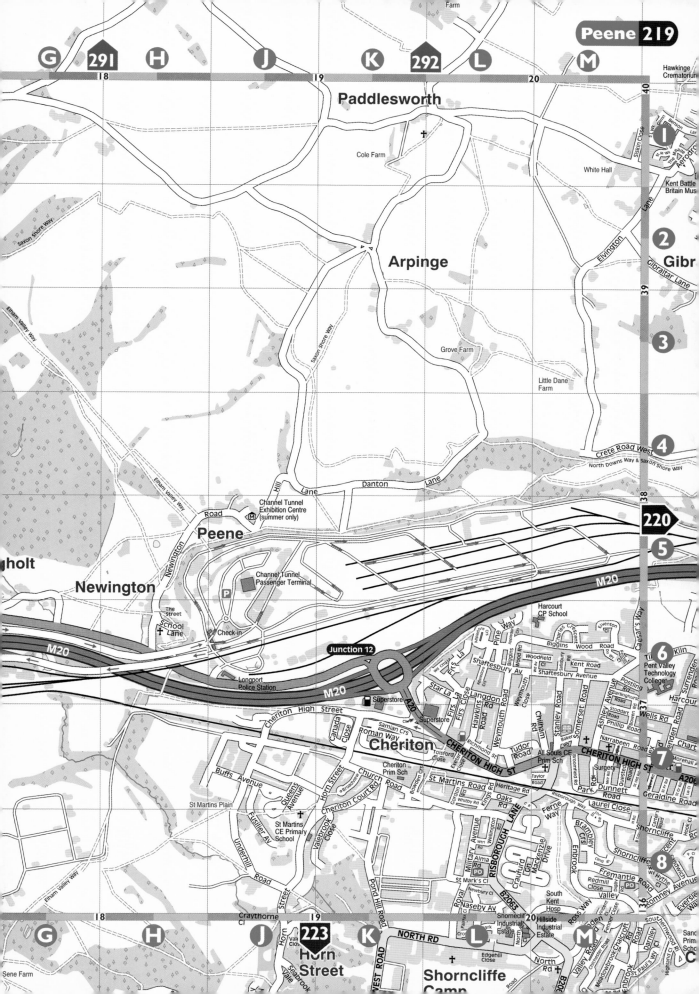

G 291 H J K 292 L M

Paddlesworth

Cole Farm

White Hall

Hawkinge Crematorium

1

Kent Battle Britain Mus

Arpinge

2 Gibr

Elvington

Gibraltar Lane

3

Grove Farm

Little Dane Farm

Saxon Shore Way

Crete Road West 4

North Downs Way & saxon shore way

Elham Valley Way

Danton Lane

Hill Lane

Channel Tunnel Exhibition Centre (summer only)

Road

Newington

Road

Peene

Newington

gholt

38 220 5

M20

The Street

School Lane

Check-in

Channel Tunnel Passenger Terminal

P

Junction 12

Longport Police Station

M20

M20

M20

Superstore

A20

Cheriton High Street

Cheriton

Canada Close

Roman Way

Samian Crs

Tolsford Cl

Superstore

Harcourt CP School

Harcourt CP School

Pine Way

Firs La

Shaftesbury Av

Biggins Wood Road

Woodfield Rd

Kent Road

Shaftesbury Avenue

Postling Road

Pent Valley Technology College

6

Til Kiln

Harcour

Wells Rd

Chart

Star La

Langdon Rd

Hawkins Road

Firs Close

Weymouth Close

Stanley Road

Somerset Road

Ashley Avenue

Darlinghurst Road

Phillip Road

CHERITON HIGH ST

Richmond St

Chilham Rd

Tudor Road

All Souls CE Prim Sch

Baker

Surgery

Narrabeen Rd

CHERITON HIGH ST 7 A20

Dunnett Road

Geraldine Road

Morehall

Morehall

Buffs Avenue

Queens Avenue

Horn Street

Church Road

Cheriton Court Road

Cheriton Prim Sch

St Martins Road

Kings Rd

Oaks Rd

Heritage Rd

Taylor Road

Park

Laurel Close

Ferne Way

Shorncliffe

Shorncliffe

Brambley Crs

8

St Martins Plain

Fusilier Av

Valerook Close

St Martins CE Primary School

Broadwell

Whitby Rd

Gordon Rd

Elsie Rd

Wellington Rd

Military Avenue

Alma Rd PO

Mackenzie Drive

Risborough Way

Crauford Cl

St Mark's Cl

Newbury Cl

South Kent Hosp

Fremantie Road

Redmill Close

PO

Hybe

Romney Road

Valley

Eversl

Underhill Road

Street

Craythorne Cl

Vale Close

Horn Street

Seabrook Vale

Royal Military

Naseby Av

B2063

Pond Hill Road

WEST ROAD

NORTH RD

Shorncliff Industrial Estate

Hillside Industrial Estate

North Rd

Sand Prim Sch

Chalcroft

Valley Road

Sene Farm

G 18 H J 19 223 Horn Street K L M

North Rd

Shorncliffe Camp

Edgehill Close

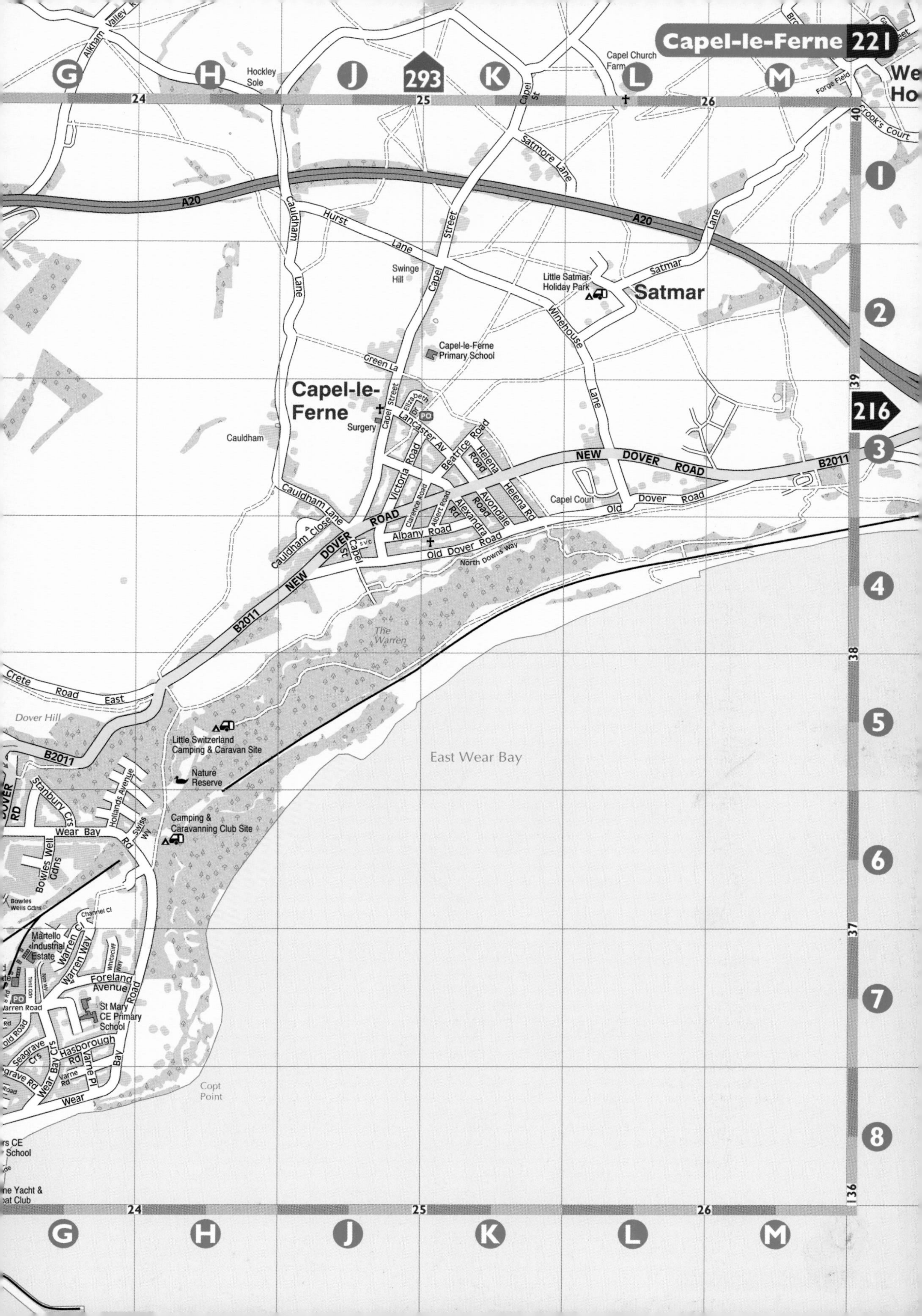

G H J 293 K L M

24 25 26

I

Capel Church Farm

Forge Field

A20

Satmore Lane

Satmar Lane

Little Satmar Holiday Park

Satmar

2

39

216

3

B2011

Swinge Hill

Cauldham Lane

Hurst Lane

Capel Street

Green La

Capel-le-Ferne Primary School

Winehouse Lane

Capel-le-Ferne

Cauldham

Surgery

PO

Elizabeth

Lancaster Av

Victoria Road

Clarence Road

Capel Street

Albert Road

Beatrice Road

Helena Road

Alexandra Rd

Avondale Rd

Helena Rd

NEW DOVER ROAD

Capel Court

Old Dover Road

NEW DOVER ROAD

Cauldham Lane

Cauldham Close

svc

Capel St

Albany Road

Old Dover Road

North Downs Way

4

38

The Warren

Crete Road East

Dover Hill

B2011

Little Switzerland Camping & Caravan Site

Nature Reserve

East Wear Bay

5

DOVER RD

Stanbury Crs

Hollands Avenue

Swiss Wy

Wear Bay

Bowles Well Gdns

Bowles Wells Gdns

Channel Cl

Camping & Caravanning Club Site

6

37

Martello Industrial Estate

Warren Way

Whitecliff

Whitecliff Road

Foreland Avenue

Warren Road

PO

St Mary CE Primary School

7

Old Road

Seagrave Rd

Wear Bay Crs

Hasborough Rd

Varne Pl

Varne Rd

Wear

Copt Point

8

36

rs CE School

e Yacht & oat Club

G H J K L M

24 25 26

We Ho

Foreign

A   B   326   C   D   E   327   F

589   90   91

Peasmarsh Place

Church Lane

1

Church Lane

Clayton Farm

Leasam House

Leasam

22

2

21

TN31

Marley

River Tillingham

Denton Close

Henley Cl

Road

Ferring Cl

Avenue

3

Pottingfield

Po

Lea

Nutley

Marl

Cooper Rd

B20

The Link

Tilling Green Inf Sch

Mason Rd

Tillingham Lane

West undercliff

Asheridan Avenue

4

Tillingham Farm

20

UDIMORE ROAD

Gillshaw Farm

Cadborough Farm

B2089

5

UDIMORE ROAD

Cadborough Cliff

1066 Country Walk

Oast House Drive

B2089

The Hammonds

UDIMORE ROAD

B2089

Watlands

Dumb Woman's Lane

6

B2089

UDIMORE ROAD

1066 Country Walk

19

7

Cock Marling

Winchelsea Lane

Roadend

Rye Marsh Farm

8

LC

Winchelsea Station

Station Road

18

Farm

589   90   91

A   B   C   D   E   F

River Brede

Ferry

1066 Country Walk

ROYAL MILL ROAD

FERRY HILL

TANYARD LANE

1 grid square represents 500 metres

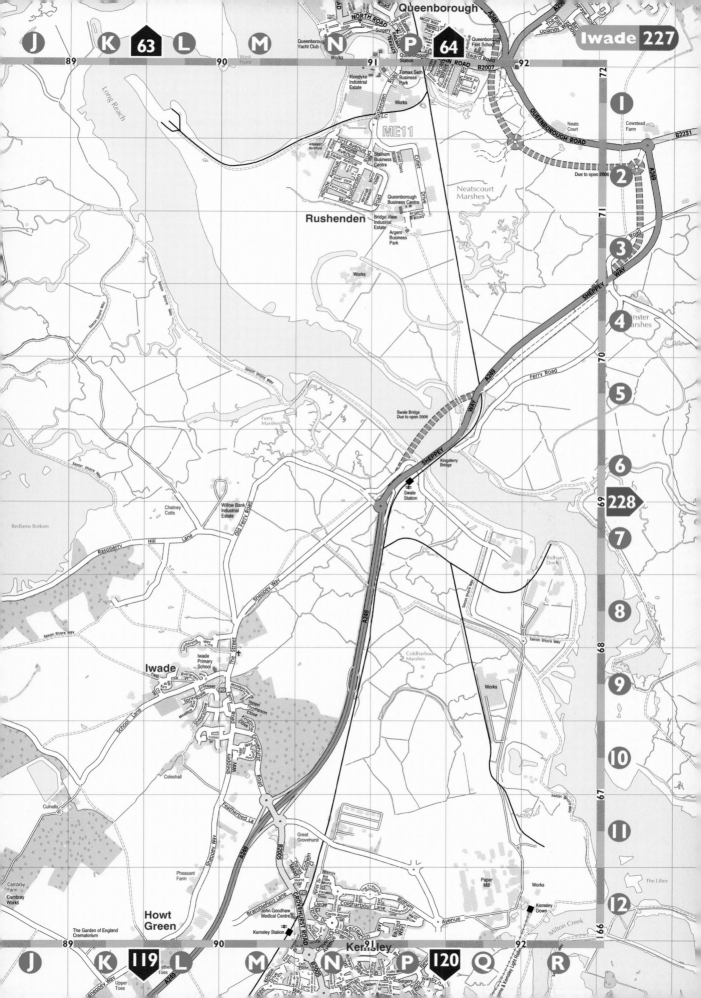

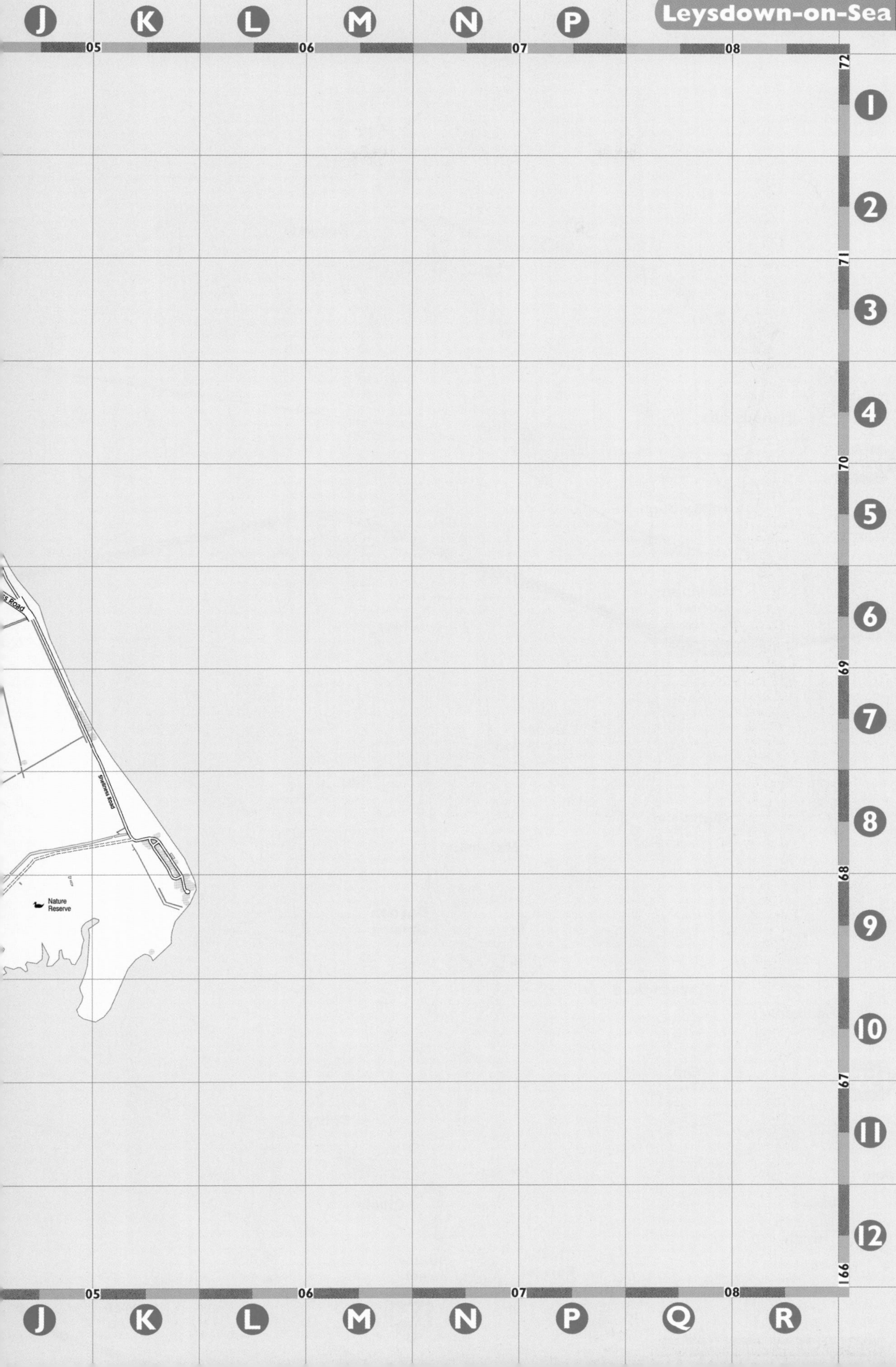

05 06 07 08

1

2

3

4

5

6

7

8

9

10

11

12

Nature
Reserve

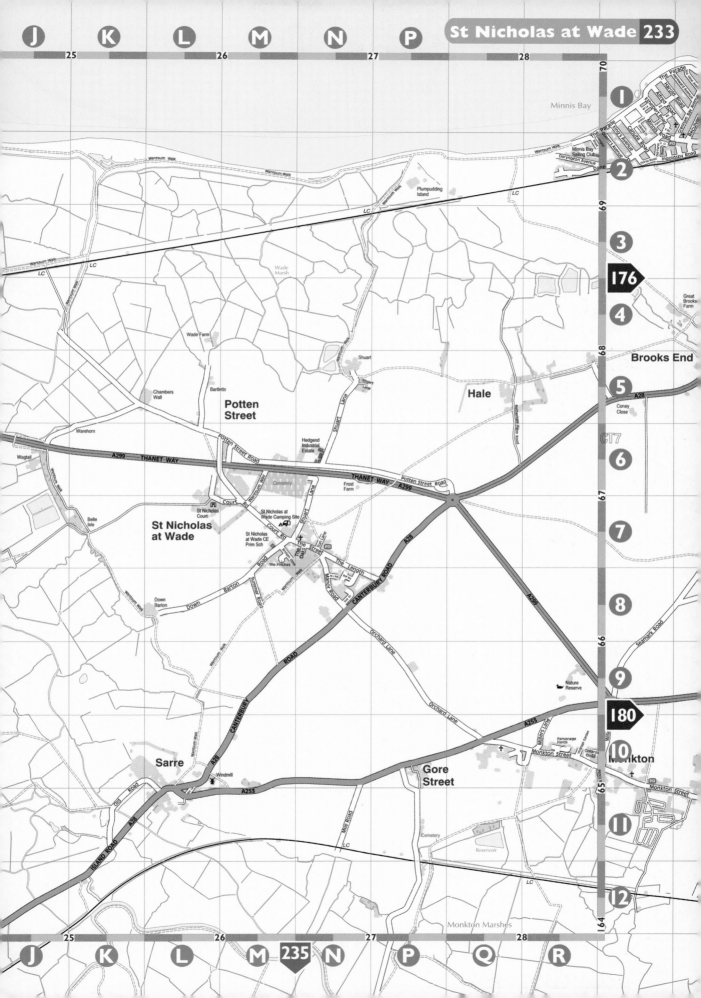

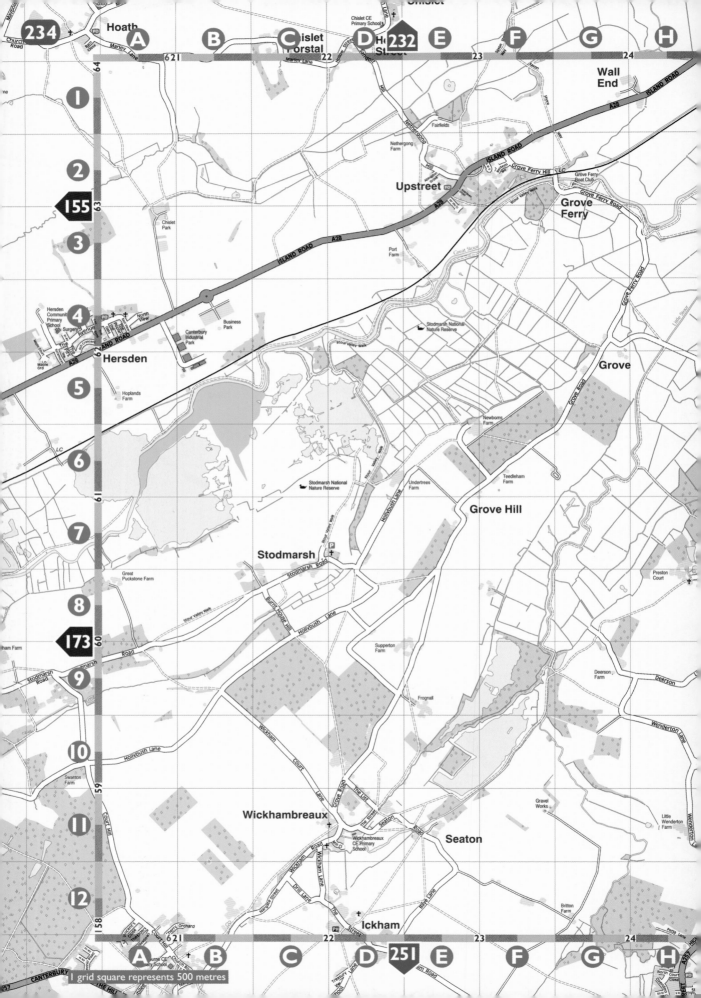

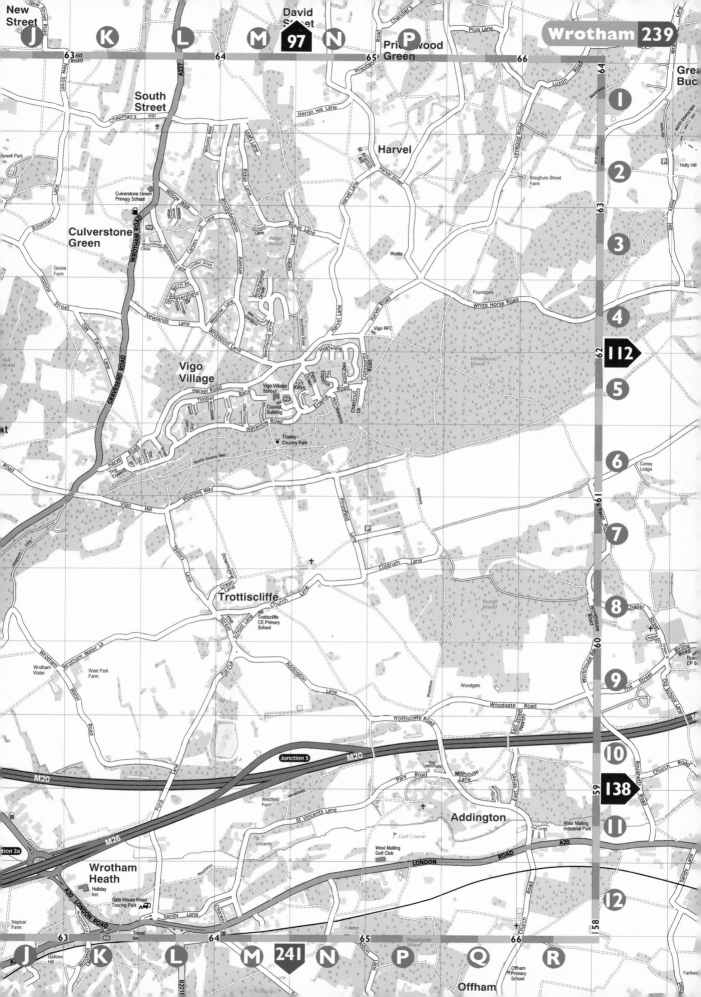

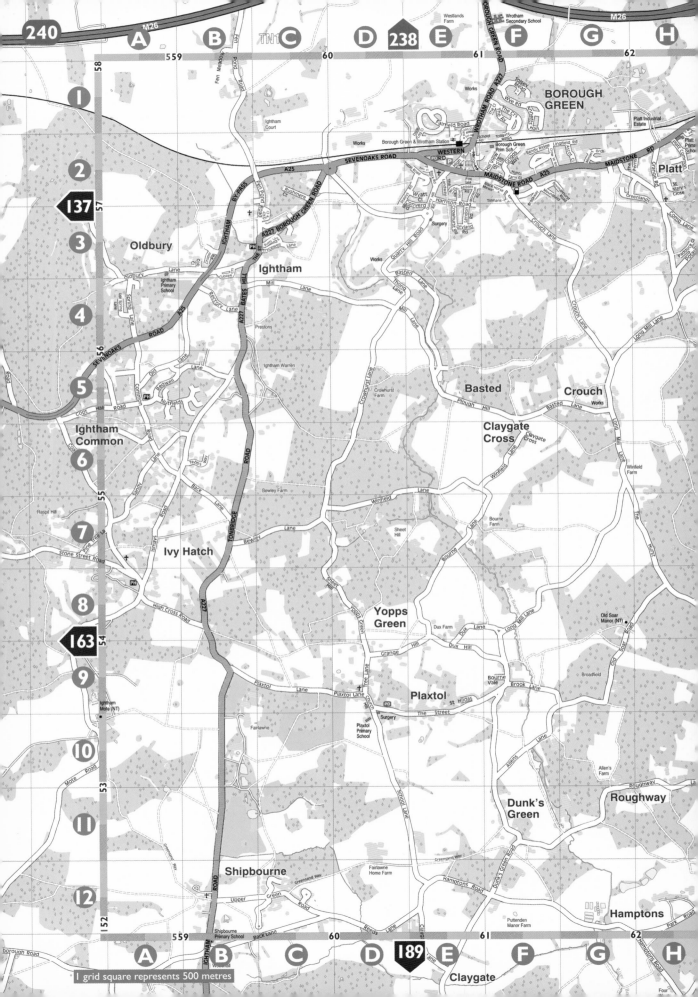

Pested

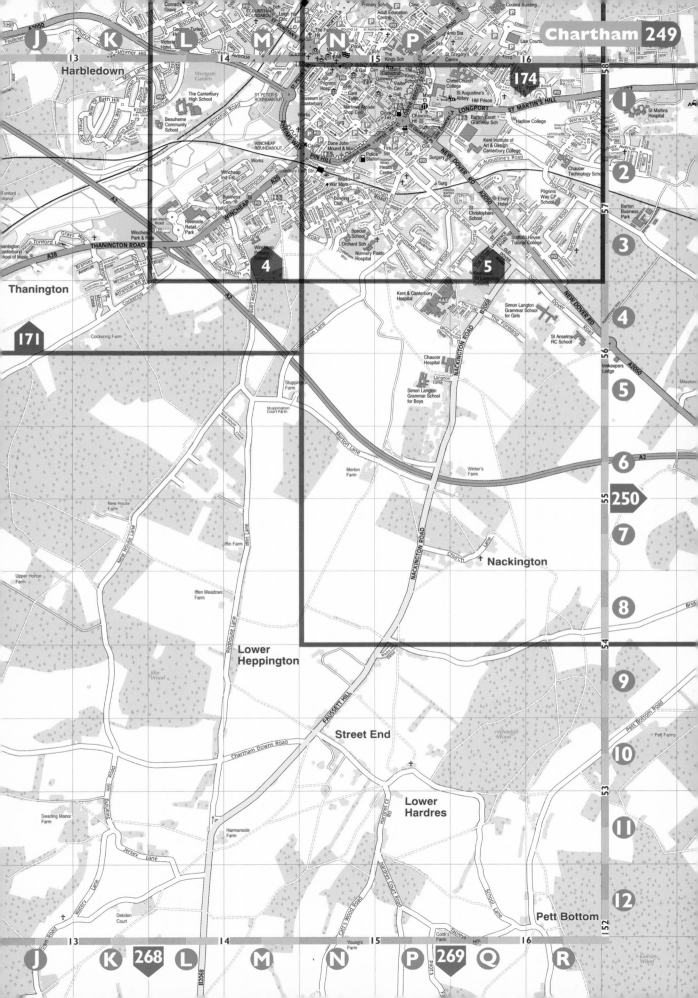

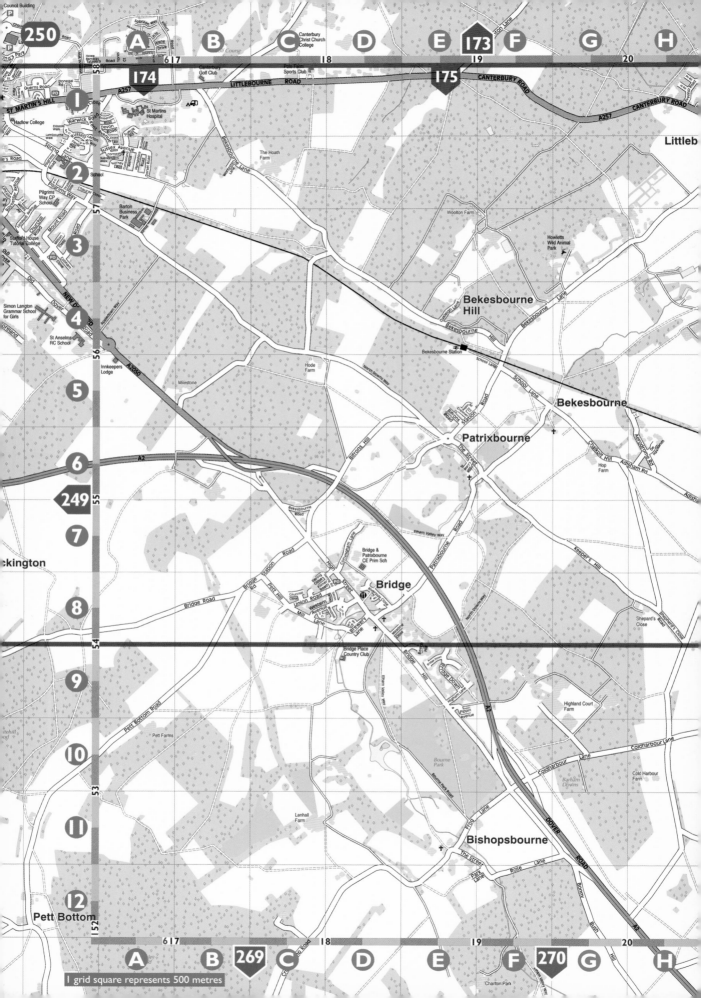

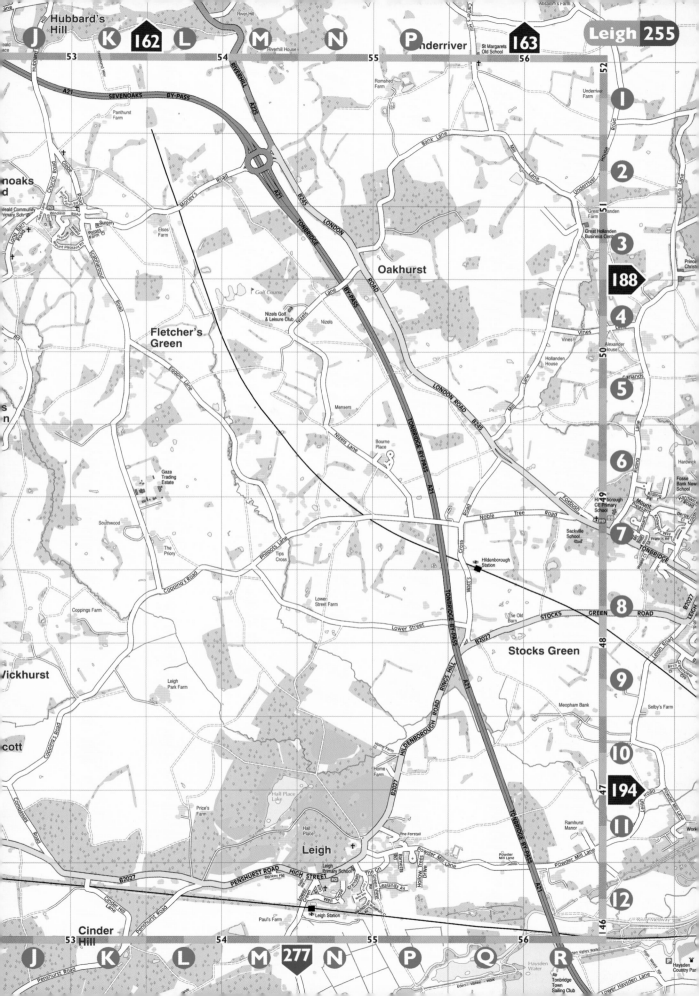

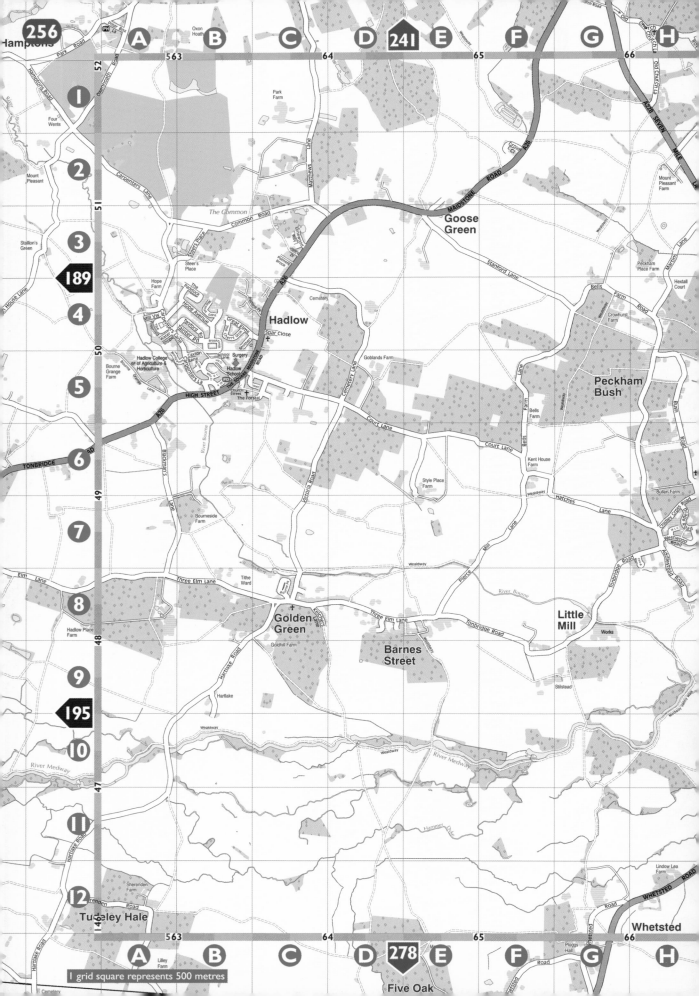

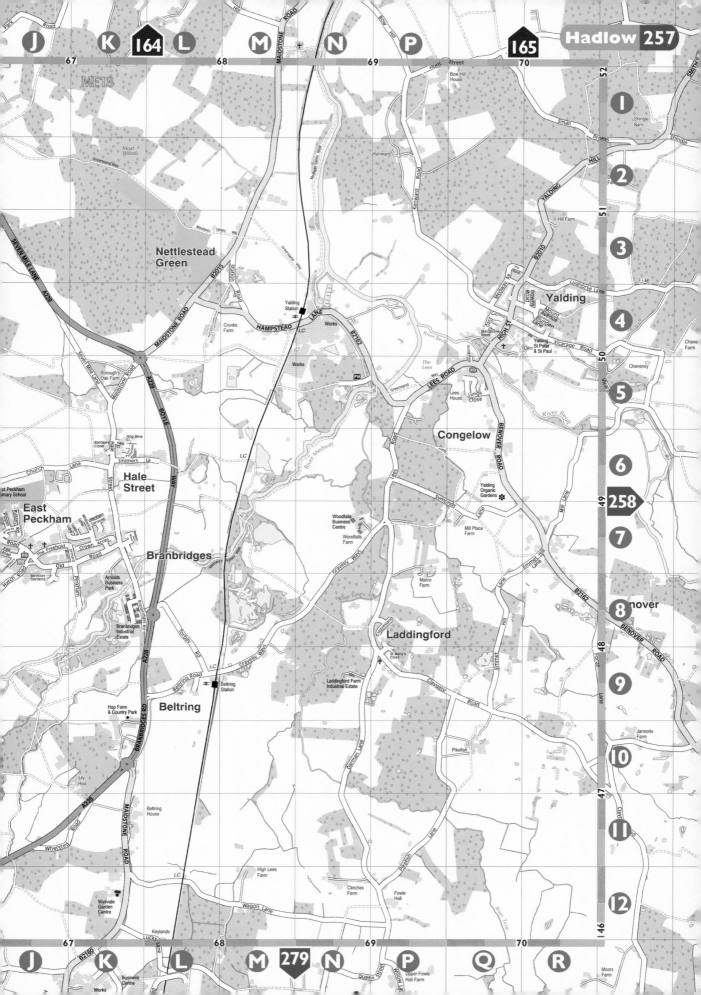

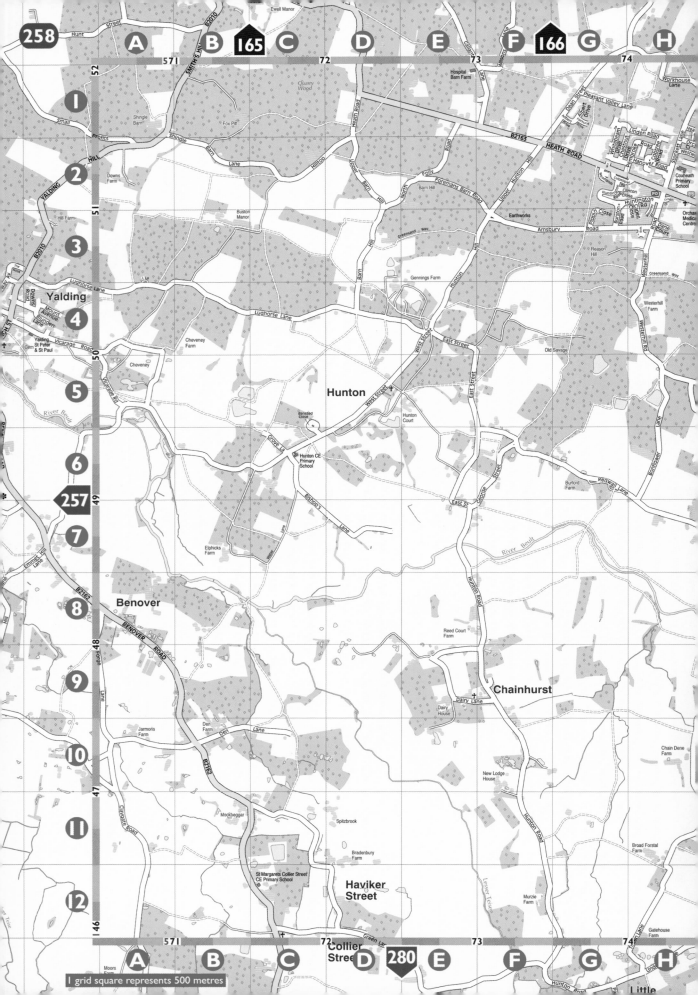

I grid square represents 500 metres

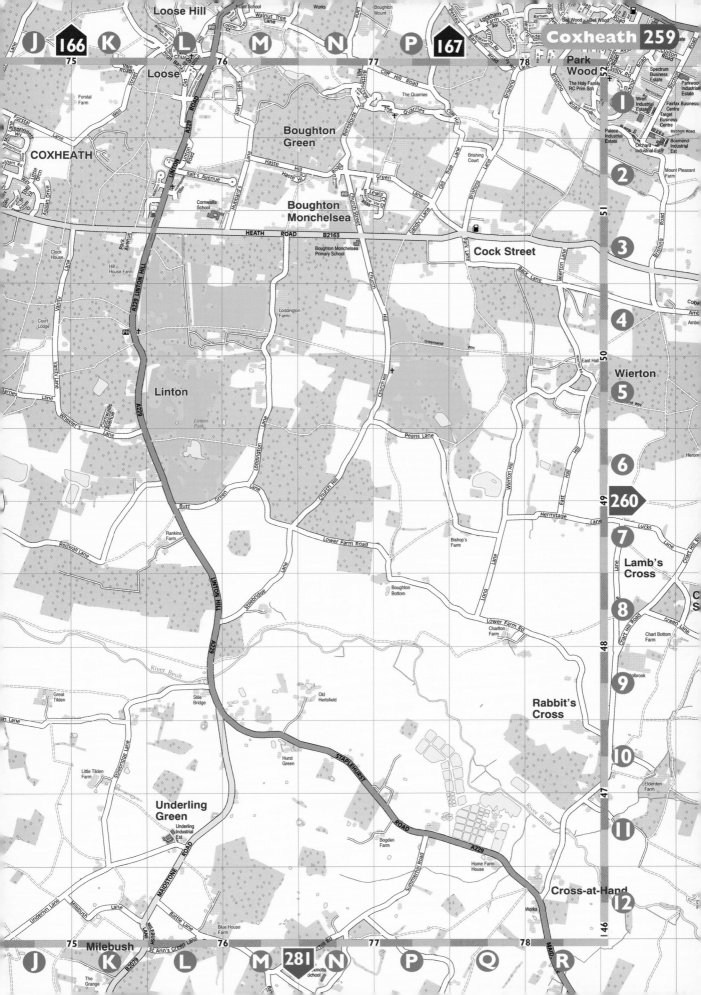

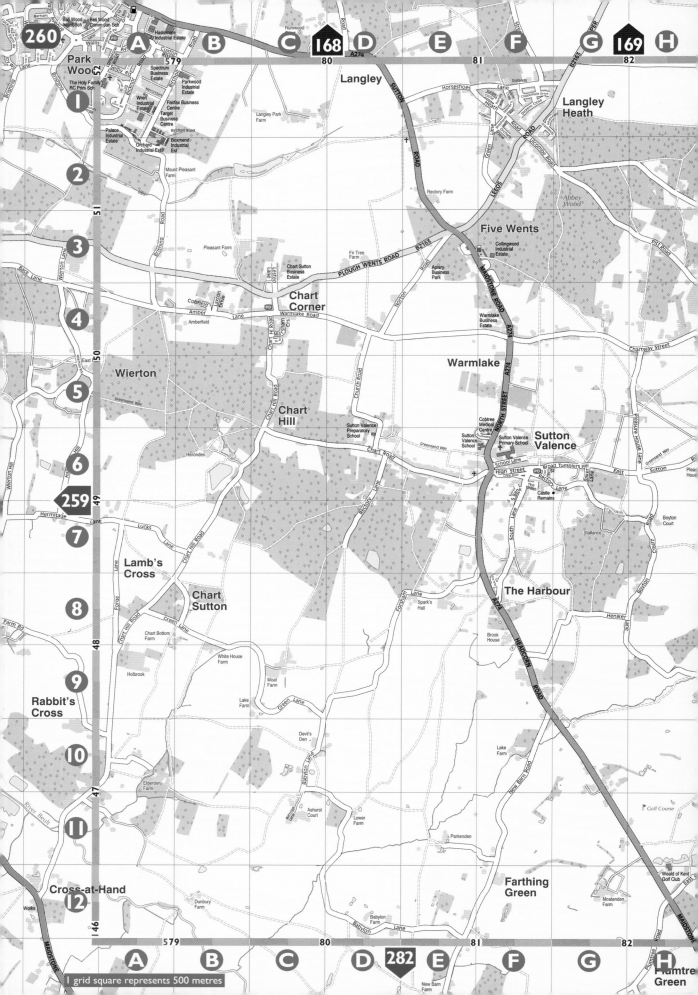

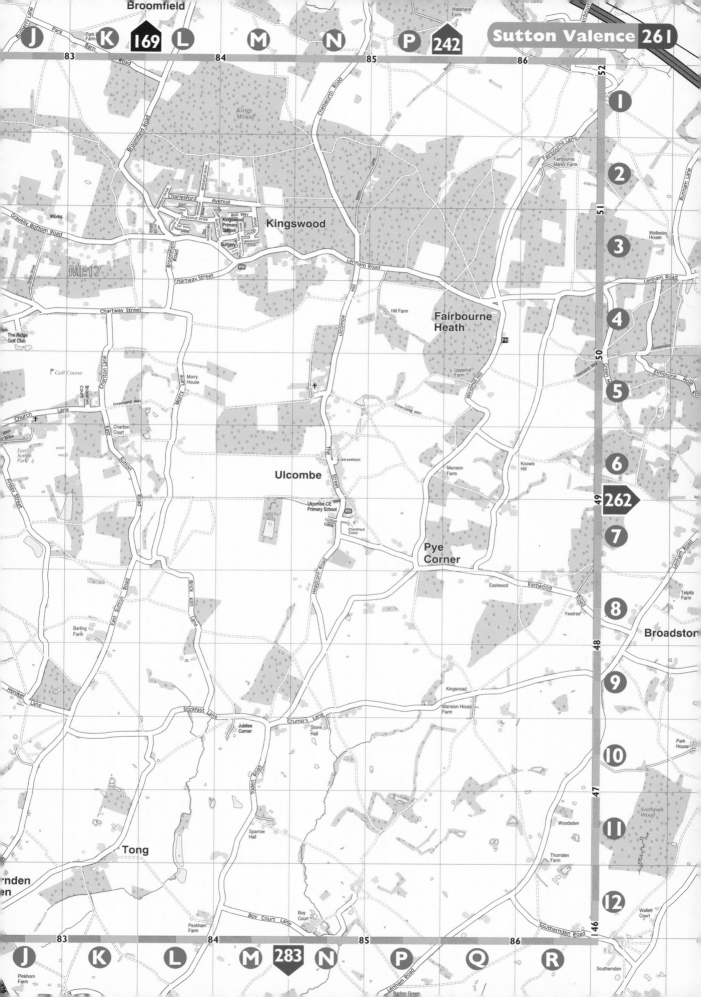

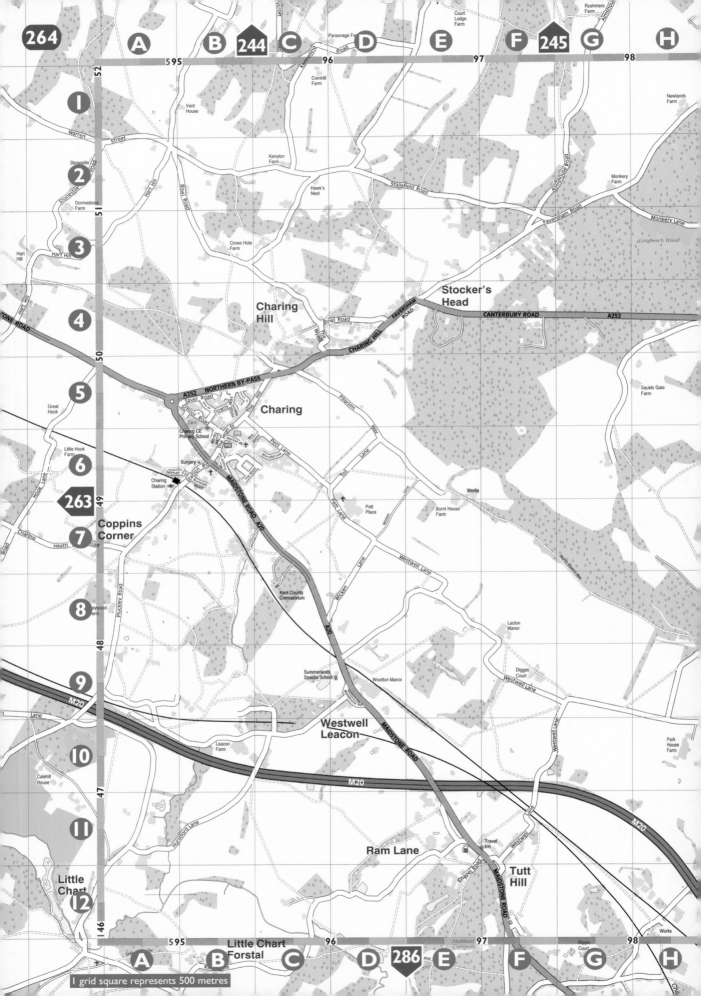

15   16   17   18   52

Young's Farm

Cook's Farm

Pilot's Farm

Bow Hill

Upper Hardres Court

Broxhall Farm

Broxhall Road

Hardres Court Road

Bursted Manor

Bursted Wood

Bursted Hill

The Manor House

Pett Bottom Road

Gorsley Wood

Wooddate

Langham Park Farm

Pheasants Hall Road

Crowe Camp Road

Charlton

Charlton Wood

1

2

3

51

Reed Farm

Marley

Jesses Lane

Marley Lane

Marley Lane

4

50

Lynsore Bottom

Hardres Road

The St

Marley Hill

Homestead Farm

Hardres Court Road

Stelling Minnis CE Primary School

Westwood

Marley Lane

Covet Lane

Covet Lane

Covet Wood

5

6

270

7

49

Bossingham

Atchester Wood

Lynsore Court

Pett Bottom Road

Palmstead

Dane Farm

Covert Wood

8

48

Bossingham Road

Split Lane

High Chimney Farm

Pagfield Wood Road

Redoak

Elham Valley Way

9

10

47

Stelling Minnis

Fryarne Park

Little Wildage

Bladbean

11

Wingmor

Bossingham Road

Farthingsole Farm

Jacques Court

Elham Valley Way

12

46

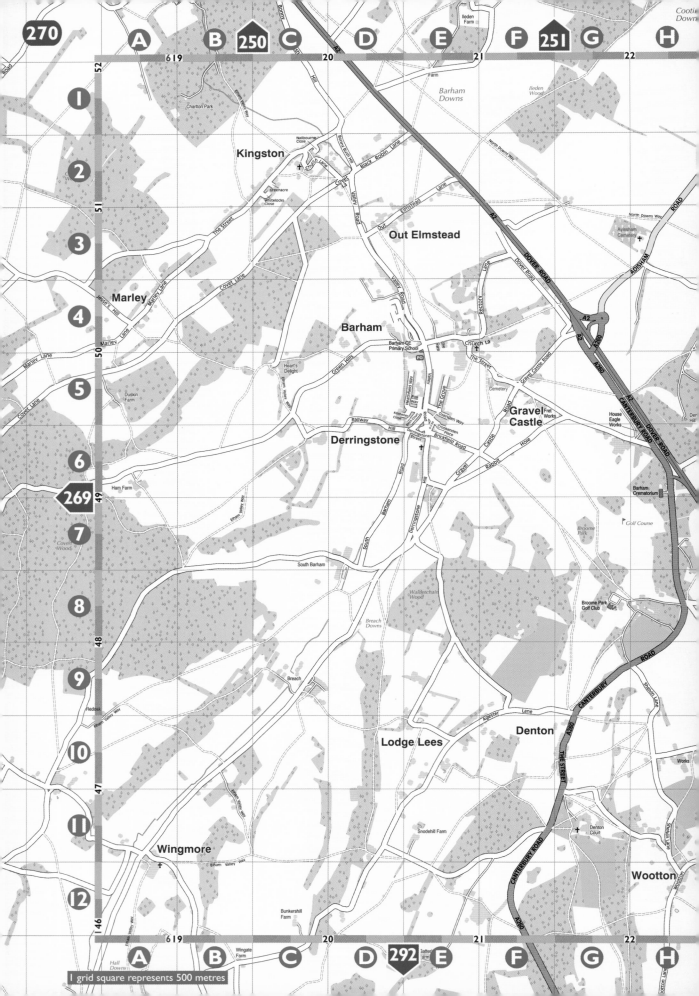

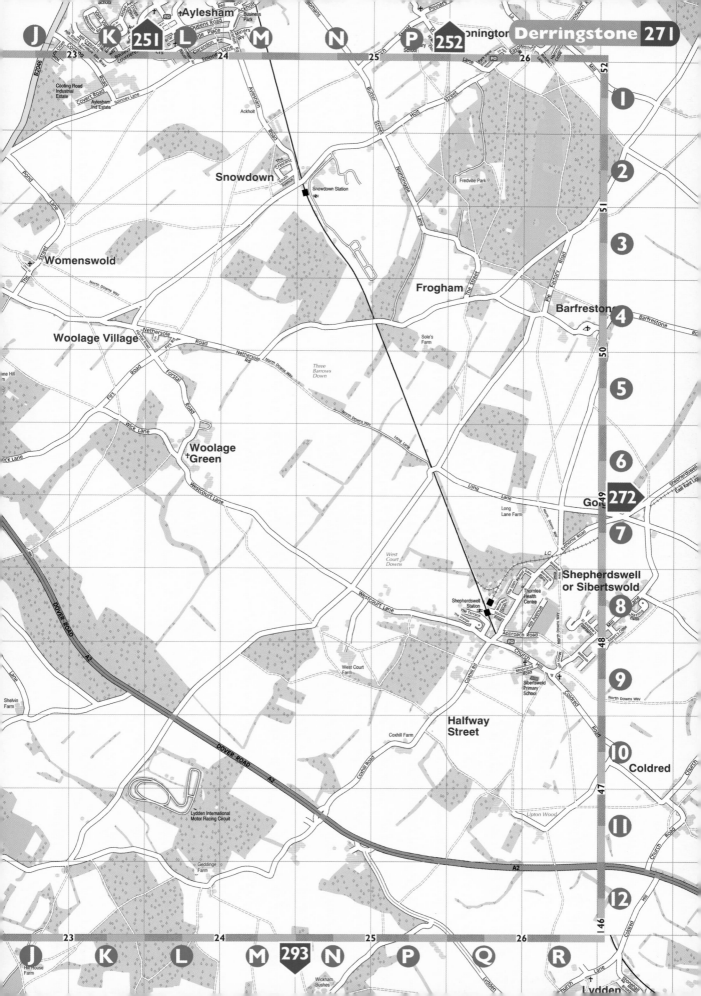

J K **251** L M N P **252** onington

23 24 25 26 52

1

2

51

3

Snowdown

Snowdown Station Fredville Park

4 Barfreston Barfreston Rd

Womenswold Frogham The Street 50

Nethersole Sole's Farm

Woolage Village Nethersole Rd Three Barrows Down

North Downs Way

5

Woolage
+Green **6**

Long Lane **272** Go...

Westcourt Lane Long Lane Farm 49

7

West Court Downs LC

Shepherdswell
or Sibertswold East Kent

8 9

Westcourt Lane Shepherdswell Station Thornlea Health Centre

The Terrace Approach Road 48

West Court Farm Church Hill **9**

Dover Road A2 Sibertswold Primary School Coldred Road

Halfway Street North Downs Way

Coxhill Farm **10** Coldred

Shelvin Farm Coxhill Road 47

11

Lydden International Motor Racing Circuit Upton Wood Church Road

Geddinge Farm A2 **12**

23 24 25 26 46

J K L M **293** N P Q R

Hill House Farm Wickham Bushes Lydden

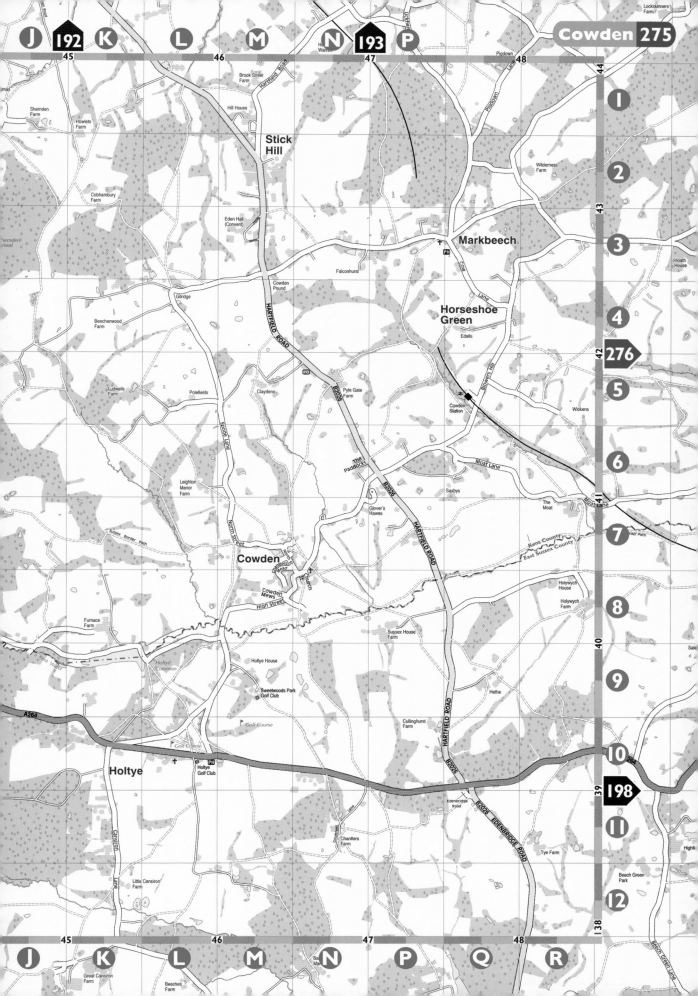

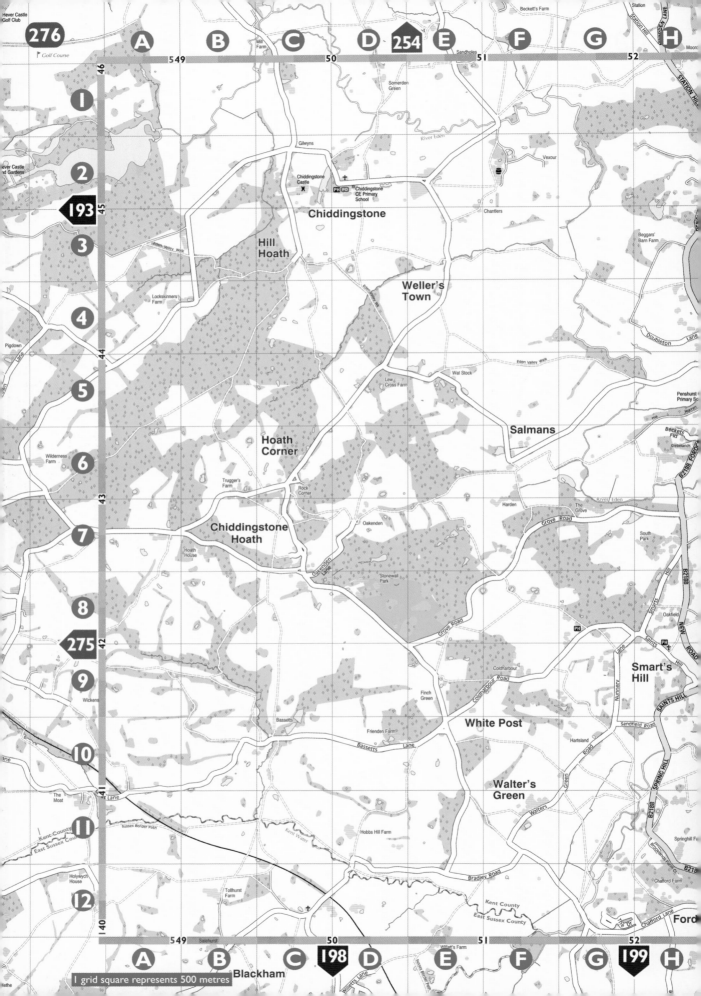

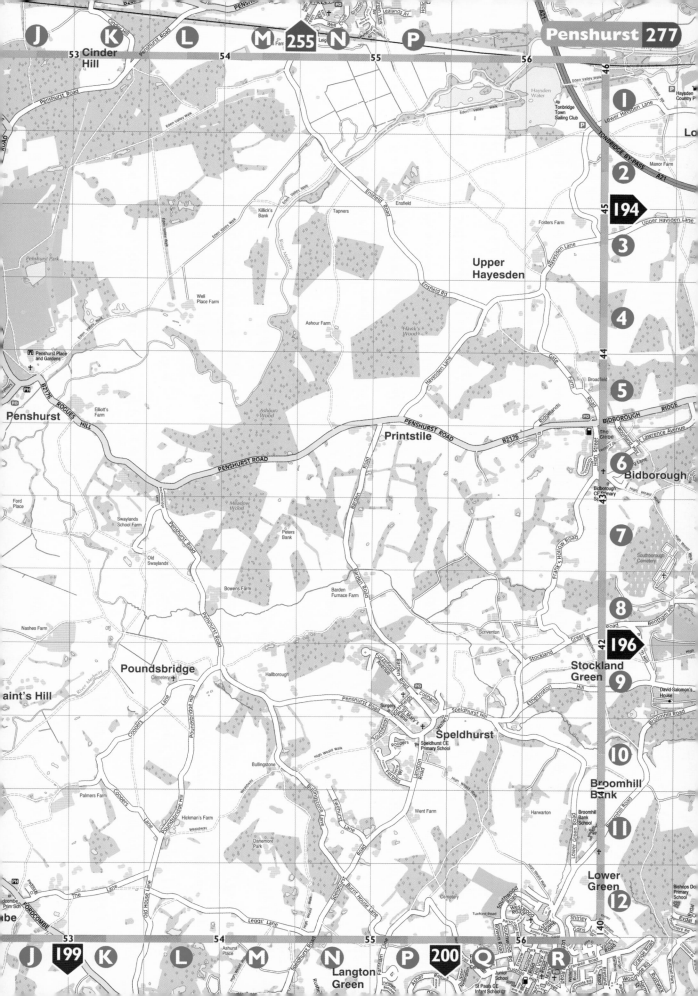

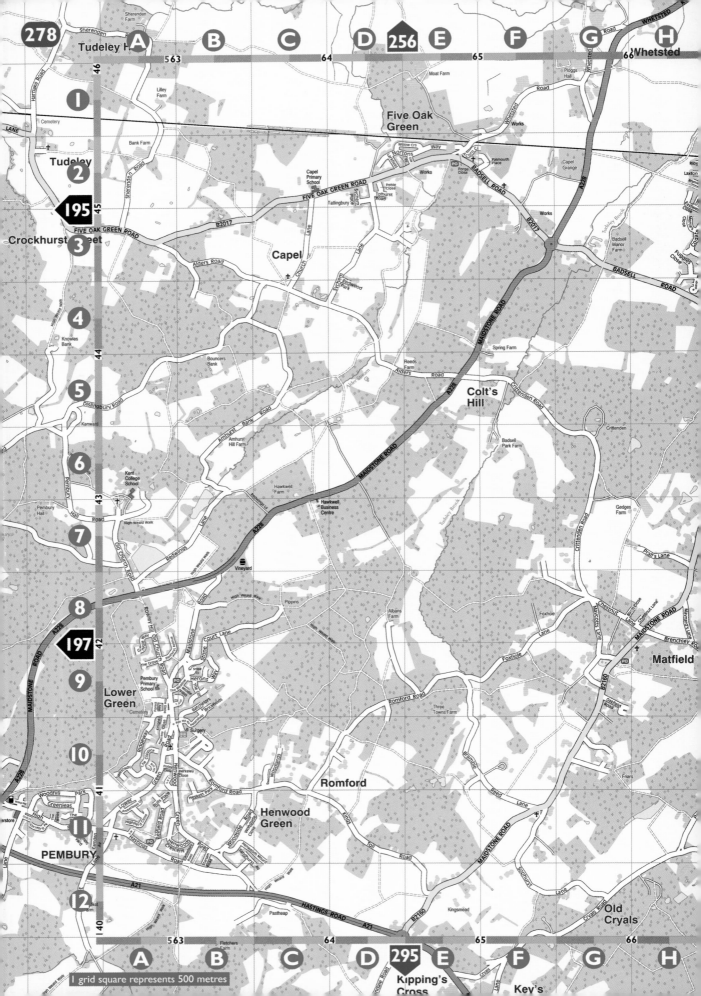

67 68 69 70

Queen Street

PADDOCK WOOD

Mile Oak

Pearson's Green

Castle Hill

Palmer's Green

Brenchley

Petteridge Chillmill

Horsmonden

The Corner

280

67 68 69 70

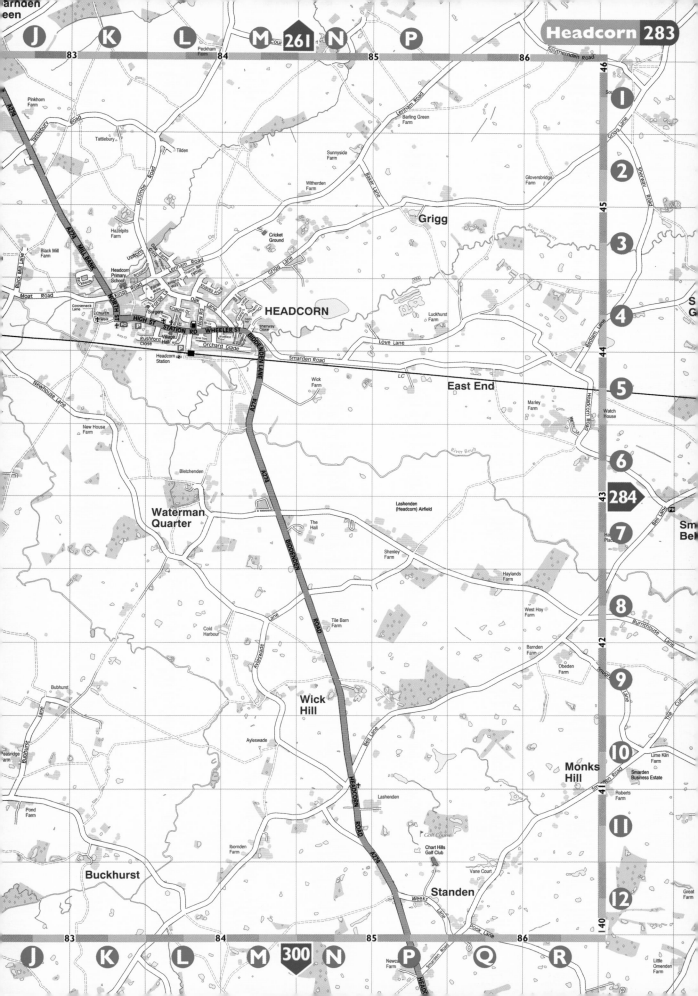

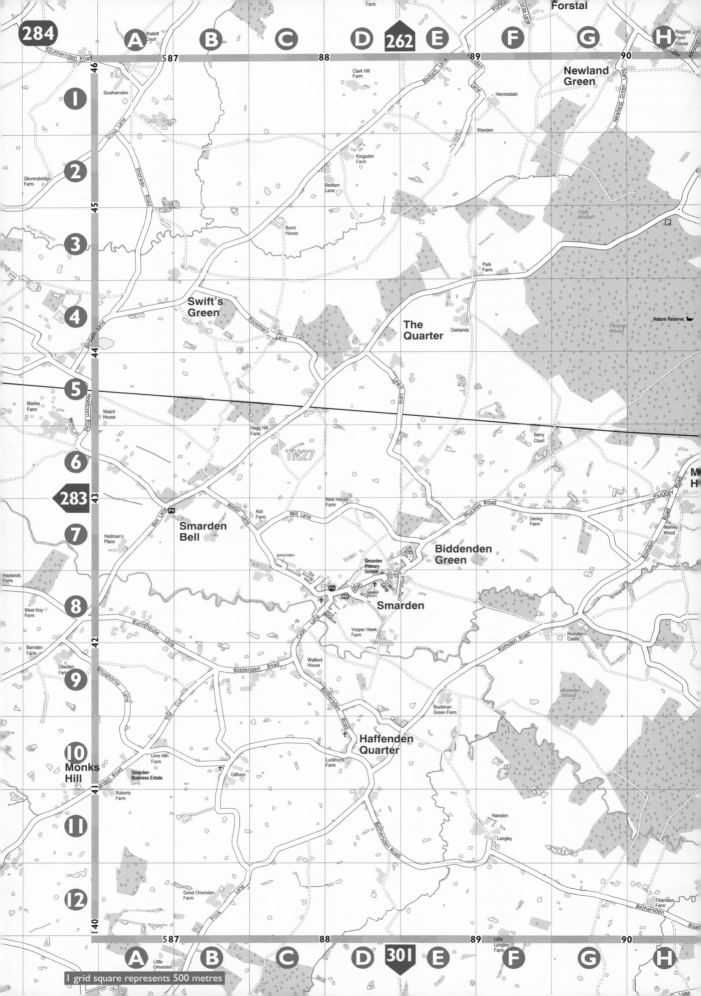

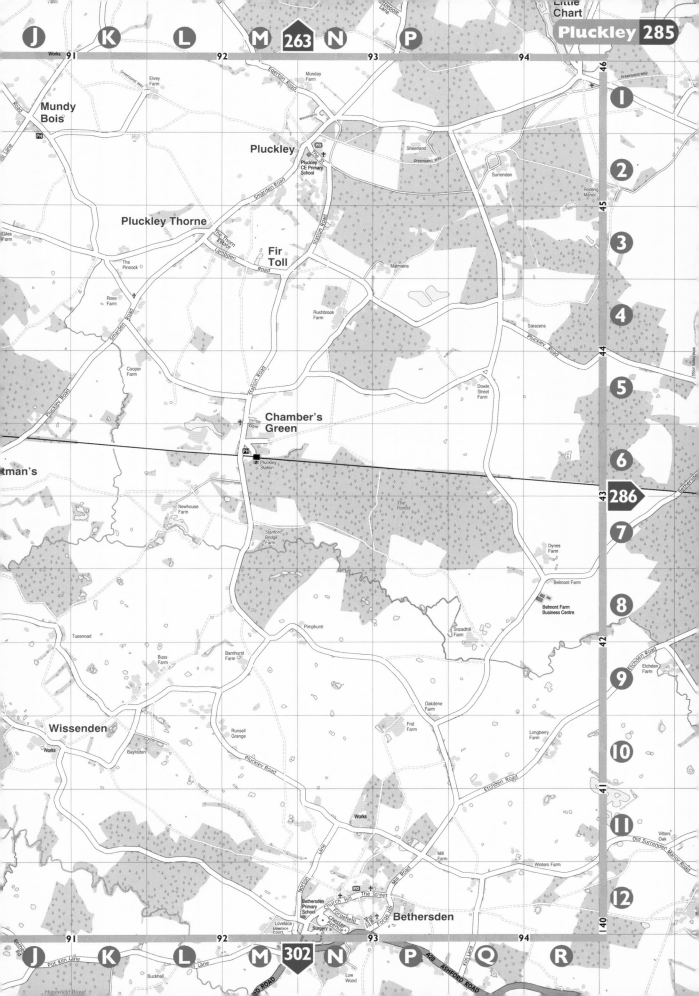

07   08   09   10   46

1

45   **Evington**

Hastingleigh

3

4

44

Brook

Troy Town

5

6

43   **290**

7

8

42   **Brabourne**

9

Bircholt Forstal

10

41

11

Brabourne Lees

12

Ridgeway

40

Coombe Manor

Amage Farm

Lyddendane Farm

West Down

North Downs Way

Broad Downs

Nature Reserve

The Street

Cold Blow

The Street

Crabtree Farm

Court Lodge

Fishponds Farm

Brabourne Road

Hampton

South Hill Farm

Kingsmill Down

Hampton Lane

Beddlestone Farm

Bulltown Farm

North Downs Way

North Downs Way

Cadman's Wood

Elmtree Farm

Hampton Lane

Hampton Lane

North Downs Way

The Hall

Brabourne Coomb

Penstock Hall

The Street

Scot's Lane

TN25

Fords Water

Brabourne CE Primary School

Canterbury Road

Charmington Lane

Seeley Farm

Manor Pound Lane

Bircholt Court

Lees Road

Pound Lane

Park Farm

Brockham Farm

Water Farm

Prospect Way

The Pound House

Woolpack Hill

Smeeth CP School

Church Road

The Ridgeway

Pound Lane

Southenay Farm

Heminge Farm

Lodge House

Priory Lane

Wheelbarrow Town

Elhampan Wood

Jacques Court

Grimsacre Farm

Oxroad Farm

Park Gate

Rural Heritage Centre

North Elham

Exted

Elham

Old Hospital

Park La

High Street

Duck Street

Cock La

Surgery

Vicarage La

Elham CE Primary School

Cemetery

Chapel Lane

Rhodes Minnis

Loner Mount Farm

Collards Lane

Canterbury Road

White Horse Lane

Magpie Lane

kbeggar

High Minnis

Park House

Millhill Farm

292

Berefourstal Farm

Wick Farm

Longage Hill

Boyke Lane

Ottinge

Shuttlesfield Lane

Mounts Court Farm

Longage Farm

Sibton Park School

Great Shuttlesfield Farm

Yewtree Cross

Woodland Road

Brady Road

Canterbury Road

Etchinghill Golf Club

Ethelburga Drive

Silverlands

Surgery

Skeete Road

Dog Kennel Lane

Palm Tree Way

Lyminge CE Primary School

Lyminge

High St

Nash Hill

Station Road

Mayfield Road

Greenbanks

Surgery

Shuttlesfield

Broad Street

Rushling Wood

15   16   17   18
J   K   218   L   M   N   P   Q   219   R   Pa
Newbarn

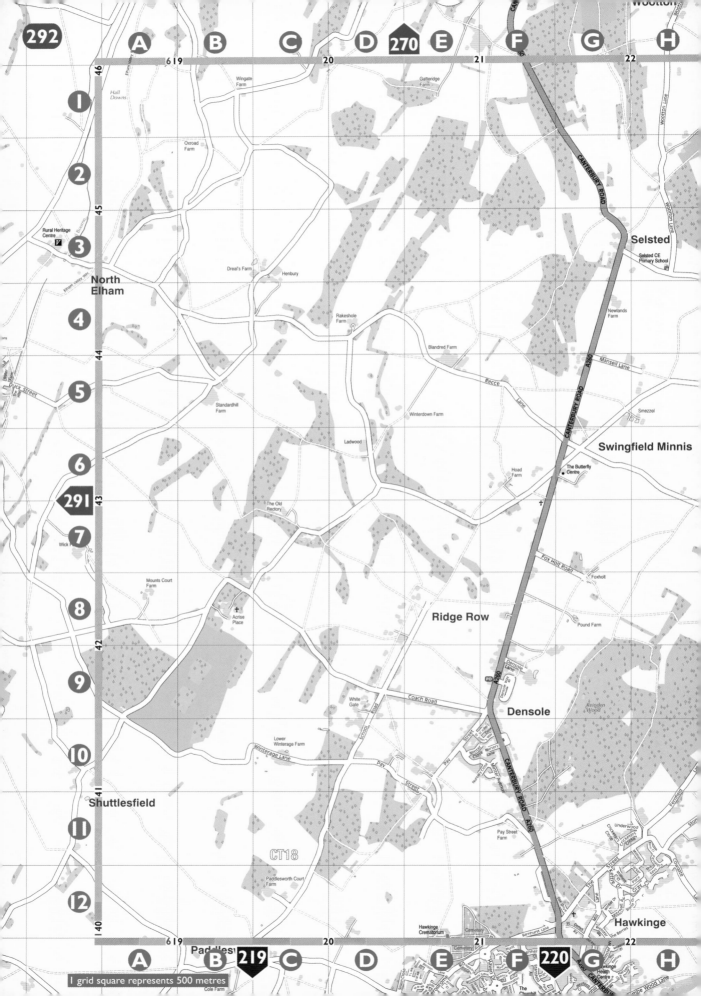

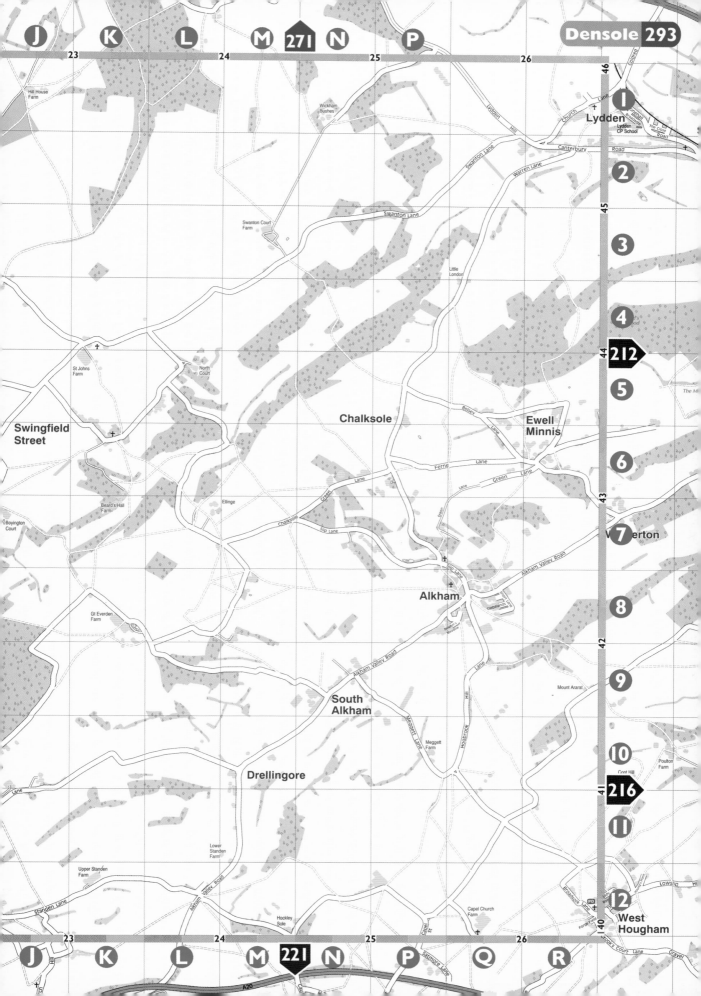

J K L M **271** N P

23 24 25 26

46

1

Lydden

2

45

3

4

44 ▶**212**

5

6

43

▶**7** Werton

Swingfield
Street

Chalksole

Ewell
Minnis

8

42

9

10

41 ▶**216**

Drellingore

South
Alkham

Alkham

11

12

West
Hougham

40

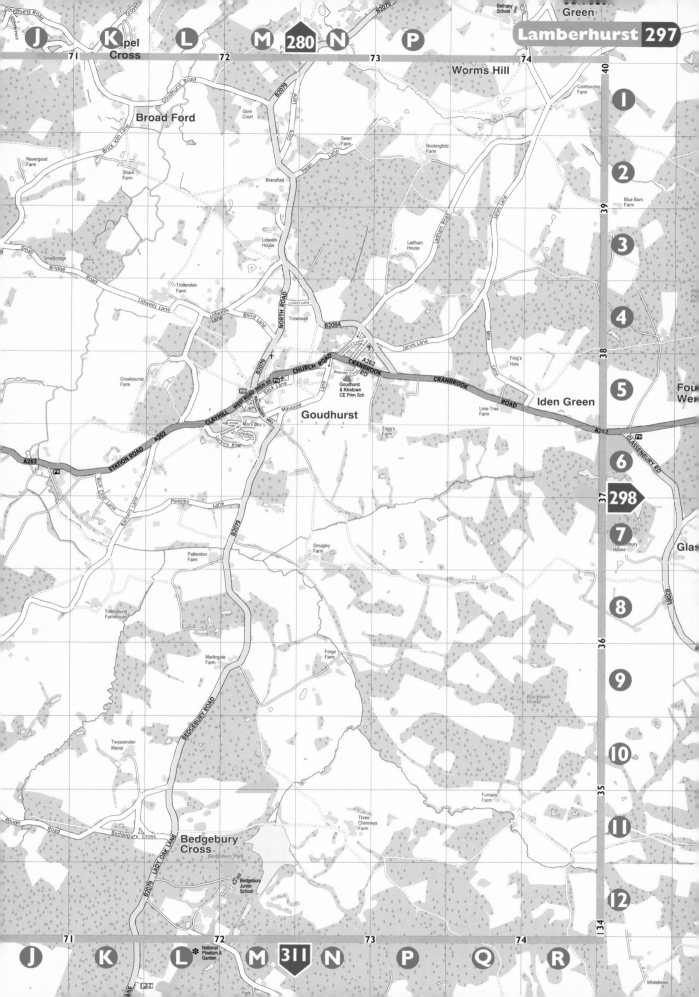

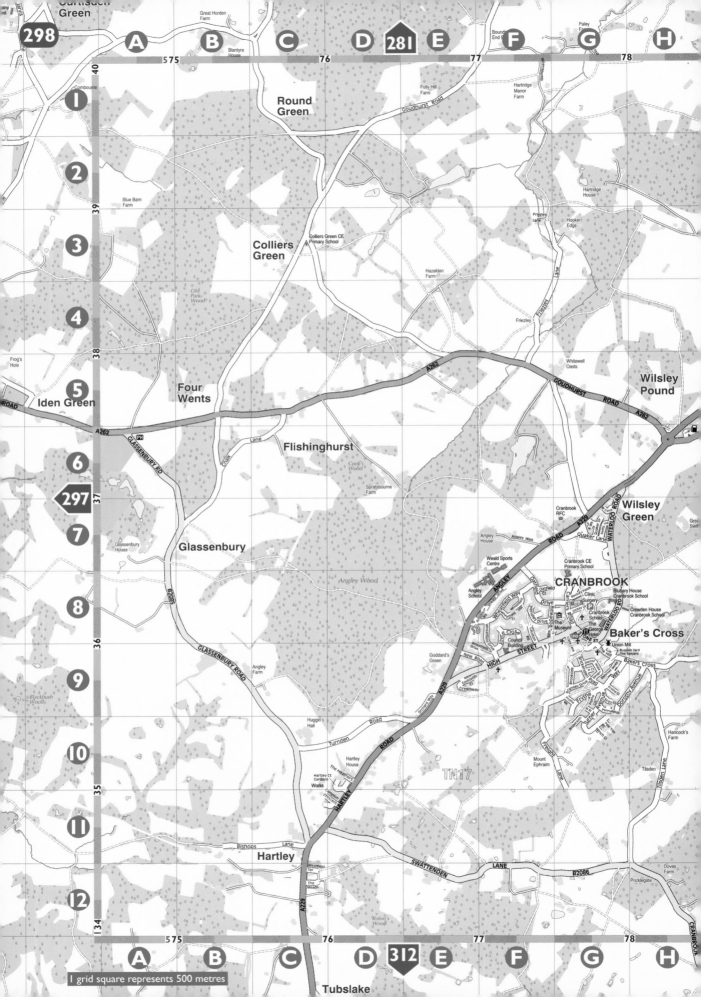

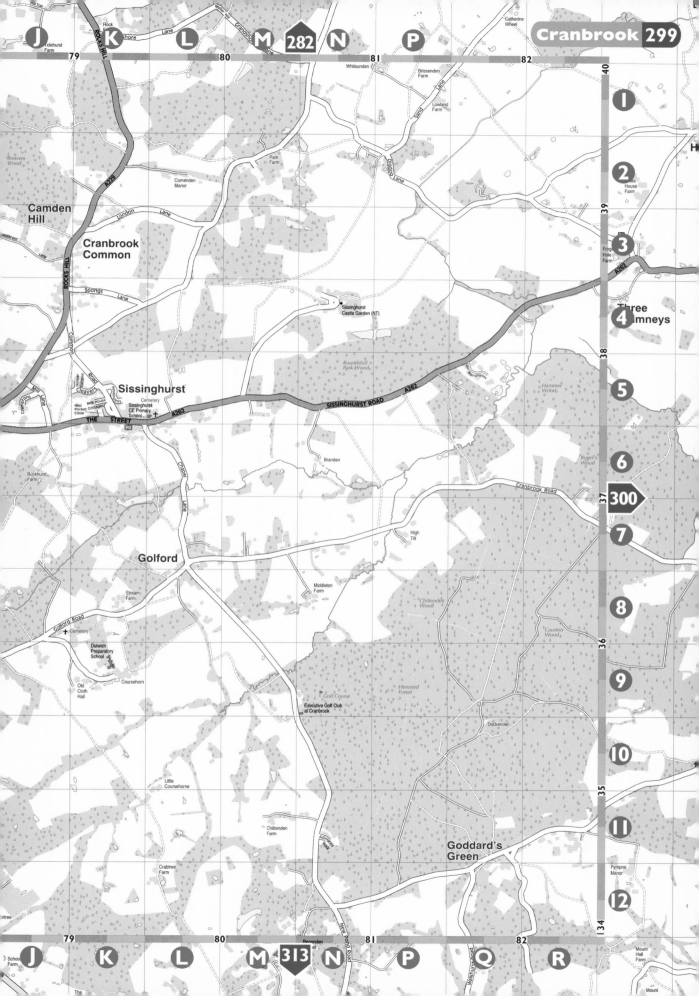

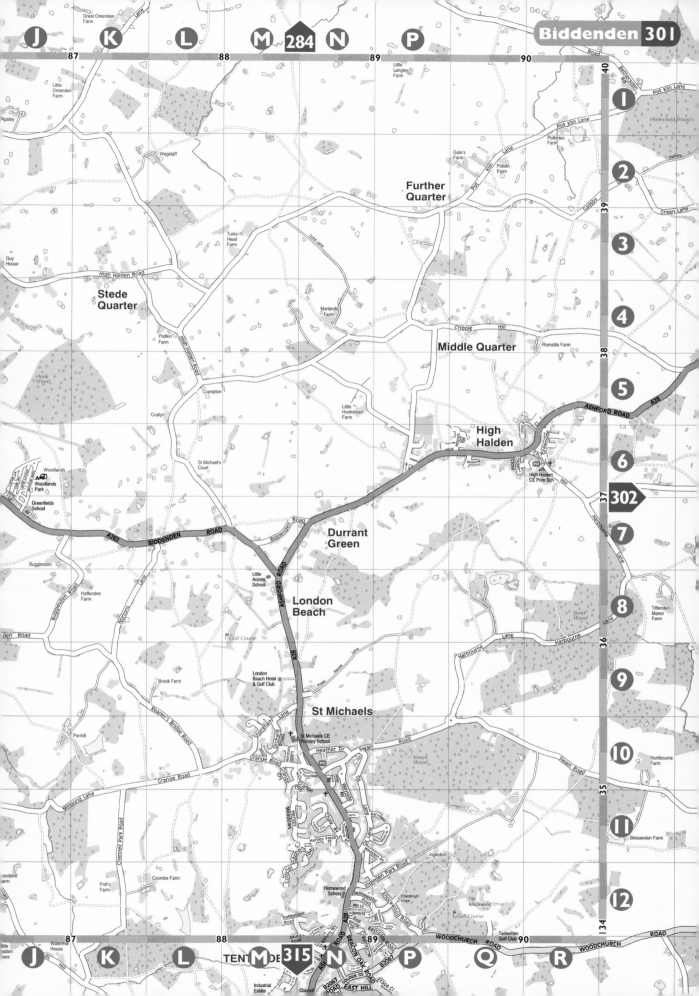

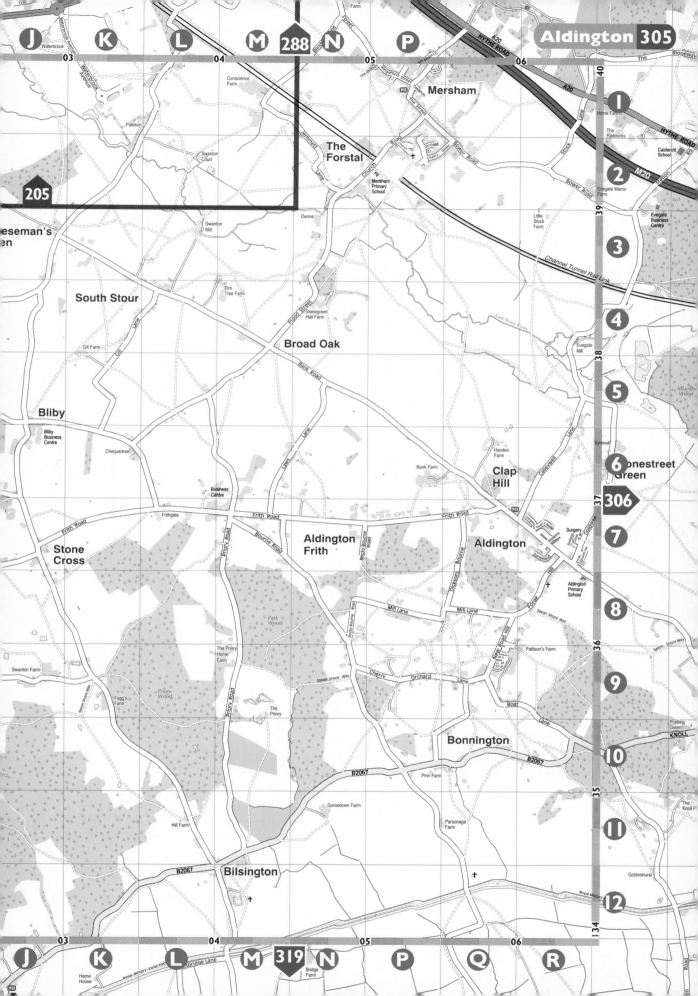

J K L M **288** N P

03 04 05 06 40

205

I
2
3
4
5
6 onestreet Green
306
7
8
9
KNOLL
10
II
12

J K L M **319** N P Q R

03 04 05 06 134

Waterbrook
Watercook Avenue
Pattison
Swanton Court
Conscience Farm
Swanton Mill
Denne

Mersham
The Forstal
Mersham Primary School
Home Farm
The Paddocks
Caldecott School
Evegate Manor Farm
Evegate Business Centre

eseman's en

South Stour
Elm Tree Farm
Flood Street
Stonegreen Hall Farm
Broad Oak
Channel Tunnel Rail Link
East Stour River
Evegate Mill
Black Wood

Gill Farm
Gill Lane
Bank Road
Bliby
Bliby Business Centre
Chequertree
Lauts Lane
Bank Farm
Handen Farm
Clap Hill
Caleywell Lane
Symnell

Business Centre
Frith Road
Frith Road
Frithgate
Frith Road
306
Surgery
7

Stone Cross
Frith Road
Priory Road
Bourne Road
Aldington Frith
Rocky Bourne Road
Dicksons
Aldington
Ecore Hill
Aldington Primary School
8

Park Wood
The Priory Home Farm
Mill Lane
Mill Lane
Saxon Shore Way
Pattison's Farm
9

Swanton Farm
Saxon Shore Way
Fagg's Farm
Priory Wood
Priory Road
The Priory
Saxon Shore Way
Cherry Orchard Lane
Boat Lane
Bonnington
B2067
Postling Green
The Knoll

Hill Farm
B2067
Pinn Farm
Gorsedown Farm
Parsonage Farm
Goldenhurst
II

B2067
Bilsington
Royal Military Canal Path
12

Herne House
Ebridge Lane
Bridge Farm

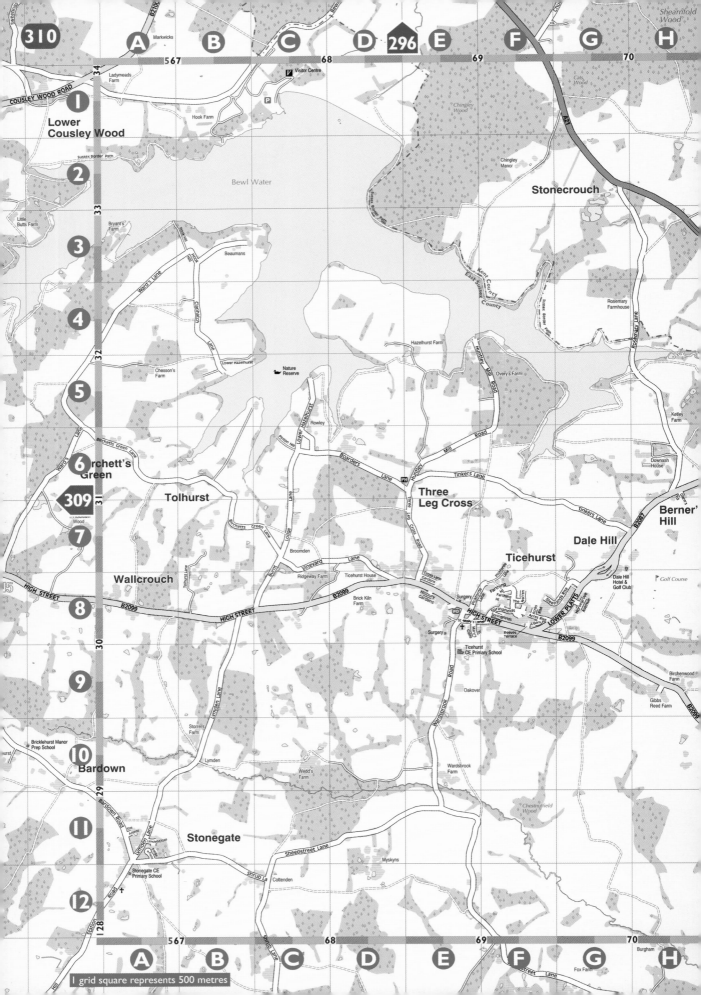

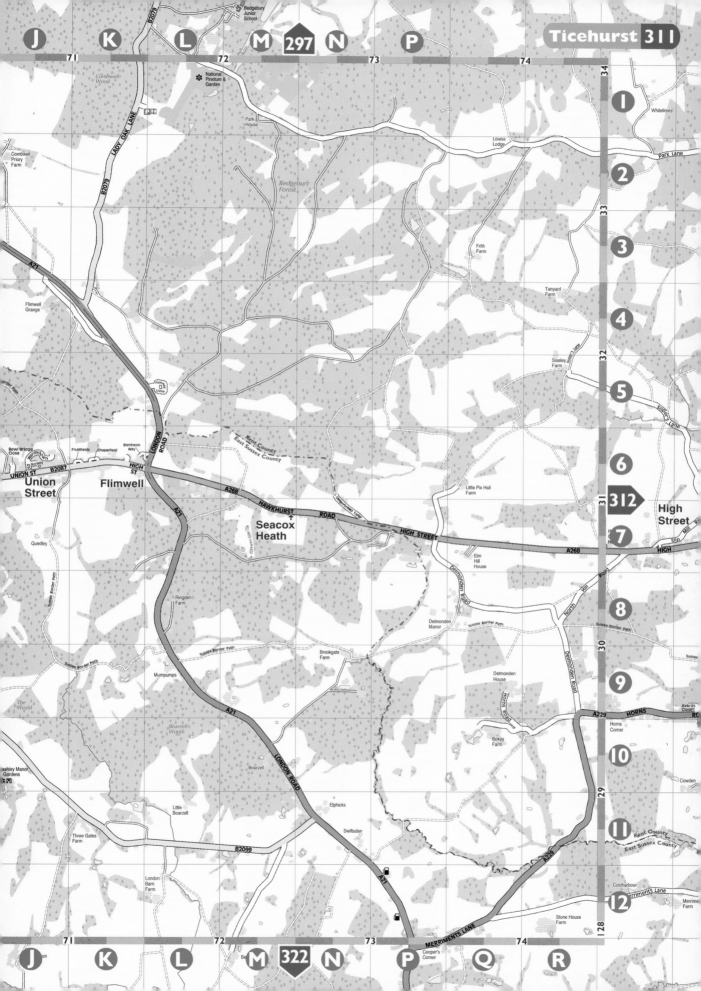

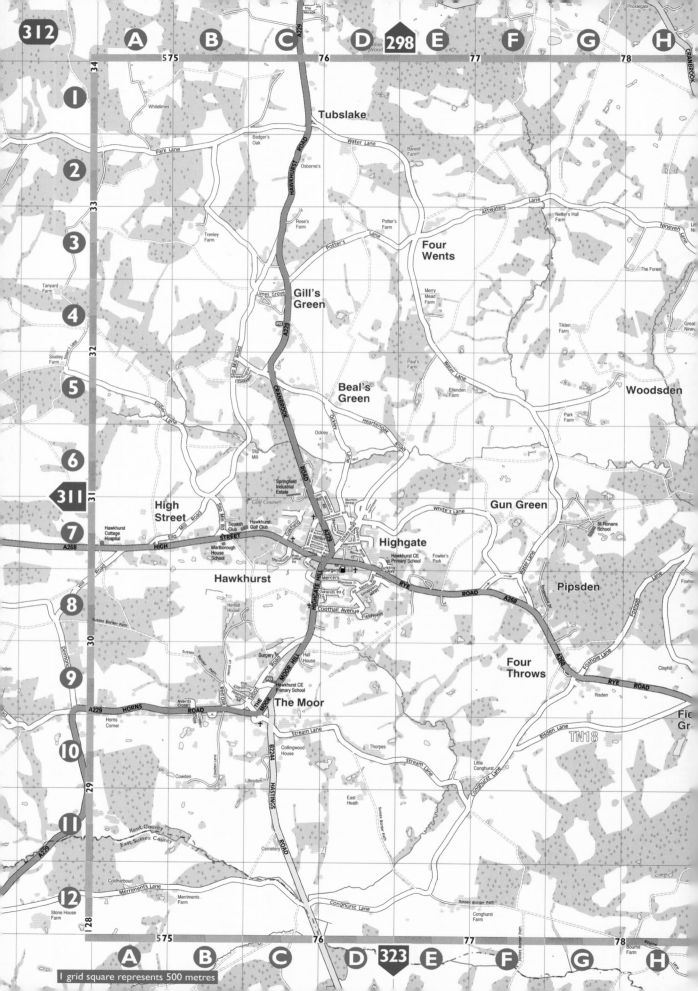

A B C A229 D 298 E F G H CRANBROOK

575 76 77 78

1 Whitelimes Tubslake

Park Lane Badger's Oak Water Lane Baretill Farm

2 Osborne's HAWKHURST ROAD

Attwaters Lane Netter's Hall Farm Nineveh La

3 Trenley Farm Rose's Farm Potter's Lane Four Wents The Forest

Limes Grove Gill's Green Merry Mead Farm Tilden Farm Great Nineveh

4 Tanyard Farm Potter's Lane A229 Paul's Farm Ellenden Farm Woodsden

Siseley Farm CRANBROOK Beal's Green Water Lane

5 Cooper's Lane Ockley Heartenoak Road Park Farm

6 Slip Mill ROAD Ockley

311 Springfield Industrial Estate Gun Green St Ronans School

High Street Golf Course Murton White's Lane

7 Hawkhurst Cottage Hospital Slip Mill Rd Squash Club Hawkhurst Golf Club Manchester Rd Highgate Fowler's Park

A268 HIGH STREET Marlborough House School Hawkhurst CE Primary School

8 Hawkhurst Hensill House HIGHGATE HILL Mercers RYE ROAD A268 Pipsden Foxhole La Foxholm

Sussex Border Path Copthall Avenue Fieldways

9 Delmonde Surgery Hall House MOOR HILL Four Throws Risden RYE ROAD

The Chestnuts Hawkhurst CE Primary School Risden Lane TN18

Red Oak THE MOOR The Moor Clayhill

A229 HORNS ROAD Stream Lane Thorpes Little Conghurst

Horns Corner Awards Close Collingwood House Conghurst Lane Field Gr

10 Cowden Croechen Lane Lillesden Stream Lane

Sussex Border Path

11 Kent County East Sussex County East Heath

A229 HASTINGS ROAD Cemetery

12 Coldharbour Merriments Lane Conghurst Lane Conghurst Farm

Stone House Farm Merriments Farm Sussex Border Path Bourne Fa

A B C 76 D 323 E F 77 G 78 H

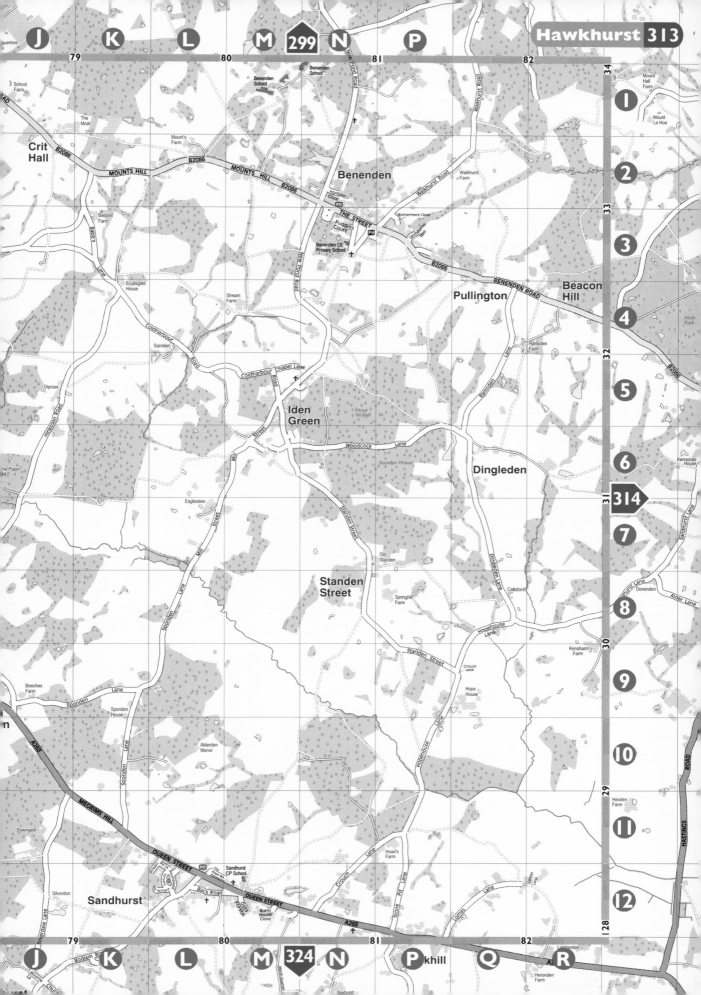

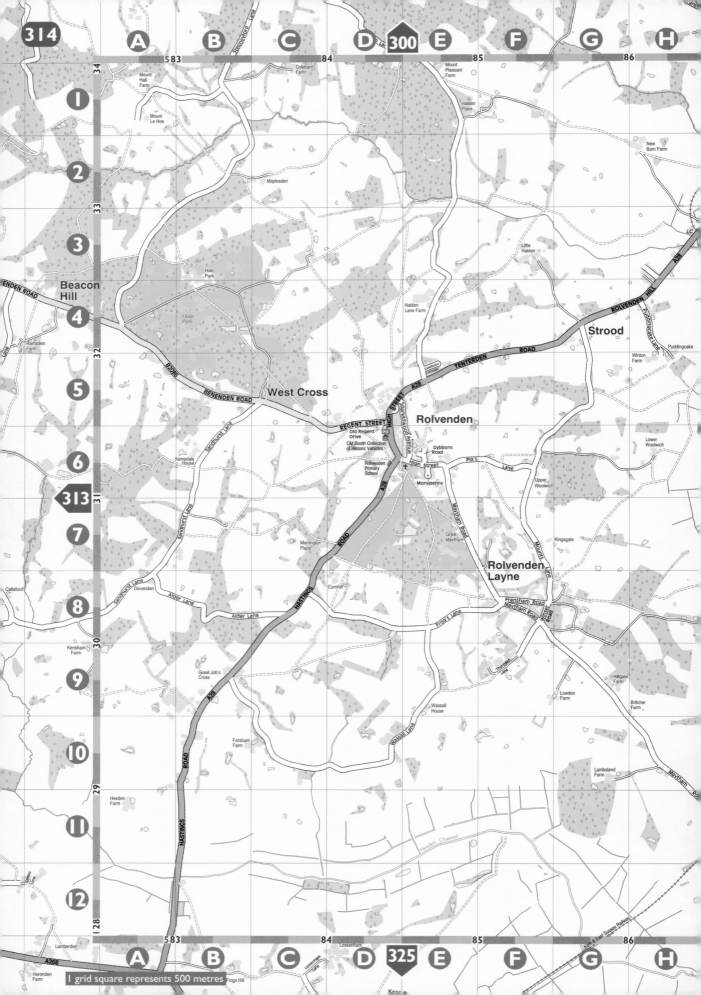

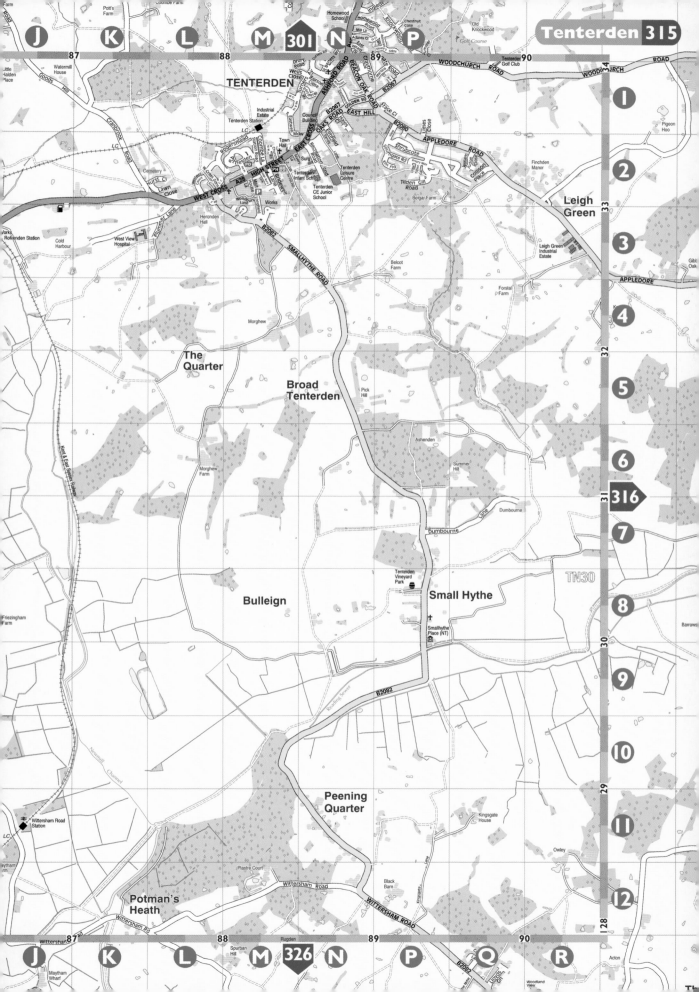

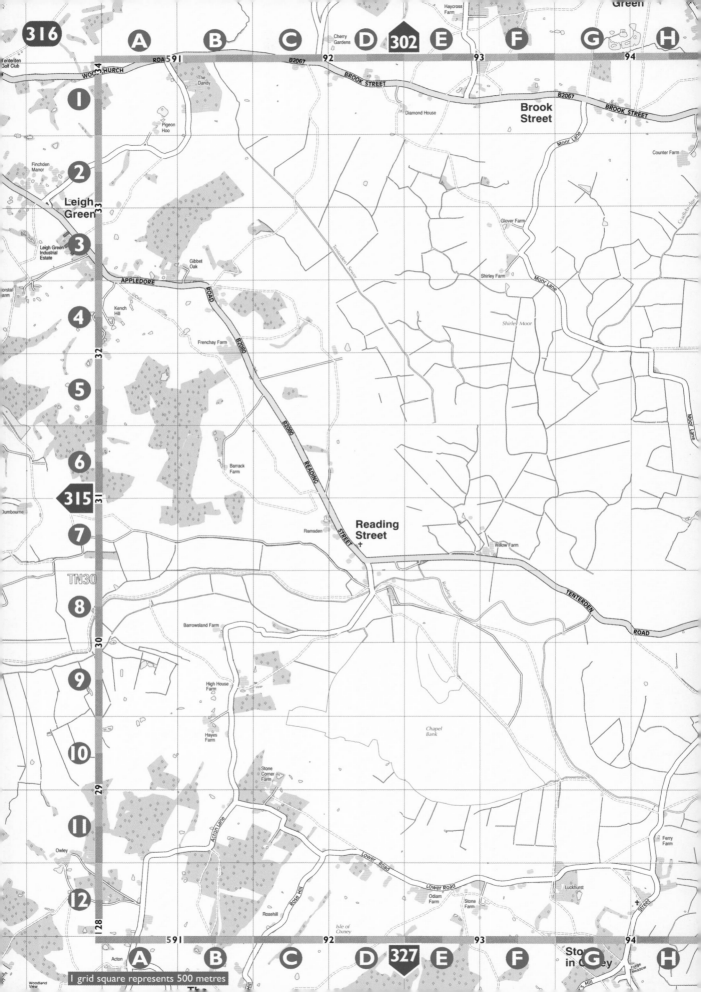

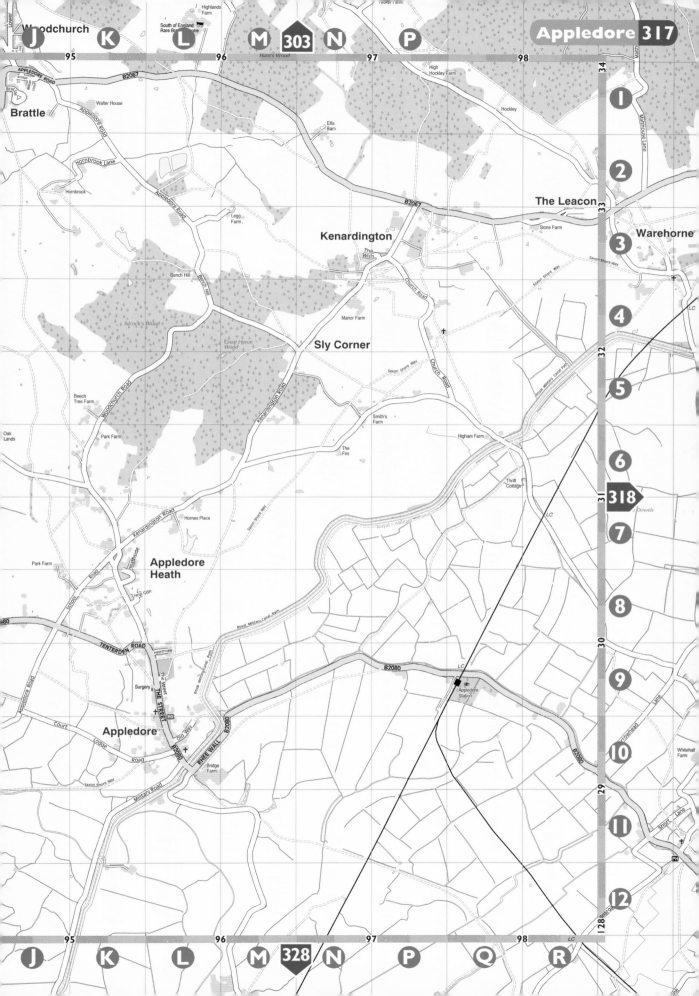

Woodchurch

J K L M 303 N P

Brattle

Walter House

Hornbrook Lane

Appledore Road

B2067

Bridge

Hornbrook

Appledore Road

Highlands Farm

South of England Rare Breeds Centre

Hunt's Wood

Ellis Barn

High Hockley Farm

Hockley

1

2

The Leacon

Warehorne

Stone Farm

Saxon Shore Way

3

Bench Hill

Silcock's Wood

Great Heron Wood

Legg Farm

Kenardington

The Wish

Church Road

Manor Farm

Sly Corner

Saxon Shore Way

Church Road

Smith's Farm

Higham Farm

Royal Military Canal Path

4

5

6

7

8

9

10

11

12

318

Dowels

Thrift Cottage

LC

Beech Tree Farm

Park Farm

Oak Lands

Woodchurch Road

Kenardington Road

Hornes Place

Saxon Shore Way

The Firs

Park Farm

School Road

Heathside

Hop Gdn

Appledore Heath

Kenardington Road

Royal Military Canal Path

Royal Military Canal

Royal Military Canal Path

B2080

LC

Appledore Station

LC

B2080

Crownhead Lane

Whitehall Farm

Short Lane

PH

Appledore Road

TENTERDEN ROAD

Hawthorn

Surgery

The Street

THE STREET

20

Appledore

Court Lodge

Road

Saxon Shore Way

Old Way

B2080

RHEE WALL

Bridge Farm

B2080

Military Road

95 96 97 98

J K L M 328 N P Q R

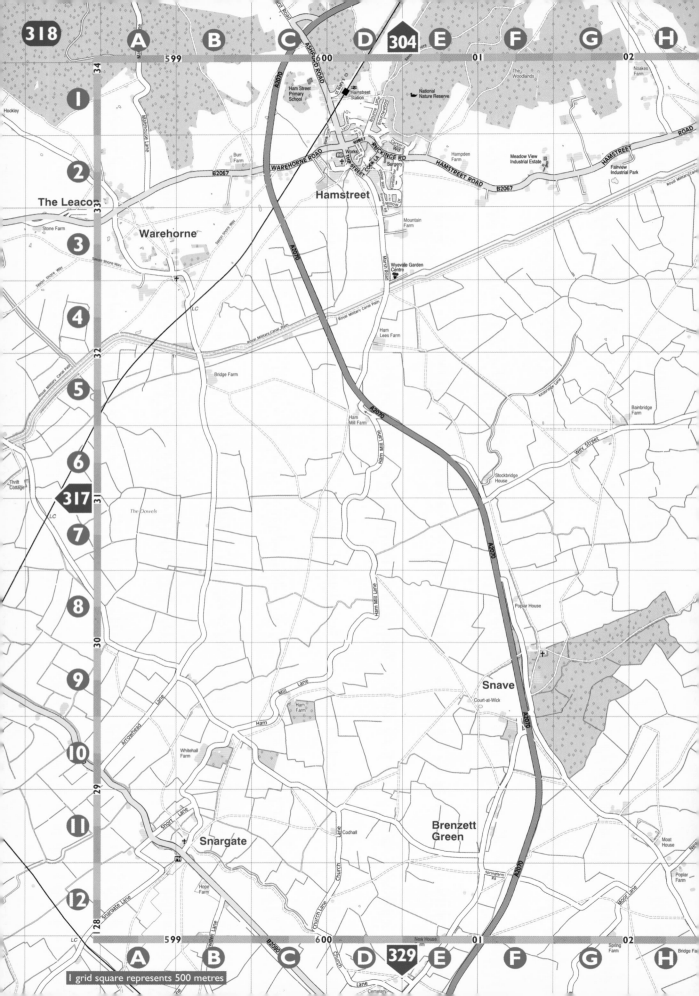

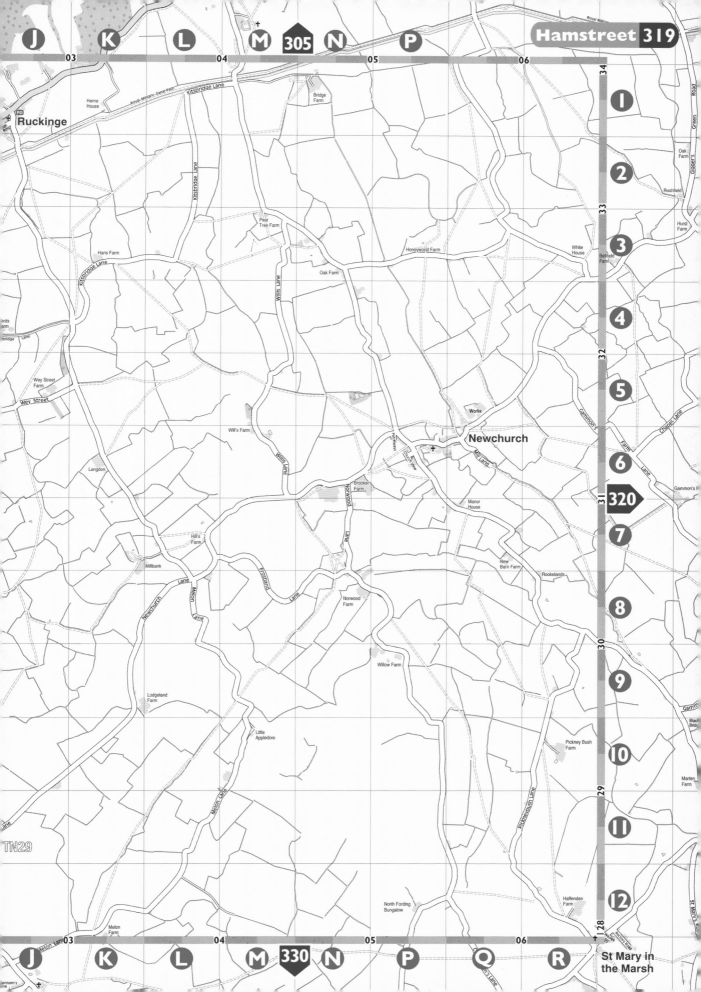

A   B   C   D 306 E   F   G   H

607   08   09   10

34

1
2
3
4
5
6
319 31
7
8
9
10
11
12

33

32

30

29

28

607   08   09   10

A   B   C 331 D   E   F   G   H

Royal Military Canal Path
Saxon Shore Way

College Farm
Tontine Farm

Green Road
Lower Wall
Lower Wall Road

Oak Farm
Gigger's
Abbott's Court

Rushfield
Lower Wall Road
Tame Lane

Hurst Farm

Bellfield Farm

Tame Lane Cottage

Church

The Green
Burmarsh

Eastbridge House
Church Road
Church Road

Chapel Lane
Forty Acre Cottage

Gammon's
Farm Lane

Gammon's Farm
Newbarn

Orgarswick Farm

New Barn Farm

Chapel Cottage Farm

Rookelands

Eastbridge Road
Sutton Farm

Dymchurch Prim Sch

Gammon's Farm Lane

Blackmanstone Bridge

Dymchurch Station
Dymchurch Surgery

Pickney Bush

Tatman Farm
Dymchurch Martello Tower

Marten Farm
Selinge Farm

St Mary's Road

Pickneybush Lane

Treloar

Dymchurch Railway

St Mary's Bay

DYMCHURCH ROAD

Copsden Road

St Mary in the Marsh

1 grid square represents 500 metres

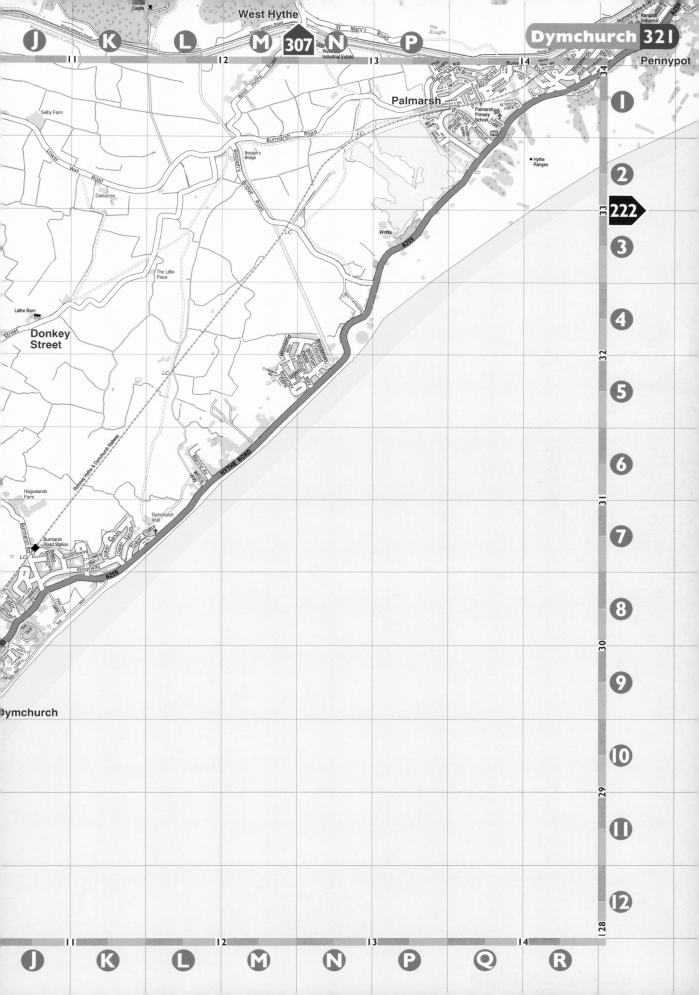

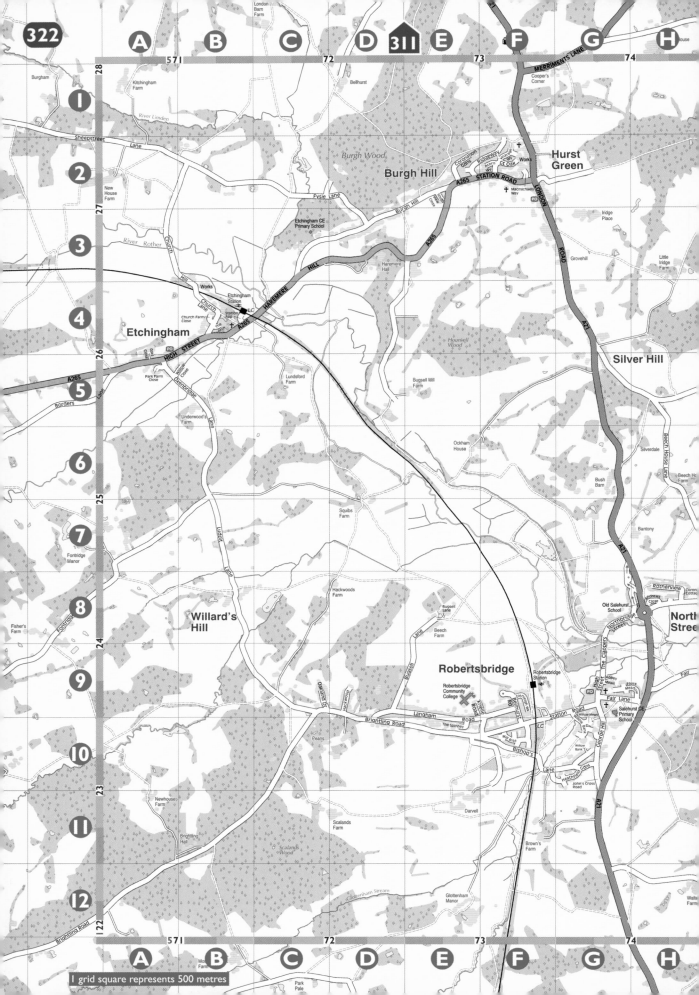

J K L M N P
75 76 77 78

312

Coldharbour
Merriments Lane
Merriments Farm
Congh...
Conghurst Farm
Sussex Border Path
28
Silverden
S

I
Sandhurst Cross
Bourne Farm
Bourne Lane
Church Road
Bodiam

2
Brickhurst Wood
B2244
27
Bodiam Road

3
Northlands
Kent County
East Sussex County

4
Climsett's Farm
High Wigsell
South Park
Neals
Elms Farm
Lower Northlands Farm
Levetts Lane
Bodiam Manor School
Court Lodge
26
Sussex Border Path

Boarsney Farm
Bourne Lane
Castle Road B2244
Bodiam CE Primary School
Bodiam

5
Bodiam Castle (NT)

Bourne Farm

6
New House
Bodiam Bridge

Haiselman's Farm
Park Farm
Bodiam Station
LC
25
324
Kent & East Sussex

Bocks Hill
Higham House
Ockham
7
Sussex Border Path

alehurst
dge
Lane
Moat Farm
Quarry Farm
Udiam
Dagg
8
Snagsha

Bocks Hill
24
Shoreham

Lane
Redlands
River Rother
Madamses Farm
Prawl... Farm
9

Fowlbrook Wood
Eyelids
10

Park Farm
Hollow Wall Farm
23

Lordship Wood
11

TN32
Staple Cross MCP Prim Sch
She...
Mill
B2165
Co...
Gre...

Poppinghole Lane
Forge Lane
Handset Farm
Cricketers Field
Staplecros...
12

The Grange
22

75 76 77 78
J K L M N P Q R
B2...
B...

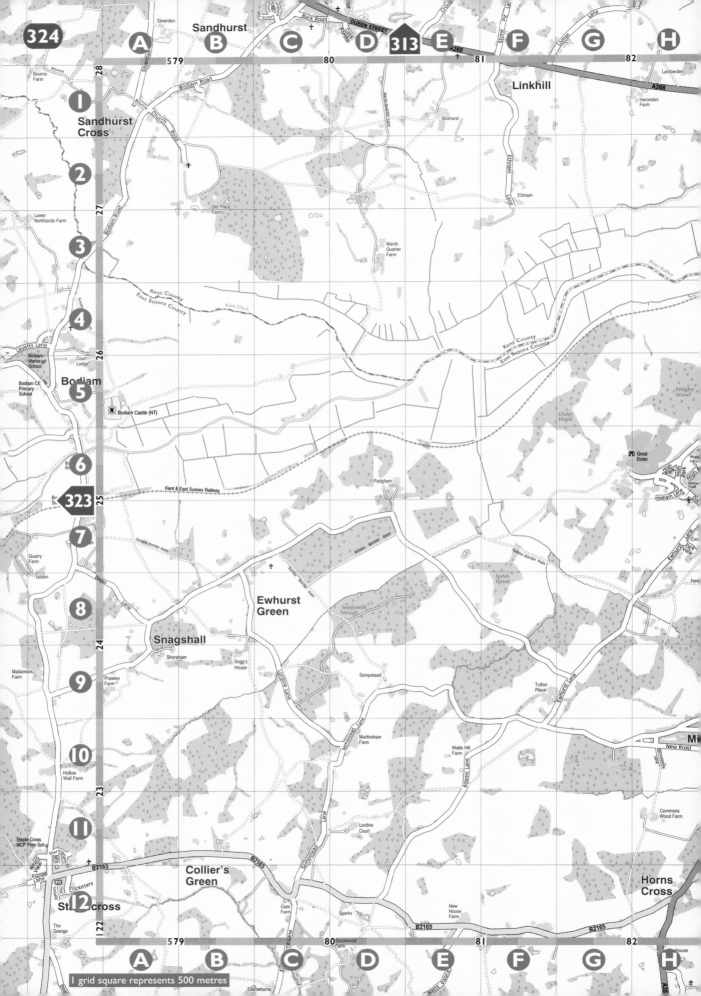

The Stocks

Stone in Oxney

Isle of Oxney

Rosehill
Rose Hill
B2082
Wittersham Road
STOCKS
ROAD
Acton

Holman's Farm

Tophill Farm

RYE
ROAD
B2082

Rother Levels

Newbridge Farm

Kent County
East Sussex County

Great Prawls Farm

Oxenden

Lower Road
Odiam Farm
Stone Farm
Luckhurst

Catt Farm

Top Road

Church Hill
Knock Hill

Mackley Farm

Cliff Farm

Stone Cliff

Cliff Marsh Farm

Forge Meadow

Saxon Shore Way

Royal Military Canal
Military
Stone Bridge

Royal Military Canal Path

Five Watering Sewer

Sussex Border Path
River Rother

Thornsdale

WITTERSHAM ROAD
B2082

Corkwood Farm

Oxenbridge
GARDNER'S HILL
WITTERSHAM RD

Baron's Grange

Readers Lane

WITTERSHAM LANE

Grove Lane
The Elms

Bosney Farm

Boonshill

Military Road

Saxon Shore Way

Church Lane
B2082
Iden
MAIN STREET
IDEN ROAD B2082

Coldharbour Lane

Iden Park

Playden Lane

Houghton Lane

Randolph Lane

Mockbeggar

Brabands
RYE ROAD

Broomhill Lodge Hotel

Bowler's Town

St Michaels CE Primary School

School Lane

Houghton Green Lane

Scots Float

Union Channel

LC

Houghton Green

Saltbarn Farm

Military Road

A259

East Su...

LC

328 ▶

I 1 2 3 4 5 6 7 8 9 10 11 12

28 27 26 25 24 23 22

91 92 93 94

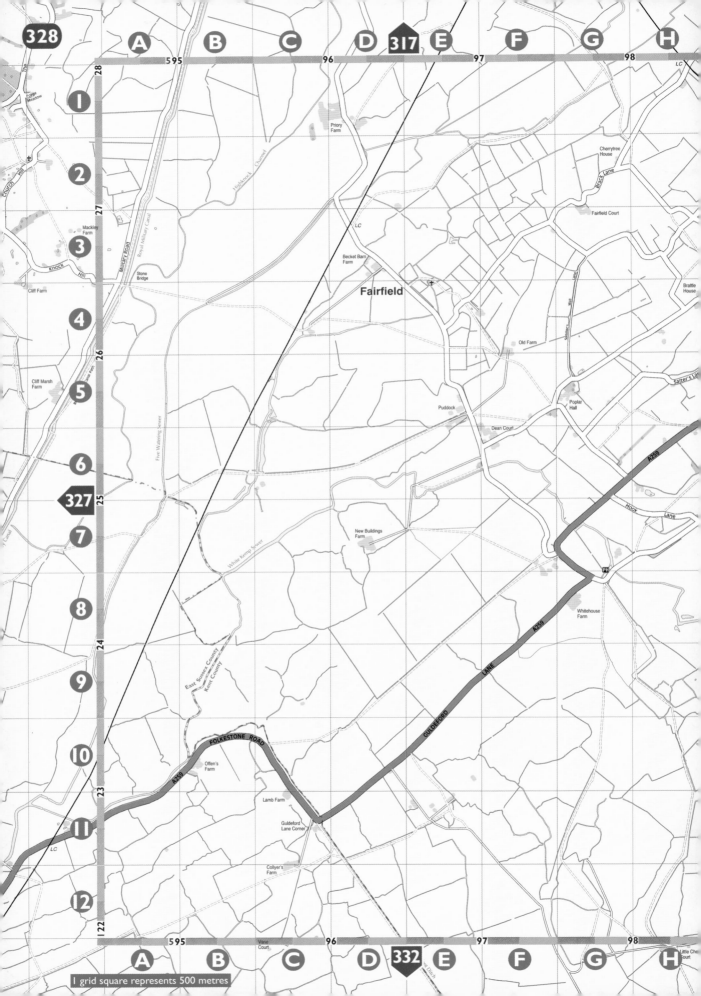

A   B   C   D   317   E   F   G   H

595   96   97   98

Fairfield

327

FOLKESTONE ROAD

GULDEFORD LANE A259

A259

A   B   C   D   332   E   F   G   H

595   96   97   98

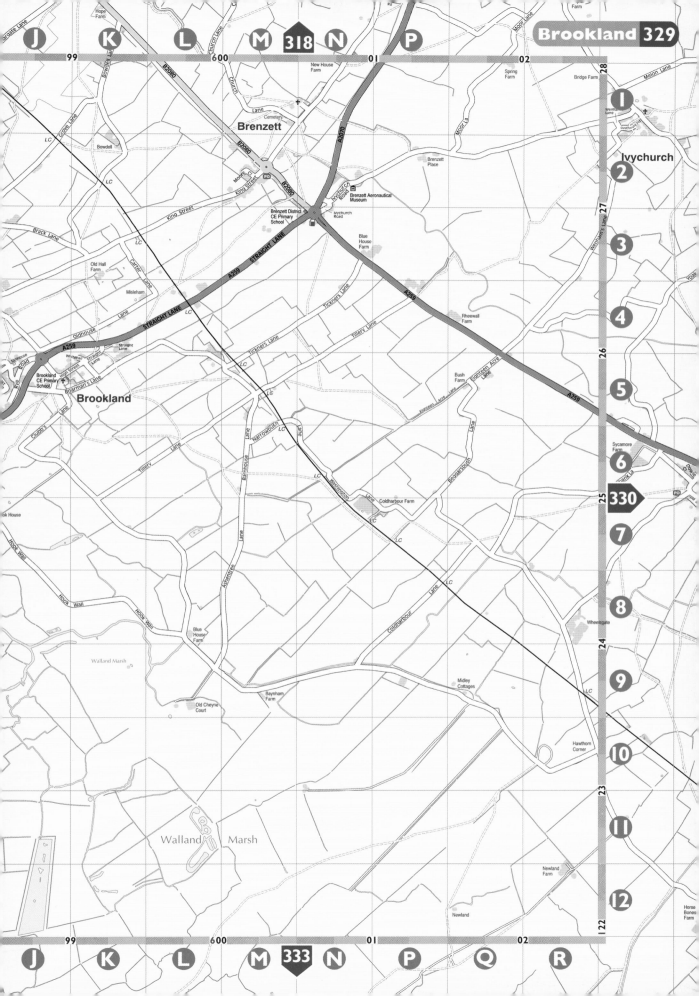

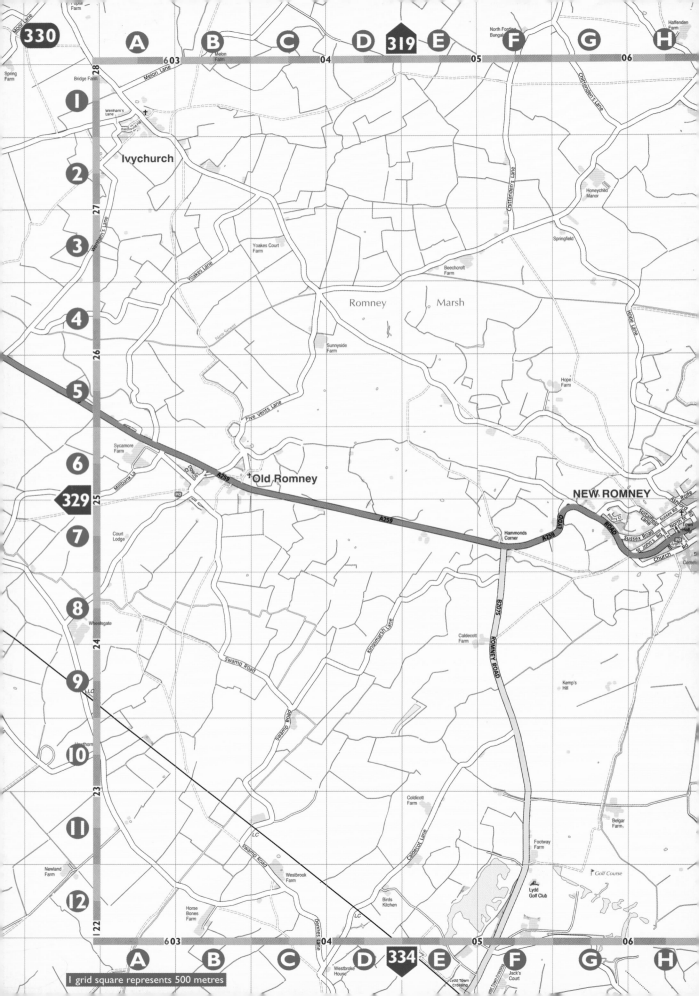

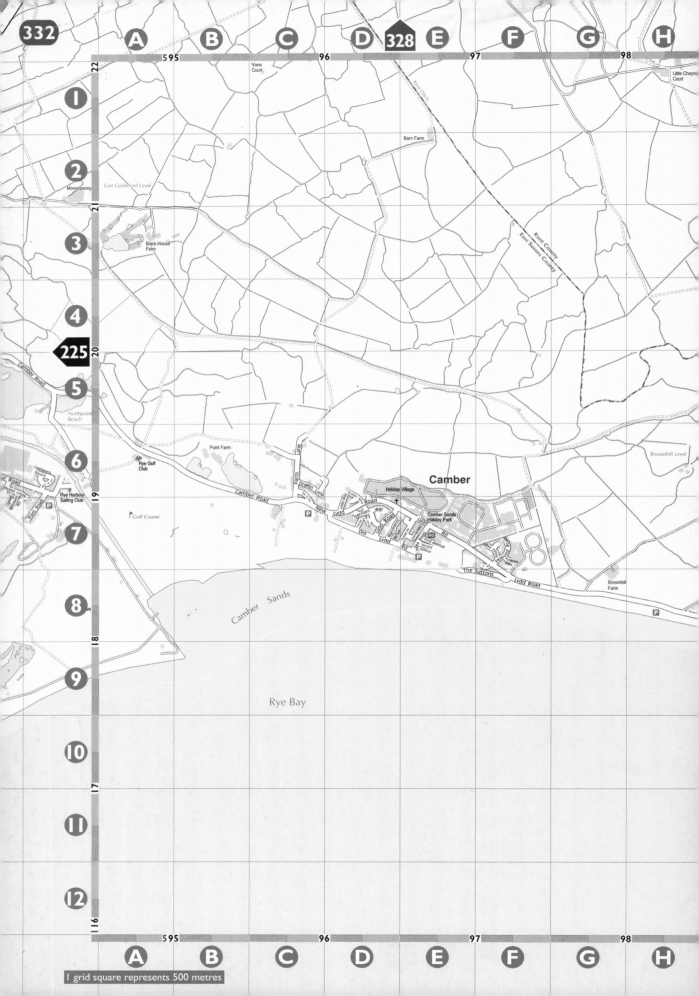

A   B   C   D   328   E   F   G   H

595   96   97   98

22

I

Vane
Court

Little Cheyne
Court

2

Moneypenny

East Guldeford Level

21

Barn Farm

Kent Ditch

3

Black House
Farm

Kent County
East Sussex County

4

225

20

Camber Road

5

Northpoint
Beach

Broomhill Level

6

Rye Golf
Club

Point Farm

Camber

Rye Harbour
Sailing Club

19

Camber Road

Farm
Draflin Lane

Holiday Village

New

Lydd

Road

Camber Sands
Holiday Park

7

Golf Course

Old

P

P

Lydd
Rd

First Avenue

Broomhill
Farm

8

Camber   Sands

The Suttons

Lydd Road

P

18

9

Rye Bay

10

17

11

12

16

595   96   97   98

A   B   C   D   E   F   G   H

1 grid square represents 500 metres

Horse
Bone
Farm

Newland

1
2
3
4
5
6
334
7
8
9
10
11
12

Lower
Agney

Little Scotney

Red
House

Kent County
East Sussex County

Scotney
Court

Jury's
Gap
Road

The Forelands

Holmstone

Jury's Gap

Lydd Road

Jury's Gap Road

Jury's Gut Sewer

Jury's Gap Road

South
Brooks

Midrips

Denge Marsh

Lydd
Ranges

The
Wicks

East Sussex County
Kent County

roomhill Sands

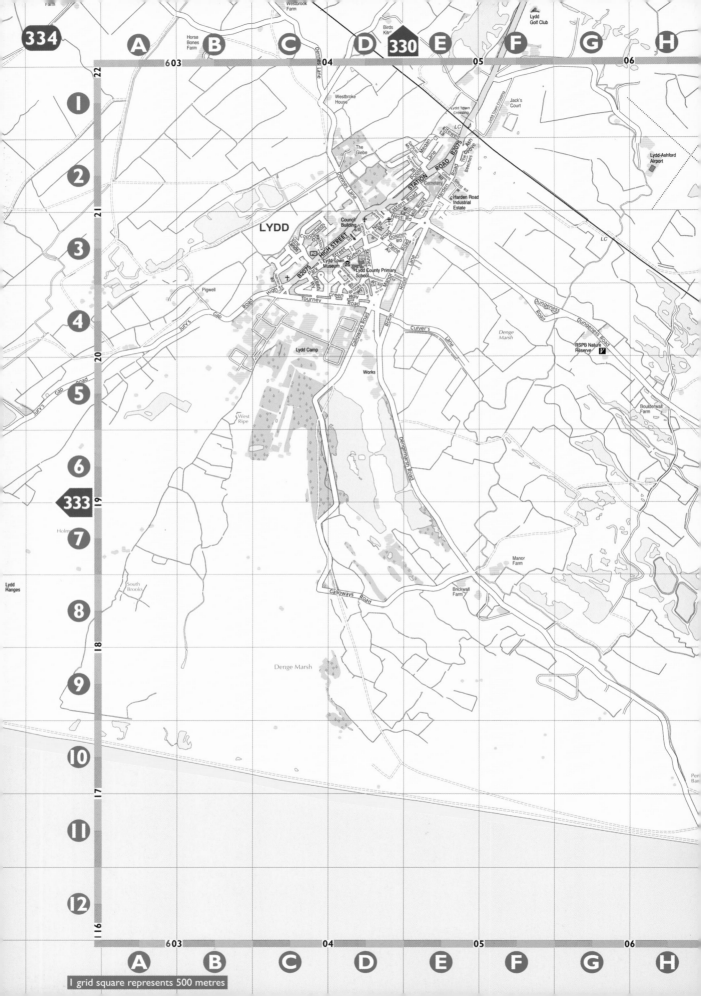

330

A   B   C   D   E   F   G   H

I
2
3
4
5
6
7
8
9
10
II
12

LYDD

HIGH STREET

Lydd Town Museum
Lydd County Primary School
Council Building

Harden Road Industrial Estate

STATION ROAD

Lydd Golf Club

Lydd-Ashford Airport

Jack's Court

Lydd Town Crossing

The Glebe

Pigwell

Jury's Gap Road

Lydd Camp

West Ripe

Works

Culver's Lane

Denge Marsh

Dungeness Road

RSPB Nature Reserve

Boulderwall Farm

Galloways Road

Denge Marsh

Manor Farm

Brickwall Farm

Lydd Ranges

South Brooks

Horse Bones Farm

Dennes Lane

Westbroke House

Westbrook Farm

Birds Kitchen

1 grid square represents 500 metres

A   B   C   D   E   F   G   H

07   08   09   10

1
2
3
4
5
6
7
8
9
10
11
12

22
21
20
19
18
17
116

Lade

Lydd-on-Sea

Holiday Village

Romney Sands Station

Beachmont Close

Prior Road

Channon Road

Derville Road

Walter Rd

Coleville Crs

Taylor Road

Fort Crs

Williamson

Lade Road

North Road

Coast Drive

Penlands Road

The Parade

Ballards Rd

Seaview Rd

Roberts

LC

P

LC

Hull Rd

LC

RSPB Reserve

Dungeness Road

Halfway Bush

Works

Kerton Road

Penlands Road Centre

Nature Reserve

Open Pits

Denge Beach

COAST Drive

Battery Road

Penlands Road South

LC

The Pilot

LC

LC

Dungeness Road

Romney Hythe & Dymchurch Railway

LC

Dungeness Station

Dungeness Power Stations' Visitor Centre

Dungeness Power Station

Reservoir Av

Transformer Av

Dungeness Road

Old Lighthouse

Dungeness

Abbey Gate 141 C2
Abbey Wood 29 J3
Acol 180 E2
Addington 104 F1
Addington 239 Q11
Addiscombe 87 G3
Adisham 251 N9
Aldington 305 Q7
Aldington Frith 305 N7
Alkham 293 P8
Allhallows 41 L6
Allhallows-on-Sea 42 A3
Allington 140 E5
Anerley 69 H6
Anvil Green 268 A6
Aperfield 132 E3
Appledore 317 K10
Appledore Heath 317 L7
Arpinge 219 K2
Ash 95 M8
Ash 236 B12
Ashbank 169 J6
Ashford 2 D7
Ashley 272 H7
Ashurst 198 E3
Avery Hill 48 D4
Aycliff 217 H4
Aylesford 140 A2
Aylesham 251 Q12
Badgers Mount 109 G3
Badlesmere 246 B8
Bagham 247 P10
Baker's Cross 298 G8
Balls Green 198 C8
Bapchild 120 F6
Barden Park 194 C4
Bardown 309 R10
Barfrestone 271 R4
Barham 270 D4
Barming Heath 166 A2
Barnehurst 50 E1
Barnes Cray 51 J2
Barnes Street 256 D9
Barnfield 263 M9
Barnsole 252 G3
Barrow Green 121 L6
Barrowhill 306 H6
Basted 240 E5
Bayley's Hill 254 F1
Bay View 230 C3
Beacon Hill 313 R4
Beal's Green 312 D5
Bean 53 J8
Bearsted 168 C3
Beckenham 70 B7
Beckley 325 P9
Bedgebury Cross 297 L11
Bekesbourne 175 L5
Bekesbourne Hill 175 J4
Bell Green 46 A8
Bellingham 70 B1
Bells Yew Green 294 G8
Beltinge 129 L5
Beltring 257 L9
Belvedere 30 C4
Benenden 313 N2
Benover 258 A8
Bermondsey 25 G1
Berner's Hill 310 H7
Berry's Green 132 F2
Berwick 307 M9
Bessels Green 20 A3
Best Beech Hill 308 H6
Bethersden 285 P12
Betsham 78 A1
Betteshanger 253 N11
Bexley 49 K2
Bexleyheath 50 A2
Bexon 145 J5
Bickley 71 M6
Bicknor 144 D7
Bidborough 196 A2
Biddenden 300 D3
Biddenden Green 284 E7
Biggin 35 K5
Biggin Hill 132 A3
Bilsington 305 M12
Bilting 266 F5
Birchden 199 L7
Birchett's Green 309 R6
Birchington 176 F6
Bircholt Forstal 289 L10
Birling 112 C7
Bishopsbourne 250 E11
Bishopstone 232 A4
Bitchet Green 163 J4
Blacketts 121 J3
Blackfen 49 G4
Blackham 198 B1
Blackheath 27 G8
Blackheath Park 47 H2
Bladbean 269 Q11
Blean 153 C7
Bliby 305 J5
Blue Bell Hill 114 D4
Blue Town 64 A2
Bluetown 146 C8
Bobbing 119 J2
Bockhanger 202 E5
Bodiam 323 R5
Bodsham 290 B1
Bonnington 305 Q10
Borden 119 H7
Borough Green 240 F1
The Borough 24 D1
Borstal 100 C3
Bossingham 269 K7
Bossington 251 N6
Bottom Pond 145 L7
Bough Beech 254 A11
Boughton Aluph 266 C8
Boughton Corner 266 D9
Boughton Green 259 M2
Boughton Lees 266 A10
Boughton Malherbe 262 D5
Boughton Monchelsea 259 M3
Boughton Street 151 H6
Boughton-under-Blean 151 G5
Bowler's Town 327 L11
Bowmans 51 G5
Boxley 141 L3
Boyden Gate 232 D9
Brabourne 289 R9
Brabourne Lees 289 M12
Bramling 251 N3
Branbridges 257 L7
Brasted 160 A2
Brasted Chart 160 A6
Brattle 317 J1
Breach 118 A1
Bredgar 145 H4
Bredhurst 116 C4
Brenchley 279 M9
The Brents 123 L8
Brenzett 329 M1
Brenzett Green 318 E11
Bridge 175 H8
Brissenden Green 302 G3
Brixton 44 B2
Broad Ford 297 K1
Broad Green 86 C3
Broadham Green 184 D2
Broad Oak 172 E2
Broad Oak 305 M4
Broadstairs 179 K8
Broadstone 262 A8
Broad Street 83 K1
Broad Street 143 J7
Broad Street 290 C12
Broad Street 291 L12
Broad Tenterden 315 M5
Broadwater Down 201 G5
Brockley 46 A3
Bromley 71 J6
Bromley Common 89 L2
Bromley Green 304 B7
Bromley Park 70 F5
Brompton 7 G1
Bromstone 183 H2
Brook 289 J4
Brookland 329 K5
Brooks End 180 A1
Brook Street 194 D6
Brook Street 316 F1
Broomfield 129 L7
Broomfield 169 K8
Broom Hill 91 G3
Broomhill 235 J12
Broomhill Bank 277 R11
Broom Street 124 E7
Buckhurst 283 K12
Buckland 213 K7
Buckland Valley 213 J5
Bulleign 315 M8
Bullockstone 154 E1
Burgh Hill 322 D2
Burham 114 A4
Burham Court 113 L4
Burmarsh 320 H5
Burrswood 199 H5
Buttsole 253 N8
Bybrook 202 F6
Cage Green 194 F1
Calcott 154 F7
Camber 332 E6
Camberwell 25 G7
Camden Hill 299 J3
Camden Park 23 K6
Camer 97 K2
Canterbury 4 B4
Capel 278 C3
Capel Cross 280 B12
Capel-le-Ferne 221 J3
Capstone 101 L6
Castle Hill 279 P8
Catford 46 D6
Cellarhill 121 K8
Chadwell St Mary 35 G2
Chafford Hundred 33 M2
Chainhurst 258 F9
Chalk 56 B6
Chalksole 293 N5
Chalkwell 119 K5
Challock 265 P3
Chamber's Green 285 M6
Charcott 254 H10
Charing 264 C5
Charing Heath 263 P6
Charing Hill 264 C4
Charlton 27 L4
Chart Corner 260 C4
Chartham 248 F7
Chartham Hatch 170 E7
Chart Hill 260 C5
Chart Sutton 260 B8
The Chart 160 A8
Chatham 6 E5
Chattenden 58 F8
Cheeseman's Green 304 H3
Cheeseman's Green 304 H3
Chegworth 242 A11
Chelsfield 91 M8
Chelsham 130 F3
Cheriton 219 K7
Chesley 118 B6
Chestfield 127 L5
Chestnut Street 118 F5
Chevening 134 E5
Chiddingstone 276 C3
Chiddingstone Causeway 254 G11
Chiddingstone Hoath 276 B7
Childsbridge 136 E5
Chilham 247 N9
Chillenden 252 F9
Chillmill 279 K11
Chilmington Green 286 H12
Chilton 16 B6
Chipstead 135 H8
Chislehurst 72 D4
Chislehurst West 72 B3
Chislet 232 E12
Chislet Forstal 232 C12
Chitty 232 E11
Church Hougham 216 C4
Church Street 57 L4
Church Whitfield 273 J12
Cinder Hill 255 K12
Clapham Hill 126 E8
Clap Hill 305 Q6
Clapper Hill 300 E8
Claygate 189 J1
Claygate 280 B4
Claygate Cross 240 F6
Clayhill 325 M10
Claypits 252 B5
Clement Street 75 L3
Cliffe 38 D7
Cliffe Woods 58 D6
Cliffs End 182 A7
Cliftonville 15 M4
Cobham 80 A8
Cock Street 259 Q3
Coldblow 50 D7
Cold Harbour 119 G3
Coldharbour 31 H3
Coldharbour 188 D4
Coldred 272 A10
Colliers Green 298 C3
Collier's Green 324 B12
Collier Street 280 D1
Colt's Hill 278 E5
Combe 308 H11
Comp 241 L3
Coney Hall 88 F7
Congelow 257 P6
Conyer 121 M3
Cooling 39 G8
Coolinge 10 A7
Cooling Street 58 E4
Coombe 253 L1
Coomb Hill 97 M7
Cooper's Corner 254 A5
Cooper Street 236 D9
Coppins Corner 263 R7
Cop Street 236 B9
Copton 149 L7
The Corner 280 A9
Court-at-Street 306 F10
Cousley Wood 309 P2
Cousley Wood 309 P2
Cowden 275 M7
Coxheath 259 J2
Crabble 212 F7
Cranbrook 298 G8
Cranbrook Common 299 K3
Crayford 51 H3
Crit Hall 313 J2
Crit Hall 313 J2
Crockenhill 92 D2
Crockham Hill 186 D3
Crockhurst Street 195 L7
Crofton 90 E5
Cross-at-Hand 259 R12
Cross Keys 161 L5
Crouch 150 F8
Crouch 240 G5
Crowdleham 137 H2
Crowhurst 190 E2
Crowhurst Lane End 184 B8
Croydon 86 E6
Crundale 267 L6
Crystal Palace 69 H3
Cubitt Town 26 D3
Cudham 133 J1
Culmers 124 F8
Culverstone Green 239 K3
Curteis' Corner 300 F2
Curtisden Green 280 H12
Cuxton 99 K3
Dale Hill 310 G7
Danaway 118 D7
Dane Street 247 L11
Daniel's Water 286 C9
Darenth 76 D2
Dargate 151 L1
Dargate Common 151 M2
Dartford 51 K5
David Street 97 H8
Davington 149 H1
Deal 209 K4
Dean Bottom 77 J7
Deans Bottom 144 D4
Deans Hill 144 E3
Dean Street 166 E7
Deerton Street 122 B7
Dene Park 189 G4
Denny Bottom 22 A5
Densole 292 F9
Denstroude 152 D5
Denton 55 M5
Denton 270 F10
Deptford 26 A5
Derringstone 270 D6
Derry Downs 91 L2
Detling 142 C4
Dingleden 313 Q6
Ditton 139 K3
Doddington 244 B2
Donkey Street 321 J4
Dormansland 274 A4
Dover 8 F6
Downe 106 E5
Downham 70 E2
The Down 296 A10
The Down 296 A10
Drellingore 293 M10
Dryhill 161 G2
Dulwich 45 G7
Dulwich Village 44 F5
Dumpton 183 H3
Dungate 146 C6
Dungeness 335 P11
Dunkirk 151 L7
Dunk's Green 240 F11
Dunn Street 116 B5
Dunn Street 265 K8
Dunton Green 135 K5
Durgates 309 J4
Durlock 180 F8
Durlock 252 G1
Durrant Green 301 N7
Dymchurch 321 J9
Each End 236 E12
East Barming 165 M4
Eastchurch 229 M2
East Dulwich 45 H3
East End 65 M6
East End 283 P5
East End 300 C10
East Farleigh 166 C6
East Guldeford 225 L2
East Hill 111 G3
East Langdon 210 B8
Eastling 244 G3
East Malling 139 J7
East Malling Heath 164 F2
East Peckham 257 J7
Eastry 253 N7
East Stourmouth 235 N4
East Street 236 E11
East Studdal 273 M5
East Tilbury 36 C3
Eastwell Park 265 Q10
East Wickham 29 H7
Eccles 114 B8
Eddington 128 F6
Edenbridge 192 B3
Eden Park 70 A8
Egerton 262 H10
Egerton Forstal 262 G12
Elham 291 P4
Elmers End 69 L7
Elmstead 71 M2
Elmsted 290 C3
Elmstone 235 M8
Eltham 47 M4
Elvington 272 D4
Erith 31 G4
Erriottwood 146 F6
Etchingham 322 A4
Etchinghill 218 D2
Evington 290 A2
Ewell Minnis 293 R5
Ewhurst Green 324 C8
Exted 291 N4
Eyhorne Street 169 J3
Eynsford 93 M5
Eythorne 272 C6
Fairbourne Heath 261 P4
Fairfield 328 D4
Fairseat 238 H6
Falconwood 48 F2
Fant 12 A7
Farleigh 104 E8
Farleigh Court 104 F8
Farleigh Green 165 M7
Farnborough 90 C8
Farningham 94 B3
Farthing Corner 116 F2
Farthing Green 260 F12
Farthingloe 217 G4
Faversham 149 M1
Fawkham Green 95 J6
Felderland 206 A5
Fenn Street 60 B2
Ferndale 23 K2
Fickleshole 105 K8
Field Green 312 H9
Finglesham 208 B1
Fir Toll 285 M3
Five Oak Green 278 D1
Five Wents 260 F3
Flackley Ash 326 C10
Fleet Downs 52 C7
Flemings 253 J3
Fletcher's Green 255 L4
Flimwell 311 K6
Flishinghurst 298 C6
Folkestone 11 K7
Foots Cray 73 J3
Force Green 159 K2
Ford 155 M1
Fordcombe 276 H12
Fordwich 173 H5
Forestdale 104 D3
Forest Hill 45 L6
Forstal 140 D3
The Forstal 305 N2
Fostall 151 H2
Fosten Green 300 C8
Four Elms 187 H8
Four Oaks 122 F8
Four Oaks 325 R8
Four Throws 312 F9
Four Wents 298 B5
Four Wents 312 E3
Foxbury 72 E2
Foxendown 97 K5
Frant 294 B10
French Street 159 L8
Frindsbury 19 K2
Friningham 143 G4
Frinsted 243 K2
Frittenden 282 G10
Frogham 271 P4
Froghole 186 E2
Frogholt 218 F5
Further Quarter 301 P2
Gadshill 81 K3
Garlinge 177 K6
Garlinge Green 248 F11
Gibraltar 220 A2
Gillingham 7 G2
Gill's Green 312 C4
Glassenbury 298 B7
Goathurst Common 161 G8
Goddard's Green 299 Q11
Godden Green 163 G3
Goddington 91 K6
Godinton Park 204 A1
Godmersham 267 J3
Golden Green 256 C8
Golford 299 K7
Golgotha 271 R7
Goodley Stock 159 G8
Goodnestone 150 E2
Goodnestone 252 C8
Goose Green 256 E3
Goose Green 300 D5
Gore 253 M6
Gore Street 233 P10
Gosmere 246 C2
Goudhurst 297 N5
Gover Hill 241 K11
Grafty Green 262 B7
Grain 43 K7
Grange 84 C7
Gravel Castle 270 F5
Graveney 124 E7
Gravesend 55 J3
Grays 34 A6
Great Bower 246 F11
Great Buckland 112 B1
Great Chart 286 H8
Great Cheveney 280 F8
Great Mongeham 208 D6
Greatness 136 C6
Great Pattenden 280 F3
Great Stonar 237 J10
Greatstone-on-Sea 331 L11
Greenhill 128 E7
Green Hill 168 C5
Greenhithe 53 G2
Green Street Green 77 H3
Green Street Green 107 K2
Greenwich 26 E4
Greet 244 A6
Grigg 283 P3
Groombridge 199 H6
Grove 234 G5
Grove End 145 K2
Grove Ferry 234 G3
Grove Green 141 L8
Grove Hill 234 E7
Grove Park 47 K8
Groves 252 E2
Grubb Street 77 J5
Guilton 235 R12
Gun Green 312 F7
Gushmere 246 H2
Guston 213 M3
Hacklinge 206 D7
Hadlow 256 C4
Hadlow Stair 195 K1
Haffenden Quarter 284 D10
Haine 182 C3
Hale 101 L5
Hale 233 Q5
Hales Place 172 B6
Hale Street 257 K6
Halfway Houses 64 F6
Halfway Street 271 Q10
Halling 99 J8
Hall's Green 254 H5
Halstead 108 F6
Ham 206 A7
Ham Green 226 A7
Ham Green 326 F4
Ham Hill 113 H7
Hammerwood 274 G10
Hammill 253 K5
Hampton 128 C4
Hamptons 240 G12
Hamsey Green 130 B1
Hamstreet 318 C2
Hanging Bank 254 A2
Harbledown 171 J5
Harbourland 141 J4
The Harbour 260 F8
Hareplain 300 B2
Harman's Corner 119 J7
Harrietsham 242 E11
Hartley 96 A1
Hartley 298 C11
Hartley Green 95 M1
Hartlip 103 L8
Harvel 239 P2
Hassell Street 267 P11
Hastingleigh 289 Q3
Haviker Street 258 D12
Hawkenbury 23 L8
Hawkenbury 282 D2
Hawkhurst 312 B8
Hawkinge 292 G12
Hawley 75 M2
Hawthorn Corner 232 B6
Haxted 192 A5
Hayes 89 J3
Hazel Street 144 B6
Hazel Street 296 F2
Hazelwood 107 H5
Headcorn 283 M4
Hearnden Green 260 H12
Hearts Delight 119 J8
Heath Side 51 G7
Heaverham 137 K3
Hempstead 101 M8
Hemsted 290 G9
Henhurst 79 M5
Henley Street 98 A2
Henwood Green 278 C11
Herne 155 G1
Herne Bay 128 F5
Herne Common 155 G2
Herne Hill 44 D4
Herne Pound 241 R7
Hernhill 151 J3
Heronden 253 K8
Hersden 234 A5
Hever 193 K7
Hextable 75 H4
Hickmans Green 151 H7
Hicks Forstal 155 H5
Higham 81 K1
Higham Wood 189 J7
High Brooms 196 F5
Highgate 312 D7
High Halden 301 Q6
High Halstow 59 M2
Highstead 232 B8
Highsted 146 A2
Highstreet 152 A3
High Street 312 A7
Hildenborough 188 B7
Hilden Park 194 B1
Hillborough 232 B5
Hill Green 117 K4
Hill Hoath 276 C3
Hill Hoath 276 C3
Hill Park 159 G1
Hill Street 290 C1
Hinxhill 288 E8
Hither Green 46 F4
Hoaden 235 N9
Hoath 232 A12
Hoath Corner 276 C6
Hockenden 74 C7
Hockley 245 M6
Hodsoll Street 238 H3
Hogben's Hill 246 F3
Holborough 113 H3
Holland 185 H3
Hollingbourne 169 M3
Hollow Street 232 D12
Hollybushes 243 P1
Holt Hill 139 L5
Holtye 275 K10
Honey Hill 152 F6
Honor Oak 45 L4
Honor Oak Park 45 M4
Hoo 180 C7
Hook Green 75 G1
Hook Green 78 A3
Hook Green 97 H2
Hook Green 295 Q9
Hoo St Werburgh 59 K7
Horns Cross 53 G4
Horns Cross 324 H12
Horns Green 133 K3
Horn Street 112 F7
Horn Street 223 J1
Horsalls 242 G7
Horseshoe Green 275 P4
Horsmonden 279 P11
Horton 248 G6
Horton Kirby 76 E8
Hosey Hill 159 K6
Hothfield 286 F2
Houghton Green 327 N12
How Green 193 L3
Howt Green 227 L12
Hubbard's Hill 162 A8
Hucking 143 M4
Hulberry 93 J5
Hungershall Park 22 A8
Hunters Forstal 129 J8
Hunton 258 D5
Hurst Green 184 F2
Hurst Green 322 F2
Hythe 222 D4
Ickham 234 D12
Ide Hill 187 M1
Iden 327 L9
Iden Green 297 R5
Iden Green 313 M5
Ightham 240 C3
Ightham Common 163 M2
Isle of Dogs 26 D3
Istead Rise 78 F4
Ivychurch 330 A2
Ivy Hatch 240 A7
Iwade 227 L9
Joyden's Wood 75 G1
Jury's Gap 333 K8
Kearnsey 212 D5
Kempe's Corner 203 L1
Kemsing 136 E3
Kemsley 120 A1
Kemsley Street 116 D4
Kenardington 317 N3
Kennington 203 H5
Kent Street 164 A3
Keston 89 L7
Keston Mark 89 L6
Kettle Corner 166 A5
Kevingtown 92 A2
Keycol 118 F3
Key's Green 295 P1
Key Street 119 H4
Kidbrooke 27 K8
Kilndown 296 H11
Kingsdown 146 E5
Kingsdown 211 J4
Kings Farm 55 K8
Kingsgate 179 K4
Kings Hill 164 C1
Kingsnorth 60 E7
Kingsnorth 204 D8
Kingston 270 B2
Kingswood 261 M3
Kipping's Cross 295 M1
Kippington 20 E8
Kit's Coty 114 D5
Knatts Valley 111 K4
Knave's Ash 155 K4
Knight's Hill 44 D6
Knockhall 53 J3
Knockholt 133 M3
Knockmill 111 K6
Knowlton 252 H10

Knox Bridge 282 B11
Laddingford 257 P8
Lade 335 M3
Ladywell 46 B2
Lakeside 33 H3
Lamberhurst 296 C8
Lamberhurst Quarter 295 Q3
Lambeth 24 B2
Lamb's Cross 260 A8
Lane End 76 E2
Langley 260 D1
Langley Heath 260 G1
Langton Green 200 A1
Larkfield 139 H3
The Leacon 317 R2
Leadingcross Green 262 F2
Leaveland 245 R9
Leaves Green 106 C5
Lee 47 G4
Leeds 169 H6
The Lees 265 M4
Leigh 255 N11
Leigh Green 315 R3
Lenham 243 L12
Lenham Forstal 263 L4
Lenham Heath 263 L5
Lessness Heath 30 C5
Lett's Green 133 L2
Lewes Heath 296 H2
Lewisham 46 D2
Lewson Street 148 A2
Leybourne 138 F2
Leysdown-on-Sea 230 G3
Lidsing 115 M4
Lilyvale 306 E2
Limpsfield 157 L5
Limpsfield Chart 186 A1
Limpsfield Common 158 A8
Linford 36 A1
Lingfield Common 190 E7
Linkhill 324 F1
Linton 259 L5
Little Bayham 295 L9
Littlebourne 175 M2
Little Chart 263 R12
Little Chart Forstal 286 B1
Little Cheveney Fm 280 D5
Little Mill 256 G8
Little Mongeham 208 B7
Little Pattenden 280 H1
Little Preston 140 B4
Littlestone-on-Sea 331 L6
Little Thurrock 34 D3
Liverton Street 262 C4
Livesey Street 165 H3
Locksbottom 90 C6
Lodge Lees 270 D10
London Beach 301 M8
Longfield 78 A7
Longfield Hill 78 E8
Longford 135 J6
Longlands 48 D8
Loose 259 L1
Loose Hill 167 G8
Lords Wood 115 K3
Lower Bitchet 163 H4
Lower Bush 99 G2
Lower Cousley Wood 309 R1
Lower Cox Street 116 E7
Lower Eythorne 272 C5
Lower Goldstone 236 C6
Lower Green 277 R12
Lower Halstow 226 D10
Lower Hardres 249 P11
Lower Hartlip 117 M1
Lower Haysden 194 B5
Lower Heppington 294 M9
Lower Herne 129 G8
Lower Higham 57 L7
Lower Island 126 D4
Lower Rainham 102 F2
Lower Stoke 41 K8
Lower Sydenham 69 L1
Lower Twydall 84 D8
Lower Upnor 83 G2
Low Street 36 A5
Loyterton 147 L4
Luddesdown 98 A4
Lunsford 138 F1
Luton 101 J4
Luxted 106 F8
Lydd 334 C3
Lydden 182 B1
Lydden 293 R1
Lydd-on-Sea 335 M4
Lyewood Common 198 C6
Lymbridge Green 290 E5
Lyminge 291 L11
Lympne 307 M10
Lynsore Bottom 269 M5
Lynsted 147 H3
Mabledon 194 C7
Maidstone 12 C5
Maltman's Hill 284 H6
Manston 181 M4
Maplescombe 94 C8
Marden 280 H4
Marden Beech 280 G6
Marden Thorn 281 M7
Margate 14 D4
Marine Town 64 E4
Markbeech 275 Q3
Marley 208 B1
Marley 270 A4
Marlpit Hill 192 C1
Marshborough 253 N2
Marsh Green 192 C8
Marshside 232 C8
Martin 210 C7
Martin Mill 210 D8
Matfield 278 H9
Maxted Street 290 E3
Maxton 217 H3
Maypole 50 F6
Maypole 108 E1
Maypole 155 M3
Medhurst Row 193 J3
Meopham 97 G5
Meopham Green 97 H6
Meopham Station 97 J1
Meresborough 103 H8
Mereworth 241 P9
Merle Common 185 H6
Mersham 305 P1
Middle Quarter 301 P4
Middle Stoke 61 K1
Milebush 281 K1
Mile Oak 279 M5
Mile Town 64 B3
Millbank 232 A10
Mill Corner 324 H10
Millhall 139 K3
Mill Hill 209 G6
Mill Street 138 F6
Millwall 26 B2
Milstead 145 M7
Milton 55 L4
Milton Regis 119 K4
Minster 65 J6
Minster 180 F7
Mockbeggar 58 B8
Modest Corner 196 B3
Molash 266 A1
Monks Hill 283 R10
Monks Orchard 87 K3
Monkton 180 A6
Moon's Green 326 D2
Moorhouse Bank 158 F6
Moorstock 306 H3
Moor Street 103 J6
The Moor 312 C9
Morehall 10 B2
Mottingham 47 K7
Mountain Street 247 N11
Mount Pleasant 180 E5
Mowshurst 192 F1
Muckingford 36 A2
Mundy Bois 285 J1
Murston 120 D5
Naccolt 288 F4
Nackington 174 C7
Napchester 273 J10
Nash 106 A1
Nash Street 79 G6
Neames Forstal 247 J2
Nettlestead 164 D7
Nettlestead Green 257 L3
New Addington 105 J2
New Ash Green 96 B5
New Barn 78 C6
Newbarn 218 C1
New Beckenham 69 M3
New Charlton 27 L3
Newchurch 319 Q6
New Cross 25 M8
New Cross Gate 25 M7
New Eltham 48 C7
Newenden 325 L2
New House 54 F7
New Hythe 139 J1
Newingreen 307 M8
Newington 16 C1
Newington 24 B2
Newington 118 D3
Newington 219 G5
Newland Green 284 G1
Newnham 244 E1
New Romney 330 G6
New Street 96 E8
New Town 52 A4
New Town 99 H7
New Town 138 C4
Noah's Arks 136 F5
Noke Street 82 D1
Nonington 252 C12
Norbury 68 C6
Northbourne 208 B5
Northbridge Street 322 H8
North Cray 50 B8
Northdown 179 G4
North Elham 291 R4
North End 31 G7
Northfleet 54 D3
Northfleet Green 78 D2
North Halling 99 H6
Northiam 325 J7
North Leigh 268 F10
North Street 60 F4
North Street 149 L8
Northumberland Heath 30 D6
Northwood 182 D2
North Woolwich 27 M1
Norton Ash 148 B1
Norwood New Town 68 E3
Nunhead 45 K2
Oad Street 118 F8
Oakhurst 255 P3
Oare 123 H7
Offham 241 Q1
Old Bexley 50 B5
Oldbury 240 A3
Old Cryals 278 G12
Old Romney 330 C6
Old Tree 232 B10
Old Wives Lees 247 P7
Orpington 91 H5
Orsett Heath 35 G1
Ospringe 149 H3
Otford 135 M3
Otham 168 B6
Otham Hole 168 D7
Otterden Place 244 E8
Otterham Quay 103 K3
Ottinge 291 M8
Out Elmstead 270 D3
Oversland 247 L2
Oxted 157 J7
Paddlesworth 112 E4
Paddlesworth 219 K1
Paddock 265 K4
Paddock Wood 279 L3
Pains Hill 185 K1
Painter's Forstal 148 F6
Palmarsh 321 P1
Palmer's Green 279 N9
Palmstead 269 N8
Paramour Street 236 A6
Park Corner 199 M8
Parker's Green 189 K7
Park Farm 204 F7
Parkgate 300 G11
Park Langley 88 D2
Park Wood 116 D2
Park Wood 167 M8
Parrock Farm 55 L8
Patrixbourne 175 J6
Payden Street 243 R9
Pean Hill 152 F3
Pearson's Green 279 P6
Peasmarsh 326 D11
Peckham 25 J8
Peckham Bush 256 G5
Pedlinge 307 Q9
Peene 219 H5
Peening Quarter 315 N11
Pegwell 16 B8
Pell Green 309 N2
Pembles Cross 262 F10
Pembury 197 M7
Penenden Heath 141 K6
Penge 69 K4
Pennypot 222 A4
Penshurst 277 J5
Perry 235 K10
Perry Street 55 G5
Perrywood 246 G5
Pested 265 N1
Petham 268 F1
Pett Bottom 249 R12
Petteridge 279 J11
Pettings 238 G2
Petts Wood 72 E8
Pineham 213 L1
Pipsden 312 G8
Pittswood 189 K5
Pizien Well 164 C6
Plaistow 71 H3
Platt 240 H2
Platt's Heath 262 C4
Plaxtol 240 E9
Playden 225 H1
Pluckley 285 M2
Pluckley Thorne 285 K3
Plucks Gutter 235 P2
Plumford 149 H7
Plumstead 28 D4
Plumstead Common 29 G5
Plumtree Green 282 H1
Pollhill 242 C12
Pootings 186 F6
Postling 307 R3
Potman's Heath 315 K12
Potten Street 233 M5
Potters Corner 202 B5
Potter's Forstal 262 E11
Poundsbridge 277 K9
Poverest 73 H8
Powder Mills 194 B2
Pratling Street 140 C1
Pratt's Bottom 108 A4
Preston 149 L3
Preston 235 J7
Priestwood 97 J8
Priestwood Green 97 K8
Printstile 277 P6
Puddledock 74 E3
Puddledock 187 H3
Pullington 313 Q4
Purfleet 32 B4
Pye Corner 261 P7
The Quarter 284 E4
The Quarter 315 L5
Queenborough 64 B8
Queen Street 279 N1
Rabbit's Cross 259 R9
Radfall 127 K8
Radfield 121 H7
Rainham 103 H6
Ram Lane 264 D11
Ramsden 91 K4
Ramsgate 17 L6
Ramslye 200 E4
Ratling 251 Q9
Reading Street 179 K5
Reading Street 316 D7
Reculver 232 E2
Red Hill 165 G4
Rhodes Minnis 291 K6
Richborough Port 237 L5
Ridge Row 292 E8
Ridgeway 289 K12
Ridley 238 G1
Ringlestone 140 E6
Ringlestone 242 G5
Ringwould 211 H4
Ripper's Cross 286 C5
Ripple 210 E1
Riseden 296 H8
River 212 E6
Riverhead 20 A1
Riverview Park 80 B1
Robertsbridge 322 E9
Robhurst 302 D11
Rochester 19 G5
Rockrobin 309 J2
The Rocks 139 H8
Rodmersham 146 E1
Rodmersham Green 146 C2
Rolvenden 314 E5
Rolvenden Layne 314 F7
Romford 278 C10
Romney Street 110 E6
Rooks Hill 163 H6
Roseacre 168 B1
Rosherville 55 G3
Rotherhithe 25 L2
Rough Common 171 J2
Roughway 240 G11
Round Green 298 C1
Round Street 79 L8
Rowling 252 F7
Rowling Street 304 H7
Rowling Street 304 H7
Royal British Legion Village 140 A5
Royal Tunbridge Wells 22 C6
Ruckinge 319 J1
Rushenden 227 N3
Rusher's Cross 308 E11
Rushmore Hill 108 B7
Rusthall 200 D1
Ruxley 73 M3
Ryarsh 138 B1
Rye 225 H3
Rye Foreign 326 H12
Rye Harbour 225 L7
St Johns 26 B8
St John's 135 M8
St John's 196 C7
St Lawrence 16 E3
St Leonard's Street 138 B6
St Margaret's at Cliffe 214 F3
St Mary Cray 91 K1
St Mary in the Marsh 331 J1
St Mary's Bay 331 P2
St Mary's Hoo 40 D7
St Mary's Island 83 H3
St Michaels 301 N9
St Nicholas at Wade 233 L7
St Paul's Cray 73 H6
St Peters 179 G8
Saint's Hill 277 J9
Salehurst 322 H8
Salmans 276 F6
Saltwood 222 B1
Sandgate 223 M2
Sandhurst 313 K12
Sandhurst Cross 323 R1
Sandling 141 G4
Sandown Park 197 J7
Sandway 262 E2
Sandwich 236 H12
Sandwich Bay Estate 207 G1
Sarre 233 L10
Satmar 221 L2
Scragged Oak 116 E6
Scrapsgate 65 H4
Seabrook 223 H3
Seacox Heath 311 M7
Seal 136 F7
Seasalter 126 B6
Seaton 234 E11
Seed 244 E3
Selgrove 149 K7
Selhurst 86 E1
Sellindge 306 H4
Selling 246 H3
Selsdon 104 B4
Selson 253 M6
Selsted 292 G3
Sevenoaks 21 K7
Sevenoaks Common 161 M7
Sevenoaks Weald 254 H2
Sevington 205 L5
Shadoxhurst 303 P5
Shalmsford Street 248 B7
Sharnal Street 60 B4
Shatterling 235 M12
Sheerness 64 D2
Sheldwich 246 B3
Sheldwich Lees 246 C4
Shelvingford 232 B10
Shepherdswell or Sibertswold 271 R8
Shepway 167 K5
Sherwood Park 197 H7
Shipbourne 240 B12
Shirkoak 302 H8
Shirley 87 K5
Sholden 209 G3
Shooters Hill 28 D7
Shoreham 109 K5
Shorncliffe Camp 223 L1
Shorne 80 F2
Shorne Ridgeway 80 E4
Shortlands 70 F7
Shottenden 247 J8
Shover's Green 309 P7
Shuttlesfield 291 R11
Sidcup 73 J1
Silver Hill 322 G5
Silver Street 145 G3
Silvertown 27 K1
Singleton 204 A4
Singlewell 79 K3
Sinkhurst Green 282 F8
Sissinghurst 299 K5
Sittingbourne 120 B7
Sixmile 290 G4
Skeete 290 G10
Slade 244 B8
Slade Green 31 H8
Sleeches Cross 294 A11
Sly Corner 317 N4
Small Hythe 315 P8
Smarden 284 D8
Smarden Bell 284 B7
Smart's Hill 276 G9
Smeeth 306 B1
Snagshall 324 A8
Snargate 318 B11
Snave 318 F9
Snipeshill 120 D6
Snodland 112 F4
Snowdown 271 L2
Sole Street 97 K1
Sole Street 267 Q6
South Alkham 293 N9
South Ashford 204 C3
Southborough 90 A2
Southborough 196 D4
South Darenth 76 E5
Southend 70 D1
Southfleet 78 C3
South Godstone 184 A8
South Green 144 B4
South Norwood 68 E7
South Stifford 33 L4
South Stour 305 K4
South Street 117 L6
South Street 127 H6
South Street 132 E5
South Street 239 K1
South Street 247 L1
South Willesborough 205 G5
Sparrow's Green 309 L4
Speed Gate 95 G5
Speldhurst 277 P10
Spitals Cross 192 D2
Spring Park 88 B5
Stalisfield Green 244 G11
Standen 283 P12
Standen Street 313 N8
Stanford 307 N4
Stanhope 204 C6
Stanstead 238 D5
Staple 252 F3
Staplecross 323 R12
Staplehurst 282 A5
Staplestreet 151 G4
Starvecrow 188 F5
Statenborough 253 P5
Stede Quarter 301 K4
Stelling Minnis 269 J11
Stick Hill 275 M2
Stiff Street 145 G2
Stockbury 117 M5
Stocker's Head 264 E4
Stockland Green 277 R9
Stocks Green 255 Q9
The Stocks 327 K1
Stodmarsh 234 C7
Stoke 61 H2
Stone 53 G3
Stonebridge Green 263 K8
Stonebridge Green 263 K8
Stone Cross 199 G3
Stone Cross 253 R2
Stone Cross 305 J7
Stone Cross 309 M6
Stonecrouch 310 F2
Stonegate 310 B11
Stonehall 212 B1
Stone Hill 306 F3
Stonehill Green 74 D3
Stone in Oxney 327 Q1
Stone Street 163 K3
Stonestreet Green 306 A6
Stonewood 53 L8
Stowting 290 D9
Stowting Common 290 D5
Strawberry Hill 200 E5
Street End 249 N10
Strood 18 D4
Strood 314 G4
Stubb's Cross 304 A3
Studdal 273 K6
Studd Hill 128 B6
Sturry 172 F3
Styants Bottom 137 L7
Summerfield 252 G4
Sundridge 71 K3
Sundridge 160 E2
Sutton 210 B2
Sutton at Hone 76 B4
Sutton Valence 260 F6
Swalecliffe 127 M2
Swanley 74 F5
Swanley Village 75 H6
Swanscombe 54 A3
Swanton Street 145 G6
Swift's Green 284 B4
Swingfield Minnis 292 G6
Swingfield Street 293 J6
Sydenham 69 L2
Tanden 302 B4
Tandridge 184 B3
Tankerton 127 H2
Tatsfield 132 C6
Teasley Mead 198 D2
Temple Ewell 212 F4
Temple Hill 51 L2
Tenterden 315 M1
Teston 165 H6
Teynham 121 K6
Teynham Street 122 A5
Thanington 171 J8
Thong 80 B3
Thornton Heath 68 C7
Three Chimneys 300 A4
Three Leg Cross 310 E7
Throwley 245 N5
Throwley Forstal 245 M8
Thurnham 142 D5
Ticehurst 310 F7
Tidebrook 308 G9
Tilbury 35 H7
Tilmanstone 272 H2
Timberden Bottom 109 K4
Titsey 158 B3
Tolhurst 310 A7
Tonbridge 194 F4
Tong 261 K11
Tonge Corner 121 G2
Tong Green 245 L8
Tovil 12 C9
Tower Hamlets 217 H1
Townland Green 302 G12
Toy's Hill 187 K2
Trench Wood 188 D6
Trottiscliffe 239 M8
Troy Town 19 K9
Troy Town 186 A8
Troy Town 289 K4
Tubslake 312 C1
Tudeley 195 M6
Tudeley Hale 195 M4
Tulse Hill 44 C6
Tunbridge Hill 60 E4
Tunstall 145 L1
Turner's Green 309 K3
Tutt Hill 264 F12
Twenties 177 M6
Twitham 252 D3
Twitton 135 K2
Twydall 102 C3
Tyler Hill 153 M7
Tyler's Green 156 A8
Ulcombe 261 M6
Underlining Green 259 L11
Underriver 162 F8
Under the Wood 232 C7
Union Street 311 J6
Upchurch 226 A9
Upper Bush 99 G3
Upper Deal 209 G5
Upper Elmers End 88 A1
Upper Goldstone 236 B8
Upper Halling 98 E8
Upper Harbledown 171 G4
Upper Hardres Court 269 J3
Upper Haysden 277 Q3
Upper Norwood 68 E5
Upper Rodmersham 146 D3
Upper Shirley 87 K7
Upper Sydenham 69 H1
Upper Upnor 82 F4
Upstreet 234 D2
Upton 183 J1
The Valley 244 G9
Vigo Village 239 L5
Wadhurst 309 K5
Wainscott 82 D3
Walderslade 115 G2
Wallcrouch 310 A8
Wall End 234 G1
Walmer 209 K7
Walter's Green 276 F10
Waltham 268 A7
Walworth 24 D5
Wandle Park 86 B5
Wanshurst Green 281 M2
Warden 230 D1
Ware 235 Q7
Warehorne 318 A3
Ware Street 142 C8
Warlingham 130 C4
Warmlake 260 E5
Warren Street 244 A10
The Warren 202 C6
Waterham 125 K7
Wateringbury 164 D6
Waterman Quarter 283 L7
Waterside 191 G6
Way 181 H6
Wayfield 101 J6
Weavering Street 168 A1
Weddington 236 A10
Weller's Town 276 D4
Well Hill 92 C8
Welling 49 J1
Well Street 138 F7
Westbere 173 K2
Westbrook 177 K3
West Cliffe 214 E3
West Court 55 M7
West Cross 314 C5
West Dulwich 44 E7
Wested Fm 92 F3
West End 154 B1
West End 244 A2
Westenhanger 307 L6
Westerham 159 J5
Western Heights 217 J3
West Farleigh 165 J7
Westfield Sole 115 K6
Westgate on Sea 177 G4
West Heath 29 L5
West Hougham 216 A4
West Hythe 307 M12
West Kingsdown 111 L2
West Langdon 273 L10
West Malling 138 C6
Westmarsh 235 Q5
West Minster 64 A5
West Norwood 68 D1
West Peckham 241 N11
West Stourmouth 235 L3
West Street 38 B8
West Street 206 B8
West Street 243 M8
West Thurrock 33 H4
West Tilbury 35 M5
Westwell 265 K9
Westwell Leacon 264 C10
West Wickham 88 E4
Westwood 77 K4
Westwood 178 E8
Westwood 269 P5
West Yoke 95 L6
Wetham Green 226 A8
Whatsole Street 290 C4
Wheelbarrow Town 291 K1
Whetsted 256 H12
Whitehill 149 H6
White Oak 74 F6
White Post 276 E10
Whitfield 213 J1
Whitley Row 161 G7
Whitstable 126 E2
Wichling 243 R4
Wickhambreaux 234 B11

Wick Hill	283	N9
Wickhurst	255	J9
Widmore	71	L6
Wierton	260	A5
Wigmore	116	D1
Wildernesse	136	D8
Wilgate Green	245	Q3
Willard's Hill	322	B8
Willesborough	3	H8
Willesborough Lees	3	K5
Willington	168	A4
Wilmington	75	J1

Wilsley Green	298	G7
Wilsley Pound	298	H5
Winchet Hill	280	G11
Windmill Hill	103	K2
Wingham	252	A2
Wingham Green	251	J2
Wingham Well	251	P3
Wingmore	270	A11
Winkhurst Green	254	C5
Winterbourne	247	M1
Wissenden	285	J10
Winthersdane	288	G1

Wittersham	326	G2
Woldingham	156	F1
Woldingham Garden Village	130	E7
Wolverton	212	A7
Womenswold	271	J3
Woodchurch	303	J12
Woodland	290	H10
Woodlands	111	H7
Woodnesborough	253	M3
Woodsden	312	H5
Wood's Green	309	L1
Woodside	87	H2

Woodside Green	243	M9
Woodstock	145	M3
Woola Green	271	L6
Woolage Village	271	J4
Woolwich	28	B5
Wootton	270	H12
Wormshill	242	H2
Worms Hill	297	Q1
Worten	286	F6
Worth	206	C4
Wouldham	99	K8
Wrotham	238	F10

Wrotham Heath	239	K12
Wye	266	G12
Wyebanks	244	C7
Yalding	257	R4
Yardhurst	286	B10
Yelsted	117	H4
Yewhedges	245	J5
Yewtree Cross	291	M9
Yopps Green	240	D8
Yorkletts	152	A2

USING THE STREET INDEX

Street names are listed alphabetically. Each street name is followed by its postal town or area locality, the Postcode District, the page number, and the reference to the square in which the name is found.

Standard index entries are shown as follows:

Abbess Cl *BRXS/STRHM* SW2 ....**44** C6

Street names and selected addresses not shown on the map due to scale restrictions are shown in the index with an asterisk:

Abbey Pl *DART* DA1 * **51** L3

GENERAL ABBREVIATIONS

ACC	ACCESS
ALY	ALLEY
AP	APPROACH
AR	ARCADE
ASS	ASSOCIATION
AV	AVENUE
BCH	BEACH
BLDS	BUILDINGS
BND	BEND
BNK	BANK
BR	BRIDGE
BRK	BROOK
BTM	BOTTOM
BUS	BUSINESS
BVD	BOULEVARD
BY	BYPASS
CATH	CATHEDRAL
CEM	CEMETERY
CEN	CENTRE
CFT	CROFT
CH	CHURCH
CHA	CHASE
CHYD	CHURCHYARD
CIR	CIRCLE
CIRC	CIRCUS
CL	CLOSE
CLFS	CLIFFS
CMP	CAMP
CNR	CORNER
CO	COUNTY
COLL	COLLEGE
COM	COMMON
COMM	COMMISSION
CON	CONVENT
COT	COTTAGE
COTS	COTTAGES
CP	CAPE
CPS	COPSE
CR	CREEK
CREM	CREMATORIUM
CRS	CRESCENT
CSWY	CAUSEWAY
CT	COURT
CTRL	CENTRAL
CTS	COURTS

CTYD	COURTYARD
CUTT	CUTTINGS
CV	COVE
CYN	CANYON
DEPT	DEPARTMENT
DALE	DALE
DM	DAM
DR	DRIVE
DRO	DROVE
DRY	DRIVEWAY
DWGS	DWELLINGS
E	EAST
EMB	EMBANKMENT
EMBY	EMBASSY
ESP	ESPLANADE
EST	ESTATE
EX	EXCHANGE
EXPY	EXPRESSWAY
EXT	EXTENSION
F/O	FLYOVER
FC	FOOTBALL CLUB
FK	FORK
FLD	FIELD
FLDS	FIELDS
FLS	FALLS
FLS	FLATS
FM	FARM
FT	FORT
FWY	FREEWAY
FY	FERRY
GA	GATE
GAL	GALLERY
GDN	GARDEN
GDNS	GARDENS
GLD	GLADE
GLN	GLEN
GN	GREEN
GND	GROUND
GRA	GRANGE
GRG	GARAGE
GT	GREAT
GTWY	GATEWAY
GV	GROVE
HGR	HIGHER
HL	HILL

HLS	HILLS
HO	HOUSE
HOL	HOLLOW
HOSP	HOSPITAL
HRB	HARBOUR
HTH	HEATH
HTS	HEIGHTS
HVN	HAVEN
HWY	HIGHWAY
IMP	IMPERIAL
IN	INLET
IND EST	INDUSTRIAL ESTATE
INF	INFIRMARY
INFO	INFORMATION
INT	INTERCHANGE
IS	ISLAND
JCT	JUNCTION
JTY	JETTY
KG	KING
KNL	KNOLL
L	LAKE
LA	LANE
LDG	LODGE
LGT	LIGHT
LK	LOCK
LKS	LAKES
LNDG	LANDING
LTL	LITTLE
LWR	LOWER
MAG	MAGISTRATE
MAN	MANSIONS
MD	MEAD
MDW	MEADOWS
MEM	MEMORIAL
MKT	MARKET
MKTS	MARKETS
ML	MALL
ML	MILL
MNR	MANOR
MS	MEWS
MSN	MISSION
MT	MOUNT
MTN	MOUNTAIN
MTS	MOUNTAINS
MUS	MUSEUM

MWY	MOTORWAY
N	NORTH
NE	NORTH EAST
NW	NORTH WEST
O/P	OVERPASS
OFF	OFFICE
ORCH	ORCHARD
OV	OVAL
PAL	PALACE
PAS	PASSAGE
PAV	PAVILION
PDE	PARADE
PH	PUBLIC HOUSE
PK	PARK
PKWY	PARKWAY
PL	PLACE
PLN	PLAIN
PLNS	PLAINS
PLZ	PLAZA
POL	POLICE STATION
PR	PRINCE
PREC	PRECINCT
PREP	PREPARATORY
PRIM	PRIMARY
PROM	PROMENADE
PRS	PRINCESS
PRT	PORT
PT	POINT
PTH	PATH
PZ	PIAZZA
QD	QUADRANT
QU	QUEEN
QY	QUAY
R	RIVER
RBT	ROUNDABOUT
RD	ROAD
RDG	RIDGE
REP	REPUBLIC
RES	RESERVOIR
RFC	RUGBY FOOTBALL CLUB
RI	RISE
RP	RAMP
RW	ROW
S	SOUTH
SCH	SCHOOL

SE	SOUTH EAST
SER	SERVICE AREA
SH	SHORE
SHOP	SHOPPING
SKWY	SKYWAY
SMT	SUMMIT
SOC	SOCIETY
SP	SPUR
SPR	SPRING
SQ	SQUARE
ST	STREET
STN	STATION
STR	STREAM
STRD	STRAND
SW	SOUTH WEST
TDG	TRADING
TER	TERRACE
THWY	THROUGHWAY
TNL	TUNNEL
TOLL	TOLLWAY
TPK	TURNPIKE
TR	TRACK
TRL	TRAIL
TWR	TOWER
U/P	UNDERPASS
UNI	UNIVERSITY
UPR	UPPER
V	VALE
VA	VALLEY
VIAD	VIADUCT
VIL	VILLA
VIS	VISTA
VLG	VILLAGE
VLS	VILLAS
VW	VIEW
W	WEST
WD	WOOD
WHF	WHARF
WK	WALK
WKS	WALKS
WLS	WELLS
WY	WAY
YD	YARD
YHA	YOUTH HOSTEL

POSTCODE TOWNS AND AREA ABBREVIATIONS

ABYW	Abbey Wood
ASH	Ashford (Kent)
BECK	Beckenham
BELV	Belvedere
BERM/RHTH	Bermondsey/Rotherhithe
BFN/LL	Blackfen/Longlands
BGR/WK	Borough Green/West Kingsdown
BH/WHM	Biggin Hill/Westerham
BKHTH/KID	Blackheath/Kidbrooke
BMLY	Bromley
BRCH	Birchington
BRDST	Broadstairs
BROCKY	Brockley
BRXN/ST	Brixton north/Stockwell
BRXS/STRHM	Brixton south/Streatham Hill
BUR/ETCH	Burwash/Etchingham
BXLY	Bexley
BXLYHN	Bexleyheath north
BXLYHS	Bexleyheath south
CAN/RD	Canning Town/Royal Docks
CANT	Canterbury
CANTW/ST	Canterbury west/Sturry
CAT	Catford
CDW/CHF	Chadwell St Mary/Chafford Hundred
CHARL	Charlton
CHAT	Chatham
CHST	Chislehurst
CMBW	Camberwell
CRBK	Cranbrook

CROW	Crowborough
CROY/NA	Swanley
CROY/NA	Mitcham
CTHM	Sanderstead/Selsdon
DART	Dartford
DEAL	Deal
DEPT	Deptford
DIT/AY	Ditton/Aylesford
DUL	Dulwich
DVE/WH	Dover east/Whitfield
DVW	Dover west
E/WMAL	East & West Malling
EDEN	Edenbridge
EDUL	East Dulwich
EGRIN	East Grinstead
ELTH/MOT	Eltham/Mottingham
ERITH	Erith
ERITHM	Erith Marshes
EYN	Eynsford
FAV	Faversham
FOLK	Folkestone
FOLKN	Folkestone north
FSTH	Forest Hill
GDST	Godstone
GILL	Gillingham
GNWCH	Greenwich
GRAYS	Grays
GRH	Greenhithe
GVE	Gravesend east
GVW	Gravesend west
HART	Hartley
HAWK	Hawkhurst
HAYES	Hayes

HB	Herne Bay
HDCN	Headcorn
HNHL	Herne Hill
HOO/HM	Hoo St Werburgh/Higham
HRTF	Hartfield
HYTHE	Hythe
IOS	Isle of Sheppey
KEN/WIL	Kennington/Willesborough
LBTH	Lambeth
LEE/GVPK	Lee/Grove Park
LEW	Lewisham
LING	Lingfield
LYDD	Lydd
MAID/BEAR	Maidstone/Bearsted
MAID/SHEP	Maidstone/Shepway
MAIDW	Maidstone west
MARG	Margate
MAYF	Mayfield
MEO	Meopham
MSTR	Minster
MTCM	Mitcham
NROM	New Romney
NRWD	Norwood
NWCR	New Cross
ORP	Orpington
OXTED	Oxted
PECK	Peckham
PGE/AN	Penge/Anerley
POP/IOD	Poplar/Isle of Dogs
PUR	Purfleet
QBOR	Queenborough
RAIN	Rainham (Gt Lon)

RAM	Ramsgate
RASHE	Rural Ashford east
RASHW	Rural Ashford west
RBTBR	Robertsbridge
RCANTE	Rural Canterbury east
RCANTW	Rural Canterbury west
RDART	Rural Dartford
RDV	Rural Dover
RFOLK	Rural Folkestone
RHAM	Rainham (Kent)
RMAID	Rural Maidstone
ROCH	Rochester
RRTW	Rural Royal Tunbridge Wells
RSEV	Rural Sevenoaks
RSIT	Rural Sittingbourne
RTON	Rural Tonbridge
RTW	Royal Tunbridge Wells
RTWE/PEM	Royal Tunbridge Wells east/Pembury
RYE	Rye
SAND/SEL	Croydon/New Addington
SBGH/RUST	Southborough/Rusthall
SCUP	Sidcup
SEV	Sevenoaks
SIT	Sittingbourne
SLH/COR	Stanford-le-Hope/Corringham
SNOD	Snodland
SNWD	South Norwood
SOCK/AV	South Ockendon/Aveley
STH/RUST	Southborough/Rusthall
STHWK	Southwark

STMC/STPC	St Mary Cray/St Paul's Cray
STPH/PW	Staplehurst/Paddock Wood
STRD	Strood
STRHM/NOR	Streatham/Norbury
SWCH	Sandwich
SWCM	Swanscombe
SYD	Sydenham
TENT	Tenterden
THHTH	Thornton Heath
THMD	Thamesmead
TIL	Tilbury
TON	Tonbridge
TONN	Tonbridge north
VX/NE	Vauxhall/Nine Elms
WADH	Wadhurst
WALD	Walderslade
WALW	Walworth
WAP	Wapping
WARL	Warlingham
WBY/YAL	Wateringbury/Yalding
WELL	Welling
WGOS	Westgate on Sea
WLGTN	Wallington
WNWD	West Norwood
WOOL/PLUM	Woolwich/Plumstead
WSEA	Winchelsea
WSTB	Whitstable
WTHK	West Thurrock
WWKM	West Wickham

I

1 Av WOOL/PLUM SE18 28 C2

A

Abbess Cl BRXS/STRHM SW2 44 C6
Abbey Brewery Ct
E/WMAL ME19 * 138 D5
Abbey Cl DEAL CT14 209 H4
IOS ME12 65 L7
Abbey Ct WGOS CT8 177 G6
Abbey Crs BELV DA17 30 B3
Abbey Dr BXLY DA5 50 F7
Abbeyfield Est
BERM/RHTH SE16 25 K3
Abbeyfield Rd
BERM/RHTH SE16 25 K3
Abbey Flds FAV ME13 149 M2
Abbey Gdns BERM/RHTH SE16 25 H3
CANTW/ST CT2 172 B6
Abbey Gv ABYW SE2 29 J3
MSTR CT12 180 F8
RAM CT11 16 C8
Abbeyhill Rd BFN/LL DA15 49 K6
Abbey La BECK BR3 70 B4
Abbey Ms RBTBR TN32 322 G9
Abbey Mt BELV DA17 30 A4
Abbey Pk BECK BR3 70 B4
Abbey Pl DART DA1 * 51 L3
FAV ME13 149 L1
Abbey Rd BELV DA17 29 L3
BXLYHS DA6 49 M2
CROY/NA CR0 86 C6
FAV ME13 149 L1
GRH DA9 53 K3
GVE DA12 55 M6
RDV CT15 212 C8
RHAM ME8 102 B3
SAND/SEL CR2 104 C4
STRD ME2 18 C1
Abbey St FAV ME13 149 L1
STHWK SE1 25 G2
Abbey Ter ABYW SE2 29 K2
Abbeyview Dr IOS ME12 65 J7
Abbey Wy KEN/WIL TN24 3 L5
Abbey Wood Rd ABYW SE2 29 J3
E/WMAL ME19 138 B8
Abbots Barton Wk CANT CT1 5 H7
Abbotsbury Ms PECK SE15 45 K1
Abbotsbury Rd WWKM BR4 89 G5
Abbots Cl STMC/STPC BR5 90 D4
Abbots Ct HOO/HM ME3 * 60 B8
Abbots Court Rd HOO/HM ME3 84 A1
Abbots Fld MAIDW ME16 166 C3
Abbots Gn CROY/NA CR0 104 C1
Abbotshall Rd CAT SE6 46 E6
Abbots Hl FAV ME13 148 F4
RAM CT11 17 K6
Abbots Pk BRXS/STRHM SW2 44 B6
Abbots Pl CANT CT1 4 F3
Abbots Rd FAV ME13 149 M2
The Abbots DVW CT17 8 A4
Abbots Wk CTHM CR3 130 A8
RASHE TN25 266 F11
Abbots Wy BECK BR3 87 M1
Abbotswell Rd BROCKY SE4 46 A3
Abbotswood Cl BELV DA17 29 M2
Abbotswood Rd EDUL SE22 44 F2
Abbott Dr RSIT ME9 * 145 L3
Abbott Rd BGR/WK TN15 240 E2
FOLK CT20 11 L3
Abbotts Cl ROCH ME1 100 C2
SWLY BR8 75 H8
Abbott's Wk BXLYHN DA7 29 L6
Abercorn Cl SAND/SEL CR2 104 C6
Abercorn Wy STHWK SE1 25 H4
Aberdare Cl WWKM BR4 88 D5
Aberdeen Cl RCANTE CT3 234 E2
Aberdeen Rd CROY/NA CR0 86 D7
Aberdeen Ter BKHTH/KID SE3 26 E8
Aberdour St STHWK SE1 24 F3
Aberford Gdns
WOOL/PLUM SE18 27 M7
Abergeldie Rd LEE/GVPK SE12 47 J4
Abernethy Rd LEW SE13 46 F2
Abery St WOOL/PLUM SE18 28 F3
Abigail Crs WALD ME5 115 H4
Abingdon Cl STHWK SE1 * 25 G4
Abingdon Gv RCANTE CT3 234 E2
Abingdon Rd MAIDW ME16 166 A3
Abingdon Wy ORP BR6 91 J7
Abinger Cl BMLY BR1 71 M7
CROY/NA CR0 105 H1
Abinger Dr NRWD SE19 68 D4
WALD ME5 115 L3
Abinger Gv DEPT SE8 26 A5
Ablett St BERM/RHTH SE16 25 K4
Acacia Cl DEPT SE8 25 M3
STMC/STPC BR5 90 E1
Acacia Gdns WWKM BR4 88 D5
Acacia Gv DUL SE21 44 E7
Acacia Rd BECK BR3 70 A7
DART DA1 51 K6
GRH DA9 52 F4
Acacia Wy BFN/LL DA15 49 G6
Academy Dr GILL ME7 102 A5
Academy Gdns CROY/NA CR0 87 G4
Academy Pl WOOL/PLUM SE18 28 A7
Academy Rd WOOL/PLUM SE18 28 B6
Acanthus Dr STHWK SE1 25 H4
Acer Av RTWE/PEM TN2 201 K5
Acer Rd BH/WHM TN16 132 C2
Achilles Cl STHWK SE1 25 H4
Achilles Rd WALD ME5 115 K3
Achilles St NWCR SE14 25 M6
Ackholt Rd RCANTE CT3 251 R12
Ackroyd Rd FSTH SE23 45 L5
Acland Cl WOOL/PLUM SE18 28 E6
Acland Crs CMBW SE5 44 E2
Acol Hl BRCH CT7 180 E1
Acorn Cl ASH TN23 204 F8
CHST BR7 72 D2
STPH/PW TN12 278 E2
Acorn Gdns NRWD SE19 69 G5
Acorn Gv DIT/AY ME20 139 L5
Acorn Pde PECK SE15 * 25 J6
Acorn Pl MAID/SHEP ME15 167 M7
Acorn Rd DART DA1 51 G3
GILL ME7 102 A1
The Acorns HDCN TN27 284 C8
SEV TN13 20 E3
WADH TN5 310 A11
Acorn St IOS ME12 64 D4
Acorn Wy BUR/ETCH TN19 322 F2
FSTH SE23 45 L8
ORP BR6 90 C7
Acorn Wharf Rd ROCH ME1 19 K5
Acott Flds WBY/YAL ME18 257 Q4
Acre Cl ROCH ME1 100 F4
Acre Dr EDUL SE22 45 H2
Acre Gv STRD ME2 113 H1
Acre La BRXS/STRHM SW2 44 A2
Acres Ri WADH TN5 310 F8
The Acre DVE/WH CT16 213 G1
Acton La TENT TN30 316 B11
Acton Rd WSTB CT5 126 E4
Acworth Pl DART DA1 * 51 K4
Adair Cl SNWD SE25 69 J7
Adam Cl CAT SE6 46 B8
FSTH SE23 45 K7
RMAID ME17 259 J3
Adams Cl TENT TN30 301 N12
Adams Ct WALD ME5 * 101 J7
Adams La RYE TN31 324 E10
Adamson Wy BECK BR3 88 D1
Adamsrill Rd SYD SE26 69 L1
Adams Rd BECK BR3 87 M1
Adams Sq BXLYHS DA6 49 M1
Adams Wy SNWD SE25 87 G2
Adare Wk STRHM/NOR SW16 44 A8
Ada Rd CANT CT1 4 B8
CMBW SE5 24 F6
Adbert Dr MAID/SHEP ME15 258 G1
Addelam Cl DEAL CT14 209 H5
Addelam Rd DEAL CT14 209 H5
Adderley Gdns ELTH/MOT SE9 72 B1
Addington Gv SYD SE26 69 M1
Addington La E/WMAL ME19 239 N9
Addington Pl RAM CT11 17 J7
Addington Rd CROY/NA CR0 86 B4
MARG CT9 15 G4
SAND/SEL CR2 104 B3
SIT ME10 119 M6
WWKM BR4 88 D7
Addington Sq CMBW SE5 24 D6
MARG CT9 15 G5
Addington St MARG CT9 15 G4
RAM CT11 17 H7
STHWK SE1 * 24 A1
Addington Village Rd
CROY/NA CR0 104 E1
Addiscombe Av CROY/NA CR0 87 H3
Addiscombe Court Rd
CROY/NA CR0 86 F4
Addiscombe Gdns MARG CT9 15 H7
Addiscombe Gv CROY/NA CR0 86 E5
Addiscombe Rd CROY/NA CR0 86 F5
MARG CT9 15 H8
Addison Cl E/WMAL ME19 139 G4
STMC/STPC BR5 90 D2
Addison Dr LEE/GVPK SE12 47 J3
Addison Gdns GRAYS RM17 34 D3
Addison Rd HAYES BR2 89 L1
SNWD SE25 69 H8
Addison's Cl CROY/NA CR0 88 A5
Addlestead Rd STPH/PW TN12 256 H8
Adelaide Av BROCKY SE4 46 B2
Adelaide Dr SIT ME10 119 K5
Adelaide Gdns IOS ME12 64 E7
RAM CT11 17 J7
Adelaide Pl CANT CT1 4 E5
Adelaide Rd CHST BR7 72 C2
GILL ME7 7 K6
RDV CT15 272 C5
TIL RM18 35 G7
The Adelaide HOO/HM ME3 57 K7
Adenmore Rd CAT SE6 46 B5
Adie Rd NROM TN28 331 L10
Adie Rd North NROM TN28 331 L10
Adisham Downs Rd
RCANTE CT3 251 M7
Adisham Dr MAIDW ME16 140 C6
Adisham Gn SIT ME10 120 A1
Adisham Rd RCANTE CT3 251 R4
RCANTE CT3 270 H3
RCANTW CT4 175 M6
Adisham Wy MARG CT9 178 F4
Admaston Rd
WOOL/PLUM SE18 28 D6
Admers Wy MEO DA13 239 N5
Admiral Cl STMC/STPC BR5 73 L8
Admiral Moore Dr
DIT/AY ME20 140 A4
Admiral Seymour Rd
ELTH/MOT SE9 48 A2
Admiral's Ga GNWCH SE10 26 C7
Admiral St DEPT SE8 26 B7
Admirals Wk CRBK TN17 299 N11
GRH DA9 53 J3
HYTHE CT21 * 222 D4
IOS ME12 64 F7
TENT TN30 301 P12
Admirals Wy POP/IOD E14 26 C1
Admiralty Cl FAV ME13 149 J1
Admiralty Ms DEAL CT14 209 L5
Admiralty Rd STRD ME2 83 G4
Admiralty Ter STRD ME2 83 G4
Admiralty Wk WSTB CT5 126 B6
Admiral Wy E/WMAL ME19 164 B4
Adolf St CAT SE6 70 B1
Adolphus St DEPT SE8 26 A6
Adrian Ct WGOS CT8 * 177 H4
Adrian Ms WGOS CT8 * 177 J4
Adrian Sq WGOS CT8 177 H4
Adrian St DVW CT17 8 D6
Adstock Wy GRAYS RM17 34 A3
Advance Rd WNWD SE27 68 D1
Advice Av CDW/CHF RM16 34 B1
Adys Rd PECK SE15 45 G1
Aerodrome Rd RCANTW CT4 175 M6
RFOLK CT18 220 A1
Afghan Rd BRDST CT10 179 J5
CHAT ME4 6 B6
Agaton Rd ELTH/MOT SE9 48 D7
Agester La RCANTW CT4 270 F10
Agnew Rd FSTH SE23 45 M5
Ailsworth La RYE TN31 * 225 H3
Ainsborough Av MARG CT9 178 F5
Ainsdale Cl FOLKN CT19 220 B6
ORP BR6 90 E4
Ainsdale Dr STHWK SE1 25 H4
Ainsty St BERM/RHTH SE16 * 25 K1
Ainsworth Cl CMBW SE5 * 24 F8
Ainsworth Rd CROY/NA CR0 86 C4
Aintree Cl GVE DA12 55 J8
Aintree Rd WALD ME5 115 K2
Airedale Cl MARG CT9 15 J6
RDART DA2 52 D6
Airfield Vw IOS ME12 229 M5
Aisher Wy SEV TN13 135 K7
Aislibie Rd LEW SE13 46 F2
Aisne Dr CANT CT1 172 E8
Aitken Rd CAT SE6 46 C7
Ajax Rd ROCH ME1 100 D6
Akabusi Cl SNWD SE25 87 H2
Akehurst La BGR/WK TN15 21 J7
Akerman Rd CMBW SE5 24 C7
Alabama St WOOL/PLUM SE18 28 E6
Alamein Av WALD ME5 101 G6
Alamein Cl DVE/WH CT16 214 A7
Alamein Gdns RDART DA2 52 E5
Alamein Rd SWCM DA10 53 L4
Alanbrooke GVE DA12 55 K5
Alan Cl DART DA1 51 K2
Alanthus Cl LEE/GVPK SE12 47 G4
Albacore Crs LEW SE13 46 C4
Alban Crs EYN DA4 94 B4
Albany Cl BXLY DA5 49 K5
TON TN9 195 G6
Albany Dr HB CT6 128 E4
Albany Hl RTWE/PEM TN2 23 K2
Albany Ms BMLY BR1 71 H3
WALW SE17 24 D5
Albany Pl DVW CT17 8 D5
Albany Rd BELV DA17 30 A5
BXLY DA5 49 K5
CHAT ME4 101 J3
CHST BR7 72 C2
CMBW SE5 24 E5
GILL ME7 7 M6
RFOLK CT18 221 J4
ROCH ME1 100 D2
SIT ME10 119 M6
TIL RM18 35 H7
Albany St MAID/BEAR ME14 13 J2
Albany Ter CHAT ME4 6 B6
Albatross Av STRD ME2 81 K7
Albatross Gdns SAND/SEL CR2 104 C5
Albatross St WOOL/PLUM SE18 28 F6
Albemarle Cl GRAYS RM17 34 B1
Albemarle Pk BECK BR3 * 70 C5
Albemarle Rd BECK BR3 70 C5
KEN/WIL TN24 3 J8
WALD ME5 115 K3
Alberta Cl DVE/WH CT16 213 J6
Alberta Est WALW SE17 24 C4
Alberta Rd BXLYHN DA7 30 D7
Alberta St WALW SE17 24 C4
Albert Av VX/NE SW8 24 A6
Albert Cl CDW/CHF RM16 34 D2
Albert Ct RAM CT11 * 17 J6
WSTB CT5 * 126 E3
Albert Dr MAID/SHEP ME15 258 G1
Albert La HYTHE CT21 222 C4
Albert Ms BROCKY SE4 * 46 A2
Albert Murray Cl GVE DA12 55 K5
Albert Pl STRD ME2 19 H3
Albert Reed Gdns
MAID/SHEP ME15 12 D9
Albert Rd BELV DA17 30 A4
BRDST CT10 179 H6
BXLY DA5 50 B4
CAN/RD E16 28 B1
CANT CT1 5 J5
CHAT ME4 6 E8
DEAL CT14 209 K3
DVE/WH CT16 8 C2
ELTH/MOT SE9 47 M8
FOLKN CT19 11 J2
GILL ME7 7 J5
HAYES BR2 89 L1
HYTHE CT21 222 C4
KEN/WIL TN24 2 B3
MARG CT9 14 C5
ORP BR6 91 H8
PGE/AN SE20 69 L4
RAM CT11 17 M4
RDART DA2 51 K8
RFOLK CT18 221 K4
ROCH ME1 100 D2
SNWD SE25 69 J8
STMC/STPC BR5 91 J2
SWCM DA10 54 A4
TON TN9 194 E4
WARL CR6 130 D3
Albert Sq VX/NE SW8 24 A6
Albert St MAID/BEAR ME14 12 F1
RAM CT11 17 J7
RTW TN1 23 G3
WSTB CT5 126 E3
Albert Ter IOS ME12 * 66 B8
MARG CT9 14 E4
Albert Wy PECK SE15 25 J6
Albion Cl HB CT6 155 H1
Albion Ct RAM CT11 17 K5
Albion Est BERM/RHTH SE16 * 25 K1
Albion La HB CT6 155 H1
Albion Ms RAM CT11 17 L6
Albion Mews Rd FOLK CT20 11 J6
Albion Pl CANT CT1 5 H3
FAV ME13 149 K2
IOS ME12 64 D3
KEN/WIL TN24 205 H4
MAID/BEAR ME14 13 J4
MARG CT9 * 15 G3
RAM CT11 17 K6
SNWD SE25 * 69 H7
Albion Rd BRCH CT7 176 D6
BRDST CT10 179 J7
BXLYHS DA6 50 A2
DEAL CT14 209 L1
FOLKN CT19 11 K2
GVE DA12 55 K5
MARG CT9 15 K3
RAM CT11 17 L4
RTW TN1 23 H2
STPH/PW TN12 281 J4
SWCH CT13 253 M7
WALD ME5 115 J3
Albion St BERM/RHTH SE16 25 K1
BRDST CT10 183 L1
CROY/NA CR0 86 C4
Albion Ter GVE DA12 55 K4
SIT ME10 * 119 M3
Albion Vls FOLK CT20 11 K6
Albion Villas Rd FSTH SE23 45 K8
Albion Wy EDEN TN8 192 D1
LEW SE13 46 D2
Albrighton Rd EDUL SE22 44 F1
Albuhera Sq CANT CT1 172 E8
Albury Av BXLYHN DA7 29 M8
Albury Cl WALD ME5 115 L3
Albury St DEPT SE8 26 B5
Albyfield BMLY BR1 72 A7
Albyn Rd DEPT SE8 26 C8
Aldbridge St WALW SE17 24 F4
Aldebert Ter VX/NE SW8 24 A6
Aldeburgh St GNWCH SE10 27 H4
Alder Cl IOS ME12 64 B5
PECK SE15 25 G5
RTWE/PEM TN2 196 F4
Aldergate La HYTHE CT21 306 H12
Alderholt Wy PECK SE15 * 24 F6
Alder La CRBK TN17 314 A8
Alderman Cl DART DA1 50 F5
Aldermary Rd BMLY BR1 71 H5
Aldermoor Rd CAT SE6 46 A8
Alderney Ms STHWK SE1 24 E2
Alderney Rd ERITH DA8 31 H6
Alder Rd FOLKN CT19 11 G2
SCUP DA14 48 F8
Aldersford Cl BROCKY SE4 45 L2
Aldersgrove Av ELTH/MOT SE9 47 K8
Aldershot Rd WALD ME5 101 H6
Aldershot Ter
WOOL/PLUM SE18 * 28 B6
Aldersmead Av CROY/NA CR0 87 L2
Alders Meadow TON TN9 194 C3
Aldersmead Rd BECK BR3 69 M4
Alders Rd RTON TN11 278 B3
The Alders WBY/YAL ME18 241 Q10
WWKM BR4 88 C4
Alderton Rd CROY/NA CR0 87 G3
HNHL SE24 44 D1
Alder Wy SWLY BR8 74 E6
Alderwood Rd ELTH/MOT SE9 48 E4
Aldington Cl WALD ME5 101 J8
Aldington La
MAID/BEAR ME14 142 E5
Aldington Rd HYTHE CT21 306 H10
MAID/BEAR ME14 168 A1
WOOL/PLUM SE18 27 L2
Aldon Cl MAID/BEAR ME14 13 M1
Aldon La E/WMAL ME19 241 N1
Aldred Rd FAV ME13 149 K3
Aldrich Crs CROY/NA CR0 105 H3
Aldridge Cl HB CT6 128 C6
Aldwick Cl CHST BR7 48 E8
Aldwick Rd CROY/NA CR0 86 A6
Aldworth Gv LEW SE13 46 D4
Alec Pemble Cl KEN/WIL TN24 203 H6
Alen Sq STPH/PW TN12 282 A5
Alers Rd BXLYHS DA6 49 L3
Alexander Cl BFN/LL DA15 48 F3
HAYES BR2 89 H4
SWCH CT13 237 J12
Alexander Ct SIT ME10 * 119 M4
Alexander Dr FAV ME13 149 J2
Alexander Evans Ms FSTH SE23 45 L7
Alexander Gv E/WMAL ME19 164 C2
Alexander Rd BXLYHN DA7 29 L8
CHST BR7 72 C3
GRH DA9 53 K3
Alexander Ter ABYW SE2 * 29 J4
Alexandra Av GILL ME7 101 M1
WARL CR6 130 E3
Alexandra Cl CDW/CHF RM16 35 J1
SIT ME10 119 M2
SWLY BR8 74 F6
Alexandra Cottages
NWCR SE14 26 A7
Alexandra Crs BMLY BR1 71 G3
Alexandra Dr NRWD SE19 68 F2
Alexandra Gdns FOLK CT20 11 K6
Alexandra Gln WALD ME5 115 H4
Alexandra Pl CROY/NA CR0 86 F4
DVE/WH CT16 8 A1
SNWD SE25 86 E1
Alexandra Rd BH/WHM TN16 132 A5
BRCH CT7 176 D8
BRDST CT10 183 L1
CHAT ME4 101 J3
CROY/NA CR0 86 F4
DEAL CT14 209 L7
DEAL CT14 211 K4
ERITH DA8 31 G5
GVE DA12 55 M5
IOS ME12 64 E3
MARG CT9 14 F8
RAM CT11 17 H3
RFOLK CT18 221 K3
SYD SE26 69 L3
TIL RM18 35 G8
WARL CR6 130 D3
WSTB CT5 126 D5
Alexandra St FOLKN CT19 11 L2
MAID/BEAR ME14 12 F1
NWCR SE14 25 M6
Alexandra Ter MARG CT9 14 F7
Alexandra Wk EYN DA4 * 76 E6
Alexandra Wy TIL RM18 36 C3
Alexandria Dr HB CT6 128 D4
Alex Hughes Cl SNOD ME6 113 G7
Alexis St BERM/RHTH SE16 25 H3
Alford Gn CROY/NA CR0 105 J1
Alford Rd ERITH DA8 30 D4
Alfred Cl CANT CT1 171 K7
CHAT ME4 101 J3
Alfred Pl GVW DA11 55 G6
Alfred Rd BELV DA17 30 A4
BRCH CT7 176 A5
CANT CT1 171 K7
DVE/WH CT16 213 J7
GVW DA11 55 J7
KEN/WIL TN24 205 G4
MARG CT9 15 L6
NROM TN28 331 M10
RDART DA2 76 A1
SNWD SE25 87 H1
Alfred St GRAYS RM17 34 D5
Alfriston Cl DART DA1 50 F4
Alfriston Gv E/WMAL ME19 164 D2
Algernon Rd LEW SE13 46 C2
Algiers Rd LEW SE13 46 B2
Alice St STHWK SE1 24 F2
Alice Thompson Cl
LEE/GVPK SE12 47 K7
Alice Walker Cl HNHL SE24 * 44 C2
Alicia Av MARG CT9 177 K5
Alison Cl CROY/NA CR0 87 L4
DVE/WH CT16 213 H3
Alison Crs DVE/WH CT16 213 H3
Alkerden La GRH DA9 53 K4
Alkham Cl MARG CT9 179 J3
Alkham Rd MAID/BEAR ME14 13 L3
RDV CT15 212 C5
Alkham Valley Rd
RFOLK CT18 220 E2
RFOLK CT18 293 N9
Allan Cl STH/RUST TN4 200 D1
Allandale Pl ORP BR6 91 L6
Allandale Rd RTWE/PEM TN2 197 G7
Alland Grange La MSTR CT12 181 H4
Allan Rd WSTB CT5 125 M2
Allard Cl STMC/STPC BR5 91 K3
Allardyce St BRXN/ST SW9 44 A2
Allen Av WGOS CT8 176 F6
Allenby Av DEAL CT14 209 J4
Allenby Crs GRAYS RM17 34 C4
Allenby Rd BH/WHM TN16 132 D3
FSTH SE23 45 M8
MSTR CT12 182 E3
Allen Cl WALD ME5 101 K7
Allen Ct IOS ME12 65 H8
Allendale Cl CMBW SE5 24 E8
RDART DA2 52 E6
SYD SE26 69 L2
Allendale St FOLKN CT19 11 J2
Allen Fld ASH TN23 204 C3
Allen Rd BECK BR3 69 L6
CROY/NA CR0 86 A3
Allens STPH/PW TN12 * 281 J4
Allens La BGR/WK TN15 240 F10
Allen St MAID/BEAR ME14 13 H2
Allenswood Rd ELTH/MOT SE9 47 M1
Allerford Rd CAT SE6 70 C1
Alleyn Crs DUL SE21 44 E7
Alleyn Pk DUL SE21 44 E7
Alleyn Rd DUL SE21 44 E8
Allhallows Rd HOO/HM ME3 41 K8
Alliance Rd RAM CT11 17 L6
WOOL/PLUM SE18 29 H5
Alliance Wy STPH/PW TN12 279 J3
Allington Dr STRD ME2 18 B2
TONN TN10 189 K8
Allington Gdns WBY/YAL ME18 164 E6
Allington Rd ORP BR6 90 F5
RHAM ME8 102 B2
STPH/PW TN12 279 J2
Allington Wy MAIDW ME16 140 C7
Allison Av GILL ME7 101 M4
Allison Cl GNWCH SE10 26 D7
Allison Gv DUL SE21 44 F6
Allnutt Mill Cl MAID/SHEP ME15 12 C9
Alloa Rd DEPT SE8 25 L4
Allotment La SEV TN13 21 K1
All Saints' Av MARG CT9 14 B7
All Saints Cl SWCM DA10 54 A3
WSTB CT5 126 F4
All Saints Dr BKHTH/KID SE3 27 G8
All Saints La CANT CT1 4 F4
All Saints Ri STH/RUST TN4 * 196 D7
All Saints' Rd GVW DA11 55 G6
HAWK TN18 312 D8
SIT ME10 120 D5
STH/RUST TN4 196 D7
Allsworth Cl RSIT ME9 118 C3
Allwood Cl SYD SE26 69 L1
Alma Gv STHWK SE1 25 G3
Alma Pl CANT CT1 * 5 H2
NRWD SE19 69 G4
RAM CT11 17 K5
STRD ME2 18 F4
THHTH CR7 86 B1
Alma Rd DIT/AY ME20 * 114 A7
E/WMAL ME19 138 B5
FOLK CT20 219 L8
HB CT6 129 J4
IOS ME12 64 D3
MARG CT9 15 G7
RAM CT11 17 J4
SCUP DA14 49 H8
STMC/STPC BR5 91 L5
SWCM DA10 53 M3
Alma St CANT CT1 5 H2
IOS ME12 64 E3
The Alma GVE DA12 * 80 A1
Almond Cl BRDST CT10 182 F1
CDW/CHF RM16 35 H2
HAYES BR2 90 B3
WSTB CT5 127 L4
Almond Ct RCANTW CT4 248 F8
Almond Dr SWLY BR8 74 E7
Almond Gv GILL ME7 116 B1
Almond Rd BERM/RHTH SE16 25 J3
RDART DA2 52 D5
The Almonds
MAID/BEAR ME14 168 B1
Almond Tree Cl IOS ME12 64 B5
Almond Wy HAYES BR2 90 B3
Almon Pl ROCH ME1 19 L8
Almshouse Rd FAV ME13 245 M11
Alnwick Rd LEE/GVPK SE12 47 J5
Alnwick Ter LEE/GVPK SE12 47 J5
Alpha Cl HOO/HM ME3 60 E6
Alpha Gv POP/IOD E14 26 B1
Alpha Rd BRCH CT7 176 D6
CROY/NA CR0 86 F4
NWCR SE14 26 A7
RAM CT11 17 G6
Alpha St PECK SE15 25 H8
Alpine Cl CROY/NA CR0 86 F6
Alpine Copse BMLY BR1 72 B6
Alpine Rd BERM/RHTH SE16 25 K3
Alsace Rd WALW SE17 24 F4
Alsager Av QBOR ME11 227 N2
Alscot Rd BERM/RHTH SE16 25 G2
Alscot Wy STHWK SE1 25 G3
Alsike Rd BELV DA17 29 L2
Alsops Rd KEN/WIL TN24 205 H4
Alston Cl IOS ME12 65 K6
Altash Wy ELTH/MOT SE9 48 A7
Alton Av E/WMAL ME19 164 C3
Alton Cl BXLY DA5 49 M6
Alton Gdns BECK BR3 70 B4
Alton Ms GILL ME7 * 7 K6
Alton Rd CROY/NA CR0 86 B7
Altyre Cl BECK BR3 88 A1
Altyre Rd CROY/NA CR0 86 E5
Altyre Wy BECK BR3 88 A1
Aluric Cl CDW/CHF RM16 35 J3
Alverstone Gdns
ELTH/MOT SE9 48 C6
Alverston Gdns SNWD SE25 86 F1
Alverton St DEPT SE8 26 A4
Alvey St WALW SE17 24 F4
Alvis Av HB CT6 128 B5
Alwold Crs LEE/GVPK SE12 47 K4
Alwyn Cl CROY/NA CR0 105 G2
Amage Rd RASHE TN25 289 K2
Amanda Cl WALD ME5 114 F2
Amar Ct WOOL/PLUM SE18 29 G3
Amardeep Ct
WOOL/PLUM SE18 29 G4
Ambassador Sq POP/IOD E14 26 C3
Amber Cl RSIT ME9 121 L7
Ambergate St WALW SE17 24 C4
Amber La RMAID ME17 260 B4
Amberleaze Dr
RTWE/PEM TN2 278 A11
Amberley Cl ORP BR6 91 G8
Amberley Ct SCUP DA14 73 K2
Amberley Gv CROY/NA CR0 87 G3
SYD SE26 69 J1
Amberley Rd ABYW SE2 29 L5
Amblecote Cl LEE/GVPK SE12 47 J8
Amblecote Meadow
LEE/GVPK SE12 47 J8
Amblecote Mdw
LEE/GVPK SE12 * 47 J8
Amblecote Rd LEE/GVPK SE12 47 J8
Ambleside BMLY BR1 70 E3
SIT ME10 120 D6
Ambleside Av BECK BR3 87 M1
Ambleside Gdns
SAND/SEL CR2 104 C4
Ambleside Rd BXLYHN DA7 30 B8
Ambley Gn GILL ME7 102 B5
Ambley Rd GILL ME7 102 C5
Ambrook Rd BELV DA17 30 B2
Ambrose Cl DART DA1 51 G2
ORP BR6 91 G6
Ambrose Hl WALD ME5 7 J9
Ambrose St BERM/RHTH SE16 25 J3
Amelia St WALW SE17 24 C4
Amels Hl RSIT ME9 144 A1
Amersham Gv NWCR SE14 26 A6
Amersham Rd CROY/NA CR0 86 D2
NWCR SE14 26 A7
Amersham V NWCR SE14 26 A6
Ames Av MAID/BEAR ME14 168 B1
Amesbury Rd BMLY BR1 71 L7
Ames Rd SWCM DA10 53 M4
Amethyst Av WALD ME5 100 F7
Amethyst Ct ORP BR6 107 K1
Amherst Cl MAIDW ME16 12 B3
MARG CT9 178 F4
STMC/STPC BR5 73 H8
Amherst Dr STMC/STPC BR5 73 G8
Amherst Hl GILL ME7 6 E2
SEV TN13 20 C2
Amherst Pl SEV TN13 20 C2
Amherst Redoubt GILL ME7 6 E3
Amherst Rd ROCH ME1 100 E2
SEV TN13 21 H1
STH/RUST TN4 22 F1
Amhurst Bank Rd
RTWE/PEM TN2 278 C5
Amina Wy BERM/RHTH SE16 25 H2
Amos Cl FAV ME13 246 B4
HB CT6 129 K6
Amott Rd PECK SE15 45 H1
Ampere Wy CROY/NA CR0 86 A4
Ampleforth Cl ORP BR6 91 K7
Ampleforth Rd ABYW SE2 29 J1
Amroth Cl FSTH SE23 45 J6
Amsbury Rd MAID/SHEP ME15 258 F3
Amsterdam Rd POP/IOD E14 26 D2
Amy Rd OXTED RH8 157 K7

Amyruth Rd BROCKY SE4....46 B3
Anatase Cl SIT ME10....119 K2
Ancaster Rd BECK BR3....69 L7
Ancaster St WOOL/PLUM SE18....28 F6
Anchorage Cl HOO/HM ME3....61 K2
Anchor Bvd DART DA1 *....
Anchor & Hope La CHARL SE7....27 K3
Anchor La IOS ME12....2 C4
Anchor Rd ROCH ME1....100 D4
Anchor St BERM/RHTH SE16....25 J1
Ancona Rd WOOL/PLUM SE18....28 E4
Ancress Cl CANTW/ST CAT3....172 G5
Andace Park Gdns BMLY BR1 *....71 K5
Anderson Wy BELV DA17....30 C1
Andover Rd ORP BR6....90 F4
Andrea Av CDW/CHF RM16....34 A1
Andrew Broughton Wy
  MAID/BEAR ME14....13 J4
Andrew Cl DART DA1....50 E3
Andrews Rd RBTBR TN32....322 H8
Andrews Cl
  RTWE/PEM TN2....23 L1
  STMC/STPC BR5....23 H7
Andrews Pl BXLY DA5....75 H1
Andrews Wk WALW SE17....24 F8
Andwell Cl ABYW SE2....29 J1
Anerley Cl MAIDW ME16....140 C6
Anerley Gv NRWD SE19....69 G4
Anerley Hl NRWD SE19....69 G5
Anerley Pk PGE/AN SE20....69 J4
Anerley Park Rd PGE/AN SE20....69 H4
Anerley Rd NRWD SE19....69 H4
Anerley Station Rd
  PGE/AN SE20....69 J5
Anerley V NRWD SE19....69 H4
Angelica Gdns CROY/NA CRO....87 L4
Angle Rd WTHK RM20....33 L5
Anglesea Av WOOL/PLUM SE18....28 D5
Anglesea Rd STMC/STPC BR5....91 K2
  WOOL/PLUM SE18....28 C5
Anglesey Av MAID/SHEP ME15....167 H7
Anglesey Cl WALD ME5....101 H4
Angley Ct STPH/PW TN12....279 R12
Angley Rd CRBK TN17....298 C8
Angley Wk CRBK TN17....298 C7
Angus St NWCR SE14....25 M6
Ankerdine Crs
  WOOL/PLUM SE18....28 C7
Annandale Rd BFN/LL DA15....28 A7
  CROY/NA CRO....87 H5
  GNWCH SE10....26 C5
Anna Pk BRCH CT7....176 D6
Anne Boleyn Cl IOS ME12....229 P2
Anne Cl BRCH CT7....176 E6
Anne Compton Ms
  LEE/GVPK SE12....47 G5
Anne Figg Cl WTHK RM20....19 K9
Anne Green Wk CANT CT1....5 H4
Anne Heart Cl WTHK RM20....33 L3
Anne of Cleves Rd DART DA1....51 L3
Anne Roper Cl NROM TN28....331 M7
Annesley Dr CROY/NA CRO....88 A6
Annesley Rd BKHTH/KID SE5....27 J7
Annetts Hall BGR/WK TN15....240 F12
Annie Rd SNOD ME6....113 G7
Ann Moss Wy
  BERM/RHTH SE16....25 K2
Ann's Rd RAM CT11....17 J3
Ann St WOOL/PLUM SE18....28 L4
Annsworthy Av THHTH CR7....68 E7
Ansdell Rd PECK SE15....25 K8
Ansell Av CHAT ME4....101 H3
Anselm Cl CROY/NA CRO....87 K4
  SIT ME10....119 M5
Anstee Rd DVW CT17....8 A2
Ansford Rd BMLY BR1....70 D7
Ansley Cl SAND/SEL CR2....104 A8
Anson Av E/WMAL ME19....164 A2
Anson Cl BRDST CT10....182 F2
  WALD ME5....101 K7
Anstridge Rd ELTH/MOT SE9....48 E4
Antelope Av CDW/CHF RM16....34 A2
Anthony Rd WOOL/PLUM SE18....28 J2
Anthony Cl SEV TN13....135 K2
Anthony Crs WSTB CT5....126 C7
Anthony Rd SNWD SE25....69 H7
  WELL DA16....29 H7
Anthonys La STRD ME2....82 F5
Anthonys Wy STRD ME2....82 F5
Antolin Wy MSTR CT12....182 D2
Antonius Ct ASH TN23....204 D6
Anvil Cl BRCH CT7....176 D7
Apex Cl DVE/WH CT16....213 M7
Aperfield Rd BH/WHM TN16....132 D3
  ERITH DA8....31 G5
Apex Cl BECK BR3....70 C5
Apollo Av BMLY BR1....71 J1
Apollo Wy CHAT ME4....83 K3
  WOOL/PLUM SE18....28 E2
Apostle Wy THHTH CR7....68 C6
Appach Rd BRXS/STRHM SW2....44 A1
Appleby Cl ROCH ME1....100 E6
Apple Cl RFOLK CT18....220 C1
  SNOD ME6....113 G7
Applecross Cl ROCH ME1....100 E6
Appledore Av BXLYHN DA7....30 D7
  IOS ME12....64 C5
Appledore Cl HAYES BR2....89 L7
  MARG CT9....178 E4
Appledore Crs BFN/LL DA15....48 F8
  FOLKN CT19....219 L6
Appledore Rd RASHW TN26....317 J1
  RASHW TN26....317 H5
  RHAM ME8....102 B2
  TENT TN30....315 Q2
Appledown Wy CANT CT1....174 L4
Appleford Dr IOS ME12....65 G6
Applegarth CROY/NA CRO....105 G2
Applegarth Dr DART DA1....51 M7
Applegarth Pk WSTB CT5....126 B3
Apple Orch SWLY BR8....74 F8
Appleshaw Cl GVW DA11....79 G3
Appleton Cl BXLYHN DA7....30 D7
Appleton Dr RDART DA2....51 J8
Appleton Rd ELTH/MOT SE9....47 M1
Appletons RTON TN11....256 C5
Apple Tree Cl MAIDW ME16....166 A3
Apple Tree La RTWE/PEM TN2....197 J5
Appold St ERITH DA8....31 G5
Approach Rd DVW CT17....217 H1
  MARG CT9....15 G2
  RDV CT15....271 J4
  WARL CR6....132 E4
Approach Rd South
  LYDD TN29....335 M11
The Approach ORP BR6....91 G5

April Cl ORP BR6....91 G8
April Gln FSTH SE23....45 L8
April Ri WSTB CT5....126 C6
Apsley Rd SNWD SE25....69 J8
Apsley St ASH TN23....
  STH/RUST TN4....200 E1
Arabin Rd BROCKY SE4....45 M2
Aragon Cl ASH TN23....204 B4
  CROY/NA CRO....105 K4
  HAYES BR2....90 A4
Arbor Cl BECK BR3....70
Arborfield Cl BRXS/STRHM SW2....44 A2
Arbroath Rd ELTH/MOT SE9....47 M1
Arbrook La STMC/STPC BR5....73 H7
Arbuthnot La DEAL DA5....49 H4
Arbuthnot Rd NWCR SE14....25 L8
Arcade Chambers
  ELTH/MOT SE9 *....48 B4
The Arcade ELTH/MOT SE9 *....48 B4
Arthur St ERITH DA8....31 G6
Arcadian Av BXLY DA5....49 M4
Arcadian Cl BXLY DA5....49 M4
Arcadian Rd BXLY DA5....49 M5
Arcadia Rd MEO DA13....79 G5
Archangel St BERM/RHTH SE16....25 J1
Archates Av CDW/CHF RM16....34 B2
Archbishop's Pl
  BRXS/STRHM SW2....44 A2
Archcliffe Rd DVW CT17....217 K4
Archdale Rd EDUL SE22....45 G3
Archer Rd FOLKN CT19....11 K2
  SNWD SE25....69 J5
  STMC/STPC BR5....91 H2
  WALD ME5....101 J1
Archer's Court Rd
  DVE/WH CT16....213 J1
Archer Sq DEPT SE8....25 M5
Archer Wy SWLY BR8....75 G7
Archery Rd ELTH/MOT SE9....48 A3
Archery Sq DEAL CT14....209 L6
Arch St STHWK SE1....24 D2
Archway Rd IOS ME12....64 B2
  RAM CT11....17 J6
Arcon Cl ASH TN23....204 C4
Arcon Rd ASH TN23....204 C4
Arcus Rd BMLY BR1....70 F3
Ardbeg Rd HNHL SE24....44 E1
Arden Cl CANT CT1 *....5 L6
Arden Crs POP/IOD E14....26 D2
Arden Dr KEN/WIL TN24....2 D2
Arden Gv ORP BR6....90 C7
Ardenlee Dr MAID/BEAR ME14....13 L4
Arden Rd FAV ME13....149 M2
Ardenrun LING RH7....190 B5
Arden St GILL ME7....7 J4
Ardent Av DEAL CT14....209 K5
Ardent Cl SNWD SE25....68 F8
Ardfern Av STRHM/NOR SW16....68 B7
Ardfillan Rd CAT SE6....46 E6
Ardgowan Rd CAT SE6....46 F6
Ardingly Cl CROY/NA CRO....87 L6
Ardington Cl FSTH SE23....45 L6
Ardlui Rd WNWD SE27....44 D7
Ardmere Rd LEW SE13....46 E4
Ardoch Rd CAT SE6....46 F6
Arethusa Pl GRH DA9....53 J2
Arethusa Rd ROCH ME1....100 P5
Argent Cl OBOR ME11....227 J7
Argent St GRAYS RM17....33 M5
Argent Ter WALD ME5 *....101 L1
Argent Wy SIT ME10....119 K3
Argles Ct GRH DA9....53 J2
Argyle Cl MARG CT9....14 B9
Argyle Cl ROCH ME1....100 F6
Argyle Gdns MARG CT9....14 A7
Argyle Rd SEV TN13....121 J7
  STH/RUST TN4....196 D5
  WSTB CT5....126 E4
Argyle Wy STHWK SE1....25 H4
Argyll Cl BRXN/ST SW9....44 A1
Argyll Dr RAM CT11....183 J4
Argyll Rd WOOL/PLUM SE18....28 D2
Arica Rd BROCKY SE4....45 M2
Ariel Ct GVE DA12....55 A1
Ark Av CDW/CHF RM16....34 A1
Arkell Av NRWD SE19....68 C4
Arkindale Rd CAT SE6....46 E7
Ark La DEAL CT14....209 K2
Arklow Rd NWCR SE14....26 A5
Arklow Sq RAM CT11....17 L5
Arkwright Rd TIL RM18....35 L3
Arlingford Rd
  BRXS/STRHM SW2....44 B1
Arlington Cl BFN/LL DA15....48 F5
  LEW SE13....46 E4
Arlington Gdns MARG CT9....178 F5
Arlington Pde
  BRXS/STRHM SW2 *....44 A2
Arlington Sq MARG CT9....14 A7
Armada Cl NROM TN28....331 M8
Armada Ct CHAT ME4 *....100 F4
Armadale Vls RAM CT11 *....16 E6
Armada St DEPT SE8....25 M5
Armada Wy CHAT ME4....6 C3
Armitage Rd GNWCH SE10....27 G4
Armor Rd PUR RM19....32 E3
Armoury Dr GVE DA12....55 K5
Armoury Rd DEPT SE8....26 B5
Armstrong Cl BMLY BR1....71 M7
  RSEV TN14....135
Armstrong Rd
  MAID/SHEP ME15....167 H4
  WOOL/PLUM SE18....28 H4
Armstrong Sq HB CT6....128 B6
Armytage Rd HOO/HM ME3....83 M1
Arne Cl TONN TN10....189 H7
Arne Gv ORP BR6....91 G6
Arne Wy BKHTH/KID SE3....47 G2
Angask Rd CAT SE6....46 E5
Arnheim Pl POP/IOD E14....26 C1
Arnhem Dr CROY/NA CRO....105 J5
  WALD ME5....101 G6
Arnold Av MEO DA13....97 J5
Arnolde Cl STRD ME2....82 F6
Arnold Est STHWK SE1 *....25 G1
Arnold Pl TIL RM18....35 L3
Arnold Rd GVE DA12....55 K7
  RAM CT11....15 G5
  RCANTW CT4....248 D7
Arnolds La RDART DA2....76 A3
Arnould Av CMBW SE5....44 E5
Arnsberg Wy BXLYHN DA7....50 B3
Arnside Rd BXLYHN DA7....30 D5
Arnside St WALW SE17....24 D5
Arnulf St CAT SE6....46 F4
Arnull's Rd STRHM/NOR SW16....68 C3
Arodene Rd BRXS/STRHM SW2....44 A1
Arolla Rd HB CT6....129 K5
Aragon Gdns WWKM BR4....88 D2
Arran Cl ERITH DA8....30 E5
Arran Rd CAT SE6....46 E7
  MAID/SHEP ME15....167 K7
Arrol Rd BECK BR3....69 K7
Arrowhead La RASHW TN26....318 A10

Arsenal Rd ELTH/MOT SE9....28 A7
Arsenal Wy CAN/RD E16....28 B1
Artemis Cl GVE DA12....55 M5
Arterial Rd North Stifford
  CDW/CHF RM16....33 M1
Arterial Rd Purfleet PUR RM19....32 F3
Arterial Rd West Thurrock
  WTHK RM20....33 G2
Arthurdon Rd LEW SE13....46 C3
Arthur Gv WOOL/PLUM SE18....28 H3
Arthur Kennedy Cl FAV ME13....151 L4
Arthur Rd BH/WHM TN16....132 B1
  BRCH CT7....176 A5
  DEAL CT14....209 H6
  HYTHE CT21....222 D4
  MARG CT9....15 J3
  RHAM ME8....102 F5
  ROCH ME1....100 D3
Arthur Salmon Cl FAV ME13....151 H1
Arthur St ERITH DA8....31 G6
  FOLKN CT19....11 L2
  GRAYS RM17....34 D5
  GVW DA11....55 H5
  SEV TN13....21 J1
Artichoke Pl CMBW SE5 *....24 F7
Artillery Gdns CANT CT1 *....5 H3
Artillery Pl WOOL/PLUM SE18....28 A4
Artillery Rd CANT CT11....17 K4
Artillery Rw GVE DA12....55 K5
Arun TIL RM18....36 B3
Arundel Av SIT ME10....119 M8
Arundel Cl BXLY DA5....50 A4
  CROY/NA CRO *....86 C6
  TON TN9....194 C6
  WALD ME5....115 K4
Arundel Dr ORP BR6....91 J8
Arundel Rd CROY/NA CRO....86 C5
  DART DA1....51 K2
  MARG CT9....15 J5
  MSTR CT12....182 A6
  RTW TN1....23 J3
Arundel St MAID/BEAR ME14....141 J7
Aschurch Rd CROY/NA CRO....87 G3
Ascot Cl BGR/WK TN15....240 C2
  WALD ME5....115 K5
Ascot Gdns WGOS CT8....177 H6
Ascot Rd GVW DA11....55 J8
  STMC/STPC BR5....73 J5
  WSTB CT5....236 H11
Ashbee Cl SNOD ME6....113 J4
Ashbee Gdns HB CT6....129 K4
Ashborne Cl KEN/WIL TN24....203 G5
Ashbourne Av BXLYHN DA7....30 B5
Ashbourne Cl WALD ME5....115 K4
Ashbourne Ri ORP BR6....90 E7
Ashburnham Gv GNWCH SE10....26 D6
Ashburnham Pl GNWCH SE10....26 C6
Ashburnham Retreat
  GNWCH SE10....26 C6
Ashburnham Rd BELV DA17....30 C6
  MAID/BEAR ME14....141 J5
  RAM CT11....16 E5
  TON TN9....194 F7
Ashburn Ms GILL ME7 *....101 M2
Ashburton Av CROY/NA CRO....87 M1
Ashburton Cl CROY/NA CRO....87 H1
  KEN/WIL TN24....3 G5
Ashburton Gdns CROY/NA CRO....87 H1
Ashburton Rd CROY/NA CRO....87 H1
Ashby Ct BMLY BR1....71 M3
Ashby Cl STRD ME2 *....113 H1
Ashby Ms BROCKY SE4....46 A1
Ashby Rd NWCR SE14....26 A6
Ashby's Cl EDEN TN8....192 A5
Ash Cl BRDST CT10....182 F1
  DIT/AY ME20....139 M4
  DVW CT17....212 F6
  EDEN TN8....192 C4
  HB CT6....128 B8
  LING RH7....190 H4
  PGE/AN SE20....69 K6
  RHAM ME8....102 C2
  RTWE/PEM TN2....201 L5
  SCUP DA14....49 J8
  STMC/STPC BR5....90 E1
  SWLY BR8....74 B3
  WALD ME5....101 K4
Ash Close Vls SWCH CT13 *....253 J3
Ashcombe Dr EDEN TN8....192 C1
Ashcroft Av BFN/LL DA15....49 H4
Ashcroft Crs BFN/LL DA15....49 H4
Ashcroft Rd HOO/HM ME3....82 C5
  STPH/PW TN12....279 L4
Ashdale Rd LEE/GVPK SE12....47 J6
Ashden Wk TONN TN10....188 E5
Ashdown Cl BECK BR3....70 C6
  BXLY DA5....50 D5
  HB CT6....128 C4
  MAIDW ME16....12 E4
  STH/RUST TN4....22 C4
Ashdown Crs NROM TN28....331 M8
Ashdown Fld RCANTW CT4....248 H4
Ashdown Gdns SAND/SEL CR2....130 A4
Ashdown Rd RSIT ME9....243 M1
Ashenden HDCN TN27....284 C7
Ashenden Av RYE TN31....224 F5
Ashenden Cl CANT CT1....171 K8
  MEO DA13....82 D3
Ashenden Wk RTWE/PEM TN2....197 H5
Ashen Dr DART DA1....51 H1
Ashen Grove Rd
  BGR/WK TN15....111 G4
Ashen Tree La DVE/WH CT16....8 E4
Ashentree La LYDD TN29....329 M8
Ashen V SAND/SEL CR2....104 A4
Asher Reeds RRTW TN3....200 B1
Ash La RTON TN11....189 H4
Ashfield Cl BECK BR3....70 A6
Ashfield La CHST BR7....72 C2
Ashford Dr RMAID ME17....261 G3
Ashford Rd ASH TN23....286 C6
  ASH TN23....204 C6
  FAV ME13....149 K4
  FAV ME13....246 A4
  FAV ME13....246 B5
  HYTHE CT21....307 P2
  MAID/BEAR ME14....13 M5
  NROM TN28....330 H1
  RASHE TN25....306 C4
  RASHE TN25....307 M7
  RASHW TN26....319 F11
  RASHW TN26....301 K6
  RASHW TN26....303 K2
  RASHW TN26....304 C5
  RASHW TN26....318 D5
  RCANTW CT4....248 D6
  RCANTW CT4....267 K3
  RMAID ME17....169 L5
  RMAID ME17....242 D11
  RMAID ME17....243 N12
  RMAID ME17....263 N2
  RMAID ME17....301 N6
  SWCH CT13....234 E2
Ash Gv LYDD TN29....334 C2

MAIDW ME16....140 D7
PGE/AN SE20....69 K6
SEV TN13....161 M5
Ashington Cl SIT ME10....119 K4
Ash Keys MEO DA13....239 N5
Ash La BGR/WK TN15....238 B5
Ashlar Pl WOOL/PLUM SE18....28 E3
Ashleigh Cl DEAL CT14....239 L4
Ashleigh Gdns HDCN TN27....283 L3
Ashleigh Rd PGE/AN SE20....69 J7
Ashley Cl IOS ME12....64 D8
  MSTR CT12....182 E3
  SEV TN12....21 G4
Ashley Gv ORP BR6....91 J5
  STH/RUST TN4....277 R12
Ashley La CROY/NA CRO....86 C7
Ashley Park Rd STH/RUST TN4....277 R12
Ashley Rd RHAM ME8....102 D3
Ashling Rd CROY/NA CRO....87 H4
Ashmead Cl MAID ME5....115 K2
Ashmead Ga BMLY BR1....71 K5
Ashmead Rd DEPT SE8....26 B7
Ashmead St DEPT SE8....26 B8
Ash Mdw KEN/WIL TN24....205 H4
Ashmere Av BECK BR3....70 E6
Ashmere Cl CROY/NA CRO....87 G1
Ashmere Gv BRXS/STRHM SW2....44 A1
Ashmole Vx VX/NE SW8....24 A5
Ashmore Cl PECK SE15....25 J6
Ashmore Gv WELL DA16....48 E1
Ash Platt BGR/WK TN15....136 D7
Ashridge Crs WOOL/PLUM SE18....28 F6
Ash Rd BH/WHM TN16....159 J3
  CROY/NA CRO....88 B3
  DART DA1....51 L6
  GVE DA12....55 M7
  HART DA3....77 M7
  ORP BR6....107 M2
  RCANTE CT3....251 N12
  RDART DA2....76 A1
  STRD ME2....18 D6
  SWCH CT13....236 H11
Ashtead Dr RSIT ME9....120 E7
Ashton Cl DEAL CT14....209 H7
Ashton Ms BRDST CT10 *....183 L1
Ashton Wy E/WMAL ME19....138 B4
Ash Tree Cl BGR/WK TN15....111 L3
  CROY/NA CRO....87 M2
  LYDD TN29....331 N2
Ashtree Cl ORP BR6....90 C7
Ash Tree Dr BGR/WK TN15....111 L3
Ash Tree La CHAT ME4....100 A3
Ash Tree Rd FOLKN CT19....11 M4
Ash Tree Rd CROY/NA CRO....87 M1
Ashurst Av WSTB CT5....126 C6
Ashurst Cl DART DA1....51 G1
  PGE/AN SE20....69 J5
Ashurst Gdns
  BRXS/STRHM SW2 *....44 B6
  MARG CT9....179 H2
Ashurst Rd MAID/BEAR ME14....13 J5
  RRTW TN3....199 J8
Ashurst Wk CROY/NA CRO....87 J5
Ashwater Rd LEE/GVPK SE12....47 H6
Ashwood WARL CR6....130 B6
Ashwood Cl HOO/HM ME3....83 J3
Ashwood Gdns CROY/NA CRO....105 K2
Ashworth Av BGR/WK TN15 *....111 K2
Ashworth Cl CMBW SE5....24 F7
Askern Cl BXLYHS DA6....49 L2
Askes Ct ASH TN23....204 D6
Askews Farm Rd GRAYS RM17....33 M4
Asolando Dr WALW SE17 *....24 D7
Aspdin Rd GVW DA11....54 E8
Aspen Cl LYDD TN29....331 N2
  ORP BR6....91 L5
  SWLY BR8....74 F5
Aspen Copse BMLY BR1....72 A6
Aspen Dr ASH TN23....202 A8
Aspen Gn ERITHM DA18....30 A2
Aspen Rd HB CT6....154 F2
  RCANTW CT4....248 F8
Aspen Wy RTWE/PEM TN2....196 F4
Aspian Dr RHAID ME17....279 J3
Aspinall Cl RCANTW CT4....175 J5
Aspinall Rd BROCKY SE4....45 L1
Asquith Rd RHAM ME8....102 D7
Astbury Rd PECK SE15....25 L7
Aster Rd HOO/HM ME3....83 M2
Astley GRAYS RM17....34 A5
Astley Av DVE/WH CT16....8 A2
Astley Gdns FOLKN CT19....10 C3
Astley St MAID/BEAR ME14....13 H4
Aston Cl SCUP DA14....49 H8
  WALD ME5....115 J3
Astor Av DVW CT17....217 J1
Astor Dr DEAL CT14....209 K4
Astoria Wk BRXN/ST SW9....44 B1
Astor Rd BGR/WK TN15....111 K1
  BRDST CT10....179 M2
Astra Dr GVE DA12....55 M7
Astrid Rd DEAL CT14....209 H7
Asylum Rd PECK SE15....25 J6
Athelney St CAT SE6....46 D8
Athelstan Gn RMAID ME17....169 K3
Athelstan Pl DEAL CT14....209 K5
Athelstan Rd CANT CT1....171 K8
  CHAT ME4....100 F3
  FAV ME13....149 J3
  MARG CT9....15 J5
Athelstan Wy STMC/STPC BR5....73 H5
Athenlay Rd PECK SE15....45 L5
Atherton Gdns CDW/CHF RM16....35 K3
Athlone Rd BRXS/STRHM SW2....44 A2
Athol Pl FAV ME13....149 H1
Athol Rd ASH TN23....204 C6
  ERITH DA8....30 D7
Athol Ter DVE/WH CT16....126 F3
Atkins Cl WWKM BR4....88 E6
Atkinson Cl ORP BR6....91 L8
Atkinson Wk KEN/WIL TN24....203 J6
Atlantic Cl SWCM DA10....53 M3
Atlantic Rd BRXN/ST SW9....44 B3
Atlas Gdns CHARL SE7....27 G4
Atlas Rd DART DA1....51 L2
Atterbury Cl BH/WHM TN16....159 J4
Attlee Av RCANTE CT3....251 P12
Attlee Cl CROY/NA CRO....86 D2
Attlee Dr DART DA1....52 B3
Attlee Rd GRAYS RM17....34 C3
Attwaters La HAWK TN18....312 F3
Attwood Cl SAND/SEL CR2....104 A8
Atwell Rd PECK SE15 *....25 J1
Atwood Av RCANTE CT3....251 N6
Aubretia Cl RSIT ME9....119 M6
Aubyn Hl WNWD SE27....68 D1

Auckland Av MSTR CT12....16 A1
Auckland Cl NRWD SE19....69 G5
  TIL RM18....35 H8
Auckland Dr SIT ME10....119 K6
Auckland Hl WNWD SE27....68 D1
Auckland Ri NRWD SE19....68 F5
Auckland Rd NRWD SE19....69 G5
  RTW TN1....196 F7
Aucklands Gdns NRWD SE19....68 F5
Auckland St LBTH SE11....24 A7
Acuba Vls WELL DA16 *....49 J1
Auden Rd DIT/AY ME20....139 H1
Audley Av GILL ME7....101 M4
  MARG CT9....177 K4
  TON TN9....194 C3
Audley Dr SAND/SEL CR2....130 B1
Audley Ri TON TN9....194 C3
Audley Rd FOLK CT20....10 F5
Audrey Cl BECK BR3....88 C2
Auger Cl RSIT ME9....103 M8
Augusta Cl GILL ME7....83 K6
Augusta Gdns FOLK CT20....11 G7
Augusta Pl RAM CT11....17 L5
Augusta Rd RAM CT11....17 L5
Augustine Rd GVE DA12....55 J5
  IOS ME12....180 E7
  MSTR CT12....180 E7
  STMC/STPC BR5....73 L4
Augustus Wk ASH TN23....204 C6
Aulton Pl LBTH SE11....24 B4
Aurelia Gdns THHTH CR7....86 A1
Aurellus Cl ASH TN23....204 C6
Austen Cl GRH DA9....53 K4
  TIL RM18....35 K8
Austen Rd ERITH DA8....30 C6
Austens Orch TENT TN30 *....315 M2
Austen Wy DIT/AY ME20....139 H1
Austin Av HAYES BR2....89 M2
  HB CT6....128 A5
Austin Cl CAT SE6....46 F1
  SIT ME10....120 B1
  WALD ME5....115 J3
Austin Rd ASH TN23....204 C5
  GVW DA11....55 G6
  STMC/STPC BR5....91 H2
Austins La SWCH CT13....237 K12
Austral Cl BFN/LL DA15....49 G8
Austral St LBTH SE11....24 C6
Autumn Gld MAID/BEAR ME14....115 L5
Autumn Gv BMLY BR1....71 J3
Avalon Cl ORP BR6....91 L5
Avalon Rd ORP BR6....91 L5
Avard Gdns ORP BR6....90 D7
Avards Cl HAWK TN18....312 D5
Avebury Av RAM CT11....183 K5
  TON TN9....194 C4
Avebury Rd ORP BR6....90 E8
Aveley Cl ERITH DA8....31 G5
Aveline St LBTH SE11....24 A4
Aveling Cl HOO/HM ME3....82 L7
Avent Wk RSIT ME9....120 F7
Avenue Du Puy TON TN9....194 H4
Avenue Gdns BECK BR3....178 F3
Avenue Le Puy TON TN9....194 H4
Avenue Ldg GRAYS RM17....34 C4
Avenue of Remembrance
  SIT ME10....120 A1
Avenue Park Rd WNWD SE27....44 D7
Avenue Rd BH/WHM TN16....132 D4
  BXLYHS DA6....49 M1
  DVE/WH CT16....8 D7
  ERITH DA8....30 D6
  HB CT6....128 C4
  RAM CT11....17 L4
  SEV TN13....21 J5
  SNWD SE25....69 H6
The Avenue BECK BR3....70 C5
  BGR/WK TN15....240 F1
  BH/WHM TN16....132 E8
  BMLY BR1....71 L7
  BXLY DA5....49 L5
  CHAT ME4....83 K3
  CROY/NA CRO....87 J8
  DEAL CT14....209 K2
  DIT/AY ME20....139 M4
  DVE/WH CT16....212 F4
  EGRIN RH19....274 A8
  GNWCH SE10....26 D3
  GRH DA9....53 J2
  GVW DA11....55 H5
  MARG CT9....15 G2
  ORP BR6....91 G5
  RCANTE CT3....155 N8
  RDV CT15....215 G3
  STMC/STPC BR5....73 J4
  TON TN9....194 C3
  WWKM BR4....88 B2
Averenches Rd
  MAID/BEAR ME14....142 A8
Avereng Gdns FOLKN CT19....10 D3
Avereng Rd FOLKN CT19....10 D3
Averil Gv STRHM/NOR SW16....68 D1
Avery Cl HOO/HM ME3....41 M4
  MAID/SHEP ME15....167 J3
Avery Hill Rd ELTH/MOT SE9....48 D4
Avery Wk MAID/SHEP ME15....168 B3
Avery Wy HOO/HM ME3....41 L5
Aviemore Cl BECK BR3....88 D7
Aviemore Gdns
  MAID/BEAR ME14....168 A1
Aviemore Wy BECK BR3....87 M1
Avignon Cl BROCKY SE4....45 L2
Avington Cl MAID/SHEP ME15....167 J3
Avington Gv PGE/AN SE20....69 K4
Avington Wy PECK SE15....25 J6
Avocet Cl STHWK SE1....25 G4
Avon Cl CANT CT1....5 M1
  GVE DA12....55 L7
  TONN TN10....188 D7
Avondale Cl MAID/SHEP ME15....167 H5
Avondale Pavement
  STHWK SE1 *....25 H4
Avondale Ri PECK SE15....45 G1
Avondale Rd BMLY BR1....70 F3
  ELTH/MOT SE9....47 M7
  GILL ME7....7 H5
  RFOLK CT18....221 K3
  WELL DA16....29 H4
Avondale Sq STHWK SE1....25 H4
Avonley Rd NWCR SE14....25 L6
Avonmouth Rd DART DA1....51 L3
Avonmouth St STHWK SE1....24 D2
Avon Rd BROCKY SE4....46 A1
Avonstowe Cl ORP BR6....90 C5
Avon St RTW TN1....23 L5
Awliscombe Rd WELL DA16....29 H5
Axis Ct GNWCH SE10....26 E3
Axminster Crs WELL DA16....29 J4
Axtane MEO DA13....78 A4
Axtane Cl EYN DA4....76 B4
Aycliffe Cl BMLY BR1....72 A4
Ayelands HART DA3....95 M5
Ayelands La HART DA3....95 M5

Aylesbury Rd HAYES BR2 ...71 H7
  RASHE TN25 ...202 E4
  WALW SE17 ...24 E4
Aylesford Av BECK BR3 ...87 H1
Aylesford Crs RHAM ME8 ...102 B2
Aylesford Pl KEN/WIL TN24 ...205 H4
Aylesford Rd ORP BR6 ...90 F3
  RCANTE CT3 ...271 N1
Ayleswade La HDCN TN27 ...283 M9
Aylett Rd SNWD SE25 ...69 H4
Aylewyn Gn SIT ME10 ...120 A1
Aylton Est BERM/RHTH SE16 * ...25 K1
Aylward Rd FSTH SE23 ...45 L2
Aylwin Est STHWK SE1 * ...24 F2
Ayliscombe Angle ORP BR6 ...91 H7
Ayres St STHWK SE1 * ...24 E1
Aysgarth Rd DUL SE21 ...44 E4
Ayton Rd RAM CT11 ...16 F6
Aytoun Pl BRXN/ST SW9 ...44 A8
Aytoun Rd BRXN/ST SW9 ...44 A8
Azalea Dr SWLY BR8 ...74 E8
Azenby Rd PECK SE15 ...45 M8
Azof St GNWCH SE10 ...26 F3

B

Babbacombe Rd BMLY BR1 ...71 J5
Babb's La CRBK TN17 ...313 K3
Babs Oak Hi CANTW/ST CT2 ...173 J3
Babylon La RMAID ME17 ...260 C11
Backfields ROCH ME1 ...19 H9
Back La BGR/WK TN15 ...162 F2
  BGR/WK TN15 ...240 F3
  BXLY DA5 ...50 B5
  CRBK TN17 ...297 N5
  IOS ME12 ...65 L7
  PUR RM19 ...32 F3
  RMAID ME17 ...259 R5
  RSEV TN14 ...161 G6
  RTON TN11 ...188 F1
  SEV TN13 ...161 J2
  STPH/PW TN12 ...279 N11
Backley Gdns SNWD SE25 ...87 H2
Back Rd HAWK TN18 ...313 L12
  SCUP DA14 ...73 H1
Back St (East) DVE/WH CT16 * ...7
Back St FOLKN CT19... ...11 M5
  RMAID ME17 ...168 F7
Bacon Gv STHWK SE1 ...25 L7
Baddlesmere Rd WSTB CT5 ...127 L1
Baden Pl STHWK SE1 ...24 E1
Baden Powell Rd SEV TN13 ...135 K3
Baden Rd GILL ME7 ...83 L6
Bader Cl S WALD ME5 ...101 H6
Bader Wk GVW DA11 ...54 F8
Badger Cl CANTW/ST CT2 ...153 H6
Badgers Cl RAM CT11 * ...16 F6
Badgers Copse ORP BR6 ...91 G5
Badgers Cft ELTH/MOT SE9 ...48 B8
Badgers Holt RTWE/PEM TN2 ...197 H6
Badgers La WARL CR6 ...130 B5
Badgers Mt CDW/CHF RM16 ...35 G5
Badgers Ri DEAL CT14 ...211 K1
  DVW CT17 ...8 F4
  RSEV TN14 ...108 F4
Badgers Rd SEV TN13 ...109 H4
Badlesmere Cl ASH TN23 ...204 B5
Badlow Cl ERITH DA8 ...30 C6
Bad Munstereifel Rd ASH TN23 ...204 E6
Badsell Rd STPH/PW TN12 ...278 F17
Badsworth Rd CMBW SE5 ...24 D6
Baffin Cl CHAT ME4 ...101 G3
Bagham La RCANTW CT4 ...247 Q9
Bagham Rd RCANTW CT4 ...247 P9
Bagley House WOOL/PLUM SE18 * ...27 L8
Bagshill Rd FAV ME13 ...245 Q5
Bagshot Cf WOOL/PLUM SE18 * ...28 B7
Bagshot Rd WALW SE17 ...24 E1
Baildon St DEPT SE8 ...26 A6
Bailey Cl PUR RM19 ...32 E3
Bailey Dr GILL ME7 ...102 F3
Bailey House WOOL/PLUM SE18 * ...27 M6
Bailey Pl SYD SE26 ...69 K3
Baileys Fld ASH TN23 ...204 C2
Baillemore Ct RAM CT11 * ...183 J4
Baines Cl CROY/NA CR0 ...104 B3
Baird Gdns NRWD SE19 ...68 F1
Baird's Hl BRDST CT10 ...179 J7
Bairdsley Cl BRDST CT10 ...179 J7
Baizdon Rd BKHTH/KID SE3 ...26 F8
Baker Cl RSIT ME9 ...121 K6
Baker Hill Cl GVW DA11 ...79 G1
Baker La HDCN TN27 ...283 P10
  RMAID ME17 ...260 C6
Baker Ms ORP BR6 ...107 J1
Baker Rd FOLKN CT19 ...219 M7
  WOOL/PLUM SE18 ...27 M6
Bakers Av BGR/WK TN15 ...111 K3
Bakers La CANTW/ST CT2 ...171 K6
  LING RH7 ...190 F8
Bakers Cross CRBK TN17 ...298 H9
Bakers La RCANTW CT4 ...247 P5
Bakers Md BDCH RH9 ...156 B8
Baker St ROCH ME1 ...100 D7
  ROCH ME1 ...114 A4
Baker's Wk ROCH ME1 ...19 H1
Bakery Cl BRXN/ST SW9 * ...24 M1
Balaclava La WADH TN5 ...309 M3
Balaclava Rd SURB KT6 ...63 K3
Balas Dr SIT ME10 ...119 K3
Balcaskie Rd ELTH/MOT SE9 ...48 A3
Balchen Rd BKHTH/KID SE3 ...27 H6
Balchier Rd EDUL SE22 ...45 J4
Balcomb Crs MARG CT9 ...178 F5
Balcombe Rd CRBK TN17 ...297 N5
Balder Ri LEE/GVPK SE12 ...47 L7
Baldock Rd WADH TN5 ...309 K5
Baldric Rd FOLK CT20 ...10 C6
Baldwin Crs CMBW SE5 ...24 D6
Baldwin Rd IOS ME12 ...54 F1
  NROM TN28 ...331 L12
Baldwin Ter FOLKN CT19 ...11 L2
Baldwyn's Pk BXLY DA5 ...50 E7
Baldwyn's Rd BXLY DA5 ...50 E7
Balfour Cl CHAT ME4 ...100 A5
  DEAL CT14 ...209 K7
  DVE/WH CT16 ...8 A1
  GRAYS RM17 ...34 D3
  HAYES BR2 ...89 L1
  SNWD SE25 ...69 H8
Balfour St STHWK SE1 ...24 E1
Balgonie Rd BECK BR3 ...69 M7
Balgowan St WOOL/PLUM SE18 ...29 G3
Baliol Rd WSTB CT5 ...126 F3
Ballamore Rd BMLY BR1 ...47 M8
Ballard Cl STPH/PW TN12 ...280 H3
Ballard Rd NROM TN28 ...331 L12
Ballards La OXTED RH8 ...158 B7
Ballards Wy SAND/SEL CR2 ...104 B1
Ballard Wy STPH/PW TN12 ...279 L2

Ballast Quay GNWCH SE10 ...26 E4
Ballater Rd SAND/SEL CR2 ...87 G4
Ballens Rd WALD ME5 ...115 K2
Ballina St FSTH SE23 ...45 L5
Balliol Rd BRDST CT10 ...179 J6
  WELL DA16 ...29 J8
Balloch Rd CAT SE6 ...46 F7
Ballow Cl CMBW SE5 * ...24 E6
Balmer Cl RHAM ME8 ...102 A6
Balmoral Av BECK BR3 ...69 M6
Balmoral Gdns BXLY DA5 ...50 A5
Balmoral Rd RAM CT11 ...17 L5
Balmoral Rd BXLYHN DA7 ...30 D7
  DEAL CT14 ...211 L3
  EYN DA4 ...76 B4
  GILL ME7 ...7 L3
  MARG CT9 ...177 L5
Baltic Rd TON TN9 ...194 E6
Baltimore Pl WELL DA16 ...29 G8
Bamford Cl BMLY BR1 ...71 J5
Bamford Rd BMLY BR1 ...70 E2
Bamford Wy DEAL CT14 ...209 K5
Bampton Rd FSTH SE23 ...45 L8
Banavie Gdns BECK BR3 ...70 B5
Banbury Vls MEO DA13 ...78 A3
Bancroft Rd BKHTH/KID SE3 ...27 K4
Bankside HART DA3 ...77 M8
Bancroft Gdns ORP BR6 ...91 H5
Bancroft La E/WMAL ME19 ...164 D3
Bancroft Rd BGR/WK TN15 ...238 C10
Banfield Rd PECK SE15 ...45 J1
Bangor St ROCH ME1 ...81 L7
Bankfields HDCN TN27 ...283 K4
Bankfield Wy CRBK TN17 ...297 N6
Bankfoot Rd BMLY BR1 ...70 F1
Bankhurst Rd CAT SE6 ...46 A5
Bank La BGR/WK TN15 ...255 P2
Bank Rd RASHE TN25 ...305 N5
Bank Side RASHW TN26 ...318 D1
Bankside GVW DA11 ...54 D4
  SEV TN13 ...135 J7
  WADH TN5 ...309 L4
  WALD ME5 ...101 H5
Bankside Cl BH/WHM TN16 ...132 B4
  RDART DA2 ...74 A1
Banks La BXLYHS DA6 ...50 A2
Banks Rd ASH TN23 ...204 D4
  STRD ME2 ...19 G2
The Banks BRDST CT10 ...179 J7
Bank St ASH TN23 ...2 B5
  CHAT ME4 ...7 L2
  CRBK TN17 ...298 G8
  FAV ME13 ...149 K2
  GVE DA12 ...55 J4
  HYTHE TN21 ...222 D3
  MAID/SHEP ME15 ...12 D3
  SEV TN13 ...21 J7
  TON TN9 ...194 E3
Bankton Rd BRXS/STRHM SW2 ...44 B6
Bankwell Rd LEW SE13 ...47 G3
Banky Fields Cl RHAM ME8 ...103 J4
Banky Meadow MAIDW ME16 ...166 A2
Banner Cl PUR RM19 ...32 E3
Banner Farm Rd RTWE/PEM TN2 ...23 H8
Banner Wy IOS ME12 ...64 D1
Banning St GNWCH SE10 ...26 F4
  STRD ME2 ...19 G2
Bannister Cl BRXS/STRHM SW2 ...44 B6
Bannister Gdns STMC/STPC BR5 ...73 K7
Bannister Hl RSIT ME9 ...119 J7
Bannister Rd MAID/BEAR ME14 ...141 H6
Bannockburn Rd WOOL/PLUM SE18 ...28 C3
Banstead St PECK SE15 ...45 K1
Bantry St CMBW SE5 ...24 E6
Banwell Rd BXLY DA5 ...49 L6
Banyard St BERM/RHTH SE16 ...25 J2
Bapchild Pl STMC/STPC BR5 ...73 J5
Barberry Av WALD ME5 ...100 H4
Barchester Wy TONN TN10 ...189 L1
Barclay Av TONN TN10 ...195 L1
Barclay Rd CROY/NA CR0 ...86 C7
Barclay Wy WTHK RM20 ...33 L4
Barcombe Cl CHST BR7 ...73 H7
Bardell Ter ROCH ME1 ...19 K7
Barden Park Rd TON TN9 ...194 D4
Barden Rd RRTW TN3 ...277 N6
  TON TN9 ...194 D4
Barden St WOOL/PLUM SE18 ...28 D6
Bardolph Av CROY/NA CR0 ...104 B3
Bardown Rd WADH TN5 ...309 Q9
Bardsley Cl CROY/NA CR0 ...87 G6
  STPH/PW TN12 ...257 K6
Bardsley La GNWCH SE10 ...26 F4
Barfield EYN DA4 ...76 C5
Barfield Rd BMLY BR1 ...72 B1
Barfleur La DEPT SE8 ...26 A6
Barfleur Mnr GILL ME7 * ...6 E1
Barforth Rd PECK SE15 ...45 J1
Barfrestone Cl MAID/SHEP ME15 ...12 E3
Barfrestone Wy PGE/AN SE20 ...69 J5
Bargate Cl WOOL/PLUM SE18 ...29 J5
Bargates ASH TN23 ...204 B5
Barge House Rd CAN/RD E16 ...28 C2
Barge Ms SIT ME10 * ...119 L5
Bargrove Cl PGE/AN SE20 ...69 H4
Bargrove Crs CAT SE6 ...46 C7
Bargrove Rd MAID/BEAR ME14 ...13 M2
Barham Cl CHST BR7 ...72 C2
  GVE DA12 ...56 A6
  HAYES BR2 ...89 H4
  MAID/SHEP ME15 ...167 M8
Barham Rd CHST BR7 ...72 C2
  CROY/NA CR0 ...2 A7
  DART DA1 ...52 B5
Barham's Mill Rd HDCN TN27 ...262 F10
Baring Cl LEE/GVPK SE12 ...47 L1
Baring Rd CROY/NA CR0 ...87 K1
  LEE/GVPK SE12 ...47 J2
Bark Burr Rd CDW/CHF RM16 ...34 A1
Barker Rd MAID/BEAR ME14 ...12 L6
Barkers Ct SIT ME10 ...119 L5
Barkis Cl ROCH ME1 ...100 E6
Barkway Dr ORP BR6 ...106 B6
Barkworth Rd BERM/RHTH SE16 ...25 J4
Barler Pl OBOR TN7 ...64 B8
Barley Cl HB CT6 ...129 L7
  RDV CT15 ...210 D7
Barleycorn E/WMAL ME19 ...138 L4
Barleycorn Dr RHAM ME8 ...102 B7
Barley Flds MAID/BEAR ME14 ...167 L1
Barleymow Cl WALD ME5 ...101 K4
Barley Wy ASH TN23 ...204 D4
Barling Cl WALD ME5 ...114 D4
Barlow Rd RHAM ME8 ...102 F8
Barlow Dr BKHTH/KID SE3 ...47 H1
Barlow St WALW SE17 ...24 E1
Barmeston Rd CAT SE6 ...46 E7
Barming Rd E/WMAL ME19 ...165 J1
Barmouth Rd CROY/NA CR0 ...87 L5
Barnaby Ter ROCH ME1 * ...100 D3

Barnard Cl CHST BR7 ...72 E5
Barnard Rd WARL CR6 ...131 G5
Barnberry Cl RCANTE CT3 ...204 B5
Barn Cl RCANTE CT3 ...155 M4
  RSIT ME9 ...119 L1
  WSTB CT5 ...152 A2
Barncroft Cl MAID/BEAR ME14 ...168 A4
Barncroft Dr GILL ME7 ...116 A1
Barned Ct MAID/BEAR ME14 ...166 A4
Barnehurst Av BXLYHN DA7 ...30 D7
Barnehurst Cl ERITH DA8 ...30 D7
Barnehurst Rd BXLYHN DA7 ...30 D8
Barn End Dr RDART DA2 ...75 K1
Barn End La SWLY BR8 ...75 K3
Barnes Av MARG CT9 ...177 J4
Barnes Cl RAM CT11 ...149 H1
Barnes Cray Rd DART DA1 ...51 H2
Barnesdale Crs STMC/STPC BR5 ...91 H1
Barnes La RMAID ME17 ...259 J5
Barnes Ter DEPT SE8 ...26 A4
Barnes Wk STPH/PW TN12 ...281 J4
Barnet's Cl CANTW/ST CT2 ...172 E1
Barnet's Av ERITH DA8 ...31 G8
Barnett Fld ASH TN23 ...204 C3
Barnetts Cl RTWE/PEM TN2 ...196 F8
Barnetts Rd RTON TN11 ...255 P11
Barnett's Shaw OXTED RH8 ...157 J5
Barnet Wood Rd HAYES BR2 ...89 K5
Barney CHARL SE7 ...27 K4
Barnfield GVW DA11 ...55 H7
  HB CT6 ...128 D7
  RTWE/PEM TN2 ...201 L6
  TENT TN30 ...278 D10
  WALD ME5 ...101 H5
Barnfield Av CROY/NA CR0 ...87 J4
  CROY/NA CR0 ...88 A3
Barnfield Cl BRXN/ST SW9 ...44 A8
  HART DA3 ...78 E7
  SWLY BR8 ...92 D3
Barnfield Crs BGR/WK TN15 ...136 D3
Barnfield Gdns WOOL/PLUM SE18 * ...28 C5
  BH/WHM TN16 ...132 C6
  FAV ME13 ...149 K1
  FOLKN CT19 ...220 D6
  SEV TN13 ...161 J1
  STMC/STPC BR5 ...73 L7
  WOOL/PLUM SE18 ...28 C5
Barnfield Rd OXTED RH8 ...185 N4
Barnfield Wood Cl BECK BR3 ...88 E2
Barnfield Wood Rd BECK BR3 ...88 E2
Barnham St STHWK SE1 ...24 F1
Barn Hl MAID/SHEP ME15 ...258 D3
Barnhouse La LYDD TN29 ...329 M6
Barnhill Av HAYES BR2 ...89 H1
Barnhurst Rd MAID/BEAR ME14 ...141 H6
Barn Meadow STPH/PW TN12 ...281 R5
  STRD ME2 ...18 D2
Barnmead Rd BECK BR3 ...69 L5
Barnock Cl DART DA1 ...50 F5
Barnsdale Av POP/IOD E14 ...26 C3
Barnsley Cl IOS ME12 ...64 D1
Barnsole Rd GILL ME7 ...7 M4
  RCANTE CT3 ...252 G4
Barnstaple La LEW SE13 ...46 D2
The Barn GRAYS RM17 * ...34 E3
Barntye Cl RDV CT15 ...213 M3
Barnwell Cl KEN/WIL TN24 ...205 K5
Barnwell Rd DART DA1 ...52 A1
  BRXS/STRHM SW2 ...44 B4
Barnwood Cl ROCH ME1 ...100 C5
Baron Cl GILL ME7 ...83 M6
  MAID/BEAR ME14 ...142 A8
Baron's Pl STHWK SE1 ...24 B1
Baron's Wk CROY/NA CR0 ...87 M2
Barque Ms DEPT SE8 ...26 A5
Barrack Cnr SEV TN13 ...21 J7
Barrack Hl HYTHE TN21 ...222 B3
Barrack Rd CHAT ME4 ...83 J5
Barrack Rw GVW DA11 ...55 J4
Barrel Arch Cl STPH/PW TN12 ...280 H3
  SEV TN13 ...135 J6
Barretts Rd TENT TN30 ...278 D10
  EDEN TN8 ...276 D10
Barrett Rd ELTH/MOT SE9 ...47 L6
Barretts Rd RTON TN11 ...23 J7
  RTWE/PEM TN2 ...23 H7
  SEV TN13 ...21 K2
Barriedale NWCR SE14 ...26 A9
Barrie Dr DIT/AY ME20 ...139 G1
Barrier Point Rd CAN/RD E16 ...28 A3
Barrier Rd CHAT ME4 ...6 D3
Barrington Cl WALD ME5 ...101 G8
Barrington Crs BRCH CT7 ...176 E6
Barrington Rd BRXN/ST SW9 ...44 B4
  BXLYHN DA7 ...29 L8
Barrington Vls WOOL/PLUM SE18 ...28 B7
Barrington Rd NRWD SE19 ...68 F1
Barrowfields WALD ME5 ...115 L4
Barrow Green Rd GDST RH9 ...184 B5
  OXTED RH8 ...157 N7
Barrow Gv SIT ME10 ...119 L6
Barrow Hill Ri RASHE TN25 ...307 J6
Barrow La RRTW TN3 ...200 A4
Barrow Rd CROY/NA CR0 ...86 B8
Barrows Cl BRCH CT7 ...176 D7
Barr Rd GVE DA12 ...56 A7
Barry Av BXLYHN DA7 ...29 M6
Barry Cl CDW/CHF RM16 ...35 G5
Barry Rd EDUL SE22 ...45 H4
Barset Rd PECK SE15 ...45 K1
Barsons Cl PGE/AN SE20 ...69 K4
Barstow Crs BRXS/STRHM SW2 ...44 A6
Barth Ms WOOL/PLUM SE18 ...28 D3
Bartholomew Cl HYTHE CT21 ...222 C3
Bartholomew St DVE/WH CT16 ...8 C3
Bartholomew Wy SWLY BR8 ...74 F7
Bartlett Cl WALD ME5 ...115 K4
Bartlett Rd BH/WHM TN16 ...159 H4
  GVW DA11 ...55 H5
Bartletts Cl IOS ME12 ...64 D8
Bartletts Cl SAND/SEL CR2 ...86 A8
Bartley Mill Rd RRTW TN3 ...295 N4
Barton Cl BXLYHS DA6 ...49 M3
Barton Hill Dr IOS ME12 ...228 C2
Barton Hill Rd ASH TN23 ...200 A4
Barton Mill Rd CANT CT1 ...172 C2
Barton Rd RFOLK CT18 ...291 L10
  DVE/WH CT16 ...213 K7

  EYN DA4 ...76 C5
  MAID/SHEP ME15 ...13 H8
  STRD ME2 ...19 K1
Barton View Ter DVE/WH CT16 ...8 A1
Bartram Rd BROCKY SE4 ...45 M4
Barts Cl BECK BR3 ...88 B1
Barville Rd RDV CT15 ...272 F4
Barward Cl WOOL/PLUM SE18 ...28 B3
Barwick Rd DVW CT17 ...213 G8
Barwood Av WWKM BR4 ...88 C4
Bascombe Dr DART DA1 ...50 F5
Bascome St BRXS/STRHM SW2 ...44 B4
Basevi Wy DEPT SE8 ...26 B5
Bashford Barn La RSIT ME9 ...145 H4
Basi Cl STRD ME2 ...82 D4
Basildon Rd ABYW SE2 ...29 H4
Basil Gdns CROY/NA CR0 ...87 L4
Basin Rd BXLYHN DA7 ...29 M8
  WNWD SE27 ...68 D2
Basil Ter MAID/SHEP ME15 * ...167 H4
Basing Cl MAID/SHEP ME15 ...12 D1
Basing Dr BXLY DA5 ...50 A4
Baskerville KEN/WIL TN24 ...2 B2
Basket Gdns ELTH/MOT SE9 ...47 M3
Basmere Cl MAID/BEAR ME14 ...13 L1
Bassano St EDUL SE22 ...45 G5
Bassant Rd WOOL/PLUM SE18 ...29 J7
Bassett Cl HYTHE CT21 ...222 F1
Bassett Gdns RTWE/PEM TN2 ...222 F1
Bassett Rd SIT ME10 ...119 L5
Bassetts Cl ORP BR6 ...90 C7
Bassetts La CROW TN6 ...308 C7
Bassetts Wy ORP BR6 ...90 C7
Basted La BGR/WK TN15 ...240 E4
Basted Ml BGR/WK TN15 ...240 E4
Bastion Rd ABYW SE2 ...29 H4
  DVW CT17 ...8
Baston Manor Rd WWKM BR4 ...89 G4
Baston Rd HAYES BR2 ...89 H5
Bata Av RI RM18 ...36 C4
Batavia Rd NWCR SE14 ...26 B9
Batchelors RTWE/PEM TN2 ...278 E9
Batchelor St CHAT ME4 ...6 F6
Batchwood Gn STMC/STPC BR5 ...73 H8
Bates Cl DIT/AY ME20 ...139 H2
Bates Crs CROY/NA CR0 ...86 C7
Bates Hl BGR/WK TN15 ...240 B4
Bath Cl PECK SE15 ...25 L7
Bath Hard OXTED RH8 ...185 M8
Bath Ms KEN/WIL TN24 * ...205 M8
Bath Pl MARG CT9 ...15 H4
Bath St DART DA1 ...51 J2
  KEN/WIL TN24 ...205 L4
  MARG CT9 ...15 H4
Bath Ter STHWK SE1 ...24 D1
Bathurst Cl MSTR CT12 ...182 D4
Bathurst Rd FOLK CT20 ...10 B6
  STPH/PW TN12 ...281 R6
  STPH/PW TN12 ...112 F1
Bathway WOOL/PLUM SE18 ...28 D3
Baton Cl PUR RM19 ...32 E3
Batteries Cl RSIT ME9 ...147 J1
Battersby Rd CAT SE6 ...46 E7
Battery Point HYTHE CT21 ...223 J3
Battery Rd LYDD TN29 ...335 N7
  THMD SE28 ...28 F6
Battlefields MAID/BEAR ME14 ...238 C10
Battlemeen Rd HOO/HM ME3 ...58 C5
Battle St GVE DA12 ...98 B3
Batt's Rd GVE DA12 ...98 B3
Baudwin Rd CAT SE6 ...46 F7
Baugh Rd SCUP DA14 ...73 K2
Bavent Rd CMBW SE5 ...24 E6
Bawdale Rd EDUL SE22 ...45 G3
Bawden Cl CANTW/ST CT2 ...172 B5
Bawtree Rd NWCR SE14 ...26 B9
Baxendale St KEN/WIL TN24 ...205 G4
Baxter Wy WOOL/PLUM SE18 ...164 E6
Bayards WARL CR6 ...130 B4
Baye La RCANTE CT3 ...234 E12
Bayfield Cl BXLYHN DA7 ...29 L8
Bayfield Rd ELTH/MOT SE9 ...47 L3
Bayford Rd SIT ME10 ...120 B5
Bayhall Rd RTWE/PEM TN2 ...23 H8
Bayham Rd RRTW TN3 ...294 H9
  RTWE/PEM TN2 ...23 J7
  SEV TN13 ...21 K2
Bay Hl RDV CT15 ...215 H4
Bayle Cl FOLK CT20 ...11 L6
The Bayle FOLK CT20 ...11 L6
Bayley's Hl RSEV TN14 ...254 F11
Baylis Rd STHWK SE1 ...24 B1
Bayly Rd DART DA1 ...52 B4
Bay Manor La WTHK RM20 ...33 G3
Baynham Cl BXLY DA5 ...50 A4
Bays Cl SYD SE26 ...69 K5
Bayswater Dr RHAM ME8 ...116 F1
Baytree Cl BFN/LL DA15 ...49 G6
  BMLY BR1 ...71 L5
Baytree Rd BRXS/STRHM SW2 ...44 A4
Bay View Gdns IOS ME12 ...230 C4
Bay View Hts BRDST CT7 * ...179 L5
Bay View Rd BRDST CT10 ...183 J5
Bayview Rd DEAL CT14 ...211 K5
  WSTB CT5 ...126 A3
Baywell WOOL/PLUM SE18 ...28 B7
Bazes Shaw HART DA3 ...96 A1
Beacham Cl CHARL SE7 ...27 L5
Beach Ap IOS ME12 ...230 D4
Beach Av BRCH CT7 ...176 C5
Beachborough Rd BMLY BR1 ...70 D1
  FOLKN CT19 ...220 A2
Beach Cl CRBK TN17 ...299 N12
Beach House Ms WGOS CT8 * ...177 J6
Beach Houses MARG CT9 * ...14 B5
Beach Ri MARG CT9 ...177 J6
Beach Rd LYDD TN29 ...321 P10
  MARG CT9 ...177 L5
Beach St DEAL CT14 ...209 H6
  FOLKN CT19... ...11 M5
  HB CT6 ...129 H4
  IOS ME12 ...64 C7
Beach Ter IOS ME12 * ...64 C7
The Beach DEAL CT14 ...209 H6
Beach Wk WSTB CT5 ...126 A2
Beacon Av HB CT6 ...129 J5
Beacon Cl RHAM ME8 ...102 D4
Beacon Dr RDART DA2 ...53 K6
Beaconfields SEV TN13 ...20 D7
Beacon Ga PECK SE15 ...45 L1
Beacon Hl HB CT6 ...129 J4
  LING RH7 ...274 F11
  PUR RM19 ...32 C4
  WALD ME5 ...101 H3
Beacon Hill La HOO/HM ME3 ...39 P3
Beacon La SWCH CT13 ...253 L8
Beacon Oak Rd TENT TN30 ...315 N1
Beacon Ri SEV TN13 ...20 E9

Beacon Rd BRDST CT10 ...179 J6
  ERITH DA8 ...31 H1
  HB CT6 ...129 H5
  SEV TN13 ...46 E4
  RMAID ME17 ...243 K12
  WALD ME5 ...101 H3
Beaconsfield Av DVE/WH CT16 ...8 B1
  GILL ME7 ...7 J3
Beaconsfield Cl BKHTH/KID SE3 ...27 H5
Beaconsfield Gdns BRDST CT10 ...179 J8
Beaconsfield Rd BKHTH/KID SE3 ...27 H5
  BMLY BR1 ...71 L2
  BXLY DA5 ...50 F7
  CANTW/ST CT2 ...172 A7
  CHAT ME4 ...6 D9
  CROY/NA CR0 ...86 E2
  DEAL CT14 ...209 L4
  DVE/WH CT16... ...8 A3
  ELTH/MOT SE9 ...47 M8
  MAID/SHEP ME15 ...12 D9
  SIT ME10 ...120 D6
  WALW SE17 ...24 E5
The Beacons RMAID ME17 ...258 H5
Beacon Wk HB CT6 ...129 H4
Beacon Wy HYTHE TN21 ...307 L10
Beadles La OXTED RH8 ...157 J8
Beadman St WNWD SE27 ...68 C1
Beadnell Rd FSTH SE23 ...45 L6
Beadon Rd HAYES BR2 ...71 H8
Beagles Cl STMC/STPC BR5 ...91 L5
Beagles Wood Rd RTWE/PEM TN2 ...278 B10
Beal Cl WELL DA16 ...29 K6
Beales La RYE TN31 ...325 J7
Beaman Cl CRBK TN17 ...297 N5
Beamish Rd STMC/STPC BR5 ...91 K3
Beamont Cl MSTR CT12 ...181 J4
The Beams MAID/SHEP ME15 ...167 M4
Bean Cl ASH TN23 ...286 H9
Beane Cft GVE DA12 ...56 A6
Beaney's La FAV ME13 ...246 G8
Bean La RDART DA2 ...53 J8
Bean Rd BXLYHS DA6 ...49 L2
  GRH DA9 ...53 J4
Beanshaw ELTH/MOT SE9 ...72 B1
Beardsell St NRWD SE19 ...68 G3
Bear's La RASHW TN26 ...286 G6
Bearstead Ri BROCKY SE4 ...46 A3
Bearsted Cl RHAM ME8 ...102 A6
Bearsted Rd MAID/BEAR ME14 ...141 K6
Beaton Cl GRH DA9 ...53 J2
Beatrice Gdns GVW DA11 ...54 F7
Beatrice Hills Cl KEN/WIL TN24 ...203 H6
Beatrice Ms LYDD TN29 ...335 M1
Beatrice Rd MARG CT9 ...157 K6
  OXTED RH8 ...157 K6
  RROCH CT18 ...221 K3
  STHWK SE1 ...25 H3
Beatty Av GILL ME7 ...102 A2
Beatty Cl FOLKN CT19 ...220 E6
Beatty Rd FOLKN CT19 ...220 E6
  ROCH ME1 ...100 E5
Beauchamp Av KEN/WIL TN24 ...2 C4
Beauchamp Cl KEN/WIL TN24 ...2 B4
Beauchamps La RDV CT15 ...252 C12
Beaufighter Rd E/WMAL ME19 ...241 K6
Beaufort Av MSTR CT12 ...16 C2
Beaufort Cl CDW/CHF RM16 ...34 A4
Beaufort Rd STRD ME2 ...18 B1
Beaufort Wk MAID/SHEP ME15 ...259 R1
Beaufoy Cl DVW CT17 ...213 H8
Beaufoy Ter DVW CT17 ...213 H8
Beaufoy Wk LBTH SE11 ...24 A3
Beaulieu Av SYD SE26 ...69 J3
Beaulieu Cl CMBW SE5 ...45 G2
Beaulieu Ri ROCH ME1 ...100 A4
Beaulieu Rd TONN TN10 ...194 D1
Beaulieu Wk MAID/SHEP ME16 * ...240 D6
Beaumanor HB CT6 ...129 J5
Beaumont Davy Cl FAV ME13 ...149 K4
Beaumont Dr GVW DA11 ...54 F5
Beaumont Rd MAIDW ME16 ...68 D3
  NRWD SE19 ...68 D3
  STMC/STPC BR5 ...90 E2
Beaumont St HB CT6 ...129 J5
Beaumont Ter FAV ME13 ...149 L5
  LEW SE13 * ...47 G5
Beauval Rd EDUL SE22 ...45 G4
Beauvoir Dr SIT ME10 ...120 E1
Beauworth Pk MAID/SHEP ME15 ...167 M5
Beauxfield DVE/WH CT16 ...213 H2
Beaverbank Rd ELTH/MOT SE9 ...48 E6
Beaver Cl PGE/AN SE20 * ...69 G7
Beaver Ct ASH TN23 ...204 D4
Beaver La ASH TN23 ...204 D4
  MAIDW ME16 ...140 C7
Beaverwood Rd CHST BR7 ...72 E5
Beazley Ct KEN/WIL TN24 ...205 G4
Bebbington Rd WOOL/PLUM SE18 ...28 F3
Beblets Cl ORP BR6 ...91 G8
Beck Cl LEW SE13 ...26 C7
Beck Ct BECK BR3 ...69 J2
Beckenham Dr MAIDW ME16 ...140 E6
Beckenham Gv HAYES BR2 ...70 E6
Beckenham Hill Rd BECK BR3 ...70 C3
Beckenham Pk RHAM ME8 * ...103 J5
Beckenham Place Pk BECK BR3 ...70 C3
Beckenham Rd BECK BR3 ...69 L5
  WWKM BR4 ...88 C3
Becket Av CANTW/ST CT2 ...209 K1
Becket Cl DEAL CT14 ...209 K1
  RCANTE CT3 ...236 A11
  SNWD SE25 ...87 H2
Becket Ct HDCN TN27 ...283 L4
Becket Ms CANTW/ST CT2 ...172 E1
Beckets Cl RASHE TN25 ...289 Q3
Beckett Rd RTON TN11 ...276 H2
Becketts St STHWK SE1 ...24 E2
Beckett Cl BELV DA17 ...29 H1
Becketts Cl ORP BR6 ...91 G6
Becketts St FAV ME13 ...149 K2
Beckett Wk BECK BR3 ...69 J1
Beckford Dr STMC/STPC BR5 ...90 D3
Beckford Pl WALW SE17 ...24 D1
Beckley Cl ASH TN23 ...204 C1
Beck La BECK BR3 ...69 J4
Beck Rd CRBK TN17 ...299 N12
Beck River Pk BECK BR3 ...70 A5
Beckley Ms WALD ME5 ...101 G8
Beckley Pl RASHE TN25 ...307 N5
Beckley Rd IOS ME12 ...64 D1
Beckton Rd CANT CT1 ...5 M9
Beckwith Rd HNHL SE24 ...44 F1
Becksbourne Cl MAID/BEAR ME14 ...141 H5

Becks Rd SCUP DA14 ...49 H8
Beck Wy BECK BR3 ...70 A7
Beckway St WALW SE17 ...24 F3
Beckwith Gn FOLK CT20 * ...219 H10
Beckwith Rd HNHL SE24 ...44 E4
Beckworth Pl MAIDW ME16 * ...166 C2
Becondale Rd NRWD SE19 ...68 A4
Becton Pl ERITH DA8 ...30 C4
Beddington Gn
  STMC/STPC BR5 ...73 G5
Beddington Pk
  STMC/STPC BR5 ...72 F5
Beddington Ter CROY/NA CRO * ...86 A7
Beddlestead La WARL CR6 ...131 L4
Beddow Wy DIT/AY ME20 ...140 C3
Bedens Rd SCUP DA14 ...73 M3
Bedford Av RHAM ME8 ...102 A4
Bedford Pk CROY/NA CRO ...86 D4
Bedford Pl CROY/NA CRO ...86 E4
  MAIDW ME16 ...2
Bedford Rd BFN/LL DA15 ...48 F8
  DART DA1 ...52 B3
  GRAYS RM17 ...34 C4
  GVW DA11 ...55 G7
  ORP BR6 ...91 J5
  STH/RUST TN4 ...196 D4
Bedford Sq MSTR CT12 * ...182 E3
Bedford Ter RTW TN1 ...22 E7
Bedgebury Rd BRCH CT7 ...182 E5
Bedgebury Cl MAID/BEAR ME14..13 M1
  ROCH ME1 ...100 E5
Bedgebury Cross CRBK TN17 ...297 L11
Bedgebury Rd CRBK TN17 ...297 K10
  ELTH/MOT SE9 ...47 L2
Bedingfield Wy RFOLK CT18 ...291 L10
Bedivere Rd BMLY BR1 ...47 K5
Bedlam Court La MSTR CT12 ...180 F8
Bedlam La HDCN TN27 ...283 R4
  HDCN TN27 ...284 A4
Bedlington Sq FAV ME13 * ...149 L2
Bedlow Wy CROY/NA CRO ...86 A7
Bedonwell Rd BELV DA17 ...29 M5
  BXLYHN DA7 ...
Bedser Ct THHTH CR7 * ...68 D7
  VX/NE SW8 * ...24 A5
Bedson Rd RHAM ME8 ...103 J4
Bedwardine Rd NRWD SE19 ...68 A4
Bedwell Rd BELV DA17 ...30 B4
Bedwin Cl ROCH ME1 ...100 E6
Beecham La TONN TN10 ...189 H7
Beech Av BFN/LL DA15 ...49 H5
  BH/WHM TN16 ...132 C1
  RCANTW CT4 ...248 G8
  SWLY BR8 ...75 G8
Beech Cl DEPT SE8 ...26 A5
  FAV ME13 ...149 J2
  FOLKN CT19 ...11 L5
Beech Copse BMLY BR1 ...72 A4
  SAND/SEL CR2 ...86 F8
Beech Ct ELTH/MOT SE9 * ...86 C3
  RASHE TN25 ...265 M4
Beechcroft CHST BR7 ...72 B4
  WSTB CT5 ...127 L4
Beechcroft Av BXLYHN DA7 ...30 E7
  TIL RM18 ...36 B3
Beechcroft Cl ORP BR6 ...90 E7
  STRHM/NOR SW16 ...68 A2
Beechcroft Gdns RAM CT11 ...17 M2
Beechcroft Rd ORP BR6 ...90 E7
Beechdale Rd
  BRXS/STRHM SW2 ...44 A3
Beech Dell HAYES BR2 ...90 A4
Beech Dr BRDST CT10 ...182 F1
  MAIDW ME16 ...140 D8
  RASHW TN26 ...286 F3
  RDV CT15 ...272 C5
Beechen Bank Rd WALD ME5 ...115 H4
Beechenlea La SWLY BR8 ...75 H4
Beechen Pl FSTH SE23 ...45 K1
The Beeches DIT/AY ME20 ...139 M4
  HART DA3 ...78 D6
  LYDD TN29 ...334 E2
  MEO DA13 ...239 M1
  RTWE/PEM TN2 ...23 J8
  SWLY BR8 ...75 G3
  TIL RM18 ...35 J8
  WALD ME5 ...115 H1
Beech Farm Rd WARL CR6 ...131 J6
Beechfield Rd BMLY BR1 ...71 K6
  CAT SE6 ...45 J1
  ERITH DA8 ...30 F6
Beech Green Cl RDV CT15 ...272 D6
Beech Green La HRTF TN ...198 A5
Beech Gv HOO/HM ME3 ...81 J2
  MSTR CT12 ...181 M8
  SOCK/AV RM15 ...32 D1
Beech Hl RCANTW CT4 ...250 E9
Beechhill Rd ELTH/MOT SE9 ...48 A5
Beech House La RBTBR TN32 ...322 H6
Beech House Rd CROY/NA CRO ...86 A7
Beech Hurst Cl RTWE/PEM TN2 ...278 A10
Beech Hurst Ct
  MAID/SHEP ME15 * ...13 J9
Beeching Cl WALD ME5 ...115 J4
Beechings Gn RHAM ME8 ...102 D2
Beechings Wy RHAM ME8 ...102 B1
Beechin Wood La
  BGR/WK TN15 ...240 C4
Beechlands Cl HART DA3 ...78 B8
Beech La HAWK TN18 ...325 M2
  STPH/PW TN12 ...295 F2
Beechmont Cl BMLY BR1 ...70 D8
Beechmont Rd TONN TN10 ...188 E7
Beechmont Rd SEV TN13 ...162 A4
Beechmore Dr WALD ME5 ...115 H3
Beecholme Rd KEN/WIL TN24 ...202 F6
Beech Rd BH/WHM TN16 ...
  DART DA1 ...51 L6
  E/WMAL ME19 ...139 H1
  HOO/HM ME3 ...83 M2
  ORP BR6 ...107 M2
  SEV TN13 ...21 H6
  STPH/PW TN12 ...280 C6
  STRD ME2 ...18 C6
  WBY/YAL ME15 ...241 Q7
Beech St RTW TN1 ...22 E7
Beech Sw STPH/PW TN12 * ...257 J7
Beech Wk DART DA1 ...51 L6
Beechway BXLY DA5 ...49 L6
Beech Wy SAND/SEL CR2 ...104 C2
Beechwood Av SAND/SEL CR2 ...104 B5
  ORP BR6 ...107 L4
  SIT ME10 ...119 M3
  THHTH CR7 ...68 C4
  WALD ME5 ...
Beechwood Cl DVE/WH CT16 ...272 G12
  LYDD TN29 ...329 N2
Beechwood Ct DEAL CT14 * ...209 K4
Beechwood Crs BXLYHN DA7 ...49 K8
Beechwood Dr HAYES BR2 ...89 L7
  MEO DA13 ...239 M4
Beechwood Gdns MEO DA13 ...239 M4
Beechwood La WARL CR6 ...130 C5
Beechwood Ms
  RTWE/PEM TN2 ...201 M1
Beechwood Ri CHST BR7 ...72 B2
Beechwood Rd MAIDW ME16 ...166 A2
Beechy Lees Rd RSEV TN14 ...136 C3

Beecroft Cl CANTW/ST CT2 ...172 B5
Beecroft La BROCKY SE4 ...45 M3
Beecroft Ms BROCKY SE4 ...45 M3
Beecroft Rd BROCKY SE4 ...45 M3
Beehive Pl BRXN/ST SW9 ...44 B1
Beeken Dene ORP BR6 ...90 D7
Beer Cart La CANT CT1 ...4
Beesfield La EYN DA4 ...94 B4
Begbie Rd BKHTH/KID SE3 ...27 J1
Beggarsbush La LYDD TN29 ...329 Q6
Beggars La BH/WHM TN16 ...159 J3
Begonia Av RHAM ME8 ...102 B3
Beke Rd RHAM ME8 ...116 L1
Bekesbourne Gn
  RCANTE CT3 ...251 J4
  RCANTW CT3 ...251 J4
Bekesbourne Rd RCANTW CT4 ...175 G7
Bekesbourne La RCANTE CT3 ...174 F2
Belcaire Cl HYTHE CT21 ...307 M10
Belcroft Cl BMLY BR1 ...71 G4
Beldam Haw RSEV TN14 ...108 F5
Belfast Rd SNWD SE25 ...69 J8
Belfield Rd RTWE/PEM TN2 ...278 A11
  RTWE/PEM TN2 ...201 K5
Belford Gv WOOL/PLUM SE18 ...28 A3
Belfort Rd PECK SE15 ...25 K4
Belfry Cl RAM CT11 ...17 K4
Belgrave Cl DVW CT17 ...217 J2
  IOS ME12 ...64 D5
  MARC CT9 ...14 E5
  RTW TN1 ...23 G3
  SNWD SE25 ...69 G8
Belgrave St DIT/AY ME20 ...114 A7
Belgravia Gdns BMLY BR1 ...70 F3
Belgrove RTW TN1 ...22 F7
Belinda Ct FOLKN CT19 ...10 L1
Belinda Rd BRXN/ST SW9 ...44 L1
Bellamaine Cl THMD SE28 ...29
Bellamy Cl POP/IOD E14 ...26 B1
Bell Chapel Cl ASH TN23 ...204 D5
Bell Cl GRH DA9 ...53 G3
Bell Crs ROCH ME1 ...114 A5
Bell-Davies Dr MSTR CT12 ...181 K4
Bellefield Rd BRXN/ST SW9 ...91 J1
Bellefields Rd BRXN/ST SW9 ...44 A1
Belle Friday Cl RSIT ME9 ...121 K7
Bellegrove Cl WELL DA16 ...29 G4
Bellegrove Rd WELL DA16 ...28 D8
Bellenden Rd PECK SE15 ...25 G6
Bellevue Av RAM CT11 ...15 L5
Bellevue Pk THHTH CR7 ...68 D7
Belle Vue Rd RFOLK CT18 ...129 J4
  ORP BR6 ...106 F4
Bellevue Rd BXLYHS DA6 ...50 A3
  IOS ME12 ...65 K6
  RAM CT11 ...17 L5
  WSTB CT5 ...127 G5
Bellevue St FOLK CT20 ...11 K4
Bell Farm Gdns MAIDW ME16 ...166 A3
Bell Farm La IOS ME12 ...66
Bellfield CROY/NA CRO ...104 A7
Bellflower Av RSIT ME9 ...228 D1
Bell Gdns STMC/STPC BR5 ...91 K1
Bell Gn CAT SE6 ...69 M1
Bell Green La SYD SE26 ...70 A1
Bell Gv RCANTE CT3 ...251 P12
Bellhurst Rd RBTBR TN32 ...322 F10
Bellingham Gn CAT SE6 ...46 B8
Bellingham La DIT/AY ME20 ...139 J2
Bellingham Wy DIT/AY ME20 ...139 J3
Bell La DIT/AY ME20 ...283 N10
  HDCN TN27 ...115 H4
  MAID/BEAR ME14 ...114 A8
  ROCH ME1 ...281 R6
  STPH/PW TN12 ...237 K12
  SWCH CT13 ...
Bellman Av GVE DA12 ...55 M6
Bellmeadow
  MAID/SHEP ME15 ...167 M7
Bell Meadow NRWD SE19 ...68 A4
Bello Ct BRXS/STRHM SW2 ...44 C6
Bellot St GNWCH SE10 ...26 F4
Bell Pde WWKM BR4 * ...88 D3
Bellring Ct BELV DA17 ...30 B5
  SIT ME10 ...119 M7
Bells Farm La RTON TN11 ...256 F6
Bells Farm Rd STPH/PW TN12 ...256 H4
Bell's La HOO/HM ME3 ...315 L6
  TENT TN30 ...315 M2
Bell St WOOL/PLUM SE18 ...27 H1
Belltrees Gv STRHM/NOR SW16 ..68 C1
Bell Water Ga
  WOOL/PLUM SE18 ...28 B2
Bell Wy RMAID ME17 ...261 M3
Bellwood Ct HOO/HM ME3 ...60 D7
Bellwood Rd PECK SE15 ...45 L2
Bell Yard Ms STHWK SE1 ...24 F1
Belmont DEAL CT14 ...209 J8
Belmont Cl MAIDW ME16 ...166 A3
Belmont Gv LEW SE13 ...46 E2
Belmont Hl LEW SE13 ...46 E2
Belmont La CHST BR7 ...72 C2
Belmont Pde CHST BR7 * ...72 C2
Belmont Pk LEW SE13 ...46 E2
Belmont Park Cl LEW SE13 ...46 E2
Belmont Pl ASH TN23 ...204 E4
  KEN/WIL TN24 ...2
Belmont Rd BECK BR3 ...69 M6
  BRDST CT10 ...183 H1
  CHST BR7 ...72 C2
  ERITH DA8 ...30 C4
  FAV ME13 ...149 K3
  GILL ME7 ...34 A4
  IOS ME12 ...64 F7
  KEN/WIL TN24 ...203 H5
  RAM CT11 ...17 H4
  SIT ME10 ...119 M6
  SNWD SE25 ...87 J3
  WGOS CT8 ...177 J5
  WHTB CT5 ...126 E4
Belmont St RAM CT11 ...17 K4
Belmont Vls BRDST CT10 * ...179 H7
Belmore Pk KEN/WIL TN24 ...2
Belnor Av RSIT ME9 ...226 G12
Belsey La RFOLK CT15 ...293 Q6
Belson Rd WOOL/PLUM SE18 ...28 A5
Beltana Dr GVE DA12 ...79 M1
Beltinge Rd HB CT6 ...129 M4
Belton Cl WHTB CT5 ...126 F5
Belton Rd SCUP DA14 ...73 L3
Beltring Rd STH/RUST TN4 ...196 D7
  STPH/PW TN12 ...257 J7
Beltwood Rd BELV DA17 ...30 A3
Beluncle Halt HOO/HM ME3 * ...60 C1
Belvedere Buildings
  STHWK SE1 ...24 D1
Belvedere Cl FAV ME13 ...149 L1
  GVE DA12 ...55 K6
Belvedere Rd BELV DA17 ...30 A2
Belvedere Ms PECK SE15 ...45 K1
Belvedere Rd BH/WHM TN16 ...132 C4
  BRDST CT10 ...183 H1
  BXLYHN DA7 ...50 A1

FAV ME13 ...149 L1
NRWD SE19 ...68 A4
STHWK SE1 ...24 A1
Benacre Rd WSTB CT5 ...126 E7
Benares Rd WOOL/PLUM SE18 ...29 J5
Benbow Rd DEPT SE8 ...26
Benbury Cl BMLY BR1 ...70 D2
Bench Hl TENT TN30 ...317 L1
Bench St DVE/WH CT16 ...8 D5
Bencurtis Pk WWKM BR4 ...88 E4
Benden Rd STPH/PW TN12 ...282 A5
Bendmore Av ABYW SE2 ...29 H4
Bendon Wy RHAM ME8 ...102 A3
Benedict Cl ORP BR6 ...90 F6
  STRD ME2 ...113 J1
Benedict Rd BRXN/ST SW9 ...44 A1
Beneden Gn HAYES BR2 ...90 A5
Benenden Rd CRBK TN17 ...313 P5
  HDCN TN27 ...300
  STRD ME2 ...82 D3
Bengal Rd MSTR CT12 ...182 D5
Benhall Mill Rd RRTW TN3 ...294 E5
Benhill Rd CMBW SE5 ...25 G6
Benhurst Cl SAND/SEL CR2 ...104 A3
Benhurst Gdns SAND/SEL CR2 ...104 A3
Benin St LEW SE13 ...46 F5
Bennells Av WSTB CT5 ...127 J3
Bennett Cl WELL DA16 ...29 H8
  RAM CT11 ...17 L5
Bennett Gv LEW SE13 ...26 E8
Bennett Pk BKHTH/KID SE3 ...47 H1
Bennett Rd BRXN/ST SW9 ...44 B1
  CROY/NA CRO ...86 C3
Bennetts Av BGR/WK TN15 ...238 B6
  CROY/NA CRO ...86 C3
Bennetts Copse CHST BR7 ...71 M3
Bennett Wy RDART DA2 ...76 E1
Benover Rd WBY/YAL ME18 ...257 Q6
Bensham Cl THHTH CR7 ...68 D8
Bensham Gv THHTH CR7 ...68 D7
Bensham La CROY/NA CRO ...86 C5
  THHTH CR7 ...
Bensham Manor Rd
  THHTH CR7 ...68 D8
Ben Smith Wy
  BERM/RHTH SE16 ...25 H2
Benson Cl RFOLK CT18 ...220 A1
Benson Rd CROY/NA CRO ...86 B6
  FSTH SE23 ...45 K5
  GRAYS RM17 ...34 C5
Bensted Rd RTWE/PEM TN2 ...201 K5
Bensted Cl MAID/SHEP ME15 ...258 C5
Bensted Gv FAV ME13 ...149 G5
Bentham Rd RRTW TN3 ...196 A4
Bentley Av HB CT6 ...128 C5
Bentley Cl DIT/AY ME20 ...140 A4
  HART DA3 ...78 D7
  WALD ME5 ...115 J3
Bentley Rd KEN/WIL TN24 ...205 J4
Bentley's Meadow
  BGR/WK TN15 ...
Bentley St GVE DA12 ...55 M4
Benton's La WNWD SE27 ...68
Benton's Ri WNWD SE27 ...68 D2
Berwick Cl BERM/RHTH SE16 ...25 H1
Berber Pde WOOL/PLUM SE18 * ...27 M6
Berber Rd STRD ME2 ...19 G2
Bercta Rd ELTH/MOT SE9 ...48 C7
Berengrave La RHAM ME8 ...102 F4
Berens Rd STMC/STPC BR5 ...91 K1
Berens Wy CHST BR7 ...73 G8
Beresford Av CHAT ME4 ...100 F3
Beresford Ct BRCH CT7 * ...176 C5
Beresford Dr BMLY BR1 ...72 A7
Beresford Gap BRCH CT7 ...176 C5
Beresford Gdns MARC CT9 ...178 F2
Beresford Rd CRBK TN17 ...297 P3
  DIT/AY ME20 ...114 D6
  DVW CT17 ...212 F6
  GILL ME7 ...7
  GVW DA11 ...54 D5
  RAM CT11 ...17 H6
  WSTB CT5 ...127 H5
Beresford Sq
  WOOL/PLUM SE18 ...28 C3
Berger Cl STMC/STPC BR5 ...91 K1
Bergland Pk STRD ME2 ...19 H1
Berkeley Av BXLYHN DA7 ...29 L7
Berkeley Cl FAV ME13 ...151 L2
  FOLKN CT19 * ...220 D2
  ORP BR6 ...90 E7
  ROCH ME1 ...100 C5
  RTWE/PEM TN2 ...278 B10
Berkeley Ct SIT ME10 ...119 L6
Berkeley Crs DART DA1 ...52 A4
Berkeley Mt CHAT ME4 * ...6
Berkeley Pl RTW TN1 * ...22 F7
Berkeley Rd BRCH CT7 ...176 C5
  RTW TN1 ...22 F7
The Berkeleys SNWD SE25 * ...69 G4
Berkeley Ter TIL RM18 * ...35 H6
Berkhampstead Rd BELV DA17 ...30 B4
Berkley Rd GVE DA12 ...55 J4
Berkley Rw GVE DA12 ...55 J4
Berkshire Cl WALD ME5 ...101 K5
Bermondsey St STHWK SE1 ...24 F1
Bermondsey Wall East
  BERM/RHTH SE16 ...25 J1
Bermondsey Wall West
  BERM/RHTH SE16 ...25 H1
Bermuda Rd TIL RM18 ...35 H1
Bernard Ashley Dr CHARL SE7 ...27 J7
Bernards Gdns RDV CT15 ...271 R9
Bernard St GVE DA12 ...55 J4
Bernay's Gv BRXN/ST SW9 ...44 A4
Berne Rd THHTH CR7 ...68 C4
Berney Rd CROY/NA CRO ...86 C1
Berridge Rd IOS ME12 ...65
  NRWD SE19 ...68
Berry La DUL SE21 ...44 E6
Berryman's La SYD SE26 ...69 L1
Berry's Green Rd
  BH/WHM TN16 ...133 G2
Berry's Hill BH/WHM TN16 ...133 G1
Bersham La SIT ME10 ...120
Bersted La CDW/CHF RM16 ...34 A2
Berthon St DEPT SE8 ...26 B6
Bertie Rd SYD SE26 ...69 L1
Bertrand St LEW SE13 ...46 D2
Berwick Crs BFN/LL DA15 ...48 F5
Berwick Rd WELL DA16 ...29 H8
Berwick Wy RSEV TN14 ...136 C3

Berwyn Gv MAID/SHEP ME15 ...167 H7
Berwyn Rd HNHL SE24 ...44 C6
Besant Placee PECK SE15 ...45 G6
Bessels Green Rd SEV TN13 ...161 J1
Bessels Meadow SEV TN13 ...161 J2
Bessemer Rd CMBW SE5 ...24 D8
Besson St NWCR SE14 ...25 M7
Best La CANT CT1 ...4
Best St CHAT ME4 ...6
Best Ter SWLY BR8 * ...92 D1
Bestwood St DEPT SE8 ...26 B5
Beta Rd HOO/HM ME3 ...60 D8
Betchworth Av ROC/NA CRO ...105 H3
Betenson Av SEV TN13 ...135 L8
Bethany Cl DEAL CT14 ...209 K1
Bethel Rd SEV TN13 ...21 K2
  WELL DA16 ...29 K1
Bethersden Cl BECK BR3 ...70 A4
Bethersden Rd HDCN TN27 ...284 C9
  RASHW TN26 ...284 H12
  RASHW TN26 ...286 B1
  RASHW TN26 ...302 H5
  RASHW TN26 ...303 N4
Bethwin Rd CMBW SE5 ...24 D6
Betjeman Cl DIT/AY ME20 ...139 G2
Betony Cl CROY/NA CRO ...87 L4
Betsham Rd ERITH DA8 ...31 G6
  MAID/SHEP ME15 ...168 A7
  MEO DA13 ...77 M2
  SWCM DA10 ...53 M5
Betterton Dr SCUP DA14 ...49 M7
Bettescombe Rd RHAM ME8 ...102 E6
Betts Cl BECK BR3 ...69 J6
Betts Wy PGE/AN SE20 ...69 J6
Beulah Av THHTH CR7 ...68 D6
Beulah Crs THHTH CR7 ...68 D5
Beulah Gv CROY/NA CRO ...86 D2
Beulah Hl NRWD SE19 ...68 D3
Beulah Rd RTW TN1 ...23 H7
  SUT SM1 ...
Beulah Wk CTHM CR3 * ...130 D6
Beult Meadow HDCN TN27 ...284 D8
Beult Rd DART DA1 ...51 H1
Bevan Ct CROY/NA CRO ...86 B1
Bevan Pl SWLY BR8 ...75 G8
Bevan Rd ABYW SE2 ...29 J4
Bevans Cl GRH DA9 ...53 K4
Bevan Wy RCANTE CT3 ...251 P12
Beverley Av BFN/LL DA15 ...49 G5
Beverley Cl RHAM ME8 ...103 G5
Beverley Ct BROCKY SE4 ...46 A1
Beverley Crs TON TN9 ...194 C6
Beverley Gdns LYDD TN29 ...321 M5
Beverley Rd BXLYHN DA7 ...30 C8
  CANTW/ST CT2 ...4
  HAYES BR2 ...89 M5
  MAIDW ME16 ...166 A3
  PGE/AN SE20 ...69 J6
Beverley Wy MSTR CT12 ...16 E1
Beverly Cl BRCH CT7 * ...176 E5
Beverstone Rd
  BRXS/STRHM SW2 ...44 A3
  THHTH CR7 ...68 B8
Bevill Cl SNWD SE25 ...69 H4
Bevington Rd BECK BR3 ...69 M5
Bevington St BERM/RHTH SE16 ...25 H1
Bevis Cl RDART DA2 ...52
Bewick Ms PECK SE15 ...25
Bewl Bridge Cl WADH TN5 ...311 J6
Bewlbridge La WADH TN5 ...296 D12
Bewley La BGR/WK TN15 ...240 C3
Bewley St DEPT SE8 ...26 C8
Bewlys Rd WNWD SE27 ...68 C2
Bewsbury Crs DVE/WH CT16 ...213 G2
Bewsbury Cross La
  DVE/WH CT16 ...213 G2
Bexhill Dr GRAYS RM17 ...33 M5
Bexhill Rd BROCKY SE4 ...46 A4
  ELTH/MOT SE9 ...48 C4
Bexley Cl DART DA1 ...50 F3
Bexley High St BXLY DA5 ...50 B4
Bexley La DART DA1 ...50 F3
  SCUP DA14 ...49 M7
Bexley Rd ELTH/MOT SE9 ...48 D4
  ERITH DA8 ...30 D6
Bexon La RSIT ME9 ...145 H4
Bhutan Rd HB CT6 ...129 H3
Bianca Rd PECK SE15 ...25 G5
Bibury Cl PECK SE15 ...24 F6
Bickles Yd STHWK SE1 ...24 F1
Bickley Crs BMLY BR1 ...71 M4
Bickley Park Rd BMLY BR1 ...72 A4
Bickley Rd BMLY BR1 ...71 L3
Bickmore Wy TON TN9 ...194 F2
Bicknell Rd CMBW SE5 ...44 E4
Bicknor Cl CANTW/ST CT2 ...172 D1
Bicknor La RSIT ME9 ...144 E2
Bicknor Rd MAID/SHEP ME15 ...260 A1
  ORP BR6 ...90 F7
Bidborough Cl HAYES BR2 ...89 G1
Bidborough Rdg
  STH/RUST TN4 ...196 A1
Biddenden Cl
  MAID/SHEP ME15 ...168 A2
  MARC CT9 ...178 F4
Biddenden La HDCN TN27 ...283 M6
  HDCN TN27 ...301 L2
Biddenden Wy ELTH/MOT SE9 ...72 B1
Bideford Rd BMLY BR1 ...71 H5
  WELL DA16 ...29 J5
Bidwell St PECK SE15 ...25 J7
Bifrons Hl RCANTW CT4 ...175 H6
Bifrons Rd RCANTW CT4 ...175 H5
Bigbury Rd CANTW/ST CT2 ...170 F6
Biggin Hl NRWD SE19 ...68 C4
Biggin La GRAYS RM17 ...35 G3
Biggins Wood Rd FOLKN CT19 ...219 M6
Biggin Wy NRWD SE19 ...68 C4
Bigginwood Rd
  STRHM/NOR SW16 ...68 C4
Bignell Rd WOOL/PLUM SE18 ...28 C4
Bilberry Cl MAID/BEAR ME14 ...141 M8
Billet Rd BGR/WK TN15 ...95 K7
Bill Hamling Cl ELTH/MOT SE9 ...48 A2
Billingford Cl BROCKY SE4 ...45 L2
Billings HART DA3 ...96 B6
Billington Gdns KEN/WIL TN24 ...203 H5
Billington Rd NWCR SE14 ...25 M7
Bill St Rd STRD ME2 ...19 J1
Billson St POP/IOD E14 ...26 E4
Bilsington Cl WALD ME5 ...101 J8
Bilton Rd ERITH DA8 ...31 H5
Binbury La MAID/BEAR ME14 ...143 G1
Bindon Blood Rd
  DVE/WH CT16 ...213 H4
The Bines STPH/PW TN12 ...279 K4
Binfield Rd SAND/SEL CR2 ...87 G8
Bingham Rd CROY/NA CRO ...87 H8
  STRD ME2 ...82 E5
Bingley Cl SNOD ME6 ...113 G5
Bingley Rd ROCH ME1 ...5
Binland Gv WALD ME5 ...115 G5
Binney Rd HOO/HM ME3 ...41 L5
Binnie Yd BRDST CT10 ...183 J3
Binsey Wk ABYW SE2 ...29 J2
Birbetts Rd ELTH/MOT SE9 ...48 A7
Birchanger Rd SNWD SE25 ...87 H1

Birch Cl BRDST CT10 ...182 F2
  EYN DA4 ...93 L6
  HART DA3 ...78 D6
  KEN/WIL TN24 ...2
  RTON TN11 ...194 A3
  RTWE/PEM TN2 ...197 D6
  STH/RUST TN4 ...21 H2
  STPH/PW TN12 ...278 A8
Birch Ct RAM CT11 * ...17 G3
  RCANTW CT4 ...270 E5
Birch Crs DIT/AY ME20 ...115 L5
Birch Dr WALD ME5 ...115 J4
The Birches CHARL SE7 ...27 J5
  CMBW SE5 ...44 E7
  ORP BR6 ...107 B7
  SWLY BR8 ...74 F6
  TON TN9 ...194 C6
Birchett La RASHW TN26 ...304 B10
Birchetts Av RRTW TN3 ...199 N3
Birchetts Green La WADH TN5 ...309 K6
Birchfield Rd MAID/SHEP ME15 ...167 J3
Birchfields MAID ME5 ...115 H2
Birch Gv GILL ME7 ...102 D8
  LEE/GVPK SE12 ...47 G5
  WELL DA16 ...49 L7
Birch Hl CROY/NA CRO ...87 L4
Birch Rd HOO/HM ME3 ...83 M2
  STPH/PW TN12 ...279 K3
  WSTB CT5 ...127 K5
Birch Tree Av WWKM BR4 ...89 G8
Birch Tree Wy CROY/NA CRO ...87 L4
  MAID/SHEP ME15 ...13 J7
Birch Vls FOLK CT20 * ...223 L2
Birchway BGR/WK TN15 ...111 L3
Birch Wy RTWE/PEM TN2 ...197 L2
  WARL CR6 ...130 C4
Birchwood Av BECK BR3 ...70 A6
  SCUP DA14 ...49 L8
  STH/RUST TN4 ...196 B2
Birchwood Dr RDART DA2 ...74 A7
Birchwood La RSEV TN14 ...134 E2
Birchwood Park Av SWLY BR8 ...74 F5
Birchwood Ri MAIDW ME16 ...140 D8
  RDART DA2 ...74 A7
  STMC/STPC BR5 ...72 E8
Birchwood Ter SWLY BR8 * ...74 F5
Birchwood Wk CANTW/ST CT2 ...171 M3
Birdbrook Rd BKHTH/KID SE3 ...47 L5
Birdham Cl BMLY BR1 ...89 M1
Bird House La ORP BR6 ...106 F4
Birdhurst Av SAND/SEL CR2 ...86 E7
Birdhurst Rd SAND/SEL CR2 ...86 E7
Birdhurst Ri SAND/SEL CR2 ...86 E6
Birds in Bush Rd PECK SE15 ...25 H6
Bird-in-Hand La BMLY BR1 ...71 L6
Bird-in-Hand Ms FSTH SE23 ...45 K7
Bird in Hand St RRTW TN3 ...199 N5
Bird La WADH TN5 ...308 G5
Birds Av MARC CT9 ...177 J6
Birdwood Av DEAL CT14 ...209 H4
Birdwood Cl SAND/SEL CR2 ...104 B5
Birkbeck Hl DUL SE21 ...44 C4
Birkbeck Pl DUL SE21 ...44 C4
Birkbeck Rd BECK BR3 ...69 L6
  SCUP DA14 ...49 H8
Birkdale Cl BERM/RHTH SE16 * ...25 J4
  ORP BR6 ...90 E3
  WSTB CT5 ...127 L5
Birkdale Ct MAIDW ME16 * ...12 D1
Birkdale Gdns FOLKN CT19 ...220 B6
  HB CT6 ...128 E7
Birkdale Gdns CROY/NA CRO ...87 L4
Birken Rd RTWE/PEM TN2 ...197 G2
Birkhall Cl WALD ME5 ...101 H8
Birkhall Rd CAT SE6 ...46 C6
Birling Av MAID/BEAR ME14 ...168 B1
  RHAM ME8 ...102 A4
Birling Dr RTWE/PEM TN2 ...201 L2
Birling Hl MEO DA13 ...112 A4
Birling Pk E/WMAL ME19 ...112 A1
Birling Park Av
  RTWE/PEM TN2 ...201 L2
Birling Rd E/WMAL ME19 ...112 A1
  E/WMAL ME19 ...138 D2
  ERITH DA8 ...30 C6
  KEN/WIL TN24 ...2
  RTWE/PEM TN2 ...201 J2
  SNOD ME6 ...113 H5
Birling Road Rookery Hl
  SNOD ME6 ...113 G6
Birnam Sq MAIDW ME16 * ...12 C5
Bittrick Dr GRH DA9 ...97 G12
Biscoe Wy LEW SE13 ...46 F2
Bisenden Rd CROY/NA CRO ...86 F6
Bishop Butt Cl ORP BR6 ...91 G6
Bishop Crs SIT ME10 * ...119 M4
Bishopden Ct CANTW/ST CT2 * ...171 K1
Bishop Jenner Ct
  RCANTE CT3 * ...235 K2
Bishop La RSIT ME9 ...103 M2
Bishop Cl BRDST CT10 ...179 L7
Bishops Cl ELTH/MOT SE9 ...48 D7
  WBY/YAL ME18 ...164 D7
Bishops Ct GRH DA9 ...52 F8
Bishop's Down STH/RUST TN4 ...22 B6
Bishop's Down Park Rd
  STH/RUST TN4 ...22 A3
Bishop's Down Rd
  STH/RUST TN4 ...22 B6
Bishops Gn ASH TN23 ...204 A4
  BMLY BR1 ...71 K5
Bishops La CRBK TN17 ...298 C15
  MAID/SHEP ME15 ...258 D7
  RBTBR TN32 ...322 F10
Bishops Md CMBW SE5 * ...24 F6
Bishops Ms TON TN9 ...194 F5
Bishops Rd CROY/NA CRO ...86 B6
Bishops Oak Ride TONN TN10 ...188 D7
Bishops Ter LBTH SE11 ...24 B6
  MAID/SHEP ME15 * ...12 D1
Bishopsthorpe Rd SYD SE26 ...69 K1
Bishopstone Dr HB CT6 ...129 G3
Bishopstone La HB CT6 ...232 B3
Bishops Wk CHST BR7 ...72 C5
  CROY/NA CRO ...
Bishops Wy CANTW/ST CT2 ...4
  MAIDW ME16 ...12 C5
Bishopswood ASH TN23 ...204 F8
Bisky Bar RYE TN31 * ...326 E11
Bittern Cl RFOLK CT18 ...220
Bittern St STHWK SE1 ...24 D1

Bixley La RYE TN31 325 P12
Blackberry Fld STMC/STPC BR5 73 H5
Blackberry Wy STPH/PW TN12 279 K3
WSTB CT5 127 J5
Blackbrook La HAYES BR2 90 B1
Black Bull Rd FOLKN CT19 11 J3
Blackburn Rd HB CT6 128 C7
Blackdown Dr KEN/WIL TN24 2 B1
Blackdown Ter
WOOL/PLUM SE18 * 28 A7
Black Eagle Cl BH/WHM TN16 159 H5
BH/WHM TN16 160 A5
Blacketts Rd RSIT ME9 121 G3
Blackfen Pde BFN/LL DA15 * 49 H4
Blackfen Rd BFN/LL DA15 49 G3
Blackfriars Rd STHWK SE1 24 C1
Blackfriars St CANT CT1 4 F3
Black Griffin La CANT CT1 4 E4
Blackhall La BGR/WK TN15 211 M2
Blackheath Av GNWCH SE10 26 F6
Blackheath Gv BKHTH/KID SE3 27 G8
Blackheath Hl GNWCH SE10 26 D7
Blackheath Pk BKHTH/KID SE3 27 H8
Blackheath Ri LEW SE13 26 D8
Blackheath Rd GNWCH SE10 26 C7
Blackheath V BKHTH/KID SE3 26 F8
Black Horse Ct STHWK SE1 24 E2
Blackhorse La CROY/NA CR0 87 H3
Black Horse Ms BGR/WK TN15 240 F2
Blackhorse Rd DEPT SE8 25 M5
Black Horse Rd SCUP DA14 73 H1
Blackhouse Hl HYTHE CT21 222 F1
Blackhouse Ri HYTHE CT21 222 E2
Blackhurst La RTWE/PEM TN2 197 K6
Blacklands E/WMAL ME19 139 G6
Blacklands Dr E/WMAL ME19 139 G5
Blacklands Rd CAT SE6 70 D1
Blackman Cl HOO/HM ME3 59 L6
Blackmans Cl DART DA1 51 K6
Blackman's La RTON TN11 256 A7
WARL CR6 105 K8
Blackmanstone Br LYDD TN29 320 B10
Blackmanstone Wy
DIT/AY ME20 140 C6
Blackmead SEV TN13 135 K7
Black Mill La HDCN TN27 283 J4
Blackmore Rd GRAYS RM17 34 D4
Blackness La HAYES BR2 106 C3
Blackpool Rd PECK SE15 25 J8
Black Prince Rd LBTH SE11 24 A3
Black Robin La RCANTW CT4 270 D2
Black Rock Gdns GILL ME7 116 C1
Blackshots La CDW/CHF RM16 34 E1
Blacksmith Dr
MAID/BEAR ME14 141 L8
Blacksmiths Hl SAND/SEL CR2 104 A7
Blacksmiths La STMC/STPC BR5 91 K1
WADH TN5 309 M5
Blacksole La BGR/WK TN15 238 E10
Blacksole Rd BGR/WK TN15 238 E10
Black Swan Yd STHWK SE1 24 F1
Blacks Yd SEV TN13 21 H6
Blackthorn Av
RTWE/PEM TN2 196 F4
WALD ME5 115 H2
Blackthorn Cl BGR/WK TN15 111 L3
Blackthorn Dr DIT/AY ME20 139 J3
Blackthorne Av CROY/NA CR0 87 K4
Blackthorne Rd RHAM ME8 103 H5
Blackthorn Gv BXLYHN DA7 49 M1
Blackthorn Rd BH/WHM TN16 132 D2
Blackthorn Wy ASH TN23 204 F8
Blacktree Ms BRXN/ST SW9 * 44 B1
Blackwall La GNWCH SE10 26 F4
Blackwall Rd KEN/WIL TN24 203 M6
Blackwall Rd North
KEN/WIL TN24 3 M4
Blackwall Rd South
KEN/WIL TN24 3 M5
Blackwater St EDUL SE22 45 G3
Blackwood St WALW SE17 24 E4
Bladindon Dr BXLY DA5 49 L5
Blagdon Rd LEW SE13 46 C4
Blair Cl BFN/LL DA15 48 F3
Blair Dr SEV TN13 21 H2
Blake Cl DEAL CT14 211 J1
WELL DA16 28 F7
Blake Ct KEN/WIL TN24 3 K9
Blake Dr DIT/AY ME20 139 G1
Blake Gdns DART DA1 52 A2
Blakemore Rd THHTH CR7 86 A1
Blakemore Wy BELV DA17 29 M2
Blakeney Av BECK BR3 70 A5
Blakeney Cl MAID/BEAR ME14 168 C1
Blakeney Rd BECK BR3 70 A5
Blaker Av ROCH ME1 100 F4
Blaker Ct CHARL SE7 * 27 K6
Blake Rd CROY/NA CR0 86 F5
Blake's Gn WWKM BR4 88 D3
Blakes Rd PECK SE15 25 G8
Blake Wy RTWE/PEM TN2 197 G6
Blanchard Cl ELTH/MOT SE9 47 M8
Blanch Cl PECK SE15 25 K6
Blanchedowne CMBW SE5 44 E2
Blanchman's Rd WARL CR6 130 D4
Bland Dr RFOLK CT18 292 H12
Blandford Av BECK BR3 69 M6
Blandford Gdns SIT ME10 119 M8
Blandford Rd BECK BR3 69 L6
Bland St ELTH/MOT SE9 47 L2
Blanmerle Rd ELTH/MOT SE9 48 C6
Blann Cl ELTH/MOT SE9 47 L4
Blashford St LEW SE13 46 E5
Blatcher Cl IOS ME12 65 J7
Blatchford Cl E/WMAL ME19 139 G4
Blatchington Rd RTW TN1 22 F9
Blaxland Cl FAV ME13 123 J8
Bleak Hill La WOOL/PLUM SE18 29 G5
Bleak Rd LYDD TN29 334 D3
Bleakwood Rd WALD ME5 101 G8
Blean Gv PGE/AN SE20 69 K4
Blean Hl CANTW/ST CT2 153 H8
Blean Rd RHAM ME8 102 D3
Blean Sq MAID/BEAR ME14 * 141 L7
Blean View Rd HB CT6 128 B7
Blendon Dr BXLY DA5 49 L4
Blendon Rd BXLY DA5 49 L4
MAID/BEAR ME14 13 L2
Blendon Ter WOOL/PLUM SE18 28 D4
Blendworth Wy PECK SE15 24 F6
Blenheim Av CANT CT1 172 E8
FAV ME13 149 M4
ROCH ME1 6 A9
Blenheim Cl BRDST CT10 183 G2
DART DA1 51 K4
HB CT6 129 H8
MAID/SHEP ME15 168 A2
MEO DA13 97 H5
Blenheim Ct BFN/LL DA15 48 E8
Blenheim Dr DVE/WH CT16 213 K6
RFOLK CT18 220 B1
WELL DA16 29 G7
Blenheim Gdns
BRXS/STRHM SW2 44 A4
Blenheim Gv GVE DA12 55 K5
PECK SE15 25 G8
Blenheim Pl FOLK CT20 10 B7
Blenheim Rd BFN/LL DA15 49 K6
DART DA1 51 K4
DEAL CT14 209 L4
E/WMAL ME19 164 A2
HAYES BR2 71 M8
NROM TN28 331 M7
ORP BR6 91 K5
PGE/AN SE20 69 K4
Blenheim Wy WADH TN5 311 K6
Blessington Rd LEW SE13 46 E2
Bletchingly Cl THHTH CR7 68 C8
Bligh Rd GVW DA11 55 H4
Blighs Ct SEV TN13 21 H6
Bligh's Rd SEV TN13 21 H6
Blighs Wk SEV TN13 21 H6
Bligh Wy STRD ME2 81 K7
Blindgrooms La RASHW TN26 303 R4
Blindhouse La RASHE TN25 307 M2
Blind La CRBK TN17 297 M4
GILL ME7 116 B4
KEN/WIL TN24 288 E12
RASHE TN25 265 N4
Blind Mary's La RSIT ME9 144 F5
Blissett St GNWCH SE10 26 D7
Bliss Wy TONN TN10 189 H8
Blithdale Rd ABYW SE2 29 H3
Blockhouse Rd GRAYS RM17 34 D5
Blockmakers Ct CHAT ME4 101 J4
Bloomfield Rd HAYES BR2 89 L1
WOOL/PLUM SE18 28 C4
Bloom Gv WNWD SE27 44 C8
Bloomhall Rd NRWD SE19 68 E2
Bloomsbury Rd RAM CT11 16 E6
Bloomsbury Wk
MAID/BEAR ME14 * 13 H4
Bloomsbury Wy
KEN/WIL TN24 202 E5
Bloors La RHAM ME8 102 F3
Bloors Wharf Rd RHAM ME8 102 F1
Blossom Cl SAND/SEL CR2 87 G8
Blowers Grove Wd GILL ME7 116 C2
Blowers Hl EDEN TN8 275 Q5
Bloxam Gdns ELTH/MOT SE9 47 M3
Blucher Rd CMBW SE5 24 D6
Blue Anchor La
BERM/RHTH SE16 25 H3
TIL RM18 35 M3
Bluebell Cl ASH TN23 204 F6
GILL ME7 84 A7
ORP BR6 90 D5
SYD SE26 69 G1
Bluebell Rd ASH TN23 204 F8
Bluebell Wks STPH/PW TN12 279 K4
Blueberry La RSEV TN14 134 B2
Bluebird Wy THMD SE28 28 E1
Blue Boar La ROCH ME1 100 F1
Blue Coat La CRBK TN17 297 L7
Bluehouse Gdns OXTED RH8 157 M6
Blue House La HYTHE CT21 218 C6
Bluehouse La OXTED RH8 157 K6
Blue Line La KEN/WIL TN24 2 B3
Blue Lion Pl STHWK SE1 24 F2
Blue Riband Est CROY/NA CR0 * 86 C5
Bluett St MAID/BEAR ME14 13 H1
Bluewater Pkwy GRH DA9 53 G6
Blunden La WBY/YAL ME18 257 R4
Blunt Rd CROY/NA CR0 86 E8
Blunts Rd ELTH/MOT SE9 48 B3
Blythe Cl CAT SE6 46 A5
Blythe Ct HYTHE CT21 * 222 E3
Blythe Hl CAT SE6 46 A5
STMC/STPC BR5 73 G5
Blythe Hill La CAT SE6 46 A5
Blythe Hill Pl FSTH SE23 * 45 M5
Blythe Rd MAID/SHEP ME15 13 K5
Blytheswood Pl
STRHM/NOR SW16 68 A1
Blythe V CAT SE6 46 A6
Blyth Rd BMLY BR1 71 G5
Boakes Meadow RSEV TN14 109 L5
Boarders La WADH TN5 310 D6
Boarley La MAID/BEAR ME14 141 G4
Boarman's La LYDD TN29 329 K5
Boatemah Wk BRXN/ST SW9 24 B8
Boathouse Wk PECK SE15 25 G6
Boat La RASHE TN25 305 Q9
Boat Lifter Wy
BERM/RHTH SE16 25 M3
Bob Amor Cl FAV ME13 149 M2
Bobbing Hl RSIT ME9 119 H4
Bobbin Lodge Hl RCANTW CT4 248 C8
Bob Marley Wy BRXN/ST SW9 44 B2
Bockham La RASHE TN25 288 F10
Bockhanger La KEN/WIL TN24 202 F5
Bocking Cl WADH TN5 309 K5
Bockingford La
MAID/SHEP ME15 166 F5
Bocks Hl RBTBR TN32 323 K6
Bodell Cl CDW/CHF RM16 34 C1
Bodenham Rd FOLK CT20 10 C6
Bodiam Br RBTBR TN32 323 R6
Bodiam Cl RHAM ME8 102 D3
Bodiam Ct MAIDW ME16 12 E7
Bodiam Rd HAWK TN18 324 A3
Bodkins Cl RMAID ME17 167 L8
Bodle Av SWCM DA10 53 M4
Bodmin Cl STMC/STPC BR5 91 K4
Bodsham Crs
MAID/SHEP ME15 168 C2
Bofors House
WOOL/PLUM SE18 * 27 M6
Bogle Rd RSIT ME9 147 K2
Bognor Dr HB CT6 128 E5
Bognor Rd WELL DA16 29 L7
Bogshole La HB CT6 129 L6
WSTB CT5 152 E1
Bolden St DEPT SE8 26 C8
Bolderwood Wy WWKM BR4 88 C5
Boley Hl ROCH ME1 19 J6
Boleyn Av MARG CT9 177 K4
Boleyn Cl CDW/CHF RM16 34 A2
Boleyn Ct CANT CT1 * 5 J5
Boleyn Gdns WWKM BR4 88 C5
Boleyn Rd BGR/WK TN15 136 D3
Boleyn Wy SWCM DA10 53 M5
Bolina Rd BERM/RHTH SE16 25 K4
Bolner Cl WALD ME5 115 G3
Bolney St VX/NE SW8 24 A6
Bolton Crs CMBW SE5 24 C6
Bolton Gdns BMLY BR1 71 G2
Bolton Rd FOLKN CT19 11 K3
Bolton St RAM CT11 17 G3
Bolts Hl RCANTW CT4 248 D7
Bombay St BERM/RHTH SE16 25 J3
Bombers La BH/WHM TN16 133 J6
Bonar Pl CHST BR7 71 M4
Bonar Rd PECK SE15 25 H6
Bonaventure Ct GVE DA12 80 A1
Bonchester Cl CHST BR7 72 B4
Bond Cl RSEV TN14 134 C1
Bondfield Cl STH/RUST TN4 196 D4
Bondfield Rd E/WMAL ME19 139 G5
Bond La ASH TN23 304 E3
Bond Rd ASH TN23 204 D3
RHAM ME8 116 F1
WARL CR6 130 C4
Bond St GRAYS RM17 34 D5
Boneashe La BGR/WK TN15 241 J3
Boneta Rd WOOL/PLUM SE18 28 A2
Bonetta Ct IOS ME12 64 C5
Bonfield Rd LEW SE13 46 D2
Bonflower La RMAID ME17 258 H6
Bonham Dr SIT ME10 120 B4
Bonham Rd BRXS/STRHM SW2 44 A3
Bonita Ms BROCKY SE4 45 L1
Bonner Wk CDW/CHF RM16 * 34 A2
Bonney Wy SWLY BR8 74 F6
Bonnington Rd
MAID/BEAR ME14 141 K7
Bonnington Sq VX/NE SW8 24 A5
Bonny Bush Hl RCANTW CT4 250 G12
Bonsor Rd FOLKN CT19 11 H2
Bonsor St CMBW SE5 24 F6
Bonville Rd BMLY BR1 71 G2
Boones Rd LEW SE13 46 F2
Boone St LEW SE13 46 F2
Boord St GNWCH SE10 26 F2
Boormans Ms
WBY/YAL ME18 * 164 F6
Bootham Cl STRD ME2 99 L1
Booth Pl MARG CT9 15 H3
Booth Rd CHAT ME4 6 D9
CROY/NA CR0 * 86 C5
Borden La RSIT ME9 119 J7
Border Crs SYD SE26 69 J2
Border Gdns CROY/NA CR0 88 C7
Border Rd SYD SE26 69 J2
Borders La BUR/ETCH TN19 322 A5
Bordyke TON TN9 194 F3
Boresisle TENT TN30 * 301 N11
Borgard House
WOOL/PLUM SE18 * 27 M6
Borgard Rd WOOL/PLUM SE18 28 A3
Borkwood Pk ORP BR6 91 G7
Borkwood Wy ORP BR6 90 F7
Borland Cl GRH DA9 53 H3
Borland Rd PECK SE15 45 K2
Bornefields ASH TN23 204 D4
Borough CANT CT1 5 G3
Borough Green Rd
BGR/WK TN15 238 F12
BGR/WK TN15 240 C3
Borough High St STHWK SE1 24 D1
Borough Hl CROY/NA CR0 86 C6
Borough Rd BH/WHM TN16 132 C7
GILL ME7 7 L6
QBOR ME11 227 Q1
STHWK SE1 24 C2
Borough Sq STHWK SE1 * 24 D1
Borrett Cl WALW SE17 24 D4
Borrowdale Av RAM CT11 16 A5
Borstal Hl WSTB CT5 126 D5
Borstal Rd ROCH ME1 100 C2
Borstal St ROCH ME1 100 B3
Borthwick St DEPT SE8 26 B4
Bosbury Rd CAT SE6 46 D8
Boscobel Cl BMLY BR1 72 A6
Boscombe Av GRAYS RM17 34 E3
Boscombe Rd FOLKN CT19 11 H3
Bosney Banks RDV CT15 212 B2
Bossingham Rd RCANTW CT4 269 J8
Bossington Rd RCANTE CT3 251 N8
Boss St STHWK SE1 25 G1
Bostall Heath ABYW SE2 * 29 K4
Bostall Hl ABYW SE2 29 J4
Bostall La ABYW SE2 29 J4
Bostall Manorway ABYW SE2 29 J3
Bostall Park Av BXLYHN DA7 29 M6
Bostall Rd STMC/STPC BR5 73 J4
Boston Cl DVE/WH CT16 213 J6
Boston Gdns RHAM ME8 102 D4
Boston Rd CROY/NA CR0 86 A2
WALD ME5 115 J3
Bosville Av SEV TN13 20 E3
Bosville Dr SEV TN13 20 E2
Bosville Rd SEV TN13 20 E3
Boswell Cl STMC/STPC BR5 91 K2
Boswell Rd THHTH CR7 68 D8
Botany TON TN9 194 F4
Botany Bay La CHST BR7 72 D6
Botany Cl IOS ME12 64 C4
Botany Rd BRDST CT10 179 J3
Botany Ter PUR RM19 * 32 B4
Botany Wy PUR RM19 32 C4
Bothwell Rd CROY/NA CR0 105 H4
Botolph's Br HYTHE CT21 321 M2
Botolph's Bridge Rd
HYTHE CT21 321 M3
Botsom La BGR/WK TN15 111 H1
Bottlescrew Hl RMAID ME17 259 N1
Bottles La RSIT ME9 146 B4
Bottom Pond Rd RSIT ME9 145 J8
Bott Rd RDART DA2 76 A1
Boucher Dr GVW DA11 55 G8
Boughton Av BRDST CT10 183 K4
HAYES BR2 89 G3
Boughton By FAV ME13 151 K7
Boughton La
MAID/SHEP ME15 167 J6
Boughton Pde
MAID/SHEP ME15 * 167 H6
Boughton Rd RMAID ME17 262 D5
THMD SE28 28 F2
Boulevard Courrieres
RCANTE CT3 271 K1
The Boulevard KEN/WIL TN24 205 J5
Boulogne Rd CROY/NA CR0 86 D2
Boulthurst Wy OXTED RH8 185 H2
Boundary Cl IOS ME12 65 M7
Boundary Ct CANT CT1 * 5 K9
Boundary La WALW SE17 24 D5
Boundary Rd BFN/LL DA15 48 F3
DEAL CT14 211 L3
HYTHE CT21 222 B4
RAM CT11 17 J4
RTWE/PEM TN2 23 L9
Boundary Rw STHWK SE1 24 C1
Boundary St ERITH DA8 31 G6
The Boundary CANT CT1 4 A8
RRTW TN3 200 E2
Boundary Wy CROY/NA CR0 88 B8
Boundfield Rd CAT SE6 46 F8
Bounds La FAV ME13 151 H6
Bounds Oak Wy
STH/RUST TN4 196 B2
The Bounds DIT/AY ME20 139 M4
Bourchier Cl SEV TN13 21 H8
Bourdon Rd PGE/AN SE20 69 K6
Bournbrook Rd
BKHTH/KID SE3 47 L1
Bourne Cl TON TN9 195 G2
Bourne Ct RAM CT11 16 C3
Bourne Grange La RTON TN11 256 A5
Bourne Gv SIT ME10 119 K4
Bourne La BGR/WK TN15 240 E7
HAWK TN18 323 R1
RASHW TN26 318 D1
RBTBR TN32 323 L5
TON TN9 194 F2
Bourne Lodge Cl
CANTW/ST CT2 153 H6
Bourne Md BXLY DA5 50 D3
Bournemouth Cl PECK SE15 25 H8
Bournemouth Dr HB CT6 128 E4
Bournemouth Gdns
FOLKN CT19 11 H3
Bournemouth Rd FOLKN CT19 11 H3
PECK SE15 25 H8
Bourne Pde BXLY DA5 * 50 C5
Bourne Pk RTON TN11 256 C8
Bourne Park Rd RCANTW CT4 250 E10
Bourne Place Ctyd
RTON TN11 * 255 P6
Bourne Place Mdw
RTON TN11 * 255 P6
Bourne Rd BXLY DA5 50 D4
GVE DA12 56 A7
HAYES BR2 71 L8
RASHE TN25 305 M7
Bournes Cl CANTW/ST CT2 173 G2
Bourneside Gdns CAT SE6 70 D2
Bourneside Ter RMAID ME17 * 169 L3
Bournes Pl RASHW TN26 303 J11
Bourne St CROY/NA CR0 86 C5
Bourne V BGR/WK TN15 240 F9
HAYES BR2 89 H4
Bourne Wy HAYES BR2 89 H5
SWLY BR8 74 D7
Bournewood RASHW TN26 318 D1
Bournewood Cl
MAID/SHEP ME15 168 A4
Bournewood Rd
STMC/STPC BR5 91 J3
WOOL/PLUM SE18 29 H6
Bournville Av CHAT ME4 101 G4
Bournville Rd CAT SE6 46 B5
Bousfield Rd NWCR SE14 25 L8
Boutique Hall LEW SE13 * 46 D2
Bouverie Pl FOLK CT20 11 J6
Bouverie Rd West FOLK CT20 10 D7
Bouverie Sq FOLK CT20 11 J6
Bovarde Av E/WMAL ME19 164 D2
Boveney Rd FSTH SE23 45 L5
Bovill Rd FSTH SE23 45 L5
Bow Arrow La DART DA1 52 B4
Bowater Pl BKHTH/KID SE3 27 J6
Bowater Rd WOOL/PLUM SE18 27 L2
Bowdell La LYDD TN29 318 B12
Bowden Crs FOLK CT20 219 K7
Bowden St LBTH SE11 24 B4
Bowditch DEPT SE8 26 A4
Bowen Dr DUL SE21 44 F8
Bowen Rd FOLKN CT19 219 M7
STH/RUST TN4 277 Q12
Bowens Fld ASH TN23 2 A7
Bowenswood CROY/NA CR0 104 E3
Bowens Wd CROY/NA CR0 * 104 E3
Bower Av GNWCH SE10 26 F7
Bower Cl MAIDW ME16 12 C5
Bowerland La LING RH7 190 E5
RCANTW CT4 247 P7
Bower La EYN DA4 93 M6
MAIDW ME16 12 C6
Bowerman Av NWCR SE14 25 M5
Bowerman Rd CDW/CHF RM16 35 H3
Bower Mount Rd MAIDW ME16 12 B6
Bower Pl MAIDW ME16 12 C7
Bower Rd RASHE TN25 305 R2
SWLY BR8 75 H4
Bowers Av GVW DA11 79 G1
Bowers Rd RSEV TN14 109 L5
Bower St MAIDW ME16 12 C5
Bower Ter MAIDW ME16 12 D6
Bowes Av MARG CT9 177 K4
Bowes Cl BFN/LL DA15 49 J4
Bowesden La GVE DA12 81 G4
Bowes La HB CT6 129 H6
Bowes Rd STRD ME2 19 H2
Bowes Vls DEAL CT14 * 253 R5
Bowes Wd HART DA3 96 A6
Bowford Av BXLYHN DA7 29 M7
Bow Hl RCANTW CT4 269 J3
WBY/YAL ME18 164 F8
Bowhill Cl BRXN/ST SW9 24 B6
Bowland Cl HB CT6 129 K7
Bowles Well Gdns FOLKN CT19 221 G6
Bowles Wells Gdns FOLKN CT19 11 M1
Bowley Cl NRWD SE19 * 69 G3
Bowley La NRWD SE19 69 G2
RMAID ME17 262 G6
Bowl Fld RASHE TN25 289 Q3
Bowling Green La DEAL CT14 209 J4
Bowling Green Pl STHWK SE1 24 E1
Bowling Green Rw
WOOL/PLUM SE18 * 28 A3
Bowling Green St LBTH SE11 24 B5
Bowling Green Ter DVW CT17 8 C5
Bowling St SWCH CT13 237 J12
Bowl Rd HDCN TN27 264 B2
Bowls Pl STPH/PW TN12 279 K2
Bowman Cl WALD ME5 101 K8
Bowmans Lea FSTH SE23 45 K5
Bowmans Rd DART DA1 51 G5
Bowmead ELTH/MOT SE9 48 A7
Bown Cl TIL RM18 35 J8
Bowness Rd BXLYHN DA7 30 C8
CAT SE6 46 C5
Bow Rd WBY/YAL ME18 164 F6
Bowser Cl DEAL CT14 209 G5
Bow Ter WBY/YAL ME18 164 F6
Bowyer Pl CMBW SE5 24 D6
Bowyer Rd WSTB CT5 126 A6
Bowyer St CMBW SE5 24 D6
Bowzell Rd RSEV TN14 254 H3
Boxall Rd DUL SE21 44 F4
Boxford Cl SAND/SEL CR2 104 C6
Boxgrove Rd ABYW SE2 29 K2
Box La FAV ME13 148 E8
Boxley ASH TN23 204 C3
Boxley Cl IOS ME12 64 C6
MAID/BEAR ME14 141 J5
Boxley Rd MAID/BEAR ME14 13 G1
WALD ME5 115 J4
Boxted La RSIT ME9 226 B12
Boxwood Wy WARL CR6 130 C3
Boyard Rd WOOL/PLUM SE18 28 C4
Boyces Hl RSIT ME9 118 E3
Boy Court La HDCN TN27 261 M12
Boyden Gate Hl RCANTE CT3 252 D9
Boyes La RCANTE CT3 252 C7
Boyfield St STHWK SE1 24 C1
Boyke La RCANTW CT4 291 N7
Boyland Rd BMLY BR1 71 G2
Boyle Wy STPH/PW TN12 257 L6
Boyne Pk STH/RUST TN4 22 D3
Boyne Rd LEW SE13 46 E1
RDV CT15 211 H8
Boys Hall Rd KEN/WIL TN24 205 J4
Boyson Rd WALW SE17 24 D5
Boystown Pl SWCH CT13 253 N6
Boyton Court Rd RMAID ME17 260 H8
Brabazon Rd IOS ME12 229 M5
Brabner Cl FOLKN CT19 220 F5
Brabourne Av RHAM ME8 102 D1
Brabourne Cl CANTW/ST CT2 172 B5
NRWD SE19 68 F2
Brabourne Crs BXLYHN DA7 30 A5
Brabourne Gdns FOLK CT20 219 M8
Brabourne La RASHE TN25 290 D7
Brabourne Ri BECK BR3 88 E1
Brabourne Rd RASHE TN25 289 M4
Brabourn Gv PECK SE15 25 K8
Bracewood Gdns CROY/NA CR0 87 G6
Bracken Av CROY/NA CR0 88 B6
Bracken Cl KEN/WIL TN24 202 F5
RTWE/PEM TN2 197 H8
Bracken Ct BRDST CT10 * 179 H8
Brackendene BXLY DA5 74 F1
Bracken Hl WALD ME5 115 H4
Bracken Hill Cl BMLY BR1 71 G5
Bracken Hill La BMLY BR1 71 G5
Bracken Lea WALD ME5 101 K4
Bracken Rd RTWE/PEM TN2 197 H8
The Brackens ORP BR6 91 H8
Bracken Wk TONN TN10 188 E7
Brack La LYDD TN29 328 G2
Brackley Cl MAID/BEAR ME14 13 L3
Brackley Rd BECK BR3 70 A4
Brackondale Av MEO DA13 79 G5
Brackwood Cl RHAM ME8 102 E8
Bracondale Rd ABYW SE2 29 H3
Bradbourne La DIT/AY ME20 139 J4
Bradbourne Park Rd SEV TN13 20 F2
Bradbourne Pkwy
DIT/AY ME20 139 H4
Bradbourne Rd BXLY DA5 50 B5
GRAYS RM17 34 C5
SEV TN13 21 G1
Bradbourne Vale Rd SEV TN13 135 L8
Bradbridge Gn ASH TN23 204 A3
Braddick Cl MAID/SHEP ME15 167 J8
Braddyll St GNWCH SE10 26 F4
Bradenham Av WELL DA16 49 H2
Bradenham Cl WALW SE17 24 E5
Bradfield Av RSIT ME9 121 L7
Bradfield Rd CAN/RD E16 27 H1
KEN/WIL TN24 202 E6
Bradfields Av WALD ME5 101 G7
Bradfields Av West WALD ME5 101 G8
Bradford Cl HAYES BR2 90 A4
SYD SE26 69 J1
Bradfords Cl CHAT ME4 83 J3
Bradford St TON TN9 194 E4
Bradgate Rd CAT SE6 46 C4
Brading Rd BRXS/STRHM SW2 44 A5
CROY/NA CR0 86 A2
Bradleigh Av GRAYS RM17 34 D3
Bradley Dr SIT ME10 119 M7
Bradley Rd FOLKN CT19 221 G7
MSTR CT12 16 F1
NRWD SE19 68 D3
RRTW TN3 276 F12
STRD ME2 98 F8
Bradshaw Cl RSIT ME9 103 M2
Bradshaws Cl SNWD SE25 69 H7
Bradstone Av FOLKN CT19 11 J3
Bradstone New Rd FOLK CT20 11 K4
Bradstone Rd FOLK CT20 11 K4
Bradstow Wy BRDST CT10 179 K8
Brady Rd RFOLK CT18 291 L10
Braeburn Wy E/WMAL ME19 164 C2
Braemar Av BXLYHN DA7 50 D2
THHTH CR7 68 C7
Braemar Gdns BFN/LL DA15 48 E8
WWKM BR4 88 D4
Braeside BECK BR3 70 B2
Braeside Av SEV TN13 20 D4
Braeside Cl SEV TN13 20 C3
Braeside Crs BXLYHN DA7 50 D2
The Braes HOO/HM ME3 81 K2
Braesyde Cl BELV DA17 30 A3
Brafferton Rd CROY/NA CR0 86 D7
Braganza St WALW SE17 24 C4
Braggs La HB CT6 154 E3
Braidwood Rd CAT SE6 46 E6
Brailsford Rd
BRXS/STRHM SW2 44 B4
Brake Av WALD ME5 100 F8
Brakefield Rd MEO DA13 78 C3
Brakes Pl BGR/WK TN15 111 K1
Bramber Wy WARL CR6 130 E2
Bramble Av RDART DA2 53 K8
Bramble Bank MEO DA13 239 L6
Bramblebury Rd
WOOL/PLUM SE18 28 E4
Bramble Cl BECK BR3 88 D1
CROY/NA CR0 88 B7
MAIDW ME16 166 C2
RASHE TN25 266 E10
RTON TN11 194 C1
Bramble Cft ERITH DA8 30 D3
Brambledown FOLKN CT19 11 K3
HART DA3 78 A8
WALD ME5 101 J5
Brambledown Cl HAYES BR2 88 F2
Bramblefield Cl HART DA3 77 M7
Bramblefield La SIT ME10 227 M12
Bramblefields Cl HB CT6 129 J7
Bramblehill Rd FAV ME13 149 K1
Bramble La RASHE TN25 266 E10
SEV TN13 162 A6
Bramble Reed La
STPH/PW TN12 278 F11
Brambletree Crs ROCH ME1 100 A3
Brambletree Whf ROCH ME1 * 99 M3
Bramble Wk RTWE/PEM TN2 * 197 G6
Brambley Crs FOLK CT20 219 M8
Brambling Ri SIT ME10 * 119 M3
Bramcote Gv BERM/RHTH SE16 25 K4
Bramdean Crs LEE/GVPK SE12 47 H6
Bramdean Gdns
LEE/GVPK SE12 47 H6
Bramerton Rd BECK BR3 70 A7
Bramhope La CHARL SE7 27 J5
Bramley Av CANT CT1 171 K7
FAV ME13 149 M3
Bramley Cl IOS ME12 229 N2
MEO DA13 79 G4
ORP BR6 90 C4
RHAM ME8 103 J5
SAND/SEL CR2 86 C8
SWLY BR8 74 F8
Bramley Ct STPH/PW TN12 280 G3
Bramley Crs MAID/SHEP ME15 168 A2
Bramley Dr CRBK TN17 298 C9
Bramley Gdns ASH TN23 204 D5
DVE/WH CT16 * 213 G2
HB CT6 129 L7
RMAID ME17 259 J2
STPH/PW TN12 278 H2
Bramley Hl SAND/SEL CR2 86 D7
Bramley Hyrst SAND/SEL CR2 * 86 D8
Bramley Pl DART DA1 51 H2
Bramley Ri STRD ME2 18 B2
Bramley Rd SNOD ME6 113 H5
STPH/PW TN12 257 J7
Bramleys HDCN TN27 283 L4
Bramley Wy E/WMAL ME19 164 B3
IOS ME12 229 N2
WWKM BR4 88 C5
Bramling Rd RCANTW CT4 251 J7
Brampton Bank RTON TN11 * 278 B3
Brampton Rd BXLYHN DA7 29 L5
CROY/NA CR0 87 G3
Bramshaw Rd CANTW/ST CT2 171 M3
Bramshot Av CHARL SE7 27 J5
Bramshott Cl MAIDW ME16 140 D7
Bramston Rd IOS ME12 65 K7
Branbridges Rd
STPH/PW TN12 257 K8
Branch Rd RCANTW CT4 247 P9
Branch St CMBW SE5 24 F6
DVE/WH CT16 8 B2
Brandon Est WALW SE17 24 C5
Brandon Rd DART DA1 52 B5
MSTR CT12 182 D4
Brandon St GVW DA11 55 J5
WALW SE17 24 D3
Brandon Wy BRCH CT7 176 E7

Brandram Ms LEW SE13 * ...46 F2
Brandram Rd LEW SE13 ...46 F1
Brands Hatch Pk HART DA3 * ...95 H6
Brands Hatch Rd BGR/WK TN15...95 H6
Brand St GNWCH SE10 ...26 C6
Brangbourne Rd BMLY BR1 ...71 J1
Brangton Rd LBTH SE11 ...24 A4
Branscombe St LEW SE13 ...46 C1
Bransell Cl SWLY BR8 ...92 D2
Bransgore Cl RHAM ME8 ...103 E4
Branston Crs STMC/STPC BR5...90 E4
Brantingham Cl TON TN9 ...194 C6
Branton Rd GRH DA9 ...53 G4
Brantwood Av ERITH DA8 ...30 D6
Brantwood Rd BXLYHS DA7 ...30 C8
    HNHL SE24 ...44 D3
Brasenose Rd GILL ME7 ...101 H2
Brasier Ct IOS ME12 ...65 H8
Brassey Av BRDST CT10 ...183 J2
Brassey Dr DIT/AY ME20 ...139 L5
Brassey Hl OXTED RH8 ...157 M8
Brassey Hl OXTED RH8 ...157 M7
Brasted Cl BXLYHS DA6...49 L3
    SYD SE26 ...69 K1
Brasted Ct RSEV TN14...82 B4
Brasted Hl RSEV TN14 ...133 M6
Brasted Hill Rd BH/WHM TN16...116 J4
Brasted La RSEV TN14 ...133 M5
Brasted Rd BH/WHM TN16...159 K4
    ERITH DA8 ...30 F6
Brattle RASHW TN26 ...317 J1
Brattle Wd SEV TN13 ...162 B7
Braundton Av BFN/LL DA15...49 G6
Braunstone Dr MAIDW ME16 ...140 A4
Braxfield Rd BROCKY SE4...45 M2
Braybrooke Gdns NRWD SE19...68 F4
Bray Crs BERM/RHTH SE16 ...25 L1
Bray Gdns MAID/SHEP ME15...167 G8
Braywood Rd ELTH/MOT SE9 ...48 A1
Breach La RSIT ME9 ...118 A1
Breach Rd WTHK RM20...
Breadlands Cl KEN/WIL TN24 ...3 J9
Breadlands Rd KEN/WIL TN24 ...3 J9
Breakneck Hl GRH DA9...53 J3
Breakspears Dr
    STMC/STPC BR5 ...73 H5
Breakspears Ms BROCKY SE4 ...26 A1
Breakspears Rd BROCKY SE4...46 A1
Brecon Cha IOS ME12 ...65 K6
Brecon Ri KEN/WIL TN24 ...2 A1
Brecon Sq MSTR CT12 ...182 D4
Bredgar Cl ASH TN23 ...204 C6
    MAID/BEAR ME14 ...13 K2
Bredgar Rd RHAM ME8 ...102 B1
Bredhurst Cl IOS ME12 ...64 C6
    PGE/AN SE20 ...69 K3
Bredhurst Rd RHAM ME8...102 C8
Bredon Rd CROY/NA CRO...87 G3
Breedon Av STH/RUST TN4...196 C4
Bremner Cl SWLY BR8...75 H8
Brenchley Av DEAL CT14 ...209 G5
    GVW DA11 ...79 J2
Brenchley Cl ASH TN23...204 B5
    CHST BR7 ...72 B5
    HAYES BR2 ...89 J1
    MEO ME1 ...100 E3
Brenchley Gdns FSTH SE23 ...45 K4
Brenchley Rd MAID/SHEP ME15...12 F3
    RHAM ME8 ...102 C3
    SIT ME10 ...117 L1
    STMC/STPC BR5 ...72 F5
    STPH/PW TN12 ...278 H9
    STPH/PW TN12 ...279 Q12
Brendon SCUP DA14 * ...73 H1
Brendon Av WALD ME5 ...115 H4
Brendon Cl ERITH DA8 ...30 F7
    RTWE/PEM TN2 ...23 L2
Brendon Dr KEN/WIL TN24 ...2 B2
Brendon Rd CHST BR7 ...72 C8
Brenley Gdns ELTH/MOT SE9 ...47 L2
Brenley La FAV ME13 ...150 D6
Brennan Rd TIL RM18 ...35 J5
Brent Cl BXLY DA5 ...49 M6
    RDART DA2 ...52 C4
    WALD ME5 ...100 F8
Brentfield Rd DART DA1...52 C2
Brent Hl FAV ME13 ...149 K1
Brentlands Dr DART DA1 ...52 A5
Brent La DART DA1 ...52 A5
Brent Rd FAV ME13 ...149 K1
    SAND/SEL CR2 ...104 A3
    WOOL/PLUM SE18 ...28 C6
The Brent DART DA1 ...52 C5
    TONN TN10 ...188 F2
Brent Wy DART DA1 ...52 C4
Brentwood Cl ELTH/MOT SE9 ...48 D6
Brentwood Rd CDW/CHF RM16...35 J3
Brenzett Cl WALD ME5 ...101 J4
Bretland Rd STH/RUST TN4 ...200 D1
Breton Rd ROCH ME1 ...100 D3
Brettell St WALW SE17 ...24 E7
Bretts Ct CANT CT1 ...4 E7
Brevet Cl PUR RM19 ...33 K4
Brewer Cl HOO/HM ME3 ...58 C6
Brewers Fld RDART DA2...75 K1
Brewers Hl OXTED CT20 ...222
Brewers Pl RCANTW CT4 * ...236 B10
Brewers Rd GVE DA12...80 D5
Brewer St DEAL CT14 ...209 G5
    MAID/BEAR ME14 ...13 G3
    RRTW TN3 ...296 B5
Brewery La RCANTW CT4 ...175 J6
    SEV TN15 ...21 J6
Brewery Rd HAYES BR2 ...89 M4
    SIT ME10 ...119 M3
    WOOL/PLUM SE18 ...28 E4
Brewery Sq RCANTE CT3 ...235 L8
Brewhouse La RASHE TN25 ...266 A9
Brewhouse Rd
    WOOL/PLUM SE18 ...28 A3
Brewhouse Yd GVE DA12 ...12 E5
Brian Crs STH/RUST TN4...196 E4
Briant St NWCR SE14 ...25 L7
Briar Av STRHM/NOR SW16...63 H8
Briar Cl DIT/AY ME20 ...139 H3
    DVW CT17 ...213 G7
    KEN/WIL TN24 ...202 F1
    RASHE TN25 * ...266 E10
    RCANTE CT3 ...251 Q12
    WARL CR6 ...130 F2
Briar Dl HOO/HM ME3...81 J2
Briarfield Cl BXLYHS DA7...30 D8
Briar Flds MAID/BEAR ME14 ...141 M8
Briar Gdns HAYES BR2 ...89 G4
Briar La CROY/NA CRO ...106 B1
Briar Rd BXLY DA5 ...50 E8
Briars Rd LYDD TN29 ...331 N2
The Briars BGR/WK TN15 ...111 J1
    WSTB CT5 * ...126 D7
Briars Wy HART DA3 ...96 B1
Briarswood Wy ORP BR6 ...91 G8
Briar Wk TONN TN10 ...188 F2

Briary Cl MARG CT9 ...177 J5
Briary Ct SCUP DA14 ...73 J2
Briary Gdns BMLY BR1 ...71 J2
Brice Av RCANTW CT4 ...248 D8
Brice Rd HOO/HM ME3 ...81 J2
Brick Ct GRAYS RM17 * ...34 B5
Brickenden Rd CRBK TN17 ...298 G9
Brickfield Cottages
    WOOL/PLUM SE18 ...29 G6
Brickfield Farm HART DA3...78 B7
Brickfield Farm Gdns ORP BR6...90 B7
Brickfield La FAV ME13 ...150 F7
Brickfield Rd RCANTW CT4 ...246 E6
    THHTH CR7 ...68 C5
Brickfields E/WMAL ME19 ...138 C4
    RTWE/PEM TN2 ...278 B9
Brick Field Vw STRD ME2...82 D4
Brick Kiln La OXTED RH8 ...158 A1
    RMAID ME17 ...261 L8
    STPH/PW TN12 ...296 H5
Brickwood Cl SYD SE26 ...45 J8
Brickwood Rd CROY/NA CRO ...86 B7
Brickworks Cl TON TN9 ...194 D6
Brideale Cl PECK SE15 * ...25 G5
Bridewain St STHWK SE1 ...25 G2
Bridewell La FAV ME13 ...150 F7
The Bridge Ap WSTB CT5 ...126 F4
Bridge Cl GRH DA9 ...53 H2
    HYTHE CT21 ...222 B3
    RASHW TN26 ...317 J1
    TON TN9 ...194 F5
Bridge Ct GRAYS RM17 * ...34 C5
Bridge Down RCANTW CT4 ...250 B4
Bridgefield Rd WSTB CT5 ...127 J2
Bridgeford Wy RCANTW CT4...175 H8
Bridge Hl DEAL CT14 ...208 D1
Bridge House SIT ME10 * ...120 B5
Bridgelands Cl BECK BR3 ...70 A4
Bridgeman Ct HYTHE CT21 * ...222 C3
Bridge Mdw NWCR SE14 ...25 L5
Bridge Mill Wy
    MAID/SHEP ME15 ...12 B9
Bridgen Rd BXLY DA5 ...49 M5
Bridge Pl CROY/NA CRO ...86 E4
    DIT/AY ME20 ...140 A3
Bridge Rd ASH TN23 ...204 C1
    BECK BR3 ...70 A4
    BXLYHN DA7 ...49 M1
    DEAL CT14 ...209 L2
    ERITH DA8 ...31 H7
    FAV ME13 ...149 K1
    GILL ME7 ...7
    GRAYS RM17 ...34 C5
    IOS ME12 ...64 C2
    MARG CT9 ...177 K5
    RASHE TN25 ...289 L12
    RCANTW CT4 ...174 F5
    ROCH ME1 ...100 D3
    STMC/STPC BR5 ...91 G7
Bridge Rw CROY/NA CRO * ...2 B4
Bridges Dr DART DA1 ...52 C3
Bridgeside DEAL CT14 ...209 K3
Bridge St DVE CT16 ...8
    FOLKN CT19 ...11 L2
    MAID/SHEP ME15 ...167 C8
    RASHE TN25 ...266 F11
Bridge Ter LEW SE13 * ...46 E2
Bridgetown Cl NRWD SE19 ...68 A4
Bridge Vw GRH DA9 ...53 J2
Bridgewater Cl CHST BR7 ...72 F7
Bridgewater Pl E/WMAL ME19...138 D7
Bridgewater Rd IOS ME12 ...64 C5
Bridgewood Cl PGE/AN SE20 ...69 J4
Bridle Cl CROY/NA CRO ...88 B8
Bridle Wy CROY/NA CRO ...88 B8
    HB CT6 ...128 F6
    HYTHE CT21 ...223 H2
    ORP BR6 ...90 D7
Bridleway Gdns BRDST CT10...183 J3
Bridleway La ASH TN23 ...204 E2
Bridlington Cl BH/WHM TN16...132 A5
Bridport Rd THHTH CR7 ...68 B2
Brief St CMBW SE5 ...24 C7
Brier Cl CDW/CHF RM16 ...35 K1
Brier Cl WALD ME5 ...101 K5
Brierley CROY/NA CRO ...105 L2
Brierley Cl SNWD SE25 ...69 H4
Brier Rd SIT ME10 ...119 H4
Brigade St BKHTH/KID SE3 * ...27 J5
Bright Cl BELV DA17 ...29 L3
Brightfield Rd LEE/GVPK SE12 ...46 E4
Brightlands CVW DA11 ...78 F1
Brightling Rd BROCKY SE4...46 A4
    RBTBR TN32 ...322 D10
Brightlingsea Rd SWCH CT13 ...206 E1
Brighton Rd BRXN/ST SW9...44 A4
Brighton Ter BRXN/ST SW9 ...44 A4
Bright Rdg CHAT ME4 ...6
Brightside Rd LEW SE13...46 E4
Bright's Pl RHAM CT1 ...17 L4
Brightwell Cl CROY/NA CRO ...86 B4
Brig Ms DEPT SE8 ...26 B5
Brigstock Rd BELV DA17 ...30 C3
    THHTH CR7 ...86 C1
Brimfield Rd PUR RM19 ...32 E3
Brimpsfield Cl ABYW SE2 ...29 J2
The Brimp HOO/HM ME3 ...41 L4
Brimstone Cl ORP BR6 ...108 B2
Brimstone Hl RMAID ME17 ...97 K5
Brindle Ga BFN/LL DA15 ...48 F8
Brindle Gv RAM CT11 ...17 M1
Brindles Cl TIL RM18 ...36 B3
Brindle Wy WALD ME5 ...115 K4
Brindley Cl BXLYHN DA7 ...50 A1
Brindley St NWCR SE14 ...26 A7
Brindley Wy BMLY BR1 ...71 J2
Brinkburn Cl ABYW SE2 ...29 H3
Brinkers Crs WADH TN5 ...309 M7
Brinklow Crs
    WOOL/PLUM SE18 ...28 C6
Brionne Gdns TON TN9 ...195 H5
Brisbane Av SIT ME10 ...119 K5
Brisbane Dr MSTR CT12 ...182 D2
Brisbane Rd CHAT ME4 ...6
Brisbane St CMBW SE5 ...24 C7
Briset Rd ELTH/MOT SE9 ...47 L2
Brishing La MAID/SHEP ME15...167 M8
Brishing Rd MAID/SHEP ME15...167 M8
    RMAID ME17 ...259 R1
Brisley Rd RASHE TN25 ...304 C6
Brissenden Cl NROM TN28...331 K6
Bristol Cl STRD ME2 ...82 A3
Bristol Pl RAM CT11 ...17 H5
Bristol Rd CANT CT1 ...55 L8
    GVE DA12 ...12 C4
Bristow Rd BXLYHN DA7 ...29 M7
    NRWD SE19 ...68 B4
Britannia Cl ERITH DA8 * ...31 G6
    SIT ME10 ...119 H1
    STRD ME2 ...113 H1
Britannia Dr GVE DA12 ...80 A2
Britannia La ASH TN23 ...204 D6

Britannia Rd DEAL CT14 ...209 L1
    HOO/HM ME3 ...60 B2
    POP/IOD E14 ...26 C3
Briton Ct IOS ME12 ...64 C4
Briton Rd FAV ME13 ...149 K2
Britten Cl HYTHE CT21 ...222 B3
    TONN TN10 ...189 G7
Brittenden Pde ORP BR6 * ...107 L1
Britton Cl LEW SE13 ...46 E5
Britton St CLKNW EC1M * ...7 J3
Brixham Rd WELL DA16 ...29 L7
Brixton Hl BRXS/STRHM SW2 ...44 A4
Brixton Ov BRXN/ST SW9 ...44 B5
Brixton Rd LBTH SE11 ...24 B5
Brixton Station Rd
    BRXN/ST SW9 ...44 B1
Brixton Water La
    BRXS/STRHM SW2 ...212 L4
Broadacre RDV CT15 ...121 L7
Broad Bridge Cl BKHTH/KID SE3...27 H6
Broadcloth CRBK TN17 ...298 G10
Broadcoombe SAND/SEL CR2 ...104 C2
Broadcroft RTWE/PEM TN2 ...201 L5
Broadcroft Rd STMC/STPC BR5 ...90 E4
Broad Ditch Rd MEO DA13 ...78 D4
Broadeaves Cl SAND/SEL CR2...86 F8
Broadfield La MAID/BEAR ME14...142 C5
Broadfield Crs FOLK CT20 ...10 C5
Broadfield Rd CAT SE6 ...46 F6
    FOLK CT20 ...10 C5
    MAID/SHEP ME15 ...167 H5
Broad Green Av CROY/NA CRO...86 D5
Broad Gv RTWE/PEM TN2 ...201 H4
Broadham Green Rd
    OXTED RH8 ...184 E3
Broadham Pl OXTED RH8 ...184 E3
Broadheath Dr CHST BR7 ...72 A4
Broadhoath Rd BXLYHS DA6...163 K4
Broadhurst Dr KEN/WIL TN24...203 J4
Broadlands CANT/ST CT2 ...173 C5
    GRAYS RM17 ...34 A4
Broadlands Av NROM TN28...331 H6
Broadlands Crs NROM TN28...331 H6
Broadlands Dr WALD ME5 ...115 J1
    WARL CR6 ...130 B5
Broadlands Rd BMLY BR1 ...71 J1
Broad La DEAL CT14 ...208 B3
    BECK BR3 ...70 A4
    RDART DA2 ...75 J1
    RRTW TN3 ...199 H2
Broad Lawn ELTH/MOT SE9 ...48 B7
Broadley Av BRCH CT7 ...176 D3
Broad Rd MARG CT9 ...179 G5
Broadmead ASH TN23 ...204 B8
    CAT SE6 ...46 B8
    RTWE/PEM TN2 ...200 F5
Broadmead Av
    RTWE/PEM TN2 ...201 G5
Broadmead Rd FOLKN CT19 ...11 H4
Broadmere Ter MAIDW ME16 * ...12 E4
Broadoak AV WALD ME19 ...138 E5
Broad Oak RRTW TN3 ...199 J7
    STPH/PW TN12 ...279 M9
Broadoak Av
    MAID/SHEP ME15 ...167 J4
Broadoak Cl RDART DA2 ...76 B3
Broad Oak Cl RTWE/PEM TN2 ...201 H4
    STMC/STPC BR5 ...90 F3
    STPH/PW TN12 ...279 M9
Broad Oak Rd CANTW/ST CT2 ...172 D5
Broadoak Rd ERITH DA8 ...30 E6
    RSIT ME9 ...145 L2
Broad Oaks Wy HAYES BR2 ...89 G1
Broadsole La RDV CT15 ...293 H12
Broadstairs Rd BRDST CT10 ...179 H6
Broad St CANT CT1 ...209 L3
    DEAL CT14 ...209 L3
    IOS ME12 ...64 C3
    MARG CT9 ...14 C3
    RAM CT11 ...17 J5
    RASHE TN25 ...290 B12
    RMAID ME17 ...260 F6
Broad Street Hl RMAID ME17 ...143 H5
Broadview FOLK CT20 ...219 K7
Broadview Av CDW/CHF RM16...34 B7
Broadwater RHAM ME8 ...102 F5
Broadwater Down
    RTWE/PEM TN2 ...201 G5
Broadwater Forest La
    RRTW TN3 ...199 M7
Broadwater La RTWE/PEM TN2...22 C9
Broadwater Ri
    RTWE/PEM TN2 ...201 G4
Broadwater Rd E/WMAL ME19...138 C7
    WOOL/PLUM SE18 ...28 M2
Broadwood Av CROY/NA CRO...86 E6
Broadway Cl SAND/SEL CR2 ...104 A8
The Broadway BRDST CT10...183 J1
    HB CT6 ...128 D4
    IOS ME12 ...65 J4
    RTON TN11 ...256 H5
Broadwood GVW DA11 ...79 J1
Broadwood Rd HOO/HM ME3 ...83 G1
Brockdene Dr HAYES BR2 ...89 M1
Brockenhurst Av
    MAID/SHEP ME15 ...167 J4
Brockenhurst Cl
    CANTW/ST CT2 ...172 D5
    RHAM ME8 ...102 D8
Brockenhurst Rd CROY/NA CRO...87 J3
    RAM CT11 ...17 M3
Brockett Cl CDW/CHF RM16...35 H2
Brockham Crs CROY/NA CRO ...105 J2
Brockham Dr
    BRXS/STRHM SW2 ...44 A5
Brockhill Rd HYTHE CT21 ...222 C4
Brockill Crs BROCKY SE4...45 M2
Brocklebank Rd CHARL SE7 ...27 J3
Brocklehurst St NWCR SE14 ...25 L7
Brocklesby Rd SNWD SE25 ...69 J4
Brockley Cross BROCKY SE4...45 M1
Brockley Gv BROCKY SE4 ...46 A3
Brockley Hall Rd BROCKY SE4...45 M4
Brockley Ms BROCKY SE4...45 M4
Brockley Pk FSTH SE23 ...45 M5
Brockley Rd BROCKY SE4...45 M5
Brockley Vw FSTH SE23 ...45 M4
Brockley Wy FSTH SE23 ...45 L5
Brockman Crs LYDD TN29 ...321 N4
Brockman Ri BMLY BR1 ...70 E8
Brockman Rd FOLK CT20 ...10 C4
Brockman's Cl MSTR CT12...180 E6

Brock St PECK SE15 * ...45 K1
Brockway BGR/WK TN15 ...240 F1
Brockwell Av BECK BR3 ...88 D1
Brockwell Ct BRXN/ST SW5 * ...91
Brockwell St STMC/STPC BR5 ...91 G1
Brockwell Park Gdns
    HNHL SE24 ...44 C5
Brodie St STHWK SE1 ...25 G2
Brodrick Gv ABYW SE2 ...29 J3
Brogdale Pl FAV ME13 ...149 J4
Brogdale Rd FAV ME13 ...149 J4
Brogden Crs RMAID ME17 ...169 G6
Brograve Gdns BECK BR3 ...70 C6
Broke Farm Dr ORP BR6 ...108 B3
Brokes Wy STH/RUST TN4...196 F4
Bromar Rd CMBW SE5 ...44 E1
Brome House
    WOOL/PLUM SE18 * ...27 M6
Brome Rd ELTH/MOT SE9 ...48 A1
Bromfield Cl OXTED RH8 ...185 H3
Bromhedge ELTH/MOT SE9 ...48 A3
Bromholm Rd ABYW SE2 ...29 J2
Bromley GRAYS RM17 ...34 A5
Bromley Cl MAID/BEAR ME14...142 C3
    RHAM ME8 ...115 J1
Bromley Common HAYES BR2...89 M3
Bromley Crs HAYES BR2 ...71 G7
Bromley Gdns HAYES BR2 ...71 G6
Bromley Green Rd
    RASHW TN26 ...304 C7
Bromley Gv HAYES BR2 ...70 E6
Bromley Hl BMLY BR1 ...70 E4
Bromley La CHST BR7 ...72 D4
Bromley Rd BECK BR3 ...70 B5
    CAT SE6 ...46 C8
    CHST BR7 ...72 D7
Bromley Ter
    WOOL/PLUM SE18 * ...28 B7
Bromstone Rd BRDST CT10...183 H7
Bromington Cl WALD ME5 ...101 H8
Bronte Cl DIT/AY ME20 ...139 G2
    ERITH DA8 ...30 C6
    TIL RM18 ...35 K8
Bronte Gv DART DA1 ...52 A2
Bronte Vw GVE DA12 ...12 D5
Bronti Cl WALW SE17 ...24 E7
Bronze Age Wy BELV DA17 ...30 D2
Bronze St DEPT SE8 ...26 B6
Brook CHAT ME4 ...6 E6
Brookbank MAID/BEAR ME14...141 H5
Brookbank Rd LEW SE13 ...46 C1
Brook Cl EGRIN RH19 ...274 A12
    HB CT6 ...128 D4
    HYTHE CT21 ...223 J2
Brook Ct BECK BR3 * ...70 A5
Brookdale BXLY DA5 ...49 M4
    CAT SE6 ...46 C5
Brookdene Rd
    WOOL/PLUM SE18 ...28 F3
Brook Dr LBTH SE11 ...24 C3
Brooke Av MARG CT9 ...177 L6
Brooke Dr GVE DA12 ...56 C7
Brook End OXTED RH8 * ...185 H3
Brookend Rd BFN/LL DA15 ...48 F6
Brookfield BGR/WK TN15 ...136 D3
Brookfield Cl DIT/AY ME20 ...139 H1
Brookfield Pl DIT/AY ME20 ...213 J7
Brookfield Rd ASH TN23 ...204 B2
    DVE/WH CT16 ...213 H6
Brookfields RTON TN11 ...256 B4
Brook Hill OXTED RH8 ...185 H3
Brook Hill Cl WOOL/PLUM SE18...28 C4
Brookhurst Gdns
    STH/RUST TN4 ...196 B2
Brooklands DART DA1 ...51 M6
    HDCN TN27 ...283 J1
Brooklands Av BFN/LL DA15...48 E7
Brooklands Cl CANT/ST CT2 ...173 C9
Brooklands Farm Cl
    RRTW TN3 ...276 H11
Brooklands Pk BKHTH/KID SE3...47 H1
Brooklands Rd DIT/AY ME20 ...139 H2
Brook La BR BXLY DA5 ...49 L3
    BKHTH/KID SE3 ...27 J8
    BMLY BR1 ...71 H3
    BXLY DA5 ...49 L3
    HB CT6 ...232 C4
    MSTR CT12 ...237 J1
    RASHE TN25 ...307 K3
    SNOD ME6 ...113 H7
    TON TN9 ...195 G3
Brooklyn Av SNWD SE25 ...69 J8
Brooklyn Paddock GILL ME7...7 L1
Brooklyn Rd SNWD SE25 ...69 J8
Brooklyn Vls STPH/PW TN12 * ...280 H4
Brookmead RTON TN11 ...194 A1
Brookmead Cl ORP BR6 ...91 J5
Brookmead Rd HOO/HM ME3 ...58 C6
Brookmill Rd DEPT SE8 ...26 B7
Brook Rd DIT/AY ME20 ...138 F1
    FAV ME13 ...149 K1
    GVW DA11 ...79 J1
    RTWE/PEM TN2 ...196 F6
    SWLY BR8 ...74 F2
    THHTH CR7 ...68 C3
Brooks Cl STPH/PW TN12 ...281 K5
Brooks Cl ELTH/MOT SE9 ...48 B8
Brookside CROY/NA CRO ...104 C2
Brookside Ms MAID/SHEP ME15...12 C9
Brookside Rd MEO DA13 ...78 C9
Brookside Wy CROY/NA CRO...87 J6
Brooks Pl MAID/BEAR ME14 ...13 H4
Brook St BELV DA17 ...30 C4
    SNOD ME6 ...113 J6
    SWCH CT13 ...253 P7
    TENT TN30 ...316 C5
    TON TN9 ...194 D5
The Brook CHAT ME4 ...6 E5
Brookway BKHTH/KID SE3 ...47 H1
Brookwood Cl HAYES BR2 ...89 K2
Broom Av STMC/STPC BR5 ...73 J6
Broom Bank WARL CR6 ...131 M5
Broom Cl HAYES BR2 ...89 M2
Broomcroft RHAM ME8 ...102

Broomfield Crs MARG CT9 ...179 J3
Broomfield Ga WSTB CT5 ...127 L8
Broomfield Rd BECK BR3 ...69 L8
    BXLYHS DA6 ...50 B3
    FAV ME13 ...123 K8
    FOLKN CT19 ...219 M7
    HB CT6 ...129 K8
    RMAID ME17 ...261 L1
    SEV TN13 ...13 L9
    SWCM DA10 ...53 M4
Broomfields HART DA3 ...95 M1
Broomgrove Rd BRXN/ST SW9...44 A8
Broomhill Park Rd
    STH/RUST TN4 ...196 B5
Broomhill Ri BXLYHS DA6...50 B3
Broomhill Rd DART DA1 ...51 J4
    ORP BR6 ...91 H5
    RRTW TN3 ...196 F3
Broom Hill Rd STRD ME2 ...18 C1
Broomhills MEO DA13 ...77 M8
Broomlands La OXTED RH8 ...158 D5
Broom Md BXLYHS DA6 ...50 B4
Broom Pk RRTW TN3 ...199 H8
Broom Rd CROY/NA CRO ...88 B6
    STMC/STPC BR5 ...120 C8
Broomshaw Rd MAIDW ME16...166 A2
Broomwood Cl BXLY DA5 ...50 E7
    CROY/NA CRO ...87 L1
Broomwood Rd
    STMC/STPC BR5 ...73 J8
Broseley Gv SYD SE26 ...69 G7
Broster Gdns SNWD SE25 ...69 H2
Broughton Cl ASH TN23 * ...204 B8
Broughton Dr BRXN/ST SW9...44 B2
Broughton Rd ORP BR6 ...90 F7
    THHTH CR7 ...86 B2
Brow Cl STMC/STPC BR5 ...91 J4
Brow Crs STMC/STPC BR5 ...91 K4
Browndens Rd STRD ME2 ...112 F1
Brownelow Copse WALD ME5 ...115 H4
Brownhill Cl WALD ME5 ...115 H4
Brownhill Rd CAT SE6 ...46 D6
Browning Cl DIT/AY ME20 ...139 G1
    WELL DA16 ...28 F7
Browning Pl FOLKN CT19 ...220 F6
Browning Rd DART DA1 ...52 A2
Brownings EDEN TN8 ...192 D1
Brownings Orch RSIT ME9 ...146 B2
Browning St WALW SE17 ...24 D7
Brownlow Rd CROY/NA CRO ...86 F8
Brown Rd GVE DA12 ...55 M9
Brownspring Dr ELTH/MOT SE9...48 C8
Brown St RHAM ME8 ...102 F4
Broxbourne Rd ORP BR6 ...91 G4
Broxhall Rd RCANTW CT4 ...269 K6
Broxholm Rd WNWD SE27 ...44 D8
Broxted Rd CAT SE6 ...46 A7
    WELL DA16 ...29 J7
Bruce Dr SAND/SEL CR2 ...104 C7
Bruce Gv ORP BR6 ...91 H4
Bruces Wharf Rd GRAYS RM17...34 A5
The Brucks WBY/YAL ME18 ...164 H6
Bruford Ct DEPT SE8 ...26 B6
Brundell Far RCANTW CT4 * ...248 C7
Brunel Cl CHAT ME4 * ...83 H6
Brunel Cl NRWD SE19 ...69 G3
    TIL RM18 ...35 J8
Brunel House
    WOOL/PLUM SE18 * ...27 M6
Brunel Rd BERM/RHTH SE16 ...25 K1
Brunel Wy CHAT ME4 ...83 G6
Brunswick Cl BXLYHS DA6 ...49 L2
Brunswick Ct STHWK SE1 ...24 F1
Brunswick Fld KENT SE9 * ...121
Brunswick Gdns
    DVE/WH CT16 ...213 J4
Brunswick Pk CMBW SE5 ...24 E7
Brunswick Pl NRWD SE19 ...69 H4
Brunswick Quay
    BERM/RHTH SE16 ...25 L2
Brunswick Rd ASH TN23 ...204 C1
    BRCH CT7 ...176 D8
    BXLYHS DA6 ...49 L2
Brunswick Sq HB CT6 ...128 F4
Brunswick St East
    DEAL CT14 * ...209 L3
    RTWT TN1 * ...22 F7
Brunswick St
    MAID/SHEP ME15 ...13 G4
    RAM CT11 ...17 K5
Brunswick Vls CMBW SE5 ...24 F7
Brunswick Wk GVE DA12 ...55 L4
Bruton Cl CHST BR7 ...72 A6
Bryan Rd BERM/RHTH SE16 ...26 A1
Bryanston Rd TIL RM18 ...35 K8
Bryant Cl WBY/YAL ME18 ...164 H2
Bryant Rd STRD ME2 ...112 E7
Bryant St CHAT ME4 ...6 D2
Bryden Cl SYD SE26 ...69 M2
Brymore Cl CANT CT1 ...5 L1
Brymore Rd CANT CT1 ...5 L1
Bryony Dr ASH TN23 ...204 E5
Bubblestone Rd RSEV TN14 ...136 A2
Buchan Rd PECK SE15 ...45 K1
Buckden Cl LEE/GVPK SE12 ...47 G4
Buckham Thorns Rd
    BH/WHM TN16 ...159 H4
Buckhole Farm Rd
    HOO/HM ME3 ...59 K1
Buckhurst Av BGR/WK TN15 ...21 J1
Buckhurst Dr MARG CT9 ...179 J3
Buckhurst La BGR/WK TN15 ...21 J1
    WADH TN5 ...308 F5
Buckhurst Rd BH/WHM TN16...153 H4
Buckingham Av THHTH CR7 ...68 A8
    WELL DA16 ...48 F2
Buckingham Cl STMC/STPC BR5...90 C3
Buckingham Dr CHST BR7 ...72 C2
Buckingham Gdns THHTH CR7 ...68 B2
Buckingham La FSTH SE23 ...45 M5
    GILL ME7 ...7 H3
Buckingham Rd BRDST CT10 * ...183 L1
    GILL ME7 ...7 H3
    GVW DA11 ...79 H1
    MARG CT9 ...14 C3
    RTWT TN1 ...23 J3
    WSTB CT5 ...127 L8
Buckingham Rw
    MAID/SHEP ME15 ...167 M6
Buckland Av DVE/WH CT16 ...213 H4
Buckland Cl WALD ME5 * ...115 H4
Buckland La MAIDW ME16 ...12 C3
    MEO DA13 ...77 G8
Buckland Rd ASH TN23 ...204 B2
    RCANTE CT3 ...252 E6
    HOO/HM ME3 ...58 A1
    MAIDW ME16 ...12 C3
    MEO DA13 ...77 G8
    ORP BR6 ...90 F7
Buckleigh Wy NRWD SE19 ...69 G5
Bucklers Ct IOS ME12 ...64 C3
    RTWE/PEM TN2 ...230 D1
Buckles Cl RHAM ME8 ...102
Buckley Cl DART DA1 ...31 L6
Bucknall Wy BECK BR3 ...70 C4

Buckner Rd BRXS/STRHM SW2 ...44 A2
Bucks Cross Rd GVW DA11 ...55 G8
Bucksford La ASH TN23 ...286 H10
Buckstone Cl FSTH SE23 ...45 K4
Buck St RASHE TN25 ...265 P3
 IOS ME12 ...228 D1
Buckthorne Rd BROCKY SE4 ...45 M4
Buddens Gn RYE TN31 ...325 Q9
Buddle Dr IOS ME12 ...64 F6
Budd's La TENT TN30 ...326 H3
Budgin's HI ORP BR6 ...108 A6
Budleigh's HI ASH TN23 ...29 K7
Buenos Ayres MARC CT9 ...14 C5
Buffs Av FOLK CT20 ...219 J7
Bugglesden Rd HDCN TN27 ...300 H8
Bug HI WARL CR6 ...130 C6
Bugsbys Wy GNWCH SE10 ...26 F1
Bugsell La RBTBR TN32 ...322 E9
Builders Sq RCANTE CT3 * ...251 K1
Bulganak Rd THHTH CR7 ...68 D8
Bullace Rw CMBW SE5 ...24 D6
Bull Aly WELL DA16 ...49 J1
Bullar Cl PECK SE15 ...25 H6
Bullbanks Rd BELV DA17 ...30 D3
Bull Cl CDW/CHF RM16 ...34 A1
Bulleid Pl ASH TN23 ...205 G4
Buller Rd CHAT ME4 ...8 D9
 THHTH CR7 ...68 E7
Buller's Av HB CT6 ...128 F5
Bullers Wood Dr CHST BR7 ...71 H5
Bull Flds SNOD ME6 ...113 H5
Bullfinch Cl SEV TN13 ...135 J8
 STPH/PW TN12 ...279 K4
Bullfinch Dene SEV TN13 ...135 L3
Bullfinch La SEV TN13 ...20 A1
Bullfinch Rd SAND/SEL CR2 ...104 C4
Bull HI RMAID ME17 ...263 K4
Bullingstone La RRTW TN3 ...277 N11
Bullion Cl STPH/PW TN12 ...278 L3
Bullivant Cl GRH DA9 ...53 H3
Bull La BGR/WK TN15 ...238 F10
 CHST BR7 ...72 E4
 DIT/AY ME20 ...151 C4
 FAV ME13 ...151 G4
 HOO/HM ME3 ...57 L6
 RASHW TN26 ...302 C1
 RSIT ME9 ...117 M4
Bullockstone Rd HB CT6 ...128 E1
Bull Orch MAIDW ME16 ...166 A3
Bull Rd C/WMAL ME19 ...112 D8
Bullrush Cl CROY/NA CR0 ...86 F7
Bulls Pl RTWE/PEM TN2 ...278 A11
Bullwark St DVW CT17 ...8 A9
Bull Yd GVE DA12 ...55 J4
 PECK SE15 ...25 H7
The Bull Yd ASH TN23 * ...2 B4
Bulrush Cl WALD ME5 ...115 G2
The Bulrushes ASH TN23 ...286 H9
Bulwark Rd DEAL CT14 ...209 L6
Bumbles Cl ROCH ME1 ...64 B8
Bunce Court Rd FAV ME13 ...204 C10
Bungalow Rd SNWD SE25 ...68 F8
The Bungalows SWCH CT13 * ...253 N4
 WTHK RM20 * ...33 H5
The Bungalow BRDST CT10 * ...178 F4
Bunker's HI DVW CT17 ...213 H7
 SCUP DA14 ...50 A8
Bunkers Hill Av DVW CT17 ...213 H8
Bunkers Hill Rd DVW CT17 ...213 H8
Bunkley Meadow
 RASHW TN26 ...318 D2
Bunkley Ter RASHW TN26 * ...318 D2
Bunny HI GVE DA12 * ...80 F3
Bunny La RRTW TN3 ...200 F9
Bunters Hill Rd HOO/HM ME3 ...58 M8
Bunton St WOOL/PLUM SE18 ...28 B2
Burbage Cl STHWK SE1 ...24 E2
Burbage Rd HNHL SE24 ...44 F4
Burberry La RMAID ME17 ...169 J8
Burcharbro Rd ABYW SE2 ...29 L5
Burch Av SWCH CT13 ...206 A1
Burchell Rd PECK SE15 ...25 J7
Burdens HDCN TN27 ...283 L4
Burden Cl GVE DA12 ...80 F1
Burdett Cl SCUP DA14 ...51 J6
Burdett Rd CROY/NA CR0 ...86 E2
 STH/RUST TN4 ...200 C1
Burdock Cl CROY/NA CR0 ...87 L4
Bure TIL RM18 ...36 D2
Burfield Dr WARL CR6 ...130 B5
Burford Rd BMLY BR1 ...71 M8
 CAT SE6 ...46 A7
Burford Wy CROY/NA CR0 ...105 J4
Burgate CANT CT1 * ...5 G4
Burgate La CANT CT1 ...5 G5
Burgess Cl DART DA1 ...51 L1
 MSTR CT12 ...180 F6
Burgess Gn DEAL CT14 ...208 F1
Burgess Hall Dr RMAID ME17 ...169 G7
Burgess Rd RCANTE CT3 ...251 R11
 STRD ME2 ...19 H1
Burge St STHWK SE1 ...24 E4
Burghclere Dr MAIDW ME16 ...166 C3
Burghfield Rd GVW DA11 ...79 G4
Burghill Rd SYD SE26 ...69 L1
Burgh HI BUR/ETCH TN19 ...322 E3
Burgos Gv GNWCH SE10 ...26 C7
Burgoyne Barracks
 FOLK CT20 * ...223 K1
Burgoyne Hts DVE/WH CT16 ...213 M7
Burgoyne Rd BRXN/ST SW9 ...44 A1
 SNWD SE25 ...69 G8
Burham Rd PGE/AN SE20 ...69 G4
Burham Rd ROCH ME1 ...99 M6
Burial Ground La
 MAID/SHEP ME15 ...12 C9
Burkeston Cl SIT ME10 ...120 B1
Burleigh Av BFN/LL DA15 ...49 G3
Burleigh Cl STRD ME2 ...18 A1
Burleigh Dr MAID/BEAR ME14 ...141 G4
Burleigh Gdns MARC CT9 ...14 C4
Burleigh Wk CAT SE6 ...46 D6
Burley Rd SIT ME10 ...119 M5
Burlings La RSEV TN14 ...133 L5
Burlington Av BFN/LL DA15 ...49 G3
Burlington Cl ORP BR6 ...90 C4
Burlington Dr HB CT6 ...129 L4
Burlington Gdns MARC CT9 ...14 C4
Burlington House
 DVE/WH CT16 * ...8 E5
Burma Crs CANT CT1 ...172 D8
Burman Cl RDART DA2 ...52 C5
Burmarsh Cl WALD ME5 ...101 J4
Burmarsh Rd HYTHE TN21 ...321 N1
 LYDD TN29 ...331 R7
Burma Ter NRWD SE19 * ...68 F2
Burma Wy WALD ME5 ...101 J4
Burnaby Rd GVW DA11 ...54 F9
Burnell Av WELL DA16 ...29 H8
Burnell Wk STHWK SE1 * ...25 G4
Burnett Rd ERITH DA8 ...31 L5
Burnett St GNWCH SE10 ...26 D6
Burnham Cl SIT ME10 ...119 M1

 STHWK SE1 ...25 G3
Burnham Crs DART DA1 ...51 K2
Burnham Gdns CROY/NA CR0 ...87 G3
Burnham La DART DA1 ...51 L3
 SCUP DA14 ...49 M7
Burnham Ter DART DA1 * ...51 K2
Burnham Wk RHAM ME8 ...116 F2
Burnham Wy SYD SE26 ...70 A2
Burnhill Rd BECK BR3 ...70 F1
Burnley Rd BRXN/ST SW9 ...24 A1
 WTHK RM20 ...33 J3
Burns Av BFN/LL DA15 ...49 J4
Burns Cl ERITH DA8 ...31 G7
 WELL DA16 ...49 G1
Burns Crs TOV TN11 ...194 D6
Burns Pl TIL RM18 ...35 J7
Burn's Rd GILL ME7 ...83 K6
 MAIDW ME16 ...166 D3
Burnt Ash Hl LEE/GVPK SE12 ...47 H5
Burnt Ash La BMLY BR1 ...71 J4
Burnt Ash Rd LEE/GVPK SE12 ...139 M5
Burnt Ash St LEE/GVPK SE12 ...47 G4
Burnt House Cl HAWK TN18 ...324 A9
 STRD ME2 ...82 D3
Burnt House HI RCANTE CT3 ...234 F8
Burnthouse La HDCN TN27 ...284 A9
Burnt House La RDART DA2 ...75 M1
 RRTW TN3 ...277 N12
Burnt Lodge La WADH TN5 ...310 C3
Burnt Oak La BFN/LL DA15 ...49 H4
Burnt Oak Ter GILL ME7 ...7 J7
Burntwick Dr RSIT ME9 ...226 C10
Burnt Oast Rd FAV ME13 ...151 H6
Burntwood Rd SEV TN13 ...162 A5
Burntwood Vw NRWD SE19 * ...69 G3
Burrage Gv WOOL/PLUM SE18 ...28 C3
Burrage Pl WOOL/PLUM SE18 ...28 C4
Burrage Rd WOOL/PLUM SE18 ...28 C4
Burr Bank Ter RDART DA2 * ...75 K1
Burr Cl BXLYHN DA7 ...50 A3
Burrell Cl CROY/NA CR0 ...87 M2
Burrell Rw BECK BR3 ...70 F1
Burrells Whf POP/IOD E14 ...26 C4
Burrfield Dr STMC/STPC BR5 ...91 K2
Burrow Rd EDUL SE22 ...44 F2
 FOLKN CT19 ...11 M3
Burrows La HOO/HM ME3 ...61 K2
Burrows Ms STHWK SE1 ...24 C1
The Burrs SIT ME10 ...120 A1
Burrstock Wy RHAM ME8 ...103 H5
Burrswood Vls RRTW TN3 * ...199 N8
Bursdon Cl BFN/LL DA15 ...49 H4
Bursill Crs MSTR CT12 ...16 C1
Burslem Rd RTWE/PEM TN2 ...197 H7
Bursted Hl RCANTW CT4 ...269 L3
Burston Rd RMAID ME17 ...258 C10
Burton Cl FOLKN CT19 ...220 B6
 HOO/HM ME3 ...82 D1
 THHTH CR7 ...68 E7
Burton Flds HB CT6 ...129 L3
Burton Gv WALW SE17 ...24 E5
Burton La BRXN/ST SW9 ...24 A1
Burton Rd BRXN/ST SW9 ...24 A1
 KEN/WIL TN24 ...203 G5
Burtwell La WNWD SE27 ...68 E1
Burwash Cl STMC/STPC BR5 ...91 K1
Burwash Rd WOOL/PLUM SE18 ...28 C3
Burwood Av HAYES BR2 ...89 J5
Busbridge Rd
 MAID/SHEP ME15 ...166 F6
 SNOD ME6 ...112 F6
Bush Av MSTR CT12 ...16 C1
Bushbaby Cl STHWK SE1 * ...24 F2
Bush Cl RSIT ME9 ...145 L1
Bushell Cl BRXS/STRHM SW2 ...44 A1
Bushell Wy CHST BR7 ...72 B2
Bushey Av STMC/STPC BR5 ...90 F1
Bushey Hill Rd CMBW SE5 ...25 J7
Bushey Cft OXTED RH8 ...157 H9
Busheyfields Rd HB CT6 ...155 G3
Bushey Hill Rd CMBW SE5 ...25 J7
Bushey Lees BFN/LL DA15 * ...49 G4
Bushey Rd CROY/NA CR0 ...88 D3
Bushey Wy BECK BR3 ...88 B3
Bush House
 WOOL/PLUM SE18 * ...27 M6
Bushmeadow Rd RHAM ME8 ...103 G3
Bushmoor Crs
 WOOL/PLUM SE18 ...28 C6
Bush Rd BERM/RHTH SE16 ...25 H6
 STPH/PW TN12 ...256 H6
 STRD ME2 ...99 G2
Bush Wk DIT/AY ME20 ...140 B3
Bushwood Dr STHWK SE1 ...25 G3
Bushy Gill RRTW TN3 ...177 Q5
Bushy Gv RMAID ME17 ...261 M5
Bushy Hill Rd CANTW/ST CT2 ...173 K5
Bushy Royds KEN/WIL TN24 ...205 G3
Busty La BGR/WK TN15 ...240 F3
Butcher Cl STPH/PW TN12 ...281 M6
Butchers La BGR/WK TN15 ...95 L1
 RDV CT15 ...252 D12
 WBY/YAL ME18 ...241 G2
Butchers Yd ORP BR6 * ...108 E6
Butchery La CANT CT1 ...4 H7
The Butchery SWCH CT13 ...237 K12
Bute Rd CROY/NA CR0 ...86 B4
Butlers & Colonial Whf
 STHWK SE1 ...25 G1
Butlers Dene Rd CTHM CR3 ...130 E4
Butler's Hl FAV ME13 ...151 L2
Butlers Pl HART DA3 * ...95 M4
Butteel Cl GRAYS RM17 * ...K4
Butterfield Cl STPH/PW TN12 ...279 K4
Butterfield Cl
 BERM/RHTH SE16 * ...25 H1
Butterfield House
 WOOL/PLUM SE18 * ...27 M6
Butterfly Av DART DA1 ...52 A8
Butterfly La ELTH/MOT SE9 ...48 C4
 WARL CR6 ...130 D6
Buttermere Av DART DA1 * ...52 A7
Buttermere Cl FOLKN CT19 ...10 F2
 GILL ME7 ...84 A8
 STHWK SE1 ...25 G4
Buttermere Gdns RCANTE CT3 ...251 Q11
Buttermere Rd STMC/STPC BR5 ...73 G6
Butternut Copse ASH TN23 ...202 A6
Butterside Rd ASH TN23 ...204 B3
Butter St RDV CT15 ...271 N1
Butterworth Ter WALW SE17 * ...24 E7
Butt Field Rd ASH TN23 ...204 B3
Butt Green La RMAID ME17 ...259 M8
Butt Haw HOO/HM ME3 ...59 M8
Buttmarsh Cl
 WOOL/PLUM SE18 ...28 C4
Button Dr HOO/HM ME3 ...41 J8
Button La MAID/SHEP ME15 ...168 C7
Button Rd CDW/CHF RM16 ...34 A4
Button St SWLY BR8 ...75 J4
Butts Rd BMLY BR1 ...70 B4
The Butts RSEV TN14 ...136 A5
 SIT ME10 ...120 A5
 SWCH CT13 ...237 J12
Buttway La HOO/HM ME3 ...38 D7

Buxted Rd EDUL SE22 ...44 F1
Buxton Cl MAID/SHEP ME15 ...167 H5
Buxton Rd CDW/CHF RM16 ...34 A1
 SCUP DA14 ...49 L8
 WELL DA16 ...28 F8
Bybrook Ct KEN/WIL TN24 ...202 F7
Bybrook Fld FOLK CT20 ...223 M2
Bybrook Rd KEN/WIL TN24 ...172 E8
Bybrook Wy FOLK CT20 ...223 M1
Bychurch Pl MAID/SHEP ME15 * ...1 J7
Bycliffe Ms GVW DA11 * ...55 G5
Bycliffe Ter GVW DA11 * ...55 G5
Bycroft St PGE/AN SE20 ...69 G4
Byfield Cl BERM/RHTH SE16 ...25 M1
Bygrove CROY/NA CR0 ...106 A1
Byland Cl ABYW SE2 ...29 J3
Byllan Rd DVW CT17 ...213 J5
Byne Rd SYD SE26 ...69 K3
Byng Rd STH/RUST TN4 ...190 B2
Byng St POP/IOD E14 ...26 A2
Bynon Av BXLYHN DA7 ...49 M1
Byrneside RTON TN11 ...194 B1
Byron Av MARC CT9 ...15 H5
Byron Cl CANT CT1 ...5 L7
 PGE/AN SE20 ...69 J7
 SYD SE26 ...69 M1
Byron Crs DVE/WH CT16 ...213 J5
Byron Dr ERITH DA8 ...30 C6
Byron Gdns TIL RM18 ...35 K7
Byron Rd DART DA1 ...52 C2
 GILL ME7 ...7 J7
 MAID/BEAR ME14 ...141 K4
 SAND/SEL CR2 ...104 A4
Bysing Wood Rd FAV ME13 ...123 H8
Bythorne Ct RHAM ME8 ...103 J4
Bythorn Rd BRXN/ST SW9 ...44 A1
Bywood Av CROY/NA CR0 ...87 K2

C

Cabbage Stalk Lane
 STH/RUST TN4 ...22 A8
Cable Pl GNWCH SE10 ...26 D7
Cables Cl BELV DA17 ...30 D2
Cacket's La RSEV TN14 ...133 J3
Cactus Cl CMBW SE5 ...24 D1
Cadborough Cliff RYE TN31 ...224 E5
Cadbury Wy BERM/RHTH SE16 ...172 E8
Cade La SEV TN13 ...162 B6
Cade Rd ASH TN23 ...204 D4
 GNWCH SE10 ...26 E7
Cades Orch FAV ME13 ...148 E6
Cadet Dr STHWK SE1 ...25 G5
Cadet Pl GNWCH SE10 ...26 F4
Cadiz St WALW SE17 ...24 E7
Cadlocks Hl RSEV TN14 ...108 E4
Cadman Cl BRXN/ST SW9 ...24 C6
Cadman La CANTW/ST CT2 ...171 M2
 STRD ME2 ...18 A2
Cadogan Av RDART DA2 ...52 E5
Cadogan Gdns PGE/AN SE20 ...69 J7
Cadogan Rd WOOL/PLUM SE18 ...28 D7
Cadwallion Rd ELTH/MOT SE9 ...48 C7
Caerleon Cl SCUP DA14 ...73 M5
Caernarvon Dr
 MAID/SHEP ME15 ...167 G4
Caesar Av RASH TN23 ...204 C7
Caesar's Wy FOLKN CT19 ...219 M6
Cage Green Rd TONN TN10 ...188 F8
Cage La HDCN TN27 ...284 F8
Cagney Cl HOO/HM ME3 ...82 D7
Cahir St POP/IOD E14 ...26 B4
Cairndale Cl BMLY BR1 ...71 G4
Cairns Cl DART DA1 ...52 A5
Cairns Rd BTSEA SW11 ...44 C5
Caister New Rd CROY/NA CR0 ...86 C5
Caistor Rd TOON TN9 ...198 E4
Caithness Gdns BFN/LL DA15 ...49 G4
Calais Hl CANTW/ST CT2 ...153 L7
Calais St CMBW SE5 ...24 C7
Calcraft Ms CANT CT1 ...5 J1
Calcraft Wy GRH DA9 ...53 K3
Calcutta Rd TIL RM18 ...35 H6
Caldecote Cl RHAM ME8 ...103 J4
Caldecot Av LYDD TN29 ...330 E11
Caldecot Rd CMBW SE5 ...24 C8
Calder Rd MAID/BEAR ME14 ...140 F6
Calderwood St
 WOOL/PLUM SE18 ...28 B3
Caldew Av RHAM ME8 ...102 D4
Caldew St CMBW SE5 ...24 D6
Caldwell St BRXN/ST SW9 ...24 B6
Caldy Rd BELV DA17 ...30 C2
Caleb St STHWK SE1 ...24 D1
Caledonian Wharf Rd
 POP/IOD E14 ...26 E3
Caledon Ter CANT CT1 ...5 L7
Calehill Cl MAID/BEAR ME14 ...141 K7
Caley Rd RTWE/PEM TN2 ...197 G3
Calfstock La EYN DA4 ...92 A8
Calgary Ter DVE/WH CT16 * ...213 J6
Calidore Cl BRXS/STRHM SW2 ...44 A1
Caling Cft HART DA3 ...96 A4
Caliph Cl GVE DA12 ...56 A8
Calland St POP/IOD E14 ...26 C3
Callander Rd CAT SE6 ...46 A1
Callaways La RSIT ME9 ...118 C3
Calley Down Crs CROY/NA CR0 ...105 R6
Callis Court Rd BRDST CT10 ...178 F3
Callisto Ct MAIDW ME16 ...166 A3
Calmington Rd CMBW SE5 ...24 F5
Calmont Rd BMLY BR1 ...70 B4
Calshot Av CDW/CHF RM16 ...34 A1
Calton Av DUL SE21 ...45 G3
Calverden Rd MSTR CT12 ...16 B1
Calverley Cl BECK BR3 ...70 C3
Calverley Ct RTW TN1 ...23 H6
Calverley Pk RTW TN1 ...23 H6
Calverley Park Crs RTW TN1 ...23 H5
Calverley Park Gdns RTW TN1 ...23 H5
Calverley Rd RTW TN1 ...23 G4
Calvert Cl BELV DA17 ...30 D3
 SCUP DA14 ...73 M3
Calvert Dr BXLY DA5 ...50 B4
Calvert Rd GNWCH SE10 ...27 G4
Calvin Cl STMC/STPC BR5 ...73 J1
Calydon Rd CHARL SE7 ...27 G5
Calypso Cl PECK SE15 ...25 G6
Calypso Wy BERM/RHTH SE16 ...26 C2
Camber Rd RYE TN31 ...225 L2
 RYE TN31 ...332 E12
Cambert Wy BKHTH/KID SE3 ...47 J2
Camberwell Church St
 CMBW SE5 ...24 E7
Camberwell Glebe CMBW SE5 ...24 E7
Camberwell Gn CMBW SE5 ...24 D7
Camberwell Gv CMBW SE5 ...24 E8
Camberwell La RSEV TN14 ...254 A1
Camberwell New Rd
 CMBW SE5 ...24 C6

Camberwell Rd CMBW SE5 ...24 D5
Camberwell Station Rd
 CMBW SE5 ...24 D7
Camborne Rd CROY/NA CR0 ...87 G6
 SCUP DA14 ...49 L8
 WELL DA16 ...28 F8
Cambourne Av WGOS CT8 ...177 G5
Cambrai Ct CANT CT1 ...172 E3
Cambray Av ROCH ME1 ...100 A3
Cambria Av BFN/LL DA15 ...48 E6
Cambria Crs GVE DA12 ...79 M1
Cambrian Av STH/RUST TN4 ...196 A1
Cambrian Gv GVW DA11 ...55 H5
Cambria Rd HNHL SE24 ...44 D2
Cambridge Av WELL DA16 ...49 G2
Cambridge Barracks Rd
 WOOL/PLUM SE18 ...28 A3
Cambridge Cl BRCH CT7 ...176 D3
Cambridge Crs
 MAID/SHEP ME15 ...167 L6
Cambridge Dr LEE/GVPK SE12 ...47 H3
Cambridge Gdns
 CDW/CHF RM16 * ...35 H3
 FOLK CT20 ...11 J3
 RTWE/PEM TN2 ...23 J6
Cambridge Gn ELTH/MOT SE9 ...48 C6
Cambridge Gv PGE/AN SE20 * ...69 H7
Cambridge Rd BMLY BR1 ...71 H4
 CANT CT1 ...4 E7
 DEAL CT14 ...209 L6
 DVW CT17 ...8 D7
 FAV ME13 ...149 J3
 PGE/AN SE20 ...69 H7
 RHAM ME8 ...102 D7
 SCUP DA14 ...72 E1
 STRD ME2 ...18 A2
Cambridge Rw
 WOOL/PLUM SE18 ...28 C4
Cambridge St RTWE/PEM TN2 ...23 J6
 FOLK CT20 ...11 J5
 MARC CT9 ...15 M6
Cambridge Ter CHAT ME4 ...6 C5
Cambridge Wy CANT CT1 ...4 E7
Camdale Rd WOOL/PLUM SE18 ...29 G6
Camden Av RTWE/PEM TN2 ...197 M7
Camden Cl CDW/CHF RM16 ...34 ...
 CHST BR7 ...72 D2
 GVW DA11 ...54 D6
 WALD ME5 ...101 J3
Camden Crs DVE/WH CT16 ...8 D7
Camden Gdns THHTH CR7 ...68 C3
Camden Gv CHST BR7 ...72 C3
Camden HI RTW TN1 ...23 H6
Camden Pk RTW TN1 ...23 J6
Camden Park Rd CHST BR7 ...72 B3
Camden Rd BRDST CT10 ...179 H6
 BXLY DA5 ...50 A6
 CDW/CHF RM16 ...33 M2
 GILL ME7 ...7 H3
 RAM CT11 ...17 H5
 RTW TN1 ...23 H6
 SEV TN13 ...153 H1
Camden Sq RAM CT11 ...17 K5
Camden St MAID/BEAR ME14 ...13 G3
Camden Ter KEN/WIL TN24 ...3 G7
Camden Wy CHST BR7 ...72 B3
 THHTH CR7 ...68 C3
Camelia Cl MARC CT9 * ...177 L4
Camellia Cl RHAM ME8 ...102 E2
Camellia Ct WOOL/PLUM SE18 * ...28 A3
Camelot Cl BH/WHM TN16 ...132 B7
 WOOL/PLUM SE18 ...28 B3
Cameron Cl BXLY DA5 ...50 C6
Cameron Rd CROY/NA CR0 ...86 C3
 HAYES BR2 ...71 J7
Cameron Ter LEE/GVPK SE12 * ...47 J3
Camer Park Rd MEO DA13 ...97 J3
Camer Rd MEO DA13 ...97 K3
Camer St MEO DA13 ...97 J3
Camilla Rd BERM/RHTH SE16 ...25 H3
Camille Cl SNWD SE25 ...69 G7
Camlan Rd BMLY BR1 ...71 G1
Campbell Cl HB CT6 ...129 K6
 WOOL/PLUM SE18 ...28 B6
Campbell Rd CROY/NA CR0 ...86 C3
 DEAL CT14 ...209 L6
 GVW DA11 ...55 H6
 MAID/SHEP ME15 ...13 H7
 STH/RUST TN4 ...190 B1
Campden Rd SAND/SEL CR2 ...86 F6
Campfield Rd ELTH/MOT SE9 ...47 L7
Camp Hl RTON TN11 ...254 H10
Campion Cl GVW DA11 ...78 C1
 SAND/SEL CR2 ...86 F7
 WALD ME5 ...114 C2
Campion Crs CRBK TN17 ...298 D11
Campions Dr EDEN TN8 ...192 D2
Campleshon Rd RHAM ME8 ...102 E4
Camplin St NWCR SE14 ...25 M6
Camp Rd CTHM CR3 ...130 D7
Campshill Pl LEW SE13 ...46 D3
Campshill Rd LEW SE13 ...46 D3
Campus Wy GILL ME7 ...102 B5
Camp Wy MAID/SHEP ME15 ...167 H5
Camrose Av ERITH DA8 ...30 C5
Camrose Cl CROY/NA CR0 ...87 M4
Camrose St ABYW SE2 ...29 L5
Canada Cl RFOLK CT18 ...219 K7
Canada Farm Rd EYN DA4 ...95 J1
Canada Rd DEAL CT14 ...209 K5
 ERITH DA8 ...31 G4
Canada St BERM/RHTH SE16 ...25 K1
Canadian Av CAT SE6 ...46 A6
 GILL ME7 ...101 M1
Canal Ap DEPT SE8 ...25 M5
Canal Basin GVE DA12 ...55 J5
Canal Cv PECK SE15 ...25 H6
Canal Rd GVE DA12 ...55 J5
 HOO/HM ME3 ...57 H7
 STRD ME2 ...19 H1
Canal St CMBW SE5 ...24 D5
Canal Wk CROY/NA CR0 ...86 D5
Canberra Gdns LEE/GVPK SE12 ...119 K5
Canberra Rd ABYW SE2 ...29 L5
 CHARL SE7 ...27 G6
Canberra Sq TIL RM18 ...35 J7
Canbury Ms SYD SE26 ...45 M8
Canbury Pth STMC/STPC BR5 ...73 J1
Cancell Rd BRXN/ST SW9 ...24 C6
Canham Rd SNWD SE25 ...68 F7
Canning Cross CMBW SE5 ...24 E8
Canning Rd CROY/NA CR0 ...87 G6
Canning St MAID/BEAR ME14 * ...13 H4
Cannington Rd RAM CT11 ...17 G2
Cannonbury Rd RAM CT11 ...195 G3
Cannongate Av HYTHE TN21 ...222 D2
Cannongate Gdns
 HYTHE CT21 ...222 E2
Cannongate Rd HYTHE CT21 ...222 E2
Cannon La TON TN9 ...195 G3

Cannon Pl CHARL SE7 ...27 M4
Cannon Rd BXLYHN DA7 ...29 M7
 RAM CT11 ...17 H5
Cannon St DEAL CT14 ...209 L6
 DVE/WH CT16 ...8 D3
 LYDD TN29 ...334 D3
 NROM TN28 ...331 R4
Cannon Beck Rd
 BERM/RHTH SE16 ...25 K1
Canonbie Rd FSTH SE23 ...45 K5
Canon Cl ROCH ME1 ...100 C3
Canon Gn RCANTE CT3 * ...251 R2
Canon La WBY/YAL ME18 ...164 D7
Canon Murnane Rd
 STHWK SE1 ...25 G2
Canon Rd BMLY BR1 ...71 K4
Canons Gate Rd DVE/WH CT16 ...8 F4
Canon's Wk CROY/NA CR0 ...87 L6
Canon Woods Wy
 KEN/WIL TN24 ...203 J5
Cansiron La EDEN TN8 ...275 K12
Canterbury Av BFN/LL DA15 ...49 K1
Canterbury Cl BECK BR3 ...70 C5
 BRDST CT10 ...179 G8
 CMBW SE5 ...24 D8
 DART DA1 ...52 B5
Canterbury Crs BRXN/ST SW9 ...44 B1
 TONN TN10 ...189 G3
Canterbury Gv WNWD SE27 ...44 F8
Canterbury HI CANTW/ST CT2 ...153 L7
Canterbury La CANT CT1 ...5 G5
 RHAM ME8 ...103 K4
Canterbury Pl WALW SE17 ...24 C5
Canterbury Rd BRCH CT7 ...233 M10
 CROY/NA CR0 ...86 A3
 FAV ME13 ...149 G6
 FAV ME13 ...150 F6
 FOLKN CT19 ...11 K2
 GVE DA12 ...55 K7
 HB CT6 ...155 G2
 KEN/WIL TN24 ...203 J5
 RASHE TN25 ...264 C4
 RASHE TN25 ...266 G6
 RASHE TN25 ...289 M12
 RCANTE CT3 ...251 K1
 RCANTW CT4 ...247 R9
 RCANTW CT4 ...266 H5
 RCANTW CT4 ...270 F12
 RCANTW CT4 ...291 P6
 RDV CT15 ...293 K2
 RFOLK CT18 ...220 L5
 RFOLK CT18 ...291 M10
 RFOLK CT18 ...292 F10
 RTWE/PEM TN2 ...23 B11
 SIT ME10 ...120 C6
 WSTB CT5 ...126 E5
Canterbury Rd Birchington
 BRCH CT7 ...176 D7
Canterbury Rd East RAM CT11 ...16 B6
Canterbury Rd Margate
 MARC CT9 ...177 L4
Canterbury Rd West
 MSTR CT12 ...182 A6
Canterbury Rd Westgate
 WGOS CT8 ...177 G5
Canterbury St GILL ME7 ...7 G4
 WTHK RM20 ...32 F7
Cantley Gdns NRWD SE19 ...68 F3
Cantwell Rd WOOL/PLUM SE18 ...28 C6
Canute Rd BRCH CT7 ...176 A5
 DEAL CT14 ...207 K8
 FAV ME13 ...149 K3
Capel Av WLGTN SM6 ...204 C2
Capel Cl ASH TN23 ...204 C2
 BRDST CT10 ...179 J4
 HAYES BR2 ...89 M4
 RHAM ME8 ...102 D2
Capel Court Pk RFOLK CT18 * ...258 F1
Capel La RMAID ME17 ...258 F1
Capell Pl RDART DA2 ...52 K1
Capel Rd FAV ME13 ...149 G2
 RASHW TN4 ...268 D1
 RCANTW CT4 ...268 D1
Capel St RFOLK CT18 ...220 M7
Capri Rd CROY/NA CR0 ...87 G3
Capstan Ct GRH DA9 ...52 D2
Capstan Rd DEPT SE8 ...26 A3
Capstan Sq POP/IOD E14 ...26 E3
Capstone Rd BMLY BR1 ...71 J1
 WALD ME5 ...101 L4
Caradoc St GNWCH SE10 ...26 F5
The Caravan Site
 SOCK/AV RM15 ...32 E2
Caravel Cl CDW/CHF RM16 ...34 A2
Caravel Ms DEPT SE8 * ...26 A5
Carberry Rd NRWD SE19 ...68 F3
Cardale St POP/IOD E14 ...26 E2
Carden Rd PECK SE15 ...25 J5
Cardens Rd HOO/HM ME3 ...58 C5
Cardiff Cl WOOL/PLUM SE18 ...28 E6
Cardigan Cl HOO/HM ME3 ...60 A4
Cardigan Rd BKHTH/KID SE3 * ...24 B4
Cardinal Bourne St
 STHWK SE1 ...24 E4
Cardinal Cl CHST BR7 ...72 E2
 IOS ME12 ...195 L6
 TON TN9 ...195 L6
Cardinal Rd CDW/CHF RM16 ...33 M2
Cardinal Wy E/WMAL ME19 ...112 E2
Cardine Cl SIT ME10 ...119 M2
Cardine Ms PECK SE15 ...25 J6
Carew Rd THHTH CR7 ...68 C7
Carew St CMBW SE5 ...24 D8
Carew Wy STMC/STPC BR5 ...91 K4
Carey Cl NROM TN28 ...331 J7
Carey's Fld SEV TN13 ...135 K6
The Carfax SYD SE26 * ...45 K8
Cargreen Rd SNWD SE25 ...68 F3
Carholme Rd FSTH SE23 ...46 A6
Caring La RMAID ME17 ...168 E3
Caring Rd MAID/SHEP ME15 ...168 G1
Carisbrooke Av BXLY DA5 ...49 M6
Carisbrooke Dr MAIDW ME16 ...12 B3
Carisbrooke Gdns PECK SE15 * ...25 G6
Carisbrooke Rd HAYES BR2 ...71 K8
 STRD ME2 ...81 M1
Carleton Pl EYN DA4 ...76 D8
Carleton Rd DART DA1 ...52 A6
Carlisle La STHWK SE1 ...24 A2
Carlisle Rd DART DA1 ...52 B4
Carlsden Cl DVE/WH CT16 ...213 H6
Carlton Av BRDST CT10 ...179 K8
 GILL ME7 ...101 M1
 IOS ME12 ...64 C4
 RAM CT11 ...17 H6
Carlton Crs RTW TN1 ...23 J4
 WALD ME5 ...101 L5
Carlton Gdns
 MAID/SHEP ME15 ...167 J5
Carlton Gn SCUP DA14 * ...73 G1

Carlton Gv PECK SE15 .....25 J7
Carlton Hl HB CT6 .....128 D5
Carlton Ldg RTW TN1 * 23 J4
Carlton Pde SEV TN13 .....136 B8
Carlton Rd WGOS CT8 .....5 E7
Carlton Rd ASH TN23 .....204 D1
  CDW/CHF RM16 .....35 G1
  DEAL CT14 .....211 K3
  ERITH DA8 .....7 J4
  RTW TN1 .....23 J4
  SCUP DA14 .....73 G2
  WELL DA16 .....3 E3
  WSTB CT5 .....152 E3
Carlton Rd East WGOS CT8 .....177 G5
Carncke Gdns ELTH/MOT SE9 * 47 M5
Carnoustie CI WSTB CT5 .....127 M5
Caroland CI RASHE TN25 .....289 L12
Carolina Rd THHTH CR7 .....68 C6
Caroline CI CROY/NA CR0 .....86 F7
  STRHM/NOR SW16 .....44 A8
  WSTB CT5 .....126 C1
Caroline Gdns PECK SE15 * 25 J6
  MAIDW ME16 .....140 E6
Caroline Sq DART DA1 .....9 T9
Carolyn Dr ORP BR6 .....91 H6
Carpeaux CI CHAT ME4 * 6 E4
Carpenters CI ROCH ME1 .....6 A9
Carpenters La RCANTW TN11 .....256 C2
  STPH/PW TN12 .....281 Q2
Carpinus CI WALD ME5 .....115 J4
Carr Gv WOOL/PLUM SE18 * 27 M3
The Carriageway CANTW/ST CT2 .....4 C3
Carrick Dr SEV TN13 .....21 G7
Carrick Ms DEPT SE8 .....25 B5
Carriers PI RRTW TN3 .....198 C4
Carriers Rd CRBK TN17 .....298 C8
Carrill Wy BELV DA17 .....29 L3
Carrington Dr CROY/NA CR0 .....87 M3
  GILL ME7 .....84 A7
Carrington Rd DART DA1 .....52 A4
Carroll CI STRD ME2 .....113 H1
Carroll Gdns DIT/AY ME20 .....139 L5
Carronade PI
  WOOL/PLUM SE18 .....28 E2
Carroun Rd VX/NE SW8 .....24 A6
Carroway's Rd MARG CT9 .....15 G4
Carrsington Gdns DART DA1 .....51 L7
Carson Rd DUL SE21 .....44 E4
Carstairs Rd CAT SE6 .....46 D8
Carston CI LEE/GVPK SE12 .....47 L1
Carswell Rd CAT SE6 .....46 D5
Cartel CI PUR RM19 .....32 E3
Carter Av BGR/WK TN15 * 111 K2
Carter La LYDD TN29 .....329 L14
Carter PI WALW SE17 .....24 D4
Carter's Rd BGR/WK TN15 .....163 G8
Carters Hill La MEO DA13 .....239 J4
Carters Rd FOLK CT20 .....10 A4
Carter St WALW SE17 .....24 D5
Carter's Wd RASHW TN26 .....318 C12
Cart La GRAYS RM17 .....34 C4
Cartmel Rd BXLYHN DA7 .....30 B7
Carton CI ROCH ME1 .....100 D3
Carton Rd HOO/HM ME3 .....81 J2
Cartwright I RCANTE CT3 .....235 R11
Carver Dr RSIT ME9 .....145 L3
Carver Rd HNHL SE24 .....44 D4
Carville Av STH/RUST TN4 .....196 C4
Carvoran Wy RHAM ME8 .....102 D8
Cascade CROY/NA CR0 .....86 D2
Cascades CROY/NA CR0 .....69 H8
Casella Rd NWCR SE14 .....25 L6
Casewick Rd WNWD SE27 .....44 B2
Casino Av HNHL SE24 .....44 D3
Caslocke St FAV ME15 .....149 K2
Caspian St CMBW SE5 .....24 F6
Caspian Wy SWCM DA10 .....53 M3
Cassilda Rd ABYW SE2 .....28 A4
Cassino Sq DVE/WH CT16 .....213 M7
Cassland Rd THHTH CR7 .....68 A1
Casslee Rd CAT SE6 .....46 A5
Casstine CI SWLY BR8 .....53 G7
Casterbridge Rd
  BKHTH/KID SE3 .....47 H1
Castfield EI HOO/HM ME3 .....58 F3
Castilion Rd CAT SE6 .....46 A7
Castlands Rd CAT SE6 .....46 A7
Castle Av BRDST CT10 .....179 L4
  DVE/WH CT16 .....8 C1
  HYTHE CT21 .....222 C2
  ROCH ME1 .....100 D1
Castle Bay FOLK CT20 .....223 G2
Castlebrook CI LBTH SE11 .....24 E7
Castle CI HAYES BR2 .....70 E7
  HYTHE CT21 .....307 M11
Castlecombe Rd ELTH/MOT SE9 .....65 M1
Castle CI SYD SE26 .....69 M1
Castle Dene MAID/BEAR ME14 .....140 F4
Castledine Rd PGE/AN SE20 .....69 J4
Castle Dr BGR/WK TN15 .....136 D5
  DVE/WH CT16 .....213 G2
Castle Farm Rd RSEV TN14 .....109 L3
Castle Fld TON TN9 * 194 B1
Castlefields MEO DA13 .....79 G5
Castleford Av ELTH/MOT SE9 .....48 C6
Castle HI FOLKN CT19 .....220 B6
  HART DA3 .....95 M1
  MAID/BEAR ME14 .....142 C4
  ROCH ME1 .....19 J6
  RTON TN11 * 256 A3
Castle Hill Av CROY/NA CR0 .....105 G4
  FOLK CT20 .....11 G5
Castle Hill CI ROCH ME1 * 19 J6
Castle Hill Rd DVE/WH CT16 .....8 F3
Castle Hurst RBTBR TN32 .....323 N5
Castle La GVE DA12 .....56 C2
Castlemaine Av MAID ME7 .....83 M7
  SAND/SEL CR2 .....87 G8
Castle Mayne Av BRCH CT7 .....181 G2
Castle Md CMBW SE5 * 24 D6
Castlemere Av QBOR ME11 .....64 C5
Castle Ms DEAL CT14 .....209 J5
Castlemount Rd DVE/WH CT16 .....8 D1
  EYN DA4 .....110 A1
  FOLK CT20 .....11 G6
  GRAYS RM17 .....34 C4
  HYTHE CT21 .....222 C1
  MAIDW ME16 .....140 E5
  SIT ME10 .....120 C4

STH/RUST TN4 .....22 D5
SWCM DA10 .....54 A4
WSTB CT5 .....126 E5
Castle Rough La SIT ME10 .....229 N12
Castle Rw CANT CT1 * 4 B4
Castle Rd ASH TN23 .....2 E4
  CANT CT1 .....4 C5
  DVE/WH CT16 .....8 B2
  GRH DA9 .....53 H3
  QBOR ME11 .....64 B8
  ROCH ME1 .....113 K1
  RTW TN1 .....23 J4
  STH/RUST TN4 .....196 B5
  STRD ME2 .....82 F4
  SWCM DA10 .....54 A4
  TON TN9 .....194 F3
Castle Ter RTON TN11 * 256 A3
Castleton Av BXLYHN DA7 .....30 E7
Castleton CI CROY/NA CR0 .....87 M2
Castleton Rd ELTH/MOT SE9 .....47 L4
Castle Vw RTON TN11 * 256 A3
Castle View Rd STRD ME2 .....18 D5
Castle Wk MAID ME15 .....309 K5
  E/WMAL ME19 .....138 F2
Castlewood Dr ELTH/MOT SE9 .....28 E8
Catalina Av CDW/CHF RM16 .....34 A1
Catalpa CI LEW SE13 .....46 E4
Caterfield La LING RH7 .....191 N12
Caterham By-Pass CTHM CR3 .....130 F8
Caterham St LEW SE13 .....46 D1
Catesby St WALW SE17 .....24 E7
Catford Broadway CAT SE6 .....46 C5
Catford HI CAT SE6 .....46 C5
Catford Island CAT SE6 * 46 C5
Catford Rd CAT SE6 .....46 C6
Catharine CI CDW/CHF RM16 .....34 A1
Cathay St BERM/RHTH SE16 .....25 J1
Cathcart Dr ORP BR6 .....90 F5
Cathay Rd BERM/RHTH SE16 .....25 J1
Catherine CI MAIDW ME16 .....166 C1
Catherine Gv GNWCH SE10 .....26 C4
Catherine PI RTW TN1 .....23 G4
Catherine St ROCH ME1 .....100 E2
Catherine Wy BRDST CT10 .....179 K7
Catkin CI WALD ME5 .....115 J4
Catlin Gdns CDST RH9 .....156 D4
Catling St BERM/RHTH SE16 .....25 H4
Catlyn CI E/WMAL ME19 .....139 J4
Cator CI CROY/NA CR0 .....105 K8
Cator Crs CROY/NA CR0 .....105 K8
Cator La BECK BR3 .....70 A1
Cator Rd SYD SE26 .....69 G1
Cator St PECK SE15 .....25 G6
Catsole HI RCANTE CT3 * 252 G3
Catterick Rd WALD ME5 .....115 L3
Cattistock Rd ELTH/MOT SE9 .....71 H1
Cattle Market SWCH CT13 .....237 J12
Catt's HI STPH/PW TN12 .....279 M5
Catt's Wood Rd RCANTW CT4 .....249 N12
Cauldham CI RFOLK CT18 .....221 H4
Cauldham La RFOLK CT18 .....221 J1
Caulfield Rd PECK SE15 .....25 J8
Causeway Br SOCK/AV RM15 .....32 F2
The Causeway CANTW/ST CT2 .....4 A2
Causton Rd CRBK TN17 .....298 F8
Cave HI MAID/SHEP ME15 .....167 G4
Cave La RCANTE CT3 .....252 D7
Cavell Crs DART DA1 .....52 B2
Cavell Sq DEAL CT14 .....209 L4
Cavell Wy SIT ME10 .....119 L4
Cavenagh Rd RDV CT15 .....215 J3
Cavendish Av BFN/LL DA15 .....49 H5
  ERITH DA8 .....30 B5
  GILL ME7 .....83 M2
  SEV TN13 .....136 B8
  WELL DA16 .....49 G1
Cavendish CI TONN TN10 .....189 G6
Cavendish Dr RTWE/PEM TN2 .....23 M5
  HB CT6 .....128 A3
  ROCH ME1 .....100 A1
Cavendish Sq HART DA3 .....77 J5
Cavendish St IS N1 .....17 J5
Cavendish Wy
  MAID/SHEP ME15 .....168 B2
  WWKM BR4 .....88 C4
Caversham CI RHAM ME8 .....103 G2
Cavour Rd FAV ME13 .....149 K2
  IOS ME12 .....64 B2
Cawmore St NRWD SE19 .....68 A3
Caxton CI HART DA3 .....78 A8
  TENT TN30 .....315 L2
Caxton La OXTED RH8 .....185 M1
  RTON TN11 .....256 C6
The Caxtons CMBW SE5 * 24 C6
Caygill CI HAYES BR2 .....71 G8
Cayser Dr RMAID ME17 .....261 M3
Caysers Crt STPH/PW TN12 .....256 K9
Cazeneuve St ROCH ME1 .....19 K9
Cecil Av CDW/CHF RM16 .....34 A1
  IOS ME12 .....64 B2
  RHAM ME8 .....102 B3
  STRD ME2 .....19 G3
Cecil CI HB CT6 .....129 H5
  KEN/WIL TN24 .....2 B3
Cecilia Gv BRDST CT10 .....179 L7
Cecilia Rd RAM CT11 .....17 K2
Cecil Pk HB CT6 .....129 H5
Cecil Rd DEAL CT14 .....211 L2
  GVW DA11 .....55 G6
  ROCH ME1 .....100 D2
Cecil Sq MARG CT9 .....14 F2
Cecil St MARG CT9 .....14 F2
Cecil Wy HAYES BR2 .....89 H4
Cedar Av BFN/LL DA15 .....49 H5
  GVE DA12 .....56 C2
Cedar CI ASH TN23 .....202 B8
  BRDST CT10 .....179 J6
  DIT/AY ME20 .....139 L5
  DUL SE21 .....44 E4
  HAYES BR2 .....89 M6
  MARG CT9 .....15 G4
  MEO DA13 .....97 H2
  SIT ME10 .....120 C4
  SWLY BR8 .....74 D6
  WARL CR6 .....130 C4
Cedar Copse BMLY BR1 .....71 K2
Cedar Crs CHARL SE7 * 27 H7
  ELTH/MOT SE9 * 47 M4
  HAYES BR2 .....89 M6
  LYDD TN29 .....331 N2
  TONN TN10 .....188 F2
Cedar Dr EDEN TN8 .....192 C5
  EYN DA4 .....76 C6
  MAIDW ME16 .....166 A1
Cedar Gdns RSIT ME9 * 117 M5
Cedar Gv BXLY DA5 .....49 J5
  GILL ME7 .....102 A2
Cedarhurst BMLY BR1 * 70 F4
Cedarhurst Dr ELTH/MOT SE9 .....47 J4
Cedar La HDCN TN27 .....301 J7
Cedar Mt ELTH/MOT SE9 * 47 K4
Cedar Rdg RTWE/PEM TN2 .....197 G8
Cedar Rd BMLY BR1 .....71 K6
  CANTW/ST CT2 .....173 F3

CDW/CHF RM16 .....35 H2
CROY/NA CR0 .....86 F5
DART DA1 .....51 H7
ERITH DA8 .....31 H7
Cedars CI LEW SE13 .....46 E1
Cedars Rd BECK BR3 .....69 M6
The Cedars SIT ME10 .....120 C5
  STPH/PW TN12 .....279 M2
Cedar Ter DVE/WH CT16 * 213 K4
Cedar Tree Gv WNWD SE27 .....68 C2
Cedarview DART DA1 * 171 K4
  STRHM/NOR SW16 .....68 A3
Cedric Rd ELTH/MOT SE9 .....48 D8
Ceil Vls DEAL CT14 * 206 C5
Celandine CI CDW/CHF RM16 .....33 M1
Celestial Gdns LEW SE13 .....46 E1
Celestine CI WALD ME5 .....115 H4
Celia Av BGR/WK TN15 * 111 K1
Celt CI SIT ME10 .....120 A1
Celtic Av HAYES BR2 .....70 F7
Celtic Rd DEAL CT14 .....209 H7
Cement Block Cottages
  STRHM/NOR SW16 * 44 A3
Cemetery La CHARL SE7 .....27 M5
  KEN/WIL TN24 .....202 F7
  RTON TN11 .....256 D5
Cemetery Rd ABYW SE2 .....28 A5
  SNOD ME6 .....113 G4
Centaur St STHWK SE1 .....24 A1
Centenary Gdns SWCH CT13 .....253 G4
Centenary Walk-Canterbury
  RCANTW 170 C1
Centenary Walk-Maidstone
  DIT/AY ME20 .....114 B7
  MAID/BEAR ME14 .....12 E1
Centenary Walk-Rochester
  ROCH ME1 .....100 B3
Central Av GVE DA12 .....55 J7
  HB CT6 .....128 A6
  SIT ME10 .....120 A6
  SOCK/AV RM15 .....32 D1
  TIL RM18 .....35 H7
  WELL DA16 .....29 H3
  WTHK RM20 .....33 J5
Central HI NRWD SE19 .....68 D2
Central Ldg PECK SE15 * 239 V7
Central Pde CROY/NA CR0 .....105 H4
  HB CT6 .....128 C4
  PGE/AN SE20 * 69 L4
  SCUP DA14 * 49 H7
Central Park Gdns ROCH ME1 .....69 G4
Central Rd DART DA1 .....51 M3
  DIT/AY ME20 .....139 J1
  RAM CT11 .....17 L1
  STRD ME2 .....18 B2
Central Ter BECK BR3 * 69 J5
  HOO/HM ME3 .....59 G7
Central Wy OXTED RH8 .....157 J5
Centre Common Rd CHST BR7 .....72 D4
Centre Ct STRD ME2 * 82 F6
Centre St BETH E2 .....25 L1
  HART DA3 .....95 M6
The Centre MARG CT9 .....14 F2
Centurion Wy ERITH DA18 .....30 A2
Centurion Sq
  WOOL/PLUM SE18 * 27 M6
Centurion Wk ASH TN23 .....204 E7
Centurion Wy PUR RM19 .....32 A3
Century Rd RAM CT11 .....17 M2
Ceres Rd WOOL/PLUM SE18 .....29 H3
Cerise Rd PECK SE15 .....25 H7
Cerne Rd GVE DA12 .....56 A8
Cervia Wy GVE DA12 .....56 A8
Chada Av GILL ME7 .....101 M2
Chadd Dr BMLY BR1 .....71 J4
Chadfield Rd TIL RM18 .....35 H6
Chadwell By-Pass GRAYS RM17 .....35 G4
Chadwell HI CDW/CHF RM16 .....35 J4
Chadwell Rd GRAYS RM17 .....34 F7
Chadwick CI GVW DA11 .....54 F7
Chadwick Rd PECK SE15 .....25 G6
Chaffe's La RSIT ME9 * 103 M3
Chaffes Ter RSIT ME9 * 103 M3
Chafford Av CROY/NA CR0 .....87 L1
Chaffinch CI ORP BR6 .....91 H3
Chaffinch Dr ASH TN23 .....204 F5
Chaffinch Rd BECK BR3 .....69 M5
Chaffinch Wy STPH/PW TN12 .....279 J4
Chafford La RRTW TN3 .....276 H12
The Chain SWCH CT13 .....237 H12
Chalcombe Rd ABYW SE2 .....29 L2
Chalcroft Rd FOLK CT20 .....223 M4
  LEW SE13 .....46 F3
Chalet CI RDART DA2 .....51 J6
Chalfont Dr HB CT6 .....129 H5
  RHAM ME8 .....102 D3
Chalfont Rd SNWD SE25 .....69 G5
Chalford Rd DUL SE21 .....68 E1
Chalgrove Ms RSIT ME9 * 99 H8
Chalice Wy GRH DA9 .....52 F2
Chalk Av TENT TN30 .....301 N11
Chalk CI GRAYS RM17 * 34 C5
Chalkenden Av RHAM ME8 .....102 B3
Chalkenden CI PGE/AN SE20 .....69 J4
Chalket La RMAID ME17 .....245 G8
Chalk HI MEO DA13 * 97 H1
Chalk Hill Rd DEAL CT14 .....211 K4
Chalk La CRBK TN17 .....298 C6
Chalk Pit Av STMC/STPC BR5 .....73 K7
Chalk Pit HI CHAT ME4 .....6 D6
  RCANTE CT3 .....252 H4
Chalkpit HI RCANTW CT4 .....175 L6
Chalkpit La OXTED RH8 .....157 H5
Chalkpit Wd OXTED RH8 .....157 H5
Chalk Rd GVE DA12 .....56 B6
  HOO/HM ME3 .....81 K7
  QBOR ME11 * 64 B8
Chalksole Green La RDV CT15 .....293 N6
Chalkstone CI WELL DA16 .....29 H7
Chalkways RSEV TN14 .....136 D2
Chalkwell Rd SIT ME10 .....119 L5
Chalky Bank GVW DA11 .....54 D7
Chalky Bank Rd RHAM ME8 .....103 J2
Chalky Rd RSIT ME9 .....118 C7
Challenge CI GVE DA12 .....56 A8
Challenger CI SIT ME10 .....119 M2
Challice Wy BRXS/STRHM SW2 .....44 A6
Challin St PGE/AN SE20 .....69 K6
Challock CI BH/WHM TN16 .....132 C4
Challock Rd CAT SE6 .....46 C4
Challock Wk
  MAID/BEAR ME14 * 141 K7
Chalmers Rd WALW SE17 * 24 F7
Chalmers Wy RHAM ME8 .....102 B1
Chalsey Rd BROCKY SE4 .....46 A2
Chamberlain Av MAIDW ME16 .....166 C3

Chamberlain CI
  WOOL/PLUM SE18 .....28 E2
Chamberlain Ct RHAM ME8 * 102 C4
Chamberlain Crs WWKM BR4 .....88 C4
Chamberlain Dr HB CT6 .....128 C5
Chamberlain Rd CHAT ME4 .....7 G9
  DVW CT17 .....217 H1
Chambers CI GRH DA9 .....53 H3
Chambers St BERM/RHTH SE16 .....25 H1
Champion Crs SYD SE26 .....69 H1
Champion Gv CMBW SE5 .....44 E1
Champion HI CMBW SE5 .....44 E1
Champion Pk CMBW SE5 .....44 E1
Champion Rd SYD SE26 .....69 H1
Champness CI WNWD SE27 .....68 E1
Chance CI CDW/CHF RM16 .....34 A2
Chancel CI BGR/WK TN15 .....111 K1
Chancellor Gv DUL SE21 .....44 D5
Chancellor Wy SEV TN13 .....20 F1
Chancelot Rd ABYW SE2 .....29 J3
Chance Meadow RDV CT15 .....214 A3
Chancery La BECK BR3 .....70 C6
  MAID/SHEP ME15 .....13 J5
Chancery Rd HOO/HM ME3 .....38 C8
Chandlers CI LEE/GVPK SE12 * 47 J7
Chandlers Dr ERITH DA8 .....30 B5
Chandler's HI MEO DA13 .....97 K8
Chandler's Ms POP/IOD E14 .....26 B1
Chandler Wy PECK SE15 .....25 G6
Chandos Ct RTW TN1 .....23 J2
Chandos Sq BRDST CT10 .....183 L1
Chandos Ter RAM CT11 * 17 J4
Channel CI FOLKN CT19 .....221 G6
Channel Lea DEAL CT14 .....209 K8
Channel View Ct RAM CT11 * 17 M5
Channel View Rd DVW CT17 .....8 B8
Channon Rd LYDD TN29 .....335 M2
Chantiers HI STPH/PW TN12 .....279 K5
Chanters Md EDEN TN8 .....275 M8
Chantrey CI SCUP DA14 .....75 K2
Chantry Av HART DA3 .....89 L1
Chantry PI STPH/PW TN12 .....280 H4
Chantry Rd STPH/PW TN12 .....280 H4
Chapel CI DART DA1 .....69 M1
  E/WMAL ME19 .....112 A8
  WTHK RM20 .....33 J5
Chapel Ct STHWK SE1 .....24 E1
  WOOL/PLUM SE18 * 29 C5
Chapel Farm Rd
  ELTH/MOT SE9 .....48 A8
Chapel Fld RYE TN31 .....324 H6
Chapelfield WADH TN5 .....311 K6
Chapel Hill CI MARG CT9 .....178 C6
  MARG CT9 .....178 D6
  RDV CT15 .....272 D6
Chapel Hill CI MARG CT9 .....178 C6
Chapel House St POP/IOD E14 .....26 C2
Chapel La CANTW/ST CT2 .....153 H6
  CANTW/ST CT2 .....172 G2
  CRBK TN17 .....313 N5
  CRBK TN17 .....210 E1
  DEAL CT14 .....210 E1
  GILL ME7 .....116 B1
  HDCN TN27 .....262 E11
  RAM CT11 .....16 E5
  RASHW TN26 .....260 F6
  RMAID ME17 .....260 F6
  SNOD ME6 .....113 H5
  WARL CR6 .....130 C4
  WNWD SE27 * 68 A3
Chapel Pk SIT ME10 * 120 D3
  RAM CT11 .....17 H5
  STH/RUST TN4 .....22 D7
Chapel Place La RAM CT11 * 17 H5
Chapel Rd BXLYHN DA7 .....30 D1
  DEAL CT14 .....209 L6
  DVE/WH CT16 .....213 H1
  HOO/HM ME3 .....43 J8
  LYDD TN29 .....320 H10
  OXTED RH8 .....158 B3
  RAM CT11 .....16 E5
  RASHW TN26 .....260 F6
  RMAID ME17 .....260 F6
  SNOD ME6 .....113 H5
  WARL CR6 .....130 C4
  WNWD SE27 .....68 A3
Chapel Rw BGR/WK TN15 .....240 B3
  HOO/HM ME3 .....61 K1
Chapel St DEAL CT14 .....209 L6
  E/WMAL ME19 .....112 A8
  FAV ME13 .....149 L3
  HYTHE CT21 .....222 C1
  IOS ME12 .....64 B2
The Chapel MAIDW ME16 * 166 C2
Chapel Vw SAND/SEL CR2 .....104 B2
Chapel Wood Rd HART DA3 .....95 M5
Chaplin CI HOO/HM ME3 .....45 H6
  STHWK SE1 * 24 B1
Chapman Av
  MAID/SHEP ME15 .....167 M5
  CROY/NA CR0 .....86 B4
Chapmans CI RASHE TN25 .....265 P3
Chapman's HI BGR/WK TN15 .....239 K1
  RCANTE CT3 .....232 A12
Chapman's La E/WMAL ME19 .....139 G6
  SWLY BR8 .....74 D6
Chapman Wy E/WMAL ME19 .....139 G5
  RTWE/PEM TN2 .....196 F5
Chappell Wy SIT ME10 .....119 L2
Chapter Rd STRD ME2 .....18 C3
  WALW SE17 .....24 C4
Charing Crs WGOS CT8 .....5 G6
Charing Heath Rd HDCN TN27 .....263 J3
Charing HI HDCN TN27 .....264 D1
Charing Rd RHAM ME8 .....102 D2
Chariot Wy STRD ME2 .....99 H2
Charlbury CI MAIDW ME16 .....166 D1
Charldane Rd ELTH/MOT SE9 .....65 J4
Charlecote Gv SYD SE26 .....69 J1
Charles CI SCUP DA14 .....73 J1
  SNOD ME6 * 113 H5
Charles Drayson Ct FAV ME13 * 149 M2

Charles Dr STRD ME2 .....99 J1
Charlesfield ELTH/MOT SE9 .....47 J5
Charlesford Av RMAID ME17 .....261 M2
Charles Grinling Wk
  WOOL/PLUM SE18 .....28 D3
Charles Haller St
  BRXS/STRHM SW2 * 44 B5
Charles Rd DEAL CT14 .....209 J5
  RAM CT11 .....17 J2
  RSEV TN14 .....109 G4
Charles St CHAT ME4 .....6 D4
  CROY/NA CR0 .....86 C6
  GRAYS RM17 .....34 C5
  GRH DA9 .....53 G3
  HB CT6 .....129 G4
  IOS ME12 .....64 B2
  MAIDW ME16 .....4 B6
  STH/RUST TN4 .....196 B5
  STRD ME2 .....18 F4
Charleston St WALW SE17 .....24 D4
Charlesworth Dr BRCH CT7 .....176 G6
Charleville Circ SYD SE26 .....69 G1
Charlieville Rd ERITH DA8 .....30 D6
Charlock CI MAIDW ME16 .....140 E5
Charlotte CI BXLYHS DA6 * 49 M4
  WALD ME5 .....101 J7
Charlotte Dr RHAM ME8 .....102 D4
Charlotte Ms CANT CT1 * 4 B6
Charlotte Pde FSTH SE23 .....45 M1
Charlotte Pk BMLY BR1 * 71 M7
  WTHK RM20 .....33 J5
Charlotte PI MARG CT9 .....15 G5
Charlotte Sq MARG CT9 * 15 L4
Charlotte St FOLK CT20 .....11 L4
  SIT ME10 .....119 M4
Charlton Ar DVE/WH CT16 * 8 D3
Charlton Av DVE/WH CT16 * 8 C1
Charlton Centre High St
  DVE/WH CT16 * 8 D3
Charlton Church La CHARL SE7 .....27 H5
Charlton CI KEN/WIL TN24 .....3 H9
  MSTR CT12 .....182 C2
Charlton Dene CHARL SE7 .....27 L4
Charlton Dr BH/WHM TN16 .....132 C3
Charlton Gn DVE/WH CT16 * 8 D3
Charlton La CHARL SE7 .....27 L4
  MAID/SHEP ME15 .....165 H6
  RMAID ME17 .....261 M5
Charlton Park La CHARL SE7 .....27 L6
Charlton Park Rd CHARL SE7 .....27 L5
Charlton Rd BKHTH/KID SE3 .....27 J5
The Charltons FAV ME13 .....151 G2
Charlton St MAIDW ME20 .....166 E5
Charlton's Wy STH/RUST TN4 .....200 F4
Charlwood CROY/NA CR0 .....104 C3
Charminster ASH TN23 .....204 B5
Charminster Rd ELTH/MOT SE9 .....1 H1
Charmouth Rd MAID DA16 .....29 K7
The Charne ORP BR6 .....108 A4
The Charne SEV TN14 .....135 M3
Charnock WSTB CT5 .....127 L4
Charnwood SWLY BR8 .....74 A7
Charnwood Gdns POP/IOD E14 .....26 A5
Charnwood Rd HB CT6 .....129 J8
  SNWD SE25 .....68 F6
Charolais CI CANTW/ST CT2 .....172 E2
Charrington Rd CROY/NA CR0 .....86 C5
Charsley Rd CAT SE6 .....46 C7
Chart CI CROY/NA CR0 .....87 K2
  FAV ME13 .....149 J2
  HAYES BR2 .....70 F5
Charter Dr BXLY DA5 .....49 H5
Charterhouse Dr SEV TN13 .....20 F2
Charterhouse Rd ORP BR6 .....91 H4
Charters CI NRWD SE19 .....68 C1
Charter St CHAT ME4 .....6 A9
  GILL ME7 .....83 M7
Chartham Downs Rd
  RCANTW 249 M10
Chartham Gv WNWD SE27 .....44 B8
Chartham Rd SNWD SE25 .....69 J7
Chartham Ter RAM CT11 * 17 J7
Chart Hill Rd RMAID ME17 .....260 B2
Chart La BH/WHM TN16 .....160 H3
Charton CI BXLY DA5 .....30 A5
Chart PI RHAM ME8 .....116 D2
Chart Rd ASH TN23 .....204 A5
  FOLKN CT19 .....10 A2
  RMAID ME17 .....260 D6
Chart Vw BGR/WK TN15 .....136 D5
Chartway SEV TN13 .....21 J5
Chartway St RMAID ME17 .....260 H4
Chartwell Av WSTB CT5 .....129 G5
Chartwell CI CHST BR7 .....48 C7
  CROY/NA CR0 .....86 E4
  STRD ME2 .....82 C2
Chartwell Ct CHAT ME4 * 6 E4
Chartwell Dr MAIDW ME16 * 166 C1
  ORP BR6 .....108 A3
Chartwell Gv SIT ME10 .....119 K6
Chartwell Wy PGE/AN SE20 .....69 J5
Charwood STRHM/NOR SW16 * 68 C3
Chasemore Gdns CROY/NA CR0 .....86 A4
Chase Sq GVE DA12 * 55 G4
The Chase BGR/WK TN15 .....136 D2
  BMLY BR1 .....71 J7
  BXLYHN DA7 .....50 C1
  ORP BR6 .....107 M5
  RAM CT11 * 102 B3
  RHAM ME8 .....102 B3
  ROCH ME1 .....100 E4
  STRHM/NOR SW16 .....68 B2
  TONN TN10 .....188 D4
  WTHK RM20 .....33 J5
Chastilian Rd DART DA1 .....51 J5
Chater CI DEAL CT14 .....209 K5
Chatfield Rd CROY/NA CR0 .....86 B6
Chatham Av HAYES BR2 .....89 H4
Chatham Gv CHAT ME4 .....101 G4
Chatham HI CHAT ME4 .....7 J4
Chatham Hill Rd RSEV TN14 .....136 B8
Chatham PI RAM CT11 * 17 J2
Chatham Rd DIT/AY ME20 .....114 C3
Chatham St WALW SE17 .....24 E6
  WOOL/PLUM SE18 .....28 C2
Chatsworth Av BFN/LL DA15 .....49 H6
  BMLY BR1 .....71 J2
Chatsworth Dr WWKM BR4 .....89 G5
Chatsworth Dr WSTB ME10 .....119 J4
  STRD ME2 .....82 C2
Chatsworth Rd CROY/NA CR0 .....86 C2
  GILL ME7 .....83 L1
  MAID ME7 .....7 G2
Chatsworth Wy WNWD SE27 .....44 C8
Chattenden
  MAID/BEAR ME14 .....141 J6
Chattenden La HOO/HM ME3 .....83 J1
Chatterton Rd HAYES BR2 .....89 L1
Chaucer Av WSTB CT5 .....127 L4
Chaucer CI CANT CT1 .....5 M7
  FAV ME13 .....82 H2
  TIL RM18 .....35 J6
Chaucer Crs DVE/WH CT16 .....213 L6
Chaucer Dr STHWK SE1 * 25 G4
Chaucer Gdns TON TN9 .....194 D2

Chaucer Gn CROY/NA CR0 ....87 J3
Chaucer Ms CANTW/ST CT2 ..171 G4
Chaucer Pk DART DA1 ....52 A5
Chaucer Rd BFN/LL DA15 ....49 K6
  BRDST CT10 ...183 K2
  CANT CT1 .....5 L3
  GILL ME7 .....L3
  GVW DA11 .....54 E8
  HNHL SE24 ....44 C3
  RDV CT15 .....272 C4
  SIT ME10 .....119 L6
  WELL DA16 ....29 G4
Chaucer Wy DART DA1 ....52 B2
  DIT/AY ME20 .139 H1
Chaundrye CI ELTH/MOT SE9 .48 A1
Chave Rd DART DA1 ....51 M8
Cheam St PECK SE15 * 45 J1
Cheddar CI KEN/WIL TN24 ...A1
Cheeselands HDCN TN27 .....300 E5
Cheesmans CI MSTR CT12 ....180 F8
Chegwell Dr WALD ME5 ......115 J1
Chegworth Gdns SIT ME10 ...119 M8
Chegworth Rd RMAID ME17 ...242 A10
Cheldoc Ri CHAT ME4 ....83 K3
Chelford Rd BMLY BR1 ......70 C2
Chellows La LING RH7 ......191 G3
Chelmar Rd CHAT ME4 ....7 C6
Chelmer Rd CDW/CHF RM16 ...35 M7
Chelmsford Rd STRD ME2 ....81 L7
Chelsea Rd CANT CT1 ....172 D5
Chelsfield Gdns SYD SE26 ..45 K4
Chelsfield HI ORP BR6 .....108 B3
Chelsfield La RSEV TN14 ...109 G5
  STMC/STPC BR5 ....91 L3
Chelsham Court Rd WARL CR6 131 J4
Chelsworth Dr
  WOOL/PLUM SE18 ...28 E5
Cheltenham CI CVE DA12 ....79 K2
  MAID/SHEP ME15 * ...168 A4
Cheltenham Rd ORP BR6 .....91 H6
  PECK SE15 ....45 K2
Cheney CI RHAM ME8 ....102 B4
Cheney HI RSIT ME9 ....146 B4
Cheney Rd FAV ME13 ....150 A2
Chenies CI RTWE/PEM TN2 ...201 H5
  RDART DA2 ....74 F11
Chennell Park Rd TENT TN30 301 K12
Chepstow CI CROY/NA CR0 ...86 F6
Chepstow Rd CROY/NA CR0 ...86 F6
Chequer La RCANTE CT3 .....236 A11
Chequers CI MEO DA13 ......78 F6
  STMC/STPC BR5 ....73 G8
  WALD ME5 ....115 H4
Chequers Ct STRD ME2 ......82 B4
Chequers HI RCANTW CT4 ....268 F5
Chequers Orch RCANTW CT4 * 268 G3
Chequers Pk RASHE TN25 ....266 F12
Chequers Rd IOS ME12 ......65 M7
Cherbourg Crs WALD ME5 ....101 K4
Cheriton Av HAYES BR2 .....89 G1
  MSTR CT12 ....16 D2
Cheriton Court Rd FOLK CT20 219 K4
Cheriton Dr WOOL/PLUM SE18 28 B5
Cheriton Gdns FOLK CT20 ...11 H5
Cheriton High St RFOLK CT18 219 J7
Cheriton Int FOLKN CT19 ...219 K5
Cheriton PI DEAL CT14 * ...209 L6
  FOLK CT20 ....11 H5
Cheriton Rd DEAL CT14 .....209 L5
  FOLK CT20 ....11 H5
  FOLKN CT19 ....10 A3
  RHAM ME8 ....102 E6
Cheriton Wy MAIDW ME16 ....140 D6
The Cherries MAIDW ME16 ...166 A3
Cherry Amber CI RHAM ME8 ..103 G5
Cherry Av CANTW/ST CT2 ....171 G3
  SWLY BR8 ....74 E7
Cherrybrook Rd CANTW/ST CT2 74 B5
Cherry CI BRXS/STRHM SW2 * 44 B5
  SIT ME10 ....119 L3
Cherrycot Ri ORP BR6 ......90 D7
Cherrydown Av SCUP DA14 ...49 L1
Cherry Dr CANTW/ST CT2 ....4 A1
Cherry Flds SIT ME10 ......119 H4
Cherry Garden Crs
  RASHE TN25 ....266 G11
Cherry Garden La FOLKN CT19 10 B1
  RASHE TN25 ....266 G11
  RCANTE CT3 ....236 B12
Cherrygarden La RDV CT15 ..252 D9
Cherry Garden Rd
  CANTW/ST CT2 ....4 A1
Cherry Gdns BRDST CT10 ....182 F2
  HB CT6 ....128 F6
  NROM TN28 ....331 L7
  RCANTW CT4 ....291 Q4
  RSIT ME9 ....121 K1
Cherry Garden St
  BERM/RHTH SE16 ...25 J1
Cherry Glebe RASHE TN25 ...305 P2
Cherry Gv RDV CT15 ....272 D3
  TONN TN10 ....189 H8
Cherry Hill Ct RSIT ME9 * .118 D3
Cherry Hill Gdns CROY/NA CR0 86 E6
Cherry Orch CHARL SE7 .....27 K5
  DIT/AY ME20 ......139 K5
  RASHW TN26 ....302 H10
  RCANTE CT3 ....234 B12
  RCANTW CT4 ....247 P7
  TENT TN30 ....315 M3
  WSTB CT5 ....127 K5
Cherry Orchard CI
  STMC/STPC BR5 ....91 K1
Cherry Orchard Gdns
  CROY/NA CR0 ......86 E4
Cherry Orchard La
  RASHE TN25 ....305 Q9
Cherry Orchard Rd
  CROY/NA CR0 ......86 E5
  HAYES BR2 ....89 M5
The Cherry Orch RTON TN11 .256 F4
Cherry Orchard Wy
  MAIDW ME16 ....166 C2
Cherry Rd HOO/HM ME3 * 83 M2
Cherry Tree Av DVE/WH CT16 * A1
Cherry Tree CI RSIT ME9 ...146 A2
Cherry Tree Ct CHARL SE7 * 27 K5
Cherry Tree Gdns DVE/WH CT16 *
Cherry Tree Gn SAND/SEL CR2 104 A8
Cherry Tree Gv BGR/WK TN15 * 111 K4
Cherry Tree Rd RDART DA2 ..51 K6
  HDCN TN27 ....263 P6
  RHAM ME8 ....103 G5
  RTWE/PEM TN2 .....200 F4
Cherry Trees HART DA3 .....96 A2
Cherry Tree Ter STHWK SE1 * 25
Cherry Tree Wk BECK BR3 ...70
  WWKM BR4
Cherry Wk HOO/HM RM16 .....H2
  HAYES BR2 89
Cherry Waye RDV CT15 ......272 F6
Cherrywood Dr GVW DA11 ....78 F1
Chertsey Crs CROY/NA CR0 ..105 H4

Cherville La RCANTE CT3 ...251 M2
Chervilles MAIDW ME16 .....166 B3
Cherwell CI TONN TN10 .....194 E1
Cheseman St SYD SE26 ......45 J8
Chesfield CI RTON TN11 * ..256 C5
Chesham Av HAYES BR2 ......90 C5
Chesham Crs PGE/AN SE20 ...69 K5
Chesham Dr RHAM ME8 ....102 F7
Chesham Rd PGE/AN SE20 ....69 K6
  WARL CR6 ....130 F2
Cheshire Rd MAID/SHEP ME15 167 M3
Cheshunt CI RHAM ME8 ......97 H2
Cheshunt Rd BELV DA17 .....30 B4
Chesney Crs CROY/NA CR0 ...105 H2
Chessenden La HDCN TN27 ...284 E8
Chessington Av BXLYHN DA7 .29 M6
Chessington Wy WWKM BR4 ...88 C5
Chester Av RASHW TN26 .....285 N12
  RTWE/PEM TN2 .....23 M7
Chester CI CDW/CHF RM16 ...33 M8
  STRD ME2 ....82 B2
Chesterfield CI STMC/STPC BR5 73 L8
Chesterfield Dr DART DA1 ..51 J3
Chester Rd BFN/LL DA15 ....48 F3
  GILL ME7 ....7 M9
  WGOS CT8 ....177 J3
Chesterfield Gdns
  GNWCH SE10 * 26 E6
Chesterfield Gv EDUL SE22 .45 G6
Chesterfield Wy PECK SE15 .25 K6
Chester Rd BFN/LL DA15 ....48 F3
  GILL ME7 ....7 M9
  WGOS CT8 ....177 J3
Chesterton Rd DIT/AY ME20 139 G1
  HOO/HM ME3 ....38 C8
Chester Wy LBTH SE11 ......B3
Chestfield CI RHAM ME8 ....102 F5
Chestfield Rd WSTB CT5 ....127 K6
Chestnut Av BH/WHM TN16 ..132 C6
  CANTW/ST CT2 .....153 H7
  CDW/CHF RM16 .....34 C1
  GRH DA9 ....53 G3
  STH/RUST TN4 .....196 E5
  STPH/PW TN12 .....281 R5
  WALD ME5 ....114 F2
  WWKM BR4 ....88 D4
Chestnut CI ASH TN23 .....202 B8
  BFN/LL DA15 ......49 H1
  CAT SE6 ....70 D11
  DVE/WH CT16 ......213 H1
  E/WMAL ME19 ......164 B3
  EDEN TN8 ....192 C5
  EGRIN RH19 ....274 A12
  GVW DA11 ....55 G4
  HYTHE CT21 ....321 R1
  NWCR SE14 ....26 A7
  ORP BR6 ....91 H8
  RMAID ME17 ....248 G8
  STH/RUST TN4 .....196 E5
  STRHM/NOR SW16 ...68 B3
  TENT TN30 ....301 P12
Chestnut Copse OXTED RH8 .185 J3
Chestnut Ct FAV ME13 .....151 G4
  RTWE/PEM TN2 .....201 H5
Chestnut Dr BRDST CT10 ...183 G1
  BXLYHN DA7 ....49 L1
  CANTW/ST CT2 .....173 J5
  DEAL CT14 ....206 B5
  HB CT6 ....128 E2
  RMAID ME17 ....258 H2
  RMAID ME17 ....261 L3
Chestnut Gv RDART DA2 ....74 B2
  SAND/SEL CR2 .....104 A2
Chestnut La ASH TN23 .....204 C2
  MEO DA13 ....239 N5
  SEV TN13 ....21 G4
  STPH/PW TN12 .....278 F5
Chestnut PI SYD SE26 .....69 G5
Chestnut Rd WOOL/PLUM SE18 28 F4
Chestnut Rd DART DA1 .....51 L6
  STRD ME2 ....82 A6
  WNWD SE27 ....44 C8
Chestnuts RASHE TN25 .....289 L12
The Chestnuts BECK BR3 * .69 L7
  E/WMAL ME19 ......239 P10
  HAWK TN18 ....312 C9
  RASHE TN25 * 289 L12
Chestnut St RSIT ME9 .....118 F5
Chestnut Ter HYTHE CT21 * 222 B4
Chestnut Wk BGR/WK TN15 * 112
  TON TN9 ....194 C5
Chestnut Wood La RSIT ME9 118 F5
Cheston Av CROY/NA CR0 ...87 M4
Cheswick CI DART DA1 .....51 G2
Chesworth CI ERITH DA8 ...30 C7
Chetney CI STRD ME2 ......81 K6
Chetney Vw RSIT ME9 ......227 L9
Chettle CI STHWK SE1 .....24 A5
Chevalier Rd DVE/WH CT16 .217 H2
Cheval St POP/IOD E14 ....26 B2
Cheveney Wk HAYES BR2 ....71 H7
Chevening CI WALD ME5 ....101 H4
Chevening La RSEV TN14 ...134 D2
Chevening Rd GNWCH SE10 ..27 G4
  NRWD SE19 ....68 A4
  RSEV TN14 ....134 L9
The Chevenings SCUP DA14 .49 J8
Cheviot CI BXLYHN DA7 ....50 F8
  DART DA1 ....51 L8
  TON TN9 ....194 F1
Cheviot Gdns
  MAID/SHEP ME15 ...168 B4
Cheviot Rd WNWD SE27 .....68 G2
Cheviot Wy KEN/WIL TN24 ..2 C1
Cheyne CI HAYES BR2 ......89 M6
  SIT ME10 ....119 L3
Cheyne Rd IOS ME12 ......229 N2
Cheyne Wk CROY/NA CR0 ....87 H5
  MEO DA13 ....97 H5
Chicago Av GILL ME7 .....83 M8
Chichele Gdns CROY/NA CR0 86 F7
Chichele Rd OXTED RH8 ....157 K6
Chicheley St STHWK SE1 ...24 A1
Chichester CI ASH TN23 ..2 A7
  BKHTH/KID SE3 ....27 J3
  CDW/CHF RM16 .....33 L5
  RHAM ME8 ....103 H5
Chichester Dr SEV TN13 ..20 D7
Chichester Ri GVE DA12 ..79 L1
Chichester Rd CROY/NA CR0 86 F6
  FOLK CT20 ....223 M1
  GRH DA9 ....53 G3
  NROM TN28 ....331 L6
  TON TN9 ....194 E5
Chichester Wy POP/IOD E14 26 E3
Chickenden La STPH/PW TN12 282
Chickfield Gdns WALD ME5 .101 K3
Chicks La CRBK TN17 ......296 G11
Chiddingfold La RSIT ME9 *
Chiddingstone Av BXLYHN DA7 30 A5
Chiddingstone CI
  MAID/SHEP ME15 ...168 A7
Chidley Cross Rd
  STPH/PW TN12 .....256 H7
Chieftain CI GILL ME7 ....102 C2
Chieftain Dr PUR RM19 ....32 B2
Chievley Dr RTWE/PEM TN2 .201 K4

Chieveley Pde BXLYHN DA7 * 50 C1
Chieveley Rd BXLYHN DA7 ..50 C1
Chiffinch Gdns GVW DA11 ..54 F8
Childeric Rd NWCR SE14 ...25 M6
Childers St DEPT SE8 .....25 M5
Childsbridge La BGR/WK TN15 136 E3
Childsbridge Wy
  BGR/WK TN15 ......136 E3
Childs Crs SWCM DA10 .....53 L4
Childscroft Rd RHAM ME8 ..103 G3
Childs Rd NRWD SE19 * 68 F3
Childs Wy BGR/WK TN15 ....238 E10
Chilham Av WGOS CT8 ......177 G6
Chilham CI BXLY DA5 ......50 A5
  CHAT ME4 ....6 D7
Chilham Rd ELTH/MOT SE9 ..71 M1
  FOLKN CT19 ....219 M7
  MAIDW ME16 ....140 D6
  RHAM ME8 ....102 D2
Chillenden CI CANTW/ST CT2 153 H7
Chillington St
  MAID/SHEP ME14 ..141 G7
Chilliwack Rd HOO/HM ME3 .59 G8
Chilston CI STH/RUST TN4 .22 F1
Chilston Rd RMAID ME17 ...243 H1
  STH/RUST TN4 .....22 F1
Chiltern Av BH/WHM TN16 ..132 C6
  BGR/WK TN15 ......240 D9
Chiltern CI BXLYHN DA7 ...30 E4
  CROY/NA CR0 ......86 F6
  MAID/SHEP ME15 ...168 A4
Chiltern End KEN/WIL TN24 2 A4
Chiltern Gdns HAYES BR2 ..71 G5
Chiltern Rd DVW CT17 .....217 G5
Chiltern Wy RTWE/PEM TN2 .23 L3
  TON TN9 ....194 F1
Chilthorne CI CAT SE6 ....46 A5
Chilton Av RDV CT15 ......212 C6
  SIT ME10 ....120 B6
Chilton Ct RHAM ME8 ......102 F2
Chilton Dr HOO/HM ME3 ....81 H1
Chilton Fld RCANTE CT3 ...236 A11
Chilton Gdns RCANTE CT3 ..236 A11
Chilton Gv DEPT SE8 ......25 L3
Chilton La RAM CT11 ......16 B7
Chilton PI RCANTE CT3 ....236 A11
Chilton Rd CDW/CHF RM16 ..35 L7
  RCANTE CT3 ....236 A12
Chilton Wy DVW CT17 ......212 H6
Chilver St GNWCH SE10 ....27 G4
The Chimes KEN/WIL TN24 ..2 A1
China Hall Ms BERM/RHTH SE16 25 K3
Chinbrook Crs LEE/GVPK SE12 47 J3
Chinbrook Rd ELTH/MOT SE9 47 K3
Chineham Wy CANT CT1 4
Chingley CI BMLY BR1 70
Chipka St POP/IOD E14 ....26 D1
Chipley St NWCR SE14 .....25 M6
Chipman's Wy MSTR CT12 ..180 B6
Chippendale CI WALD ME5 ..115 G4
Chippendayle Dr RMAID ME17 242 E11
Chipperfield Rd
  STMC/STPC BR5 ....73 J7
Chipstead Av THHTH CR7 ..68 C8
Chipstead CI MAIDW ME16 ..12 A1
  NRWD SE19 ....69 G4
Chipstead La SEV TN13 ....135 U3
Chipstead Pk SEV TN13 ....135 H8
Chipstead Park CI SEV TN13 135 H8
Chipstead Rd ERITH DA8 ...30 A7
  MBLAR W1H 116 A1
Chisholm Rd CROY/NA CR0 ..86 F5
Chislehurst CI
  MAID/SHEP ME15 ...168 A7
Chislehurst High St CHST BR7 72 C5
Chislehurst Rd BMLY BR1 ..71 H6
  ORP BR6 ....91 H3
  SCUP DA14 ....71 H5
  STMC/STPC BR5 ....72 F5
Chislet CI BECK BR3 ......70 B4
Chislet Rd HB CT6 ....128 F4
Chislett CI RASHE TN25 ...307 K5
Chismall Rd DVW CT17 .....212 F5
Chiswell Sq BKHTH/KID SE3 27 J8
Chiswick CI CROY/NA CR0 ..86 A5
Chittenden's La LYDD TN29 330 F7
Chitty La RCANTE CT3 .....232 E11
Chorleywood Crs
  STMC/STPC BR5 ....73 G6
Choumert Gv PECK SE15 ....45 J1
Choumert Rd PECK SE15 ....45 G1
Chrismill La MAID/BEAR ME14 169 L3
Christ Church Av ERITH DA8 30 C5
  RTW TN1 ....22 F4
Christ Church Rd FOLK CT20 11 H5
  GVE DA12 ....79 K1
Christchurch Rd ASH TN23 .2 A7
  BECK BR3 * 70 B6
  DART DA1 ....51 K5
  TIL RM18 ....35 H7
Christchurch Wy
  DVE/WH CT16 ......213 J6
  GNWCH SE10 ....26 F4
Christian Flds
  STRHM/NOR SW16 ...68 B4
Christian Fields Av GVE DA12 79 K1
Christie CI WALD ME5 .....101 J2
Christie Dr DIT/AY ME20 ..139 L7
  SNWD SE25 ....87 H1
Christies Av RSEV TN14 ...108 F3
Christmas La HOO/HM ME3 ..59 M8
Christmas St GILL ME7 ....83 M6
Christopher Bushell Wy
  DVE/WH CT16 ......213 J6
  GNWCH SE10 ....26 F4
Christopher CI BFN/LL DA15 49 H7
Christy Rd BH/WHM TN16 ..132 B1
Chrysler Av HB CT6 ....128 B5
Chryssell Rd BRXN/ST SW9 .44 B6
Chubworthy St NWCR SE14 ..25 M5
Chudleigh Rd BROCKY SE4 ..46 A3
Chudleigh St HDCN TN27 ...300 F6
Chulsa Rd SYD SE26 ......69 J2
Chumleigh Gdns CMBW SE5 * 24 F4
Chumleigh St CMBW SE5 ...24 F4
Church Aly GVE DA12 .....79 L1
Church Ap DUL SE21 ......44 E8
  NROM TN28 ....330 F6
Church Av BECK BR3 ......70 B5
  SCUP DA14 ....49 H2
Churchbury Rd ELTH/MOT SE9 47 L5
Church Cliff DEAL CT14 ...211 L3
Church CI HOO/HM ME3 ....38 D2
  RASHE TN25 ....305 P2
  STPH/PW TN12 .....279 R10
  WBY/YAL ME18 .....241 M9
Church Court Gv BRDST CT10 183 J3
Church Crs RMAID ME17 ...242 G11
Church Cft DART DA1 .....51 L7
Churchdown BMLY BR1 .....70 F4
Church Dr WWKM BR4 ......88 D2
Church Farm CI
  BUR/ETCH TN19 ....322 D4
  HOO/HM ME3 ....83 M1
Church Farm Rd RSIT ME9 .146 B3
Church Farm Wy SWCH CT13 253 M3
Church Fld DART DA1 .....51 L7
  EDEN TN8 ....192 D4

RASHE TN25 ....307 N4
SEV TN13 ....20 C1
SNOD ME6 ....113 J4
Churchfield PI MARG CT9 ..14 F5
Churchfield Rd WELL DA16 .49 H1
Churchfields BRDST CT10 ..179 J6
Church Flds E/WMAL ME19 .138 C5
Churchfields GNWCH SE10 ..26 D5
Churchfields Rd BECK BR3 .69 J2
Churchfields Ter ROCH ME1 19 H9
Churchfields Rd RASHE TN25 266 F11
Church Gn BRXN/ST SW9 * .24 B8
  RMAID ME17 * 169 M2
  STPH/PW TN12 .....280 H3
  STRD ME2 ....81 R7
Church Gv LEW SE13 ......46 C2
Church Hts HYTHE CT21 * ..222 D3
Church HI ASH TN23 ......204 D8
  ASH TN23 ....304 F4
  BGR/WK TN15 ......240 D9
  BH/WHM TN16 ......132 C6
  BUR/ETCH TN19 ....322 B4
  CANTW/ST CT2 .....171 K6
  DART DA1 ....50 F2
  DART DA1 ....51 L8
  DVE/WH CT16 ......212 E4
  FAV ME13 ....151 H4
  HDCN TN27 ....263 M6
  ORP BR6 ....91 H3
  RAM CT11 ....17 G5
  RASHE TN25 ....289 L12
  RASHW TN26 ....301 K6
  RCANTW CT4 ....247 N9
  RDV CT15 ....210 B1
  RDV CT15 ....271 R9
  RDV CT15 ....272 D5
  RFOLK CT18 ....220 E1
  RMAID ME17 ....259 P5
  RMAID ME17 ....259 P5
  RRTW TN3 ....296 D7
  RSEV TN14 ....133 H1
  RSIT ME9 ....144 A2
  RTON TN11 ....188 J7
  RTW TN1 ....22 E5
  SCUP DA14 ....73 H2
  SIT ME10 ....120 C4
  STH/RUST TN4 .....196 C3
  STPH/PW TN12 .....279 L4
  SWCM DA10 ....54 A4
  SWLY BR8 ....75 J5
  TENT TN30 ....315 M2
  TIL RM18 ....34 F5
  WARL CR6 ....130 B3
  WBY/YAL ME18 .....241 N11
  WELL DA16 ....29 G4
Church Rw CHST BR7 ......72 D5
Churchsettle La WADH TN5 .309 H10
Churchside MEO DA13 .....239 M5
Churchside CI BH/WHM TN16 132 B4
Church Sq BRDST CT10 ....183 L1
  RMAID ME17 ....225 H4
  RYE TN31 225
Church St BGR/WK TN15 ...136 F6
  BRDST CT10 ....179 J6
  CANTW/ST CT2 .....4 E5
  CHAT ME4 * 6 E5
  CROY/NA CR0 ......86 D7
  DEAL CT14 ....209 J7
  DVE/WH CT16 ......213 J7
  EDEN TN8 ....191 H6
  EDEN TN8 ....275 N8
  FAV ME13 ....149 L1
  FOLK CT20 ....11 K6
  GILL ME7 ....83 M7
  GRAYS RM17 ....34 D5
  GVW DA11 ....38 G2
  HOO/HM ME3 ....57 K6
  HOO/HM ME3 ....58 C1
  HOO/HM ME3 ....59 M8
  MAID/BEAR ME14 ..13 C4
  MAID/SHEP ME15 ..12 D9
  MARG CT9 ....15 G6
  MEO DA13 ....78 B2
  MSTR CT12 ....180 F8
  RASHE TN25 ....266 F11
  RASHE TN25 ....252 B12
  RASHE TN25 ....259 N6
  RBTBR TN32 ....322 H8
  RCANTE CT3 ....232 D12
  RCANTE CT3 ....235 K4
  RCANTE CT3 ....235 L2
  RCANTE CT3 ....251 N8
  RCANTW CT4 ....174 B7
  RCANTW CT4 ....268 B7
  RCANTW CT4 ....268 A7
  RCANTW CT4 ....270 C2
  RCANTW CT4 ....270 F4
  RDV CT15 ....216 C5
  RDV CT15 ....273 L10
  RDV CT15 ....293 R1
  RMAID ME17 ....242 G11
  RMAID ME17 ....261 K5
  RSIT ME9 ....117 M5
  RSIT ME9 ....118 C3
  RTON TN11 ....278 C3
  RYE TN31 ....325 K9
  RYE TN31 ....325 M9
  RYE TN31 ....326 F12
  RYE TN31 ....327 L9
  TON TN9 ....194 D5
  WARL CR6 ....130 C3
  WBY/YAL ME18 .....241 R12
  WSTB CT5 ....126 F2
Church St (St Pauls) CANT CT1 5 L4
Church Ter BGR/WK TN15 * .136 F6
  LEW SE13 ....46 F1
  WALD ME5 ....101 K5
Church v FSTH SE23 ......45 K7
Church Vw HB CT6 ....129 L5
  HDCN TN27 ....300 F6
  LYDD TN29 ....319 P6
  RASHE TN25 ....305 R7
  SOCK/AV RM15 .....32 C1
Church Wk DART DA1 ......51 L8
  MAIDW ME16 ....139 H6
  GVE DA12 ....55 L5
  HDCN TN27 ....285 G4
  RCANTW CT4 * 291 G5
Church Whitfield Rd
  RDV CT15 ....273 J12
Church Wood CI
  STMC/STPC BR5 ....171 L3
Churchwood Dr WSTB CT5 ..127 L4
Churchyard ASH TN23 .....2 B5
Churchyard Rw LBTH SE11 ..24 D3
Churn La STPH/PW TN12 ...279 N6
Churston Ct
  BRXS/STRHM SW2 * 44 C6
Chute CI RHAM ME8 ....116 L1
Clyngton CI BFN/LL DA15 ..49 G8
Ciceley Rd PECK SE15 ....25 H7
Cicely Rd FSTH SE23 .....J7
Cimba Wd GVE DA12 ......79 M1
Cinderford Wy BMLY BR1 ..70 F1
Cinder Hill La RTON TN11 .255 L2
Cinder Hill Wd
  STPH/PW TN12 * ...278 F8

Cinnabar Cl *WALD* ME5 * 115 H4
Cinnabar Dr *SIT* ME10 119 K3
Cinnamon Cl *PECK* SE15 25 G6
Cinque Ports Av *HYTHE* CT21 222 C4
Cinque Ports Rd *NROM* TN28 331 K8
Cinque Ports St *RYE* TN31 225 G4
Cintra Pk *NRWD* SE19 69 G4
Circular Rd *DEAL* CT14 208 B2
Circular Wy *WOOL/PLUM* SE18 28 A5
Circus St *GNWCH* SE10 26 D6
Cirrus Crs *GVE* DA12 79 M2
Citadel Crs *DVW* CT17 8 A8
Citadel Pl *LBTH* SE11 24 A4
Citadel Rd *DVW* CT17 8 A8
Citroen Cl *HB* CT6 128 C5
Citron Ter *PECK* SE15 * 45 J1
City Vw *CANTW/ST* CT2 171 K5
City Wk *STHWK* SE1 24 F2
City Wy *ROCH* ME1 100 E1
Civic Sq *TIL* RM18 35 H8
Civic Wy *RTW* TN1 22 F4
Clacket La *BH/WHM* TN16 158 D2
Clack St *BERM/RHTH* SE16 25 K1
Claire Cswy *GRH* DA9 * 52 F2
Claire Ct *BRDST* CT10 179 L8
Claire Pl *POP/IOD* E14 26 B2
Clancy Gdns *CRBK* TN17 298 E8
Clandon Rd *WALD* ME5 115 L4
Clandon St *DEPT* SE8 26 B8
Clanricarde Gdns *RTW* TN1 22 F5
Clanricarde Rd *RTW* TN1 22 F5
Clanwilliam Rd *DEAL* CT14 209 L4
Clapham Hl *WSTB* CT5 126 E8
Claphatch La *WADH* TN5 310 B4
Clapper La *STPH/PW* TN12 281 Q5
The Clappers *RBTBR* TN32 322 G9
Clara Pl *WOOL/PLUM* SE18 28 B3
Clare Av *TON* TN9 194 C4
Clare Cswy *GRH* DA9 52 F2
Clare Cnr *ELTH/MOT* SE9 48 C5
Clare Ct *CTHM* CR3 156 F1
Clare Dr *HB* CT6 128 D7
Clare La *E/WMAL* ME19 138 F5
Claremont Cl
BRXS/STRHM SW2 44 A6
CDW/CHF RM16 34 D2
ORP BR6 90 B7
SAND/SEL CR2 130 A1
Claremont Crs *DART* DA1 50 F2
Claremont Gdns *RAM* CT11 16 E5
RTW TN1 23 H7
Claremont Pl *CANT* CT1 4 D7
CRBK TN17 * 313 M5
Claremont Rd *BMLY* BR1 71 M8
CROY/NA CR0 87 H4
DEAL CT14 209 J4
DEAL CT14 211 K3
FOLK CT20 11 H5
MAID/BEAR ME14 13 K3
RTW TN1 23 G7
SWLY BR8 74 F4
Claremont St *GNWCH* SE10 26 C5
HB CT6 128 D6
Claremont Vls *CMBW* SE5 * 24 E6
Claremont Wy *CHAT* ME4 6 D7
Clarence Av *HAYES* BR2 71 M8
MARG CT9 179 G3
Clarence Ct *MAID/BEAR* ME14 167 M1
Clarence Crs *SCUP* DA14 49 J8
Clarence Gdns *IOS* ME12 230 C2
Clarence Pl *DEAL* CT14 209 L2
DVW CT17 * 8 D9
GVE DA12 55 J5
Clarence Rd *BH/WHM* TN16 132 E4
BMLY BR1 71 M7
BXLYHS DA6 49 M2
CHAT ME4 101 J3
CROY/NA CR0 86 E3
DEAL CT14 209 L6
DEPT SE8 26 C5
ELTH/MOT SE9 47 M7
GRAYS RM17 34 C5
HB CT6 128 E4
RAM CT11 16 D7
RFOLK CT18 221 J4
RTW TN1 22 F5
SCUP DA14 49 J8
Clarence Rw *GVE* DA12 55 J5
RTW TN1 22 F5
Clarence St *FOLK* CT20 11 K4
HB CT6 128 F4
Clarendon Cl
MAID/BEAR ME14 168 B1
SIT ME10 120 A8
STMC/STPC BR5 73 H7
Clarendon Dr *STRD* ME2 82 B4
Clarendon Gdns *RAM* CT11 17 H6
RDART DA2 52 E6
RTWE/PEM TN2 201 H4
Clarendon Gn *STMC/STPC* BR5 73 H7
Clarendon Gv *STMC/STPC* BR5 73 H8
Clarendon Ms *BRDST* CT10 183 K1
NROM TN28 331 K5
Clarendon Pth *STMC/STPC* BR5 73 H8
Clarendon Pl *DVW* CT17 8 A6
MAID/SHEP ME15 * 13 H5
RDART DA2 74 E2
SEV TN13 * 20 F6
Clarendon Ri *LEW* SE13 46 D1
Clarendon Rd *BRDST* CT10 183 K1
CROY/NA CR0 86 C5
DVW CT17 8 B6
GVE DA12 55 K4
MARG CT9 15 J4
RCANTE CT3 251 Q12
SEV TN13 20 F6
Clarendon St *DVW* CT17 217 J2
HB CT6 128 D5
Clarendon Wy *CHST* BR7 73 G7
RTWE/PEM TN2 201 G4
Clarens St *CAT* SE6 46 A7
Clare Rd *NWCR* SE14 26 A8
WSTB CT5 126 F3
Claret Gdns *SNWD* SE25 68 F8
Clareville Rd *STMC/STPC* BR5 90 D5
Clare Wy *BXLYHN* DA7 29 M7
SEV TN13 162 B6
Clarewood Dr *E/WMAL* ME19 138 F5
Claribel Rd *BRXN/ST* SW9 24 C8
Claridge Cl *GILL* ME7 116 A1
Claridge Ms *HYTHE* CT21 * 222 D3
Clarkbourne Dr *GRAYS* RM17 34 E5
Clark Cl *ERITH* DA8 31 H7
Clarke Crs *KEN/WIL* TN24 203 J7
Clarke's Cl *DEAL* CT14 209 G5
Clarkes Green Rd
BGR/WK TN15 110 F8
Clark Ms *DIT/AY* ME20 140 A4
Clark Rd *NROM* TN28 331 M9
Clarks La *RSEV* TN14 108 E6
WARL CR6 158 A1
Claston Cl *DART* DA1 50 F2
Claude Rd *PECK* SE15 25 J8
Claude St *POP/IOD* E14 26 B3
Claudian Wy *CDW/CHF* RM16 35 J2
Claudius Gv *ASH* TN23 204 C6
Clavadal Rd *STPH/PW* TN12 279 K2
Clavell Cl *RHAM* ME8 116 E2
Clavell St *GNWCH* SE10 26 D5
Claverdale Rd
BRXS/STRHM SW2 44 A5
Claxfield Rd *RSIT* ME9 147 H2
Claybank Gv *LEW* SE13 46 C1
Claybridge Rd *LEE/GVPK* SE12 71 K1
Claydown Ms
WOOL/PLUM SE18 28 B4
Clayfarm Rd *ELTH/MOT* SE9 48 D7
Clayford *LING* RH7 274 A3
Claygate *ASH* TN23 204 B6
MAID/SHEP ME15 167 L4
RMAID ME17 169 L3
Claygate Crs *CROY/NA* CR0 105 H1
Claygate Cross *BGR/WK* TN15 240 F6
Claygate La *RTON* TN11 240 E12
Claygate Rd *STPH/PW* TN12 258 A11
WBY/YAL ME18 257 Q9
Clayhill *CRBK* TN17 297 M5
Clayhill Crs *ELTH/MOT* SE9 71 L1
Clay Hill Rd *RRTW* TN3 295 Q5
Claylands Pl *BRXN/ST* SW9 24 B6
Claylands Rd *VX/NE* SW8 24 A5
Clayton Croft Rd *RDART* DA2 51 H7
Clayton Dr *DEPT* SE8 25 M4
Clayton Md *GDST* RH9 156 A8
Clayton Ms *GNWCH* SE10 26 E7
Clayton Rd *PECK* SE15 25 H7
Clayton's La *RRTW* TN3 198 F4
Clayton St *LBTH* SE11 24 B5
Claytonville Ter *BELV* DA17 * 30 D1
Clay Wood Cl *ORP* BR6 90 F3
Claywood La *RDART* DA2 53 L8
Clayworth Cl *BFN/LL* DA15 49 J4
Cleanthus Cl *WOOL/PLUM* SE18 28 C7
Cleanthus Rd
WOOL/PLUM SE18 28 C7
Clearmount Dr *HDCN* TN27 264 B5
Clearway *BGR/WK* TN15 239 M12
Cleave Av *ORP* BR6 107 K1
Cleaverholme Cl *SNWD* SE25 87 J2
Cleaver La *RAM* CT11 17 J5
Cleave Rd *GILL* ME7 101 M3
Cleavers *CRBK* TN17 299 K5
Cleaver Sq *LBTH* SE11 24 B4
Cleaver St *LBTH* SE11 24 B4
Cleavesland *WBY/YAL* ME18 257 P8
Cleeve Av *RTWE/PEM* TN2 23 M8
Cleeve Ct *E/WMAL* ME19 164 C3
Cleeve Hl *FSTH* SE23 45 J6
Cleeve Park Gdns *SCUP* DA14 49 J7
Clematis Av *RHAM* ME8 102 C8
Clement Cl *CANT* CT1 5 J2
SIT ME10 119 M1
Clement Ct *MAIDW* ME16 12 B2
Clementine Cl *HB* CT6 129 L5
Clement Rd *BECK* BR3 69 L6
Clements Rd *BERM/RHTH* SE16 25 H2
MSTR CT12 182 F3
Clement St *SWLY* BR8 75 L3
Clenches Farm La *SEV* TN13 20 E9
Clenches Farm Rd *SEV* TN13 20 F9
Clendon Wy *WOOL/PLUM* SE18 28 E3
Clennam St *STHWK* SE1 * 24 D1
Clerke Dr *SIT* ME10 120 B1
Clerks Fld *HDCN* TN27 283 L4
Clermont Cl *GILL* ME7 116 B1
Clevedon Ct *RASHE* TN25 265 M3
Clevedon Rd *PGE/AN* SE20 69 L5
Cleveland *RTWE/PEM* TN2 23 L3
Cleveland Cl *DVE/WH* CT16 213 J6
Cleveland Rd *GILL* ME7 7 M1
WELL DA16 29 G8
Clevely Cl *CHARL* SE7 27 L3
Cleve Rd *SCUP* DA14 49 L8
Cleves Crs *CROY/NA* CR0 105 H5
Cleves Rd *BGR/WK* TN15 136 D3
Cleves Wy *ASH* TN23 204 B3
Clewson Ri *MAID/BEAR* ME14 141 J5
Cliff Av *HB* CT6 129 K4
Cliff Cl *HYTHE* CT21 222 E2
Cliff Dr *HB* CT6 128 D5
IOS ME12 230 D1
Cliffe Av *MARG* CT9 177 L4
Cliffe Rd *DEAL* CT14 211 L3
SAND/SEL CR2 86 E8
STRD ME2 19 G1
Cliff Fld *WGOS* CT8 176 F5
Cliff Gdns *IOS* ME12 65 M6
Cliff Hl *RMAID* ME17 259 Q1
Cliff Hill Rd *RMAID* ME17 259 P1
Clifford Av *CHST* BR7 72 A3
Clifford Dr *BRXN/ST* SW9 44 C2
Clifford Gdns *DEAL* CT14 209 H7
Clifford Rd *CDW/CHF* RM16 34 A1
SNWD SE25 69 H8
WSTB CT5 127 G5
Cliff Reach *GRH* DA9 52 F4
Cliff Rd *BRCH* CT7 176 B5
BRDST CT10 179 L6
FOLK CT20 10 C8
HYTHE CT21 222 F2
WSTB CT5 127 G2
Cliff Sea Gv *HB* CT6 128 D5
Cliffs End Gv *MSTR* CT12 182 A8
Cliffs End Rd *MSTR* CT12 182 A8
Cliffside Dr *BRDST* CT10 183 K4
Cliff St *RAM* CT11 17 J7
Cliff Ter *DEPT* SE8 26 B8
MARG CT9 15 H2
Clifftown Gdns *HB* CT6 128 C5
Cliff View Gdns *IOS* ME12 230 C4
Cliffview Rd *LEW* SE13 46 B1
Cliff View Rd *MSTR* CT12 182 A7
Clifton Cl *MAID/BEAR* ME14 13 K2
ORP BR6 90 D8
STRD ME2 18 C5
Clifton Ct *BECK* BR3 * 70 C5
Clifton Crs *FOLK* CT20 10 F8
PECK SE15 25 J6
Clifton Gdns *CANTW/ST* CT2 4 B1
FOLK CT20 11 H7
MARG CT9 15 H4
Clifton Gv *GVW* DA11 55 J5
Clifton Lawn *RAM* CT11 * 17 H8
Clifton Marine Pde *GVW* DA11 55 H4
Clifton Ms *SNWD* SE25 68 F8
Clifton Pl *BERM/RHTH* SE16 25 K1
MARG CT9 15 J3
RTW TN1 23 G7
Clifton Ri *NWCR* SE14 25 M6
Clifton Rd *FOLK* CT20 11 G7
GILL ME7 83 K6
GVW DA11 55 H4
MARG CT9 15 J4
RAM CT11 16 D3
RTWE/PEM TN2 196 F6
SCUP DA14 72 F1
SNWD SE25 68 F8
WELL DA16 49 K1
WSTB CT5 126 E5
Clifton St *MARG* CT9 15 H3
Cliftonville Av *MARG* CT9 15 K5
MSTR CT12 16 D1
Cliftonville Ms *MARG* CT9 15 K2
Clifton Wy *PECK* SE15 25 K6
Clinch St *HOO/HM* ME3 40 A8
Clinton Av *STRD* ME2 81 L5
WELL DA16 49 H2
Clinton Cl *RMAID* ME17 258 G2
Clinton La *EDEN* TN8 193 L2
Clinton Ter *DEPT* SE8 * 26 B5
Clints La *RCANTW* CT4 270 H8
Clipper Bvd *GRH* DA9 52 F2
Clipper Bvd West *GRH* DA9 52 E1
Clipper Cl *BERM/RHTH* SE16 25 L1
STRD ME2 82 F6
Clipper Ct *STRD* ME2 * 82 F6
Clipper Crs *GVE* DA12 80 A1
Clipper Wy *LEW* SE13 46 D2
Clive Av *DART* DA1 51 G4
Cliveden Cl *MAIDW* ME16 140 E6
Clive Dennis Ct *KEN/WIL* TN24 3 H6
Clive Rd *BELV* DA17 30 B3
DUL SE21 44 E8
GVW DA11 55 J4
MARG CT9 178 D8
MSTR CT12 182 A7
ROCH ME1 100 D2
SIT ME10 119 J4
Clockhouse *ASH* TN23 204 B2
RTWE/PEM TN2 197 J7
Clockhouse La *CDW/CHF* RM16 33 M2
Clock House La *SEV* TN13 20 F1
Clockhouse Pk *RASHE* TN25 265 N3
Clock House Rd *BECK* BR3 69 M7
Cloister Gdns *SNWD* SE25 87 J2
Cloisterham Rd *ROCH* ME1 100 E6
Cloisters *SIT* ME10 * 119 M5
Cloisters Av *HAYES* BR2 90 A1
The Cloisters *RAM* CT11 17 G8
Cloonmore Av *ORP* BR6 91 G8
The Close *ASH* TN23 204 B4
BECK BR3 69 M8
BGR/WK TN15 240 C3
BGR/WK TN15 240 F1
BH/WHM TN16 * 133 G2
BXLY DA5 50 B4
CANTW/ST CT2 172 A5
CDW/CHF RM16 34 C1
E/WMAL ME19 112 C8
EDEN TN8 254 B11
FAV ME13 149 K3
FOLKN CT19 220 F5
HART DA3 78 C6
HYTHE CT21 222 C1
RASHE TN25 266 F12
RCANTW CT4 * 175 G8
RDART DA2 51 K8
RDV CT15 212 A1
ROCH ME1 19 J9
RRTW TN3 199 K7
RYE TN31 224 F3
SCUP DA14 73 J2
SEV TN13 20 B4
SNWD SE25 * 87 H2
STMC/STPC BR5 90 F2
Cloth Hall Gdns *HDCN* TN27 300 F3
Clothworkers Rd
WOOL/PLUM SE18 28 E6
Cloudberry Cl *MAIDW* ME16 12 B1
Cloudesley Cl *ROCH* ME1 100 C4
Cloudesley Rd *BXLYHN* DA7 30 A7
ERITH DA8 31 G7
Clovelly Av *WARL* CR6 130 A4
Clovelly Dr *IOS* ME12 65 J5
Clovelly Rd *BXLYHN* DA7 29 M5
WSTB CT5 126 E6
Clovelly Wy *ORP* BR6 91 G2
Clover Bank Vw *WALD* ME5 101 J7
Cloverdale Gdns *BFN/LL* DA15 49 G4
Clover Lay *RHAM* ME8 103 J3
Clover Ri *WSTB* CT5 127 J4
Clover Rd *HOO/HM* ME3 83 M2
The Clovers *GVW* DA11 78 F1
Clover St *CHAT* ME4 6 D6
Clover Ter *MAID/SHEP* ME15 * 167 L5
Clover Wy *STPH/PW* TN12 279 K4
Clowders Rd *CAT* SE6 46 A8
Clowes Ct *CANTW/ST* CT2 * 171 K1
Clubb's La *LYDD* TN29 329 J6
Club Gardens Rd *HAYES* BR2 89 H3
Cluny Est *STHWK* SE1 24 F2
Cluny Pl *STHWK* SE1 24 F2
Cluny Rd *FAV* ME13 150 A2
Clyde *TIL* RM18 36 D3
Clyde Av *SAND/SEL* CR2 130 A1
Clyde Rd *CROY/NA* CR0 87 G5
TONN TN10 188 F8
Clyde St *CANT* CT1 * 5 H2
DEPT SE8 26 A5
IOS ME12 64 E3
Clyde Ter *FSTH* SE23 45 K7
Clyde V *FSTH* SE23 45 K7
Clydon Cl *ERITH* DA8 30 F5
Clynton Wy *ASH* TN23 204 D4
Coach Dr *RASHW* TN26 286 F2
The Coach Dr *MEO* DA13 239 K6
Coach & Horses Pas
RTWE/PEM TN2 22 E8
Coach House Ms *FSTH* SE23 45 K4
NWCR SE14 * 25 L7
Coach Rd *BGR/WK* TN15 163 M2
HDCN TN27 262 H8
RFOLK CT18 292 E9
STH/RUST TN4 200 D2
The Coachyard *MAIDW* ME16 166 C2
Coalpit La *RSIT* ME9 243 P3
Coal Post Cl *ORP* BR6 107 L2
Coast Dr *LYDD* TN29 331 N3
LYDD TN29 335 N4
NROM TN28 331 M9
Coastguard Sq *RYE* TN31 225 M6
Coast Rd *NROM* TN28 331 N5
Coates Hill Rd *BMLY* BR1 72 B6
Coats Av *IOS* ME12 64 B5
Cobay Cl *HYTHE* CT21 222 E3
Cobb Cl *STRD* ME2 81 L5
Cobbets Wy *EDEN* TN8 192 D5
Cobbett Cl *E/WMAL* ME19 139 G5
Cobbett Rd *ELTH/MOT* SE9 47 M1
Cobbett's Ride
RTWE/PEM TN2 201 G4
Cobbett St *VX/NE* SW8 24 A6
Cobblers Bridge Rd *HB* CT6 128 E5
Cobblestone Pl *CROY/NA* CR0 86 D4
Cobblestones *GILL* ME7 102 A8
Cobbs Cl *STPH/PW* TN12 279 J3
WBY/YAL ME18 164 F6
Cobbs Hl *RCANTW* CT4 247 P7
Cobbs Ms *FOLK* CT20 11 H6
Cobbs Pl *MARG* CT9 14 F3
Cob Cl *BGR/WK* TN15 240 B3
Cobden Ms *SYD* SE26 69 J2
Cobden Pl *CANT* CT1 5 G3
Cobden Rd *CHAT* ME4 7 H9
HYTHE CT21 222 C4
ORP BR6 90 E7
SEV TN13 21 J2
SNWD SE25 87 H1
Cobdown Cl *DIT/AY* ME20 139 J3
Cobdown Gv *RHAM* ME8 103 H3
Cob Dr *GVE* DA12 80 F2
Cobfield *RMAID* ME17 260 B4
Cobham *CDW/CHF* RM16 34 C1
Cobham Av *SIT* ME10 119 M8
Cobhambury Rd *GVE* DA12 80 B8
Cobham Cha *FAV* ME13 149 J1
Cobham Cl *BFN/LL* DA15 49 J4
CANT CT1 5 M9
GRH DA9 53 J4
HAYES BR2 89 M3
MAIDW ME16 12 C4
STRD ME2 18 B3
Cobham Dr *E/WMAL* ME19 164 D2
Cobham Pl *BXLYHS* DA6 49 L3
Cobham Ri *GILL* ME7 83 M8
Cobhams *RRTW* TN3 277 P9
Cobham St *GVW* DA11 55 H5
Cobham Ter *GRH* DA9 * 53 J3
GVW DA11 * 55 G6
Cobland Rd *LEE/GVPK* SE12 71 K1
Cobourg Rd *CMBW* SE5 25 G5
Cobsden Cl *LYDD* TN29 331 P1
Cobsden Rd *LYDD* TN29 331 N1
Cobtree Cl *WALD* ME5 101 K5
Cobtree Rd *RMAID* ME17 258 H2
Coburg Crs *BRXS/STRHM* SW2 44 A6
Cockerhurst Rd *RSEV* TN14 109 K3
Cockering Rd *RCANTW* CT4 248 E8
Cock La *RASHW* TN26 318 D2
RCANTW CT4 291 Q5
Cockmannings La
STMC/STPC BR5 91 L4
Cockmannings Rd
STMC/STPC BR5 91 L3
Cockmount La *WADH* TN5 309 L4
Cockreed La *NROM* TN28 331 J6
Cocksett Av *ORP* BR6 107 K1
Cocksure La *SCUP* DA14 74 B1
Codrington Crs *GVE* DA12 79 K2
Codrington Gdns *GVE* DA12 79 L2
Codrington Hl *FSTH* SE23 45 M5
Codrington Rd *RAM* CT11 17 G6
Coe Av *SNWD* SE25 87 H2
Coffey St *DEPT* SE8 26 B6
Cogans Ter *CANT* CT1 4 C8
Cogate Rd *STPH/PW* TN12 278 H3
Coggins Mill Rd *MAYF* TN20 308 D12
Coinston Av *RAM* CT11 16 A5
Cokers La *DUL* SE21 44 D6
Colburn Rd *BRDST* CT10 183 K4
Colby Rd *NRWD* SE19 68 F2
Colchester Cl *WALD* ME5 101 G6
Cold Arbor Rd *SEV* TN13 161 J2
Coldbath St *LEW* SE13 26 C8
Coldblow *DEAL* CT14 209 H8
Cold Blow Crs *BXLY* DA5 50 E6
Coldblow La *MAID/BEAR* ME14 143 H4
NWCR SE14 25 L6
Coldbridge La *RMAID* ME17 262 C8
Cold Harbour *CANT* CT1 5 H1
Coldharbour Crest
ELTH/MOT SE9 * 48 B8
Cold Harbour La *RSIT* ME9 119 G3
Coldharbour La *BRXN/ST* SW9 44 B2
DIT/AY ME20 140 B4
LYDD TN29 329 P8
MAID/BEAR ME14 143 J4
RAIN RM13 31 J2
RASHE TN25 266 H11
RCANTW CT4 250 F10
RTON TN11 188 B7
RYE TN31 327 K9
SIT ME10 227 N12
Coldharbour Pl *CMBW* SE5 24 D8
Coldharbour Rd *CRBK* TN17 313 K4
CROY/NA CR0 86 B8
GVW DA11 54 F7
Cold Harbour Rd *RMAID* ME17 244 C12
Coldharbour Rd *RTON* TN11 276 F9
Coldharbour Wy *CROY/NA* CR0 86 B8
Coldred Hl *RDV* CT15 212 A1
Coldred Rd *MAID/SHEP* ME15 260 A1
RDV CT15 271 R9
RDV CT15 272 C9
Coldrum La *E/WMAL* ME19 239 P8
Coldshott *OXTED* RH8 185 H3
Coldswood Rd *MSTR* CT12 182 B3
Cole Av *CDW/CHF* RM16 35 K3
Colebrook Ri *HAYES* BR2 70 F6
Colebrook Rd *STH/RUST* TN4 196 F6
Colebrook St *ERITH* DA8 31 G5
Coleby Pth *CMBW* SE5 * 24 E6
Colegate Dr *MAID/BEAR* ME14 168 D1
Colegates Cl *FAV* ME13 123 H7
Colegates Ct *FAV* ME13 123 J7
Colegates Rd *FAV* ME13 123 H7
Colegrove Rd *PECK* SE15 25 G5
Coleman Cl *SNWD* SE25 69 H6
Coleman Crs *MSTR* CT12 182 F4
Coleman Dr *SIT* ME10 227 N12
Coleman Rd *BELV* DA17 30 B2
CMBW SE5 24 F6
Colemans Cl *LYDD* TN29 334 E3
Colemans Heath
ELTH/MOT SE9 48 B8
Coleman's Stairs Rd *BRCH* CT7 176 D5
Coleman's Yd *RAM* CT11 17 J6
Colenso Vls *STPH/PW* TN12 * 280 H3
Colepits Wood Rd
ELTH/MOT SE9 48 E3
Coleraine Rd *BKHTH/KID* SE3 27 H5
Coleridge Cl *DIT/AY* ME20 139 H1
Coleridge Gdns *RCANTE* CT3 251 Q11
Coleridge Rd *CROY/NA* CR0 87 K3
DART DA1 52 B2
TIL RM18 35 K8
Coleridge Wy *ORP* BR6 91 H2
Cole Rd *FAV* ME13 149 M2
Colesburg Rd *BECK* BR3 70 A7
Coleshall Cl *MAID/SHEP* ME15 168 A7
Coles La *BH/WHM* TN16 160 B1
Cole St *STHWK* SE1 24 D1
Cole Ter *RMAID* ME17 * 243 K12
Colets Orch *RSEV* TN14 136 A2
Colette Cl *BRDST* CT10 179 K3
Coleville Crs *LYDD* TN29 335 M2
Colewood Dr *STRD* ME2 81 J5
Colewood Rd *WSTB* CT5 127 M2
Colfe & Hatcliffe Glebe
LEW SE13 * 46 C3
Colfe Rd *FSTH* SE23 45 M6
Colfe Wy *SIT* ME10 120 B1
Colin Blythe Rd *TONN* TN10 189 J8
Colin Chapman Wy *HART* DA3 95 G6
Colin Cl *CROY/NA* CR0 88 A6
RDART DA2 52 C4
WWKM BR4 89 G6
Colin's Wy *HYTHE* CT21 223 H2
Collard Cl *HB* CT6 129 J5
Collard Rd *KEN/WIL* TN24 205 K4
Collards Cl *MSTR* CT12 233 R10
Collards La *RCANTW* CT4 291 N6
College Ap *GNWCH* SE10 26 D5
College Av *GILL* ME7 7 H5
GRAYS RM17 34 C3
MAID/SHEP ME15 12 F7
TON TN9 194 D6
College Ct *MAID/SHEP* ME15 * 13 G7
College Dr *RTWE/PEM* TN2 23 L3
College Gn *NRWD* SE19 68 F4
College Park Cl *LEW* SE13 46 E2
College Pl *GRH* DA9 53 K2
College Rd *BMLY* BR1 71 H5
CANT CT1 5 J4
CHAT ME4 83 H6
CROY/NA CR0 86 E5
DEAL CT14 209 L1
DIT/AY ME20 139 J2
DUL SE21 44 F5
GRAYS RM17 34 D3
GVW DA11 54 C3
MAID/SHEP ME15 12 F8
MARG CT9 15 G8
NRWD SE19 69 G2
RAM CT11 17 J1
SIT ME10 119 L7
SWLY BR8 74 F4
College Rw *DVW* CT17 * 217 J2
College Vw *ELTH/MOT* SE9 47 L6
College Wk *MAID/SHEP* ME15 13 G7
MARG CT9 14 F4
College Wy *RCANTE* CT3 251 R2
College Yd *ROCH* ME1 19 J6
Coller Crs *RDART* DA2 76 F2
Collet Rd *BGR/WK* TN15 136 D3
Collett Rd *BERM/RHTH* SE16 25 H2
Collet Wk *RHAM* ME8 116 E1
Collie Dr *ASH* TN23 204 B6
Colliers Water La *THHTH* CR7 86 B1
Colliers Wd *HAYES* BR2 89 L8
Collindale Av *BFN/LL* DA15 49 H6
ERITH DA8 30 C5
Collingbourne *ASH* TN23 204 B5
Collington Cl *GVW* DA11 54 F5
Collington St *GNWCH* SE10 * 26 E4
Collington Ter
MAID/SHEP ME15 260 A1
Collingtree Rd *SYD* SE26 69 K1
Collingwood Cl *BRDST* CT10 183 H1
Colling Wood Cl *PGE/AN* SE20 69 J5
Collingwood Cl *WGOS* CT8 177 G6
Collingwood Ri *FOLK* CT20 219 M8
Collingwood Rd *DIT/AY* ME20 114 D6
RDV CT15 215 G1
WSTB CT5 126 D4
Collingwood Rd East
RDV CT15 211 H8
Collinson St *STHWK* SE1 24 D1
Collinson Wk *STHWK* SE1 * 24 D1
Collins Rd *HB* CT6 128 D7
Collins St *BKHTH/KID* SE3 26 F8
Collison Pl *TENT* TN30 315 Q2
Collis St *STRD* ME2 18 F1
Coll's Rd *PECK* SE15 25 K7
Collyer Pl *PECK* SE15 25 H7
Colman Pde
MAID/BEAR ME14 * 13 G4
Colmore Ms *PECK* SE15 25 J7
Colnbrook St *STHWK* SE1 24 C2
Colne *TIL* RM18 36 D2
Colne Rd *TONN* TN10 188 E8
Colney Rd *DART* DA1 52 A4
Colombo Sq *MSTR* CT12 182 D4
Colomb St *GNWCH* SE10 26 F4
Colonel's La *FAV* ME13 151 H6
Colonel Stephens Wy
TENT TN30 301 N11
Colonel's Wy *STH/RUST* TN4 196 D3
The Colonnade *DEPT* SE8 * 26 A3
STHWK SE1 * 24 B1
Colorado Cl *DVE/WH* CT16 213 J6
Colson Dr *RSIT* ME9 227 L10
Colson Rd *CROY/NA* CR0 86 E5
Coltness Crs *ABYW* SE2 29 J4
Colton Crs *DVE/WH* CT16 213 J5
Coltsfoot Ct *GRAYS* RM17 34 E5
Coltsfoot Dr *MAID/BEAR* ME14 168 A1
Coltsfoot La *OXTED* RH8 185 G3
Colts Hill Pl *STPH/PW* TN12 * 278 E4
Coltstead *HART* DA3 95 M6
Columbia Av *WSTB* CT5 126 C6
Columbia Wharf Rd
GRAYS RM17 34 B5
Columbine Cl *E/WMAL* ME19 139 G4
STRD ME2 18 A3
WSTB CT5 126 D7
Columbine Rd *E/WMAL* ME19 139 G4
STRD ME2 18 A4
Columbine Wy *LEW* SE13 * 26 D8
Columbus Av *MSTR* CT12 181 G4
Colveiw Ct *ELTH/MOT* SE9 47 L6
Colvin Cl *SYD* SE26 69 K2
Colvin Rd *THHTH* CR7 86 B1
Colwell Rd *EDUL* SE22 45 G3
Colworth Gv *WALW* SE17 24 D3
Colworth Rd *CROY/NA* CR0 87 H4
Colyer Cl *ELTH/MOT* SE9 48 C7
Colyer Rd *GVW* DA11 54 E7
Colyers Cl *ERITH* DA8 30 E7
Colyers La *ERITH* DA8 30 D7
Colyton Cl *WELL* DA16 29 L7
Colyton La *STRHM/NOR* SW16 68 B2
Colyton Rd *EDUL* SE22 45 J3
Combe Av *BKHTH/KID* SE3 27 G6
Combe Bank Dr *RSEV* TN14 160 D1
Combedale Rd *GNWCH* SE10 27 H4
Comber Gv *CMBW* SE5 24 D6
Combermere Rd *BRXN/ST* SW9 44 A1
Combeside *WOOL/PLUM* SE18 29 G6
Combwell Crs *ABYW* SE2 29 H2
Comerford Rd *BROCKY* SE4 45 M2
Comet Cl *PUR* RM19 32 B3
Comet Pl *DEPT* SE8 26 B6
Comet St *DEPT* SE8 26 B6
Comforts Farm Av *OXTED* RH8 185 G3
Comfrey Ct *GRAYS* RM17 34 E5
Command Rd
MAID/BEAR ME14 141 G5
Commerce Wy *CROY/NA* CR0 86 A6
EDEN TN8 192 D2
Commercial Pl *GVE* DA12 55 K4
Commercial Quay *DVW* CT17 8 D7
Commercial Rd *RTW* TN1 23 H2
STPH/PW TN12 279 K2
STRD ME2 18 F4
TON TN9 194 F5
Commercial Wy *PECK* SE15 25 H6
Commerell Pl *GNWCH* SE10 27 G4
Commerell St *GNWCH* SE10 26 F4
Commissioners Ct *CHAT* ME4 6 D2
Commissioner's Rd *STRD* ME2 19 J1
Commodore Pde
STRHM/NOR SW16 * 68 A4
Commodore Rd
MAID/BEAR ME14 13 L2
Common La *DVW* CT17 212 F6
HOO/HM ME3 38 D7
RDART DA2 51 H7
Common Rd *BGR/WK* TN15 240 A6
CRBK TN17 299 K5
HOO/HM ME3 82 C1
ROCH ME1 114 C3
RTON TN11 256 C3
Commonside *HAYES* BR2 89 K7
The Common *ROCH* ME1 19 K5
STH/RUST TN4 22 D5
Common Vw *STH/RUST* TN4 200 D2
Common Wall *HOO/HM* ME3 38 E7
Commonwealth Cl *SIT* ME10 120 C6
Commonwealth Wy *ABYW* SE2 29 J4
Commority Rd *MEO* DA13 239 N5
Communications Pk
STRD ME2 * 18 E7
Como Rd *FSTH* SE23 45 M7
Compass Cl *ROCH* ME1 100 D4

Compasses Rd RTON TN11 255 J11
The Compasses HOO/HM ME3 * 38 C7
Comp La BGR/WK TN15 240 H3
E/WMAL ME19 241 M2
Comport Gn CROY/NA CR0 105 K6
Compton Cl WALD ME5 115 L3
Compton Pl ERITH DA8 31 G5
Compton Rd CROY/NA CR0 87 J4
Comus Pl WALW SE17 24 F3
Concanon Rd
BRXS/STRHM SW2 44 A2
Concord Av WALD ME5 100 F8
Concord Cl RTWE/PEM TN2 * 23 K3
STPH/PW TN12 278 H3
Condor Cl IOS ME12 230 D2
Condover Crs
WOOL/PLUM SE18 28 C6
Conduit Hl RYE TN31 225 H3
Conduit La SAND/SEL CR2 87 H8
Conduit Rd WOOL/PLUM SE18 28 C4
Conduit St FAV ME13 * 149 L1
Coney Banks FAV ME13 * 124 D7
Coneyburrow Rd
RTWE/PEM TN2 197 H8
Coneybury Cl WARL CR6 130 A5
Coney Hall Pde WWKM BR4 * 88 F6
Coney Hill Rd WWKM BR4 88 F5
Coney Wy VX/NE SW8 24 A5
Conference Rd ABYW SE2 29 K3
Conghurst La HAWK TN18 312 D12
Congleton Gv
WOOL/PLUM SE18 28 D4
Congo Rd WOOL/PLUM SE18 28 E4
Congress Rd ABYW SE2 29 K3
Congreve Rd ELTH/MOT SE9 48 A1
Congreve St WALW SE17 24 F3
Conifer Av HART DA3 95 M2
Conifer Cl ORP BR6 90 E7
Conifer Dr MEO DA13 239 L3
WALD ME5 115 L4
Conifer Gdns
STRHM/NOR SW16 44 A8
The Conifers DEAL CT14 209 H7
Conifer Wy SWLY BR8 74 D5
Conington Rd LEW SE13 26 C8
Conisborough Crs CAT SE6 46 D8
Coniscliffe Cl CHST BR7 72 B5
Coniston Av STH/RUST TN4 22 A2
WELL DA16 48 F1
Coniston Cl BXLYHN DA7 30 D7
DART DA1 51 J6
ERITH DA8 30 F6
GILL ME7 84 B7
Coniston Dr RCANTE CT3 251 Q11
Coniston Rd BMLY BR1 70 F3
BXLYHN DA7 30 D7
CROY/NA CR0 87 H3
FOLKN CT19 10 F2
Conker Cl ASH TN23 204 F8
Conley St GNWCH SE10 * 26 F4
Connaught Av CDW/CHF RM16 34 C1
Connaught Cl
MAID/SHEP ME15 260 A1
Connaught Gdns MARG CT9 15 G7
Connaught Ms WALD ME5 7 J9
WOOL/PLUM SE18 28 B4
Connaught Rd CHAT ME4 101 J3
DVE/WH CT16 8 C1
FOLK CT20 11 J5
GILL ME7 7 L3
MARG CT9 15 G7
SIT ME10 119 M6
WOOL/PLUM SE18 28 B4
Connaught Wy STH/RUST TN4 22 C1
Conrad Av CANT CT1 172 D6
Conrad Cl CDW/CHF RM16 34 C1
RHAM ME8 116 E1
Conrad Gdns CDW/CHF RM16 34 B1
Consort Cl MAID/BEAR ME14 13 K3
Consort Rd PECK SE15 25 J8
Cons St STHWK SE1 24 B1
Constable Rd BRCH CT7 176 D5
GVW DA11 54 F8
TONN TN10 * 189 H8
Constable's Rd DVE/WH CT16 8 F2
Constable Wk DUL SE21 44 F8
Constance Crs HAYES BR2 89 G4
Constance Rd CROY/NA CR0 86 C3
Constantine Rd ASH TN23 204 C6
Constitutional Hill Rd
STH/RUST TN4 196 B4
Constitution Hl CHAT ME4 7 G9
GVE DA12 55 K6
SNOD ME6 113 G5
Constitution Ri
WOOL/PLUM SE18 28 B7
Constitution Rd WALD ME5 7 H8
Consul Gdns SWLY BR8 * 75 H4
Content St WALW SE17 24 D3
Contessa Cl ORP BR6 90 F8
Convalescent La CRBK TN17 298 H3
Convent Cl BECK BR3 70 D4
RDV CT15 215 H3
Convent Hl NRWD SE19 68 D3
Convent Rd BRDST CT10 179 K4
Convent Wk RAM CT11 16 C8
Conway Cl BRCH CT7 176 B6
STRD ME2 81 M4
Conway Gdns GRAYS RM17 34 C6
Conway Ms GILL ME7 6 E2
Conway Rd MAIDW ME16 140 D7
WOOL/PLUM SE18 28 E3
Conyerd Rd BGR/WK TN15 240 E3
Conyer Rd RSIT ME9 121 L6
Conyngham Cl MSTR CT12 182 E3
Conyngham La RCANTW CT4 175 H7
Conyngham Rd HB CT6 129 L3
MSTR CT12 180 F8
Cooden Cl BMLY BR1 71 J4
RHAM ME8 103 H3
Cook Cl GRH DA9 53 J2
WALD ME5 101 K7
Cooke Cl CDW/CHF RM16 33 M2
Cookham Dene Cl CHST BR7 72 E5
Cookham Hl ROCH ME1 100 B3
Cookham Rd SWLY BR8 74 B5
Cookham Wood Rd
ROCH ME1 100 C5
Cookhill Rd ABYW SE2 29 J1
Cooks La SIT ME10 119 M3
Cook's Lea SWCH CT13 253 N7
Cookson Gv ERITH DA8 30 C6
Cooks Rd WALW SE17 24 C5
Cooks Whf ROCH ME1 6 A5
Cooling Cl MAID/BEAR ME14 141 K7
Cooling Common
HOO/HM ME3 58 D5
Cooling La FOLK CT20 10 B4
Coolinge Rd FOLK CT20 11 H5
Cooling Rd HOO/HM ME3 58 C1
HOO/HM ME3 59 K2
STRD ME2 82 C3
Cooling St HOO/HM ME3 58 E3
Coombe Av CROY/NA CR0 86 F7
RSEV TN14 136 A6
Coombe Cl DVW CT17 213 H8
SNOD ME6 113 H6
WALD ME5 115 J2
Coombe Dr SIT ME10 120 D5
Coombe Farm La HOO/HM ME3 40 F7
Coombe Lands TENT TN30 326 G1
Coombe La CROY/NA CR0 87 J8
RCANTE CT3 236 B12
TENT TN30 315 M2
WADH TN5 308 H10
Coombe Lea BMLY BR1 71 M7
Coombe Ldg CHARL SE7 27 K5
Coombe Rd CROY/NA CR0 87 G7
DVW CT17 213 G8
FOLKN CT19 10 B3
GVE DA12 55 K7
HOO/HM ME3 59 M8
MAID/SHEP ME15 12 F9
RDV CT15 216 E1
RSEV TN14 136 B1
SAND/SEL CR2 86 F7
SYD SE26 69 J1
Coombe Valley Rd DVW CT17 217 H1
Coombe Wy RFOLK CT18 220 D2
Coombe Wood La RFOLK CT18 220 C1
Coomb Fld EDEN TN8 192 D5
Coombfield Dr RDART DA2 76 E1
Coombs Cl RYE TN31 325 R8
Cooper Cl GRH DA9 52 F3
STHWK SE1 24 B1
Cooper Rd CROY/NA CR0 86 B8
RYE TN31 224 F4
SNOD ME6 113 G7
WALD ME5 115 H2
Coopers Cl EYN DA4 76 D5
Coopers Dr BXLY DA5 50 F7
Cooper Shaw Rd TIL RM18 35 L6
Coopers La LEE/GVPK SE12 47 J7
RASHE TN25 306 F3
RTON TN11 277 K10
Coopers Ms BECK BR3 70 B6
Cooper's Rd GVW DA11 54 F6
STHWK SE1 25 G4
Cooper Street Dro
RCANTE CT3 236 D9
Cooper's Yd NRWD SE19 68 F3
Coote Rd BXLYHN DA7 30 A7
Cooting La RCANTE CT3 251 N10
Cooting Rd RCANTE CT3 271 K1
Copeland Rd PECK SE15 25 H8
Copeman Cl SYD SE26 69 K2
Copenhagen Rd GILL ME7 7 J4
Copers Cope Rd BECK BR3 70 B5
Cope St BERM/RHTH SE16 25 L3
Copgate Pth STRHM/NOR SW16 68 A3
Copinger Cl CANTW/ST CT2 172 B5
Copland Av IOS ME12 65 K7
Coplands Ri RYE TN31 325 J6
Copleston Rd PECK SE15 45 G1
Copley Cl WALW SE17 24 C5
Copley Dene BMLY BR1 71 L5
Copley Pk STRHM/NOR SW16 68 A3
Coppards La RYE TN31 325 K5
Coppelia Rd BKHTH/KID SE3 47 G2
Copperas St DEPT SE8 26 C5
Copper Beech Cl GVE DA12 55 L5
STMC/STPC BR5 91 K1
Copper Cl NRWD SE19 69 G4
Copperfield Cl GVE DA12 56 B6
KEN/WIL TN24 202 F6
Copperfield Crs STRD ME2 81 K3
Copperfield Dr RMAID ME17 260 F1
Copperfield Rd ROCH ME1 100 D3
Copperfields BGR/WK TN15 136 E3
LYDD TN29 334 C3
The Copperfields ROCH ME1 * 19 G9
Copperfield St STHWK SE1 24 C1
Copperfields Wk
BGR/WK TN15 136 E3
Copperfield Wy CHST BR7 72 D3
Coppergate CANTW/ST CT2 4 E1
GILL ME7 102 A8
Coppergate Cl BMLY BR1 71 J5
Copperhouse La GILL ME7 84 C7
Copperhouse Rd STRD ME2 81 K6
Copper La STPH/PW TN12 281 L4
Copperpenny Dr GILL ME7 116 C2
Copper Tree Ct
MAID/SHEP ME15 167 H8
Copperwood KEN/WIL TN24 2 D1
Coppice Cl BECK BR3 70 C8
Coppice Ct GILL ME7 116 C1
Coppice Rd WALD ME5 115 K3
The Coppice BGR/WK TN15 163 J4
BXLY DA5 50 E8
CANTW/ST CT2 173 G3
DIT/AY ME20 139 M4
MEO DA13 239 L5
RTWE/PEM TN2 278 A10
Coppice Vw MAID/BEAR ME14 141 M7
Copping Cl CROY/NA CR0 86 F7
Copping's Rd RTON TN11 255 J10
Coppins La RSIT ME9 119 J7
The Coppins CROY/NA CR0 105 G1
Coppin St DEAL CT14 209 L3
Copse Av WWKM BR4 88 C6
Copse Bank BGR/WK TN15 136 E6
Copse Cl CHARL SE7 27 J5
ROCH ME1 100 F4
Copsehill DIT/AY ME20 138 F3
Copse Rd RTON TN11 194 B1
Copse Side HART DA3 77 M7
The Copse ASH TN23 202 B8
HOO/HM ME3 83 M2
Copse Vw SAND/SEL CR2 104 D3
Copsewood Cl BFN/LL DA15 48 F4
Copsewood Wy
MAID/SHEP ME15 168 B2
Cop Street Rd RCANTE CT3 236 A11
Copt Cl CANTW/ST CT2 173 G2
Coptefield Dr BELV DA17 29 L2
Copthall HAWK TN18 * 325 L2
Copthall Av HAWK TN18 312 D8
Copthall Gdns FOLK CT20 11 J5
Copt Hall Rd BGR/WK TN15 163 M1
MEO DA13 79 J8
Copthorne Av HAYES BR2 90 A5
Coralline Wk ABYW SE2 29 K1
Coral St STHWK SE1 24 B1
Corbett Cl CROY/NA CR0 105 J6
Corbett's La BERM/RHTH SE16 25 K3
Corbylands Rd BFN/LL DA15 48 F6
Cordelia Cl HNHL SE24 44 C2
Cordelia Crs ROCH ME1 100 B3
Cordingham Rd WSTB CT5 126 B7
Cordwell Rd LEW SE13 46 E3
Corelli Rd BKHTH/KID SE3 27 M7
Corinthian Manorway
ERITH DA8 30 E3
Corinthian Rd ERITH DA8 30 E3
Cork La STPH/PW TN12 281 Q10
Corkscrew Hl WWKM BR4 88 D5
Cork St DIT/AY ME20 114 A7
Corkwell St CHAT ME4 6 B8
Cormont Rd CMBW SE5 24 C7
Cormorant Cl STRD ME2 81 K6
Cormorant Wy HB CT6 232 A5
Cornbrook Rd HYTHE CT21 321 Q1
Cornelis Dr MSTR CT12 180 E8
Cornell Cl SCUP DA14 73 M3
Corner Farm Rd
STPH/PW TN12 281 R5
Corner Fld ASH TN23 204 E6
Corner Fielde
BRXS/STRHM SW2 * 44 A6
Corner Gn BKHTH/KID SE3 27 H8
Corner House Buildings
HYTHE CT21 * 222 C3
Cornes Cl KEN/WIL TN24 3 L7
Cornfield Wy TONN TN10 189 G7
Cornflower Cl
MAID/BEAR ME14 167 M1
Cornflower La CROY/NA CR0 87 L4
Cornflower Ter EDUL SE22 45 J4
Cornford Cl HAYES BR2 89 H1
RTWE/PEM TN2 197 L7
Cornford La RTWE/PEM TN2 201 M1
RTWE/PEM TN2 294 E1
Cornford Pk RTWE/PEM TN2 197 M7
Cornford Rd BRCH CT7 176 D7
Cornforth Cl STPH/PW TN12 282 A5
Cornforth Dr RSIT ME9 * 145 L3
Cornhill RAM CT11 17 J7
The Corniche FOLK CT20 223 K2
Cornish Gv PGE/AN SE20 69 J5
Corn Mill Dr ORP BR6 91 G3
Cornmill La LEW SE13 46 C1
Cornwall Av RAM CT11 17 M2
WELL DA16 48 F1
Cornwall Cl MAID/SHEP ME15 167 M6
Cornwall Crs ROCH ME1 113 K1
Cornwall Dr STMC/STPC BR5 73 K4
Cornwall Gdns CANT CT1 174 E2
MARG CT9 15 M4
SNWD SE25 * 69 G8
Cornwallis Av BFN/LL DA15 48 E7
CHAT ME4 100 F4
FOLKN CT19 10 E1
GILL ME7 102 A1
HB CT6 129 K6
RCANTE CT3 251 Q12
RMAID ME17 259 K6
TONN TN10 195 H1
Cornwallis Cir WSTB CT5 126 D4
Cornwallis Cl ERITH DA8 31 G5
FOLKN CT19 10 E3
KEN/WIL TN24 205 L4
Cornwallis Gdns BRDST CT10 179 K7
Cornwallis Rd MAIDW ME16 12 B5
WOOL/PLUM SE18 28 D3
Cornwallis Wk ELTH/MOT SE9 48 A1
Cornwall Rd CROY/NA CR0 86 C5
DART DA1 52 A1
DEAL CT14 209 K6
GILL ME7 7 K1
HB CT6 128 C7
ROCH ME1 100 D2
STHWK SE1 24 B1
Cornwall Sq LBTH SE11 * 24 B4
Cornwell Av GVE DA12 55 K8
Corona Rd LEE/GVPK SE12 47 H5
Corona Ter SNOD ME6 113 G7
Coronation Av TIL RM18 36 D3
Coronation Cl BRDST CT10 179 H6
BXLY DA5 49 L4
Coronation Cottages
RBTBR TN32 322 H8
Coronation Crs MARG CT9 177 L5
QBOR ME11 64 A8
Coronation Dr ASH TN23 286 H8
IOS ME12 230 C3
Coronation Gdns
BUR/ETCH TN19 322 E2
Coronation Rd HOO/HM ME3 43 J8
IOS ME12 64 D4
RAM CT11 17 G6
WALD ME5 7 K9
Coronation St LYDD TN29 334 D3
Corone Cl FOLKN CT19 10 C1
Corporation Rd GILL ME7 7 M1
Corporation St ROCH ME1 19 K6
Corral Cl WALD ME5 7 L9
Corrance Gn MAID/SHEP ME15 167 H5
Correnden Rd RTON TN11 194 D2
Cortland Cl SIT ME10 119 M3
Cortland Ms SIT ME10 119 M3
Corunna Cl HYTHE CT21 222 C3
Corunna Pl DVE/WH CT16 213 M6
Cory's Rd ROCH ME1 19 L6
Cosbycote Av HNHL SE24 44 D3
Cosedge Crs CROY/NA CR0 86 B8
Cossack St ROCH ME1 100 D2
Cossall Wk PECK SE15 25 J7
Cosser St STHWK SE1 24 B2
Cossington Rd CANT CT1 5 H6
WALD ME5 115 J4
Costa St PECK SE15 25 H8
Costells Meadow
BH/WHM TN16 159 J4
Cotelands CROY/NA CR0 86 F6
Cotford Rd THHTH CR7 68 D8
Cotham St WALW SE17 24 D3
Cotherstone Rd
BRXS/STRHM SW2 44 A6
Cot La HDCN TN27 300 G2
Cotleigh Av BXLY DA5 49 L7
Cotmandene Crs
STMC/STPC BR5 73 J6
Cotman's Ash La
BGR/WK TN15 137 J1
Cotman Wy STPH/PW TN12 256 H7
Coton Rd WELL DA16 49 H1
Cotswold Cl BXLYHN DA7 30 F7
KEN/WIL TN24 2 B1
Cotswold Gdns
MAID/SHEP ME15 168 B4
Cotswold Ri ORP BR6 91 G2
Cotswold St WNWD SE27 68 C1
Cottage Av HAYES BR2 89 M4
Cottage Field Cl SCUP DA14 49 K6
Cottage Gn CMBW SE5 24 E6
Cottage Rd CHAT ME4 6 D1
RAM CT11 17 K6
Cottage Rw SWCH CT13 237 J12
Cottages Crs SEV TN13 135 K6
Cottall Av CHAT ME4 6 C9
Cottenham Cl E/WMAL ME19 139 G6
Cottesbrook St NWCR SE14 25 M6
Cottesloe Ms STHWK SE1 24 B2
Cottingham Rd PGE/AN SE20 69 L4
VX/NE SW8 24 A6
Cottington Rd MSTR CT12 181 M8
Cottington St LBTH SE11 24 B4
Cottongrass Cl CROY/NA CR0 87 L4
Cotton Hl BMLY BR1 70 E1
Cotton La GRH DA9 52 E3
Cotton Rd CANT CT1 4 B7
Couchman Green La
STPH/PW TN12 282 A3
Coulgate St BROCKY SE4 45 M1
Coulman St GILL ME7 7 M4
Coulson Gv DEAL CT14 208 B4
Coulter Rd ASH TN23 204 B6
HB CT6 128 C7
Coulters Cl MAID/BEAR ME14 167 L1
Coulton Av GVW DA11 54 F5
Coultrip Cl IOS ME12 66 C8
Council Av GVW DA11 54 D4
Councillor St CMBW SE5 24 D6
Countess Fld LYDD TN29 320 H9
Country Ways HDCN TN27 263 N2
County Ga CHST BR7 48 D8
County Gv CMBW SE5 24 D7
E/WMAL ME19 138 C5
County Rd MAID/BEAR ME14 13 G3
THHTH CR7 68 C6
County Sq ASH TN23 2 B4
County St STHWK SE1 24 E2
Coupland Pl WOOL/PLUM SE18 28 D4
The Course ELTH/MOT SE9 48 B8
Court Ap FOLK CT20 11 G6
Court Av BELV DA17 30 A4
Court Crs SWLY BR8 74 F8
Court Downs Rd BECK BR3 70 C6
Court Dr CROY/NA CR0 86 A7
MAIDW ME16 12 A3
Courtenay Dr BECK BR3 70 E6
CDW/CHF RM16 34 A2
Courtenay Rd CANTW/ST CT2 151 M4
DEAL CT14 209 K1
MAID/SHEP ME15 12 E9
PGE/AN SE20 69 L4
Courtenay Sq LBTH SE11 * 24 B4
Courtenay St LBTH SE11 24 A4
Courteney Rd RHAM ME8 102 C5
Courtenwell RRTW TN3 * 199 M1
Court Farm Rd ELTH/MOT SE9 47 L7
Courtfield Av WALD ME5 115 K2
Courtfield Ri WWKM BR4 88 E6
Court Hall QBOR ME11 64 A8
Court Hl RCANTE CT3 234 A12
Courthill Rd LEW SE13 46 D3
Courthope STPH/PW TN12 279 K3
Courthope Av WADH TN5 309 L5
Court House Farm RDV CT15 252 D12
Courtland Av DVE/WH CT16 213 H3
STRHM/NOR SW16 68 A4
Courtland Dr DVE/WH CT16 212 F5
Courtlands DEAL CT14 211 L3
RTON TN11 194 D2
WBY/YAL ME18 165 H5
Courtlands Av HAYES BR2 88 F4
LEE/GVPK SE12 47 J3
Courtlands Cl MSTR CT12 182 A8
Courtlands Wy WGOS CT8 177 J4
Court La DUL SE21 45 G5
MAID/BEAR ME14 116 D8
RCANTE CT3 234 H8
RTON TN11 256 D6
Court Lane Gdns DUL SE21 44 F5
Courtleet Dr BXLYHN DA7 30 C7
Court Lodge Farm
WBY/YAL ME18 * 164 F6
Court Lodge Rd GILL ME7 84 A7
RASHW TN26 317 K10
Courtmead Cl HNHL SE24 44 D4
Court Meadow RHAM ME8 * 102 C3
Court Mdw RCANTE CT3 251 J1
Court Mt BRCH CT7 * 176 D7
Courtney Cl NRWD SE19 * 68 F3
Courtney Rd CDW/CHF RM16 35 K1
CROY/NA CR0 86 B6
Courtrai Rd BROCKY SE4 45 M4
Court Rd BRCH CT7 233 M7
DEAL CT14 209 H8
ELTH/MOT SE9 48 A6
RDART DA2 76 F2
ROCH ME1 113 L4
SIT ME10 119 M2
SNWD SE25 69 G6
STH/RUST TN4 22 B3
Court Rd (Orpington By-Pass)
ORP BR6 91 J6
Courtside SYD SE26 * 45 K8
The Courts MARG CT9 177 K4
Court St BMLY BR1 71 H6
FAV ME13 149 L2
The Court WARL CR6 130 D4
Court Tree Dr IOS ME12 66 C8
Courtwood Dr SEV TN13 20 E4
Courtwood La CROY/NA CR0 104 E4
Courtwood Vls RDV CT15 * 271 Q9
Court Wurtin Beaver La
ASH TN23 204 D4
Court Yd ELTH/MOT SE9 47 M4
The Courtyard
BH/WHM TN16 * 159 J4
BRG/WK TN15 238 H3
EGRIN RH19 274 A12
GILL ME7 * 102 B5
KEN/WIL TN24 205 H5
RCANTE CT3 * 252 F3
The Court Yd RHAM ME8 * 103 G4
Courtyard Ms STMC/STPC BR5 73 H4
Cousley Wood Rd WADH TN5 309 M3
Couthurst Rd BKHTH/KID SE3 27 J5
Coutts Av GVE DA12 80 F1
Coventon La DEAL CT14 206 B3
Coventry Cl STRD ME2 81 L7
Coventry Gdns HB CT6 129 M4
Coventry Rd SNWD SE25 69 H8
TONN TN10 189 G8
Coverack Cl CROY/NA CR0 87 M3
Coverdale Av
MAID/SHEP ME15 167 L7
Coverdale Cl WALD ME5 101 J6
Coverdale Gdns CROY/NA CR0 87 G6
Covert Rd RCANTE CT3 271 K1
The Covert MEO DA13 239 K6
NRWD SE19 * 69 G4
ORP BR6 90 F2
WALD ME5 115 H4
Covesfield GVW DA11 55 G4
Covet La RCANTW CT4 269 Q7
RCANTW CT4 270 B4
Covet Wood Cl STMC/STPC BR5 91 G2
Covey Hall Rd SNOD ME6 113 H5
Covington Gdns
STRHM/NOR SW16 68 C4
Covington Wy
STRHM/NOR SW16 68 C4
Cowbeck Cl RHAM ME8 102 E7
Cowden Cl HAWK TN18 312 B10
Cowden La HAWK TN18 312 B10
Cowden Ms EDEN TN8 275 M8
Cowden Rd MAID/BEAR ME14 13 M2
ORP BR6 91 G3
Cowden St CAT SE6 70 B1
Cowdray Rd DEAL CT14 209 H6
Cowdray Sq DEAL CT14 209 J6
Cowdrey Cl KEN/WIL TN24 205 K4
MAIDW ME16 166 C4
ROCH ME1 100 C3
Cowdrey Ct DART DA1 51 J5
Cowdrey Pl CANT CT1 5 J8
Cowgate Hl DVW CT17 8 C5
Cowgate La RFOLK CT18 292 H12
Cow La CANT CT1 4 B7
DVW CT17 217 H2
EDEN TN8 275 Q4
Cowley Av GRH DA9 53 G3
Cowley Cl SAND/SEL CR2 104 B3
Cowley Ri MARG CT9 178 F5
Cowley Rd BRXN/ST SW9 24 B7
Cowper Av TIL RM18 35 J7
Cowper Cl HAYES BR2 71 L8
WELL DA16 49 H3
Cowper Rd BELV DA17 30 A3
DEAL CT14 209 J4
DVW CT17 212 F7
GILL ME7 7 L7
HAYES BR2 71 L8
MARG CT9 15 G6
SIT ME10 120 C5
Cowstead Rd RSIT ME9 117 L2
Coxes Av MSTR CT12 182 E2
Coxes La MSTR CT12 182 E2
Coxett Hl FAV ME13 148 E4
Cox Gdns RHAM ME8 102 B3
Coxhill Crs DVW CT17 212 E6
Coxhill Gdns DVW CT17 212 E6
Coxhill Rd RDV CT15 271 N10
Coxmount Rd CHARL SE7 27 L4
Coxon Dr CDW/CHF RM16 33 M2
Cox's Cl SNOD ME6 113 G5
Coxson Wy STHWK SE1 25 G1
Cox St MAID/BEAR ME14 116 D8
Coxwell Rd NRWD SE19 68 F4
WOOL/PLUM SE18 28 E4
Cozenton Cl RHAM ME8 102 F4
Crabble Av DVW CT17 213 H7
Crabble Cl DVW CT17 213 G7
Crabble Hl DVW CT17 213 H6
Crabble La DVW CT17 212 F8
Crabble Mdw DVW CT17 213 H7
Crabble Rd DVW CT17 213 H6
Crabbs Croft Cl ORP BR6 * 90 D8
Crab Hl BECK BR3 70 E4
Crabtree Cl E/WMAL ME19 164 B3
Crabtree La RMAID ME17 263 L5
Crabtree Manorway South
BELV DA17 30 D2
Crabtree Rd RHAM ME8 102 E5
Craddock Dr CANT CT1 5 J2
Craddock Rd CANT CT1 5 J3
Craddock Wy RHAM ME8 102 E8
Cradducks La STPH/PW TN12 282 C5
Cradle Bridge Dr KEN/WIL TN24 3 H5
Cradles Rd RSIT ME9 117 K4
Cradley Rd ELTH/MOT SE9 48 E6
Crafford St DVE/WH CT16 8 C3
Craigen Av CROY/NA CR0 87 J4
Craigerne Rd BKHTH/KID SE3 27 J6
Craigholm WOOL/PLUM SE18 28 B8
Craignair Rd BRXS/STRHM SW2 44 A5
Craignish Av STRHM/NOR SW16 68 A6
Craigton Rd ELTH/MOT SE9 48 A2
Crail Rw WALW SE17 24 E3
Crampton Rd PGE/AN SE20 69 K3
Cramptons CRBK TN17 299 J5
Crampton's Rd RSEV TN14 136 A6
Crampton St WALW SE17 24 C3
Cranborne Av
MAID/SHEP ME15 167 K5
Cranbourne Cl RAM CT11 17 M2
Cranbrook Cl HAYES BR2 89 H2
MAID/SHEP ME15 168 A6
MARG CT9 179 H4
RHAM ME8 102 D2
Cranbrook Dr SIT ME10 119 L8
Cranbrook Rd BXLYHN DA7 30 A7
CRBK TN17 282 A11
CRBK TN17 297 N5
CRBK TN17 298 H12
CRBK TN17 313 J2
DEPT SE8 26 B8
HAWK TN18 312 C4
HDCN TN27 299 R6
HDCN TN27 300 D8
STPH/PW TN12 282 A10
TENT TN30 315 K2
THHTH CR7 68 D6
Crandalls RTON TN11 255 N12
Crandon Wk EYN DA4 * 76 F6
Crane La CRBK TN17 298 G8
Crane Md BERM/RHTH SE16 25 L4
Crane St PECK SE15 25 G7
Cranfield Rd BROCKY SE4 46 A1
Cranfield Rw STHWK SE1 * 24 C2
Cranford Cl RHAM ME8 102 E4
Cranford Rd DART DA1 51 M6
TONN TN10 189 K8
Cranleigh Cl BXLY DA5 * 50 C4
ORP BR6 91 H6
PGE/AN SE20 69 J6
Cranleigh Dr DVE/WH CT16 213 H2
SWLY BR8 74 F8
Cranleigh Gdns MAIDW ME16 140 D6
ROCH ME1 100 E2
SNWD SE25 68 F7
WSTB CT5 126 F5
Cranmer Cl RCANTW CT4 175 J5
WARL CR6 130 D3
Cranmer Ct MAID/SHEP ME15 167 J5
Cranmere Ct STRD ME2 19 J2
Cranmer Gdns WARL CR6 130 D3
Cranmer Rd BRXN/ST SW9 24 B6
CROY/NA CR0 86 C6
SEV TN13 20 A2
Cranmore Rd BMLY BR1 46 F8
CHST BR7 72 A2
Cranston Rd FSTH SE23 45 M6
Cranswick Rd
BERM/RHTH SE16 25 J4
Crantock Rd CAT SE6 46 D7
Cranwell Rd STH/RUST TN4 200 D1
Cranworth Gdns BRXN/ST SW9 24 B7
Craster Rd BRXS/STRHM SW2 44 A5
Crathie Rd LEE/GVPK SE12 47 J4
Craufurd Gn FOLK CT20 219 L8
Craven Cl MARG CT9 14 A9
Craven Rd CROY/NA CR0 87 J4
ORP BR6 91 L6
Crawford Gdns MARG CT9 15 L5
Crawford Rd BRDST CT10 179 J8
CMBW SE5 24 D8
Crawfords SWLY BR8 74 F4
Crawshay Cl SEV TN13 20 E2
Crawthew Gv EDUL SE22 45 G2
Cray Av STMC/STPC BR5 91 J1
Craybrooke Rd SCUP DA14 73 J1
Crayburne MEO DA13 78 A2
Craybury End ELTH/MOT SE9 48 D7
Cray Cl DART DA1 51 H3
Craydene Rd ERITH DA8 31 G7
Crayford Cl MAID/BEAR ME14 13 L1
Crayford High St DART DA1 50 F3
Crayford Rd DART DA1 51 G3
Crayford Wy DART DA1 51 H2
Craylands STMC/STPC BR5 73 K7
Craylands La SWCM DA10 53 M4
Craylands Sq SWCM DA10 53 L3
Crayleigh Ter SCUP DA14 * 73 K3
Cray Rd BELV DA17 30 B5
SCUP DA14 73 K3
SWLY BR8 92 D2
Crays Pde STMC/STPC BR5 * 73 K6
Craythorne TENT TN30 301 N12
Craythorne Cl HYTHE CT21 223 J1
NROM TN28 331 K5
Craythorne La NROM TN28 331 J6
Cray Valley Rd STMC/STPC BR5 91 H1
Creasy Est STHWK SE1 * 24 F2
Crebor St EDUL SE22 45 H4
Credenhall Dr HAYES BR2 90 A4
Credon Rd BERM/RHTH SE16 25 J4
Credo Wy WTHK RM20 33 J5
Creek Rd DEPT SE8 26 B5
Creekside DEPT SE8 26 B6

The Creek GVW DA11 ....54 C3
Creeland Gv CAT SE6 ....46 A6
Cremer Cl RCANTW CT4 ....248 D7
Cremer Pl FAV ME13 ....149 H1
Cremers Rd GVW DA11 ....120 C4
Cremorne Pk STH/RUST TN4 ....196 D4
Crescent Av SIT ME10 ....55 G5
Crescent Ct CT2 ....25 M3
Crescent Dr STMC/STPC BR5 ....90 D2
Crescent Gdns CROY/NA CRO 74 D6
Crescent Rd BECK BR3 ....70 C6
  BFN/LL DA15 ....70 B5
  BMLY BR1 ....71 H4
  BRCH CT7 ....176 D6
  BRDST CT10 ....179 L5
  ERITH DA8 ....31 H4
  FAV ME13 ....149 L2
  MARG CT9 ....14 C5
  RAM CT11 ....16 F5
  RTW TN1 ....23 G5
  SOCK/AV RM15 ....32 D1
  WOOL/PLUM SE18 ....28 C4
The Crescent BECK BR3 ....70 B5
  BGR/WK TN15 ....240 F1
  BXLY DA5 ....49 K5
  CANTW/ST CT2 ....172 A6
  CHAT ME4 ....83 J4
  CTHM CR3 ....156 F1
  FAV ME13 ....151 H1
  FOLK CT20 ....223 M2
  GRH DA9 ....55 K4
  GVW DA11 ....55 G3
  HART 77 M7
  IOS ME12 ....64 F7
  MAID/BEAR ME14 ....141 G1
  RCANTW CT4 ....248 E8
  RDV CT15 ....215 H4
  RDV CT15 ....209 M7
  RDV CT15 ....272 D6
  RSIT ME9 ....121 L1
  SCUP DA14 ....73 G1
  SEV TN13 ....136 C8
  SIT ME10 ....227 N12
  SNWD SE25 ....86 E2
  STH/RUST TN4 ....196 D4
  SWCH CT13 ....253 R3
  TON TN9 ....194 E3
  WWKM BR4 ....88 F2
Crescent Vw SOCK/AV RM15 ....32 D1
Crescent Wy BROCKY SE4 ....46 B1
  ORP BR6 ....90 F8
  STRHM/NOR SW16 ....68 A4
  WALD ME5 ....100 B3
Crescent Wood Rd SYD SE26 ....45 H8
Cressey Ct CHAT ME4 ....6 B6
Cressfield ASH TN23 ....204 C2
Cressingham Rd LEW SE13 ....46 D1
Cress Wy FAV ME13 ....149 H2
Cresswell Pk BKHTH/KID SE3 ....47 L5
Cresswell Rd SNWD SE25 ....69 H8
Crest Av GRAYS RM17 ....34 C5
Crest Cl RSEV TN14 ....109 G5
Cresthill Av GRAYS RM17 ....34 D4
Crest Rd HAYES BR2 ....89 J1
  ROCH ME1 ....100 D4
  SAND/SEL CR2 ....104 A2
Crest Vw GRH DA9
Crest View Dr STMC/STPC BR5 ....90 C1
Crestway WALD ME5 ....101 J5
Creswell Dr BECK BR3 ....88 C1
Crete Hall Rd GVW DA11 ....54 F4
Crete Rd East RFOLK CT18 ....220 D4
Crete Rd West FOLKN CT19 ....219 M4
Creteway Cl FOLKN CT19 ....220 F5
Creve Coeur Cl MAID/BEAR ME14 ....142 B8
Crewdson Rd BRXN/ST SW9 ....44 A6
Crewe's Av WARL CR6 ....130 B2
Crewe's Cl WARL CR6 ....130 B2
Crewe's La WARL CR6 ....130 C2
Crews St POP/IOD E14 ....26 B3
Crewys Rd PECK SE15 ....25 J8
Cricketers Cl ERITH DA8 ....30 F4
  RFOLK CT18 ....292 H11
  RMAID ME17 ....242 E11
  SIT ME10 ....227 N13
Cricketers Dr MEO DA13 ....97 H6
Cricketers Fld RBTBR TN32 ....323 R12
Cricketers Wk SYD SE26 ....69 G1
Cricket Ground Rd CHST BR7 ....72 C5
Cricket St DEPT SE8 ....69 M3
Crimond Av LYDD TN29 ....321 N16
Crimscott St STHWK SE1 ....24 F6
Crinan Ct BRDST CT10 * 183 J4
Crinan La RASHW TN26 ....303 N4
Criol Rd RASHW TN26 ....303 Q2
Cripple Hi RASHW TN26 ....301 G4
Cripple St MAID/SHEP ME15 ....167 P12
Cripps Cl RCANTE CT3 ....251 P12
Crismill Rd MAID/BEAR ME14 ....168 F2
Crispe Rd RHAM ME8 ....116 E1
Crispe Park Cl BRCH CT7 ....176 E6
Crispe Rd BRCH CT7 ....176 D6
Crispin Cl FAV ME13 ....149 L1
Crispin Rd RMAID ME17 ....258 H2
Crispin St STRD ME2 ....18 A2
Crispin Wy E/WMAL ME19 ....148 F2
Crittenden Rd STPH/PW TN12 ....278 F5
Crittle's Ct WADH TN5 ....309 L5
Crockenhall Wy MEO DA13 ....78 D2
Crockenhill La STMC/STPC BR5 ....91 L1
Crockenhill La SWLY BR8 ....93 H3
Crocken Hill Rd HDCN TN27 ....262 G11
Crockham Ct STMC/STPC BR5 ....91 K1
Crockham La FAV ME13 ....151 L3
Crockham Wy ELTH/MOT SE9 ....72 B1
Crockshard Hi RCANTE CT3 ....252 A5
Crockshard La RCANTE CT3 ....252 A5
Crocus Cl CROY/NA CRO 87 L4
Croft Av WWKM BR4 ....88 D4
Croft Cl BELV DA17 ....30 A4
  CHST BR7 ....72 A4
  RMAID ME17 ....261 L1
  TONN TN10 ....189 J8
  WALD ME5 ....115 K4
Croft Ct EDEN TN8 ....144 D1
Croft Gdns RMAID ME16 ....243 L12
Croft La EDEN TN8 ....192 D4
  FOLK CT20 ....10 B4
Crofton Av BXLY DA5 ....49 G5
  ORP BR6 ....90 B7
Crofton Cl KEN/WIL TN24 ....202 F5
Crofton Gate Wy BROCKY SE4 ....45 M3
Crofton La STMC/STPC BR5 ....90 D8
Crofton Park Rd BROCKY SE4 ....46 B1
Crofton Rd BH/WHM TN16 ....159 G4
  CMBW SE5 ....24 F8
  CROY/NA CRO 86 B7
  ORP BR6 ....90 B7
  WGOS CT8 ....177 H6
Croft Rd BH/WHM TN16 ....159 G4

  BMLY BR1 ....71 H3
  CTHM CR3 ....130 E8
  KEN/WIL TN24 ....2 D1
  STRHM/NOR SW16 ....68 A2
Croft Rd Flats KEN/WIL TN24 * 2 B2
Croftside MEO DA13 ....239 M5
Croft's Pl BRDST CT10 * 183 L1
Croft St DEPT SE8 ....25 M3
The Croft E/WMAL ME19 ....138 F8
  SWLY BR8 ....74 F1
  SEV TN13 ....20 C5
Croftwood ASH TN23 ....204 E3
Croham Park Av SAND/SEL CR2 ....87 G8
Croham Rd SAND/SEL CR2 ....86 F8
Croham Valley Rd SAND/SEL CR2 ....104 A2
Cromer Rd SIT ME10 ....145 M1
  SNWD SE25 ....69 J7
  STRD ME2 ....19 G1
Cromer St TON TN9 ....194 D4
Cromford Cl ORP BR6 ....90 E7
Cromlix Cl CHST BR7 ....72 C6
Crompton Gdns MAID/SHEP ME15 ....13 J8
Cromwell Av HAYES BR2 ....71 J7
Cromwell Cl HAYES BR2 ....71 J7
Cromwell Park Pl FOLK CT20 ....223 L1
Cromwell Rd BECK BR3 ....69 M6
  BRXN/ST SW9 ....44 C7
  CANT CT1 ....5 G8
  CROY/NA CRO 86 D3
  GRAYS RM17 ....34 E4
  IOS ME12 ....64 A6
  MAID/BEAR ME14 ....13 H3
  RTWE/PEM TN2 ....23 J4
  WSTB CT5 ....126 E4
Cromwell Ter CHAT ME4 ....6 E4
Cronin Dr DIT/AY ME20 ....139 G1
Cronin St PECK SE15 ....25 J6
Crooked La GVE DA12 ....55 L7
Crooked S Rd RCANTW CT4 ....210 F2
Crooke Rd DEPT SE8 ....25 M3
Crook Log BXLYHN DA7 ....49 L1
Crook Rd STPH/PW TN12 ....281 M8
Crook's Court La RDV CT15 ....216 A3
Crookston Rd ELTH/MOT SE9 ....48 C1
Croom's Hi GNWCH SE10 ....26 E6
Croom's Hill Gv GNWCH SE10 ....26 E6
Crosby Rw STHWK SE1 ....24 L1
Crosier Cl WOOL/PLUM SE18 ....27 M7
Crosier Rd GILL ME7 ....7 M3
Crossbrook Rd BXHTH/KID SE3 * 27 M8
Cross Dr RMAID ME17 ....261 J4
Crossfield Cl DEPT SE8 ....26 B6
Crossfield St DEPT SE8 ....26 B6
Crossford St BRXN/ST SW9 ....24 A5
Cross La BXLY DA5 ....245 M10
  FAV ME13 ....151 K3
  SIT ME10 ....119 M3
Cross La East GVE DA12 ....55 L7
Cross Lane Gdns WADH TN5 ....310 E12
Cross La West GVW DA11 ....55 L7
Crosslet St WALW SE17 ....17 J6
Crosslet V GNWCH SE10 ....26 C7
Crossley Av HB CT6 ....128 C5
Crossley Cl BH/WHM TN16 ....159 G1
Crossmead ELTH/MOT SE9 ....48 A6
Cross Rd BRCH CT7 ....176 D5
  CMBW SE5 ....24 F8
  CROY/NA CRO 86 F8
  DART DA1 ....51 K4
  DEAL CT14 ....209 M7
  GVW DA11 ....55 J7
  HAYES BR2 ....89 M5
  MAID/BEAR ME14 ....13 G3
  STRD ME2 ....19 G2
Crossthwaite Av HNHL SE24 ....44 D1
Crosswall Quay DVW CT17 ....9 G8
Cross Wy ROCH ME1 ....100 C2
Crossways BH/WHM TN16 ....132 B4
  CANTW/ST CT2 ....172 B5
  SAND/SEL CR2 ....104 B5
  SIT ME10 ....119 M3
Crossways Av MARG CT9 ....178 C3
Crossways Bvd GRH DA9 ....52 D2
Crossways La LYDD TN29 ....321 K7
Crossways Rd BECK BR3 ....70 B8
The Crossway ELTH/MOT SE9 ....200 B8
  STH/RUST TN4 ....200 B8
Crothall Hvn KEN/WIL TN24 * 2 B3
Crouch Cl BECK BR3 ....70 B8
Crouch Cft ELTH/MOT SE9 ....48 B8
Crouch Hill Ct RSIT ME9 ....226 D10
Crouch House Rd EDEN TN8 ....192 B2
Crouch La BGR/WK TN15 ....240 C4
  FAV ME13 ....151 K3
  HAWK TN18 ....313 N12
Crouchman Cl CDW/CHF RM16 ....34 E1
Crouchmans Cl SYD SE26 ....45 G8
Crouch Rd GRAYS RM17 ....35 K4
Crowborough Cl WARL CR6 ....130 D4
Crowborough Rd KEN/WIL TN24 ....205 J5
Crowbridge Rd KEN/WIL TN24 ....205 J5
Crow Dr RSEV TN14 ....135 H1
Crow Hi BRDST CT10 ....179 K6
  ORP BR6 ....108 E4
Crow Hill Rd BGR/WK TN15 ....240 F2
  MARG CT9 ....177 L5
Crowhurst Cl BRXN/ST SW9 ....24 B5
Crowhurst Cl BGR/WK TN15 ....95 J2
  BGR/WK TN15 ....240 D5
  LING RH7 ....184 B8
Crowhurst Md GDST RH9 ....156 F3
Crowhurst Rd BGR/WK TN15 ....240 E7
  LING RH7 ....190 E7
Crowhurst Village Rd LING RH7 ....190 F3
Crowhurst Wy STMC/STPC BR5 ....91 K1
Crowland Rd THHTH CR7 * 68 D3
Crow La ROCH ME1 ....19 K8
Crowley Crs CROY/NA CRO 86 D4
Crown Acres STPH/PW TN12 ....257 N7
Crown Cl ORP BR6 ....90 B7
Crown Dl NRWD SE19 ....68 D3
Crownfield Rd ASH TN23 ....204 D4
Crownfields MAID/BEAR ME14 ....167 M1
  SEV TN13 ....21 G1
Crown Gdns CANTW/ST CT2 ....4 C4
Crown Hl CROY/NA CRO * 86 D5
Crown Hill Rd HB CT6 ....128 C5

Crown La CHST BR7 ....72 D5
  GVE DA12 ....80 F1
  HAYES BR2 ....89 L1
  RCANTW CT4 ....268 H11
Crown Lane Gdns WNWD SE27 * 68 B2
Crown Lane Sp HAYES BR2 ....89 L2
Crown Quay La SIT ME10 ....120 L2
Crown Rd EDEN TN8 ....192 B2
  GRAYS RM17 ....34 B5
  ORP BR6 ....91 H4
  RSEV TN14 ....109 L4
  SIT ME10 ....119 M4
Crownstone Rd BRXS/STRHM SW2 ....44 B3
Crown St CMBW SE5 ....24 F6
  GILL ME7 ....7 G1
Crown Whf STRD ME2 * 82 F6
Crown Woods Wy ELTH/MOT SE9 ....48 E3
Crowson Camp Rd RCANTW CT4 ....269 Q1
Crowstone Rd CDW/CHF RM16 ....34 D5
Crowther Cl STPH/PW TN12 ....281 P9
Crowther Rd SNWD SE25 ....69 H8
Crowton Ct MEO DA13 * 113 J5
Croxley Cl STMC/STPC BR5 ....73 H7
Croxley Gn STMC/STPC BR5 ....73 J7
Croxted Cl DUL SE21 ....44 D5
Croxted Rd DUL SE21 ....44 E7
Croyde Cl ELTH/MOT SE9 ....48 E5
Croydon Ct WALD ME5 ....115 K4
The Croydon F/O CROY/NA CRO * 86 C7
Croydon Gv CROY/NA CRO 86 C7
Croydon Rd BH/WHM TN16 ....159 G4
  CROY/NA CRO 87 L1
  PGE/AN SE20 ....69 J6
  WARL CR6 ....131 J2
  WWKM BR4 ....88 F6
Crozier Dr SAND/SEL CR2 ....104 A4
Crucifix La STHWK SE1 ....24 F1
Cruden Rd GVE DA12 ....55 L8
Crumpsall St ABYW SE2 ....29 K3
Crump's La RMAID ME17 ....261 N10
Crundale Cl ASH TN23 ....204 C4
Crundale Rd RHAM ME8 ....102 D2
Crundale Wy MARG CT9 ....179 H3
Crundwell Rd STH/RUST TN4 ....196 C4
Crusader Cl GILL ME7 ....102 B5
  PUR RM19 ....32 B3
Crusader Gdns CROY/NA CRO 86 F6
Crusoe Rd ERITH DA8 ....30 A4
Crutches La BFN/LL DA15 ....48 B3
Crutchley Rd CAT SE6 ....46 F7
Cryalls La RSIT ME9 ....119 J6
Cryals Rd STPH/PW TN12 ....295 P1
Cryol Rd ASH TN23 ....204 C4
Crystal Palace NRWD SE19 ....69 H4
Crystal Palace Pde NRWD SE19 ....69 G3
Crystal Palace Park Rd SYD SE26 ....69 H2
Crystal Palace Rd EDUL SE22 ....45 G4
Crystal Ter NRWD SE19 ....68 E3
Cuba St POP/IOD E14 ....26 C2
Cubitt St CROY/NA CRO 86 A8
Cuckolds Green Rd HOO/HM ME3 ....80 C6
Cuckoo La ASH TN23 ....204 D4
  CDW/CHF RM16 ....34 A1
  HYTHE CT21 ....218 A3
  RTON TN1 ....189 K6
  STPH/PW TN12 ....296 B3
Cuckoowood Av MAID/BEAR ME14 ....141 G4
Cudham Cl MAID/BEAR ME14 ....13 J2
Cudham Dr CROY/NA CRO 105 G2
Cudham Gdns MARG CT9 ....179 H3
Cudham La North RSEV TN14 ....107 H8
Cudham La South RSEV TN14 ....133 H1
Cudham Park Rd RSEV TN14 ....107 K4
Cudham Rd BH/WHM TN16 ....132 D5
  ORP BR6 ....106 D5
Cudham St CAT SE6 ....46 D5
Cudworth Rd KEN/WIL TN24 ....205 G4
Cuff Crs ELTH/MOT SE9 ....47 M4
Cugley Rd RDART DA2 ....52 D5
Culcroft HART DA3 ....76 D5
Culford Rd CDW/CHF RM16 ....34 D1
Cullens Hi RCANTW CT4 ....291 G6
Cullet Dr QBOR ME11 ....227 P2
Culling's Hl STHWK SE1 ....45 G4
Culloden Rd BFN/LL DA15 ....48 D5
Culmers Ter MAID/BEAR ME13 * 124 F8
Culmore Rd PECK SE15 ....25 J6
Culpeper Cl RHAM ME8 ....116 E1
Culpepper Cl MAID/BEAR ME17 ....169 G3
Culpeppers CRBK TN17 ....297 M6
Culpepper Cl CANTW/ST CT2 ....172 B5
Culpepper Rd RHAM ME8 ....116 E1
  RMAID ME17 ....261 J4
Culverden Av STH/RUST TN4 ....196 C7
Culverden Down STH/RUST TN4 ....22 B2
Culverden Pk STPH/PW TN12 * 22 B1
Culverden Park Rd STH/RUST TN4 ....22 D1
Culverden Sq RTW TN1 ....22 F2
Culverden St RTW TN1 ....22 F3
Culver Dr OXTED RH8 ....157 K3
Culverhouse Gdns STRHM/NOR SW16 ....68 A1
Culverley Rd CAT SE6 ....46 C6
Culverstone Cl HAYES BR2 ....88 B8
Culvey Ct HART DA3 ....95 M1
Cumberland Av BRDST CT10 ....179 K8
  CANT CT1 ....174 E2
  GVE DA12 ....55 L8
  MAID/SHEP ME15 ....167 L5
  WELL DA16 ....48 D4
Cumberland Dr BXLYHN DA7 ....29 M6
Cumberland Gdns STRHM/NOR SW16 ....68 A1
Cumberland Ms LBTH SE11 * 24 B4
Cumberland Pl CAT SE6 ....47 G6
Cumberland Rd CDW/CHF RM16 ....33 M1
  GILL ME7 ....83 K6
  HAYES BR2 ....70 B8
  MARG CT9 ....15 L3
  RAM CT11 ....17 G3
  SNWD SE25 ....69 J2
Cumberland Ter PGE/AN SE20 * 69 J3
Cumberland Yd RTW TN1 ....22 F7
Cumberlow Av SNWD SE25 ....69 H3
Cumberow La BXLYHN DA7 ....29 L6
Cumnor Cl BRXN/ST SW9 ....24 A7
Cunningham Cl STH/RUST TN4 ....196 E6
  WWKM BR4 ....88 D2
Cunningham Crs BRCH CT7 ....176 C5
  WALD ME5 ....101 H5
Cunningham Rd STH/RUST TN4 ....196 E6
Cupola Cl BMLY BR1 ....71 J3
Curates Wk DART DA1 ....51 L8

Curlew Av RSIT ME9 ....226 C10
Curlew Cl SAND/SEL CR2 ....104 C5
Curlew Crs STRD ME2 ....81 K2
The Curlews GVE DA12 ....55 G1
Curlew Ct RAM CT11 ....16 E7
Curlinge Ct RAM CT11 ....16 E7
Curling La GRAYS RM17 ....34 A4
Curness St LEW SE13 ....46 D2
Curnick's La WNWD SE27 ....68 D1
Curran Av BFN/LL DA15 ....49 G5
Currie Rd STH/RUST TN4 ....196 D7
Curteis Rd TENT TN30 ....301 N12
Curtis Field Rd STRHM/NOR SW16 ....68 A1
Curtis La RCANTW CT4 ....268 G11
Curtismill Cl STMC/STPC BR5 ....73 J7
Curtismill Wy STMC/STPC BR5 ....73 J7
Curtis Rd KEN/WIL TN24 ....205 H4
Curtis St STHWK SE1 ....25 G5
Curtis Wy ME13 * 149 K2
  STHWK SE1 ....25 G5
Curtis Wood Park Rd HB CT6 ....155 H2
Curtis Wood Rd HB CT6 ....155 G2
Curzon Cl DEAL CT14 ....209 K6
  ORP BR6 ....90 E7
Curzon Dr GRAYS RM17 ....34 C6
Curzon Rd CHAT ME4 ....6 D8
  DVW CT17 ....217 J1
  MAID/BEAR ME14 ....141 H7
  THHTH CR7 ....86 B2
Cushman Rd CANT CT1 ....6 C8
Custom House Quay DVW CT17 * 8 C8
Custom House Reach BERM/RHTH SE16 * 26 A2
Cutbush Cl RMAID ME17 ....242 E11
Cutbush & Corrall Ct MAID/BEAR ME14 * 13 J4
Cutcombe Rd CMBW SE5 ....24 D8
Cuthbert Gdns SNWD SE25 ....68 F7
Cuthbert Rd CROY/NA CRO 73 J7
  WGOS CT8 ....177 H5
Cutmore St GVW DA11 ....55 J5
Cutter Cl STRD ME2 ....83 G2
Cutter Ridge Rd MEO DA13 ....98 D4
The Cut HDCN TN27 ....284 A10
  STHWK SE1 ....24 B1
The Cuttings MSTR CT12 ....17 G1
Cutty Sark Cl CEH DA9 * 53 H3
Cuxton Cl BXLYHS DA6 ....49 H5
Cuxton Rd MAID/SHEP ME15 ....168 A8
  STRD ME2 ....18 B9
Cyclamen Rd SWLY BR8 ....74 E1
Cygnet Cl DIT/AY ME20 ....139 H3
Cygnet Cl WALD ME5 ....115 K3
Cygnet Gdns SNWD SE25 ....69 H4
Cygnet Wy ASH TN23 ....204 C2
Cylinder Rd HYTHE CT21 ....222 C1
Cypress Av ASH TN23 ....204 D3
  HOO/HM ME3 ....83 M2
Cypress Cl GILL ME7 * 84 A7
  WSTB CT5 ....126 A7
Cypress Ct GILL ME7 * 84 A7
Cypress Gdns BROCKY SE4 ....45 M3
Cypress Gv ORP BR6 ....272 C5
  RTWE/PEM TN2 ....201 K5
Cypress Rd SNWD SE25 ....68 F6
  STRD ME2 ....82 D4
Cypress Tree Cl BFN/LL DA15 ....49 G6
Cyprus Pl RYE TN31 ....332 H4
Cyprus Rd FAV ME13 ....149 M2
Cyrena Rd EDUL SE22 ....45 G3
Cyril Rd BXLYHN DA7 ....29 M8
  ORP BR6 ....91 H3
Czar St DEPT SE8 ....26 B3

D

Dabbling Cl ERITH DA8 * 31 J6
Dabin Crs GNWCH SE10 ....26 D7
Dacca St DEPT SE8 ....26 A5
Dacre Gdns LEW SE13 * 46 F2
Dacre Pk LEW SE13 ....46 F1
Dacre Pl LEW SE13 ....46 F1
Dacres Est FSTH SE23 ....45 J2
Dacre Rd FSTH SE23
Daerwood Hi HAYES BR2 ....90 A4
Daffodil Cl CROY/NA CRO 87 L4
Daffodil Rd STRD ME2 ....18 A2
Dagg La STPH/PW TN12 ....258 F9
Daglish Cl LEW SE13 ....46 E4
Dagmar Rd CHAT ME4 ....101 J3
  CMBW SE5 ....24 F7
  SNWD SE25 ....68 F8
Dagnall Pk SNWD SE25 ....86 F1
Dagnall Rd SNWD SE25 ....86 F1
Dagonet Rd BMLY BR1 ....47 H8
Dahlia Dr SWLY BR8 ....75 G6
Dahlia Rd ABYW SE2 ....29 J4
Daimler Av HB CT6 ....128 C6
Dainford Cl BMLY BR1 ....70 E2
Dairsie Rd ELTH/MOT SE9 ....48 B1
Dairy Cl BMLY BR1 * 71 J4
  EYN DA4 ....76 C4
  THHTH CR7 ....68 D6
Dairy La EDEN TN8 ....186 C6
  STPH/PW TN12 ....258 F9
  WOOL/PLUM SE18 ....28 A5
Dairy Pl STPH/PW TN12 * 258 F9
Daisy Cl CROY/NA CRO 87 L4
Dalberg Rd BRXS/STRHM SW2 ....44 B3
Dalby Rd ABYW SE2 ....29 L2
Dalby Sq MARG CT9 ....15 J3
Dale Cl BKHTH/KID SE3 ....47 J1
  DART DA1 ....51 G4
Dale Ct WALD ME5 ....115 H3
Dale Park Av CROY/NA CRO 87 G6
Dale Rd DART DA1 ....51 G4
  MEO DA13 ....78 B1
  ROCH ME1 ....100 D2
  SWLY BR8 ....93 G7
  WALW SE17 ....24 C5
Daleside ORP BR6 ....91 H8
Daleside ORP BR6 ....107 N12
Dale St CHAT ME4 ....6 C8
  RTW TN1 ....23 L1
The Dale HAYES BR2 ....89 L2
Dale Vw ERITH DA8 ....31 H8
Dale Wk MEO DA13 ....202 F4
Dalewood SIT ME10 ....55 G5
Dale Wood Rd ORP BR6 ....90 F3
Dalison Ct STRD ME2 ....82 C3
Dalkeith Rd DUL SE21 ....44 D6
Dallas-Brett Crs FOLKN CT19 ....220 F3
Dallas Rd SYD SE26 ....69 J1
Dallinger Rd BRCH CT7 ....176 C5
  LEE/GVPK SE12 ....47 G4
Dalmain Rd FSTH SE23 ....45 L6
Dalmally Rd CROY/NA CRO 87 G3
Dalmeny Av MARG CT9 ....179 G4
  STRHM/NOR SW16 ....68 D2
Dalmeny Rd ERITH DA8 ....30 D7
Dalmeny Ter HYTHE CT21 * 222 D3
Dalmore Rd DUL SE21 ....44 D7

Dalrymple Rd BROCKY SE4 ....45 M2
Daltons Rd ORP BR6 ....90 F8
Daltons Rd BMLY BR1 ....92 A3
Dalton St GILL ME7 ....7 J2
  WNWD SE27 ....24 C7
Dalwood St CMBW SE5 ....24 F7
Dalyell Rd BRXN/ST SW9 ....44 A1
Damerham Cl CANTW/ST CT2 ....171 M2
Damien Cl CHAT ME4 ....101 H3
Damigos Rd GVE DA12 ....56 A6
Damon Cl SCUP DA14 ....49 H8
Damsel Cl BERM/RHTH SE16 * 25 H1
Damson Dr HOO/HM ME3 ....81 L2
Danby St PECK SE15 ....45 G4
Dando Crs BKHTH/KID SE3 ....47 L3
Dandridge Cl GNWCH SE10 ....27 G4
Dan Dr FAV ME13 ....149 H1
Danebury CROY/NA CRO 105 G1
Daneby Rd CAT SE6 ....46 D8
Dane Cl BXLY DA5 ....50 B5
  ORP BR6 ....90 E8
  RSIT ME9 ....105 L8
  WALD ME5 ....115 K3
Dane Ct MAID/BEAR ME17 ....258 H6
Dane Court Gdns BRDST CT10 ....179 H3
Danecourt Gdns CROY/NA CRO 87 G6
Dane Court Rd BRDST CT10 ....178 F3
Dane Crs RAM CT11 ....17 J3
Danedale Av IOS ME12 ....66 A7
Dane End Rd WGOS CT8 ....177 G5
Dane Gdns MARG CT9 ....15 M9
Dane Hl MARG CT9 ....15 G5
Dane Hill Gv MARG CT9 ....15 G5
Dane Hill Rw MARG CT9 ....15 H5
Danehurst WGOS CT8 * 177 H5
Dane John Ct CANT CT1 * 4 C8
Dane John Ms CANT CT1 * 4 C8
Dane La RSIT ME9 ....105 L8
Danemore TENT TN30 ....315 N11
Dane Mt MARG CT9 ....15 H4
Dane Park Rd MARG CT9 ....15 H4
Dane Park Vls MARG CT9 * 15 J4
Dane Rd BRCH CT7 ....233 L6
  MARG CT9 ....15 H5
  RAM CT11 ....17 J3
  SEV TN13 ....135 K3
  WARL CR6 ....130 C3
Danes Cl GVW DA11 ....54 F4
Danescombe LEE/GVPK SE12 ....47 H6
Danes Ct DVE/WH CT16 ....213 L4
Danes Dr IOS ME12 ....230 C4
Danes Hl GILL ME7 ....84 B7
Danesmead Ter WALD ME5 * 115 H2
Daneswood Av CAT SE6 ....46 E8
Dane Valley Rd BRDST CT10 ....179 G6
  MARG CT9 ....15 G4
Daneville Rd CMBW SE5 ....24 E7
Daniel Cl CDW/CHF RM16 ....33 J2
  CDW/CHF RM16 ....35 J2
Daniel Gdns PECK SE15 ....25 H6
Daniels Ct WSTB CT5 ....126 D4
Daniels La WARL CR6 ....130 E2
Daniel's Rd PECK SE15 ....45 K1
Daniel Wy RYE TN31 ....332 G1
Danley Rd IOS ME12 ....64 F6
Danns La WBY/VAL ME18 ....164 B5
Dansington Rd WELL DA16 ....48 C4
Danson Crs WELL DA16 ....49 J4
Danson La WELL DA16 ....49 J4
Danson Md WELL DA16 ....49 K1
Danson Rd BXLYHS DA6 ....49 J5
  BXLY DA5 ....49 J4
Danson U/P BFN/LL DA15 ....49 J4
Danson Wy RHAM ME8 ....102 A4
Dante Pl LBTH SE11 * 24 C3
Dante Rd LBTH SE11 ....24 C3
Danvers Rd TON TN9 ....194 E4
Darby Gdns HOO/HM ME3 ....81 J2
Darby Pl FOLK CT20 ....11 J4
Darby Rd FOLK CT20 ....11 J4
Darby's La WADH TN5 ....309 N7
D'Arcy Pl HAYES BR2 ....71 H8
Darent Av SEV TN13 ....135 H8
Darenth Av TONN TN10 ....135 H8
Darenth Dr GVE DA12 ....56 C6
Darenth Gdns BH/WHM TN16 ....159 J5
Darenth Hl RDART DA2 ....76 C2
Darenth La SEV TN13 ....135 H7
Darenth Park Av RDART DA2 ....52 F7
Darenth Rd DART DA1 ....51 M4
  MAID/BEAR ME14 ....13 J7
  WELL DA16 ....48 B2
Darenth Rd South RDART DA2 ....52 F7
Darenth Wy RSEV TN14 ....109 M5
Darenth Wood Rd RDART DA2 ....52 F7
Darent Md EYN DA4 ....76 D1
Darent Valley Pth DART DA1 ....31 J2
  EYN DA4 ....94 C1
  SEV TN13 ....135 H7
Darfield Rd BROCKY SE4 ....46 A3
Dargate Cl MAIDW ME16 ....140 D6
  NRWD SE19 ....69 G2
Dargate Rd WSTB CT5 ....152 A3
Dargets Rd WALD ME5 ....115 H2
Dark Hl FAV ME13 ....149 J1
Darland Av GILL ME7 ....101 K3
Darley Cl CROY/NA CRO 87 G2
Darlinghurst Rd FOLKN CT19 ....219 M6
Darling Rd BROCKY SE4 ....46 B1
Darlington Dr IOS ME12 ....65 G7
Darlington Rd WNWD SE27 ....68 C1
Darlton Cl DART DA1 ....51 G1
Darman La STPH/PW TN12 ....257 M3
Darnets Fld RSEV TN14 ....135 L3
Darnley Rd BRDST CT10 ....183 J5
  FOLK CT20 ....10 B2
  GVW DA11 ....55 H5
Darnley St GVW DA11 ....55 H5
Darns Hl SWLY BR8 ....92 D3
Darracott Cl DEAL CT14 ....209 J4
Darrell Rd EDUL SE22 ....45 H3
Darren Gdns BRDST CT10 ....183 H4
Darrick Wood Rd ORP BR6 ....90 D6
Darset Av FOLK CT20 ....18 B5
Dartford Rd BXLY DA5 ....50 D6
  DART DA1 ....51 H4
  EYN DA4 ....94 B1
  SEV TN13 ....21 J4
Dartmoor Wk POP/IOD E14 * 26 B3
Dartmouth Gv GNWCH SE10 ....26 E8
Dartmouth Hl GNWCH SE10 ....26 E8
Dartmouth Pl FSTH SE23 ....45 K3
Dartmouth Rd HAYES BR2 ....88 A3
  SYD SE26 ....69 H2
Dartmouth Rw GNWCH SE10 ....26 E8
Dartmouth Ter GNWCH SE10 ....26 E8
Dartnell Rd CROY/NA CRO 87 G3
Dartview Cl GRAYS RM17 ....35 K4
Darwin Cl ORP BR6 ....90 D7

Darwin Ct *ROCH* ME1 *	...19	L8
Darwin Dr *TONN* TN10	...189	G7
Darwin Rd *BRCH* CT7	...176	D5
TIL RM18	...35	C2
WELL DA16	...49	G1
Darwin St *WALW* SE17	...24	C9
Daryngton Av *BRCH* CT7	...233	R2
Dashmonden Cl *MRDN* ME2	...82	D3
Dashwood Cl *BXLYHS* DA6	...50	B5
Dashwood Rd *GVW* DA11	...45	H6
Dassett Rd *WWWD* SE27	...68	C2
Datchelor Pl *CMBW* SE5 *	...24	A7
Datchet Rd *CAT* SE6	...44	A8
Date St *WALW* SE17	...24	D4
Davenport Av *GILL* ME7	...83	M7
Davenport Rd *LEW* SE13	...46	C4
SCUP DA14	...49	L7
Davern Cl *GNWCH* SE10	...27	G3
Davey St *PECK* SE15	...25	G5
David Av *MARG* CT9	...179	J8
Davidge St *STHWK* SE1 *	...24	C1
Davids Cl *BRDST* CT10	...183	L12
Davidson Rd *CANTW/ST* CT2	...4	B2
CROY/NA CR0	...87	J6
David's Rd *FSTH* SE23	...45	K6
Davie Cl *IOS* ME12	...64	C5
Davington Hl *FAV* ME13	...149	K1
Davis Av *DART* CT14	...149	H5
GVW DA11	...54	F6
Davis Cl *SEV* TN13	...136	B8
Davy's Pl *GVE* DA12	...79	M3
Dawell Dr *BH/WHM* TN16	...132	B3
Dawes Cl *GRH* DA9	...53	G3
Dawes Rd *CDW/CHF* RM16	...34	A2
Dawes St *WALW* SE17	...7	J4
Dawn Ri *IOS* ME12	...67	G2
Dawn Av *STMC/STPC* BR5	...73	J4
Dawson Cl *WOOL/PLUM* SE18	...28	D3
Dawson Dr *SWLY* BR8	...74	F4
Dawson Rd *FOLKN* CT19	...11	K3
Dawsons Rw *MAID* ME13 *	...149	H3
Daysbrook Rd	
BRXS/STRHM SW2	...44	A6
Days La *BFN/LL* DA15	...48	F5
Daytona Wy *HB* CT6	...128	C6
Dayton Dr *ERITH* DA8	...31	L5
Dayton Gv *PECK* SE15	...25	K7
Dayton Rd *FAV* ME13	...246	B6
Deacon Cl *STRD* ME2	...18	B2
Deacons Leas *ORP* BR6	...90	E7
Deacons Wy *MAID/SHEP* SE17	...24	E7
Deadmans La *RYE* TN31	...225	H3
Deakin Leas *TON* TN4	...194	H6
Deakins Ter *ORP* BR6	...91	H3
Deal Castle Rd *DEAL* CT14	...209	H4
Deal Porters Wy	
BERM/RHTH SE16	...25	K2
Deal Rd *DEAL* CT14	...208	B4
Deals Gtwy *DEPT* SE8	...26	A4
The Deals *RYE* TN31	...225	C4
Deal Wk *BRXN/ST* SW9	...24	D1
Deane Cft *HB* CT6	...129	J7
Deane Cl *WSTB* CT5	...126	F6
Deanery Rd *EDEN* TN8	...186	D4
Deanfield Gdns *CROY/NA* CR0 *	...2	E11
Dean Hl *RCANTE* CT3	...268	E11
Dean La *MEO* DA13	...97	L1
Dean Md *FOLKN* CT19	...220	C6
Dean Rd *CROY/NA* CR0	...86	E7
SIT ME10	...119	M3
STRD ME2	...18	C2
Dean's Buildings *WALW* SE17	...24	F7
Deans Cl *CROY/NA* CR0	...87	G6
Deans Ct *TON* TN9	...194	E5
Deans Gate Cl *FSTH* SE23	...45	L8
Deans Hill Rd *RSIT* ME9	...144	F4
Dean St *MAID/SHEP* ME15	...258	C1
Deans Wk *ASH* TN23	...204	C4
Deansway Av *CANTW/ST* CT2	...172	F2
Deanwood Dr *RHAM* ME8	...102	E7
Deanwood Dr *DVW* CT17	...212	F6
Deborah Cl *ISTW* TW7	...127	L5
Debrabant Cl *ERITH* DA8	...30	C5
De Burgh Hl *DVW* CT17	...8	A2
De Burgh St *DVW* CT17	...8	B3
Decima St *STHWK* SE1	...24	F1
Decimus Cl *SNWD* SE25 *	...87	H9
Decoy Hill Rd *HOO/HM* ME3	...40	A7
De Crespigny Pk *CMBW* SE5	...24	B8
Deedes Cl *HYTHE* CT21	...222	D2
Deepdene Av *HAYES* BR2	...71	G8
Deepdene *WADH* TN5	...309	L3
Deepdene Gdns	
BRXS/STRHM SW2	...44	A5
Deepdene Rd *HNHL* SE24	...44	D2
WELL DA16	...49	H1
Deerbrook Rd	
BRXS/STRHM SW2	...44	C6
Deerdale Rd *HNHL* SE24	...44	D7
Deerhurst Ct *HART* DA3	...78	D7
Deerhurst Gdns *MAID* ME16	...12	C2
Deerhurst Rd	
STRHM/NOR SW16	...68	A2
Deering Cl *CHAT* ME4	...83	J3
Deerleap La *RSEV* TN14	...108	L7
Deer Park Wy *WWKM* BR4	...89	G5
Deerson La *RCANTE* CT3	...234	H9
Deerton St *RSIT* ME9	...122	B7
Defiant Cl *MAID* ME5	...101	J7
Defoe Cl *WALD* ME5	...101	J1
Defoe Pde *CDW/CHF* RM16	...35	J2
Defoe Rd *BERM/RHTH* SE16	...26	A1
De Frene Rd *SYD* SE26	...69	L1
Degema Rd *CHST* BR7	...72	C2
De Havilland Ct *RFOLK* CT18	...220	C1
Delaware Av *HAYES* BR2	...71	G8
Deepdene *WADH* TN5	...309	L3
Deepdene Gdns	
BRXS/STRHM SW2	...44	A5
De Havillands *WOOL/PLUM* SE18	...28	C5
De Havilland Dr	
WOOL/PLUM SE18	...28	C5
Dekker Rd *DUL* SE21	...44	F4
Delacourt Cl *MSTR* CT12	...181	M8
Delacourt Rd *BKHTH/KID* SE3	...27	J6
Delafield Rd *CHARL* SE7	...27	J5
GRAYS RM17	...34	E4
Delaford Rd *BERM/RHTH* SE16	...25	M1
Delagarde Rd *BH/WHM* TN16	...159	K2
Delamere Crs *CROY/NA* CR0	...87	K2
Delamark Rd *IOS* ME12	...64	D3
Delane Rd *DEAL* CT14	...209	H4
De-l'Angle Rw *RCANTW* CT4	...248	E6
De Lapre Cl *STMC/STPC* BR5	...91	J1
Delargy Cl *CDW/CHF* RM16	...35	J2
Delarue Rd *RTON* TN11	...189	G5
De Laune St *WALW* SE17	...24	C5
Delaware Av *CANTW/ST* CT2	...173	G5
Delawyk Crs *HNHL* SE24	...44	E3
Delce Rd *ROCH* ME1	...19	L6
Delce La *STPH/PW* TN12	...258	C10
Delfside *SWCH* CT13	...206	B1
Delf St *SWCH* CT13	...237	J12
Del Gdns *SNOD* ME6 *	...113	H5
Delisle Rd *THMD* SE28	...28	C1
Delius Dr *TONN* TN10	...189	J7
Dell Dr *RTWE/PEM* TN2	...23	L3
Dellfield Cl *BECK* BR3	...70	D5

Dell Rd *GRAYS* RM17	...34	C3
The Dell *ABYW* SE2	...29	H4
BECK BR3 *	...70	B4
EGRN RH19	...274	A12
GRH DA9	...53	J3
NRWD SE19	...69	G5
Delmaney Cl *BRDST* CT10	...179	L3
Delme Crs *BKHTH/KID* SE3	...27	J8
Delmey Cl *CROY/NA* CR0	...87	G6
Delmonden Rd *HAWK* TN18	...311	Q7
Deloraine St *DEPT* SE8	...26	B7
De Luci Rd *ERITH* DA8	...30	D4
De Lucy St *ABYW* SE2	...29	J5
Delverton Rd *WALW* SE17	...24	C4
De Mere Cl *RHAM* ME8	...102	C3
Demozay Dr *RFOLK* CT18	...220	B1
Denbeigh Dr *TONN* TN10	...189	G7
Denberry Dr *SCUP* DA14	...49	L8
Denbigh Av *RHAM* ME8	...102	E4
Denbigh Cl *CHST* BR7	...72	A5
SIT ME10	...119	M2
Denbigh Pl *ASH* TN23 *	...2	B9
Denbigh Rd *MSTR* CT12	...16	A1
STH/RUST TN4	...196	F6
Denbridge Rd *BMLY* BR1	...72	A6
Dence Cl *HB* CT6	...129	J4
Dence Pk *HB* CT6	...129	J4
Den Cl *BECK* BR3	...70	E8
Dencorra Wy *ASH* TN23	...204	D2
Dene Av *BFN/LL* DA15	...49	J5
Dene Cl *BROCKY* SE4	...45	M1
HAYES BR2	...89	J1
RDART DA2	...74	F1
Denecroft Gdns *GRAYS* RM17	...34	E2
Dene Dr *HART* DA3	...78	C6
ORP BR6	...91	J1
Dene Farm La *RCANTE* CT3	...251	J5
Dene Holm Rd *GVW* DA11	...54	E8
Dene Lodge Cl *BGR/WK* TN15	...240	F1
Dene Rd *DART* DA1	...52	A5
Denesway *MEO* DA13	...97	H2
The Dene *CANT* CT1	...174	C4
CROY/NA CR0	...87	L7
HYTHE CT21 *	...222	D3
RASHW TN26	...285	N12
SEV TN13	...171	H8
Dene Wk *DART* TN23 *	...77	M7
Dene Wy *RRTW* TN3	...277	P10
Dengemarsh Rd *LYDD* TN29	...334	G6
Dengrove Pk *CANTW/ST* CT2 *	...172	E3
Denham Cl *LYDD* TN29	...321	N4
Denham Rd *RSIT* ME9	...118	C2
Denham Wy *RYE* TN31	...332	D7
Denison Ms *HOO/HM* ME3	...61	K1
Deniston Av *BXLY* DA5	...49	L6
Den La *STPH/PW* TN12	...258	C10
Denman Rd *PECK* SE15	...25	G5
Denmark Hl *HNHL* SE24	...44	E2
Denmark Rd *BMLY* BR1	...71	J1
CMBW SE5	...24	D7
RAM CT11	...17	K4
SNWD SE25	...87	H5
Denmark St *FOLKN* CT19	...11	L2
Denmark Ter *ASH* TN23 *	...2	C8
Denmead Rd *CROY/NA* CR0	...86	C4
Denne Cl *CANTW/ST* CT2	...173	G1
Denne Manor La *RCANTW* CT4	...246	H10
Dennes La *LYDD* TN29	...330	C12
LYDD TN29	...330	C12
Dennes Mill Cl *RASHE* TN25	...266	E11
Dennett Rd *CROY/NA* CR0	...86	B3
Denness Rd *ASH* TN23	...204	E4
Dennett's Gv *NWCR* SE14	...25	L8
Dennettsland Rd *EDEN* TN8	...186	D4
Dennett's Rd *NWCR* SE14	...25	L8
Denning Av *CROY/NA* CR0	...86	B8
Denning Cl *MAID* ME16	...166	C1
Dennis Rd *GVW* DA11	...15	H8
Dennis Wy *FOLKN* CT19	...219	M6
Denny Crs *LBTH* SE11	...24	B4
Denny St *LBTH* SE11	...24	B4
Den Rd *HAYES* BR2	...70	E8
Densole Cl *BECK* BR3 *	...69	M5
Densole La *RFOLK* CT18	...292	F9
Denstead Ct *CANTW/ST* CT2 *	...171	K1
Denstead La *RCANTW* CT4	...170	A1
Denstead Oast *RCANTW* CT4	...170	A1
Denstroude La *CANTW/ST* CT2	...152	F2
Dental Cl *SIT* ME10	...119	H5
Dental Rd *SIT* ME10	...119	H5
Dent-de-Lion Cl *MARG* CT9	...177	K5
Dent-de-Lion Rd *MARG* CT9	...177	K5
Denton Court Rd *GVE* DA12	...55	M6
WELL DA16	...29	K6
Denton Rd *BXLY* DA5	...50	B5
Denton St *GVE* DA12	...55	M5
Denton Ter *BXLY* DA5 *	...50	B5
Denton Wy *MARG* CT9	...178	F4
Denver Rd *DART* DA1	...51	H5
Depot St *CMBW* SE5	...24	C6
Deptford Br *GNWCH* SE10	...26	A7
Deptford Broadway *DEPT* SE8	...26	A7
Deptford Church St *DEPT* SE8	...26	A6
Deptford Gn *DEPT* SE8	...26	A6
Deptford High St *DEPT* SE8	...26	A6
Deptford Whf *DEPT* SE8	...26	A4
Derby Cl *RTON* TN11	...188	B7
Derby Hl *FSTH* SE23	...45	K7
Derby Hill Crs *FSTH* SE23	...45	K7
Derby Rd *CROY/NA* CR0	...86	B5
MAID/SHEP ME15	...167	K5
WALD ME5	...101	M3
Derby Road Br *GRAYS* RM17	...34	C4
Derek Walcott Cl *HNHL* SE24 *	...44	D1
Dering Cl *HDCN* TN27	...175	D8
Dering Pl *CROY/NA* CR0	...86	D7
HB CT6	...129	J5
KEN/WIL TN24	...2	C1
RCANTW CT4	...175	G8
Dering Wy *GVE* DA12	...56	A2
Deringwood Dr	
MAID/SHEP ME15	...168	B3
Deringwood Pde	
MAID/SHEP ME15 *	...168	B3
Dermody Gdns *LEW* SE13 *	...46	E4
Dermody Rd *LEW* SE13	...46	E4
Dernier Rd *RTON* TN11	...194	F1
Deronda Rd *BRXS/STRHM* SW2	...44	D2
Derrick Gdns *CHARL* SE7	...27	K2
Derrick Rd *BECK* BR3	...70	B2
Derringstone Hl *RCANTW* CT4	...263	P2
Derringstone St *RCANTW* CT4	...270	E6
Derry Downs *STMC/STPC* BR5	...91	K3
Derville Rd *LYDD* TN29	...335	M2
Derwent Av *RAM* CT11	...16	C5
Derwent Cl *DART* DA2	...51	J4
Derwent Crs *BXLYHN* DA7	...30	B8
Derwent Dr *STH/RUST* TN4	...22	D7
STMC/STPC BR5	...90	B7

Derwent Gv *EDUL* SE22	...45	G2
Derwent Rd *PGE/AN* SE20	...69	H6
TONN TN10	...188	D7
Derwent St *GNWCH* SE10	...26	F4
Derwent Wy *RCANTE* CT3	...251	Q11
Desenfans Rd *DUL* SE21	...44	F4
Desmond Crs *FAV* ME13 *	...150	B5
Desmond St *NWCR* SE14	...25	M5
Desmond Tutu Dr *FSTH* SE23	...45	M6
D'Este Rd *RAM* CT11	...17	J3
Detillens La *OXTED* RH8	...157	M7
Detling Av *GVE* DA12	...79	M3
Detling Cl *IOS* ME12	...64	C5
Detling Hl *MAID/BEAR* ME14	...142	B4
Detling Rd *BMLY* BR1	...71	K7
ERITH DA8	...30	E6
GVW DA11	...54	E6
Devema Cl *CHST* BR7	...72	B5
Devenish Rd *ABYW* SE2	...29	H1
Devereux Cl *BECK* BR3	...88	D1
Deverell St *STHWK* SE1	...24	E2
Devon Av *DEAL* CT14	...209	G4
Devon Cl *RHAM* ME8	...103	G4
WALD ME5	...101	K4
Devon Gdns *BRCH* CT7	...176	C7
Devon Rd *CANT* CT1	...5	M7
EYN DA4	...76	C5
FOLKN CT19	...11	J4
MAID/SHEP ME15	...167	K4
Devonshire Av *DART* DA1	...51	J4
Devonshire Cl *RTWE/PEM* TN2	...201	J3
Devonshire Dr *GNWCH* SE10	...26	C7
Devonshire Gdns *MARG* CT9	...15	M4
SLH/COR SS17	...36	B2
Devonshire Gv *PECK* SE15	...25	J5
Devonshire Rd *BXLYHS* DA6	...33	M5
CDW/CHF RM16	...33	M3
CROY/NA CR0	...86	D5
DVW CT17	...8	D5
ELTH/MOT SE9	...47	M7
FSTH SE23	...45	L5
GILL ME7	...83	K6
ORP BR6	...91	H3
Devonshire Sq *HAYES* BR2	...71	H1
Devonshire Ter *BRDST* CT10	...183	L1
EDUL SE22 *	...45	H2
Devonshire Wy *CROY/NA* CR0	...88	C1
Devon St *PECK* SE15	...25	J5
Dewar St *PECK* SE15	...25	H1
Dewbury Cl *CHAT* ME4	...83	J4
Dewhurst La *WADH* TN5	...308	H11
Dewlands Av *RDART* DA2	...52	C5
Dexter Cl *GRAYS* RM17	...34	B2
Dexter La *RYE* TN31	...325	P5
D'Eynsford Rd *CMBW* SE5	...24	D7
Dhekelia Cl *MAID/BEAR* ME14	...141	H6
Dial Cl *GILL* ME7	...21	M5
GRH DA9	...53	K1
Dial Rd *GILL* ME7	...84	A7
Diameter Rd *STMC/STPC* BR5	...90	C3
Diamond Cl *DART* DA1	...51	J4
Diamond Ct *IOS* ME12	...64	C5
Diamond Rd *GILL* ME7	...21	M8
Diamond St *PECK* SE15	...25	F6
Diamond Vls *NROM* TN28 *	...330	C2
Diana Cl *CDW/CHF* RM16	...34	A2
DEPT SE8	...26	A6
SCUP DA14	...49	M7
Diana Gdns *DEAL* CT14	...209	H4
Diana Rd *CHAT* ME4	...84	F9
Dianthus Cl *ABYW* SE2 *	...29	J4
Dibden La *RSEV* TN14	...20	A4
Dibdin Rd *DEAL* CT14	...209	L2
Dickens Av *CANT* CT1	...172	D7
DART DA1	...52	B2
RAM CT11	...16	B2
Dickens Cl *ERITH* DA8	...30	B8
HART DA3	...95	M1
RMAID ME17	...260	F1
Dickens Dr *CHST* BR7	...72	D3
E/WMAL ME19	...139	G4
Dickens Est *BERM/RHTH* SE16 *	...25	H2
Dickensian Cl *HOO/HM* ME3	...61	H2
Dickenson's La *SNWD* SE25	...87	H3
Dickenson's Rd *SNWD* SE25	...87	H2
Dickens Rd *BRDST* CT10	...179	M6
GVE DA12	...55	M6
MAID/BEAR ME14	...140	F2
ROCH ME1	...100	D3
Dickens Sq *STHWK* SE1 *	...24	D2
Dickens Wk *HOO/HM* ME3 *	...59	C1
Dickens Wd Cl *NRWD* SE19	...68	C4
Dickley La *RMAID* ME17	...242	H11
Dickson House	
WOOL/PLUM SE18 *	...27	M6
Dickson Rd *DVW* CT17	...8	C5
ELTH/MOT SE9	...47	M1
Dicksons Bourne *RASHE* TN25	...305	Q8
Dieu Stone La *DVE/WH* CT16	...9	H4
Digby Cl *CROY/NA* CR0	...87	G6
Digby Rd *FOLK* CT20	...219	M8
Digdog La *CRBK* TN17	...299	P9
Dignals Cl *RHAM* ME8	...103	G3
Dilhorne Rd *LEE/GVPK* SE12	...47	H4
Diligent Dr *SIT* ME10	...120	A2
Dillon Wy *RTWE/PEM* TN2	...197	G7
Dillwyn Cl *SYD* SE26	...70	A1
Dilly Fields Wd *HOO/HM* ME3	...82	B2
Dillywood La *HOO/HM* ME3	...81	M3
Dilnot Wy *DEAL* CT14	...209	H4
Dimmock Cl *STPH/PW* TN12	...279	L13
Dingleden La *DEN* TN17	...313	Q8
Dingwall Av *CROY/NA* CR0	...86	D5
Dingwall Rd *CROY/NA* CR0	...86	D5
Dinsdale Gdns *SNWD* SE25	...68	C8
Dinsdale Rd *BKHTH/KID* SE3	...27	G5
Dippers Cl *BGR/WK* TN15	...136	E5
Discovery Rd	
MAID/SHEP ME15	...168	B3
Discovery Wk *CANT* CT1	...5	M6
Dislingham Cl *RTON* TN11	...197	L5
Disney Pl *STHWK* SE1 *	...24	D1
Disney St *STHWK* SE1 *	...24	D1
Disraeli Cl *MAID/SHEP* ME15	...167	M8
Distin St *LBTH* SE11	...24	B6
Dittisham Rd *ELTH/MOT* SE9	...71	H1
Ditton Court Cl *DIT/AY* ME20 *	...139	J4
Dittoncroft Cl *SAND/SEL* CR2	...86	F7
Ditton Pl *PGE/AN* SE20 *	...69	J4
PGE/AN SE20	...69	J4
Ditton Rd *BXLYHS* DA6	...50	A1
Dixon Cl *MAID/SHEP* ME15	...12	D6
Dixon Pl *WWKM* BR4	...88	D7
Dixon Rd *NWCR* SE14	...25	M7
SNWD SE25	...87	G3
Dixwell Cl *RHAM* ME8	...102	C3
Dixwell Rd *FOLK* CT20	...11	G2
Dobbie Cl *SIT* ME10	...119	M3
Dobell Rd *ELTH/MOT* SE9	...48	A3
Dobson Rd *GVE* DA12	...79	M2

Dock Approach Rd	
GRAYS RM17	...34	F4
Dockers Tanner Rd	
POP/IOD E14	...26	B3
Dock Exit Rd *DVE/WH* CT16	...9	J4
Dockhead *STHWK* SE1	...25	H1
Dock Head Rd *CHAT* ME4	...83	H1
Dock Hill Av *BERM/RHTH* SE16	...12	C5
Dockley Rd *BERM/RHTH* SE16	...25	H2
Dock Rd *CHAT* ME4	...83	H1
GRAYS RM17	...34	F6
Doctor Hope's Rd *CRBK* TN17	...298	G9
Doctors *SYD* SE26	...69	G9
Dodbrooke Rd *WNWD* SE27	...44	B8
Doddington Cl *MAIDW* ME16	...12	C5
Doddington Pl *WALW* SE17	...24	C5
Doddington Rd *RHAM* ME8	...102	D3
Dodd Rd *TONN* TN10	...189	H6
Dodds La *DVE/WH* CT16	...213	H6
Dodson St *STHWK* SE1 *	...24	B1
Doebury Wk *WOOL/PLUM* SE18 *	...29	H5
Doggeral Acre *WSTB* CT5 *	...127	G6
Doggets Cl *EDEN* TN8	...192	D5
Doggett Rd *CAT* SE6	...46	B5
Doggetts Ms *RHAM* ME3	...43	J7
Doggett's Sq *STRD* ME2	...19	H4
Dog Kennel Hl *EDUL* SE22	...44	F1
Dog Kennel La *RFOLK* CT18	...291	L11
Dogwood Cl *GVW* DA11	...78	F2
WALD ME5	...101	L5
Dola Av *DEAL* CT14	...209	J3
Dolben Ct *DEPT* SE8 *	...26	A5
Dolland St *LBTH* SE11	...24	A4
Dolman St *BRXN/ST* SW9	...44	C2
Dolphin Cl *BRDST* CT10	...179	K3
Dolphin Dr *RHAM* ME8	...102	F8
Dolphin La *DVE/WH* CT16	...8	E5
Dolphin Pk *SIT* ME10 *	...120	C4
Dolphin Pas *DVE/WH* CT16	...8	E5
Dolphin Rd *LYDD* TN29	...334	E3
SIT ME10	...120	C4
Dolphins Rd *FOLKN* CT19	...220	D6
Dolphin St *DEAL* CT14	...209	L2
HB CT6	...128	F4
Dolphin Wy *WTHK* RM20	...32	F4
Dombey Cl *HOO/HM* ME3	...81	K2
ROCH ME1 *	...100	D3
Dome Hill Pk *SYD* SE26	...69	G1
Domett Cl *CMBW* SE5	...44	D2
Dominion Rd *CROY/NA* CR0	...87	G3
Domneva Rd *MSTR* CT12	...180	E7
WGOS CT8	...177	G5
Domonic Dr *ELTH/MOT* SE9	...48	C8
Donald Biggs Dr *GVE* DA12	...55	L5
Donald Moor Av *RSIT* ME9	...121	K7
Donald Rd *CROY/NA* CR0	...86	A2
Donaldson Rd	
WOOL/PLUM SE18	...28	B7
Doncaster Cl	
MAID/SHEP ME15	...168	A7
Doncella Cl *CDW/CHF* RM16	...33	K3
Donegal Rd *CANT* CT1	...5	L4
Donemore Dr *SIT* ME10	...120	A1
Donet Cl *RHAM* ME8	...103	H2
Dongola Rd *STRD* ME2	...18	B4
Donkey Av *EDUL* SE22	...45	H5
Donkey Fld *RTON* TN11	...255	M12
Donkey La *EYN* DA4	...94	C5
RCANTE CT3	...251	M9
Dunnage St *SLYD* TN29	...320	H5
Donnay Cl *ESTH* ME12	...16	C4
Donnahay Rd *MSTR* CT12	...182	A5
Donnella Ct *CDW/CHF* RM16	...33	L2
Don Phelan Cl *CMBW* SE5	...24	D7
Doon Brae *STH/RUST* TN4	...196	D3
Dorado Gdns *ORP* BR6	...91	L6
Doran Gv *WOOL/PLUM* SE18	...28	F6
Dorcas Gdns *BRDST* CT10	...179	K7
Dorchester Av *BXLY* DA5	...49	L6
Dorchester Cl *DART* DA1	...58	C6
HOO/HM ME3	...61	K2
STMC/STPC BR5	...73	J4
Dorchester Dr *HNHL* SE24	...44	D1
Dorchester Rd *GVE* DA12	...55	L8
Dorcis Av *BXLYHN* DA7	...29	M8
Dorian Ct *WARL* CR6 *	...130	A5
Doria Av *STH/RUST* TN4	...196	C4
Doric Cl *STH/RUST* TN4	...196	C4
Doric Ct *RAM* CT11	...16	F8
Dorin Ct *WARL* CR6 *	...130	A5
Doris Av *BXLYHN* DA7	...30	D7
Doris Vls *SWCH* CT13 *	...237	K12
Dorking Cl *DEPT* SE8	...26	A5
Dorking Rd *RTW* TN1	...196	A5
Dorman Av North *RCANTE* CT3	...251	Q12
Dorman Av South	
RCANTE CT3	...251	Q12
Dormers Dr *MEO* DA13	...97	J3
Dornberg Cl *BKHTH/KID* SE3	...27	H6
Dornberg Rd *BKHTH/KID* SE3 *	...27	J5
Dornden Dr *RRTW* TN3	...200	B1
Dornden Gdns *WALD* ME5	...115	J3
Dorney Ri *STMC/STPC* BR5	...73	G8
Dornton Rd *SAND/SEL* CR2	...86	F5
Dorothy Av *CRBK* TN17	...298	H9
Dorothy Dr *MSTR* CT12	...182	E2
Dorothy Evans Cl *BXLYHN* DA7	...50	C2
Dorrington Wy *BECK* BR3	...88	D1
Dorrit St *STHWK* SE1 *	...24	D1
Dorrit Wy *CHST* BR7	...72	D5
ROCH ME1	...100	E3
Dorset Av *WELL* DA16	...49	G4
Dorset Cl *WSTB* CT5	...126	C6
Dorset Crs *GVE* DA12	...55	M8
Dorset Gdns *MAID/SHEP* ME15	...167	K4
DEAL CT14 *	...209	K7
STRHM/NOR SW16	...68	A8
Dorset Rd *BECK* BR3	...69	L2
CANT CT1	...174	E2
ELTH/MOT SE9	...47	M7
IOS ME12	...64	D3
VX/NE SW8	...24	C6
Dorset Sq *RHAM* ME8	...102	E4
Dorset St *SEV* TN13	...21	J7
Dorset Wy *MAID/SHEP* ME15	...167	K5
Dorton Cl *PECK* SE15	...25	F6
Dorton Dr *BGR/WK* TN15	...136	E2
Dorville Rd *LEE/GVPK* SE12	...47	H3
Dothill Rd *WOOL/PLUM* SE18	...28	F7
Dotterel Cl *WALD* ME5	...115	U4
Doubleday Dr *RSIT* ME9	...120	C7
Doubleton La *RTON* TN11	...276	H4
Douglas Av *HYTHE* CT21	...222	D3
WSTB CT5	...126	F4
Douglas Cl *BRDST* CT10	...179	M6
CDW/CHF RM16	...33	M2
Douglas Pth *POP/IOD* E14	...26	D4
Douglas Rd *POP/IOD* E14 *	...26	B2
DEAL CT14	...209	H4
DVW CT17	...217	J1
HB CT6	...129	M5
MAIDW ME16	...12	D7
RMAID ME17	...243	J12
TON TN9	...194	D5
WELL DA16	...49	H1
Douglas Wy *NWCR* SE14	...26	A6

Douro Cl *CANT* CT1	...172	D5
Douro Pl *DVE/WH* CT16	...8	D7
Dour Side *DVW* CT17	...213	H6
Dour St *DVW* CT17	...8	E5
Doust Wy *ROCH* ME1	...19	M8
Dove Cl *ASH* TN23	...204	F8
CDW/CHF RM16	...33	M2
HYTHE CT21	...321	C1
SAND/SEL CR2	...104	C5
WALD ME5	...101	J7
WSTB CT5	...126	C6
Dovedale *BRCH* CT7	...176	B6
Dovedale Cl *WELL* DA16	...29	H7
Dovedale Ct *BRCH* CT7	...176	E6
KEN/WIL TN24 *	...2	A3
Dovedale Rd *EDUL* SE22	...45	J3
RDART DA2	...52	D6
Doveney Cl *STMC/STPC* BR5	...73	L8
Dovercourt Rd *THHTH* CR7	...68	B8
Dovercourt Rd *EDUL* SE22	...44	F8
Dover Hl *FOLKN* CT19	...220	F5
Dove Rd *TONN* TN10	...188	D7
Dover Patrol *BKHTH/KID* SE3	...27	J1
Dover Pl *DEAL* CT14	...211	G5
DEAL CT14	...253	N9
FOLK CT20	...11	G5
GVW DA11	...54	F6
NRWD SE19	...250	C12
RCANTW CT4	...213	M5
SWCH CT13	...253	N8
WOOL/PLUM SE18	...28	D3
Dover Rd East *GVW* DA11	...54	F5
Dover Rd *CANT* CT1	...5	G6
MAIDW ME16	...166	D3
SIT ME10	...119	M5
Doves Cl *HAYES* BR2	...89	H1
Doves Cft *RSIT* ME9	...145	K2
Doveton Rd *SAND/SEL* CR2	...86	E6
Dowanhill Rd *CAT* SE6	...46	E6
Dowding Rd *BH/WHM* TN16	...132	B4
Dowding Wy *RTWE/PEM* TN2	...197	H4
Dower House Crs	
STH/RUST TN4	...196	B2
Dowgate Cl *TON* TN9	...195	G6
Dowlas St *CMBW* SE5	...24	F6
Dowle Cl *LYDD* TN29	...330	B6
Dowlerville Rd *ORP* BR6	...107	L1
Dowling Cl *SNOD* ME6	...112	F6
The Downage *GVW* DA11	...55	H7
Down Av *RRTW* TN3	...296	B10
Downbanka Av *BXLYHN* DA7	...233	M8
Down Barton Rd *BRCH* CT7	...204	B6
Down Ct *ASH* TN23	...204	B6
Downderry Rd *BMLY* BR1	...46	E8
Downe Av *RSEV* TN14	...107	H6
Downe Cl *WELL* DA16	...29	K6
Downe *WOOL/PLUM* SE18	...28	C5
Downer Ct *ROCH* ME1	...100	F5
Downe Rd *HAYES* BR2	...106	C3
RSEV TN14	...107	H8
Downham Wy *BMLY* BR1	...70	B1
Downhill Cl *DVE/WH* CT16 *	...212	E13
The Downings *HB* CT6	...129	H7
Downland Ct *KEN/WIL* TN24 *	...2	A3
Downlands *DEAL* CT14	...242	G11
RMAID ME17	...242	G11
Downland Wk *WALD* ME5	...101	H8
Downleys Cl *ELTH/MOT* SE9	...47	M7
Downman Rd *ELTH/MOT* SE9	...47	M1
Downs Av *CHST* BR7	...72	A2
DART DA1	...52	B5
WSTB CT5	...126	B5
Downs Bridge Rd *BECK* BR3	...70	F1
Downs Cl *HDCN* TN27	...264	B5
HDCN TN27	...283	M4
MAID/BEAR ME14	...141	H4
RDV CT15	...273	L5
RFOLK CT18	...219	C7
SIT ME10	...119	M5
Downs Hl *BECK* BR3	...70	F1
Downside *BECK* BR3 *	...70	B5
FOLKN CT19	...11	H1
RCANTW CT4 *	...175	M4
RDV CT15	...215	H3
STRD ME2	...18	E3
Downs Rd *BECK* BR3	...70	C1
DEAL CT14	...209	G7
FOLKN CT19	...220	D5
MAID/BEAR ME14	...141	H5
MEO DA13	...78	E2
RAM CT11	...16	B7
RDV CT15	...273	M5
THHTH CR7	...68	A6
WBY/WAL ME18	...257	P4
The Downs *RAM* CT11	...17	J7
RCANTE CT3	...235	K7
RCANTW CT4	...248	E8
WALD ME5	...114	C4
Downs Vw *ROCH* ME1	...114	A4
Downsview *E/WMAL* ME19	...239	M7
WALD ME5	...101	K5
Downsview Cl *SWLY* BR8	...75	G7
Downsview Gdns *NRWD* SE19	...68	B5
Downs View Rd	
MAID/BEAR ME14	...141	H5
Downsview Rd *NRWD* SE19	...68	B5
SEV TN13	...20	C7
Downs Wy *HDCN* TN27	...283	M4
OXTED RH8	...157	K5
RASHE TN25	...306	H4
Downs Wd *MEO* DA13	...239	L5
Downton Av	
BRXS/STRHM SW2	...44	A7
Downtown Rd	
BERM/RHTH SE16	...25	M1
Dowson Cl *CMBW* SE5 *	...44	E2
Doyce St *STHWK* SE1 *	...24	D1
Doyle Cl *ERITH* DA8	...50	D1
Doyle Rd *SNWD* SE25	...87	H5
Dracic St *WALW* SE17	...24	D5
Draco St *WALW* SE17	...24	D5
Draffin La *RYE* TN31	...332	G6
Drage Rd *STPH/PW* TN12	...256	H2
Dragonfly Wy *RFOLK* CT18	...220	C5
Dragon Rd *PECK* SE15	...24	F5
Dragoon Rd *DEPT* SE8	...26	A4
Drainless Rd *SWCH* CT13	...253	M5
Drake Av *IOS* ME12	...65	L8
LYDD TN29	...345	J1
Drakefell Rd *NWCR* SE14	...25	L8
Drake Ms *HAYES* BR2	...71	K8
Drake Rd *BROCKY* SE4	...46	B1
CDW/CHF RM16	...33	M1
CROY/NA CR0	...86	A3
KEN/WIL TN24	...205	K4
Drake's Av *STRD* ME2	...18	D1

Drakes Cl RSIT ME9 103 M3
Drakes Lee NROM TN28 331 M8
Draper Cl BELV DA17 30 A3
Drapers Av MARG CT9 15 H8
Drapers Cl MARG CT9 15 J9
Draper St STH/RUST TN4 196 C3
Drappers Wy BERM/RHTH SE16 25 H3
Draven Cl HAYES BR2 89 G3
Drawbridge Cl
MAID/SHEP ME15 167 M5
Drawell Cl WOOL/PLUM SE18 28 F4
Dray Corner Rd HDCN TN27 282 H2
Draycott Cl CMBW SE5 24 E6
Dray Ct RTON TN11 256 B5
Dray's Fld RSIT ME9 242 H2
Drayton Av ORP BR6 90 C4
Drayton Cl HOO/HM ME3 59 M2
Drayton Rd CROY/NA CR0 86 C5
TON TN9 194 F5
Dreadnought Av IOS ME12 65 H7
Dreadnought St GNWCH SE10 26 F2
Dressington Av BROCKY SE4 46 B4
Drewery Ct BKHTH/KID SE3 * 46 F1
Drewery Dr RHAM ME8 102 D8
Drew La DEAL CT14 209 K5
Driffield Gdns STH/RUST TN4 194 B6
The Drift HAYES BR2 89 L6
Drill La RCANTE CT3 234 C12
The Drive BECK BR3 70 B6
BXLY DA5 49 L5
CANT CT1 5 J9
CHST BR7 73 G5
ERITH DA8 30 C6
GVE DA12 79 L1
HART DA3 78 C7
ORP BR6 91 G5
RRTW TN3 276 G12
RTWE/PEM TN2 201 H4
SCUP DA14 49 J8
SEV TN13 21 G5
THHTH CR7 68 E8
TON TN9 194 E6
WSTB CT5 127 L5
WWKM BR4 88 E3
Droitwich Cl SYD SE26 45 H8
Drop Redoubt Rd DVW CT17 8 B7
Drove Rd IOS ME12 64 F5
Drovers Pl PECK SE15 25 J6
Drovers Rd SAND/SEL CR2 86 E8
The Drove CANTW/ST CT2 173 H5
DEAL CT14 208 B4
DVE/WH CT16 213 H1
WSTB CT5 127 L5
The Drove Wy MEO DA13 78 F4
The Droveway RDV CT15 215 J3
Druce Rd DUL SE21 44 F4
Drudgeon Wy RDART DA2 53 J8
Druid St STHWK SE1 24 F1
Druids Wy HAYES BR2 70 E8
Drum La ASH TN23 2 B4
Drum Major Dr DEAL CT14 209 J6
Drummond Cl ERITH DA8 30 F7
Drummond Rd
BERM/RHTH SE16 25 J2
CROY/NA CR0 86 D5
Drury Crs CROY/NA CR0 86 B5
Drury Rd TENT TN30 315 M1
Dry Bank Ct TONN TN10 194 E1
Drybeck Av RAM CT11 182 C6
Dryden Cl CANT CT1 5 M7
Dryden Pl TIL RM18 35 J7
Dryden Rd DVE/WH CT16 213 J6
WOOL/PLUM SE18 29 G7
Dryden Wy ORP BR6 91 H4
Dryhill La RSEV TN14 161 G1
Dry Hill Park Crs TONN TN10 194 F2
Dry Hill Park Rd TONN TN10 194 E2
Dryhill Rd BELV DA17 30 A5
Dry Hill Rd TONN TN10 194 E2
Dryland Av ORP BR6 91 G7
Dryland Rd BGR/WK TN15 240 E3
SNOD ME6 113 G5
Drywall SIT ME10 * 120 C3
Duarte Pl CDW/CHF RM16 34 A2
Duchess Cl STRD ME2 18 A2
Duchess of Kent Ct
DIT/AY ME20 * 139 M4
Duchess of Kent Dr
WALD ME5 115 J2
Duchess' Wk BGR/WK TN15 21 M8
Ducketts Rd DART DA1 51 G3
Duck La CANT CT1 5 G2
RASHW TN26 303 N6
Duckpit Rd RCANTW CT4 268 D8
Duck St RCANTW CT4 291 R5
Duckworth Cl KEN/WIL TN24 205 L4
Duddington Cl ELTH/MOT SE9 71 L1
Dudely Rd GVW DA11 54 E5
Dudley Av WGOS CT8 176 F5
Dudley Cl CDW/CHF RM16 33 M1
Dudley Rd FOLKN CT19 11 M4
KEN/WIL TN24 203 H6
RTW TN1 22 E4
Dudrich Ms EDUL SE22 45 G3
Dudsbury Rd DART DA1 51 J4
Duffield Cl CDW/CHF RM16 34 A2
Dufrey Pl CMBW SE5 * 24 E6
Duggan Dr CHST BR7 71 M3
Duke Humphrey Rd
BKHTH/KID SE3 26 F8
Dukes Av CDW/CHF RM16 34 B2
Dukes Hl CTHM CR3 130 D6
Dukes Meadow RASHW TN26 318 D2
RTON TN11 254 G11
Dukes Meadow Dr GILL ME7 102 A7
Dukes Orch BXLY DA5 50 D6
Dukes Rd RTW TN1 23 J2
Dukesthorpe Rd SYD SE26 69 L1
Duke St DEAL CT14 209 L2
MARG CT9 14 F3
Dukes Wk MAID/SHEP ME15 13 H5
Dukes Wy WWKM BR4 88 F6
Dukeswood WSTB CT5 127 L8
Dully Rd RSIT ME9 146 E5
Dulverton Rd ELTH/MOT SE9 48 D7
SAND/SEL CR2 104 B4
Dulwich Common DUL SE21 44 E6
The Dulwich Oaks DUL SE21 * 45 G8
Dulwich Rd HNHL SE24 44 B3
Dulwich Village DUL SE21 44 E4
Dulwich Wood Av NRWD SE19 68 F2
Dulwich Wood Pk NRWD SE19 68 F1
Dumbourne La TENT TN30 315 Q7
Dumbreck Rd ELTH/MOT SE9 48 B2
Dumb Woman's La RYE TN31 224 C6
Dumergue Av QBOR ME11 64 C8
Dumpton Gap Rd BRDST CT10 183 K3
Dumpton La RAM CT11 17 K1
Dumpton Park Dr RAM CT11 17 M3
Dumpton Park Rd RAM CT11 17 J3
Dunbar Av BECK BR3 69 M8
STRHM/NOR SW16 68 B6
Dunbar St WNWD SE27 44 D8
Dunblane Rd ELTH/MOT SE9 47 M1
Duncan Cl WSTB CT5 126 E6
Duncan Dr BRCH CT7 176 B5
Duncan Rd GILL ME7 7 L4
RAM CT11 17 G6
WSTB CT5 126 E6
Duncombe Hl FSTH SE23 45 M5
Duncrievie Rd LEW SE13 46 E4
Duncroft WOOL/PLUM SE18 28 F6
Dundale Rd RRTW TN3 294 H5
STPH/PW TN12 295 M1
Dundalk Rd BROCKY SE4 45 M1
Dundas Rd PECK SE15 25 K8
Dundee Rd SNWD SE25 87 J1
Dundein Dr DVE/WH CT16 213 J6
Dundonald Rd RAM CT11 16 F5
Dunedin Cl SIT ME10 119 K6
Dunedin Rd MSTR CT12 182 C4
Dunelm Gv WNWD SE27 68 D1
Dunera Dr MAID/BEAR ME14 141 G6
Dunes Av RYE TN31 332 E7
Dunes Rd NROM TN28 331 L10
Dunfield Rd CAT SE6 70 C2
Dungeness Rd LYDD TN29 334 G4
LYDD TN29 335 L6
Dunheved Cl THHTH CR7 86 B2
Dunheved Rd North
THHTH CR7 86 B2
Dunheved Rd South
THHTH CR7 86 B2
Dunheved Rd West THHTH CR7 86 B2
Dunkeld Rd SNWD SE25 68 E8
Dunkery Ri KEN/WIL TN24 2 A1
Dunkery Rd ELTH/MOT SE9 71 L1
Dunkin Rd DART DA1 52 B2
Dunkirk Cl GVE DA12 79 K2
LYDD TN29 320 G10
Dunkirk Dr WALD ME5 101 G7
Dunkirk Rd FAV ME13 247 M2
Dunkirk Rd North FAV ME13 151 J7
Dunkirk Rd South FAV ME13 151 J8
Dunkirk Sq RDV CT15 214 A6
Dunkirk St WNWD SE27 * 68 D1
Dunk's Green Rd RTON TN11 240 F12
Dunley Dr CROY/NA CR0 105 H1
Dunlin Dr CHAT ME4 83 K3
Dunlop Pl BERM/RHTH SE16 25 G2
Dunlop Rd TIL RM18 35 G7
Dunnett Rd FOLKN CT19 219 M7
Dunning's La ROCH ME1 19 K9
The Dunnings MAIDW ME16 166 B3
Dunnock Rd RASHE TN25 202 E4
Dunn Street Rd GILL ME7 116 B5
Dunoon Ct RAM CT11 * 183 J4
Dunoon Gdns FSTH SE23 * 45 L5
Dunoon Rd FSTH SE23 45 K5
Dunsfold Wy CROY/NA CR0 105 H2
Dunstall Cl LYDD TN29 320 F12
Dunstall Gdns LYDD TN29 320 F12
Dunstall La LYDD TN29 320 F12
Dunstall Welling Est
WELL DA16 * 29 J8
Dunstan Av WGOS CT8 177 G6
Dunstan Gld STMC/STPC BR5 * 90 E2
Dunstan Gv STH/RUST TN4 196 E7
Dunstan Rd STH/RUST TN4 196 E7
Dunstan's Gv EDUL SE22 45 J4
Dunstan's Rd EDUL SE22 45 H5
Dunster Ter
MAID/SHEP ME15 * 167 M5
Dunsterville Wy STHWK SE1 24 E1
Dunton Rd STHWK SE1 25 G3
Dunvegan Rd ELTH/MOT SE9 48 A2
Dunwich Rd BXLYHN DA7 30 A7
Duppas Av CROY/NA CR0 86 C7
Duppas Hill Rd CROY/NA CR0 86 B7
Duppas Hill Ter CROY/NA CR0 86 C6
Duppas Rd CROY/NA CR0 86 B6
Dupree Rd CHARL SE7 27 J4
Dura Den Cl BECK BR3 70 C4
Durand Gdns BRXN/ST SW9 24 A7
Durant Rd SWLY BR8 75 H3
Durban Crs DVE/WH CT16 213 K5
Durban Rd BECK BR3 70 A6
MARG CT9 15 J7
WNWD SE27 68 D1
Durfey Pl CMBW SE5 24 E6
Durham Av HAYES BR2 71 G8
Durham Cl CANT CT1 4 F8
DVW CT17 8 C5
MAID/SHEP ME15 167 L4
Durham Hl BMLY BR1 71 G1
DVW CT17 8 C5
Durham Ri WOOL/PLUM SE18 28 D4
Durham Rd HAYES BR2 71 H8
RHAM ME8 102 D6
SCUP DA14 73 J2
Durham St LBTH SE11 24 A4
Durham Ter PGE/AN SE20 * 69 J4
Duriun Wy ERITH DA8 31 J6
Durley Gdns ORP BR6 91 J7
Durlock MSTR CT12 180 F8
Durlock Av RAM CT11 16 D8
Durlock Rd RCANTE CT3 252 F3
The Durlocks FOLKN CT19 11 M5
Durndale La GVW DA11 78 F1
Durnford Cl CANTW/ST CT2 171 M3
Durning Rd NRWD SE19 68 E2
Durrant Wy ORP BR6 90 E8
SWCM DA10 53 M5
Durrell Gdns WALD ME5 101 K4
Dursley Cl BKHTH/KID SE3 27 K8
Dursley Gdns BKHTH/KID SE3 27 L7
Dursley Rd BKHTH/KID SE3 27 K8
Dutton St GNWCH SE10 26 D7
Duval Dr ROCH ME1 100 F5
Dux Court Rd HOO/HM ME3 59 K5
Dux Hl BGR/WK TN15 240 E9
Dux La BGR/WK TN15 240 E8
Dwelly La LING RH7 191 K1
Dyke Dr STMC/STPC BR5 91 K3
Dyke Rd FOLKN CT19 11 M5
Dykes Wy HAYES BR2 71 G7
Dykewood Cl BXLY DA5 50 E8
Dylan Rd BELV DA17 30 B2
Dylways CMBW SE5 44 E2
Dymchurch Cl ORP BR6 90 F7
Dymchurch Rd HYTHE CT21 321 R1
LYDD TN29 320 G12
NROM TN28 331 K5
Dyneley Rd LEE/GVPK SE12 71 K1
Dynes Rd BGR/WK TN15 136 D3
Dynevor Rd STH/RUST TN4 196 F6
Dyngley Cl SIT ME10 119 M2

E

Eadred Wy SIT ME10 227 P12
Eagle Cl BERM/RHTH SE16 25 J4
DIT/AY ME20 139 H3
Eagle Hl NRWD SE19 68 E3
RAM CT11 17 H4
Eagle Rd RYE TN31 225 H3
Eagles Cl SIT ME10 120 D5
Eagles Dr BH/WHM TN16 132 C4
Eaglesfield Rd
WOOL/PLUM SE18 28 C7
Eagles Rd GRH DA9 53 J2
Eaglestone Cl BGR/WK TN15 240 F1
Eagle Wy GVW DA11 54 B3
Ealdham Sq ELTH/MOT SE9 47 K2
Ealham Cl CANT CT1 174 C4
KEN/WIL TN24 3 L9
Ealing Cl WALD ME5 115 J1
Eardemont Cl DART DA1 51 G2
Eardley Rd BELV DA17 30 B4
SEV TN13 21 G5
Earl Cl WALD ME5 115 J1
Earl Ri WOOL/PLUM SE18 28 E4
Earl Rd GVW DA11 54 F7
Earl's Av FOLK CT20 10 F7
KEN/WIL TN24 3 J6
Earlsfield RASHE TN25 305 R7
Earlsfield Rd HYTHE CT21 222 E3
Earlshall Rd ELTH/MOT SE9 48 A2
Earlsmead Crs MSTR CT12 181 M8
Earl's Rd STH/RUST TN4 22 C3
Earlsthorpe Rd SYD SE26 69 L1
Earl St MAID/BEAR ME14 12 F4
Earlswood Av THHTH CR7 86 B1
Earlswood St GNWCH SE10 26 F4
Earlsworth Rd KEN/WIL TN24 205 G5
Easole Hts RDV CT15 252 C12
Easole St RDV CT15 252 D12
Eason Vls STPH/PW TN12 * 281 J3
East Av CROY/NA CR0 86 A8
Eastbridge Rd LYDD TN29 320 G9
Eastbrook Pl DVE/WH CT16 * 8 E4
Eastbrook Rd BKHTH/KID SE3 27 J7
Eastbury Rd STMC/STPC BR5 90 E2
Eastchurch Rd IOS ME12 66 B8
MARG CT9 179 H3
East Cliff DVE/WH CT16 9 G4
FOLKN CT19 11 M4
RYE TN31 225 H4
East Cliff Gdns FOLKN CT19 11 M4
East Cliff Pde HB CT6 129 H4
East Cliff Pas FOLKN CT19 11 M4
East Cliff Rd STH/RUST TN4 196 D7
Eastcombe Av CHARL SE7 27 J5
Eastcote ORP BR6 91 G4
Eastcote Rd WELL DA16 28 E8
East Ct MAID/SHEP ME15 * 167 H4
Eastcourt Gn RHAM ME8 102 C2
Eastcourt La GILL ME7 84 D8
RHAM ME8 102 C3
East Cross TENT TN30 315 N2
Eastdown Pk LEW SE13 46 E2
East Dr STMC/STPC BR5 91 J2
East Dulwich Gv EDUL SE22 44 F3
East Dulwich Rd EDUL SE22 45 H2
Easterfields E/WMAL ME19 139 K8
Eastern Av ASH TN23 204 D1
IOS ME12 64 E6
QBOR ME11 227 Q1
SOCK/AV RM15 32 D1
WTHK RM20 33 G4
Eastern Docks Rbt
DVE/WH CT16 9 H4
Eastern Esp BRDST CT10 179 L7
MARG CT9 15 L3
Eastern Gdns KEN/WIL TN24 3 H9
Eastern Rd BROCKY SE4 46 B2
GILL ME7 84 A7
LYDD TN29 334 E2
Eastern Vw BH/WHM TN16 132 B3
Eastern Wy ERITHM DA18 30 B1
GRAYS RM17 34 B5
THMD SE28 29 H1
Easter Wy GDST RH9 184 A8
East Ferry Rd POP/IOD E14 26 D2
Eastfield Gdns TONN TN10 189 H8
Eastfield Rd BRCH CT7 176 D6
Eastfields FOLKN CT19 11 L3
Eastgate ROCH ME1 19 L8
Eastgate Cl HB CT6 129 J6
Eastgate Ct ROCH ME1 19 K7
Eastgate Rd TENT TN30 301 N12
Eastgate Ter ROCH ME1 19 K7
East Gn SIT ME10 227 P12
East Hall Hl RMAID ME17 259 R7
East Hall La SIT ME10 120 D4
East Hall Rd STMC/STPC BR5 91 M3
East Hl ASH TN23 2 D4
BH/WHM TN16 132 A4
DART DA1 52 A5
EYN DA4 76 E5
OXTED RH8 157 L7
TENT TN30 315 N1
East Hill Dr DART DA1 52 A5
East Hill Rd BGR/WK TN15 111 G6
OXTED RH8 157 K7
East Holme ERITH DA8 30 E7
East India Wy CROY/NA CR0 87 G4
East Kent Av GVW DA11 54 D4
Eastlake Rd CMBW SE5 24 C8
Eastlands Cl OXTED RH8 157 J5
STH/RUST TN4 200 F5
Eastlands Crs EDUL SE22 45 G4
Eastlands Rd STH/RUST TN4 200 F5
Eastlands Wy OXTED RH8 157 J5
East La BERM/RHTH SE16 25 H1
IOS ME12 * 64 B3
East Langdon Rd RDV CT15 213 M3
Eastleigh Rd BXLYHN DA7 30 D8
Eastling Cl RHAM ME8 102 E2
Eastling Rd FAV ME13 244 H3
FAV ME13 245 J3
East Lodge Rd ASH TN23 202 B8
Eastmead Av ASH TN23 2 C8
Eastmead Cl BMLY BR1 71 M6
Eastmearn Rd DUL SE21 44 D7
East Ml GVW DA11 55 G4
East Milton Rd GVE DA12 55 L5
Eastmoor Pl WOOL/PLUM SE18 27 L2
Eastmoor St CHARL SE7 27 L3
East Mountain La RASHE TN25 203 J4
Eastney Rd CROY/NA CR0 86 C4
Eastney St GNWCH SE10 26 E4
Eastnor Rd ELTH/MOT SE9 48 D6
East Northdown Cl MARG CT9 179 H4
East Park Rd DIT/AY ME20 140 B4
East Parkside WARL CR6 130 F2
East Pl WNWD SE27 68 D1
East Rp DVE/WH CT16 9 K3
East Rd CHAT ME4 83 H6
FOLK CT20 223 L2
MSTR CT12 237 K5
WELL DA16 29 J8
East Rochester Wy
BFN/LL DA15 48 F3
DART DA1 50 E5
East Roman Ditch
DVE/WH CT16 9 G3
East Rw ROCH ME1 19 K8
Eastry Av HAYES BR2 89 G2
Eastry Cl ASH TN23 204 C5
MAIDW ME16 140 D6
Eastry Ct RCANTE CT3 * 251 Q12
Eastry Ms SWCH CT13 * 253 N7
Eastry Rd ERITH DA8 30 B6
East St ASH TN23 2 A5
BMLY BR1 71 H6
BXLYHN DA7 50 B2
CANT CT1 172 D6
CHAT ME4 6 F8
DVW CT17 8 A3
E/WMAL ME19 239 R11
FAV ME13 149 L2
FOLKN CT19 11 M5
GILL ME7 7 L2
HB CT6 129 H4
MAID/SHEP ME15 258 E5
RMAID ME17 242 F12
RYE TN31 225 H4
SIT ME10 120 B6
SNOD ME6 113 J5
TON TN9 194 F3
WALW SE17 24 D4
WTHK RM20 33 M5
East St (North) E/WMAL ME19 239 R10
East Surrey Gv PECK SE15 25 G6
East Sutton Rd HDCN TN27 260 H12
RMAID ME17 260 H6
East Ter BFN/LL DA15 * 48 F6
GVE DA12 55 K4
East Thurrock Rd GRAYS RM17 34 C5
East Tilbury Rd SLH/COR SS17 36 B1
East Vw LYDD TN29 * 329 J5
RCANTE CT3 234 A4
Eastview Av WOOL/PLUM SE18 28 F6
East Vls RCANTW CT4 * 247 Q6
East Wy CROY/NA CR0 87 M5
Eastway HAYES BR2 89 H3
East Weald Dr TENT TN30 301 N12
East Well TENT TN30 * 315 M2
Eastwell Barn Ms TENT TN30 315 M1
Eastwell Cl BECK BR3 69 M5
MAID/BEAR ME14 13 L2
RASHW TN26 303 Q4
STPH/PW TN12 278 H3
Eastwell Mdw TENT TN30 315 M2
Eastwood Rd RMAID ME17 261 R8
SIT ME10 119 L4
Eaton Dr BRXN/ST SW9 44 C2
Eaton Hl MARG CT9 14 F5
Eaton Rd DVW CT17 217 J2
MARG CT9 14 F5
SCUP DA14 49 L7
Eaves Rd DVW CT17 217 H2
Ebbisham Dr VX/NE SW8 24 A5
Ebbsfleet La MSTR CT12 237 K2
Ebdon Wy BKHTH/KID SE3 47 J1
Ebley Cl PECK SE15 25 G5
Ebsworth St FSTH SE23 45 L5
Ebury Cl HAYES BR2 89 M6
Ecclesbourne Rd THHTH CR7 86 D1
Eccles Rw DIT/AY ME20 114 A7
Eccleston Cl ORP BR6 * 90 E4
Eccleston Rd MAIDW ME16 12 E8
Echo Cl MAID/SHEP ME15 168 A7
Echo Ct GVE DA12 55 K7
Eclipse Dr SIT ME10 119 M1
Ector Rd CAT SE6 46 F7
Eddington Cl
MAID/SHEP ME15 167 J7
Eddington La HB CT6 128 E6
Eddystone Rd BROCKY SE4 45 M3
Eden Av WALD ME5 101 G6
Edenbridge Cl
BERM/RHTH SE16 * 25 J4
STMC/STPC BR5 73 L8
Edenbridge Dr IOS ME12 64 C5
Edenbridge Rd EDEN TN8 275 Q11
Eden Cl BXLY DA5 74 E1
Edendale Rd BXLYHN DA7 30 E7
Eden Farm La E/WMAL ME19 138 E6
Edenfield BRCH CT7 176 E6
Eden Pde BECK BR3 * 69 M8
Eden Park Av BECK BR3 70 A8
Eden Pl GVE DA12 55 J5
Eden Rd BECK BR3 69 M8
BXLY DA5 74 D1
CROY/NA CR0 86 E7
HOO/HM ME3 59 M1
RTW TN1 22 F8
WNWD SE27 68 C2
WSTB CT5 126 B6
Eden Valley Wk EDEN TN8 192 A7
EDEN TN8 276 B3
RTON TN11 277 K4
Eden Wk RTW TN1 22 F8
Eden Wy BECK BR3 88 B1
WARL CR6 130 D4
Ederline Av STRHM/NOR SW16 68 A7
Edgar Cl SWLY BR8 75 G7
WSTB CT5 127 L2
Edgar Kail Wy CMBW SE5 44 F1
Edgar Rd BGR/WK TN15 136 D3
BH/WHM TN16 132 C7
CANT CT1 5 J3
DVW CT17 213 J8
MARG CT9 15 J3
MSTR CT12 180 E7
Edgeborough Wy BMLY BR1 71 L5
Edgebury CHST BR7 72 C1
Edgecoombe SAND/SEL CR2 104 C3
Edge End Rd BRDST CT10 183 J1
Edgefield Cl DART DA1 52 C6
Edge Hl WOOL/PLUM SE18 28 C5
Edgehill Cl FOLK CT20 223 L1
Edgehill Gdns MEO DA13 79 G5
Edgehill Rd CHST BR7 48 D8
Edgeler Ct SNOD ME6 113 G6
Edgepoint Cl WNWD SE27 * 68 C2
Edgeway CHAT ME4 83 J3
Edgewood Dr ORP BR6 91 G8
Edgewood Gn CROY/NA CR0 87 L4
Edgeworth Rd ELTH/MOT SE9 47 K2
Edgington Wy SCUP DA14 73 K4
Edinburgh Ms TIL RM18 35 J8
Edinburgh Rd CHAT ME4 101 K3
GILL ME7 7 K4
HOO/HM ME3 43 H8
KEN/WIL TN24 2 B4
MARG CT9 177 L5
Edinburgh Sq
MAID/SHEP ME15 167 K7
Edington Rd ABYW SE2 29 J2
Edison Gv WOOL/PLUM SE18 29 G6
Edison Rd HAYES BR2 71 H6
WELL DA16 29 G7
Edith Cavell Wy
WOOL/PLUM SE18 27 M7
Edith Nesbit Wk ELTH/MOT SE9 47 M2
Edith Rd FAV ME13 149 K3
ORP BR6 91 H8
RAM CT11 16 E7
SNWD SE25 86 E1
WGOS CT8 177 J4
Ediva Rd MEO DA13 97 H1
Edmanson Av MARG CT9 177 K4
Edmund Cl MAIDW ME16 166 B2
MEO DA13 97 H1
Edmund Halley Wy
GNWCH SE10 26 F1
Edmund Rd CDW/CHF RM16 33 L1
STMC/STPC BR5 91 K2
WELL DA16 49 H1
Edmunds Av STMC/STPC BR5 73 L7
Edmund St CMBW SE5 24 E6
RCANTE CT3 251 R1
Edna Rd MAID/BEAR ME14 141 G6
Edred Rd DVW CT17 217 J1
Edric Rd NWCR SE14 25 L6
Edridge Rd CROY/NA CR0 86 D6
Edward Cl CDW/CHF RM16 33 L1
Edward Ct WALD ME5 * 101 K4
Edward Dr BRCH CT7 176 E6
Edward Pl DEPT SE8 26 A5
Edward Rd BH/WHM TN16 132 D4
BMLY BR1 71 J4
CANT CT1 5 H5
CHST BR7 72 C2
CROY/NA CR0 86 F3
DEAL CT14 211 K3
FOLKN CT19 11 J2
PGE/AN SE20 69 L4
QBOR ME11 64 C8
Edwards Cl RHAM ME8 102 D8
Edwards Ct EYN DA4 93 M6
Edwards Gdns SWLY BR8 74 E8
Edwards Rd BELV DA17 30 B3
DVE/WH CT16 8 D4
Edward St CHAT ME4 6 F8
DEPT SE8 26 A5
NWCR SE14 25 M6
STH/RUST TN4 200 C1
STRD ME2 19 G3
Edward's Wy LEW SE13 46 B3
Edward Tyler Rd
LEE/GVPK SE12 47 J7
Edward Wk E/WMAL ME19 139 G5
Edwina Av IOS ME12 65 H6
Edwin Cl BXLYHN DA7 30 A5
Edwin Hall Pl LEW SE13 46 E4
Edwin Petty Pl RDART DA2 * 52 D5
Edwin Rd RDART DA2 51 J8
RHAM ME8 102 D5
Edwin St GVE DA12 55 J5
Edyngham Cl SIT ME10 120 B1
Effingham Crs DVW CT17 8 C4
Effingham Rd CROY/NA CR0 86 A3
LEW SE13 46 F3
Effingham St DVW CT17 8 C4
RAM CT11 17 J6
Effra Pde BRXS/STRHM SW2 44 B3
Effra Rd BRXS/STRHM SW2 44 B3
Egbert Rd BRCH CT7 176 A5
FAV ME13 149 J3
MSTR CT12 180 E7
WGOS CT8 177 H4
Egdean Wk SEV TN13 21 J3
Egerton Av SWLY BR8 75 G5
Egerton Cl DART DA1 51 J6
Egerton Dr GNWCH SE10 26 C7
MARG CT9 179 H3
Egerton House Rd HDCN TN27 262 H9
Egerton Rd DVE/WH CT16 212 F5
HDCN TN27 263 L12
HDCN TN27 263 N6
MAID/BEAR ME14 140 F6
SNWD SE25 68 F7
Egerton Vls FOLKN CT19 * 220 F6
Eggarton La RCANTW CT4 267 K3
Eggpie La RTON TN11 255 L5
Eggringe ASH TN23 204 B2
Eglantine La EYN DA4 94 C2
Eglinton Hl WOOL/PLUM SE18 28 C5
Eglinton Rd SWCM DA10 54 A4
WOOL/PLUM SE18 28 B5
Eglise Rd WARL CR6 130 D3
Egmont St NWCR SE14 25 L6
Egremont Rd
MAID/SHEP ME15 168 A3
WNWD SE27 44 B8
Egret Cl CHAT ME4 83 J3
Eider Cl HB CT6 128 E7
Eighteen Acre La LYDD TN29 329 Q5
Eileen Rd SNWD SE25 86 E1
Elaine Av STRD ME2 18 B4
Elam Cl CMBW SE5 24 C8
Elam St CMBW SE5 24 C8
Eland Rd CROY/NA CR0 86 C6
Elba Pl WALW SE17 24 D3
Elborough Rd SNWD SE25 87 H1
Elcot Av PECK SE15 25 J6
Elder Cl BFN/LL DA15 49 G6
HOO/HM ME3 83 M2
RMAID ME17 261 L3
Elder Ct RHAM ME8 102 C7
Elder Oak Cl PGE/AN SE20 69 J5
Elder Rd WNWD SE27 68 D2
Elderslie Cl BECK BR3 88 B2
Elderslie Rd ELTH/MOT SE9 48 B3
The Elders RCANTE CT3 251 J1
Elderton Rd SYD SE26 69 M1
Eldon Av CROY/NA CR0 87 K5
Eldon Pk SNWD SE25 69 J8
Eldon Pl BRDST CT10 * 183 L1
Eldon St CHAT ME4 6 E5
Eldon Wy STPH/PW TN12 279 J2
Eldred Dr STMC/STPC BR5 91 L5
Eleanor Dr SIT ME10 120 A1
Electric Av BRXN/ST SW9 44 B2
Electric La BRXN/ST SW9 * 44 B2
Elephant & Castle STHWK SE1 * 24 C3
Elephant La BERM/RHTH SE16 25 K1
Elephant Rd WALW SE17 24 D3
Elfindale Rd HNHL SE24 44 D3
Elford Cl BKHTH/KID SE3 47 K2
Elford Rd HOO/HM ME3 38 C8
Elfrida Cl MARG CT9 178 F5
Elfrida Crs CAT SE6 70 B1
Elgal Cl ORP BR6 90 C8
Elgar Cl DEPT SE8 26 B6
TONN TN10 189 H7
Elgar Gdns TIL RM18 35 H7
Elgar Pl RAM CT11 17 H4
Elgar St BERM/RHTH SE16 25 M1
Elgin Rd CROY/NA CR0 87 G5
Elham Cl BMLY BR1 71 L4
MARG CT9 178 F4
RHAM ME8 102 C3
Elham Rd CANT CT1 4 C8
Elham Valley Wy HYTHE CT21 218 B7
RCANTW CT4 175 J7
RCANTW CT4 269 R10
RCANTW CT4 291 N8
RCANTW CT4 292 A1
RFOLK CT18 291 N10
Elham Wy BRDST CT10 183 K3
Elias Pl LBTH SE11 24 B5
Elibank Rd ELTH/MOT SE9 48 B2
Elim Est STHWK SE1 * 24 E2
Elim St STHWK SE1 24 E2
Eliot Bank FSTH SE23 45 J7
Eliot Hl LEW SE13 26 D8
Eliot Pk LEW SE13 26 D8
Eliot Pl BKHTH/KID SE3 26 F8
Eliot Rd DART DA1 52 C3
Eliot V BKHTH/KID SE3 26 E8
Elizabeth Carter Av DEAL CT14 209 G5
Elizabeth Cl TIL RM18 35 J8
Elizabeth Ct RHAM ME8 102 D4
Elizabeth Dr RFOLK CT18 221 J3
Elizabeth Gdns HYTHE CT21 222 C4
Elizabeth Kemp Ct MSTR CT12 16 F1
Elizabeth Pl EYN DA4 * 94 A2
Elizabeth Rd CDW/CHF RM16 34 A2
DVW CT17 8 C9
RAM CT11 17 L5
Elizabeth Smith Ct
E/WMAL ME19 * 139 G6
Elizabeth St GRH DA9 52 F3
Elizabeth Wy HB CT6 129 J6
NRWD SE19 68 E4
STMC/STPC BR5 91 K1
Elland Rd PECK SE15 45 K2

Ellen Av RAM CT11 .....183 H4
Ellenborough Rd SCUP DA14 .....73 L3
Ellen Cl BMLY BR1 .....71 L5
Ellenden Ct CANTW/ST CT2 * 171 K1
Ellens Rd DEAL CT14 .....208 F4
Ellenswood Cl
 MAID/SHEP ME15 .....168 B4
Ellenwhorne La RBTBR TN32 .324 C12
Ellerdale St LEW SE13 .....46 C1
Ellerman Rd TIL RM18 .....35 J8
Ellery Rd NRWD SE19 .....68 E4
Ellery St PECK SE15 .....25 J3
Ellesmere Av BECK BR3 .....70 C5
Ellesmere Dr SAND/SEL CR2 .104 A8
Ellesmere Ms NROM TN28 .....331 J6
Ellice Rd OXTED RH8 .....157 L7
Ellingham Leas
 MAID/SHEP ME15 .....167 K5
Ellingham Wy ASH TN23 .....204 B4
Ellington Av MARG CT9 .....177 L5
Ellington Pl RAM CT11 .....17 F5
Ellington Rd RAM CT11 .....16 F5
Elliot Cl CANT CT1 .....172 F5
Elliots Pl FAV ME13 .....149 L2
Elliotts La BH/WHM TN16 .....160 F1
Elliotts Pl FAV ME13 * 149 L2
Elliott's Rw LBTH SE11 .....24 C6
Elliott St GVE DA12 .....55 L5
Ellis Cl ELTH/MOT SE9 .....48 D7
Elliscombe Mt CHARL SE7 * 27 K5
Elliscombe Rd CHARL SE7 .....27 K4
Ellis Dr NROM TN28 .....331 K4
Ellison Cl WSTB CT5 .....127 K4
Ellison Rd BFN/LL DA15 .....48 B6
Ellisons Wk CANT CT1 .....7 M5
Ellison Wy RHAM ME8 .....103 H3
Ellis Rd WSTB CT5 .....127 K4
 HB CT6 .....129 K7
Elm Av RAM CT11 .....17 H6
Elmbank Dr BMLY BR1 .....71 L5
Elmbourne Dr BXLY DA5 .....49 M5
Elmbrook Gdns ELTH/MOT SE9 .47 M2
Elm Cl DART DA1 .....51 K6
 HDCN ME17 .....263 J10
 HOO/HM ME3 .....81 K2
 WARL CR6 .....130 C3
Elm Ct GILL ME7 * 115 M2
 HYTHE CT21 .....307 F12
Elmcourt Rd WNWD SE27 * 7 C7
Elms Cr E/WMAL ME19 .....139 G5
Elmcroft Av BFN/LL DA15 .....49 G5
Elmcroft Rd ORP BR6 .....91 H3
Elmdene BECK BR3 .....88 A1
Elmdene Rd WOOL/PLUM SE18 .28 E4
Elm Dr SWLY BR8 .....74 E6
Elmer Rd CAT SE6 .....46 E5
Elmers End Rd BECK BR3 .....69 H8
Elmerside Rd BECK BR3 .....69 M8
Elmers Rd CROY/NA CR0 .....88 A1
Elmfield RHAM ME8 .....102 B2
 TENT TN30 .....315 N1
Elmfield Cl GVW DA11 .....55 J6
 RSEV TN14 .....255 J3
Elmfield Ct RMAID ME17 * 258 H2
Elmfield Pk BMLY BR1 .....71 H1
Elmfield Rd BMLY BR1 .....71 H1
Elm Gdns HYTHE CT21 .....222 F3
Elm Gv ERITH DA8 .....30 E6
 MAID/SHEP ME15 .....13 J7
 MSTR CT12 .....182 A4
 ORP BR6 .....91 G4
 PECK SE15 .....25 J3
 RTON TN11 .....194 C1
 SIT ME10 .....120 C5
 WGOS CT8 .....177 H5
Elmgrove Rd CROY/NA CR0 .....87 J3
Elmhurst BELV DA17 .....29 M5
Elmhurst Av RTWE/PEM TN2 .278 A9
Elmhurst La RASHE TN25 .....202 B7
Elmhurst Gdns ROCH ME1 .....100 E2
Elmhurst Rd ELTH/MOT SE9 .....47 M7
Elmington Cl BXLY DA5 .....49 L6
Elmington Est CMBW SE5 .....24 E6
Elmington Rd CMBW SE5 .....24 E6
Elmira St LEW SE13 .....46 C1
Elm La CAT SE6 .....46 A2
 IOS ME12 .....65 K8
 TON TN9 .....194 F2
Elmlee Cl CHST BR7 .....72 A3
Elmleigh Rd RCANTE CT3 .....251 K1
Elmley Rd IOS ME12 .....228 G2
Elmley St WOOL/PLUM SE18 .....28 E4
Elmley Wy MARG CT9 .....178 C6
Elm Pde SCUP DA14 * 73 H1
Elm Pk BRXS/STRHM SW2 .....44 F5
Elmpark Gdns SAND/SEL CR2 .104 B4
Elm Park Gdns SNWD SE25 .....69 G2
Elm Rd BECK BR3 .....70 A6
 BH/WHM TN16 .....159 K4
 DART DA1 .....51 J5
 ERITH DA8 .....31 H7
 FOLKN CT19 .....11 L2
 GRAYS RM17 .....34 D5
 GRH DA9 .....52 F4
 GVE DA12 .....55 K8
 HOO/HM ME3 .....83 M2
 LYDD TN29 .....331 N2
 ORP BR6 .....107 M2
 RCANTE CT3 .....251 P12
 SCUP DA14 .....73 H1
 STH/RUST TN4 .....196 C4
 THHTH CR7 .....68 C8
 WARL CR6 .....130 C3
Elms Av RAM CT11 .....17 H6
Elmscott Rd BMLY BR1 .....70 E2
Elms HI RDV CT15 .....216 D3
Elmshurst Gdns TONN TN10 .188 E4
Elmside CROY/NA CR0 .....105 G5
Elmsmead RYE TN31 .....327 L9
Elmstead Av CHST BR7 .....72 A3
Elmstead Gld CHST BR7 .....72 A3
Elmstead La CHST BR7 .....72 A4
Elmstead Pl FOLK CT20 .....11 L4
Elmstead Rd ERITH DA8 .....30 E7
Elmsted Crs WELL DA16 .....29 K5
The Elms RCANTE CT3 .....155 M8
Elmstone Cl MAIDW ME16 .....166 F4
Elmstone Gdns MARG CT9 .179 H3
Elmstone Hole Rd
 RMAID ME17 .....262 B5
Elmstone La RAM ME16 .....166 B1
 RHAM ME8 .....102 B5
Elmstone Rd RAM CT11 .....17 G4
Elmstone Ter STMC/STPC BR5 * .91 J7
Elms Vale Rd DVW CT17 .....217 H4
 RDV CT15 .....216 E3
Elm Ter ELTH/MOT SE9 .....48 D7
 RAM RM20 .....33 J1
Elmton La RDV CT15 .....272 D3
Elm Tree Cl ASHF TN23 .....204 B4
Elm Tree Ct CHART ME4 * 6 C7
Elm Tree Dr ROCH ME1 .....100 B3
Elm Wk DIT/AT ME20 .....139 M4
 ORP BR6 .....90 A6

Elmwood Av BRDST CT10 .....179 K5
Elmwood Cl BRDST CT10 .....179 J6
Elmwood Dr BXLY DA5 .....49 M5
Elmwood Rd CROY/NA CR0 .....86 B6
 HNHL SE24 .....44 F1
 HOO/HM ME3 .....59 G7
Elm Wd West WSTB CT5 .....127 K3
Elmworth Gv DUL SE21 .....44 E2
Elphick's Pl RTWE/PEM TN2 .201 L5
Elrick Cl ERITH DA8 .....30 F5
Elsa Rd WELL DA16 .....29 G8
Elsiemaud Rd BROCKY SE4 .....46 A3
Elsie Rd EDUL SE22 .....45 J3
Elsinore Rd FSTH SE23 .....45 M6
Elstan Wy CROY/NA CR0 .....87 M3
Elsted St WALW SE17 .....24 C7
Elstow Cl ELTH/MOT SE9 .....48 B3
Elstree Gdns BELV DA17 .....29 M3
Elstree Hl BMLY BR1 .....70 F4
Elswick Rd LEW SE13 .....26 C5
Eltham Cl BFN/LL DA15 .....49 K3
Eltham Green Rd
 ELTH/MOT SE9 .....47 K3
Eltham High St ELTH/MOT SE9 .48 A4
Eltham Hl ELTH/MOT SE9 .....47 L3
Elthruda Rd LEW SE13 .....46 E4
Eltham Palace Rd
 ELTH/MOT SE9 .....47 L4
Eltham Park Gdns
 ELTH/MOT SE9 .....48 A3
Eltham Rd ELTH/MOT SE9 .....47 K3
Elton Cl KUTN/CMB KT2 .....9 H8
Elton Pl STNW/STAM N16 .....7 L1
Elton Rd KUTN/CMB KT2 .....9 J6
Elverland La FAV ME13 .....148 C3
Elverton St WEST SW1P 23 G6
Elvina Gn HAYES BR2 .....89 G1
Elvington La RFOLK CT18 .....219 M2
Elvino Rd SYD SE26 .....69 J2
Elwick Rd ASH TN23 .....2 B5
Elwill Wy BECK BR3 .....70 B3
 MEO DA13 .....79 G5
Elwyn Gdns LEE/GVPK SE12 .....47 H5
Ely Cl ERITH DA8 .....31 G8
 RHAM ME8 .....102 A2
Ely Cl RTW TN1 * 23 C4
Ely Gdns TON TN9 .....195 G1
Ely Rd CROY/NA CR0 .....86 F1
Elysian Wy STMC/STPC BR5 .....90 F3
Embassy Cl GILL ME7 .....102 A4
Embassy Ct SCUP DA14 .....49 G8
Emba St BERM/RHTH SE16 .....25 H1
Ember Cl STMC/STPC BR5 .....90 C3
Embleton Rd LEW SE13 .....46 C2
Emerald Cl ROCH ME1 .....100 E2
Emerald Vw IOS ME12 .....230 D1
Emersons Rd SWLY BR8 .....75 G3
Emerton Cl BXLYHS DA6 .....49 H5
Emery St STHWK SE1 .....24 B2
Emes Rd ERITH DA8 .....30 D6
Emily Jackson Cl SEV TN13 .....21 G5
Emily Rd WALD ME17 .....101 J7
Emmerson Gdns WSTB CT5 .....127 K2
Emmetfield La WBY/YAL ME18 .257 Q9
Emmett Hill La WBY/YAL ME18 .257 Q8
Emmetts Rd BH/WHM TN16 .....160 F2
Empire Ter MARG CT9 .....15 L1
Empress Dr CHST BR7 .....72 C3
Empress Gdns IOS ME12 .....230 D1
Empress Rd GVE DA12 .....55 M5
Empress St WALW SE17 .....24 D5
Emsworth Gv
 MAID/BEAR ME14 .....141 L7
Emsworth St
 BRXS/STRHM SW2 .....44 A1
Enbrook Rd FOLK CT20 .....223 A7
Enbrook Va FOLK CT20 .....219 M8
Encombe FOLK CT20 .....11 H3
Endeavour Pk BGR/WK TN15 * .239 M12
Enderby St GNWCH SE10 .....26 F4
Endsleigh Rd SAND/SEL CR2 .104 B6
Endwell Rd BROCKY SE4 .....25 M8
Endymion Rd
 BRXS/STRHM SW2 .....44 A1
Enfield Rd DEAL CT14 .....209 L2
Engadine Cl CROY/NA CR0 .....87 G6
Engate St LEW SE13 .....46 D2
Engineer Cl WOOL/PLUM SE18 .28 E6
Englefield Cl CROY/NA CR0 .....86 D2
 STMC/STPC BR5 .....73 G8
Englefield Crs HOO/HM ME3 .....58 C6
 STMC/STPC BR5 .....91 H1
Englefield Pth STMC/STPC BR5 .73 H1
Engleheart Rd CAT SE6 .....46 E5
Englehurst RASHE TN25 .....202 B7
Enmore Av SNWD SE25 .....87 H1
Enmore Rd SNWD SE25 .....87 H1
Ennerdale FAV ME13 .....149 M3
Ennerdale Gdns RCANTE CT3 .251 Q11
Ennerdale Rd BXLYHN DA7 .....30 C4
 LEW SE13 .....46 D2
Ennersdale Rd LEW SE13 .....46 E4
Ennis Rd WOOL/PLUM SE18 .....28 C5
Ensfield Rd RTON TN11 .....277 L1
Enslin Rd ELTH/MOT SE9 .....48 B4
Enterprise Cl CROY/NA CR0 .....86 B1
 STRD ME2 .....19 M2
Enterprise Pk
 MAID/SHEP ME15 .....167 H4
Enterprise Wy DEPT SE8 * 26 A3
Enterprize Wy DEPT SE8 * 26 A3
Enticott Cl WSTB CT5 .....127 H4
Epaul La ROCH ME1 .....19 L4
Epping Cl HB CT6 .....129 M1
 POP/IOD E14 .....26 D5
Epple Bay Av BRCH CT7 .....176 B5
Epple Bay Rd BRCH CT7 .....176 B5
Epple Rd BRCH CT7 .....176 B5
Epps Cl STRD ME2 * 19 H2
Epps Rd SIT ME10 .....119 M6
Epsom Cl BXLYHN DA7 .....50 C1
 E/WMAL ME19 .....138 C1
Epsom Rd CROY/NA CR0 * 87 H4
Erebus Dr WOOL/PLUM SE18 .....28 A7
Eresby Dr BECK BR3 .....88 B4
Erica Gdns CROY/NA CR0 .....88 F1
Eric Rd DVW CT17 .....213 J7
Eridge Green Cl
 STMC/STPC BR5 .....91 K1
Eridge Rd RRTW TN3 .....199 J3
Erindale WOOL/PLUM SE18 .....28 E7
Erindale Ter WOOL/PLUM SE18 .28 E7
Erith Ct PUR RM19 .....32 C1
Erith High St ERITH DA8 .....30 D4
Erith Rd BELV DA17 .....30 C5
Erith St DVW CT17 .....213 J7
Erlanger Rd NWCR SE14 .....25 L1
Ermine Rd LEW SE13 .....46 C1
Ermington Rd ELTH/MOT SE9 .....48 E7
Ernest Av WNWD SE27 .....68 A6
Ernest Cl BMLY BR1 .....70 F4
Ernest Dr MAIDW ME16 .....140 C4
Ernest Gv BECK BR3 .....88 A1
Ernest Rd CHAT ME4 .....6 C7
Ernwell Rd FOLKN CT19 .....11 K2
Errington Rd CDW/CHF RM16 .....35 J2

Ersham Rd CANT CT1 .....5 H6
Erskine Park Rd RRTW TN4 .....200 C1
Erskine Rd MEO DA13 .....239 N5
Erwood Rd CHARL SE7 .....27 M4
Erskine Ter STH/NOR SW16 .....68 B2
Escreet Gv WOOL/PLUM SE18 .28 D3
Eshcol Rd HOO/HM ME3 .....60 D7
Esher Cl BXLY DA5 .....49 M6
Eskdale Av RAM CT11 .....16 B5
Eskdale Rd BXLYHN DA7 .....30 B8
Eskmont Rdg NRWD SE19 .....68 B3
Esmeralda Rd STHWK SE1 * 25 H3
Esmonde Dr MSTR CT12 .....181 J5
Esplanade DVW CT17 .....8 B7
 ROCH ME1 .....19 H8
Esplanade Quay DVW CT17 .....8 B7
The Esplanade ROCH ME1 .....19 H7
Essella Pk KEN/WIL TN24 .....3 K4
Essella Rd KEN/WIL TN24 .....3 K4
Essenden Rd BELV DA17 .....30 B4
Essenford Rd ASH TN23 .....205 G4
Essex Av RBI CT6 .....128 C5
Essex Gv NRWD SE19 .....68 B3
Essex Rd BRCH CT7 .....176 C2
 SLH/COR SS17 .....36 B1
Essex Gv NRWD SE19 .....68 B3
Essex Cl RTWE/PEM TN2 .....201 L5
Essex Rd CANT CT1 .....174 E2
 DART DA1 * 51 L4
 GVW DA11 .....55 H6
 HART DA3 .....77 J3
 MAID/SHEP ME15 .....167 M7
 STRD ME2 .....99 H3
 WGOS CT8 .....177 J5
 WTHK RM20 .....33 H5
Essex St WSTB CT5 .....126 E5
Estcourt Rd SNWD SE25 .....87 J2
Estelle Cl ROCH ME1 .....100 B3
Estella Cl STMC/STPC BR5 .....73 J1
Estoria Cl BRXS/STRHM SW2 .....44 B5
Estridge Wy TONN TN10 .....189 J8
Estuary Cl IOS ME12 .....64 C9
Estuary Rd IOS ME12 .....65 E5
Etchden Rd RASHW TN26 .....285 Q11
 RASHW TN26 .....286 A9
Etfield Gv SCUP DA14 .....73 J2
Ethelbert Cl HAYES BR2 .....71 H4
Ethelbert Crs MARG CT9 .....15 J1
Ethelbert Gdns MARG CT9 .....15 J1
Ethelbert Rd BMLY BR1 .....71 H7
 BRCH CT7 .....176 B5
 CANT CT1 .....5 H9
 DEAL CT14 .....207 L3
 ERITH DA8 .....30 C6
 FAV ME13 .....149 J3
 FOLKN CT19 .....11 K1
 MARG CT9 .....15 J1
 RAM CT11 .....15 J1
 RDART DA2 .....75 M1
 ROCH ME1 .....100 D1
 STMC/STPC BR5 .....73 J1
Ethelbert Sq WGOS CT8 .....177 H4
Ethelbert Ter MARG CT9 .....15 J1
 WGOS CT8 .....177 H4
Ethelburga Dr RFOLK CT18 .291 L10
Ethelred Cl FAV ME13 .....149 K3
Ethelred St WALW SE17 .....24 D5
Etheridge Rd BRDST CT10 .....179 J8
Etheredge Cl STMC/STPC BR5 .91 H1
Etherington Hl RRTW TN3 .....277 N9
Etherow St EDUL SE22 .....45 H4
Etherstone Rd
 STRHM/NOR SW16 .....68 A1
Ethnam La HAWK TN18 .....324 F2
Ethnard Rd PECK SE15 .....25 J6
Ethronvi Rd BXLYHN DA7 .....49 M1
Eton Cl WALD ME5 .....115 G1
Eton Gv LEW SE13 .....46 F1
Eton Rd ORP BR6 .....91 J7
Eton Wy DART DA1 .....51 K2
Etta St DEPT SE8 .....25 M5
Ettrick Ter HYTHE CT21 * 222 F3
Euclid Wy WTHK RM20 .....33 J1
Europa Rd BERM/RHTH SE16 .....25 H4
Euralink Wy SIT ME10 .....120 B5
Europa Pk WTHK RM20 * 33 K5
Eustace PI WOOL/PLUM SE18 .....28 A3
Euston Rd CROY/NA CR0 .....86 A6
Evandale Rd BRXN/ST SW9 .....24 B8
Evans Cl GRH DA9 .....53 H3
Evans Rd CAT SE6 .....46 F5
 KEN/WIL TN24 .....205 K4
Eveline Lowe Est
 BERM/RHTH SE16 .....25 H2
Evelyn Cl STRD ME2 .....19 J3
Evelyn Est DEPT SE8 .....25 M5
Evelyn Gdns GDST RH9 .....156 B9
Evelyn Rd MAIDW ME16 .....12 D7
 RSEV TN14 .....136 F2
Evelyn St DEPT SE8 .....25 M4
Evenden Rd MEO DA13 .....97 H3
Evenhill Rd RCANTE CT3 .....175 M1
Everard Av HAYES BR2 .....89 H4
Everard Wy FAV ME13 .....149 L5
Everest Cl GVW DA11 .....54 F8
Everest Dr HOO/HM ME3 .....83 M1
Everest La STRD ME2 .....82 A7
Everest Ms HOO/HM ME3 .....83 M1
Everest PI SWLY BR8 .....75 J3
Everest Rd ELTH/MOT SE9 .....47 M3
Everglade BH/WHM TN16 .....159 L2
Everglade Cl HART DA3 .....78 A8
The Everglades GILL ME7 .....102 A7
Evergreen Cl E/WMAL ME19 .138 C1
 IOS ME12 .....230 B3
 HOO/HM ME3 .....69 K4
 PGE/AN SE20 .....69 K4
 RSIT ME9 .....227 L1
Eversley Av BXLYHN DA7 .....30 D7
Eversley Cl MAIDW ME16 .....140 D7
Eversley Cross BXLYHN DA7 .....30 D7
Eversley Rd CHARL SE7 .....27 H5
 HYTHE CT21 .....223 H2
 NRWD SE19 .....68 B2
Eversley Wy CROY/NA CR0 .....88 D2
 FOLK CT20 .....10 C5
Everthorpe Rd PECK SE15 .....45 G1
Everton Rd CROY/NA CR0 .....87 G1
Evesham Rd GVE DA12 .....55 H6
Evison Cl DVE/WH CT16 .....213 J7
Evry Rd SCUP DA14 .....73 J3
Ewart Rd FSTH SE23 .....45 L5
Ewell Av MAID/SHEP ME15 .....165 L4
Ewell La MAID/SHEP ME15 .....165 L5
Ewellhurst La RRTW TN3 .....277 N11
Ewen Crs BRXS/STRHM SW2 .....44 C5
Ewenny Rd ORP BR6 * 108 B3
Ewhurst Cl ASH TN23 .....204 B4
Ewhurst La RYE TN31 .....324 G9
Ewhurst Rd BROCKY SE4 .....46 B4

Ewins Cl STPH/PW TN12 .....279 K3
Exbury Rd CAT SE6 .....46 B7
Exedown Rd BGR/WK TN15 .238 B9
Exenborder FOLK CT20 .....219 M4
 TON TN9 .....195 G1
Exeter Cl CROY/NA CR0 .....55 L8
 GVE DA12 .....55 L8
 WELL DA16 .....29 G8
Exeter Wy NWCR SE14 .....26 A7
Exford Rd LEE/GVPK SE12 .....47 J6
Exford Rd LEE/GVPK SE12 .....47 J7
Exmoor Ri KEN/WIL TN24 .....2 A1
Exmouth Rd GILL ME7 .....83 K3
 GRAYS RM17 .....34 C5
 WELL DA16 .....29 K7
Exon St WALW SE17 .....24 D7
Exton Gdns
 MAID/BEAR ME14 .....142 A8
Eyhorne St RMAID ME17 .....169 K4
Eylewood Rd WNWD SE27 .....68 D2
Eynella Rd DUL SE21 .....45 G5
Eynsford Crs SCUP DA14 .....49 K6
 STMC/STPC BR5 .....90 D3
Eynsford Ri EYN DA4 .....93 L7
Eynsford Rd EYN DA4 .....94 A4
 GRH DA9 .....53 K3
 MAIDW ME16 .....140 C6
 SWLY DR8 .....92 B7
Eynsham Dr ABYW SE2 .....29 J2
Eynswood Dr SCUP DA14 .....73 J2
Eythorne Rd BRXN/ST SW9 .....24 B7
Eythorne Rd RCANTE CT3 .....203 C6
 RDV CT15 .....271 R7

F

The Facade FSTH SE23 * 45 K7
Fackenden La BGR/WK TN15 .110 F7
Factory La CROY/NA CR0 .....86 B5
Factory PI POP/IOD E14 .....26 D4
Factory Rd CAN/RD E16 .....28 A1
 GVW DA11 .....54 D4
Faesten Wy BXLY DA5 .....50 F8
Fagus Cl WALD ME5 .....115 J4
Fairacre BRDST CT10 .....183 H1
Fairacres CROY/NA CR0 .....104 A8
Fairacres Cl HB CT6 .....129 K5
Fairbank Av ORP BR6 .....90 C5
Fairbourne La RMAID ME17 .242 D12
Fairby HI HART DA3 .....95 M1
Fairby La HART DA3 .....95 M2
Fairby Rd LEE/GVPK SE12 .....47 J3
Fairchildes Av CROY/NA CR0 .105 J6
Fairchildes Rd WARL CR6 .....131 J6
Faircrouch La WADH TN5 .....308 H5
Fairfax Cl FOLK CT20 .....223 L1
 RHAM ME8 .....102 E8
Fairfax Dr HB CT6 .....232 A4
Fairfax Gdns BKHTH/KID SE3 .27 K7
Fairfax Rd GRAYS RM17 .....34 C4
 TIL RM18 .....35 C7
Fairfield DEAL CT14 .....209 G3
 GVE DA12 .....79 M2
 RCANTW CT4 .....291 Q4
Fairfield Av BFN/LL DA15 .....23 K1
 BGR/WK TN15 .....136 F4
 NROM TN28 .....330 H6
Fairfield Crs TON TN9 .....194 F5
Fairfield Gv CHARL SE7 .....27 L5
Fairfield Pk BRDST CT10 .....183 H1
Fairfield Pth BECK BR3 .....70 B6
 BXLYHN DA7 .....30 A8
 CROY/NA CR0 .....86 E6
 MSTR CT12 .....180 E6
 STMC/STPC BR5 .....90 E3
Fairfields CAT SE6 .....46 D3
Fairfield Ter RASHW TN26 .....318 D2
Fairfield Wy RTON TN11 .....188 B4
Fairford Av BXLYHN DA7 .....30 C3
 CROY/NA CR0 .....87 L1
Fairford Cl CROY/NA CR0 .....87 L1
Fairglen Rd WADH TN5 .....308 G6
Fairgreen Rd THHTH CR7 .....86 C1
Fairhaven Av CROY/NA CR0 .....87 L1
Fairholme Rd CROY/NA CR0 .....86 B3
Fairhurst Dr MAID/SHEP ME15 .258 C11
Fairlands Av THHTH CR7 .....86 A1
Fair La RBTBR TN32 .....322 H9
Fairlawn CHARL SE7 .....27 K6
 WSTB CT5 .....127 L4
Fairlawn Av BXLYHN DA7 .....29 L4
Fairlawn Cl WBY/YAL ME18 .165 N1
Fairlawn Ct CHARL SE7 * 27 K6
Fairlawn Pk SYD SE26 .....69 M2
Fairlawn Rd MSTR CT12 .....182 C2
Fairlead Rd ROCH ME1 .....100 E4
Fairleas SIT ME10 .....120 E7
Fairlie Gdns FSTH SE23 .....45 K5
Fairlight Av NROM TN28 .....330 F7
Fairlight Cl STH/RUST TN4 .....196 B3
Fairlight Cross HART DA3 .....78 A7
Fairlight Rd HYTHE CT21 .....222 B2
Fairlight Ter NROM TN28 * 330 F7
Fairman's La STPH/PW TN12 .279 L11
Fairmead BMLY BR1 .....72 A1
Fairmeadow MAID/BEAR ME14 .12 F2
Fair Meadow RYE TN31 .....225 L4
Fairmead Rd CROY/NA CR0 .....86 B3
 EDEN TN8 .....186 D4
Fairmile Rd RTWE/PEM TN2 .197 H4
Fairmont Cl BELV DA17 .....30 A4
Fairmount Rd
 BRXS/STRHM SW2 .....44 A4
Fairoak Cl STMC/STPC BR5 .....90 C3
Fairoak Dr ELTH/MOT SE9 .....48 G4
Fairoaks HB CT6 .....129 J5
Fairseat La BGR/WK TN15 .....238 G4
Fair St BRDST CT10 .....183 H1
Fairthorn Rd CHARL SE7 .....27 H6
Fairtrough Rd ORP BR6 .....108 A7
Fairview ERITH DA8 .....31 G6
 HART DA3 .....95 J6
 HAWK TN18 .....312 C7
 RSIT ME9 .....226 D11
Fairview Av RHAM ME8 .....102 A4
Fairview Cl MARG CT9 .....15 J4
 RTON TN11 .....194 C1
 SYD SE26 .....69 L5
Fairview Dr HOO/HM ME3 .....81 J1
 ORP BR6 .....107 K7
Fairview Gdns CANTW/ST CT2 .173 H5
 DEAL CT14 .....209 H7
 MEO DA13 .....97 J1
Fairview Pl BRXS/STRHM SW2 .44 A5

Fairview Rd MEO DA13 .....78 E4
 RDV CT15 .....272 C4
 SIT ME10 .....120 B6
 STRHM/NOR SW16 .....68 A5
Fairwater BXLYHS DA6 .....49 M3
Fairway BXLYHS DA6 .....49 M3
 STMC/STPC BR5 .....90 F2
Fairway Av FOLKN CT19 .....10 C1
Fairway Cl CROY/NA CR0 .....87 M1
 LYDD TN29 .....331 N2
 ROCH ME1 .....100 D4
Fairway Crs WSTB CT5 .....126 B6
Fairway Dr RDART DA2 .....52 C5
Fairway Gdns BECK BR3 .....88 C2
The Fairway FAV ME13 .....149 H3
 STH/RUST TN4 .....196 B6
The Fairway BMLY BR1 .....72 A1
 DEAL CT14 .....209 K1
 GVW DA11 .....55 H7
 HB CT6 .....128 E7
 HYTHE CT21 .....222 D4
 LYDD TN29 .....320 F12
 NROM TN28 .....331 L1
 ROCH ME1 .....100 D4
 SIT ME10 .....119 M8
Fairwy Rd SYD SE26 .....45 M8
Falcon Av BMLY BR1 .....71 M7
 GRAYS RM17 .....34 C5
 HB CT6 .....128 E7
Falcon Gdns IOS ME12 .....65 L6
Falcon Ms CWV DA11 .....54 F6
Falcons Cl BH/WHM TN16 .....132 C5
Falcon Wy ASH TN23 .....204 B4
Falconwood Av WELL DA16 .....28 E8
Falconwood Rd CROY/NA CR0 .104 F2
Falkland Park Av SNWD SE25 .....68 F2
Falkland Pl WALD ME5 .....114 F4
Fallow Ct STHWK SE1 * 25 H4
Fallowfield RDART DA2 .....51 M8
 SIT ME10 .....120 B7
 WALD ME5 .....101 J5
Fallowfield Cl
 MAID/BEAR ME14 .....167 M1
Falmouth Cl LEE/GVPK SE12 .....47 G3
Falmouth Pl STPH/PW TN12 .278 F12
Falmouth Rd STHWK SE1 .....24 D2
Falstaff Ct CHART SE1 .....24 C5
Fambridge Cl SYD SE26 .....70 A1
Fanconi Rd WALD ME5 .....115 J2
Fane Wy RHAM ME8 .....116 A1
Fanns Ri PUR RM19 .....32 B5
Fanshawe Rd CDW/CHF RM16 * .35 H2
Fans La RSIT ME9 .....227 L9
The Fan DVE/WH CT16 .....9 A3
Fant La MAID/SHEP ME15 .....166 B2
Fant Wy MAID/SHEP ME15 .....166 A3
Faraday Av SCUP DA14 .....49 J7
Faraday Ride TONN TN10 .....189 J7
Faraday Rd MAID/BEAR ME14 .141 K6
 WELL DA16 .....29 G8
Faraday Wy STMC/STPC BR5 .....73 J8
 WOOL/PLUM SE18 .....27 G4
Farringdon Av HAYES BR2 .....90 C2
Farjeon Rd BKHTH/KID SE3 .....27 L7
Farleigh Av HAYES BR2 .....89 G3
Farleigh Court Rd
 CROY/NA CR0 .....86 A5
 WARL CR6 .....104 F8
Farleigh Dean Crs
 CROY/NA CR0 .....105 G5
Farleigh HI MAID/SHEP ME15 .166 F4
Farleigh La MAIDW ME16 .....166 B6
Farleigh Rd CANTW/ST CT2 .172 B6
 WARL CR6 .....130 D3
Farley Cl RASHW TN26 .....303 P4
 WALD ME5 .....115 L3
Farleycroft BH/WHM TN16 .159 G4
Farley Nursery BH/WHM TN16 .159 H4
Farley Pk OXTED RH8 .....157 J8
Farley Pl SNWD SE25 .....69 H5
Farley Rd CAT SE6 .....46 D5
 GVE DA12 .....56 A5
 MARG CT9 .....178 C8
 SAND/SEL CR2 .....104 A2
Farleys Wy RYE TN31 .....326 E11
Farlow Cl GVW DA11 .....55 H7
Farm Av SWLY BR8 .....74 D7
Farm Cl ASH TN23 .....204 A4
 WWKM BR4 .....89 G4
Farmcombe La RTW TN1 .....23 H8
Farmcombe Rd RTW TN1 .....23 H8
Farmcote Rd LEE/GVPK SE12 .....47 H7
Farm Crs SIT ME10 .....120 B7
Farmcroft GVW DA11 .....55 H7
Farmdale Rd CHARL SE7 .....27 L5
Farmdale Av ROCH ME1 .....100 A3
Farmdale Pl GNWCH SE10 .....27 H4
Farm Dr CROY/NA CR0 .....88 A3
Farmer Cl HYTHE CT21 .....222 B4
 RMAID ME17 .....169 H1
Farmers Rd CMBW SE5 .....24 C7
Farmfield Rd BMLY BR1 .....70 E2
Farm Gdns RYE TN31 .....326 F11
Farm Ground Cl TON TN9 .....195 H5
Farm Hill Av SYD SE26 .....82 A4
Farm Holt HART DA3 .....96 A4
Farmhouse Cl RCANTW CT4 * .270 E6
Farm House La WSTB CT5 .....127 K1
Farmland Wk CHST BR7 .....72 C2
Farm La CROY/NA CR0 .....88 A3
 DEAL CT14 .....209 G3
 RTON TN11 .....194 D1
 RYE TN31 .....332 C6
 WTHK RM20 .....33 M5
Farm PI DART DA1 .....51 J2
Farm Rd CDW/CHF RM16 .....35 G1
 RASHW TN26 .....318 E3
 RSEV TN14 .....136 B6
 TIL RM18 .....35 D7
 WALD ME5 .....130 D2
Farmstead Dr EDEN TN8 .....192 G2
Farmstead Rd CAT SE6 .....70 C1
Farm V BXLY DA5 .....50 C4
Farnaby Dr SEV TN13 .....20 F7
Farnaby Rd BMLY BR1 .....70 D5
 ELTH/MOT SE9 .....47 K2
Farnborough Av
 SAND/SEL CR2 .....104 D7
Farnborough Cl
 MAIDW ME16 .....166 D3
Farnborough Common
 ORP BR6 .....90 A6
Farnborough Crs HAYES BR2 .89 G4
 SAND/SEL CR2 .....104 D7
Farnborough HI ORP BR6 .....90 F8
Farnborough Wy ORP BR6 .....107 F5
 PECK SE15 .....25 F6
Farncombe St
 BERM/RHTH SE16 .....25 H1
Farncombe La RTWE/PEM TN2 .213 J9
Farne Cl MAID/SHEP ME15 .....167 M1
Farnham Beeches RRTW TN3 .103 J4
 RRTW TN3 .....200 B1
Farnham La RRTW TN3 .....200 B1

Farnham Pl RRTW TN3 200 B2
Farnham Rd WELL DA16 29 K8
Farnham Royal LBTH SE11 24 A4
Farningham Cl
MAID/BEAR ME14 141 K7
Farningham Hill Rd SWLY BR8 93 K1
Farnley Rd THHTH CR7 68 E8
Farnol Rd DART DA1 52 B3
Faro Cl BMLY BR1 72 B6
Farquhar Rd NRWD SE19 69 G2
Farquharson Rd CROY/NA CR0 86 D3
Farraday Cl ROCH ME1 100 E5
Farrance Ct RTW TN1 * 23 H4
Farrant Cl ORP BR6 107 M2
Farrar Rd BRCH CT7 176 D7
Farren Rd FSTH SE23 45 M7
Farrers Wk ASH TN23 204 E7
Farrier Cl BMLY BR1 71 L7
MAID/BEAR ME14 141 L8
RASHE TN25 202 C6
The Farriers EDEN TN8 192 D2
Farriers Cl GVE DA12 56 A6
Farriers Ct RHAM ME8 103 K5
Farrier St DEAL CT14 209 L2
Farrington Av STMC/STPC BR5 73 J7
Farrington Pl CHST BR7 72 E4
Farrow La NWCR SE14 25 K6
Farrow Pl BERM/RHTH SE16 25 M2
Fartherwell Av E/WMAL ME19 138 B5
Fartherwell Rd E/WMAL ME19 138 A6
Farthing Aly STHWK SE1 * 25 H1
Farthingfield BGR/WK TN15 238 F10
Farthing Hl WADH TN5 310 F8
Farthingloe Rd DVW CT17 217 H3
Farthings Ct CANTW/ST CT2 * 171 K1
Farthing St ORP BR6 106 E2
Farwell Rd SCUP DA14 73 J1
Farwig La BMLY BR1 71 H5
Fashoda Rd HAYES BR2 71 L8
Fauchon's Cl
MAID/BEAR ME14 168 A2
Fauchon's La
MAID/BEAR ME14 168 A2
Faulkners La CANTW/ST CT2 171 J4
Faulkner St NWCR SE14 25 K7
Faunce St WALW SE17 24 C5
Faussett Hl RCANTW CT4 249 N10
Faustina Dr ASH TN23 204 C7
Faversham Reach FAV ME13 149 L1
Faversham Rd BECK BR3 70 A6
CAT SE6 46 A5
FAV ME13 148 D4
FAV ME13 245 N12
FAV ME13 264 G3
HDCN TN27 264 D4
RASHE TN25 202 F3
RASHE TN25 265 R10
RASHE TN25 265 R6
RCANTW CT4 246 A12
RMAID ME17 243 L12
RSIT ME9 148 A8
RSIT ME9 243 Q5
RSIT ME9 244 A3
WSTB CT5 125 K3
Favourite Rd WSTB CT5 126 B7
Fawcett Cl STRHM/NOR SW16 68 B1
Fawcett Rd CROY/NA CR0 86 C6
Fawkes Av DART DA1 52 A7
Fawkham Av HART DA3 78 D7
Fawkham Green Rd HART DA3 95 J6
Fawkham Rd BGR/WK TN15 95 G7
HART DA3 77 L8
Fawley Cl MAID/BEAR ME14 140 F6
Fawnbrake Av HNHL SE24 44 C3
Faygate Crs BXLYHS DA6 50 B3
Faygate Rd BRXS/STRHM SW2 44 A7
Fayre Meadow RBTBR TN32 322 H9
Fearon St GNWCH SE10 27 H4
Featherbed La CROY/NA CR0 104 E2
FAV ME13 226 G1
RSIT ME9 227 M11
Featherby Rd GILL ME7 84 B8
RHAM ME8 102 B2
Feathers Pl GNWCH SE10 26 E5
Featherstone Av FSTH SE23 45 J7
Featley Rd BRXN/ST SW9 44 C1
Federation Rd ABYW SE2 29 K3
Feenan Hwy TIL RM18 35 J7
Felborough Cl RCANTW CT4 247 P9
Felbridge Cl STRHM/NOR SW16 68 B1
Felday Rd LEW SE13 46 C4
Felderland Cl DEAL CT14 253 R4
RMAID ME17 167 M8
Felderland Dr RMAID ME17 167 M8
Felderland La SWCH CT13 253 R5
Felderland Rd RMAID ME17 167 M8
Feldspar Cl SIT ME10 119 L3
WALD ME5 115 G4
Felhampton Rd ELTH/MOT SE9 48 C8
Felicia Wy CDW/CHF RM16 35 J3
Felipe Rd CDW/CHF RM16 33 K3
Felix Pl BRXS/STRHM SW2 44 B3
Felixstowe Rd ABYW SE2 29 K2
Felbrigg Rd EDUL SE22 45 G3
Fell Md STPH/PW TN12 257 J7
Fellmongers Yd CROY/NA CR0 86 D6
Fellowes Wy RTON TN11 188 B8
Fell Rd CROY/NA CR0 86 D6
Felltram Wy CHARL SE7 27 H4
Felmingham Rd PGE/AN SE20 69 K6
Felspar Cl WOOL/PLUM SE18 29 G4
Felstead Rd ORP BR6 91 H5
Felton Cl STMC/STPC BR5 90 C2
Felton Lea SCUP DA14 73 G2
Fendall St STHWK SE1 * 24 F2
Fendyke Rd ABYW SE2 29 L3
Fen Gv BFN/LL DA15 49 G4
Fenham Rd PECK SE15 25 H6
Fen Meadow BGR/WK TN15 238 B12
Fenn Cl BMLY BR1 71 H3
Fennel Cl CROY/NA CR0 87 L4
MAIDW ME16 166 C2
ROCH ME1 100 C2
Fennell St WOOL/PLUM SE18 28 B5
Fenner Cl BERM/RHTH SE16 25 J3
FOLK CT20 223 M1
Fenner Rd CDW/CHF RM16 33 K2
Fenning St STHWK SE1 * 24 F1
Fen Pond Rd BGR/WK TN15 238 B12
BGR/WK TN15 240 B1
Fens Wy SWLY BR8 75 H3
Fenton Cl BRXN/ST SW9 * 24 A8
CHST BR7 72 A2
Fenton Ct DEAL CT14 209 J3
Fenton Rd CDW/CHF RM16 33 M2
Fenwick Gv PECK SE15 45 H1
Fenwick Rd PECK SE15 45 H1
Ferbies RRTW TN3 277 P10
Ferdinand Ter RRTW TN3 * 199 K6
Ferguson Av GVE DA12 79 K1
Ferguson Cl BECK BR3 70 D7
HYTHE CT21 223 G3
Ferguson's Cl POP/IOD E14 26 B3
Fermor Rd FSTH SE23 45 M6
Fernbank EYN DA4 * 94 A5
Fernbank Cl WALD ME5 114 F4
Fern Bank Crs FOLKN CT19 11 K2
Fernbrook Rd LEW SE13 46 F4
Fern Cl ERITH DA8 31 J7
RFOLK CT18 292 H11
WARL CR6 130 D4
WSTB CT5 127 K4
Ferndale BMLY BR1 71 K6
RTWE/PEM TN2 23 K3
Ferndale Cl BXLYHN DA7 29 M7
IOS ME12 64 E7
RTWE/PEM TN2 23 K3
Ferndale Ct BRCH CT7 * 176 D7
Ferndale Point
RTWE/PEM TN2 * 23 K3
Ferndale Rd GILL ME7 83 M8
GVE DA12 55 J7
SNWD SE25 87 J1
Ferndale Wy ORP BR6 90 E8
Ferndell Av BXLY DA5 50 E8
Ferndene HART DA3 78 E7
Ferndene Rd HNHL SE24 44 D2
Fern Down MEO DA13 239 N5
Ferndown Av ORP BR6 90 E4
Ferndown Cl GILL ME7 102 B8
Ferndown Rd ELTH/MOT SE9 47 L5
Ferne La RDV CT15 293 Q6
Ferne Wy FOLK CT20 219 M8
Fernfield RFOLK CT18 292 H12
Fernfield La RFOLK CT18 292 H11
Fernham Rd THHTH CR7 68 D8
Fernheath Wy RDART DA2 74 E2
Fernhill Rd MAIDW ME16 166 B3
Fernholme Rd PECK SE15 45 L3
Fernholt TONN TN10 188 F6
Fernhurst Crs STH/RUST TN4 196 D3
Fernhurst Rd CROY/NA CR0 87 H3
Fernlea Av HB CT6 128 F5
Fernleigh Cl CROY/NA CR0 86 B7
FAV ME13 151 J6
Fernleigh Ri DIT/AY ME20 139 J3
Fernleigh Ter SIT ME10 * 119 L7
Ferns Cl SAND/SEL CR2 104 A4
Fernside La SEV TN13 162 B7
The Ferns BGR/WK TN15 240 H2
DIT/AY ME20 139 J4
RTW TN1 23 J4
Fern Wk STHWK SE1 25 H4
Fernwood Cl BMLY BR1 71 K6
Ferranti Cl WOOL/PLUM SE18 27 L2
Ferrey Ms BRXN/ST SW9 24 B8
Ferrier Cl RHAM ME8 116 F1
Ferring Cl RYE TN31 224 F3
Ferrings DUL SE21 44 F7
Ferris Av CROY/NA CR0 88 A6
Ferris Rd EDUL SE22 45 H2
Ferry La ROCH ME1 113 K1
Ferry Rd IOS ME12 227 R5
RSIT ME9 227 M9
RYE TN31 225 G4
STRD ME2 113 H1
TIL RM18 35 H8
Ferry St POP/IOD E14 26 D4
Ferry Vw QBOR ME11 227 N2
Feryby Rd CDW/CHF RM16 35 J2
Festival Av HART DA3 78 E7
Festival Cl BXLY DA5 49 L6
ERITH DA8 31 G6
Ffinch Cl DIT/AY ME20 139 L5
Ffinch St DEPT SE8 26 B6
Fiddlers Cl GRH DA9 53 J2
Fiddling La RASHE TN25 290 B10
Field Av CANT CT1 172 E6
Field Cl BMLY BR1 71 K6
SAND/SEL CR2 104 A8
WALD ME5 100 F7
Field Ct OXTED RH8 157 K6
Field Dr EDEN TN8 192 E2
Field End KEN/WIL TN24 3 L6
Field End Pl FAV ME13 151 H6
Fielding Av TIL RM18 35 J7
Fielding Dr DIT/AY ME20 139 H2
The Fieldings FSTH SE23 45 K6
SIT ME10 119 M7
Fielding St FAV ME13 * 149 K2
WALW SE17 24 D4
Field Mill Rd HDCN TN27 263 L8
Field Rd BGR/WK TN15 96 F8
MEO DA13 97 G7
Fieldside Cl ORP BR6 90 D7
Fields La WBY/YAL ME18 164 F6
Field Vw ASH TN23 204 D7
WSTB CT5 126 C6
Field View Cl IOS ME12 64 D7
Field Wy CROY/NA CR0 105 G2
Fieldway STMC/STPC BR5 90 E2
Fieldways HAWK TN18 312 D8
Fieldworks Rd CHAT ME4 83 H6
Fiennes Wy SEV TN13 162 B5
Fiesta Wk CANT CT1 5 M6
Fife Rd HB CT6 128 C7
Fifield Pth FSTH SE23 45 L8
Fifth Av MARG CT9 15 M2
WTHK RM20 33 H5
Fig Tree Rd BRDST CT10 179 J6
Fig Tree Wk RDV CT15 * 272 D6
Fiji Ter MAID/BEAR ME14 141 H6
Filborough Wy GVE DA12 56 C6
Filer Rd IOS ME12 64 F6
Filey Cl BH/WHM TN16 132 A5
Filmer La RSEV TN14 136 D7
Filmer Rd RCANTW CT4 175 G8
Filston La RSEV TN14 133 J2
Finchale Rd ABYW SE2 29 J2
Finch Av WNWD SE27 68 E1
The Finches BRCH CT7 233 M7
SIT ME10 120 B6
Finch Gv HYTHE CT21 321 Q1
Finchley Cl DART DA1 52 B4
Finchley Rd GRAYS RM17 34 C5
Finch Ms DEAL CT14 209 K5
PECK SE15 * 25 G7
Findlay Cl RHAM ME8 102 E8
Fingal St GNWCH SE10 27 G4
Finglesham Cl STMC/STPC BR5 91 L4
Finglesham Ct
MAID/SHEP ME15 167 K5
Finland Rd BROCKY SE4 45 M1
Finland St BERM/RHTH SE16 25 M2
Finlay Cl FAV ME13 149 J2
Finn Farm Ct ASH TN23 304 G4
Finsbury Rd RAM CT11 17 J4
Finsbury Wy BXLY DA5 50 A4
Finsen Rd HNHL SE24 44 D2
Fintonagh Dr
MAID/BEAR ME14 141 J6
Finucane Dr STMC/STPC BR5 91 K3
Finwell Rd RHAM ME8 103 H3
Firbank Gdns MARG CT9 178 A6
Firbank Rd PECK SE15 25 J8
Firbanks WSTB CT5 127 G5
Fir Ct KEN/WIL TN24 3 K7
Fircroft Wy EDEN TN8 192 D2
Fir Dene ORP BR6 90 A6
Firecrest Cl HART DA3 78 C7
Firethorn Cl GILL ME7 83 M7
Firhill Rd CAT SE6 46 B8
Firmin Av RMAID ME17 167 L8
Firmingers Rd ORP BR6 92 C8
Firmin Rd DART DA1 51 K3
Firsby Av CROY/NA CR0 87 L4
Firs Cl DIT/AY ME20 139 M4
FOLKN CT19 219 L7
FSTH SE23 45 L5
Firside Gv BFN/LL DA15 49 G6
Firs La FOLKN CT19 219 L7
Firs Rd RCANTW CT4 271 L4
First Av BRDST CT10 179 J3
BXLYHN DA7 29 K6
CHAT ME4 101 K3
GVW DA11 54 F6
IOS ME12 64 D4
IOS ME12 66 F8
MARG CT9 15 L2
QBOR ME11 227 N2
RYE TN31 332 E7
WTHK RM20 33 H5
The Firs BXLY DA5 50 E6
DEAL CT14 * 209 K1
ORP BR6 * 108 F1
RCANTE CT3 155 M8
First La MAID/SHEP ME15 168 F3
First St RRTW TN3 200 A2
Firtree Cl CANTW/ST CT2 171 H2
Fir Tree Cl ORP BR6 91 G8
RAM CT11 16 E6
RTON TN11 * 188 B8
STPH/PW TN12 282 A6
Fir Tree Gdns CROY/NA CR0 88 B7
Fir Tree Gv GILL ME7 116 C4
WALD ME5 115 L4
Fir Tree Hl SWCH CT13 253 N3
Fir Tree Rd STH/RUST TN4 22 C6
Fisher Cl CROY/NA CR0 87 G4
HYTHE CT21 222 E4
Fishermans Dr
BERM/RHTH SE16 25 L1
Fishermen's Hl GVW DA11 54 C3
Fisher Rd CANTW/ST CT2 4 A3
WALD ME5 101 J6
Fishers Cl STPH/PW TN12 282 A4
Fishers Ct NWCR SE14 25 L7
Fishers Rd STPH/PW TN12 282 A4
Fisher St MAID/BEAR ME14 13 G1
SWCH CT13 237 K12
Fisher Street Rd FAV ME13 246 D7
Fishmarket Rd RYE TN31 225 H4
Fishmonger's La DVE/WH CT16 * 8 E5
Fishponds Rd HAYES BR2 89 L8
Fitzalan St LBTH SE11 24 A3
Fitzgerald Av HB CT6 128 D6
Fitzjames Av CROY/NA CR0 87 H5
Fitzmary Av MARG CT9 177 K4
Fitzroy Av BRDST CT10 179 K3
MARG CT9 15 L7
MSTR CT12 182 E3
Fitzroy Gdns NRWD SE19 68 F4
Fitzroy Rd WSTB CT5 127 G2
Fitzwalter Ct DVE/WH CT16 * 213 J5
Fitzwilliam Rd
MAID/BEAR ME14 142 A8
Fiveacre Cl THHTH CR7 86 B2
Fiveash Rd GVW DA11 55 G5
Five Bells La ROCH ME1 * 19 M9
Five Elms Rd HAYES BR2 89 K6
Five Fields La EDEN TN8 193 K1
Five Oak Green Rd RTON TN11 278 A3
TON TN9 195 J6
Five Oak La STPH/PW TN12 281 N8
Five Oak Ms BMLY BR1 47 H8
Five Vents La LYDD TN29 330 C5
Fiveways Cnr ELTH/MOT SE9 48 C7
Five Ways Ct CHAT ME4 6 F7
Fiveways Ri DEAL CT14 209 G4
Fiveways Rd BRXN/ST SW9 24 B8
Five Wents SWLY BR8 75 H6
Five Wents Vls
STPH/PW TN12 * 278 G8
Flack Gdns HOO/HM ME3 59 M8
Flag Cl CROY/NA CR0 87 L4
Flamborough Cl
BH/WHM TN16 132 A5
Flamingo Cl WALD ME5 101 H6
Flamingo Dr HB CT6 128 F6
Flamsteed Rd CHARL SE7 27 M4
Flanders Cl SIT ME10 227 N12
Flanders Fld RASHE TN25 305 P1
Flavell Ms GNWCH SE10 26 F4
Flax Court La RDV CT15 272 D6
Flaxman Dr MAIDW ME16 140 D7
Flaxman Rd CMBW SE5 24 C8
Flaxmans Ct GILL ME7 6 E1
Flaxmore Pl STH/RUST TN4 196 D3
Flaxpond Rd ASH TN23 204 C4
Flaxton Rd WOOL/PLUM SE18 28 E7
Fleet Av IOS ME12 64 C4
RDART DA2 52 D6
Fleetdale Pde RDART DA2 * 52 D6
Fleet Rd GVW DA11 54 D8
RDART DA2 52 D6
RDV CT15 211 H8
ROCH ME1 100 E4
Fleets La CANTW/ST CT2 153 L6
Fleet Ter CAT SE6 * 46 D5
Fleetwood Av HB CT6 128 E5
Fleetwood Cl CROY/NA CR0 87 G6
IOS ME12 65 J7
Fleming Ct CROY/NA CR0 86 B8
Fleming Gdns TIL RM18 35 K7
Fleming Rd CDW/CHF RM16 33 K3
RCANTE CT3 252 H3
WALW SE17 24 C5
Fleming Wy FOLKN CT19 220 E5
Fletcher Rd STPH/PW TN12 281 R6
Fletchers Cl HAYES BR2 71 J8
Fletching Rd CHARL SE7 27 L5
Flete Rd MARG CT9 178 A8
Flimwell ASH TN23 204 A5
Flimwell Cl BMLY BR1 70 F2
WADH TN5 311 L5
Flint Cl ORP BR6 107 L2
SIT ME10 119 M1
Flint Down Cl STMC/STPC BR5 * 73 H5
Flint Gn WALD ME5 115 K3
Flint La RMAID ME17 243 L9
Flintmill Crs BKHTH/KID SE3 27 M8
ELTH/MOT SE9 47 M1
Flinton St WALW SE17 24 F4
Flint St WALW SE17 24 E3
WTHK RM20 33 J5
The Floats SEV TN13 135 K7
Flockton St BERM/RHTH SE16 25 H1
Flodden Rd CMBW SE5 24 D7
Flood Hatch MAID/SHEP ME15 12 B9
Flood La FAV ME13 149 K2
Flood St RASHE TN25 305 N4
Flora Gdns CROY/NA CR0 105 H5
Florance La RRTW TN3 199 J7
Flora Rd RAM CT11 17 K3
Flora St BELV DA17 30 A4
Florence Av WSTB CT5 126 B6
Florence Cl WTHK RM20 33 M5
Florence Rd ABYW SE2 29 K2
BECK BR3 69 L6
BMLY BR1 71 H5
MAIDW ME16 12 D7
NWCR SE14 26 A7
RAM CT11 16 F7
Florence St STRD ME2 19 H2
Florence Ter NWCR SE14 26 A7
Florida Cl DVE/WH CT16 213 J6
Florida Rd THHTH CR7 68 C5
Florin Dr ROCH ME1 100 C1
Flowerfield RSEV TN14 135 L3
Flowerhill Wy MEO DA13 78 F4
Flower La GDST RH9 156 C7
Floyd Rd CHARL SE7 27 K4
Fludyer St LEW SE13 46 F2
Flume End MAIDW ME16 12 B9
The Flyers Wy BH/WHM TN16 159 J4
Flying Horse La DVE/WH CT16 * 8 E5
Foads Hl MSTR CT12 182 A7
Foads La MSTR CT12 182 A8
Foalhurst Cl TONN TN10 195 H1
Focal Point Rd DVE/WH CT16 213 G5
Foley Cl KEN/WIL TN24 205 K4
Foley Rd BH/WHM TN16 132 C4
Foley St MAID/BEAR ME14 13 H2
Folkestone Rd DVW CT17 217 J2
RDV CT15 216 F4
RYE TN31 328 A10
Folks Wood Wy HYTHE CT21 307 M10
Folly Rd FOLK CT20 11 M3
Folly Wall POP/IOD E14 26 D1
Fonblanque Rd IOS ME12 * 64 D3
Fontaine Rd STRHM/NOR SW16 68 A3
Fontwell Cl MAID/SHEP ME15 168 A7
Fontwell Dr HAYES BR2 90 B1
Foord Cl RDART DA2 52 F7
Foord Rd RMAID ME17 243 L12
Foord Rd North FOLKN CT19 11 J3
Foord Rd South FOLK CT20 11 K5
Foord St ROCH ME1 19 K9
Footbury Hill Rd ORP BR6 91 H3
Foots Cray High St SCUP DA14 73 K3
Foots Cray La BXLY DA5 49 K6
Footscray Rd ELTH/MOT SE9 48 B4
Forbes Rd FAV ME13 149 K3
Force Green La
BH/WHM TN16 159 J2
Ford Cl HB CT6 128 B5
RCANTW CT4 175 G8
THHTH CR7 86 C2
Fordcombe Cl
MAID/SHEP ME15 168 A6
Fordcombe Rd RRTW TN3 277 J12
RTON TN11 276 H6
Fordcroft Rd STMC/STPC BR5 91 J1
Forde Av BMLY BR1 71 K7
Fordel Rd CAT SE6 46 E6
Ford Hl RCANTE CT3 155 M2
Fordingbridge Cl
MAIDW ME16 140 C8
Ford La BGR/WK TN15 239 L11
E/WMAL ME19 239 M9
Ford Manor Rd LING RH7 274 B3
Fordmill Rd CAT SE6 46 B7
Fordoun Rd BRDST CT10 179 J8
Ford Rd GVW DA11 54 C3
Ford Wy ASH TN23 204 C2
Fordwich Cl MAIDW ME16 140 C6
ORP BR6 91 G3
Fordwich Dr HOO/HM ME3 82 B3
Fordwich Gv BRDST CT10 179 H6
Fordwich Pl SWCH CT13 206 A1
Fordwich Rd CANTW/ST CT2 173 G5
Fordyce Rd LEW SE13 46 D4
Foreland Av FOLKN CT19 221 G7
MARG CT9 179 G3
Foreland Ct RAM CT11 * 17 G8
Foreland Hts BRDST CT10 179 L6
Foreland Rd RDV CT15 215 H5
Forelands Sq DEAL CT14 209 J6
Foreland St WOOL/PLUM SE18 28 E3
The Foreland CANT CT1 174 C4
Foremans Barn Rd
MAID/SHEP ME15 258 F2
Foreness Cl MARG CT9 179 K2
Forestall Meadow ASH TN23 204 D7
Forest Av ASH TN23 202 B7
Forest Cl CHST BR7 72 B5
Forestdale Rd WALD ME5 115 H5
Forest Dene RTWE/PEM TN2 201 K4
Forest Dr HAYES BR2 89 M7
WALD ME5 115 G3
Forester Rd PECK SE15 45 J2
Foresters Cl WALD ME5 115 G3
Foresters Crs BXLYHN DA7 50 C2
Foresters Wy FOLK CT20 11 J5
Forest Gv TONN TN10 188 F8
Forest Hl MAID/SHEP ME15 167 G4
Forest Hill Rd EDUL SE22 45 J4
Forestholme Cl FSTH SE23 45 K7
SYD SE26 69 K2
Forest Rdg BECK BR3 70 B7
HAYES BR2 89 M7
Forest Rd ERITH DA8 31 H7
RTWE/PEM TN2 23 M7
STPH/PW TN12 279 K3
Forest Wy BFN/LL DA15 48 E5
E/WMAL ME19 164 B2
HRTF TN7 198 D7
RTWE/PEM TN2 201 K4
RTWE/PEM TN2 278 A9
STMC/STPC BR5 91 H1
Forge Cl CANTW/ST CT2 173 G4
FAV ME13 * 149 L3
HAYES BR2 89 H4
RASHE TN25 307 J5
RDV CT15 272 D6
STPH/PW TN12 278 E2
Forge Ct RHAM ME8 103 H2
Forge Cft EDEN TN8 192 D4
Forgefield BH/WHM TN16 132 C2
RASHW TN26 285 N12
Forge Fld RDV CT15 293 R12
WADH TN5 310 A11
Forgefields HB CT6 155 H1
Forge Hl RASHE TN25 305 R8
RASHW TN26 285 P12
Forge La ASH TN23 2 A4
BGR/WK TN15 111 M4
DVE/WH CT16 213 H1
EYN DA4 76 D8
GILL ME7 83 M7
GILL ME7 116 B4
GVE DA12 56 A7
GVE DA12 80 F2
HDCN TN27 262 F12
HDCN TN27 283 L4
HOO/HM ME3 59 L2
HOO/HM ME3 81 K2
MAID/BEAR ME14 141 K2
MAID/SHEP ME15 166 C6
RBTBR TN32 323 R12
RCANTE CT3 232 D9
RDV CT15 210 B4
RMAID ME17 169 G6
RMAID ME17 260 A8
RSIT ME9 226 A10
WBY/YAL ME18 241 M11
WBY/YAL ME18 257 R9
WBY/YAL ME18 258 A9
Forge Meadow RMAID ME17 242 E11
TENT TN30 327 R1
Forge Mdw HDCN TN27 283 L4
Forge Meads TENT TN30 326 H2
Forge Ms CROY/NA CR0 88 B8
Forge Pth DVE/WH CT16 213 H1
Forge Pl GVE DA12 * 56 A6
Forge Rd SIT ME10 119 M3
STH/RUST TN4 196 C4
Forge Wy RSEV TN14 109 L5
STPH/PW TN12 279 K2
Formby Rd STRD ME2 99 H7
The Forrens CANT CT1 * 5 G3
Forrester Cl CANT CT1 5 L1
Forrester Pth SYD SE26 69 K1
Forresters Pl ASH TN23 * 2 C9
Forrest Gdns
STRHM/NOR SW16 68 A7
Forsham La RMAID ME17 260 E8
Forson Cl TENT TN30 315 N1
Forstal Cl HAYES BR2 71 H7
Forstall RRTW TN3 200 B1
Forstal La RMAID ME17 259 J2
The Forstall RTON TN11 255 P11
Forstal Rd DIT/AY ME20 140 B3
HDCN TN27 262 F12
RCANTW CT4 271 L5
The Forstal RASHE TN25 266 F11
RCANTE CT3 235 J7
RTON TN11 256 B5
RTWE/PEM TN2 278 B9
Forstal Vls HDCN TN27 * 262 F12
Forster Rd BECK BR3 69 M7
Forsters RMAID ME17 260 F1
Forsyte Crs NRWD SE19 68 F5
Forsyth Cl E/WMAL ME19 139 H4
Forsyth Gdns WALW SE17 24 C5
Fort Bridgewood ROCH ME1 * 100 C6
Fort Burgoyne Rd
DVE/WH CT16 8 F1
Fort Cl LYDD TN29 335 M3
Fort Crs MARG CT9 15 G2
Fort Hl MARG CT9 14 F3
Fort Lower Prom MARG CT9 15 G2
Fort Paragon MARG CT9 15 H2
Fort Pitt Hl CHAT ME4 6 A6
Fort Pitt St CHAT ME4 6 B7
Fort Rd BRDST CT10 183 L1
HYTHE CT21 222 B3
MARG CT9 14 F3
RSEV TN14 135 H1
STHWK SE1 25 G3
TIL RM18 55 J2
Fortrye Cl GVW DA11 54 F7
Fort St ROCH ME1 100 E1
Fortuna Ct RAM CT11 17 H4
Fortune Pl STHWK SE1 25 G4
Fortune Wy E/WMAL ME19 164 C2
Forty Acres Hl IOS ME12 228 F1
Forty Acres Rd CANTW/ST CT2 4 D2
Forum Magnum Sq
STHWK SE1 * 24 A1
Forward Wy ROCH ME1 100 D7
Foss Av CROY/NA CR0 86 B8
Fossdene Rd CHARL SE7 27 J4
Fosse Bank TON TN9 194 D6
Fosse Bank Cl TON TN9 194 D6
Fosse Rd TON TN9 194 E3
Fossil Rd LEW SE13 46 B1
Fossington Rd BELV DA17 29 L3
Fostall Gn ASH TN23 204 C4
Fostall Rd FAV ME13 123 K8
Fosten La HDCN TN27 300 D5
Foster Clarke Dr
MAID/SHEP ME15 167 L8
Foster Cl FOLKN CT19 219 M6
Foster Ct SWCH CT13 * 206 A2
Fosterdown GDST RH9 156 A7
Foster Rd KEN/WIL TN24 205 K5
Foster's Av BRDST CT10 179 H6
Fosters Cl CHST BR7 72 A2
Foster's Ct SWCH CT13 206 B2
Foster St MAID/SHEP ME15 13 G6
Foster Wy DEAL CT14 209 J4
Fostington Wy WALD ME5 115 G4
Fougeres Wy KEN/WIL TN24 202 D7
Foulds Cl RHAM ME8 116 C1
Foulsham Rd THHTH CR7 68 D7
Founders Gdns NRWD SE19 68 D4
Foundry Whf ROCH ME1 6 A5
Fountain Dr NRWD SE19 69 G1
Fountain Green Sq
BERM/RHTH SE16 25 H1
Fountain La MAIDW ME16 166 B3
Fountain Pl BRXN/ST SW9 24 B7
Fountain Rd STRD ME2 81 M4
THHTH CR7 68 D6
Fountains Cl KEN/WIL TN24 3 L6
Fountain St SIT ME10 119 M5
Fountain Wk GVW DA11 55 G4
Four Elms Hl HOO/HM ME3 82 F2
Four Elms Rd EDEN TN8 192 D3
Four Horseshoes Pk
FAV ME13 * 124 E8
Four Oaks Rd HDCN TN27 282 G3
Fourth Av GILL ME7 101 M1
IOS ME12 67 G7
WTHK RM20 33 H5
Fourwents Rd HOO/HM ME3 59 L7
Fowey Cl WALD ME5 101 K8
Fowler Cl RHAM ME8 116 D2
SCUP DA14 73 M2
Foxberry Rd BROCKY SE4 45 M2
Foxborough Cl SWCH CT13 253 N3
Foxborough Gdns BROCKY SE4 46 B4
Foxborough Hl SWCH CT13 253 N3
Foxborough La MSTR CT12 180 F7
Foxburrow Cl RHAM ME8 102 E8
Foxbury Av CHST BR7 72 E3
Foxbury Cl BMLY BR1 71 J3
ORP BR6 91 H8
Foxbury Dr ORP BR6 107 M1
Foxbury Rd BMLY BR1 71 J3
Foxbush RTON TN11 255 R7
Fox Cl ORP BR6 91 H8
RFOLK CT18 291 L10
Foxcombe CROY/NA CR0 105 G1
Foxcroft Rd WOOL/PLUM SE18 28 C7
Foxden Dr MAID/SHEP ME15 168 A4
Foxdene Rd WSTB CT5 126 A7
Foxdown Cl CANTW/ST CT2 171 L3
Foxearth Cl BH/WHM TN16 132 D4
Foxearth Rd SAND/SEL CR2 104 B4
Foxearth Sp SAND/SEL CR2 104 B3
Foxendown La MEO DA13 97 J4
Foxes Dl BKHTH/KID SE3 47 H1
HAYES BR2 70 E7
Foxes Gn CDW/CHF RM16 35 H1
Foxfield Rd ORP BR6 90 E5
Foxglove Cl BFN/LL DA15 49 H4
Foxglove Crs WALD ME5 114 F1
Foxglove Gn KEN/WIL TN24 3 K5
Foxglove Ri MAID/BEAR ME14 140 F6
Foxglove Rd KEN/WIL TN24 3 H6
Foxglove Rw STRD ME2 * 99 G8
The Foxgloves STPH/PW TN12 279 L4
Foxgrove SIT ME10 119 M2
Foxgrove Av BECK BR3 70 C4
Foxgrove Rd BECK BR3 70 D4
WSTB CT5 127 H3
Fox Hl NRWD SE19 69 G4
SIT ME10 120 E6
Fox Hill Gdns NRWD SE19 * 68 F4
Foxhole La HAWK TN18 312 H8
STPH/PW TN12 278 F9
WADH TN5 309 N6

Foxhole Rd ELTH/MOT SE9 47 M3
Fox Hollow Cl
WOOL/PLUM SE18 28 F4
Fox Hollow Dr BXLYHN DA7 49 L1
Fox Holt Rd RDV CT15 292 F7
Foxhome Cl CHST BR7 72 B3
Fox House Rd BELV DA17 30 C3
Fox La HAYES BR2 89 J8
Fox Lea BGR/WK TN15 240 E2
Foxley Rd CMBW SE5 24 B6
QBOR ME11 64 B8
THHTH CR7 68 C8
Foxley Sq BRXN/ST SW9 * 24 C6
Fox Manor Wy WTHK RM20 33 J5
Fox's Cross Hl WSTB CT5 152 B2
Fox's Cross Rd WSTB CT5 152 C2
Fox St GILL ME7 7 J2
Foxton Rd WTHK RM20 33 L5
Fox Wy RCANTW CT4 270 E5
Foxwell St BROCKY SE4 45 M1
Foxwood Gv GVW DA11 54 F6
ORP BR6 108 B4
Foxwood Rd BKHTH/KID SE3 47 G2
RDART DA2 53 J8
Foxwood Wy HART DA3 78 E6
Foyle Rd BKHTH/KID SE3 27 G5
Framley Rd TONN TN10 189 J8
Framlingham Crs
ELTH/MOT SE9 71 M1
Frampton Rd HYTHE CT21 222 B3
Francemary Rd LEW SE13 46 B3
France Rd DVE/WH CT16 213 H4
Frances Gdns RAM CT11 17 M3
Frances St WOOL/PLUM SE18 28 A3
Francis Av BXLYHN DA7 30 B8
SWCH CT13 207 H2
Francis Barber Cl
STRHM/NOR SW16 * 68 A1
Francis Dr WALD ME5 115 H3
Francis La MAID/SHEP ME15 168 A8
Francis Ms LEE/GVPK SE12 * 47 G4
Francis Rd ASH TN23 2 A9
BRDST CT10 179 L6
CROY/NA CR0 86 C3
DART DA1 51 L3
RTON TN11 188 A7
STMC/STPC BR5 73 L7
Frankapps Cl RSIT ME9 118 C3
Frank Burton Cl CHARL SE7 27 J4
Frank Dixon Cl DUL SE21 44 F5
Frank Dixon Wy DUL SE21 44 F6
Frank Edinger Cl
KEN/WIL TN24 203 G7
Frankfield Ri RTWE/PEM TN2 201 G4
Frankfurt Rd HNHL SE24 44 D3
Frankham St DEPT SE8 26 B6
Frankland Cl BERM/RHTH SE16 25 J2
Franklin Cl LEW SE13 26 C7
WNWD SE27 44 C8
Franklin Dr MAID/BEAR ME14 167 L1
Franklin Rd BXLY DA5 50 F7
BXLYHN DA7 29 M7
GILL ME7 7 L4
GVE DA12 79 L2
PGE/AN SE20 69 K4
Franklyn Rd CANTW/ST CT2 171 K6
Franks Ct RHAM ME8 102 C4
Frank's Hollow Rd RRTW TN3 277 R8
Franks La EYN DA4 94 C1
Franks Wood Av
STMC/STPC BR5 90 C1
Frank Woolley Rd TONN TN10 189 J8
Fransfield Gv SYD SE26 45 J8
Frant Cl PGE/AN SE20 69 K4
Frant Fld EDEN TN8 192 E4
Frant Green Rd RRTW TN3 294 A10
Frant Rd RRTW TN3 201 H7
RTWE/PEM TN2 22 E9
THHTH CR7 86 C1
Fraser Cl BXLY DA5 50 D6
Fraser Rd ERITH DA8 30 D4
Frazier St STHWK SE1 24 B1
Frean St BERM/RHTH SE16 25 H2
Freathy La RASHE TN25 202 F3
Freda Cl BRDST CT10 183 J4
Freda Corbett Cl PECK SE15 25 H6
Frederick Crs BRXN/ST SW9 24 C6
Frederick Gdns CROY/NA CR0 86 C2
Frederick Pl WOOL/PLUM SE18 28 C4
Frederick Rd DEAL CT14 209 H6
GILL ME7 7 J6
WALW SE17 24 C5
Frederick St SIT ME10 119 M5
The Freedown RDV CT15 215 H2
Free Heath Rd RRTW TN3 295 P10
The Freehold RTON TN11 256 A4
STPH/PW TN12 257 J7
Freelands Av SAND/SEL CR2 104 C3
Freelands Gv BMLY BR1 71 J5
Freelands Rd BMLY BR1 71 J5
SNOD ME6 112 F5
Freeland Wy ERITH DA8 31 H7
Freeman Gdns CHAT ME4 101 G4
Freeman Rd GVE DA12 55 M8
Freeman's Cl WSTB CT5 126 B7
Freeman's Rd MSTR CT12 180 E7
Freemantle St WALW SE17 24 F4
Freeman Wy
MAID/SHEP ME15 167 M6
Freemason's Rd CROY/NA CR0 86 F4
Freemen's Wy DEAL CT14 209 J6
Freesia Cl GILL ME7 84 A7
ORP BR6 91 G8
Freethorpe Cl NRWD SE19 68 F5
Freight La CRBK TN17 298 G10
Freightmaster Est RAIN RM13 * 31 H3
Fremantle Rd BELV DA17 30 B3
FOLK CT20 219 M8
Fremlin Cl STH/RUST TN4 200 C1
Fremlins Rd MAID/BEAR ME14 168 D1
Frencham Cl CANTW/ST CT2 172 B5
Frendsbury Rd BROCKY SE4 45 M2
Frensham Cl SIT ME10 120 C5
Frensham Dr CROY/NA CR0 105 H2
Frensham Rd BFN/LL DA15 48 E7
CRBK TN17 314 F8
Frensham St PECK SE15 25 H5
Frensham Wk WALD ME5 115 G4
Freshfield Cl LEW SE13 46 E2
Freshfield La HYTHE CT21 222 B1
Freshfields CROY/NA CR0 88 A3
Freshland Rd MAIDW ME16 166 C1
Freshlands HB CT6 129 M4
Freshwater Cl HB CT6 128 C6
Freshwater Rd WALD ME5 101 J6
Freshwood Cl BECK BR3 70 C5
Freta Rd BXLYHS DA6 50 A3
Frewen Cl RYE TN31 325 J6
Friar Ms WNWD SE27 44 C8
Friar Rd STMC/STPC BR5 91 H1
Friars Av WALD ME5 115 G3
Friars Cl WSTB CT5 127 G4
Friars Ct MAID/BEAR ME14 * 13 J4
Friars Md POP/IOD E14 26 D2
Friars Ms ELTH/MOT SE9 48 B3
The Friars CANT CT1 4 E4
HOO/HM ME3 * 60 A1
Friars Wk ABYW SE2 29 L4
Friars Wy DVE/WH CT16 213 H6
RTWE/PEM TN2 197 G7
Friarswood CROY/NA CR0 104 D3
Friars Wd CROY/NA CR0 * 104 D3
Friary Est PECK SE15 * 25 H6
Friary Pl STRD ME2 19 G3
Friary Rd PECK SE15 25 H6
Friary Wy CANTW/ST CT2 171 L3
Friday Rd ERITH DA8 30 E4
Friday St RMAID ME17 261 J7
Friendly Cl MARG CT9 179 G4
Friendly Pl GNWCH SE10 26 C7
Friendly St DEPT SE8 26 B7
Friendly Street Ms DEPT SE8 26 B8
Friends Av MARG CT9 179 G5
Friends' Rd CROY/NA CR0 86 E6
Friern Rd EDUL SE22 45 H4
Friesian Wy KEN/WIL TN24 202 F4
Friezland Rd STH/RUST TN4 200 E4
Friezley La CRBK TN17 298 G3
Frigate Ms DEPT SE8 26 B5
Frimley Cl CROY/NA CR0 105 H2
Frimley Ct SCUP DA14 73 K2
Frimley Crs CROY/NA CR0 105 H2
Frindsbury Hl STRD ME2 82 D4
Frindsbury Rd STRD ME2 19 J1
Frinstead Gv STMC/STPC BR5 73 L8
Frinstead Wk MAIDW ME16 140 C6
Frinsted Cl RHAM ME8 102 D2
Frinsted Rd ERITH DA8 30 E6
RSIT ME9 145 M8
Frinton Rd SCUP DA14 49 M7
Friston Wy ROCH ME1 100 E5
Friswell Pl BXLYHN DA7 50 B2
Frith Rd CROY/NA CR0 86 D5
DVE/WH CT16 8 B1
RASHE TN25 305 K7
Frithwood Cl
MAID/SHEP ME15 168 A4
Frittenden Cl ASH TN23 204 B5
Frittenden Rd STPH/PW TN12 282 B7
STRD ME2 82 E4
Frobisher Cl SIT ME10 119 M2
Frobisher Gdns ROCH ME1 100 D3
Frobisher Rd ERITH DA8 31 H6
Frobisher Wy GRH DA9 53 J2
GVE DA12 79 M2
Froghole La EDEN TN8 186 F3
Frog La E/WMAL ME19 138 D5
RCANTW CT4 250 F11
RTW TN1 22 F7
Frogley Rd EDUL SE22 45 G2
Frognal Av SCUP DA14 73 H3
Frognal Cl RSIT ME9 121 J7
Frognal Gdns RSIT ME9 121 J7
Frognal La RSIT ME9 121 J7
Frognal Pl SCUP DA14 73 J2
Frogs Hole La CRBK TN17 300 D11
Frog's La CRBK TN17 314 E8
Froissart Rd ELTH/MOT SE9 47 M3
Frome TIL RM18 36 D3
Front Brents FAV ME13 149 L1
Front Rd RASHW TN26 302 H12
Front St DEAL CT14 211 G4
The Front RDV CT15 215 H5
Frost Crs WALD ME5 101 H6
Frostland La LYDD TN29 319 N8
Froyle Cl MAIDW ME16 140 D7
Fruiterer's Cl RSIT ME9 146 B2
Fruitfields WADH TN5 311 K6
Fry Cl HOO/HM ME3 43 H7
Fryston Av CROY/NA CR0 87 H5
Frythe Cl CRBK TN17 298 G9
Frythe Crs CRBK TN17 298 G9
Frythe Wk CRBK TN17 298 G9
Frythe Wy CRBK TN17 298 G9
Fuchsia St ABYW SE2 29 J4
Fuggles Cl STPH/PW TN12 278 H3
Fuggles Ct CRBK TN17 313 N3
Fulbert Dr MAID/BEAR ME14 142 A8
Fulbert Rd DVE/WH CT16 213 J4
Fulford St BERM/RHTH SE16 25 J1
Fulham Av MARG CT9 177 L6
Fuller Cl ORP BR6 91 G8
WADH TN5 309 K5
Fullers Cl MAID/BEAR ME14 168 B1
Fullers Hl BH/WHM TN16 159 J4
Fullers La RYE TN31 325 J7
Fuller's Wd CROY/NA CR0 88 B8
Fullerton Rd CROY/NA CR0 87 G3
Fulmar Dr EGRIN RH19 274 A10
Fulmar Rd STRD ME2 81 L8
Fulmar Wy HB CT6 232 A5
Fulsam Pl MARG CT9 14 C6
Fulston Pl SIT ME10 120 B6
Fulthorp Rd BKHTH/KID SE3 27 H8
Fulwich Rd DART DA1 52 A4
Furfield Cl MAID/SHEP ME15 167 M8
Furley Rd PECK SE15 25 H6
Furnace Av RRTW TN3 296 B10
Furnace La RRTW TN3 295 R9
RRTW TN3 296 A9
RYE TN31 325 M12
STPH/PW TN12 279 P9
Furneaux Av WNWD SE27 68 C2
Furner Cl DART DA1 51 G1
Furness Cl CDW/CHF RM16 35 J4
Furnival Ct RTWE/PEM TN2 * 201 G5
Furrell's Rd ROCH ME1 19 L8
Furtherfield Cl CROY/NA CR0 86 B2
Further Field STPH/PW TN12 281 R4
Further Green Rd CAT SE6 46 F5
Furzefield Av RRTW TN3 277 P9
Furzefield Cl CHST BR7 72 C3
Furzefield Rd BKHTH/KID SE3 27 J5
Furze Hill Crs IOS ME12 64 E7
Furzehill Sq STMC/STPC BR5 73 J8
Furze Rd THHTH CR7 68 D7
Fusilier Av FOLK CT20 219 J8
Future Ct STRD ME2 * 82 F5
Fyfe Wy BMLY BR1 71 H6
Fyfield Cl BECK BR3 70 E8
Fyfield Rd BRXN/ST SW9 44 B1
Fysie La BUR/ETCH TN19 322 D2

G

Gabion Av PUR RM19 32 E3
Gable Cl DART DA1 51 H3
Gable Ct SYD SE26 69 J1
Gable Ms HAYES BR2 89 M5
Gables Cl CMBW SE5 24 F7
LEE/GVPK SE12 47 H6
The Gables GRAYS RM17 * 34 A3
HART DA3 78 D6
NRWD SE19 * 68 F5
Gabriel Gdns GVE DA12 79 M2
Gabriel's Hl MAID/BEAR ME14 13 G4
Gabrielspring Rd EYN DA4 94 E5
Gabriel Spring Rd (East)
EYN DA4 94 F5
Gabriel St FSTH SE23 45 L5
Gadby Rd SIT ME10 119 K4
Gadsby La RASHW TN26 301 R3
Gads Hill Pl HOO/HM ME3 * 81 J2
Gagetown Ter
MAID/BEAR ME14 141 G6
Gain Hl STPH/PW TN12 * 258 A11
Gainsboro Rd BRCH CT7 176 C5
Gainsborough Av DART DA1 51 K3
MARG CT9 178 F5
TIL RM18 35 H7
Gainsborough Cl BECK BR3 70 B4
FOLKN CT19 10 C1
RHAM ME8 102 E7
SIT ME10 119 J4
Gainsborough Dr GVW DA11 54 E8
HB CT6 129 M4
MAIDW ME16 * 166 C1
Gainsborough Gdns
TONN TN10 189 H8
Gainsborough Ms DUL SE21 44 D6
SYD SE26 * 45 J8
Gainsborough Sq BXLYHN DA7 49 L1
Gainsford St STHWK SE1 25 G1
Gairloch Rd CMBW SE5 24 F8
Gaist Av CTHM CR3 130 A8
Gaitskell Rd ELTH/MOT SE9 48 D6
Gaitskell Wy STHWK SE1 24 D1
Galahad Av STRD ME2 18 A5
Galahad Rd BMLY BR1 47 H8
Galatea Sq PECK SE15 45 J1
Galbraith St POP/IOD E14 26 D2
Galena Cl SIT ME10 119 K3
WALD ME5 115 H4
Gallants La MAID/SHEP ME15 166 A7
Galleon Bvd GRH DA9 52 E2
Galleon Cl BERM/RHTH SE16 25 K1
ERITH DA8 30 E3
ROCH ME1 100 D5
Galleon Rd CDW/CHF RM16 33 J3
Galleon Wy STRD ME2 83 G2
Gallery Rd DUL SE21 44 E6
Galley Dr RSIT ME9 * 145 L3
Galley Hill Rd GVW DA11 54 A3
Galleywall Rd
BERM/RHTH SE16 25 J3
Galliard St SWCH CT13 206 B1
Gallions Rd CHARL SE7 27 J3
Gallions View Rd THMD SE28 28 F1
Gallon Cl CHARL SE7 27 K3
The Gallops MEO DA13 239 L6
The Gallop SAND/SEL CR2 104 A2
Gallosson Rd WOOL/PLUM SE18 28 F3
Galloway Dr DART DA1 50 F5
RASHE TN25 202 F3
Galloway Pth CROY/NA CR0 86 E7
Galloways Rd LYDD TN29 334 D4
Gallus Sq BKHTH/KID SE3 47 J1
Gallwey Av BRCH CT7 176 B6
Galsworthy Crs
BKHTH/KID SE3 * 27 K7
Galsworthy Rd TIL RM18 35 K7
Galway Cl BERM/RHTH SE16 * 25 J4
Galway Rd IOS ME12 64 D3
Gamma Rd HOO/HM ME3 60 E6
Gammon's Farm La
LYDD TN29 319 R6
LYDD TN29 320 A6
Gandolfi St PECK SE15 * 24 F5
Gandy's La RMAID ME17 259 P3
Gange Ms FAV ME13 * 149 L2
Gangers Hl GDST RH9 156 E5
Gann Rd WSTB CT5 127 G3
The Gap CANT CT1 174 C4
CANTW/ST CT2 153 H6
Garden Av BXLYHN DA7 50 A1
Garden Cl CANTW/ST CT2 171 H3
LEE/GVPK SE12 47 J8
MAID/SHEP ME15 167 M6
Garden Ct ROCH ME1 99 K8
SEV TN13 * 136 C8
Gardeners Quay SWCH CT13 * 237 K12
Gardeners Rd CROY/NA CR0 86 C4
Gardenia Cl STRD ME2 82 C4
Garden La BMLY BR1 71 J3
BRXS/STRHM SW2 44 A6
Garden of England Pk
RMAID ME17 * 242 C10
Garden Pl KEN/WIL TN24 203 H5
RDART DA2 51 L8
Garden Rd BMLY BR1 71 J4
FOLKN CT19 11 J2
PGE/AN SE20 69 K5
RTW TN1 23 H3
SEV TN13 21 L1
TON TN9 195 G3
Garden Rw GVW DA11 55 G8
STHWK SE1 24 C2
The Gardens BECK BR3 70 D6
EDUL SE22 45 H2
RMAID ME17 * 258 H2
Garden St GILL ME7 6 E1
RTW TN1 23 H4
Garden Wk BECK BR3 70 A5
Garden Wy E/WMAL ME19 164 A3
Gardiner Cl STMC/STPC BR5 73 K6
Gardiner House
WOOL/PLUM SE18 * 27 M6
Gardiner St GILL ME7 7 K2
Gardner's Hl RYE TN31 327 L7
Gardyne Ms TON TN9 194 E5
Gareth Gv BMLY BR1 71 H1
Garfield Pl FAV ME13 149 L2
Garfield Rd GILL ME7 7 M1
MARG CT9 14 C5
Gargery Cl GVE DA12 56 A6
Garibaldi St WOOL/PLUM SE18 28 F3
Garland Rd WOOL/PLUM SE18 28 E6
Garlands RTON TN11 188 A5
Garlies Rd FSTH SE23 45 M8
Garlinge Green Rd
RCANTW CT4 248 G11
Garlinge Rd STH/RUST TN4 196 D4
Garner Dr E/WMAL ME19 139 H4
Garnet Rd THHTH CR7 68 D8
Garnett Cl ELTH/MOT SE9 48 A1
Garnies Cl PECK SE15 25 G6
Garrard Av MARG CT9 177 L5
Garrard Cl BXLYHN DA7 50 B1
CHST BR7 72 C2
Garrick Crs CROY/NA CR0 86 F5
Garrick Dr WOOL/PLUM SE18 28 E2
Garrick St GVW DA11 55 J4
Garrington Cl
MAID/BEAR ME14 141 K7
Garrison Cl WOOL/PLUM SE18 28 B6
Garrison Rd IOS ME12 64 B2
Garrolds Cl SWLY BR8 74 E6
Garrow HART DA3 78 C7
Garside Cl WOOL/PLUM SE18 28 E2
Garsington Ms BROCKY SE4 46 A1
Garthorne Rd FSTH SE23 45 L5
Garth Rd SEV TN13 162 B6
Garton Wy ASH TN23 286 H10
Garvock Dr SEV TN13 20 F9
Gascoigne Rd CROY/NA CR0 105 H4
Gascoyne Cl MAID/SHEP ME15 168 C3
Gascoyne Dr DART DA1 51 G1
Gasholder Pl LBTH SE11 24 A4
Gas House Rd ROCH ME1 19 K4
Gas Rd SIT ME10 120 A4
Gasson Rd SWCM DA10 53 M4
Gassons Rd SNOD ME6 112 F5
Gas St CANT CT1 4 E6
Gasworks La ASH TN23 2 A6
Gataker St BERM/RHTH SE16 25 J2
Gatcombe Cl MAIDW ME16 140 C8
WALD ME5 101 H8
Gateacre Rd WSTB CT5 126 B7
Gate Farm Rd RRTW TN3 277 R5
Gatefield Cottages CRBK TN17 314 E5
Gatekeeper Cha RHAM ME8 103 G5
Gateley Rd BRXN/ST SW9 44 A1
Gates Ct WALW SE17 * 24 D4
Gates Green Rd WWKM BR4 89 H7
Gatestone Rd NRWD SE19 68 F3
Gateway WALW SE17 24 D5
Gateway Pde GVE DA12 * 80 A1
The Gateway DVE/WH CT16 8 E5
Gatland La MAIDW ME16 166 C3
Gatling Rd ABYW SE2 29 H4
Gatonby St PECK SE15 25 G7
Gattons Wy SCUP DA14 74 A1
Gatwick Rd GVE DA12 55 J7
Gault Cl MAID/SHEP ME15 168 B3
Gaunt's Cl DEAL CT14 209 H5
Gaunt St STHWK SE1 24 C2
Gautrey Rd PECK SE15 25 K8
Gavel St WALW SE17 * 24 E3
Gaverick St POP/IOD E14 26 B3
Gavestone Crs LEE/GVPK SE12 47 J6
Gavestone Rd LEE/GVPK SE12 47 J5
Gayhurst Cl RHAM ME8 102 E7
Gayhurst Dr SIT ME10 119 K4
Gaylor Rd TIL RM18 34 F7
Gaynesford Rd FSTH SE23 45 L7
Gaywood Cl BRXS/STRHM SW2 44 A6
Gaywood St STHWK SE1 24 C2
Gaza St WALW SE17 24 C4
Gazedown LYDD TN29 331 N2
Gaze Hill Av SIT ME10 120 B6
Gazelle Gld GVE DA12 80 A2
Gean Cl WALD ME5 115 H4
Geddes Pl BXLYHN DA7 50 B2
Gedge's Hl STPH/PW TN12 279 J5
Gedling Pl STHWK SE1 25 G2
Geldart Rd PECK SE15 25 J6
Gellatly Rd PECK SE15 25 K8
General Wolfe Rd GNWCH SE10 26 E7
Genesta Av WSTB CT5 126 C6
Genesta Cl SIT ME10 119 M2
Genesta Gld GVE DA12 80 B2
Genesta Rd WOOL/PLUM SE18 28 C5
Geneva Av RHAM ME8 102 B3
Geneva Dr BRXN/ST SW9 44 B2
Geneva Rd THHTH CR7 86 D1
Genoa Rd PGE/AN SE20 69 K5
Gentian Cl MAID/BEAR ME14 141 M8
Geoffrey Cl CMBW SE5 24 D8
Geoffrey Rd BROCKY SE4 46 A1
George Beard Rd DEPT SE8 26 A3
George Groves Rd
PGE/AN SE20 69 H5
George Gurr Crs FOLKN CT19 220 E5
George Hl RBTBR TN32 322 G10
George Hill Rd BRDST CT10 179 J4
George La FOLK CT20 11 K6
HAYES BR2 89 J4
LEW SE13 46 D4
NROM TN28 331 J6
RMAID ME17 169 H6
ROCH ME1 19 K6
George Mathers Rd
LBTH SE11 * 24 C3
George Pk MARG CT9 177 L4
George Parris Ct IOS ME12 * 65 K7
George Roche Rd CANT CT1 4 F8
George Rw BERM/RHTH SE16 25 H1
George's Av WSTB CT5 126 B6
George's Rd BH/WHM TN16 132 C6
George St ASH TN23 2 B7
CROY/NA CR0 86 E5
DEAL CT14 209 L2
DVW CT17 213 J8
GRAYS RM17 34 B5
MAID/SHEP ME15 13 G7
RAM CT11 17 J6
RTWE/PEM TN2 23 J6
SIT ME10 120 C6
STPH/PW TN12 281 R3
TON TN9 194 E5
WADH TN5 309 L4
George Summers Cl STRD ME2 82 F5
Georgetown Cl NRWD SE19 68 E2
Georgette Pl GNWCH SE10 26 D6
George V Av MARG CT9 14 A8
George Williams Wy
KEN/WIL TN24 203 H7
George Wood Cl LYDD TN29 334 D3
Georgian Cl HAYES BR2 89 J4
Georgian Dr RMAID ME17 259 J2
Georgian Wy RHAM ME8 116 D1
Georgia Rd THHTH CR7 68 C5
Geraint Rd BMLY BR1 47 H8
Gerald Av CHAT ME4 101 G3
Geraldine Rd FOLKN CT19 10 A3
Geraldine St LBTH SE11 24 C2
Gerald Rd GVE DA12 55 M5
Gerards Cl BERM/RHTH SE16 25 K5
Gerda Rd ELTH/MOT SE9 48 C7
Gerdview Dr RDART DA2 75 K1
Gerrard Av ROCH ME1 100 E5
Gerrards Dr SIT ME10 120 A7
Gerridge St STHWK SE1 24 B2
Gertrude Rd BELV DA17 30 B3
Gervase St PECK SE15 25 J6
Ghent St CAT SE6 46 B7
Ghyll Side Rd RYE TN31 325 J6
Giant Arches Rd HNHL SE24 44 D5
Gibbet La STPH/PW TN12 279 Q11
Gibbetts RRTW TN3 200 A2
Gibbon Rd PECK SE15 25 K8
Gibbons Rd SIT ME10 119 J4
Gibbs Av NRWD SE19 68 E3
Gibbs Brook La OXTED RH8 184 E4
Gibbs Cl NRWD SE19 * 68 E2
Gibbs Hl HDCN TN27 283 M4
WBY/YAL ME18 164 C8
Gibbs Sq NRWD SE19 * 68 E2
Gibraltar Av GILL ME7 83 H6
Gibraltar Hl CHAT ME4 6 C6
Gibraltar La MAID/BEAR ME14 140 F5
RFOLK CT18 220 A2
Gibraltar Sq RDV CT15 213 M6
Gibson Cl GVW DA11 55 G8
Gibson Dr E/WMAL ME19 164 A1
Gibson Rd LBTH SE11 24 A3
Gibson's Hl STRHM/NOR SW16 68 B4
Gibson St GNWCH SE10 26 F4
SIT ME10 119 M5
Giddyhorn La MAIDW ME16 12 A1
Gideon Cl BELV DA17 30 C3
Giffin St DEPT SE8 26 B6
Gifford Cl GILL ME7 102 D1
Giffordside CDW/CHF RM16 35 J4
Gigger's Green Rd
RASHE TN25 320 B2
Giggs Hl STMC/STPC BR5 73 H6
Gighill Rd DIT/AY ME20 139 G2
Gilbert Cl GILL ME7 102 B8
SWCM DA10 53 L4
WOOL/PLUM SE18 28 A7
Gilbert Rd BELV DA17 30 B2
BMLY BR1 71 H4
CDW/CHF RM16 33 K2
LBTH SE11 24 B3
RAM CT11 17 G3
Gilbert Rw GVW DA11 * 55 G7
Gilbert Wy CANT CT1 4 C9
Gilbourne Rd
WOOL/PLUM SE18 29 G5
Gilchrist Av HB CT6 128 D7
Gildenhill Rd SWLY BR8 75 K4
Gildersome St
WOOL/PLUM SE18 28 B5
Giles Coppice NRWD SE19 69 G1
Giles Gdns MARG CT9 15 G8
Giles La CANTW/ST CT2 171 K2
Giles Young Ct SIT ME10 * 119 M4
Gilford Rd DEAL CT14 209 K4
Gilham Gv DEAL CT14 209 J5
Gilkes Crs DUL SE21 44 F4
Gilkes Pl DUL SE21 44 F4
Gill Av STRD ME2 82 E2
Gill Crs GVW DA11 55 G8
Gillett Rd LYDD TN29 334 E2
THHTH CR7 68 E8
Gilletts La E/WMAL ME19 139 H7
Gillian St LEW SE13 46 C3
Gillies Rd BGR/WK TN15 94 F8
Gillingham Gn GILL ME7 83 M7
Gillingham Rd GILL ME7 7 K5
Gillison Wk BERM/RHTH SE16 * 25 H2
Gill La RASHE TN25 305 K5
RASHW TN26 304 F11
Gillman Cl RFOLK CT18 220 A1
Gillmans Rd STMC/STPC BR5 91 J4
Gills Ct STRD ME2 * 82 F5
Gill's Rd EYN DA4 76 F5
The Gill RTWE/PEM TN2 278 B9
Gilmore Rd LEW SE13 46 E2
Gilroy Wy STMC/STPC BR5 91 J3
Gilsland Rd THHTH CR7 68 E8
Gilton Rd CAT SE6 46 F8
Gimble Wy RTWE/PEM TN2 278 A9
Gingerbread La HAWK TN18 311 N7
Ginsbury Cl STRD ME2 6 A2
Gipps Cross La RRTW TN3 200 A2
Gipsy Hl NRWD SE19 68 F2
Gipsy La GRAYS RM17 34 D5
Gipsy Rd WELL DA16 29 L8
WNWD SE27 68 E1
Gipsy Road Gdns WNWD SE27 68 D1
Giraud Dr FAV ME13 149 J1
Girton Gdns CROY/NA CR0 88 B6
Girton Rd SYD SE26 69 L2
Gittens Cl BMLY BR1 71 G1
Glack Rd DEAL CT14 209 G5
Glade Gdns CROY/NA CR0 87 M3
Gladeside CROY/NA CR0 87 L3
The Glades EGRIN RH19 274 A12
GVE DA12 79 L3
The Glade BMLY BR1 71 L6
CHARL SE7 27 K6
CROY/NA CR0 87 L1
DEAL CT14 209 G3
SEV TN13 21 G2
WALD ME5 115 H3
WWKM BR4 88 C6
Gladiator St FSTH SE23 45 M4
Gladstone Dr SIT ME10 120 D6
Gladstone Ms PGE/AN SE20 69 K4
Gladstone Rd BRDST CT10 183 J2
CHAT ME4 6 B9
CROY/NA CR0 86 E3
DART DA1 52 A4
DEAL CT14 209 K5
FOLKN CT19 11 L2
KEN/WIL TN24 205 H5
MAID/BEAR ME14 141 H7
MARG CT9 14 F7
ORP BR6 90 D8
STH/RUST TN4 200 C1
TON TN9 194 E4
WSTB CT5 126 E4
Gladstone St STHWK SE1 24 C2
Gladstone Ter WNWD SE27 * 68 D1
Gladwell Rd BMLY BR1 71 H3
Gladwyn Cl RHAM ME8 116 E1
Glaisher St DEPT SE8 26 C5
Glamford Rd STRD ME2 81 L8
Glamis Cl WALD ME5 101 H8
Glanfield Rd BECK BR3 70 A8
Glanville Rd GILL ME7 7 M4
HAYES BR2 71 J7
STRD ME2 18 F3
Glarn's Yd WADH TN5 310 H6
Glasbrook Rd ELTH/MOT SE9 47 L5
Glassenbury Rd CRBK TN17 298 A6
Glasshill St STHWK SE1 24 C1
Glassmill La HAYES BR2 71 G6
Glass Yd WOOL/PLUM SE18 28 B2
Glastonbury Cl STMC/STPC BR5 91 K4
Glazebrook Cl DUL SE21 44 E7
Gleaming Wood Dr
MAID/BEAR ME14 115 L5
Gleaners Cl MAID/BEAR ME14 167 M1
Gleanings Ms ROCH ME1 * 19 J8
Glebe Cl HDCN TN27 284 E7
RDV CT15 215 G4
Glebe Ct BKHTH/KID SE3 * 46 F1
The Glebefield SEV TN13 20 C2
Glebe Gdns MARG CT9 177 L5
RMAID ME17 243 M12
Glebe House Dr HAYES BR2 89 J4
Glebeland HDCN TN27 263 J9
Glebelands DART DA1 51 G2
HDCN TN27 300 E4
RCANTE CT3 235 R12
RDV CT15 293 Q8
RRTW TN3 277 R6
RTON TN11 276 H6
Glebelands Cl CMBW SE5 * 44 F1
Glebe La MAIDW ME16 166 A4
SEV TN13 21 H9
SIT ME10 120 C7
Glebe Meadow
WBY/YAL ME18 164 E6
Glebe Pl EYN DA4 76 D8
Glebe Rd BMLY BR1 71 H5
GILL ME7 101 M2
GVW DA11 55 G6
MARG CT9 177 L5
RSEV TN14 255 K2
WARL CR6 130 C3
The Glebe BKHTH/KID SE3 46 F1
CHST BR7 72 D5
HDCN TN27 264 C6
RTWE/PEM TN2 278 A9
STH/RUST TN4 196 A2
STRD ME2 99 K3
Glebe Wy ERITH DA8 30 F5
KEN/WIL TN24 203 G4
WSTB CT5 126 E5
WWKM BR4 88 E5
Gleeson Dr ORP BR6 91 G8
Glenaffric Av POP/IOD E14 26 D3
Glenalvon Wy
WOOL/PLUM SE18 27 M3
Glen Av HB CT6 129 K4
Glenbarr Cl ELTH/MOT SE9 48 C1
Glenbervie Dr HB CT6 129 M4
Glenbow Rd BMLY BR1 70 F3

Glenbrook Cl HB CT6 129 L4
Glenbrook Gv SIT ME10 119 M2
Glencoe Rd CHAT ME4 6 E9
MARG CT9 15 K6
Glendale SWLY BR8 93 G1
Glendale Cl ELTH/MOT SE9 48 B1
Glen Dale Ms BECK BR3 70 C5
Glendale Rd ERITH DA8 30 D3
GVW DA11 78 F1
IOS ME12 65 J6
Glendall St BRXN/ST SW9 44 A1
Glendower Crs ORP BR6 91 H2
Glendown Rd ABYW SE2 29 H4
Gleneagles Cl
BERM/RHTH SE16 * 25 J4
ORP BR6 90 E4
Gleneagles Dr
MAID/SHEP ME15 167 G4
Glenesk Rd ELTH/MOT SE9 48 B2
Glenfarg Rd CAT SE6 46 E6
Glenfield Rd DVE/WH CT16 213 J6
Glenfinlas Wy CMBW SE5 24 C6
Glenforth St GNWCH SE10 27 G3
Glengall Br POP/IOD E14 26 C2
Glengall Gv POP/IOD E14 26 C2
Glengall Rd BXLYHN DA7 49 M1
PECK SE15 25 G5
Glengall Ter PECK SE15 25 G5
Glen Gdns CROY/NA CR0 86 B6
Glengarnock Av POP/IOD E14 26 D3
Glengarry Rd EDUL SE22 44 F2
Glen Gv DVW CT17 217 J2
Glenhead Cl ELTH/MOT SE9 48 C1
Glenhouse Rd ELTH/MOT SE9 48 B3
Glenhurst Av BXLY DA5 50 A6
Glenhurst Ri NRWD SE19 68 D4
Glen Iris Av CANTW/ST CT2 171 K3
Glen Iris Cl CANTW/ST CT2 171 K3
Glenister Rd GNWCH SE10 27 G4
Glenlea Rd ELTH/MOT SE9 48 B3
Glenleigh Wk RBTBR TN32 322 F9
Glenluce Rd BKHTH/KID SE3 47 J1
Glenluge Rd BKHTH/KID SE3 27 H5
Glenlyon Rd ELTH/MOT SE9 48 B3
Glenmore Pk RTWE/PEM TN2 201 G5
Glenmore Rd WELL DA16 29 G7
Glennie Rd WNWD SE27 44 B8
Glen Rd DEAL CT14 211 K2
Glenrosa Gdns GVE DA12 80 A2
Glensdale Rd BROCKY SE4 46 A1
Glenshiel Rd ELTH/MOT SE9 48 B3
Glenside WSTB CT5 127 H5
Glenside Av CANT CT1 172 C7
Glen Ter POP/IOD E14 26 D1
The Glen CROY/NA CR0 87 L6
HAYES BR2 70 F6
IOS ME12 65 K6
ORP BR6 90 A6
RDV CT15 271 Q8
Glenthorne Av CROY/NA CR0 87 K4
Glenton Rd LEW SE13 46 F2
Glentrammon Av ORP BR6 107 L1
Glentrammon Cl ORP BR6 107 L1
Glentrammon Gdns ORP BR6 107 L1
Glentrammon Rd ORP BR6 107 L1
Glenure Rd ELTH/MOT SE9 48 B3
Glenview ABYW SE2 29 L5
Glen Vw GVE DA12 55 K6
Glen View Rd BMLY BR1 71 L6
Glenville Gv DEPT SE8 26 A6
Glenwood TENT TN30 * 301 N10
Glenwood Cl GILL ME7 102 A6
MAIDW ME16 140 D8
TENT TN30 301 N10
WALD ME5 101 K4
Glenwood Dr IOS ME12 65 J6
Glenwood Rd CAT SE6 46 A6
Glenwood Rw NRWD SE19 * 69 G5
Glenwood Wy CROY/NA CR0 87 L2
Glenworth Av POP/IOD E14 26 E3
Glimpsing Gn ERITHM DA18 29 M2
Glistening Gld RHAM ME8 102 F7
Gload Crs STMC/STPC BR5 91 L5
Globe La CHAT ME4 6 C4
Globe St STHWK SE1 24 E1
Gloster Cl RFOLK CT18 220 C2
Gloster Ropewalk DVW CT17 217 K4
Gloster Ter FOLK CT20 * 223 L3
Gloster Wy DVW CT17 217 K4
Gloucester Av BFN/LL DA15 48 F7
BRDST CT10 183 J2
CDW/CHF RM16 34 D1
MARG CT9 179 G3
TIL RM18 36 D4
WELL DA16 49 G3
Gloucester Circ GNWCH SE10 26 D6
Gloucester Cl RHAM ME8 103 H5
Gloucester Ms NROM TN28 331 K5
Gloucester Pde BFN/LL DA15 * 49 H3
Gloucester Pl FOLK CT20 11 J5
Gloucester Rd BELV DA17 30 A4
CROY/NA CR0 86 E3
DART DA1 51 J4
GVE DA12 79 K1
MAID/SHEP ME15 167 L5
WADH TN5 309 L3
WSTB CT5 127 G3
Glover Cl ABYW SE2 29 K3
SIT ME10 227 N12
Glover Rd KEN/WIL TN24 3 H7
Glovers Cl BH/WHM TN16 132 A2
Glovers Crs SIT ME10 * 120 A6
Gloxinia Rd MEO DA13 78 C3
Glyn Cl SNWD SE25 68 F6
Glyn Davies Cl SEV TN13 135 K6
Glyndebourne Pk ORP BR6 90 C6
Glynde Rd BXLYHN DA7 49 M1
Glynde St BROCKY SE4 46 A4
Glyndon Rd WOOL/PLUM SE18 28 D3
Glyn Dr SCUP DA14 73 J1
Glyn St LBTH SE11 24 A4
Goad Av WALD ME5 115 J2
Goat Lees La KEN/WIL TN24 203 G4
Goatsfield Rd BH/WHM TN16 132 B6
Gobery Hl RCANTE CT3 235 J12
Goddard Rd BECK BR3 69 L8
Goddards Cl CRBK TN17 298 E9
Godden Cl RYE TN31 325 K6
Godden Rd CANTW/ST CT2 172 B5
SNOD ME6 113 G5
Godden Wy RHAM ME8 102 B1
Goddings Dr ROCH ME1 100 B2
Goddington Cha ORP BR6 91 J7
Goddington La ORP BR6 91 H6
RMAID ME17 242 D10
Goddington Rd STRD ME2 19 G1
Godfrey Evans Cl TONN TN10 189 J8
Godfrey Gdns RCANTW CT4 248 G8
Godfrey Hl WOOL/PLUM SE18 27 M3
Godfrey Rd WOOL/PLUM SE18 28 A3
Godfrey Wk ASH TN23 2 B8
Godinton La RASHW TN26 286 H4
Godinton Rd ASH TN23 2 A5
Godinton Wy ASH TN23 204 D1
Godman Rd CDW/CHF RM16 35 J2
PECK SE15 * 25 J8
Godric Crs CROY/NA CR0 105 J4
Godson Rd CROY/NA CR0 86 B6
Godstone Hl GDST RH9 156 A6
Godstone Rd CTHM CR3 156 A4
GDST RH9 184 C1
LING RH7 190 D8
OXTED RH8 157 H8
Godstow Rd ABYW SE2 29 K1
Godwin Bungalows
MARG CT9 * 15 L3
Godwin Cl SIT ME10 227 N12
Godwin Rd CANT CT1 171 K7
DVE/WH CT16 9 G3
HAYES BR2 71 K7
MARG CT9 15 K4
Godwyne Cl DVE/WH CT16 8 D3
Godwyne Ct DVE/WH CT16 * 8 D2
Godwyne Rd DVE/WH CT16 8 D3
Godwyn Gdns FOLK CT20 10 D6
Godwyn Rd DEAL CT14 209 K1
FOLK CT20 10 D5
Goffers Rd BKHTH/KID SE3 26 F8
Cogway RCANTW CT4 268 E8
Goldace GRAYS RM17 34 A5
Goldcrest Dr CHAT ME4 83 K3
Goldcrest Wy CROY/NA CR0 105 J3
Golden Acre La WGOS CT8 177 G6
Golden Cl WGOS CT8 177 G6
Golden Hl WSTB CT5 127 G6
Golden Hind Pl DEPT SE8 * 26 A3
Golden Sq TENT TN30 315 N1
Golden St DEAL CT14 209 L2
Golden Wood Cl WALD ME5 115 L5
Goldfinch Cl DIT/AY ME20 139 H3
FAV ME13 123 K8
HB CT6 129 K7
ORP BR6 91 H8
STPH/PW TN12 279 K4
Goldfinch Rd SAND/SEL CR2 104 D4
THMD SE28 28 E2
Gold Hl RASHE TN25 265 J10
Golding Cl DIT/AY ME20 139 K4
ROCH ME1 100 F4
Golding Gdns STPH/PW TN12 257 K7
Golding Rd SEV TN13 136 B8
Goldings STPH/PW TN12 278 H4
Goldings Cl E/WMAL ME19 164 B3
The Goldings RHAM ME8 102 D5
Goldsel Rd SWLY BR8 74 F8
Goldsmid Rd TON TN9 194 F6
Goldsmid St WOOL/PLUM SE18 28 F4
Goldsmith GRAYS RM17 34 A5
Goldsmith Ct TENT TN30 301 N12
Goldsmith Rd PECK SE15 25 H7
RHAM ME8 102 F8
Goldsmiths Whf GRAYS RM17 * 34 B6
Goldstone Dro RCANTE CT3 236 C5
Goldstone Wk WALD ME5 115 H4
Gold St GVE DA12 97 M1
Goldsworth Dr STRD ME2 82 B4
Goldsworthy Gdns
BERM/RHTH SE16 25 K3
Goldthorne Cl
MAID/BEAR ME14 13 L4
Goldups La FAV ME13 246 G8
Goldwell Cl RASHE TN25 305 R7
Goldwell La RASHE TN25 305 R7
RASHE TN25 306 A7
RASHW TN26 286 E8
Goldwell Rd THHTH CR7 68 A8
Golf Cl STRHM/NOR SW16 68 B5
Golf Ct DEAL CT14 * 207 K8
Golf Links Av GVW DA11 79 J2
Golford Rd CRBK TN17 299 K8
Golf Rd BMLY BR1 72 B7
DEAL CT14 207 K8
Golf Road Pl DEAL CT14 209 K1
Gollogly Ter CHARL SE7 27 K4
Gomm Rd BERM/RHTH SE16 25 K2
Gonson St DEPT SE8 26 C5
Gonville Rd THHTH CR7 86 A1
Gooch Cl MAIDW ME16 140 E5
Goodall Cl RHAM ME8 102 F8
Goodban Sq RCANTE CT3 236 A12
Goodbury Rd BGR/WK TN15 111 G7
Goodcheap La KEN/WIL TN24 288 E7
Goodfellow Wy DVE/WH CT16 8 C3
Goodhart Wy WWKM BR4 88 F2
Goodhew Rd SNWD SE25 87 H2
Goodley Stock Rd EDEN TN8 159 G7
Goodmead Rd ORP BR6 91 H3
Goodnestone Hl RCANTE CT3 252 C6
Goodnestone Rd RCANTE CT3 252 A3
SIT ME10 120 C6
Goodrich Rd EDUL SE22 45 G4
Goods Hl TENT TN30 315 J1
Goods Station Rd RTW TN1 23 G3
Goodtrees La EDEN TN8 275 N11
Goodwin Av WSTB CT5 127 L3
Goodwin Cl BERM/RHTH SE16 25 G2
EDEN TN8 192 C3
Goodwin Dr MAID/BEAR ME14 141 J5
SCUP DA14 49 L7
Goodwin Pk MARG CT9 178 C8
Goodwin Rd CROY/NA CR0 86 C8
HOO/HM ME3 58 C6
RAM CT11 16 C8
RDV CT15 215 G5
Goodwood Cl HOO/HM ME3 59 M2
MAID/SHEP ME15 168 A7
Goodwood Crs GVE DA12 79 K3
Goodwood Pde BECK BR3 * 69 M8
Goodwood Rd NWCR SE14 25 M6
Goodworth Rd BGR/WK TN15 238 E10
Goosander Wy
WOOL/PLUM SE18 28 E2
Gooseberry La RYE TN31 324 H10
Goose Cl WALD ME5 101 H6
Goosefields FAV ME13 124 E8
Goose Green Cl STMC/STPC BR5 73 H6
Gooseneck La HDCN TN27 283 K4
Gordon Av QBOR ME11 227 P1
Gordonbrock Rd BROCKY SE4 46 B3
Gordon Cl KEN/WIL TN24 2 F5
SIT ME10 120 D5
TIL RM18 36 E6
Gordon Crs CROY/NA CR0 86 F4
Gordon Gv CMBW SE5 24 C8
WGOS CT8 177 H4
Gordon Pl GVE DA12 55 K4
RYE TN31 * 225 L6
Gordon Prom East GVE DA12 55 L4
Gordon Rd BECK BR3 70 A7
BELV DA17 30 D3
BFN/LL DA15 48 F3
CANT CT1 4 D6
CDW/CHF RM16 34 F1
CHAT ME4 6 F9
DART DA1 51 L5
FAV ME13 149 M1
FOLK CT20 219 L7
GILL ME7 83 H6
GILL ME7 83 M8
GVW DA11 54 F5
HB CT6 129 G5
HOO/HM ME3 59 L8
MARG CT9 15 K3
PECK SE15 25 J8
RAM CT11 17 H3
SEV TN13 21 G6
STH/RUST TN4 196 F6
STRD ME2 18 E2
WSTB CT5 126 E6
Gordon Sq BRCH CT7 176 C6
FAV ME13 149 M2
Gordons Wy OXTED RH8 157 J6
Gordon Ter LYDD TN29 * 334 D4
ROCH ME1 19 J9
Gordon Wy BMLY BR1 71 H5
Gore Court Rd
MAID/SHEP ME15 168 A8
SIT ME10 119 M7
Gore End Cl BRCH CT7 176 B6
Gore Green Rd HOO/HM ME3 57 L7
Gore La CRBK TN17 297 M2
RASHW TN26 301 N3
SWCH CT13 253 N7
Gore Ms CANT CT1 5 K1
Gore Rd RDART DA2 52 E7
RSIT ME9 145 G4
SWCH CT13 253 N6
Goretop La DEAL CT14 206 D4
Gorham Cl SNOD ME6 113 G6
Gorham Dr MAID/SHEP ME15 168 B4
TON TN9 195 H5
Gorman Rd WOOL/PLUM SE18 28 A3
Gorrell Rd WSTB CT5 126 F5
Gorringe Av EYN DA4 76 E6
Gorse Av WALD ME5 114 F1
Gorse Crs DIT/AY ME20 139 L5
Gorse La HB CT6 129 K7
Gorse Rd CROY/NA CR0 88 B6
RTWE/PEM TN2 197 H8
SIT ME10 120 D4
STMC/STPC BR5 92 B5
STRD ME2 18 D1
Gorse Wy HART DA3 96 A1
Gorse Wood Rd HART DA3 96 A1
Gorst St GILL ME7 7 K4
Goschen Rd DVW CT17 217 J1
Gosfield Rd HB CT6 129 H5
Gosling Wy BRXN/ST SW9 24 B7
Gosport Wy PECK SE15 25 G6
Gossage Rd WOOL/PLUM SE18 28 E4
Gosselin St WSTB CT5 126 F5
Goss Hall La RCANTE CT3 236 D11
Goss Hl SWLY BR8 75 K3
Gosshill Rd CHST BR7 72 B6
Gossington Cl CHST BR7 72 C1
Gosterwood St DEPT SE8 25 M5
Goston Gdns THHTH CR7 68 B7
Goteley Mere KEN/WIL TN24 202 F4
Gothic Cl DART DA1 51 L8
DEAL CT14 209 J8
Goudhurst Cl CANTW/ST CT2 172 B5
MAIDW ME16 12 D4
Goudhurst Rd BMLY BR1 70 F2
CRBK TN17 298 E1
CRBK TN17 298 H5
RHAM ME8 102 C2
STPH/PW TN12 280 A12
STPH/PW TN12 280 H4
STPH/PW TN12 281 Q9
Gouge Av GVW DA11 54 F6
Gough Rd FOLK CT20 223 M2
Goulding Gdns THHTH CR7 68 D6
Gould Rd WALD ME5 115 J2
Gourock Rd ELTH/MOT SE9 48 B3
Gover Hl WBY/YAL ME18 241 K11
Gover Vw WBY/YAL ME18 241 K10
Gowers La CDW/CHF RM16 35 G1
Gowland Pl BECK BR3 70 A6
Gowlett Rd PECK SE15 45 H1
Gowlland Cl CROY/NA CR0 87 H3
Grace Av BXLYHN DA7 30 A8
Grace Cl ELTH/MOT SE9 47 L8
Grace Hl FOLK CT20 11 J4
Grace Meadow DVE/WH CT16 213 H2
Grace Rd CROY/NA CR0 86 D2
IOS ME12 64 B4
Grace's Ms CMBW SE5 24 F8
Grace's Rd CMBW SE5 24 F8
Gracious La SEV TN13 161 M8
Gracious Lane Br
BGR/WK TN15 136 F2
Gracious Lane End RSEV TN14 161 L8
The Gradient SYD SE26 69 H1
Graduate Pl STHWK SE1 24 E2
Grafton Av ROCH ME1 100 F5
Grafton Ri HB CT6 128 D6
Grafton Rd BRDST CT10 179 H5
CROY/NA CR0 86 B4
SIT ME10 120 A5
Graham Cl CROY/NA CR0 88 B5
Graham Rd BXLYHN DA7 50 A2
Graham Ter BFN/LL DA15 * 49 J4
Grainey Fld RSIT ME9 117 M1
Grain Rd HOO/HM ME3 61 K1
HOO/HM ME3 62 E2
RHAM ME8 116 D2
Grampian Cl ORP BR6 91 G2
RTWE/PEM TN2 23 M2
Grampian Wy
MAID/SHEP ME15 168 B4
Grampion Cl KEN/WIL TN24 2 C1
Gramsci Wy CAT SE6 46 C8
Gram's Rd DEAL CT14 211 K1
Granada St MAID/SHEP ME15 * 13 G5
Granary STPH/PW TN12 279 L3
Granary Cl MAID/BEAR ME14 141 M8
RHAM ME8 103 G4
Granary Court Rd RASHE TN25 289 P12
Granby Rd ELTH/MOT SE9 28 A8
GVW DA11 54 E4
WOOL/PLUM SE18 28 C2
Grand Depot Rd
WOOL/PLUM SE18 28 B4
Grand Dr HB CT6 128 D5
Grand Pde NROM TN28 331 M9
Grandshore La CRBK TN17 282 B12
Grandsire Gdns HOO/HM ME3 59 M7
Grand View Av BH/WHM TN16 132 B3
Grange Av SNWD SE25 68 F6
Grangecliffe Gdns SNWD SE25 68 F6
Grange Cl BFN/LL DA15 49 H8
BH/WHM TN16 159 J4
E/WMAL ME19 138 D3
EDEN TN8 192 D4
Grange Crs RDART DA2 52 C4
TENT TN30 301 M10
Grange Dr CHST BR7 71 M3
ORP BR6 108 B3
Grange Gdns SNWD SE25 68 F6
STH/RUST TN4 200 E1
Grange Hl BGR/WK TN15 240 E9
SNWD SE25 68 F6
WALD ME5 7 H8
Grangehill Pl ELTH/MOT SE9 48 A1
Grangehill Rd ELTH/MOT SE9 48 A2
Grange La DUL SE21 45 G7
HART DA3 96 C3
MAID/BEAR ME14 141 G4
Grangemill Rd CAT SE6 46 B8
Grangemill Wy CAT SE6 46 B7
Grange Park Rd THHTH CR7 68 E7
Grange Rd BGR/WK TN15 240 H2
BRDST CT10 179 J7
DEAL CT14 209 J4
FOLKN CT19 219 M7
GILL ME7 83 M7
GRAYS RM17 34 C5
GVW DA11 55 H5
HB CT6 129 J5
HYTHE CT21 222 C1
ORP BR6 90 D5
RAM CT11 16 F4
SEV TN13 161 M5
SNWD SE25 68 E7
STH/RUST TN4 200 E1
STHWK SE1 24 F2
STRD ME2 19 H3
TENT TN30 301 M10
The Grange BGR/WK TN15 111 L3
CROY/NA CR0 88 A5
E/WMAL ME19 139 H6
EYN DA4 76 E5
RDV CT15 271 Q8
STHWK SE1 25 G2
WSTB CT5 126 B7
Grange Wk STHWK SE1 24 F2
Grange Walk Ms STHWK SE1 25 G2
Grange Wy BRDST CT10 183 J3
ERITH DA8 31 J6
HART DA3 96 A2
ROCH ME1 100 D2
Grangeways Cl GVW DA11 79 G1
Grangewood BXLY DA5 50 A6
Grangewood Av
CDW/CHF RM16 34 F2
Grangewood La BECK BR3 70 A3
Grange Yd STHWK SE1 25 G2
Granite St WOOL/PLUM SE18 29 G4
Grant Cl BRDST CT10 179 H7
GILL ME7 102 C4
Grant Dr MAID/SHEP ME15 167 L7
Grantham Av DEAL CT14 209 H4
Grantley Cl ASH TN23 204 D4
Granton Rd SCUP DA14 73 J3
Grant Rd CROY/NA CR0 87 G4
HOO/HM ME3 82 E2
Grants Hl CRBK TN17 * 313 P3
Grants La OXTED RH8 185 L7
Granville Ar BRXN/ST SW9 * 44 B2
Granville Av BRDST CT10 183 L2
MSTR CT12 182 E4
Granville Cl CROY/NA CR0 86 F5
FAV ME13 149 K2
Granville Dr HB CT6 128 C7
Granville Farm Ms RAM CT11 * 17 M4
Granville Gdns
STRHM/NOR SW16 68 A5
Granville Gv LEW SE13 46 D1
Granville Marina Ct RAM CT11 * 17 M5
Granville Ms SCUP DA14 73 H1
Granville Pde FOLK CT20 223 M2
Granville Pk LEW SE13 46 D1
Granville Pl IOS ME12 64 D3
Granville Rd BH/WHM TN16 159 H4
BRDST CT10 183 L2
DEAL CT14 209 K7
DEAL CT14 211 L6
GILL ME7 83 M8
GVW DA11 55 G5
IOS ME12 64 C3
MAID/BEAR ME14 141 H7
OXTED RH8 157 L7
RDV CT15 215 J3
RTW TN1 23 J2
SCUP DA14 73 H1
SEV TN13 20 F5
WELL DA16 49 K1
Granville Rd East FOLK CT20 10 A9
Granville Sq PECK SE15 * 24 F6
Granville St DEAL CT14 209 L4
DVE/WH CT16 8 B2
Graphite Sq LBTH SE11 * 24 A4
Grapple Rd MAID/BEAR ME14 141 H6
Grasdene Rd WOOL/PLUM SE18 29 H6
Grasmere Av ORP BR6 90 C6
RAM CT11 16 A5
Grasmere Gdns FOLKN CT19 10 F1
ORP BR6 90 C6
Grasmere Gv STRD ME2 82 D3
Grasmere Rd BMLY BR1 71 G5
BXLYHN DA7 30 D7
KEN/WIL TN24 202 F5
ORP BR6 90 C6
SNWD SE25 87 J2
STRHM/NOR SW16 68 A2
WSTB CT5 127 H5
Grasmere Wy RCANTE CT3 251 Q11
Grassington Rd SCUP DA14 73 H1
Grasslands RMAID ME17 260 F1
Grassmere DIT/AY ME20 138 F4
LYDD TN29 331 M2
Grassmount FSTH SE23 45 J7
Grassy Gld GILL ME7 102 C7
Grassy La SEV TN13 162 A5
Grately Wy PECK SE15 * 24 F6
Gravel Castle Rd RCANTW CT4 270 F6
Gravel Hl BXLYHS DA6 50 C3
CROY/NA CR0 104 C1
FAV ME13 244 F9
Gravel Hill Cl BXLY DA5 50 C4
Gravel La RDV CT15 216 A5
Gravelly Bottom Rd
RMAID ME17 261 J3
Gravelly Fld ASH TN23 286 H9
Gravelly Ways WBY/YAL ME18 257 M9
Gravel Pit Wy ORP BR6 91 H5
Gravel Rd EYN DA4 76 C4
HAYES BR2 89 M5
Gravel Wk ASH TN23 2 A3
CANT CT1 4 F5
ROCH ME1 19 K8
Gravelwood Cl CHST BR7 48 D8
Graveney Cl HOO/HM ME3 58 D6
Graveney Gv PGE/AN SE20 69 K4
Graveney Rd FAV ME13 150 A2
MAID/SHEP ME15 168 A6
Gravesend Rd BGR/WK TN15 238 G9
GVE DA12 80 F1
MEO DA13 239 K5
STRD ME2 18 C2
Gray Cl RFOLK CT18 292 H12
Grayland Cl BMLY BR1 71 L5
Graylands GRAYS RM17 * 33 M5
Graylen Cl DEAL CT14 209 K2
Graylings Ct SIT ME10 119 K7
The Graylings ROCH ME1 100 C2
Grayne Av HOO/HM ME3 43 J8
Grays End Cl CDW/CHF RM16 34 B2
Grays Farm Rd STMC/STPC BR5 73 J5
Grayshott Cl SIT ME10 120 A6
Grays Rd BH/WHM TN16 133 G7
Graystone Rd WSTB CT5 127 H2
Gray St STHWK SE1 24 B1
Grays Wy CANT CT1 171 J7
Grazeley Cl BXLYHS DA6 50 D3
Great Bounds Dr
STH/RUST TN4 196 B2
Great Brooms Rd
STH/RUST TN4 196 E5
Great Brownings SYD SE26 69 G1
Great Conduit St
HYTHE CT21 * 222 D3
Great Courtlands RRTW TN3 200 B2
Great Cross Av GNWCH SE10 26 F6
Great Dover St STHWK SE1 24 E1
Great Elms RTON TN11 256 B4
Great Elms Rd HAYES BR2 71 K8
Greatfield Cl LEW SE13 46 B2
Great Footway RRTW TN3 200 A1
Great Gatton Cl CROY/NA CR0 87 M3
Great Hall Ar RTW TN1 * 22 F6
Great Harry Dr ELTH/MOT SE9 48 B8
Great Lines GILL ME7 6 F3
Great Maze Pond STHWK SE1 24 E1
Greatness La RSEV TN14 136 B7
Greatness Rd RSEV TN14 136 B7
Great Oak BUR/ETCH TN19 322 F2
Great Queen St DART DA1 52 A4
Great South Av CHAT ME4 101 H4
Great Spilmans EDUL SE22 44 F3
Great Stour Pl CANTW/ST CT2 * 4 E2
Great Suffolk St STHWK SE1 24 C1
Great Thrift STMC/STPC BR5 72 D8
Great Till Cl RSEV TN14 135 K2
Greatwood CHST BR7 72 B4
Grebe Cl HOO/HM ME3 61 K1
RFOLK CT18 220 B1
Grebe Crs HYTHE CT21 321 Q1
Grebe Crest WTHK RM20 33 H3
Grecian Crs NRWD SE19 68 C3
Grecian Rd RTW TN1 23 G7
Grecian St MAID/BEAR ME14 13 H1
Greenacre RCANTW CT4 270 C2
Greenacre Cl SWLY BR8 74 F8
WALD ME5 101 H8
Greenacre Dr DEAL CT14 209 K8
Green Acres CROY/NA CR0 87 G6
RDV CT15 272 E6
SCUP DA14 * 73 G1
Greenacres ELTH/MOT SE9 48 B4
OXTED RH8 157 K5
Greenacres Cl ORP BR6 90 D7
Greenacre Sq
BERM/RHTH SE16 * 25 L1
Greenbank KEN/WIL TN24 203 G5
WALD ME5 101 J5
Green Bank Cl GILL ME7 * 102 B8
Greenbanks DART DA1 51 M7
RFOLK CT18 291 M11
Greenbay Rd CHARL SE7 27 L6
Greenborough Cl
MAID/SHEP ME15 167 M7
Green Chain Wk BECK BR3 70 D4
CHARL SE7 27 L3
ELTH/MOT SE9 48 C3
SYD SE26 69 L3
Green Cl HAYES BR2 70 F7
RFOLK CT18 220 C1
ROCH ME1 100 E3
Green Cloth Ms CANT CT1 5 J1
Green Ct FOLKN CT19 220 F6
RCANTW CT4 175 H8
Green Court Av CROY/NA CR0 87 J5
Green Court Gdns
CROY/NA CR0 87 J5
Greencourt Rd STMC/STPC BR5 90 F1
Green Court Rd SWLY BR8 92 E2
Greencroft ASH TN23 204 A5
Green Dl EDUL SE22 44 F3
Greendale Wk GVW DA11 54 F8
Green Dell CANTW/ST CT2 172 A5
Green Farm Cl ORP BR6 91 G8
Green Farm La GVE DA12 56 F8
Greenfell Man DEPT SE8 * 26 A4
Greenfield EDEN TN8 192 E4
Greenfield Cl DIT/AY ME20 114 B7
STH/RUST TN4 277 R12
Greenfield Dr BMLY BR1 71 K6
Greenfield Gdns
STMC/STPC BR5 90 D3
Greenfield Rd FOLKN CT19 11 L1
GILL ME7 7 M2
MSTR CT12 182 F3
RDART DA2 74 E2
Greenfields MAID/SHEP ME15 167 M5
RASHE TN25 307 K3
Greenfields Cl HOO/HM ME3 82 E2
Greenfinches GILL ME7 102 A7
HART DA3 78 C7
Greenfrith Dr TONN TN10 188 E6
Green Gdns ORP BR6 90 D8
Greenham Cl STHWK SE1 24 B1
Green Hedges TENT TN30 315 N1
Green Hl MAID/SHEP ME15 168 C4
ORP BR6 106 D6
WOOL/PLUM SE18 28 A4
Greenhill STPH/PW TN12 281 R4
Greenhill Av CTHM CR3 130 A7
Greenhill Cl MSTR CT12 180 E6
Greenhill Gdns HB CT6 128 E6
MSTR CT12 180 E6
Green Hill La RMAID ME17 262 A5
Greenhill La HDCN TN27 284 H2
WARL CR6 130 D3
Greenhill Rd GVW DA11 55 G7
HB CT6 128 E6
RSEV TN14 136 B1
Green Hills RCANTW CT4 270 D5
Greenhithe MAID/SHEP ME15 12 F7
Greenhithe Cl ELTH/MOT SE9 48 F5
Greenhill STPH/PW TN12 281 R4
Greenholm Rd ELTH/MOT SE9 48 C3
Green House La CANTW/ST CT2 4 C1
Green Hundred Rd PECK SE15 25 H5
Greenhurst La OXTED RH8 185 H2
Greenhurst Rd WNWD SE27 68 B2
Greening St ABYW SE2 29 K3
Greenland Ms DEPT SE8 25 L4
Greenland Quay
BERM/RHTH SE16 25 L3
Greenlands BGR/WK TN15 240 H2
Green Lands GVE DA12 97 L1
Green La ASH TN23 204 B6
BRDST CT10 179 H8
CRBK TN17 300 B11
DEAL CT14 209 J8
DVE/WH CT16 212 F4
DVE/WH CT16 213 J7
E/WMAL ME19 239 M8
EDEN TN8 187 K6
ELTH/MOT SE9 48 B7
ELTH/MOT SE9 72 C1
FOLKN CT19 11 L1
HDCN TN27 284 D8
HOO/HM ME3 38 C7
HOO/HM ME3 43 J7
HYTHE CT21 222 B3
MARG CT9 179 H4
MEO DA13 97 J3
PGE/AN SE20 69 L4
RASHE TN25 265 M3
RASHW TN26 302 A3
RCANTE CT3 252 G6
RCANTW CT4 247 P7
RDV CT15 211 G8
RDV CT15 272 E6
RDV CT15 293 P7
RFOLK CT18 221 J2
RFOLK CT18 290 G8
RMAID ME17 259 P2
RMAID ME17 260 A8
RMAID ME17 260 F2
RMAID ME17 262 C4
RSIT ME9 118 A8
RSIT ME9 146 C2

STPH/PW TN12 ....258 D12
STPH/PW TN12 ....279 L4
THHTH CR7 ....
WSTB CT5 ....126 C5
Green Lane Av HYTHE CT21 ....222 A3
Green Lane Gdns THHTH CR7 ....68 C5
The Green La RTON TN11 ....255 N12
Greenlaw St WOOL/PLUM SE18 ....28 C3
Greenleaf Cl
BRXS/STRHM SW2 * 44 B5
Greenlees RTWE/PEM TN2 ....197 M7
Green Leas WSTB CT5 ....127 L4
Greenleigh Av STMC/STPC BR5...73 J3
Greenly Wy NROM TN28 ....331 K7
Greenmead Cl SNWD SE25 ....87 H1
Green Mdw LYDD TN29 ....321 J7
Greenoak Ri BH/WHM TN16 ....132 B4
Green Porch Cl SIT ME10 ....120 A2
Green Rd BRCH CT7 ....176 C5
STPH/PW TN12 ....279 R12
Greensand Rd
MAID/SHEP ME15 ....168 B3
Green Sands
MAID/BEAR ME14 ....115 K5
Greensand Wy EDEN TN8 ....159 H8
HDCN TN27 ....262 H9
HDCN TN27 ....285 K1
MAID/SHEP ME15 ....13 J6
OXTED RH8 ....258 C5
RASHW TN26 ....286 A1
RASHW TN26 ....303 K9
RMAID ME17 ....258 H3
RMAID ME17 ....259 G4
RMAID ME17 ....260 H6
RSEV TN14 ....254 B1
RTON TN11 ....240 A12
RTON TN11 ....241 K12
SEV TN13 ....241 P7
WBY/YAL ME18 ....241 P11
WBY/YAL ME18 ....257 C8
Greens End WOOL/PLUM SE18 ....28 C3
Greenside BXLY DA5 ....49 M6
MAID/SHEP ME15 ....13 J6
RASHW TN26 ....301 R6
SWLY BR8 ....74 E6
Greenside Cl CAT SE6 ....46 E7
Greenside Rd CROY/NA CRO 86 D3
Greensland Cl ASH TN23 ....204 A7
ASH TN23 ....286 C9
RASHW TN26 ....286 F4
RASHW TN26 ....304 C5
Greensleeves Wy
E/WMAL ME19 ....164 D2
Greensole La LASTR CT12 ....182 B5
Green St GILL ME7 ....7 J3
Green Street Green Rd
DART DA1 ....51 L1
Greenstreet Hi NWCR SE14 * 45 L1
The Green BGR/WK TN15 * 111 L4
BH/WHM TN16 ....159 J4
BH/WHM TN16 ....30 B2
BXLYHN DA7 ....30 B7
CANTW/ST CT2 ....153 H7
CANTW/ST CT2 * 170 F7
CROY/NA CRO 104 E3
CTHM CR3 ....156 F1
HAYES BR2 ....89 H3
HYTHE CT21 ....222 C1
LYDD TN29 ....329 H5
MSTR CT12 ....182 A4
ORP BR6 * 108 B4
RASHE TN25 ....266 F11
RCANTE CT3 * 235 K1
RCANTE CT3 ....251 J2
RCANTW CT4 ....248 E6
RCANTW CT4 ....271 K4
RDART DA2 ....52 E7
RRTW TN3 ....199 M2
RSIT ME9 ....226 C10
RTON TN11 ....255 N12
SCUP DA14 ....73 J4
SEV TN13 ....136 C8
STMC/STPC BR5 ....73 J4
WELL DA16 ....48 F2
Greentrees Av TONN TN10 ....189 J8
Green V BXLYHS DA6 ....49 H5
Greenvale Gdns RHAM ME8 ....102 C3
Greenvale Rd ELTH/MOT SE9 ....48 A2
Greenview Av BECK BR3 ....87 M2
Green View Av RTON TN11 ....255 N12
Greenview Crs RTON TN11 ....194 B1
Green Wk DART DA1 ....51 G2
Green Wy ELTH/MOT SE9 ....47 L3
HART DA3 ....95 M1
HAYES BR2 ....89 K7
LYDD TN29 ....334 G4
MAIDW ME16 ....166 C2
RTWE/PEM TN2 ....197 H5
Greenway BH/WHM TN16 ....132 B6
CHST BR7 ....72 B2
CRBK TN17 ....298 E9
FAV ME13 ....149 J1
WALD ME5 ....100 E7
Greenway Court Rd
RMAID ME17 ....169 M3
RMAID ME17 ....242 A7
Greenway Gdns CROY/NA CRO 88 A4
Greenway La RMAID ME17 ....242 B10
Greenways BECK BR3 ....70 B6
HART DA3 ....78 E7
MAID/BEAR ME14 ....142 A8
RSIT ME9 ....15 L6
SIT ME10 ....120 C6
The Greenways
STPH/PW TN12 ....279 J4
The Greenway OXTED RH8 ....185 N4
Greenwell Cl GDST RH9 ....156 A8
Greenwich Church St
GNWCH SE10 * 26 D5
Greenwich Cl MAIDW ME16 ....12 A4
WALD ME5 ....115 J1
Greenwich Foot Tnl
GNWCH SE10 ....26 D4
Greenwich Hts
WOOL/PLUM SE18 * 27 M6
Greenwich High Rd
GNWCH SE10 ....26 D6
Greenwich Park St
GNWCH SE10 * 26 E5
Greenwich Quay DEPT SE8 ....26 D7
Greenwich South St
GNWCH SE10 ....26 C7
Greenwich Vw POP/IOD E14 ....26 C2
Greenwood Cl BFN/LL DA15 ....49 H7
STMC/STPC BR5 ....90 D4
Greenwood Rd BXLY DA5 ....74 E1
CROY/NA CRO 86 C3
Greenwood Wy SEV TN13 ....136 A2
Greggs Wood Rd
RTWE/PEM TN2 ....197 H5
Gregor Ms BKHTH/KID SE3 * 27 H7
Gregory Cl RHAM ME8 ....116 F1
Gregory Crs ELTH/MOT SE9 ....47 L5
Gregory Ter WALW SE17 * 24 C5
Grenaby Av CROY/NA CRO 86 E3

Grenaby Rd CROY/NA CRO 86 E3
Grenada Rd CHARL SE7 ....27 K6
Grenade St POP/IOD E14 ....
Grenadier RTON TN11 ....188 B2
Grenadier Cl RHAM ME8 ....103 G3
Grenard Cl PECK SE15 * 25 H6
Grenham Bay Av BRCH CT7 ....176 B6
Grenham Rd BRCH CT7 ....176 B5
Grenville Cl MEO DA13 ....97 H5
Grenville Gdns BRCH CT7 ....176 B5
CROY/NA CRO 105 H4
Grenville Rd CDW/CHF RM16 ....33 J4
CROY/NA CRO 105 H4
Gresham Cl BXLY DA5 ....49 M4
OXTED RH8 ....157 L7
RHAM ME8 ....103 G4
Gresham Rd BECK BR3 ....69 M6
BRXN/ST SW9 ....
OXTED RH8 ....157 L7
RMAID ME17 ....259 J2
SNWD SE25 * 69 H8
Greshams Wy EDEN TN8 ....192 B3
Gresswell Cl SCUP DA14 ....49 H8
Greville Av SAND/SEL CR2 ....104 C4
Greybury La EDEN TN8 ....274 G2
Greycot Rd BECK BR3 ....70 B2
Greyfriars Cl MAIDW ME16 ....12 A6
Greyhound La CDW/CHF RM16 ....35 H1
Greyhound Rd DART DA1 ....50 F4
Greyladies Gdns GNWCH SE10 * 26 D8
Greys Park Cl HAYES BR2 ....89 K8
Greystone Cl SAND/SEL CR2 ....104 B5
Greystone Pk RSEV TN14 ....160 D3
Greystones Cl BGR/WK TN15 ....136 D3
Greystones Rd
MAID/SHEP ME15 ....168 B3
MSTR CT12 ....182 A8
Grey Wethers
MAID/BEAR ME14 ....140 F1
Grey Willow Gdns ASH TN23 ....204 A3
Gribble Bridge La RHAM TN27 ....300 H6
Grice Av BH/WHM TN16 ....106 A7
Grice Cl RFOLK CT18 ....220 G1
Grierson Rd FSTH SE23 ....45 M4
Grieves Cl GVW DA11 ....55 G8
Griffin Cl GILL ME7 ....84 A7
Griffin Manor Wy THMD SE28 ....28 E3
Griffin Rd WOOL/PLUM SE18 ....28 E4
The Griffins CDW/CHF RM16 ....34 C1
Griffin St STHWK SE1 * 209 L2
Griffin Wk CRH DA9 ....53 G3
Grifon Cl CDW/CHF RM16 ....33 K2
Grifon Rd CDW/CHF RM16 ....33 K2
Grigg La HDCN TN27 ....283 M3
Grigg's Pl STHWK SE1 * 24 F2
Griggs Rd BGR/WK TN15 ....240 E5
Grimsby Av CAN/RD E16 ....28 C1
Grimsel Pth CMBW SE5 ....24 C4
Grimshill Cl CANTW/ST CT2 * 171 N1
Grimshill Rd WSTB CT5 ....126 E6
Grimston Av FOLK CT20 ....10 E6
Grimston Gdns FOLK CT20 ....10 E6
Grimthorpe Av CROY/NA CRO 87 H6
Grimwade Av CROY/NA CRO 87 M6
Grindall Cl CROY/NA CRO * 86 D7
Grindal St STHWK SE1 * 24 B1
Grindley Gdns CROY/NA CRO * 87 L2
Grinling Pl DEPT SE8 ....26 B5
Grinsell Hi MSTR CT12 ....181 H7
Grinstead Rd DEPT SE8 ....25 M4
Grisbrook Farm Cl LYDD TN29 ....334 B13
Grizedale Cl ROCH ME1 ....100 E5
Gromenfield RRTW TN3 ....199 H5
Groombridge Dr GILL ME7 ....84 F2
Groombridge Hi RRTW TN3 ....199 K5
Groombridge Rd RRTW TN3 ....199 H5
Groombridge Sq
MAID/SHEP ME15 * 168 B3
Groom Cl HAYES BR2 ....71 J8
Groom Wy RMAID ME17 ....243 M12
Grosmont Rd
WOOL/PLUM SE18 ....29 G4
Grosvenor Av ROCH ME1 ....82 C5
Grosvenor Br RTW TN1 ....23 H1
Grosvenor Gdns MARG CT9 ....14 F5
Grosvenor Hi MARG CT9 ....14 F5
Grosvenor Pk CMBW SE5 ....24 D6
RTW TN1 ....22 F3
Grosvenor Rd BELV DA17 ....30 A5
BRDST CT10 ....183 K1
BXLYHS DA6 ....49 L5
GILL ME7 ....102 A4
KEN/WIL TN24 ....202 F4
RAM CT11 ....16 E5
RTW TN1 ....22 F3
SNWD SE25 ....69 H8
STMC/STPC BR5 ....90 F2
WSTB CT5 ....126 F3
WWKM BR4 ....88 F7
Grosvenor Ter CMBW SE5 ....24 D6
Grosvenor Wk RTW TN1 ....22 F3
Grosvenor Wharf Rd
POP/IOD E14 ....26 E3
Grote's Buildings
BKHTH/KID SE3 ....26 F8
Grote's Pl BKHTH/KID SE3 * 26 F8
Grotto Ct STHWK SE1 * 24 D1
Grotto Gdns MARG CT9 ....15 H4
Grotto Hi MARG CT9 ....15 H4
Grotto Rd MARG CT9 ....15 H4
Groveland Av
STRHM/NOR SW16 ....68 A4
Groveland Rd BECK BR3 ....70 A4
Grovelands RMAID ME17 ....243 M12
Grovelands Cl CMBW SE5 ....24 F6
Grovelands Rd STMC/STPC BR5 ....73 H4
Grovelands Wy GRAYS RM17 ....34 A4
Grove La CMBW SE5 ....24 F6
LYDD TN29 ....329 K1

MAID/SHEP ME15 ....258 C6
RYE TN31 ....327 M9
Grove Market Pl
ELTH/MOT SE9 * 48 A4
Grove Park Av WSTB CT5 ....24 F4
Grove Park Rd SIT ME10 ....119 H4
Grove Pk FAV ME13 ....149 K5
Grove Rd BELV DA17 ....30 A5
BGR/WK TN15 ....136 F8
BH/WHM TN16 ....132 B6
BXLYHN DA7 ....30 B7
CHAT ME4 ....7 H9
DEAL CT14 ....209 L6
EDEN TN8 ....276 B6
FAV ME13 ....246 G5
FOLK CT20 ....11 L4
GILL ME7 ....84 B7
GRAYS RM17 ....34 C5
GVW DA11 ....54 C3
LING RH7 ....
MAID/SHEP ME15 ....190 F8
RAM CT11 ....17 G6
RCANTE CT3 ....234 D11
RCANTE CT3 ....234 E5
RCANTE CT3 ....252 E3
RSEV TN14 ....136 F3
RTON TN11 ....276 C2
RTWE/PEM TN2 ....278 A9
RYE TN31 ....329 J5
SCUP DA14 ....73 M2
SWCM DA10 ....55 M3
SWLY BR8 ....75 J7
WGOS CT8 ....177 J5
WWKM BR4 ....88 D6
Grove V CHST BR7 ....72 B3
EDUL SE22 ....44 F2
Groveway BRXN/ST SW9 ....24 A7
IOS ME12 ....230 A7
Grovewood Dr
MAID/BEAR ME14 ....167 M1
Grub La OXTED RH8 ....158 H1
Grummant Rd PECK SE15 ....25 G3
Grummock Dr RAM CT11 ....16 C5
Grundy's Hi RAM CT11 ....17 G4
Guardian Av CDW/CHF RM16 ....33 L1
Guardian Ct RHAM ME8 ....102 D4
Gubyon Av HNHL SE24 * 44 D3
Guernsey Gv HNHL SE24 ....44 D5
Guernsey Wy KEN/WIL TN24 ....202 F4
Guestwick TONN TN10 ....189 J7
Guibal Rd LEE/GVPK SE12 ....47 J6
Guildables La OXTED RH8 ....185 M4
Guildcount La SWCH CT13 ....233 J12
Guildford Av MARG CT9 ....177 G5
Guildford Gdns STRD ME2 ....81 H5
Guildford Lawn RAM CT11 ....17 J6
Guildford Rd CANT CT1 ....4 E2
CROY/NA CRO 86 E2
Guildhall St CANT CT1 ....4 F4
Guildhall St North FOLKN CT19 ....11 J4
Guild Rd CHARL SE7 ....27 L6
ERITH DA8 ....31 G6
Guilford Av DVE/WH CT16 ....213 H1
Guilford Rd SWCH CT13 ....207 G1
Guillat Av RSIT ME9 ....145 L3
Guilton RCANTE CT3 ....235 R12
Guiness Dr HOO/HM ME3 ....82 C5
Guinness Ct CROY/NA CRO * 87 J5
STHWK SE1 * 24 F1
Guinness Sq STHWK SE1 * 24 E1
Guldeford La LYDD TN29 ....328 E10
Guldeford Rd RYE TN31 ....225 K3
Gullands RMAID ME17 ....260 F1
Gulliver Rd BFN/LL DA15 ....48 E7
Gulliver St BERM/RHTH SE16 ....26 A2
Gumley Rd WTHK RM20 ....33 L5
Gumping Rd STMC/STPC BR5 ....90 D5
Gun Back La STPH/PW TN12 ....279 R12
Gundulph Rd CHAT ME4 ....7 K4
HAYES BR2 ....71 K7
Gundulph Sq ROCH ME1 ....19 J6
Gunfleet Cl GVE DA12 ....55 M5
Gun Hi TIL RM18 ....35 L5
Gunlands STPH/PW TN12 ....279 R11
Gunn Rd SWCM DA10 ....53 M4
Gun Tower Ms ROCH ME1 ....100 C1
Gunyard Ms WOOL/PLUM SE18 * 27 M6
Gurdon Rd CHARL SE7 ....27 H4
Curling Rd RDV CT15 ....211 G8
Gurney Crs CROY/NA CRO 86 A4
Gushmere FAV ME13 ....246 H2
Guston Rd MAID/BEAR ME14 ....141 L2
Guthrie Gdns DVW CT17 ....212 F6
Guy Cl BRDST CT10 ....
Guy Cl BFN/LL DA15 ....49 L6
Guy St STHWK SE1 * 24 E1
Gwillim Cl BFN/LL DA15 ....49 H6
Gwydor Rd BECK BR3 ....69 J5
Gwydyr Rd HAYES BR2 ....71 J5
Gwynne Av CROY/NA CRO 87 L6
Gwynn Rd GVW DA11 ....54 D7
Gwyn Rd MSTR CT12 ....182 F9
Gybbon Ri STPH/PW TN12 ....281 R6
Gybbons Rd CRBK TN17 ....314 E6
Gylcote Cl CMBW SE5 ....44 E2
Gypsy Wy HOO/HM ME3 ....59 M2

H

Habington Cl CMBW SE5 * 24 E6
Habitat Cl PECK SE15 ....25 H4
Hackfield Rd ASH TN23 ....204 C2
Hackford Rd BRXN/ST SW9 ....24 A7
Hackford Wk BRXN/ST SW9 ....24 A7
Hackington Crs BECK BR3 ....70 B3
Hackington Rd
CANTW/ST CT2 ....153 L4

Hackington Ter
CANTW/ST CT2 ....171 M3
Hackling Hi DEAL CT14 ....206 D7
Hackney Rd MAIDW ME16 ....166 D3
Hackwood RBTBR TN32 ....322 D9
Hadden Rd THMD SE28 ....28 F8
Haddington Rd BMLY BR1 ....46 E8
Haddon Gv BFN/LL DA15 ....49 H5
Haddon Rd STMC/STPC BR5 ....91 K1
Haden St GNWCH SE10 ....26 C5
Hadleigh Cl HAYES BR2 ....116 B2
Hadleigh Gdns HB CT6 ....129 J4
Hadley Cl MEO DA13 ....97 J5
Hadley Rd BELV DA17 ....30 A5
Hadlow Castle RTON TN11 * 256 C5
Hadlow Dr MARG CT9 ....179 H3
Hadlow Pk RTON TN11 ....256 C5
Hadlow Rd MAID/BEAR ME14 ....13 L2
SCUP DA14 ....73 H1
TON TN9 ....194 F3
TONN TN10 ....189 L6
WELL DA16 ....29 K6
Hadlow Rd East TONN TN10 ....189 L7
Hadlow Stair Rd TONN TN10 ....195 J1
Hadlow Wy MEO DA13 ....78 F4
Hadrian Gdns ASH TN23 ....204 D5
Hadrian St GNWCH SE10 ....26 F4
Haffenden Cl STPH/PW TN12 ....281 J3
Haffenden Rd TENT TN30 ....301 M12
Hafton Rd CAT SE6 ....46 F6
Ha-Ha Rd WOOL/PLUM SE18 ....28 A7
Haig Av CHAT ME4 ....101 H5
GILL ME7 ....101 M1
ROCH ME1 ....100 E4
Haig Gdns GVE DA12 ....55 K5
Haig Rd BH/WHM TN16 ....132 D3
THHTH CR7 ....35 H2
Haig Ter BXLYHN DA6 ....49 K4
DEAL CT14 ....209 K5
Hailey Rd ERITH DA18 ....29 M3
Hailsham Av BRXS/STRHM SW2 ....44 A7
Hailstone Cl RTON TN11 ....256 D5
Haimo Rd ELTH/MOT SE9 ....47 L3
Hainault Av BRDST CT10 ....183 M1
Haine Rd MSTR CT12 ....182 C6
Hainford Cl BROCKY SE4 ....45 L2
Hainthorpe Rd WNWD SE27 ....44 C8
Halcot Av BXLYHS DA6 ....50 B2
Haldane Gdns GVW DA11 ....54 D6
Halden Cl MAID/SHEP ME15 ....168 A7
Halden La CRBK TN17 ....300 D12
Hale Cl ORP BR6 ....90 D7
Hale House WOOL/PLUM SE18 * 135 L3
Hale La RSEV TN14 ....135 L2
Hale Oak Rd EDEN TN8 ....254 H4
RSEV TN14 ....254 H4
Hale Rd HOO/HM ME3 ....58 D6
Hales Cl TENT TN30 ....315 M1
Hales Dr CANTW/ST CT2 ....172 A1
Hales Rd SIT ME10 ....119 J4
Hale St DEPT SE8 ....26 L8
Halesworth Rd LEW SE13 ....46 F2
Haleys Pl ROCH ME1 ....114 B5
Halfmile Ride MARG CT9 ....178 B12
RTON TN11 ....188 A7
Halford Cl HB CT6 ....129 J7
Halfpence La GVE DA12 ....80 C7
Halfpenny Cl MAID/BEAR ME14 ....166 B3
Halfway Ct PUR RM19 ....33 K3
Halfway Rd IOS ME12 ....64 E5
Halfway St BFN/LL DA15 ....48 E6
Half Yoke MAIDW ME16 ....166 C5
Halifax Cl WALD ME5 ....101 J7
Halifield Dr BELV DA17 ....29 M4
Haliburton Cl CHST BR7 ....72 A2
Hall Av KEN/WIL TN24 ....203 J5
Hall Cl SIT ME10 ....119 M5
Hallcroft Ct RAM CT11 ....16 E5
Hall Dr SYD SE26 ....69 K2
Hallett Wk CANT CT1 ....5 G1
Halford Wy DART DA1 ....51 K4
BH/ER/WK TN15 * 30 C2
OXTED RH8 ....184 E2
Halliday Cl HYTHE CT21 * 222 B3
Halliday Dr DEAL CT14 ....209 K6
Halliday Rd LEW SE13 ....46 C2
Halliwell Rd BRXS/STRHM SW2 ....44 A4
Hall Place Crs BXLY DA5 ....50 C3
DIT ME20 ....140 A4
HOO/HM ME3 ....40 D7
ROCH ME1 ....113 K2
SOCK/AV RM15 ....32 C1
WALD ME5 ....115 K2
Hallsfield Rd WALD ME5 ....114 E2
Hall's Hole Rd RTWE/PEM TN2 ....23 M6
Hallsland Wy OXTED RH8 ....185 G3
Hall Ter SOCK/AV RM15 ....32 E1
The Hall BKHTH/KID SE3 ....47 H1
Hallwards STPH/PW TN12 ....281 R7
Hallwood Cl RHAM ME8 ....102 B8
Halons Rd ELTH/MOT SE9 ....48 B5
Halpin Pl WALW SE17 ....24 E5
Halsbrook Rd CMBW SE5 ....24 E5
Halsmere Rd CMBW SE5 ....24 C6
Halstatt Rd DEAL CT14 ....209 H6
Halstead Cl CANTW/ST CT2 ....172 B5
CROY/NA CRO 86 E7
Halstead Gdns MARG CT9 ....179 J3
Halstead La RSEV TN14 ....134 D1
Halstead Rd ERITH DA8 ....30 F7
Halstow Cl MAID/SHEP ME15 ....167 J8
Halstow Rd GNWCH SE10 ....27 H4
Halstow Wy ASH TN23 ....204 C3
Halt Dr TIL RM18 ....36 B3
Halton Rd CDW/CHF RM16 ....33 M2
Halt Robin Rd BELV DA17 ....30 C3
The Halt RCANTW CT4 ....291 Q5
WSTB CT5 ....127 C6
Hambledon WALW SE17 * 24 E5
Hambledon Cl MAIDW ME16 ....166 C2
Hambledon Gdns SNWD SE25 ....69 H7
Hambledon Pl DUL SE21 ....45 G6
Hambledown Rd
ELTH/MOT SE9 ....48 B5
Hamble Rd TONN TN10 ....188 D7
Hambro Av HAYES BR2 ....89 H4
Hambrook Cl RCANTW CT4 ....247 N5
Hambrook La RCANTW CT4 ....247 N10
Hambrook Wk SIT ME10 ....120 A1
The Hamele RCANTW CT4 ....173 G4
Hamelin Rd GILL ME7 ....102 A5
Hamfield Rd GVW DA11 ....54 D6
Hamfield Cl OXTED RH8 ....157 H5
Hamfield Rd GVW DA11 ....334 E2
Hamilton Cl BERM/RHTH SE16 ....25 M1
MSTR CT12 ....182 D4
NROM TN28 ....331 M8
Hamilton Ct ROCH ME1 * 100 C1
Hamilton Crs SIT ME10 ....119 K6
Hamilton Rd BFN/LL DA15 ....73 H1
BXLYHN DA7 ....29 M8

DEAL CT14 ....209 J5
DVW CT17 ....217 H1
GILL ME7 ....83 L9
KEN/WIL TN24 ....205 G5
LYDD TN29 ....334 D1
WNWD SE27 ....68 D1
WSTB CT5 ....126 E4
Hamilton Sq STHWK SE1 * 24 F1
Hamilton St DEPT SE8 ....26 B5
Ham La GILL ME7 ....115 M2
RMAID ME17 ....243 K12
Hamlea Cl BKHTH/KID SE3 ....47 H3
Hamlet Cl LEW SE13 ....46 E2
Hamlet Rd NRWD SE19 ....69 G4
The Hamlet CMBW SE5 ....44 E1
Hamlet Wy STHWK SE1 * 24 E1
Hamlin Rd SEV TN13 ....135 K7
Hamlyn Gdns NRWD SE19 ....68 G5
Hammelton Rd BMLY BR1 ....71 H5
Ham Mill La LYDD TN29 ....318 C10
Hammond Cl RDV CT15 ....252 D12
Hammonds Hawk TN18 ....312 D7
Hammond's Rd FOLK CT20 ....219 M8
Hammonds Sq SNOD ME6 ....113 H5
Hamond Hi CHAT ME4 ....6 B5
Hampden Av BECK BR3 ....69 M6
Hampden La ASH TN23 ....204 D1
Hampden Ms ASH TN23 ....204 D5
BECK BR3 ....69 M6
GRAYS RM17 ....34 C4
Hampshire Cl WALD ME5 ....101 K6
Hampshire Drive Rd
MAID/SHEP ME15 ....167 K5
Hampshire Rd CANT CT1 ....174 E2
Hampson Wy
MAID/BEAR ME14 ....168 B1
VX/NE SW8 ....24 A7
Hampstead La WBY/YAL ME18 ....257 N4
Hampton Cl HB CT6 ....128 B6
WALD ME5 ....101 H8
Hampton Crs GVE DA12 ....55 M7
Hampton Gdns HB CT6 ....128 B6
Hampton La RASHW TN26 ....289 J7
Hampton Pier Av HB CT6 ....128 C5
Hampton Rd CROY/NA CRO 86 D2
MAID/BEAR ME14 ....13 L1
Hamptons Rd RTON TN11 ....240 G12
Hampton St WALW SE17 ....24 C3
Hampton V HYTHE CT21 ....223 H1
Ham River Hi HOO/HM ME3 ....58 B7
Ham Rd FAV ME13 ....123 K8
Hamsey Green Gdns
WARL CR6 ....130 B2
Hamsey Wy SAND/SEL CR2 ....130 A3
Ham Shades Cl BFN/LL DA15 ....49 G8
Ham Shades La WSTB CT5 ....127 H4
Hamstreet Rd RASHE TN25 ....318 H2
RASHW TN26 ....304 D13
Ham Vw CROY/NA CRO 87 M2
Hanbury Cl WBY/YAL ME18 ....164 F6
Hanbury Dr BH/WHM TN16 ....106 A3
Hancock Cl STRD ME2 ....82 C4
Hancock Rd NRWD SE19 ....68 E5
Hancocks Fld DEAL CT14 ....209 H4
Handcroft Rd CROY/NA CRO 86 C4
Handel Crs TIL RM18 ....36 H5
Handel Rd LEW SE13 ....46 E3
Handforth Rd BRXN/ST SW9 ....24 B6
Hang Grove Hi ORP BR6 ....107 J7
Hangman's La DEAL CT14 ....210 E4
RDV CT15 ....214 B3
Hankey Pl STHWK SE1 * 24 E1
Hanley Pl BECK BR3 ....70 B4
Hanmer Wy STPH/PW TN12 ....281 J7
Hannah Ct FAV ME13 ....
Hannah Mary Wy STHWK SE1 * 25 H5
Hannen Rd WNWD SE27 * 44 C8
Hannibal Wy CROY/NA CRO 86 A8
Hanover Cl DEAL CT14 ....209 L7
MARG CT9 ....
SIT ME10 ....119 M7
Hanover Dr CHST BR7 ....72 D1
RHAM ME8 ....116 F1
Hanover Gdns LBTH SE11 ....24 B4
Hanover Gn DIT/AV ME20 * 139 G2
Hanover Pk PECK SE15 ....25 H7
Hanover Rd RMAID ME17 ....258 A2
RTW TN1 ....22 F1
Hanover Sq HB CT6 ....129 G6
Hanover St CROY/NA CRO 86 C6
HB CT6 ....129 G4
Hanover Wy BXLYHN DA7 ....49 G4
Hansler Rd EDUL SE22 ....45 G3
Hanslett's La FAV ME13 ....148 D6
Hansol Rd BXLYHS DA6 ....49 M3
Hansom Ter BMLY BR1 * 71 J5
Hanson Cl BECK BR3 ....70 C2
Hanway RHAM ME8 ....102 B3
Harbex Cl BXLY DA5 ....50 C5
Harbinger Rd POP/IOD E14 ....26 C3
Harbledown Gdns MARG CT9 ....179 J2
Harbledown Pk
CANTW/ST CT2 ....171 K4
Harbledown Pl STMC/STPC BR5 ....73 K8
Harbord Cl CMBW SE5 ....24 E8
Harborough Av BFN/LL DA15 ....48 F5
Harborough Rd
STRHM/NOR SW16 ....68 A1
Harbour Approach Rd
........11 L6
Harbourland Cl
MAID/BEAR ME14 ....141 J5
Harbour Ms WSTB CT5 * 126 E1
Harbourne La RASHW TN26 ....301 Q9
Harbour Pde RAM CT11 ....17 J5
Harbour Rd CMBW SE5 ....24 E8
RYE TN31 ....225 H6
Harbour St BRDST CT10 ....183 L1
FOLK CT20 ....11 L6
RAM CT11 ....17 K6
WSTB CT5 ....126 E1
The Harbour RMAID ME17 ....260 F1
Harbour View Rd DVW CT17 ....217 J1
Harcourt Av BFN/LL DA15 ....49 K4
Harcourt Cl ERITH DA8 ....31 G6
Harcourt Dr CANTW/ST CT2 ....4 B1
HB CT6 ....128 C5
Harcourt Gdns RHAM ME8 ....116 F1
Harcourt Rd BROCKY SE4 ....45 L2
BXLYHS DA6 ....49 M2
FOLKN CT19 ....10 A1
THHTH CR7 ....87 H2
Hardcastle Cl SNWD SE25 ....87 H4
Hardcourts Cl WWKM BR4 ....88 E2
Hardel Wk BRXS/STRHM SW2 ....44 B5
Harden Wk BRXS/STRHM SW2 ....44 B5
Hardens Manorway
WOOL/PLUM SE18 ....28 L2
Harders Rd PECK SE15 ....25 J1
Hardie Cl E/WMAL ME19 * 139 G4
Harding Cl CROY/NA CRO 87 G6
WALW SE17 ....24 D5

Hardinge Av STH/RUST TN4 196 B2
Hardinge Cl RHAM ME8 116 D1
Hardinge Rd KEN/WIL TN24 2 C3
Hardinge St WOOL/PLUM SE18 28 C2
Harding Rd BXLYHN DA7 30 A8
CDW/CHF RM16 35 H2
Hardings La PGE/AN SE20 69 L3
Hardman Rd CHARL SE7 27 J4
Hardres Court Rd
RCANTW CT4 249 P12
RCANTW CT4 269 J7
Hardres Rd RAM CT11 17 K4
Hardres St RAM CT11 17 K5
Hardres Ter STMC/STPC BR5 * 91 L5
Hards Town CHAT ME4 6 F6
Hardwick Crs DART DA1 52 C4
Hardwicke Rd DVW CT17 217 J3
Hardwick Rd FOLK CT20 10 C6
RTON TN11 188 B7
Hardwidge St STHWK SE1 24 F1
Hardy Av GVW DA11 54 F7
Hardy Cl BERM/RHTH SE16 25 L1
CANTW/ST CT2 171 K4
KEN/WIL TN24 205 K4
WALD ME5 101 J7
Hardy Gv DART DA1 52 B2
Hardy Rd BKHTH/KID SE3 27 G5
NROM TN28 331 L10
RDV CT15 214 F1
Hardy St MAID/BEAR ME14 13 G1
Harebell Cl IOS ME12 228 D1
MAID/BEAR ME14 141 M8
Hare & Billet Rd BKHTH/KID SE3 26 E7
Harebrook RAM CT11 17 L3
Haredale Cl ROCH ME1 100 E6
Haredale Rd HNHL SE24 44 D2
Haredon Cl FSTH SE23 45 K5
Harefield Ms BROCKY SE4 46 A1
Harefield Rd BROCKY SE4 46 A1
SCUP DA14 49 L7
STRHM/NOR SW16 68 A4
Haremere Hl BUR/ETCH TN19 322 C4
Hares Bank CROY/NA CR0 105 J4
Harescroft RTWE/PEM TN2 201 G6
Hare St WOOL/PLUM SE18 28 B2
Hare Ter WTHK RM20 * 33 L4
Harewood Gdns
SAND/SEL CR2 130 A1
Harfield Gdns CMBW SE5 * 44 F1
Harfst Wy SWLY BR8 74 D5
Hargate Cl RTWE/PEM TN2 201 G6
Hargood Rd BKHTH/KID SE3 27 K7
Hargwyne St BRXN/ST SW9 44 A1
Harkness Dr CANTW/ST CT2 4 B1
Harland Av BFN/LL DA15 48 E8
CROY/NA CR0 87 G6
Harland Rd LEE/GVPK SE12 47 H6
Harlands Gv ORP BR6 90 C7
Harland Wy STH/RUST TN4 196 C2
Harlech Cl STRD ME2 82 A4
Harlescott Rd PECK SE15 45 L2
Harleyford BMLY BR1 71 J5
Harleyford Rd LBTH SE11 24 A5
Harley Gdns ORP BR6 90 F7
Harlinger St WOOL/PLUM SE18 27 M2
Harlington Rd BXLYHN DA7 49 M1
Harman Av GVW DA11 79 J2
HYTHE CT21 307 L10
Harman Cl STHWK SE1 * 25 H4
Harman Dr BFN/LL DA15 49 G4
Harmans Dr EGRIN RH19 274 A12
Harmans Md EGRIN RH19 274 A12
Harmer Rd SWCM DA10 54 A4
Harmer St GVE DA12 55 K4
Harmers Wy HDCN TN27 263 J10
Harmony St STH/RUST TN4 200 E1
Harmony Wy HAYES BR2 71 H6
Harmsworth Gdns
BRDST CT10 179 K8
Harmsworth Ms STHWK SE1 24 B2
Harmsworth St WALW SE17 24 C4
Harness Rd THMD SE28 29 H1
Harnet St SWCH CT13 237 K12
Harnetts Cl SWLY BR8 * 92 E3
Harold Av BELV DA17 30 A4
GILL ME7 101 M1
WGOS CT8 177 H5
Harold Ct FAV ME13 149 K3
Harold Est STHWK SE1 * 24 F2
Harold Rd BRCH CT7 176 A5
DEAL CT14 209 K1
MARG CT9 15 L4
NRWD SE19 68 E4
RDART DA2 76 A1
SIT ME10 120 C5
STRD ME2 99 J2
Harold's Rd DVE/WH CT16 8 F3
Harold St DVE/WH CT16 8 E3
QBOR ME11 227 P1
Harpenden Rd WNWD SE27 44 C7
Harper Cl CDW/CHF RM16 33 K4
Harper Rd STHWK SE1 24 D2
Harp Farm Rd
MAID/BEAR ME14 115 K6
Harple La MAID/BEAR ME14 142 A4
Harps Av IOS ME12 65 J7
Harpswood La HYTHE CT21 222 B2
Harptree Dr WALD ME5 101 G8
Harraden Rd BKHTH/KID SE3 27 K7
Harrap Cha GRAYS RM17 34 A4
Harrier Dr SIT ME10 120 B7
Harrier Ms THMD SE28 28 E1
Harries Rd RTWE/PEM TN2 197 G6
Harriet Cl BRXS/STRHM SW2 44 B5
Harriet Dr ROCH ME1 100 B2
Harriet Gdns CROY/NA CR0 87 H5
Harringe La RASHE TN25 306 G4
Harrington Rd SNWD SE25 69 H8
Harrington Wy
WOOL/PLUM SE18 27 L2
Harriot Cl FOLKN CT19 220 C6
Harriott Cl GNWCH SE10 27 G3
Harris Cl GVW DA11 54 F8
Harris Ct GILL ME7 102 A3
Harrison Dr HOO/HM ME3 59 M1
RMAID ME17 242 F11
Harrison Rd BGR/WK TN15 240 E3
RAM CT11 17 G7
Harrison's Ri CROY/NA CR0 86 C6
Harrisons Whf PUR RM19 32 B4
Harrison Ter FAV ME13 * 123 J7
Harrison Wy SEV TN13 20 F1
Harris Rd BXLYHN DA7 29 M7
IOS ME12 64 D3
Harris's Aly RCANTE CT3 251 R2
Harris St CMBW SE5 24 E6
Harrowby Gdns GVW DA11 54 F7
Harrow Ct RSIT ME9 117 L5
Harrow Dene BRDST CT10 179 H8
Harrow Gdns ORP BR6 91 J7
WARL CR6 130 E2
Harrow Manor Wy ABYW SE2 29 K3
Harrow Rd GILL ME7 102 A7
RSEV TN14 134 D1
WARL CR6 130 E1
Harrow Wy ASH TN23 204 B6
MAID/BEAR ME14 141 M8
Harrriets Cnr WSTB CT5 152 B1
Harry Pay Cl KEN/WIL TN24 203 H7
Harrys Rd RSIT ME9 121 K6
Harry Wells Rd HB CT6 128 C6
Hart Cl RFOLK CT18 220 B1
Hart Cnr WTHK RM20 * 33 L4
Hart Dyke Rd STMC/STPC BR5 91 K5
SWLY BR8 74 E8
Hartfield Cl TONN TN10 189 H8
Hartfield Crs WWKM BR4 89 H6
Hartfield Gv PGE/AN SE20 69 J5
Hartfield Pl GVW DA11 54 E5
Hartfield Rd EDEN TN8 275 M1
WWKM BR4 89 H7
Hartford Rd BXLY DA5 50 B4
Hart Hl HDCN TN27 263 R4
Harting Rd ELTH/MOT SE9 71 M1
Hartington Cl ORP BR6 90 D8
Hartington St CHAT ME4 6 E7
Hartlake Rd RTON TN11 195 M5
RTON TN11 256 B9
Hartlands Cl BXLY DA5 50 A4
Hartland Wy CROY/NA CR0 87 M5
Hartley Bottom Rd HART DA3 96 C4
Hartley Cl BMLY BR1 72 A6
MAID/SHEP ME15 168 A7
Hartley Court Gdns
CRBK TN17 298 C10
Hartley Hl HART DA3 96 B4
Hartley Ms RHAM ME8 102 C3
Hartley Rd BH/WHM TN16 159 J3
CRBK TN17 298 D11
CROY/NA CR0 86 D3
HART DA3 77 M6
WELL DA16 29 K6
Hartlip Cl IOS ME12 64 C6
Hartlip Hl RSIT ME9 103 M6
Hartnokes HAWK TN18 312 D7
Hartnup St MAIDW ME16 166 D3
Harton Cl BMLY BR1 71 L5
Harton St DEPT SE8 26 B7
Hartpiece Cl RHAM ME8 103 G3
Hartscroft CROY/NA CR0 104 D3
Hartsdown Pk MARG CT9 * 14 C7
Hartsdown Rd MARG CT9 14 B6
Hart Shaw HART DA3 78 C6
Hartshill Rd GVW DA11 55 G7
Hartsland Rd SEV TN13 21 K3
Hart's La NWCR SE14 25 M6
Hartslock Dr ABYW SE2 29 L1
Hartsmead Rd ELTH/MOT SE9 48 A7
Hart St MAIDW ME16 12 E7
Hartville Rd WOOL/PLUM SE18 28 F3
Harty Av RHAM ME8 116 C2
Harty Ferry Rd IOS ME12 230 A4
Harty Ferry Vw WSTB CT5 126 D7
Harty Ter IOS ME12 * 66 B8
Harvard Rd LEW SE13 46 D3
Harvel Av STRD ME2 18 B3
Harvel Cl CHST BR7 73 H7
Harvel Crs ABYW SE2 29 L4
Harvel La MEO DA13 239 N2
Harvel Rd MEO DA13 239 K6
Harvel St MEO DA13 239 P2
Harvest Bank Rd WWKM BR4 89 H6
Harvesters Cl RHAM ME8 102 F7
Harvesters Wy
MAID/BEAR ME14 167 L1
Harvest Rdg E/WMAL ME19 138 E3
Harvest Rd TONN TN10 189 G7
Harvest Wy ASH TN23 204 A4
RFOLK CT18 220 C1
SWLY BR8 92 D3
Harvey CDW/CHF RM16 34 C1
Harvey Av DEAL CT14 209 K6
Harvey Dr SIT ME10 120 B7
WSTB CT5 127 J4
Harvey Gdns CHARL SE7 27 L4
Harvey Pl FOLK CT20 11 L4
Harvey Rd CMBW SE5 24 E7
KEN/WIL TN24 3 J6
RHAM ME8 102 F5
Harvey St FOLK CT20 11 L4
Harville Rd RASHE TN25 203 M1
Harvill Rd SCUP DA14 73 L2
Harwich St WSTB CT5 126 E5
Harwick Dr NROM TN28 331 K5
Harwood Av BMLY BR1 71 J6
Harwood Rd RHAM ME8 103 J4
Hasborough Rd FOLKN CT19 221 G7
Hascombe Ter CMBW SE5 * 24 E8
Haseley End FSTH SE23 * 45 K5
Haseltine Rd SYD SE26 70 A1
Haskard Cl RFOLK CT18 220 A1
Haslam St PECK SE15 25 G7
Haslemere Rd BXLYHN DA7 30 A8
THHTH CR7 86 C1
Hasletts Cl RTW TN1 196 E7
Haslewood Cl HDCN TN27 284 E7
Hassall Reach CANT CT1 171 J7
Hassell St RASHE TN25 267 P12
Hassendean Rd BKHTH/KID SE3 27 J5
Hassocks Cl SYD SE26 45 J8
Hassock Wd HAYES BR2 89 L7
Hasted Cl GRH DA9 53 K4
Hasted Rd CHARL SE7 27 L4
HOO/HM ME3 82 B3
RSIT ME9 118 C2
Hasteds RMAID ME17 169 K3
Haste Hill Cl MAID/SHEP ME15 259 M2
Haste Hill Rd
MAID/SHEP ME15 259 M2
Hastings Av MARG CT9 15 K6
Hastings Cl PECK SE15 * 25 H6
WTHK RM20 33 M5
Hastings Pl SWCH CT13 206 A1
Hastings Rd CROY/NA CR0 87 G4
HAWK TN18 312 C11
HAWK TN18 314 B11
HAYES BR2 89 M4
MAID/SHEP ME15 13 J6
RTWE/PEM TN2 278 B11
Hastings St WOOL/PLUM SE18 28 D2
Hatcham Park Ms NWCR SE14 25 L7
Hatcham Park Rd NWCR SE14 25 L7
Hatcham Rd PECK SE15 25 K5
Hatcher's Ms STHWK SE1 24 F1
Hatches La RTON TN11 256 G7
Hatch La RCANTW CT4 170 D8
Hatch Rd RMAID ME17 243 K12
Hatch St FAV ME13 149 K2
Hatcliffe Cl BKHTH/KID SE3 47 G1
Hatcliffe St GNWCH SE10 27 G4
Hatfield Ct BKHTH/KID SE3 * 27 H6
Hatfield Rd CDW/CHF RM16 33 L4
MARG CT9 14 B5
RAM CT11 17 G5
STRD ME2 18 F1
Hatham Green La
BGR/WK TN15 238 C4
Hathaway Cl HAYES BR2 90 A4
Hathaway Ct ROCH ME1 19 H8
Hathaway Rd CROY/NA CR0 86 C3
GRAYS RM17 34 C3
Hatherall Rd MAID/BEAR ME14 13 K1
Hatherley Crs SCUP DA14 49 H7
Hatherley Rd SCUP DA14 49 H8
Hathern Gdns ELTH/MOT SE9 72 B1
Hathorne Cl PECK SE15 25 J8
Hathway St PECK SE15 25 K8
Hatmill La STPH/PW TN12 279 L10
Hatteraick St BERM/RHTH SE16 25 K1
Hattersfield Cl BELV DA17 30 A3
Hatton Cl CDW/CHF RM16 33 L2
GVW DA11 54 F8
WOOL/PLUM SE18 28 E6
Hatton Rd CROY/NA CR0 86 B4
WALD ME5 115 K2
Havannah St POP/IOD E14 26 B1
Havelock Rd BELV DA17 * 30 A3
CROY/NA CR0 87 G5
DART DA1 51 J5
DEAL CT14 209 K6
GVW DA11 55 G6
HAYES BR2 71 K8
TON TN9 194 E2
Havelock St CANT CT1 5 H4
Havelock Wk FSTH SE23 45 K6
Haven Cl ELTH/MOT SE9 48 A8
MEO DA13 79 G5
ROCH ME1 100 D3
SCUP DA14 73 K3
SWLY BR8 75 G6
Haven Dr HB CT6 232 A3
RFOLK CT18 220 B1
Havengore Av GVE DA12 55 M5
Haven Hl BGR/WK TN15 238 F2
Haven Pl CDW/CHF RM16 34 D1
Haven St HOO/HM ME3 58 D8
The Haven DEAL CT14 * 211 L3
GRAYS RM17 35 G3
HYTHE CT21 321 P1
Haventhorpe KEN/WIL TN24 2 C2
Haven Wy CHAT ME4 83 J4
Havering Cl RTWE/PEM TN2 197 J7
Haverthwaite Rd ORP BR6 90 E6
Havil St CMBW SE5 24 F7
Havisham Cl ROCH ME1 * 100 E3
Havisham Pl NRWD SE19 68 C3
Havisham Rd GVE DA12 56 B6
Hawarden Gv HNHL SE24 44 D5
Hawarden Pl RCANTE CT3 * 251 R2
Hawbeck Rd RHAM ME8 116 D2
Hawden Cl RTON TN11 194 C1
Hawden La RTON TN11 194 C2
Hawden Rd TON TN9 194 E3
Hawe Cl CANTW/ST CT2 172 B5
Hawe Farm Wy HB CT6 129 J7
Hawe La CANTW/ST CT2 173 H2
Hawes Av RAM CT11 16 C5
Hawes La WWKM BR4 88 D4
Hawes Rd BMLY BR1 71 J5
Hawfield Bank ORP BR6 91 L6
Hawk Cnr WTHK RM20 * 33 L4
Hawkenbury Cl
RTWE/PEM TN2 23 L8
Hawkenbury Md
RTWE/PEM TN2 23 L9
Hawkenbury Ri HOO/HM ME3 82 C3
Hawkenbury Rd
RTWE/PEM TN2 23 M9
STPH/PW TN12 282 E2
Hawkenbury Vls
STPH/PW TN12 * 282 D3
Hawke Pl BERM/RHTH SE16 * 25 L1
Hawke Rd NRWD SE19 68 E3
Hawkesbury St DVW CT17 8 C9
Hawkes Cl GRAYS RM17 34 C5
Hawkesfield Rd FSTH SE23 45 M7
Hawkes Pl SEV TN13 161 M5
Hawkes Rd DIT/AY ME20 114 A8
Hawkhurst Cl BRCH CT7 176 E5
Hawkhurst Rd
BUR/ETCH TN19 311 N7
CRBK TN17 298 C12
HAWK TN18 312 C2
RHAM ME8 102 B2
Hawkhurst Wy BRDST CT10 183 K3
WWKM BR4 88 C5
Hawkins Av GVE DA12 79 K1
Hawkins Cl CHAT ME4 6 E2
SIT ME10 119 M3
Hawkins Dr CDW/CHF RM16 33 L1
Hawkins Rd FOLKN CT19 219 L7
Hawkins Ter CHARL SE7 27 M4
Hawkins Wy CAT SE6 70 B2
Hawkley Gdns WNWD SE27 44 C7
Hawkridge Dr GRAYS RM17 34 E4
Hawksbrook La BECK BR3 88 D2
Hawksdown DEAL CT14 211 J1
Hawksdown Rd DEAL CT14 211 K1
Hawkshead Cl BMLY BR1 70 F4
Hawks Hill La RSIT ME9 145 K5
Hawkshill Rd DEAL CT14 211 L1
Hawkslade Rd PECK SE15 45 L3
Hawk's La CANT CT1 4 E4
Hawks Ms GNWCH SE10 * 26 D6
Hawksmoor Cl
WOOL/PLUM SE18 28 F4
Hawkstone Est
BERM/RHTH SE16 25 K3
Hawkstone Rd
BERM/RHTH SE16 25 K3
Hawks Wy ASH TN23 204 B4
Hawkwood MAIDW ME16 140 C8
Hawkwood Cl ROCH ME1 19 M8
Hawkwood La CHST BR7 72 D5
Hawley Rd DART DA1 51 M7
Hawley Sq MARG CT9 14 F5
Hawley St MARG CT9 14 F4
Hawley Ter RDART DA2 * 76 B1
Hawley V RDART DA2 * 76 B2
Hawser Rd ROCH ME1 100 D4
Hawstead La ORP BR6 92 A8
Hawstead Rd LEW SE13 46 C4
Hawthorn RASHW TN26 317 L9
Hawthorn Av CANTW/ST CT2 172 B7
IOS ME12 64 B5
THHTH CR7 68 C5
Hawthorn Cl DVW CT17 212 F7
EDEN TN8 192 C3
GVE DA12 79 J1
HYTHE CT21 * 321 R1
LYDD TN29 331 N2
RAM CT11 183 H4
STMC/STPC BR5 90 E2
Hawthorn Cnr HB CT6 232 B6
Hawthorn Crs SAND/SEL CR2 104 B5
Hawthornden Cl
E/WMAL ME19 164 D2
Hawthorndene Cl HAYES BR2 * 89 G5
Hawthorndene Rd HAYES BR2 89 H5
Hawthorn Dr WWKM BR4 88 F7
Hawthorne Av BH/WHM TN16 132 C1
RHAM ME8 102 D3
Hawthorne Cl BMLY BR1 72 A7
RDV CT15 272 E6
Hawthorne Rd BMLY BR1 72 A7
Hawthorn Gv PGE/AN SE20 69 J5
Hawthorn La SEV TN13 135 L8
Hawthorn Pl ERITH DA8 30 D4
Hawthorn Rd ASH TN23 204 E7
BXLYHS DA6 * 50 A2
DART DA1 51 L7
SIT ME10 119 M5
STRD ME2 18 A6
Hawthorns HART DA3 78 A8
WALD ME5 * 115 G4
The Hawthorns BRDST CT10 182 F1
DIT/AY ME20 139 M4
OXTED RH8 185 H3
Hawthorn Ter BFN/LL DA15 49 G4
Hawthorn Wk RTWE/PEM TN2 197 H5
TONN TN10 188 F6
Haxted Rd BMLY BR1 71 J5
LING RH7 190 F6
Haydens Cl STMC/STPC BR5 91 K3
Haydens Ms TON TN9 194 F2
The Haydens TON TN9 194 F2
Haydon Cl MAIDW ME16 166 C1
Hayes Cha WWKM BR4 88 E2
Hayes Cl HAYES BR2 89 H5
HOO/HM ME3 81 K2
WTHK RM20 33 K5
Hayesden La RRTW TN3 277 Q5
Hayesford Park Dr HAYES BR2 89 G1
Hayes Gdn HAYES BR2 89 H5
Hayes Gv EDUL SE22 45 G1
Hayes Hl HAYES BR2 88 F4
Hayes Hill Rd HAYES BR2 89 G4
Hayes La BECK BR3 70 E7
HAYES BR2 89 H2
RSIT ME9 144 A3
Hayes Mead Rd HAYES BR2 88 F4
Hayes Plat RYE TN31 325 K8
Hayes Rd HAYES BR2 71 H8
RDART DA2 52 F5
Hayes St HAYES BR2 89 J4
Hayes Ter GVE DA12 * 80 F2
Hayes Wy BECK BR3 70 D8
Hayes Wood Av HAYES BR2 89 J4
Hayfield E/WMAL ME19 138 E3
Hayfield Rd STMC/STPC BR5 91 H1
Hayfields WALD ME5 115 L3
Hay Hl DEAL CT14 253 Q8
Hay La DEAL CT14 253 R7
Hayle TIL RM18 36 D2
Hayle Mill Rd
MAID/SHEP ME15 167 G5
Hayle Pl MAID/SHEP ME15 * 167 G5
Hayle Rd MAID/SHEP ME15 13 G7
Hayles St LBTH SE11 24 C3
Hayley Cl STRD ME2 99 K3
Haymakers La ASH TN23 204 A3
Haymans Hl STPH/PW TN12 280 A10
Hayman Wk DIT/AY ME20 * 114 A7
Haymen St CHAT ME4 6 B8
Haymerle Rd STHWK SE1 25 H5
Hayne Rd BECK BR3 70 A6
Haynes Cl BKHTH/KID SE3 46 F1
Haynes La NRWD SE19 68 F3
Haynes Rd GVW DA11 55 G8
Hay Pl SWLY BR8 * 92 D2
Hayrick Cl MAID/BEAR ME14 141 M8
Haysel SIT ME10 120 B7
Haysleigh Gdns PGE/AN SE20 69 H6
Hays Rd SNOD ME6 113 G7
Hayton Rd RASHE TN25 307 M4
Haywain Cl ASH TN23 204 B6
MAID/BEAR ME14 168 A1
STPH/PW TN12 279 K4
Hayward Av STRD ME2 19 G2
Hayward Cl DART DA1 50 E3
DEAL CT14 209 H5
KEN/WIL TN24 3 M9
Hayward Dr DART DA1 52 A8
Haywardens LING RH7 190 E8
Hayward's Cl NROM TN28 331 J7
Hayward's Hl FAV ME13 245 N5
Haywood Pl CDW/CHF RM16 * 35 K1
Haywood Ri ORP BR6 90 F8
Haywood Rd HAYES BR2 71 L8
Hazebrouck Rd FAV ME13 149 H2
Hazel Av HOO/HM ME3 83 M2
MAIDW ME16 140 D8
Hazelbank RRTW TN3 200 A2
Hazelbank Rd CAT SE6 46 E7
Hazel Cl CROY/NA CR0 87 L3
RDV CT15 272 D6
Hazelden Cl BGR/WK TN15 111 M3
Hazeldene Rd WELL DA16 29 K8
Hazeldon Rd BROCKY SE4 45 M3
Hazeldown Cl DVW CT17 212 F7
Hazel Dr ERITH DA8 31 H7
Hazel End SWLY BR8 92 F1
Hazel Gdns CDW/CHF RM16 34 F2
Hazel Gv ORP BR6 90 C5
SYD SE26 69 L1
WALD ME5 101 J5
Hazel Hts RASHE TN25 202 B6
Hazelhurst BECK BR3 70 E5
Hazelmere Rd STMC/STPC BR5 72 D8
Hazelmere Wy HAYES BR2 89 H2
Hazel Rd DART DA1 51 L7
ERITH DA8 31 H7
Hazel Shaw TONN TN10 188 F7
The Hazels RHAM ME8 102 C8
Hazel Street Rd RSIT ME9 144 B5
Hazel Wk HAYES BR2 90 B2
Hazel Wy STHWK SE1 * 25 G3
Hazelwood TIL RM18 36 B3
Hazelwood Cl RTWE/PEM TN2 197 G5
Hazelwood Dr MAIDW ME16 166 C1
Hazelwood Gv SAND/SEL CR2 104 A8
Hazelwood Hts OXTED RH8 185 H1
Hazelwood Meadow
SWCH CT13 206 A2
Hazelwood Rd OXTED RH8 185 J2
RSEV TN14 107 J6
Hazen Rd E/WMAL ME19 164 C2
Hazledean Rd CROY/NA CR0 86 E5
Hazlemere Dr GILL ME7 84 B8
HB CT6 129 L4
Hazlemere Rd WSTB CT5 126 B6
Hazling Dane RDV CT15 272 A8
Hazlitt Dr MAIDW ME16 12 A2
Headcorn Dr CANTW/ST CT2 172 B5
Headcorn Gdns MARG CT9 179 H3
Headcorn Rd BMLY BR1 71 G2
HDCN TN27 283 N11
HDCN TN27 283 R6
RHAM ME8 102 C1
RMAID ME17 260 F9
RMAID ME17 261 N8
RMAID ME17 262 B6
STPH/PW TN12 282 C4
THHTH CR7 68 A8
Head Hl FAV ME13 150 E3
Head Hill Rd FAV ME13 150 E1
Headingley Rd MAIDW ME16 140 C7
Headley Av WLGTN SM6 86 A8
Headley Dr CROY/NA CR0 105 H2
The Head Race
MAID/SHEP ME15 12 B9
Heaf Gdns DIT/AY ME20 * 140 A4
Heald St NWCR SE14 26 A7
Healy Dr ORP BR6 91 G7
Heansill La HAWK TN18 312 B9
Heard Wy SIT ME10 120 C4
Hearn's Buildings WALW SE17 24 E3
Hearns Cl STMC/STPC BR5 73 K8
Hearns Rd STMC/STPC BR5 73 K8
Heartenoak Rd HAWK TN18 312 E6
Heart In Hand Rd HB CT6 232 A7
Hearts Delight La RCANTE CT3 235 J10
Hearts Delight Rd RSIT ME9 119 J8
Heath Av BXLYHN DA7 29 L5
Heath Cl CANTW/ST CT2 173 G2
STMC/STPC BR5 91 K2
SWLY BR8 74 F6
Heathclose Av DART DA1 51 J5
Heathclose Rd DART DA1 51 H6
Heathcote Cl DIT/AY ME20 140 A3
Heathdene Dr BELV DA17 30 C3
Heathdene Rd
STRHM/NOR SW16 68 A4
Heathedge SYD SE26 * 45 J7
Heathend Rd BXLY DA5 50 F6
Heatherbank CHST BR7 72 B6
ELTH/MOT SE9 28 A8
Heather Bank STPH/PW TN12 279 L3
Heatherbank Cl DART DA1 50 F4
Heather Cl LEW SE13 46 E5
MARG CT9 14 B8
SIT ME10 120 B6
WALD ME5 115 G1
Heather Dr DART DA1 51 H5
MAID/SHEP ME15 13 J9
TENT TN30 301 N10
Heather End SWLY BR8 92 E1
Heather Rd LEE/GVPK SE12 47 H7
Heatherset Gdns
STRHM/NOR SW16 68 A4
Heatherside Rd SCUP DA14 49 K8
The Heathers CRBK TN17 298 D10
Heather Wk TONN TN10 188 E7
Heather Wy SAND/SEL CR2 104 C3
Heatherwood Cl RMAID ME17 261 M3
Heathfield CHST BR7 72 D3
RMAID ME17 260 G1
Heathfield Av DVE/WH CT16 213 J7
MAID/BEAR ME14 141 K6
Heathfield Cl HAYES BR2 89 K8
MAID/BEAR ME14 141 J6
WALD ME5 101 J6
Heathfield Gdns
CROY/NA CR0 * 86 D7
RBTBR TN32 322 G10
Heathfield La CHST BR7 72 D3
Heathfield Rd BMLY BR1 71 G4
BXLYHS DA6 50 A2
CROY/NA CR0 86 E8
HAYES BR2 89 K8
KEN/WIL TN24 2 D2
MAID/BEAR ME14 141 J6
SEV TN13 135 L8
Heathfield Ter SWLY BR8 * 74 E6
WOOL/PLUM SE18 28 F5
Heathfield V SAND/SEL CR2 104 C3
Heathfield Wy RCANTW CT4 270 E5
Heath Gdns DART DA1 * 51 K6
Heath Gv MAIDW ME16 166 B3
PGE/AN SE20 69 K4
Heathlands Ri DART DA1 51 J5
Heath La BKHTH/KID SE3 26 E8
DART DA1 51 K6
Heathlee Rd BKHTH/KID SE3 47 G2
DART DA1 50 F4
Heathley End CHST BR7 72 D3
Heathorn St MAID/BEAR ME14 13 J2
Heath Park Dr BMLY BR1 71 M7
Heath Ri HAYES BR2 89 H2
Heath Rd BXLY DA5 50 D6
CDW/CHF RM16 35 G1
DART DA1 51 G4
MAID/SHEP ME15 258 D1
MAIDW ME16 166 A2
RMAID ME17 259 N3
RMAID ME17 260 F1
THHTH CR7 68 D7
Heathside RASHW TN26 317 K8
Heath Side STMC/STPC BR5 90 D4
Heathside Av BXLYHN DA7 29 M8
RMAID ME17 258 H1
Heath St DART DA1 51 L5
The Heath E/WMAL ME19 138 F8
Heathview Av DART DA1 50 F4
Heathview Crs DART DA1 51 H5
Heath View Dr ABYW SE2 29 L5
Heath View Gdns
CDW/CHF RM16 34 D1
Heath View Rd CDW/CHF RM16 34 D1
Heathview Rd THHTH CR7 68 B8
Heath Vls WOOL/PLUM SE18 29 G4
Heathway BKHTH/KID SE3 27 H6
CROY/NA CR0 88 A6
Heath Wy ERITH DA8 30 D7
Heathwood Dr RAM CT11 183 H4
Heathwood Gdns CHARL SE7 27 M3
SWLY BR8 74 D6
Heathwood Pde SWLY BR8 * 74 D6
Heathwood Wk BXLY DA5 50 F6
Heaton Rd CANT CT1 4 D8
PECK SE15 45 J1
Heaverham Rd BGR/WK TN15 137 G3
Heavitree Cl WOOL/PLUM SE18 28 E4
Heavitree Rd
WOOL/PLUM SE18 28 E4
Heber Rd EDUL SE22 45 G4
Hectorage Rd TON TN9 194 F5
Hector St WOOL/PLUM SE18 * 28 F3
Hedge Place Rd GRH DA9 53 G4
Hedgerows ASH TN23 204 A4
The Hedgerows GVW DA11 54 F7
The Hedgerow
MAID/BEAR ME14 141 M8
Hedger St LBTH SE11 24 C3
The Hedges MAID/BEAR ME14 141 H6
Hedgley St LEE/GVPK SE12 47 G3
Hedingham Rd CDW/CHF RM16 33 K4
Hedley Av WTHK RM20 33 K5
Hedley St MAID/BEAR ME14 13 H3
Heeley Cl RSIT ME9 * 145 L3
Heel La CANTW/ST CT2 172 D1
Heel Rd FAV ME13 245 M10
Heighton Gdns CROY/NA CR0 86 C8
Heights Ter DVW CT17 8 A8
The Heights BECK BR3 * 70 D4
CHARL SE7 27 K4
SEV TN13 * 20 B1
WSTB CT5 126 D6
Heiron St WALW SE17 24 C5
Helder Gv LEE/GVPK SE12 47 G5
Helding Cl HB CT6 129 J7
Helena Av MARG CT9 14 F8
Helena Corniche FOLK CT20 223 K2
Helena Rd RFOLK CT18 221 K3
Helen Cl DART DA1 51 J5
Helen Keller Cl TONN TN10 * 195 G1
Helen St WOOL/PLUM SE18 * 28 C3
Helen Thompson Cl RSIT ME9 227 M9
Heligan Cl ORP BR6 91 G7
Helix Gdns BRXS/STRHM SW2 44 A4
Helix Rd BRXS/STRHM SW2 44 A4
Helleborine GRAYS RM17 34 A4
Hellyar Ct ROCH ME1 * 19 K9
Helmdon Cl MSTR CT12 182 F3
Helsinki Sq BERM/RHTH SE16 26 A2
Helvellyn Av RAM CT11 16 C4
Helvetia St CAT SE6 46 A7
Hemmings Cl SCUP DA14 49 J7
Hempstead La RSIT ME9 120 F6
Hempstead Rd GILL ME7 116 A2
Hempstead Va GILL ME7 * 116 B2
Hempstead Valley Dr
GILL ME7 102 B7
Hempsted St ASH TN23 * 2 B5
Hemp Wk WALW SE17 24 E3

Hemsted Rd ERITH DA8 30 F7
Henbane Cl MAID/BEAR ME14 141 M8
Henderson Dr DART DA1 52 B2
Henderson Rd BH/WHM TN16 106 B6
CROY/NA CR0 86 E2
Hendley Dr CRBK TN17 298 F8
Hendre Rd STHWK SE1 24 F3
Hendy Rd SNOD ME6 113 J5
Heneage Crs CROY/NA CR0 105 H4
Henfield Cl BXLY DA5 50 B4
Hengest Rd DEAL CT14 209 L2
Hengist Av MARG CT9 15 L7
Hengist Ct MAID/BEAR ME14 * 13 H4
Hengist Rd BRCH CT7 233 R2
ERITH DA8 30 D6
LEE/GVPK SE12 47 J5
WGOS CT8 177 G5
Hengist Wy HAYES BR2 70 E8
Hengrave Rd FSTH SE23 45 K5
Hengrove Ct BXLY DA5 49 M6
Henham Gdns STPH/PW TN12 257 K7
Henhurst Rd MEO DA13 79 L6
Heniker La RMAID ME17 260 G8
Henley Cl BERM/RHTH SE16 * 25 K1
RHAM ME8 102 E5
RTWE/PEM TN2 23 K3
RYE TN31 224 F3
WALD ME5 101 H7
Henley Deane GVW DA11 78 F1
Henley Dr BERM/RHTH SE16 25 G3
Henley Flds MAID/BEAR ME14 141 M7
TENT TN30 301 N11
Henley Mdw TENT TN30 301 M11
Henley Rd CAN/RD E16 28 A1
STPH/PW TN12 279 K2
Henley St MEO DA13 98 A2
Hennel Cl FSTH SE23 45 K8
Henrietta Cl DEPT SE8 26 B5
Henry Cooper Wy
ELTH/MOT SE9 47 L8
Henryson Rd BROCKY SE4 46 B3
Henry St BMLY BR1 71 J5
CHAT ME4 7 G8
GRAYS RM17 34 D5
RHAM ME8 103 H4
Hensford Gdns SYD SE26 69 J1
Henshaw St WALW SE17 24 E3
Hensil La HAWK TN18 312 B9
Henslowe Rd EDUL SE22 45 H3
Henson Cl ORP BR6 90 C5
Henville Rd BMLY BR1 71 J5
Henwick Rd ELTH/MOT SE9 47 L1
Henwood KEN/WIL TN24 2 E2
Henwood Green Rd
RTWE/PEM TN2 278 B11
Henwoods Crs
RTWE/PEM TN2 278 B11
Henwoods Mt RTWE/PEM TN2 278 B11
Hepburn Cl CDW/CHF RM16 33 L3
Hepburn Gdns HAYES BR2 89 G4
Heralds Pl LBTH SE11 * 24 C3
Herbert Pl WOOL/PLUM SE18 28 C5
Herbert Rd BXLYHN DA7 29 M8
CHAT ME4 6 E8
HAYES BR2 89 L1
KEN/WIL TN24 205 G5
RAM CT11 16 E6
RHAM ME8 102 F5
SWCM DA10 54 A4
SWLY BR8 75 J3
WOOL/PLUM SE18 28 C6
Herberts Ct HOO/HM ME3 * 61 K1
Herbert St DVW CT17 213 J8
Hercules Rd STHWK SE1 24 A2
Herdsdown HOO/HM ME3 59 L8
Herdson Rd FOLK CT20 10 C5
Hereford Cl KEN/WIL TN24 202 F4
Hereford Gdns BRCH CT7 176 C6
Hereford Pl NWCR SE14 * 26 A6
Hereford Retreat PECK SE15 25 H6
Hereford Rd MAID/SHEP ME15 167 K6
Hereson Rd RAM CT11 17 L3
Hereward Av BRCH CT7 176 A5
Heritage Cl WSTB CT5 126 B7
Heritage Dr GILL ME7 102 A4
Heritage Gdns DVE/WH CT16 8 E3
Heritage Hl HAYES BR2 89 K8
Heritage Rd FOLK CT20 219 L7
WALD ME5 101 H7
Herman Ter CHAT ME4 6 E7
Hermitage Cl HYTHE CT21 222 C3
Hermitage Ct MAIDW ME16 140 A8
Hermitage Gdns NRWD SE19 68 D4
Hermitage La CROY/NA CR0 87 G3
DIT/AY ME20 140 A6
MAID/BEAR ME14 142 C2
RMAID ME17 259 R7
STRHM/NOR SW16 68 A4
Hermitage Rd HOO/HM ME3 81 K2
NRWD SE19 68 E3
The Hermitage FSTH SE23 45 K6
LEW SE13 * 26 D8
Herne Av HB CT6 129 H5
Herne Bay Rd CANTW/ST CT2 172 F2
RCANTE CT3 154 F8
WSTB CT5 127 K2
Herne Dr HB CT6 128 D7
Herne Hl HNHL SE24 44 D3
Herne Hill Rd HNHL SE24 44 D1
Herne Pl HNHL SE24 44 C4
Herne Rd RHAM ME8 102 D3
Herne St HB CT6 129 H8
Herneville Gdns HB CT6 129 J5
Heron Cl RSIT ME9 226 C10
Heron Ct HAYES BR2 71 K8
Heron Crs SCUP DA14 72 F1
Herondale SAND/SEL CR2 104 C3
Heronden Rd
MAID/SHEP ME15 260 A1
SWCH CT13 253 K8
Heron Dr IOS ME12 65 J8
Heron Forstal Av RFOLK CT18 220 C2
Herongate Rd SWLY BR8 74 F3
Heron Hl BELV DA17 30 A3
Heron Hill La MEO DA13 239 N1
Heron Rd CROY/NA CR0 * 86 F4
DIT/AY ME20 139 G4
HNHL SE24 44 D2
Heron's Brook RASHE TN25 288 E3
Herons Cl RCANTW CT4 247 P9
Heron's Wy HYTHE CT21 321 P1
RTWE/PEM TN2 278 B9
Heron Wk ASH TN23 * 204 B3
Heron Wy HOO/HM ME3 61 K1
WALD ME5 101 H7
WTHK RM20 33 J4
Herringham Rd CHARL SE7 27 K2
Herschell Rd BRCH CT7 176 C5
FSTH SE23 45 L5
Herschell Rd East DEAL CT14 209 K6
Herschell Rd West DEAL CT14 209 K6
Herschell Sq DEAL CT14 209 K6
Hertford Pl RAM CT11 17 J7
Hertford St RAM CT11 17 H7
Herts Crs MAID/SHEP ME15 259 L2
Herying Cl STRD ME2 113 J1
Hesiers Hl WARL CR6 131 K3
Hesiers Rd WARL CR6 131 K2
Hesketh Av RDART DA2 52 C6
Heskett Pk RTWE/PEM TN2 278 B11
Hesperus Crs POP/IOD E14 26 C3
Hestia Wy ASH TN23 204 B6
Heston St DEPT SE8 26 A7
Hevelius Cl GNWCH SE10 27 G4
Hever Av BGR/WK TN15 111 K1
Hever Cl MAID/SHEP ME15 168 A7
Hever Court Rd GVE DA12 79 K3
Hever Cft ELTH/MOT SE9 72 B1
STRD ME2 18 C7
Hever Gdns BMLY BR1 72 B6
MAIDW ME16 12 C7
Heverham Rd
WOOL/PLUM SE18 28 F3
Hever Pl CANTW/ST CT2 172 B6
SIT ME10 119 K6
Hever Rd BGR/WK TN15 111 K1
EDEN TN8 193 H6
Heversham Rd BXLYHN DA7 30 B8
Hever Wood Rd BGR/WK TN15 111 K2
Hewett Pl SWLY BR8 74 E8
Hewitt Cl CROY/NA CR0 88 B6
GILL ME7 84 A7
MAIDW ME16 140 E6
Hewitt Rd DVE/WH CT16 8 C2
Hewitts Pl KEN/WIL TN24 3 K6
Hewitts Rd ORP BR6 108 E2
Hexal Rd CAT SE6 46 F8
Hexham Rd WNWD SE27 44 D7
Hextable Cl ASH TN23 204 C5
MAIDW ME16 140 D6
Heybridge Av
STRHM/NOR SW16 68 A3
Heyford Cl RFOLK CT18 220 C1
Heygate St WALW SE17 24 D3
Hibbs Cl SWLY BR8 74 E6
Hibernia Dr GVE DA12 56 A8
Hibernia St RAM CT11 17 K5
Hichisson Rd PECK SE15 45 K3
Hickin Cl CHARL SE7 27 L3
Hickin St POP/IOD E14 26 D2
Hickory Dell GILL ME7 102 B8
Hicks Forstal Rd RCANTE CT3 155 G5
Hicks St DEPT SE8 25 M4
Hidden Meadow FAV ME13 * 149 K2
Higham Cl MAID/SHEP ME15 12 C9
Higham Gdns TONN TN10 189 J8
Higham La RCANTW CT4 250 E9
RTON TN11 189 H4
RYE TN31 324 H7
Higham Rd HOO/HM ME3 58 B1
HOO/HM ME3 82 E2
Higham School Rd TONN TN10 189 H7
Higham Vw MAID/BEAR ME14 140 F1
High Ash Cl TIL RM18 36 B2
High Bank ROCH ME1 100 E3
High Banks MAID/SHEP ME15 167 G8
Highbanks Cl WELL DA16 29 H6
Highbarrow Rd CROY/NA CR0 87 G4
High Beeches ORP BR6 107 M1
RTWE/PEM TN2 197 G7
SCUP DA14 73 M2
Highberry E/WMAL ME19 138 F3
Highbourne Pk RMAID ME17 243 R12
Highbrook Rd BKHTH/KID SE3 47 L1
High Broom Crs WWKM BR4 88 C3
High Brooms Rd
STH/RUST TN4 196 F5
Highbury Av THHTH CR7 68 B6
Highbury Cl WWKM BR4 88 C5
Highbury Gdns MSTR CT12 * 182 E3
High Bury La TENT TN30 315 M2
Highclere St SYD SE26 69 M1
Highcombe CHARL SE7 27 J5
Highcombe Cl ELTH/MOT SE9 47 L6
High Cross Rd BGR/WK TN15 240 A8
Highcross Rd MEO DA13 77 L3
Highdaun Dr
STRHM/NOR SW16 68 A8
High Dewar Rd RHAM ME8 103 H5
High Dr CTHM CR3 130 E8
High Elms RHAM ME8 102 F3
High Elms Rd ORP BR6 107 H3
Highfield Av ERITH DA8 30 D5
ORP BR6 107 L1
Highfield Cl CANTW/ST CT2 171 J2
HAWK TN18 312 D8
HYTHE CT21 222 B1
LEW SE13 46 E4
MSTR CT12 182 E2
RHAM ME8 102 E6
RTWE/PEM TN2 278 A11
Highfield Dr HAYES BR2 70 F8
WWKM BR4 88 C6
Highfield Gdns CDW/CHF RM16 34 E1
MARG CT9 14 B7
Highfield Hl NRWD SE19 68 E4
Highfield La KEN/WIL TN24 205 M5
Highfield Rd BGR/WK TN15 136 D2
BH/WHM TN16 132 B3
BMLY BR1 72 A8
BXLYHS DA6 50 A3
DART DA1 51 L5
IOS ME12 64 F7
KEN/WIL TN24 3 L9
MSTR CT12 182 E2
RHAM ME8 102 E6
STH/RUST TN4 196 F6
STMC/STPC BR5 73 G7
Highfield Rd North DART DA1 51 L4
Highfield Rd South DART DA1 51 L5
Highfields Av HB CT6 129 K5
Highfields Rd EDEN TN8 186 D8
Highfields Vw HB CT6 129 K5
High Firs SWLY BR8 74 F8
Highgate Hl HAWK TN18 312 D8
Highgate Rd WSTB CT5 127 J4
High Gv BMLY BR1 71 K5
WOOL/PLUM SE18 28 E6
Highgrove RTWE/PEM TN2 201 H5
Highgrove Cl CHST BR7 71 M5
Highgrove Rd WALD ME5 101 H8
High Halden Rd HDCN TN27 300 G4
HDCN TN27 301 K3
High Hilden Cl RTON TN11 194 D1
High House La CDW/CHF RM16 35 L2
RTON TN11 189 L4
Highland Cl FOLK CT20 10 A7
Highland Cft BECK BR3 70 C2
Highland Rd BMLY BR1 71 G5
BXLYHS DA6 50 B3
MAID/SHEP ME15 167 M6
NRWD SE19 68 F3
RCANTW CT4 248 E7
RSEV TN14 109 G5
Highlands Cl STRD ME2 81 L7
Highlands Crs LYDD TN29 331 P1
Highlands Hl SWLY BR8 75 H6
Highlands Pk BGR/WK TN15 136 D7
Highlands Rd STMC/STPC BR5 91 J3
Highland Ter LEW SE13 * 46 C1
High La CTHM CR3 130 E5
High Level Dr SYD SE26 69 H1
High Limes NRWD SE19 * 68 F3
Highmead WOOL/PLUM SE18 29 G6
High Md WWKM BR4 88 E5
High Meadow RYE TN31 324 H6
High Minnis RCANTW CT4 291 J2
Highmore Rd BKHTH/KID SE3 26 F6
High Oak Hl RSIT ME9 118 F1
High Pk RYE TN31 324 H6
High Pines WARL CR6 130 B5
High Point ELTH/MOT SE9 48 C8
High Rdg CRBK TN17 297 M6
Highridge GILL ME7 102 A4
HYTHE CT21 223 H2
Highridge Cl MAID/BEAR ME14 142 A8
High Rd RDART DA2 51 K8
High Rocks La RRTW TN3 200 D4
Highshore Rd PECK SE15 25 H8
High Snoad Wd RASHE TN25 265 M3
Highstead Crs ERITH DA8 30 F7
Highsted Rd RSIT ME9 146 A2
SIT ME10 120 B8
High St ASH TN23 2 C4
BECK BR3 70 B6
BGR/WK TN15 136 E7
BGR/WK TN15 136 F3
BGR/WK TN15 238 F10
BGR/WK TN15 240 E2
BH/WHM TN16 159 H5
BH/WHM TN16 160 B2
BMLY BR1 71 H7
BRDST CT10 179 H8
BUR/ETCH TN19 322 B4
CANT CT1 4 F4
CANTW/ST CT2 173 H5
CHAT ME4 6 E6
CRBK TN17 297 M5
CRBK TN17 298 F9
CRBK TN17 314 E6
CROY/NA CR0 86 D6
DART DA1 51 M4
DEAL CT14 209 L3
DIT/AY ME20 140 A2
DVE/WH CT16 8 B3
DVE/WH CT16 212 E4
E/WMAL ME19 138 D5
E/WMAL ME19 139 H7
EDEN TN8 192 D4
EDEN TN8 275 M8
EYN DA4 93 M5
GILL ME7 6 E1
GILL ME7 7 K3
GRAYS RM17 34 B5
GRH DA9 53 J2
GVE DA12 55 J4
GVW DA11 54 C4
HAWK TN18 311 P7
HAWK TN18 312 B7
HB CT6 129 G4
HDCN TN27 283 L4
HDCN TN27 284 D8
HDCN TN27 300 F4
HOO/HM ME3 43 J7
HOO/HM ME3 61 K1
HYTHE CT21 222 D3
IOS ME12 64 C2
IOS ME12 65 L7
IOS ME12 229 N2
LYDD TN29 320 H10
LYDD TN29 329 J5
LYDD TN29 334 C4
MAID/BEAR ME14 12 F5
MARG CT9 15 G6
MSTR CT12 180 F7
MSTR CT12 181 M5
NROM TN28 331 J7
ORP BR6 90 D8
ORP BR6 91 J3
ORP BR6 106 F5
OXTED RH8 157 J8
OXTED RH8 158 A6
PGE/AN SE20 69 K4
PUR RM19 32 A4
QBOR ME11 64 A8
RAM CT11 17 G4
RASHE TN25 266 F11
RBTBR TN32 322 G9
RCANTE CT3 251 J2
RCANTE CT3 251 R2
RCANTW CT4 175 G7
RCANTW CT4 291 Q4
RDART DA2 53 J8
RDV CT15 215 G3
RFOLK CT18 291 M11
RHAM ME8 103 G5
RMAID ME17 260 F6
RMAID ME17 262 G1
ROCH ME1 19 M9
ROCH ME1 113 K1
RRTW TN3 294 B9
RRTW TN3 296 B9
RSEV TN14 109 L4
RSEV TN14 135 M2
RSIT ME9 118 C3
RTON TN11 255 N12
RTON TN11 256 B5
RTW TN1 22 F7
RTWE/PEM TN2 197 M7
RYE TN31 225 H4
SCUP DA14 73 H1
SEV TN13 21 J7
SIT ME10 119 M3
SNOD ME6 113 H5
SNWD SE25 69 G8
STH/RUST TN4 277 R6
STMC/STPC BR5 73 K8
STPH/PW TN12 279 L9
STPH/PW TN12 281 J3
STPH/PW TN12 282 A6
STRD ME2 18 F3
STRD ME2 99 H8
SWCH CT13 237 K12
SWCH CT13 253 N7
SWCM DA10 54 A3
SWLY BR8 74 F7
TENT TN30 315 M2
THHTH CR7 68 D8
TON TN9 194 F4
WADH TN5 309 L4
WADH TN5 309 R8
WADH TN5 311 K6
WBY/YAL ME18 257 Q4
WSTB CT5 126 E3
WWKM BR4 88 C4
Highstreet Rd FAV ME13 125 K7
High Street St Lawrence
RAM CT11 16 D5
The High St HDCN TN27 264 B6
High Tor Cl BMLY BR1 71 J4
High Trees BRXS/STRHM SW2 44 B6
CROY/NA CR0 87 M4
High Trees Cl KEN/WIL TN24 3 L7
High Vw HOO/HM ME3 81 K1
Highview MEO DA13 239 N5
High View Av GRAYS RM17 34 D4
HB CT6 128 C4
WLGTN SM6 86 A8
Highview Cl FAV ME13 151 J6
High View Cl NRWD SE19 69 G6
Highview Dr WALD ME5 100 E8
High View Gdns GRAYS RM17 34 D4
High View Rd NRWD SE19 68 E3
Highview Rd IOS ME12 65 K6
SCUP DA14 73 J1
Highview Ter DART DA1 * 51 L3
The Highway ORP BR6 91 J8
High Weald Wk RRTW TN3 199 K6
RRTW TN3 277 N10
RTON TN11 197 M2
RTWE/PEM TN2 197 G4
RTWE/PEM TN2 201 M4
RTWE/PEM TN2 278 A12
RTWE/PEM TN2 294 H1
STH/RUST TN4 22 C8
STH/RUST TN4 196 F3
STPH/PW TN12 278 C12
TON TN9 195 H6
Highwood Cl ORP BR6 90 D5
Highwood Dr ORP BR6 90 D5
Highwoods Cl HOO/HM ME3 81 J1
High Woods La RTWE/PEM TN2 23 M7
Hilary Cl BXLYHN DA7 30 C7
HB CT6 129 K5
Hilary Gdns ROCH ME1 100 A3
Hilbert Cl RTWE/PEM TN2 23 K2
Hilbert Rd RTWE/PEM TN2 23 K1
Hilborough Wy ORP BR6 90 E8
Hilda Lockert Wk BRXN/ST SW9 24 C8
Hilda May Av SWLY BR8 74 F7
Hilda Rd CHAT ME4 6 E8
IOS ME12 64 E7
Hilda Ter BRXN/ST SW9 * 24 B8
Hilda Vale Rd ORP BR6 90 B7
Hilden Av RTON TN11 194 C1
Hildenborough Crs
MAIDW ME16 140 C6
Hildenborough Gdns
BMLY BR1 70 F3
Hildenborough Rd RTON TN11 188 C1
RTON TN11 255 P11
Hilden Dr ERITH DA8 31 J6
Hildenlea Pl HAYES BR2 70 F6
Hilden Park Rd RTON TN11 194 C1
Hilders Cl EDEN TN8 192 C1
Hildersham Cl BRDST CT10 179 H7
Hilders La EDEN TN8 192 A1
Hillary Av GVW DA11 54 F8
Hillary Rd MAID/BEAR ME14 141 H6
Hill Av RDV CT15 271 R8
Hillbeck Cl PECK SE15 25 K6
Hillborough Av SEV TN13 21 M1
Hillborough Dr HB CT6 232 A4
Hillborough Gv WALD ME5 115 H2
Hill Brow BMLY BR1 71 L5
DART DA1 51 G4
MAID/BEAR ME14 142 B8
SIT ME10 119 L7
Hillbrow Av CANTW/ST CT2 173 G2
HB CT6 129 J7
Hillbrow Cl BXLY DA5 74 E1
Hillbrow Ct OXTED RH8 157 J8
Hillbrow La ASH TN23 204 C2
Hillbrow Rd ASH TN23 204 D3
BMLY BR1 70 F4
RAM CT11 17 G3
Hill Bunker's BELV DA17 30 B3
Hillbury Cl WARL CR6 130 A4
Hillbury Gdns WADH TN5 310 E8
WARL CR6 130 B4
Hill Cha WALD ME5 114 F2
Hill Cl CHST BR7 72 C2
MEO DA13 78 F4
Hill Cnr RRTW TN3 277 J12
Hillcote Av STRHM/NOR SW16 68 B4
Hill Ct HOO/HM ME3 83 G1
Hillcourt Rd EDUL SE22 45 J4
Hill Crs BXLY DA5 50 D6
RCANTE CT3 251 P12
Hill Crest BFN/LL DA15 49 H5
SEV TN13 20 E1
STH/RUST TN4 196 E5
Hillcrest ASH TN23 286 G9
CMBW SE5 * 44 E2
EDEN TN8 187 J8
RYE TN31 225 G2
Hillcrest Av WTHK RM20 33 H5
Hillcrest Cl BECK BR3 88 A2
KEN/WIL TN24 203 H5
SYD SE26 69 H1
Hillcrest Dr GRH DA9 53 H3
RTWE/PEM TN2 197 G6
STRD ME2 99 K3
Hillcrest Gdns DEAL CT14 209 H7
RAM CT11 16 D6
Hillcrest Rd BH/WHM TN16 132 C2
BMLY BR1 71 H1
CHAT ME4 6 C9
DART DA1 50 F5
DEAL CT14 211 K5
EDEN TN8 192 D1
HYTHE CT21 222 C2
ORP BR6 91 H5
RCANTE CT3 175 M1
Hillcrest Vw BECK BR3 88 A2
Hillcroft Rd HB CT6 129 J6
Hilden Shaw
MAID/SHEP ME15 167 H5
Hilldown Rd HAYES BR2 88 F4
Hill Dr STRHM/NOR SW16 68 A7
SWCH CT13 253 N6
Hilldrop Rd BMLY BR1 71 J3
Hill End ORP BR6 91 G5
WOOL/PLUM SE18 28 B7
Hiller Cl BRDST CT10 179 K7
Hillery Cl WALW SE17 24 E3
Hillfield Rd SEV TN13 135 K6
Hillgarth STH/RUST TN4 196 D5
Hill Green Rd RSIT ME9 117 K5
Hill House Dr CDW/CHF RM16 35 J4
MSTR CT12 180 F6
Hill House Rd RDART DA2 52 D5
STRHM/NOR SW16 68 A2
Hillier Gdns CROY/NA CR0 86 B8
Hillingdale BH/WHM TN16 132 A4
Hillingdon Av SEV TN13 136 B7
Hillingdon Ri SEV TN13 136 C8
Hillingdon Rd BXLYHN DA7 50 D1
GVW DA11 55 J7
Hillingdon St WALW SE17 24 C5
Hill La RFOLK CT18 219 J4
Hillman Av HB CT6 128 B5
Hillmead Dr BRXN/ST SW9 44 C2
Hillmore Gv SYD SE26 69 L2
Hill Pk KEN/WIL TN24 205 M4
Hillreach WOOL/PLUM SE18 28 A4
Hill Ri RDART DA2 76 E2
Hill Rd DART DA1 51 M7
FOLKN CT19 220 F5
ROCH ME1 99 M8
Hillsboro Rd EDUL SE22 44 F3
Hillsgrove Cl WELL DA16 29 K6
Hill Shaw HART DA3 96 A2
Hillshaw Crs STRD ME2 18 A7
Hillside EYN DA4 94 A3
GRAYS RM17 34 E3
RDART DA2 76 F2
TON TN9 194 D6
Hillside Av CANTW/ST CT2 171 K4
GVE DA12 55 L7
QBOR ME11 227 N2
STRD ME2 19 H1
Hillside Ct STRD ME2 * 18 E3
SWLY BR8 75 H8
WBY/YAL ME18 164 F6
Hillside Dr GVE DA12 55 L7
Hillside Gdns
BRXS/STRHM SW2 * 44 B7
Hillside La HAYES BR2 89 H5
Hillside Rd BGR/WK TN15 136 E3
BH/WHM TN16 132 D5
BRXS/STRHM SW2 44 A7
CHAT ME4 6 F6
CROY/NA CR0 86 C8
DART DA1 51 H4
DVW CT17 213 H7
FAV ME13 244 H11
HAYES BR2 71 G7
IOS ME12 65 J6
SEV TN13 21 L2
WSTB CT5 127 H4
Hillside St HYTHE CT21 222 C3
Hillside Ter FAV ME13 * 149 K2
GVE DA12 * 55 J6
The Hillside ORP BR6 108 A3
Hills La BGR/WK TN15 111 G6
Hills Pl STRD ME2 * 98 F8
Hill's Ter CHAT ME4 6 C7
Hill St RASHE TN25 290 C3
RTW TN1 23 G2
The Hill CRBK TN17 298 G9
GVW DA11 54 D4
HDCN TN27 264 C5
RCANTE CT3 175 M1
Hill Top CRBK TN17 281 K12
Hilltop MAID/SHEP ME15 258 C2
TON TN9 194 E6
WSTB CT5 * 126 E6
Hilltop Dr RYE TN31 225 G2
Hilltop Gdns DART DA1 52 A3
ORP BR6 90 F5
Hilltop Rd IOS ME12 65 H8
STRD ME2 82 D4
WTHK RM20 33 H5
Hilltop Wk CTHM CR3 130 D6
Hill Vw BGR/WK TN15 240 F2
KEN/WIL TN24 2 D2
Hill View Cl BGR/WK TN15 240 F2
Hillview Crs ORP BR6 90 F4
Hill View Dr WELL DA16 28 F8
Hill View Rd HART DA3 78 C7
ORP BR6 91 G4
RTON TN11 188 C8
STH/RUST TN4 200 D1
Hillview Rd CANTW/ST CT2 171 K3
CHST BR7 72 B2
WSTB CT5 126 E5
Hill View Wy WALD ME5 100 F8
Hillworth BECK BR3 * 70 C6
Hillworth Rd BRXS/STRHM SW2 44 B5
Hillyard St BRXN/ST SW9 24 B7
Hillydeal Rd RSEV TN14 136 B1
Hillyfield Cl STRD ME2 82 A4
Hillyfield Rd ASH TN23 204 D3
Hilly Flds BROCKY SE4 * 46 B2
Hilly Fields Crs BROCKY SE4 46 B2
Hillyfields Ri ASH TN23 204 D3
Hilton Cl FAV ME13 149 L3
Hilton Dr SIT ME10 119 J3
Hilton Rd ASH TN23 204 C1
HOO/HM ME3 58 C6
Hilton Wy SAND/SEL CR2 130 A1
Hinchcliffe Wy MARG CT9 179 G5
Hinckley Rd EDUL SE22 45 H2
Hind Cl LYDD TN29 320 H9
Hind Crs ERITH DA8 30 D6
Hinde Cl SIT ME10 120 A2
Hindmans Rd EDUL SE22 45 H3
Hindsley's Pl FSTH SE23 45 K7
Hind Ter WTHK RM20 * 33 L5
Hines Ter WALD ME5 * 101 K4
Hinksden Rd CRBK TN17 313 J6
Hinksey Pth ABYW SE2 29 L2
Hinstock Rd WOOL/PLUM SE18 28 D6
Hinton Cl ELTH/MOT SE9 47 M6
Hinton Crs GILL ME7 102 B7
Hinton Rd BRXN/ST SW9 44 C1
Hinxhill Rd KEN/WIL TN24 205 M3
Hirst Cl DVE/WH CT16 213 J5
Hitchen Hatch La SEV TN13 20 F3
Hither Chantlers RRTW TN3 200 B2
Hither Farm Rd BKHTH/KID SE3 47 K1
Hither Fld HDCN TN27 264 B6
Hitherfield Rd
STRHM/NOR SW16 44 A7
Hither Green La LEW SE13 46 D3
Hitherwood Dr DUL SE21 69 G1
Hive La GVW DA11 54 C4
Hoaden Rw RCANTE CT3 * 235 N9
Hoades Wood Rd
CANTW/ST CT2 173 H2
Hoads Wood Gdns
RASHE TN25 202 B5
Hoath Cl GILL ME7 102 B6
Hoath La RHAM ME8 102 C6
Hoath Meadow
STPH/PW TN12 * 279 R11
Hoath Rd RCANTE CT3 173 J2
Hoath Wy RHAM ME8 102 C5
Hobart Crs DVE/WH CT16 213 J7
Hobart Gdns SIT ME10 119 K5
THHTH CR7 68 E7
Hobart Rd MSTR CT12 182 D4
TIL RM18 35 H7
Hobbs La RYE TN31 326 A7
Hobbs Rd WNWD SE27 68 D1
Hoblands End CHST BR7 72 F3
Hockenden La SWLY BR8 74 B7
Hockeredge Gdns WGOS CT8 177 J5
Hockers Cl MAID/BEAR ME14 142 B5
Hockers La MAID/BEAR ME14 142 A6
Hoddesdon Rd BELV DA17 30 B4
Hodges Cl CDW/CHF RM16 33 L4
Hodgson Crs SNOD ME6 113 H5
Hodgson Rd WSTB CT5 125 M2
Hodister Cl CMBW SE5 24 D6
Hodsoll St BGR/WK TN15 239 J4
Hodson Crs STMC/STPC BR5 91 L2
Hoffmann Gdns
SAND/SEL CR2 104 A2
Hogarth Cl HB CT6 129 M4
Hogarth Crs CROY/NA CR0 86 D3
Hogbarn La RMAID ME17 242 H7
Hogben Cl RFOLK CT18 291 L10
Hogbrook Hill La RDV CT15 293 Q10
Hogg La CDW/CHF RM16 34 B2
RCANTW CT4 268 H3
Hog Gn RCANTW CT4 291 Q5
Hog Hl MAID/BEAR ME14 168 C1
Hog Hole La RRTW TN3 295 R11
Hognore La BGR/WK TN15 239 J7
Hogtrough Hl BH/WHM TN16 133 M8
Hogtrough La OXTED RH8 157 G6
Holbeach Gdns BFN/LL DA15 48 F4
Holbeach Rd CAT SE6 46 B5
Holbeam Rd FAV ME13 245 K8
Holbeck Rw PECK SE15 25 H6
Holborn La CHAT ME4 6 C4
Holborough Rd SNOD ME6 113 H5
Holbourn Cl HB CT6 155 J1
Holbrook Dr MSTR CT12 182 E4
Holbrook La CHST BR7 72 E4
Holbrook Wy HAYES BR2 90 A2
Holburne Cl BKHTH/KID SE3 27 K7
Holburne Gdns BKHTH/KID SE3 27 L7

Holburne Rd BKHTH/KID SE3 ....27 K7
Holcombe Cl BH/WHM TN16 ....159 J4
Holcombe Rd CHAT ME4 ....6 D9
  ROCH ME1 ....100 D2
Holcote Cl BELV DA17 ....29 M2
Holdenby Rd BROCKY SE4 ....45 M3
Holden Cl WALD ME5 ....101 K7
Holden Park Rd
  STH/RUST TN4 ....196 C5
Holden Rd STH/RUST TN4 ....196 B4
Holder Cl WALD ME5 ....101 K7
Holderness Wy WNWD SE27 ....68 C2
Holding St RHAM ME2 ....102 F2
Hole La EDEN TN8 ....186 B7
Holford Rd TIL RM18 ....35 L3
Holford St TON TN9 ....194 E4
Holgate St CHARL SE7 ....27 J5
Holland Crs OXTED RH8 ....179 K5
  HAYES BR2 ....89 J5
  IOS ME12 ....64 C4
Holland Dr FSTH SE23 ....45 M8
Holland Gv BRXN/ST SW9 ....24 B6
Holland La OXTED RH8 ....185 K5
Holland Rd MAID/BEAR ME14 ....13 H5
  OXTED RH8 ....185 H5
  SNWD SE25 ....87 H1
  WALD ME5 ....114 F9
Hollands Av FOLKN CT19 ....221 G6
Hollands Cl GVE DA12 ....80 F2
Holland Wy HAYES BR2 ....89 G5
Hollicondane Rd RAM CT11 ....17 J3
Hollies Av BFN/LL DA15 ....49 G2
Hollies Ct STRHM/NOR SW16 ....68 B3
The Hollies HART DA3 ....78 D7
Holligrave Rd BMLY BR1 ....71 H5
Hollin Cl STH/RUST TN4 ....22 A7
Hollingbourne Av BXLYHN DA7 ....30 A7
Hollingbourne Hl RMAID ME17 ....242 A5
Hollingbourne Rd HNHL SE24 ....44 D3
  MAID ME8 ....102 D2
Hollingsworth Rd
  SAND/SEL CR2 ....104 A3
Hollington Pl KEN/WIL TN24 ....2 B3
Hollingworth Rd
  MAID/SHEP ME15 ....168 A8
  STMC/STPC BR5 ....90 C3
Hollingworth Wy
  BH/WHM TN16 ....159 J4
Hollis Pl GRAYS RM17 ....34 B2
Hollman Gdns
  STRHM/NOR SW16 ....68 C3
Hollowfield Av GRAYS RM17 ....34 E3
Hollow La CANT CT1 ....4 C9
  LING RH7 ....274 C1
  RSIT ME9 ....103 L8
  SNOD ME6 ....113 G6
Hollowmede CANT CT1 ....4 C8
Hollow Rd RCANTE CT3 ....232 C11
Hollow St RCANTE CT3 ....232 D11
The Hollow
  MAID/SHEP ME15 * 165 M7
Hollow Trees Dr RTON TN11 ....255 P12
Hollow Wood Rd DVW CT17 ....216 F1
Holly Bank STPH/PW TN12 ....279 L9
Hollybrake Cl CHST BR7 ....72 E4
Hollybush Cl SEV TN13 ....161 K4
Hollybush La ORP BR6 ....108 F1
  RCANTE CT3 ....234 A10
Holly Bush La SEV TN13 ....21 K4
Hollybush Rd GVE DA12 ....55 M3
Hollybush Ter NRWD SE19 ....68 F3
Holly Cl BECK BR3 ....70 D8
  BRDST CT10 ....183 J1
  FOLKN CT19 ....220 F6
  GILL ME7 ....83 M7
  HYTHE CT21 * 222 E2
  SWCH CT13 ....253 P7
  WALD ME5 ....101 K4
Holly Crs BECK BR3 ....88 A1
Hollycroft Cl SAND/SEL CR2 ....86 F6
Hollydale Dr HAYES BR2 ....90 A6
Hollydale Rd PECK SE15 ....25 K8
Hollydene Rd WADH TN5 ....309 L3
Holly Farm Rd
  MAID/SHEP ME15 ....168 D2
Holly Gdns BXLYHN DA7 ....50 D2
  MAID/BEAR ME14 * 12 F2
  MARG CT9 ....178 F3
Holly Gv PECK SE15 ....25 G8
Holly Hedge Ter LEW SE13 ....46 B5
Holly Hl MEO DA13 ....112 A2
  FAV ME13 ....151 L4
Holly La BELV DA17 ....30 C4
  FAV ME13 ....151 L4
Holly Mdw ASH TN23 ....202 A8
Hollymount Cl GNWCH SE10 ....26 D7
Holly Rd DART DA1 ....51 N1
  LYDD TN29 ....331 N1
  ORP BR6 ....107 M2
  RAM CT11 ....17 J2
  STRD ME2 ....18 B6
Hollyshaw Cl RTWE/PEM TN2 ....23 J7
Hollytree Av SWLY BR8 ....74 F6
Holly Tree Ho RMAID ME17 ....261 M3
Hollytree Pl HOO/HM ME3 ....73 L1
Hollytree Pde SCUP DA14 * 73 L1
Holly Vls MAID/SHEP ME15 * 165 M7
  STPH/PW TN12 * 278 F10
Hollywood La BGR/WK TN15 ....111 L5
  STRD ME2 ....82 C2
Hollywoods CROY/NA CR0 ....104 E4
Hollywood Wy ERITH DA8 ....31 J7
Holman Ms CANT CT1 ....5 G6
Holmbury Av CROY/NA CR0 ....104 E2
Holmbury Mnr SCUP DA14 * 73 H1
Holmbury Pk CHST BR7 ....71 M4
Holmcroft Rd HAYES BR2 ....90 A1
Holmdale Av CHST BR7 ....72 A1
Holmdene Av HNHL SE24 ....44 D3
Holmdene Cl BECK BR3 ....70 D6
Holmdene Cl BMLY BR1 ....71 M7
Holme Lacey Rd
  LEE/GVPK SE12 ....47 G4
Holme Oak Cl CANT CT1 ....4 F8
Holmes Cl EDUL SE22 ....45 H2
  HOO/HM ME3 ....59 M2
Holmesdale Cl
  MAID/SHEP ME15 ....259 L2
  SNWD SE25 ....69 G2
  WADH TN5 ....309 K4
Holmesdale Hl EYN DA4 ....76 D3
Holmesdale Rd BXLYHN DA7 ....29 L8
  CROY/NA CR0 ....86 E1
  EYN DA4 ....76 D5
  SEV TN13 ....21 L3
  SNWD SE25 ....68 D5
Holmesdale Ter FOLK CT20 ....11 L6
Holmesley Rd BROCKY SE4 ....45 M4
Holme Ter STHWK SE1 * 7 L3
Holmestone Rd RDV CT15 ....212 F8
Holmewood Gdns
  BRXS/STRHM SW2 ....44 A5
Holmewood Rdg RRTW TN3 ....200 A2
Holmewood Rd SNWD SE25 ....68 F7
  STH/RUST TN4 ....196 F6
Holmhurst Cl STH/RUST TN4 ....22 B4

Holmhurst Rd BELV DA17 ....30 C4
Holmlea Cl KEN/WIL TN24 ....3 H6
Holmleigh Av DART DA1 ....51 K2
Holm Mill La RMAID ME17 ....242 C11
Holm Oak Gdns BRDST CT10 ....183 J1
  RHAM ME8 ....102 F3
Holmscroft Rd HB CT6 ....129 L4
Holmsdale Gv BXLYHN DA7 ....30 F5
Holmside Cl GILL ME7 ....101 M3
Holmside Av IOS ME12 ....64 E7
Holmwood Rd ASH TN23 ....204 B4
Holness Rd RCANTE CT3 ....236 A11
Holstein Wy ERITH DA18 ....29 L2
Holton Cl BRCH CT7 ....176 D7
Holt St RDV CT15 ....271 Q1
Holt Wood La DIT/AY ME20 ....139 L5
Holtwood Cl RASHE ME15 * 13 J6
Holtye Crs MAID/SHEP ME15 ....13 J6
Holtye Pl EGRIN RH19 ....274 A10
Holtye Rd EGRIN RH19 ....274 A9
Holwood Park Av
  BECK BR3 * 90 A7
Holyoake St CMBW SE5 ....24 E6
Holyoake Ter SEV TN13 ....20 F3
Holyoak Rd LBTH SE11 ....24 C3
Holyrood Dr IOS ME12 ....65 H8
Holyrood Gdns CDW/CHF RM16 ....35 J2
Holywell Av FOLKN CT19 ....220 D5
Holywell Cl BERM/RHTH SE16 * 25 J4
  BKHTH/KID SE3 ....27 H5
  ORP BR6 ....91 H7
Holywell La RSIT ME9 ....226 A11
Homecroft Rd SYD SE26 ....69 K2
Home Farm Cl RTON TN11 ....255 P10
Home Farm La
  RTWE/PEM TN2 ....197 J4
Homefield Av DEAL CT14 ....209 H3
Homefield Cl STMC/STPC BR5 ....73 J8
  SWLY BR8 ....75 J4
Homefield Dr RHAM ME8 ....103 J3
Homefield Ms BECK BR3 * 70 F3
Homefield Ri ORP BR6 ....91 H4
Homefield Rd BMLY BR1 ....71 K5
  SEV TN13 ....20 B3
  WARL CR6 ....130 B5
Homefield Rw DEAL CT14 * 209 H3
  DIT/AY ME20 ....139 J4
  LBTH SE11 ....24 B3
  STPH/PW TN12 ....279 J4
Homeland Cl ASH TN23 ....202 C8
Homelands La RASHE ME15 ....307 J4
Homemead Cl DEAL CT14 ....209 G6
Homemead Dr NRWD SE19 ....68 F4
Home Lea ORP BR6 ....91 G8
Homeleigh Rd MSTR CT12 ....182 G2
  PECK SE15 ....45 L2
Homemead MEO DA13 ....97 H2
Homemead Rd HAYES BR2 ....90 A1
Home Pk OXTED RH8 ....185 H4
Home Pk Cl BXLYHN DA7 ....30 C4
Homer Dr POP/IOD E14 ....26 B3
Homer Rd CROY/NA CR0 ....87 L1
Homersham CANT CT1 ....4 F2
Homesdale Rd HAYES BR2 ....71 K8
  ORP BR6 ....90 F3
Homeside Farm RCANTW CT4 ....269 J7
Homestall Cl CANTW/ST CT2 * 171 K1
Homestall La FAV ME13 ....150 C4
Homestall Rd EDUL SE22 ....45 K3
  RSIT ME9 ....147 L6
Homestead ASH TN23 ....204 A4
Homestead Cl MARG CT9 ....15 H3
Homestead Ct DEAL CT14 * 208 F3
  DEAL CT14 ....209 H5
Homestead La RDV CT15 ....273 H1
Homestead Rd EDEN TN8 ....186 B6
  ORP BR6 ....108 A2
The Homestead DART DA1 * 51 K4
  RHAM ME8 * 103 H3
  RRTW TN3 ....199 R5
Homestead Vw RSIT ME9 ....119 J7
Homestead Village RAM CT11 ....16 E2
Homestead Wy CROY/NA CR0 ....105 H4
Homewise Wy SWT ME10 ....120 C5
Homewards Rd HOO/HM ME3 ....41 J4
Homewood Av SIT ME10 ....119 L6
Homewood Crs CHST BR7 ....72 F3
Homewood Gdns SNWD SE25 * 86 F1
Homewood Rd CANTW/ST CT2 * 173 H5
  RRTW TN3 ....200 A2
  TENT TN30 ....301 N12

Hoopers Rd ROCH ME1 ....19 K9
Hop Bine Cl STPH/PW TN12 ....257 K6
Hop Av RTON TN11 * 256 F6
Hope Cl LEE/GVPK SE12 ....47 J7
Hopedale Rd CHARL SE7 ....27 J5
Hopehouse La HAWK TN18 ....313 P10
Hopgarden Rd TDWN TN10 ....189 G8
Hop Garden La CANT CT1 * 5 H8
Hoppers Av ASH TN23 ....204 A3
Hop Pocket Cl CRBK TN17 ....299 K5
Hop Pocket La STPH/PW TN12 ....279 K2
Hopsons Pl IOS ME12 ....64 D3
Hopton Rd WOOL/PLUM SE18 ....28 C2
Hopwood Gdns
  STH/RUST TN4 ....196 D7
Hopwood Rd WALW SE17 ....24 C5
Horatio Pl HAWK TN18 * 100 C1
Hordle Prom East PECK SE15 ....25 G6
Hordle Prom North PECK SE15 ....24 F6
Hordle Prom West PECK SE15 ....24 F6
Horizon Cl STH/RUST TN4 ....196 B5
Horley Cl BXLYHS DA6 ....50 B3
Horley Rd ELTH/MOT SE9 ....70 B3
Hornash La RASHW TN26 ....303 R5
Hornbeam Av RTWE/PEM TN2 ....197 G4
  WALD ME5 ....115 J3
Hornbeam Cl ASH TN23 ....202 C8
  DIT/AY ME20 ....139 J4
  LBTH SE11 ....24 B3
  STPH/PW TN12 ....279 J4
Hornbeams MEO DA13 ....239 N5
Hornbeam Wy HAYES BR2 ....90 B2
Hornbrook La TENT TN30 ....317 K2
Horncastle Cl LEE/GVPK SE12 ....47 H5
Horncastle Rd LEE/GVPK SE12 ....47 H5
Horne House
  WOOL/PLUM SE18 * 27 M6
Hornet Cl BRDST CT10 ....183 J3
Hornfair Rd CHARL SE7 ....27 J7
Horn Hl RSIT ME9 ....145 M7
Horniman Dr FSTH SE23 ....45 J6
Horniman Gdns FSTH SE23 * 45 J6
Horning Cl ELTH/MOT SE9 ....71 M1
Horn La GNWCH SE10 ....27 H6
Horn Link Wy GNWCH SE10 ....27 H3
Horn Park Cl LEE/GVPK SE12 ....47 J3
Horn Park La LEE/GVPK SE12 ....47 J3
Hornshay St PECK SE15 ....25 K5
Horns La WBY/YAL ME18 ....241 Q8
Horns Ldg TOWN TN10 * 189 G6
Horns Lodge La RTON TN11 ....188 D5
Horn's Oak Rd MEO DA13 ....97 J7
Horns Rd HAWK TN18 ....311 Q10
  HAWK TN18 ....312 B9
Horn St HYTHE CT21 ....223 J2
Horsa Rd BRCH CT7 ....176 A6
  DEAL CT14 ....209 L1
  ERITH DA8 ....31 J3
  LEE/GVPK SE12 ....47 K5
Horsebridge Rd WSTB CT5 ....126 D3
Horsecroft Cl ORP BR6 ....91 J4
Horseferry Rd GNWCH SE10 ....26 D5
Horsegrove Av WADH TN5 ....310 G8
Horselees Rd FAV ME13 ....247 M1
Horsell Rd STMC/STPC BR5 ....73 J8
Horseshoe Cl GILL ME7 ....102 A8
  MAID/BEAR ME14 ....141 M8
  POP/IOD E14 ....26 A7
Horseshoe La RTWE/PEM TN2 ....197 J4
Horseshoes La RMAID ME17 ....260 F1
Horsewash La ROCH ME1 ....19 J5
Horsfield Gdns ELTH/MOT SE9 ....47 M3
Horsfield Rd ELTH/MOT SE9 ....47 M3
Horsford Cl RDART DA2 ....52 D5
Horsford Rd BRXS/STRHM SW2 ....44 A3
Horsham La RHAM ME8 ....103 L2
Horsham Rd BXLYHS DA6 ....50 C3
The Horshams HB CT6 ....129 L4
Horsley Cl RFOLK CT18 ....220 L3
Horsley Dr CROY/NA CR0 ....105 H2
Horsley Rd BMLY BR1 ....71 J5
  ROCH ME1 ....19 H9
Horsley St WALW SE17 ....25 J8
Horsmans Pl DART DA1 * 51 M5
Horsman St CMBW SE5 ....24 E5
Horsmonden Cl ORP BR6 ....90 F3
Horsmonden Rd BROCKY SE4 ....46 A3
  STPH/PW TN12 ....279 M10
Horsted Av CHAT ME4 ....100 F4
Horsted Wy ROCH ME1 ....100 E6
Horton Downs
  MAID/SHEP ME15 ....168 A4
Horton Pl BH/WHM TN16 ....159 J4
Horton Rd EYN DA4 ....76 D7
Hortons Cl CRBK TN17 ....313 N5
Horton St LEW SE13 ....46 B5
Hortons Wy BH/WHM TN16 ....159 J4
Horton Wy CROY/NA CR0 ....87 L1
  EYN DA4 ....94 A3
Horwood Cl ROCH ME1 ....100 C5
Hoselands Vw HART DA3 ....77 N8
Hoser Av LEE/GVPK SE12 ....47 H7
Hoser Gdns BRCH CT7 ....176 C6
Hosey Common La
  BH/WHM TN16 ....159 K8
Hosey Common Rd
  BH/WHM TN16 ....159 K7
Hosey Hl BH/WHM TN16 ....159 K5
Hoskins Rd OXTED RH8 ....157 K7
Hoskins St GNWCH SE10 ....27 G5
Hoskins Wk OXTED RH8 ....157 K7
Hospital La CANT CT1 ....4 D3
  ROCH ME1 ....6 D1
Hospital Rd RMAID ME17 ....169 M5
Hospital Wy LEW SE13 ....46 D5
Hostier Cl STRD ME2 ....82 C1
Hotel Rd RDV CT15 ....215 J3
  RHAM ME8 ....102 A3
Hotham Cl EYN DA4 ....76 B4
  SWLY BR8 ....75 J1
Hothfield Pl BERM/RHTH SE16 ....25 J1
Hothfield Rd RHAM ME8 ....103 J1
Hotspur St LBTH SE11 ....24 B6
Hottsfield HART DA3 ....77 M1
Hougham Court La RDV CT15 ....216 B6
Houghton Av RTON TN11 ....116 F9

Houghton Green La RYE TN31 ....327 N12
Houghton La RYE TN31 ....327 N10
House Fld KEN/WIL TN24 ....3 L5
Housefield Rd FAV ME13 ....245 L11
Houselands Rd TON TN9 ....194 D3
Houseman Wy CMBW SE5 ....24 E6
Houston Rd FSTH SE23 ....45 M7
Hove Cl GRAYS RM17 ....34 A5
Hovenden Cl CANTW/ST CT2 ....172 B5
Hovendens CRBK TN17 ....299 L5
Hoveton Av BXLY DA5 ....49 K6
  ROCH ME1 ....100 E2
  SIT ME10 ....119 L6
Howard Cl IOS ME12 ....65 E2
Howard Dr MAIDW ME16 ....140 C2
Howard Gdns RTWE/PEM TN2 ....22 E9
Howard Rd BMLY BR1 ....71 H4
  BRDST CT10 ....183 J2
  CDW/CHF RM16 ....35 J2
  DART DA1 ....52 B2
  E/WMAL ME19 ....139 G5
  PGE/AN SE20 ....69 J1
  SNWD SE25 ....87 H1
Howards Crest Cl BECK BR3 ....70 B3
Howarth Rd ABYW SE2 ....29 H4
Howberry Rd THHTH CR7 ....68 B5
Howbury Cl ERITH DA8 ....31 H8
Howbury Rd PECK SE15 ....45 K1
Howden Rd SNWD SE25 ....69 G6
Howden St PECK SE15 ....45 H1
Howe Barracks CANT CT1 ....5 M3
Howells Cl BGR/WK TN15 ....111 K1
Howell Wk WALW SE17 ....24 C7
Howerd Wy WOOL/PLUM SE18 ....27 M7
Howfield La RASHW TN26 ....170 A8
How Green La EDEN TN8 ....193 M4
Howland Ms CANT CT1 * 4 C9
Howland Rd STPH/PW TN12 ....281 L5
Howland Vls STPH/PW TN12 * 281 L4
Howletts Rd HNHL SE24 ....44 E3
Howley Rd CROY/NA CR0 ....86 C6
Howlsmere Cl HNHL SE24 ....44 D2
Howson Rd BROCKY SE4 ....45 M2
Howt Gn SIT ME10 * 227 L12
Hoxton Cl ASH TN23 ....204 A3
Hoyland Cl PECK SE15 * 25 J6
The Hoystings Cl CANT CT1 ....5 H7
Hoy Ter WTHK RM20 * 33 J1
Hubbard Rd WNWD SE27 ....68 D1
Hubbards Hl RMAID ME17 ....243 Q12
  SEV TN13 ....255 J1
Hubble Dr MAID/SHEP ME15 ....167 M6
Hubert Wy BRDST CT10 ....179 H4
Huckleberry Cl WALD ME5 ....115 J2
Hucksteps Rw RYE TN31 ....225 H4
Hudson Cl CANTW/ST CT2 ....173 G3
  DVE/WH CT16 ....213 J4
  RHAM ME8 ....102 F4
Hudson Pl WOOL/PLUM SE18 ....28 C4
Hudson Rd BXLYHN DA7 ....30 C2
  CANT CT1 ....5 H4
Huggins Pl BRXS/STRHM SW2 ....44 A4
Hughes Dr STRD ME2 ....82 F3
Hughes Rd CDW/CHF RM16 ....35 J2
Hughes Wk CROY/NA CR0 ....86 D3
Hugh Price Cl SIT ME10 ....120 C4
Hugin Av BRDST CT10 ....179 H6
Hulkes La ROCH ME1 ....6 E3
Hull Rd LYDD TN29 ....335 M3
Hulme Pl STHWK SE1 * 24 D1
Hulsewood Cl RDART DA2 ....51 J8
Humber Av HB CT6 ....128 A3
Humber Crs STRD ME2 ....18 A2
Humber Rd BKHTH/KID SE3 ....27 H5
  DART DA1 ....51 J3
Humboldt Cl RTWE/PEM TN2 ....23 L1
Hume Av TIL RM18 ....55 J1
Hume Cl TIL RM18 ....55 H1
Humphrey St STHWK SE1 ....25 J4
Hundreds Cl WGOS CT8 ....177 G5
Hunger Hatch La HDCN TN27 ....263 P8
Hungerfield Pk STH/RUST TN4 ....22 H4
Hungershall Park Cl
  STH/RUST TN4 ....22 A8
Hunsdon Dr SEV TN13 ....21 H3
Hunsdon Rd NWCR SE14 ....25 L6
Hunstanton Cl RHAM ME8 ....116 F7
Hunt Cl BKHTH/KID SE3 * 27 H8
  RFOLK CT18 ....220 B1
Hunter Av KEN/WIL TN24 ....3 H9
  STHWK SE1 * 24 F2
Hunter Cl CMBW SE5 ....24 F8
Hunter Rd KEN/WIL TN24 ....3 H7
  THHTH CR7 ....68 B2
Hunters Bank RCANTW CT4 ....291 P5
Hunters Cha GDST RH9 ....184 A1
  HB CT6 ....129 K1
  WSTB CT5 ....126 F6
Hunters Cl BXLY DA5 ....50 B3
Huntersfield Cl WALD ME5 ....115 H3
Hunters Forstal Rd HB CT6 ....129 J1
Hunters Gv ORP BR6 ....90 D7
Hunters Meadow NRWD SE19 ....68 C1
Hunters Wk DEAL CT14 ....209 H4
  RSEV TN14 ....108 A3
Hunters Wy CROY/NA CR0 ....86 F7
  FAV ME13 ....246 B4
  RTWE/PEM TN2 ....201 G4
Hunters West
  WALD ME5 ....101 L3
Hunter Wy EDEN TN8 ....192 D2

Hurricane House
  WOOL/PLUM SE18 * 27 M6
Hurricane Rd E/WMAL ME19 ....164 A2
Hurstbourne Rd FSTH SE23 ....45 M6
Hurst Cl HAYES BR2 ....89 C4
  STPH/PW TN12 ....282 A5
  TENT TN30 ....315 L2
  WALD ME5 ....100 F7
Hurstdene Av HAYES BR2 ....89 H1
Hurst Farm Rd RSEV TN14 ....255 K2
Hurst Green Cl OXTED RH8 ....185 M7
Hurst Gv MSTR CT12 ....16 E1
Hurst Hl WALD ME5 ....114 F9
The Hurstings MAIDW ME16 ....12 B8
Hurstlands OXTED RH8 ....185 M7
Hurst La ABYW SE2 ....29 L4
  HDCN TN27 ....263 P9
  RFOLK CT18 ....221 J1
  RSEV TN14 ....255 N12
  SIT ME10 ....227 N12
Hurst Pl ABYW SE2 ....29 K4
  DART DA1 ....51 K4
  RHAM ME8 ....103 J5
Hurst Rd BFN/LL DA15 ....49 J3
  CROY/NA CR0 ....86 E8
  ERITH DA8 ....30 E8
Hurst Springs BXLY DA5 ....49 M6
Hurst St HNHL SE24 ....44 C4
The Hurst BGR/WK TN15 ....240 H7
  RTWE/PEM TN2 ....197 H6
Hurst Vls STPH/PW TN12 ....281 J4
Hurst Wy MAIDW ME16 ....166 A3
  SEV TN13 ....162 B5
Hurstwood WALD ME5 ....114 F9
Hurstwood Av BXLY DA5 ....49 M6
  ERITH DA8 ....30 F7
Hurstwood Dr BMLY BR1 ....72 A2
Hurstwood La STH/RUST TN4 ....22 A4
Hurstwood Pk STH/RUST TN4 ....22 C4
Hurstwood Rd GILL ME7 ....116 C4
Husheath Hl CRBK TN17 ....281 L11
Husseywell Crs HAYES BR2 ....89 H4
Hustlings Dr IOS ME12 ....65 G6
Hutchingson's
  CROY/NA CR0 ....105 H5
Hutching's St POP/IOD E14 ....26 B1
Hutsford Cl RHAM ME8 ....102 B8
Huxbear St BROCKY SE4 ....45 M4
Huxley Ct ROCH ME1 * 19 G3
Huxley Rd WELL DA16 ....49 G1
Hyacinth Rd STRD ME2 ....81 L7
Hybrid Cl ROCH ME1 ....100 L4
Hyde Dr STMC/STPC BR5 ....73 J8
Hyde Pl RCANTE CT3 ....251 Q12
Hyde Rd BXLYHN DA7 ....30 C2
  MAIDW ME16 ....140 E6
Hyder Rd CDW/CHF RM16 ....35 J2
Hydes Orch HDCN TN27 ....283 M4
Hyde St DEPT SE8 ....26 C6
The Hyde RCANTW CT4 ....248 D7
Hyde V GNWCH SE10 ....26 D6
Hylton St WOOL/PLUM SE18 ....29 G3
Hyndewood FSTH SE23 ....45 L8
Hyndman St PECK SE15 ....25 J5
Hyperion Dr STRD ME2 ....82 A4
Hyson Rd BERM/RHTH SE16 ....25 J4
Hythe Av BXLYHN DA7 ....29 M6
Hythe Cl FOLK CT20 ....11 G1
  STH/RUST TN4 ....196 D4
  STMC/STPC BR5 ....73 K8
Hythe Pl SWCH CT13 ....206 B1
Hythe Rd THHTH CR7 ....68 C3
  KEN/WIL TN24 ....2 C7
  LYDD TN29 ....320 H9
  RASHE TN25 ....288 G12
  SIT ME10 ....119 H3
  THHTH CR7 ....68 E6
Hythe St DART DA1 ....51 M4

I

Ian's Wk HYTHE CT21 ....223 H2
Ibis Cl WSTB CT5 ....126 C7
Icehouse Wd OXTED RH8 ....184 F1
Ickleton Rd ELTH/MOT SE9 ....71 M1
Ide Hill Rd RSEV TN14 ....254 A3
Iden Cl HAYES BR2 ....70 F7
Iden Crs STPH/PW TN12 ....281 K7
Iden La HDCN TN27 ....282 D6
Iden Rd RYE TN31 ....327 L11
  STRD ME2 ....82 D4
Idenwood Cl RHAM ME8 ....102 E7
Idleigh Court Rd HART DA3 ....96 C5
Idmiston Rd WNWD SE27 ....44 D8
Idonia St DEPT SE8 ....26 A6
Iffin La RCANTW CT4 ....249 M7
Ifield Cl MAID/SHEP ME15 ....168 A3
Ifield Wy GVE DA12 ....79 L3
Ightham By-Pass
  BGR/WK TN15 ....240 C2
Ightham Rd ERITH DA8 ....30 B6
  RTON TN11 ....240 B12
Ildersly Gv DUL SE21 ....44 E3
Ilderton Rd BERM/RHTH SE16 ....25 K5
Ilex Cl FOLKN CT19 ....10 C3
Ilex Wy STRHM/NOR SW16 ....68 B2
Ilfracombe Rd BMLY BR1 ....47 G8
Iliffe St WALW SE17 ....24 C4
Iliffe Yd WALW SE17 ....24 C4
Ilkley Rd NRWD SE19 ....68 E3
Illustrious Cl WALD ME5 ....101 H8
Imbert Cl NROM TN28 ....331 K7
Impala Gdns STH/RUST TN4 ....196 B4
Imperial Av IOS ME12 ....65 L6
Imperial Dr GVE DA12 ....80 A2
Imperial Ms IOS ME12 ....230 D2
Imperial Pl CHST BR7 ....72 B5
Imperial Rd GILL ME7 ....7 J6
Imperial Wy ASH TN23 ....286 H10
  CHST BR7 ....72 D8
Impton La WALD ME5 ....115 J3
Inca Dr ELTH/MOT SE9 ....48 C5
Ince Rd CANTW/ST CT2 ....173 G2
Inchmery Rd CAT SE6 ....46 F7
Independents Rd
  BKHTH/KID SE3 ....47 G1
Indescon Ct POP/IOD E14 ....26 C1
Indus Rd CHARL SE7 ....27 H7
Infant House
  WOOL/PLUM SE18 * 27 M6
Ingatestone Rd SNWD SE25 ....87 J2
Ingle Cl SAND/SEL CR2 ....104 C3
Ingham Rd SAND/SEL CR2 ....104 B3
Ingleborough La
  BGR/WK TN15 ....
Ingleborough St BRXN/ST SW9 ....24 B6
Ingleby Rd CDW/CHF RM16 ....35 J2
Ingleby Wy CHST BR7 ....72 B3
Ingle Cl BRCH CT7 ....
Ingleden Cl SIT ME10 ....120 A1

Ingleden Park Rd TENT TN30 301 N12
Ingledew Rd WOOL/PLUM SE18 28 E4
Inglemere Rd FSTH SE23 45 L8
Ingle Rd CHAT ME4 6 C9
Ingleside Cl BECK BR3 70 B4
Ingleside Gv BKHTH/KID SE3 27 G5
Ingles La FOLK CT20 11 J5
Ingles Rd FOLK CT20 11 G6
Ingleton Av WELL DA16 49 H3
Ingleton St BRXN/ST SW9 24 B8
Inglewood CROY/NA CR0 104 D3
SWLY BR8 * 74 F6
Inglewood Cl POP/IOD E14 26 B3
Inglewood Copse BMLY BR1 71 M6
Inglewood Rd BXLYHN DA7 50 E2
Inglis Rd CROY/NA CR0 87 G4
Inglis St CMBW SE5 24 C7
Ingoldsby Rd BRCH CT7 176 A6
CANT CT1 4 A9
FOLKN CT19 11 L1
GVE DA12 55 M6
Ingram Cl LBTH SE11 24 A3
Ingram Rd DART DA1 51 M6
GILL ME7 83 M8
GRAYS RM17 34 D3
THHTH CR7 68 D5
Ingress Park Av GRH DA9 53 K3
Ingress Ter MEO DA13 * 78 A1
Inigo Jones Rd CHARL SE7 27 L6
Inner Lines GILL ME7 6 F1
Innes St PECK SE15 24 F6
Innes Yd CROY/NA CR0 86 D6
Institute Rd CHAT ME4 6 F6
FAV ME13 149 L2
Instone Rd DART DA1 51 L5
Inverary Ct RAM CT11 * 183 H4
Inverine Rd CHARL SE7 27 J4
Invermore Pl
WOOL/PLUM SE18 28 D3
Inverness Ter BRDST CT10 183 K2
Inverton Rd PECK SE15 45 L2
Invicta Cl CHST BR7 72 B2
Invicta Ct SIT ME10 120 A2
Invicta Pde SCUP DA14 * 73 J1
Invicta Rd BKHTH/KID SE3 27 H6
FOLKN CT19 11 K1
IOS ME12 64 D3
MARG CT9 15 M9
RDART DA2 52 C4
WSTB CT5 127 G4
Inville Rd WALW SE17 24 E4
Inwood Cl CROY/NA CR0 87 M5
Iona Cl CAT SE6 46 B5
WALD ME5 115 L4
Iona Rd MAID/SHEP ME15 167 H6
Ionia Wk GVE DA12 56 A8
Irchester St RAM CT11 17 L5
Irchester Vls RAM CT11 * 17 L5
Irene Rd ORP BR6 91 G3
Ireton Pl GRAYS RM17 34 B3
Iris Av BXLY DA5 49 M4
Iris Cl CROY/NA CR0 87 L4
WALD ME5 115 H5
Iris Crs BXLYHN DA7 30 A5
Iron Bar La CANT CT1 5 G5
Iron Mill La DART DA1 51 G2
Iron Mill Pl DART DA1 51 G2
Ironside Cl BERM/RHTH SE16 25 L1
WALD ME5 101 H5
Ironstones RRTW TN3 200 C2
Irvine Dr MARG CT9 178 F5
Irvine Rd HOO/HM ME3 81 J2
Irvine Wy ORP BR6 91 G3
Irving Gv BRXN/ST SW9 24 A8
Irving Wy SWLY BR8 74 E6
Irwell Est BERM/RHTH SE16 * 25 K1
Irwin Av WOOL/PLUM SE18 28 F6
Isaac Wy STHWK SE1 24 D1
Isabella Dr ORP BR6 90 D7
Isabel St BRXN/ST SW9 24 A7
Isambard Ms POP/IOD E14 26 D2
Isis Cl HYTHE CT21 307 M10
Island Rd BERM/RHTH SE16 25 L3
CANTW/ST CT2 173 H3
RCANTE CT3 173 M1
RCANTE CT3 233 K12
Island Wall WSTB CT5 126 D4
Island Wy East CHAT ME4 83 J4
Island Wy West CHAT ME4 83 J3
Isla Rd WOOL/PLUM SE18 28 D5
Islehurst Cl CHST BR7 72 B5
Islingham Farm Rd
HOO/HM ME3 82 D2
Ismays Rd BGR/WK TN15 240 A7
Istead Ri MEO DA13 79 G4
Itchingwood Common Rd
OXTED RH8 185 K3
Ivanhoe Rd CMBW SE5 45 G1
HB CT6 129 H5
WGOS CT8 177 H4
Ivedon Rd WELL DA16 29 K8
Ivens Wy RMAID ME17 242 E11
Iverhurst Cl BXLYHS DA6 49 L3
Iversgate Cl RHAM ME8 103 G3
Ivers Wy CROY/NA CR0 105 G2
Ives Rd TON TN9 194 C4
Ivor Gv ELTH/MOT SE9 48 C6
Ivory Cl FAV ME13 123 H8
Ivorydown BMLY BR1 71 H1
Ivy Bower Cl GRH DA9 53 J3
Ivychurch Cl PGE/AN SE20 69 J4
Ivychurch Gdns MARG CT9 179 H3
Ivy Church La STHWK SE1 * 25 G4
Ivychurch Rd LYDD TN29 329 N3
Ivy Cl DART DA1 52 B4
GVE DA12 79 K1
RFOLK CT18 218 D2
RMAID ME17 261 L3
Ivy Cottage Hl MSTR CT12 181 H6
Ivy Ct CANTW/ST CT2 153 M7
STHWK SE1 * 25 H4
Ivydale Rd BROCKY SE4 45 L1
Ivyday Gv STRHM/NOR SW16 44 A8
Ivy House La SEV TN13 135 J3
Ivy House Rd WSTB CT5 127 G4
Ivy La CANT CT1 5 H5
RAM CT11 17 H7
RRTW TN3 294 F8
RSEV TN14 134 D2
Ivymount Rd WNWD SE27 44 B8
Ivy Pl CANT CT1 4 D7
ROCH ME1 * 100 B3
Ivy Rd BROCKY SE4 46 A2
Ivy St RHAM ME8 103 G5
Ivy Wy FOLKN CT19 220 F6
Izane Rd BXLYHS DA6 50 A2

J

Jaarlen Rd LYDD TN29 334 C3
Jacinth Dr SIT ME10 119 K3
Jackass La GDST RH9 184 A1
HAYES BR2 106 A1
Jack Bailey Rw FAV ME13 * 151 H3
Jacklin Cl WALD ME5 115 G2
Jackson Av ROCH ME1 100 F5
Jackson Cl GRH DA9 53 G3
RHAM ME8 102 D4
Jackson Rd CANT CT1 4 C6
HAYES BR2 89 M5
Jacksons La TENT TN30 315 M2
Jackson's Pl CROY/NA CR0 86 E4
Jackson St WOOL/PLUM SE18 28 B5
Jackson's Wy CROY/NA CR0 88 B6
Jacob Cl MARG CT9 178 B6
Jacob's La HOO/HM ME3 60 D7
Jacob St STHWK SE1 25 G1
Jacob Yd FAV ME13 * 149 L2
Jade Cl SIT ME10 119 K2
Jaffray Rd HAYES BR2 71 L8
Jaggard Wy STPH/PW TN12 281 R6
Jagger Cl RDART DA2 52 D5
Jago Cl WOOL/PLUM SE18 28 D5
Jago Wk CMBW SE5 24 E6
Jail La BH/WHM TN16 132 C1
Jamaica Rd STHWK SE1 25 G1
THHTH CR7 86 C2
Jamaica Ter MAID/BEAR ME14 141 H6
James Allchin Gdns
KEN/WIL TN24 203 J7
James Av BGR/WK TN15 * 111 K2
James Cl RCANTE CT3 236 A11
RFOLK CT18 291 M10
James Hall Gdns DEAL CT14 209 K6
James Haney Dr
KEN/WIL TN24 203 J6
James Joyes Wk HNHL SE24 * 44 C2
James Rd DART DA1 51 H5
STRD ME2 99 J3
James St ASH TN23 204 D1
CHAT ME4 6 D6
FOLKN CT19 11 K2
GILL ME7 7 K2
IOS ME12 64 E3
MAID/BEAR ME14 13 G2
RAM CT11 17 H7
ROCH ME1 19 K9
James Watt Wy ERITH DA8 30 F5
James Whatman Ct
MAID/SHEP ME15 * 13 L6
James Whatman Wy
MAID/BEAR ME14 12 E2
Janet St POP/IOD E14 26 B2
Janeway Pl BERM/RHTH SE16 25 J1
Janeway St BERM/RHTH SE16 25 H1
Japonica Cl WALD ME5 115 K3
Jarman's Fld RASHE TN25 266 G11
Jarrett Av STRD ME2 82 E3
Jarrett Cl BRXS/STRHM SW2 44 C6
Jarretts Cl RYE TN31 225 H4
Jarrow Rd BERM/RHTH SE16 25 K3
Jarvis Dr KEN/WIL TN24 205 K4
Jarvis La CRBK TN17 280 G12
Jarvis Pl TENT TN30 301 N10
Jarvis Rd EDUL SE22 44 F2
Jarvist Pl DEAL CT14 211 L3
Jasmine Cl E/WMAL ME19 139 G5
HAYES BR2 90 C5
RCANTW CT4 248 F8
Jasmine Ct LEE/GVPK SE12 47 H4
Jasmine Gdns CROY/NA CR0 88 C6
Jasmine Gv PGE/AN SE20 69 J5
Jasmine Pl RCANTE CT3 * 251 R1
Jasmine Rd E/WMAL ME19 139 G5
Jasmine Vls STPH/PW TN12 * 280 H4
Jason Wk ELTH/MOT SE9 72 B1
Jasper Av ROCH ME1 100 D3
Jasper Rd NRWD SE19 69 G3
Javelin Rd E/WMAL ME19 164 A2
Jay Gdns CHST BR7 72 A1
Jayne Wk WSTB CT5 126 C7
Jefferson Cl ASH TN23 204 C2
Jefferson Dr RHAM ME8 102 D4
Jefferson Rd IOS ME12 64 E4
Jefferstone Gdns LYDD TN29 331 M1
Jefferstone La LYDD TN29 331 L1
Jeffery St GILL ME7 7 L3
Jeffrey Cl STPH/PW TN12 281 R5
Jeffrey St MAID/BEAR ME14 13 H3
Jeken Rd ELTH/MOT SE9 47 K2
Jelf Rd BRXS/STRHM SW2 44 B3
Jellicoe Av GVE DA12 55 K8
Jellicoe Cl KEN/WIL TN24 205 K4
Jemmett La RASHE TN25 305 N2
Jemmett Rd ASH TN23 204 D3
Jenkins' Dl CHAT ME4 6 D8
Jenkins Dr MAID/SHEP ME15 167 M8
Jenner Cl SCUP DA14 73 H1
Jenner Rd ROCH ME1 100 D1
Jenner's Wy LYDD TN29 331 M2
Jenner Wy DIT/AY ME20 114 A7
Jennett Rd CROY/NA CR0 86 B6
Jennifer Ct HOO/HM ME3 * 59 M8
Jennifer Gdns MARG CT9 178 F5
Jennifer Rd BMLY BR1 47 G8
Jennings Rd EDUL SE22 45 G4
Jenningtree Rd ERITH DA8 31 J6
Jenningtree Wy BELV DA17 30 D1
Jenson Wy NRWD SE19 69 G4
Jenton Av BXLYHN DA7 29 M7
Jephson St CMBW SE5 24 E7
Jerningham Rd NWCR SE14 25 M8
Jerome Rd DIT/AY ME20 139 G1
Jerrard St LEW SE13 46 C1
Jersey Cl RASHE TN25 202 F3
Jersey Dr STMC/STPC BR5 90 E2
Jersey La RCANTW CT4 249 L11
Jersey Rd STRD ME2 18 E2
Jerviston Gdns
STRHM/NOR SW16 68 B3
Jervois House
WOOL/PLUM SE18 * 27 M6
Jeskyns Rd MEO DA13 79 L6
Jesmond Rd CROY/NA CR0 87 G3
Jesmond St FOLKN CT19 11 J3
Jessamine Pl RDART DA2 52 D5
Jessamine Ter SWLY BR8 * 74 D5
Jesse's Hl RCANTW CT4 269 R4
Jessett Cl ERITH DA8 30 E3
Jessica Ms CANT CT1 5 J2
SIT ME10 119 M2
Jesson Cl LYDD TN29 331 P1
Jessup Cl WOOL/PLUM SE18 28 D3
Jesuit Cl CANTW/ST CT2 172 B5
Jetty Rd HOO/HM ME3 60 E6
IOS ME12 64 A2
IOS ME12 230 D2
Jetty Wk GRAYS RM17 34 B5
Jevington Wy
LEE/GVPK SE12 47 J6
Jewell Gv STPH/PW TN12 281 J4
Jewels Hl WARL CR6 105 M6
Jewry La CANT CT1 4 F4
Jews Wk SYD SE26 69 J1
Jeyes Rd GILL ME7 7 J6
Jezreels Rd GILL ME7 7 L8
Jim Bradley Cl
WOOL/PLUM SE18 28 B3
Jiniwin Rd ROCH ME1 100 E6
Joan Crs ELTH/MOT SE9 47 L5
Jocelyn St PECK SE15 25 H7
Jockey La CRBK TN17 298 G8
Jodane Rd DEPT SE8 26 A3
Jodrell Wy WTHK RM20 33 G4
Johanna St STHWK SE1 24 B1
Johannesburg Rd
DVE/WH CT16 213 K5
John Badger Cl KEN/WIL TN24 203 H6
John Dutton Wy
KEN/WIL TN24 * 203 H7
John Felton Rd
BERM/RHTH SE16 * 25 H1
John Hall Cl FAV ME13 123 J7
John Harrison Wy
BERM/RHTH SE16 25 L2
GNWCH SE10 27 G2
John Maurice Cl STHWK SE1 24 E3
John McKenna Wk
BERM/RHTH SE16 * 25 H2
John Newington Cl
KEN/WIL TN24 203 H6
John Penn St LEW SE13 26 C7
John Roll Wy BERM/RHTH SE16 25 H2
John Ruskin St CMBW SE5 24 C6
Johns Cl HART DA3 96 A1
John's Cross Rd RBTBR TN32 322 G10
Johnsdale OXTED RH8 157 L7
John's Gn SWCH CT13 253 R3
John Silkin La DEPT SE8 25 L4
Johnson Av GILL ME7 83 K6
Johnson Cl GVW DA11 54 E8
KEN/WIL TN24 205 K4
Johnson Ct FAV ME13 123 J8
Johnson Rd CROY/NA CR0 86 E3
HAYES BR2 89 L1
SIT ME10 119 L5
Johnsons Av RSEV TN14 109 G4
Johnsons Wy GRH DA9 53 K4
Johnsons Whf GRH DA9 * 53 H2
Johnson Wy IOS ME12 65 H6
John's Rd BH/WHM TN16 132 C6
MEO DA13 97 G1
John's Ter CROY/NA CR0 86 F4
Johnston Cl BRXN/ST SW9 24 A7
John St BRDST CT10 * 183 L1
GRAYS RM17 34 D5
MAID/BEAR ME14 141 H7
ROCH ME1 19 K9
SNWD SE25 69 H8
STH/RUST TN4 22 E1
John Tapping Cl DEAL CT14 209 J8
John William Cl WTHK RM20 33 L4
John Williams Cl NWCR SE14 25 L5
John Wilson St
WOOL/PLUM SE18 28 B3
John Wooley Cl LEW SE13 * 46 F2
Joiners Arms Yd CMBW SE5 * 24 E7
Joiners Ct CHAT ME4 101 J3
Jointon Rd FOLK CT20 10 F6
Jonas Dr WADH TN5 309 K4
Jonas La WADH TN5 309 L3
Jonathan St LBTH SE11 24 A4
Jordan Cl MAID/SHEP ME15 167 M8
Joseph Hardcastle Cl
NWCR SE14 25 L6
Josephine Av
BRXS/STRHM SW2 44 A3
Josling Cl GRAYS RM17 34 A5
Joslin Rd PUR RM19 32 D4
Joss Gap Rd BRDST CT10 179 L4
Jowett St PECK SE15 25 G6
Joyce Cl CRBK TN17 298 F9
Joyce Green La DART DA1 31 L7
Joyden's Wood Rd BXLY DA5 74 E1
Joyes Cl DVE/WH CT16 213 H2
FOLKN CT19 220 F6
Joyes Rd DVE/WH CT16 213 H2
FOLKN CT19 11 L1
Joy La WSTB CT5 126 B6
Joy Rd GVE DA12 55 K6
Joy Wd RMAID ME17 167 L8
Jubilee Cl GRH DA9 53 K4
HYTHE CT21 321 Q1
Jubilee Crs BGR/WK TN15 240 B4
GVE DA12 55 M7
QBOR ME11 64 A8
Jubilee Fld TENT TN30 326 H1
Jubilee Ri BGR/WK TN15 136 E7
Jubilee Rd DEAL CT14 206 C6
ORP BR6 108 F1
RCANTE CT3 251 J1
SWCH CT13 206 A1
WTHK RM20 33 J5
Jubilee St SIT ME10 119 M4
Jubilee Ter GILL ME7 7 J1
The Jubilee GNWCH SE10 * 26 C6
Jubilee Wy DVE/WH CT16 214 B7
SCUP DA14 49 H7
Jubilee Wy (Elevated Rd)
DVE/WH CT16 9 J3
Judd Rd FAV ME13 149 H2
TON TN9 194 E6
Judeth Gdns GVE DA12 79 M2
Judkins Cl WALD ME5 101 K7
Juglans Rd ORP BR6 91 H4
Julian Pl POP/IOD E14 26 C4
Julian Rd FOLKN CT19 10 F4
ORP BR6 107 M1
Julians Cl SEV TN13 161 M5
Julians Wy SEV TN13 161 M5
Julian Tayler Pth FSTH SE23 * 45 J7
Julie Cl BRDST CT10 179 K7
Julien Pl KEN/WIL TN24 3 L9
Juliette Wy PUR RM19 32 A1
Junction Ap LEW SE13 46 D1
Junction Rd DART DA1 51 L4
GILL ME7 7 M6
RBTBR TN32 323 M3
Juniper Cl ASH TN23 204 B1
BH/WHM TN16 132 D3
CANT CT1 5 G9
MAIDW ME16 140 C7
RTWE/PEM TN2 197 G4
WALD ME5 115 H1
Juno Wy NWCR SE14 25 L5
Jupiter La ASH TN23 204 B6
Jurgens Rd PUR RM19 * 32 D3
Jury's Gap Rd LYDD TN29 333 L7
LYDD TN29 334 B4
Jury St GVE DA12 55 J4
Jutland Cl HOO/HM ME3 41 L6
Jutland Rd CAT SE6 46 D5
Juxon St LBTH SE11 24 A3

K

Kake St RCANTW CT4 268 B6
Kale Rd ERITHM DA18 29 L1
Kangley Bridge Rd SYD SE26 70 A2
Karen Ct BMLY BR1 71 G5
ELTH/MOT SE9 47 K3
Karloff Wy HOO/HM ME3 82 C3
Kashgar Rd WOOL/PLUM SE18 29 G4
Kashmir Rd CHARL SE7 27 L6
Katharine St CROY/NA CR0 86 D6
Katherine Ct WALD ME5 115 J3
Katherine Gdns ELTH/MOT SE9 47 L2
Katherine Rd EDEN TN8 192 D5
Kay St WELL DA16 29 J7
Kearsney Abbey Vls
DVE/WH CT16 * 212 E5
Keary Rd SWCM DA10 54 A5
Keat Farm Cl HB CT6 232 A4
Keating Cl ROCH ME1 100 B2
Keats Cl STHWK SE1 * 25 G3
Keats Gdns TIL RM18 35 J8
Keats Rd BELV DA17 30 D2
DIT/AY ME20 139 G2
WELL DA16 28 F7
Keats Wy CROY/NA CR0 87 K2
Kechill Gdns HAYES BR2 89 H3
Keddow's Cl HYTHE CT21 321 Q1
Kedleston Dr STMC/STPC BR5 91 G2
Keeble Cl WOOL/PLUM SE18 * 28 C5
Keedonwood Rd BMLY BR1 70 F1
Keefe Cl WALD ME5 114 E4
Keeley Ms GILL ME7 * 101 M2
Keeley Rd CROY/NA CR0 86 D5
Keel Gdns STH/RUST TN4 196 B5
Keeling Rd ELTH/MOT SE9 47 L3
Keemor Cl WOOL/PLUM SE18 * 28 B6
Keen's Rd CROY/NA CR0 86 D7
Keeper's Hl RCANTW CT4 175 L7
The Keep BKHTH/KID SE3 27 H8
Keesey St WALW SE17 24 E5
Keetons Rd BERM/RHTH SE16 25 J2
Keightley Dr ELTH/MOT SE9 48 D6
Keith Av EYN DA4 76 C3
MSTR CT12 16 A2
Keith Park Crs BH/WHM TN16 106 B6
Kelbrook Rd BKHTH/KID SE3 27 M8
Kelchers La RTON TN11 256 C8
Kellaway Rd BKHTH/KID SE3 27 L7
WALD ME5 115 H3
Kellerton Rd LEW SE13 46 F3
Kellett Rd BRXS/STRHM SW2 44 B2
Kelling Gdns CROY/NA CR0 86 C3
Kellner Rd THMD SE28 29 G2
Kell St STHWK SE1 24 C2
Kelly Av PECK SE15 25 G7
Kelly Dr GILL ME7 83 K6
Kelmore Gv EDUL SE22 45 H2
Kelsall Cl BKHTH/KID SE3 27 J8
Kelsey La BECK BR3 70 B7
Kelsey Park Av BECK BR3 70 C7
Kelsey Park Rd BECK BR3 70 B6
Kelsey Rd STMC/STPC BR5 73 J6
Kelsey Sq BECK BR3 70 B6
Kelsey Wy BECK BR3 70 B7
Kelso Dr GVE DA12 80 A1
Kelvedon Rd DEAL CT14 209 K7
Kelvin Cl TONN TN10 189 G6
Kelvin Gv SYD SE26 45 J8
Kelvington Cl CROY/NA CR0 87 M3
Kelvington Rd PECK SE15 45 L3
Kelvin Pde ORP BR6 90 F4
Kelvin Rd TIL RM18 35 H8
WELL DA16 49 H1
Kemble Cl RTWE/PEM TN2 197 H6
Kemble Dr HAYES BR2 89 M6
Kemble Rd CROY/NA CR0 86 C6
FSTH SE23 45 L6
Kembleside Rd BH/WHM TN16 132 B4
Kemerton Rd BECK BR3 70 C6
CMBW SE5 44 D1
CROY/NA CR0 87 G3
Kemnal Rd CHST BR7 72 D3
Kemp Cl WALD ME5 114 F1
Kempes Pl RASHE TN25 * 266 F11
Kemp Gdns CROY/NA CR0 86 D2
Kemp Rd WSTB CT5 127 K3
Kempsford Rd LBTH SE11 24 B3
Kempthorne Rd DEPT SE8 25 M3
Kempthorne St GVW DA11 * 55 J4
Kempton Cl ERITH DA8 30 D5
WALD ME5 115 K2
Kempton Wk CROY/NA CR0 87 M2
Kempt St WOOL/PLUM SE18 28 B5
Kemsdale Rd FAV ME13 151 G3
Kemsing Cl BXLY DA5 49 M5
THHTH CR7 * 68 D8
Kemsing Gdns CANTW/ST CT2 172 C5
Kemsing Rd BGR/WK TN15 238 A11
GNWCH SE10 27 H4
Kemsley Cl GRH DA9 53 J4
GVW DA11 79 G1
Kemsley Rd BH/WHM TN16 132 C5
Kemsley Street Rd
MAID/BEAR ME14 116 D4
Kenardington Rd
RASHW TN26 317 L7
Kenbrook KEN/WIL TN24 202 F4
Kenbury St CMBW SE5 24 D8
Kendal Cl CMBW SE5 24 C6
RAM CT11 16 C6
Kendal Dr TON TN9 194 F3
Kendale CDW/CHF RM16 35 J2
Kendale Rd BMLY BR1 70 F2
Kendall Av BECK BR3 69 M6
E/WMAL ME19 164 D2
Kendall Rd BECK BR3 69 M6
WOOL/PLUM SE18 27 M7
Kendal Meadow WSTB CT5 127 L4
Kendal Pk STH/RUST TN4 22 A2
Kendal Ri BRDST CT10 179 K8
Kendal Wy RHAM ME8 102 E5
Kender St NWCR SE14 25 K6
Kenfield Rd RCANTW CT4 248 H11
Kenilworth Cl RDV CT15 215 H3
Kenilworth Ct SIT ME10 119 K4
Kenilworth Dr RHAM ME8 102 E7
Kenilworth Gdns
WOOL/PLUM SE18 28 C8
Kenilworth Rd PGE/AN SE20 69 L5
STMC/STPC BR5 90 D2
Kenley Cl BXLY DA5 50 B5
CHST BR7 72 F7
Kenley Gdns THHTH CR7 68 C8
Kenmare Rd THHTH CR7 86 B2
Kenmere Rd WELL DA16 29 K8
Kennard Cl ROCH ME1 100 A3
Kennedy Cl FAV ME13 123 L8
STMC/STPC BR5 90 E4
Kennedy Dr DEAL CT14 209 J7
Kennedy Gdns SEV TN13 21 L2
Kennedy Wk WALW SE17 * 24 E3
Kennel Barn Rd RSIT ME9 144 D4
Kennel Hl RDV CT15 272 G7
Kennelling Rd FAV ME13 244 H12
Kennel Wood Crs
CROY/NA CR0 105 J5
Kennet Rd DART DA1 51 H1
TONN TN10 188 F8
Kennett Dr DEAL CT14 209 H7
Kennett La RASHE TN25 307 N5
Kenning St BERM/RHTH SE16 25 K1
Kennings Wy LBTH SE11 24 B4
Kennington Cl
MAID/SHEP ME15 168 A5
RHAM ME8 102 C1
Kennington Gv LBTH SE11 24 A5
Kennington La LBTH SE11 24 A4
Kennington Ov LBTH SE11 24 A5
Kennington Park Gdns
LBTH SE11 24 C5
Kennington Park Pl
WALW SE17 24 B5
Kennington Park Rd LBTH SE11 24 B5
Kennington Pl KEN/WIL TN24 203 G4
Kennington Rd KEN/WIL TN24 3 M5
LBTH SE11 24 B2
Kensington Av THHTH CR7 68 B5
Kensington Ct GRAYS RM17 * 34 D5
Kensington Rd CANT CT1 172 D5
Kent Av CANT CT1 5 M5
IOS ME12 65 J7
KEN/WIL TN24 2 A3
MAID/SHEP ME15 167 K4
SIT ME10 119 L6
WELL DA16 49 G3
Kent Cl BGR/WK TN15 * 111 K2
ORP BR6 107 K1
ROCH ME1 100 D5
STPH/PW TN12 279 K3
Kent Gdns BRCH CT7 176 D6
Kent Gate Wy CROY/NA CR0 104 E1
Kent Hatch Rd OXTED RH8 158 B8
Kent House La BECK BR3 69 M3
Kent House Rd BECK BR3 69 L4
Kentish Gdns RTWE/PEM TN2 200 F5
Kentish Rd BELV DA17 30 B3
Kentish Wy BMLY BR1 71 J6
Kentlea Rd THMD SE28 28 F1
Kentmere Av RAM CT11 182 C6
Kentmere Rd
WOOL/PLUM SE18 28 F3
Kenton Gdns MSTR CT12 180 E7
Kent Pl RAM CT11 17 L6
Kent Rd DART DA1 51 M4
FOLKN CT19 219 M6
GRAYS RM17 34 D5
GVW DA11 55 H6
HART DA3 77 L6
IOS ME12 64 C4
MARG CT9 15 M8
SNOD ME6 113 H7
STH/RUST TN4 196 D7
STMC/STPC BR5 91 J2
STRD ME2 99 H7
WWKM BR4 88 C4
Kent St WBY/YAL ME18 241 R7
WSTB CT5 126 E5
Kent Ter HOO/HM ME3 * 57 L6
MEO DA13 * 97 H6
RAM CT11 17 L6
RHAM ME8 103 K3
Kent Vw SOCK/AV RM15 32 D1
Kent View Dr IOS ME12 229 N4
Kentwell Cl BROCKY SE4 * 45 M2
Kenward Ct RTON TN11 256 B5
Kenward Rd ELTH/MOT SE9 47 K3
MAIDW ME16 140 D8
WBY/YAL ME18 257 P2
Kenwood Av HART DA3 78 D7
WALD ME5 115 H1
Kenwood Dr BECK BR3 70 D7
Kenwyn Rd DART DA1 51 L3
Kenya Rd CHARL SE7 27 L6
Kenya Ter MAID/BEAR ME14 141 H6
Kerfield Crs CMBW SE5 24 E7
Kerfield Pl CMBW SE5 24 E7
Kerry Av PUR RM19 32 A1
Kerry Hill Wy
MAID/BEAR ME14 140 F7
Kerry Pth NWCR SE14 26 A5
Kerry Rd NWCR SE14 26 A5
Kersey Dr SAND/SEL CR2 104 B6
Kershaw Cl CDW/CHF RM16 33 K2
Kerton Rd LYDD TN29 335 N6
Kesteven Cl STRD ME2 99 H8
Keston Av HAYES BR2 89 K8
Keston Cl WELL DA16 29 K6
Keston Ct RHAM ME8 * 102 B3
Keston Gdns HAYES BR2 89 K7
Keston Park Cl HAYES BR2 90 A7
Keston Rd PECK SE15 45 H1
THHTH CR7 86 A2
Kestrel Av HNHL SE24 44 C3
Kestrel Cl SIT ME10 120 B7
Kestrel Pl NWCR SE14 * 25 M5
Kestrel Rd WALD ME5 115 K3
Kestrel Wy CROY/NA CR0 105 J3
Keswick Cl TON TN9 194 F3
Keswick Dr MAIDW ME16 140 D8
Keswick Rd BXLYHN DA7 30 B8
ORP BR6 91 G4
SIT ME10 120 D6
WWKM BR4 88 F5
Ketridge La WBY/YAL ME18 164 E3
Kettle Dr RFOLK CT18 292 G12
Kettle Hl FAV ME13 245 J5
Kettle Hill Rd FAV ME13 244 H4
FAV ME13 245 J4
Kettle La MAID/SHEP ME15 165 M6
Kettlewell Ct SWLY BR8 75 G6
Kevin Dr RAM CT11 16 C7
Kevington Cl STMC/STPC BR5 73 G8
Kevington Dr CHST BR7 73 G8
Kewlands MAID/BEAR ME14 13 M1
Keycol Hl RSIT ME9 118 F4
Keyes Av CHAT ME4 101 G3
Keyes Gdns TON TN9 194 C6
Keyes Pl FOLKN CT19 220 F6
Keyes Rd DART DA1 52 B2
Keymer Cl BH/WHM TN16 132 B2
Keymer Rd BRXS/STRHM SW2 44 A7
Keynsham Gdns ELTH/MOT SE9 47 M3
Keynsham Rd ELTH/MOT SE9 47 L3
Keyse Rd STHWK SE1 25 G2
The Keys RFOLK CT18 292 H12
Key St SIT ME10 119 H4
Keyworth Cl STPH/PW TN12 279 J3
Keyworth Ms CANT CT1 5 J1
Keyworth St STHWK SE1 24 C2
Kezia St DEPT SE8 25 M4
Khartoum Pl GVE DA12 55 K4
Khartoum Rd CHAT ME4 6 E2
Khartoum Sq DVE/WH CT16 213 H3
Khyber Rd GILL ME7 83 J6
Kibbles La STH/RUST TN4 196 B5
Kibworth St VX/NE SW8 24 A6
Kidbrooke Gdns
BKHTH/KID SE3 27 H8
Kidbrooke Gv BKHTH/KID SE3 27 H7
Kidbrooke La ELTH/MOT SE9 47 M2
Kidbrooke Park Cl
BKHTH/KID SE3 27 J7
Kidbrooke Park Rd
BKHTH/KID SE3 27 J8
ELTH/MOT SE9 47 J3
Kidbrooke Wy BKHTH/KID SE3 27 J8
Kidderminster Pl CROY/NA CR0 86 C4
Kidderminster Rd
CROY/NA CR0 86 C4
Kidd Pl CHARL SE7 27 M4
Kilbride Ct BRDST CT10 * 183 J4
Kilgour Rd FSTH SE23 45 M4
Killearn Rd CAT SE6 46 E6
Killewarren Wy
STMC/STPC BR5 91 K3
Killick Cl SEV TN13 135 K7
Killick Rd HOO/HM ME3 59 L8
Kilmartin Av STRHM/NOR SW16 68 B7
Kilmorie Rd FSTH SE23 45 M6
Kiln Barn Rd DIT/AY ME20 139 K5
Kilnbridge Cl
MAID/SHEP ME15 166 C6
Kiln Cl RASHE TN25 265 N4
SIT ME10 120 B6

Kilndown GVE DA12 79 K3
Kilndown Cl ASH TN23 204 B5
MAIDW ME15 140 D6
Kilndown Gdns CANTW/ST CT2 172 B5
MARG CT9 179 H3
Kiln Dr RYE TN31 225 G4
Kiln Fld TENT TN30 315 P2
Kiln La RASHW TN26 305 P9
RTON TN11 255 N12
Kiln Rd RASHE TN25 305 Q9
Kiln Wy GRAYS RM17 34 A4
STPH/PW TN12 279 K4
Kilnwood RSEV TN14 108 E7
Kimbell Pl ELTH/MOT SE9 47 K2
Kimberley Av PECK SE15 25 J8
Kimberley Cl DVE/WH CT16 213 K6
Kimberley Dr SCUP DA14 49 J7
Kimberley Gv WSTB CT5 126 A7
Kimberley Rd BRCH CT7 69 C6
CROY/NA CR0 86 C2
GILL ME7 7 L7
MSTR CT12 182 D4
Kimbolton Cl LEE/GVPK SE12 47 G4
Kimmeridge Gdns ELTH/MOT SE9 71 M1
Kimmeridge Rd ELTH/MOT SE9 71 M1
Kimpton Rd CMBW SE5 24 E7
Kinburn St BERM/RHTH SE16 * 25 L1
Kincaid Rd PECK SE15 25 J6
Kincraig Dr SEV TN13 20 F3
Kinfauns Rd BRXS/STRHM SW2 44 B2
King Alfred Av CAT SE6 46 B8
King Arthur Cl PECK SE15 25 K6
King Arthur Rd MSTR CT12 182 A6
King Arthur's Dr STRD ME2 82 B4
Kingcup Cl CROY/NA CR0 87 L4
King Edward St WSTB CT5 126 E4
King Edward Dr CDW/CHF RM16 34 F2
King Edward Rd BRCH CT7 176 D8
CHAT ME4 6 C9
DEAL CT14 209 K1
GILL ME7 84 A7
GRH DA9 53 H3
MAID/SHEP ME15 13 L7
RAM CT11 16 E6
ROCH ME1 19 J8
King Edward the Third Ms BERM/RHTH STHWK SE1 25 J1
King Edward Wk STHWK SE1 24 B2
Kingfield Rd HB CT6 128 E6
Kingfisher Av HYTHE CT21 232 K4
Kingfisher Cl KEN/WIL TN24 205 K4
MARG CT9 177 L5
RSIT ME9 227 M10
STMC/STPC BR5 73 L8
WSTB CT5 126 D6
Kingfisher Dr GRH DA9 53 H3
WALD ME5 101 K6
Kingfisher Gdns SAND/SEL CR2 104 C4
Kingfisher Rd DIT/AY ME20 139 G3
Kingfisher Wk BRDST CT10 * 179 J8
Kingfisher Wy CROY/NA CR0 87 L1
King Gdns CROY/NA CR0 86 A8
King Garth Ms FSTH SE23 45 K7
King George Rd WALD ME5 114 F4
King George St GNWCH SE10 26 D6
George VI HII RTW TN1 23 J1
George VI Av TIL RM18 36 C3
King Harolds Wy BXLYHN DA7 29 L6
King Henry Ms ORP BR6 91 G8
King Henry's Dr CROY/NA CR0 104 D5
King Hl E/WMAL ME19 138 B8
King James St STHWK SE1 24 C1
King John's Wk ELTH/MOT SE9 47 M5
Kinglake Est WALW SE17 * 24 E6
Kinglake St WALW SE17 25 J7
King Lear's Wy DVW CT17 * 217 J4
King & Queen Cl ELTH/MOT SE9 71 M1
King & Queen St WALW SE17 24 D6
Kings Acre MAID/SHEP ME15 168 B4
Kingsand Rd LEE/GVPK SE12 47 G3
King's Av ASH TN23 204 D1
BMLY BR1 71 G3
BRCH CT7 176 A5
BRDST CT10 179 J6
MSTR CT12 16 D1
ROCH ME1 100 D2
RYE TN31 225 J3
SWCH CT13 207 G2
WSTB CT5 126 D6
King's Bank La RYE TN31 325 N11
King's Bastion GILL ME7 6 F4
Kings Bench St STHWK SE1 24 C1
Kingsbridge Ct POP/IOD E14 26 B4
Kings Cha MAID/BEAR ME14 3 M5
Kings Cl DART DA1 50 F2
DEAL CT14 211 K4
Kingscote Rd CROY/NA CR0 87 J3
King's Ct STHWK SE1 * 24 C1
Kingsdale Rd PGE/AN SE20 69 L5
WOOL/PLUM SE18 29 G5
Kingsdown Chambers WSTB CT5 * 127 G2
Kingsdown Cl BERM/RHTH SE16 * 25 J4
GILL ME7 116 C1
GVE DA12 56 A6
MAIDW ME16 140 C4
Kingsdown Hi DEAL CT14 211 K6
Kingsdown Pk DEAL CT14 * 211 L4
WSTB CT5 127 G3
Kingsdown Rd DEAL CT14 209 L7
RDV CT15 215 G3
RSIT ME9 146 D6
Kingsdown Wy HAYES BR2 89 H2
Kings Dr GVE DA12 55 J8
Kingsferry Br RSIT ME9 227 P6
Kingsfield Rd HB CT6 129 J7
Kingsfield Ter DART DA1 * 51 L4
Kingsford St KEN/WIL TN24 288 E12
RASHE TN25 305 P9
Kingsford Ter ASH TN23 * 204 D5
Kingsgate Av BRDST CT10 179 J4
Kingsgate Bay BRDST CT10 179 K3
Kingsgate Cl BXLYHN DA7 29 M1
MAIDW ME16 140 A3
STMC/STPC BR5 73 K7
Kingsgate La TENT TN30 315 P12
Kingsground ELTH/MOT SE9 47 M5
King's Gv PECK SE15 25 J7
Kings Hall Ms LEW SE13 46 C1
Kings Hall Rd BECK BR3 46 E8
King's Head Wy IOS ME12 68 F5
Kingshill Av WOOL/PLUM SE18 28 F5
Kingshill Dr HOO/HM ME3 59 M7
Kingsholm Gdns ELTH/MOT SE9 47 K6
Kingshurst Rd LEE/GVPK SE12 47 H5
Kingsingfield Rd BGR/WK TN15 211 K2
Kingsingfield Rd BGR/WK TN15 111 K2
Kings Keep HAYES BR2 * 70 F7

Kingsland Gdns DEAL CT14 211 J1
Kingsland Gv HDCN TN27 283 L4
Kingsland Hollow LYDD TN29 331 P1
Kingsland La HDCN TN27 262 H12
RASHE TN25 202 C4
Kings La STPH/PW TN12 280 B2
Kingsleigh Wk HAYES BR2 * 71 G3
Kingsley Av DART DA1 52 B3
Kingsley Ms CHST BR7 72 C3
MAID/SHEP ME15 13 H6
ORP BR6 107 L1
WSTB CT5 126 B3
Kingsley Rd CDW/CHF RM16 35 H3
Kingsley Wood Dr ELTH/MOT SE9 48 A8
Kingslyn Crs NRWD SE19 68 F7
Kingsman St WOOL/PLUM SE18 28 A3
Kingsmarsh La LYDD TN29 330 D9
FOLKN CT19 220 C6
Kingsmead Cl BFN/LL DA15 49 H7
Kingsmead Ct CANTW/ST CT2 * 172 B7
Kings Meadow KEN/WIL TN24 203 H4
Kingsmead Pk STPH/PW TN12 279 L3
Kingsmead Rd BRXS/STRHM SW2 44 B3
Kings Ms CANT CT1 * 5 J7
RAM CT11 17 G6
Kings Mill Cl SIT ME10 119 M4
Kingsnorth Gdns FOLK CT20 11 G5
Kingsnorth Rd ASH TN23 204 D5
FAV ME13 149 K3
RHAM ME8 102 D1
Kingsoak Ms WALD ME5 115 G1
King's Orch ELTH/MOT SE9 47 M4
ROCH ME1 19 K7
Kings Pde ASH TN23 * 2 B7
King's Pk CANT CT1 * 5 J4
Kings Reach MAID/SHEP ME15 167 L5
Kingsridge Gdns DART DA1 51 H5
Kings Rd BH/WHM TN16 132 B3
BRCH CT7 176 D7
DVW CT17 217 H2
FAV ME13 149 K3
FOLK CT20 219 L7
HB CT6 128 F5
HDCN TN27 283 K4
IOS ME12 65 J8
ORP BR6 91 G7
RAM CT11 17 G3
RCANTE CT3 251 Q12
SNWD SE25 69 H7
TON TN9 194 F5
WALD ME5 101 K6
Kings Ropewalk DVW CT17 * 217 J4
Kings Rw MAID/SHEP ME15 * 167 H4
Kings Standing Wy RTWE/PEM TN2 197 J3
King Stairs Cl BERM/RHTH SE16 25 J7
Kingsthorpe Rd SYD SE26 69 L1
Kings Toll Rd RTWE/PEM TN3 278 D11
Kingston Av MARG CT9 177 L6
Kingston Cl DVW CT17 215 G6
HB CT6 129 M4
MSTR CT12 182 E4
Kingston Crs BECK BR3 70 A2
WALD ME5 115 J1
Kingston Dr MAID/SHEP ME15 167 H5
Kingston Pde ASH RM17 * 34 C3
Kingston Sq NRWD SE19 68 C1
King St CANT CT1 4 F3
CANTW/ST CT2 173 G5
CHAT ME4 6 C5
DEAL CT14 209 K3
DVE/WH CT16 8 D5
E/WMAL ME19 138 C5
GILL ME7 7 K3
GVE DA12 55 J4
IOS ME12 64 B3
LYDD TN29 329 M2
MAID/BEAR ME14 13 H4
MARG CT9 14 F2
RAM CT11 17 G3
ROCH ME1 19 K9
SIT ME10 119 M4
SWCH CT13 237 K12
Kings Wk MAID/BEAR ME14 13 J1
SAND/SEL CR2 104 A4
Kings Wy CROY/NA CR0 86 A8
Kingsway LYDD TN29 321 K7
STMC/STPC BR5 90 E1
WALD ME5 101 L4
WKM BR4 70 F2
Kingsway Av SAND/SEL CR2 104 B3
Kingswear Gdns STRD ME2 19 H4
Kingswood Av BELV DA17 30 A3
CHAT ME4 100 F3
HAYES BR2 70 F7
SAND/SEL CR2 130 A1
SWCH CT13 75 G8
THHTH CR7 68 B1
Kingswood Cl DART DA1 51 K4
ORP BR6 90 E3
RTWE/PEM TN2 23 H1
Kingswood Ct LEW SE13 46 C3
Kingswood Dr NRWD SE19 68 C1
Kingswood La WARL CR6 130 B1
Kingswood Pl LEW SE13 46 F3
Kingswood Rd GILL ME7 * 7 G7
HAYES BR2 70 F7
PGE/AN SE20 69 K3
ROCH ME1 114 D7
RTWE/PEM TN2 23 K5
SEV TN13 135 K7
Kingswood Vls DVW CT17 * 213 K7
Kingswood Wy SAND/SEL CR2 104 C6
Kingsworth Cl BECK BR3 87 M1
King William La GNWCH SE10 26 F4
King William Rd GILL ME7 23 K6
King William Wk GNWCH SE10 26 D5
Kinlet Rd WOOL/PLUM SE18 28 C8
Kinnaird Av BMLY BR1 71 J2
Kinnaird Cl BMLY BR1 71 J2
Kinnings Rw TON TN9 194 F3
Kinross Cl WALD ME5 101 J6
Kinsale Rd PECK SE15 45 H1
Kintyre Cl STRHM/NOR SW16 68 A6
Kinveachy Gdns CHARL SE7 27 M4
Kinver Rd SYD SE26 69 J2
Kipling Av TIL RM18 35 J2
Kipling Dr DIT/AY ME20 139 G3
Kipling Est STHWK SE1 * 24 E1
Kipling Rd ASH TN23 204 A4
BXLYHN DA7 29 H2
DART DA1 51 L1
Kipling St STHWK SE1 24 E1
Kipping Cl RFOLK CT18 220 A2
Kippington Dr ELTH/MOT SE9 47 M3
Kippington Rd SEV TN13 20 F7
Kirby Cl BRDST CT10 * 298 C19
Kirby Est BERM/RHTH SE16 * 25 J1
Kirby Gv STHWK SE1 * 24 F1
Kirby La HOO/HM ME3 58 F8

RDART DA2 52 D5
Kirby's La CANTW/ST CT2 4 E3
Kirkdale SYD SE26 45 J7
Kirkdale Cl WALD ME5 115 L4
Kirkdale Cnr SYD SE26 * 45 J8
Kirkdale Rd MAID/SHEP ME15 167 G1
RTW TN1 23 F5
Kirkham St WOOL/PLUM SE18 28 F5
Kirkham Cl STPH/PW TN12 279 F14
Kirkland Cl BFN/LL DA15 48 F4
Kirkland Ter BECK BR3 70 B3
Kirk La WOOL/PLUM SE18 28 D6
Kirklees Rd THHTH CR7 68 B5
Kirkside Rd BKHTH/KID SE3 27 H5
Kirkstone Av RAM CT11 182 C6
Kirkstone Wy BMLY BR1 70 F1
Kirkwood Rd PECK SE15 25 J8
Kirtley Rd SYD SE26 69 M1
Kirton Cl RFOLK CT18 220 A1
Kirwyn Wy CMBW SE5 24 D6
Kitchener Av CHAT ME4 101 G4
GVE DA12 79 K1
Kitchener Cl RCANTW CT4 270 D5
Kitchener Rd DVW CT17 217 H2
HOO/HM ME3 83 C1
STRD ME2 18 F1
THHTH CR7 68 C2
Kite Farm WSTB CT5 127 L2
Kite La STPH/PW TN12 279 K11
Kitewell La LYDD TN29 334 E1
Kither Rd ASH TN23 204 D4
Kit Hill FAV ME13 247 J1
Kit Hill Rd WALD ME5 114 F2
Kitley Gdns NRWD SE19 69 G5
Kitsbridge La RASHW TN26 318 G5
RASHW TN26 319 K4
Kitson Rd CMBW SE5 24 D5
SAND/SEL CR2 104 D4
Kitto Rd NWCR SE14 25 L8
Knapdale Cl FSTH SE23 45 K3
Knapmill Rd CAT SE6 46 B7
Knapmill Wy CAT SE6 46 B7
Knatchbull Rd CMBW SE5 24 C7
Knatchbull Wy RASHE TN25 289 M12
Knatts La BGR/WK TN15 111 K5
Knatts Valley Rd EYN DA4 111 H1
Knaves Acre HDCN TN27 283 L4
Knave Wood Rd BGR/WK TN15 136 D3
Knee Hl ABYW SE2 29 K4
Knee Hill Crs ABYW SE2 29 K4
Knelle Rd RBTBR TN32 322 E9
Kneller Rd BROCKY SE4 45 M2
Knight Av CANTW/ST CT2 171 K5
GILL ME7 7 M1
Knighthead Point POP/IOD E14 * 26 B1
Knighton Park Rd SYD SE26 69 M1
Knighton Rd RSEV TN14 135 L3
Knightrider Ct MAID/SHEP ME15 * 13 C6
Knightrider St MAID/SHEP ME15 * 13 C6
SWCH CT13 237 K12
Knight's Av BRDST CT10 179 L7
Knightsbridge La STH/RUST TN4 22 C2
RTWE/PEM TN2 278 A10
Knights Cft HART DA3 96 A7
Knightsfield Rd SIT ME10 119 L2
Knights Hl WNWD SE27 68 C2
Knight's Hill Sq WNWD SE27 68 C1
Knights Manor Wy DART DA1 52 A4
RMAID ME17 242 F11
Knights Pk RTWE/PEM TN2 197 J3
Knights Pl RTWE/PEM TN2 278 A10
Knights Rdg ORP BR6 91 J8
Knight's Rd RTWE/PEM TN2 278 A10
HOO/HM ME3 59 L7
Knights Templar DVW CT17 * 217 J4
Knights Wk LBTH SE11 24 C5
Knights Wy CROY/NA CR0 213 H6
HDCN TN27 283 L4
RTWE/PEM TN2 197 J3
Knockhall Cha GRH DA9 53 K3
Knockhall Rd GRH DA9 53 K4
Knock Hl TENT TN30 327 R5
Knockholt Rd ELTH/MOT SE9 47 L6
MARG CT9 179 H2
RSEV TN14 108 B8
Knock Mill La BGR/WK TN15 111 M7
Knock Rd ASH TN23 204 D4
Knockwood Rd TENT TN30 301 P12
Knold Pk MARG CT9 14 E9
Knole Cl CROY/NA CR0 * 87 G2
Knole La BGR/WK TN15 111 K5
Knole Rd DART DA1 51 H5
SEV TN13 21 L3
WALD ME5 115 K3
The Knole ELTH/MOT SE9 72 F1
FAV ME13 149 J2
MEO DA13 78 F4
Knole Wy BGR/WK TN15 21 J6
Knoll Hl RASHE TN25 306 B10
Knoll La ASH TN23 204 B4
Knoll Pl DEAL CT14 209 K8
Knoll Ri ORP BR6 91 G4
Knoll Rd BXLY DA5 50 B5
BXLYHN DA7 29 K7
SCUP DA14 50 B2
The Knoll BECK BR3 70 C5
HAYES BR2 89 H6
Knoll Wy IOS ME12 230 C1
Knolly's Cl STRHM/NOR SW16 44 B8
Knolly's Rd STRHM/NOR SW16 44 B8
Knott Cl MAID/BEAR ME14 141 H7
Knott Crs KEN/WIL TN24 205 L4
Knott's La CANT CT1 5 J3
RDV CT15 215 G5
Knotts Pl SEV TN13 20 E6
Knowle Av BXLYHN DA7 29 M6
Knowle Cl BRXN/ST SW9 44 F2
RRTW TN3 199 M4
Knowle La STPH/PW TN12 279 N6
Knowle Rd HAYES BR2 89 M5
MAID/BEAR ME14 141 H7
ROCH ME1 19 G3
STPH/PW TN12 279 N6
Knowles Gdns HDCN TN27 283 L4
Knowles Hill Crs LEW SE13 46 D4
Knowlton Gn HAYES BR2 89 H6
Knowlton Wk CANT CT1 5 M3
Knowsley Wy RTON TN11 188 E10
Knoyle St NWCR SE14 25 M5
Kohima Pl DVE/WH CT16 214 A4
Koonowla Cl BH/WHM TN16 130 A5
Kooringa WARL CR6 130 A5
Kossuth St GNWCH SE10 26 F4
Kuala Gdns STRHM/NOR SW16 68 A5

Kydbrook Cl STMC/STPC BR5 90 D3
Kyetop Wk RHAM ME8 102 E2
Kymbeline Ct DEAL CT14 209 J5
Kynaston Av THHTH CR7 86 D1
Kynaston Crs THHTH CR7 86 D1
Kynaston Rd BMLY BR1 71 H2
STMC/STPC BR5 91 J3
THHTH CR7 86 D1

L

La Belle Alliance Sq RAM CT11 17 L5
Labour-in-Vain Rd BGR/WK TN15 238 C7
Laburnum Av DART DA1 51 K6
SWCH CT15 206 A1
SWLY BR8
Laburnum Av DVE/WH CT16 212 F5
Laburnum Dr DIT/AY ME20 139 G3
Laburnum Gdns CROY/NA CR0 87 L3
Laburnum Gv CWW DA11 54 E5
Laburnum La CANTW/ST CT2 173 J2
Laburnum Pl ELTH/MOT SE9 * 48 B3
SIT ME10 119 M5
Laburnum Rd STRD ME2 18 A2
Laburnum Wy HAYES BR2 90 B2
Lacebark Cl BFN/LL DA15 64 F7
Lacey Cl RMAID ME17 260 F1
Laceys La RMAID ME17 258 H6
Lacock Gdns MAID/SHEP ME15 167 H4
Lacon Rd EDUL SE22 45 H3
Lacton Oast STMC/STPC BR5 205 L3
Lacton Wy KEN/WIL TN24 3 M9
Lacy Cl MAIDW ME16 140 C6
Ladas Rd WNWD SE27 68 D1
Ladbrooke Crs SCUP DA14 49 L8
Ladbrook Rd SNWD SE25 68 E7
Ladds La SNOD ME6 113 H9
Lade Fort Crs LYDD TN29 335 M9
Ladham Rd CRBK TN17 297 P3
Ladyclose Av HOO/HM ME3 58 F8
Ladycroft Gdns ORP BR6 90 D8
Ladycroft Rd LEW SE13 46 C1
Ladycroft Wy ORP BR6 90 C1
Ladyfields GVW DA11 79 G1
Ladyfields Cl RSIT ME9 146 A4
Lady Garne Rd RDV CT15 216 A4
Ladygrove CROY/NA CR0 104 D5
Lady Oak La CRBK TN17 297 L12
CRBK TN17 311 K2
Lady's Gift Rd STH/RUST TN4 196 B5
Ladyship Ter EDUL SE22 * 45 J3
Ladysmith Gv WSTB CT5 126 A3
Ladysmith Rd ELTH/MOT SE9 48 B4
WSTB CT5 126 A3
Lady Vane Cl HOO/HM ME3 58 C3
Ladywell DVE/WH CT16 8 C8
Ladywell Rd LEW SE13 46 C3
Ladywood Av STMC/STPC BR5 90 F1
Ladywood Rd CANTW/ST CT2 173 G2
RDART DA2 76 F2
STRD ME2 99 J3
Lady Wootton's Gn CANT CT1 5 H4
Lafone St STHWK SE1 25 L1
Lagonda Wy DART DA1 51 K2
Lagoon Rd STMC/STPC BR5 91 J1
Lagos Av MSTR CT12 16 B1
Lairdale Cl DUL SE21 44 D6
Laird Av CDW/CHF RM16 34 E1
Lakedale Rd WOOL/PLUM SE18 28 E4
Lake Dr HOO/HM ME3 58 C3
Lakehall Gdns THHTH CR7 86 C1
Lakehall Rd THHTH CR7 86 C1
Lakelands MAID/SHEP ME15 167 H6
RMAID ME17 242 F11
Lakemead ASH TN23 204 B4
Lake Ri WTHK RM20 33 H3
Lake Rd CROY/NA CR0 88 A5
DIT/AY ME20 139 M3
STH/RUST TN4 22 C2
Laker Rd ROCH ME1 100 D7
Lakeside ASH TN23 * 204 B2
BECK BR3 70 C2
RTWE/PEM TN2 197 H7
SNOD ME6 113 H7
Lakeside Cl BFN/LL DA15 49 K3
EDEN TN8 254 A9
SNWD SE25 69 H7
Lakeside Dr HAYES BR2 89 H6
Lakes Rd HAYES BR2 89 K8
Lake St CROW TN6 308 D11
MAYF TN6 308 D11
Lakeswood Rd STMC/STPC BR5 90 D3
Lake View Rd SEV TN13 20 E2
Lakeview Rd WELL DA16 48 D3
WNWD SE27 68 B2
Lakewood Dr RHAM ME8 102 D7
Laking Av BRDST CT10 179 K6
Laleham Gdns MARG CT9 15 G5
Laleham Rd CAT SE6 46 D5
MARG CT9 15 L7
Laleham Wk MARG CT9 15 L7
Lamberde Cl STRD ME2 * 113 H1
Lamberde Dr SEV TN13 135 J4
Lambardes Rd SEV TN13 135 J4
Lambardes DEAL CT14 211 K3
Lambardes Cl ORP BR6 108 B5
Lamb Cl TIL RM18 35 K8
Lambden Rd HDCN TN27 285 M3
Lamberhurst Cl STMC/STPC BR5 91 L4
RHAM ME8 102 D7
Lamberhurst By RRTW TN3 296 D9
Lamberhurst Rd RRTW TN3 296 D5
STPH/PW TN12 279 R11
STPH/PW TN12 296 G1
WNWD SE27 68 B1
Lamberhurst Wy MARG CT9 179 J2
Lambersart Cl RTWE/PEM TN2 197 H5
Lambert Cl BH/WHM TN16 132 C3
Lambert Rd BRXS/STRHM SW2 44 C3
MAID/BEAR ME14 141 H7
ROCH ME1 19 G3
STPH/PW TN12 279 N6
Lambert's Pl CROY/NA CR0 * 87 L8
Lambert's Rd STHWK SE1 24 D1
Lambert's Yd TON TN9 194 E4
Lambeth High St LBTH SE11 24 A3
Lambeth Palace Rd STHWK SE1 24 A3
Lambeth Rd CANT CT1 172 D5
CROY/NA CR0 86 A5
STHWK SE1 24 B3
Lambeth Wk Open Space LBTH SE11 24 A3
Lambeth Wk LBTH SE11 24 B3
Lambfrith Gv GILL ME7 116 C2
Lambkin Cl CANT CT1 172 D5
Lambourne Dr E/WMAL ME19 164 A3

Lambourne Gv BERM/RHTH SE16 25 L3
Lambourne Pl BKHTH/KID SE3 * 27 J3
RHAM ME8 103 H3
Lambourne Rd MAID/SHEP ME15 168 A3
Lambourne Wk CANT CT1 5 L5
Lambourn Wy RTWE/PEM TN2 201 L4
WALD ME5 115 K3
Lambs Bank TON TN9 194 D6
Lambscroft Av ELTH/MOT SE9 48 K8
Lambsfrith Gv GILL ME7 116 C2
Lamb's Wk WSTB CT5 126 C1
Lambton Rd DVW CT17 213 H8
Lamb Wk STHWK SE1 24 F1
Lamerock Rd BMLY BR1 71 G1
Lamerton St DEPT SE8 26 B5
Laming Rd BRCH CT7 176 E7
Lamlash St LBTH SE11 24 C5
Lammas Dr SIT ME10 119 M5
Lammas Ga FAV ME13 149 L1
Lamorbey Cl BFN/LL DA15 49 G4
Lamorbey Pk BFN/LL DA15 * 49 G6
Lamorna Cl GVE DA12 55 L8
Lamorna Cl ORP BR6 91 H5
Lampeter Rw RRTW TN3 199 M4
Lamplighters Cl DART DA1 52 A4
Lampmead Rd LEW SE13 46 A1
Lamport Cl WOOL/PLUM SE18 28 A3
Lanbury Rd PECK SE15 45 L2
Lancashire Rd MAID/SHEP ME15 167 M5
WNWD SE27 44 C7
Lancaster Av HAYES BR2 71 G8
MSTR CT12 182 E4
RASHW TN26 318 C11
Lancaster Ct HART DA3 * 102 D6
HB CT6 129 L4
Lancaster House WOOL/PLUM SE18 * 4 F7
Lancaster Rd CANT CT1 4 C1
DVW CT17 8 C5
SNWD SE25 69 H7
WTHK RM20 33 L3
Lancaster St STHWK SE1 24 C1
Lancaster Wy E/WMAL ME19 164 A3
Lance Cl SIT ME10 120 A1
Lancelot Av STRD ME2 18 A4
Lancelot Cl DART DA1 * 209 H7
STRD ME2 18 A4
Lancelot Rd WELL DA16 48 B4
Lances Cl MEO DA13 97 H3
Lancet La MAID/SHEP ME15 167 G1
Lancey Cl CHARL SE7 27 L3
Lanchester Cl HB CT6 128 B5
Lanchester Wy NWCR SE14 25 K7
Lancing Rd CROY/NA CR0 86 A2
ORP BR6 91 J5
Landale Gdns DART DA1 51 K6
Landau Ter HAYES BR2 89 M6
Landau Wy ERITH DA8 31 L4
Landbury Wk RASHE TN25 202 C4
Landcroft Rd EDUL SE22 45 G4
Landells Rd EDUL SE22 45 G4
Lander Rd GRAYS RM17 34 E4
Landgate RYE TN31 225 H3
Landmann Wy NWCR SE14 25 L5
Landon Rd HB CT6 129 K4
Landor Ct GILL ME7 116 E1
Landrail Rd RSIT ME9 226 C10
Landscape Rd WARL CR6 130 A5
Landseer Av GVW DA11 54 E8
Landseer Cl TONN TN10 189 H7
ORP BR6 91 J8
Landstead Rd WOOL/PLUM SE18 28 G6
Landway BGR/WK TN15 136 E6
Land Wy HOO/HM ME3 58 B5
The Landway BGR/WK TN15 136 F6
BGR/WK TN15 240 E2
MAID/BEAR ME14 168 A3
STMC/STPC BR5 73 G7
Lane Av GRH DA9 53 K4
Lane End BXLYHN DA7 29 L5
WTHK RM20 33 H3
Lane End BXLYHN DA7 29 C1
Lanercost Rd BRXS/STRHM SW2 44 B3
Lanes Av GVW DA11 55 G8
Laneside CHST BR7 72 C2
The Lanes MSTR CT12 181 G7
The Lane BKHTH/KID SE3 47 H1
RDV CT15 214 A3
RRTW TN3 277 K12
Lanfranc Gdns CANTW/ST CT2 171 K4
Lanfranc Rd DEAL CT14 209 K1
Langafel Cl HART DA3 77 M6
Langbrook Rd BKHTH/KID SE3 47 L3
Lang Ct WSTB CT5 127 K2
Langdale ASH TN23 204 B5
Langdale Av RAM CT11 16 B5
Langdale Cl ORP BR6 90 C6
Langdale Dr MAIDW ME16 140 C4
THHTH CR7 68 B3
Langdale Ri MAIDW ME16 140 C4
Langdale Rd GNWCH SE10 26 D6
THHTH CR7 68 B3
Langdon Av RCANTE CT3 236 B12
Langdon Cl RDV CT15 215 G4
Langdon House WOOL/PLUM SE18 * 27 M6
Langdon Pl FOLKN CT19 11 M6
HAYES BR2 71 J7
Langdon Shaw SCUP DA14 73 G2
Langdon Wy STHWK SE1 25 L8
Langford Gn CMBW SE5 44 H1
Langford Pl SCUP DA14 49 H8
Langham Cl MARG CT9 177 L2
Langham Gv MAIDW ME16 176 C8
Langham Park Pl HAYES BR2 71 G8
Langham Rd RBTBR TN32 322 E10
Langhorn Rd ASH TN23 204 D4
RRTW TN3 200 B1
Langhorne Gdns FOLK CT20 11 H7
Langland Gdns CROY/NA CR0 88 A5
Langlands Dr RDART DA2 76 F2
Langley Ct BECK BR3 * 70 C5
Langley Gdns MARG CT9 179 H2
STMC/STPC BR5 90 C2
HAYES BR2 89 L4
Langley Rd BECK BR3 69 L3
SAND/SEL CR2 104 C3
SIT ME10 120 A3
WELL DA16 48 C5
Langley Wy WWKM BR4 70 F1
Langley Wd BECK BR3 * 88 F1
Langmead St WNWD SE27 68 C1
Langney Dr RAM CT11 16 B5
Langport Rd NROM TN28 331 L6
Langston Hughes Cl HNHL SE24 * 44 C12
Langthorne Crs GRAYS RM17 34 D4
Langton Cl MAID/BEAR ME14 3 H3
Langton La RYE TN31 174 A1
Langton Ri FSTH SE23 45 J5
Langton Rd BRXN/ST SW9 44 G2
RRTW TN3 200 A2
Langton Wy BKHTH/KID SE3 27 J4

CDW/CHF RM16 .....35 K3
CROY/NA SE20 .....86 F7
Langworth Cl RDART DA2 .....51 E3
Lanier Rd LEW SE13 .....46 D4
Lankester Parker Rd
ROCH ME1 .....100 D7
Lankton Cl BECK BR3 .....70 D7
Lannoy Rd ELTH/MOT SE9 .....48 D6
Lanridge Rd ABYW SE2 .....29 K6
Lansbury Crs DART DA1 .....52 B3
Lansdowne Av BXLYHN DA7 .....29 K6
ORP BR6 .....90 C4
Lansdowne HI WWND SE27 .....44 F8
Lansdowne La CHARL SE7 .....27 L4
Lansdowne Ms CHARL SE7 .....27 L4
Lansdowne Ms SE19 .....68 M8
STHWK SE1 .....24 E2
Lansdowne PI NRWD SE19 .....69 J1
Lansdowne Rd BMLY BR1 .....71 H4
CHAT ME4 .....100 F3
CROY/NA CR0 .....86 C6
RTW TN1 .....23 L5
SEV TN13 .....21 L1
TON TN9 .....194 E3
Lansdowne Sq GVW DA11 .....55 G4
Lansdowne Wood Cl
WNWD SE27 .....44 F8
Lansdown Pl GVW DA11 .....55 G6
Lansdown Rd CANT CT1 .....5 D7
SCUP DA14 .....49 H8
SIT ME10 .....120 D5
TIL RM18 .....37 H4
Lanterns Ct POP/IOD E14 .....26 B2
Lanthorne Ct BRDST CT10 * 179 L7
Lanthorne Ms RTW TN1 .....23 G5
Lanthorne Rd BRDST CT10 .....179 K7
RTW TN1 .....23 G5
Lant St STHWK SE1 .....24 D1
Lanvanor Rd PECK SE15 .....25 H3
Lapis Cl GVE DA12 .....54 C6
La Providence ROCH ME1 * 19 J7
Lapwing Cl CROY/NA CR0 .....104 D4
ERITH DA8 * 31 J6
IOS ME12 .....65 K8
Lapwing Dr ASH TN23 .....205 G8
RSIT ME9 .....226 C10
Lapwing Rd HOO/HM ME3 .....43 J6
Lapwings HART DA3 .....78 C7
Lapworth Ct ORP BR6 .....91 K5
Lara Cl LEW SE13 .....46 D4
Larch Cl BRDST CT10 .....183 G1
DEPT SE8 .....26 A5
DIT/AY ME20 .....139 J3
WARL CR6 .....130 D5
Larch Crs HOO/HM ME3 .....83 M2
Larch Dene ORP BR6 .....90 B5
The Larches ECRIN RH19 .....274 A1
FAV ME15 .....149 H1
HOO/HM ME3 .....81 K2
WSTB CT5 .....126 D5
Larch Gv BFN/LL DA15 .....49 G6
STPH/PW TN12 .....279 J3
Larch Rd DART DA1 .....51 K6
RDV CT15 .....272 C4
Larch Ter IOS ME12 * 64 B5
Larch Tree Wy CROY/NA CR0 .....88 B6
Larch Wk KEN/WIL TN24 .....202 F5
Larch Wy HAYES BR2 .....90 B3
Larchwood Rd ELTH/MOT SE9 .....48 C7
Larcombe Cl CROY/NA CR0 .....3 G7
Larcom St WALW SE17 .....24 D3
Larissa St WALW SE17 * 24 E4
Larkbere Rd SYD SE26 .....69 M1
Larkey Vw RCANTW CT4 .....248 M1
Larkfield Av GILL ME7 .....101 M3
SIT ME10 .....119 M3
Larkfield Cl DIT/AY ME20 * 139 H1
Larkfield Rd DIT/AY ME20 .....139 H4
SCUP DA14 .....49 G8
SEV TN13 .....161 H1
Larkfields GVW DA11 .....55 G4
Larkhill Ter WOOL/PLUM SE18 * 28 B6
Larkin Cl BRCH CT7 * 82 C3
Larking Dr MAIDW ME16 .....140 E6
Larscliff Ct BRCH CT7 * 4 A8
Larks Fld HART DA3 .....78 A3
Larksfield Rd FAV ME15 .....123 K8
Larkspur Cl E/WMAL ME19 .....139 H4
ORP BR6 .....91 K5
Larkstore Pk STPH/PW TN12 * 280 F1
WALD ME5 .....114 F1
Larkswood Cl ERITH DA8 .....31 H7
Larkwell La HART DA3 .....78 A3
Larner Rd ERITH DA8 .....30 F6
Lasacelles Rd DUW CT17 .....217 H5
Laser Quay STRD ME2 * 19 M5
Lassa Rd ELTH/MOT SE9 .....47 M5
Lassell St GNWCH SE10 .....26 E6
La-Tene DEAL CT14 .....209 J7
Latham Cl BH/WHM TN16 .....132 B2
RDART DA2 .....52 F7
Latham Rd BXLYHS DA6 .....50 B3
Latham's Wy CROY/NA CR0 .....86 A1
Latimer Cl HB CT6 .....128 C7
Latimer PI GILL ME7 .....23 K6
Latimer Rd CROY/NA CR0 * 86 C5
Latona Dr GVE DA12 .....55 M5
Latona Rd PECK SE15 .....25 H5
La Tourne Gdns ORP BR6 .....107 J5
Latymers RTON TN11 .....277 J5
Laud St CROY/NA CR0 .....86 C6
SE11 .....24 A4
Launcelot Rd BMLY BR1 .....71 H1
Launcelot St STHWK SE1 * 24 A2
Launch Wy POP/IOD E14 .....26 D2
Launder Wy MAID/SHEP ME15 .....12 G2
Laundry Rd MSTR CT12 .....181 G9
Laura Dr SWLY BR8 .....75 H4
Laura PI FAV ME13 * 151 L2
Laureate Cl MARG CT9 .....55 K7
Laurel Av GVE DA12 .....55 K7
LYDD TN29 .....331 L9
Laurel Bank STH/RUST TN4 .....196 E3
Laurel Cl DART DA1 .....51 K6
FOLK CT20 .....219 M7
SCUP DA14 .....49 G8
Laurel Crs CROY/NA CR0 .....88 B6
Laurel Dr OXTED RH8 .....185 G1
Laurel Gv PGE/AN SE20 .....69 J4
RMAID ME17 * .....
SYD SE26 .....69 L3
Laurel PI FAV ME13 * 151 L2
Laurel Rd GILL ME7 .....83 K6
RTWE/PEM TN2 .....197 G2
The Laurels CMBW SE5 * 24 C6
DART 78 C7
MAIDW ME16 .....52 B7
RDART DA2 * 51 K8
Laurel Vis STPH/PW TN12 * 280 H4
Laurel Wy RCANTW CT4 .....248 M1
Laureston PI DVE/WH CT16 .....8 E3

Laurie Gray Av WALD ME5 .....114 E4
Laurie Gv NWCR SE14 .....25 M7
Laurier Rd CROY/NA CR0 .....87 G2
Lauriston Ct CAT CT11 .....16 E2
PECK SE15 .....25 K7
Lausanne Rd MARG CT9 .....15 G5
PECK SE15 .....25 K7
Lausanne Ter MARG CT9 * 15 G5
Lavenda Cl GILL ME7 .....116 B1
Lavender Cl E/WMAL ME19 .....139 G5
HAYES BR2 .....90 M2
MARG CT9 .....14 B8
Lavender Ct SIT ME10 .....120 B6
Lavender Gdns WADH TN5 .....310 F8
Lavender HI SWLY BR8 .....74 E7
TON TN9 .....194 F5
Lavender La MSTR CT12 .....181 M8
Lavender Ms CANT CT1 .....4 A1
Lavender Rd CROY/NA CR0 .....86 A2
E/WMAL ME19 .....139 G5
Lavenders Rd E/WMAL ME19 .....138 D6
Lavender Wy CROY/NA CR0 .....87 G2
Lavernock Rd BXLY DA5 .....50 A2
Laverstoke Gdns MAIDW ME16 .....140 D5
Lavington Rd CROY/NA CR0 .....86 A2
Lavinia Rd DART DA1 .....52 A4
Lawdon Gdns CROY/NA CR0 * 86 C7
Lawford Gdns DART DA1 .....51 K3
Lawley Ct MSTR CT12 .....182 F4
Lawn Cl BMLY BR1 .....71 J4
CHAT ME4 .....101 J3
SWLY BR8 .....74 D6
TENT TN30 .....
Lawn House Cl POP/IOD E14 .....26 D1
Lawn Pk SEV TN13 .....162 A5
Lawn Rd BECK BR3 .....70 A8
BRDST CT10 .....183 K1
DEAL CT14 .....209 K8
GVW DA11 .....54 D4
TENT TN30 .....194 E5
Lawns Crs GRAYS RM17 .....34 E5
Lawns PI GRAYS RM17 * 34 E5
The Lawns BKHTH/KID SE3 * 47 L1
NRWD SE19 .....68 E5
SCUP DA14 .....73 J1
STPH/PW TN12 .....279 L9
Lawn Ter BKHTH/KID SE3 .....47 L1
Lawrence Sq GVW DA11 * 55 G8
Lawrence Cl FOLKN CT19 .....11 M2
MAID/SHEP ME15 .....167 H6
Lawrence Ct FOLKN CT19 .....11 M2
Lawrence Dr GVE DA12 .....80 D5
Lawrence Gdns HB CT6 .....129 K5
TIL RM18 .....35 J2
Lawrence Hill Gdns DART DA1 .....51 K4
Lawrence Hill Rd DART DA1 .....51 K4
Lawrence Rd ERITH DA8 .....30 C6
SNWD SE25 .....
TONN TN10 .....189 H7
WWKM BR4 .....89 H7
Lawrence St GILL ME7 .....7 J3
Lawrie Park Crs SYD SE26 .....69 J3
Lawrie Park Gdns SYD SE26 .....69 J3
Lawrie Park Rd SYD SE26 .....69 K3
Laws Cl THHTH CR7 .....68 E8
Laws La RASHE TN25 .....305 N6
Lawson Cl GILL ME7 * 84 A1
Lawson Gdns DART DA1 .....51 K3
Lawson Rd DART DA1 .....51 K3
Law St STHWK SE1 .....24 E2
Laxey Rd ORP BR6 .....107 L5
The Laxey MAID/SHEP ME15 * 166 F4
Laxley Cl CMBW SE5 .....24 C6
Laxton Cl MAID/SHEP ME15 .....168 A3
Laxton Dr RMAID ME17 .....260 B4
Laxton Gdns STPH/PW TN12 .....278 D2
Laxton Wy CANT CT1 .....5 M6
FAV ME13 .....149 M4
SIT ME10 .....119 L3
WSTB CT5 .....127 K4
Layard Rd BERM/RHTH SE16 .....25 J3
Layard Sq BERM/RHTH SE16 .....25 J3
Layfield Rd GILL ME7 .....84 A4
Layhams Rd HAYES BR2 .....105 H2
WWKM BR4 .....88 F7
Laylam Cl BRDST CT10 .....179 J7
Laymarsh Cl DART DA1 .....30 A2
Layton Crs CROY/NA CR0 .....86 B6
Layzell Wk ELTH/MOT SE9 .....47 L6
Lea Av RYE TN31 .....224 F5
Lea Cl HYTHE CT21 .....222 C1
Leacon Rd ASH TN23 .....204 C2
Leafield Cl STRHM/NOR SW16 .....68 C3
Leafield La SCUP DA14 .....74 A1
Leafy Gld RHAM ME8 .....102 C7
Leafy Gv HAYES BR2 .....105 G3
Leafy La MEO DA13 .....239 M1
Leafy Oak Rd LEE/GVPK SE12 .....71 K1
Leafy Wy CROY/NA CR0 .....87 G6
Leahurst Rd LEW SE13 .....46 F4
Leake St STHWK SE1 .....24 A1
Lealands Av RTON TN11 .....255 P12
Lealands Cl RRTW TN3 .....199 K6
Leaman Cl HOO/HM ME3 .....60 A1
Leamington Av BMLY BR1 .....71 J1
ORP BR6 .....90 F7
Leamington Rd BMLY BR1 .....71 J1
Leander Dr GVE DA12 .....80 A1
Leander Rd BRXS/STRHM SW2 .....44 A1
ROCH ME1 .....100 D4
THHTH CR7 .....68 M4
Lea Rd BECK BR3 .....70 B6
CDW/CHF RM16 .....35 H2
SEV TN13 .....162 B5
Learoyd Rd NROM TN28 .....331 K8
Leasam La RYE TN31 .....224 F2
Leas Dl ELTH/MOT SE9 .....48 D3
Leas Gn BRDST CT10 .....183 G1
CHST BR7 .....73 G3
Leas La WARL CR6 .....130 C4
Leas Rd DEAL CT14 .....209 J4
WARL CR6 .....130 C4
The Leas DEAL CT14 .....335 M2
FAV ME13 .....149 J1
FOLK CT20 .....11 L6
IOS ME12 .....65 J4
WADH TN5 .....309 M3
WSTB CT5 .....127 H7
Leatherbottle Gn ERITHM DA18 * 30 A2
Leathermarket Ct STHWK SE1 * 24 F1
Leathermarket St STHWK SE1 .....24 F1
Leather Rd BERM/RHTH SE16 .....25 K4
Leathwell Rd DEPT SE8 .....26 B7
Lea Vw DART DA1 .....50 B1
Leaveland Cl ASH TN23 .....204 F8
BECK BR3 .....70 B2
Leaves Green Crs HAYES BR2 .....106 C4
Leaves Green Rd HAYES BR2 .....106 C5
Lebanon Gdns BH/WHM TN16 .....132 C4
Lebanon Rd CROY/NA CR0 .....86 D7

Lebrun Sq BKHTH/KID SE3 .....47 J2
Leckwith Av ABYW SE2 .....29 M5
Leconfield Cl TON TN9 .....194 C1
Leda Rd WOOL/PLUM SE18 .....28 A2
Ledbury Rd CROY/NA CR0 .....86 D7
Ledbury St PECK SE15 .....25 H6
Ledgers Rd WARL CR6 .....130 E2
Ledrington Rd NRWD SE19 .....69 G5
Lee Church St LEW SE13 .....46 F2
Leeds Ct CHAT ME4 .....91 H5
Leeds House Ms RTON TN11 * 256 H5
Leeds Rd RHAM ME8 .....102 C2
Lee Gn STMC/STPC BR5 .....91 H1
Lee High Rd LEW SE13 .....46 E2
Lee Pk BKHTH/KID SE3 .....47 G2
Lee Rd BKHTH/KID SE3 .....47 G2
SNOD ME6 .....113 H5
The Lees FAV ME13 .....289 L12
Lees Court Rd FAV ME13 .....246 B4
Leeson HI CHST BR7 .....72 F7
Leesons Wy STMC/STPC BR5 .....73 G6
Lees Rel KEN/WIL TN24 .....3 J6
RASHE TN25 .....289 M10
WBY/YAL ME18 .....257 Q5
The Lees CROY/NA CR0 .....88 A5
Lewes Av BRYN ME7 * .....
Lewes Cl GRAYS RM17 .....34 B6
Lewes Rd BMLY BR1 .....71 L6
Lewing Cl ORP BR6 .....90 F4
Lewin Rd BXLYHS DA6 .....49 M2
Lewis Cl FAV ME13 .....149 H2
Lewis Ct ASH TN23 * 204 C4
Lewis Court Dr RMAID ME17 .....259 N2
Lewis Crs MARG CT9 .....15 H3
Lewisham High St LEW SE13 .....46 C4
Lewisham Pk LEW SE13 .....46 D3
Lewisham Rd DVW CT17 .....212 F6
LEW SE13 .....26 C7
Lewisham Wy BROCKY SE4 .....26 A6
Lewis Ms SNOD ME6 .....113 G7
Lewis Rd NEO DA13 .....79 G5
SWCM DA10 .....53 M4
WELL DA16 .....49 K8
Lewson Street Rd RSIT ME9 .....147 M1
Leybank RTON TN11 .....194 B1
Leybourne Cl HAYES BR2 .....89 L5
WALD ME5 .....115 H3
Leybourne Dell CRBK TN17 .....313 H3
Leybourne Rd MARG CT9 .....177 G5
Leybourne St STRD ME2 .....18 G2
Leybourne Wy DIT/AY ME20 .....139 H1
Leyburn Rd BRDST CT10 .....183 L3
IOS ME12 .....229 C3
Leyburn Gdns CROY/NA CR0 .....86 D5
Leyburn House
WOOL/PLUM SE18 * 27 M6
Leycroft Cl CANTW/ST CT2 .....171 M2
Leycroft Gdns ERITH DA8 .....31 J7
Leydenhatch La SWLY BR8 .....74 E5
Leyhill Cl SWLY BR8 .....92 F1
Leyland Rd LEE/GVPK SE12 .....47 G3
Leylang Rd NWCR SE14 .....25 L6
Leysdown Av BXLYHN DA7 .....50 D2
Leysdown Rd IOS ME12 .....229 M3
IOS ME12 .....229 M3
Leysdown Wy WSTB CT5 .....126 F3
Leyton Av GILL ME7 .....101 M4
Leyton Cross Rd RDART DA2 .....51 J8
Leywood Rd MEO DA13 .....239 R1
Lezayre Rd ORP BR6 .....107 L1
Liardet St NWCR SE14 .....25 M7
Liberty St BRXN/ST SW9 .....24 A5
Library St STHWK SE1 .....24 C1
Libya Ter MAID/BEAR ME14 .....141 H6
Lichfield Rd DVE/WH CT16 .....213 G2
Lichfield Wy SAND/SEL CR2 .....104 A7
Lidcote Gdns BRXN/ST SW9 * 24 A6
Liddon Rd BMLY BR1 .....71 K7
Lidgate Rd PECK SE15 * 25 F6
Lidsing Rd MAID/BEAR ME14 .....141 K1
Lidwells La CRBK TN17 .....297 J3
Liege Cl SIT ME10 .....227 N12
Liffler Rd WOOL/PLUM SE18 .....28 D5
Lighterman's Rd POP/IOD E14 .....26 B1
Lighthouse Rd RDV CT15 .....215 G5
Lilac Av SWLY BR8 .....74 E7
Lilac Gdns CROY/NA CR0 .....88 B1
SWLY BR8 .....74 E7
Lilac Gv E/WMAL ME19 .....139 H5
Lilac PI LBTH SE11 .....24 A3
Lilac Rd STRD ME2 .....18 C2
Lilah Ms HAYES BR2 .....71 G6
Lila PI SWLY BR8 .....74 F8
Lilburne Gdns ELTH/MOT SE9 .....47 M3
Lilburne Rd ELTH/MOT SE9 .....24 C3
Lilford Rd BRXN/ST SW9 .....24 B6
Lilian Barker Cl LEE/GVPK SE12 .....47 H3
Lilechurch Rd HOO/HM ME3 .....58 E5
Lillian Rd RAM CT11 .....17 J3
Lillian Vis STPH/PW TN12 * 280 H4
Lilleiburn E/WMAL ME19 .....138 E3
Lillie Rd BH/WHM TN16 .....132 C4
Limden Cl WADH TN5 .....310 A11
Lime Av GVW DA11 .....54 E5
Lime Cl ASH TN23 .....202 C8
BMLY BR1 .....71 G1
RRTW TN3 .....294 A10
STPH/PW TN12 .....280 H3
Lime Ct RHAM ME8 .....116 D2
Lime Crs E/WMAL ME19 .....139 H6
Lime Gv BFN/LL DA15 .....49 G4
HDCN TN27 .....301 J6
IOS ME12 .....64 D9
ORP BR6 .....90 E7
SIT ME10 .....120 B5
WARL CR6 .....130 D5
Limeharbour POP/IOD E14 .....26 C2
Lime Hill Rd RTW TN1 .....22 F4
Limehouse Whf ROCH ME1 * 19 J5
Lime Kiln Dr CHARL SE7 .....27 J5
Lime Kiln Rd CANT CT1 .....6 C3
Limekiln Rbt DVW CT17 .....8 C9
Limekiln St DVW CT17 .....8 C9
Lime Pit La RSEV TN14 .....135 H3
Limes Av CROY/NA CR0 .....86 A6
PGE/AN SE20 .....69 J4
Limes Cl TENT TN30 .....315 P2
Limesford Rd PECK SE15 .....45 M1
Limes Gv HAWK TN18 .....312 C4
Limes Rd BECK BR3 .....70 D2
CROY/NA CR0 .....86 C2
DVE/WH CT16 .....10 B1
FOLKN CT19 .....10 D6
Limes Rw ORP BR6 .....106 E7
The Limes ASH TN23 .....204 F6
EDEN TN8 .....192 G4
EYN DA4 * 94 A3
PUR RM19 .....32 D5

Limestone Wk ABYW SE2 .....29 L1
Limes Wk PECK SE15 * 45 L6
Lime Tree Cl TON TN9 .....194 F1
Lime Tree Rd BRCH CT7 .....53 H6
Limetree Cl BRXS/STRHM SW2 .....44 A3
WALD ME5 .....171 J6
Lime Tree Gv CROY/NA CR0 .....88 A6
Lime Trees STPH/PW TN12 .....281 M5
Lime Tree Ter CAT SE6 * 46 A6
Lime Tree Wk SEV TN13 .....21 H7
WWKM BR4 .....89 G7
Limewood Cl BECK BR3 .....88 D1
Limewood Rd ERITH DA8 .....30 D6
Limpsfield Av THHTH CR7 .....68 A1
Limpsfield Rd SAND/SEL CR2 .....104 A8
WARL CR6 .....130 B2
Linacre Cl PECK SE15 .....45 J1
The Linces DVE/WH CT16 .....213 J5
Linchmere Rd LEE/GVPK SE12 .....47 G5
Lincoln Av CANT CT1 .....5 K7
Lincoln Cl ERITH DA8 .....31 L8
Lincoln Gdns BRCH CT7 .....176 C6
Lincoln Green Rd
STMC/STPC BR5 .....91 G1
Lincoln Rd ERITH DA8 .....31 G1
MAID/SHEP ME15 .....167 K5
SCUP DA14 .....73 J2
SNWD SE25 .....69 J7
Lincombe Rd BMLY BR1 .....47 G8
Lincon Rd GILL ME7 .....
Lindal Rd BROCKY SE4 .....46 A3
Linden Av BRDST CT10 .....179 J5
DART DA1 .....51 K6
HB CT6 .....128 C7
THHTH CR7 .....68 C8
WSTB CT5 .....127 G5
Linden Cha CANTW/ST CT2 4
Linden Chase Rd SEV TN13 .....21 G1
Linden Cl ORP BR6 .....91 H8
PUR RM19 .....32 D5
RTWE/PEM TN2 .....22 D9
SIT ME10 .....119 L6
STPH/PW TN12 .....279 K3
WGOS CT8 .....177 H6
Linden Crs FOLKN CT19 .....11 G3
Linden Dr ORP BR6 .....107 G5
Lindenfield CHST BR7 .....72 C6
Linden Gdns RTWE/PEM TN2 .....22 D9
Linden Gv CANTW/ST CT2 4
PECK SE15 .....45 J1
SYD SE26 .....69 K3
WARL CR6 .....130 E2
Linden Leas WWKM BR4 .....88 E5
Linden Park Rd RTWE/PEM TN2 .....22 D9
Linden Rd GILL ME7 .....83 M8
KEN/WIL TN24 .....
RCANTW CT4 .....248 F4
RMAID ME17 .....258 F12
WGOS CT8 .....177 H6
Linden Sq SEV TN13 .....135 K8
The Lindens CROY/NA CR0 .....105 H1
DIT/AY ME20 .....139 M4
Lindenthorpe Rd BRDST CT10 .....179 J7
Lindfield Rd CROY/NA CR0 .....87 G2
Lindisfarne Cl GVE DA12 .....55 M7
Lindisfarne Gdns MAIDW ME16 .....12 H1
Lindley Est PECK SE15 * 25 H6
Lindley Rd GDST RH9 .....156 B8
Lindo St PECK SE15 .....25 K8
Lindridge Cl HB CT6 .....155 H1
Lindridge La STPH/PW TN12 .....281 P4
Lindsell St GNWCH SE10 .....26 D7
Lindsey Cl BMLY BR1 .....71 K3
Lind St DEPT SE8 .....26 C8
Lindway WNWD SE27 .....68 A2
Lineacre Cl RHAM ME8 .....102 C7
Lines Ter CHAT ME4 .....6 E1
Linford Rd CDW/CHF RM16 .....35 J3
Lingards Rd LEW SE13 .....46 D2
Lingey Cl BFN/LL DA15 .....49 G5
Lingfield Av RDART DA2 .....52 C5
Lingfield Common Rd
LING RH7 .....190 D8
Lingfield Crs ELTH/MOT SE9 .....48 D2
Lingfield Rd BCR/WK TN15 .....192 B5
EDEN TN8 .....192 B5
GVE DA12 .....55 J7
Lingley Dr STRD ME2 .....82 D3
Ling Rd ERITH DA8 .....30 D6
Lingrove Rd BRCH CT7 .....176 C6
Link Fld HAYES BR2 .....89 H7
Link Hill La HDCN TN27 .....262 G11
Link La CANT CT1 .....6 B6
Link Rd CANTW/ST CT2 * 153 G7
Links Cl ASH TN23 * 207 K8
Links Ct DEAL CT14 * .....
Links Crs LYDD TN29 .....331 K5
Linksfield Rd WGOS CT8 .....177 G6
Links Gdns STRHM/NOR SW16 .....68 B3
Links Rd DEAL CT14 .....209 K1
WWKM BR4 .....88 E5
The Links E/WMAL ME19 .....139 R11
WALD ME5 .....101 J5
Links Vw DART DA1 .....51 K6
Links View Rd CROY/NA CR0 .....88 B2
Links Wy BECK BR3 .....88 B2
LYDD TN29 .....319 R9
NROM TN28 .....331 K5
RYE TN31 .....332 D7
Linksway FOLKN CT19 .....220 E5
Linksway Cl FOLKN CT19 .....220 C4
The Link RTON TN31 .....
Link Wy HAYES BR2 .....89 H7
RTWE/PEM TN2 .....197 M5
Linkway DIT/AY ME20 .....139 K4
RSIT ME9 .....227 L3
Linley Cl TIL RM18 .....36 C4
Linley Rd BRDST CT10 .....179 H6
Linnell Rd CMBW SE5 .....24 F7
Linnet Av STPH/PW TN12 .....281 N5
WSTB CT5 .....127 G6
Linnet Cl SAND/SEL CR2 .....104 C4
Linnet Wy PUR RM19 .....32 C4
Linsey St BERM/RHTH SE16 .....25 H3
Linslade Rd ORP BR6 .....107 M1
Linton CHARL SE7 .....
WELL DA16 .....29 H7
Linton Dann Cl HOO/HM ME3 .....59 L4
Linton Gld CROY/NA CR0 .....104 D4
Linton Gore RMAID ME17 .....258 C12
Linton Rd MAID/SHEP ME15 .....259 M3
Linwood Av STRD ME2 .....18 A2
Linwood Cl CMBW SE5 .....25 J8
Lion Cl BROCKY SE4 .....46 B4
Lion Ct RSIT ME9 * 121 P7
Lionel Gdns ELTH/MOT SE9 .....47 L5
Lionel Rd ELTH/MOT SE9 .....47 L5
TON TN9 .....194 D6
Lion Fld FAV ME13 .....149 H2
Lion Rd BXLYHS DA6 .....49 M4
CROY/NA CR0 .....86 C2
Lions Cl ELTH/MOT SE9 .....47 K8
Lion's Rd NROM TN28 .....330 H7
Lion St RYE TN31 .....225 L9
Lion Yd CLAT CT16 * 236 A12
Lion Yd FAV ME13 .....148 H1
Liphook Crs FSTH SE23 .....45 K5
Liphook Wy MAIDW ME16 .....140 D5

Lipscombe Rd RTWE/PEM TN2 197 G7
Liptraps La RTWE/PEM TN2 197 G6
Lipwell Hl HOO/HM ME3 59 J1
Lisford St PECK SE15 25 G7
Liskeard Gdns BKHTH/KID SE3 27 H7
Lisle Cl GVE DA12 56 C7
Lisle Pl GRAYS RM17 34 B2
Lismore Cl MAID/SHEP ME15 167 H6
Lismore Rd HB CT6 129 L4
WSTB CT5 127 J5
Liss Rd SWCH CT13 253 M8
Lister Cl DEAL CT14 209 K4
DVW CT17 213 J8
E/WMAL ME19 139 G5
Lister Rd MARG CT9 15 J9
TIL RM18 35 H8
Lister Wy FOLK CT20 10 B8
Listmas Rd CHAT ME4 7 G8
Listowel Cl BRXN/ST SW9 24 B6
The List RCANTE CT3 234 D11
Little Acre BECK BR3 70 B7
Little Aly EDEN TN8 192 C8
Little Av DEAL CT14 209 G5
Little Birches BFN/LL DA15 48 F7
Little Bornes DUL SE21 68 F1
Little Boundes Cl
STH/RUST TN4 196 B2
Littlebourne Av RHAM ME8 102 C1
Littlebourne Rd
MAID/BEAR ME14 141 K7
RCANTE CT3 174 F1
Littlebrook Cl ASH TN23 202 D8
CROY/NA CR0 87 L2
Littlebrook Manor Wy
DART DA1 52 B3
Little Brook Rd ASH TN23 202 D8
Little Brownings FSTH SE23 45 J7
Little Browns La EDEN TN8 191 M1
Little Buckland Av
MAIDW ME16 12 B1
Little Chequers RASHE TN25 266 F11
Little Copse Cl RCANTW CT4 248 F8
Little Ct WWKM BR4 88 F5
Littlecourt Rd SEV TN13 20 E4
Littlecroft ELTH/MOT SE9 48 B1
MEO DA13 78 F4
Littledale ABYW SE2 29 H5
Little Dorrit Ct STHWK SE1 24 D1
Little Fld STPH/PW TN12 281 R5
Littlefield Rd RHAM ME8 103 J3
Little Flds RTON TN11 * 256 B5
Little Footway RRTW TN3 200 A2
Little Glovers SIT ME10 120 A6
Little Harts Heath
STPH/PW TN12 * 281 L10
Little Heath CHARL SE7 27 M5
Little Heath Rd BXLYHN DA7 30 A7
Littleheath Rd SAND/SEL CR2 104 A3
Little John Av WALD ME5 115 G3
Littlejohn Rd STMC/STPC BR5 91 H2
Little Julians Hl SEV TN13 161 M5
Little London Ct STHWK SE1 * 25 G1
Little Lullenden LING RH7 190 E8
Little Mallett RRTW TN3 199 M2
Little Market Rw E/WMAL ME19 138 F3
Little Md FOLKN CT19 10 D1
Little Meadow CANTW/ST CT2 170 F4
Littlemede ELTH/MOT SE9 48 B8
Littlemore Rd ABYW SE2 29 H1
Little Mount Sion RTW TN1 22 F7
Little Oakham Ct HOO/HM ME3 61 K1
Little Orch RMAID ME17 259 J2
Little Oxley DIT/AY ME20 138 F3
Little Paddocks WSTB CT5 127 L6
Little Pk WADH TN5 309 K4
Little Queen St DART DA1 52 A5
Little Redlands BMLY BR1 71 M6
Little Robhurst RASHW TN26 301 R6
Littlestone Cl BECK BR3 70 B3
Littlestone Rd NROM TN28 331 M8
Little Thrift STMC/STPC BR5 72 D8
Little Tilden Gill TENT TN30 315 P2
Little Walton SWCH CT13 253 P6
Littlewood LEW SE13 46 D3
Little Wd SEV TN13 136 B8
Little Wood Cl STMC/STPC BR5 73 H5
Liverpool Gv WALW SE17 24 E4
Liverpool Lawn RAM CT11 17 J7
Liverpool Rd DEAL CT14 209 K8
THHTH CR7 68 D7
Livesey Cl WOOL/PLUM SE18 28 D2
Livesey Pl PECK SE15 25 H5
Livesey St WBY/YAL ME18 165 H4
Livingstone Buildings GILL ME7 * 7 M4
Livingstone Circ GILL ME7 7 M4
Livingstone Cl LYDD TN29 321 N5
Livingstone Gdns GVE DA12 79 L2
Livingstone Rd BRDST CT10 179 H7
GILL ME7 83 M8
GVE DA12 79 L2
THHTH CR7 68 E6
Lizban St BKHTH/KID SE3 27 J6
Llanover Rd WOOL/PLUM SE18 28 B6
Llewellyn St BERM/RHTH SE16 25 H1
Lloyd Park Av CROY/NA CR0 87 G7
Lloyd Rd BRDST CT10 179 K8
Lloyds Gn TENT TN30 326 G1
Lloyd's Pl BKHTH/KID SE3 * 26 F8
Lloyds Wy BECK BR3 87 M1
Lloyd Vls BROCKY SE4 26 B8
Loampit Hl LEW SE13 26 B8
Loampits Cl TON TN9 195 G2
Loampit V LEW SE13 46 C1
Lobelia Cl GILL ME7 83 M8
Locarno Av RHAM ME8 102 B3
Lochaber Rd LEW SE13 46 F2
Lochat Rd HOO/HM ME3 58 F7
Lochmere Cl ERITH DA8 30 C5
Lock Cha LEW SE13 46 F1
Lockesley Dr STMC/STPC BR5 91 G2
Lockham Farm Av
MAID/SHEP ME15 167 L8
Lockholt Cl ASH TN23 202 B8
Lockington Cl TON TN9 194 C6
Lockington Gv ROCH ME1 19 J8
Lock La MAIDW ME16 140 E4
Lockmead Rd LEW SE13 46 D1
Lockside TON TN9 194 F3
Locksley Cl WALD ME5 114 F3
Lock St GILL ME7 7 J3
Lockswood MAIDW ME16 140 E6
Locks Yd BGR/WK TN15 * 21 J7
Lockwood Cl SYD SE26 69 L1
Lockwood Sq
BERM/RHTH SE16 25 J2
Lockyer Est STHWK SE1 * 24 E1
Lockyer Pl BH/WHM TN16 * 159 J4
Lockyer Rd PUR RM19 32 D4
Lockyers Hl MEO DA13 97 M8
Lockyer St STHWK SE1 24 E1
Loddington La RMAID ME17 259 M6
Loder Cl RMAID ME17 243 J12
Loder St PECK SE15 25 K6
Lodge Av CROY/NA CR0 86 A6
DART DA1 51 K4
Lodge Cl ORP BR6 91 J4
WBY/YAL ME18 164 E5
Lodge Ct GVE DA12 80 F3
Lodge Crs ORP BR6 91 J4
Lodge Field Rd HB CT6 154 B2
WSTB CT5 127 L4
Lodge Gdns BECK BR3 88 A1
RMAID ME17 261 N7
Lodge Hl HOO/HM ME3 59 G7
WELL DA16 29 J6
Lodge Hill La HOO/HM ME3 59 G5
Lodge La BH/WHM TN16 159 H5
BXLY DA5 49 L4
CDW/CHF RM16 34 C2
CROY/NA CR0 105 G2
GVE DA12 80 C8
RRTW TN3 200 B5
Lodge Oak La TON TN9 195 G5
Lodge Rd BMLY BR1 71 K4
CROY/NA CR0 86 C2
MAID/BEAR ME14 141 L8
STPH/PW TN12 281 R4
TON TN9 194 E3
Lodge Wk WARL CR6 130 F2
Lodge Wood Dr RASHE TN25 202 C6
Loewen Rd CDW/CHF RM16 35 H2
Loftie St BERM/RHTH SE16 25 H1
Logs Hl CHST BR7 71 M5
Logs Hill Cl CHST BR7 71 M5
Lollard St LBTH SE11 24 B3
Loman St STHWK SE1 24 C1
Lomas Cl CROY/NA CR0 105 H2
Lomas La HAWK TN18 313 R12
Lomas Rd SIT ME10 120 E5
Lombard St EYN DA4 76 D8
MARG CT9 14 F3
Lombard Wall CHARL SE7 27 J2
Lombardy Cl GILL ME7 102 B7
Lombardy Dr MAID/BEAR ME14 13 M4
Lomond Gdns SAND/SEL CR2 104 D2
Lomond Gv CMBW SE5 24 E6
Loncroft Rd CMBW SE5 24 F5
Londonderry Pde ERITH DA8 * 30 E6
London La BMLY BR1 71 H4
CRBK TN17 299 L3
London Loop CROY/NA CR0 87 L6
SAND/SEL CR2 104 C3
London Rd BGR/WK TN15 238 A5
BGR/WK TN15 255 N3
BH/WHM TN16 159 H1
BMLY BR1 71 G4
BUR/ETCH TN19 311 M10
CANTW/ST CT2 4 B3
CROY/NA CR0 86 C4
DART DA1 50 E3
DEAL CT14 209 J4
DIT/AY ME20 139 J4
DVE/WH CT16 8 A1
E/WMAL ME19 139 G4
E/WMAL ME19 239 P12
EYN DA4 93 L2
FAV ME13 149 J3
FAV ME13 170 A3
FSTH SE23 45 K6
GRAYS RM17 34 B5
GRH DA9 53 K3
GVW DA11 54 E4
HYTHE CT21 222 A2
MAIDW ME16 12 A1
PUR RM19 32 B2
RAM CT11 16 D7
RBTBR TN32 322 G7
RDART DA2 52 D5
RDV CT15 212 C3
RHAM ME8 103 K6
RSEV TN14 108 E3
RSIT ME9 118 A2
RSIT ME9 121 H7
RTON TN11 194 D2
RTON TN11 255 N4
SEV TN13 20 D3
SIT ME10 119 K4
STH/RUST TN4 22 E5
STH/RUST TN4 196 C1
STHWK SE1 24 C2
STRD ME2 18 E3
STRHM/NOR SW16 68 A6
SWLY BR8 74 D6
THHTH CR7 86 B2
TIL RM18 35 J8
TONN TN10 194 E2
WADH TN5 311 L6
WTHK RM20 33 L5
London Rd Purfleet PUR RM19 32 C5
London Rd (River)
DVE/WH CT16 212 F5
London Rd Rocky Hl
MAIDW ME16 12 D5
London Rd Temple Ewell
DVE/WH CT16 212 D4
London Rd West Thurrock
WTHK RM20 32 F5
London St FOLK CT20 11 L4
Lone Barn Rd RMAID ME17 243 Q9
Lonefield RASHW TN26 303 Q4
Lonewood Wy RTON TN11 256 C3
Long Acre STMC/STPC BR5 91 L5
Longacre WSTB CT5 127 L4
Long Acre Cl CANTW/ST CT2 4 D1
Longacre Rd ASH TN23 204 A4
Longage Hl RCANTW CT4 291 K7
Long Barn Rd RSEV TN14 255 J3
The Long Barrow
KEN/WIL TN24 205 H6
Long Beech ASH TN23 204 B2
Longbridge KEN/WIL TN24 205 L2
Longbridge Ter HYTHE CT21 * 222 B4
Longbridge Wy LEW SE13 46 D3
Longbury Cl STMC/STPC BR5 73 J7
Longbury Dr STMC/STPC BR5 73 J7
Long Catlis Rd RHAM ME8 116 E1
Long Ct PUR RM19 32 B3
Longcroft ELTH/MOT SE9 48 B8
Longdon Wd HAYES BR2 89 M7
Longdown Rd CAT SE6 70 B1
Long Dr SWCH CT13 253 P7
Longfellow Rd GILL ME7 7 J8
Longfellow Wy STHWK SE1 25 G3
Longfield BMLY BR1 71 G5
TENT TN30 315 M2
Longfield Av HART DA3 78 D6
HOO/HM ME3 59 M1
Longfield Cl WSTB CT5 127 L3
Longfield Crs SYD SE26 45 K8
Longfield Est STHWK SE1 * 25 G3
Longfield Pl MAID/SHEP ME15 167 J5
Longfield Rd DVW CT17 217 J3
MEO DA13 96 F1
RTWE/PEM TN2 197 J4
Longfields Dr
MAID/BEAR ME14 142 B8
Longford Cl RHAM ME8 103 H5
Longford Ter FOLK CT20 11 J7
Longford Wy FOLK CT20 11 J7
Longham Copse
MAID/SHEP ME15 168 A4
Longheath Gdns
CROY/NA CR0 87 K1
Long Hl CTHM CR3 130 D7
RCANTW CT4 247 P7
Longhill Av GILL ME7 7 G7
Longhill Rd CAT SE6 46 E7
Longhouse Rd CDW/CHF RM16 35 J2
Longhurst Dr WALD ME5 115 G3
Longhurst Rd CROY/NA CR0 87 J2
LEW SE13 46 F3
Longlands Park Crs
BFN/LL DA15 48 F8
Longlands Rd BFN/LL DA15 48 F8
Long La BXLYHN DA7 29 M6
CDW/CHF RM16 34 B1
CROY/NA CR0 87 K2
RDV CT15 271 Q7
RMAID ME17 259 Q8
STHWK SE1 24 E1
Longleigh La ABYW SE2 29 K5
Long Length ASH TN23 204 A8
Longley Rd CROY/NA CR0 86 C3
RHAM ME8 103 G4
ROCH ME1 100 D2
Longley St STHWK SE1 25 H3
Long Market CANT CT1 5 G4
Longmarsh Vw EYN DA4 76 C5
Longmead CHST BR7 72 B6
Longmead Cl HB CT6 128 D6
Longmead Dr SCUP DA14 49 L7
Longmeade GVE DA12 56 A6
Longmeadow SEV TN13 135 J7
Long Meadow Cl BECK BR3 88 D3
Longmeadow Rd BFN/LL DA15 48 F6
Long Meadow Wy
CANTW/ST CT2 172 A5
Long Meads RRTW TN3 200 C2
Long Mead Wy TONN TN10 188 E8
Longmete Rd RCANTE CT3 235 L8
Long Mill La BGR/WK TN15 240 F8
Longmore Dr IOS ME12 229 M4
Longparish Cl
MAID/SHEP ME15 168 A6
Long Pond Rd BKHTH/KID SE3 26 F7
Longport CANT CT1 5 J5
Long Reach Cl WSTB CT5 126 D7
Longreach Rd ERITH DA8 31 J6
Long Rede La MAIDW ME16 166 A2
Longridge SIT ME10 120 C7
Longridge Vls
STPH/PW TN12 * 281 K6
Long Rock WSTB CT5 127 K2
Longsfield RASHE TN25 305 R7
Longshaw Rd
MAID/SHEP ME15 260 A1
Longshore DEPT SE8 26 A3
Long Slip RRTW TN3 200 B2
Longtail Ri HB CT6 128 F7
Longton Av SYD SE26 69 H1
Longton Gv SYD SE26 69 J1
Longtye Dr WSTB CT5 127 K6
Longview Wy RTWE/PEM TN2 197 G5
Longville Rd LBTH SE11 24 C3
Longwalk MEO DA13 78 F5
Long Wk STHWK SE1 24 F2
Longwood WALD ME5 115 J5
Lonsdale Av MARG CT9 178 F2
Lonsdale Cl ELTH/MOT SE9 47 L8
Lonsdale Crs RDART DA2 52 D7
Lonsdale Dr RHAM ME8 102 F7
SIT ME10 119 K4
Lonsdale Gdns RTW TN1 22 F5
STRHM/NOR SW16 68 A8
Lonsdale Rd BXLYHN DA7 30 A8
SNWD SE25 69 J8
Lookers La HYTHE CT21 222 C2
Loop Court Ms SWCH CT13 237 J12
Loop Rd CHST BR7 72 D3
Loop St SWCH CT13 237 J12
Loose Down Rd FAV ME13 245 Q10
Loose Rd MAID/SHEP ME15 13 J9
Lord Chatham's Ride
RSEV TN14 134 C3
Lord Holland La BRXN/ST SW9 * 24 B8
Lordine La RBTBR TN32 324 C9
Lords Cl DUL SE21 44 D7
RSIT ME9 120 F7
Lordship La EDUL SE22 45 G4
Lord St GVE DA12 55 J5
Lordswood Cl RDART DA2 76 F1
Lords Wood Cl WALD ME5 115 J3
Lords Wood La WALD ME5 101 J8
Lord Warden Av DEAL CT14 209 L7
Lord Warden Sq DVW CT17 8 D9
Lord Warwick St
WOOL/PLUM SE18 28 A2
Lorimar Ct SIT ME10 119 K2
Lorina Rd MSTR CT12 16 E2
Lorn Ct BRXN/ST SW9 24 B8
Lorne Av CROY/NA CR0 87 L3
Lorne Gdns CROY/NA CR0 87 M3
Lorne Rd DVE/WH CT16 213 J8
RAM CT11 16 F6
Lorn Rd BRXN/ST SW9 24 A8
Lorrimore Rd WALW SE17 24 C5
Lorrimore Sq WALW SE17 24 C5
Lorton Cl GVE DA12 55 M7
Lossenham La HAWK TN18 325 L2
Lothian Rd BRXN/ST SW9 24 C7
Lotus Rd BH/WHM TN16 132 E4
Loudon Ct ASH TN23 202 B8
Loudon Wy ASH TN23 202 B8
Loughborough Pk
BRXN/ST SW9 44 C2
Loughborough Rd
BRXN/ST SW9 24 C8
Loughborough St LBTH SE11 24 A4
Louis Cl CHST BR7 72 A1
Louise Bennett Cl HNHL SE24 * 44 C2
Louisville Av GILL ME7 7 M6
Louvain Rd RDART DA2 52 F5
Lovegrove St STHWK SE1 25 H4
Lovelace Av HAYES BR2 90 B2
Lovelace Cl BGR/WK TN15 111 K1
RHAM ME8 102 E8
Lovelace Ct RASHW TN26 285 M12
Lovelace Gn ELTH/MOT SE9 48 A1
Lovelace Rd DUL SE21 44 D7
Love La BXLY DA5 50 B4
CANT CT1 5 H5
FAV ME13 150 A3
HDCN TN27 283 P4
IOS ME12 65 L6
MARG CT9 14 F3
RCANTE CT3 251 Q7
ROCH ME1 19 J7
RYE TN31 225 G3
SNWD SE25 69 J7
SOCK/AV RM15 32 D1
TIL RM18 36 D5
WBY/YAL ME18 164 E6
WOOL/PLUM SE18 28 B3
Lovel Av WELL DA16 29 H8
Lovelinch Cl PECK SE15 25 K5
Lovell Pl BERM/RHTH SE16 25 M2
Lovell Rd CANTW/ST CT2 171 J2
IOS ME12 65 H8
Lovers La CRBK TN17 297 M4
GRH DA9 53 L2
Love Wk CMBW SE5 24 E8
Lovibonds Av ORP BR6 90 C6
Low Cl GRH DA9 53 H3
Lowden Rd HNHL SE24 44 C2
Lower Addiscombe Rd
CROY/NA CR0 86 E4
Lower Bell La DIT/AY ME20 139 J3
Lower Blackhouse Hl
HYTHE CT21 222 E3
Lower Bloors La RHAM ME8 102 F3
Lower Boxley Rd
MAID/BEAR ME14 12 F2
Lower Bridge St CANT CT1 5 G5
Lower Camden CHST BR7 72 A5
Lower Chantry La CANT CT1 5 H6
Lower Church St
CROY/NA CR0 * 86 C5
Lower Coombe St
CROY/NA CR0 86 D7
Lower Crs SLH/COR SS17 36 B2
Lower Cft SWLY BR8 75 G8
Lower Denmark Rd ASH TN23 2 C8
Lower Ensden Rd
RCANTW CT4 247 P5
Lower Fant Rd MAIDW ME16 12 C7
Lower Farm Rd RMAID ME17 259 N7
Lower Gravel Rd HAYES BR2 89 M4
Lower Gn RTON TN11 255 N12
Lower Green Rd RRTW TN3 277 R11
RTWE/PEM TN2 278 A11
STH/RUST TN4 200 D1
Lower Hartlip Rd RSIT ME9 117 L1
Lower Haysden La TON TN9 194 A5
Lower Hazelhurst WADH TN5 310 C6
Lower Herne Rd HB CT6 154 F1
Lower Higham Rd GVE DA12 56 A6
Lower High St WADH TN5 309 N7
Lower Lees Rd RCANTW CT4 247 Q7
Lower Marsh STHWK SE1 24 A1
Lower Mill La DEAL CT14 209 K4
Lower Northdown Av
MARG CT9 15 L5
Lower Norton La RSIT ME9 148 B1
Lower Park Rd BELV DA17 30 B2
Lower Platts WADH TN5 310 G8
Lower Rainham Rd GILL ME7 84 B7
RHAM ME8 103 J2
Lower Range Rd GVE DA12 55 M5
Lower Rd BELV DA17 30 D2
BERM/RHTH SE16 25 K2
DVE/WH CT16 212 E4
FAV ME13 149 H2
GVE DA12 56 F7
GVW DA11 54 B2
IOS ME12 228 C1
IOS ME12 228 H1
IOS ME12 229 L2
MAID/SHEP ME15 13 K7
MAID/SHEP ME15 165 L6
RASHW TN26 303 J12
RCANTE CT3 252 G3
RMAID ME17 260 F6
RSIT ME9 121 G6
RSIT ME9 122 A7
STMC/STPC BR5 91 J2
SWLY BR8 75 J4
TENT TN30 316 E12
TIL RM18 55 H2
Lower Rochester Rd
HOO/HM ME3 57 L7
Lower Sandgate Rd FOLK CT20 11 H8
Lower Sands LYDD TN29 321 K7
Lower Santon La RCANTE CT3 235 M6
Lower Station Rd DART DA1 50 F4
Lower Stone St
MAID/SHEP ME15 13 G5
Lower St DEAL CT14 272 H3
RMAID ME17 169 H6
RTON TN11 255 P8
SWCH CT13 253 N8
Lower Tovil MAID/SHEP ME15 12 C9
Lower Twydall La GILL ME7 102 D1
Lower Vicarage Rd
KEN/WIL TN24 202 F4
Lower Wall Rd HYTHE CT21 321 K2
RASHE TN25 320 C2
Lower Warren Rd WALD ME5 114 F7
Lower Woodlands Rd GILL ME7 84 A7
Lowfield Rd IOS ME12 64 F7
Lowfield St DART DA1 51 M5
Low Meadow STRD ME2 99 H8
The Lowry TON TN9 194 E5
Lowslip Hl RDV CT15 216 A4
Low Street La TIL RM18 36 A4
Lowther Hl FSTH SE23 45 M5
Lowther Rd DVW CT17 217 J1
Lowth Rd CMBW SE5 24 D8
Loxford Ldg FOLK CT20 * 223 L3
Loxley Cl SYD SE26 69 L2
Loxton Rd FSTH SE23 45 L6
Loxwood Cl DVE/WH CT16 213 J2
STMC/STPC BR5 91 L5
Lubbock Cl MAID/SHEP ME15 167 M8
Lubbock Rd CHST BR7 72 A4
Lubbock St NWCR SE14 25 K6
Lucas Crs GRH DA9 53 J3
Lucas Rd GRAYS RM17 34 B2
PGE/AN SE20 69 K3
SNOD ME6 112 F6
Lucas Shadwell Wy RYE TN31 225 L7
Lucas St DEPT SE8 26 B8
Lucerne Dr WSTB CT5 126 A7
Lucerne La RDV CT15 210 D7
Lucerne Rd ORP BR6 91 G4
THHTH CR7 86 C1
Lucerne St MAID/BEAR ME14 13 H3
Lucey Rd BERM/RHTH SE16 25 H2
Lucey Wy BERM/RHTH SE16 25 H2
Lucilina Dr EDEN TN8 192 D5
Lucilla Av ASH TN23 204 C7
Luckhurst Gdns MARG CT9 179 H2
Luckhurst Rd DVW CT17 212 F6
KEN/WIL TN24 205 K4
Lucknow Cl RDV CT15 214 A6
Lucknow Rd STPH/PW TN12 279 K1
Lucknow St WOOL/PLUM SE18 28 F6
Lucks Hl E/WMAL ME19 138 E5
Lucks La RMAID ME17 260 A7
STPH/PW TN12 257 L12
Lucks Wy STPH/PW TN12 280 G3
Lucorn Cl LEE/GVPK SE12 47 G4
Lucy Av FOLKN CT19 10 E1
Lucy's Hl HYTHE CT21 222 C3
Luddenham Cl ASH TN23 204 C5
MAID/BEAR ME14 13 M1
Luddesdon Rd ERITH DA8 30 B6
Luddesdown Rd MEO DA13 98 C3
Ludford Cl CROY/NA CR0 86 C7
Ludgate Rd RSIT ME9 146 F5
Ludlow Cl HAYES BR2 71 H7
Ludlow Pl GRAYS RM17 34 C2
Ludpit La BUR/ETCH TN19 322 B7
Luffield Rd ABYW SE2 29 J2
Luffman Rd LEE/GVPK SE12 47 J8
Lugard Rd PECK SE15 25 J8
Lughorse La WBY/YAL ME18 257 R4
WBY/YAL ME18 258 A4
Lukes Cl DVW CT17 213 H8
Lullarook Cl BH/WHM TN16 132 B2
Lullingstone Av SWLY BR8 75 G7
Lullingstone Cl GILL ME7 116 C2
STMC/STPC BR5 73 J4
Lullingstone Crs
STMC/STPC BR5 73 H4
Lullingstone La EYN DA4 93 K6
LEW SE13 46 E4
Lullingstone Rd BELV DA17 30 A5
MAIDW ME16 140 D6
Lullington Garth BMLY BR1 * 70 F4
Lullington Rd PGE/AN SE20 69 H4
Lulworth Rd ELTH/MOT SE9 47 M7
PECK SE15 * 25 J8
WELL DA16 29 G8
Lumley Cl BELV DA17 30 B5
Lumsden Ter CHAT ME4 6 B6
Lunar Cl BH/WHM TN16 132 C2
Luna Rd THHTH CR7 68 D7
Lunedale Rd RDART DA2 52 D6
Lunghurst Rd CTHM CR3 130 F7
Lunham Rd NRWD SE19 68 F3
Lunsford La DIT/AY ME20 113 G8
Lupin Cl BRXS/STRHM SW2 44 C7
CROY/NA CR0 87 L4
Lupton Cl LEE/GVPK SE12 71 J1
Lurkins Ri CRBK TN17 297 M6
Lushington Rd CAT SE6 70 C2
MAID/BEAR ME14 140 F6
Lusted Hall La BH/WHM TN16 132 B6
Luton Av BRDST CT10 183 J2
Luton Ct BRDST CT10 183 J2
Luton High St WALD ME5 101 K3
Luton Pl GNWCH SE10 26 D6
Luton Rd CHAT ME4 7 G7
FAV ME13 149 M2
SCUP DA14 49 K8
Lutwyche Rd FSTH SE23 46 A7
Luxfield Rd ELTH/MOT SE9 47 M6
Luxford St BERM/RHTH SE16 25 L3
Luxmore St BROCKY SE4 26 A7
Luxon Rd MEO DA13 239 R1
Luxor St CMBW SE5 44 D1
Luxted Rd ORP BR6 106 F6
Lyall Av DUL SE21 68 F1
Lyall Wy RHAM ME8 116 E1
Lychfield Dr STRD ME2 18 F1
Lych Gate Rd ORP BR6 91 H4
Lyconby Gdns CROY/NA CR0 87 M3
Lydbrook Cl SIT ME10 119 K5
Lydd Cl BFN/LL DA15 48 F8
Lydden Hl RDV CT15 293 Q1
Lydd Rd BXLYHN DA7 30 A6
NROM TN28 330 G7
RYE TN31 332 D7
WALD ME5 101 J8
Lydd Town Crossing
LYDD TN29 334 F1
Lydens La EDEN TN8 193 G7
Lydhurst Av BRXS/STRHM SW2 44 A7
Lydia Rd DEAL CT14 209 H7
ERITH DA8 31 G5
Lydos Cl LYDD TN29 335 M4
Lydstep Rd CHST BR7 72 B1
Lyell Cl HYTHE CT21 222 B4
Lyell Rd BRCH CT7 176 C6
Lyford St WOOL/PLUM SE18 27 M3
Lyle Cl STRD ME2 19 G1
Lyle Ct MAIDW ME16 140 D8
Lyle Pk SEV TN13 21 H2
Lymden La WADH TN5 310 B10
Lyme Farm Rd LEE/GVPK SE12 47 H2
Lymer Av NRWD SE19 69 G2
Lyme Rd WELL DA16 29 J7
Lyminge Cl RHAM ME8 102 D3
SCUP DA14 73 G1
Lyminge Wy MARG CT9 178 F4
Lymington Ct
MAID/SHEP ME15 260 A1
Lymington Rd WGOS CT8 177 G6
Lympne Hl HYTHE CT21 307 M12
Lympstone Gdns PECK SE15 25 H6
Lyncourt BKHTH/KID SE3 * 26 E8
Lyndale Cl BKHTH/KID SE3 27 G5
Lynden Wy SWLY BR8 74 D7
Lyndhurst Av MARG CT9 15 L5
RHAM ME8 102 D6
Lyndhurst Cl BXLYHN DA7 50 C1
CANTW/ST CT2 171 M2
CROY/NA CR0 87 G6
ORP BR6 90 C7
Lyndhurst Dr SEV TN13 20 B4
Lyndhurst Gv CMBW SE5 24 F8
SIT ME10 119 M7
Lyndhurst Leys HAYES BR2 * 70 E6
Lyndhurst Prior SNWD SE25 * 68 F7
Lyndhurst Rd BRDST CT10 179 K8
BXLYHN DA7 50 C1
DVW CT17 212 F7
LYDD TN29 320 H10
MAID/SHEP ME15 167 K5
RAM CT11 17 M4
THHTH CR7 68 B8
Lyndhurst Sq PECK SE15 25 G7
Lyndhurst Wy MEO DA13 78 F5
PECK SE15 25 G7
Lyndon Av BFN/LL DA15 49 G3
Lyndon Rd BELV DA17 30 B3
Lyndon Wy RFOLK CT18 291 M10
Lynette Av STRD ME2 82 B4
Lyngate Ct MARG CT9 179 G3
Lyngs Cl WBY/YAL ME18 257 Q5
Lynmead Cl EDEN TN8 192 C1
Lynmere Rd WELL DA16 29 J8
Lynmouth Dr IOS ME12 65 K6
Lynmouth Ri STMC/STPC BR5 73 J8
Lynne Cl ORP BR6 107 L1
SAND/SEL CR2 104 B5
Lynors Av STRD ME2 82 B3
Lynstead Cl BMLY BR1 71 K6
Lynsted Cl ASH TN23 204 C5
BXLYHS DA6 50 C3
Lynsted Ct BECK BR3 69 M6
Lynsted Gdns ELTH/MOT SE9 47 L2
Lynsted La RSIT ME9 147 J2
Lynsted Rd IOS ME12 64 F6
RHAM ME8 102 C2
Lynton Av STMC/STPC BR5 73 J8
Lynton Dr WALD ME5 115 J2
Lynton Est STHWK SE1 * 25 H3
Lynton Pde MARG CT9 * 15 K4
Lynton Rd CROY/NA CR0 86 B2
GVW DA11 55 H6
HYTHE CT21 222 D4
STHWK SE1 25 G3
Lynton Rd South GVW DA11 55 H6
Lynwood FOLKN CT19 11 G2
RRTW TN3 199 K7
Lynwood Gdns CROY/NA CR0 86 A7
Lynwood Gv ORP BR6 90 F3
Lyons Crs TON TN9 194 F3
Lyoth Rd STMC/STPC BR5 90 D5
Lypeatt Ct CANTW/ST CT2 * 171 K1
Lyric Ms SYD SE26 69 K1
Lysander Cl BRDST CT10 182 F2
RCANTW CT4 175 M5
Lysander Rd E/WMAL ME19 164 A2
Lysander Wk RFOLK CT18 220 B1
Lysander Wy ORP BR6 90 D6
Lytchet Rd BMLY BR1 71 H4
Lytcott Gv EDUL SE22 45 G3
Lytham Av HB CT6 128 E8
Lytham St WALW SE17 24 E4
Lytton Rd CDW/CHF RM16 35 H3
Lyveden Rd BKHTH/KID SE3 27 J6

M

Mabel Rd SWLY BR8 75 H3
Maberley Crs NRWD SE19 69 H4
Maberley Rd BECK BR3 69 L7
NRWD SE19 69 G5
Mabledon Av KEN/WIL TN24 2 F6
Mabledon Cl NROM TN28 331 J7
Mabledon Rd TON TN9 194 D5
Macarthur Ter CHARL SE7 * 27 L5
Macaulay Cl DIT/AY ME20 139 H1
Macbean St WOOL/PLUM SE18 28 B2
Macclesfield Rd SNWD SE25 87 J1
Macdonald Pde WSTB CT5 126 B6
Macdonald Rd DVW CT17 213 H8
GILL ME7 7 L1
Mace La ASH TN23 2 E4
RSEV TN14 107 J7
Machell Rd PECK SE15 45 K1
Mackenders Cl DIT/AY ME20 114 A7
Mackenders La DIT/AY ME20 114 B7
Mackenzie Dr FOLK CT20 219 M8
Mackenzie Rd BECK BR3 69 M5
Mackenzie Ter DVE/WH CT16 * 213 J6
Mackenzie Wy GVE DA12 79 L3
Mackerel Hl RYE TN31 326 C9
Mackie Rd BRXS/STRHM SW2 44 B5
Mackintosh Cl HOO/HM ME3 59 M1
Macklands Wy RHAM ME8 103 H3
Macks Rd BERM/RHTH SE16 25 H3
Maclean Rd FSTH SE23 45 M4
Maclean Ter GVE DA12 * 56 A7
Macleod Cl GRAYS RM17 34 E3
Macleod House
WOOL/PLUM SE18 * 27 M6
Macleod St WALW SE17 24 D4
Macmichaels Wy
BUR/ETCH TN19 322 F2
Macoma Rd WOOL/PLUM SE18 28 E5
Macoma Ter WOOL/PLUM SE18 28 E5
Maconochies Rd
POP/IOD E14 * 26 C4
Macquarie Wy POP/IOD E14 26 C3
Madan Cl BH/WHM TN16 159 K3
Madan Rd BH/WHM TN16 159 J3
Mada Rd ORP BR6 90 C6
Madden Av WALD ME5 100 F8
Madden Cl SWCM DA10 53 M4
Maddocks Cl SCUP DA14 73 L3
Maddock Wy WALW SE17 24 C5
Madeira Av BMLY BR1 70 F5
Madeira Pk RTW TN1 22 F8
Madeira Rd MARG CT9 15 J4
NROM TN28 331 N7
Madeira Wk RAM CT11 17 K6
Madeline Rd PGE/AN SE20 69 H4
Madginford Cl
MAID/SHEP ME15 168 B3
Madginford Rd
MAID/SHEP ME15 168 A3
Madison Crs WELL DA16 29 K6
Madison Gdns BXLYHN DA7 29 K6
Madison Wy SEV TN13 20 D2
Madron St STHWK SE1 24 F4
Maesmaur Rd BH/WHM TN16 132 C7
Mafeking Rd WALD ME5 115 G2
Magazine Rd KEN/WIL TN24 2 B3
Magdala Rd BRDST CT10 179 H7
DVW CT17 213 J8
Magdalen Cl GILL ME7 116 B1
Magdalen Ct BRDST CT10 179 K8
CANT CT1 5 H7
Magdelan Gv ORP BR6 91 J7
Magee St LBTH SE11 24 B5
Magness Rd DEAL CT14 209 H7
Magnet Rd WTHK RM20 33 K5
Magnolia Av MARG CT9 179 G3
RHAM ME8 102 C8
Magnolia Dr BH/WHM TN16 132 C2
RCANTW CT4 248 G9
Magpie Cl DIT/AY ME20 139 H4
Magpie Ct IOS ME12 65 H7
Magpie Hall Cl HAYES BR2 89 M2
Magpie Hall La HAYES BR2 89 M3
Magpie Hall Rd CHAT ME4 6 F9
RASHW TN26 304 A3
Magpie La MAID/BEAR ME14 117 G4
RCANTW CT4 291 L6
Magpie Pl NWCR SE14 * 25 M5
Maguire St STHWK SE1 25 G1
Magwitch Cl ROCH ME1 100 C1
Maida Rd BELV DA17 30 B2
CHAT ME4 7 H9
Maida Vale Rd DART DA1 51 H4
Maiden Erlegh Av BXLY DA5 49 M6
Maiden La CANT CT1 4 B8
DART DA1 51 H2
Maidenstone Hl GNWCH SE10 26 D7
Maidstone Rd ASH TN23 202 D8
BGR/WK TN15 137 G8
BGR/WK TN15 240 H2
CHAT ME4 6 C6
GILL ME7 116 C3
HDCN TN27 260 H12
HDCN TN27 263 Q4
HDCN TN27 264 D9
HDCN TN27 264 E10
HDCN TN27 282 H1
RMAID ME17 243 L12
RMAID ME17 260 F4
ROCH ME1 100 C6
RSIT ME9 118 C8
RTON TN11 256 C5
RTWE/PEM TN2 197 M5
RTWE/PEM TN2 278 B9
SCUP DA14 73 L3
SEV TN13 20 B1
SIT ME10 119 H3
STPH/PW TN12 278 E12
STPH/PW TN12 278 E5
STPH/PW TN12 279 J3
STPH/PW TN12 279 Q12
STPH/PW TN12 280 A9
STPH/PW TN12 281 K2
STPH/PW TN12 281 R3
SWLY BR8 74 C5
WALD ME5 100 E7
WBY/YAL ME18 257 M3
The Mailyns RHAM ME8 102 D6
Main Barracks
WOOL/PLUM SE18 * 28 A4
Maine Cl DVE/WH CT16 213 J6
Main Ga TIL RM18 * 35 G8
Main Gate Rd CHAT ME4 83 G6
Mainridge Rd CHST BR7 72 B1
Main Rd BFN/LL DA15 48 F8
BH/WHM TN16 132 C2
EDEN TN8 186 C8
EYN DA4 76 C3
EYN DA4 93 M2
HART DA3 78 D8
HOO/HM ME3 59 J8
HOO/HM ME3 60 E6
HOO/HM ME3 83 G1
IOS ME12 64 B2
ORP BR6 * 108 B3
QBOR ME11 64 B8
RDART DA2 77 K5
RSEV TN14 133 M4
RSEV TN14 160 D2
STMC/STPC BR5 73 K5
SWLY BR8 75 G5
SWLY BR8 92 D2
Main Road Gorse Hl EYN DA4 94 C4
Main St CHAT ME4 83 J3
RYE TN31 325 J8
RYE TN31 326 E11
RYE TN31 327 L9
Maismore St PECK SE15 25 H5
Maison Dieu Rd DVE/WH CT16 8 C3
Maitland Cl GNWCH SE10 26 C6
Maitland Ct FAV ME13 123 J8
Maitland Rd SYD SE26 69 L3
Majendie Rd WOOL/PLUM SE18 28 E4
Major Cl BRXN/ST SW9 44 C1
WSTB CT5 126 C7
Major Rd BERM/RHTH SE16 * 25 H2
Major York's Rd STH/RUST TN4 22 B6
Makenade Av FAV ME13 149 L4
Malabar St POP/IOD E14 26 B1
Malan Cl BH/WHM TN16 132 D3
Malcolm Cl PGE/AN SE20 * 69 K4
Malcolm Rd PGE/AN SE20 69 K4
SNWD SE25 87 H2
Malcolm Sargent Rd
ASH TN23 204 E5
Malden Av SNWD SE25 69 J8
Malden Dr MAID/BEAR ME14 141 G5
Maldon Cl CMBW SE5 * 44 F1
Maley Av WNWD SE27 44 C7
Malfort Rd CMBW SE5 44 F1
Malham Dr MARG CT9 15 K7
Malham Rd FSTH SE23 45 L6
Mallams Ms BRXN/ST SW9 44 B1
Mallard Cl DART DA1 52 A3
HB CT6 128 F7
Mallard Ct IOS ME12 65 H7
Mallard Rd SAND/SEL CR2 104 C4
Mallards KEN/WIL TN24 205 G4
Mallards Wy MAID/SHEP ME15 168 B3
Mallard Wk CROY/NA CR0 87 L1
Mallard Wy HOO/HM ME3 61 J1
Mallet Rd LEW SE13 46 E4
Malling Cl CROY/NA CR0 * 87 K2
Mallingdene Cl HOO/HM ME3 58 C5
Malling Rd DIT/AY ME20 112 F8
SNOD ME6 113 H6
WBY/YAL ME18 241 R8
Mallings Dr MAID/BEAR ME14 168 E1
Mallings La MAID/BEAR ME14 168 D1
Malling Ter MAIDW ME16 166 D1
Malling Wy HAYES BR2 89 G3
Mallory Cl BECK BR3 69 M6
BROCKY SE4 45 M2
MSTR CT12 182 F3
Mallow Cl CROY/NA CR0 87 L4
GVW DA11 78 F1
Mallow Ct GRAYS RM17 34 E5
The Mall DVE/WH CT16 * 8 B3
FAV ME13 149 K3
GILL ME7 * 7 J2
Mallys Pl EYN DA4 76 D5
Malmains Cl BECK BR3 88 E1
Malmains Rd DVW CT17 217 H2
Malmains Wy BECK BR3 70 D8
Malmaynes Hall Rd
HOO/HM ME3 60 D2
Malmeady Ct DEAL CT14 * 209 H8
Malpas Rd BROCKY SE4 26 A8
CDW/CHF RM16 35 K2
Malta Av WALD ME5 101 H6
Malta Rd TIL RM18 35 G8
Malta Ter MAID/BEAR ME14 141 H6
Maltby Cl ORP BR6 91 H4
Maltby St STHWK SE1 25 G2
Malthouse Cl RMAID ME17 243 L12
Malthouse Hl HYTHE CT21 222 C3
MAID/SHEP ME15 259 L1
Malthouse La GVE DA12 80 F2
RASHW TN26 318 A2
RYE TN31 326 E11
Malt House La TENT TN30 315 M2
Malthouse Rd BGR/WK TN15 238 E4
CANTW/ST CT2 4 F1
Maltings Cl RTON TN11 256 B5
Malting's Pl STHWK SE1 24 F1
The Maltings CANT CT1 * 5 H5
DEAL CT14 211 J1
MAID/BEAR ME14 141 M8
ORP BR6 91 G4
OXTED RH8 185 C1
RCANTE CT3 251 J2
RHAM ME8 103 H5
RMAID ME17 259 N1
RTON TN11 * 256 B5
SNWD SE25 * 68 F7
Malt Ms ROCH ME1 19 J7
Malton Ms WOOL/PLUM SE18 28 F5
Malton St WOOL/PLUM SE18 28 F5
Malton Wy RTWE/PEM TN2 197 J7
Malt St STHWK SE1 25 H5
Malus Cl WALD ME5 115 H4
Malvern Av BXLYHN DA7 29 M6
Malvern Meadow
DVE/WH CT16 212 F4
Malvern Pk HB CT6 129 L5
Malvern Rd DVE/WH CT16 212 F4
DVW CT17 8 A5
GILL ME7 101 M3
GRAYS RM17 34 F3
KEN/WIL TN24 2 B1
ORP BR6 91 J7
THHTH CR7 68 B8
Malvina Av GVE DA12 55 J7
Malyons Rd LEW SE13 46 C3
SWLY BR8 75 G4
Malyons Ter LEW SE13 46 C3
Mamignot Cl
MAID/BEAR ME14 142 A8
Manaton Cl PECK SE15 45 J1
Manchester Cl WALD ME5 101 K7
Manchester Gv POP/IOD E14 26 D4
Manchester Rd POP/IOD E14 26 D4
THHTH CR7 68 D7
Manciple Cl CANTW/ST CT2 171 K6
Manciple St STHWK SE1 24 E1
Mandarin La HB CT6 128 F7
Mandela St BRXN/ST SW9 24 B6
Mandela Wy STHWK SE1 24 F3
Mandeville Rd CANTW/ST CT2 4 D1
Mangers La DVE/WH CT16 213 H7
Mangers Pl DVE/WH CT16 213 H6
Mangold Wy ERITHM DA18 29 L2
Mangravet Av
MAID/SHEP ME15 167 K6
Manilla St POP/IOD E14 26 B1
Manister Rd ABYW SE2 29 H2
Manley Cl DVE/WH CT16 213 H2
Mann Cl CROY/NA CR0 86 D6
Mannering Cl DVW CT17 213 G6
Manning Rd STMC/STPC BR5 91 L1
Mannock Rd DART DA1 52 A1
Manns Hl RCANTW CT4 269 K7
Mann Sq TON TN9 195 G6
Manor Av BROCKY SE4 26 A8
DEAL CT14 209 J5
Manorbrook BKHTH/KID SE3 47 H2
Manor Cl CANT CT1 171 K8
DART DA1 50 E2
DEAL CT14 209 H5
GDST RH9 184 A8
GVE DA12 56 C7
HB CT6 232 A3
MAID/BEAR ME14 168 C2
QBOR ME11 227 N2
RDART DA2 51 H8
STH/RUST TN4 22 B4
WARL CR6 130 D3
Manor Ct MAID/BEAR ME14 168 C2
MEO DA13 97 L1
Manor Dr BRCH CT7 176 C7
HART DA3 96 B2
Manor Est BERM/RHTH SE16 25 J3
Manor Farm Cl HYTHE CT21 307 M9
Manor Farm Rd
STRHM/NOR SW16 68 B6
Manorfield ASH TN23 204 B3
Manor Fld GVE DA12 80 F2
Manorfields Cl CHST BR7 73 G7
Manor Forstal HART DA3 96 A6
Manor Gdns WALD ME5 115 G1
Manor Gv BECK BR3 70 C6
PECK SE15 25 K5
SIT ME10 119 M6
TONN TN10 194 F2
Manor House Dr ASH TN23 204 F7
MAIDW ME16 12 A6
Manor House Gdns
EDEN TN8 192 D4
Manor La HART DA3 95 K3
LEW SE13 46 F3
ROCH ME1 100 A2
Manor Lane Ter LEW SE13 46 F2
Manor Lea Rd BRCH CT7 233 N8
Manor Leaze RASHE TN25 289 N12
Manor Ms DEAL CT14 211 G4
Manor Mt FSTH SE23 45 K6
Manor Pk CHST BR7 72 E6
LEW SE13 46 E3
STH/RUST TN4 22 B5
Manor Park Cl WWKM BR4 88 C4
Manor Park Rd CHST BR7 72 D5
WWKM BR4 88 C4
Manor Pl CHST BR7 72 E6
WALW SE17 24 D4
Manor Pound La RASHE TN25 289 M10
Manor Ri DVW CT17 217 H3
MAID/BEAR ME14 168 C2
Manor Rd BECK BR3 70 B6
BFN/LL DA15 49 G8
BGR/WK TN15 111 L5
BH/WHM TN16 132 D6
BRCH CT7 233 N8
BXLY DA5 50 C6
CHAT ME4 6 C5
DART DA1 50 F2
DEAL CT14 209 H5
DVW CT17 217 H3
EDEN TN8 192 C4
ERITH DA8 31 G5
FOLK CT20 11 H5
GRAYS RM17 34 D5
GVE DA12 * 54 J4
HART DA3 96 D1
HB CT6 232 A3
LYDD TN29 334 E3
MEO DA13 97 K1
QBOR ME11 227 N2
RSEV TN14 160 C2
RSIT ME9 146 A8
SNWD SE25 69 H8
STH/RUST TN4 200 D1
SWCM DA10 53 M5
TIL RM18 35 H8
WSTB CT5 127 H2
WTHK RM20 33 K5
WWKM BR4 88 C5
Manor Rw TENT TN30 * 315 M2
Manor St GILL ME7 6 E1
Manor Vw HART DA3 * 96 B2
Manor Wy ASH TN23 202 D8
BECK BR3 70 B7
BKHTH/KID SE3 47 H2
BXLY DA5 50 B6
BXLYHN DA7 50 E1
GRAYS RM17 34 D6
GVW DA11 54 B1
HAYES BR2 89 M2
IOS ME12 67 K7
IOS ME12 230 G3
STMC/STPC BR5 72 D8
SWCM DA10 53 M2
Manse Fld RASHE TN25 289 M12
Mansel Dr ROCH ME1 100 B3
Mansell La RDV CT15 292 G5
Mansergh Cl WOOL/PLUM SE18 27 M6
Manse Wy SWLY BR8 75 H8
Mansfield Cl STMC/STPC BR5 91 L3
Mansfield Rd SWLY BR8 74 F3
Mansfield Wk MAIDW ME16 12 B8
Mansion Gdns DVE/WH CT16 213 H5
Mansion House Cl HDCN TN27 300 F3
Mansion Rw GILL ME7 6 F1
Manston Cl PGE/AN SE20 69 K5
Manston Court Rd MARG CT9 182 B1
MSTR CT12 181 M5
Manston Rd MARG CT9 178 A7
MSTR CT12 16 B3
MSTR CT12 181 H3
Manthorpe Rd
WOOL/PLUM SE18 28 D4
Mantle Rd BROCKY SE4 45 M1
Mantles Hl DEAL CT14 208 E8
Manton Rd ABYW SE2 29 H3
The Manwarings
STPH/PW TN12 279 R11
Manwood Av CANTW/ST CT2 172 A6
Manwood Cl SIT ME10 120 A7
Manwood Rd BROCKY SE4 46 A4
SWCH CT13 206 B1
Maple Av GILL ME7 83 M8
MAIDW ME16 140 D7
Maple Cl ASH TN23 204 A1
CANTW/ST CT2 171 H3
DIT/AY ME20 139 H3
MARG CT9 179 H4
RTWE/PEM TN2 22 E9
STMC/STPC BR5 90 E1
SWLY BR8 74 F6
Maple Ct RCANTE CT3 155 M8
Maple Crs BFN/LL DA15 49 H4
Mapledale Av CROY/NA CR0 87 J6
Maple Dr EGRIN RH19 274 A12
LYDD TN29 331 N2
Maple Gdns RCANTE CT3 173 M1
Maple Leaf Dr BFN/LL DA15 49 G6
Maple Leaf Sq
BERM/RHTH SE16 * 25 L1
Maple Ms STRHM/NOR SW16 68 A2
Maple Rd DART DA1 51 K6
GRAYS RM17 34 D5
GVE DA12 79 K1
HOO/HM ME3 83 M2
PGE/AN SE20 69 K4
STRD ME2 18 C5
Maplescombe La EYN DA4 94 B6
Maplesden STPH/PW TN12 * 281 J4
Maplesden Cl MAIDW ME16 166 A2
Maplestead Rd
BRXS/STRHM SW2 44 A5
The Maples BRDST CT10 182 F1
HART DA3 78 C7
IOS ME12 65 J7
Maple St IOS ME12 64 D4
Maplethorpe Rd THHTH CR7 68 B8
Mapleton Cl HAYES BR2 89 H1
Mapleton Rd BH/WHM TN16 159 K8
EDEN TN8 187 H5
Maple Tree Pl BKHTH/KID SE3 27 M7
Maplins Cl RHAM ME8 * 103 G4
Mara Ct CHAT ME4 * 101 G4
Maran Wy ERITHM DA18 29 L2
Marathon Paddock GILL ME7 7 M5
Marathon Wy THMD SE28 29 G1
Marbrook Ct LEE/GVPK SE12 47 K8
Marcella Rd BRXN/ST SW9 24 B8
Marcellina Wy ORP BR6 90 F6
Marcet Rd DART DA1 51 K3
Marchants STPH/PW TN12 * 278 G9
Marchants Dr RYE TN31 332 D7
Marchant St NWCR SE14 25 M5
Marchwood Cl CMBW SE5 24 F6
Marcia Rd STHWK SE1 24 F3
Marconi Rd GVW DA11 54 E8
Marconi Wy ROCH ME1 100 E6
Marcus Garvey Ms EDUL SE22 45 J4
Marcus Garvey Wy
BRXN/ST SW9 44 B2
Marcus Rd DART DA1 51 H5
Mardale Cl RHAM ME8 103 H4
Mardell Rd CROY/NA CR0 87 L1
Marden Av HAYES BR2 89 H2
MSTR CT12 16 D3
Marden Crs BXLY DA5 50 D3
CROY/NA CR0 86 A2
Marden Rd CROY/NA CR0 86 A2
STPH/PW TN12 281 N4
STRD ME2 82 D4
Marden Sq BERM/RHTH SE16 25 J2
Mardol Rd KEN/WIL TN24 202 F6
Mardyke Vw SOCK/AV RM15 * 32 F2
Marechal Niel Av BFN/LL DA15 48 E8
Marechal Niel Pde
BFN/LL DA15 * 48 E8
Maresfield CROY/NA CR0 86 F6
Maresfield Cl DVE/WH CT16 213 J7
Margaret Gardner Dr
ELTH/MOT SE9 48 A7
Margaret Rd BXLY DA5 49 L4
Margarets Rd RDV CT15 211 H7
Margaret St FOLK CT20 11 L5
Margate Cl GILL ME7 83 M7
Margate Hl BRCH CT7 180 E2
Margate Rd BRDST CT10 182 E1
HB CT6 129 M7
Margetts La ROCH ME1 113 L4
Margetts Pl STRD ME2 83 H2
Maria Cl BERM/RHTH SE16 25 H3
Marian Av IOS ME12 65 H6
Marian Sq STPH/PW TN12 282 A5
Marie Curie CMBW SE5 * 24 F7
Marie Manor Wy RDART DA2 * 52 D8
Marigold St BERM/RHTH SE16 25 J1
Marigold Wy CROY/NA CR0 87 L4
Marilyn Crs BRCH CT7 176 E6
Marina Ct DEAL CT14 * 209 L1
Marina Dr DART DA1 52 B6
GVW DA11 55 G5
IOS ME12 65 H6
WELL DA16 28 F8
Marina Esp RAM CT11 17 M5
Marina Rd RAM CT11 17 M5
The Marina DEAL CT14 209 L1
Marine Av LYDD TN29 321 L6
Marine Ct PUR RM19 32 A3
Marine Crs FOLK CT20 11 K7
WSTB CT5 127 K2
Marine Dr BRDST CT10 179 K2
HOO/HM ME3 83 M2
MARG CT9 14 E4
WOOL/PLUM SE18 28 A3
Marine Gap WSTB CT5 126 D4
Marine Gdns MARG CT9 14 E5
Marine Pde DVE/WH CT16 8 E6
FOLK CT20 11 L6
IOS ME12 64 E3
NROM TN28 331 M8
WSTB CT5 127 G2
Marine Parade Ms FOLK CT20 11 L6
Marine Pl IOS ME12 * 64 E3
Marine Rd DEAL CT14 209 L5
Mariners Lea BRDST CT10 183 G1
Mariners Ms POP/IOD E14 26 E3
The Mariners ROCH ME1 * 19 H9
Mariners Wy GVW DA11 54 F5
Marine St BERM/RHTH SE16 25 H2
Marine Ter FOLK CT20 11 L6
MARG CT9 14 D5
Marine Vw CHAT ME4 83 J4
Marine Walk St HYTHE CT21 * 222 D3
Marion Cl WALD ME5 115 H3
Marion Crs MAID/SHEP ME15 167 J4
STMC/STPC BR5 91 J1
Marion Rd CROY/NA CR0 86 D1
Marischal Rd LEW SE13 46 E1
Marisco Cl CDW/CHF RM16 35 J3
Maritime Av HB CT6 129 K5
Maritime Cl GRH DA9 53 J3
STRD ME2 19 M1
Maritime Ga GVW DA11 54 F5
Maritime Quay POP/IOD E14 26 B4
Maritime Wy CHAT ME4 83 J4
Marjan Cl DVW CT17 213 H8
Mark Av RAM CT11 16 C8
Mark Cl BXLYHN DA7 29 M7
HAYES BR2 89 M7
Market Buildings
MAID/BEAR ME14 12 F4
Market Hl HYTHE CT21 * 222 D3
Market Meadow
STMC/STPC BR5 73 K8
Market Pde BMLY BR1 * 71 H5
SCUP DA14 * 73 H1
SNWD SE25 * 69 H8
Market Pl BERM/RHTH SE16 * 25 H3
BXLYHN DA7 50 B2
DART DA1 51 M5
HDCN TN27 264 B6
MARG CT9 14 F3
RCANTE CT3 251 Q12
TIL RM18 * 35 H8
Market Rd RYE TN31 225 G4
Market Sq BH/WHM TN16 159 H5
BMLY BR1 71 H6
RTW TN1 * 23 G4
Market St DART DA1 51 M5
DEAL CT14 209 L3
FAV ME13 149 L2
HB CT6 129 G4
MARG CT9 14 F3
RTWE/PEM TN2 * 22 E7
RYE TN31 225 H4
STPH/PW TN12 282 A4
SWCH CT13 237 K12
WOOL/PLUM SE18 28 B3
Market Vw RCANTE CT3 251 Q12
Market Wy BH/WHM TN16 159 J4
CANTW/ST CT2 172 B7
Market Yard Ms STHWK SE1 24 F2
Markfield CROY/NA CR0 104 E5
Markfield Rd CTHM CR3 156 A4
Markland Rd DVW CT17 217 H2
Mark La GVE DA12 55 M5
Marks Rd WARL CR6 130 D4
Marks Sq GVW DA11 79 G1
Markstone Ter ORP BR6 * 91 H3
Mark St CHAT ME4 6 F9
Mark Wy SWLY BR8 93 H1
Markwell Cl SYD SE26 69 J1
Marlborough Cl BRDST CT10 183 H2
CDW/CHF RM16 34 D1
NROM TN28 331 L6
ORP BR6 91 G3
STH/RUST TN4 22 B4
WALW SE17 * 24 C3
Marlborough Crs SEV TN13 20 A4
Marlborough Gv STHWK SE1 25 H4
Marlborough La CHARL SE7 27 K5
Marlborough Ms BRXN/ST SW9 44 A2
Marlborough Pde
MAIDW ME16 * 166 A3
Marlborough Park Av
BFN/LL DA15 49 H6
Marlborough Rd BXLYHN DA7 49 L1
DART DA1 51 K4
DEAL CT14 209 H7
GILL ME7 7 H4
HAYES BR2 71 K8
MARG CT9 14 F7
RAM CT11 17 H6
RDV CT15 217 G2
WOOL/PLUM SE18 28 C2
WSTB CT5 126 E8
Marlborough Wy
KEN/WIL TN24 203 J4
Marle Place Rd
STPH/PW TN12 279 M12
Marler Rd FOLKN CT19 219 M7
FSTH SE23 46 A6
Marley Av BXLYHN DA7 29 L5
Marley Ct CANTW/ST CT2 * 171 K1
Marley La DEAL CT14 208 B2
HDCN TN27 283 R6
RCANTE CT3 234 C1
RCANTW CT4 269 R5
Marley Rd BERM/RHTH SE16 * 25 L3
HOO/HM ME3 59 L7
RMAID ME17 242 H11
RYE TN31 224 F3
Marley Wy ROCH ME1 100 D3
Marlhurst EDEN TN8 192 C1
Marlings Cl CHST BR7 72 F8
Marlings Park Av CHST BR7 72 F8
Marling Wy GVE DA12 79 M2
Marlow Av PUR RM19 32 B3
Marlow Cl PGE/AN SE20 69 J7
WSTB CT5 127 J4
Marlow Copse WALD ME5 115 G4
Marlowe Av CANT CT1 4 F6
Marlowe Cl CHST BR7 72 E3
Marlowe Rd ASH TN23 2 A4
DIT/AY ME20 139 H2
DVE/WH CT16 213 J6
MARG CT9 15 M9
The Marlowes DART DA1 50 E2
Marlow Mdw CANTW/ST CT2 * 173 G4
Marlow Rd PGE/AN SE20 69 J7
Marlow Wy BERM/RHTH SE16 25 L1
Marlpit Cl EDEN TN8 192 D1
The Marlpit WADH TN5 309 L4
Marlton St GNWCH SE10 27 G4
Marlwood Cl BFN/LL DA15 48 F7
Marmadon Rd
WOOL/PLUM SE18 29 G3
Marmont Rd PECK SE15 25 H7
Marmora Rd EDUL SE22 45 K4
Marne Av WELL DA16 49 H1
Marnfield Crs
BRXS/STRHM SW2 44 A6
Marnock Rd BROCKY SE4 46 A3
Maroons Wy CAT SE6 70 B2
Marquis Dr GILL ME7 116 C2
Marrabon Cl BFN/LL DA15 49 H6
Marr Cl IOS ME12 65 G6
Marriott Rd DART DA1 52 B5
Marrose Av MSTR CT12 182 E2
Marsala Rd LEW SE13 46 C2
Marsden Rd PECK SE15 45 G1
Marsden Wy ORP BR6 91 G7
Marshall Crs BRDST CT10 183 H1
QBOR ME11 227 N2
Marshall Gdns RTON TN11 256 B4
Marshall Rd RHAM ME8 102 D4
Marshalls Gv WOOL/PLUM SE18 27 M3
Marshalls Land TENT TN30 301 M10
Marshall's Pl BERM/RHTH SE16 25 G2
Marshall St FOLKN CT19 11 L1
Marshalsea Rd STHWK SE1 24 D1
Marsham Cl CHST BR7 * 72 C2
Marsham Crs RMAID ME17 260 C4
Marsham St MAID/BEAR ME14 13 H4
Marsham Wy STRD ME2 99 H8
Marshborough Rd SWCH CT13 253 N2
Marshbrook Cl BKHTH/KID SE3 47 L1
Marsh Crs HOO/HM ME3 59 M1
NROM TN28 331 J7
Marsh Farm Rd MSTR CT12 236 F1
Marshfield St POP/IOD E14 26 D2
Marshfoot Rd GRAYS RM17 35 H4
Marsh Green Rd EDEN TN8 274 G1
Marshlands LYDD TN29 320 G11
Marshlands Cl LYDD TN29 320 G10
Marshland Vw HOO/HM ME3 41 K8
Marsh La DEAL CT14 209 H3
HOO/HM ME3 38 C7
RSIT ME9 122 A5
Marsh Quarter La HAWK TN18 324 D1
Marsh Ri SIT ME10 227 P12
Marsh Rd RASHW TN26 318 D3
STRD ME2 99 J8
Marsh St DART DA1 32 B8
POP/IOD E14 * 26 C3
STRD ME2 19 H3
Marsh Ter STMC/STPC BR5 * 73 L8
Marsh Vw GVE DA12 56 A6
HYTHE CT21 321 P1
Marsh Wall POP/IOD E14 26 B1
Marsh Wy DIT/AY ME20 139 H1
Marshwood Cl CANT CT1 172 D6
Marsland Cl WALW SE17 24 C4
Marstan Cl RSIT ME9 103 M3
Marston Cl WALD ME5 114 F2
Marston Dr MAID/BEAR ME14 13 K3
WARL CR6 130 D4
Marston Wy NRWD SE19 68 C4
Martara Ms WALW SE17 24 D4
Martello Cl RYE TN31 225 G5
Martello Dr HYTHE CT21 307 R12
Martello Rd FOLK CT20 11 M3
Martello Ter FOLK CT20 10 A9
Martell Rd DUL SE21 44 E8
Marten Rd FOLK CT20 10 E5
Martens Av BXLYHN DA7 50 D2

Martens Cl BXLYHN DA7 50 D2
Martha Cl FOLKN CT19 10 E1
Martin Bowes Rd
ELTH/MOT SE9 48 A1
Martin Cl SAND/SEL CR2 104 C5
WARL CR6 130 A2
Martin Ct GILL ME7 116 B2
Martin Crs CROY/NA CR0 86 A4
Martindale Av ORP BR6 91 H8
Martindale Cl CANT CT1 4 F7
Martin Dale Crs RDV CT15 210 D7
Martin Dene BXLYHS DA6 50 A3
Martindown Rd WSTB CT5 126 D6
Martin Hardie Wy TONN TN10 189 H8
Martin Ri BXLYHS DA6 50 A3
Martin Rd RDART DA2 51 K8
STRD ME2 19 G2
Martins Cl HOO/HM ME3 57 L7
MSTR CT12 182 F3
STMC/STPC BR5 73 L7
TENT TN30 315 P1
WWKM BR4 88 E5
Martins La STPH/PW TN12 256 H3
Martin Sq DIT/AY ME20 139 H4
Martin's Rd HAYES BR2 70 F6
Martin's Shaw SEV TN13 135 H8
The Martins RASHW TN26 302 B5
SYD SE26 69 J2
Martin's Wy HYTHE CT21 321 Q1
Marton Cl CAT SE6 46 B8
Martyrs' Field Rd CANT CT1 4 D7
Marvels Cl LEE/GVPK SE12 47 J7
Marvels La LEE/GVPK SE12 47 J7
Marwell BH/WHM TN16 159 G4
Marwell Cl WWKM BR4 89 G5
Marwood Cl WELL DA16 49 J1
Mary Ann Buildings DEPT SE8 26 B5
Marybank WOOL/PLUM SE18 28 A3
Mary Datchelor Cl CMBW SE5 24 E7
Mary Day's CRBK TN17 297 M6
Mary Dukes Pl
MAID/SHEP ME15 * 13 J6
Maryfield Cl BXLY DA5 50 F8
Mary Green Wk CANT CT1 5 J1
Maryland Ct RHAM ME8 102 F8
Maryland Dr MAIDW ME16 166 A3
Maryland Gv CANT CT1 5 K9
Maryland Rd RTWE/PEM TN2 23 L9
THHTH CR7 68 C5
Mary Last Cl SNOD ME6 112 F6
Mary Lawrencson Pl
BKHTH/KID SE3 27 G6
Marylee Wy LBTH SE11 24 A3
Maryon Gv WOOL/PLUM SE18 27 M3
Maryon Rd CHARL SE7 27 M3
Mary Rd DEAL CT14 209 H6
Mary Rose Cl CDW/CHF RM16 33 K3
DART DA1 52 D2
Mary Stamford Gn RYE TN31 225 M6
Mascall's Court La
STPH/PW TN12 279 M5
Mascall's Court Rd
STPH/PW TN12 279 J4
Mascalls Pk STPH/PW TN12 279 J4
Mascalls Rd CHARL SE7 27 K5
Masefield Cl ERITH DA8 31 G7
Masefield Dr HOO/HM ME3 58 C5
Masefield Rd CDW/CHF RM16 34 F1
DART DA1 52 C3
GVW DA11 54 E8
Masefield Vw ORP BR6 90 D6
Masefield Wy TON TN9 194 C5
Maskall Cl BRXS/STRHM SW2 * 44 B6
Mason Cl BERM/RHTH SE16 25 H4
BXLYHN DA7 50 C1
Mason Rd RYE TN31 224 F4
Mason's Av CROY/NA CR0 86 D6
Masons Hl HAYES BR2 71 J8
WOOL/PLUM SE18 28 C3
Mason's Ri BRDST CT10 179 K8
Masons Rd DVW CT17 213 H8
Mason St WALW SE17 24 E3
Massinger St STHWK SE1 24 F3
Master Cl OXTED RH8 157 K7
Master Gunners Pl
WOOL/PLUM SE18 27 M7
Masters Dr BERM/RHTH SE16 25 J4
Masters La E/WMAL ME19 112 C8
Masthead Cl GRH DA9 52 D2
Masthouse Ter POP/IOD E14 26 B3
Mast House Ter POP/IOD E14 * 26 B3
Mastmaker Rd POP/IOD E14 26 B1
Matchless Dr WOOL/PLUM SE18 28 B6
Matfield Cl HAYES BR2 89 H1
Matfield Crs MAID/BEAR ME14 13 L2
Matfield Rd BELV DA17 30 B5
Matham Gv EDUL SE22 45 G2
Matilda Cl GILL ME7 102 C5
NRWD SE19 68 E4
Matterdale Gdns
MAIDW ME16 165 M3
Matthews Cl DEAL CT14 209 K3
Matthews Ct GILL ME7 * 7 L4
Matthew's Gdns
CROY/NA CR0 105 J5
Matthews La RTON TN11 256 C2
Matthew's Pl DVE/WH CT16 8 B2
Matthews Rd HB CT6 128 D7
Mattingly Wy PECK SE15 25 G6
Mattinson Pl RSIT ME9 242 G2
Matts Hill Rd RSIT ME9 116 F3
Maud Cashmore Wy
WOOL/PLUM SE18 28 A2
Maude Rd CMBW SE5 24 F8
SWLY BR8 75 H3
Maudslay Rd ELTH/MOT SE9 48 A1
Maugham Ct WSTB CT5 126 E5
Maunder Cl CDW/CHF RM16 33 L3
Maunders Cl WALD ME5 101 K5
Maunsell Pl KEN/WIL TN24 205 G4
Mauritius Rd GNWCH SE10 26 F3
Mavelstone Rd BMLY BR1 71 L5
Mawbey Pl STHWK SE1 25 G4
Mawbey Rd STHWK SE1 25 G4
Maxey Rd WOOL/PLUM SE18 28 D3
Maximfeldt Rd ERITH DA8 30 F4
Maximilian Dr STRD ME2 113 J1
Maxim Rd DART DA1 50 F3
ERITH DA8 30 F4
Maxine Gdns BRDST CT10 179 J8
Maxted Rd PECK SE15 45 G1
Maxton Cl MAID/BEAR ME14 142 A8
Maxton Rd DVW CT17 217 H3
Maxwell Dr MAIDW ME16 140 C7
Maxwell Gdns ORP BR6 91 G6
Maxwell Pl DEAL CT14 209 K5
Maxwell Rd GILL ME7 6 E3
WELL DA16 49 H2
Maya Cl PECK SE15 25 J8
Mayall Rd BRXN/ST SW9 44 C3
May Av GVW DA11 55 G6
STMC/STPC BR5 91 J1
Maybourne Cl SYD SE26 * 69 J3
Maybury Av RDART DA2 52 C6
Maybury Cl STMC/STPC BR5 90 C1
Maycotts La STPH/PW TN12 278 G8
Maycroft Av GRAYS RM17 34 E4
Maycroft Gdns GRAYS RM17 34 E4
Mayday Gdns BKHTH/KID SE3 27 M8
Mayday Rd THHTH CR7 86 C2
Maydowns Rd WSTB CT5 127 L3
Mayefield Rd THHTH CR7 68 A8
Mayerne Rd ELTH/MOT SE9 47 L3
Mayers Rd DEAL CT14 209 H8
Mayes Cl SWLY BR8 75 H8
WARL CR6 130 C4
Mayeswood Rd LEE/GVPK SE12 71 K1
Mayfair STRD ME2 19 J1
Mayfair Av BXLYHN DA7 49 L7
MAID/SHEP ME15 167 H5
Mayfair Cl BECK BR3 70 C5
Mayfair Rd DART DA1 51 L3
Mayfield BXLYHN DA7 50 A1
LING RH7 274 A4
SWCM DA10 53 M4
Mayfield Av DVE/WH CT16 213 J7
ORP BR6 91 G4
Mayfield Cl PGE/AN SE20 * 69 J5
RHAM ME8 102 F3
WALD ME5 115 H4
Mayfield Crs THHTH CR7 68 A8
Mayfield Gdns DVE/WH CT16 213 J7
Mayfield La WADH TN5 308 H6
Mayfield Pk WADH TN5 309 J4
Mayfield Rd BELV DA17 30 D3
BMLY BR1 89 M1
DVE/WH CT16 213 H2
GVW DA11 55 G6
HB CT6 129 H6
RFOLK CT18 291 M11
STH/RUST TN4 22 D4
Mayfields CDW/CHF RM16 34 D1
Mayfield Vls SCUP DA14 * 73 L3
Mayflower Cl BERM/RHTH SE16 25 L3
Mayflower Rd CDW/CHF RM16 33 K4
Mayflower St
BERM/RHTH SE16 25 K1
Mayfly Cl STMC/STPC BR5 73 L8
Mayfly Dr RFOLK CT18 220 B1
Mayford Cl BECK BR3 69 L7
Mayford Rd WALD ME5 115 L3
Mayforth Gdns RAM CT11 16 C7
Mayhew Cl ASH TN23 204 D3
Mayhill Rd CHARL SE7 27 J5
Maylam Gdns RSIT ME9 119 J5
Maylands Dr SCUP DA14 49 M8
Maymills SWCH CT13 * 253 N7
Maynard Av MARG CT9 177 L5
Maynard Cl ERITH DA8 31 G6
Maynard Pl WALD ME5 * 101 M9
Maynard Rd CANT CT1 4 B7
Maynards STPH/PW TN12 280 H4
Maynard's La STPH/PW TN12 278 H8
Mayo Rd CROY/NA CR0 86 E1
Mayow Rd SYD SE26 69 L1
Maypits ASH TN23 204 C3
May Pl STPH/PW TN12 * 281 L3
Mayplace Av DART DA1 51 H2
Mayplace Cl BXLYHN DA7 50 C1
Mayplace La WOOL/PLUM SE18 28 C5
Mayplace Rd BXLYHN DA7 50 D1
Mayplace Rd East BXLYHN DA7 50 D1
Mayplace Rd West BXLYHN DA7 50 B2
Maypole Crs ERITH DA8 31 L5
Maypole Dr E/WMAL ME19 164 D2
Maypole Gv RFOLK CT18 * 292 G12
Maypole La CRBK TN17 297 N5
RCANTE CT3 155 M3
Maypole Rd GVE DA12 56 A6
ORP BR6 108 E1
RCANTE CT3 155 L4
May Rd GILL ME7 7 H5
RDART DA2 76 A1
ROCH ME1 100 D2
May's Buildings Ms
GNWCH SE10 26 E6
May's Hill Rd HAYES BR2 70 F6
Mays Rd RAM CT11 16 F6
May St HB CT6 232 A5
SNOD ME6 113 J5
STRD ME2 99 J3
May Ter GILL ME7 83 H6
Maytham Rd CRBK TN17 314 F8
Maythorne Cottages LEW SE13 46 E4
Mayton La CANTW/ST CT2 154 D8
Maytree Wk
BRXS/STRHM SW2 * 44 B7
Mayville Rd BRDST CT10 179 H7
Mayweed Av WALD ME5 114 F1
Maywood Cl BECK BR3 * 70 C4
Maze Hl BKHTH/KID SE3 27 G6
GNWCH SE10 26 F5
McAlpine Crs
MAID/SHEP ME15 259 L2
McAuley Cl ELTH/MOT SE9 48 B3
STHWK SE1 24 B2
McCabe Cl STPH/PW TN12 281 K7
McCall Crs CHARL SE7 27 M4
McCarthy Av CANTW/ST CT2 173 G2
McClean Wk IOS ME12 229 L5
McCoid Wy STHWK SE1 * 24 D1
McCudden Rd DART DA1 52 A1
McCudden Rw GILL ME7 6 E1
McDermott Rd BGR/WK TN15 240 E2
PECK SE15 45 H1
McKenzie Cl DIT/AY ME20 140 A5
McKenzie Rd WALD ME5 115 H2
McKerrell Rd PECK SE15 25 H7
McKillop Wy SCUP DA14 73 K4
McKinlay Ct BRCH CT7 * 176 A5
McLeod Rd ABYW SE2 29 K3
McMillan Cl GVE DA12 79 K1
McMillan St DEPT SE8 * 26 B5
McNeil Rd CMBW SE5 24 F8
Mead Cl CDW/CHF RM16 34 C1
SWLY BR8 93 H1
Mead Crs DART DA1 51 L6
Meadcroft Rd LBTH SE11 24 B5
Meades Cl LING RH7 274 A4
STPH/PW TN12 280 G3
The Meades LING RH7 274 A4
The Meade RFOLK CT18 220 A1
Meadfield Rd MEO DA13 97 H5
Meadow Av CROY/NA CR0 87 L2
Meadowbank BKHTH/KID SE3 47 G1
Meadow Bank E/WMAL ME19 138 D5
RTON TN11 255 N12
Meadow Bank Cl
BGR/WK TN15 111 L3
Meadowbank Rd CHAT ME4 6 F6
Meadowbrook FOLK CT20 223 M1
OXTED RH8 157 H8
Meadowbrook Cl
KEN/WIL TN24 203 G5
Meadowbrook Ct FOLK CT20 * 223 M1
Meadowbrook Rd
KEN/WIL TN24 203 G5
Meadow Cl BXLYHS DA6 50 A3
CAT SE6 70 B2
CHST BR7 72 C2
HB CT6 129 K5
RCANTW CT4 175 H8
RCANTW CT4 247 R9
RFOLK CT18 220 C1
RSIT ME9 227 L9
SEV TN13 20 E2
SLH/COR SS17 36 B2
STRD ME2 112 F1
WALD ME5 101 G8
Meadow Ct BGR/WK TN15 238 E10
MARG CT9 * 15 L7
RASHE TN25 307 N7
RHAM ME8 102 C3
Meadowcourt Rd
BKHTH/KID SE3 47 G2
Meadow Crs STRD ME2 112 F1
Meadow Cft BMLY BR1 72 A7
Meadowcroft Farm
RDART DA2 * 77 J4
Meadowdown
MAID/BEAR ME14 167 M1
Meadowdown Cl GILL ME7 116 B1
Meadow Gv RASHE TN25 307 J5
Meadow Hill Rd RTW TN1 23 G7
Meadowlands BGR/WK TN15 136 E6
OXTED RH8 185 H4
Meadow La EDEN TN8 192 C1
LEE/GVPK SE12 47 K8
MEO DA13 239 M4
Meadow Ms VX/NE SW8 24 A5
Meadow Ri RSIT ME9 227 L9
Meadow Rd ASH TN23 202 D7
CANTW/ST CT2 171 K3
CANTW/ST CT2 173 G3
GVW DA11 54 D6
GVW DA11 55 H7
HAYES BR2 70 F5
MARG CT9 177 L4
RRTW TN3 199 J6
RTW TN1 22 F3
STH/RUST TN4 196 C4
STH/RUST TN4 200 D1
TON TN9 194 D5
VX/NE SW8 24 A6
Meadow Rw STHWK SE1 24 D2
Meadowside DART DA1 51 M6
ELTH/MOT SE9 47 K2
The Meadows HB CT6 129 K7
HDCN TN27 300 E3
MAID/SHEP ME15 12 C9
NROM TN28 331 K7
ORP BR6 108 B1
RSEV TN14 108 E7
SIT ME10 120 A7
TENT TN30 326 G1
WARL CR6 130 C3
Meadow Stile CROY/NA CR0 86 D6
Meadowsweet Vw CHAT ME4 83 J3
The Meadow CHST BR7 72 D3
RTWE/PEM TN2 278 B9
Meadow Vw BFN/LL DA15 49 J4
HOO/HM ME3 * 41 M4
RASHW TN26 286 E3
RSIT ME9 * 226 C10
SWLY BR8 * 92 E2
WALD ME5 101 G8
Meadowview Rd BXLY DA5 49 M4
CAT SE6 70 B1
Meadow View Rd RDV CT15 271 R8
RMAID ME17 259 N2
THHTH CR7 86 C1
Meadow Wk MAID/SHEP ME15 13 J6
RDART DA2 75 K1
SNOD ME6 113 G6
WSTB CT5 126 D6
Meadow Wy HYTHE CT21 321 Q1
ORP BR6 90 B6
RDART DA2 52 D5
RDV CT15 272 D5
STPH/PW TN12 281 J3
Mead Pl CROY/NA CR0 86 C4
Mead Rd CHST BR7 72 D3
DART DA1 51 L6
EDEN TN8 192 E6
FOLKN CT19 11 J2
GVW DA11 55 J7
KEN/WIL TN24 205 H4
Mead Rw STHWK SE1 24 B2
The Meads Av SIT ME10 119 L2
Meadside Cl BECK BR3 69 M5
Meadside Wk WALD ME5 101 G7
The Meads CRBK TN17 298 C12
RTWE/PEM TN2 23 K8
Meads Wy LYDD TN29 331 M2
The Mead BECK BR3 70 D6
E/WMAL ME19 138 F5
HART DA3 95 M5
WWKM BR4 88 E4
Meadvale Rd CROY/NA CR0 87 G3
Mead Wall HOO/HM ME3 37 L5
Mead Wy CANTW/ST CT2 4 D3
CROY/NA CR0 87 M5
HAYES BR2 89 H2
Meadway BECK BR3 70 D5
DVW CT17 212 E6
GRAYS RM17 34 E3
RSEV TN14 108 E7
RTON TN11 188 B8
WARL CR6 130 B2
The Meadway BKHTH/KID SE3 26 E8
ORP BR6 91 J8
SEV TN13 20 D1
Meaford Wy PGE/AN SE20 69 J4
Meakin Est STHWK SE1 * 24 F2
Meath Cl STMC/STPC BR5 91 J1
Medbury Rd GVE DA12 56 A6
Medebourne Cl BKHTH/KID SE3 47 H1
Medhurst Crs GVE DA12 56 A8
Medhurst Gdns GVE DA12 56 A8
Medick Ct GRAYS RM17 34 F5
Medina Av WSTB CT5 126 C6
Medina Rd DIT/AY ME20 139 K4
GRAYS RM17 34 E4
TONN TN10 188 F7
Medlar Cl RSIT ME9 145 H3
Medlar Gv GILL ME7 116 B1
Medlar Rd GRAYS RM17 34 E5
The Medlars MAID/BEAR ME14 141 L7
MEO DA13 97 H2
Medlar St CMBW SE5 24 D7
Medora Rd BRXS/STRHM SW2 44 A4
Medusa Rd LEW SE13 46 C4
Medway Av HOO/HM ME3 39 M1
WBY/YAL ME18 257 Q4
Medway Br STRD ME2 99 M2
Medway Cl CROY/NA CR0 87 K2
SIT ME10 119 L5
Medway Gdns CHAT ME4 83 G6
Medway Mdw STPH/PW TN12 257 K7
Medway Rd DART DA1 51 H1
GILL ME7 83 K6
IOS ME12 64 C4
RTW TN1 23 H1
Medway St CHAT ME4 6 C4
MAID/BEAR ME14 12 F5
Medway Ter WBY/YAL ME18 * 164 E7
Medway Valley Wk
DIT/AY ME20 113 L8
MAIDW ME16 140 E4
STPH/PW TN12 256 H9
WBY/YAL ME18 257 M3
Medway Vw RTON TN11 * 256 C8
Medway Wharf Rd TON TN9 194 F4
Medwin St BRXN/ST SW9 44 A2
Meehan Rd NROM TN28 331 M10
Meehan Rd South
NROM TN28 331 L10
Meerbrook Rd BKHTH/KID SE3 47 K1
Meeres Court La SIT ME10 120 D4
Meeson's Cl FAV ME13 244 H3
Meeson's La GRAYS RM17 34 A3
Meeting House La CHAT ME4 6 D5
PECK SE15 25 J7
Meeting St RAM CT11 17 J5
Megan Cl LYDD TN29 334 E2
Meggett La RDV CT15 293 P10
Megone Cl RFOLK CT18 220 B1
Megrims Hl HAWK TN18 313 K11
Meirscourt Rd RHAM ME8 116 F1
Melanda Cl CHST BR7 72 A2
Melanie Cl BXLYHN DA7 29 M7
Melba Gdns TIL RM18 35 H6
Melbourne Av DVE/WH CT16 213 J4
MSTR CT12 16 C1
Melbourne Cl ORP BR6 90 F3
Melbourne Gv EDUL SE22 44 F2
Melbourne Ms BRXN/ST SW9 24 B7
CAT SE6 46 D5
Melbourne Rd CHAT ME4 6 F8
TIL RM18 34 F7
Melbourne Sq BRXN/ST SW9 24 B7
Melbourne Ter EDUL SE22 * 44 F2
Melbury Cl CHST BR7 72 A3
Melbury Dr CMBW SE5 24 F6
Melbury Ms NROM TN28 331 K5
Meldrum Cl OXTED RH8 185 G2
STMC/STPC BR5 91 K2
Melfield Gdns CAT SE6 70 C1
Melfont Av THHTH CR7 68 C7
Melford Dr MAIDW ME16 166 D1
Melford Rd EDUL SE22 45 H6
Melfort Rd THHTH CR7 68 C7
Melior Pl STHWK SE1 * 24 F1
Melior St STHWK SE1 24 E1
Meliot Rd CAT SE6 46 E7
Mellanby Cl BRCH CT7 176 D7
Melliker La MEO DA13 97 G2
Melling St WOOL/PLUM SE18 28 F5
Mellish St POP/IOD E14 26 B2
Mellor Rw SIT ME10 227 N12
Mells Crs ELTH/MOT SE9 72 A1
Mell St GNWCH SE10 26 F4
Melody Cl IOS ME12 230 D1
RHAM ME8 116 D1
Melody Rd BH/WHM TN16 132 B4
Melon La RASHW TN26 319 L8
Melon Rd PECK SE15 25 H7
Melrose Av DART DA1 50 F5
STRHM/NOR SW16 68 A7
Melrose Cl LEE/GVPK SE12 47 H6
MAID/SHEP ME15 167 H6
Melrose Crs ORP BR6 90 E7
Melrose Rd BH/WHM TN16 132 B2
Melrose Vls BECK BR3 * 70 B6
Melsetter Cl BRCH CT7 * 176 E6
Melthorpe Gdns
WOOL/PLUM SE18 27 L7
Melville Av SAND/SEL CR2 104 G8
Melville Ct CHAT ME4 6 D1
DEPT SE8 25 L3
Melville Lea SWCH CT13 253 P2
Melville Rd MAID/SHEP ME15 13 H6
SCUP DA14 49 K7
Melvin Rd PGE/AN SE20 69 K5
Memel Pl RAM CT11 17 H6
Mendfield St FAV ME13 149 K2
Mendip Cl SYD SE26 69 K1
Mendip Ri KEN/WIL TN24 2 A1
Mendip Rd BXLYHN DA7 30 F7
Mendip Wk RTWE/PEM TN2 23 L2
Menin Rd SIT ME10 227 N12
Menlo Gdns NRWD SE19 68 E4
Mentmore Rd MSTR CT12 182 F2
Menzies Av DEAL CT14 209 J8
Menzies Ct IOS ME12 65 H8
Menzies Rd DVE/WH CT16 213 H4
Meopham Ct MEO DA13 * 97 J4
Mepham St STHWK SE1 24 B1
Mera Dr BXLYHN DA7 50 B1
Merbury Cl LEW SE13 46 D3
Merbury St WOOL/PLUM SE18 28 C2
Mercator Pl POP/IOD E14 26 B4
Mercator Rd LEW SE13 46 E3
Mercer Dr RMAID ME17 242 G11
Mercers HAWK TN18 312 D8
RRTW TN3 200 B2
Mercers Cl GNWCH SE10 27 G3
STPH/PW TN12 278 H3
Mercers Pl E/WMAL ME19 164 B3
Mercer St RTW TN1 23 G2
Mercer Wy RMAID ME17 260 C4
Mercery La CANT CT1 4 F4
Merchant Pl STPH/PW TN12 280 H4
Merchants Cl SNWD SE25 69 H8
Merchants Wy CANTW/ST CT2 171 K6
Merchiston Rd CAT SE6 46 E7
Merchland Rd ELTH/MOT SE9 48 D6
Mercia Gv LEW SE13 46 D1
Mercury Cl ROCH ME1 100 B3
Mercury Wy NWCR SE14 25 L5
Mercy Ter LEW SE13 46 C3
Merebank La WLGTN SM6 86 A8
Mere Cl ORP BR6 90 C5
Meredith Cl RMAID ME17 169 G6
Meredith Ms BROCKY SE4 * 46 A2
Meredith Rd CDW/CHF RM16 35 H3
Mere End CROY/NA CR0 87 L3
Mere Ga MARG CT9 14 E7
Meresborough La RHAM ME8 103 H8
Meresborough Rd RHAM ME8 117 G1
Mereside ORP BR6 90 B5
Meretone Cl BROCKY SE4 45 M2
Merewood Cl BMLY BR1 72 B6
Merewood Gdns CROY/NA CR0 87 L3
Merewood Rd BXLYHN DA7 30 D8
Mereworth Cl HAYES BR2 89 G1
RHAM ME8 102 B2
Mereworth Dr
WOOL/PLUM SE18 28 C6
Mereworth Rd STH/RUST TN4 196 D7
WBY/YAL ME18 241 N11
Meriden Cl BMLY BR1 71 L4
Meridian Pk STRD ME2 * 6 B1
Meridian Rd CHARL SE7 27 L6
Merifield Rd ELTH/MOT SE9 47 K2
Merileys Cl HART DA3 78 D7
Merino Wy ASH TN23 204 B6
Merivale Gv WALD ME5 115 J1
Merleburgh Dr SIT ME10 120 A1
Merle Common Rd
OXTED RH8 185 H6
Merlewood SEV TN13 21 G2
Merlewood Dr CHST BR7 72 A5
Merlin Av DIT/AY ME20 139 G3
Merlin Cl CROY/NA CR0 86 F7
SIT ME10 120 B6
TONN TN10 195 H1
Merlin Gv BECK BR3 70 A8
Merlin Rd WELL DA16 49 H2
Merlin Rd North WELL DA16 49 H2
Merlin Vls MARG CT9 * 15 H2
Mermaid Cl GVW DA11 54 E5
WALD ME5 101 H7
Mermaid Ct STHWK SE1 24 E1
Mermaid St RYE TN31 225 G4
Mermerus Gdns GVE DA12 80 A1
Merrals Wood Ct STRD ME2 * 81 L8
Merrals Wood Rd STRD ME2 81 L8
Merredene St
BRXS/STRHM SW2 44 A4
Merrick Sq STHWK SE1 24 E2
Merrilees Rd BFN/LL DA15 48 F5
Merriman Rd BKHTH/KID SE3 27 K7
Merrimans Vw WALD ME5 * 7 J9
Merriments La
BUR/ETCH TN19 311 Q12
Merrion Cl STH/RUST TN4 196 E6
Merrion Wy STH/RUST TN4 196 E6
Merritt Rd BROCKY SE4 46 A3
NROM TN28 331 M11
Merrivale Hts BRDST CT10 183 K2
Merrow St WALW SE17 24 E4
Merrow Wk WALW SE17 24 E4
Merrow Wy CROY/NA CR0 105 H1
Merry Boys Rd HOO/HM ME3 58 C5
Merrydown Wy CHST BR7 71 M5
Merryfield BKHTH/KID SE3 27 G8
Merryfields STRD ME2 82 B4
Merryfields Cl HART DA3 78 A8
Merryfield Wy CAT SE6 46 C5
Merryhills Cl BH/WHM TN16 132 C2
Merryweather Cl DART DA1 52 A4
Mersey Rd TONN TN10 188 E8
Mersham Pl PGE/AN SE20 69 J5
THHTH CR7 68 E6
Mersham Rd THHTH CR7 68 E7
Merton Av HART DA3 77 M8
Merton Cl WALD ME5 115 K1
Merton Gdns STMC/STPC BR5 90 C1
Merton La CANT CT1 174 A6
Merton Pl CDW/CHF RM16 35 H3
Merton Rd MAID/SHEP ME15 168 A3
SNWD SE25 87 G1
Merttins Rd PECK SE15 45 L2
Mervan Rd BRXS/STRHM SW2 44 B2
Mervyn Av ELTH/MOT SE9 48 D8
Meryl Gdns DEAL CT14 209 K8
Mesne Wy RSEV TN14 109 L6
Messent Rd ELTH/MOT SE9 47 K3
Messeter Pl ELTH/MOT SE9 48 B4
Meteor Av WSTB CT5 126 C6
Meteor Cl SIT ME10 119 M1
Meteor Rd E/WMAL ME19 164 A2
Methley St LBTH SE11 24 B4
Methuen Rd BELV DA17 30 C3
BXLYHS DA6 50 A2
Metropole Rd East FOLK CT20 10 E8
Metropole Rd West FOLK CT20 10 E8
Meverall Av MSTR CT12 182 A8
Mews Ct GILL ME7 102 A3
Mewsend BH/WHM TN16 132 C4
The Mews BECK BR3 * 70 B5
MAIDW ME16 * 12 D3
RTWE/PEM TN2 197 M7
SEV TN13 * 20 F4
SIT ME10 120 A6
STRD ME2 18 D4
STRHM/NOR SW16 * 68 A5
Meyer Rd ERITH DA8 30 D5
Meyrick Rd IOS ME12 64 D3
Micawber Cl WALD ME5 115 H4
Michael Av RAM CT11 183 K5
Michael Gdns GVE DA12 79 M3
Michael Rd SNWD SE25 68 F7
Michaels Cl LEW SE13 46 F1
Michaels La HART DA3 95 J5
Micheldever Rd LEW SE13 46 F4
Michelle Gdns MARG CT9 177 K5
Michel Wk WOOL/PLUM SE18 28 C4
Mickleburgh Av HB CT6 129 J6
Mickleburgh Hl HB CT6 129 J5
Mickleham Cl STMC/STPC BR5 73 G6
Mickleham Rd STMC/STPC BR5 73 G5
Mickleham Wy CROY/NA CR0 105 J2
Middelburg Sq FOLK CT20 11 J6
Middle Cl ASH TN23 286 H8
Middle Deal Rd DEAL CT14 209 H4
Middle Fld RTWE/PEM TN2 278 B9
Middlefields CROY/NA CR0 104 D3
RHAM ME8 103 H5
Middle La BGR/WK TN15 136 E7
Middle Md FOLKN CT19 10 E1
Middle Mill Rd E/WMAL ME19 139 G6
Middle Park Av ELTH/MOT SE9 47 L5
Middle Rd RRTW TN3 294 F8
Middle Rw ASH TN23 2 C4
FAV ME13 149 L2
MAID/BEAR ME14 12 F5
Middlesex Rd
MAID/SHEP ME15 167 L6
Middle St ASH TN23 2 B5
CROY/NA CR0 86 D5
DEAL CT14 209 L3
GILL ME7 6 E1
Middleton Av SCUP DA14 73 K3
Middleton Cl RHAM ME8 116 F1
Middleton Dr BERM/RHTH SE16 25 L1
Middleton Wy LEW SE13 46 E2
Middletune Av SIT ME10 119 M2
Middle Wk RTWE/PEM TN2 197 H5
Middle Wall WSTB CT5 126 E3
Middle Wy SIT ME10 120 C6
Middlings Ri SEV TN13 20 D8
The Middlings SEV TN13 20 D8
Middlings Wd SEV TN13 20 D6
Midfield Av BXLYHN DA7 50 D1
SWLY BR8 75 H3
Midfield Wy STMC/STPC BR5 73 J5
Midholm Rd CROY/NA CR0 87 M6
Midhurst Av CROY/NA CR0 86 B3
Midhurst Hl BXLYHS DA6 50 B3
Midley Cl MAIDW ME16 140 D6
Midship Point POP/IOD E14 * 26 B1
Midsummer Hl KEN/WIL TN24 203 G5
Midsummer Rd SNOD ME6 112 F5
The Midway STH/RUST TN4 200 E3
Midwinter Cl WELL DA16 49 H1
Mierscourt Cl RHAM ME8 103 H5
Mierscourt Rd RHAM ME8 102 F8
Milborough Crs LEE/GVPK SE12 46 F4
Milbourne Gv SIT ME10 119 M2
Milburn Rd GILL ME7 83 K6
Milcote St STHWK SE1 24 C1
Mildmay Pl RSEV TN14 109 L5
Mildred Cl DART DA1 52 B4
Mildred Rd ERITH DA8 30 F4
Milebush La STPH/PW TN12 259 J12
Mile La CRBK TN17 297 Q5
Mile Oak Rd STPH/PW TN12 279 M5
Mile Rd RCANTE CT3 233 N11
Miles Ct RCANTE CT3 * 251 R1
Miles La GDST RH9 184 B6
Miles Pl ROCH ME1 100 B2
Milestone Cl FOLKN CT19 220 B6
Milestone Rd DEAL CT14 209 J4
NRWD SE19 69 G3
Mile Stone Rd RDART DA2 52 C4
Miles Wy BRCH CT7 176 C6
Milford Cl ABYW SE2 29 M5
MAIDW ME16 140 D8
Milford Ms STRHM/NOR SW16 44 A8
Military Rd CANT CT1 5 J2
CHAT ME4 6 D4
DVW CT17 8 C5
FOLK CT20 10 A9

HYTHE CT21 ...222 B3
RAM CT11 ...17 H8
RASHW TN26 ...317 K11
RYE TN31 ...327 N12
TENT TN30 ...328 A3
Milk House Cottages
  CRBK TN17 ...299 K5
Milking La ORP BR6 ...106 D6
Milk St BMLY BR1 ...71 J3
Milkwell Yd CMBW SE5 ...24 D7
Milkwood Rd HNHL SE24 ...44 C5
Millais PI TIL RM18 ...35 H6
Millais Rd DVE/WH CT16 ...8 A1
Millars Meadow LEE/GVPK SE12 ...47 H3
Mill Bank HDCN TN27 ...283 K3
Millbank La LYDD TN29 ...330 A6
Millbank Rd ASH TN23 ...204 C6
Mill Bay FOLK CT20 ...11 K5
Millbro SWLY BR8 ...75 H5
Millbrook E/WMAL ME19 ...138 E4
  HYTHE CT21 ...222 E8
Millbrook Av WELL DA16 ...48 E2
Millbrook CI MAID/SHEP ME15 ...12 E2
Millbrook Meadow ASH TN23 ...204 B2
Millbrook Rd BRXN/ST SW9 ...44 C1
Mill Brook Rd STMC/STPC BR5 ...73 K8
Mill CI DVW CT17 ...213 G7
  RBTBR TN32 ...323 R11
  RCANTE CT3 ...234 D11
  RMAID ME17 ...262 G1
  STRD ME2 ...82 C4
  SWCH CT13 ...236 H11
Mill Cottages RAM CT11 ...17 H8
Mill Ct KEN/WIL TN24 ...2 E5
Mill Crs TON TN9 ...195 G5
Millcroft Rd HOO/HM ME3 ...58 C1
Milldale CI DEAL CT14 ...209 J5
Millennium CI POP/IOD E14 ...26 D6
Millennium Sq STHWK SE1 ...25 G1
Millennium Ter CANT CT1 * ...171 K7
Millennium Wy BRDST CT10 ...182 F1
  CNWCH SE10 ...26 F1
  IOS ME12 ...64 C3
Millen Rd SIT ME10 ...119 M4
Millens Rw FAV ME13 ...246 A6
Miller Av CANTW/ST CT2 ...4 A4
Miller CI BMLY BR1 ...71 J4
  KEN/WIL TN24 ...2 E5
  SIT ME10 ...120 B1
Miller Ct IOS ME12 ...65 H6
Miller Rd CROY/NA CR0 ...86 A4
  GVE DA12 ...56 B7
Millers Ct WSTB CT5 ...126 E6
Millers La MSTR CT12 ...233 K10
Millersthumb CRBK TN17 ...281 P12
Millers Wk MAD13 ...97 H6
Miller Wy STRD ME2 ...82 C5
Miller's Yd CANT CT1 * ...4 D7
  RCANTE CT3 ...236 B12
Millfield ASH TN23 ...204 A2
  FOLK CT20 ...11 H6
  HART DA3 ...95 M5
  RASHW TN26 ...301 Q6
  RDV CT15 ...215 G5
  RFOLK CT18 ...292 H11
  SIT ME10 ...120 A6
Millfield CI RFOLK CT18 ...292 G12
Millfield Dr GVW DA11 ...54 F7
Millfield La HART DA3 ...95 M4
Millfield Mnr WSTB CT5 ...126 F4
Millfield Rd BGR/WK TN15 ...111 J1
  ...149 M2
  MSTR CT12 ...112
Millfields RDV CT15 ...271 R9
  WALD ME5 ...115 L3
Millfields CI STMC/STPC BR5 ...73 J8
Mill Fields Rd HYTHE CT21 ...222 A3
Millfordhope Rd STRD ME2 ...81 K6
Mill Gdns SYD SE26 ...69 J1
Mill Gn SWCH CT13 ...253 M7
  MAID/BEAR ME14 ...13 L3
Milsted Rd RHAM ME8 ...102 D3
Mill Hall Rd DIT/AY ME20 ...139 L2
Millharbour POP/IOD E14 ...26 C2
Mill HI ASH TN23 * ...204 C3
  ASH TN23 ...304 C3
  DEAL CT14 ...209 H6
  EDEN TN8 ...192 E6
Mill Hill La GVE DA12 ...80 E2
Millhouse La E/WMAL ME19 ...239 Q10
Millhouse PI WNWD SE27 ...68 C1
Mill La BGR/WK TN15 ...240 C4
  BGR/WK TN15 ...255 R2
  BH/WHM TN16 ...159 H4
  BRCH CT7 ...176 C7
  CANT CT1 * ...4 F3
  CANTW/ST CT2 ...171 K5
  CRBK TN17 ...282 F10
  CRBK TN17 ...299 J5
  DEAL CT14 ...206 A5
  DEAL CT14 ...208 A3
  DVE/WH CT16 ...213 J5
  EYN DA4 ...93 M4
  HB CT6 ...129 J6
  HDCN TN27 ...284 C7
  KEN/WIL TN24 ...2 L7
  LYDD TN29 ...319 Q6
  LYDD TN29 ...334 D5
  MARG CT9 ...14 F5
  ORP BR6 ...106 C4
  OXTED RH8 ...185 Q2
  OXTED RH8 ...186 A1
  RASHE TN25 ...305 Q8
  RCANTE CT3 ...235 L7
  RCANTW CT4 ...175 G8
  RCANTW CT4 ...269 Q10
  RCANTW CT4 * ...270 F2
  RDV CT15 ...271 R1
  RDV CT15 ...272 A8
  RFOLK CT18 ...292 G12
  RMAID ME17 ...259 J2
  RSEV TN14 ...109 L4
  RSEV TN14 ...136 F3
  RSIT ME9 ...103 M7
  RSIT ME9 ...147 J4
  RTON TN9 ...255 Q5
  RYE TN31 ...326 C10
  SNOD ME6 ...113 J4
  STPH/PW TN12 ...280 A8
  STPH/PW TN12 ...282 D8
  SWCH CT13 ...253 J7
  TENT TN30 ...301 N12
  TON TN9 ...194 F3
  WALD ME5 ...101 K4
  WALD ME5 ...114 A4
  WBY/YAL ME18 ...164 E5
  WBY/YAL ME18 ...257 B4
  WOOL/PLUM SE18 ...28 B4
  WTHK RM20 ...33 L4
Millmark Gv NWCR SE14 ...25 M8
Millmead Gdns MARG CT9 ...179 G4

Mill Meadow Yd MAIDW ME16 * ...12 E3
Millmead Rd MARG CT9 ...15 M7
Mill Ms DEAL CT14 ...209 J5
Mill PI CHST BR7 ...72 B5
  DART DA1 ...51 H2
Mill Pond CI SEV TN13 ...136 C7
Millpond Est
  BERM/RHTH SE16 * ...25 J1
Millpond La RCANTE CT3 ...300 G11
Mill Pond Rd DART DA1 ...51 M4
Mill Race DVW CT17 ...213 G6
Mill Ri RBTBR TN32 ...322 F10
Mill Rd RCANTW/ST CT2 ...172 F3
  DEAL CT14 ...209 K4
  ERITH DA8 ...30 D6
  GILL ME7 ...7 J1
  GVW DA11 ...54 E7
  HYTHE CT21 ...222 E8
  LYDD TN29 ...320 H10
  LYDD TN29 ...334 E3
  PUR RM19 ...32 C5
  RASHW TN26 ...285 P12
  RCANTE CT3 ...232 A12
  RCANTE CT3 ...251 P3
  RCANTE CT3 ...252 G4
  RDART DA2 ...76 A1
  RYE TN31 ...225 H2
  SEV TN13 ...135 K7
  STRD ME2 ...19 G1
Mill Rw BRCH CT7 ...176 C7
  BXLY DA5 ...50 C5
Mills CI DART DA1 ...51 H2
Mills Crs BGR/WK TN15 ...136 D3
Mill Shaw OXTED RH8 ...185 Q2
Mills Rd DIT/AY ME20 ...139 M6
Mills Ter CHAT ME4 ...6 F2
Millstock Ter
  MAID/SHEP ME15 * ...12 C9
Mill Stone CI EYN DA4 ...76 D6
Millstone Ms EYN DA4 ...76 D5
Millstream CI FAV ME13 ...149 K2
  RRTW TN3 ...198 E3
  WSTB CT5 ...126 C3
Millstream Rd STHWK SE1 ...25 G1
Mill Stream Wy WALD ME5 * ...114 F3
Millstrood Rd WSTB CT5 ...126 F5
Mill Ter RCANTW CT4 * ...248 E6
Mill V HAYES BR2 ...71 H7
Mill Vw KEN/WIL TN24 ...3 J9
  RASHW TN26 ...302 H10
  RTON TN11 ...256 A4
Mill View Gdns CROY/NA CR0 ...87 L6
Mill Vw HB CT6 ...129 H8
Mill Wk MAIDW ME16 ...166 B2
Millwall Dock Rd POP/IOD E14 ...26 B2
Mill Wall PI SWCH CT13 ...206 B1
Mill Wy SIT ME10 ...119 M4
Millwood Ct CHAT ME4 * ...6 B1
Millwood Rd ORP BR6 ...73 L1
  STMC/STPC BR5 ...73 K7
Milne CI RDV CT15 ...272 E4
Milne Gdns ELTH/MOT SE9 * ...48 C5
Milne Pk East CROY/NA CR0 ...105 J5
Milne Pk West CROY/NA CR0 ...105 J5
Milner CI RDV CT15 ...272 D8
Milner Crs RCANTE CT3 ...251 Q12
Milne Rd KEN/WIL TN24 ...3 K9
Milner Rd GILL ME7 ...83 L6
  RDV CT15 ...272 C4
  THHTH CR7 ...68 D7
  WSTB CT5 ...126 B7
Milners RMAID ME17 ...169 G7
Milo Rd EDUL SE22 ...45 G4
Milroy Av GVW DA11 ...54 F7
Milstead CI IOS ME12 ...64 C5
  MAID/BEAR ME14 ...13 L3
Milsted Rd RHAM ME8 ...102 D3
Milton Av CROY/NA CR0 ...86 F3
Milton Court Rd NWCR SE14 ...25 M6
Milton Dr RTWE/PEM TN2 ...197 G6
  TON TN9 ...194 C7
Milton Gdns TIL RM18 ...35 J7
Milton Hall Rd GVE DA12 ...55 J7
Milton La HDCN TN27 ...284 C7
Milton La E/WMAL ME19 ...164 C2
Milton PI GVE DA12 ...55 K4
Milton Rd ASH TN23 ...204 A4
  BELV DA17 ...30 B3
  CANT CT1 ...4 F3
  CRBK TN17 ...299 J5
  CROY/NA CR0 ...86 B6
  DEAL CT14 ...206 A5
  DVE/WH CT16 ...213 J5
  GILL ME7 ...7 H1
  GRAYS RM17 ...34 C3
  GVE DA12 ...55 J4
  HNHL SE24 ...44 D3
  SEV TN13 ...135 K5
  SWCM DA10 ...53 M4
Milton Sq MARG CT9 ...15 G6
Milton St MAIDW ME16 ...166 D5
  SWCM DA10 ...53 M4
Milverton St LBTH SE11 ...24 E4
Milverton Wy ELTH/MOT SE9 ...72 K1
Mimms Ter STPH/PW TN12 * ...279 K2
Mimosa CI ORP BR6 ...91 K6
Mina Rd WALW SE17 ...24 F4
Minard Rd CAT SE6 ...46 E6
Mincers CI WALD ME5 ...115 K5
Minden Rd PGE/AN SE20 ...69 J2
Mindeheim Av EGRIN RH19 ...274 A11
Minehead Rd
  STRHM/NOR SW16 ...68 A2
Mineral St WOOL/PLUM SE18 ...28 A3
Miners Wy RCANTE CT3 ...251 P3
Minerva Av BRXN/ST SW9 ...44 C1
Minerva Rd STRD ME2 ...18 E2
Minet Rd CMBW SE5 ...24 C8
Ministry Wy ELTH/MOT SE9 ...48 C5
Minnis La RDV CT15 ...215 G2
Minnis Rd BRCH CT7 ...176 B5
Minnis Ter DVW CT17 ...213 H7
Minnis Wy DEAL CT14 ...206 A3
Minnow Rd SIT ME10 ...227 N12
Minor Canon Rw ROCH ME1 ...19 J7
Minshull PI BECK BR3 ...70 B1
Minster CI BRDST CT10 ...183 J3
Minster Dr CROY/NA CR0 ...86 D3
  HB CT6 ...128 E5
  IOS ME12 ...65 G7
Minster Rd BMLY BR1 ...71 J4
  BRCH CT7 ...180 C3
  FAV ME13 ...149 M2
  IOS ME12 ...65 G7

RAM CT11 ...16 D8
RHAM ME8 ...102 D2
Mintching Wood La RSIT ME9 ...146 A7
Minter Av RFOLK CT18 ...292 F10
Minter CI RFOLK CT18 ...292 F10
Interne Rd SIT ME10 ...119 K7
Minters Orch BGR/WK TN15 ...240 C7
Mint St STHWK SE1 ...24 D1
The Mint CANTW/ST CT2 * ...171 K4
  RYE TN31 ...225 J3
Mint Wk CROY/NA CR0 ...86 D6
  WARL CR6 ...150 C3
The Mint Yd CANT CT1 * ...5 H5
Miranda Ct IOS ME12 ...64 C4
Mirfield St CHARL SE7 ...27 L4
Miriam Rd WOOL/PLUM SE18 ...28 F4
  HOO/HM ME3 ...59 L8
Miskin Rd DART DA1 ...51 K5
Miskin Wy GVE DA12 ...79 L3
Misling La RCANTW CT4 ...290 F5
Mission PI PECK SE15 ...25 J7
Mistletoe CI CROY/NA CR0 ...87 L4
Mitcham Rd CROY/NA CR0 ...86 B3
  LYDD TN29 ...320 H10
Mitchell Av CHAT ME4 ...101 J3
Mitchell CI ABYW SE2 ...29 K4
  BELV DA17 ...30 D2
  DART DA1 ...51 M7
  RMAID ME17 ...243 K12
Mitchell Rd E/WMAL ME19 ...164 A3
  ORP BR6 ...91 J7
Mitchell Wy BMLY BR1 ...71 H5
Mitchell Wy BRXN/ST SW9 ...111 K2
  CANTW/ST CT2 ...172 B5
Mitre Ct TON TN9 ...194 F3
Mitre Rd ROCH ME1 ...19 G6
  STHWK SE1 ...24 B1
Moat CI ORP BR6 ...107 L1
Moat La ELTH/MOT SE9 * ...48 A4
Moat Cft WELL DA16 ...49 K1
Moat Farm RTWE/PEM TN2 ...201 H6
Moat Farm CI FOLK CT19 ...11 H1
Moat Farm Rd FOLK CT19 ...11 H1
  HOO/HM ME3 ...40 D7
Moatfield Meadow ASH TN23 ...204 E7
Moat La CANTW/ST CT2 ...171 J1
  CANTW/ST CT2 ...173 G6
  EDEN TN8 ...275 R7
  EDEN TN8 ...276 A11
  ERITH DA8 ...31 G2
  RCANTE CT3 ...236 B12
Moat PI BRXN/ST SW9 ...44 A1
Moat Rd HDCN TN27 ...283 A1
Moat Sole SWCH CT13 ...237 J12
Moat Wy QBOR ME11 ...64 B8
Mockbeggar La CRBK TN17 ...300 B10
Mocket Dr BRDST CT10 ...183 J3
Mock La ASH TN23 ...286 C11
Model Farm CI ELTH/MOT SE9 ...47 M8
Moffat Rd THHTH CR7 ...68 D7
Moiety Rd POP/IOD E14 ...26 B1
Moira CI ELTH/MOT SE9 ...48 A2
Molash Rd RCANTE CT3 ...73 L8
Mole CI ELTH/MOT SE9 * ...73 G7
Molehill Rd RDV CT15 ...272 E4
Molescroft ELTH/MOT SE9 * ...127 L6
Molescroft Wy TON TN9 ...194 C6
Moles Md EDEN TN8 ...192 D3
Molesworth St LEW SE13 ...46 D1
Molineux Rd MSTR CT12 ...180 E7
Molland CI RCANTE CT3 ...235 R11
Molland Lea RCANTE CT3 ...235 R11
Molland Lea RCANTE CT3 ...235 R11
Mollison Ri GVE DA12 ...79 M2
Molloy Rd RASHW TN26 ...303 Q4
Molyneux Park Gdns
  STH/RUST TN4 ...22 D4
Molyneux Park Rd
  STH/RUST TN4 ...22 B3
Monarch CI TIL RM18 ...35 J8
  WALD ME5 ...101 H7
  WWKM BR4 ...89 G7
Monarch Ms WNWD SE27 ...68 B2
Monarch Rd BELV DA17 ...30 B2
Mona Rd PECK SE15 ...25 K8
Monastery Av WNWD SE27 ...
Monastery St CANT CT1 ...5 H5
Monckton's Av
  MAID/BEAR ME14 ...140 F6
Monckton's Dr
  MAID/BEAR ME14 ...140 F6
Monckton's La
  MAID/BEAR ME14 ...140 F6
Monclar Rd CMBW SE5 ...44 E2
Moncrieff St PECK SE15 ...25 H8
Moncrif Rd MAID/BEAR ME14 ...168 C1
Mongeham Church CI
  DEAL CT14 ...208 E5
Mongeham Rd DEAL CT14 ...208 E7
Monica CI FAV ME13 ...149 K3
Monins Rd DVW CT17 ...217 J7
Monivea Rd BECK BR3 ...46 F8
Monkdown MAID/SHEP ME15 ...168 B4
Monkery La RASHE TN25 ...264 E8
Monks CI ABYW SE2 ...29 L3
  CANTW/ST CT2 ...172 B7
  FAV ME13 ...149 J1
Monkshill Rd FAV ME13 ...125 H7
Monks La OXTED RH8 ...185 N2
  WADH TN5 ...309 N2
Monks Orch DART DA1 ...51 M4
Monks Orchard Rd BECK BR3 ...88 B4
Monks St WOOL/PLUM SE18 ...28 B3
Monks Wk HDCN TN27 ...264 B6
  MEO DA13 ...78 B3
  TON TN9 ...194 B3
Monks Wy BECK BR3 ...88 C6
  DVE/WH CT16 ...213 H6
  RYE TN31 ...325 J5
  STMC/STPC BR5 ...90 D4
Monk Ter FSTH SE23 ...46 A7
Monkton Court La RDV CT15 ...272 E6
Monkton Gdns MARG CT9 ...179 G4
Monkton PI RAM CT11 ...17 H5
Monkton Rd BGR/WK TN15 ...240 C5
  WELL DA16 ...48 B3
Monkton St LBTH SE11 ...24 B3
  MSTR CT12 ...233 R10
Monkwood CI ROCH ME1 ...100 B1
Monmouth CI RHAM ME8 ...102 E3
  WELL DA16 ...49 H2
Monnow Rd WNWCR SE14 * ...
Monson Rd NWCR SE14 ...25 L6
  RTW TN1 ...23 G4
Monson Wy RTW TN1 ...23 G4
Mons Wy HAYES BR2 ...89 G4
Montacute Gdns
  RTWE/PEM TN2 ...22 D8
Montacute Rd CAT SE6 ...46 A5
  CROY/NA CR0 ...105 K6
  RTWE/PEM TN2 ...22 E9
Montague Av BROCKY SE4 ...46 A4
Montague CI SWLY BR8 ...75 G8

Montague Ct IOS ME12 ...64 C4
Montague PI SWLY BR8 * ...75 G8
Montague Rd CROY/NA CR0 ...86 C5
  RAM CT11 ...17 K3
Montague Sq NWCR SE14 ...25 M6
Montague St HB CT6 ...128 E4
Montana Gdns CAT SE6 ...70 A2
Montbelle Rd ELTH/MOT SE9 ...48 C8
Montbretia CI STMC/STPC BR5 ...73 K8
Montcalm CI HAYES BR2 ...89 J7
Montcalm Rd CHARL SE7 ...27 L6
Montcalm Ter DVE/WH CT16 * ...213 J6
Monteagle Wy PECK SE15 ...45 J2
Montefiore Av RAM CT11 ...17 M1
Montefiore Cottages
  RAM CT11 ...17 L3
Monteith CI RRTW TN3 ...200 E3
Montem CI FSTH SE23 ...46 A5
Monterey CI BXLY DA5 ...50 D7
Montford CI RASHW TN26 ...204 C4
  CANTW/ST CT2 ...172 B5
Montfort Dr E/WMAL ME19 ...164 A3
Montfort Rd BGR/WK TN15 ...136 D3
  STRD ME2 ...18 D3
  WALD ME5 ...114 F3
Montgomerie Ms FSTH SE23 ...45 K5
Montgomery Av WALD ME5 ...101 H6
Montgomery CI BFN/LL DA15 ...48 D5
Montgomery Rd EYN DA4 ...76 B5
  GILL ME7 ...7 J7
  STH/RUST TN4 ...196 F6
Montgomery Wy FOLKN CT19 ...220 B7
  WSTB CT5 ...126 E7
Montpelier Ga MAIDW ME16 * ...140 C8
Montpelier Rd PECK SE15 ...25 L7
  BXLY DA5 ...71
Montpelier V BKHTH/KID SE3 ...27 G4
Montpelier W BKHTH/KID SE3 ...27 G4
Montrave Rd PGE/AN SE20 ...69 K3
Montreal CI DVE/WH CT16 ...213 J6
Montreal Rd SEV TN13 ...20 B2
  TIL RM18 ...55 H1
Montrose Av BFN/LL DA15 ...49 H5
  WELL DA16 ...48 E4
Montrose CI WELL DA16 ...48 E4
Montrose Rd FSTH SE23 ...45 L5
Mont St Aignan Wy EDEN TN8 ...192 D4
Montserrat CI NRWD SE19 ...68 E2
Monument Wy KEN/WIL TN24 ...205 J6
Monypenny CRBK TN17 ...314 G6
Monypenny CI RTON TN11 ...256 B5
Moon La RDV CT15 ...271 R9
Moon's La LEE/GVPK SE12 * ...47 L1
Moonstone Dr WALD ME5 ...115 J3
Moorcroft Gdns HAYES BR2 ...89 M4
Moorden CI RTON TN11 ...254 H12
Moordown WOOL/PLUM SE18 ...28 C7
Moore Av TIL RM18 ...35 J8
  WTHK RM20 ...33 M4
Moore CI LYDD TN29 ...329 M2
Mooreland Rd BMLY BR1 ...71 G4
Moore Rd NRWD SE19 ...68 D3
  SWCM DA10 ...53 M4
Moore St STRD ME2 ...18 F1
Moorfield CANTW/ST CT2 ...172 A5
Moorfield Rd ORP BR6 ...91 L2
Moorhead Wy BKHTH/KID SE3 ...47 J2
Moorhen CI ERITH DA8 ...31 J7
Moor HI HAWK TN18 ...312 C9
Moorhouse Rd OXTED RH8 ...158 F1
Mooring Rd ROCH ME1 ...100 B4
The Moorings
  MAID/SHEP ME15 * ...13 C5
  RSIT ME9 ...121 M3
Moorland Rd BRXN/ST SW9 ...44 C1
  RDV CT15 ...271 R9
Moor La LYDD TN29 ...318 H12
  LYDD TN29 ...329 Q2
  TENT TN30 ...316 H4
  TENT TN30 ...316 H6
Moor Park CI RHAM ME8 ...103 H5
The Moor Rd RSEV TN14 ...138 A3
Moorside Rd BMLY BR1 ...70 F1
Moorstock La RASHE TN25 ...306 H3
Moor St RHAM ME8 ...103 H3
The Moor HAWK TN18 ...312 C9
Moorwell Dr RDV CT15 ...271 R9
Morant Dr CDW/CHF RM16 ...35 J2
Morants Court Rd RSEV TN14 ...135 H4
Moray Av BRXN/ST SW9 ...44 A1
Mordaunt Av WGOS CT8 ...177 H5
Morden HI LEW SE13 ...26 D6
Morden Rd BKHTH/KID SE3 ...27 H7
Morden Road Ms
  BKHTH/KID SE3 ...27 H8
Morden St LEW SE13 ...26 C7
  ROCH ME1 ...19 J9
Morden Wharf Rd GNWCH SE10 ...26 D4
Mordred Rd CAT SE6 ...46 F7
Morecambe St POP/IOD E14 ...26 C4
  WALW SE17 ...24 D4
Morehall CI FOLKN CT19 ...10 A3
Morelands Av CDW/CHF RM16 ...34 C2
Morel Ct SEV TN13 ...135 H1
Morello CI RSIT ME9 ...121 K7
  SWLY BR8 ...88 E8
Moremead Rd CAT SE6 ...69 M4
Morement Rd HOO/HM ME3 ...59 L7
Morena St CAT SE6 ...46 F6
Moreton St DART DA1 ...51 J3
Moreton Rd SAND/SEL CR2 ...86 C8
Moreton Ter RASHW TN26 ...303 P4
Morewood CI SEV TN13 ...135 J5
Morgan Kirby Gdns
  FAV ME13 ...246 C4
Morgan Kirby's Gdn FAV ME13 ...246 C4
Morgan Rd BMLY BR1 ...71 H4
  STRD ME2 ...18 F2
Morhen CI SNOD ME6 ...112 H4
Morkyns Wk DUL SE21 * ...45 G4
Morland Av CROY/NA CR0 ...86 F4
Morland CI HART DA3 ...51 J3
Morland Dr RRTW TN3 ...200 E3
  STRD ME2 ...18
Morland Rd CROY/NA CR0 ...87 G4
  PGE/AN SE20 ...69 K4
Morley CI ORP BR6 ...90 F3
Morley Dr STPH/PW TN12 ...279 K11
Morley Rd CHST BR7 ...71 K2
  LEW SE13 ...46 C2
  TON TN9 ...195 G4
Morley Sq CDW/CHF RM16 ...35 H3
Morley's Rd RSEV TN14 ...255 M1
Morley St STHWK SE1 ...24 B2
Morna Rd CMBW SE5 ...24 D8
Mornington Av BMLY BR1 ...71 K7
Mornington CI BXLY DA5 ...50 E4
Mornington Ms CMBW SE5 ...24 D8
Mornington Rd DEPT SE8 ...26

Morris Av HB CT6 ...128 A5
Morris CI CROY/NA CR0 ...87 K2
  E/WMAL ME19 ...139 G4
  ORP BR6 ...90 F6
Morris Ct GILL ME7 ...84 A8
Morris Court CI RSIT ME9 ...120 E3
Morris Gdns DART DA1 ...52 B5
Morrison Rd FOLK CT20 ...11 M5
Morry La RMAID ME17 ...261 L5
Mortimer CI ASH TN23 ...204 E4
Mortimer Rd BH/WHM TN16 ...106 B6
  DVE/WH CT16 ...9 E3
  ERITH DA8 ...30 E5
Mortimers Av HOO/HM ME3 ...59 J5
Mortimer St HB CT6 ...129 G4
Mortlake CI CROY/NA CR0 ...86 A6
Morton CI MAID/SHEP ME15 ...167 G3
Morton PI STHWK SE1 ...24 B2
Morvale CI BELV DA17 ...30 A3
Morval Rd BRXS/STRHM SW2 ...44 B3
Moselle Rd BH/WHM TN16 ...132 D8
Mosquito Rd E/WMAL ME19 ...164 A2
Moss Bank GRAYS RM17 ...34 A4
Mossbank WALD ME5 ...115 H2
Mossdown CI BELV DA17 ...30 B3
Mossend Ms RAM CT11 ...183 H5
Moss Gdns SAND/SEL CR2 ...104 C2
Mosslea Rd BMLY BR2 ...89 L1
  PGE/AN SE20 ...69 J3
Moss Wy RDART DA2 ...76 A4
Mossy Gld RHAM ME8 ...102 H7
Mostyn Rd BRXN/ST SW9 ...24
  MAID/BEAR ME14 ...13 L4
Mosul Wy HAYES BR2 ...89 M3
Mosyer Dr STMC/STPC BR5 ...91 L5
Mote Av MAID/SHEP ME15 ...13 J6
Mote Pk MAID/SHEP ME15 ...167 L4
Mote Rd BGR/WK TN15 ...163 M6
  MAID/SHEP ME15 ...13 H6
Motherwell Wy WTHK RM20 ...33 H4
Moth House
  WOOL/PLUM SE18 * ...27 M6
Motney Hill Rd RHAM ME8 ...103 H1
Mottingham Gdns
  ELTH/MOT SE9 ...47 L6
Mottingham La ELTH/MOT SE9 ...47 K6
Mottingham Rd ELTH/MOT SE9 ...47 M8
Mottisfont Rd ABYW SE2 ...29 J2
Mouchotte CI BH/WHM TN16 ...106 A6
Moultain HI SWLY BR8 ...75 H8
Mountacre CI SYD SE26 ...69 G1
Mount Adon Pk EDUL SE22 ...45 H5
Mountain CI RCANTW CT4 ...238 E10
Mountain St RCANTW CT4 ...247 N11
Mount Ash Rd SYD SE26 ...69 G1
Mount Av WBY/YAL ME18 ...257 A4
Mountbatten Av HOO/HM ME3 ...81 K1
  WALD ME5 ...101 H6
Mountbatten CI NRWD SE19 ...68 F2
  WOOL/PLUM SE18 ...28 E5
Mountbatten Wy RASHE TN25 ...289 M11
Mount Castle La RMAID ME17 ...263 K4
Mount Charles Wk
  RCANTW CT4 * ...175 G8
Mount CI BMLY BR1 ...71 M5
  SEV TN13 ...20 D1
Mount Ct WWKM BR4 ...88 F5
Mount Culver Av SCUP DA14 ...73 L3
Mount Dr MAID/BEAR ME14 ...168 C1
Mounteaun Gdns
  STRHM/NOR SW16 ...44 A8
Mount Edgcumbe Rd
  STH/RUST TN4 ...22 E5
Mount Ephraim RTW TN1 ...22 E4
Mount Ephraim La
  STH/RUST TN4 ...22 E4
Mount Ephraim Rd RTW TN1 ...22 F4
Mount Fld FAV ME13 ...149 J3
  OBOR ME11 ...64 B8
Mountfield CI LEW SE13 ...46 E5
  MEO DA13 ...239
Mountfield Gdns RTW TN1 ...23 G5
Mountfield Pk TON TN9 ...194 F6
Mountfield Rd NROM TN28 ...331 K8
  RTW TN1 ...23 G6
Mountfield Ter CAT SE6 ...46 F6
Mountfield Wy STMC/STPC BR5 ...73 K8
  WGOS CT8 ...177 G7
Mount Gdns SYD SE26 ...69 J8
Mount Green Av MSTR CT12 ...182 A5
Mount Harry Rd SEV TN13 ...20 D1
Mounthurst Rd HAYES BR2 ...89 H3
Mountjoy CI THMD SE28 ...28 F7
Mount Lodge Ter ROCH ME1 * ...100
Mount Nod Rd
  STRHM/NOR SW16 ...44 A8
Mount Pleasant
  BH/WHM TN16 ...132 C3
  CANTW/ST CT2 ...153 C7
  CHAT ME4 ...7 G7
  DIT/AY ME20 ...140
  DVW CT17 * ...7 J3
  RTON TN11 ...188 A7
  STPH/PW TN12 ...279 J3
  TENT TN30 ...315 P1
  WADH TN5 ...309 L4
Mount Pleasant Av RTW TN1 ...23 G5
Mountpleasant Dr RFOLK CT18 ...291 M10
Mount Pleasant Dr
  MAID/BEAR ME14 ...142 A4
Mount Pleasant La RRTW TN3 ...296 B7
Mount Pleasant PI
  WOOL/PLUM SE18 ...28 E4
Mount Pleasant Rd DART DA1 ...52 A4
  FOLK CT20 ...11 K4
  LEW SE13 ...46 D4
  RSEV TN14 ...255 K3
  RTW TN1 ...22 F4
Mount Rd FSTH SE23 ...45 L7
Mount Rd BXLYHS DA6 ...49 M3
  CANT CT1 ...5 H?
  CHAT ME4 ...6 D8
  DART DA1 ...51 J2
  DVW CT17 ...217 H4
  NRWD SE19 * ...68 A2
  ROCH ME1 ...100 B3
Mountsfield CI MAIDW ME16 ...12 E?
Mounts Hill CRBK TN17 ...313 K2
Mount Sion RTW TN1 ...22 F4
Mounts La CRBK TN17 ...314 F8
Mounts Pond Rd
  BKHTH/KID SE3 ...26 E8
Mount Rd GRH DA9 ...53 J4
Mount St HYTHE CT21 ...222 D?
Mount Vw RASHE TN25 ...306
The Mount BMLY BR1 ...71 M5
  BXLYHS DA6 ...50 C3
  CHAT ME4 ...6 D7
  FAV ME13 ...149 J3
  STH/RUST TN4 ...277 R6
Mountview RSIT ME9 ...119
Mount View Ct CHAT ME4 * ...6 D7
Mountview Rd ORP BR6 ...91 H3

Mount Vls WNWD SE27 ...44 C8
Mountwood Cl SAND/SEL CR2 ...104 A4
Mowbray Rd NRWD SE19 ...69 G5
Mowll St BRXN/ST SW9 ...24 B6
Moyes Cl MSTR CT12 ...182 A8
Moyle Cl HYTHE CT21 ...222 D4
Mozart Ct CHAT ME4 ...18 B7
Muckingford Rd TIL RM18 ...36 A3
Muggeridge Cl SAND/SEL CR2 ...25 J4
Muirfield Cl BERM/RHTH SE16 * ...25 J4
Muirfield Crs POP/IOD E14 ...26 D6
Muirkirk Rd CAT SE6 ...46 D6
Muir Rd MAID/SHEP ME15 ...13 G7
  RAM CT11 ...17 M2
Mulberry Cl GILL ME7 ...116 B1
  MEO DA13 ...97 J2
  RAM CT11 ...17 L3
  RTWE/PEM TN2 ...197 G4
Mulberry Ct CANT CT1 ...4 E5
  HYTHE CT21 ...222 E2
Mulberry Dr PUR RM19 ...32 A3
Mulberry Fld SWCH CT13 ...237 J12
Mulberry Hl RCANTW CT4 ...247 Q8
Mulberry La CROY/NA CR0 ...87 G4
Mulberry Ms NWCR SE14 ...26 A7
Mulberry Pl ELTH/MOT SE9 ...47 L2
Mulberry Rd ASH TN23 ...202 A8
  GVW DA11 ...78 F1
Mulberry Wy BELV DA17 ...30 D1
Mulgrave Rd CROY/NA CR0 ...86 E6
  WOOL/PLUM SE18 ...28 A3
Mullein Ct GRAYS RM17 ...34 E5
Multon Rd BGR/WK TN15 ...111 K1
Mulvaney Wy STHWK SE1 * ...24 A2
Mumford Mills GNWCH SE10 ...26 D7
Mumford Rd HNHL SE24 ...44 C7
Muncies Ms CAT SE6 ...46 D7
Mundania Rd EDUL SE22 ...45 J4
Munday Bois Rd HDCN TN27 ...262 H12
Munford Dr SWCM DA10 ...54 A5
Mungo Park Rd GVE DA12 ...79 L2
Mungo Park Wy STMC/STPC BR5 ...91 K3
Munnery Wy ORP BR6 ...90 K6
Munn's La RSIT ME9 ...103 M7
Munsgore La RSIT ME9 ...118 F7
Munton Rd WALW SE17 ...25 J5
Murchison Av BXLY DA5 ...49 L6
Murdock St PECK SE15 ...25 J5
Murillo Rd LEW SE13 ...46 E2
Murphy St STHWK SE1 ...24 A1
Murrain Dr MAID/SHEP ME15 ...168 B4
Murray Av BMLY BR1 ...71 J7
Murrey House WOOL/PLUM SE18 * ...27 M6
Murray Rd STMC/STPC BR5 ...91 H3
  STRD ME2 ...82 C4
Murston Rd SIT ME10 ...120 C6
Murthwaite Ct IOS ME12 ...65 H8
Murton-neale Cl HAWK TN18 ...312 H1
Murton Pl FAV ME13 ...124 F8
Muscatel Pl CMBW SE5 ...24 F7
Muschamp Rd PECK SE15 ...45 G1
Muscovy Ms RASHE TN25 ...202 E3
Muscovy Wy HB CT6 ...128 F6
Musgrave Cl MSTR CT12 ...181 J3
Musgrave Rd ASH TN23 ...204 D5
Musgrove Rd NWCR SE14 ...25 L7
Musket La RMAID ME17 ...169 J3
Mussenden La EYN DA4 ...94 E2
Mustang Rd E/WMAL ME19 ...164 A4
Mustards Rd IOS ME12 ...230 C4
Mutrix Gdns MARG CT9 ...177 K4
Mutrix Rd MARG CT9 ...177 L5
Mutton La LING RH7 ...274 A3
Mutton La FAV ME13 ...149 H4
Myatt Rd BRXN/ST SW9 ...24 C7
Mycenae Rd BKHTH/KID SE3 ...27 H5
Myers La NWCR SE14 ...25 J5
Mylis Cl SYD SE26 ...69 J1
Mymms Cl WWKM BR4 ...127 K5
Myra St ABYW SE2 ...48 B7
Myron Pl LEW SE13 ...46 D1
Myrtle Aly WOOL/PLUM SE18 ...28 B2
Myrtle Cl ERITH DA8 ...30 F6
Myrtle Crs WALD ME5 ...101 L4
Myrtledene Rd ABYW SE2 ...29 H7
Myrtle Gn ASH TN23 ...202 A7
Myrtle Gv E/WMAL ME19 ...204 B5
  SOCK/AV RM15 ...32 D1
Myrtle Pl RDART DA2 ...52 C6
Myrtle Rd CROY/NA CR0 ...88 B6
  DART DA1 ...11 L2
The Myrtles IOS ME12 * ...65 G3
Myrtle Vls NROM TN28 * ...330 H7
  STPH/PW TN12 * ...280 H4
Mystole La RCANTW CT4 ...248 C8
Mystole Rd RCANTW CT4 ...248 C9
Myton Rd DUL SE21 ...44 E8

N

Nackington Rd RCANTW CT4 ...174 B8
Nadine St CHARL SE7 ...27 K4
Nags Head La ROCH ME1 ...19 M9
  WELL DA16 ...49 J1
Nailbourne Cl RCANTW CT4 ...270 C2
Naildown Cl HYTHE CT21 ...223 H2
Naildown Rd HYTHE CT21 ...223 H2
Nairn Ct TIL RM18 * ...35 H5
Nairne Cl RASHW TN26 ...303 P5
Nairne Gv SEA SE22 ...44 E3
Namba Roy Cl STRHM/NOR SW16 ...68 A8
Namton Dr STRHM/NOR SW16 ...68 A8
Namur Pl RDV CT15 ...214 A6
Nansen Rd GVE DA12 ...79 J8
Napchester Rd DVE/WH CT16 ...213 H4
  RDV CT15 ...273 J12
Napier Av POP/IOD E14 ...32 B4
Napier Barracks FOLK CT20 * ...223 K1
Napier Cl DEPT SE8 ...25 L5
  SIT ME10 ...119 K5
Napier Ct LEE/GVPK SE12 ...47 J3
Napier Gdns HYTHE CT21 ...222 D4
Napier Rd BELV DA17 ...30 A3
  BRDST CT10 ...179 H1
  DVE/WH CT16 ...213 H6
  GILL ME7 ...7 L1
  GVW DA11 ...55 G6
  HAYES BR2 ...71 J1
  RTWE/PEM TN2 ...22 A6
  SNOD ME6 ...113 H6
Napier Ter IOS ME12 * ...64 B7
Napleton Rd FAV ME13 ...149 K2
  RAM CT11 ...16 B7
Napoleon Dr STPH/PW TN12 ...281 J4
Napwood Cl RHAM ME8 ...116 B1
Nares Rd RHAM ME8 ...116 E1
Nargate St RCANTE CT3 ...234 C12
Narrabeen Rd FOLKN CT19 ...219 M7
Narrow Boat Cl THMD SE28 ...28 E1

Narrowbush La LYDD TN29 ...329 N6
Narrow La WARL CR6 ...130 A5
Narrow Wy HAYES BR2 ...89 M2
Naseby Av FOLK CT20 ...219 L8
Naseby Rd NRWD SE19 ...68 E3
Nash Bank MEO DA13 ...79 C6
Nash Ct CANT CT1 ...115 K3
Nash Court Gdns MARG CT9 ...15 C9
Nash Court Rd MARG CT9 ...15 C9
Nash Cft MEO DA13 ...78 F1
Nashenden Farm La ROCH ME1 ...100 A4
Nashenden La ROCH ME1 ...100 A4
Nash Gdns BRDST CT10 ...183 L1
Nash Gn BMLY BR1 ...71 H4
Nash Hl RFOLK CT18 ...291 N11
Nash La HAYES BR2 ...105 M1
  MARG CT9 ...178 C6
Nash Rd BROCKY SE4 ...45 M2
  MARG CT9 ...14 F1
  RCANTE CT3 ...235 K11
Nash St MEO DA13 ...79 H6
Nasmyth Rd BRCH CT7 ...176 D5
Natal Rd CHAT ME4 ...18 C7
Nathan Wy THMD SE28 ...29 H1
National Ter BERM/RHTH SE16 * ...25 J1
Nativity Cl SIT ME10 ...119 M5
Nat's La RASHE TN25 ...288 H4
Nautilus Cl IOS ME12 ...65 J2
Nautilus Dr IOS ME12 ...65 H8
Naylands MARG CT9 ...14 C6
Naylor Rd PECK SE15 ...25 J6
Nazareth Cl PECK SE15 ...25 J8
Nealden St BRXN/ST SW9 ...44 A1
Neale St CHAT ME4 ...18 C7
Neal's Place Rd CANTW/ST CT2 ...171 K5
Neal Ter FSTH SE23 * ...45 L6
Neame Rd BRCH CT7 ...176 D6
Neason Wy FOLKN CT19 ...221 G7
Neate St CMBW SE5 ...24 E5
Neath Ct MAID/SHEP ME15 * ...167 M5
Neb La OXTED RH8 ...184 D1
Nebraska St STHWK SE1 ...24 D1
Neckinger BERM/RHTH SE16 ...25 G2
Neckinger St BERM/RHTH SE16 ...25 G2
Neckinger St STHWK SE1 ...25 G1
Nectarine Wy LEW SE13 ...26 C8
Needleman St BERM/RHTH SE16 ...25 J1
Neills Rd RRTW TN3 ...295 Q11
Nelgarde Rd CAT SE6 ...46 B5
Nelldale Rd BERM/RHTH SE16 ...25 J3
Nellington Rd RRTW TN3 ...200 E1
Nello James Gdns WNWD SE27 ...68 E1
Nelson Av IOS ME12 ...65 L7
  TON TN9 ...194 D4
Nelson Cl BH/WHM TN16 ...132 D5
  CROY/NA CR0 ...86 B5
  IOS ME12 ...64 D5
  KEN/WIL TN24 ...205 L3
Nelson Crs RAM CT11 ...17 J7
Nelson Mandela Rd BKHTH/KID SE3 ...47 K1
Nelson Park Rd RDV CT15 ...211 K1
Nelson Pl BRDST CT10 ...179 L8
  SCUP DA14 ...73 G1
Nelson Rd BELV DA17 ...30 A3
  DART DA1 ...51 K4
  GILL ME7 ...7 L1
  GNWCH SE10 ...26 D5
  GVW DA11 ...55 G7
  HAYES BR2 ...71 J1
  ROCH ME1 ...113 M1
  RTWE/PEM TN2 ...22 L8
  SCUP DA14 ...73 G1
  WSTB CT5 ...126 D4
Nelson Sq STHWK SE1 ...24 C1
Nelson St DEAL CT14 ...209 L2
  FAV ME13 ...149 K3
  SIT RTW TN1 ...22 B7
Nelson Ter DVE/WH CT16 ...213 J6
  WALD ME5 ...101 K4
Nepicar La BGR/WK TN15 ...238 H10
Neptune Gr STRD ME2 ...82 F6
Neptune Gap WSTB CT5 * ...126 E3
Neptune Ter BERM/RHTH SE16 ...25 K2
Neptune Wy STRD ME2 ...6 B1
Nesbit Cl BKHTH/KID SE3 ...46 F1
Nesbit Rd ELTH/MOT SE9 ...47 L2
Nesbitt Sq NRWD SE19 * ...68 F4
Ness Rd ERITH DA8 ...31 L5
Ness St BERM/RHTH SE16 ...25 H2
The Ness CANT CT1 ...174 B4
Nestor Ct WBY/YAL ME18 ...165 H1
Nether Av NROM TN28 ...331 L8
Netherby Rd FSTH SE23 ...45 K5
Nethercourt Farm Rd RAM CT11 ...16 C5
Nethercourt Gdns RAM CT11 ...16 C6
Nethercourt Hl RAM CT11 ...16 C6
Nethergong Hl RCANTE CT3 ...234 E2
Netherhale Farm Rd BRCH CT7 ...233 Q6
Nethern Court Rd CTHM CR3 ...156 F1
Nethersole Cl CANTW/ST CT2 ...172 B5
Nethersole Rd RCANTW CT4 ...271 K4
Netley Cl CROY/NA CR0 ...105 N2
  MAID/BEAR ME14 ...141 L7
  PECK SE15 ...25 H6
Nettlefield Pl WNWD SE27 ...44 D1
Nettlefold Pl WNWD SE27 ...44 D1
Nettlepole La HDCN TN27 ...263 P12
Nettlestead Cl BECK BR3 ...70 A4
Nettlestead La WBY/YAL ME18 ...164 B2
Nettleton Rd NWCR SE14 ...25 L6
Neuchatel Rd CAT SE6 ...46 A7
Nevada St GNWCH SE10 ...26 D6
Nevell Rd CDW/CHF RM16 ...35 J2
Nevell Rd E/WMAL ME19 ...138 D4
Neville Cl BFN/LL DA15 ...73 G1
  MAID/BEAR ME14 ...141 L7
  PECK SE15 ...25 H6
Neville Rd B MEO DA13 * ...97 H1
  CROY/NA CR0 ...86 B9
Nevill Gdns DEAL CT14 ...209 J8
Nevill Pl RTWE/PEM TN2 ...201 J4
Nevill Pk RTW TN1 ...22 A6
Nevill Rdg STH/RUST TN4 ...200 E3
Nevill Rd SNOD ME6 ...113 H6
Nevill St RTW TN1 ...22 C6
Nevill Ter RTWE/PEM TN2 ...22 D8
New Acres Rd THMD SE28 ...28 F1
Newark Yd STRD ME2 ...19 H1
Newbarn La STH/RUST TN4 ...133 J2
New Barn Rd MEO DA13 ...78 D2
  RMAID ME17 ...260 F11
  SWLY BR8 ...74 F5
New Barns Rd MAID/BEAR ME14 ...141 H5

Newbery Rd ERITH DA8 ...31 G7
Newbridge Av SIT ME10 ...119 M2
Newburgh Rd GRAYS RM17 ...34 E4
Newburn Rd MAID/BEAR ME16 ...140 E7
Newbury Cl BRCH CT7 ...176 E7
  FOLK CT20 ...219 L8
  HOO/HM ME3 ...58 C5
Newbury La WADH TN5 ...309 P1
Newbury Rd HAYES BR2 ...71 H7
  STPH/PW TN12 ...279 K3
  SWLY BR8 ...75 J8
New Butt La DEPT SE8 * ...26 B7
Newcastle Hl RAM CT11 ...17 K5
New Church La LYDD TN29 ...318 H11
  LYDD TN29 ...319 J9
New Church Rd MAID/SHEP ME15 ...167 H4
  STH/RUST TN4 ...22 C2
Newcomen Rd STHWK SE1 ...24 E1
New Concordia Whf STHWK SE1 * ...25 G1
New Covenant Pl ROCH ME1 ...19 M9
New Cross Rd NWCR SE14 ...25 M7
New Cross St MARG CT9 ...14 C4
New Cut CHAT ME4 ...6 B5
  MAID/SHEP ME15 ...166 E6
New Cut Rd MAID/BEAR ME14 ...167 L1
  RCANTW CT4 ...247 N8
Newdigate STRHM/NOR SW16 * ...68 B1
New Dover Rd CANT CT1 ...5 J4
  RFOLK CT18 ...221 J4
Newenden Cl ASH TN23 ...204 C5
Newenden Rd STRD ME2 ...82 D3
New England Rd STH/RUST TN4 ...196 D6
New Farm La HAYES BR2 ...71 H7
New Farthingdale LING RH7 ...274 A5
New Ferry Ap WOOL/PLUM SE18 ...28 B2
New Forest La RCANTW CT4 ...247 N6
New Gardens Rd RSIT ME9 ...121 K4
Newgate CROY/NA CR0 ...86 D9
Newgate Gap MARG CT9 ...15 K2
Newgate Lower Prom MARG CT9 ...15 J2
Newgate Prom MARG CT9 ...15 J2
New Green Pl BRXS/STRHM SW2 ...44 B5
  NRWD SE19 ...68 F3
New Hall Cl LYDD TN29 ...320 H9
New Hall Farm La HOO/HM ME3 ...41 J7
Newham's Rw STHWK SE1 ...24 F1
Newhaven Gdns ELTH/MOT SE9 ...47 L2
Newhaven La SNWD SE25 ...86 B1
New House Cl CANT CT1 ...249 M6
New House La GVW DA11 ...55 J6
Newhouse La HAYES BR2 ...246 C2
  HDCN TN27 ...283 J5
New House La RCANTW CT4 ...249 M6
New House Ter EDEN TN8 * ...192 D3
New Hythe La DIT/AY ME20 ...139 H1
Newick Cl BXLY DA5 ...50 C4
Newing Cl RCANTE CT3 ...175 M1
  RCANTE CT3 ...251 J1
Newing Gn BMLY BR1 ...71 L4
Newington Butts LBTH SE11 ...24 C3
Newington Cswy STHWK SE1 ...24 D2
Newington Rd MSTR CT12 ...16 E4
  RAM CT11 ...16 E4
  RFOLK CT18 ...219 H5
Newington Wk MAID/BEAR ME14 * ...141 K7
Newitt Rd HOO/HM ME3 ...59 L8
New Kent Rd STHWK SE1 ...24 D2
New King St DEPT SE8 ...26 B5
Newland Green La HDCN TN27 ...284 G1
Newland Rd IOS ME12 ...64 A0
  DVE/WH CT16 ...213 J3
  RRTW TN3 ...200 E1
Newlands Av SIT ME10 ...119 J5
Newlands Dr DEAL CT14 ...211 J1
Newlands Farm Rd HOO/HM ME3 ...40 C2
Newlands La MEO DA13 ...239 L4
  MSTR CT12 ...183 G3
Newlands Pk SYD SE26 ...69 K3
Newlands Ri STH/RUST TN4 ...196 D7
Newlands Rd HDCN TN27 ...263 Q8
  STRHM/NOR SW16 ...68 A2
  STH/RUST TN4 ...196 D7
Newlands Wd CROY/NA CR0 ...104 E3
Newlands Woods CROY/NA CR0 * ...104 E3
New La LYDD TN29 ...334 F9
New Lodge Dr OXTED RH8 ...157 L6
New Lydd Rd RYE TN31 ...332 D9
New Lydenburg St CHARL SE7 ...27 J2
Newlyn Cl ORP BR6 ...91 G7
Newlyn Dr STPH/PW TN12 ...282 A4
Newlyn Rd WELL DA16 ...29 J8
Newlyn's Meadow RDV CT15 ...293 L6
Newman Dr SIT ME10 ...120 B3
Newman Rd BMLY BR1 ...71 J4
  CROY/NA CR0 ...86 A3
  RCANTE CT3 ...251 P12
Newmans Cl BRDST CT10 ...179 K1
New Mill Rd STMC/STPC BR5 ...73 K5
Newnham Dr RHAM ME8 ...102 D3
  THHTH CR7 ...68 C6
Newnham Av FAV ME13 ...244 H5
Newnham Pl CDW/CHF RM16 ...35 J3
Newnhams Cl BMLY BR1 ...72 A7
Newnham St CHAT ME4 ...6 E4
Newnham Ter STHWK SE1 ...24 B2
New Place Sq BERM/RHTH SE16 * ...25 J2
New Pond Rd CRBK TN17 ...299 N12
  CRBK TN17 ...313 M3
Newports SWLY BR8 ...92 E3
Newport St LBTH SE11 ...24 B3
New Pound La WBY/YAL ME18 ...241 H9
Newquay Rd CAT SE6 ...46 C7
New Rectory La ASH TN23 ...204 C3
New Rents ASH TN23 ...2 C6
New Rd ABYW SE2 ...29 H7
  CANTW/ST CT2 ...154 A6
  CANTW/ST CT2 ...170 D2
  CHAT ME4 ...6 D7
  CRBK TN17 ...298 F9
  DIT/AY ME20 ...139 H4
  EYN DA4 ...76 D6
  GDST RH9 ...184 B9
  GRAYS RM17 ...34 C5
  GVW DA11 ...78 F1
  HDCN TN27 ...265 K11
  HDCN TN27 ...283 L4
  HOO/HM ME3 ...58 D7
  HYTHE CT21 ...222 C7
  IOS ME12 ...64 D5
  IOS ME12 ...65 J2
  MEO DA13 ...97 J2
  ORP BR6 ...91 H3
  OXTED RH8 ...158 A8

  RCANTW CT4 ...291 Q5
  RDV CT15 ...272 D8
  RMAID ME17 ...168 D3
  ROCH ME1 ...114 A5
  RSEV TN14 ...160 C2
  RTON TN11 ...276 H7
  RYE TN31 ...225 J3
  RYE TN31 ...324 H10
  STPH/PW TN12 ...279 K3
  SWLY BR8 ...75 J8
  TON TN9 ...194 J8
New Road Hl HAYES BR2 ...106 D3
New Romney Pl SWCH CT13 * ...206 A1
New Ruttington La CANT CT1 ...5 J2
New Stairs CHAT ME4 ...6 C2
Newstead Av ORP BR6 ...90 F7
Newstead Rd LEE/GVPK SE12 ...47 G5
New St BGR/WK TN15 ...239 J1
  BH/WHM TN16 ...159 H5
  CANT CT1 ...4 D7
  CHAT ME4 ...6 B4
  DEAL CT14 ...209 L2
  DVE/WH CT16 ...8 D7
  FOLK CT20 ...8 K4
  IOS ME12 ...64 D7
  KEN/WIL TN24 ...2 D7
  LYDD TN29 ...334 D3
  MARG CT9 ...14 F1
  RCANTE CT3 ...236 B12
  SWCH CT13 ...206 B1
New Street Hl BMLY BR1 ...71 M4
New Street Rd MEO DA13 ...96 D6
New Swan Yd GVE DA12 * ...55 J4
Newton Abbot Rd GVW DA11 ...55 G7
Newton Av TONN TN10 ...189 G6
Newton Cl MAIDW ME16 ...12 B6
  WALD ME5 ...115 K3
Newton Gdns STPH/PW TN12 ...279 J2
Newton Pl POP/IOD E14 ...26 E2
Newton Rd FAV ME13 ...149 L2
  RTW TN1 ...22 F4
  TIL RM18 ...35 H8
  WELL DA16 ...49 H1
  WSTB CT5 ...127 J3
Newton's Ct GRH DA9 ...52 E3
Newton Ter HAYES BR2 ...89 L2
Newton Willows RRTW TN3 ...199 K6
New Town Gn KEN/WIL TN24 ...2 E7
New Town Rd ASH TN23 ...2 D7
New Town St CANT CT1 ...4 D8
  RCANTW CT4 ...170 D8
New Union Cl POP/IOD E14 ...26 D2
New Wharf Rd TON TN9 ...194 E3
New Winchelsea Rd RYE TN31 ...225 J2
New Years Cl RSEV TN14 ...133 L2
Nicholas Cl MAIDW ME16 ...166 B2
Nicholas Ct BRDST CT10 ...179 M1
Nicholas Rd CROY/NA CR0 ...86 A3
  RASHE TN25 ...202 D4
Nichol La BMLY BR1 ...71 H4
Nicholls Dr BRDST CT10 ...183 J3
Nicholson House WOOL/PLUM SE18 * ...27 M6
Nicholson Rd CROY/NA CR0 ...87 G4
Nicklaus Dr WALD ME5 ...115 G2
Nickle Bank RCANTW CT4 * ...248 B5
Nickleby Cl ROCH ME1 ...100 D3
Nickleby Rd GVE DA12 ...56 B6
Nickle Ga RCANTW CT4 * ...248 B6
Nickle Wood Rd RASHW TN26 ...303 R7
Nicolson Rd STMC/STPC BR5 ...91 K4
Niederwald Rd SYD SE26 ...45 H1
Nigel Rd PECK SE15 ...45 J1
Nigeria Rd CHARL SE7 ...27 K6
Nightingale Av HYTHE CT21 ...321 Q1
  WSTB CT5 ...126 C7
Nightingale Cl BH/WHM TN16 ...132 D3
  GVW DA11 ...78 D1
  KEN/WIL TN24 ...205 K4
  RCANTW CT4 ...170 D7
  RHAM ME8 ...102 F7
Nightingale Cnr STMC/STPC BR5 * ...73 L8
Nightingale Gv STRD ME2 ...81 G4
Nightingale Gv LEW SE13 ...46 F3
Nightingale Ms BMLY BR1 ...71 K6
  RDV CT15 ...271 P3
  RSEV TN14 ...161 G8
Nightingale Ms LBTH SE11 * ...24 C3
Nightingale Pl MARG CT9 ...15 G4
  WOOL/PLUM SE18 ...28 B5
The Nightingales CRBK TN17 ...299 P3
Nightingale V WOOL/PLUM SE18 ...28 B5
Nightingale Wy SWLY BR8 ...74 F7
Nile Rd GILL ME7 ...7 K5
Nile St DEPT SE8 ...26 A5
Nine Acres Cl HYTHE CT21 ...179 K7
  KEN/WIL TN24 ...202 H2
Nine Acres Rd STRD ME2 ...18 H2
Nine Ash La FAV ME13 ...150 D6
Nine Elms Gv GVW DA11 ...55 H6
Ninehams Rd BH/WHM TN16 ...132 A4
Nineveh La HAWK TN18 ...312 H1
Ninhams Wd ORP BR6 ...90 B7
Ninn La BGR/WK TN15 ...283 R7
Nisbet Wk SCUP DA14 ...73 H1
Niven Cl HOO/HM ME3 ...59 M8
Nixon Av MSTR CT12 ...182 A8
Nizels La RTON TN11 ...255 N4
No1 St WOOL/PLUM SE18 ...28 A2
No2 St WOOL/PLUM SE18 ...28 A2
Noah's Ark BGR/WK TN15 ...137 G4
Noah's Ark Rd DVW CT17 ...217 H2
Noakes Meadow ASH TN23 ...204 C5
Nobel Cl RSIT ME9 ...121 K7
Nobel Ct FAV ME13 ...149 J2
Noble Ct MARG CT9 ...15 G4
Noble Gdns MARG CT9 ...177 K5
Noble Tree Rd RTON TN11 ...256 A6
Nonsuch Cl CANT CT1 ...5 M5
The Nook WBY/YAL ME18 ...257 Q3
Norah La HOO/HM ME3 ...81 J7
Norbury Av STRHM/NOR SW16 ...68 B4
Norbury Ct STRHM/NOR SW16 ...68 B5
Norbury Crs STRHM/NOR SW16 ...68 C5
Norbury Hl STRHM/NOR SW16 ...68 B2
Norbury Rd THHTH CR7 ...68 C6
Norcrofts Gdns EDUL SE22 ...45 H2
Nordenfeldt Rd ERITH DA8 ...30 E4
Nore Cl GILL ME7 ...101 M4
  IOS ME12 ...64 D7
Noreen Av IOS ME12 ...65 L7
Norfield Rd RDART DA2 ...74 D1

Norfolk Cl DART DA1 ...52 B3
  WALD ME5 ...115 K2
Norfolk Crs BFN/LL DA15 ...48 F5
Norfolk Dr ASH TN23 ...204 D3
Norfolk Gdns BXLYHN DA7 ...30 A7
Norfolk Pl CDW/CHF RM16 ...33 N4
  WELL DA16 ...29 H8
Norfolk Rd CANT CT1 ...4 D7
  GVE DA12 ...55 L5
  MAID/SHEP ME15 ...167 K5
  MARG CT9 ...15 J2
  RTW TN1 ...23 G7
  THHTH CR7 ...68 D2
  TON TN9 ...194 D5
Norfolk Sq MSTR CT12 ...182 A8
Norfolk St WSTB CT5 ...126 C5
Norheads La BH/WHM TN16 ...131 M4
Norhyrst Av SNWD SE25 ...69 G5
Norington La CHST BR7 ...72 C5
Norlands Ga CHST BR7 ...72 C5
Norman Cl MAID/BEAR ME14 ...141 H5
  ORP BR6 ...90 F7
  RHAM ME8 ...116 C1
  RSEV TN14 ...136 C3
  STRD ME2 ...18 D9
Normandy Cl SYD SE26 ...45 K7
Normandy Rd BRXN/ST SW9 ...24 B7
Normanhurst Av WELL DA16 ...49 L2
Normanhurst Rd BGR/WK TN15 ...240 C5
  BRXS/STRHM SW2 ...44 A7
  STMC/STPC BR5 ...73 K5
Norman Pde SCUP DA14 ...49 K8
Norman Rd ASH TN23 ...204 H8
  BELV DA17 ...30 C1
  BRDST CT10 ...179 H1
  CANT CT1 ...4 D7
  DART DA1 ...51 M6
  E/WMAL ME19 ...138 A2
  FAV ME13 ...149 K2
  GNWCH SE10 ...26 C6
  RAM CT11 ...17 L5
  RDV CT15 ...215 J3
  RTW TN1 ...23 H7
  SNOD ME6 ...113 H7
  THHTH CR7 ...86 D1
  WGOS CT8 ...177 J4
Normans Cl GVW DA11 ...55 H5
Normans La EDEN TN8 ...191 M5
Norman St MSTR CT12 ...18 B1
  RSEV TN14 ...160 D8
Normanton Rd FSTH SE23 ...45 L7
Normington Cl STRHM/NOR SW16 ...68 B2
Norreys Rd RHAM ME8 ...102 D3
Norrie Rd BRCH CT7 ...176 D7
Norrington Md FOLKN CT19 ...220 D3
Norris Rd MAID/SHEP ME15 ...167 H7
Norris Wy DART DA1 ...51 G2
Norstead Gdns STH/RUST TN4 ...196 D6
Norsted La ORP BR6 ...108 A3
Northall Rd BXLYHN DA7 ...30 D7
Northampton Quay DVW CT17 ...8 D7
Northampton Rd CROY/NA CR0 ...87 H5
North Ash Rd HART DA3 ...95 M8
North Av RAM CT11 ...17 H6
North Bank Cl STRD ME2 ...18 D2
North Barrack Rd DEAL CT14 ...209 L6
Northbourne HAYES BR2 ...89 H3
Northbourne Av DVW CT17 ...217 G4
Northbourne Rd DEAL CT14 ...204 D3
  DEAL CT14 ...273 M4
  RHAM ME8 ...102 C2
Northborough Rd STRHM/NOR SW16 ...68 D1
Northbridge St RBTBR TN32 ...322 C8
Northbrooke La KEN/WIL TN24 ...2 D7
Northbrook Rd CROY/NA CR0 ...86 D1
  LEW SE13 ...46 F3
Northcliffe Gdns BRDST CT10 ...179 K6
North Cl BXLYHN DA6 ...49 G5
  FOLK CT20 ...223 L1
Northcote Rd CROY/NA CR0 ...86 C2
  DEAL CT14 ...209 L4
  DEAL CT14 ...211 L5
  GVW DA11 ...55 L5
  SCUP DA14 ...72 F1
  STRD ME2 ...18 E4
  TON TN9 ...194 D5
North Ct MAID/SHEP ME15 * ...167 H4
North Court Cl RCANTE CT3 ...251 K4
North Court Rd DEAL CT14 ...272 H1
North Cray Rd BXLY DA5 ...50 A3
  SCUP DA14 ...73 H4
North Crs RMAID ME17 ...259 J4
North Cross Rd EDUL SE22 ...45 G2
North Dane Wy WALD ME5 ...101 L2
Northdown KEN/WIL TN24 ...2 D7
  RSIT ME9 ...118 D6
North Down STPH/PW TN12 ...281 K5
Northdown Ar MARG CT9 * ...15 J2
Northdown Cl MAID/BEAR ME14 ...141 J7
  STPH/PW TN12 ...279 J3
Northdown Hl BRDST CT10 ...179 G6
Northdown Pde MARG CT9 * ...15 L2
Northdown Rd BGR/WK TN15 ...136 D5
  BRDST CT10 ...179 G6
  GDST RH9 ...156 F3
  HART DA3 ...77 M8
  MARG CT9 ...15 J3
  WELL DA16 ...29 H8
North Downs Cl RCANTW CT4 ...247 N7
Northdowns Cl RDV CT15 ...273 J7
North Downs Crs CROY/NA CR0 ...105 G6
North Downs Rd CROY/NA CR0 ...105 G6
North Downs Wy BGR/WK TN15 ...238 D5
  CANT CT1 ...9 G1
  CANTW/ST CT2 ...171 H5
  DVW CT17 ...8 D7
  E/WMAL ME19 ...239 L6
  GDST RH9 ...156 E6
  HDCN TN27 ...263 Q3
  HYTHE CT21 ...307 R1
  MAID/BEAR ME14 ...141 M1
  MEO DA13 ...239 M6
  OXTED RH8 ...157 M1
  RASHE TN25 ...264 G8
  RASHE TN25 ...289 R7
  RCANTW CT4 ...175 J8
  RCANTW CT4 ...247 N8
  RDV CT15 ...271 N6
  RFOLK CT18 ...221 L1
  RMAID ME17 ...143 J7
  RMAID ME17 ...242 A5
  SEV TN13 ...143 L11

STRD ME2 99 G4
North Downs Wy & Saxon Shore Wy
FOLKN CT19 220 C4
Northdown Vw RMAID ME17 242 G11
Northdown Wy MARG CT9 178 F4
North Dr BECK BR3 70 C8
ORP BR6 90 F7
North Eastling Rd RSIT ME9 245 J1
North End CROY/NA CR0 86 D5
North End La ORP BR6 107 G3
Northend Rd ERITH DA8 31 G7
Northern By-Pass HDCN TN27 264 B5
North Farm La
RTWE/PEM TN2 197 H4
North Farm Rd
RTWE/PEM TN2 196 F6
Northfield HART DA3 78 A7
Northfield Av STMC/STPC BR5 91 K2
Northfield Cl BMLY BR1 71 M5
Northfields GRAYS RM17 34 D3
MAIDW ME16 166 A3
RRTW TN3 277 P9
Northfleet Cl
MAID/BEAR ME14 13 M2
North Folly Rd
MAID/SHEP ME15 258 E2
North Foreland Av
BRDST CT10 179 L6
North Foreland Rd
BRDST CT10 179 L6
North Frith RTON TN11 * 189 J4
Northgate CANT CT1 5 G3
ROCH ME1 19 K6
Northgate Borough CANT CT1 5 H2
Northgrove Rd HAWK TN18 312 D7
North Hill Rd HAWK TN18 311 R8
HAWK TN18 312 A8
North Holmes Rd CANT CT1 5 J3
North Kent Av GVW DA11 54 D4
Northlands HYTHE CT21 * 222 D3
Northlands Av ORP BR6 90 F7
Northlands St CMBW SE5 24 D8
North La CANTW/ST CT2 4 E3
FAV ME13 149 K2
FAV ME13 247 L1
North Lea DEAL CT14 209 K2
Northleigh Cl
MAID/SHEP ME15 167 H7
North Lockside CHAT ME4 * 83 J5
North Lyminge La RFOLK CT18 291 N10
North Meadow E/WMAL ME19 241 Q2
North Military Rd DVW CT17 8 B6
Northolme Cl CDW/CHF RM16 * 34 D2
Northolme Ri ORP BR6 90 F5
Northover BMLY BR1 47 G8
North Pk ELTH/MOT SE9 48 A4
North Pasley Rd CHAT ME4 83 J6
North Peckham Est PECK SE15 25 G6
North Pends KEN/WIL TN24 203 H5
North Pole La HAYES BR2 105 M1
North Pole Rd WBY/YAL ME18 165 J3
North Pondside CHAT ME4 * 83 H5
North Pondside Rd CHAT ME4 83 H5
Northridge RYE TN31 324 H7
Northridge Rd GVE DA12 55 K8
North Riding HART DA3 78 E7
North Rd BELV DA17 30 C2
BMLY BR1 71 J5
CHAT ME4 83 H5
CRBK TN17 297 M5
DART DA1 51 G4
DEAL CT14 211 L3
DVW CT17 8 A4
FOLK CT20 223 K1
HOO/HM ME3 38 C7
HYTHE CT21 222 D3
MSTR CT12 237 K4
PUR RM19 32 D3
QBOR ME11 64 A8
SWCH CT13 207 H1
WOOL/PLUM SE18 28 F3
WWKM BR4 88 C4
North Rd West HYTHE CT21 222 B2
North Salts RYE TN31 225 H3
North Several BKHTH/KID SE3 * 26 E8
Northside Rd BMLY BR1 71 H5
Northside Three CHAT ME4 * 83 K5
Northstead Rd
BRXS/STRHM SW2 44 B7
North St ASH TN23 2 C4
BMLY BR1 71 H5
BXLYHN DA7 50 B2
DART DA1 51 L5
DEAL CT14 209 L2
DVW CT17 217 J2
EDEN TN8 275 M7
FOLKN CT19 11 M5
GVE DA12 55 J5
HB CT6 129 G4
HDCN TN27 283 K4
HDCN TN27 300 F3
MAIDW ME16 165 M3
NROM TN28 330 H7
RMAID ME17 260 F6
RTWE/PEM TN2 23 J5
SIT ME10 119 M2
STRD ME2 19 G3
North Trench TONN TN10 * 188 F7
Northumberland Av
KEN/WIL TN24 203 G6
MARG CT9 178 F4
RHAM ME8 102 F4
WELL DA16 48 F2
Northumberland Cl ERITH DA8 30 D6
Northumberland Ct
MAID/SHEP ME15 * 167 L6
Northumberland Gdns
BMLY BR1 72 B8
Northumberland Pk ERITH DA8 30 D6
Northumberland Rd
MAID/SHEP ME15 167 M5
MEO DA13 79 G4
SLH/COR SS17 36 A1
Northumberland Wy
ERITH DA8 30 D7
North Vw MAID/SHEP ME15 167 J4
RCANTE CT3 234 A4
RRTW TN3 * 277 P9
Northview SWLY BR8 74 F6
North View Av TIL RM18 35 H7
North View Rd SEV TN13 136 B7
North Wk CROY/NA CR0 88 C8
Northwall Ms DEAL CT14 209 K2
Northwall Quay DVW CT17 8 D8
Northwall Rd DEAL CT14 209 K2
North Wy DEAL CT14 208 B2
MAID/BEAR ME14 141 J6
Northway Rd CMBW SE5 44 D1
CROY/NA CR0 87 G2
Northwood CDW/CHF RM16 35 J1
Northwood Av HOO/HM ME3 59 M1
Northwood Dr SIT ME10 120 A8
Northwood Pl ERITHM DA18 30 A2
Northwood Rd BRDST CT10 182 F2
FSTH SE23 46 A6
THHTH CR7 68 D6
TONN TN10 188 E7
WSTB CT5 126 F3
Norton Av HB CT6 155 H1
Norton Crs TONN TN10 188 E6
Norton Dr MSTR CT12 180 E7
Norton Gv WALD ME5 114 F1
Norton La RASHW TN26 285 N12
Norton Rd RMAID ME17 260 E4
RSIT ME9 147 L5
STH/RUST TN4 196 D4
Nortons La HDCN TN27 301 K8
Nortons Wy STPH/PW TN12 278 E2
Norval Gn BRXN/ST SW9 * 24 B8
Norview Rd WSTB CT5 126 C6
Norway Dro RDV CT15 211 H8
Norway Ga BERM/RHTH SE16 25 M2
Norway St GNWCH SE10 26 C5
Norway Ter MAID/BEAR ME14 141 G6
Norwich Av TONN TN10 189 G8
Norwich Cl STRD ME2 81 L7
Norwich Pl BXLYHS DA6 50 B2
Norwich Rd THHTH CR7 68 D7
Norwood Cl HOO/HM ME3 58 C1
Norwood Gdns ASH TN23 2 A4
Norwood High St WNWD SE27 44 C8
Norwood La LYDD TN29 319 N7
MEO DA13 97 J1
Norwood Park Rd WNWD SE27 68 D2
Norwood Ri IOS ME12 65 K6
Norwood Rd HNHL SE24 44 C6
Norwood St ASH TN23 2 B5
Notley St CANT CT1 5 H2
CMBW SE5 24 E6
Notley Ter CANT CT1 * 5 H2
Notson Rd SNWD SE25 69 J8
Nottidge Rd STH/RUST TN4 200 E4
Nottingham Av
MAID/SHEP ME15 167 L7
Nottingham Rd BRCH CT7 176 C8
SAND/SEL CR2 86 D8
Nouds La RSIT ME9 147 L2
Nouds Rd RSIT ME9 147 L1
Novar Cl ORP BR6 91 G3
Nova Rd CROY/NA CR0 86 C4
Novar Rd ELTH/MOT SE9 48 D6
The Nower RSEV TN14 133 L6
RSEV TN14 134 C2
Nubia Wy BMLY BR1 70 F1
Nuding Cl LEW SE13 46 B1
Nuffield Rd SWLY BR8 75 H3
Nugent Rd SNWD SE25 69 G7
Nunappleton Wy OXTED RH8 185 H2
Nunhead Gv PECK SE15 45 J1
Nunhead La PECK SE15 45 J1
Nunnery Flds CANT CT1 5 G8
Nunnery La RTON TN11 276 G9
Nunnery Rd CANT CT1 4 F8
Nunnington Cl ELTH/MOT SE9 47 M8
Nunns Wy GRAYS RM17 34 E3
Nursery Av BXLYHN DA7 50 A1
CROY/NA CR0 87 L5
MAID/BEAR ME14 168 C2
MAIDW ME16 140 C7
Nursery Cl BROCKY SE4 26 A8
CROY/NA CR0 87 L5
IOS ME12 64 E4
ORP BR6 91 G3
RAM CT11 16 E4
RDART DA2 52 D5
RFOLK CT18 292 E10
SEV TN13 21 J1
SWLY BR8 74 D6
TONN TN10 195 H1
WADH TN5 311 J6
WSTB CT5 127 H4
Nursery Est HB CT6 * 128 D6
Nursery Flds BRCH CT7 180 E2
HYTHE CT21 222 A3
Nursery Gdns CHST BR7 72 C3
HOO/HM ME3 59 M8
MARG CT9 179 H4
Nurserylands HB CT6 129 G6
Nursery La DVE/WH CT16 213 G2
FAV ME13 246 C4
RFOLK CT18 292 F10
Nursery Pl SEV TN13 135 J8
Nursery Rd BRXN/ST SW9 44 A2
DIT/AY ME20 139 K4
MEO DA13 97 H1
RHAM ME8 102 E5
STH/RUST TN4 196 E5
STPH/PW TN12 279 J1
THHTH CR7 68 E8
Nursery Rw WALW SE17 24 E3
The Nursery ERITH DA8 31 G6
Nursery Wk CANTW/ST CT2 4 D1
Nursery Wy OXTED RH8 * 157 K7
Nurstead Av HART DA3 78 E7
Nurstead Church La MEO DA13 79 H8
Nurstead La HART DA3 78 E8
Nurstead Rd ERITH DA8 30 B6
Nutberry Av CDW/CHF RM16 34 B1
Nutberry Cl CDW/CHF RM16 34 B1
RSIT ME9 121 L7
Nutbrook St PECK SE15 45 G1
Nutcroft Rd PECK SE15 25 J6
Nutfield Cl WALD ME5 101 J5
Nutfield Rd EDUL SE22 45 G3
THHTH CR7 68 C8
Nutfields BGR/WK TN15 240 B5
SIT ME10 120 C6
Nutfield Wy ORP BR6 90 B5
Nuthatch HART DA3 78 C7
Nuthatch Gdns THMD SE28 28 E1
Nuthurst Av BRXS/STRHM SW2 44 A7
Nutley Cl KEN/WIL TN24 2 D2
RYE TN31 224 F3
SWLY BR8 75 G5
Nutmead Cl BXLY DA5 50 D6
Nut Tree Cl ORP BR6 91 L6
Nutts Av IOS ME12 230 F3
Nutt St PECK SE15 25 G6
Nutwood Cl MAID/BEAR ME14 167 M1
Nuxley Rd BELV DA17 30 A5
Nyanza St WOOL/PLUM SE18 28 E5
Nynehead St NWCR SE14 25 M6
Nyon Gv FSTH SE23 46 A7

O

Oakapple Cl SAND/SEL CR2 104 A8
Oakapple La MAIDW ME16 166 B2
Oak Av CROY/NA CR0 88 B5
GILL ME7 83 M7
HDCN TN27 301 J6
IOS ME12 65 M7
RDV CT15 272 E8
SEV TN13 162 A6
Oakbank CROY/NA CR0 105 H1
Oakbank Gv HNHL SE24 44 D2
Oakbrook Cl BMLY BR1 71 J1
Oak Bungalows LYDD TN29 * 334 D3
Oak Caer RASHE TN25 305 Q9
Oak Cl DART DA1 50 F2
HOO/HM ME3 83 M2
Oak Cottage Cl CAT SE6 46 F6
Oakcroft Rd LEW SE13 26 E8
Oakdale La EDEN TN8 186 D3
Oakdale Rd HB CT6 129 H5
PECK SE15 45 K1
STH/RUST TN4 22 C3
Oakdene Av CHST BR7 72 B2
ERITH DA8 30 D5
Oakdene Rd MSTR CT12 16 E1
SEV TN13 20 F1
STMC/STPC BR5 91 H2
Oakden St LBTH SE11 24 B3
Oak Dr DIT/AY ME20 139 H3
HOO/HM ME3 81 J2
LYDD TN29 331 N2
RFOLK CT18 292 G12
Oak End Cl STH/RUST TN4 196 D3
Oakenden La EDEN TN8 276 C8
Oakenden Rd MEO DA13 97 M4
Oakenpole ASH TN23 204 B2
Oakey La STHWK SE1 * 24 B2
Oak Farm Gdns HDCN TN27 283 L3
Oak Farm La BGR/WK TN15 239 K5
Oakfield CRBK TN17 * 314 F8
HAWK TN18 312 C7
Oakfield Ct MSTR CT12 16 D2
Oakfield Court Rd
RTWE/PEM TN2 23 H6
Oakfield Gdns BECK BR3 88 B1
Oakfield La HAYES BR2 89 K7
RDART DA2 51 H7
Oakfield Park Rd DART DA1 51 L7
Oakfield Pl DART DA1 51 L7
Oakfield Rd CROY/NA CR0 86 D4
EDEN TN8 192 C1
KEN/WIL TN24 203 G7
PGE/AN SE20 69 J5
STPH/PW TN12 278 G9
Oakfields SEV TN13 21 H9
SIT ME10 119 K6
The Oakfield RYE TN31 225 G1
Oak Gdns CROY/NA CR0 88 B5
Oak Gv RDV CT15 272 C3
WWKM BR4 88 D5
Oak Grove Rd PGE/AN SE20 69 K5
Oakham Cl CAT SE6 * 46 A7
Oakham Dr HAYES BR2 71 H8
Oak Hl SWCH CT13 253 N3
Oakhill Rd BECK BR3 70 D6
ORP BR6 91 G5
PUR RM19 32 C4
Oak Hill Rd SEV TN13 20 F7
Oakhouse Rd BXLYHS DA6 50 B3
Oakhurst Av BXLYHN DA7 29 M6
Oakhurst Cl CHST BR7 72 A5
WALD ME5 115 G2
Oakhurst Gdns BXLYHN DA7 29 M6
Oakhurst Gv EDUL SE22 45 H2
Oakland Ct HB CT6 * 128 F4
MSTR CT12 181 M8
Oakland Dr RBTBR TN32 322 C9
Oaklands ASH TN23 204 C2
RASHE TN25 305 P1
Oaklands Av BFN/LL DA15 49 G5
BRDST CT10 179 H8
THHTH CR7 68 B8
WWKM BR4 88 C6
Oaklands Cl BGR/WK TN15 111 K1
BXLYHS DA6 50 A3
STMC/STPC BR5 90 F2
Oaklands La BH/WHM TN16 132 B1
Oaklands Rd BMLY BR1 70 F4
BXLYHS DA6 50 A2
GVW DA11 79 G1
HAWK TN18 312 D8
RDART DA2 52 C6
RRTW TN3 199 J7
Oaklands Wy CANTW/ST CT2 173 J2
RTON TN11 194 C1
Oak La HDCN TN27 283 L4
IOS ME12 65 M7
LYDD TN29 334 C3
RSIT ME9 103 L4
SEV TN13 21 H9
Oaklea Rd STPH/PW TN12 279 J4
Oakleigh Cl SWLY BR8 74 F7
WALD ME5 114 F3
Oakleigh Ct OXTED RH8 * 157 K7
STPH/PW TN12 279 Q11
Oakleigh Gdns ORP BR6 90 F7
Oakleigh La RCANTW CT4 175 J4
Oakleigh Park Av CHST BR7 72 B6
Oakley Cl WTHK RM20 33 K5
Oakley Dr BFN/LL DA15 48 E7
HAYES BR2 89 M6
LEW SE13 46 E4
Oakley Pk BFN/LL DA15 49 K5
Oakley Pl STHWK SE1 25 G4
Oakley Rd HAYES BR2 89 M6
SNWD SE25 87 J1
Oak Lodge Dr WWKM BR4 88 C3
Oak Lodge La BH/WHM TN16 159 J3
Oak Lodge Rd NROM TN28 * 331 J6
Oakmead MEO DA13 97 H5
TONN TN10 188 F7
Oakmead Av HAYES BR2 89 H2
Oakmere Rd ABYW SE2 29 H5
Oakmore Gdns STMC/STPC BR5 73 K8
Oakridge BRDST CT10 179 K4
Oak Rdg RASHE TN25 319 J1
Oakridge Rd BMLY BR1 70 F1
Oak Rd BH/WHM TN16 159 J3
ERITH DA8 30 D6
ERITH DA8 31 H7
GRAYS RM17 34 D5
GRH DA9 52 F4
GVE DA12 55 J8
HOO/HM ME3 83 M2
ORP BR6 107 M2
RTWE/PEM TN2 197 G6
SIT ME10 120 D4
STPH/PW TN12 278 E2
STRD ME2 18 B6
Oaks Av HB CT6 128 E7
NRWD SE19 68 F2
Oaks Cl BUR/ETCH TN19 322 A4
Oaks Dene WALD ME5 115 G4
Oaksford Av SYD SE26 45 J8
Oaks Forstal HAWK TN18 313 M12
Oakshade Rd BMLY BR1 70 E1
Oakshaw OXTED RH8 157 J5
Oakside Rd RCANTE CT3 251 P12
Oaks La CROY/NA CR0 87 K6
Oaks Pk CANTW/ST CT2 171 J2
Oaks Rd CROY/NA CR0 87 J8
FOLK CT20 219 L7
TENT TN30 315 N2
The Oaks BRCH CT7 233 N7
BRDST CT10 179 J6
DIT/AY ME20 139 M4
HAYES BR2 * 90 B2
RCANTE CT3 234 A4
RDART DA2 52 C4
SWLY BR8 74 F6
WOOL/PLUM SE18 28 D4
WSTB CT5 126 C7
Oak St DEAL CT14 209 L3
Oaks Vw HYTHE CT21 321 P1
Oak Ter WALD ME5 * 115 H3
Oak Tree Av GRH DA9 53 G5
MAID/SHEP ME15 167 K6
Oak Tree Cl RTW TN1 22 F9
STPH/PW TN12 * 281 J4
Oak Tree Gdns BMLY BR1 71 J2
Oak Tree Gv MARG CT9 177 K5
Oak Tree Rd ASH TN23 204 C3
Oakum Ct CHAT ME4 101 J3
Oakvale Cl DVW CT17 217 J2
Oak Vw EDEN TN8 192 C3
Oakview Gv CROY/NA CR0 87 M4
Oakview Rd CAT SE6 70 C2
Oak Wk HYTHE CT21 222 D3
Oak Warren SEV TN13 161 M7
Oak Wy CROY/NA CR0 87 L2
Oakway HAYES BR2 70 E6
Oakway Cl BXLY DA5 49 M4
Oakways ELTH/MOT SE9 48 C4
Oakwood MARG CT9 * 178 F5
Oakwood Av BECK BR3 70 D6
HAYES BR2 71 J7
Oakwood Cl CHST BR7 72 A3
DART DA1 52 C6
LEW SE13 46 E4
Oakwood Ct MAIDW ME16 12 B6
Oakwood Dr BXLYHN DA7 50 D2
NRWD SE19 68 E3
SEV TN13 21 G3
WSTB CT5 127 H4
Oakwood Gdns ORP BR6 90 D5
Oakwood Ms WSTB CT5 * 126 E6
Oakwood Pk MAIDW ME16 * 166 D2
Oakwood Pl CROY/NA CR0 86 B2
Oakwood Ri HART DA3 77 M7
RTWE/PEM TN2 197 H6
Oakwood Rd CANTW/ST CT2 173 H2
CROY/NA CR0 86 B2
MAIDW ME16 166 D2
ORP BR6 90 D5
Oakwood Ter SIT ME10 * 120 D5
Oakwood Vls RAM CT11 * 183 H4
Oare Rd FAV ME13 123 J8
Oast Cl RTWE/PEM TN2 197 G6
Oast Ct MARG CT9 15 H8
SIT ME10 119 M7
WBY/YAL ME18 257 Q4
Oast House Dr RYE TN31 224 E5
Oasthouse Fld LYDD TN29 330 A1
Oast House Wy
STMC/STPC BR5 73 J8
Oast La FAV ME13 245 P11
RTON TN11 194 D1
Oast Meadow KEN/WIL TN24 3 K6
Oast Rd OXTED RH8 185 G1
The Oast CANT CT1 * 5 J9
Oastview RHAM ME8 103 H5
Oast Vw STPH/PW TN12 279 R12
Oast Wy HART DA3 95 M2
Oaten Hl CANT CT1 5 G6
Oaten Hill Pl CANT CT1 5 G6
Oates Cl HAYES BR2 70 E7
Oatfield Cl CRBK TN17 298 F8
Oatfield Dr CRBK TN17 298 F8
Oatfield Rd ORP BR6 91 G4
The Oaze WSTB CT5 126 D7
Oban Rd SNWD SE25 68 E8
Oborne Cl HNHL SE24 44 C3
Occupation La
WOOL/PLUM SE18 28 C7
Occupation Rd WALW SE17 24 D4
Ocean Cl BRCH CT7 176 E5
Ocean Ter IOS ME12 * 65 L6
Ocean Vw BRDST CT10 183 K4
Ocelot Ct WALD ME5 7 H8
Ockham Dr STMC/STPC BR5 73 H4
Ockley La HAWK TN18 312 D6
Ockley Rd CROY/NA CR0 86 A3
HAWK TN18 312 D7
Ockleys Md GDST RH9 156 B7
Ockman La RYE TN31 * 225 H4
Octavia Ct WALD ME5 * 115 J2
Octavian Dr HYTHE CT21 307 M10
Octavius St DEPT SE8 26 B6
Odeon Pde ELTH/MOT SE9 * 47 M2
Odessa St BERM/RHTH SE16 26 A2
Odiham Dr MAIDW ME16 140 D6
Odo Rd DVW CT17 217 J1
Offenham Rd ELTH/MOT SE9 72 A1
Offen's Dr STPH/PW TN12 281 R6
Offham Rd E/WMAL ME19 138 B6
Officers Ter CHAT ME4 83 G6
Offley Cl MARG CT9 178 F4
Offley Rd BRXN/ST SW9 24 B6
Ogilby St WOOL/PLUM SE18 28 A3
Oglander Rd PECK SE15 45 G2
Okehampton Cl KEN/WIL TN24 203 J4
Okehampton Crs WELL DA16 29 J7
Olantigh Rd RASHE TN25 266 G9
Olave Rd MARG CT9 15 K7
Old Ash Cl KEN/WIL TN24 202 F6
Old Ashford Rd HDCN TN27 264 B6
RMAID ME17 243 M12
Old Badgins Rd FAV ME13 245 R3
The Old Bailey RMAID ME17 242 F11
Old Bakery Cl LYDD TN29 * 331 N1
Old Bakery Ms FAV ME13 * 151 G6
Old Barn Cl BGR/WK TN15 136 F3
GILL ME7 102 A7
TON TN9 194 C5
Old Barn Rd E/WMAL ME19 138 E3
Old Barn Wy BXLYHN DA7 50 E2
Old Bexley La BXLY DA5 50 F7
Old Billet La IOS ME12 66 D7
Old Boundary Rd MARG CT9 177 J4
Old Bridge Rd WSTB CT5 126 F4
Old Bromley Rd BMLY BR1 70 E2
Oldbury Cl STMC/STPC BR5 73 L8
Oldbury La BGR/WK TN15 240 A4
Oldbury Vls BGR/WK TN15 * 240 A4
The Old Carriageway
GILL ME7 116 A2
SEV TN13 161 H1
Old Chapel Rd SWLY BR8 92 D3
Old Charlton Rd DVE/WH CT16 213 L7
Old Chatham Rd DIT/AY ME20 114 E7
MAID/BEAR ME14 140 F4
Old Church La WBY/YAL ME18 256 H1
Old Church Rd RCANTW CT4 248 G8
ROCH ME1 113 L4
RTWE/PEM TN2 278 A7
WBY/YAL ME18 241 R12
Old Coach Rd BGR/WK TN15 238 D9
Old Court Hl RDV CT15 252 B12
The Old Courthouse CHAT ME4 * 6 C5
The Old Ctyd BMLY BR1 71 J5
Old Crossing Rd MARG CT9 177 L4
Old Dairy Cl RAM CT11 17 L4
Old Dartford Rd EYN DA4 94 A2
Old Dover Rd BKHTH/KID SE3 27 H6
CANT CT1 5 G6
RFOLK CT18 221 K4
Old Downs HART DA3 95 M1
Old Dr MAID/SHEP ME15 167 G7
Old Farleigh Rd SAND/SEL CR2 104 B4
WARL CR6 130 E1
Old Farm Av BFN/LL DA15 48 E6
Old Farm Gdns SWLY BR8 75 G7
Old Farm Rd BRCH CT7 176 A6
Old Farm Rd East BFN/LL DA15 49 H7
Old Farm Rd West BFN/LL DA15 49 G7
Old Ferry Rd RSIT ME9 227 M7
Oldfield Cl BMLY BR1 72 A8
MAID/SHEP ME15 167 M4
RHAM ME8 102 E5
Oldfield Dr ROCH ME1 99 K8
Oldfield Gv DEPT SE8 25 L3
Oldfield Rd BMLY BR1 72 A8
BXLYHN DA7 29 M8
Old Fold WSTB CT5 127 K5
Old Folkestone Rd DVW CT17 217 H5
Old Forge La RSIT ME9 144 A5
Old Forge Wy SCUP DA14 73 J1
Old Garden Ct RCANTW CT4 248 F8
Old Gardens Cl
RTWE/PEM TN2 201 J5
The Old Gdn SEV TN13 161 J1
Old Gate Rd FAV ME13 149 J2
Old George Ct HOO/HM ME3 * 83 G1
Old Green Rd BRDST CT10 179 J6
MARG CT9 178 F4
Old Hadlow Rd TONN TN10 195 H1
Old Hall Dr MSTR CT12 181 M8
Old Ham La RMAID ME17 243 J12
Oldhawe Hl HB CT6 155 L1
The Old High St FOLK CT20 11 K5
Old Hl CHST BR7 72 B5
ORP BR6 107 K1
Old Hockley Rd FAV ME13 245 M7
Old Homesdale Rd HAYES BR2 71 K8
Old Hook Rd IOS ME12 229 J4
The Old Hop Gdn RYE TN31 326 F11
Oldhouse La LYDD TN29 329 K4
Old House La RRTW TN3 277 L12
Old House Rd RSIT ME9 117 M1
Old Jamaica Rd STHWK SE1 25 H2
Old James St PECK SE15 45 J1
Old Kent Rd PECK SE15 25 J5
STHWK SE1 24 F4
STPH/PW TN12 279 K3
Old Kingsdown Cl
BRDST CT10 * 183 H2
Old Lain RMAID ME17 242 G11
Old La BGR/WK TN15 240 B5
BH/WHM TN16 132 C7
OXTED RH8 157 L8
Old Lenham Rd RSIT ME9 243 Q6
Old London Rd BGR/WK TN15 238 E9
HYTHE CT21 307 R11
RSEV TN14 134 D1
TONN TN10 * 194 F2
Old Loose Hl MAID/SHEP ME15 259 L1
Old Lydd Rd RYE TN31 332 E7
Old Maidstone Rd SCUP DA14 74 A4
Old Manor Wy BXLYHN DA7 30 E8
ELTH/MOT SE9 72 A2
Old Md FOLKN CT19 10 D1
Old Mill Cl EYN DA4 93 M4
Old Mill La DIT/AY ME20 140 D2
Old Mill Rd RMAID ME17 169 G5
WOOL/PLUM SE18 28 E5
The Old Ml RSIT ME9 * 120 F5
Old Orch ASH TN23 204 A3
HAWK TN18 313 L12
Old Orchard La E/WMAL ME19 138 E4
The Old Orch RHAM ME8 103 G5
Old Otford Rd RSEV TN14 136 A4
Old Palace STPH/PW TN12 * 279 L9
Old Palace Rd CROY/NA CR0 86 D6
Old Paradise St LBTH SE11 24 A3
Old Park Cl DVE/WH CT16 213 H5
Old Park Hl DVE/WH CT16 213 H5
Old Park Rd ABYW SE2 29 H4
DVE/WH CT16 213 J7
Old Pattens La ROCH ME1 100 E3
Old Perry St CHST BR7 72 F4
GVW DA11 54 F7
Old Pond Rd ASH TN23 204 C2
Old Post Office La
BKHTH/KID SE3 47 J1
Old Rectory Cl RASHE TN25 288 F12
RFOLK CT18 220 C1
Old Regent Dr CRBK TN17 314 D6
Old Rd BRCH CT7 233 K11
CHAT ME4 6 C6
DART DA1 50 E2
LEW SE13 46 F2
RCANTW CT4 291 Q5
STPH/PW TN12 257 K7
WBY/YAL ME18 164 C6
Old Rd East GVE DA12 55 L6
Old Rd West GVW DA11 55 G6
Old Roman Rd RDV CT15 210 D8
Old Ruttington La CANT CT1 5 H3
Old School Cl BECK BR3 69 L6
CANTW/ST CT2 173 G3
RMAID ME17 262 G1
Old School Ct HDCN TN27 262 H10
HOO/HM ME3 83 G1
SWLY BR8 74 F6
Old School Gdns MARG CT9 15 J7
Old School La E/WMAL ME19 138 A1
Old School Ms RCANTW CT4 * 248 D7
Old School Pl CROY/NA CR0 86 B7
MAID/BEAR ME14 13 H3
The Old School CRBK TN17 297 M5
FAV ME13 * 149 L2
Old School Yd BRDST CT10 * 179 H8
Old Soar Rd BGR/WK TN15 240 G9
Oldstairs Rd DEAL CT14 211 L5
Old Station Rd WADH TN5 309 K3
Oldstead Rd BMLY BR1 70 E1
Old Surrenden Manor Rd
RASHW TN26 286 B12
The Old Surrey Ms GDST RH9 * 156 B8
Old Tannery Cl TENT TN30 * 315 L2
Old Terry's Lodge Rd
BGR/WK TN15 137 L2
Old Tovil Rd MAID/SHEP ME15 12 F9
Old Town CROY/NA CR0 86 C6
Old Trafford Cl MAIDW ME16 140 C7
Old Tramyard
WOOL/PLUM SE18 28 F3
Old Tree La RMAID ME17 259 Q2
Old Tree Rd RCANTE CT3 155 M3
Old Tye Av BH/WHM TN16 132 D2
Old Valley Rd RCANTW CT4 270 E6
Old Vicarage Gdn
CANTW/ST CT2 * 173 G3
Old Vicarage Gdns
RASHE TN25 266 F11
The Old Vicarage SWCH CT13 * 253 P2
The Old Wk RSEV TN14 136 A3
Old Wardsdown WADH TN5 311 J6
Old Watling St STRD ME2 81 J5
Old Wy RASHW TN26 317 L10
Old Westhall Cl WARL CR6 130 B5
Old Woolwich Rd GNWCH SE10 26 E5
The Old Yews HART DA3 78 C7
Oleander Cl ORP BR6 90 E8
Olive Gv RAM CT11 * 17 L4
Oliver Av SNWD SE25 69 G7
Oliver Cl CHAT ME4 101 J3
WTHK RM20 33 G6
Oliver Crs EYN DA4 94 A3
Oliver Gv SNWD SE25 69 G8
Oliver Ms PECK SE15 25 H8
Olive Rd DART DA1 51 L6
Oliver Rd STPH/PW TN12 281 R6
SWLY BR8 74 E7
WTHK RM20 33 H6
Oliver Twist Cl ROCH ME1 19 G9

Olivine Cl *SIT* ME10 ...119 K2
WALD ME5 ...115 H5
Olliffe Cl *WALD* ME5 ...115 G3
Olliffe St *POP/IOD* E14 ...26 D2
Olmar St *STHWK* SE1 ...25 H5
Olney Rd *WALW* SE17 ...24 E5
Olron Crs *BXLYHN* DA6 ...49 L3
Olven Rd *WOOL/PLUM* SE18 ...29 H8
Olyffe Av *WELL* DA16 ...29 H8
Olyffe Dr *BECK* BR3 ...70 D5
Omega St *NWCR* SE14 ...26 A7
Omer Av *MARG* CT9 ...178 F3
Ommaney Rd *NWCR* SE14 ...26 A7
Ondine Rd *EDUL* SE22 ...45 G2
Onega Ga *BERM/RHTH* SE16 ...25 H1
One Tree Cl *FSTH* SE23 ...45 K4
Onslow Crs *CHST* BR7 ...72 C5
Onslow Dr *SCUP* DA14 ...49 L8
Onslow Rd *CROY/NA* CRO ...86 B3
ROCH ME1 ...100 E2
Ontario St *STHWK* SE1 ...24 C2
Opal St *LBTH* SE11 ...24 C3
Openshaw Rd *ABYW* SE2 ...29 J4
Ophir Ter *PECK* SE15 ...45 K4
Oppenheim Rd *LEW* SE13 ...26 D8
Optima Pk *CANT* CT1 * ...51 H1
Orache Dr *MAID/BEAR* ME14 ...141 M8
Orange Court La *ORP* BR6 ...106 F3
Orange Pl *BERM/RHTH* SE16 ...25 K2
Orangery La *ELTH/MOT* SE9 ...48 F4
Orange St *CANT* CT1 ...4 F4
Orange Ter *ROCH* ME1 ...19 L8
Orbital One *DART* DA1 * ...52 C7
Orbit Cl *WALD* ME5 ...115 H5
Orb St *WALW* SE17 ...24 F4
Orchard Av *BELV* DA17 ...29 M5
CROY/NA CRO ...87 M5
DART DA1 ...51 J5
DEAL CT14 ...209 J4
DIT/AY ME20 ...139 H4
GVW DA11 ...79 J2
STRD ME2 ...18 A3
Orchard Cl *BXLYHN* DA7 ...29 M7
CANTW/ST CT2 ...172 A5
DVE/WH CT16 ...213 G1
EDEN TN8 ...192 C3
FSTH SE23 ...45 K4
HART DA3 ...78 C6
MAID/SHEP ME15 * ...13 G7
MSTR CT12 ...180 E6
MSTR CT12 ...182 E2
RASHE TN25 ...305 P2
RCANTE CT3 ...251 J2
RMAID ME17 ...260 F1
RSEV TN14 ...136 B7
RTWE/PEM TN2 ...197 C6
STPH/PW TN12 ...279 Q11
WSTB CT5 ...127 C6
Orchard Crs *STPH/PW* TN12 ...279 R11
Orchard Dr *BKHTH/KID* SE3 ...26 H8
DVW CT17 ...212 F6
EDEN TN8 ...192 C3
GRAYS RM17 ...34 B3
MEO DA13 ...97 C1
NROM TN28 ...331 M7
RASHE TN25 ...202 C7
RASHE TN25 ...266 G12
RSIT ME9 ...89 M3
TONN TN10 ...189 H8
Orchard Fld *HYTHE* CT21 * ...307 R3
RASHW TN26 ...285 N12
RASHW TN26 ...302 E1
Orchard Gdns *MARG* CT9 ...177 K4
Orchard Gld *HDCN* TN27 ...283 M4
Orchard Gn *ORP* BR6 ...90 F5
Orchard Gv *CROY/NA* CRO ...87 M3
DIT/AY ME20 ...139 J3
IOS ME12 ...65 K7
ORP BR6 ...91 G5
PGE/AN SE20 ...69 H4
Orchard Hts *RASHE* TN25 ...202 C6
Orchard Hl *DART* DA1 ...52 C8
LEW SE13 ...26 C8
Orchard La *BRCH* CT7 ...233 K8
KEN/WIL TN24 ...203 H4
RASHE TN25 ...265 N3
Orchard Lea *MEO* DA13 * ...98 A1
Orchard Ms *DEAL* CT14 * ...209 L4
Orchard Pl *FAV* ME13 ...149 L2
MAIDW ME16 ...12 D6
SIT ME10 ...119 H7
STMC/STPC BR5 * ...73 K7
Orchard Ri *CROY/NA* CRO ...87 M4
RRTW TN3 ...199 J6
Orchard Ri East *BFN/LL* DA15 ...48 F3
Orchard Ri West *BFN/LL* DA15 ...48 E3
Orchard Ri *BELV* DA17 ...30 B3
BMLY BR1 ...71 J5
GVW DA11 ...54 D7
HB CT6 ...129 C6
LYDD TN29 ...320 F12
MAID/BEAR ME14 ...167 M3
MARG CT9 ...178 F1
ORP BR6 ...90 C8
ORP BR6 ...108 B3
RSEV TN14 ...135 L2
SAND/SEL CR2 ...104 A8
SCUP DA14 ...72 C1
SEV TN13 ...135 K8
STPH/PW TN12 ...279 R12
SWCH CT13 ...253 N6
SWCM DA10 ...55 M5
TENT TN30 ...301 M10
WELL DA16 ...49 J7
Orchard Rw *HB* CT6 * ...155 H1
The Orchards *CANTW/ST* CT2 ...4 D3
DART DA1 ...51 M4
MAID/SHEP ME15 ...13 G7
RHAM ME8 ...102 F6
Orchard Ter *GRH* DA9 * ...52 F3
RYE TN31* ...325 J7
The Orchard *BKHTH/KID* SE3 ...26 H8
BUR/ETCH TN19 ...322 B4
MAID/BEAR ME14 ...168 C1
SEV TN13 ...135 K7
SWLY BR8 ...74 E6
WSTB CT5 * ...126 F6
Orchard Va *HYTHE* CT21 ...222 B3
Orchard Wa *MAID/BEAR* ME14 ...142 B8
RCANTE CT3 ...236 C12
RSIT ME9 ...121 K6
TENT TN30 ...315 J3
Orchard Vls *SCUP* DA14 * ...73 L3
Orchard Wy *BGR/WK* TN15 ...136 K3
CRBK TN17 ...298 E9
CROY/NA CRO ...87 M3
IOS ME12 ...64 N4
OXTED RH8 ...185 H3
RDART DA2 ...51 J8
RYE TN31 ...325 F12
SNOD ME6 ...113 G4
STPH/PW TN12 ...279 R12
Orchid Cl *IOS* ME12 ...228 D3
SNOD ME6 ...113 G4
Orchidhurst *RTWE/PEM* TN2 ...197 N1
The Orchids *RASHE* TN25 ...305 N1
RFOLK CT18 ...218 E1

Orchis Gv *GRAYS* RM17 ...34 A3
Ordnance Crs *GNWCH* SE10 ...26 F1
Ordnance Rd *GVE* DA12 ...55 K4
WOOL/PLUM SE18 ...28 B5
Oregon Sq *ORP* BR6 ...90 E4
Orford Rd *CAT* SE6 ...46 C8
Orgarswick Av *LYDD* TN29 ...320 H10
Orgarswick Wy *LYDD* TN29 ...320 H10
Orient Pl *CANTW/ST* CT2 ...4 E2
Orient St *LBTH* SE11 ...24 C4
Oriole Wy *DIT/AY* ME20 ...139 G3
Orion Rd *ROCH* ME1 ...100 D6
Orion Wy *KEN/WIL* TN24 ...3 G8
Orissa Rd *WOOL/PLUM* SE18 ...28 H4
Orleans Rd *NRWD* SE19 ...68 E3
Orlestone Gdns *ORP* BR6 ...91 M8
Orlick Rd *GVE* DA12 ...56 C7
Ormanton Rd *SYD* SE26 ...69 H1
Ormiston Rd *GNWCH* SE10 ...27 H4
Ormond Av *ORP* BR6 ...91 J6
Ormonde Rd *FOLK* CT20 ...11 M3
FOLK CT21 ...222 D4
Ormside St *PECK* SE15 ...25 K5
Orpheus St *CMBW* SE5 ...24 E7
The Orpines *WBY/YAL* ME18 ...165 G6
Orpington By-Pass *RSEV* TN14 ...108 F3
Orpington Rd *CHST* BR7 ...72 F7
Orpines Cl *RASHE* TN25 * ...289 L11
Orr Cl *RFOLK* CT18 ...220 A1
Orsett Heath Crs
CDW/CHF RM16 ...35 H2
Orsett Rd *GRAYS* RM17 ...34 C2
Orsett St *LBTH* SE11 ...24 A4
Orwell Dit *DIT/AY* ME20 ...139 L2
Orwell Spike *E/WMAL* ME19 ...138 B8
Osberton Rd *LEE/GVPK* SE12 ...47 K5
Osborne Cl *BECK* BR3 ...69 M8
Osborne Dr
MAID/BEAR ME14 * ...142 D3
Osborne Gdns *HB* CT6 ...129 M4
THHTH CR7 ...68 C4
Osborne Rd *BELV* DA17 ...30 A4
DEAL CT14 ...211 K3
GILL ME7 ...7 J2
KEN/WIL TN24 ...3 J1
THHTH CR7 ...68 D6
Osborne Ter *MARG* CT9 ...15 H6
Osborn La *FSTH* SE23 ...45 M5
Osborn Rd *BKHTH/KID* SE3 ...47 G2
Osbourn Av *WGOS* CT8 ...177 H5
Osbourne Rd *BRDST* CT10 ...183 J1
RDART DA2 ...52 C4
Oscar Rd *BRDST* CT10 ...183 L1
Oscar St *DEPT* SE8 ...26 C7
Osgood Av *ORP* BR6 ...91 G8
Osgood Gdns *ORP* BR6 ...91 G8
Osier Fld *KEN/WIL* TN24 ...203 H4
The Osier Fld *KEN/WIL* TN24 * ...203 H4
Osier Rd *RSIT* ME9 ...121 M6
Oslac Rd *CAT* SE6 ...46 C8
Osmers Hl *WALM* TN5 ...309 M2
Osney Wy *GVE* DA12 ...56 A7
Osprey Av *WALD* ME5 ...101 M3
WSTB CT5 ...126 E6
Osprey Cl *SIT* ME10 ...120 B6
Osprey Est *BERM/RHTH* SE16 ...25 L3
Osprey Gdns *SAND/SEL* CR2 ...104 C4
Osprey Wk *DIT/AY* ME20 ...139 G4
Ospringe Cl *PGE/AN* SE20 ...69 J4
Ospringe Pl *FAV* ME13 ...149 K4
Ospringe Rd *RTWE/PEM* TN2 ...197 J2
Ospringe St *FAV* ME13 ...149 H3
Ossory Rd *STHWK* SE1 ...25 H5
Ostade Rd *BRXS/STRHM* SW2 ...44 A5
Osterberg Rd *DART* DA1 ...52 A2
Osterley Gdns *THHTH* CR7 ...68 D6
Ostlers Ct *HOO/HM* ME3 * ...81 K1
SNOD ME6 ...113 H5
Ostlers La *DEPT* SE8 ...233 L11
Oswald Pl *DVW* CT17 ...213 G6
Oswald Rd *DVW* CT17 ...213 J7
Osward *CROY/NA* CRO ...104 E4
Oswin St *LBTH* SE11 ...24 C3
Oswyth Rd *CMBW* SE5 ...24 F8
Otford Cl *BMLY* BR1 ...72 B5
BXLY DA5 ...50 C4
PGE/AN SE20 ...69 K5
Otford Crs *BROCKY* SE4 ...46 A4
Otford Rd *RSEV* TN14 ...108 F3
Otham Cl *CANTW/ST* CT2 ...172 B5
Otham La *MAID/SHEP* ME15 ...168 D5
Otham St *MAID/SHEP* ME15 ...168 G6
Othello Cl *LBTH* SE11 ...24 C4
Otlinge Rd *STMC/STPC* BR5 ...73 L8
Ottawa Crs *DVE/WH* CT16 ...213 K6
Ottawa Rd *TIL* RM18 ...35 H8
Otterbourne Pl
MAID/BEAR ME14 ...168 B2
Otterbourne Rd *CROY/NA* CRO ...86 D5
ORP BR6 ...90 F7
Otterden Cl *ASH* TN23 ...204 C5
Otterden Rd *FAV* ME13 ...244 C4
Otterden St *CAT* SE6 ...70 E1
Otterham Quay La *RHAM* ME8 ...103 H1
Otteridge Rd
MAID/BEAR ME14 ...168 B2
Otterpool La *HYTHE* CT21 ...307 K9
Otters Cl *STMC/STPC* BR5 ...73 L8
Otto Cl *SYD* SE26 ...45 J8
Otto St *WALW* SE17 ...24 C5
Otway Cl *CHAT* ME4 ...6 C4
Otway Ter *CHAT* ME4 ...6 E7
Out Elmstead La *RCANTW* ...270 C5
Outfall Av *LYDD* TN29 ...335 M11
Outram Rd *CROY/NA* CRO ...87 G6
Oval Gdns *GRAYS* RM17 ...34 D2
Oval Pl *VX/NE* SW8 ...24 A6
Oval Rd *CROY/NA* CRO ...86 A5
The Oval *BFN/LL* DA15 ...49 H5
HART DA3 ...78 D7
LYDD TN29 ...321 J8
Oval Wy *LBTH* SE11 ...24 L4
Ovenden Rd *RSEV* TN14 ...134 C6
Overbrae *BECK* BR3 ...70 B3
Overbury Av *BECK* BR3 ...70 D2
Overbury Crs *CROY/NA* CRO ...105 H4
Overcliffe *GVW* DA11 ...55 H4
Overcliff Rd *GRAYS* RM17 ...34 E4
LEW SE13 ...46 B1
Overcourt Cl *BFN/LL* DA15 ...49 J4
Overdale *RSEV* TN14 ...255 J3
Overdown Rd *CAT* SE6 ...69 L3
Overhill Rd *EDUL* SE22 ...45 H5
Overhill Wy *BECK* BR3 ...88 C1
Overland La *RCANTE* CT3 ...235 P10
Overmead *ELTH/MOT* SE9 ...48 C5
SWLY BR8 ...92 H1
Over Minnis *HART* DA3 ...96 A4
Overstand Cl *BECK* BR3 ...88 B1
Overstone Gdns *CROY/NA* CRO ...88 A3
Overton Rd *ABYW* SE2 ...29 L3
BRXN/ST SW9 ...24 B8
Overton's Yd *CROY/NA* CRO ...86 D7

Overy Liberty *DART* DA1 ...51 M5
Overy St *DART* DA1 ...51 M5
Ovett Cl *NRWD* SE19 ...68 F2
Ovex Cl *POP/IOD* E14 ...26 D2
Owen Cl *CROY/NA* CRO ...86 D2
E/WMAL ME19 ...137 G5
Owenite St *ABYW* SE2 ...29 J3
Owen Rd Cl *HYTHE* CT21 ...223 H4
Owen Sq *DEAL* CT14 ...209 J7
Owens Wy *FSTH* SE23 ...45 M5
GILL ME7 ...7 L4
Owgan Cl *CMBW* SE5 ...24 E6
Owl Cl *SAND/SEL* CR2 ...104 C4
Owletts Cl *MAID/SHEP* ME15 ...167 L5
Owl's Hatch Rd *HB* CT6 ...128 E4
Ownsted St *CROY/NA* CRO ...105 H4
Oxenbridge La
BUR/ETCH TN19 ...322 B5
Oxenden Crs *RCANTE* CT3 ...251 R1
Oxenden Park Dr *HB* CT6 ...128 B3
Oxenden Rd *FOLK* CT20 ...223 M2
Oxenford St *PECK* SE15 ...45 G1
Oxenhill Rd *BGR/WK* TN15 ...136 D5
Oxenhoath Rd *RTON* TN11 ...189 H11
Oxen Lease *ASH* TN23 ...204 B3
Oxenturn Rd *RASHE* TN25 ...266 F12
Oxestalls Rd *DEPT* SE8 ...25 M4
Oxford Av *CDW/CHF* RM16 ...35 H4
Oxford Cl *GVE* DA12 ...56 A7
Oxford Ms *BXLY* DA5 ...50 A5
Oxford Rd *CANT* CT1 ...4 C7
GILL ME7 ...7 H7
MAID/SHEP ME15 ...167 L4
NRWD SE19 ...68 E3
SCUP DA14 ...73 J2
Oxford St *MARG* CT9 ...15 C6
SNOD ME6 ...113 H5
WSTB CT5 ...126 E4
Oxford Ter *FOLK* CT20 ...11 J6
Oxhawth Crs *HAYES* BR2 ...90 C2
Ox La *TENT* TN30 ...301 N11
Ox Lea *RRTW* TN3 ...200 B2
Oxleas Cl *WELL* DA16 ...48 B1
Oxley Cl *STHWK* SE1 ...25 C4
Oxley Shaw La *E/WMAL* ME19 ...138 B8
Oxney Cl *BRCH* CT7 ...176 C6
Oxonian St *EDUL* SE22 ...45 G4
Oxted Rd *ELTH/MOT* SE9 ...184 A1
Oyster Cl *HB* CT6 ...128 C2
SIT ME10 * ...119 M3
Oyster Creek *RYE* TN31 ...225 J4
The Oysters *WSTB* CT5 * ...126 F5

P

Pacific Cl *SWCM* DA10 ...53 M3
Packer Pl *WALD* ME5 ...101 H5
Packer's La *RAM* CT11 ...17 K5
Packham Rd *GVW* DA11 ...55 G8
Packhorse Rd *SEV* TN13 ...161 H4
Packmores Rd *ELTH/MOT* SE9 ...48 E3
Padbrook *OXTED* RH8 ...157 H7
Padbrook La *RCANTE* CT3 ...185 C9
Paddlesworth Rd *SNOD* ME6 ...112 D4
Paddock Cl *BGR/WK* TN15 ...240 H1
BKHTH/KID SE3 ...47 H1
DEAL CT14 ...209 G4
EDEN TN8 ...192 D2
EYN DA4 ...76 D2
FOLK CT20 ...10 A4
LYDD TN29 ...334 C3
QBOR ME11 ...227 Q1
OXTED RH8 ...185 G1
RRTW TN3 ...277 J12
SYD SE26 ...69 L1
Paddock Gdns *NRWD* SE19 ...68 A3
Paddock Rd *BRCH* CT7 ...176 D6
BXLYHS DA6 ...49 J2
Paddocks Cl *STMC/STPC* BR5 ...73 L8
The Paddocks *ASH* TN23 ...286 H6
BRDST CT10 ...179 H4
EDEN TN8 ...192 B3
GILL ME7 ...102 A8
HB CT6 ...129 H1
MARG CT9 ...178 A7
SIT ME10 * ...119 M6
SOCK/AV RM15 * ...32 D1
STRD ME2 ...18 B1
SWCM DA10 * ...54 A3
SYD SE26 ...69 J1
The Paddock *BH/WHM* TN16 ...159 L1
CANT CT1 ...5 G5
CHAT ME4 ...6 C4
DVE/WH CT16 ...8 D7
MEO DA13 ...239 L6
RCANTE CT3 ...251 R1
RRTW TN3 * ...276 G12
RTON TN11 ...256 C3
RTWE/PEM TN2 ...197 M7
RYE TN31 ...325 J1
SIT ME10 * ...119 L7
Paddock Vw *WSTB* CT5 ...126 E6
Paddock Wy *WARL* CR6 ...130 A5
Paddock Wy *CHST* BR7 ...72 E4
OXTED RH8 ...185 G1
Padfield Rd *CMBW* SE5 ...44 D1
Pad's Hl *MAID/SHEP* ME15 ...13 H4
Padsole La *MAID/SHEP* ME15 ...13 L4
Padstow Cl *ORP* BR6 ...91 G7
Padua Rd *PGE/AN* SE20 ...69 K6
Padwell La *ASH* TN23 ...286 H9
Paffard Cl *CANTW/ST* CT2 ...173 J2
Pageant Cl *TIL* RM18 ...35 K7
Pageant Wk *CROY/NA* CRO ...86 A7
Page Crs *CROY/NA* CRO ...86 C2
ERITH DA8 ...30 B6
Page Heath La *BMLY* BR1 ...71 J1
Page Heath Vls *BMLY* BR1 ...71 J1
Pagehurst Rd *CROY/NA* CRO ...87 H1
STPH/PW TN12 ...281 P6
Page Pl *RFOLK* CT18 ...220 E5
Page's Wk *STHWK* SE1 ...25 G3
Paget Gdns *CHST* BR7 ...72 C5
Paget Rd *WOOL/PLUM* SE18 ...28 B6
Paget Rw *GILL* ME7 ...7 J3
Paget Ter *WOOL/PLUM* SE18 ...28 C5
Pagette Wy *GRAYS* RM17 ...34 A6
Pagitt St *CHAT* ME4 ...6 E5
Pagnell St *NWCR* SE14 ...26 A6
Pagoda Gdns *BKHTH/KID* SE3 ...26 E8
Paiges Farm Cl *RSEV* TN14 ...255 J3
Paine Av *LYDD* TN29 ...334 D3
Painesfield Cl *LYDD* TN29 ...320 H1
Pains Hl *OXTED* RH8 ...185 M5
Painters Ash La *GVW* DA11 ...54 E8
Painter's Forstal Rd *FAV* ME13 ...148 A3
Palace Av *MAID/SHEP* ME15 ...13 L4
Palace Cha *BRDST* CT10 ...179 H4
Palace Cl *MARG* CT9 * ...179 G3
OXTED RH8 ...157 L6
RFOLK CT18 ...220 B3
Palace Ct *DUL* SE21 * ...44 E8
SYD SE26 * ...69 J1
Palace Gdns *BMLY* BR1 ...71 J1
Palace Gn *CROY/NA* CRO ...104 F7
Palace Rd *BH/WHM* TN16 ...132 F4
BMLY BR1 ...71 J1
BRXS/STRHM SW2 ...44 A6

NRWD SE19 ...69 G4
Palace Sq *NRWD* SE19 ...69 G4
Palace Vw *BMLY* BR1 ...71 J2
CROY/NA CRO ...88 A7
LEE/GVPK SE12 ...47 H7
Palewell Cl *STMC/STPC* BR5 ...73 J6
Palfrey Pl *BRXN/ST* SW9 ...24 A7
Pallant Wy *ORP* BR6 ...90 B7
Pallet Wy *WOOL/PLUM* SE18 ...28 A7
Palmar Crs *BXLYHN* DA7 ...50 B1
Palmar Rd *BXLYHN* DA7 ...30 B8
MAIDW ME16 ...12 A1
Palmarsh Rd *STMC/STPC* BR5 ...73 L8
Palm Av *SCUP* DA14 ...73 L3
Palm Bay Av *MARG* CT9 ...178 F2
Palm Bay Gdns *MARG* CT9 ...178 F2
Palmeira Rd *BXLYHN* DA7 ...49 L1
Palmer Av *GVE* DA12 ...49 L1
Palmer Cl *HB* CT6 ...155 J1
WWKM BR4 ...88 C5
Palmer Crs *MARG* CT9 ...178 F5
Palmer Rd *RCANTE* CT3 ...251 R2
Palmers Brook *RTON* TN11 ...256 C3
Palmers Cross Hi
...171 H4
Palmers Green La
STPH/PW TN12 ...279 N9
Palmers Orch *RSEV* TN14 ...109 J3
Palmers Rd *STRHM/NOR* SW16 ...68 A8
Palmerston Av *BRDST* CT10 ...183 L2
Palmerston Crs
WOOL/PLUM SE18 ...28 D5
Palmerston Gdns *WTHK* RM20 ...33 L4
Palmerston Rd *DVE/WH* CT16 * ...213 H6
CROY/NA CRO ...86 E1
ORP BR6 ...90 D7
WTHK RM20 ...33 L4
Palmerston St *FOLK* CT19 ...11 J1
Palm Tree Cl *RFOLK* CT18 ...272 E6
Palm Tree Wy *RFOLK* CT18 ...291 L10
Palting Wy *FOLK* CT20 ...10 A5
Panfield Rd *ABYW* SE2 ...29 H2
Pankhurst Rd *HOO/HM* ME3 ...59 L7
Panmure Rd *SYD* SE26 ...45 J8
Pannell Dr *RFOLK* CT18 ...220 C3
Pannell Rd *HOO/HM* ME3 ...43 H7
Pantony La *RSIT* ME9 ...120 F7
Panter's *SWLY* BR8 ...75 G4
Pantheon Gdns *ASH* TN23 ...204 C6
The Pantiles *BMLY* BR1 ...71 M7
BXLYHN DA7 ...30 A6
RTWE/PEM TN2 ...22 E8
Panton Cl *CROY/NA* CRO ...86 D1
WALD ME5 ...115 K1
Paper La *KEN/WIL* TN24 ...205 J5
Papillons Wk *BKHTH/KID* SE3 ...27 H8
Papion Gv *WALD* ME5 ...114 F3
Papworth Cl *FOLK* CT19 ...220 B6
Papworth Wy
BRXS/STRHM SW2 ...44 B5
The Parade *BH/WHM* TN16 * ...132 B7
BRCH CT7 ...233 R7
BROCKY SE4 * ...26 A7
CROY/NA CRO * ...86 A8
DART DA1 * ...51 G3
EDUL SE22 * ...44 F1
FOLK CT20 ...11 L5
GVE DA12 ...55 J7
HART DA3 * ...95 M1
KEN/WIL TN24 ...205 J6
MARG CT9 ...14 F3
MEO DA13 * ...97 H3
NROM TN28 ...335 M1
PGE/AN SE20 * ...69 K5
RAM CT11 * ...183 H5
SIT ME10 ...119 A7
SOCK/AV RM15 * ...32 D1
STRD ME2 ...18 B1
SWCM DA10 * ...54 A3
SYD SE26 ...69 J1
Paradise *RAM* CT11 ...17 H5
Paradise Rw *SWCH* CT13 ...237 J12
Paradise St *BERM/RHTH* SE16 ...25 J1
Paragon *RAM* CT11 ...17 J5
Paragon Cl *MARG* CT9 * ...15 H2
Paragon Ms *STHWK* SE1 * ...24 E3
Paragon Pl *BKHTH/KID* SE3 ...27 G8
The Paragon *BKHTH/KID* SE3 ...27 H8
Paraker Wy *HYTHE* CT21 ...223 J2
Parbrook Rd *HOO/HM* ME3 ...60 C4
Parbury Rd *FSTH* SE23 ...45 M4
Parchmere Rd *THHTH* CR7 ...68 C6
Parchmore Wy *THHTH* CR7 ...68 C5
Pardoner Cl *CANTW/ST* CT2 ...171 K6
Pardoner St *STHWK* SE1 ...24 F3
Pardoners Wy *DVE/WH* CT16 ...213 H6
Parfitt Wy *DVE/WH* CT16 ...213 J7
Parham Cl *CANT* CT1 ...172 C7
Parham Rd *CANT* CT1 ...172 C7
CHAT ME4 ...6 D9
Parish Gate Dr *BFN/LL* DA15 ...48 F4
Parish La *PGE/AN* SE20 ...69 L4
Parish Rd *IOS* ME12 ...65 J3
RCANTW ME12 ...248 D7
Parish Whf *WOOL/PLUM* SE18 ...27 M3
WBY/YAL ME18 ...164 A2
Park Ap *BERM/RHTH* SE16 * ...25 J1
WELL DA16 ...49 J2
Park Av *BMLY* BR1 ...71 H5
BRCH CT7 ...176 D7
BRDST CT10 ...183 H3
DEAL CT14 ...209 H4
EDEN TN8 ...192 C3
GILL ME7 ...7 G4
GVE DA12 ...55 K6
IOS ME12 ...64 F4
MAID/BEAR ME14 ...13 J1
ORP BR6 ...90 A5
ORP BR6 ...91 H6
QBOR ME11 ...227 Q1
RMAID ME17 ...259 G5
RTON TN11 ...188 C4
SIT ME10 ...119 M7
WSTB CT5 ...127 G5
WWKM BR4 ...88 D5
Park Av Ingress *GRH* DA9 ...53 K2
Park Barn Rd *RMAID* ME17 ...169 J8
Park Cha *GVW* DA11 ...78 A1
Park Cl *MARG* CT9 * ...179 G4
OXTED RH8 ...157 L6
RFOLK CT18 ...220 B3
Park Corner Rd *MEO* DA13 ...78 A1
Park Ct *DUL* SE21 * ...44 E8
SYD SE26 * ...69 J1
Park Crs *CHAT* ME4 ...101 G5

ERITH DA8 ...30 E5
Park Crescent Rd *MARG* CT9 ...15 J6
Parkcroft Rd *LEE/GVPK* SE12 ...47 G5
Parkdale Rd *WOOL/PLUM* SE18 ...28 F4
Park Dr *CHARL* SE7 ...27 M5
HART DA3 ...77 M7
RASHW TN26 ...286 E12
SIT ME10 ...119 L8
Park End *BMLY* BR1 ...71 L5
Parker Av *TIL* RM18 ...35 K7
Parker Cl *RHAM* ME8 ...102 F8
Parker Pl *RFOLK* CT18 ...292 H12
Parker Rd *CROY/NA* CRO ...86 D7
GRAYS RM17 ...34 A4
Parkers Rw *STHWK* SE1 ...25 G1
Parker Ter *FSTH* SE23 ...46 A7
Park Farm Cl *BUR/ETCH* TN19 ...322 A5
CANTW/ST CT2 ...153 M7
FOLKN TN19 ...220 D5
RASHW TN26 ...303 Q4
Park Farm Rd *BMLY* BR1 ...71 L5
E/WMAL ME19 ...239 H7
FOLKN TN19 ...220 C5
Parkfield *BGR/WK* TN15 ...162 E1
Parkfield Rd *FOLKN* TN19 ...11 H5
NWCR SE14 ...26 B8
RHAM ME8 ...103 G3
Parkfields *CROY/NA* CRO ...88 A4
STRD ME2 ...81 K6
Parkfield Wy *HAYES* BR2 ...90 A2
Park Gdns *ERITH* DA8 ...30 E3
Park Ga *BRDST* CT10 ...183 J3
Parkgate Rd *ORP* BR6 ...92 D7
Park Gv *BMLY* BR1 ...71 J1
BXLYHN DA7 ...50 D2
Park Hall Rd *DUL* SE21 ...44 E8
Park Hl *BMLY* BR1 ...71 M8
FSTH SE23 ...45 J1
MEO DA13 ...78 F8
Park Hill Ri *CROY/NA* CRO ...86 F6
Park Hill Rd *BGR/WK* TN15 ...136 D3
CROY/NA CRO ...86 F6
HAYES BR2 ...89 M2
Parkhill Rd *BFN/LL* DA15 ...48 F3
BXLY DA5 ...50 A5
Park House Gdns
STH/RUST TN4 ...196 D4
Parkhouse St *CMBW* SE5 ...24 F6
Parkhurst Gdns *BXLY* DA5 ...50 B5
Parkhurst Rd *BXLY* DA5 ...50 B5
Parkland Cl *SEV* TN13 ...135 H5
Parkland Ct *BRDST* CT10 ...179 J3
Parklands *OXTED* RH8 ...184 F1
Park La *BGR/WK* TN15 ...136 F4
BRCH CT7 ...176 D7
CROY/NA CRO ...86 D6
HAWK TN18 ...312 B2
LING RH7 ...190 F8
MAID/BEAR ME14 ...141 G6
RASHW TN26 ...288 B10
RCANTW CT4 ...250 E12
RCANTW CT4 ...291 Q4
RMAID ME17 ...259 G3
SEV TN13 ...21 J4
SWLY BR8 ...75 K6
Park Lea *DEAL* CT14 * ...209 H4
Park Ley Rd *CTHM* CR3 ...130 C6
Park Md *BFN/LL* DA15 ...49 H3
DVE/WH CT16 ...8 E4
GNWCH SE10 * ...27 G4
Park Piazza *LEW* SE13 ...46 E4
Park Pl *ASH* TN23 ...204 B4
BMLY BR1 ...71 J5
DVE/WH CT16 ...8 C3
GVE DA12 ...55 K6
KEN/WIL TN24 ...3 J1
MARG CT9 ...14 F3
SEV TN13 ...161 J1
Park Rise Rd *FSTH* SE23 ...45 M4
Park Rd *BECK* BR3 ...70 A4
BMLY BR1 ...71 J1
BRCH CT7 ...176 E7
BRDST CT10 ...72 C5
CHST BR7 ...72 C5
DART DA1 ...52 B5
DVE/WH CT16 ...212 E4
DVE/WH CT16 ...213 J7
E/WMAL ME19 ...138 C2
E/WMAL ME19 ...239 F10
FAV ME13 ...149 L3
FOLK CT20 ...11 L4
GVW DA11 ...55 J7
HB CT6 ...129 C5
HYTHE CT21 ...222 C4
IOS ME12 ...64 E4
KEN/WIL TN24 ...203 G5
LING RH7 ...190 F2
MARG CT9 ...15 J5
NROM TN28 ...331 M8
OXTED RH8 ...157 L6
QBOR ME11 ...227 Q1
RAM CT11 ...16 F4
RCANTE CT3 ...235 L6
RTON TN11 ...240 H12
SIT ME10 ...119 M6
SNWD SE25 ...68 F3
STH/RUST TN4 ...196 D3
STMC/STPC BR5 ...73 J8
STPH/PW TN12 ...281 M6
SWCM DA10 ...53 M4
SWLY BR8 ...75 G2
WARL CR6 ...105 K8
WBY/YAL ME18 ...164 A2
Park Rd North *KEN/WIL* TN24 ...3 G5
Park Rw *GNWCH* SE10 ...26 F5
Parkside *BECK* BR3 * ...70 C6
BKHTH/KID SE3 ...27 G6
CDW/CHF RM16 ...35 H4
DEAL CT14 ...209 K3
HOO/HM ME3 ...58 C6
RSEV TN14 ...108 D2
SCUP DA14 ...49 J7
Parkside Av *BMLY* BR1 ...71 M6
BXLYHN DA7 ...30 B8
TIL RM18 ...35 J8
Parkside Cl *PGE/AN* SE20 ...69 K5
Parkside Cross *BXLYHN* DA7 ...30 F8
Parkside Ms *WARL* CR6 ...130 F2
Parkside Pde *ERITH* DA8 * ...31 G8
Parkside Pl *CANT* CT1 ...172 E1
Parkside Rd *BELV* DA17 ...30 B4
Parkstone Rd *PECK* SE15 * ...25 H8
Park St *ASH* TN23 ...204 B4
CROY/NA CRO ...86 D6
DEAL CT14 ...209 L3
DVE/WH CT16 ...8 E1
LYDD TN29 ...334 E3
RTWE/PEM TN2 ...23 H4
Park Ter *GRH* DA9 ...53 K2
RSEV TN14 ...160 F2
The Park *SCUP* DA14 ...73 L3
Park Vw *KEN/WIL* TN24 ...203 G5
Park Vw *BRCH* CT7 ...176 E7
CANTW/ST CT2 ...173 J2

FOLKN CT19 220 F6
RSIT ME9 * 147 K4
RYE TN31 324 H7
RYE TN31 326 E11
Park View Cl EDEN TN8 192 C3
RCANTE CT3 252 C7
Park View Gdns GRAYS RM17 34 C4
Park View Ri RDV CT15 271 Q1
Parkview Rd CROY/NA CR0 87 H4
Park View Rd CTHM CR3 130 E8
ELTH/MOT SE9 48 C6
WELL DA16 49 L1
Park Vls RTON TN11 * 256 C4
SWCH CT13 * 253 P7
Park Vls GNWCH SE10 26 E5
Park Wy BXLY DA5 51 G8
MAID/SHEP ME15 167 J4
RMAID ME17 258 H2
Parkway CROY/NA CR0 105 H3
ERITHM DA18 29 M2
TONN TN10 189 G8
The Parkway BRCH CT7 176 E6
Parkwood BECK BR3 70 B4
RYE TN31 327 L9
Park Wood Cl ASH TN23 204 E6
Parkwood Cl BRDST CT10 183 H3
RTWE/PEM TN2 196 F7
Park Wood La STPH/PW TN12 282 D8
Parkwood Rd BH/WHM TN16 132 D7
BXLY DA5 50 A5
Park Wood Rd CANTW/ST CT2 171 K1
Parnell Cl CDW/CHF RM16 33 K4
Paroma Rd BELV DA17 30 B2
Parr Av GILL ME7 7 M1
Parr Cl CDW/CHF RM16 33 K3
Parrock Av GVE DA12 55 K6
Parrock Rd GVE DA12 55 K6
Parrock St GVE DA12 55 J5
Parrs Haed Ms ROCH ME1 * 19 K5
Parry Pl WOOL/PLUM SE18 28 C3
Parry Rd SNWD SE25 68 F7
Parsonage Cha IOS ME12 65 G8
Parsonage Cl STH/RUST TN4 277 R12
WARL CR6 130 D2
Parsonage Flds MSTR CT12 233 R10
Parsonage La EYN DA4 76 C3
RRTW TN3 296 C7
RSIT ME9 119 H1
SCUP DA14 74 A1
STRD ME2 19 K1
Parsonage Manorway
ERITH DA8 30 B5
Parsonage Rd HB CT6 129 H6
STH/RUST TN4 277 Q12
WTHK RM20 33 K5
Parsonage Stocks Rd
FAV ME13 245 R4
Parsonage St POP/IOD E14 26 D3
The Parsonage RDV CT15 * 215 G3
Parsons La RDART DA2 51 J8
Parson's Md CROY/NA CR0 86 C4
Partridge Av DIT/AY ME20 139 G2
Partridge Cl HB CT6 129 K6
Partridge Dr CHAT ME4 83 J4
ORP BR6 90 D6
Partridge Gn ELTH/MOT SE9 48 B8
Partridge La FAV ME13 149 K1
Partridge Rd SCUP DA14 48 F8
Partridges La WADH TN5 308 D4
Pascoe Rd LEW SE13 46 E3
Pasley Cl WALW SE17 24 C4
Pasley Rd GILL ME7 83 H6
Pasley Rd East CHAT ME4 83 H6
Pasley Rd West CHAT ME4 83 G6
The Passage MARG CT9 * 15 H2
Passey Pl ELTH/MOT SE9 48 A4
Pastens Rd OXTED RH8 185 K1
Pastime Cl SIT ME10 119 M1
Paston Crs LEE/GVPK SE12 47 J5
Pastor St LBTH SE11 24 C3
Pasture Rd CAT SE6 46 F6
The Pasture KEN/WIL TN24 203 G5
RFOLK CT18 220 C1
The Patch SEV TN13 135 K8
Patchways LYDD TN29 319 P6
Patmos Rd BRXN/ST SW9 24 C6
Patricia Ct WELL DA16 29 J6
Patricia Wy BRDST CT10 183 G2
Patrixbourne Av RHAM ME8 102 D3
Patrixbourne Rd RCANTW CT4 175 J7
Patrol Pl CAT SE6 46 C4
Pattenden Gdns
STPH/PW TN12 257 K6
Pattenden La STPH/PW TN12 280 G2
Pattenden Rd CAT SE6 46 A6
Pattens Cl CHAT ME4 100 F5
Pattens La CHAT ME4 100 F4
Patterdale Cl BMLY BR1 70 F3
Patterdale Rd PECK SE15 25 K6
RDART DA2 52 D6
Patterson Cl DEAL CT14 209 H5
Patterson Rd NRWD SE19 69 G3
Paulet Rd CMBW SE5 24 C8
Paul Gdns CROY/NA CR0 87 G5
Paulinus Cl STMC/STPC BR5 73 K6
Pauls Md LING RH7 190 F8
Paul's Pl DVE/WH CT16 8 B2
The Pavement TENT TN30 301 N10
WNWD SE27 * 68 D1
Pavilion Cl DEAL CT14 209 K1
Pavilion Dr SIT ME10 227 N12
Pavilion La WBY/YAL ME18 164 B5
Pavilion Meadow DVW CT17 212 E5
Pavilion Rd FOLKN CT19 11 J3
Pawleyne Cl PGE/AN SE20 69 K4
Pawson's Rd CROY/NA CR0 86 D2
Paxton Av RFOLK CT18 220 A2
Paxton Pl WNWD SE27 68 F1
Paxton Rd BMLY BR1 71 H4
FSTH SE23 45 M8
Payden St RMAID ME17 244 A9
RSIT ME9 243 R7
Payers Pk FOLK CT20 11 K5
Paynell Ct BKHTH/KID SE3 46 F1
Paynesfield Rd
BH/WHM TN16 132 C5
Payne's La MAID/SHEP ME15 167 H6
Payne St DEPT SE8 26 A5
Pays La RASHE TN25 265 J4
Pay St RFOLK CT18 292 E10
Payton Cl MARG CT9 178 C7
Payton Ms CANT CT1 5 J2
Peabody Cl CROY/NA CR0 87 K4
GNWCH SE10 * 26 C7
Peabody Est CMBW SE5 * 24 E7
HNHL SE24 44 C5
WALW SE17 * 24 E3
Peabody Hl DUL SE21 44 C6
Peabody Sq STHWK SE1 24 C1
Peace Cl SNWD SE25 68 F8
Peace St WOOL/PLUM SE18 28 B5
Peach Cft GVW DA11 54 F8
Peachum Rd BKHTH/KID SE3 27 G5
Peacock Gdns CROY/NA CR0 104 D4
Peacock Ms MAIDW ME16 * 12 E5
Peacock Ri WALD ME5 115 H1
Peacock St GVE DA12 55 K5
WALW SE17 24 C3
Peacock Yd WALW SE17 24 C3
Peafield Wood Rd
RCANTW CT4 269 P9
Peak Dr SWCH CT13 253 N6
Peak Hl SYD SE26 69 K1
Peak Hill Av SYD SE26 69 K1
Peak Hill Gdns SYD SE26 69 K1
The Peak SYD SE26 45 K8
Peal Cl HOO/HM ME3 59 M8
Peall Rd CROY/NA CR0 86 A2
Pean Court Rd WSTB CT5 152 E2
Pean Hl WSTB CT5 152 E2
Pearcefield Av FSTH SE23 45 K6
Pear Cl NWCR SE14 25 M6
Peareswood Rd ERITH DA8 31 G7
Pearfield Rd FSTH SE23 45 M8
Pearl Wy E/WMAL ME19 164 D2
Pearman Cl RHAM ME8 103 H4
Pearman St STHWK SE1 24 B1
Pear Pl STHWK SE1 24 B1
Pearse Pl RRTW TN3 296 C9
Pearse St PECK SE15 24 F5
Pearson's Av NWCR SE14 26 B7
Pearsons Green Rd
STPH/PW TN12 279 N5
STPH/PW TN12 279 P7
Pearson's Rd NWCR SE14 * 26 B7
Pearson's Wy BRDST CT10 179 H6
Pearson Wy DART DA1 52 A7
Pear Tree Av DIT/AY ME20 139 K5
Pear Tree Cl BRDST CT10 182 F1
CRBK TN17 298 G10
ERITH DA8 30 E7
SWLY BR8 74 E6
Peartree Cl HAYES BR2 89 L1
SAND/SEL CR2 104 A8
Pear Tree La GILL ME7 101 M6
LYDD TN29 321 J8
MAID/SHEP ME15 167 J7
Peartree La STRD ME2 81 H3
Peartree Pl HOO/HM ME3 * 81 J2
Peartree Rd HB CT6 129 K6
Peartree Wy GNWCH SE10 27 H3
Pease Hl BGR/WK TN15 238 E1
Peasley La CRBK TN17 297 M7
Peatfield Cl BFN/LL DA15 48 F8
Peat Wy HOO/HM ME3 42 E6
Peckarmans Wd SYD SE26 45 H8
Peckford Pl BRXN/ST SW9 24 B8
Peckham Cl STRD ME2 19 J1
Peckham Gv PECK SE15 24 F6
Peckham High St PECK SE15 25 H7
Peckham Hill St PECK SE15 25 H6
Peckham Hurst Rd
WBY/YAL ME18 241 L10
Peckham Park Rd PECK SE15 25 H6
Peckham Rd CMBW SE5 24 F7
PECK SE15 25 G7
Peckham Rye EDUL SE22 45 H2
Pedding Hl RCANTE CT3 235 N12
Pedding La RCANTE CT3 235 N12
Peel Dr SIT ME10 120 D5
Peel Rd ORP BR6 90 D7
Peel St MAID/BEAR ME14 13 G1
Peens La RMAID ME17 259 P6
Pegasus Ct GVE DA12 55 K8
Pegasus Pl LBTH SE11 * 24 B5
Pegasus Wy EGRIN RH19 274 A10
Pegden RCANTW CT4 * 291 Q4
Peggoty Cl HOO/HM ME3 81 J2
Pegley Gdns LEE/GVPK SE12 47 H7
Pegwell Av RAM CT11 16 B9
Pegwell Cl RAM CT11 16 B8
Pegwell Rd RAM CT11 16 B9
Pegwell St WOOL/PLUM SE18 28 F6
Pelham Cl CMBW SE5 44 F1
Pelham Gdns FOLK CT20 10 C4
Pelham Rd BXLYHN DA7 50 B1
GVW DA11 55 G5
PGE/AN SE20 69 K6
Pelham Rd South GVW DA11 55 G6
Pelican Cl STRD ME2 81 K7
Pelier St WALW SE17 24 D5
Pelinore Rd CAT SE6 46 F7
Pellatt Rd EDUL SE22 45 G3
Pell Cl WADH TN5 309 M3
Pellings Cl HAYES BR2 70 F7
Pellipar Rd WOOL/PLUM SE18 28 A4
Pells La BGR/WK TN15 111 M5
Pelton Rd GNWCH SE10 26 F4
Pelwood Rd RYE TN31 332 F7
Pemberton Gdns SWLY BR8 74 F7
Pemberton Rd KEN/WIL TN24 2 E5
Pemberton Sq STRD ME2 19 K1
Pemble Cl STPH/PW TN12 278 D2
Pembroke CHAT ME4 83 H5
Pembroke Av MARG CT9 177 L4
Pembroke Cl ERITH DA8 30 D3
Pembroke Gdns RHAM ME8 116 F1
Pembroke Ms NROM TN28 331 K5
SEV TN13 * 21 J6
Pembroke Pde ERITH DA8 * 30 D4
Pembroke Pl EYN DA4 76 C5
Pembroke Rd BMLY BR1 71 K6
CHAT ME4 * 83 H5
ERITH DA8 30 D4
RMAID ME17 258 H2
SEV TN13 21 H6
SNWD SE25 68 F8
TON TN9 194 D4
Pembry Cl BRXN/ST SW9 24 B7
Pembury Cl HAYES BR2 89 G3
RTWE/PEM TN2 * 278 A10
Pembury Crs SCUP DA14 49 M7
Pembury Gdns MAIDW ME16 12 B6
Pembury Gra RTWE/PEM TN2 197 K7
Pembury Gv TON TN9 194 F5
Pembury Hall Rd
RTWE/PEM TN2 197 M2
Pembury Pl RASHE TN25 202 C7
Pembury Rd BXLYHN DA7 29 M6
RTON TN11 197 K2
RTWE/PEM TN2 23 K4
SNWD SE25 69 H8
TON TN9 194 E5
Pembury St SIT ME10 119 M5
Pembury Wks RTON TN11 197 L3
Pembury Wy RHAM ME8 102 F3
Pemdevon Rd CROY/NA CR0 86 B3
Penarth St PECK SE15 25 K5
Penberth Rd CAT SE6 46 D7
Pencester Ct DVE/WH CT16 * 8 E4
Pencester Rd DVE/WH CT16 8 D4
Pencraig Wy PECK SE15 * 25 J5
Pencroft Dr DART DA1 51 K5
Penda Rd ERITH DA8 30 C6
Pendennis Rd ORP BR6 91 K5
SEV TN13 21 H2
Penderel Ms TENT TN30 315 N1
Penderry Ri CAT SE6 46 E7
Pendlebury House
WOOL/PLUM SE18 * 27 M6
Pendragon Rd BMLY BR1 47 H8
Pendrell Rd BROCKY SE4 45 M1
Pendrell St WOOL/PLUM SE18 28 E5
Penenden HART DA3 96 A5
Penenden Heath Rd
MAID/BEAR ME14 141 J6
Penenden St MAID/BEAR ME14 13 G1
Penerley Rd CAT SE6 46 C6
Penfield La RSIT ME9 146 B5
Penfold Cl CROY/NA CR0 86 B6
MAID/SHEP ME15 167 M7
WALD ME5 * 101 J6
Penfold Gdns RDV CT15 271 R8
Penfold Hl RMAID ME17 169 J5
Penfold Rd FOLKN CT19 220 F7
Penfolds Cl TONN TN10 188 F8
Penfold Wy MAID/SHEP ME15 167 G7
Penford Gdns ELTH/MOT SE9 47 L2
Penford St CMBW SE5 24 C8
Pengarth Rd BXLY DA5 49 L3
Penge La PGE/AN SE20 69 K4
Penge Rd SNWD SE25 69 H7
Penguin Cl STRD ME2 81 L7
Penhale Cl ORP BR6 91 H7
Penhall Rd CHARL SE7 27 L3
Penhill Rd BXLY DA5 49 K5
Penhurst Cl MAID/BEAR ME14 142 A8
Penhurst Pl STHWK SE1 * 24 A2
Peninsular Park Rd CHARL SE7 27 H4
Penlee Cl EDEN TN8 192 D3
Penmon Rd ABYW SE2 29 H2
Pennack Rd PECK SE15 25 G5
Pennant Rd ROCH ME1 100 D6
Penn Cl SIT ME10 120 C7
Pennethorne Rd PECK SE15 25 J6
Penney Cl DART DA1 51 L5
Penn Gdns CHST BR7 72 C6
Penn Hl ASH TN23 204 B5
Pennine Wk RTWE/PEM TN2 23 L2
Pennine Wy BXLYHN DA7 30 F7
GVW DA11 54 F8
KEN/WIL TN24 2 B1
MAID/SHEP ME15 168 B4
Pennington Cl CANTW/ST CT2 173 K2
Pennington Mnr
STH/RUST TN4 * 196 C3
Pennington Pl STH/RUST TN4 196 E3
Pennington Rd STH/RUST TN4 196 D3
Pennington Wy LEE/GVPK SE12 47 J7
Penn La BXLY DA5 49 L4
RSEV TN14 160 D5
Penns Yd RTWE/PEM TN2 197 M7
Pennybridge La MAYF TN20 308 D12
Penny Cress Gdns
MAIDW ME16 166 D2
Penny Cress Rd IOS ME12 228 D1
Pennycroft SAND/SEL CR2 104 D3
Pennyfields CRBK TN17 298 G9
Penny Pot La RCANTW CT4 248 D9
RCANTW CT4 267 Q1
Penpool La WELL DA16 49 J1
Penrith Cl BECK BR3 70 C5
Penrith Pl STRHM/NOR SW16 44 C7
Penrith Rd THHTH CR7 68 D6
Penrose Gv WALW SE17 24 D4
Penrose St WALW SE17 24 D4
Penry St STHWK SE1 * 24 F3
Penshurst Av BFN/LL DA15 49 H4
Penshurst Cl BGR/WK TN15 111 K1
CANTW/ST CT2 172 B6
HART DA3 78 E6
RHAM ME8 102 E3
Penshurst Gdns MARG CT9 179 J3
Penshurst Gn HAYES BR2 89 G1
Penshurst Ri FAV ME13 149 J1
Penshurst Rd BXLYHN DA7 30 A7
RAM CT11 17 M4
RRTW TN3 277 N9
RTON TN11 276 H3
RTON TN11 277 L9
THHTH CR7 86 C1
Penshurst Wy STMC/STPC BR5 73 K8
The Penstocks MAIDW ME16 12 B9
The Pentagon CHAT ME4 * 6 D5
Penton Pl WALW SE17 24 D4
Pentridge St PECK SE15 25 G6
Pentstemon Dr SWCM DA10 53 M3
Pent Vale Cl FOLKN CT19 10 D2
Penventon Ct TIL RM18 * 35 H8
Pen Wy TONN TN10 189 H8
Pepingstraw Cl E/WMAL ME19 241 Q2
Peppercorn Cl THHTH CR7 68 E6
Pepper Hl GVW DA11 54 D8
Peppermead Sq LEW SE13 * 46 B3
Pepper St POP/IOD E14 26 C2
STHWK SE1 24 D1
Pepys Av IOS ME12 64 C3
Pepys Cl GVW DA11 54 E8
TIL RM18 35 K7
Pepys Est DEPT SE8 25 M3
Pepys Park Est DEPT SE8 26 A3
Pepys Ri ORP BR6 91 G4
Pepys Rd NWCR SE14 25 L8
Pepy's Wy STRD ME2 18 D2
Perch La RRTW TN3 295 Q4
Percival Rd ORP BR6 90 C5
Percival Ter DVW CT17 217 J2
Percy Av BRDST CT10 179 J4
Percy Rd BRDST CT10 179 J8
BXLYHN DA7 29 M8
MARG CT9 15 J3
PGE/AN SE20 69 L5
RAM CT11 17 H3
SNWD SE25 87 G1
Percy St GRAYS RM17 34 D5
Percy Ter STH/RUST TN4 * 196 D7
Peregrine Cl HYTHE CT21 321 R1
Peregrine Ct WELL DA16 29 G7
Peregrine Dr SIT ME10 120 B6
Peregrine Gdns CROY/NA CR0 87 M5
Peregrine Rd E/WMAL ME19 164 B8
Peri Ct CANT CT1 4 E8
Perie Rw GILL ME7 6 D1
Perifield DUL SE21 44 D6
Perimeter Rd DIT/AY ME20 139 K2
Periton Rd ELTH/MOT SE9 47 L2
Periwinkle Cl SIT ME10 119 M4
Perkins Av MARG CT9 15 G8
Perkins Cl GRH DA9 53 G3
Perks Cl BKHTH/KID SE3 26 F8
Perpins Rd ELTH/MOT SE9 48 F4
Perran Cl HART DA3 78 A8
Perran Rd BRXS/STRHM SW2 44 C7
Perries Md FOLKN CT19 10 E1
Perryfield St MAID/BEAR ME14 12 F1
Perry Gv DART DA1 52 B2
Perry Hall Cl ORP BR6 91 H3
Perry Hall Rd ORP BR6 91 G2
Perry Hl CAT SE6 46 A7
HOO/HM ME3 58 D4
Perry Mnr CHST BR7 72 F3
Perrymans Cross RYE TN31 * 325 J10
Perryn Rd BERM/RHTH SE16 25 J1
Perry Ri FSTH SE23 45 M8
Perry Rd RCANTE CT3 235 K10
Perrys La ORP BR6 108 A7
Perry St CHAT ME4 6 A8
CHST BR7 72 F3
DART DA1 50 F1
GVW DA11 54 F6
MAID/BEAR ME14 142 A8
Perry V FSTH SE23 45 L7
Persant Rd CAT SE6 46 F8
Perseverance Pl
BRXN/ST SW9 * 24 B6
Perth Gdns SIT ME10 119 K5
Perth Rd BECK BR3 70 D6
Pescot Av HART DA3 78 B7
Pested Bars Rd RMAID ME17 167 K8
Pested La RASHE TN25 265 N2
Petchart Cl STRD ME2 99 K2
Peter Av OXTED RH8 157 J7
Peterboat Cl GNWCH SE10 26 F3
Peter James Cl RYE TN31 332 D7
Peters Cl WELL DA16 28 F8
Petersfield RTWE/PEM TN2 278 B10
Petersfield Dr MEO DA13 239 L4
Petersham Dr STMC/STPC BR5 73 G6
Petersham Gdns
STMC/STPC BR5 73 H6
Peterstone Rd ABYW SE2 29 J1
Peter St DEAL CT14 209 L2
DVE/WH CT16 8 B3
FOLK CT20 11 L4
Peterwood Wy CROY/NA CR0 86 A5
Petfield Cl IOS ME12 65 K7
Petham Gn RHAM ME8 102 D3
Petrel Cl HB CT6 232 A5
Petrel Wy RFOLK CT18 220 B2
Petta La RCANTE CT3 234 H12
Pett Bottom Rd RCANTW CT4 250 A9
RCANTW CT4 269 M3
Petten Cl STMC/STPC BR5 91 L4
Pettendon Dr SIT ME10 120 A1
Petten Gv STMC/STPC BR5 91 K4
Petteridge La STPH/PW TN12 278 H11
Pettfield Hill Rd FAV ME13 245 L8
Pett Hl RCANTW CT4 175 G8
Pettits Rw FAV ME13 * 149 J2
Pett La HDCN TN27 264 D7
RSIT ME9 144 B1
Pettman Cl HB CT6 129 G6
Pettman Crs THMD SE28 28 E3
Pettman Ms WSTB CT5 * 126 D3
Pett's Crs MSTR CT12 180 E8
Pett St WOOL/PLUM SE18 27 M3
Petts Wood Rd STMC/STPC BR5 90 E1
Petworth Rd BXLYHS DA6 50 B3
Peverel Dr MAID/BEAR ME14 142 A8
Peverell Rd DVE/WH CT16 213 J4
Pewter Ct CANT CT1 4 F7
Peyton Pl GNWCH SE10 26 D6
Pharos Dr DVE/WH CT16 8 E2
Pheasant La MAID/SHEP ME15 167 J6
Pheasant Rd CHAT ME4 * 101 K3
Pheasants' Hall Rd
RCANTW CT4 269 Q3
Phelps Cl BGR/WK TN15 111 K1
Phelp St WALW SE17 24 E5
Philimore Cl WOOL/PLUM SE18 28 F4
Philip Corby Cl MARG CT9 15 M5
Philip Gdns CROY/NA CR0 88 A5
Philippa Gdns ELTH/MOT SE9 47 L3
Philip Rd PECK SE15 45 H1
Philip Sydney Rd WTHK RM20 33 L4
Phillip Av SWLY BR8 74 E8
Phillippa Ct SIT ME10 119 M2
Phillip Rd FOLKN CT19 10 A2
Phillips Cl DART DA1 51 J4
Phillips Ct RHAM ME8 102 C3
Phillips Rd BRCH CT7 176 D7
Philpots La RTON TN11 255 M7
Phineas Pett Rd ELTH/MOT SE9 47 M1
Phoebeth Rd LEW SE13 46 B3
Phoenix Cl WWKM BR4 88 E5
Phoenix Ct POP/IOD E14 26 B3
Phoenix Dr HAYES BR2 89 L7
WBY/YAL ME18 164 F7
Phoenix Pk
MAID/SHEP ME15 * 260 A1
Phoenix Pl DART DA1 51 L5
Phoenix Rd PGE/AN SE20 69 K3
WALD ME5 115 J3
Phoenix Wharf Rd STHWK SE1 25 G1
Picardy Manorway BELV DA17 30 C2
Picardy Rd BELV DA17 30 B4
Picardy St BELV DA17 30 B2
Pickelden La RCANTW CT4 248 A9
Pickering Gdns SNWD SE25 87 G2
Pickering St MAID/SHEP ME15 167 H7
Pickford Cl BXLYHN DA7 29 M8
Pickforde La WADH TN5 310 F8
Pickford La BXLYHN DA7 29 M8
Pickford Rd BXLYHN DA7 49 M1
Pickhurst Gn HAYES BR2 89 G3
Pickhurst La HAYES BR2 88 F1
HAYES BR2 89 G2
Pickhurst Md HAYES BR2 89 G3
Pickhurst Pk HAYES BR2 88 F2
Pickhurst Ri WWKM BR4 88 E4
Pickle's Wy HOO/HM ME3 38 B7
Pickneybush La LYDD TN29 319 R11
Pickwick Crs ROCH ME1 100 D3
Pickwick Gdns GVW DA11 54 E8
Pickwick Rd DUL SE21 44 E5
Pickwick St STHWK SE1 24 D1
Pickwick Wy CHST BR7 72 D3
Picton Rd RAM CT11 16 F6
Picton St CMBW SE5 24 E6
Piedmont Rd
WOOL/PLUM SE18 28 E4
Pie Factory Rd RDV CT15 271 R4
Pier Approach Rd GILL ME7 83 L6
Pier Av HB CT6 128 F5
WSTB CT5 127 H2
Pierce Mill La RTON TN11 256 F7
Piermont Pl BMLY BR1 71 L6
Piermont Rd EDUL SE22 45 J3
Pierpoint Rd WSTB CT5 126 E6
Pierremont Av BRDST CT10 183 K1
Pier Rd CAN/RD E16 28 B1
CHAT ME4 83 J5
ERITH DA8 30 F5
GRH DA9 53 J2
GVW DA11 55 G4
Pier St POP/IOD E14 26 D3
The Pier DVE/WH CT16 213 G1
Pier Wy WOOL/PLUM SE18 28 C2
Pier Whf GRAYS RM17 * 34 B6
Pigdown La EDEN TN8 275 Q1
Pigeon La HB CT6 129 H7
Piggs Cnr GRAYS RM17 * 34 D2
Pigsdean Rd MEO DA13 98 C3
Pike Cl BMLY BR1 71 J2
FOLKN CT19 220 B6
Pikefish La STPH/PW TN12 257 P12
Pike Rd RDV CT15 272 F3
Pikes La LING RH7 190 F4
Pikey La E/WMAL ME19 138 E8
Pilckem Cl CANT CT1 172 E8
Pile La STPH/PW TN12 282 B5
Pilgrimage St STHWK SE1 24 E1
Pilgrim Hl WNWD SE27 68 D1
Pilgrims Ct DART DA1 52 B3
Pilgrims Lakes RMAID ME17 242 F11
Pilgrims La OXTED RH8 158 B2
RCANTW CT4 247 R8
WSTB CT5 152 C1
Pilgrim Spring FOLKN CT19 220 D5
Pilgrims Rd CANT CT1 5 L6
STRD ME2 99 G7
SWCM DA10 53 M2
Pilgrims Vw GRH DA9 53 K4
MAID/BEAR ME14 140 F2
Pilgrim's Wy BGR/WK TN15 136 D2
BGR/WK TN15 137 K2
BGR/WK TN15 238 E9
BH/WHM TN16 159 G1
CANT CT1 5 L6
DART DA1 52 C6
DIT/AY ME20 114 C7
DVE/WH CT16 213 H6
E/WMAL ME19 239 L7
EDEN TN8 192 E4
HDCN TN27 264 D6
MAID/BEAR ME14 141 K1
MAID/BEAR ME14 142 C4
RASHE TN25 265 K9
RASHE TN25 266 A10
RASHE TN25 290 D10
RMAID ME17 242 A6
RMAID ME17 242 F9
RMAID ME17 243 J10
ROCH ME1 113 M1
SAND/SEL CR2 * 87 G8
SNOD ME6 112 C4
STRD ME2 99 K2
Pilgrims Wy East RSEV TN14 136 B2
Pilgrims Wy West RSEV TN14 135 L2
Pilkington Rd ORP BR6 90 D6
PECK SE15 25 J8
Pillar Box La RTON TN11 241 J12
Pillar Box Rd BGR/WK TN15 137 K8
Pilot Cl DEPT SE8 26 A5
Pilot Rd ROCH ME1 100 D5
Pilots Av DEAL CT14 209 H5
Pilot's Farm Rd RCANTW CT4 269 K2
Pilots Pl GVE DA12 55 K4
Pilton Pl WALW SE17 24 D4
Pimpernel Cl
MAID/BEAR ME14 168 C1
Pimpernel Wy WALD ME5 114 F1
Pinchbeck Rd ORP BR6 107 L1
Pincott Pl BROCKY SE4 45 L1
Pincott Rd BXLYHS DA6 50 B3
Pincroft Wd HART DA3 78 D8
Pine Av GVE DA12 55 L6
WWKM BR4 88 C4
Pine Cl DIT/AY ME20 139 H3
PGE/AN SE20 69 K5
SWLY BR8 75 G8
Pine Coombe CROY/NA CR0 87 L7
Pinecrest Gdns ORP BR6 90 C7
Pinecroft WELL DA16 29 H6
Pine Gld ORP BR6 90 A7
Pine Gv EDEN TN8 192 C3
GILL ME7 102 B8
MAID/BEAR ME14 141 J7
Pineham Rd RDV CT15 213 L3
Pinehurst RSEV TN14 136 D7
Pinelands Cl BKHTH/KID SE3 * 27 G6
Pineneedle La SEV TN13 21 G2
Pine Pl MAID/SHEP ME15 166 F4
Pine Rdg TONN TN10 188 E7
Pine Ri MEO DA13 97 H2
Pine Rd STRD ME2 18 D6
Pinesfield La E/WMAL ME19 239 N7
Pineside Rd RCANTE CT3 175 M1
Pines Rd BMLY BR1 71 M6
The Pines BRDST CT10 182 F1
NRWD SE19 * 68 C3
Pine Tree Av CANTW/ST CT2 4 C1
Pinetree Cl WSTB CT5 127 G2
Pine Tree La BGR/WK TN15 163 M3
Pine Vw BGR/WK TN15 240 H2
Pine Wk HB CT6 129 M4
Pine Wy FOLKN CT19 219 L6
Pinewood Av BFN/LL DA15 48 F6
SEV TN13 136 C7
Pinewood Cl CROY/NA CR0 87 M6
MSTR CT12 16 E1
ORP BR6 90 E4
STPH/PW TN12 279 J3
TIL RM18 36 C2
Pinewood Dr
MAID/BEAR ME14 115 L5
ORP BR6 90 F8
Pinewood Gdns
STH/RUST TN4 196 D4
Pinewood Pl BXLY DA5 50 F7
Pinewood Rd ABYW SE2 29 L5
HAYES BR2 71 H8
RTWE/PEM TN2 23 L1
Pin Hl CANT CT1 4 E6
Pinkham STPH/PW TN12 257 K8
Pinks Hl SWLY BR8 92 F1
Pinnacle Hl BXLYHN DA7 50 C2
Pinnacle Hl North BXLYHN DA7 50 C1
The Pinnacles CHAT ME4 83 K4
Pinnell Rd ELTH/MOT SE9 47 L2
Pinners Hl RDV CT15 252 B11
Pinners La RDV CT15 252 C12
Pinnock La STPH/PW TN12 281 R8
Pinnock's Av GVW DA11 55 J6
Pintail Cl HOO/HM ME3 43 J7
Pintail Dr RSIT ME9 227 M10
The Pintails CHAT ME4 83 J4
Pintail Wy HB CT6 129 K7
Pinton Hl WADH TN5 310 C6
Pinto Wy BKHTH/KID SE3 47 J2
Pioneer Rd DVE/WH CT16 213 H6
Pioneer St PECK SE15 25 H7
Pioneer Wy SWLY BR8 74 F7
Pipers Cl WADH TN5 309 M5
Pipers Gdns CROY/NA CR0 87 M3
Piper's Green Rd
BH/WHM TN16 159 M6
Pipers La BH/WHM TN16 159 M6
Pippin Av RCANTW CT4 250 E9
Pippin Cl CROY/NA CR0 88 A4
RMAID ME17 258 G3
SIT ME10 119 L3
Pippin Cft GILL ME7 102 B7
Pippin Rd STPH/PW TN12 257 J7
The Pippins MEO DA13 97 H2
Pippin Wy E/WMAL ME19 164 B3
Piquet Rd PGE/AN SE20 69 K6
Pirbright Cl WALD ME5 115 L3
Pirbright Crs CROY/NA CR0 105 H1
Pirrip Cl GVE DA12 56 A6
Pitchfont La OXTED RH8 157 M4
Pitfield HART DA3 78 A8
Pitfield Dr MEO DA13 97 G6
Pitfold Rd LEE/GVPK SE12 47 H5
Pitlake CROY/NA CR0 86 C5
Pit La EDEN TN8 192 D1
Pitman St CMBW SE5 24 D6
Pitstock Rd RSIT ME9 146 C5
Pittlesden TENT TN30 315 M2
Pittlesden Pl TENT TN30 315 M2
Pitt Rd MAIDW ME16 166 C4
ORP BR6 90 D7
RMAID ME17 260 H3
THHTH CR7 86 D1
Pittsmead Av HAYES BR2 89 H3
Pittville Gdns SNWD SE25 69 H7
Pivington La HDCN TN27 263 M11
Pixot Hl STPH/PW TN12 279 M7
Pix's La CRBK TN17 314 F6
Pixton Wy CROY/NA CR0 104 E2
Pixwell La DEAL CT14 208 E6
Pizien Well Rd WBY/YAL ME18 164 B7
Place Farm Av ORP BR6 90 E4
Place La RASHW TN26 303 K10
RSIT ME9 103 L8

The Place RCANTW CT4 271 L4
Plain Rd FOLK CT20 10 D7
RASHE TN25 289 M12
STPH/PW TN12 280 H6
Plains Av MAID/SHEP ME15 167 J4
Plains of Waterloo RAM CT11 17 K5
Plaistow Gv BMLY BR1 71 J4
Plaistow La BMLY BR1 71 H4
Plaistow Sq
MAID/BEAR ME14 * 141 K7
Plane Av GVW DA11 54 E5
Plane St SYD SE26 45 J8
Plane Wk TONN TN10 188 F6
Plantain Pl STHWK SE1 * 24 E1
Plantation Cl GRH DA9 53 G4
RASHW TN26 286 F2
Plantation Dr STMC/STPC BR5 91 L4
Plantation La
MAID/BEAR ME14 168 B1
WARL CR6 130 D5
Plantation Rd ERITH DA8 31 H7
FAV ME13 149 K3
GILL ME7 84 B7
SWLY BR8 75 H4
WSTB CT5 127 L3
The Plantation BKHTH/KID SE3 27 H8
Plassy Rd CAT SE6 46 C5
Platt Common BGR/WK TN15 240 H2
The Platters RHAM ME8 102 D5
The Plat EDEN TN8 192 E4
RYE TN31 325 J7
Platt House La BGR/WK TN15 238 H7
Platt Mill Ter BGR/WK TN15 * 240 H2
The Platt RMAID ME17 260 F6
Plawsfield Rd BECK BR3 69 L5
Plaxdale Green Rd
BGR/WK TN15 238 D5
Plaxtol Cl BMLY BR1 71 K5
Plaxtol La BGR/WK TN15 240 B9
Plaxtol Rd ERITH DA8 30 B6
Playden La RYE TN31 327 M10
Playfield Crs EDUL SE22 44 F3
Playgreen Wy CAT SE6 70 B1
Playground Cl BECK BR3 69 L6
Playhouse Ct STHWK SE1 24 D1
Playing Flds SWCH CT13 * 253 R2
Playstool Cl RSIT ME9 118 C3
Playstool Rd RSIT ME9 118 B3
Pleasance Rd STMC/STPC BR5 73 J6
Pleasance Rd Central
LYDD TN29 335 N6
Pleasance Rd North
LYDD TN29 335 N4
Pleasance Rd South
LYDD TN29 335 N7
Pleasant Gv CROY/NA CR0 88 A6
Pleasant Rw GILL ME7 6 E1
Pleasant Valley La
MAID/SHEP ME15 258 G1
Pleasant Vw ERITH DA8 30 F4
ORP BR6 90 D8
Pleasent Pl IOS ME12 64 F7
Pleasure House La
RMAID ME17 260 H6
Plevna St POP/IOD E14 26 D2
Pleydell Av NRWD SE19 69 G4
Pleydell Gdns FOLK CT20 11 J7
NRWD SE19 * 69 G3
Plimsoll Av FOLKN CT19 220 E5
Plomley Cl RHAM ME8 116 E1
Plough Ct HB CT6 129 L7
Plough Hl BGR/WK TN15 240 F5
RDV CT15 216 C5
Plough La EDUL SE22 45 G4
WSTB CT5 127 L2
Ploughmans Wy RHAM ME8 102 F7
WALD ME5 115 H4
Plough Rd IOS ME12 66 B8
LING RH7 274 A3
Plough Wy BERM/RHTH SE16 25 L3
Plough Wents Rd
RMAID ME17 260 E3
Plover Cl HB CT6 232 A4
WALD ME5 115 L4
Plover Rd DIT/AY ME20 139 G3
IOS ME12 65 H8
Plover Wy BERM/RHTH SE16 25 M2
Plowenders Cl E/WMAL ME19 239 Q11
Pluckley Cl RHAM ME8 102 D2
Pluckley Gdns MARG CT9 179 H3
Pluckley Rd HDCN TN27 264 A8
HDCN TN27 284 F7
RASHW TN26 285 M10
RASHW TN26 285 R5
Plug La MEO DA13 97 L8
Plumbridge St GNWCH SE10 * 26 D7
Plumford Rd FAV ME13 149 H7
Plum La WOOL/PLUM SE18 28 C6
Plummer La TENT TN30 315 L3
Plumpton Wk CANT CT1 5 J2
Plumpudding La FAV ME13 151 L1
Plumstead Common Rd
WOOL/PLUM SE18 28 D5
Plumstead High St
WOOL/PLUM SE18 28 E3
Plumstead Rd
WOOL/PLUM SE18 28 D3
Plumstone Rd BRCH CT7 180 D3
Plum Tree Gdns RASHW TN26 303 J12
Plumtree Gv GILL ME7 116 B1
Plum Tree La RSIT ME9 117 J5
Plumtree Rd HDCN TN27 260 H12
Plumtrees MAIDW ME16 166 B3
Plurenden Rd RASHW TN26 302 F6
Plymouth Dr BGR/WK TN15 21 J5
Plymouth Pk BGR/WK TN15 21 K5
Plymouth Rd BMLY BR1 71 J5
CDW/CHF RM16 33 K4
Plymouth Whf POP/IOD E14 26 E3
Plympton Cl BELV DA17 29 M2
Plymstock Rd WELL DA16 29 K6
Poachers Cl WALD ME5 101 K8
Pochard Crs HB CT6 128 F6
Pocket Hl SEV TN13 161 M6
Pocock St STHWK SE1 24 C1
Podkin Wd WALD ME5 115 G5
Poets Cnr MARG CT9 15 H6
Poets Wk DEAL CT14 209 J8
Point Cl GNWCH SE10 26 D7
Point Cnr RTON TN11 * 240 E12
Pointers Cl POP/IOD E14 26 C4
Point Hl GNWCH SE10 26 D7
Polebrook Rd BKHTH/KID SE3 47 K1
Polecroft La CAT SE6 46 A7
Polesden Rd RTWE/PEM TN2 23 L8
Polesteeple Hl BH/WHM TN16 132 C3
The Poles RSIT ME9 103 M1
Polhill RSEV TN14 135 H1
Polhill Dr WALD ME5 115 G3
Police Station Rd
E/WMAL ME19 138 D5
Pollard Cl ASH TN23 204 C3
Pollard Pl WSTB CT5 * 126 D7
Pollards Hl East
STRHM/NOR SW16 68 A7
Pollards Hl North
STRHM/NOR SW16 68 A7
Pollards Oak Crs OXTED RH8 185 H2
Pollards Oak Rd OXTED RH8 185 H2
Pollards Wood Hl OXTED RH8 157 M8
Pollards Wood Rd OXTED RH8 185 J1
Polley Cl RTWE/PEM TN2 278 A10
Pollyhaugh EYN DA4 93 M6
Polo Wy WSTB CT5 127 K4
Polperro Cl ORP BR6 91 G2
Polperro Ms LBTH SE11 24 B3
Polsted Rd CAT SE6 46 A5
Polthorne Gv
WOOL/PLUM SE18 28 D3
Polytechnic St
WOOL/PLUM SE18 28 B3
Pomeroy St NWCR SE14 25 K6
Pomfret Houses
RCANTW CT4 * 248 E8
Pomfret Rd CMBW SE5 44 C1
RCANTW CT4 248 E8
Pommeus La DEAL CT14 210 E2
Poncia Rd ASH TN23 204 D4
Pond Cl BKHTH/KID SE3 27 H8
Pond Cottage La BECK BR3 88 B4
Pond Dr SIT ME10 120 B7
Pond Farm Rd RMAID ME17 143 L4
RSIT ME9 119 G8
Pondfield La GVE DA12 80 F4
Pondfield Rd HAYES BR2 88 F4
ORP BR6 90 C6
Pond Hl HOO/HM ME3 38 C7
RCANTE CT3 251 N8
Pond Hill Rd FOLK CT20 219 K8
Pond La BGR/WK TN15 163 K3
RCANTE CT3 271 J3
RDV CT15 214 E2
Pond Md EDUL SE22 44 E4
Pondmore Wy RASHE TN25 202 C7
Pond Rd BKHTH/KID SE3 47 G1
Pond Wy EGRIN RH19 274 A12
Pondwood Ri ORP BR6 90 F3
Pontefract Rd BMLY BR1 71 H2
Pontoise Cl SEV TN13 20 D1
Ponycart La RCANTW CT4 268 H10
Pook La HDCN TN27 283 Q12
HDCN TN27 300 H2
Pool Cl BECK BR3 70 B2
Pool Ct CAT SE6 46 B7
Poolmans St BERM/RHTH SE16 25 L1
Poona Rd RTW TN1 23 H7
Poorhole La BRDST CT10 178 D8
Pootings Rd EDEN TN8 186 E5
Poot La RSIT ME9 85 M7
Pope Dr STPH/PW TN12 281 R5
Pope House La TENT TN30 301 N9
Pope Rd HAYES BR2 89 L1
Popes Gv CROY/NA CR0 88 A6
Popes La CANTW/ST CT2 172 F2
OXTED RH8 185 G5
Pope's Rd BRXN/ST SW9 * 44 B2
Pope St MAIDW ME16 166 D3
RCANTW CT4 267 M1
STHWK SE1 24 F1
Popjak Rd RSIT ME9 * 145 L3
Poplar Av GVE DA12 79 K1
ORP BR6 90 C5
Poplar Cl ASH TN23 202 C8
HOO/HM ME3 83 M2
STRD ME2 18 C7
Poplar Dr HB CT6 128 D7
RDV CT15 272 C3
Poplar Gv MAIDW ME16 140 D8
Poplar La LYDD TN29 334 E2
Poplar Mt BELV DA17 30 C3
Poplar Rd BRDST CT10 179 H7
HNHL SE24 44 D2
RAM CT11 17 G5
STRD ME2 18 A8
TENT TN30 326 H2
Poplars Cl HART DA3 78 D7
The Poplars ASH TN23 * 204 D4
RCANTE CT3 234 A4
Poplar Wk CROY/NA CR0 86 D5
HNHL SE24 44 D2
MEO DA13 97 J2
Poplicans Rd STRD ME2 99 J2
Poppinghole La RBTBR TN32 323 J12
Poppy Cl BELV DA17 30 C2
GILL ME7 83 M8
HAYES BR2 89 K8
MAIDW ME16 12 B7
Poppy La CROY/NA CR0 87 K3
Poppy Meadow
STPH/PW TN12 279 K4
Popsal La RCANTE CT3 252 A3
Porchester Cl HART DA3 78 A8
MAID/SHEP ME15 167 H7
Porchester Md BECK BR3 70 C3
Porchfield Cl GVE DA12 55 K7
Porcupine Cl ELTH/MOT SE9 47 M7
Porden Rd BRXS/STRHM SW2 44 A2
Porlock St STHWK SE1 24 E1
Porrington Cl CHST BR7 72 A5
Portal Cl WNWD SE27 44 B8
Port Av GRH DA9 53 J4
Portbury Cl PECK SE15 25 H7
Portchester Cl CMBW SE5 44 D2
Port Cl MAID/BEAR ME14 142 A8
WALD ME5 115 J2
Porter Cl IOS ME12 65 H7
WTHK RM20 33 K5
Porters Cl STPH/PW TN12 279 J11
Porter's La FAV ME13 149 J7
Porters Wk RMAID ME17 260 F1
Porters Wd STPH/PW TN12 * 278 H11
Porthcawe Rd SYD SE26 69 M1
Port Hl ORP BR6 108 A6
Porthkerry Av WELL DA16 49 H2
Portland Av BFN/LL DA15 49 H4
GVE DA12 55 J7
SIT ME10 120 D5
Portland Cl HYTHE CT21 222 C3
KEN/WIL TN24 202 E4
Portland Ct RAM CT11 17 K4
Portland Crs ELTH/MOT SE9 47 M7
Portland Gv VX/NE SW8 24 A7
Portland Pl HART DA3 * 77 M7
SNOD ME6 113 H5
SNWD SE25 69 H8
Portland Rd BMLY BR1 71 K1
ELTH/MOT SE9 47 M7
GILL ME7 83 M7
GVW DA11 54 E4
GVW DA11 55 J6
HYTHE CT21 222 C3
ROCH ME1 113 K1
SNWD SE25 69 J8
Portland St CHAT ME4 6 F9
WALW SE17 24 E4
Portlight Pl WSTB CT5 126 B7
Portman Cl BXLY DA5 50 F6
BXLYHN DA7 49 L1
Portman Pk TON TN9 194 F2
Portmeadow Wk ABYW SE2 29 L1
Portree Ms GILL ME7 * 101 M2
Port Ri CHAT ME4 6 C7
Portsdown Cl MAIDW ME16 166 C3
Portsea Rd TIL RM18 35 K7
Portsmouth Cl STRD ME2 81 L7
Port Victoria Rd HOO/HM ME3 63 K2
Portway WSTB CT5 126 D5
Portway Gdns
WOOL/PLUM SE18 27 L7
Portway Rd HOO/HM ME3 58 C5
Post Barn Rd CHAT ME4 101 G3
Postern La TON TN9 195 G3
Postley Rd MAID/SHEP ME15 13 G8
Postling ASH TN23 204 B2
Postling Rd FOLKN CT19 219 M6
Postmill Cl CROY/NA CR0 87 K6
Postmill Dr MAID/SHEP ME15 167 G4
Post Office Rd HAWK TN18 312 C7
Post Office Sq RTW TN1 * 22 F6
Potash La BGR/WK TN15 240 H3
Potier St STHWK SE1 24 E2
Pot Kiln La RASHW TN26 301 R1
Potten Street Rd BRCH CT7 233 M6
Potters Cl CROY/NA CR0 87 M4
RASHE TN25 202 B5
Potter's La HAWK TN18 312 D3
Potter St SWCH CT13 237 K12
Pottery Rd BXLY DA5 50 D7
HOO/HM ME3 59 L8
Pottery St BERM/RHTH SE16 * 25 J1
Pottingfield Rd RYE TN31 224 F3
Poulders Rd SWCH CT13 253 R1
Poulters Wd HAYES BR2 89 L8
Poulton Cl DVW CT17 217 G1
Poulton La RCANTE CT3 235 R12
Pound Bank Cl BGR/WK TN15 111 L3
Pound Cl ORP BR6 90 E5
Pound Ct ASH TN23 204 D8
Pound Court Dr ORP BR6 90 E5
Poundfield Rd HAWK TN18 313 L12
Poundhurst Rd RASHW TN26 304 E9
Pound La ASH TN23 204 C7
CANTW/ST CT2 4 E3
RASHE TN25 289 N12
RCANTW CT4 266 A2
RCANTW CT4 291 Q5
RSEV TN14 134 C1
SEV TN13 21 J4
Pound Park Rd CHARL SE7 27 L3
Pound Pl ELTH/MOT SE9 48 B4
Pound Rd STPH/PW TN12 256 H7
Poundsbridge Hl RTON TN11 277 L9
Poundsbridge La RTON TN11 277 L7
Pounsley Rd SEV TN13 135 K7
Pout Rd SNOD ME6 113 G6
Poverest Rd STMC/STPC BR5 91 G1
Povey Av STRD ME2 82 D3
Powdermill Cl RTWE/PEM TN2 196 F5
Powder Mill La DART DA1 51 M7
RTON TN11 255 P12
STH/RUST TN4 196 E6
Powell Av RDART DA2 52 F7
Powell Cl DIT/AY ME20 140 B2
Powerscroft Rd SCUP DA14 73 K3
Power Station Rd IOS ME12 64 F6
Powis St WOOL/PLUM SE18 28 B2
Powlett Rd STRD ME2 82 D4
Powster Rd BMLY BR1 71 J2
Powys Cl BXLYHN DA7 29 L5
Poynder Rd TIL RM18 35 J7
Poynings Cl ORP BR6 91 K5
Poyntell Crs CHST BR7 72 E5
Poyntell Rd STPH/PW TN12 282 A5
Pragnell Rd LEE/GVPK SE12 47 J7
Prall's La STPH/PW TN12 278 H7
Pratling St DIT/AY ME20 140 C2
Pratt Wk LBTH SE11 24 A3
The Precincts CANT CT1 5 G3
ROCH ME1 19 J7
Premier Av CDW/CHF RM16 34 D1
Premier Pl DIT/AY ME20 139 M4
Prendergast Rd
BKHTH/KID SE3 46 F1
Prentis Cl SIT ME10 119 K4
Prentis Quay SIT ME10 120 A4
Prentiss Ct CHARL SE7 27 L3
Prescott Av STMC/STPC BR5 90 C2
Prescott Cl RDV CT15 213 M4
Presentation Ms
BRXS/STRHM SW2 44 A7
Prestbury Sq ELTH/MOT SE9 72 A1
Prestedge Av RAM CT11 183 H3
Prestley Dr TONN TN10 189 G6
Preston Av FAV ME13 149 M4
GILL ME7 101 M4
Preston Cl STHWK SE1 24 F3
Preston Dr BXLYHN DA7 29 L7
Preston Gv FAV ME13 149 K3
Preston Hall Gdns IOS ME12 230 D1
Preston Hl RCANTE CT3 235 J12
Preston La FAV ME13 149 K3
RCANTE CT3 235 J9
Preston Malthouse
FAV ME13 * 149 L3
Preston Pde WSTB CT5 126 A6
Preston Pk FAV ME13 149 L3
Preston Pl FAV ME13 * 149 L3
Preston Rd GVW DA11 54 F6
MSTR CT12 182 A2
NRWD SE19 68 C3
RCANTE CT3 235 J10
TON TN9 194 D4
Prestons Rd HAYES BR2 89 H6
Preston St FAV ME13 149 L3
Prestwood Cl
WOOL/PLUM SE18 29 H6
Prestwood Gdns CROY/NA CR0 86 D3
Pretoria Pde LEW SE13 * 26 B8
Pretoria Rd CANT CT1 5 K4
CHAT ME4 101 G3
GILL ME7 7 L7
Prettymans La EDEN TN8 193 H2
Price Rd CROY/NA CR0 86 C8
Price's Av MARG CT9 15 K5
RAM CT11 16 E6
Prickley Wd HAYES BR2 89 G4
Priddy's Yd CROY/NA CR0 * 86 D5
Pridham Rd THHTH CR7 68 E8
Pridmore Rd SNOD ME6 113 C5
Priest Av CANTW/ST CT2 171 K5
Priestfield Rd FSTH SE23 45 M8
GILL ME7 83 M8
Priest Flds HB CT6 232 A4
Priestfields ROCH ME1 100 C3
Priest Hl OXTED RH8 158 A7
Priestlands Park Rd
BFN/LL DA15 49 G8
Priestley Dr DIT/AY ME20 139 G1
Priest Wk WSTB CT5 127 J2
Priestwood Rd MEO DA13 239 N1
Prima Rd BRXN/ST SW9 24 B6
Primmett Cl BGR/WK TN15 111 K1
Primrose Av RHAM ME8 102 C8
Primrose Cl CAT SE6 70 D2
CHAT ME4 100 F6
Primrose Dr ASH TN23 204 E8
DIT/AY ME20 139 L5
Primrose Hl RCANTW CT4 170 B6
Primrose La CROY/NA CR0 87 K4
RSIT ME9 145 H3
Primrose Rd DVW CT17 213 H8
STRD ME2 98 F8
Primrose Ter GVE DA12 * 55 K6
Primrose Wk NWCR SE14 25 M6
STPH/PW TN12 279 K4
Primrose Wy MSTR CT12 181 M8
WSTB CT5 127 K4
Prince Andrew Rd
BRDST CT10 179 H6
Prince Arthur Rd GILL ME7 7 G1
Prince Charles Av EYN DA4 76 E6
IOS ME12 65 K7
SIT ME10 120 C7
WALD ME5 115 J1
Prince Charles Rd
BKHTH/KID SE3 27 G7
BRDST CT10 179 H6
Prince Consort Dr CHST BR7 72 E5
Prince Edward Prom
RAM CT11 16 E9
Prince Henry Rd CHARL SE7 27 L6
Prince Imperial Rd CHST BR7 72 C4
WOOL/PLUM SE18 28 A7
Prince John Rd ELTH/MOT SE9 47 M3
Prince of Orange La
GNWCH SE10 * 26 D6
Prince of Wales Pier DVW CT17 8 F8
Prince of Wales Rd
BKHTH/KID SE3 27 G7
Prince of Wales Rbt DVW CT17 8 C7
Prince of Wales Ter DEAL CT14 209 L4
Prince Rd SNWD SE25 86 F1
Prince Rupert Rd
ELTH/MOT SE9 48 A2
Princes Av IOS ME12 65 L6
MSTR CT12 16 D1
RDART DA2 52 C6
SAND/SEL CR2 130 A1
STMC/STPC BR5 90 F1
WALD ME5 115 H1
Princes Cl BRCH CT7 176 A6
SAND/SEL CR2 130 A1
SCUP DA14 49 L8
Princes Crs MARG CT9 15 G5
Princes Dr SWCH CT13 237 R12
Prince's Gdns MARG CT9 178 F3
Princes Pde HYTHE CT21 223 G3
Prince's Pln HAYES BR2 89 M3
Princes Ri LEW SE13 26 D8
Princes Rd DART DA1 51 J5
GVE DA12 79 K1
PGE/AN SE20 69 L3
RAM CT11 17 G3
RDART DA2 52 D6
SWLY BR8 75 H3
Princess Alice Wy THMD SE28 28 E1
Princess Anne Rd BRDST CT10 179 H6
Princess Av TIL RM18 36 D3
Princess Cl WSTB CT5 127 K2
Princesses Pde DART DA1 * 51 G3
Princess Margaret Av
MARG CT9 179 G3
MSTR CT12 16 B1
Princess Margaret Rd TIL RM18 36 C3
Princess Mary Av CHAT ME4 83 J6
Princess Pde ORP BR6 * 90 B6
Princess Rd CROY/NA CR0 86 D2
WSTB CT5 127 K2
Princess St BXLYHN DA7 50 A1
FOLKN CT19 11 L2
STHWK SE1 24 C2
Princes St DEAL CT14 209 L2
DVW CT17 8 D5
GVE DA12 55 J4
MAID/BEAR ME14 13 H3
MARG CT9 14 F4
RAM CT11 17 J6
ROCH ME1 100 D2
RTWE/PEM TN2 23 J6
Princes Ter HYTHE CT21 * 222 A4
Prince St DEPT SE8 26 A5
Princes Vw DART DA1 52 B6
Princes Wy CANTW/ST CT2 4 B3
CROY/NA CR0 86 A8
MAID/BEAR ME14 142 B4
WWKM BR4 89 G7
Princethorpe Rd SYD SE26 69 L1
Prince William Ct DEAL CT14 * 209 L2
Prinys Dr RHAM ME8 116 D1
Priolo Rd CHARL SE7 27 K4
Prior Cha GRAYS RM17 34 A3
Prioress Rd CANTW/ST CT2 4 A4
WNWD SE27 44 C8
Prioress St STHWK SE1 24 F2
Prior Rd LYDD TN29 335 L2
Priorsdean Cl MAIDW ME16 165 M4
Priorsford Av STMC/STPC BR5 73 H8
Prior St GNWCH SE10 26 D6
Prior's Wy EDEN TN8 * 275 M7
Priory Av STMC/STPC BR5 90 E2
Priory Cl BECK BR3 69 M7
BMLY BR1 72 A5
DART DA1 51 K3
MAID/SHEP ME15 166 C5
NROM TN28 330 G7
Priory Crs NRWD SE19 68 D4
Priory Dr ABYW SE2 29 L4
Priory Flds EYN DA4 94 A5
Priory Gdns CANT CT1 5 G8
DART DA1 51 L3
FOLK CT20 11 K6
SNWD SE25 69 G8
Priory Ga MAID/BEAR ME14 13 G3
Priory Gate Rd DVW CT17 8 B4
Priory Gv DIT/AY ME20 139 L4
DVW CT17 8 B4
TON TN9 194 E5
Priory Hl DART DA1 51 L4
DVW CT17 8 A4
Priory La EYN DA4 94 A4
RASHE TN25 306 H1
Priory Leas ELTH/MOT SE9 * 47 M6
Priory of St Jacob CANT CT1 4 B8
Priory Pk BKHTH/KID SE3 47 G1
DIT/AY ME20 * 139 K2
Priory Pl DART DA1 51 L4
Priory Rd CROY/NA CR0 86 B3
DART DA1 51 L2
DVE/WH CT16 8 C4
FAV ME13 149 J1
MAID/SHEP ME15 13 G6
RAM CT11 17 H7
RASHE TN25 305 M7
RHAM ME8 102 B3
STRD ME2 18 E5
TON TN9 194 F5
Priory Rw FAV ME13 123 K8
Priory Station Approach Rd
DVW CT17 8 B4
Priory St DVE/WH CT16 8 C4
TON TN9 194 E5
The Priory BKHTH/KID SE3 47 G1
CROY/NA CR0 * 86 B6
ORP BR6 * 91 J3
STHWK SE1 * 24 C1
Priory Wk TON TN9 194 E5
Priory Wy TENT TN30 315 P2
Pristling La STPH/PW TN12 281 N9
Pritchard Dr RFOLK CT18 220 B1
Priter Rd BERM/RHTH SE16 * 25 H2
Probert Rd BRXS/STRHM SW2 44 B3
Probyn Rd BRXS/STRHM SW2 44 C7
Proctor Wk RFOLK CT18 220 A1
The Progress Est
MAID/SHEP ME15 * 260 B1
Progress Wy CROY/NA CR0 86 A5
The Promenade IOS ME12 230 F3
Prospect Av STRD ME2 19 H1
Prospect Cl BELV DA17 30 B3
SYD SE26 69 J1
WGOS CT8 177 H6
Prospect Gdns MSTR CT12 180 E6
Prospect Gv GVE DA12 55 L5
Prospect Ms HYTHE CT21 * 222 D3
Prospect Pk STH/RUST TN4 196 C4
Prospect Pl BRCH CT7 * 233 M8
BRDST CT10 * 183 L1
CANT CT1 5 G7
DART DA1 51 M4
DVW CT17 213 J8
GRAYS RM17 * 34 C5
GVE DA12 55 L5
HAYES BR2 71 J7
MAIDW ME16 12 C7
ROCH ME1 * 100 B3
Prospect Rd BRCH CT7 176 C6
BRDST CT10 183 L1
FOLK CT20 223 L2
HYTHE CT21 222 D3
MSTR CT12 180 E7
RTWE/PEM TN2 23 H6
SEV TN13 21 J2
STH/RUST TN4 196 C4
Prospect Rw CHAT ME4 6 E7
GILL ME7 6 E2
Prospect St BERM/RHTH SE16 25 J1
Prospect Ter RAM CT11 17 J7
Prospect V WOOL/PLUM SE18 27 M3
Prospect Wy RASHE TN25 289 M12
Provender La FAV ME13 148 A3
Provender Wk FAV ME13 * 149 L1
Provender Wy
MAID/BEAR ME14 167 M1
Providence Sq STHWK SE1 25 H1
Providence St ASH TN23 2 C9
GRH DA9 53 H3
Provincial Ter PGE/AN SE20 * 69 L4
Puckle La CANT CT1 5 G8
Puddingcake La CRBK TN17 314 H4
Pudding La MAID/BEAR ME14 12 F4
RCANTE CT3 236 A12
Pudding Rd RHAM ME8 103 G5
Puddledock La BH/WHM TN16 187 H2
RDART DA2 74 F2
Puffin Cl CROY/NA CR0 87 L1
Puffin Rd HB CT6 129 M5
HOO/HM ME3 43 J8
Pullman Cl MSTR CT12 16 F1
Pullman Ms LEE/GVPK SE12 47 J8
Pullman Pl ELTH/MOT SE9 47 M3
Pulross Rd BRXN/ST SW9 44 A1
Pump Cl E/WMAL ME19 138 E4
Pump House Cl HAYES BR2 71 G6
Pump La MARG CT9 15 G4
NWCR SE14 25 K6
RHAM ME8 102 E2
Punch Cft HART DA3 95 M6
Purbeck Rd CHAT ME4 100 F3
Purbrook Est STHWK SE1 * 24 F1
Purbrook St STHWK SE1 24 F2
Purcell Av TONN TN10 189 J7
Purchas Ct CANTW/ST CT2 * 171 K1
Purchase La RASHW TN26 286 D10
Purelake Ms LEW SE13 * 46 E1
Purfleet By-Pass PUR RM19 32 D4
Purfleet Deep Whf PUR RM19 * 32 D5
Purland Rd THMD SE28 29 G1
Purley Wy CROY/NA CR0 86 A4
Purneys Rd ELTH/MOT SE9 47 L2
Purrett Rd WOOL/PLUM SE18 29 G4
Purser Wy GILL ME7 83 K6
Puttenden Rd RTON TN11 189 J3
Puttney Dr SIT ME10 120 B1
Pye Alley La WSTB CT5 152 D2
Pymers Md DUL SE21 44 D6
Pym Pl GRAYS RM17 34 B3
Pynham Cl ABYW SE2 29 H2
Pyott Ms CANT CT1 5 J2
Pyrmont Gv WNWD SE27 44 C8
Pyrus Cl WALD ME5 115 H5
Pyson's Rd MSTR CT12 182 F3
Pytchley Crs NRWD SE19 68 D3
Pytchley Rd EDUL SE22 44 F1

Q

Quadrangle Cl STHWK SE1 * 24 F3
The Quadrangle HNHL SE24 * 44 D3
Quadrant Rd THHTH CR7 68 C8
The Quadrant BXLYHN DA7 29 L6
PUR RM19 32 D3
Quaggy Wk BKHTH/KID SE3 47 H2
Quail Gdns CROY/NA CR0 104 D4
Quaker Cl SEV TN13 21 L3
Quaker Dr CRBK TN17 298 G7
Quaker La CRBK TN17 298 G7
Quakers Cl HART DA3 77 M7
Quaker's Hall La SEV TN13 21 J1
Quantock Cl RTWE/PEM TN2 23 M2
Quantock Dr KEN/WIL TN24 2 B2
Quantock Gdns MSTR CT12 182 E2
Quantock Ms PECK SE15 25 H8
Quantock Rd BXLYHN DA7 30 F8
The Quarries RMAID ME17 259 P1
Quarrington La RASHE TN25 288 G10
Quarry Bank TON TN9 194 D6
Quarry Cl OXTED RH8 157 K8
Quarry Gdns TON TN9 * 194 E5
Quarry Hl BGR/WK TN15 21 M2
GRAYS RM17 34 B4
Quarry Hill Rd BGR/WK TN15 240 E3
TON TN9 194 E5
Quarry Ms PUR RM19 32 B3
Quarry Ri TON TN9 194 D6
Quarry Rd GDST RH9 156 B6
HYTHE CT21 222 C2
MAID/SHEP ME15 13 G9
OXTED RH8 157 K8
RTW TN1 23 H2
Quarry Sq MAID/BEAR ME14 13 G2
Quarry Vw ASH TN23 204 A4
E/WMAL ME19 * 241 P2
Quarry Wk HYTHE CT21 223 H2
Quarry Wy WTHK RM20 33 G5
Quarry Wd RASHE TN25 305 R7
Quay House POP/IOD E14 * 26 B1
Quay La GRH DA9 53 J2
SWCH CT13 237 K12
Quayside CHAT ME4 83 J5
Quebec Av BH/WHM TN16 159 J4
Quebec Rd TIL RM18 35 H8
Quebec Sq BH/WHM TN16 159 J4
Quebec Ter DVE/WH CT16 213 J6
Quebec Wy BERM/RHTH SE16 25 L1
Queen Adelaide Rd
PGE/AN SE20 69 K3
Queen Anne Av HAYES BR2 71 H7
Queen Anne Ga BXLYHN DA7 49 L1
Queen Anne Rd
MAID/BEAR ME14 13 J4
Queen Bertha Rd RAM CT11 16 E7

Queen Bertha's Av BRCH CT7 176 F5
Queenborough Dr IOS ME12 65 J6
Queenborough Gdns CHST BR7 72 E3
Queenborough Rd
QBOR ME11 227 R2
Queendown Av RHAM ME8 102 E8
Queendown Rd BRCH CT7 181 J1
Queen Elizabeth Av
MARG CT9 179 G4
TIL RM18 36 D3
Queen Elizabeth II Br
WTHK RM20 32 F8
Queen Elizabeth Rd
DVE/WH CT16 9 G4
Queen Elizabeth's Dr
CROY/NA CR0 105 J4
Queen Elizabeth Sq
MAID/SHEP ME15 167 L7
Queen Elizabeth St STHWK SE1 25 G1
Queenhill Rd SAND/SEL CR2 104 A4
Queen Mary Av TIL RM18 36 D3
Queen Mary Rd NRWD SE19 68 C3
The Queen Mother Ct
ROCH ME1 100 C1
Queen's Av BRCH CT7 176 A6
BRDST CT10 179 L7
CANTW/ST CT2 4 C4
DVW CT17 217 H2
FOLK CT20 219 J7
HB CT6 129 L4
MAIDW ME16 12 B2
MARG CT9 14 F6
MSTR CT12 16 D2
SNOD ME6 113 H5
Queensbridge Dr HB CT6 128 D4
Queens Cottages WADH TN5 309 K4
Queens Ct HAWK TN18 312 D7
KEN/WIL TN24 2 C3
MARG CT9 15 K2
Queenscroft Rd ELTH/MOT SE9 47 L3
Queensdown Rd DEAL CT14 211 K5
Queen's Dr RSEV TN14 136 B6
Queen's Farm Rd GVE DA12 56 F7
Queen's Gdns DVE/WH CT16 8 D4
HB CT6 129 G4
RDART DA2 52 C6
STH/RUST TN4 196 E7
Queens Garth FSTH SE23 * 45 K7
Queens Gate Gdns CHST BR7 72 E5
Queen's Gate Rd RAM CT11 16 F4
Queens House MAIDW ME16 166 B2
Queen's Mead Rd HAYES BR2 71 G6
Queens Ms DEAL CT14 209 L3
FOLK CT20 * 223 L2
Queens Pde FAV ME13 * 149 L2
MARG CT9 15 K2
Queen's Ri DEAL CT14 211 G4
Queen's Rd BECK BR3 69 M6
BMLY BR1 71 H6
BRDST CT10 183 L1
CHST BR7 72 C3
CROY/NA CR0 86 C2
ERITH DA8 30 F5
FAV ME13 149 J2
GILL ME7 7 K5
GVE DA12 55 K8
HAWK TN18 312 D7
IOS ME12 65 L6
KEN/WIL TN24 2 C3
KEN/WIL TN24 3 M7
LYDD TN29 334 D3
MAIDW ME16 12 A4
NROM TN28 331 K7
PECK SE15 25 K7
RAM CT11 17 M4
RCANTE CT3 236 A11
RCANTE CT3 251 Q12
SNOD ME6 113 H5
STH/RUST TN4 22 F1
WALD ME5 101 L4
WELL DA16 29 J8
WGOS CT8 177 J5
WSTB CT5 127 G3
Queens Rd Upper KEN/WIL TN24 2 B2
Queens Rw WALW SE17 24 E5
Queensthorpe Ms SYD SE26 * 69 L1
Queensthorpe Rd SYD SE26 69 L1
Queen St ASH TN23 2 B5
BXLYHN DA7 50 A1
CHAT ME4 6 E5
CROY/NA CR0 86 D7
DEAL CT14 209 L3
DVE/WH CT16 8 D5
E/WMAL ME19 164 B2
ERITH DA8 * 30 F5
FOLK CT20 11 L4
GVE DA12 55 J4
HAWK TN18 313 J10
HB CT6 129 G4
MARG CT9 14 F4
RAM CT11 17 J7
ROCH ME1 19 K9
STPH/PW TN12 279 M4
Queen's Wy IOS ME12 64 B5
MAID/BEAR ME14 142 B4
Queensway HOO/HM ME3 41 L4
LYDD TN29 321 J7
LYDD TN29 334 D3
STMC/STPC BR5 90 D1
WWKM BR4 89 H7
Queenswood Av THHTH CR7 86 B1
Queenswood Rd BFN/LL DA15 49 G4
DIT/AY ME20 114 E6
FSTH SE23 45 M8
Queen Victoria Rw
DVE/WH CT16 * 8 C4
Quentin Pl LEW SE13 46 F1
Quentin Rd BKHTH/KID SE3 46 F1
Quentins Dr BH/WHM TN16 * 133 G2
Quentins Wk BH/WHM TN16 * 133 G2
Quernmore Cl BMLY BR1 71 H3
Quernmore Rd BMLY BR1 71 H3
Quern Rd DEAL CT14 209 H7
Querns Pl CANT CT1 5 K4
Querns Rd CANT CT1 5 L4
The Quern MAID/SHEP ME15 166 F4
Quested Rd FOLKN CT19 219 M7
Quested Wy RMAID ME17 242 E11
Questor DART DA1 * 52 A7
Quetta Rd MSTR CT12 182 C4
Quex Rd WGOS CT8 177 J5
Quex View Rd BRCH CT7 176 D8
Quickbourne La RYE TN31 325 L6
Quickrells Av HOO/HM ME3 38 C8
Quickstep Cl SIT ME10 120 A1
Quickthorn Crs WALD ME5 100 F8
Quiet Nook HAYES BR2 89 L6
Quilp St STHWK SE1 * 24 D1
Quilter Rd STMC/STPC BR5 91 K4
Quilter St WOOL/PLUM SE18 29 G4
Quince Orch RASHW TN26 318 D2
Quince Rd LEW SE13 26 C8
Quincewood Gdns TONN TN10 188 E6
Quinion Cl WALD ME5 115 G5
Quinnell St RHAM ME8 102 F4
Quinton Cl BECK BR3 70 D7
Quinton Rd RSIT ME9 119 K2
Quixote Crs STRD ME2 82 C4
Quorn Rd EDUL SE22 44 F2

R

Rabbit Hole RCANTW CT4 270 F6
Rabbits Rd EYN DA4 77 G6
Rablus Pl EYN DA4 * 94 A2
Racefield Cl GVE DA12 80 F3
Rackham Cl WELL DA16 29 J8
Radcliffe Rd CROY/NA CR0 87 G5
STHWK SE1 24 F2
Radcot St LBTH SE11 24 B4
Radfall Ride WSTB CT5 127 K8
Radfall Rd WSTB CT5 127 K7
Radfield Wy ELTH/MOT SE9 48 E5
Radford Rd LEW SE13 46 D4
Radleigh Gdns CHAT ME4 100 F4
Radlet Av SYD SE26 45 J8
Radley Cl BRDST CT10 179 K7
Radley Ct BERM/RHTH SE16 25 L1
Radnor Av WELL DA16 49 J3
Radnor Bridge Rd FOLK CT20 11 L4
Radnor Cliff FOLK CT20 10 C9
FOLK CT20 11 K7
Radnor Cliff Crs FOLK CT20 10 B8
Radnor Cl CHST BR7 72 F3
HB CT6 129 J8
Radnor Crs WOOL/PLUM SE18 29 H6
Radnor Park Av FOLKN CT19 10 F3
Radnor Park Crs FOLKN CT19 11 H4
Radnor Park Gdns FOLKN CT19 11 H3
Radnor Park Rd FOLKN CT19 11 H3
Radnor Pk West FOLKN CT19 10 F4
Radnor Rd PECK SE15 25 H6
Radnor St FOLKN CT19 11 M5
Radnor Wk CROY/NA CR0 87 M3
Raeburn Av DART DA1 51 J3
Raeburn Cl TONN TN10 189 H7
Raeburn Rd BFN/LL DA15 48 F4
Rafford Wy BMLY BR1 71 J6
Raggatt Pl MAID/SHEP ME15 13 K8
Ragge Wy BGR/WK TN15 136 E6
Raggleswood CHST BR7 72 B5
Rag Hill Rd BH/WHM TN16 132 C7
Raglan Ct CROY/NA CR0 86 C8
Raglan Rd BELV DA17 30 A3
HAYES BR2 71 K8
WOOL/PLUM SE18 28 D4
Ragstone Ct DIT/AY ME20 139 K5
Ragstone Hollow RASHE TN25 305 R7
Ragstone Rd
MAID/SHEP ME15 168 B3
Railton Rd HNHL SE24 44 B3
Railway Ap TON TN9 194 E5
Railway Ar BRXN/ST SW9 * 44 B2
Railway Av BERM/RHTH SE16 25 K1
WSTB CT5 126 F4
Railway Gv NWCR SE14 26 A6
Railway Hl RCANTW CT4 270 D6
Railway Pl BELV DA17 30 B2
Railway Ri EDUL SE22 44 F2
Railway Rd IOS ME12 64 C3
Railway St CHAT ME4 6 C6
GILL ME7 7 L3
GVW DA11 54 B3
Railway Ter BH/WHM TN16 159 J3
LEW SE13 46 C3
MARG CT9 * 14 D6
QBOR ME11 64 B8
Rainbow Av POP/IOD E14 26 C4
Rainbow Rd CDW/CHF RM16 33 L3
PUR RM19 32 F2
Rainbow St CMBW SE5 24 F6
Rainham Cl ELTH/MOT SE9 48 F4
MAID/SHEP ME15 167 H4
Rainham Rd GILL ME7 7 J8
Rainham Vls STPH/PW TN12 * 258 F9
Rainsborough Av DEPT SE8 25 M3
Rainton Rd CHARL SE7 27 H4
Raleigh Cl ERITH DA8 31 G5
KEN/WIL TN24 3 M9
WALD ME5 101 H7
Raleigh Gdns
BRXS/STRHM SW2 44 A4
Raleigh Ms ORP BR6 91 G8
Raleigh Rd PGE/AN SE20 69 L4
Raleigh Wy IOS ME12 64 F7
Ralph Perring Ct BECK BR3 70 B8
Ramac Wy CHARL SE7 27 J3
Ramillies Cl WALD ME5 101 H8
Ramillies Rd BFN/LL DA15 49 J4
Ram La RASHW TN26 286 B1
Rammell Ms CRBK TN17 298 G9
Rampion Cl MAID/BEAR ME14 141 M8
Ramsden Cl STMC/STPC BR5 91 K4
Ramsden La CRBK TN17 313 Q5
Ramsden Rd ERITH DA8 30 E6
ORP BR6 91 J3
Ramsey Cl CANTW/ST CT2 4 C2
Ramsey Rd THHTH CR7 86 A2
Ramsgate Rd BRDST CT10 183 J3
MARG CT9 15 G7
SWCH CT13 237 K5
Ramslye Rd STH/RUST TN4 200 E4
Ramstone Cl RASHE TN25 289 M12
Ramus Wood Av ORP BR6 90 F8
Rancliffe Gdns ELTH/MOT SE9 47 M2
Rancorn Rd MARG CT9 14 A6
Randall Cl ERITH DA8 30 D5
Randall Hill Rd BGR/WK TN15 238 E10
Randall Pl GNWCH SE10 26 D6
Randall Rd CHAT ME4 100 F4
LBTH SE11 24 A4
Randall Rw LBTH SE11 24 A3
Randall St MAID/BEAR ME14 12 F1
Randisbourne Gdns CAT SE6 * 46 C8
Randlesdown Rd CAT SE6 70 B1
Randle's La ORP BR6 108 C8
Randle Wy RSIT ME9 120 F7
Randolph Cl BXLYHN DA7 50 D1
CANT CT1 5 H8
Randolph Gdns KEN/WIL TN24 203 H6
Randolph La RYE TN31 327 L10
Randolph Rd DVW CT17 213 H8
GILL ME7 7 K4
HAYES BR2 90 A4
Randolph Sq MARG CT9 * 15 H3
Ranelagh Gdns GVW DA11 55 G5
Ranelagh Gv BRDST CT10 179 H8
Ranelagh Rd DEAL CT14 209 L4
IOS ME12 64 D3
Rangefield Rd BMLY BR1 70 F2
Range Rd GVE DA12 55 L5
HYTHE CT21 222 C5
IOS ME12 229 N4
Rangeworth Pl BFN/LL DA15 49 G8
Rankine Rd RTWE/PEM TN2 197 G6
Ranleigh Gdns BXLYHN DA7 30 A6
Ranmore Av CROY/NA CR0 87 G6
Ranmore Pth STMC/STPC BR5 73 H8
Ranscombe Cl STRD ME2 81 L8
Ransom Rd CHARL SE7 * 27 K4
Ranters La CRBK TN17 296 H9
Ranworth Cl ERITH DA8 30 F8
Raphael Av TIL RM18 35 H7
Raphael Rd GVE DA12 55 L5
Rapier Cl PUR RM19 32 A3
Rashleigh Wy EYN DA4 76 D8
Raspberry Hill La RSIT ME9 227 L7
Ratcliffe Cl LEE/GVPK SE12 47 H5
Ratcliffe Hwy HOO/HM ME3 59 J8
Rathbone Sq CROY/NA CR0 * 86 D7
Rathfern Rd CAT SE6 46 A6
Rathgar Rd BRXN/ST SW9 44 C1
Rathmore Rd CHARL SE7 27 J4
GVW DA11 55 H5
Ratling Rd RCANTE CT3 251 R11
Rattington St RCANTW CT4 248 F7
Rattray Rd BRXS/STRHM SW2 44 B2
Raul Rd PECK SE15 25 H8
Raven Cl DIT/AY ME20 139 H4
Ravencroft CDW/CHF RM16 35 J1
Ravencroft Crs ELTH/MOT SE9 48 A8
Ravenlea Rd FOLK CT20 10 D5
Ravensbourne Av HAYES BR2 70 E5
Ravensbourne Pk BROCKY SE4 46 B5
Ravensbourne Park Crs
CAT SE6 46 A5
Ravensbourne Pl DEPT SE8 26 C8
Ravensbourne Rd BMLY BR1 71 H7
CAT SE6 46 A5
DART DA1 51 H1
Ravensbury Rd
STMC/STPC BR5 73 G8
Ravenscar Rd BMLY BR1 70 F1
Ravens Cl HAYES BR2 71 G6
Ravenscourt Rd
CANTW/ST CT2 171 J2
DEAL CT14 209 K4
STMC/STPC BR5 73 H7
Ravenscroft Rd BECK BR3 69 K6
Ravensdale Gdns NRWD SE19 68 E4
Ravens Dane Cl
MAID/SHEP ME15 168 B4
Ravensdon St LBTH SE11 24 B4
Ravenshead Cl SAND/SEL CR2 104 B5
Ravenshill CHST BR7 72 C5
Ravensmead Rd HAYES BR2 70 E4
Ravens Ms BKHTH/KID SE3 * 47 H3
Ravens Wy LEE/GVPK SE12 47 H3
Ravenswood BXLY DA5 49 M6
Ravenswood Av
RTWE/PEM TN2 196 F7
STRD ME2 19 H1
WWKM BR4 88 D4
Ravenswood Crs WWKM BR4 88 D4
Ravenswood Rd CROY/NA CR0 86 C6
Ravensworth Rd
ELTH/MOT SE9 72 A1
Ravent Rd LBTH SE11 24 A3
Ravine Gv WOOL/PLUM SE18 28 F5
Rawdon Rd MAID/SHEP ME15 13 H7
RAM CT11 16 D7
Rawlings Cl BECK BR3 88 D1
ORP BR6 91 G8
Rawling St RSIT ME9 146 A5
Rawlins Cl SAND/SEL CR2 104 E2
Rawlyn Cl CDW/CHF RM16 33 K4
Ray Bell Ct BROCKY SE4 * 26 A8
Rayfield Cl HAYES BR2 89 M2
Rayfield Ct SNOD ME6 113 H4
Rayford Av LEE/GVPK SE12 47 G5
Rayford Cl DART DA1 51 K3
Rayham Rd WSTB CT5 127 H5
Ray Lamb Wy ERITH DA8 31 J5
Ray La LING RH7 190 B6
Rayleas Cl WOOL/PLUM SE18 28 C7
Rayleigh Cl MAIDW ME16 140 E6
Raymead Av THHTH CR7 86 B1
Raymere Gdns
WOOL/PLUM SE18 28 E6
Raymer Rd MAID/BEAR ME14 141 J5
Raymond Av CANT CT1 5 G7
Raymond Cl SYD SE26 69 K2
Raymond Fuller Wy
KEN/WIL TN24 203 H7
Raymond Rd BECK BR3 69 M8
Raymoor Av LYDD TN29 320 F12
Raymouth Rd
BERM/RHTH SE16 25 J3
Rayners Hl RMAID ME17 263 L1
Rays Hl EYN DA4 76 D8
Rays Rd WWKM BR4 88 D3
Reach Cl RDV CT15 215 G4
Reachfields HYTHE CT21 222 B4
Reach Rd HYTHE CT21 307 K10
RDV CT15 215 G4
Reader's Bridge Rd
TENT TN30 301 L10
Readers La RYE TN31 327 J9
Reading Cl DEAL CT14 209 J8
Reading Rd DVW CT17 217 G2
Reading St BRDST CT10 179 J5
TENT TN30 316 C5
Reading Street Rd
BRDST CT10 179 H5
Readscroft Rd RHAM ME8 102 E8
Read Wy GVE DA12 79 L2
The Rear STH/RUST TN4 * 22 E7
Reaston St NWCR SE14 25 K6
Recce La RFOLK CT18 292 F5
Record St PECK SE15 25 K5
Recreation Av SNOD ME6 113 H5
Recreation Cl
MAID/BEAR ME14 13 J1
Recreation Ground Rd
TENT TN30 315 N2
Recreation Rd HAYES BR2 71 G6
SYD SE26 69 L1
Recreation Wy SIT ME10 227 N12
Rectory Cl DART DA1 50 F2
RASHW TN26 302 H11
ROCH ME1 99 K8
SCUP DA14 73 J1
SNOD ME6 113 H5
Rectory Dr STH/RUST TN4 277 R6
Rectory Field Crs CHARL SE7 27 K6
Rectory Flds CRBK TN17 298 G8
Rectory Gdns BECK BR3 * 70 B5
CHST BR7 * 72 D5
WSTB CT5 127 L3
Rectory Gra ROCH ME1 100 D3
Rectory Gn BECK BR3 70 A5
Rectory Gv CROY/NA CR0 86 C5
Rectory La BGR/WK TN15 240 B4
BH/WHM TN16 158 D1
BH/WHM TN16 160 B2
HYTHE CT21 218 C8
MAIDW ME16 166 B4
RCANTW CT4 270 F4
RFOLK CT18 291 M11
RMAID ME17 242 F12
RMAID ME17 260 D7
RYE TN31 325 G1
RYE TN31 325 N9
SCUP DA14 73 J1
SEV TN13 21 J8
Rectory La North
E/WMAL ME19 138 E3
Rectory La South
E/WMAL ME19 138 F3
Rectory Meadow MEO DA13 78 B3
Rectory Park Rd
STPH/PW TN12 296 H3
Rectory Pl CHST BR7 * 72 D5
WOOL/PLUM SE18 28 B3
Rectory Rd BECK BR3 70 B5
BGR/WK TN15 96 D8
BRDST CT10 179 L8
DEAL CT14 209 G5
GRAYS RM17 34 E2
HAYES BR2 106 C2
HOO/HM ME3 58 B3
LYDD TN29 320 A12
SIT ME10 120 C6
SWCM DA10 53 M5
TIL RM18 35 L5
Rectory Wy KEN/WIL TN24 202 F6
Reculver Av BRCH CT7 176 B6
Reculver Cl HB CT6 232 A3
Reculver Dr HB CT6 129 M4
Reculver La HB CT6 232 C4
Reculver Rd BERM/RHTH SE16 25 L3
HB CT6 129 K5
Reculvers Rd WGOS CT8 177 J6
Redan Pl IOS ME12 * 64 E3
Redan Ter CMBW SE5 24 C8
Redbank E/WMAL ME19 138 F3
Red Barracks Rd
WOOL/PLUM SE18 28 A3
Redberry Gv SYD SE26 45 K8
Redberry Rd ASH TN23 204 E6
Redbridge Cl WALD ME5 * 101 J8
Redbridge Gdns CMBW SE5 24 F6
Redbrook St RASHW TN26 302 D7
Redbrooks Wy HYTHE CT21 222 A2
Redcar St CMBW SE5 * 24 D6
Red Cedars Rd ORP BR6 90 F3
Redcliffe La MAID/BEAR ME14 141 J6
Redcot La RCANTE CT3 173 J2
Redcross Wy STHWK SE1 24 D1
Redding Cl RDART DA2 52 F7
Reddins Rd PECK SE15 25 H6
Reddons Rd BECK BR3 69 M4
Reddy Rd ERITH DA8 31 G5
Rede Court Rd STRD ME2 18 A2
Rede Wood Rd MAIDW ME16 165 M2
Redfern Av GILL ME7 83 M8
Redfern Rd CAT SE6 46 D5
Redford Av THHTH CR7 68 A8
Redgate Dr HAYES BR2 89 J5
Redgrave Cl SNWD SE25 87 G2
Red Hl CHST BR7 72 B2
WBY/YAL ME18 164 F5
Redhill Rd BGR/WK TN15 95 M7
WGOS CT8 177 G5
Redhill Wd HART DA3 96 B7
Red House Gdns
WBY/YAL ME18 164 E6
Red House La BXLYHS DA6 49 L2
Redhouse La RCANTW CT4 249 M9
Redhouse Rd BH/WHM TN16 132 B7
Redhouse Wall DEAL CT14 207 J8
Redland Shaw ROCH ME1 100 F4
Redlands Rd SEV TN13 20 D5
Red La OXTED RH8 185 J3
Redleaf Cl BELV DA17 30 B5
RTWE/PEM TN2 197 G7
Red Lion Cl STMC/STPC BR5 91 K2
WALW SE17 24 E5
Red Lion La WOOL/PLUM SE18 28 B7
Red Lion Pl WOOL/PLUM SE18 * 28 B7
Red Lion Rw WALW SE17 24 D5
Red Lodge Crs BXLY DA5 50 E8
Red Lodge Rd BXLY DA5 50 E8
WWKM BR4 88 D4
Redmans La RSEV TN14 109 L1
Redmill Cl FOLK CT20 219 M8
Red Oak HAWK TN18 312 B9
Red Oak Cl ORP BR6 90 C6
Redoubt Wy LYDD TN29 321 N5
Redpoll Wk STPH/PW TN12 279 K4
Redpoll Wy ERITHM DA18 29 L2
Red Post Hl HNHL SE24 44 E3
Redriff Rd BERM/RHTH SE16 25 M2
Redroofs Cl BECK BR3 70 C5
Redsells Cl MAID/SHEP ME15 168 B4
Redshank Rd CHAT ME4 83 H4
Redstart Cl CROY/NA CR0 105 J4
NWCR SE14 * 25 M6
Red St MEO DA13 78 C3
Redsull Av DEAL CT14 209 H6
Red Tree Orch ASH TN23 204 B4
Redvers Rd CHAT ME4 6 E9
WARL CR6 130 C4
Redwall La RMAID ME17 258 G6
Redwell Gv E/WMAL ME19 164 D3
Redwell La BGR/WK TN15 240 B5
Redwing Cl SAND/SEL CR2 104 C5
Redwing Ct ORP BR6 91 H3
Redwing Ms CMBW SE5 24 D8
Redwing Rd WALD ME5 101 J7
Redwings La RTWE/PEM TN2 278 B7
Redwood Cl BFN/LL DA15 49 H6
CANTW/ST CT2 4 C1
WALD ME5 115 J3
Redwood Pk RTON TN11 278 D4
Redyear Ct KEN/WIL TN24 3 M6
Reed Av CANT CT1 172 D7
ORP BR6 90 F6
Reed Cl LEE/GVPK SE12 47 H3
Reed Crs ASH TN23 204 F8
Reedham Crs HOO/HM ME3 58 D6
Reedham St PECK SE15 * 25 H8
Reedland Crs FAV ME13 149 K1
Reedmace Cl ASH TN23 204 A3
Reeds Cl HB CT6 129 J5
Reeds La RTON TN11 240 D12
Reed St HOO/HM ME3 38 C7
Reedworth St LBTH SE11 24 B3
Rees Gdns CROY/NA CR0 87 G2
Reeves Cl STPH/PW TN12 281 R5
Reeves Cnr CROY/NA CR0 86 C5
Reeves Ct DIT/AY ME20 139 H4
Reeves Crs SWLY BR8 74 E7
Reeves Rd WOOL/PLUM SE18 28 C5
Reeves Ter WADH TN5 310 F8
Reeves Wy WSTB CT5 127 K4
Reform Rd CHAT ME4 7 G8
Regency Cl BGR/WK TN15 111 K1
RHAM ME8 116 D2
Regency Ct SIT ME10 119 L5
Regency Ms BECK BR3 70 D5
Regency Pl CANT CT1 5 K1
Regency Wk CROY/NA CR0 87 M2
Regency Wy BXLYHN DA7 49 L1
Regeneration Rd
BERM/RHTH SE16 * 25 L3
Regent Cl CDW/CHF RM16 34 D1
Regent Dr MAID/SHEP ME15 167 H5
Regent Pl RTWE/PEM TN2 * 23 L5
Regent Rd GILL ME7 7 H5
HNHL SE24 44 C4
Regents Ct ASH TN23 2 A4
Regents Dr HAYES BR2 89 L8
Regents Pl ASH TN23 2 A4
Regent Sq BELV DA17 30 C3
Regent St CRBK TN17 314 D6
WSTB CT5 126 E3
Regent Wy E/WMAL ME19 164 D2
Reginald Av STRD ME2 99 K2
Reginald Rd DEPT SE8 26 B6
MAIDW ME16 12 D7
Reginald Sq DEPT SE8 26 B6
Regina Rd SNWD SE25 69 H7
Regis Crs SIT ME10 120 A2
Reidhaven Rd
WOOL/PLUM SE18 28 F3
Reigate Rd BMLY BR1 47 H7
Reinden Gv MAID/SHEP ME15 168 A4
Relf Rd PECK SE15 45 H1
Reliance Ar BRXN/ST SW9 * 44 B2
Rembrandt Cl POP/IOD E14 26 E2
TONN TN10 189 H7
Rembrandt Dr GVW DA11 54 E8
Rembrandt Rd LEW SE13 46 F2
Remus Cl ASH TN23 204 C7
Rendezvous St FOLK CT20 11 K5
The Rendezvous MARG CT9 14 F3
Rendle Cl CROY/NA CR0 87 G1
Renforth St BERM/RHTH SE16 25 K1
Renfrew Rd LBTH SE11 24 C3
Rennell St LEW SE13 46 D1
Rennets Cl ELTH/MOT SE9 48 E3
Rennets Wood Rd
ELTH/MOT SE9 48 E3
Rennie Est BERM/RHTH SE16 25 J3
Renown Cl CROY/NA CR0 86 C4
Renown Rd WALD ME5 115 K3
Renshaw Cl BELV DA17 30 A5
Rentain Rd RCANTW CT4 248 E7
Renton Cl BRXS/STRHM SW2 * 44 A4
Renton Dr STMC/STPC BR5 91 L3
Rephidim St STHWK SE1 24 F2
Repository Rd
WOOL/PLUM SE18 28 A5
Repton Cl BRDST CT10 179 J7
Repton Ct BECK BR3 70 C5
Repton Manor Rd ASH TN23 202 D8
Repton Rd ORP BR6 91 H7
Repton Wy WALD ME5 115 G1
Reservoir Av LYDD TN29 335 N11
Reservoir Cl GRH DA9 53 K4
THHTH CR7 68 E7
Reservoir Rd BROCKY SE4 25 M8
WSTB CT5 126 F3
Resolution Cl WALD ME5 101 H8
Resolution Wy DEPT SE8 26 B6
Restell Cl BKHTH/KID SE3 26 F5
Rest Harrow FAV ME13 246 B4
Restharrow Rd
MAID/BEAR ME14 167 M1
Restharrow Wy CHAT ME4 83 K4
Restmore Cl HOO/HM ME3 58 B1
Restons Crs ELTH/MOT SE9 48 E4
The Retreat BRCH CT7 176 E5
GRAYS RM17 34 C5
MSTR CT12 16 C2
ORP BR6 108 A1
SEV TN13 * 21 J5
THHTH CR7 68 E8
Rettendon Dr SIT ME10 120 A1
Reveley Sq BERM/RHTH SE16 25 M1
Revell Ri WOOL/PLUM SE18 29 G5
Revelon Rd BROCKY SE4 45 M2
Revenge Rd MAID/BEAR ME14 115 K5
Reventlow Rd ELTH/MOT SE9 48 D6
Reverdy Rd STHWK SE1 25 H3
Reynard Cl BMLY BR1 72 A7
Reynard Dr NRWD SE19 69 G4
Reynard Pl NWCR SE14 * 25 M5
Reynolds Cl HB CT6 129 J5
TONN TN10 189 H7
Reynolds Flds HOO/HM ME3 57 K7
Reynolds La RCANTE CT3 232 D6
STH/RUST TN4 196 C7
Reynolds Pl BKHTH/KID SE3 27 J6
Reynolds Rd PECK SE15 45 K3
Reynolds Wy CROY/NA CR0 86 F7
Rhee Wall RASHW TN26 317 M10
Rheims Ct CANTW/ST CT2 4 A3
Rheims Wy CANTW/ST CT2 4 B3
Rhodaus Cl CANT CT1 4 F6
Rhodaus Town CANT CT1 4 F6
Rhodes Gdns BRDST CT10 179 J7
Rhode St CHAT ME4 6 E6
Rhodewood Cl
MAID/SHEP ME15 168 B4
Rhododendron Av MEO DA13 239 M3
Ribblesdale Rd RDART DA2 52 D6
Ribbon Dance Ms CMBW SE5 24 E7
Ribston Cl HAYES BR2 90 A4
Ribston Gdns STPH/PW TN12 278 H2
Rice Pde STMC/STPC BR5 * 90 E1
Richard Cl WOOL/PLUM SE18 27 M3
Richard's Cl RTON TN11 254 G11
Richardson Cl GRH DA9 53 G3
Richardson Rd STH/RUST TN4 196 D7
Richardson Wy MSTR CT12 181 M7
Richard St CHAT ME4 6 D6
ROCH ME1 100 D2
Richard Watts Ct CHAT ME4 * 6 C4
Richborne Ter VX/NE SW8 24 A6
Richborough Cl
STMC/STPC BR5 73 L8
Richborough Dr STRD ME2 82 B4
Richborough Rd SWCH CT13 236 H11
WGOS CT8 177 J6
Richborough Wy ASH TN23 204 B6
Richdore Rd RCANTW CT4 267 R7
Richmer Rd ERITH DA8 31 H6
Richmond Av MARG CT9 15 L6
Richmond Cl BH/WHM TN16 132 A5
STRD ME2 83 G4
WALD ME5 115 J1
Richmond Dr HB CT6 129 M5
NROM TN28 331 K5
SIT ME10 119 M2
Richmond Gdns
CANTW/ST CT2 171 K3
Richmond Meech Dr
KEN/WIL TN24 203 H7
Richmond Pl RTWE/PEM TN2 201 J5
WOOL/PLUM SE18 28 D3
Richmond Rd GRAYS RM17 34 D5
RAM CT11 17 G6
THHTH CR7 68 C8
WSTB CT5 127 J4
Richmond St FOLKN CT19 219 L7
HB CT6 129 G4
IOS ME12 64 E3
Richmond Wy
MAID/SHEP ME15 167 H5
Richmount Gdns
BKHTH/KID SE3 47 H1
Rickard Cl BRXS/STRHM SW2 44 B6
Ricketts Hill Rd
BH/WHM TN16 132 C4
Riddlesdale Av STH/RUST TN4 196 D7
Riddles Rd SIT ME10 119 K6
Riddons Rd LEE/GVPK SE12 47 K8
Rideout St WOOL/PLUM SE18 28 A3
Rider Cl BFN/LL DA15 48 F4
Ridge Av DART DA1 51 G4
Ridgebrook Rd BKHTH/KID SE3 47 K2
Ridge Cl THMD SE28 28 E1
Ridgecroft Cl BXLY DA5 50 D6
Ridgelands RRTW TN3 277 R5
Ridge La MEO DA13 239 N3
Ridgemount Av CROY/NA CR0 87 L5
The Ridge BXLY DA5 50 A5
CTHM CR3 157 K3
KEN/WIL TN24 203 H6
ORP BR6 90 E5
RRTW TN3 * 199 H7

Ridge Wy DART DA1 51 G4
EDEN TN8 192 D1
Ridgeway BUR/ETCH TN19 322 F2
GRAYS RM17 34 F3
HAYES BR2 89 H5
HYTHE CT21 307 M10
RDART DA2 76 F2
RTWE/PEM TN2 278 A10
WSTB CT5 127 K4
Ridgeway Av GVE DA12 55 J8
Ridgeway Cliff HB CT6 128 D4
Ridgeway Crs ORP BR6 90 F6
TONN TN10 195 G1
Ridgeway Crescent Gdns
ORP BR6 90 F5
Ridgeway Dr BMLY BR1 71 J1
Ridgeway East BFN/LL DA15 49 G3
The Ridgewaye
STH/RUST TN4 196 E4
Ridgeway Rd HB CT6 155 H2
The Ridgeway BRDST CT10 183 H2
CHAT ME4 100 F6
CROY/NA CR0 86 A6
DVW CT17 212 F7
FAV ME13 151 H6
GILL ME7 * 83 K6
GVE DA12 80 F4
MARG CT9 15 M6
RASHE TN25 289 K12
TON TN9 195 G1
Ridgeway Wk HB CT6 155 H2
Ridgeway West BFN/LL DA15 48 F3
Ridgewell Cl SYD SE26 70 A1
Ridgewood HART DA3 78 D6
Ridgway MAIDW ME16 166 C3
Ridgway Rd BRXN/ST SW9 44 C1
Ridham Av SIT ME10 227 P12
Riding Gate Rbt CANT CT1 4 F6
Riding Hl KEN/WIL TN24 202 F5
Riding La RTON TN11 188 A6
Riding Pk RTON TN11 188 A6
The Ridings BH/WHM TN16 132 D3
CANT CT1 * 5 J2
MARG CT9 179 H2
RTWE/PEM TN2 197 J7
STPH/PW TN12 279 K2
WSTB CT5 127 L4
Ridlands Gv OXTED RH8 158 D8
Ridlands La OXTED RH8 158 D8
Ridlands Ri OXTED RH8 158 D8
Ridley Cl HB CT6 155 H1
Ridley Rd HAYES BR2 71 G7
ROCH ME1 19 H9
WARL CR6 130 B4
WELL DA16 29 J7
Ridsdale Rd PGE/AN SE20 69 J5
Riefield Rd ELTH/MOT SE9 48 E2
Riesco Dr CROY/NA CR0 104 B1
Rigby Cl CROY/NA CR0 86 B6
Rigby Gdns CDW/CHF RM16 35 J3
Rigden Rd ASH TN23 204 E4
Rigshill Rd FAV ME13 244 F12
Riley Av HB CT6 128 A5
Riley Rd STHWK SE1 25 G2
Rill Wk EGRIN RH19 274 A12
Ring Cl BMLY BR1 71 J4
Ringden Av STPH/PW TN12 278 H4
Ringer's Rd BMLY BR1 71 H7
Ringlestone Crs
MAID/BEAR ME14 141 G5
Ringlestone Rd RMAID ME17 242 E5
Ringlet Rd CHAT ME4 83 J3
Ringmer Wy BMLY BR1 90 A1
Ringmore Ri FSTH SE23 45 J5
Ringold Av MSTR CT12 16 B2
Ringshall Rd CHST BR7 73 H7
Rings Hl RTON TN11 255 Q9
Ringside EDEN TN8 192 D2
Ringstead Rd CAT SE6 46 C5
Ring Wall DEAL CT14 206 F7
Ringwold Cl BECK BR3 69 M4
Ringwood Av ORP BR6 108 B4
Ringwood Cl CANTW/ST CT2 171 M2
RHAM ME8 102 E6
Ringwood Rd
MAID/SHEP ME15 167 K5
Ringwould Rd DEAL CT14 211 J4
RDV CT15 210 E5
Ripley Cl BMLY BR1 90 A1
CROY/NA CR0 105 H1
Ripley Rd BELV DA17 30 B3
KEN/WIL TN24 3 M9
Ripon Cl RHAM ME8 102 E2
Ripon Rd WOOL/PLUM SE18 28 C5
Rippersley Rd WELL DA16 29 H7
Ripple Rd DEAL CT14 210 F3
Rippolson Rd
WOOL/PLUM SE18 29 G4
Risborough Barracks
FOLK CT20 * 219 L8
Risborough La FOLK CT20 219 L8
Risborough St STHWK SE1 * 24 C1
Risborough Wy FOLK CT20 219 M7
Risden La HAWK TN18 312 G10
Risdon Cl CANTW/ST CT2 173 G3
Risdon St BERM/RHTH SE16 25 K1
Risedale Rd BXLYHN DA7 50 C1
Riseden Rd WADH TN5 308 H9
Riseldine Rd FSTH SE23 45 M4
The Rise ASH TN23 204 B4
BXLY DA5 49 K5
DART DA1 51 G2
DEAL CT14 211 K4
GILL ME7 116 B2
GVE DA12 79 M1
IOS ME12 64 D8
RDV CT15 215 J3
ROCH ME1 100 E2
RSIT ME9 119 J7
SAND/SEL CR2 104 B3
SEV TN13 162 B6
Rising Rd ASH TN23 204 D2
Ritchie Rd CROY/NA CR0 87 J2
Ritch Rd SNOD ME6 112 F5
Ritter St WOOL/PLUM SE18 28 B5
Rivendell Cl HOO/HM ME3 43 J8
River Bank Cl MAID/SHEP ME15 13 J5
Riverbank Rd BMLY BR1 47 H8
River Barge Cl POP/IOD E14 26 D1
River Cl MAID/SHEP ME15 166 C6
River Ct RCANTW CT4 248 E7
River Dl DVW CT17 213 G6
Riverdale Est TON TN9 * 195 G5
Riverdale Rd BXLY DA5 50 A5
CANT CT1 172 C6
ERITH DA8 30 C4
WOOL/PLUM SE18 29 G4
River Dr DVW CT17 213 G7
STRD ME2 18 B4
River Grove Pk BECK BR3 70 A5
Riverhead Cl MAIDW ME16 12 A1
MARG CT9 15 M7
SIT ME10 119 K6
Riverhill SEV TN13 255 M1
River Lawn Rd TON TN9 194 E4
Rivermead CHAT ME4 83 K3
River Meadow DVW CT17 213 G6
River Pde SEV TN13 * 20 B1
Riverpark Gdns HAYES BR2 70 E4
River Park Vw ORP BR6 91 J3
Rivers Cl WBY/YAL ME18 164 F6
Rivers Ct MSTR CT12 * 180 F8
Riversdale GVW DA11 54 F7
Riversdale Rd ASH TN23 2 C9
MSTR CT12 16 C1
Riverside CHARL SE7 27 J2
CHAT ME4 6 C4
DVE/WH CT16 212 D4
EDEN TN8 192 D4
EYN DA4 93 L5
RCANTW CT4 248 D6
Riverside Cl ASH TN23 204 D8
RCANTW CT4 175 H8
STMC/STPC BR5 73 K6
Riverside Est STRD ME2 * 6 B1
Riverside Ms RCANTW CT4 175 H8
Riverside Rd MSTR CT12 237 K5
SCUP DA14 49 M8
Riverside Wy DART DA1 51 M3
Rivers Rd RSIT ME9 121 L7
River St DVW CT17 212 F6
GILL ME7 6 E1
Riverview ASH TN23 204 B2
River Vw CANTW/ST CT2 173 G2
CDW/CHF RM16 35 H4
GILL ME7 102 E2
MAID/SHEP ME15 12 F8
QBOR ME11 227 N2
Riverview Pk CAT SE6 46 B7
Riverview Rd GRH DA9 * 53 H3
Riverview Ter PUR RM19 * 32 C4
River Wk TON TN9 194 E4
River Wy DIT/AY ME20 139 H1
GNWCH SE10 27 G2
River Whf BELV DA17 * 30 E1
Riverwood La CHST BR7 72 E6
Riviera Rd FOLK CT20 10 C9
The Riviera FOLK CT20 10 B9
Roach St STRD ME2 18 F4
Road of Remembrance
FOLK CT20 11 K6
Roan Ct STRD ME2 * 18 C2
Roan St GNWCH SE10 26 D5
Robert Keen Cl PECK SE15 25 H7
Robert Lowe Cl NWCR SE14 25 L6
Roberton Dr BMLY BR1 71 K6
Roberts Cl ELTH/MOT SE9 48 E6
SIT ME10 119 L2
STMC/STPC BR5 91 K1
THHTH CR7 68 E7
Roberts House
WOOL/PLUM SE18 * 27 M6
Roberts Orchard Rd
MAIDW ME16 165 M2
Robert Sq LEW SE13 46 D2
Roberts Rd BELV DA17 30 B4
NROM TN28 331 M12
RHAM ME8 102 F5
SNOD ME6 113 G5
WSTB CT5 126 A7
Robert St CROY/NA CR0 86 D6
DEAL CT14 209 L2
WOOL/PLUM SE18 28 E4
Robina Cl BXLYHS DA6 49 L2
Robin Hill Dr CHST BR7 71 M3
Robin Hood Gn
STMC/STPC BR5 91 H1
Robin Hood La BXLYHS DA6 49 M3
LYDD TN29 334 E4
WALD ME5 114 E4
Robin Hood La (Lower)
WALD ME5 114 F4
Robin Hood La (Upper)
WALD ME5 114 F4
Robinia Av GVW DA11 54 E5
Robinia Cl PGE/AN SE20 69 H5
Robin La LYDD TN29 334 D3
Robins Av RMAID ME17 243 K12
Robin's Cl HYTHE CT21 321 Q1
RMAID ME17 262 F1
Robins Gv WWKM BR4 89 H6
Robin Wy STMC/STPC BR5 73 J7
Robsart St BRXN/ST SW9 24 A8
Robson Dr DIT/AY ME20 139 L3
HOO/HM ME3 59 L8
Robson Rd WNWD SE27 44 C8
Robus Cl RFOLK CT18 291 M10
Robyns Cft GVW DA11 54 F8
Robyns Wy EDEN TN8 192 E5
SEV TN13 135 L8
Rocastle Rd BROCKY SE4 45 M3
Rocfort Rd SNOD ME6 113 H5
Rochdale Rd ABYW SE2 29 J4
RTW TN1 23 J1
Rochdale Wy DEPT SE8 26 B6
Rochester Av BMLY BR1 71 J6
CANT CT1 5 K7
ROCH ME1 100 D1
Rochester Br 19 J5
Rochester Cl BFN/LL DA15 49 J4
Rochester Ct STRD ME2 * 82 F5
Rochester Crs HOO/HM ME3 59 L7
Rochester Dr BXLY DA5 50 B4
Rochester Gdns CROY/NA CR0 86 F6
Rochester Ga ROCH ME1 * 19 L8
Rochester Rd DART DA1 52 B5
DIT/AY ME20 140 B2
GVE DA12 56 B7
ROCH ME1 113 M2
STRD ME2 99 L2
TONN TN10 195 G1
WALD ME5 114 D1
Rochester St CHAT ME4 6 B9
Rochester Wy BKHTH/KID SE3 27 J7
DART DA1 50 F5
ELTH/MOT SE9 47 M2
ELTH/MOT SE9 48 A1
Rochester Wy Relief Rd
ELTH/MOT SE9 47 M3
Rock Av GILL ME7 7 K7
Rockbourne Rd FSTH SE23 45 L6
Rock Channel RYE TN31 225 H4
Rockdale Gdns SEV TN13 * 21 H7
Rockdale Pleasance SEV TN13 * 21 J7
Rockdale Rd SEV TN13 21 H8
Rockell's Pl EDUL SE22 45 J4
Rockfield Cl OXTED RH8 185 G1
Rockfield Rd OXTED RH8 157 L8
Rock Grove Wy
BERM/RHTH SE16 25 H3
Rockhampton Rd
STRHM/NOR SW16 68 B1
Rock Hl ORP BR6 109 G1
SYD SE26 69 G1
Rock Hill Rd HDCN TN27 262 H11
Rockingham Pl HB CT6 129 J7
Rockingham St STHWK SE1 24 D2
Rockmount Rd NRWD SE19 68 E3
WOOL/PLUM SE18 29 G4
Rock Rd BGR/WK TN15 240 E2
MAID/BEAR ME14 141 H6
SIT ME10 119 M5
Rocks Cl E/WMAL ME19 139 H7
Rocks Hl CRBK TN17 299 J4
The Rocks Rd E/WMAL ME19 139 J8
Rockstone Wy MSTR CT12 182 C4
Rock Villa Rd RTW TN1 22 F4
Rockwell Gdns NRWD SE19 68 F1
Rocky Bourne Rd RASHE TN25 305 N8
Rocky Hill Ter MAIDW ME16 * 12 D5
Rocombe Crs FSTH SE23 * 45 K5
Rocque La BKHTH/KID SE3 47 G1
Roden Gdns CROY/NA CR0 86 F2
Rodeo Cl ERITH DA8 31 J7
Rodmell Rd RTWE/PEM TN2 22 F8
Rodmer Cl IOS ME12 65 K5
Rodmere St GNWCH SE10 26 F4
Rodney Av TONN TN10 195 H1
Rodney Gdns WWKM BR4 89 H7
Rodney Pl STHWK SE1 24 D3
Rodney Rd WALW SE17 24 E3
Rodney St RAM CT11 17 H7
Rodway Rd BMLY BR1 71 J5
Rodwell Rd EDUL SE22 45 G4
Roebuck Rd FAV ME13 149 H2
ROCH ME1 19 J8
Roedean Cl ORP BR6 91 J7
Roedean Rd RTWE/PEM TN2 22 F9
Roehampton Cl GVE DA12 55 M5
Roehampton Dr CHST BR7 72 D3
Roffen Rd ROCH ME1 100 D3
Roffey St POP/IOD E14 26 D1
Rogers Ct SWLY BR8 75 H8
Rogers La WARL CR6 130 E4
Rogersmead TENT TN30 315 M2
Rogers Rd GRAYS RM17 34 D3
Rogers Rough Rd CRBK TN17 296 H11
Rogerstown EDEN TN8 * 275 L9
Rogers Wood La BGR/WK TN15 95 H7
Rogues Hl RTON TN11 277 K6
Rojack Rd FSTH SE23 45 L6
Rokeby Rd BROCKY SE4 * 26 A8
Rokesby Cl WELL DA16 28 E8
Rokesley Rd DVE/WH CT16 213 J4
Roland Wy WALW SE17 24 E4
Rolfe La NROM TN28 330 H7
Rolinsden Wy HAYES BR2 89 L7
Rolleston Av STMC/STPC BR5 90 C2
Rolleston Cl STMC/STPC BR5 90 C3
Rollins St NWCR SE14 25 K5
Rollo Rd SWLY BR8 75 G4
Roll's Av IOS ME12 229 L4
Rollscourt Av HNHL SE24 44 D3
Rolls Rd STHWK SE1 25 G4
Rolt St DEPT SE8 25 M5
Rolvenden Av RHAM ME8 102 D2
Rolvenden Dr SIT ME10 119 J4
Rolvenden Gdns BMLY BR1 71 L5
Rolvenden Hl CRBK TN17 314 H4
Rolvenden Rd STRD ME2 82 D3
Roman Cl DEAL CT14 209 J3
WALD ME5 114 E4
Romanfield Rd
BRXS/STRHM SW2 44 A5
Roman Hts MAID/BEAR ME14 141 K6
Romanhurst Av HAYES BR2 70 F8
Romanhurst Gdns BECK BR3 70 F8
Roman Ri NRWD SE19 68 E3
Roman Rd CANTW/ST CT2 171 G4
EDEN TN8 192 E8
FAV ME13 149 K2
GVW DA11 54 D8
MSTR CT12 182 E3
RDART DA2 53 J7
RDV CT15 273 K9
SNOD ME6 113 G5
Roman Sq SIT ME10 120 A6
Roman Villa Rd EYN DA4 76 D3
Roman Wy ASH TN23 204 E7
CROY/NA CR0 86 C5
DART DA1 50 F3
FOLKN CT19 219 K7
RDV CT15 215 G4
RDV CT15 272 C3
STRD ME2 18 C9
Romany Ri STMC/STPC BR5 90 D4
Romany Rd RHAM ME8 102 C3
Romborough Gdns LEW SE13 46 D3
Romborough Wy LEW SE13 46 D3
Romden Rd HDCN TN27 284 F9
Rome Rd NROM TN28 330 H7
Romero Sq BKHTH/KID SE3 47 K2
Rome Ter CHAT ME4 6 D5
Romeyn Rd STRHM/NOR SW16 44 A8
Romford Rd RTWE/PEM TN2 278 B11
STPH/PW TN12 278 E9
Romilly Gdns MSTR CT12 182 F3
Rommany Rd WNWD SE27 68 E1
Romney Av FOLK CT20 10 A5
Romney Cl MAID/SHEP ME15 168 B2
Romney Ct SIT ME10 119 L4
Romney Dr BMLY BR1 71 L4
Romney Gdns BXLYHN DA7 30 A7
Romney Marsh Rd ASH TN23 2 C7
Romney Pl MAID/SHEP ME15 13 G5
Romney Rd GNWCH SE10 26 D5
GVW DA11 54 F8
KEN/WIL TN24 3 H7
LYDD TN29 330 F9
RASHW TN26 318 D3
WALD ME5 101 J8
WOOL/PLUM SE18 28 D2
Romney Wy HYTHE CT21 307 R12
TONN TN10 189 H8
Romola Rd BRXS/STRHM SW2 44 C6
Romsey Cl KEN/WIL TN24 3 L5
ORP BR6 90 D7
STRD ME2 18 A1
Romulus Gdns ASH TN23 204 C7
Ronald Cl BECK BR3 88 A1
Ronalds Ct SIT ME10 * 120 B5
Ronalds Rd BMLY BR1 71 H5
Ronaldstone Rd BFN/LL DA15 48 F4
Ronfearn Av STMC/STPC BR5 91 L1
Ron Green Ct ERITH DA8 30 E4
Ronver Rd LEE/GVPK SE12 47 H6
Roodlands La EDEN TN8 187 L7
Rookery Cl KEN/WIL TN24 202 F4
RSIT ME9 145 H3
Rookery Ct WTHK RM20 * 33 H5
Rookery Crs HOO/HM ME3 38 C7
Rookery Dr CHST BR7 72 B5
Rookery Gdns STMC/STPC BR5 91 K1
Rookery La HAYES BR2 89 L2
Rookery Ldg HOO/HM ME3 * 38 C8
Rookery Rd ORP BR6 106 E4
Rookery Rw
MAID/SHEP ME15 * 165 M7
The Rookery
STRHM/NOR SW16 * 68 A3
WTHK RM20 33 H5
Rookery Vw GRAYS RM17 34 E4
Rookesley Rd STMC/STPC BR5 91 L3
Rook La RSIT ME9 119 G3
Rookley Cl RTWE/PEM TN2 23 L7
Rooks Hl BGR/WK TN15 163 H7
Rookwood Cl GRAYS RM17 34 C3
Roonagh Ct SIT ME10 119 M7
Roopers RRTW TN3 277 P10
Roosevelt Av WALD ME5 101 G6
Roosevelt Rd DVE/WH CT16 213 J6
Ropemaker Rd
BERM/RHTH SE16 25 M1
Ropemakers Ct CHAT ME4 101 H4
Roper Cl CANTW/ST CT2 4 D2
RHAM ME8 116 D2
Roper La STHWK SE1 24 F1
Roper Rd CANTW/ST CT2 4 D2
RSIT ME9 121 L6
Ropers Ga STH/RUST TN4 22 B9
Roper's Green La HOO/HM ME3 60 B5
Roper's La HOO/HM ME3 60 A5
Roper St ELTH/MOT SE9 48 A3
The Ropery CHAT ME4 * 83 G6
Rope St BERM/RHTH SE16 25 M2
Rope Wk CHAT ME4 6 D4
Ropewalk CRBK TN17 298 G8
Rope Wk RYE TN31 225 H3
Rope Walk Ms SWCH CT13 * 206 A1
The Rope Wk HAWK TN18 313 L12
Rope Yard Rails
WOOL/PLUM SE18 28 C2
Rosamond St SYD SE26 45 J8
Rosamund Cl SAND/SEL CR2 86 E7
Roseacre OXTED RH8 185 H3
Roseacre Cl CANTW/ST CT2 4 D2
Roseacre Ct MARG CT9 179 H3
Roseacre Gdns
MAID/BEAR ME14 * 168 B2
Roseacre La MAID/BEAR ME14 168 B2
Rose Acre Rd RCANTE CT3 251 J2
Roseacre Rd WELL DA16 49 J1
Rose Av GVE DA12 55 M6
Rosebank PGE/AN SE20 69 J4
Rosebank Gdns GVW DA11 54 F6
Roseberry Gdns DART DA1 51 K5
ORP BR6 90 F6
Roseberry St BERM/RHTH SE16 25 J3
Rosebery Av BFN/LL DA15 48 F5
HB CT6 129 M4
RAM CT11 17 L1
THHTH CR7 68 D6
Rosebery Cl SIT ME10 120 E5
Rosebery Ct GVW DA11 55 G6
Rosebery Rd CHAT ME4 100 F3
GILL ME7 7 M1
GRAYS RM17 33 M5
Rosecourt Rd CROY/NA CR0 86 A2
Rosecroft Cl BH/WHM TN16 132 E4
STMC/STPC BR5 91 K2
Rosecroft Pk RRTW TN3 * 200 B1
Rose Dl ORP BR6 90 C5
Rosedale Cl ABYW SE2 29 J2
RDART DA2 52 C5
Rosedale Rd GRAYS RM17 34 E4
MARG CT9 15 J6
Rosedene Av
STRHM/NOR SW16 44 A8
Rosedene Cl DART DA1 51 K5
Rosefield SEV TN13 20 E5
Rose Gdns BRCH CT7 176 C7
HB CT6 129 K5
MSTR CT12 180 E7
RDV CT15 272 E6
Rosegarth MEO DA13 78 F5
Rose Hl RAM CT11 17 J6
TENT TN30 316 C12
Rosehill Rd BH/WHM TN16 132 B3
Rosehill Wk RTW TN1 22 E5
Roseholme MAIDW ME16 12 B8
Rosehurst Vls STH/RUST TN4 * 196 F6
Roselands DEAL CT14 209 J8
Roselands Gdns
CANTW/ST CT2 171 L3
Rose La CANT CT1 4 F5
RCANTW CT4 250 F12
RMAID ME17 263 M4
Roselare Cl BH/WHM TN16 159 J3
Roselawn Gdns MARG CT9 177 L5
Roselea Av HB CT6 129 G6
Roseleigh Av MAIDW ME16 166 D1
Roseleigh Rd SIT ME10 119 L8
Rosemary Av BRDST CT10 183 J3
IOS ME12 64 E7
Rosemary Cl OXTED RH8 185 H3
Rosemary Gdns BRDST CT10 183 J3
WSTB CT5 127 G5
Rosemary La BGR/WK TN15 239 J3
CANT CT1 4 E5
HDCN TN27 284 C4
WADH TN5 310 H4
Rosemary Rd E/WMAL ME19 139 G4
MAID/SHEP ME15 168 B2
PECK SE15 25 G6
WELL DA16 29 G7
Rosemount Cl
MAID/SHEP ME15 259 L1
Rosemount Ct STRD ME2 82 B4
Rosemount Dr BMLY BR1 72 A8
Rosendale Rd HNHL SE24 44 D5
Roseneath Pl
STRHM/NOR SW16 68 B1
Rosenheath Cl ORP BR6 108 A2
Rosenthal Rd CAT SE6 46 C4
Rosenthorpe Rd PECK SE15 45 L3
Roserton St POP/IOD E14 26 D1
The Rosery CROY/NA CR0 87 L2
Rose St GVW DA11 54 C4
IOS ME12 64 C3
ROCH ME1 100 E2
TON TN9 194 F5
Rose Ter FAV ME13 * 149 L4
HOO/HM ME3 * 43 J8
Rosetower Ct BRDST CT10 179 J5
Roseveare Rd LEE/GVPK SE12 71 K1
Rose Vls ASH TN23 * 2 C8
STPH/PW TN12 * 280 H4
Rose Wk RFOLK CT18 220 B1
WWKM BR4 88 E5
Roseway DUL SE21 44 E4
Rose Wy LEE/GVPK SE12 47 H3
Rosewell Cl PGE/AN SE20 69 J4
Rosewood RDART DA2 74 F1
Rosewood Cl SCUP DA14 49 K8
Rosewood Dr RASHE TN25 202 B7
Rosewood Ter PGE/AN SE20 * 69 K4
Rose Yd MAID/BEAR ME14 13 G4
Rosherville Wy GVW DA11 54 F5
Roslin Wy BMLY BR1 71 H2
Rossdale RTWE/PEM TN2 23 K2
Rossell Rd TIL RM18 35 G8
Rosse Ms BKHTH/KID SE3 27 J7
Rossendale Gdns FOLK CT20 11 M3
Rossendale Rd FOLK CT20 11 M3
Rossetti Rd BERM/RHTH SE16 25 J4
BRCH CT7 176 C5
Ross Gdns CANTW/ST CT2 171 H2
Ross House WOOL/PLUM SE18 * 27 M6
Rossland Cl BXLYHS DA6 50 B3
Rossland Rd MSTR CT12 16 A2
Rosslyn Cl WWKM BR4 89 G6
Rosslyn Gn MAIDW ME16 140 C8
Ross Rd DART DA1 51 H4
SNWD SE25 68 F7
Ross St ROCH ME1 19 L9
Ross Wy ELTH/MOT SE9 47 M1
FOLK CT20 223 M1
Rotary Gdns GILL ME7 102 A3
Rotary St STHWK SE1 24 C2
Rothbrook Dr KEN/WIL TN24 202 F4
Rothbury Cottages
GNWCH SE10 26 F3
Rotherhithe New Rd
BERM/RHTH SE16 25 K3
Rotherhithe Old Rd
BERM/RHTH SE16 25 L3
Rotherhithe St
BERM/RHTH SE16 25 K1
Rotherhithe Tnl
BERM/RHTH SE16 25 K1
Rothermere Cl CRBK TN17 313 P3
Rothermere Rd CROY/NA CR0 86 A8
Rother Rd TONN TN10 188 E8
Rother V WALD ME5 115 K1
Rotherview RBTBR TN32 322 H8
Rothery Ter BRXN/ST SW9 * 24 C6
Rothesay Rd SNWD SE25 68 E8
Rothley Cl TENT TN30 315 N1
Rothsay Ct BRDST CT10 * 183 J4
Rothsay St STHWK SE1 24 F2
Rothschild St WNWD SE27 68 C1
Rotterdam Dr POP/IOD E14 26 D2
Rouel Rd BERM/RHTH SE16 25 H3
Rouge La GVE DA12 55 J6
Rough Common Rd
CANTW/ST CT2 171 H3
Roughetts Rd E/WMAL ME19 138 A2
Roughetts Rw
E/WMAL ME19 * 138 A2
Roughway La RTON TN11 240 H11
Round Ash Wy HART DA3 95 M2
Roundel Cl BROCKY SE4 46 A2
RSIT ME9 121 L7
The Roundels RSIT ME9 * 147 H1
The Roundel SIT ME10 119 M7
Roundel Wy STPH/PW TN12 280 H4
Round Gv CROY/NA CR0 87 L3
Roundhay E/WMAL ME19 138 E4
Roundhay Cl FSTH SE23 45 L7
Round Hl SYD SE26 45 J7
Roundhill Rd RTWE/PEM TN2 201 L4
Roundlyn Gdns
STMC/STPC BR5 73 J8
Round St MEO DA13 79 K7
Roundtable Rd BMLY BR1 47 H8
Roundwell MAID/BEAR ME14 168 E1
Roundwood CHST BR7 72 C6
Round Wood Cl WALD ME5 115 H4
Roupell Rd BRXS/STRHM SW2 44 A6
Rouse Gdns DUL SE21 68 F1
Rover Rd WALD ME5 115 J3
Rowan Cl ASH TN23 204 B1
CANTW/ST CT2 173 G3
DIT/AY ME20 139 M4
MEO DA13 97 J2
RCANTE CT3 252 F3
STPH/PW TN12 279 J4
Rowan Ct BRDST CT10 * 179 K8
Rowan Crs DART DA1 51 K6
Rowan Gdns CROY/NA CR0 87 G6
Rowan Lea WALD ME5 101 J5
Rowan Rd BXLYHN DA7 49 M1
SWLY BR8 74 E7
Rowans Cl HART DA3 77 L6
Rowan Shaw TONN TN10 189 G7
The Rowans IOS ME12 * 65 J6
RTWE/PEM TN2 * 278 B11
Rowan Ter PGE/AN SE20 * 69 H5
Rowan Tree Rd RTWE/PEM TN2 22 B9
Rowan Wk CHAT ME4 6 B7
HAYES BR2 90 A6
Rowanwood Av BFN/LL DA15 49 H6
Rowbrocke Cl RHAM ME8 116 E2
Rowcross St STHWK SE1 25 G4
Rowden Rd BECK BR3 69 M5
Rowdow La RSEV TN14 136 C2
Rowdown Crs CROY/NA CR0 105 J3
Rowe Cl MARG CT9 178 C6
Rowena Rd WGOS CT8 177 H4
Rowetts Wy IOS ME12 229 N2
Rowland Av GILL ME7 101 M4
Rowland Cl MAIDW ME16 12 D6
WALD ME5 101 M4
Rowland Crs HB CT6 129 M5
Rowland Dr HB CT6 128 D7
Rowland Gv SYD SE26 45 J8
Rowlatt Cl RDART DA2 75 K1
Rowley Av BFN/LL DA15 49 J5
Rowley Hl RTWE/PEM TN2 278 A8
Rowmarsh Cl GVW DA11 78 E1
The Row EDEN TN8 * 192 C1
RCANTE CT3 * 236 B8
RCANTW CT4 291 Q5
Rowton Rd WOOL/PLUM SE18 28 D6
Rowzill Rd SWLY BR8 75 G3
Roxburgh Rd WGOS CT8 177 J4
WNWD SE27 68 C2
Roxley Rd LEW SE13 46 C4
Roxton Gdns CROY/NA CR0 104 E1
Royal Arsenal West
WOOL/PLUM SE18 * 28 B4
Royal Av TON TN9 194 F5
WSTB CT5 126 D8
Royal Buildings DEAL CT14 * 209 L5
Royal Cha STH/RUST TN4 22 D3
Royal Circ WNWD SE27 44 B8
Royal Cl BRDST CT10 183 H1
DEPT SE8 26 A5
ORP BR6 90 C7
Royal Ct ELTH/MOT SE9 * 48 A6
IOS ME12 * 64 D3
Royal Crs MARG CT9 14 C5
RAM CT11 * 17 H8
Royal Eagle Cl STRD ME2 82 F6
Royal Engineers' Rd
MAID/BEAR ME14 141 G7
Royal Esp MARG CT9 177 K4
RAM CT11 16 D9
Royal Harbour Ap RAM CT11 16 A8
Royal Hl GNWCH SE10 26 D6
Royal Military Av FOLK CT20 219 L8
Royal Military Canal Pth
RASHE TN25 318 H2
RASHW TN26 317 M8
TENT TN30 327 R5
Royal Military Rd HYTHE CT21 307 J12
Royal Naval Pl NWCR SE14 26 A6
Royal Oak Pl EDUL SE22 45 J4
Royal Oak Rd BXLYHS DA6 50 A3
Royal Oak Yd STHWK SE1 24 F1
Royal Pde BKHTH/KID SE3 27 G8
CHST BR7 72 D4
RAM CT11 17 J8
Royal Pier Rd GVE DA12 55 J4
Royal Pl GNWCH SE10 26 D6
Royal Rd IOS ME12 64 D3
RAM CT11 17 H7
RDART DA2 76 B2
SCUP DA14 49 L8
WALW SE17 24 C5
Royal Sovereign Av CHAT ME4 83 J6
Royal Star Ar
MAID/BEAR ME14 * 12 F5
Royal St STHWK SE1 24 A2
Royal Terrace Pier GVE DA12 * 55 K4
Royal Victoria Pl RTW TN1 23 G4
Royal West Kent Av
TONN TN10 195 G1
Roycroft Cl BRXS/STRHM SW2 * 44 B6
Roydene Rd WOOL/PLUM SE18 28 F5
Roydon Hall Rd
STPH/PW TN12 256 H1
WBY/YAL ME18 241 R12
Royds Rd KEN/WIL TN24 205 G5
Royston Gdns RDV CT15 215 G3

Royston Rd DART DA1 51 G4
MAID/SHEP ME15 168 B2
PGE/AN SE20 69 L5
Roystons Cl RHAM ME8 103 G3
Royton Av RMAID ME17 243 L12
Rubens St CAT SE6 46 A7
Rubery Dro RCANTE CT3 236 G7
Ruby St PECK SE15 25 J5
Ruby Triangle PECK SE15 * 25 J5
Ruckinge Rd RASHW TN26 318 D2
Ruckinge Wy RHAM ME8 102 D2
Ruck La STPH/PW TN12 296 F2
Ruddstreet Cl
WOOL/PLUM SE18 28 C3
Rudge Cl WALD ME5 115 L3
Rudland Rd BXLYHN DA7 50 C1
Ruffets Wd ASH TN23 204 F8
The Ruffetts SAND/SEL CR2 104 A2
Rugby Cl BRDST CT10 179 J8
WALD ME5 115 G1
Rugby Gdns ASH TN23 2 D9
Rugby Rd DVW CT17 217 H3
Ruggles Cl HOO/HM ME3 59 M2
Ruins Barn Rd RSIT ME9 145 K5
Rumfields Rd BRDST CT10 183 G1
Rumsey Rd BRXN/ST SW9 44 A1
Rumstead La
MAID/BEAR ME14 143 K3
RSIT ME9 117 L8
Rumstead Rd RSIT ME9 143 L1
Runcie Pl CANTW/ST CT2 4 B2
Runciman Cl ORP BR6 108 B4
Runham La RMAID ME17 262 C1
Runnymede Ms FAV ME13 * 149 K2
Rupack St BERM/RHTH SE16 * 25 K1
Rupert Gdns BRXN/ST SW9 24 C8
Rural Ter RASHE TN25 * 266 F11
Rural V GVW DA11 54 F5
Ruscombe Cl STH/RUST TN4 196 C3
Rusham Rd RCANTE CT3 235 L12
Rushbrook Rd ELTH/MOT SE9 48 D7
Rush Cl LYDD TN29 320 G11
WALD ME5 115 H2
Rushcroft Rd
BRXS/STRHM SW2 44 B2
Rushdean Rd STRD ME2 81 L8
Rushden Cl NRWD SE19 68 E4
Rushdene ABYW SE2 29 K2
Rushdene Wk BH/WHM TN16 132 C3
Rushdon Cl CDW/CHF RM16 34 B2
Rushenden Rd QBOR ME11 227 N2
Rushet Rd STMC/STPC BR5 73 H6
Rushetts RRTW TN3 200 A1
Rushetts Rd BGR/WK TN15 111 J2
Rushey Gn CAT SE6 46 C5
Rushey Md BROCKY SE4 46 B3
Rushford Cl HDCN TN27 283 L4
Rushford Rd BROCKY SE4 46 A4
Rushfords LING RH7 190 F7
Rushgrove St
WOOL/PLUM SE18 28 A3
Rushley Cl HAYES BR2 89 L7
Rushlye Cl RRTW TN3 294 E8
Rushmead Cl CANTW/ST CT2 171 L3
CROY/NA CR0 87 G7
Rushmead Dr
MAID/SHEP ME15 167 H6
Rushmere Ct BGR/WK TN15 240 C2
Rushmore Cl BMLY BR1 71 M7
Rushmore Hl ORP BR6 108 B4
Rusholme Gv NRWD SE19 68 F2
Rushworth St STHWK SE1 24 C1
Rushymead BGR/WK TN15 136 F4
Ruskin Av WELL DA16 49 H1
Ruskin Cl E/WMAL ME19 139 G5
Ruskin Dr ORP BR6 90 F6
WELL DA16 49 H1
Ruskin Gv DART DA1 52 B3
WELL DA16 29 H8
Ruskin Rd BELV DA17 30 B3
CDW/CHF RM16 35 H3
CROY/NA CR0 86 C5
Ruskin Wk HAYES BR2 89 M2
HNHL SE24 44 D3
Rusland Av ORP BR6 90 E6
Russel Cl BECK BR3 70 C7
Russell Cl BXLYHN DA7 50 B2
CHARL SE7 27 K6
DART DA1 51 H1
SIT ME10 119 K6
Russell Ct CHAT ME4 7 G8
Russell Dr WSTB CT5 127 L2
Russell Gv BRXN/ST SW9 24 B7
Russell Pl EYN DA4 76 B5
FAV ME13 123 J6
Russell Rd DIT/AY ME20 114 D6
FOLKN CT19 11 H2
GVE DA12 55 L4
TIL RM18 34 F7
Russells Av RHAM ME8 103 H5
Russell St DVE/WH CT16 8 E4
IOS ME12 64 C3
Russells Yd CRBK TN17 298 G9
Russell Ter EYN DA4 * 76 D8
Russel Rd GRAYS RM17 34 B3
Russet Av FAV ME13 149 M4
Russet Cl STRD ME2 18 A1
Russet Dr CROY/NA CR0 87 M4
The Russets MAIDW ME16 * 140 C8
MEO DA13 97 H2
WSTB CT5 127 L4
Russett Cl DIT/AY ME20 139 M5
ORP BR6 91 J8
Russett Rd CANT CT1 5 M5
STPH/PW TN12 257 J7
Russett Wy SWLY BR8 74 E6
Russet Wy E/WMAL ME19 164 A3
Rusthall Cl CROY/NA CR0 87 K2
Rusthall Gra STH/RUST TN4 200 E1
Rusthall High St
STH/RUST TN4 200 C1
Rusthall Pk STH/RUST TN4 22 A4
Rusthall Pl STH/RUST TN4 * 200 E2
Rusthall Rd STH/RUST TN4 200 E2
Ruston Rd WOOL/PLUM SE18 27 M2
Rust Sq CMBW SE5 24 E6
Rustwick STH/RUST TN4 200 E1
Rutherford Rd KEN/WIL TN24 202 E6
Rutherford Wy TONN TN10 189 G6
Rutherglen Rd ABYW SE2 29 H5
Ruthin Rd BKHTH/KID SE3 27 H5
Rutland Av BFN/LL DA15 49 H5
MARG CT9 178 E2
Rutland Cl BXLY DA5 49 L6
CANT CT1 174 E2
DART DA1 51 L5
Rutland Ct CHST BR7 72 B5
Rutland Gdns BRCH CT7 176 C6
CROY/NA CR0 86 F7
MARG CT9 178 F3
Rutland Ga BELV DA17 30 C4
HAYES BR2 71 G8
Rutland Pk CAT SE6 46 A7
Rutland Pl RHAM ME8 116 D2
Rutland Rd DVE/WH CT16 213 J6
Rutland Wk CAT SE6 46 A7
Rutland Wy MAID/SHEP ME15 167 M5
STMC/STPC BR5 91 K2
Rutley Cl LBTH SE11 24 C5
Rutt's Ter NWCR SE14 25 L7
Ruxley Cl SCUP DA14 73 L3
Ruxton Cl SWLY BR8 74 F7
Ruxton Ct SWLY BR8 74 F7
Ryan Cl BKHTH/KID SE3 47 J2
Ryan Dr MAID/SHEP ME15 168 B3
Ryarsh Crs ORP BR6 90 F7
Ryarsh La E/WMAL ME19 138 C4
Ryarsh Pk E/WMAL ME19 * 138 A7
Ryarsh Rd E/WMAL ME19 112 C8
Rycault Cl MAIDW ME16 12 C6
Rycaut Cl RHAM ME8 116 E2
Rycroft La RSEV TN14 161 K8
Ryculff Sq BKHTH/KID SE3 27 G8
Rydal Av RAM CT11 16 B5
Rydal Cl STH/RUST TN4 22 A2
Rydal Dr BXLYHN DA7 30 B7
STH/RUST TN4 22 A2
WWKM BR4 88 F5
Rydal Mt HAYES BR2 * 71 G8
Ryde Cl WALD ME5 101 J5
Ryder Dr BERM/RHTH SE16 25 J4
Ryders RRTW TN3 200 B2
Ryder's Av WGOS CT8 177 G5
Ryde St CANTW/ST CT2 4 C3
Rye Cl BXLY DA5 50 C4
Ryecotes Md DUL SE21 44 F6
Rye Crs STMC/STPC BR5 91 L4
Ryecroft GVE DA12 79 M2
HART DA3 78 E8
Ryecroft Rd LEW SE13 46 D3
RSEV TN14 135 M3
STMC/STPC BR5 90 E2
STRHM/NOR SW16 68 B3
Ryedale EDUL SE22 45 J4
Ryedale Ct SEV TN13 135 K7
Ryefield Rd NRWD SE19 68 D3
Ryegrass Cl WALD ME5 101 K7
Rye Hill Pk PECK SE15 45 K2
Ryelands Crs LEE/GVPK SE12 47 K4
Rye La PECK SE15 25 H8
RSEV TN14 135 L5
Rye Rd HAWK TN18 312 F8
LYDD TN29 329 J5
PECK SE15 45 L2
RYE TN31 327 K11
TENT TN30 327 K3
Rye Wk HB CT6 129 K7
Rykhill CDW/CHF RM16 35 J2
Rylandes Rd SAND/SEL CR2 104 A3
Ryland Pl FOLK CT20 11 M4
Rylands Rd KEN/WIL TN24 203 G7
Rymer Rd CROY/NA CR0 86 F3
Rymers Cl RTWE/PEM TN2 197 G6
Rymer St HNHL SE24 44 C4
Rype Cl LYDD TN29 334 D4
Rysted La BH/WHM TN16 159 H4
Ryswick Ms NROM TN28 331 K5

S

Sabina Rd CDW/CHF RM16 35 K3
Sacketts Hl BRDST CT10 178 E7
Sackville Av HAYES BR2 89 H4
Sackville Cl RASHW TN26 286 F2
SEV TN13 136 A8
Sackville Crs ASH TN23 204 D1
Sackville Rd DART DA1 51 L7
Saddington St GVE DA12 55 J5
Saddlers Cl MAID/BEAR ME14 141 M8
Saddlers Hall EYN DA4 * 93 L6
Saddlers Hl RCANTE CT3 252 C7
Saddlers Ms WSTB CT5 127 L4
Saddler's Pk EYN DA4 93 L6
Saddler's Wall La LYDD TN29 328 G4
Saddlers Wy ASH TN23 204 E7
Saddleton Gv WSTB CT5 * 126 E5
Saddleton Rd WSTB CT5 126 E5
Sadlers Cl WALD ME5 114 E3
Saffron Rd CDW/CHF RM16 33 K3
Saffron's Pl FOLK CT20 11 L5
Saffron Wy SIT ME10 120 A2
Sage Rd ROCH ME1 100 B2
Sailmakers Ct CHAT ME4 101 J3
Sail St LBTH SE11 24 A3
Sainsbury Rd NRWD SE19 68 F2
St Agnes Gdns IOS ME12 64 D4
St Agnes Pl CMBW SE5 24 C5
St Aidan's Rd EDUL SE22 45 J4
St Aidan's Wy GVE DA12 55 M8
St Albans Cl GILL ME7 83 M6
GVE DA12 55 L8
St Alban's Gdns GVE DA12 55 L8
St Alban's Rd DART DA1 52 A4
RCANTE CT3 155 M8
STRD ME2 81 K7
St Alfege Rd CHARL SE7 27 L5
St Alphege Cl WSTB CT5 126 C6
St Alphege Ct WSTB CT5 * 126 E4
St Alphege La CANT CT1 4 F3
St Alphege Rd DVE/WH CT16 8 B1
St Ambrose Gn RASHE TN25 266 F11
St Amunds Cl CAT SE6 70 B1
St Andrew Rd GILL ME7 83 L6
St Andrews Cl
BERM/RHTH SE16 * 25 J4
CANT CT1 4 D6
FOLKN CT19 220 C6
HB CT6 129 G5
MAIDW ME16 166 B3
MARG CT9 178 C6
STPH/PW TN12 279 K3
WSTB CT5 126 F6
St Andrews Ct STH/RUST TN4 196 D4
St Andrews Dr ORP BR6 91 J2
St Andrews Gdns DVW CT17 * 213 J7
RDV CT15 271 R8
St Andrew's Lees SWCH CT13 206 B1
St Andrews Pk MAIDW ME16 * 166 B2
St Andrews Park Rd
STH/RUST TN4 196 D4
St Andrew's Rd CROY/NA CR0 86 D7
DEAL CT14 209 K3
GVE DA12 * 55 J5
MAIDW ME16 166 B3
NROM TN28 331 M7
RAM CT11 17 L2
SCUP DA14 49 L8
STPH/PW TN12 279 K3
TIL RM18 34 F8
St Andrews Wy DEAL CT14 272 H2
OXTED RH8 185 M1
St Annes Ct MAIDW ME16 12 D4
St Anne's Dr HB CT6 128 E5
St Anne's Gdns MARG CT9 15 G9
St Anne's Rd ASH TN23 204 C4
WSTB CT5 127 G2
St Ann's Green La
STPH/PW TN12 281 L1
St Ann's Rd FAV ME13 149 J3
LYDD TN29 320 G10
St Anns Wy BH/WHM TN16 * 133 G2
St Anthony's Ct HAYES BR2 90 C4
St Anthony's Wy MARG CT9 178 F4
St Arvans Cl CROY/NA CR0 86 F6
St Asaph Rd BROCKY SE4 45 L1
St Aubyns Cl ORP BR6 91 G6
St Aubyns Gdns ORP BR6 91 G5
St Aubyn's Rd NRWD SE19 69 G3
St Audrey Av BXLYHN DA7 30 B8
St Augustine Rd
CDW/CHF RM16 35 J3
St Augustine's Av BMLY BR1 89 M1
MARG CT9 15 G9
St Augustine's Crs WSTB CT5 127 L2
St Augustine's Pk RAM CT11 16 F7
St Augustine's Rd BELV DA17 30 A3
CANT CT1 5 J6
DEAL CT14 209 G5
RAM CT11 17 G8
St Austell Rd BKHTH/KID SE3 26 D8
St Barnabas Cl BECK BR3 70 D6
GILL ME7 7 M7
MAIDW ME16 140 D5
RTW TN1 * 23 H2
St Bartholomew's Cl SYD SE26 69 K1
St Bartholomew's La ROCH ME1 6 A5
St Bartholomew's Ter
ROCH ME1 6 A5
St Bart's DVW CT17 * 8 A3
St Bart's Rd SWCH CT13 253 R1
St Benedict Rd SNOD ME6 112 F5
St Benedict's Av GVE DA12 55 M8
St Benedict's Lawn RAM CT11 * 17 G8
St Benet's Rd WGOS CT8 177 H6
St Benets Wy TENT TN30 301 N12
St Benjamins Dr ORP BR6 108 B3
St Bernards CROY/NA CR0 86 F6
St Bernards Cl WNWD SE27 68 E1
St Bernards Rd TONN TN10 188 F7
St Blaise Av BMLY BR1 71 J6
St Botolph Rd GVW DA11 54 E8
St Botolph's Av SEV TN13 20 F4
St Botolph's Rd SEV TN13 21 G4
St Brelades Ct EDEN TN8 * 192 B2
St Brides Cl ERITHM DA18 29 L1
St Catherines Ct RAM CT11 * 183 J4
St Catherine's Dr FAV ME13 149 L3
NWCR SE14 25 L8
St Catherine's Gv MSTR CT12 182 A4
St Cecilia Rd CDW/CHF RM16 35 J3
St Chad's Dr GVE DA12 55 M8
St Chad's Rd TIL RM18 35 H7
St Christopher Cl MARG CT9 179 G5
St Christophers Gn
BRDST CT10 * 179 J8
St Clair Cl OXTED RH8 157 H8
St Clair's Rd CROY/NA CR0 86 F5
St Clare Rd DEAL CT14 209 K8
St Clements SWCH CT13 237 K12
St Clement's Av WTHK RM20 33 H5
St Clements Cl GVW DA11 * 55 G8
IOS ME12 230 C3
St Clements Ct BRDST CT10 * 179 H8
PUR RM19 32 B3
St Clements Rd IOS ME12 * 230 D2
WGOS CT8 177 H4
WTHK RM20 33 K6
St Clements Yd EDUL SE22 * 45 G3
St Clere Hill Rd BGR/WK TN15 111 L6
St Cloud Rd WNWD SE27 68 D1
St Columba's Cl GVE DA12 55 M8
St Cosmus Cl RASHE TN25 265 N4
St Crispin's Rd WGOS CT8 177 H5
St Davids Av DVW CT17 217 H5
St Davids Cl BERM/RHTH SE16 * 25 J4
BRCH CT7 176 E5
WSTB CT5 126 F6
WWKM BR4 88 C3
St David's Crs GVE DA12 79 L1
St David's Rd DEAL CT14 209 K3
HOO/HM ME3 41 L5
RAM CT11 17 L1
STH/RUST TN4 196 E7
SWLY BR8 75 G3
St Davids Sq POP/IOD E14 26 C4
St Denis Rd WNWD SE27 68 E1
St Denys Rd RFOLK CT18 292 G12
St Donatt's Rd NWCR SE14 26 A7
St Dunstan's Cl CANTW/ST CT2 4 C2
St Dunstan's Dr GVE DA12 55 M8
St Dunstan's Rd MARG CT9 15 K5
SNWD SE25 69 G8
St Dunstan's Rbt CANTW/ST CT2 4 C2
St Dunstan's St CANTW/ST CT2 4 D2
St Dunstan's Ter CANTW/ST CT2 4 C3
St Eanswythe Wy FOLK CT20 11 K5
St Edith's Rd BGR/WK TN15 136 F4
St Edmunds Cl ABYW SE2 29 L1
St Edmunds Rd CANT CT1 4 E5
DART DA1 52 A2
DEAL CT14 208 F5
St Edwards Cl CROY/NA CR0 105 J5
St Elmos Rd BERM/RHTH SE16 25 M1
St Faith's La MAID/BEAR ME14 168 C1
St Faith's Rd HNHL SE24 44 C6
St Faith's St MAID/BEAR ME14 12 F4
St Fidelis' Rd ERITH DA8 30 E3
St Fillans Rd CAT SE6 46 D6
St Francis Av GVE DA12 79 M1
St Francis Cl DEAL CT14 208 F5
MAID/BEAR ME14 141 J7
MARG CT9 179 G5
ORP BR6 90 F2
STRD ME2 18 B5
St Francis Rd EDUL SE22 44 F2
FOLKN CT19 10 A3
MEO DA13 239 N2
St Francis Wy CDW/CHF RM16 35 K3
St George's Av GRAYS RM17 34 D3
IOS ME12 64 C5
IOS ME12 229 N3
St Georges Centre CANT CT1 5 H5
St Georges Circ STHWK SE1 24 C2
St George's Cl WSTB CT5 126 F6
St George's Ct BGR/WK TN15 238 E10
DVW CT17 * 213 H7
St Georges Crs DVW CT17 217 J4
GVE DA12 79 L1
St Georges La CANT CT1 4 F5
St George's Lees SWCH CT13 206 B1
St Georges Ms
BERM/RHTH SE16 26 A3
TON TN9 * 194 E5
St Georges Pde CAT SE6 * 46 A7
St George's Pk
RTWE/PEM TN2 201 G5
St George's Pl CANT CT1 5 G5
HYTHE CT21 321 Q1
RDV CT15 215 G3
SWCH CT13 206 C1
St George's Rd BECK BR3 70 C5
BMLY BR1 72 A6
BRDST CT10 183 K1
DEAL CT14 209 L3
FOLKN CT19 10 A3
GILL ME7 7 K1
RAM CT11 17 L2
SCUP DA14 73 L3
SEV TN13 136 A8
STHWK SE1 24 C2
STMC/STPC BR5 90 E2
SWCH CT13 206 B1
SWLY BR8 75 G8
St Georges Rd West BMLY BR1 71 M6
St George's Rbt CANT CT1 5 G5
St Georges Sq GVW DA11 * 55 J4
MAIDW ME16 12 B6
St George's St CANT CT1 4 F4
St George's Ter HB CT6 128 F4
PECK SE15 * 25 H6
St George's Wk CROY/NA CR0 86 D5
St George's Wy PECK SE15 24 F5
St German's Pl BKHTH/KID SE3 27 H8
St German's Rd FSTH SE23 45 M6
St Giles Cl ORP BR6 90 E8
St Giles Rd CMBW SE5 24 F7
DVW CT17 217 J4
St Giles Wk DVW CT17 217 J4
St Gothard Rd WNWD SE27 68 E1
St Gregory's CANT CT1 * 5 G3
St Gregory's Cl DEAL CT14 209 G5
St Gregory's Crs GVE DA12 55 M7
St Gregory's Rd CANT CT1 5 J3
St Helena Rd BERM/RHTH SE16 25 L3
St Helens Cnr
MAID/SHEP ME15 * 165 M5
St Helen's Crs
STRHM/NOR SW16 68 A5
St Helens La MAID/SHEP ME15 165 M5
St Helens Rd ERITHM DA18 29 L1
HOO/HM ME3 38 C8
IOS ME12 64 E4
STRHM/NOR SW16 68 A6
St Helier's Cl MAIDW ME16 166 C3
St Hilda Rd FOLKN CT19 219 M7
St Hildas BGR/WK TN15 240 E9
St Hilda's Rd HYTHE CT21 222 C4
St Hilda's Wy GVE DA12 55 M8
St Hugh's Rd PGE/AN SE20 69 J5
St Hugh Ter RFOLK CT18 * 220 A1
St Jacob's Pl CANT CT1 4 B8
St James' Av BRDST CT10 179 H8
MSTR CT12 182 E4
St James Cl IOS ME12 230 D1
St James' Gdns WSTB CT5 126 E5
St James La DVE/WH CT16 8 E5
RDART DA2 52 F5
St James Man STHWK SE1 * 24 B2
St James Ms POP/IOD E14 * 26 D2
St James Oaks GVW DA11 * 55 H5
St James' Pk RTW TN1 23 J2
St James' Park Rd MARG CT9 177 K5
St James Pl DART DA1 51 L4
St James Rd DEAL CT14 211 K4
HOO/HM ME3 43 J7
RTW TN1 23 J3
St James's NWCR SE14 25 M7
St James's Av BECK BR3 69 M7
GVW DA11 55 H5
St James's Cl WOOL/PLUM SE18 28 D4
St James's Crs BRXN/ST SW9 44 B1
St James's Pk CROY/NA CR0 86 D3
St James Sq HART DA3 * 77 M7
St James's Rd
BERM/RHTH SE16 25 H2
CROY/NA CR0 86 E4
GVW DA11 55 H5
SEV TN13 136 A8
St James's St GVW DA11 55 H4
St James's Ter BRCH CT7 176 E5
St James St DVE/WH CT16 8 E5
St James Ter BRCH CT7 * 176 E5
ORP BR6 * 108 B3
St James Wy BXLY DA5 50 B5
SCUP DA14 73 M2
St Jean's Rd WGOS CT8 177 H6
St John's Av MSTR CT12 16 B1
SIT ME10 120 C6
St John's Church Rd
FOLKN CT19 11 H3
St Johns Cl BH/WHM TN16 * 133 G2
HOO/HM ME3 81 K2
RFOLK CT18 292 F10
St Johns Ct GDST RH9 * 184 A8
KEN/WIL TN24 * 205 K5
St John's Crs BRXN/ST SW9 44 B1
CANTW/ST CT2 153 L6
St Johns Est STHWK SE1 * 25 G1
St John's Hl SEV TN13 21 J1
St John's La ASH TN23 2 C5
CANT CT1 4 E5
HART DA3 96 A2
St Johns Pde SCUP DA14 * 73 J1
St John's Pk BKHTH/KID SE3 27 H6
STH/RUST TN4 196 D5
St John's Pl CANT CT1 5 G2
St Johns Ri BH/WHM TN16 * 133 G2
St Johns Rd CDW/CHF RM16 35 J4
CROY/NA CR0 86 C6
DVW CT17 8 B5
ERITH DA8 30 E4
FAV ME13 149 L2
GILL ME7 7 J8
GVE DA12 55 L5
HOO/HM ME3 59 L7
HOO/HM ME3 81 K1
HYTHE CT21 222 B2
MARG CT9 15 G5
NROM TN28 330 H7
PGE/AN SE20 69 K4
RDART DA2 52 D5
RDV CT15 272 C4
SCUP DA14 73 J1
SEV TN13 136 A8
STH/RUST TN4 196 D6
STMC/STPC BR5 90 E2
WELL DA16 49 J1
WSTB CT5 127 L2
St John's St FOLK CT20 11 K4
MARG CT9 15 G5
St John's Ter WOOL/PLUM SE18 28 D5
St John's V DEPT SE8 26 B8
St John's Wy EDEN TN8 192 D2
RFOLK CT18 292 F10
ROCH ME1 100 B3
St Josephs Cl ORP BR6 91 G7
St Joseph's V BKHTH/KID SE3 26 E8
St Julian's Cl
STRHM/NOR SW16 * 68 B1
St Julian's Farm Rd
WNWD SE27 68 B1
St Julien Av CANT CT1 172 E8
St Justin Cl STMC/STPC BR5 73 L7
St Katherine Rd IOS ME12 64 F6
St Katherine's La SNOD ME6 113 G6
St Katherines Rd ERITHM DA18 29 L1
St Keverne Rd ELTH/MOT SE9 71 M1
St Kilda Rd ORP BR6 91 G4
St Kitts Ter NRWD SE19 68 F2
St Laurence Av DIT/AY ME20 140 C5
St Laurence Cl RSIT ME9 120 E7
STMC/STPC BR5 73 L7
St Lawrence Av RAM CT11 16 D9
STH/RUST TN4 196 A2
St Lawrence Cl CANT CT1 5 J8
St Lawrence Forstal CANT CT1 5 J9
St Lawrence Rd CANT CT1 5 K8
St Lawrence Ter
DVE/WH CT16 * 213 J6
St Lawrence Wy
BRXN/ST SW9 * 24 B8
St Leonards Av CHAT ME4 101 G3
St Leonards Cl GRAYS RM17 34 A5
WELL DA16 49 H1
St Leonards Ri ORP BR6 90 F7
St Leonard's Rd CROY/NA CR0 86 C6
DEAL CT14 209 J5
HYTHE CT21 222 C4
MAIDW ME16 140 D5
St Leonard's St E/WMAL ME19 138 C6
St Leonard's Wk
STRHM/NOR SW16 68 A4
St Louis Gv HB CT6 128 D5
St Louis Rd WNWD SE27 68 D1
St Lukes Av MAID/BEAR ME14 13 J3
RAM CT11 17 H2
WGOS CT8 177 H5
St Lukes Cl RDART DA2 76 F2
SNWD SE25 87 J2
SWLY BR8 74 E6
WSTB CT5 126 F6
St Lukes Rd MAID/BEAR ME14 13 J2
RAM CT11 17 K3
STH/RUST TN4 196 E7
St Luke's Wk RFOLK CT18 220 A1
St Luke's Wy HOO/HM ME3 41 L5
St Magnus Cl BRCH CT7 176 D5
St Margarets STPH/PW TN12 * 279 R11
St Margarets Av BFN/LL DA15 48 E8
BH/WHM TN16 * 133 G2
St Margaret's Banks ROCH ME1 19 M9
St Margarets Cl MAIDW ME16 166 C3
ORP BR6 91 J7
RDART DA2 52 E7
WSTB CT5 126 B7
St Margarets Ct HOO/HM ME3 * 59 M2
St Margaret's Crs GVE DA12 55 M8
St Margarets Dr DEAL CT14 209 J8
RHAM ME8 102 D8
St Margaret's Gv
WOOL/PLUM SE18 28 D5
St Margaret's Ms ROCH ME1 19 J7
St Margarets Rd BRCH CT7 181 J2
BROCKY SE4 46 A2
EYN DA4 76 F4
RDV CT15 215 H4
WGOS CT8 177 H6
St Margaret's St CANT CT1 4 F5
ROCH ME1 19 J8
St Margarets Ter RYE TN31 225 G4
WOOL/PLUM SE18 28 D4
St Mark's Av GVW DA11 54 F5
St Mark's Cl FOLK CT20 219 L8
WSTB CT5 126 F5
St Marks Ct DIT/AY ME20 * 114 A7
St Marks Houses GILL ME7 * 7 J3
St Mark's Rd HAYES BR2 71 J7
RTWE/PEM TN2 201 G6
SNWD SE25 69 H8
St Martins Av CANT CT1 5 K4
St Martins Cl CANT CT1 5 K4
DVW CT17 217 J4
ERITHM DA18 29 L1
MAID/BEAR ME14 142 B4
St Martins Dr EYN DA4 93 L6
St Martins Gdns DVW CT17 * 8 B5
St Martin's Hl CANT CT1 5 K5
St Martin's La BECK BR3 88 C1
St Martins Meadow
BH/WHM TN16 160 B1
St Martin's Pl CANT CT1 5 K4
St Martin's Rd BRXN/ST SW9 24 A8
CANT CT1 5 J4
DART DA1 52 A4
DEAL CT14 209 G5
FOLK CT20 219 L7
NROM TN28 331 J7
RDV CT15 213 M5
St Martin's Ter CANT CT1 5 J4
St Martin's Vw HB CT6 155 H1
St Marychurch St
BERM/RHTH SE16 25 K1
St Mary Newington Cl
WALW SE17 * 24 F4
St Mary's SWCH CT13 237 J12
St Mary's Av HAYES BR2 70 F7
MARG CT9 179 G4
St Mary's Church Rd
RSEV TN14 160 D3
St Mary's Cl BGR/WK TN15 240 H2
GRAYS RM17 34 E5
GVE DA12 55 K7
OXTED RH8 157 K7
RASHW TN26 318 D1
RDV CT15 252 B12
RFOLK CT18 218 E2
STMC/STPC BR5 73 J6
SWCH CT13 253 N3
SWCH CT13 253 N7
WADH TN5 310 E8
WBY/YAL ME18 257 P9
St Mary's Ct BH/WHM TN16 159 J4
CANT CT1 * 4 E5
E/WMAL ME19 * 138 C5
St Mary's Dr SEV TN13 20 B2
St Marys Est
BERM/RHTH SE16 * 25 K1
St Mary's Gdns CHAT ME4 83 J6
LBTH SE11 24 B3
LYDD TN29 320 F12
RCANTE CT3 234 F2
St Mary's Gn BH/WHM TN16 132 B4
KEN/WIL TN24 203 H4
St Mary's Gv BH/WHM TN16 132 B4
DEAL CT14 272 H1
WSTB CT5 126 A7
St Mary's La RRTW TN3 277 P9
WADH TN5 310 F8
St Mary's Meadow
RCANTE CT3 251 R2
St Marys Ms KEN/WIL TN24 3 K9
St Marys Pl RCANTE CT3 * 251 R1
St Mary's Rd BGR/WK TN15 238 F11
BRDST CT10 * 183 L1
BXLY DA5 50 D6
CDW/CHF RM16 35 J3
DEAL CT14 209 K8
FAV ME13 149 L3
GILL ME7 7 K1
GRH DA9 52 F3
HYTHE CT21 307 N12
LYDD TN29 320 B12
LYDD TN29 320 F10
MSTR CT12 180 E7
NROM TN28 331 J5
PECK SE15 25 K8
RCANTW CT4 175 J6
SNWD SE25 68 F7
STRD ME2 19 G3
SWLY BR8 74 E8
TON TN9 194 E6
St Marys Rw IOS ME12 * 65 H7
St Mary's St CANT CT1 4 E5
St Mary St WOOL/PLUM SE18 28 A3
St Mary's Vw RSIT ME9 118 D3
St Mary's Wk LBTH SE11 24 B3
St Marys Wy HART DA3 77 M7
St Matthews Dr BMLY BR1 72 A7
ROCH ME1 100 B3
St Matthew's Rd
BRXS/STRHM SW2 44 A3
St Matthew's Wy HOO/HM ME3 41 L5

St Meddens CHST BR7 * 72 E4
St Merryn Cl WOOL/PLUM SE18 28 E6
St Michaels Av MARG CT9 179 G5
St Michaels Cl BMLY BR1 71 M7
CANTW/ST CT2 171 H4
CHAT ME4 6 C8
DIT/AY ME20 140 D2
ERITHM DA18 * 29 L1
St Michaels Ct RTON TN11 * 188 B6
STRD ME2 * 19 H2
St Michaels Dr RSEV TN14 136 C2
St Michael's Pl CANTW/ST CT2 171 M3
St Michaels Ri WELL DA16 * 29 J7
St Michael's Rd BRXN/ST SW9 24 A8
CANTW/ST CT2 171 M2
CDW/CHF RM16 35 J4
CROY/NA CR0 86 D4
MAIDW ME16 12 B6
SIT ME10 119 M5
STH/RUST TN4 196 E6
WELL DA16 49 J1
St Michael's St FOLK CT20 11 L4
St Michaels Ter TENT TN30 * 301 M10
St Michael's Wk RFOLK CT18 220 A1
St Mildred's Av BRCH CT7 176 B6
BRDST CT10 183 K1
RAM CT11 16 E7
St Mildred's Cl TENT TN30 315 M2
St Mildreds Ct DEAL CT14 209 K8
St Mildred's Gdns WGOS CT8 * 177 J4
St Mildreds Pl CANT CT1 4 D7
St Mildreds Rd CAT SE6 46 F5
LEE/GVPK SE12 47 H5
MARG CT9 15 K5
MSTR CT12 180 E8
RAM CT11 16 E7
WGOS CT8 177 H4
St Monicas Rd DEAL CT14 211 L3
St Nicholas Cl CANTW/ST CT2 173 G2
DEAL CT14 209 G5
St Nicholas Dr SEV TN13 21 J8
St Nicholas Gdns STRD ME2 18 D2
St Nicholas Rd CANT CT1 171 K7
FAV ME13 149 H2
HYTHE CT21 222 C3
NROM TN28 331 M7
WOOL/PLUM SE18 29 G4
St Nicholas St DEPT SE8 26 A7
St Nicolas La CHST BR7 71 M5
St Norbert Rd BROCKY SE4 45 M2
St Olaves Est STHWK SE1 * 24 F1
St Olaves Gdns LBTH SE11 * 24 B3
St Oswald's Pl LBTH SE11 24 A4
St Oswald's Rd
STRHM/NOR SW16 68 C5
St Patrick's Cl DEAL CT14 209 K3
WSTB CT5 126 F6
St Patrick's Gdns GVE DA12 79 L1
St Patrick's Pl CDW/CHF RM16 35 J3
St Patrick's Rd DEAL CT14 209 K3
DVW CT17 217 H5
RAM CT11 17 L2
St Paul's Av FAV ME13 149 H2
St Paul's Cl CHARL SE7 27 L4
STRD ME2 81 L8
SWCM DA10 53 M5
TONN TN10 189 G8
St Paul's Cray Rd CHST BR7 72 E5
St Pauls Crs FAV ME13 151 H6
St Paul's Rd ERITH DA8 30 D6
FAV ME13 151 H6
MARG CT9 15 K3
THHTH CR7 68 D7
St Paul's St SIT ME10 119 M4
STH/RUST TN4 200 D1
St Pauls Ter CANT CT1 * 5 H5
WALW SE17 * 24 C5
St Paul's Wy FOLK CT20 10 A7
St Paul's Wood Hl
STMC/STPC BR5 72 F6
St Peters Av BH/WHM TN16 * 133 G2
St Peter's Br MAIDW ME16 12 E5
St Peters Cl CHST BR7 72 E4
DIT/AY ME20 139 J4
IOS ME12 64 D7
SWCM DA10 54 A5
St Peter's Ct BRDST CT10 179 J8
FAV ME13 149 H2
LEE/GVPK SE12 * 47 G3
St Peter's Footpath MARG CT9 15 J7
St Peter's Gdns WNWD SE27 44 B8
St Peter's Gv CANT CT1 4 E4
St Peter's La CANT CT1 4 E3
St Peter's Park Rd
BRDST CT10 179 J8
St Peters Pth ROCH ME1 * 19 K8
St Peter's Pl CANT CT1 4 D4
DIT/AY ME20 114 A7
St Peter's Rd BRDST CT10 179 H8
CDW/CHF RM16 35 J3
CROY/NA CR0 86 E7
DIT/AY ME20 139 J4
FAV ME13 151 H6
MARG CT9 15 G7
WSTB CT5 126 E3
St Peter's Rbt CANTW/ST CT2 4 D4
St Peters Rw RRTW TN3 277 J12
St Peter's St CANT CT1 4 E4
MAIDW ME16 12 E5
RTWE/PEM TN2 23 K6
SAND/SEL CR2 86 E8
SWCH CT13 237 K12
St Peter St MAIDW ME16 12 E3
ROCH ME1 19 L9
St Philip's Av MAID/SHEP ME15 13 J7
St Pier's La LING RH7 274 A1
St Quentin Rd WELL DA16 49 G1
St Radigund's Pl CANT CT1 * 5 G2
St Radigund's Rd DVW CT17 213 H8
St Radigunds St CANT CT1 4 F3
St Richard's Rd DEAL CT14 209 G5
St Ronan's Cl
MAID/SHEP ME15 * 167 K6
St Saviour's Cl FAV ME13 149 M2
FOLKN CT19 11 K1
St Saviours Est STHWK SE1 * 25 G2
St Saviour's Rd
BRXS/STRHM SW2 44 A3
CROY/NA CR0 86 D2
MAID/SHEP ME15 167 L7
Saints Cl WNWD SE27 68 C1
Saints Hl RTON TN11 276 H9
St Stephen's Cl CANTW/ST CT2 4 F1
St Stephen's Ct CANTW/ST CT2 4 F1
RTW TN1 * 23 H2
St Stephen's Crs THHTH CR7 68 B7
St Stephen's Flds
CANTW/ST CT2 * 4 F2
St Stephen's Gn
CANTW/ST CT2 172 A6
St Stephen's Gv LEW SE13 46 D1
St Stephen's Hl CANTW/ST CT2 153 M8
St Stephen's Rd CANTW/ST CT2 4 F2
St Stephen's Sq
MAID/SHEP ME15 12 D9
St Stephen's St TON TN9 194 E5
St Stephen's Ter VX/NE SW8 24 A6
St Stephen's Wk ASH TN23 204 D5
St Stephens Wy FOLK CT20 10 B7
St Stephons Ct RTW TN1 * 23 H2
Saint's Wk CDW/CHF RM16 35 K3
St Swithin's Rd WSTB CT5 127 J3
St Swithun's Rd LEW SE13 * 46 E3
St Teresa Wk CDW/CHF RM16 35 J3
St Theresa's Cl KEN/WIL TN24 2 A3
St Thomas Ct BXLY DA5 50 B5
St Thomas' Dr STMC/STPC BR5 90 D4
St Thomas Hl CANTW/ST CT2 171 K2
St Thomas Rd BELV DA17 30 D1
GVW DA11 * 54 F6
St Thomas's Av GVW DA11 55 J7
St Thomas's Pl GRAYS RM17 34 D5
St Thomas Well GVE DA12 * 80 B5
St Vincent Cl WNWD SE27 68 C2
St Vincent Rd RDV CT15 214 F2
St Vincents Av DART DA1 52 B3
St Vincent's Cl RCANTE CT3 234 A12
WSTB CT5 126 F6
St Vincents La E/WMAL ME19 239 N11
St Vincents Rd DART DA1 52 B4
St Welcume's Wy
RMAID ME17 242 F11
St Werburgh Crs HOO/HM ME3 59 L8
St William's Wy ROCH ME1 100 E2
St Winifred Rd FOLKN CT19 10 A3
St Winifred's Rd
BH/WHM TN16 132 E4
Saladin Dr PUR RM19 32 B3
Salamanca Pl LBTH SE11 24 A3
Salamanca St LBTH SE11 24 A3
Salbris Cl LYDD TN29 321 J9
Salcot Crs CROY/NA CR0 105 H4
Salcote Rd GVE DA12 79 M2
Salehurst Rd BROCKY SE4 46 A4
Salem Pl CROY/NA CR0 86 D6
GVW DA11 54 E5
Salem St MAID/SHEP ME15 13 H7
Salisbury Av BRDST CT10 183 J3
RAM CT11 17 L3
RHAM ME8 102 E5
SWLY BR8 75 H8
Salisbury Cl SIT ME10 120 D5
TONN TN10 189 G8
WALW SE17 24 E3
Salisbury Pl BRXN/ST SW9 24 C6
Salisbury Rd BXLY DA5 50 B6
CANTW/ST CT2 171 M3
CHAT ME4 6 F7
CROY/NA CR0 87 H2
DEAL CT14 209 J7
DIT/AY ME20 114 D5
DVE/WH CT16 8 C2
FOLKN CT19 219 M6
GRAYS RM17 34 D5
GVW DA11 55 G6
HAYES BR2 89 M1
HB CT6 129 J4
MAID/BEAR ME14 13 H1
RDART DA2 52 D6
RDV CT15 215 J3
RRTW TN3 200 A2
STH/RUST TN4 196 F5
TONN TN10 195 G1
WSTB CT5 126 E5
Salisbury Ter PECK SE15 45 K1
Salisbury Vls NROM TN28 * 330 H7
Salix Rd GRAYS RM17 34 E5
Sallow Cl CHAT ME4 83 K4
Sallows Shaw MEO DA13 97 K1
Sally Port GILL ME7 6 F1
Sally Port Gdns GILL ME7 6 F2
Salmestone Ri MARG CT9 14 F9
Salmestone Rd MARG CT9 14 F9
Salmon Crs IOS ME12 65 G7
Salmon Rd BELV DA17 30 B4
DART DA1 52 A1
Saltash Rd WELL DA16 29 K7
Saltbox Hl BH/WHM TN16 106 A7
Saltcote Cl DART DA1 50 F4
Saltcote St RYE TN31 225 H1
Salter Rd BERM/RHTH SE16 25 M1
Salters Cross
MAID/SHEP ME15 * 258 A4
Salter's Hl NRWD SE19 68 E2
Salters La FAV ME13 149 L4
LYDD TN29 328 H5
Saltford Cl ERITH DA8 30 F4
Salthouse Cl LYDD TN29 329 J5
Saltings Rd SNOD ME6 113 H6
The Saltings NROM TN28 331 M8
WSTB CT5 126 E3
Salt La HOO/HM ME3 58 A1
Saltoun Rd BRXS/STRHM SW2 44 B2
Salt's Av MAID/SHEP ME15 259 L2
Salts Cl WSTB CT5 126 E4
Salt's Dr BRDST CT10 179 H8
Salts La MAID/SHEP ME15 259 M1
Saltwood Cl ORP BR6 91 K7
Saltwood Gdns MARG CT9 179 H3
Saltwood Gv WALW SE17 * 24 E4
Saltwood Rd
MAID/SHEP ME15 167 G4
Samara Cl WALD ME5 115 H4
Sam Bartram Cl CHARL SE7 27 K4
Samian Crs FOLKN CT19 219 K7
Samos Rd PGE/AN SE20 69 J6
Samphire Cl MAID/BEAR ME14 167 M1
Samphire Ct DVE/WH CT16 8 E3
GRAYS RM17 34 F5
Samphire Wy CHAT ME4 83 H4
Sampson Cl BELV DA17 29 L2
Samuel Cl NWCR SE14 25 L5
WOOL/PLUM SE18 27 M3
Samuel Ms LYDD TN29 334 E2
Samuel St PECK SE15 25 G6
WOOL/PLUM SE18 28 A3
Sancroft Av CANTW/ST CT2 171 K4
Sancroft St LBTH SE11 24 B4
Sanctuary Cl BRDST CT10 183 J3
DART DA1 51 K4
DVW CT17 212 E5
Sanctuary Rd RHAM ME8 102 B2
Sanctuary St STHWK SE1 * 24 D1
The Sanctuary BXLY DA5 49 L4
Sandbach Pl WOOL/PLUM SE18 28 D4
Sandbanks Hl RDART DA2 77 K3
Sandbanks Rd FAV ME13 124 C7
Sandbourne Dr
MAID/BEAR ME14 141 G4
Sandbourne Rd BROCKY SE4 25 M8
Sandby Gn ELTH/MOT SE9 47 M1
Sandcliff Rd ERITH DA8 30 E3
Sandell St STHWK SE1 24 B1
Sand End WSTB CT5 * 126 D7
Sanderling Wy GRH DA9 53 H3
RSIT ME9 227 L9
Sandersons Av RSEV TN14 108 F4
Sanderson Wy TON TN9 195 H4
Sanderstead Rd
STMC/STPC BR5 91 J2
Sandfield Gdns THHTH CR7 68 C7
Sandfield Pl THHTH CR7 68 D7
Sandfield Rd RTON TN11 276 H10
THHTH CR7 68 C7
Sandford Rd BXLYHS DA6 49 M2
HAYES BR2 71 H8
SIT ME10 119 J4
Sandford Rw WALW SE17 24 E4
Sandgate Ct RHAM ME8 117 G1
Sandgate Hl FOLK CT20 10 B8
Sandgate Rd FOLK CT20 10 F7
WELL DA16 29 K6
Sandgate St PECK SE15 25 J5
Sandhill La HOO/HM ME3 57 L7
Sandhurst Av RTWE/PEM TN2 278 C12
Sandhurst Cl CANTW/ST CT2 172 B5
RHAM ME8 102 D2
RTWE/PEM TN2 196 F6
Sandhurst La CRBK TN17 314 A8
Sandhurst Pde CAT SE6 * 46 D6
Sandhurst Pk RTWE/PEM TN2 197 G7
Sandhurst Rd BFN/LL DA15 49 G8
BXLY DA5 49 L3
CAT SE6 46 E6
MARG CT9 179 J3
ORP BR6 91 H6
RTWE/PEM TN2 197 G6
TIL RM18 35 K8
Sandiland Crs HAYES BR2 89 G5
Sandilands CROY/NA CR0 87 H6
KEN/WIL TN24 3 H6
SEV TN13 135 J8
Sandison St PECK SE15 45 G1
Sand La CRBK TN17 282 H11
Sandle's Rd BRCH CT7 176 C6
Sandlewood Dr BRCH CT7 233 N8
Sandling La MAID/BEAR ME14 140 F4
Sandling Pl
MAID/BEAR ME14 * 141 G5
Sandling Ri ELTH/MOT SE9 48 B8
Sandling Rd HYTHE CT21 218 A7
MAID/BEAR ME14 12 F2
Sandlings Cl PECK SE15 25 J8
The Sandlings HYTHE CT21 * 321 P1
Sandling Wy CHAT ME4 83 J4
Sandown Cl DEAL CT14 207 L8
RTWE/PEM TN2 197 J7
Sandown Ct SYD SE26 * 45 J8
Sandown Dr HB CT6 128 E5
RHAM ME8 102 E6
Sandown Gv RTWE/PEM TN2 197 J7
Sandown Lees SWCH CT13 206 D1
Sandown Pk RTWE/PEM TN2 197 J8
Sandown Rd DEAL CT14 207 L8
E/WMAL ME19 138 C5
GVE DA12 79 K3
SNWD SE25 87 J1
SWCH CT13 206 D1
Sandpiper Cl BERM/RHTH SE16 26 A1
GRH DA9 53 H3
Sandpiper Dr ERITH DA8 31 J6
Sandpiper Rd RFOLK CT18 220 B2
SAND/SEL CR2 104 C5
WALD ME5 115 K3
WSTB CT5 126 C7
The Sandpipers GVE DA12 55 L7
Sandpiper Wy STMC/STPC BR5 73 L8
Sandpit Hl RCANTE CT3 232 D12
Sandpit Pl CHARL SE7 27 M4
Sandpit Rd BMLY BR1 70 F2
DART DA1 51 K2
Sandpits Rd CROY/NA CR0 87 L7
Sandringham Ct
E/WMAL ME19 * 164 B4
Sandringham Dr BXLY DA5 50 F7
WELL DA16 28 F8
Sandringham Rd BMLY BR1 71 H2
CROY/NA CR0 86 D1
RHAM ME8 116 F1
Sand Rd RRTW TN3 296 B9
Sandrock Pl CROY/NA CR0 87 L7
Sandrock Rd LEW SE13 46 B1
RTWE/PEM TN2 23 K3
Sandstone Dr SIT ME10 119 M1
Sandstone Ri
MAID/BEAR ME14 115 K5
Sandstone Rd LEE/GVPK SE12 47 J7
Sandtoft Rd CHARL SE7 27 J5
Sandway Rd RMAID ME17 262 C1
STMC/STPC BR5 73 K8
Sandwich Cl FOLK CT20 10 A4
Sandwich Rd DVE/WH CT16 213 H2
MSTR CT12 237 M2
RCANTE CT3 236 B12
RDV CT15 252 D12
RDV CT15 272 E5
SWCH CT13 253 P6
Sandwood Rd BRDST CT10 183 J4
SWCH CT13 206 A1
Sandy Bank Rd GVE DA12 55 J6
Sandy Bury ORP BR6 90 E6
Sandycroft ABYW SE2 29 H5
Sandycroft Rd STRD ME2 82 A4
Sandy Dell GILL ME7 116 B2
Sandy Hill Av WOOL/PLUM SE18 28 C4
Sandy Hill La WOOL/PLUM SE18 28 C3
Sandy Hill Rd
WOOL/PLUM SE18 28 C4
Sandyhurst La RASHE TN25 202 B5
Sandy La BGR/WK TN15 239 L12
BGR/WK TN15 240 A7
BH/WHM TN16 159 J3
CDW/CHF RM16 35 J5
E/WMAL ME19 138 B4
HYTHE CT21 223 J2
KEN/WIL TN24 205 L2
MAID/BEAR ME14 141 K4
MAID/BEAR ME14 142 C8
MEO DA13 77 M1
ORP BR6 91 H3
OXTED RH8 157 H7
OXTED RH8 158 A5
RASHW TN26 286 D10
RDART DA2 53 L8
SEV TN13 21 K2
SNOD ME6 112 F7
STMC/STPC BR5 73 L4
TENT TN30 315 N2
WTHK RM20 33 J5
Sandy Mt MAID/BEAR ME14 142 C8
Sandy Pl RASHE TN25 289 L12
Sandy Rdg BGR/WK TN15 240 F2
CHST BR7 72 B3
Sandy Wy CROY/NA CR0 88 A6
San Feliu Ct EGRIN RH19 274 A12
Sanford St NWCR SE14 25 M5
Sanger Cl MARG CT9 14 E7
Sangley Rd CAT SE6 46 C6
SNWD SE25 68 F8
Sangro Pl CANT CT1 172 E8
San Juan Dr CDW/CHF RM16 33 L3
San Marcos Dr CDW/CHF RM16 33 K4
Sansom St CMBW SE5 24 E6
Sanspareil Av IOS ME12 65 G7
Santiago Wy WTHK RM20 33 L4
Santon La RCANTE CT3 235 M5
Saperton Wk LBTH SE11 * 24 A3
Sapho Pk GVE DA12 80 A1
Saphora Cl ORP BR6 90 E8
Sapphire Cl SIT ME10 119 K2
Sapphire Rd DEPT SE8 25 M3
Saracen Cl CROY/NA CR0 86 E2
GILL ME7 102 B4
Saracen Flds WALD ME5 115 J5
Sara Crs GRH DA9 53 H2
Sara Pk GVE DA12 79 M1
Sark Cl LYDD TN29 320 H9
Sarre Pl SWCH CT13 206 A1
Sarsen Hts WALD ME5 115 G4
Sarsens Cl GVE DA12 80 A7
Sartor Rd PECK SE15 45 L2
Sassoon Cl DIT/AY ME20 139 H1
Satis Av SIT ME10 119 M2
Satmar La RFOLK CT18 221 L2
Satmore La RFOLK CT18 221 K1
Saunders Cl GVW DA11 54 F7
Saunders La RCANTE CT3 236 C12
Saunders Ness Rd POP/IOD E14 26 E3
Saunders Rd STH/RUST TN4 200 F5
WOOL/PLUM SE18 29 G4
Saunders St GILL ME7 7 J1
LBTH SE11 24 B3
Saunders Wy DART DA1 52 A7
RYE TN31 332 F7
Savage Rd WALD ME5 115 J2
Savanah Cl PECK SE15 25 G6
Savernake Dr HB CT6 129 J7
Savile Gdns CROY/NA CR0 87 G5
Saville Rw HAYES BR2 89 G4
Savoy Rd DART DA1 51 K3
Saw Lodge Fld ASH TN23 204 F7
Sawpit Rd RSIT ME9 146 C7
Sawyers Ct CHAT ME4 101 J3
Sawyer St STHWK SE1 24 D1
Saxby's La LING RH7 190 F8
Saxbys Rd BGR/WK TN15 137 J8
Saxby Wd RTON TN11 255 N12
Saxon Av IOS ME12 65 J7
Saxon Cl E/WMAL ME19 164 A3
GVW DA11 54 D8
HYTHE CT21 222 F3
RSEV TN14 135 L3
STRD ME2 82 A4
Saxonfield Cl
BRXS/STRHM SW2 44 A5
Saxon Hl BH/WHM TN16 * 159 J4
Saxon Pl EYN DA4 94 D1
STRD ME2 18 D8
Saxon Rd BMLY BR1 71 G4
CROY/NA CR0 86 E1
FAV ME13 149 K3
RAM CT11 16 C7
RCANTW CT4 175 H8
RDART DA2 75 M1
WGOS CT8 177 J4
Saxons Dr MAID/BEAR ME14 141 J6
Saxon Shore WSTB CT5 * 126 D5
Saxon Shore Wy DEAL CT14 211 L1
DVE/WH CT16 9 H3
FAV ME13 124 A8
GILL ME7 84 D7
GVE DA12 55 K4
HB CT6 232 B3
HOO/HM ME3 57 H2
HYTHE CT21 306 H12
HYTHE CT21 307 Q10
MSTR CT12 236 B2
RASHE TN25 305 K9
RASHW TN26 304 E12
RASHW TN26 317 K10
RASHW TN26 318 B3
RCANTE CT3 232 D6
RCANTE CT3 234 G2
RCANTE CT3 236 C7
RDV CT15 215 H5
RFOLK CT18 218 D1
ROCH ME1 19 K6
RSIT ME9 226 B8
RSIT ME9 227 R8
RSIT ME9 228 D12
RYE TN31 225 K1
STRD ME2 82 F5
SWCH CT13 236 H9
SWCH CT13 237 N12
TENT TN30 327 Q3
WSTB CT5 127 J2
Saxon St DVW CT17 8 C4
Saxon Wk RSIT ME9 227 L9
Saxton Cl LEW SE13 46 E1
Saxton Rd LYDD TN29 335 M4
Saxton St GILL ME7 7 J4
Saxville Rd STMC/STPC BR5 73 J7
Sayer Cl GRH DA9 53 H3
Sayer Rd HDCN TN27 264 B5
Sayers La TENT TN30 315 M2
Sayes Court Rd
STMC/STPC BR5 73 H7
Sayes Court St DEPT SE8 26 A4
Scabharbour Rd RSEV TN14 255 K4
Scadbury Gdns STMC/STPC BR5 73 H6
Scads Hill Cl ORP BR6 91 G2
Scanlons Bridge Rd
HYTHE CT21 222 B3
Scarborough Cl
BH/WHM TN16 132 B4
Scarborough Dr IOS ME12 65 K5
Scarborough La ROCH ME1 113 L4
Scarbrook Rd CROY/NA CR0 86 D6
Scarlet Cl STMC/STPC BR5 73 J8
Scarlet Rd CAT SE6 46 F8
Scarsbrook Rd BKHTH/KID SE3 47 L1
Scawen Rd DEPT SE8 25 M4
Sceales Dr MSTR CT12 182 A7
Sceptre Wy WSTB CT5 126 C6
Scholars Ri STRD ME2 81 K6
Scholey Cl STRD ME2 113 J1
School Ap BGR/WK TN15 240 E2
School Av GILL ME7 101 M1
School Cl DART DA1 51 G2
MEO DA13 97 H3
The School Cl WGOS CT8 177 H4
School Fld EDEN TN8 192 D3
Schoolfield Rd WTHK RM20 33 H5
School Hl RCANTW CT4 247 N10
RRTW TN3 296 C7
School House La
STPH/PW TN12 280 D10
School La BGR/WK TN15 111 L5
BGR/WK TN15 136 E7
CANTW/ST CT2 153 H6
E/WMAL ME19 239 M8
EYN DA4 95 G2
FAV ME13 244 G11
HB CT6 155 H1
HOO/HM ME3 57 K7
MAID/SHEP ME15 167 M4
MEO DA13 239 M3
RAM CT11 17 J5
RCANTE CT3 155 M3
RCANTE CT3 235 M4
RCANTE CT3 251 M1
RCANTE CT3 251 R2
RCANTE CT3 252 B7
RCANTE CT3 252 F3
RCANTW CT4 175 K5
RCANTW CT4 249 Q12
RDART DA2 53 K8
RFOLK CT18 219 H6
RMAID ME17 260 F6
RMAID ME17 262 C3
ROCH ME1 99 L8
RSIT ME9 118 C2
RSIT ME9 119 G6
RSIT ME9 120 E7
RSIT ME9 226 D11
RSIT ME9 227 K10
RTON TN11 240 D11
RTON TN11 256 B5
RYE TN31 326 E12
RYE TN31 327 M12
SWLY BR8 75 J4
WELL DA16 49 J1
School Ri RTWE/PEM TN2 201 G4
School Rd CHST BR7 72 D5
DEAL CT14 272 H2
FAV ME13 149 J3
GVE DA12 55 K8
HDCN TN27 264 B5
HYTHE CT21 222 C1
RASHW TN26 286 F2
RASHW TN26 302 E1
RASHW TN26 317 K8
RCANTE CT3 235 R11
RFOLK CT18 292 D10
SIT ME10 120 C6
SWCH CT13 237 J12
School Ter HAWK TN18 312 D7
Schooner Cl POP/IOD E14 26 E2
Schooner Ct GRH DA9 52 D2
Schreiber Ms GILL ME7 * 7 M4
Scimitar Cl GILL ME7 102 B4
Scocles Rd IOS ME12 65 K8
Scoles Crs BRXS/STRHM SW2 44 B6
Scoones Cl RSIT ME9 120 F7
Scords La BH/WHM TN16 187 K2
Scotby Av WALD ME5 115 J1
Scotchmen Cl IOS ME12 64 F6
Scotia Rd BRXS/STRHM SW2 44 B5
Scotland La GVE DA12 80 B6
Scotney Cl ORP BR6 90 B7
Scotsdale Cl CHST BR7 72 F8
Scotsdale Rd LEE/GVPK SE12 47 J3
Scotshall La WARL CR6 131 H1
Scot's La RASHE TN25 290 A9
Scott Av RHAM ME8 103 H5
Scott Cl DIT/AY ME20 139 K5
STRHM/NOR SW16 68 A5
Scott Crs ERITH DA8 31 G7
Scotteswood Av CHAT ME4 101 G3
Scott Lidgett Crs
BERM/RHTH SE16 25 H1
Scotton St RASHE TN25 266 G11
Scott Rd CDW/CHF RM16 35 H3
GVE DA12 79 L2
TON TN9 194 C5
Scotts Acre RYE TN31 332 D7
Scotts Av HAYES BR2 70 E6
Scott's La HAYES BR2 70 E7
Scotts Pas WOOL/PLUM SE18 * 28 C3
Scotts Rd BMLY BR1 71 H4
Scott's Ter CHAT ME4 6 C8
Scott St MAID/BEAR ME14 12 F1
Scotts Wy RTWE/PEM TN2 200 F5
SEV TN13 135 K8
Scovell Crs STHWK SE1 * 24 D1
Scovell Rd STHWK SE1 24 D1
Scragged Oak Rd
MAID/BEAR ME14 116 D8
MAID/BEAR ME14 142 C3
MAID/BEAR ME14 143 K5
Scrapsgate Rd IOS ME12 65 H6
Scraps Hl RSIT ME9 120 F5
Scratchers La EYN DA4 94 E6
Scratton Flds GVE DA12 97 L1
Scrooby St CAT SE6 46 C4
Scudders Hl HART DA3 95 K2
Scutari Rd EDUL SE22 45 J3
Scylla Rd PECK SE15 45 J1
Sea Ap IOS ME12 230 D1
Seaborough Rd
CDW/CHF RM16 35 K2
Seabourne Wy LYDD TN29 320 G10
Seabrook Ct HYTHE CT21 223 J2
Seabrook Dr WWKM BR4 88 F5
Seabrooke Ri GRAYS RM17 34 C5
Seabrook Gdns HYTHE CT21 223 H3
Seabrook Gv HYTHE CT21 223 H3
Seabrook Rd RTON TN11 194 D2
Seabrook V HYTHE CT21 223 J1
Seacourt Rd ABYW SE2 29 L1
Seacroft Rd BRDST CT10 183 K4
Seadown Cl HYTHE CT21 223 H1
Seafield Rd BRDST CT10 183 J1
RAM CT11 16 E5
WSTB CT5 127 J2
Seaford Ct ROCH ME1 * 19 H9
Seagar Rd FAV ME13 123 J8
Seager Buildings DEPT SE8 * 26 B7
Seager Rd IOS ME12 64 F3
Seagrave Crs FOLKN CT19 221 G8
Seagull Rd STRD ME2 81 L7
Sealand Ct ROCH ME1 * 19 H8
Seal Dr BGR/WK TN15 136 E7
Seal Hollow Rd SEV TN13 21 L4
Seally Rd GRAYS RM17 34 B4
Seal Rd SEV TN13 136 C7
Seamark Cl MSTR CT12 180 A7
Seamark Rd MSTR CT12 180 A5
Seapoint Rd BRDST CT10 183 L2
Searchwood Rd WARL CR6 130 A4
Searles Rd STHWK SE1 24 E3
Sea Rd BRCH CT7 176 E5
DEAL CT14 211 K3
HYTHE CT21 223 H3
RYE TN31 332 E7
Sears St CMBW SE5 24 E6
Seasalter Beach WSTB CT5 126 B6
Seasalter Cl IOS ME12 230 D1
Seasalter Cross WSTB CT5 125 M3
Seasalter La WSTB CT5 152 A1
Seasalter Rd FAV ME13 124 F7
Seaside Av IOS ME12 65 K5
Sea St HB CT6 128 C6
RDV CT15 215 H3
Seathorpe Av IOS ME12 65 K6
Seaton Av HYTHE CT21 222 C2
Seaton Cl LBTH SE11 24 C4
Seaton Rd DART DA1 51 H5
GILL ME7 101 M2
RCANTE CT3 234 E11
WELL DA16 29 K6
Seaview HOO/HM ME3 43 J8
Sea View Av BRCH CT7 176 B5
Seaview Av IOS ME12 230 G4
Sea View Cl RFOLK CT18 221 J4
Sea View Gdns IOS ME12 230 D2
Sea View Hts BRCH CT7 * 176 A5
Seaview Hts LYDD TN29 * 330 C4
Sea View Rd BRCH CT7 176 B5
BRDST CT10 179 K7
HB CT6 129 K4
MSTR CT12 182 A7
RDV CT15 215 G5
Seaview Rd GILL ME7 7 K5
NROM TN28 331 M12
Sea View Sq HB CT6 * 129 G4
Sea View Ter FOLK CT20 * 223 L2
MARG CT9 14 B5
Seaview Ter QBOR ME11 * 64 B8
RSIT ME9 * 226 C10
RYE TN31 * 225 H4
Seaview Vls BRDST CT10 * 179 J4
Seaville Dr HB CT6 129 M4
Sea Wall LYDD TN29 321 K8
WSTB CT5 126 E3

Seaway Crs LYDD TN29 331 N1
Seaway Gdns LYDD TN29 331 N1
Seaway Rd LYDD TN29 331 N1
Second Av BRDST CT10 179 K3
GILL ME7 101 M2
IOS ME12 64 C4
IOS ME12 67 G8
MARG CT9 15 L2
QBOR ME11 227 N2
RYE TN31 332 E7
WALD ME5 101 K4
WTHK RM20 33 H5
Secretan Rd ROCH ME1 100 C4
Sedan Wy WALW SE17 24 F4
Sedcombe Cl SCUP DA14 73 J1
Sedgebrook Rd BKHTH/KID SE3 27 L8
Sedge Crs WALD ME5 114 F1
Sedgehill Rd CAT SE6 70 B2
Sedgemere Rd ABYW SE2 29 K2
Sedgeway CAT SE6 47 G6
Sedgewood Cl HAYES BR2 89 G3
Sedgmoor Pl CMBW SE5 24 F6
Sedley MEO DA13 78 B2
Sedley Cl DIT/AY ME20 139 M3
HOO/HM ME3 58 D6
RHAM ME8 116 D2
Sednem Ct PECK SE15 25 H8
Seeley Dr DUL SE21 68 F1
Sefton Cl STMC/STPC BR5 73 G8
Sefton Rd CROY/NA CR0 87 H4
STMC/STPC BR5 73 G8
Segrave Rd FOLKN CT19 221 G8
Selah Dr SWLY BR8 74 D5
Selbey Cl HB CT6 129 K5
Selborne Av BXLY DA5 49 M6
Selborne Rd CMBW SE5 24 E8
CROY/NA CR0 86 F6
MARG CT9 15 M8
SCUP DA14 73 J1
Selbourne Cl HART DA3 78 E7
Selbourne Rd GILL ME7 83 L6
Selbourne Sq GDST RH9 156 B8
Selbourne Wk
MAID/SHEP ME15 168 A7
Selby Cl CHST BR7 72 B3
Selby Rd MAID/SHEP ME15 260 A1
PGE/AN SE20 69 H6
Selbys LING RH7 190 F8
Selden Rd PECK SE15 25 K8
Selhurst New Rd SNWD SE25 86 F2
Selhurst Pl CROY/NA CR0 86 F2
Selhurst Rd SNWD SE25 86 F1
Selkirk Dr ERITH DA8 30 F7
Selkirk Rd DVE/WH CT16 213 J6
Sellbourne Pk RRTW TN3 294 B9
Sellindge Cl BECK BR3 70 A4
Selling Ct FAV ME13 246 H4
Selling Rd FAV ME13 149 M4
FAV ME13 246 H3
RCANTW CT4 247 N6
Selsdon Crs SAND/SEL CR2 104 B4
Selsdon Park Rd
SAND/SEL CR2 104 D3
Selsdon Rd SAND/SEL CR2 86 E8
WNWD SE27 44 C8
Selsdon Wy POP/IOD E14 26 C2
Selsea Av HB CT6 128 E4
Selsey Crs WELL DA16 29 L7
Selstead Cl RHAM ME8 102 C4
Selway Ct DEAL CT14 209 J6
Selwood Cl IOS ME12 64 F7
Selwood Rd CROY/NA CR0 87 J5
Selworthy Rd CAT SE6 46 A8
Selwyn Crs WELL DA16 49 J2
Selwyn Dr BRDST CT10 179 H8
Selwyn Rd TIL RM18 35 G8
Semaphore Rd BRCH CT7 176 C5
Semper Rd CDW/CHF RM16 35 K1
Semple Cl MSTR CT12 180 F6
Sempstead La RBTBR TN32 324 C12
Senacre La MAID/SHEP ME15 167 M7
Senacre Sq MAID/SHEP ME15 168 A6
Senate St PECK SE15 25 K8
Seneca Rd THHTH CR7 68 D8
Sene Pk HYTHE CT21 222 E2
Senlac Cl RAM CT11 16 C7
Senlac Pl RRTW TN3 * 199 K6
Senlac Rd LEE/GVPK SE12 47 J6
Sequoia Gdns ORP BR6 91 G3
Serenaders Rd BRXN/ST SW9 24 B8
Serene Ct BRDST CT10 183 L1
Sermon Dr SWLY BR8 74 D7
Serpentine Ct SEV TN13 21 L1
Serpentine Rd SEV TN13 21 L2
Serviden Dr BMLY BR1 71 L5
Sessions House Sq
MAID/BEAR ME14 12 F2
Setchell Rd STHWK SE1 25 G3
Setchell Wy STHWK SE1 25 G3
Setford Rd WALD ME5 101 K7
Setterfield House
HYTHE CT21 * 222 E3
Setterfield Rd MARG CT9 15 G7
Settington Av WALD ME5 101 K4
Sevastopol Pl CANT CT1 172 E8
Sevenacre Rd FAV ME13 123 K8
Seven Acres SWLY BR8 92 E2
Seven Mile La BGR/WK TN15 241 L1
STPH/PW TN12 256 H2
WBY/YAL ME18 241 M6
Sevenoaks By-Pass SEV TN13 255 J1
Sevenoaks Rd BGR/WK TN15 163 M1
BGR/WK TN15 240 B4
BROCKY SE4 46 A4
ORP BR6 91 G7
ORP BR6 107 L3
RSEV TN14 108 E3
RSEV TN14 136 A2
Sevenoaks Wy STMC/STPC BR5 73 K7
Seven Stones Dr BRDST CT10 183 K4
Severn TIL RM18 36 C2
Severnake Cl POP/IOD E14 26 B3
Severn Cl TONN TN10 188 F8
Severn Rd WALD ME5 101 K8
Sevington La KEN/WIL TN24 3 K9
Sevington Pk
MAID/SHEP ME15 167 G7
Seward Rd BECK BR3 69 L6
Sewell Cl BRCH CT7 176 D7
CDW/CHF RM16 33 K4
Sewell Rd ABYW SE2 29 H2
Sexburga Dr IOS ME12 65 J5
Sextant Av POP/IOD E14 26 E3
Sextant Pk STRD ME2 * 6 A1
Sexton Rd TIL RM18 35 G7
Seymour Av MARG CT9 177 J4
WSTB CT5 126 F4
Seymour Cl HB CT6 129 J8
Seymour Dr HAYES BR2 90 A4
Seymour Gdns BROCKY SE4 45 L1
Seymour Pl CANT CT1 4 C7
SNWD SE25 69 J8
Seymour Rd CDW/CHF RM16 33 K2
GVW DA11 55 G6
RDV CT15 215 G1
RHAM ME8 103 K5
TIL RM18 35 G7
WALD ME5 7 G7
Seymour St WOOL/PLUM SE18 28 D3
Seymour Ter PGE/AN SE20 69 J5
Seymour Vls PGE/AN SE20 69 J5
Seymour Wk SWCM DA10 53 M5
Seyssel St POP/IOD E14 26 D3
Shacklands Rd RSEV TN14 109 H5
Shackleton Cl FSTH SE23 45 J7
WALD ME5 101 J7
The Shades STRD ME2 81 J6
Shadoxhurst Rd RASHW TN26 303 K9
Shad Thames STHWK SE1 25 G1
Shaftesbury Av FOLKN CT19 219 M6
Shaftesbury Cl E/WMAL ME19 139 G4
Shaftesbury Dr MAIDW ME16 166 D1
Shaftesbury La DART DA1 52 C2
Shaftesbury Rd BECK BR3 70 A6
CANTW/ST CT2 171 M2
RCANTE CT3 155 M8
STH/RUST TN4 196 D7
WSTB CT5 126 E4
Shaftsbury St RAM CT11 17 L5
Shah Pl RAM CT11 17 H4
Shakespeare Av TIL RM18 35 J8
Shakespeare Farm Rd
HOO/HM ME3 41 G6
Shakespeare Rd BRCH CT7 176 D5
BXLYHN DA7 29 M7
DART DA1 52 B2
DVW CT17 217 J3
GILL ME7 7 J7
HNHL SE24 44 C3
MARG CT9 15 G6
SIT ME10 120 B5
TON TN9 194 C5
Shakespeare Ter FOLK CT20 11 H6
Shalford Cl ORP BR6 90 D7
Shalloak Rd CANTW/ST CT2 172 E4
Shallons Rd ELTH/MOT SE9 72 C1
Shallows Rd BRDST CT10 178 F7
Shalmsford Ct RCANTW CT4 248 D7
Shalmsford Rd RCANTW CT4 247 R7
Shalmsford St RCANTW CT4 248 B7
The Shambles SEV TN13 21 J7
Shamrock Av WSTB CT5 126 C6
Shamrock Rd CROY/NA CR0 86 A2
GVE DA12 55 M5
Shandon Cl RTWE/PEM TN2 23 K4
Shand St STHWK SE1 24 F1
Shanklin Cl WALD ME5 101 K5
Shannon Gv BRXN/ST SW9 44 A2
Shannon Wy BECK BR3 70 C3
Shapland Cl HB CT6 129 K6
Shardcroft Av HNHL SE24 44 C3
Shardeloes Rd BROCKY SE4 26 A8
Shard's Sq PECK SE15 25 H5
Share & Coulter Rd WSTB CT5 127 L4
Sharfleet Dr STRD ME2 81 J6
Sharland Cl THHTH CR7 86 B2
Sharland Rd GVE DA12 55 K7
Sharman Ct SCUP DA14 73 H1
Sharnal La SNOD ME6 113 H6
Sharnal St HOO/HM ME3 60 B4
Sharnbrooke Cl WELL DA16 49 K1
Sharon Crs WALD ME5 115 G1
Sharp's Fld HDCN TN27 283 M4
Sharps Gn GILL ME7 84 E8
Sharp Wy DART DA1 52 A1
Sharratt St PECK SE15 25 K5
Sharsted Hl RSIT ME9 244 F1
Sharsted St WALW SE17 24 C4
Sharsted Wy GILL ME7 116 B2
MAID/BEAR ME14 * 142 C8
Shawbrooke Rd ELTH/MOT SE9 47 L2
Shawbury Rd EDUL SE22 45 G3
Shaw Cl HOO/HM ME3 58 C6
MAID/BEAR ME14 141 K6
Shaw Crs TIL RM18 35 J7
Shaw Cross KEN/WIL TN24 203 G6
Shawdon Av SWCH CT13 207 H2
Shawfield Pk BMLY BR1 71 L6
Shaw Rd BH/WHM TN16 132 B6
BMLY BR1 47 G8
EDUL SE22 44 F2
Shaw's Cottages FSTH SE23 45 M8
Shawstead Rd WALD ME5 101 K6
Shaws Wy ROCH ME1 100 C2
The Shaw CHST BR7 * 72 D4
RTWE/PEM TN2 23 K8
Shaxton Crs CROY/NA CR0 105 H3
Sheafe Dr CRBK TN17 298 F8
Sheal's Crs MAID/SHEP ME15 13 H9
Shearers Cl MAID/BEAR ME14 167 M1
Shearman Rd BKHTH/KID SE3 47 G2
Shearwater HART DA3 78 C7
MAIDW ME16 140 C8
Shearwater Av WSTB CT5 126 D6
Shearwater Cl STRD ME2 81 K6
Shearwater Ct IOS ME12 64 C5
Shear Wy LYDD TN29 320 H4
Shearway Rd FOLKN CT19 220 A6
Shearwood Crs DART DA1 51 G1
Sheenewood SYD SE26 69 J2
Sheen Rd STMC/STPC BR5 73 G8
Sheen Wy WLGTN SM6 86 A8
Sheepbarn La WARL CR6 105 M6
Sheepcote La STMC/STPC BR5 74 B8
Sheepfold La ASH TN23 204 F7
Sheephurst La STPH/PW TN12 280 D4
Sheepstreet La
BUR/ETCH TN19 322 A2
WADH TN5 310 C11
Sheerness Docks IOS ME12 * 64 C3
Sheerstone RSIT ME9 227 L10
Sheerwater Rd RCANTE CT3 235 L8
Sheerways FAV ME13 149 H3
Sheet Glass Rd QBOR ME11 227 P2
Sheet Hl BGR/WK TN15 240 C8
Sheffield Gdns DEAL CT14 209 K5
Sheffield Rd STH/RUST TN4 196 C3
The Sheilings BGR/WK TN15 136 E6
Shelbury Cl SCUP DA14 49 H8
Shelbury Rd EDUL SE22 45 J3
Shelden Dr RHAM ME8 103 G5
Sheldon Cl LEE/GVPK SE12 47 J3
PGE/AN SE20 69 J5
RCANTE CT3 251 R11
Sheldon Rd BXLYHN DA7 30 A7
Sheldon St CROY/NA CR0 86 D6
Sheldon Wy DIT/AY ME20 139 H2
Sheldwich Cl ASH TN23 204 C5
Sheldwich Ter HAYES BR2 * 89 M2
Shelford Ri NRWD SE19 68 F4
Shellbank La RDART DA2 77 J2
Shell Cl HAYES BR2 89 M2
Shelldrake Cl HOO/HM ME3 43 J8
Shelley Av CANT CT1 172 D7
Shelley Cl ORP BR6 90 F6
Shelley Dr WELL DA16 28 F7
Shelley Pl TIL RM18 35 J7
Shelley Ri ROCH ME1 100 B2
Shelley Rd MAIDW ME16 166 D3
Shelleys La RSEV TN14 133 M2
Shellness Rd IOS ME12 230 H4
Shellons St FOLK CT20 11 K5
Shell Rd LEW SE13 46 C1
Shelton Av WARL CR6 130 B4
Shelton Cl TONN TN10 188 F8
WARL CR6 130 B3
Shelvin La RCANTW CT4 270 H11
Shenden Cl SEV TN13 162 B6
Shenden Wy SEV TN13 162 B6
Shenley Gv MAID/BEAR ME14 141 G3
Shenley Pk HDCN TN27 * 283 M7
Shenley Rd CMBW SE5 24 F7
DART DA1 52 B4
Shepherd Cl ASH TN23 204 B6
Shepherd Dr KEN/WIL TN24 3 L9
Shepherds Cl ORP BR6 91 G6
Shepherd's Close Rd
RCANTW CT4 175 M8
Shepherdsgate CANTW/ST CT2 * 4 E2
Shepherds Ga GILL ME7 102 A8
Shepherdsgate Dr HB CT6 155 H1
Shepherds Gate Dr
MAID/BEAR ME14 141 M8
Shepherds Gn CHST BR7 72 E4
Shepherdsgrove La
EGRIN RH19 274 E8
Shepherds La DART DA1 51 H6
Shepherd's Leas
ELTH/MOT SE9 * 48 E2
Shepherd St GVW DA11 54 E5
Shepherds Wk HYTHE CT21 321 R1
RTWE/PEM TN2 23 L4
WSTB CT5 127 K5
Shepherds Wy HOO/HM ME3 61 K1
RMAID ME17 260 F1
SAND/SEL CR2 104 C2
WSTB CT5 127 K5
Shepherdswell Rd RDV CT15 272 B6
Sheppard Dr BERM/RHTH SE16 25 J4
Shepperton Cl WALD ME5 115 K1
Shepperton Rd
STMC/STPC BR5 90 D2
Sheppey Cl BRCH CT7 176 C6
ERITH DA8 31 J6
Sheppey Ct IOS ME12 * 64 E6
Sheppey Rd MAID/SHEP ME15 167 G6
Sheppey St IOS ME12 64 B3
Sheppey Vw WSTB CT5 126 D7
Sheppey Wy IOS ME12 228 A2
RSIT ME9 119 K1
RSIT ME9 227 P6
Sheppy Pl GVE DA12 55 J5
Shepway KEN/WIL TN24 203 H6
Shepway Cl FOLKN CT19 11 J3
Shepway Ct
MAID/SHEP ME15 * 167 K5
Sherard Rd ELTH/MOT SE9 47 M3
Sheraton Ct WALD ME5 115 G4
Sherborne Cl RTWE/PEM TN2 23 M8
Sherborne Gv BGR/WK TN15 136 F3
Sherborne Rd STMC/STPC BR5 91 G1
Sherbourne Cl BGR/WK TN15 111 K1
Sherbourne Dr MAIDW ME16 166 C3
STRD ME2 82 B4
Sherbrooke Cl BXLYHN DA7 50 B2
Sherenden La STPH/PW TN12 280 H9
Sherenden Rd RTON TN11 256 A12
Sherfield Rd GRAYS RM17 34 C5
Sheridan Cl MAID/BEAR ME14 140 F5
WALD ME5 101 K6
Sheridan Ct DART DA1 52 B2
Sheridan Crs CHST BR7 72 C6
Sheridan Rd BELV DA17 30 B3
BXLYHN DA7 49 M1
DVE/WH CT16 213 J6
Sheridan Wy BECK BR3 70 A5
Sheriff Dr WALD ME5 115 H3
Sheringham Cl MAIDW ME16 140 E6
RBTBR TN32 323 R12
Sheringham Rd PGE/AN SE20 69 J6
Sherington Rd CHARL SE7 27 J5
Sherlies Av ORP BR6 90 F5
Sherman Cl GILL ME7 102 C4
Sherman Rd BMLY BR1 71 H5
Shernden La EDEN TN8 192 D8
Shernolds MAID/SHEP ME15 167 J6
Sheron Cl DEAL CT14 209 H4
Sherriffs Court La MSTR CT12 180 C7
Sherway Cl HDCN TN27 283 M4
Sherway Rd HDCN TN27 284 A2
Sherwin Rd NWCR SE14 25 L7
Sherwood Av WALD ME5 115 H3
Sherwood Cl BXLY DA5 49 K4
FAV ME13 149 J1
HB CT6 129 K7
KEN/WIL TN24 203 G4
WSTB CT5 126 D7
Sherwood Ct WGOS CT8 * 177 H4
Sherwood Dr WSTB CT5 126 D7
Sherwood Gdns POP/IOD E14 26 B3
RAM CT11 183 H4
STHWK SE1 25 H4
Sherwood Pk
RTWE/PEM TN2 * 197 H8
Sherwood Park Av BFN/LL DA15 49 H5
Sherwood Pl RRTW TN3 199 M2
Sherwood Rd BRCH CT7 176 C8
CROY/NA CR0 87 J3
RTWE/PEM TN2 23 M1
WELL DA16 48 F1
Sherwoods WALD ME5 * 114 E4
Sherwood Wy
RTWE/PEM TN2 197 G7
WWKM BR4 88 D5
Shieldhall St ABYW SE2 29 K3
Shifford Pth FSTH SE23 45 L8
Shillingheld Cl
MAID/BEAR ME14 142 A8
Shimmin Rd RSIT ME9 * 145 L3
Shingle Barn La
MAID/SHEP ME15 258 B2
Shinglewell Rd ERITH DA8 30 B6
Shinners Cl SNWD SE25 87 H1
Shipbourne Rd TON TN9 194 F1
Ship Cl LYDD TN29 320 H9
Ship Field Cl BH/WHM TN16 132 B7
Ship Hl BH/WHM TN16 132 C7
Ship La ROCH ME1 6 A5
SOCK/AV RM15 32 E1
SWLY BR8 75 L5
Shipley Hills Rd MEO DA13 97 G4
Shipley Mill Cl ASH TN23 204 F7
Shipman Av CANTW/ST CT2 171 K5
Shipman Rd FSTH SE23 45 L7
Shipmans Wy DVE/WH CT16 213 H6
Ship & Mermaid Rw STHWK SE1 24 E1
Ship St DEPT SE8 26 B7
FOLKN CT19 11 J4
Shipwright Rd
BERM/RHTH SE16 25 M1
Shipwrights Av CHAT ME4 101 H3
The Shipyard FAV ME13 * 123 L8
Shirburn Cl FSTH SE23 45 K5
Shirebrook Rd BKHTH/KID SE3 27 L8
Shirehall Rd RDART DA2 75 L2
Shire La FAV ME13 244 F11
ORP BR6 106 E2
The Shires STPH/PW TN12 279 K2
Shires Wk EDEN TN8 192 D2
Shireway Cl FOLKN CT19 10 D1
Shirley Av BXLY DA5 49 L5
CROY/NA CR0 87 K4
RAM CT11 183 H3
Shirley Church Rd
CROY/NA CR0 87 L6
Shirley Cl DART DA1 51 K2
GVE DA12 56 C7
Shirley Crs BECK BR3 69 M8
Shirley Gdns STH/RUST TN4 200 D1
STH/RUST TN4 277 R12
Shirley Gv STH/RUST TN4 277 R12
Shirley Hills Rd CROY/NA CR0 87 L8
Shirley Oaks Rd CROY/NA CR0 87 L4
Shirley Park Rd CROY/NA CR0 87 J5
Shirley Rd BFN/LL DA15 48 F8
CROY/NA CR0 87 K5
Shirley Rw SNWD SE25 * 69 H6
Shirley Wy CROY/NA CR0 88 A6
MAID/SHEP ME15 168 B2
Shoebury Ter IOS ME12 * 66 B8
Sholden Bank DEAL CT14 208 F5
Sholden Gdns STMC/STPC BR5 91 K1
Sholden New Rd DEAL CT14 209 G4
Sholden Rd STRD ME2 82 D4
Shooter's Hl DVW CT17 8 A2
RDV CT15 272 D5
WOOL/PLUM SE18 28 A7
Shooters Hill Rd
BKHTH/KID SE3 26 F7
WOOL/PLUM SE18 27 M7
Shore Cl BRCH CT7 * 176 A5
HB CT6 128 C6
Shorefields RHAM ME8 103 H3
Shoregate La RSIT ME9 226 A7
Shoreham Cl CROY/NA CR0 87 K2
Shoreham La RSEV TN14 108 F6
TENT TN30 301 M10
Shoreham Pl RSEV TN14 109 M6
Shoreham Rd RSEV TN14 136 A1
STMC/STPC BR5 73 J5
Shoreham Wy HAYES BR2 89 H2
Shorehill La BGR/WK TN15 136 F1
The Shore GVW DA11 54 E3
Shorland Ct ROCH ME1 * 19 H8
Shorncliffe Crs FOLK CT20 19 A5
Shorncliffe Rd FOLK CT20 10 C5
STHWK SE1 25 G4
Shorndean St CAT SE6 46 D6
Shorne Cl BFN/LL DA15 49 J4
STMC/STPC BR5 73 L8
Shornefield Cl BMLY BR1 72 B7
Shorne Ifield Rd GVE DA12 80 C3
Shortlands Cl BELV DA17 30 A2
Shortlands Gdns HAYES BR2 70 F6
Shortlands Gv HAYES BR2 70 E7
Shortlands Rd HAYES BR2 70 E7
SIT ME10 120 B5
Short La LYDD TN29 318 B11
OXTED RH8 185 J2
RDV CT15 293 Q8
Short's Prospect IOS ME12 229 M5
Shorts Reach ROCH ME1 * 19 H8
Short St CHAT ME4 7 G8
IOS ME12 64 C3
RCANTE CT3 252 F9
STHWK SE1 24 B1
SWCH CT13 237 K12
Shorts Wy ROCH ME1 100 B3
Shortway ELTH/MOT SE9 47 M1
Shottendane Rd BRCH CT7 181 G1
Shottenden La RCANTW CT4 246 F11
Shottenden Rd FAV ME13 246 B10
GILL ME7 83 L6
RCANTW CT4 246 F9
Shottery Cl ELTH/MOT SE9 47 M8
Shovelstrode La EGRIN RH19 274 D11
Showfields Rd
RTWE/PEM TN2 201 G4
Shrapnel Cl WOOL/PLUM SE18 27 M6
Shrapnel Rd ELTH/MOT SE9 48 A1
Shrewsbury La
WOOL/PLUM SE18 28 C7
Shrewsbury Rd BECK BR3 69 M7
Shrimpton Cl RCANTW CT4 247 N6
Shroffold Rd BMLY BR1 70 F1
Shropshire Ter
MAID/SHEP ME15 167 M6
Shrubbery Rd EYN DA4 76 E5
GVE DA12 55 J6
The Shrubbery DEAL CT14 209 K8
RCANTW CT4 * 270 E4
Shrubcote TENT TN30 315 P2
Shrub Hill Rd WSTB CT5 127 L6
Shrublands Av CROY/NA CR0 88 B7
Shrublands Cl SYD SE26 45 K8
Shrublands Ct
RTWE/PEM TN2 * 23 K3
Shrub La WADH TN5 310 C12
Shrubsall Cl ELTH/MOT SE9 47 M6
Shrubsole Av IOS ME12 64 D4
Shrubsole Dr
MAID/BEAR ME14 140 F2
Shuart La BRCH CT7 233 N5
Shurland Av IOS ME12 65 J7
IOS ME12 230 G4
SIT ME10 120 A8
Shurland Gdns PECK SE15 * 25 G6
Shurlock Av SWLY BR8 74 E6
Shurlock Dr ORP BR6 90 D7
Shuttle Cl BFN/LL DA15 49 G5
Shuttlemead BXLY DA5 50 A5
Shuttle Rd BRDST CT10 183 L1
DART DA1 51 H1
Shuttlesfield La RCANTW CT4 291 N8
Sibert's Cl RDV CT15 272 A8
Sibley Cl BXLYHS DA6 49 M3
Sibthorpe Rd LEE/GVPK SE12 47 K5
Sidcup By-Pass Rd SCUP DA14 72 F1
Sidcup Hl SCUP DA14 73 J2
Sidcup Hill Gdns SCUP DA14 * 73 K2
Sidcup Pl SCUP DA14 73 H2
Sidcup Rd LEE/GVPK SE12 47 J3
Siddons Rd CROY/NA CR0 86 B6
FSTH SE23 45 M7
Sidewood Rd ELTH/MOT SE9 48 E6
Sidford Pl STHWK SE1 24 A2
The Sidings MEO DA13 * 97 H1
RFOLK CT18 291 M10
Sidmouth Rd PECK SE15 25 G7
STMC/STPC BR5 73 J8
WELL DA16 29 K6
Sidney Cl RTWE/PEM TN2 200 F5
Sidney Gdns RSEV TN14 136 B2
Sidney Rd BECK BR3 69 M6
BRXN/ST SW9 24 A8
GILL ME7 83 K6
ROCH ME1 100 B3
SNWD SE25 87 H1
Sidney St FOLKN CT19 11 L2
MAIDW ME16 166 D3
Siebert Rd BKHTH/KID SE3 27 H5
Siemens Rd WOOL/PLUM SE18 27 L2
Sienna Ct RHAM ME8 * 116 E1
Signal Ct LING RH7 190 F8
Signpost Fld RTON TN11 * 256 D8
Silchester Ct
MAID/BEAR ME14 141 K6
Silecroft Ct ASH TN23 * 204 B2
Silecroft Rd BXLYHN DA7 30 B7
Silex St STHWK SE1 24 C1
Silk Cl LEE/GVPK SE12 47 H3
Silkham Rd OXTED RH8 157 J5
Silk Mills Cl RSEV TN14 136 B7
Silk Mills Pth LEW SE13 46 D1
Silver Av BRCH CT7 176 E7
Silver Bank WALD ME5 101 H7
Silver Birch Av MEO DA13 239 L4
Silver Birch Cl CAT SE6 46 A8
RDART DA2 74 F1
Silver Birches STH/RUST TN4 * 196 E5
WALD ME5 115 H2
Silver Birch Gv ASH TN23 204 E7
Silver Cl NWCR SE14 * 25 M6
TON TN9 194 E7
Silverdale HART DA3 78 A8
MAIDW ME16 166 A3
SYD SE26 69 K1
Silverdale Av IOS ME12 65 H7
Silverdale Dr ELTH/MOT SE9 47 M7
HB CT6 129 L7
RHAM ME8 102 F6
Silverdale Gv SIT ME10 119 K6
Silverdale La HAWK TN18 313 J12
STH/RUST TN4 196 E7
Silverdale Rd BXLYHN DA7 30 C8
RAM CT11 16 B8
STH/RUST TN4 196 E7
STMC/STPC BR5 73 H7
Silver Hl CHAT ME4 6 D7
ROCH ME1 * 100 A3
Silver Hill Gdns CHAT ME4 6 D7
KEN/WIL TN24 3 M7
Silver Hill Rd KEN/WIL TN24 3 M7
Silverhurst Dr TONN TN10 188 F7
Silverlands Rd RFOLK CT18 291 M10
Silver La WWKM BR4 88 E5
Silverleigh Rd THHTH CR7 68 A8
Silverlocke Rd GRAYS RM17 34 E5
Silvermere Rd LEW SE13 46 B4
Silvermere Rw SNWD SE25 * 69 H6
Silver Rd GVE DA12 55 M7
Silverspot Cl RHAM ME8 103 G6
Silver Spring Cl ERITH DA8 30 C5
Silversted La BH/WHM TN16 133 K6
The Silvers BRDST CT10 182 F1
Silver St DEAL CT14 209 L2
RSIT ME9 145 G4
Silver Tree WALD ME5 115 H4
Silverweed Rd WALD ME5 101 G8
Silverwood Cl BECK BR3 70 B4
CROY/NA CR0 104 E3
Silvester Rd EDUL SE22 45 G3
Silvester St STHWK SE1 * 24 D1
Silwood Estate Regeneration
Area DEPT SE8 25 L4
Silwood St BERM/RHTH SE16 25 L4
Simcoe Ter DVE/WH CT16 * 213 J6
Simmonds La
MAID/SHEP ME15 168 C7
Simmonds Rd CANT CT1 4 C7
Simmons Rd WOOL/PLUM SE18 28 C4
Simms Rd STHWK SE1 25 H3
Simnel Rd LEE/GVPK SE12 47 J5
Simon Av MARG CT9 179 G3
Simone Cl BMLY BR1 71 L5
Simon's Av ASH TN23 204 C4
Simpson Rd SIT ME10 119 K4
SNOD ME6 113 H7
Simpson's Rd HAYES BR2 71 H7
Sinclair Cl RHAM ME8 102 F8
Sinclair Wy RDART DA2 76 E1
Singapore Dr GILL ME7 7 G3
Singledge Av DVE/WH CT16 213 H3
Singledge La RDV CT15 272 C10
Singles Cross RSEV TN14 * 134 C1
Single's Cross La RSEV TN14 134 B1
Single St BH/WHM TN16 133 G1
Singleton Cl CROY/NA CR0 86 D3
MSTR CT12 180 E7
Singleton Hl ASH TN23 204 A3
Singleton Rd ASH TN23 286 H8
Singlewell Rd GVW DA11 55 J8
Sion Hl RAM CT11 17 J7
Sion Houses RTW TN1 * 22 F7
Sion Wk RTW TN1 * 22 F7
Sirdar Strd GVE DA12 80 A2
Sir David's Pk STH/RUST TN4 196 B4
Sir Evelyn Rd ROCH ME1 100 C5
Sir John Hawkins Wy
CHAT ME4 6 C5
Sir John Kirk Cl CMBW SE5 24 D6
Sir John Moore Av
HYTHE CT21 222 B3
Sir John Moore Barracks
FOLK CT20 * 223 L1
Sir Thomas Longley Rd
STRD ME2 6 B1
Siskin Cl RASHE TN25 202 E4
RFOLK CT18 219 M1
Siskin Gdns STPH/PW TN12 279 K4
Sissinghurst Cl BMLY BR1 70 F2
Sissinghurst Dr MAIDW ME16 166 C1
Sissinghurst Rd CRBK TN17 299 N5
CROY/NA CR0 87 H3
HDCN TN27 300 A3
Sister Mabels Wy PECK SE15 25 H6
Sisulu Pl BRXN/ST SW9 44 B1
Sittingbourne Rd
MAID/BEAR ME14 13 J4
Siward Rd HAYES BR2 71 J7
Six Bells La SEV TN13 21 J8
Six Bells Ms RYE TN31 325 K8
Six Fields Pth TENT TN30 315 M2
Six Penny Cl EDEN TN8 192 D5
Sixth Av IOS ME12 67 H8
Skeete Rd RFOLK CT18 291 K10
Skeet Hill La STMC/STPC BR5 92 A5
Skeffington St
WOOL/PLUM SE18 28 D2
Skene Cl RHAM ME8 103 H4
Sketchley Gdns
BERM/RHTH SE16 25 L4
Skeynes Rd EDEN TN8 192 C4
Skibbs La ORP BR6 91 M6
Skid Hill La WARL CR6 131 L1
Skiffington Cl
BRXS/STRHM SW2 44 B6
Skinner Gdns CRBK TN17 299 K5
Skinner Rd LYDD TN29 334 D4
Skinners Cl DIT/AY ME20 114 B7
Skinners La EDEN TN8 192 E3
Skinner St CHAT ME4 6 D7
GILL ME7 7 J3
Skinner's Wy RMAID ME17 260 F1
Skinney La EYN DA4 76 E7
Skippers Cl GRH DA9 53 J3
Skye Cl MAID/SHEP ME15 167 H6
Skylark Wy ASH TN23 205 G8
Sladebrook Rd BKHTH/KID SE3 47 L1
Slade Cl WALD ME5 115 J3
Sladedale Rd
WOOL/PLUM SE18 28 F4
Slade Gdns ERITH DA8 31 G7
Slade Green Rd ERITH DA8 31 G7
Slade Rd FAV ME13 244 A9
Slades Cl WSTB CT5 127 K5
Slades Dr CHST BR7 48 D8
The Slade RRTW TN3 296 B10
TON TN9 194 E3
WOOL/PLUM SE18 28 F4
Slade Wk WALW SE17 24 C5
Slagrove Pl LEW SE13 46 B3
Slaithwaite Rd LEW SE13 46 D2
Slaney Rd STPH/PW TN12 282 A5
Slatin Rd STRD ME2 18 F1

Sleepers Farm Rd
CDW/CHF RM16 35 J1
Sleepers Stile Rd WADH TN5 295 Q12
Sleigh Rd CANTW/ST CT2 173 G3
Slicketts Hl CHAT ME4 * 6 E6
Slines New Rd CTHM CR3 130 C6
Slines Oak Rd CTHM CR3 130 F5
Slip La RDV CT15 293 N7
Slip Mill Rd HAWK TN18 312 B5
Slippers Pl BERM/RHTH SE16 25 J2
Slip Rd CHAT ME4 83 H5
The Slip BH/WHM TN16 159 H4
Sloane Gdns ORP BR6 90 D6
Sloane Sq HART DA3 * 77 M7
Sloane Wk CROY/NA CR0 88 A2
Sloe La BRDST CT10 178 E7
Slough Rd RSIT ME9 146 B5
Small Bridge Rd CRBK TN17 297 K4
Small Grains HART DA3 95 J6
Small Hythe Cl
MAID/SHEP ME15 168 C3
Smallhythe Rd TENT TN30 315 L2
Small Profits WBY/YAL ME18 257 R2
Smarden Cl BELV DA17 30 B4
Smarden Rd HDCN TN27 283 M5
HDCN TN27 285 K4
HDCN TN27 300 F1
Smarts Hl RTON TN11 276 H8
Smarts Rd GVE DA12 55 J8
Smeed Cl SIT ME10 120 C5
Smetham Gdns STRD ME2 82 C4
Smiles Pl LEW SE13 26 D8
Smithers Cl RTON TN11 256 B4
Smithers La STPH/PW TN12 257 L6
Smithfield Rd HOO/HM ME3 43 K8
Smithies Rd ABYW SE2 29 J3
Smith Rd WALD ME5 115 J2
Smith's Hl MAID/SHEP ME15 258 B1
Smiths La EDEN TN8 186 D3
Smiths Orch RSIT ME9 145 G4
Smith St STRD ME2 18 E5
Smithy Dr ASH TN23 204 F7
The Smithy WADH TN5 308 F6
Smugglers Leap MSTR CT12 * 180 F5
Smugglers Ms HAWK TN18 312 D8
Smuggler's Wy BRCH CT7 176 D5
Smugglers Whf GRH DA9 53 J3
Smyrks Rd WALW SE17 24 F4
Smythe Cl STH/RUST TN4 196 B2
Smythe Rd EYN DA4 76 B5
Snag La RSEV TN14 107 J6
Snakes Hl RCANTE CT3 251 R4
Snape La WADH TN5 309 K8
Snape Vw WADH TN5 309 L5
Snargate La LYDD TN29 318 A12
Snargate St DVW CT17 8 C7
Snatts Hl OXTED RH8 157 L7
Snell Gdns HB CT6 128 C7
Snelling Av GVW DA11 55 G7
Snipe Cl ERITH DA8 31 J6
RASHE TN25 202 F4
RTWE/PEM TN2 278 B9
Snoad La STPH/PW TN12 281 M9
Snodhurst Av WALD ME5 100 F8
Snodland Rd E/WMAL ME19 112 D7
Snoggers Hl FAV ME13 247 M2
Snoll Hatch Rd STPH/PW TN12 257 J8
Snowbell Rd ASH TN23 204 E7
Snowdon Av MAID/BEAR ME14 13 K3
Snowdon Cl WALD ME5 101 J6
Snowdon Pde
MAID/BEAR ME14 * 13 L3
Snowdown Cl PGE/AN SE20 69 K5
Snowdrop Cl FOLKN CT19 220 D5
Snowsfields STHWK SE1 24 E1
Snughorne La HDCN TN27 283 R9
Soames St PECK SE15 45 G1
Sobraon Wy CANT CT1 172 E8
Solar Ct RAM CT11 * 16 D9
Solefields Rd SEV TN13 162 A6
Soleoak Dr SEV TN13 162 A5
Soleshill Rd RCANTW CT4 246 H8
RCANTW CT4 247 J8
Sole St MEO DA13 97 L1
Solomon Rd RHAM ME8 103 G4
Solomons La FAV ME13 149 L2
Solomon's Pas PECK SE15 45 J2
Solomons Rd CHAT ME4 6 D5
Solway TIL RM18 36 D2
Solway Rd EDUL SE22 45 H2
Somerden Rd STMC/STPC BR5 91 L3
Somerfield Cl MAIDW ME16 * 12 B4
Somerfield La MAIDW ME16 12 B3
Somerfield Rd MAIDW ME16 12 B4
Somerfield St
BERM/RHTH SE16 25 L4
Somerford Wy
BERM/RHTH SE16 25 M1
Somerhill Av BFN/LL DA15 49 J5
Somerhill Rd TON TN9 195 G5
WELL DA16 29 J8
Somerleyton Rd BRXN/ST SW9 44 B2
Somerset Av WELL DA16 49 G3
Somerset Barracks
FOLK CT20 * 223 L1
Somerset Cl SIT ME10 119 K5
WALD ME5 101 K5
WSTB CT5 126 C6
Somerset Ct MSTR CT12 * 182 E3
Somerset Gdns LEW SE13 26 C8
STRHM/NOR SW16 68 A7
Somerset Rd CANT CT1 5 M5
DART DA1 51 J4
DEAL CT14 209 J6
FOLKN CT19 219 M7
KEN/WIL TN24 2 C4
MAID/SHEP ME15 167 K5
ORP BR6 91 H3
SLH/COR SS17 36 B1
STH/RUST TN4 196 D7
Somerset Vls RRTW TN3 * 199 K6
Somersham Rd BXLYHN DA7 29 M8
Somers Pl BRXS/STRHM SW2 44 A5
Somers Rd BRXS/STRHM SW2 44 A4
Somerton Rd PECK SE15 45 J2
Somertrees Av LEE/GVPK SE12 47 J7
Somerville Gdns STH/RUST TN4 22 D4
Somerville Rd DART DA1 52 A4
PGE/AN SE20 69 L4
Somme Ct CANT CT1 172 E8
Somner Cl CANTW/ST CT2 4 B2
Somner Wk MAID/SHEP ME15 260 A1
Sondes Cl HB CT6 129 H7
Sondes Rd DEAL CT14 209 L4
Sondes St WALW SE17 24 E5
Songhurst Cl CROY/NA CR0 86 A2
Sonning Rd CROY/NA CR0 87 H2
Sonora Wy SIT ME10 119 K3
Soper Cl FSTH SE23 45 L6
Soper's La HAWK TN18 311 R5
Sophurst La STPH/PW TN12 278 G12
Sophurst Wd STPH/PW TN12 * 278 G12
Sopwith Cl BH/WHM TN16 132 C2
Sorrel Bank CROY/NA CR0 104 D4
Sorrell Cl BRXN/ST SW9 * 24 B8
NWCR SE14 25 M6
Sorrell Rd WALD ME5 115 G1
Sorrell Wy GVW DA11 78 F1
Sortmill Rd SNOD ME6 113 J6
Sotherton KEN/WIL TN24 205 H4
Souberg Cl DEAL CT14 209 K1
Sounds Ldg SWLY BR8 92 D2
Southall Cl MSTR CT12 180 F6
Southall Pl STHWK SE1 24 E1
Southampton Wy CMBW SE5 24 E6
South Ash Rd BGR/WK TN15 238 D1
South Av RDV CT15 271 M2
RHAM ME8 102 B3
SIT ME10 120 B6
South Bank BH/WHM TN16 159 J4
HOO/HM ME3 58 C3
RMAID ME17 260 F6
STPH/PW TN12 281 R7
South Barham Rd
RCANTW CT4 270 D7
Southborough La HAYES BR2 89 M1
Southborough Rd BMLY BR1 71 M7
Southbourne ASH TN23 204 B6
HAYES BR2 89 H3
Southbourne Gdns
LEE/GVPK SE12 47 J3
Southbourne Gv WALD ME5 115 H1
Southbourne Rd FOLKN CT19 11 M4
Southbridge Pl CROY/NA CR0 86 D7
Southbridge Rd CROY/NA CR0 86 D7
Southbrook Rd LEW SE13 46 F4
South Bush La RHAM ME8 103 J7
South Canterbury Rd CANT CT1 5 G8
South Cliff Pde BRDST CT10 183 K4
South Cl BXLYHS DA6 49 L2
CANT CT1 5 G4
Southcote Rd SNWD SE25 87 J1
South Court Dr RCANTE CT3 251 R2
South Crs RMAID ME17 258 H2
Southcroft Av WELL DA16 48 F1
WWKM BR4 88 D5
Southcroft Rd ORP BR6 90 F6
South Croxted Rd DUL SE21 44 E8
Southdene RSEV TN14 108 E7
Southdown Rd CTHM CR3 130 E8
IOS ME12 64 F7
South Dr ORP BR6 90 F8
South Eastern Rd RAM CT11 16 F6
STRD ME2 19 H3
South Eden Park Rd BECK BR3 70 C8
Southenay La RASHE TN25 290 A12
RASHE TN25 306 G2
South End CROY/NA CR0 86 D8
Southend Cl ELTH/MOT SE9 48 C4
Southend Crs ELTH/MOT SE9 48 B4
Southend La CAT SE6 70 B1
Southend Rd BECK BR3 70 B5
GRAYS RM17 34 D3
Southern Av SNWD SE25 69 G7
Southernden Rd HDCN TN27 261 R12
Southerngate Wy NWCR SE14 25 M6
Southern Pl SWLY BR8 74 E8
Southern Wy FOLK CT20 11 M3
Southernwood Ri FOLK CT20 10 A6
Southey Rd BRXN/ST SW9 24 B7
Southey St PGE/AN SE20 69 L4
Southey Wk TIL RM18 35 J7
Southey Wy DIT/AY ME20 139 G1
Southfield Rd CHST BR7 73 G7
STH/RUST TN4 196 D7
Southfields ROCH ME1 100 C2
RRTW TN3 277 P10
WADH TN5 309 L3
Southfield Shaw MEO DA13 239 N4
Southfields Rd BGR/WK TN15 111 L2
CTHM CR3 156 F2
Southfields Wy STH/RUST TN4 196 E5
Southfleet Av HART DA3 78 C6
Southfleet Rd GVW DA11 55 G6
ORP BR6 90 F6
RDART DA2 77 K1
SWCM DA10 54 B5
South Ga PUR RM19 32 D3
Southgate Rd TENT TN30 315 P2
South Gipsy Rd WELL DA16 49 L1
South Green La RSIT ME9 144 A2
South Gv RTW TN1 22 F7
South Hall Cl EYN DA4 94 A3
South Hl CHST BR7 72 A3
South Hill Rd GVE DA12 55 J6
HAYES BR2 70 F7
Southholme Cl NRWD SE19 68 F5
Southill Rd CHAT ME4 6 C8
CHST BR7 71 M4
South Island Pl BRXN/ST SW9 24 A6
South Kent Av GVW DA11 54 D4
Southland Rd
WOOL/PLUM SE18 29 G6
Southlands Av ORP BR6 90 F7
Southlands Gv BMLY BR1 71 M7
Southlands La OXTED RH8 184 C4
Southlands Rd HAYES BR2 71 L8
Southland Ter PUR RM19 * 32 C4
South La RMAID ME17 260 F7
South Lea ASH TN23 204 D8
Southlees La RSIT ME9 144 A7
Southmead Cl FOLKN CT19 10 D2
South Motto ASH TN23 204 E6
South Norwood Hl SNWD SE25 68 F6
South Oak Rd
STRHM/NOR SW16 68 A1
Southold Ri ELTH/MOT SE9 48 B8
Southover BMLY BR1 71 H2
South Pk SEV TN13 21 G7
South Park Crs CAT SE6 46 F6
South Park Hill Rd
SAND/SEL CR2 86 E8
South Park Rd
MAID/SHEP ME15 167 J4
South Pondside Rd CHAT ME4 83 H5
Southport Rd
WOOL/PLUM SE18 28 E3
South Rd DEAL CT14 211 L4
DVW CT17 217 J1
ERITH DA8 31 G5
FAV ME13 149 J2
FSTH SE23 45 L7
GILL ME7 83 H6
HB CT6 129 H4
HYTHE CT21 222 D4
STPH/PW TN12 281 K4
SWCH CT13 237 K5
South Rw BKHTH/KID SE3 27 H8
Southsea Av IOS ME12 65 J4
Southsea Dr HB CT6 128 E5
South Sea St BERM/RHTH SE16 26 A2
Southspring ELTH/MOT SE9 48 E5
South Stour Av ASH TN23 2 C8
South St BMLY BR1 71 H6
CANT CT1 172 D6
DEAL CT14 209 L4
FAV ME13 150 E8
GVE DA12 55 J5
LYDD TN29 334 D3
MAIDW ME16 165 M5
MEO DA13 97 G7
QBOR ME11 64 A8
WSTB CT5 127 H5
South Street Rd RSIT ME9 117 K6
South Ter EYN DA4 * 94 A3
South Trench TONN TN10 * 188 F8
South Undercliff RYE TN31 225 H4
South V NRWD SE19 68 F3
Southvale Rd BKHTH/KID SE3 26 F8
South Vw BMLY BR1 71 K6
Southview SWLY BR8 75 G8
South View Av TIL RM18 35 H7
South View Cl BUR/ETCH TN19 322 E2
BXLY DA5 50 A4
Southview Cl SWLY BR8 75 H8
South View Ct NRWD SE19 * 68 D4
South View Gdns IOS ME12 64 D5
South View Hts WTHK RM20 * 33 K5
South View Rd RDART DA2 51 L8
STH/RUST TN4 196 E5
WADH TN5 309 L3
WSTB CT5 126 E7
WTHK RM20 33 K5
Southview Rd BMLY BR1 70 E1
CTHM CR3 157 G2
WARL CR6 130 A6
Southviews SAND/SEL CR2 104 C3
South Wk WWKM BR4 88 F6
South Wall DEAL CT14 209 J2
Southwall Rd DEAL CT14 209 J3
Southwark Bridge Rd
STHWK SE1 24 C2
Southwark Park Est
BERM/RHTH SE16 * 25 J3
Southwark Park Rd
BERM/RHTH SE16 25 G3
Southwark Pl BMLY BR1 72 A7
Southwark Rd STRD ME2 81 L7
Southwater Cl BECK BR3 70 C4
South Wy CROY/NA CR0 87 M6
PUR RM19 32 F2
Southway HAYES BR2 89 H3
Southways RMAID ME17 260 F6
Southwell Cl CDW/CHF RM16 33 K4
Southwell Rd CMBW SE5 44 D1
CROY/NA CR0 86 B2
STRD ME2 81 K7
South Wharf Rd GRAYS RM17 34 A5
Southwold Pl WGOS CT8 177 G6
Southwold Rd BXLY DA5 50 C4
Southwood MAIDW ME16 166 A3
Southwood Av STH/RUST TN4 196 D7
Southwood Cl BMLY BR1 72 A8
Southwood Gdns RAM CT11 16 D6
Southwood Hts RAM CT11 16 E6
Southwood Rd ELTH/MOT SE9 48 C7
RAM CT11 16 E6
STH/RUST TN4 277 Q12
WSTB CT5 127 J3
Sovereign Bvd GILL ME7 101 M3
Sovereigns Wy
STPH/PW TN12 280 H3
Sovereign Wy TON TN9 194 F4
Sowell St BRDST CT10 179 J8
Sowerby Cl ELTH/MOT SE9 48 A3
Spa Cl NRWD SE19 68 F5
Spade La RSIT ME9 103 K7
Spa Hl THHTH CR7 68 E5
Spanton Crs HYTHE CT21 222 B2
Spar Cl RTON TN11 256 C4
Sparepenny La EYN DA4 93 M3
Sparkeswood Av CRBK TN17 314 E6
Sparks Cl HAYES BR2 71 J8
Spa Rd BERM/RHTH SE16 25 G2
Sparrow Castle MARG CT9 15 G6
Sparrow Dr STMC/STPC BR5 90 D4
Sparrows La ELTH/MOT SE9 48 D6
Sparta St GNWCH SE10 26 D7
Speakers Ct CROY/NA CR0 * 86 E4
Spearhead Rd
MAID/BEAR ME14 141 G6
Spearman St
WOOL/PLUM SE18 * 28 B5
Spectrum Pl WALW SE17 24 E4
Speedgate Hl HART DA3 95 H5
Speedwell Av WALD ME5 114 F1
Speedwell Cl GILL ME7 83 M8
MAID/BEAR ME14 167 M1
Speedwell Rd WSTB CT5 126 C7
Speedwell St DEPT SE8 26 B6
Spekehill ELTH/MOT SE9 48 A8
Speke Rd BRDST CT10 179 H7
THHTH CR7 68 E6
Spekes Rd GILL ME7 102 B7
Spelders Hl RASHE TN25 288 H5
Speldhurst Cl ASH TN23 204 B6
HAYES BR2 89 G1
Speldhurst Ct MAIDW ME16 12 A4
Speldhurst Gdns MARG CT9 179 J2
Speldhurst Hl RRTW TN3 277 Q10
Speldhurst Rd RRTW TN3 199 M1
STH/RUST TN4 196 C5
Spelmonden Rd
STPH/PW TN12 296 G1
Spence Cl BERM/RHTH SE16 26 A1
RFOLK CT18 220 B1
Spencer Cl ORP BR6 90 F5
WALD ME5 101 H8
Spencer Ct FOLK CT20 * 223 K3
Spencer Ms RTW TN1 * 22 F7
Spencer Pl CROY/NA CR0 86 E3
Spencer Rd BMLY BR1 71 G4
BRCH CT7 176 D5
SAND/SEL CR2 86 F8
Spencer Sq RAM CT11 17 H7
Spencer St GVW DA11 55 H5
RAM CT11 17 H7
Spencer Wk TIL RM18 35 H8
Spencer Wy MAID/SHEP ME15 167 M6
Spenlow Dr WALD ME5 115 H4
Spenny La STPH/PW TN12 280 B3
Spenser Ms DUL SE21 44 E6
Spenser Rd HB CT6 129 G5
HNHL SE24 44 C3
Speranza St WOOL/PLUM SE18 29 G4
Speyside TONN TN10 188 E8
Spicer Cl CMBW SE5 24 C8
Spicers Homes SIT ME10 * 120 A6
Spices Yd CROY/NA CR0 86 D7
Spielman Rd DART DA1 52 A2
Spillett Cl FAV ME13 149 J2
The Spillway MAID/SHEP ME15 12 B9
Spindle Cl WOOL/PLUM SE18 27 M2
Spindle Gld MAID/BEAR ME14 13 M2
Spindles TIL RM18 35 H6
Spindlewood Cl WALD ME5 115 J2
Spindlewood End ASH TN23 202 A7
Spindlewood Gdns
CROY/NA CR0 86 E7
Spindrift Av POP/IOD E14 26 C3
Spinel Cl WOOL/PLUM SE18 29 G4
Spinnaker Ct ROCH ME1 * 100 D4
Spinners Cl HDCN TN27 300 F3
Spinney Cl BECK BR3 70 C8
Spinney Gdns NRWD SE19 69 G2
Spinney La RCANTE CT3 251 R12
Spinney Oak BMLY BR1 71 M6
The Spinneys BMLY BR1 72 A6
The Spinney ASH TN23 202 B8
DVW CT17 212 F7
MAID/SHEP ME15 13 K8
MARG CT9 179 H4
RBTBR TN32 322 E10
SCUP DA14 73 M2
SWLY BR8 74 F6
TON TN9 194 D6
WALD ME5 115 J4
Spinney Wy RSEV TN14 107 J5
Spire Av WSTB CT5 127 G5
Spire Cl GVE DA12 55 J6
The Spires CANTW/ST CT2 4 E1
DART DA1 51 L7
MAIDW ME16 12 A4
STRD ME2 81 L8
Spitalfield La NROM TN28 330 H7
Spital St DART DA1 51 L4
Spitfire Cl WALD ME5 101 J7
Spitfire House
WOOL/PLUM SE18 * 27 M6
Spitfire Rd E/WMAL ME19 164 A2
Spitfire Wy RFOLK CT18 220 C2
Split La RCANTW CT4 269 K8
Spode La EDEN TN8 275 M6
Sponden La HAWK TN18 313 J9
Spongs La CRBK TN17 299 K4
Sportsbank St CAT SE6 46 D5
Sportsfield MAID/BEAR ME14 13 K2
Sportsman's Cottages
E/WMAL ME19 138 C8
Spot La MAID/SHEP ME15 168 B3
Spout Hl CROY/NA CR0 88 B8
Spout La EDEN TN8 186 D4
STPH/PW TN12 279 L12
Spratling La MSTR CT12 182 C4
Spratling St MSTR CT12 182 B4
Spray Hl RRTW TN3 296 C9
Spray St WOOL/PLUM SE18 28 C3
The Sprig MAID/BEAR ME14 168 B1
Springall St PECK SE15 25 J6
Springbank Rd LEW SE13 46 F4
Springbourne Ct BECK BR3 70 D5
Springcroft HART DA3 96 B2
Spring Cross HART DA3 96 B6
Springett Cl DIT/AY ME20 114 A7
Springett Wy RMAID ME17 259 J2
Springfarm Rd LYDD TN29 318 F12
Springfield MAID/BEAR ME14 * 141 G7
OXTED RH8 157 J8
Springfield Av
MAID/BEAR ME14 140 F7
SWLY BR8 75 G8
TENT TN30 301 N11
Springfield Cl RAM CT11 183 H3
Springfield Gdns BMLY BR1 72 A8
WWKM BR4 88 C5
Springfield Gv CHARL SE7 27 K5
Springfield Pl RRTW TN3 * 199 K6
Springfield Ri SYD SE26 69 J1
Springfield Rd BMLY BR1 72 A8
BXLYHN DA7 50 C1
CDW/CHF RM16 34 F1
DIT/AY ME20 139 G1
DVE/WH CT16 * 213 J7
EDEN TN8 192 C4
GILL ME7 83 M7
MARG CT9 179 H2
RRTW TN3 199 K6
SIT ME10 119 L4
STH/RUST TN4 196 C4
SYD SE26 69 J2
THHTH CR7 68 D5
WELL DA16 49 J1
Springfields WADH TN5 310 F8
Springfield Ter CHAT ME4 * 6 C6
Springfield Wy HYTHE CT21 223 J2
STMC/STPC BR5 73 K7
Spring Gdns BH/WHM TN16 132 B4
ORP BR6 108 A1
STH/RUST TN4 * 200 C1
Spring Gv GVE DA12 55 J6
Springhead RTWE/PEM TN2 23 L1
Spring Head Rd BGR/WK TN15 136 E3
Springhead Rd ERITH DA8 31 G5
FAV ME13 123 K8
GVW DA11 54 D6
Spring Hl RRTW TN3 276 H11
RYE TN31 325 J6
SYD SE26 69 K1
Spring Hollow LYDD TN29 331 P1
Springholm Cl BH/WHM TN16 132 B4
Springhurst Cl CROY/NA CR0 88 A7
Spring La BGR/WK TN15 240 A4
CANT CT1 5 K5
CANTW/ST CT2 173 H5
HYTHE CT21 223 H1
OXTED RH8 184 E1
SNWD SE25 87 J2
STH/RUST TN4 196 A2
Spring Park Av CROY/NA CR0 87 L5
Springpark Dr BECK BR3 70 D7
Spring Park Rd CROY/NA CR0 87 L5
Springrice Rd LEW SE13 46 D4
Spring Shaw Rd
STMC/STPC BR5 73 H5
Spring Ter FOLK CT20 * 11 K5
Spring Tide Cl PECK SE15 * 25 H7
Spring V BXLYHN DA7 50 C2
GRH DA9 53 K4
MAIDW ME16 12 D5
Springvale RHAM ME8 102 D7
RSIT ME9 227 L9
Spring Vale Cl SWLY BR8 75 G4
Springvale Ct GVW DA11 * 54 D7
Spring V North DART DA1 51 L5
Spring V South DART DA1 * 51 L5
Spring Wk WSTB CT5 126 D6
Springwater Cl
WOOL/PLUM SE18 * 28 B7
Springwell Rd
STRHM/NOR SW16 68 B1
TON TN9 194 E5
Springwood Cl ASH TN23 202 B8
Springwood Dr ASH TN23 202 A8
Springwood Rd MAIDW ME16 166 B2
Sprotlands Av KEN/WIL TN24 3 J6
Sprotshill Cl SIT ME10 119 M3
Spruce Cl DIT/AY ME20 139 H3
Sprucedale Cl SWLY BR8 74 F6
Sprucedale Gdns CROY/NA CR0 87 L7
Spruce Rd BH/WHM TN16 132 C2
Sprules Rd BROCKY SE4 25 M8
Spurgeon Av NRWD SE19 68 E5
Spurgeon Rd NRWD SE19 68 E4
Spurgeon St STHWK SE1 24 E2
Spurling Rd EDUL SE22 * 45 G2
Spurrell Av RDART DA2 74 E1
Spur Rd ORP BR6 91 H5
STHWK SE1 24 B1
Spurway MAID/BEAR ME14 168 B1
Square Hl MAID/BEAR ME14 13 J5
Square Hill Rd
MAID/SHEP ME15 13 J6
The Square BH/WHM TN16 132 B6
MAID/SHEP ME15 * 258 C6
RCANTE CT3 * 251 R2
RCANTW CT4 291 Q5
RMAID ME17 * 169 G8
RMAID ME17 243 L12
RTON TN11 256 B5
SEV TN13 20 B1
SWLY BR8 * 74 E7
Squerryes Mede
BH/WHM TN16 * 159 H5
Squire Av CANTW/ST CT2 171 K5
Squires Cl STRD ME2 81 J6
Squires Ct IOS ME12 229 P2
Squires Fld SWLY BR8 75 H5
Squires Wy DVE/WH CT16 213 H6
RDART DA2 74 E1
Squires Wood Dr CHST BR7 * 72 A4
Squirrel La RASHE TN25 202 C6
Squirrel's Cha CDW/CHF RM16 35 H1
The Squirrels LEW SE13 46 E1
Squirrel Wy RTWE/PEM TN2 197 H8
Stable Cl WALD ME5 101 K8
Stable Ct FAV ME13 * 149 L3
Stabledene Wy
RTWE/PEM TN2 278 A11
Stablemead FOLKN CT19 10 D1
Stable Ms WNWD SE27 68 D2
Stables End ORP BR6 90 D6
Stables Wy LBTH SE11 24 B4
Stace Cl TENT TN30 315 P1
Stacey Cl GVE DA12 79 M2
Stacey Rd RTON TN11 194 D2
Staceys St MAID/BEAR ME14 12 F2
Stacklands Cl BGR/WK TN15 111 K1
Stack La HART DA3 96 A1
Stack Rd EYN DA4 76 E8
Stacy Pth CMBW SE5 * 24 F6
Staddon Cl BECK BR3 69 M8
Staddon Ct BECK BR3 69 M8
Stade St HYTHE CT21 222 D3
The Stade FOLKN CT19 11 M5
Stadium Rd WOOL/PLUM SE18 28 A6
Stadium Wy DART DA1 50 F4
SIT ME10 120 D3
Stadler Cl MAIDW ME16 140 E6
Staffa Rd MAID/SHEP ME15 167 H6
Staffhurst Wood Rd
OXTED RH8 185 K7
Stafford Cl ASH TN23 204 C1
CDW/CHF RM16 33 K3
GRH DA9 53 G3
SLH/COR SS17 36 B2
Stafford Gdns CROY/NA CR0 86 A8
Stafford Rd CROY/NA CR0 86 B7
RTWE/PEM TN2 201 M1
SCUP DA14 72 F1
TON TN9 194 E3
Staffordshire St PECK SE15 25 H7
RAM CT11 17 J5
Stafford St GILL ME7 7 J4
Stafford Wy SEV TN13 162 B5
Stag Rd RTWE/PEM TN2 197 G4
WALD ME5 101 J8
Stagshaw Cl MAID/SHEP ME15 13 G9
Stainer Rd TONN TN10 189 J7
Staines Ct MAID/BEAR ME14 13 G3
Stainmore Cl CHST BR7 72 E5
Stainton Rd LEW SE13 46 E5
Stairfoot La SEV TN13 135 H8
Stair Rd TONN TN10 195 J1
Stake La STRD ME2 99 H7
Staleys Rd BGR/WK TN15 240 E2
Stalham Ct GILL ME7 * 116 C1
Stalham St BERM/RHTH SE16 25 J2
Stalin Av WALD ME5 101 J5
Stalisfield Rd FAV ME13 244 G10
FAV ME13 245 M4
HDCN TN27 264 E2
Stambourne Wy NRWD SE19 68 F4
WWKM BR4 88 D6
Stamford Dr HAYES BR2 71 G8
The Stampers MAIDW ME16 12 B9
Stanam Rd RTWE/PEM TN2 278 B12
Stanbridge Rd EDEN TN8 192 C3
Stanbrook Rd ABYW SE2 29 J1
GVW DA11 55 G6
Stanbury Crs FOLKN CT19 221 G5
Stanbury Rd PECK SE15 25 J7
Stancomb Av RAM CT11 16 F8
Standard Rd BELV DA17 30 B4
BXLYHS DA6 49 M2
ORP BR6 106 F4
Standen Cl RHAM ME8 116 F1
Standen La RFOLK CT18 293 J12
Standen St CRBK TN17 313 N7
STH/RUST TN4 22 E1
Stane Wy WOOL/PLUM SE18 27 L6
Stanford Dr MAIDW ME16 166 D2
Stanford La RTON TN11 256 F4
Stanford Pl STHWK SE1 24 F3
Stanford Rd CDW/CHF RM16 34 F1
Stanford Wy STRD ME2 99 K3
Stangate Rd E/WMAL ME19 112 C5
STRD ME2 81 K6
Stanger Rd SNWD SE25 69 H8
Stangrove Rd EDEN TN8 192 D4
Stanham Pl DART DA1 51 H2
Stanham Rd DART DA1 51 K3
Stanhope Av HAYES BR2 89 H4
SIT ME10 120 B6
Stanhope Cl
BERM/RHTH SE16 * 25 L1
MAID/BEAR ME14 140 F6
Stanhope Gv BECK BR3 88 A1
Stanhope Rd ASH TN23 204 B4
BFN/LL DA15 73 H1
BXLYHN DA7 29 M8
CROY/NA CR0 86 F6
DEAL CT14 209 L3
DVE/WH CT16 213 K7
RTW TN1 23 J1
STRD ME2 18 F3
SWCM DA10 54 A3
Stanhopes OXTED RH8 158 A6
Stanhope Wy SEV TN13 135 J8
Stan La WBY/YAL ME18 241 L10
Stanley Av BECK BR3 70 D7
IOS ME12 65 L6
QBOR ME11 227 P1
Stanley Cl GRH DA9 52 F3
LYDD TN29 321 N5
STPH/PW TN12 281 R6
Stanley Ct GILL ME7 84 A8
Stanley Crs GVE DA12 79 L2
Stanley Gdns HB CT6 129 G6
Stanley Gv THHTH CR7 86 B2
Stanley Pl RAM CT11 17 J3
Stanley Rd BRDST CT10 179 J7
CROY/NA CR0 86 B3
DEAL CT14 209 L4
FOLKN CT19 219 M7
GILL ME7 7 K1
GRAYS RM17 34 C5
HAYES BR2 71 K7
HB CT6 129 G5
MARG CT9 15 K3
ORP BR6 91 G4
RAM CT11 17 G3
RTW TN1 23 H2
SCUP DA14 49 H8
SWCM DA10 54 A4
WALD ME5 101 K7
WSTB CT5 126 E6
Stanley St DEPT SE8 26 A6
Stanley Sykes Cl MARG CT9 15 L7
Stanley Ter BXLYHS DA6 * 50 B2
Stanley Wy STMC/STPC BR5 91 J1
Stanmore Ct CANT CT1 5 J7
Stanmore Rd BELV DA17 30 D3
Stanmore Ter BECK BR3 70 B6
Stannary Pl LBTH SE11 24 B4
Stannary St LBTH SE11 24 B5

Stansfeld Av RFOLK CT18 220 B1
Stansfield Rd BRXN/ST SW9 44 A1
Stanstead Cl HAYES BR2 89 G1
Stanstead Gv CAT SE6 46 A6
Stanstead Rd FSTH SE23 45 M6
Stansted Cl MAIDW ME16 140 D6
Stansted Crs BXLY DA5 49 L6
Stansted Hl BGR/WK TN15 238 F5
Stansted La BGR/WK TN15 238 B4
Stanswood Gdns CMBW SE5 24 F6
Stanton Cl STMC/STPC BR5 91 K3
Stanton Rd CROY/NA CR0 86 D3
Stanton St PECK SE15 * 25 H7
Stanton Wy SYD SE26 70 A1
Stanworth St STHWK SE1 25 G1
Staple Cl BXLY DA5 50 E8
SIT ME10 119 M3
Staple Dr STPH/PW TN12 282 A6
Stapleford Ct SEV TN13 20 D3
Staplehurst Av BRDST CT10 183 K3
Staplehurst Gdns MARG CT9 179 H2
Staplehurst Rd LEW SE13 46 E3
RHAM ME8 102 C2
SIT ME10 119 K4
STPH/PW TN12 259 N10
STPH/PW TN12 282 E8
Staple Rd RCANTE CT3 252 C3
Staplers Ct MAID/BEAR ME14 141 J5
Staple St STHWK SE1 24 E1
Staplestreet Rd FAV ME13 151 G4
Stapleton Gdns CROY/NA CR0 86 B8
Stapleton Rd BXLYHN DA7 30 A6
ORP BR6 91 G6
Stapley Rd BELV DA17 30 B4
Starbeck Cl ELTH/MOT SE9 48 B5
Starboard Av GRH DA9 53 J4
Starboard Wy POP/IOD E14 26 B2
Starborough Rd EDEN TN8 274 D1
Star Hl DART DA1 50 F3
ROCH ME1 19 L9
Star Hill Rd RSEV TN14 134 E2
Star La FOLKN CT19 219 L6
GILL ME7 102 B6
MARG CT9 178 D8
STMC/STPC BR5 73 L8
Starle Cl CANT CT1 5 J1
Starling Cl HART DA3 78 C7
Starling Rd CROY/NA CR0 87 M2
Star Mill Ct WALD ME5 * 101 L3
Star Mill La WALD ME5 101 L3
Star Rd KEN/WIL TN24 2 F5
Starts Cl ORP BR6 90 B6
Starts Hill Av ORP BR6 90 C8
Starts Hill Rd ORP BR6 90 C6
Starveacre La RSIT ME9 119 K7
State Farm Av ORP BR6 90 C7
Station Ap BECK BR3 69 M5
BGR/WK TN15 240 E2
BKHTH/KID SE3 47 J1
BRCH CT7 176 C6
BUR/ETCH TN19 322 B4
BXLYHN DA7 29 M8
BXLYHN DA7 30 D8
CAT SE6 70 A2
CHST BR7 71 M3
CHST BR7 72 B5
CROY/NA CR0 * 86 E5
DART DA1 51 M4
E/WMAL ME19 * 138 B3
EDEN TN8 192 D4
HAYES BR2 89 H4
MAIDW ME16 12 E6
MSTR CT12 180 F8
NROM TN28 331 K7
ORP BR6 91 G5
ORP BR6 91 J8
OXTED RH8 157 K7
RCANTE CT3 251 P9
RDV CT15 210 D7
RSEV TN14 136 B2
RTW TN1 22 F6
RYE TN31 225 G3
STMC/STPC BR5 73 J8
STPH/PW TN12 279 K2
STPH/PW TN12 281 R4
STRD ME2 99 H8
SWLY BR8 74 F8
WELL DA16 29 H8
Station Approach Rd
RAM CT11 16 F3
Station Buildings HAYES BR2 * 89 H4
Station Ct BGR/WK TN15 240 E2
Station Crs BKHTH/KID SE3 27 H4
Station Dr DEAL CT14 209 H8
Station Est BECK BR3 69 L8
Station Hl HAYES BR2 89 H5
RTON TN11 254 G12
Station Pde BECK BR3 * 69 L8
BMLY BR1 * 71 H5
BXLYHN DA7 * 29 M8
SEV TN13 * 20 F4
Station Pas PECK SE15 25 K7
Station Ri WNWD SE27 44 C7
Station Rd ASH TN23 2 C5
BELV DA17 30 B2
BFN/LL DA15 49 H7
BGR/WK TN15 240 E2
BH/WHM TN16 160 A1
BMLY BR1 71 H5
BRCH CT7 176 C6
BUR/ETCH TN19 322 F2
BXLYHN DA7 49 M1
CRBK TN17 297 J6
CROY/NA CR0 86 D4
CTHM CR3 130 D8
DART DA1 51 G4
DEAL CT14 209 H8
DIT/AY ME20 139 K4
DIT/AY ME20 140 A3
EDEN TN8 186 C5
EDEN TN8 192 D2
EYN DA4 76 C6
EYN DA4 93 L6
FOLKN CT19 10 B4
GRH DA9 53 H3
GVW DA11 54 C4
HART DA3 77 M7
HAYES BR2 70 F6
HB CT6 128 F6
HDCN TN27 264 B6
HDCN TN27 283 L4
HDCN TN27 285 M5
HOO/HM ME3 58 B2
HRTF TN7 198 C8
HYTHE CT21 222 E3
LEW SE13 46 D1
LING RH7 190 F8
LYDD TN29 320 G10
LYDD TN29 334 E2
MAID/BEAR ME14 12 F3
MAID/SHEP ME15 166 B6
MARG CT9 14 C5
MEO DA13 78 A1
MEO DA13 97 H1
MSTR CT12 180 F8
NROM TN28 331 K7
NRWD SE19 69 H3
ORP BR6 91 G5
PGE/AN SE20 69 K3
RASHE TN25 306 B2
RBTBR TN32 322 F10
RBTBR TN32 322 G9
RCANTE CT3 251 P8
RCANTW CT4 175 G8
RCANTW CT4 175 J5
RCANTW CT4 248 E6
RDV CT15 210 D8
RDV CT15 271 Q8
RFOLK CT18 291 M11
RHAM ME8 103 H3
RMAID ME17 242 E11
RRTW TN3 199 K6
RSEV TN14 108 E5
RSEV TN14 109 M5
RSEV TN14 136 A2
RSIT ME9 118 C3
RSIT ME9 121 K7
RYE TN31 325 J6
RYE TN31 325 L4
SCUP DA14 49 H8
SEV TN13 135 K6
SNWD SE25 69 G8
STMC/STPC BR5 73 K8
STPH/PW TN12 279 J2
STPH/PW TN12 282 A5
STRD ME2 19 H4
STRD ME2 99 K3
SWLY BR8 74 F8
TENT TN30 315 M2
TIL RM18 36 C6
WADH TN5 308 H3
WADH TN5 309 J4
WADH TN5 309 R12
WADH TN5 310 A12
WBY/YAL ME18 257 M4
WGOS CT8 177 J4
WSEA TN36 224 D8
WSTB CT5 126 F3
WWKM BR4 88 D4
Station Rd East CANT CT1 4 E6
OXTED RH8 157 K7
Station Rd North BELV DA17 30 C2
Station Rd West CANTW/ST CT2 4 E3
OXTED RH8 157 K7
Station Sq STMC/STPC BR5 90 D1
Station St SIT ME10 120 A5
Station Ter CMBW SE5 24 D7
Staunton St DEPT SE8 26 A5
Staveley Cl PECK SE15 25 K7
Steadman Cl HOO/HM ME3 57 K8
Stead St WALW SE17 24 E3
Stebondale St POP/IOD E14 26 D4
Stede Hl RMAID ME17 242 G6
Stedly SCUP DA14 * 73 H1
Stedman Cl BXLY DA5 50 F8
Steedman St WALW SE17 24 D3
Steeds Cl ASH TN23 304 D4
Steeds La RASHW TN26 304 D4
Steele Av GRH DA9 53 H3
Steele's La MEO DA13 97 G7
Steele St STRD ME2 18 F1
Steellands Ri WADH TN5 310 G8
Steep Cl ORP BR6 107 L1
Steep Hl CROY/NA CR0 86 F7
Steeple Heights Dr
BH/WHM TN16 158 C3
Steerforth Cl ROCH ME1 100 D3
Steers Pl RTON TN11 256 B3
Steers Wy BERM/RHTH SE16 25 M1
Stella Cl STPH/PW TN12 281 J4
Stelling Rd ERITH DA8 30 E6
Stembridge Rd PGE/AN SE20 69 J6
Stembrook DVE/WH CT16 8 D4
Stempe Cl RFOLK CT18 220 C2
Stenning Av TIL RM18 36 C3
Stephen Cl BRDST CT10 183 K1
ORP BR6 91 G6
Stephen Rd BXLYHN DA7 50 D1
Stephens Cl FAV ME13 149 J1
MARG CT9 177 L6
RAM CT11 16 F3
Stephenson Av TIL RM18 35 H7
Stephenson Rd
CANTW/ST CT2 172 A6
Stephen's Rd STH/RUST TN4 196 D7
Stepneyford La CRBK TN17 300 C12
Steps Hill Rd RSIT ME9 117 L7
Step Style SIT ME10 120 C7
Sterling Av MAIDW ME16 140 D8
Sterling Cl BRDST CT10 179 H8
Sterling Gdns NWCR SE14 25 M5
Sterling Rd QBOR ME11 64 B8
SIT ME10 119 L8
Sterndale Rd DART DA1 52 A5
Sternhall La PECK SE15 45 H1
Sterry St STHWK SE1 24 E1
Steucers La FSTH SE23 45 M6
Steve Biko La CAT SE6 70 B1
Stevedale Rd WELL DA16 29 K8
Steven Ct RAM CT11 * 16 C9
Stevens Cl BECK BR3 70 B3
BXLY DA5 74 E1
HDCN TN27 263 J10
RDART DA2 76 F2
SNOD ME6 113 H5
Stevenson Cl ERITH DA8 31 J6
MAID/SHEP ME15 12 F7
Stevenson Crs
BERM/RHTH SE16 25 H4
Stevenson Wy DIT/AY ME20 139 G1
Stevens Rd DIT/AY ME20 114 A7
Stevens St STHWK SE1 24 F2
Stewart Cl CHST BR7 72 C2
Stewart Rd RTWE/PEM TN2 196 F6
Stewart St POP/IOD E14 26 D1
Steyning Gv ELTH/MOT SE9 72 A1
Steynton Av BXLY DA5 49 M7
Stickens La E/WMAL ME19 138 F7
Stickfast La RMAID ME17 261 L10
RSIT ME9 226 H12
Stickland Rd BELV DA17 30 B3
Stilebridge La STPH/PW TN12 259 K10
Stiles Cl ERITH DA8 30 C4
FOLKN CT19 10 D1
HAYES BR2 90 A2
IOS ME12 65 H7
Still La STH/RUST TN4 196 C3
Stillness Rd FSTH SE23 45 M4
Stillwater Ms CHAT ME4 83 J3
Stirling Cl RHAM ME8 116 F1
ROCH ME1 100 B3
SCUP DA14 73 G1
Stirling Dr ORP BR6 91 J8
Stirling Rd E/WMAL ME19 164 A2
Stirling Wy EGRIN RH19 274 A10
MSTR CT12 182 D3
Stirling Rd KEN/WIL TN24 205 G4
Stisted Wy HDCN TN27 263 J10
Stockbury Dr MAIDW ME16 140 E6
Stockbury Gdns MARG CT9 179 H3
Stockbury Rd CROY/NA CR0 87 K2
Stockdale Gdns DEAL CT14 209 K5
Stockenbury STPH/PW TN12 257 J7
Stockers Brow RSIT ME9 146 B2
Stocker's Hl FAV ME13 150 F5
RSIT ME9 146 B2
Stockett La MAID/SHEP ME15 259 J1
RMAID ME17 258 H2
Stockfield Rd
STRHM/NOR SW16 44 A8
Stock Hl BH/WHM TN16 132 C2
Stockholm Rd
BERM/RHTH SE16 25 K4
Stockland Green Rd
RRTW TN3 277 R9
Stock La RASHE TN25 305 R2
RDART DA2 75 K1
Stocks Green Rd RTON TN11 255 R8
Stocks Rd TENT TN30 326 H2
Stockton Cl MAID/BEAR ME14 141 J5
Stockwell Av BRXN/ST SW9 44 A1
Stockwell Cl BMLY BR1 71 J6
Stockwell Gdns BRXN/ST SW9 24 A7
Stockwell Gn BRXN/ST SW9 24 A8
Stockwell La BRXN/ST SW9 24 A8
Stockwell Park Crs
BRXN/ST SW9 24 A8
Stockwell Park Rd
BRXN/ST SW9 24 B8
Stockwell Park Wk
BRXN/ST SW9 44 A1
Stockwell Rd BRXN/ST SW9 24 A8
Stockwell St GNWCH SE10 26 D5
Stockwell Ter BRXN/ST SW9 24 A7
Stodart Rd PGE/AN SE20 69 K5
Stoddards La RYE TN31 325 N8
Stoddart Rd FOLKN CT19 219 M7
Stodmarsh Rd RCANTE CT3 173 G8
RCANTE CT3 234 A9
Stofield Gdns ELTH/MOT SE9 47 L8
Stoke Rd HOO/HM ME3 41 K8
HOO/HM ME3 60 B7
Stokes Rd CROY/NA CR0 87 L2
Stombers La RFOLK CT18 292 H11
Stonar Cl RAM CT11 183 H4
SWCH CT13 237 K12
Stonar Gdns SWCH CT13 237 K11
Stondon Pk FSTH SE23 45 M5
Stoneacre Cl RHAM ME8 102 E8
Stoneacre Ct
MAID/SHEP ME15 * 167 H4
Stoneacre La
MAID/SHEP ME15 168 C6
Stone Barn Av BRCH CT7 176 D7
Stonebridge RASHE TN25 288 H4
Stone Br TENT TN30 328 A3
Stonebridge Green Rd
HDCN TN27 263 K9
Stonebridge Rd GVW DA11 54 C3
Stonebridge Vls NROM TN28 * 330 H6
Stonebridge Wy FAV ME13 149 J2
Stone Court La
RTWE/PEM TN2 278 B9
Stonecroft MEO DA13 239 M5
Stonecroft Rd ERITH DA8 30 D6
Stonecrop Cl CHAT ME4 83 K4
Stonecross Lea WALD ME5 101 J4
Stone Cross Lees SWCH CT13 206 A2
Stone Cross Rd WADH TN5 309 M6
Stonedane Ct FAV ME13 149 K1
Stonefield Cl BXLYHN DA7 50 B1
Stonefield Wy CHARL SE7 27 L6
Stone Gdns BRDST CT10 179 L8
Stonegate RASHE TN25 266 F11
Stonegate Cl STMC/STPC BR5 73 K7
Stonegate Rd WADH TN5 309 P8
Stonehall Rd RDV CT15 212 A1
Stoneheap Rd DEAL CT14 273 M4
Stone Hl RASHE TN25 306 F3
Stone Hill Rd HDCN TN27 263 J11
Stonehills Ct DUL SE21 44 F8
Stonehill Woods Pk
RDART DA2 * 74 C3
Stonehorse La HOO/HM ME3 82 B2
Stonehouse La ORP BR6 108 C3
PUR RM19 32 F4
Stone House Ms BRDST CT10 * 179 L7
Stonehouse Rd ORP BR6 108 C4
Stoneings La RSEV TN14 133 L4
Stoneleigh Park Av
CROY/NA CR0 87 L2
Stoneleigh Rd OXTED RH8 158 D8
Stoneness Rd WTHK RM20 33 J5
Stone Park Av BECK BR3 70 B8
Stone Pit La HAWK TN18 313 P12
Stone Place Rd GRH DA9 52 F3
Stone Rd BRDST CT10 179 L8
HAYES BR2 89 G1
Stone Rw RRTW TN3 * 277 J12
Stones Cross Rd SWLY BR8 92 D1
Stones End St STHWK SE1 24 D1
Stonestile Farm Rd
HDCN TN27 263 R2
Stone Stile La RCANTW CT4 247 J8
Stonestile Rd HDCN TN27 282 H2
Stone St CRBK TN17 298 G8
FAV ME13 149 K2
GVE DA12 55 J4
RASHE TN25 290 F11
RASHE TN25 307 N4
RASHE TN25 307 N8
RCANTW CT4 268 G1
RFOLK CT18 290 G11
RTW TN1 23 H3
Stone Street Rd BGR/WK TN15 163 H2
Stoneswood Rd OXTED RH8 158 A8
Stonewall Park Rd RRTW TN3 200 A2
Stonewood RDART DA2 53 K8
Stonewood Cl
STH/RUST TN4 * 196 D5
Stonewood Rd ERITH DA8 30 F4
Stoney Aly WOOL/PLUM SE18 28 B8
Stoney Bank GILL ME7 102 A4
Stoneycroft Cl LEE/GVPK SE12 47 G5
Stoney La NRWD SE19 69 G3
Stoney Rd FAV ME13 151 J6
Stony Cnr HART DA3 76 F8
Stony La ROCH ME1 100 D7
Stopes St PECK SE15 25 G6
Stopford Rd GILL ME7 7 K6
WALW SE17 24 C4
Store Rd CAN/RD E16 28 B1
Storers Quay POP/IOD E14 26 E3
Stories Ms CMBW SE5 * 24 F8
Stories Rd CMBW SE5 44 F1
Storks Rd BERM/RHTH SE16 * 25 H2
Stornaway Strd GVE DA12 80 A1
Storrington Rd CROY/NA CR0 87 G4
Storway Ct STRD ME2 * 18 F7
Stoughton Cl LBTH SE11 24 A3
Stour Cl ASH TN23 204 B2
HAYES BR2 89 K7
RCANTW CT4 248 E7
STRD ME2 18 C4
TONN TN10 188 E8
Stour Ct SWCH CT13 237 J12
Stour Crs CANT CT1 172 E6
Stourfields KEN/WIL TN24 2 E1
Stourmouth Rd RCANTE CT3 235 K6
Stour Rd CDW/CHF RM16 35 H4
DART DA1 51 H1
RCANTW CT4 248 E7
Stour St CANT CT1 4 F4
Stour Valley Cl RCANTE CT3 234 E2
Stour Valley Wk ASH TN23 286 H6
CANTW/ST CT2 4 B5
HDCN TN27 263 L9
RASHE TN25 288 E2
RASHW TN26 286 B5
RCANTE CT3 234 C7
RCANTE CT3 234 D4
RCANTW CT4 247 Q12
RCANTW CT4 267 L3
RCANTW CT4 267 N1
RMAID ME17 262 H2
SWCH CT13 237 M12
Stour Valley Wy RCANTE CT3 235 M3
Stowage DEPT SE8 26 C5
The Stowage DEPT SE8 26 B5
Stowell Av CROY/NA CR0 105 J4
Stowe Rd ORP BR6 91 J7
Stowting Hl RASHE TN25 290 D8
Stowting Rd ORP BR6 90 F7
Stradella Rd HNHL SE24 44 D4
Strafford St POP/IOD E14 26 B1
Straight La LYDD TN29 329 K5
Straightsmouth GNWCH SE10 26 D6
Strakers Hl RDV CT15 273 L5
Straker's Rd EDUL SE22 45 J2
Strand RYE TN31 225 G4
Strand Approach Rd GILL ME7 83 M6
Strand Cl MEO DA13 97 H3
Strandfield Cl
WOOL/PLUM SE18 28 F4
Strand St SWCH CT13 237 J12
The Strand DEAL CT14 209 L4
Stranger's Cl CANT CT1 171 K7
Stranger's La CANT CT1 171 K7
Strangford Pl HB CT6 129 J8
Strangford Rd WSTB CT5 127 G3
Strasbourg St MARG CT9 * 178 D7
Stratford Av RHAM ME8 102 E5
Stratford Dr MAID/SHEP ME15 167 L7
Stratford House Av BMLY BR1 71 M7
Stratford La RHAM ME8 103 G5
Stratford Rd E/WMAL ME19 138 B5
THHTH CR7 68 B8
Stratford St RTW TN1 23 J1
Strathaven Rd LEE/GVPK SE12 47 J4
Strathbrook Rd
STRHM/NOR SW16 68 A1
Strathdale STRHM/NOR SW16 68 A2
Stratheden Rd BKHTH/KID SE3 27 H7
Strathmore TIL RM18 36 D3
Strathmore Rd CROY/NA CR0 86 D3
Strathnairn St STHWK SE1 25 H3
Strathyre Av STRHM/NOR SW16 68 B7
Stratton Cl BXLYHN DA7 49 M1
Strattondale St POP/IOD E14 26 D2
Stratton Rd BXLYHN DA7 49 M1
Stratton Ter BH/WHM TN16 159 H5
Strawberry Cl RRTW TN3 200 F5
Strawberry Flds RYE TN31 324 H6
SWLY BR8 74 F6
Strawberry V TON TN9 194 F5
Straw Mill Hl
MAID/SHEP ME15 166 F4
Streamdale ABYW SE2 29 J5
Stream La HAWK TN18 312 C10
Streamline Ms EDUL SE22 45 J6
Stream Pit La HAWK TN18 313 L12
Streamside DIT/AY ME20 139 J4
Stream Side TONN TN10 189 G6
Streamside Cl HAYES BR2 71 H8
The Stream DIT/AY ME20 139 J4
Stream Wk WSTB CT5 126 E3
Stream Wy BELV DA17 30 B5
Streatfield EDEN TN8 192 E4
Streatham Common North
STRHM/NOR SW16 68 A2
Streete Court Rd WGOS CT8 177 J5
Street End Rd WALD ME5 101 J5
Streetfield HB CT6 155 J1
RMAID ME17 261 N6
Streetfield Ms BKHTH/KID SE3 27 H8
Streetfield Rd RHAM ME8 103 G4
The Street ASH TN23 286 H9
BGR/WK TN15 95 M8
BGR/WK TN15 240 C3
BGR/WK TN15 240 E10
BRCH CT7 180 E2
BRCH CT7 233 N7
CRBK TN17 282 F11
CRBK TN17 299 L5
CRBK TN17 313 N3
DEAL CT14 206 B5
DEAL CT14 208 B4
DEAL CT14 208 C1
DEAL CT14 209 G4
E/WMAL ME19 138 A1
E/WMAL ME19 239 M8
EYN DA4 76 G8
FAV ME13 123 J7
FAV ME13 151 H6
FAV ME13 244 H3
GILL ME7 116 C4
GVE DA12 80 A7
GVE DA12 80 F2
HDCN TN27 263 J10
HDCN TN27 285 N2
HOO/HM ME3 59 M2
HYTHE CT21 218 A3
HYTHE CT21 307 L11
KEN/WIL TN24 203 H4
KEN/WIL TN24 205 L3
MAID/BEAR ME14 141 K2
MAID/BEAR ME14 142 B4
MAID/BEAR ME14 168 D1
MEO DA13 97 H4
RASHE TN25 289 K3
RASHE TN25 289 Q3
RASHE TN25 289 R9
RASHE TN25 305 P1
RASHW TN26 285 N12
RASHW TN26 286 F3
RASHW TN26 303 P5
RASHW TN26 317 L9
RASHW TN26 318 D2
RCANTE CT3 234 D12
RCANTE CT3 235 K7
RCANTE CT3 235 M4
RCANTE CT3 236 A12
RCANTE CT3 251 M1
RCANTE CT3 251 N9
RCANTE CT3 252 C7
RCANTE CT3 252 F3
RCANTW CT4 175 J6
RCANTW CT4 247 N9
RCANTW CT4 250 F11
RCANTW CT4 267 J4
RCANTW CT4 268 E2
RCANTW CT4 269 K6
RCANTW CT4 270 B3
RCANTW CT4 270 F5
RCANTW CT4 270 G10
RCANTW CT4 271 J4
RDV CT15 210 B8
RDV CT15 210 C6
RDV CT15 213 M3
RDV CT15 216 A4
RDV CT15 271 G4
RDV CT15 272 E6
RFOLK CT18 219 H6
RFOLK CT18 292 G12
RMAID ME17 261 N6
RSIT ME9 103 M1
RSIT ME9 117 L1
RSIT ME9 117 M5
RSIT ME9 119 H7
RSIT ME9 120 F6
RSIT ME9 145 G4
RSIT ME9 147 H3
RSIT ME9 226 A9
RSIT ME9 226 C10
RSIT ME9 227 M9
RSIT ME9 242 H2
RSIT ME9 244 B2
STRD ME2 98 F8
SWCH CT13 253 N3
SWCH CT13 253 Q2
TENT TN30 316 H12
TENT TN30 326 G3
TENT TN30 327 R1
WBY/YAL ME18 165 H6
WBY/YAL ME18 241 Q9
Strettitt Gdns STPH/PW TN12 257 J8
Stretton Rd CROY/NA CR0 86 F3
Strickland Av DART DA1 52 A2
Strickland St DEPT SE8 26 B8
Strickland Wy ORP BR6 91 G7
Stringer Dr BRCH CT7 176 D7
Strode Crs IOS ME12 64 D3
Strode Park Rd HB CT6 129 H7
Strond Green Gdns
CROY/NA CR0 87 K3
Strond Green Wy CROY/NA CR0 87 K3
Strond St DVW CT17 8 C7
Strongbow Crs ELTH/MOT SE9 48 A3
Strongbow Rd ELTH/MOT SE9 48 A3
Stroud Green Wy CROY/NA CR0 87 K2
Stroud Rd SNWD SE25 87 H2
Strouts Rd ASH TN23 204 A4
Strover St GILL ME7 83 K6
Strumer Ct E/WMAL ME19 164 B3
Struttons Av GVW DA11 55 G7
Stuart Av HAYES BR2 89 H4
Stuart Cl MAID/BEAR ME14 13 L1
RTWE/PEM TN2 201 G5
SWLY BR8 75 G4
Stuart Ct DVW CT17 * 8 B4
Stuart Crs CROY/NA CR0 88 A6
Stuart Evans Cl WELL DA16 49 K1
Stuart Mantle Wy ERITH DA8 30 E6
Stuart Rd FOLKN CT19 11 M2
GILL ME7 7 M8
GRAYS RM17 34 C4
GVW DA11 55 H4
PECK SE15 45 K2
THHTH CR7 68 D8
WARL CR6 130 A6
WELL DA16 29 J7
Stubbs Dr BERM/RHTH SE16 25 J4
Stubbs Hl ORP BR6 108 B7
Studfall Cl HYTHE CT21 321 Q1
Studholme St PECK SE15 25 J6
Studio Cl KEN/WIL TN24 203 G5
Studland Cl BFN/LL DA15 49 G8
Studland Rd SYD SE26 69 L2
Studley Ct SCUP DA14 73 J2
Studley Crs HART DA3 78 D6
Stumble La ASH TN23 304 E4
Stumps Hill La BECK BR3 70 B3
Stuppington Court Farm
CANT CT1 249 M5
Stuppington La CANT CT1 249 M5
Sturdee Av GILL ME7 101 M1
Sturdy Cl HYTHE CT21 222 E3
Sturdy Rd PECK SE15 25 J8
Sturgeon Rd WALW SE17 24 D4
Sturges Fld CHST BR7 72 E4
Sturges Rd KEN/WIL TN24 2 B3
Sturge St STHWK SE1 24 D1
Sturla Rd CHAT ME4 6 E9
Sturmer Cl CANT CT1 5 L6
Sturry Court Ms
CANTW/ST CT2 173 G3
Sturry Hl CANTW/ST CT2 173 G3
Sturry Rd CANT CT1 5 J1
Sturry Wy RHAM ME8 102 D3
Styants Bottom Rd
BGR/WK TN15 137 L8
Style Cl RHAM ME8 116 F1
Styles Cl EDEN TN8 187 J8
Styles Gdns BRXN/ST SW9 44 C1
Styles La MAID/BEAR ME14 141 K2
Styles Wy BECK BR3 70 D8
Succombs Hl CTHM CR3 130 A6
Succombs Pl WARL CR6 130 A6
Sudbury Crs BMLY BR1 71 H2
Sudbury Gdns CROY/NA CR0 86 F7
Sudbury Pl WGOS CT8 177 G6
Sudrey St STHWK SE1 24 D1
Suffield Cl SAND/SEL CR2 104 C6
Suffield Rd PGE/AN SE20 69 K6
Suffolk Av RHAM ME8 103 G4
WGOS CT8 177 G6
Suffolk Dr ASH TN23 204 D1
Suffolk Rd CANT CT1 174 E1
DART DA1 51 M4
GVE DA12 55 L4
MAID/SHEP ME15 167 L5
SCUP DA14 73 K3
SNWD SE25 69 G8
Suffolk St WSTB CT5 126 E5
Suffolk Wy BGR/WK TN15 21 J6
Sugar Loaf Wk FOLKN CT19 220 E5
Sullivan Cl DART DA1 51 J4
Sullivan Rd LBTH SE11 24 B3
TIL RM18 35 H7
TONN TN10 189 H8
Sultan Rd WALD ME5 115 K3
Sultan St BECK BR3 69 L6
CMBW SE5 24 D6
Summer Cl HYTHE CT21 222 A3
TENT TN30 301 P12
Summerfield Av WSTB CT5 127 G4
Summerfield Rd MARG CT9 179 H3
Summerfield St LEE/GVPK SE12 47 G5
Summer Hl CANTW/ST CT2 171 K4
CHST BR7 72 B6
Summerhill HDCN TN27 282 H3
Summerhill Av STH/RUST TN4 196 C4
Summerhill Cl ORP BR6 90 F7
Summerhill Pk
KEN/WIL TN24 * 205 M4
Summerhill Rd DART DA1 51 L5
STPH/PW TN12 281 N1
Summerhouse Dr RDART DA2 74 E2
Summer La CANTW/ST CT2 153 M7
Summer Leeze KEN/WIL TN24 3 H9
Summer Leeze Gdns
KEN/WIL TN24 3 H9
Summer Rd BRCH CT7 233 M8
Summervale Rd STH/RUST TN4 22 A9
Summerville Av IOS ME12 65 G8
Summit Wy NRWD SE19 68 F4
Sumner Av PECK SE15 25 G7
Sumner Cl ORP BR6 90 D7
Sumner Gdns CROY/NA CR0 86 B4
Sumner Rd CROY/NA CR0 86 C4
PECK SE15 25 G5
Sumner Rd South
CROY/NA CR0 86 B4
Sumpter Wy FAV ME13 149 H2
Sunbeam Av HB CT6 128 A5

Sunburst Cl STPH/PW TN12 281 J4
Sunbury St WOOL/PLUM SE18 28 A2
Sun Ct ERITH DA8 31 G8
Suncroft Pl SYD SE26 45 K8
Sundale Av SAND/SEL CR2 104 B4
Sunderland Cl ROCH ME1 100 B2
Sunderland Dr RHAM ME8 103 H5
Sunderland Mt FSTH SE23 * 45 L7
Sunderland Rd FSTH SE23 45 L7
Sundew Gv RAM CT11 17 J3
Sundial Av SNWD SE25 69 G6
Sundorne Rd CHARL SE7 27 J4
Sundridge Av BMLY BR1 71 L5
WELL DA16 28 E8
Sundridge Cl CANTW/ST CT2 172 B5
DART DA1 52 B4
Sundridge Dr WALD ME5 115 H1
Sundridge Hl RSEV TN14 134 B4
STRD ME2 99 K3
Sundridge La RSEV TN14 134 A3
Sundridge Pde BMLY BR1 * 71 J4
Sundridge Rd CROY/NA CR0 87 G4
RSEV TN14 134 F6
Sunfields Pl BKHTH/KID SE3 27 J6
Sun Hl HART DA3 95 H5
Sunhill Pl RTWE/PEM TN2 * 197 M7
Sun in Sands Rbt
BKHTH/KID SE3 27 J6
Sunken Rd CROY/NA CR0 87 K8
Sunland Av BXLYHS DA6 49 M2
Sun La BKHTH/KID SE3 27 J6
BRCH CT7 233 N7
GVE DA12 55 K7
HYTHE CT21 222 D3
Sunningdale Av FOLKN CT19 220 B6
Sunningdale Cl
BERM/RHTH SE16 * 25 J4
RHAM ME8 102 E7
Sunningdale Dr RHAM ME8 102 E7
Sunningdale Rd HAYES BR2 71 M8
Sunningdale Wk HB CT6 128 E8
Sunninghill GVW DA11 54 F7
Sunninghill Rd LEW SE13 26 C8
Sunningvale Av
BH/WHM TN16 132 B1
Sunningvale Cl BH/WHM TN16 132 C2
Sunny Bank HYTHE CT21 222 A3
SIT ME10 120 C4
SNWD SE25 69 H8
WARL CR6 130 D3
Sunnybank RDV CT15 * 272 C5
Sunnycroft Rd SNWD SE25 69 H7
Sunnydale ORP BR6 90 B5
Sunnydale Rd LEE/GVPK SE12 47 J3
Sunnydene St SYD SE26 69 M1
Sunnyfields Cl RHAM ME8 102 F5
Sunnyfields Dr IOS ME12 64 D7
Sunnyhill Rd HB CT6 128 C6
Sunnymead CANTW/ST CT2 153 L6
Sunnymead Av GILL ME7 83 M8
Sunnyridge RRTW TN3 * 277 P9
Sunnyside CAT SE6 * 46 A5
Sunny Side MEO DA13 * 97 H6
Sunnyside Av IOS ME12 65 H7
Sunnyside Cl DEAL CT14 208 E8
Sunnyside Gdns SWCH CT13 253 R1
Sunnyside Rd FOLK CT20 223 L2
STH/RUST TN4 200 D1
Sun Pas BERM/RHTH SE16 25 H2
Sun Pier CHAT ME4 * 6 C5
Sunray Av CMBW SE5 44 E2
HAYES BR2 89 M2
WSTB CT5 126 C6
Sun Rd SWCM DA10 54 A4
Sunset Cl ERITH DA8 31 J6
IOS ME12 67 G7
WSTB CT5 126 D7
Sunset Gdns NRWD SE19 68 F6
Sunset Rd CMBW SE5 44 D2
THMD SE28 29 H1
Sun St CANT CT1 4 F4
Sun Ter WALD ME5 * 115 J1
Sun Valley Wy RDV CT15 272 D5
Super Abbey Est DIT/AY ME20 * 140 C3
Superior Dr ORP BR6 107 L1
Surf Crs IOS ME12 67 G7
Surrenden Rd FOLKN CT19 10 A1
STPH/PW TN12 281 R6
Surrey Canal Rd
BERM/RHTH SE16 25 K5
Surrey Cl BGR/WK TN15 * 111 K2
RTWE/PEM TN2 201 G5
Surrey Gdns BRCH CT7 176 C6
Surrey Gv WALW SE17 24 F4
Surrey Ms WNWD SE27 68 F1
Surrey Quays Rd
BERM/RHTH SE16 25 K2
Surrey Rd CANT CT1 174 E2
MAID/SHEP ME15 167 L5
MARG CT9 15 M3
PECK SE15 45 L3
WWKM BR4 88 C4
Surrey Rw STHWK SE1 24 C1
Surrey Sq WALW SE17 24 F4
Surrey St CROY/NA CR0 86 D6
Surrey Ter WALW SE17 24 F4
Surridge Gdns NRWD SE19 68 E3
Surtees Cl KEN/WIL TN24 205 H5
Susan Rd BKHTH/KID SE3 27 J8
Susan's Hl RASHW TN26 302 E11
Susan Wd CHST BR7 72 B5
Sussex Av CANT CT1 174 E2
KEN/WIL TN24 2 A3
MARG CT9 15 H7
Sussex Border Pth
BUR/ETCH TN19 311 K9
EDEN TN8 274 H6
EDEN TN8 275 L7
EDEN TN8 276 A11
HAWK TN18 311 R8
HAWK TN18 323 P1
LING RH7 274 D6
RRTW TN3 198 E1
RRTW TN3 295 J12
RYE TN31 324 F7
WADH TN5 295 J12
WADH TN5 308 E4
Sussex Cl BGR/WK TN15 * 111 K2
HB CT6 128 C5
RTWE/PEM TN2 23 J9
Sussex Dr WALD ME5 115 H1
Sussex Gdns BRCH CT7 176 C6
HB CT6 128 C5
WGOS CT8 177 J4
Sussex Gdns Walk CANT CT1 174 E2
Sussex Man WGOS CT8 * 177 J4
Sussex Ms RTWE/PEM TN2 22 E8
Sussex Rd DART DA1 52 B5
ERITH DA8 30 C6
FOLKN CT19 11 J3
MAID/SHEP ME15 167 L4
NROM TN28 330 H7
SCUP DA14 73 J2
STMC/STPC BR5 91 K2
TON TN9 194 D5
WWKM BR4 88 C4
Sussex St RAM CT11 17 K4
Sussex Ter PGE/AN SE20 * 69 K4
PUR RM19 * 32 C4
Sussex Wk CANT CT1 174 E2
Sutcliffe Rd WELL DA16 29 K8
WOOL/PLUM SE18 28 F5
Sutherland Av BH/WHM TN16 132 C3
STMC/STPC BR5 91 G2
WELL DA16 48 E2
Sutherland Cl GVE DA12 56 C7
HYTHE CT21 222 B3
Sutherland Dr BRCH CT7 176 E6
Sutherland Rd BELV DA17 30 B2
CROY/NA CR0 86 B3
DEAL CT14 209 K3
RTW TN1 23 G7
Sutherland Sq WALW SE17 24 D4
Sutherland Wk WALW SE17 24 D4
Sutlej Rd CHARL SE7 27 K6
Sutton Baron Rd RSIT ME9 145 G1
Sutton Cl BECK BR3 70 C5
FOLKN CT19 10 C1
RHAM ME8 103 H5
Sutton Ct STPH/PW TN12 280 H4
Sutton Forge STPH/PW TN12 281 J4
Sutton Gdns CROY/NA CR0 87 G1
Sutton La DEAL CT14 210 D1
Sutton Rd MAID/SHEP ME15 167 J5
RCANTE CT3 155 M8
RMAID ME17 260 E2
The Suttons RYE TN31 332 F8
Sutton St MAID/BEAR ME14 168 E2
Sutton Valence Hl
RMAID ME17 * 260 E7
Swadelands Cl RMAID ME17 243 L12
Swaffield Rd SEV TN13 136 B8
Swain Cl STRD ME2 18 C2
Swain Rd RASHW TN26 302 C11
RHAM ME8 102 C7
TENT TN30 301 N10
THHTH CR7 86 D1
Swaisland Rd DART DA1 51 J4
Swaislands Dr DART DA1 51 G3
Swale Av IOS ME12 64 C4
QBOR ME11 227 N2
Swale Br (Due to open 2006)
RSIT ME9 227 P5
Swalecliffe Av HB CT6 128 C5
Swalecliffe Court Dr
WSTB CT5 127 L3
Swalecliffe Rd WSTB CT5 127 J3
Swaledale Rd RDART DA2 52 D6
Swale Heritage Trail FAV ME13 123 H6
SIT ME10 120 D3
Swale Rd DART DA1 51 H1
STRD ME2 81 K6
Swallands Rd CAT SE6 46 B8
Swallow Av WSTB CT5 126 C6
Swallow Cl BXLYHN DA7 30 F7
CDW/CHF RM16 33 K3
GRH DA9 53 G3
MARG CT9 14 B8
NWCR SE14 25 K7
Swallow Ct HB CT6 * 155 G2
Swallowdale SAND/SEL CR2 104 C3
Swallow Dr RTWE/PEM TN2 197 J7
Swallowfield KEN/WIL TN24 205 H4
Swallowfield Rd CHARL SE7 27 J4
Swallow Ri WALD ME5 101 H8
Swallow Rd DIT/AY ME20 139 G3
Swallowtail Cl STMC/STPC BR5 73 L8
Swamp Rd LYDD TN29 330 B9
Swanbridge Rd BXLYHN DA7 30 B7
Swan Cl CROY/NA CR0 * 86 F3
SIT ME10 120 C5
STMC/STPC BR5 73 H7
Swan Cottages TENT TN30 326 G2
Swanfield Rd WSTB CT5 126 E5
Swan Gn RASHE TN25 306 H4
Swanland Dr TON TN9 194 C6
Swan La CRBK TN17 297 N2
DART DA1 51 G5
EDEN TN8 192 D1
RASHE TN25 307 J4
Swanley La SWLY BR8 75 G7
Swanley Rd WELL DA16 29 K7
Swanley Village Rd SWLY BR8 75 J5
Swan Md STHWK SE1 24 F2
Swanmead Wy TON TN9 195 G3
Swan Ms BRXN/ST SW9 24 A8
Swann Wy RFOLK CT18 220 B1
Swan Rdg EDEN TN8 192 E1
Swan Rd BERM/RHTH SE16 25 K1
WOOL/PLUM SE18 27 L2
Swanscombe St SWCM DA10 54 A4
Swanstree Av SIT ME10 120 C7
Swan St E/WMAL ME19 138 D5
STHWK SE1 24 D2
TENT TN30 326 E2
Swanton La RCANTE CT3 173 K8
RDV CT15 293 Q2
Swanton Rd ERITH DA8 30 B6
WBY/YAL ME18 241 M10
Swanzy Rd RSEV TN14 136 B6
Sward Rd STMC/STPC BR5 91 H2
Swarling Hill Rd RCANTW CT4 249 K11
Swattenden La CRBK TN17 298 E12
Swaylands Rd BELV DA17 30 B5
Swaynesland Rd OXTED RH8 186 A4
Swaynes Wy SWCH CT13 253 N7
Sweden Ga BERM/RHTH SE16 25 M3
Sweechbridge Rd HB CT6 232 B5
Sweechgate CANTW/ST CT2 172 F2
Sweeney Crs STHWK SE1 25 G1
Sweeps Hill Cl RTWE/PEM TN2 278 A10
Sweeps La STMC/STPC BR5 91 L1
Sweet Bay Crs ASH TN23 202 A8
Sweetbriar La RDV CT15 272 C4
Sweetings La RRTW TN3 295 R11
Sweetlove Pl RCANTE CT3 251 R1
Sweets La E/WMAL ME19 165 J1
Sweyne Rd SWCM DA10 53 M4
Sweyn Pl BKHTH/KID SE3 27 H8
Sweyn Rd MARG CT9 15 K3
Swievelands Rd
BH/WHM TN16 132 A5
Swift Cl DIT/AY ME20 139 H3
Swift Crs WALD ME5 101 J7
Swift Pl STRD ME2 * 82 F5
Swiftsden Wy BMLY BR1 70 F3
Swiftsure Rd CDW/CHF RM16 33 K3
Swifts Vw CRBK TN17 298 G7
Swiller's La GVE DA12 80 F2
Swinburne Av BRDST CT10 183 K2
Swinburne Crs CROY/NA CR0 87 K2
Swinburne Gdns TIL RM18 35 J8
Swinford Gdns BRXN/ST SW9 44 C1
MARG CT9 178 F5
Swingate Av HOO/HM ME3 38 C8
Swingate Cl WALD ME5 115 J3
Swingate La WOOL/PLUM SE18 28 F6
Swinton Av HOO/HM ME3 59 G8
Swires Shaw HAYES BR2 89 L7
Swiss Wy FOLKN CT19 221 H6
Switch House Av LYDD TN29 335 N11
Swithland Gdns ELTH/MOT SE9 72 A1
Sybil Phoenix Cl DEPT SE8 25 L4
Sycamore Av BFN/LL DA15 49 G4
RCANTE CT3 251 P12
Sycamore Cl BRDST CT10 182 F1
GVE DA12 55 L5
HB CT6 129 K4
HYTHE CT21 307 R12
LYDD TN29 334 E2
MARG CT9 178 A6
SAND/SEL CR2 86 F8
TIL RM18 35 H7
Sycamore Crs MAIDW ME16 140 D8
Sycamore Dr DIT/AY ME20 139 M4
SWLY BR8 74 F7
Sycamore Gdns LYDD TN29 320 H9
STPH/PW TN12 279 J4
Sycamore Gra RAM CT11 17 L1
Sycamore Gv CAT SE6 46 D4
PGE/AN SE20 69 H5
Sycamore Ms ERITH DA8 * 30 E4
Sycamore Rd DART DA1 51 L5
STRD ME2 18 B8
The Sycamores RCANTE CT3 173 M1
Sychem La RTON TN11 278 D4
Sychem Pl STPH/PW TN12 278 D2
Sydcot Dr DEAL CT14 209 K1
Sydcote DUL SE21 * 44 D7
Sydenham Av SYD SE26 69 J2
Sydenham Hl FSTH SE23 45 J7
Sydenham Pk SYD SE26 45 K8
Sydenham Park Rd FSTH SE23 45 K8
Sydenham Ri FSTH SE23 45 J7
Sydenham Rd CROY/NA CR0 86 E4
DEAL CT14 209 L2
SYD SE26 69 L2
Sydenham Station Ap
SYD SE26 69 K1
Sydmons Ct FSTH SE23 * 45 K5
Sydney Av SIT ME10 119 K5
Sydney Cooper Cl
CANTW/ST CT2 171 J3
Sydney Rd ABYW SE2 29 L2
BXLYHS DA6 49 L2
CHAT ME4 6 E8
DEAL CT14 209 H8
RAM CT11 17 L4
SCUP DA14 72 F1
TIL RM18 35 H8
WSTB CT5 126 F5
Sydney St ASH TN23 2 B9
Sylewood Cl ROCH ME1 100 C5
Sylvan Cl CDW/CHF RM16 33 M3
OXTED RH8 158 A7
SAND/SEL CR2 104 A4
Sylvan Gld WALD ME5 115 H5
Sylvan Gv PECK SE15 25 J5
Sylvan Hl NRWD SE19 68 F5
Sylvan Ms GRH DA9 53 J2
Sylvan Rd NRWD SE19 69 G5
RHAM ME8 102 D5
Sylvan Ter PECK SE15 * 25 J6
Sylvan Wy WWKM BR4 88 F7
Sylverdale Rd CROY/NA CR0 86 C6
Sylvester Av CHST BR7 72 A3
Sylvestre Cl STRD ME2 113 H1
Symmonds Dr SIT ME10 120 B4
Symonds Cl BGR/WK TN15 94 F8
Symonds La WBY/YAL ME18 257 Q7
Symonds Rd HOO/HM ME3 58 B2
Symons Av CHAT ME4 6 E9

T

Tabard Garden Est STHWK SE1 24 E1
Tabard St STHWK SE1 24 E1
Tabret Cl KEN/WIL TN24 203 G5
Tack Ms BROCKY SE4 46 B1
Tadburn Gn WALD ME5 115 J1
Taddington Wood La
WALD ME5 114 F3
Taddy Gdns MARG CT9 178 F5
Tadworth Rd KEN/WIL TN24 203 G6
Taeping St POP/IOD E14 26 C3
Taillour Cl SIT ME10 120 A2
The Tail Race MAID/SHEP ME15 12 C8
Tainter Rd RTON TN11 256 B4
Tainters Hl EDEN TN8 * 193 L7
Tait Rd CROY/NA CR0 86 F3
Talavera Rd CANT CT1 172 D8
Talbot Av HB CT6 128 C6
Talbot Pk RTWE/PEM TN2 23 L2
Talbot Pl BKHTH/KID SE3 26 F8
Talbot Rd EDUL SE22 44 F2
HAWK TN18 312 C9
MAIDW ME16 140 D7
MARG CT9 15 L5
THHTH CR7 68 E8
Talcott Pth BRXS/STRHM SW2 * 44 B6
Talfourd Pl PECK SE15 25 G7
Talfourd Rd PECK SE15 25 G7
Talisman Sq SYD SE26 69 H1
Tall Elms Cl HAYES BR2 89 G1
Tallents Cl EYN DA4 76 C4
Tallis Gv CHARL SE7 27 J5
Tall Trees STRHM/NOR SW16 68 A7
Tall Trees Cl RMAID ME17 261 L3
Tally Ho Rd RASHW TN26 303 R3
Tally Rd OXTED RH8 185 M1
Talmage Cl FSTH SE23 45 K5
Talma Rd BRXS/STRHM SW2 44 B2
Talus Cl PUR RM19 32 E3
Tamar Dr STRD ME2 18 C5
Tamarind Cl GILL ME7 116 B1
Tamar Rd TONN TN10 188 E8
Tamar St WOOL/PLUM SE18 27 M3
Tame La LYDD TN29 320 E2
Tamesis Strd GVE DA12 79 M2
Tamley La RASHE TN25 289 Q4
Tams Gdns IOS ME12 65 L7
Tamworth Pl CROY/NA CR0 * 86 D5
Tamworth Rd CROY/NA CR0 86 D5
Tandridge Dr ORP BR6 90 E4
Tandridgehill La GDST RH9 156 E6
Tandridge La LING RH7 190 A5
OXTED RH8 184 B3
Tandridge Rd WARL CR6 130 C5
Tanfield Rd CROY/NA CR0 86 D7
Tangier Cl DVE/WH CT16 213 M6
Tangier La RRTW TN3 201 J7
Tangleberry Cl BMLY BR1 72 A8
Tanglewood Cl CROY/NA CR0 87 K6
RHAM ME8 102 D7
Tangmere Cl GILL ME7 84 A8
Tanhouse La RYE TN31 326 D11
Tanhouse Rd OXTED RH8 184 E2
Tanker Hl RHAM ME8 102 E7
Tankerton Circ WSTB CT5 127 G2
Tankerton Ms WSTB CT5 126 F2
Tankerton Rd WSTB CT5 126 F2
Tankerton Ter CROY/NA CR0 * 86 A3
Tank Farm St LYDD TN29 335 N11
Tank Hill Rd PUR RM19 32 B3
Tank La PUR RM19 32 B3
Tanner's Hl DEPT SE8 26 B7
HYTHE CT21 222 D1
Tanner's Hill Gdns HYTHE CT21 222 D1
Tanners Md EDEN TN8 192 D4
Tanners Ms DEPT SE8 26 A7
Tanners St FAV ME13 149 K2
Tanner St STHWK SE1 24 F1
Tannery Cl CROY/NA CR0 87 L1
Tannery La ASH TN23 2 D5
SWCH CT13 237 J12
TON TN9 194 F4
Tannery Rd TON TN9 194 F4
The Tannery STHWK SE1 * 24 F1
Tannsfeld Rd SYD SE26 69 L2
Tanswell St STHWK SE1 * 24 B1
Tanyard HAWK TN18 313 L12
Tanyard Hl GVE DA12 80 F3
Tan Yard La BXLY DA5 * 50 B5
Tanyard La STH/RUST TN4 196 C4
The Tanyard CRBK TN17 298 G9
Tapleys Hl RCANTW CT4 249 Q12
Tappan Dr CHAT ME4 83 J3
Tappesfield Rd PECK SE15 45 K1
Tapsell's La WADH TN5 308 H4
Tara Ter BROCKY SE4 * 45 M1
Tarbert Rd EDUL SE22 44 F3
Target Firs DVE/WH CT16 212 E4
Tarleton Gdns FSTH SE23 45 J6
Tarling Cl SCUP DA14 49 J8
Tarn St STHWK SE1 24 D2
Tarnwood Pk ELTH/MOT SE9 48 A6
Tarragon Cl NWCR SE14 * 25 M6
Tarragon Gv SYD SE26 69 L3
Tarragon Rd MAIDW ME16 166 B2
Tarriff Crs DEPT SE8 26 A3
Tartane La LYDD TN29 320 H9
Tarver Rd WALW SE17 24 C4
Tarves Wy GNWCH SE10 26 C6
Tasker Cl MAID/SHEP ME15 168 C2
Tasker Rd CDW/CHF RM16 35 J2
Tassell Cl E/WMAL ME19 139 H4
Taswell Cl DVE/WH CT16 8 E3
Taswell Rd RHAM ME8 103 H4
Taswell St DVE/WH CT16 8 E3
Tates HAWK TN18 312 D8
Tates Orch HART DA3 96 A2
Tatler Cl WALD ME5 115 L3
Tatnell Rd FSTH SE23 45 M4
Tatsfield La BH/WHM TN16 132 E7
Tattersall Cl ELTH/MOT SE9 47 M3
Tattlebury La CRBK TN17 297 N5
Tattlebury Rd HDCN TN27 283 K1
Tatum St WALW SE17 24 E3
Taunton Cl BXLYHN DA7 50 E1
MAID/SHEP ME15 168 A7
Taunton Rd GVW DA11 54 B3
LEW SE13 46 F3
Taunton V GVE DA12 55 L8
Taveners Rd RHAM ME8 102 E6
Tavern Cl BGR/WK TN15 240 E2
Tavistock Cl RHAM ME8 102 F6
SIT ME10 119 L5
WALD ME5 115 G4
Tavistock Gv CROY/NA CR0 86 E3
Tavistock Rd CROY/NA CR0 86 E4
HAYES BR2 71 H8
RAM CT11 183 H4
WELL DA16 29 K7
Tavy Br ABYW SE2 29 K1
Tavy Cl LBTH SE11 24 B4
Tawny Wy BERM/RHTH SE16 25 L3
Tay Cl WALD ME5 101 J8
Tay Flds STPH/PW TN12 * 282 E2
Taylor Cl DEPT SE8 26 A5
ORP BR6 91 G7
RMAID ME17 242 E11
Taylor Rd FOLKN CT19 219 M7
LYDD TN29 335 M3
MSTR CT12 180 E7
SNOD ME6 113 G6
Taylor Rw RDART DA2 51 K8
Taylor's Buildings
WOOL/PLUM SE18 28 C3
Taylors Cl LYDD TN29 331 N2
SCUP DA14 73 G1
Taylors Hl RCANTW CT4 247 N9
Taylors La E/WMAL ME19 239 L8
HOO/HM ME3 57 J8
LYDD TN29 331 N2
STRD ME2 19 H4
SYD SE26 69 J1
Taylors Pas ASH TN23 2 B4
Taylor St STH/RUST TN4 196 C5
Taylors Yd RASHE TN25 * 266 F11
Taymount Ri FSTH SE23 45 K7
Taywood Cl KEN/WIL TN24 3 K6
Tea Garden La RRTW TN3 200 D3
Teal Av STMC/STPC BR5 73 L8
Teal Cl HOO/HM ME3 * 43 J8
SAND/SEL CR2 104 C5
Teal Dr HB CT6 128 F7
Teal Wy RSIT ME9 227 M10
Teapot La DIT/AY ME20 139 M4
Teasaucer Hl
MAID/SHEP ME15 167 G5
Teasel Cl CROY/NA CR0 87 L4
MAID/BEAR ME14 168 A1
Teasel Rd WALD ME5 115 G1
Tebbs Wy BGR/WK TN15 240 B6
Teddars Leas Rd RFOLK CT18 218 E1
Tedder Av WALD ME5 101 H6
Tedder Rd SAND/SEL CR2 104 C2
STH/RUST TN4 196 E6
Teddington Cl CANT CT1 5 J1
Teelin Cl LYDD TN29 331 N1
Teesdale Gdns SNWD SE25 68 F6
Teesdale Rd RDART DA2 52 D6
Teevan Cl CROY/NA CR0 87 H3
Teevan Rd CROY/NA CR0 87 H3
Teignmouth Rd WELL DA16 29 K8
Teise Cl RTWE/PEM TN2 23 K8
Telegraph Hl HOO/HM ME3 81 K3
Telegraph Pl POP/IOD E14 26 C3
Telegraph Rd DEAL CT14 209 J7
Telford Cl NRWD SE19 69 G3
Telford Ct FOLKN CT19 11 L2
Telford Rd CHST BR7 48 E7
Telham Av MSTR CT12 16 D3
Tell Gv EDUL SE22 45 G2
Tellson Av WOOL/PLUM SE18 27 L7
Telscombe Cl ORP BR6 90 F5
Telston La RSEV TN14 135 L3
Temeraire Hts FOLK CT20 223 K2
Temeraire St BERM/RHTH SE16 25 K1
Tempest Rd E/WMAL ME19 164 A2
Templar Dr GVW DA11 79 H2
Templar Rd DVE/WH CT16 212 E4
Templars Ct DART DA1 * 52 B3
Templar St CMBW SE5 24 C8
DVW CT17 8 A3
Temple Av CROY/NA CR0 88 A6
Temple Boat Yd STRD ME2 * 18 F6
Temple Cl ASH TN23 204 C6
DVE/WH CT16 212 E3
WOOL/PLUM SE18 28 D2
Temple Ct STRD ME2 * 18 E6
Temple Gdns SIT ME10 120 C6
STRD ME2 18 D6
Temple Hl DART DA1 52 A3
Temple Hill Sq DART DA1 52 A3
Temple Ms CANT CT1 * 4 E5
Templer Av CDW/CHF RM16 35 H3
Temple Rd CANTW/ST CT2 4 B2
CROY/NA CR0 86 E7
Templer Wy ASH TN23 202 D8
Temple Side DVE/WH CT16 212 E4
Templeton Cl THHTH CR7 68 E5
Temple Wy DEAL CT14 206 B5
E/WMAL ME19 139 G5
Ten Acre Wy RHAM ME8 103 J4
Tenby Rd WELL DA16 29 L7
Tenchley's La OXTED RH8 185 L1
Tenda Rd BERM/RHTH SE16 25 J3
Tennants Rw TIL RM18 * 34 F8
Tennison Rd SNWD SE25 69 G8
Tennis St STHWK SE1 24 E1
Tennyson Av CANT CT1 172 E6
GRAYS RM17 34 C2
HOO/HM ME3 58 C6
Tennyson Cl WELL DA16 28 F7
Tennyson Gdns RCANTE CT3 251 Q11
Tennyson Pl FOLKN CT19 11 M1
Tennyson Rd ASH TN23 204 D5
DART DA1 52 B3
GILL ME7 7 J7
PGE/AN SE20 69 L4
Tennyson Wk GVW DA11 54 E8
TIL RM18 35 J8
Ten Perch Rd CANT CT1 4 A8
Tensing Av GVW DA11 * 54 F8
Tenterden Cl ELTH/MOT SE9 72 A1
Tenterden Dr CANTW/ST CT2 172 A5
Tenterden Gdns CROY/NA CR0 87 H3
Tenterden Rd CRBK TN17 314 F5
CROY/NA CR0 87 H3
HDCN TN27 300 F10
RASHW TN26 316 H8
WALD ME5 * 101 J8
Tenterden Wy MARG CT9 * 178 F4
Tent Peg La STMC/STPC BR5 90 D1
Teredo St LEW SE13 26 C8
Terence Cl CHAT ME4 101 H3
GVE DA12 56 A7
Terlingham La RFOLK CT18 220 B3
Terminus Dr HB CT6 129 L4
Terminus Rd MAIDW ME16 166 B3
Tern Crs STRD ME2 81 K7
Terrace Rd MAIDW ME16 12 D5
RDV CT15 272 C4
SIT ME10 120 C6
The Terraces RDART DA2 52 D5
Terrace St GVE DA12 55 J4
The Terrace CANTW/ST CT2 172 A6
DEPT SE8 * 26 A3
FAV ME13 * 149 H2
FSTH SE23 * 45 M5
GVE DA12 55 K4
GVE DA12 * 80 A7
RDV CT15 271 Q8
ROCH ME1 19 K8
RTON TN11 * 256 B5
SEV TN13 135 J8
Terry's Lodge Rd
BGR/WK TN15 238 B8
Terry Wk DIT/AY ME20 138 F3
Testers Cl OXTED RH8 185 J1
Teston La MAID/SHEP ME15 165 K6
Teston Rd E/WMAL ME19 164 F3
E/WMAL ME19 241 N1
Tetty Wy HAYES BR2 71 H6
Teviot Cl WELL DA16 29 J7
Tewkesbury Av FSTH SE23 45 J6
Tewson Rd WOOL/PLUM SE18 28 F4
Teynham Cl MARG CT9 179 J3
Teynham Dr WSTB CT5 127 G3
Teynham Gn HAYES BR2 89 H1
RHAM ME8 102 B1
Teynham Rd WSTB CT5 126 F4
Teynham St RSIT ME9 122 A5
Thackeray Av TIL RM18 35 J7
Thackeray Rd DIT/AY ME20 139 H2
Thakeham Cl SYD SE26 69 J2
Thalia Cl GNWCH SE10 26 E5
Thame Rd BERM/RHTH SE16 25 L1
Thames Av HOO/HM ME3 59 M1
IOS ME12 64 C4
RHAM ME8 102 F5
Thames Cir POP/IOD E14 26 B3
Thames Dr CDW/CHF RM16 35 H4
Thames Ga DART DA1 52 B3
Thames Pth BERM/RHTH SE16 26 A2
Thames Rd DART DA1 51 H1
TONN TN10 188 F8
Thames St GNWCH SE10 26 D5
Thames Vw GRAYS RM17 35 H4
HOO/HM ME3 58 D6
Thames Wy GVW DA11 54 B4
Thamley PUR RM19 32 B3
Thanescroft Gdns
CROY/NA CR0 86 F6
Thanet Coastal Pth BRCH CT7 176 B5
BRDST CT10 179 L4
MSTR CT12 237 M2
Thanet Dr HAYES BR2 89 L6
Thanet Gdns FOLKN CT19 221 G7
Thanet Pl CROY/NA CR0 86 D7
Thanet Place Gdns
BRDST CT10 179 L7
Thanet Rd BRDST CT10 183 L1
BXLY DA5 50 B5
ERITH DA8 30 F6
MARG CT9 15 H5
RAM CT11 17 L3
WGOS CT8 177 G4
Thanet Ter RASHW TN26 * 286 F3
Thanet Vw RDV CT15 * 272 C5
Thanet Wy BRCH CT7 232 H6
FAV ME13 125 M7
FAV ME13 150 D4
HB CT6 128 E6
HB CT6 232 A6
RCANTE CT3 232 C6
Thanington Rd CANT CT1 171 K7
Thatch Barn Rd HDCN TN27 283 L3
Thatcher Rd STPH/PW TN12 281 R5
Thatchers La HOO/HM ME3 38 C8
The Thatchers MAIDW ME16 * 140 C8
Thaxted Rd ELTH/MOT SE9 48 D7
Thayers Farm Rd BECK BR3 69 M5
Theatre St HYTHE CT21 222 D3
The Courtyard HAYES BR2 106 D1
Thelma Cl GVE DA12 80 A2
Theobald Rd CROY/NA CR0 86 C5
Theobalds HAWK TN18 312 C7
Theobalds Av GRAYS RM17 34 D4
Theobald St STHWK SE1 24 E2
Theodore Cl RTWE/PEM TN2 197 H6
Theodore Pl GILL ME7 7 J3
Theodore Rd LEW SE13 46 E4
Therapia Rd EDUL SE22 45 K4
Theresa Rd HYTHE CT21 222 C4
Thermopylae Ga POP/IOD E14 26 C3
Thesiger Rd PGE/AN SE20 69 L4
Thicket Gv PGE/AN SE20 69 H4
Thicket Rd PGE/AN SE20 69 J4
Thicket Ter PGE/AN SE20 * 69 H4
Thicketts SEV TN13 21 J3
Third Av CHAT ME4 101 K4
GILL ME7 101 M2
GVW DA11 * 55 G6
IOS ME12 67 H7
MARG CT9 15 L2
WTHK RM20 33 H5
Third St RRTW TN3 200 A2
Thirlemere Cl MAIDW ME16 140 E5
Thirlmere KEN/WIL TN24 202 F5
Thirlmere Av RAM CT11 16 B5

Thirlmere Cl *GILL* ME7 84 B8
STRD ME2 82 D4
Thirlmere Gdns *RCANTE* CT3 251 Q11
Thirlmere Ri *BMLY* BR1 71 G3
Thirlmere Rd *BXLYHN* DA7 30 D8
STH/RUST TN4 22 A2
Thirsk Rd *SNWD* SE25 68 E8
Thirza Rd *DART* DA1 52 A4
Thislefield Cl *BXLY* DA5 49 L6
Thistlebank *WALD* ME5 115 H2
Thistlebrook *ABYW* SE2 29 K2
Thistledown
MAID/BEAR ME14 168 A1
STPH/PW TN12 * 278 G7
Thistledown Cl *GILL* ME7 116 B1
Thistle Dr *WSTB* CT5 126 C8
Thistle Hill Wy *IOS* ME12 65 J8
Thistlemead *CHST* BR7 72 C6
Thistle Rd *GVE* DA12 55 M5
Thistlewood Crs *CROY/NA* CR0 105 J6
Thomas Bata Av *TIL* RM18 36 C3
Thomas Dean Rd *SYD* SE26 * 70 A1
Thomas Dinwiddy Rd
LEE/GVPK SE12 47 J7
Thomas Doyle St *STHWK* SE1 24 C2
Thomas Dr *GVE* DA12 55 L7
Thomas' La *CAT* SE6 46 C5
Thomas Rd *FAV* ME13 149 K2
SIT ME10 120 C5
Thomas St *ROCH* ME1 100 D2
STH/RUST TN4 22 E1
WOOL/PLUM SE18 28 B3
Thompson Cl *DEAL* CT14 211 J1
FOLKN CT19 220 C6
RHAM ME8 103 H5
Thompson Rd *EDUL* SE22 45 G4
Thompson's Av *CMBW* SE5 * 24 D6
Thomson Cl *SNOD* ME6 113 H4
Thomson Crs *CROY/NA* CR0 86 B4
Thomson Rd *KEN/WIL* TN24 202 E6
Thong La *BGR/WK* TN15 240 D4
GVE DA12 56 B7
Thorburn Sq *STHWK* SE1 25 H3
Thornbridge Rd *DEAL* CT14 209 H6
Thorn Cl *HAYES* BR2 90 B2
WALD ME5 114 E4
Thorncombe Rd *EDUL* SE22 44 F3
Thorndale Cl *WALD* ME5 100 E8
Thornden Cl *HB* CT6 128 B7
Thornden Ct *CANTW/ST* CT2 * 171 K1
Thornden La *CRBK* TN17 314 F9
Thornden Wood Rd
CANTW/ST CT2 153 M3
Thorndike Cl *CHAT* ME4 * 101 G5
Thorndike Rd *LYDD* TN29 320 H5
Thorndon Cl *STMC/STPC* BR5 73 G6
Thorndon Rd *STMC/STPC* BR5 73 G6
Thorne Cl *ERITH* DA8 30 C5
Thorne Hl *MSTR* CT12 181 J6
Thorneloe Gdns *CROY/NA* CR0 86 C8
Thorne Rd *MSTR* CT12 180 E7
Thorne's Cl *BECK* BR3 70 D7
The Thorn Est *HDCN* TN27 285 M3
Thornet Wood Rd *BMLY* BR1 72 B7
Thorneycroft Rd *FAV* ME13 244 G12
Thornfield Gdns
RTWE/PEM TN2 197 J8
Thornford Rd *LEW* SE13 46 D3
Thorn Gdns *RAM* CT11 183 H4
Thornham Rd *RHAM* ME8 102 D2
Thornham St *GNWCH* SE10 26 C5
Thornhill Av *WOOL/PLUM* SE18 28 F6
Thornhill Pl *MAID/BEAR* ME14 13 G1
Thornhill Rd *CROY/NA* CR0 86 D3
Thorn Hill Rd *IOS* ME12 67 L8
Thorn La *RCANTW* CT4 268 F11
Thornlaw Rd *WNWD* SE27 68 B1
Thornlea *ASH* TN23 204 B1
Thorn Rd *STPH/PW* TN12 281 L6
Thornsbeach Rd *CAT* SE6 46 D6
Thornsett Pl *PGE/AN* SE20 69 J6
Thornsett Rd *PGE/AN* SE20 69 J6
Thornsett Ter *PGE/AN* SE20 * 69 J6
Thorn's Meadow
BH/WHM TN16 160 B1
Thornton Av *CROY/NA* CR0 86 A2
Thornton Cl *KEN/WIL* TN24 3 L6
Thornton Dene *BECK* BR3 70 B6
Thornton La *DEAL* CT14 253 K11
Thornton Rd *BELV* DA17 * 30 C3
BMLY BR1 71 H2
THHTH CR7 86 B1
Thornton Rw *THHTH* CR7 86 B1
Thornton St *BRXN/ST* SW9 24 B8
Thorntree Rd *CHARL* SE7 27 L4
Thornville St *DEPT* SE8 26 B7
Thornwood Rd *LEW* SE13 46 F3
Thorold Cl *SAND/SEL* CR2 104 C4
Thorold Rd *CHAT* ME4 7 G7
Thorpe Av *TONN* TN10 188 F8
Thorpe Cl *CROY/NA* CR0 105 H5
ORP BR6 90 F5
SYD SE26 * 69 L1
Thorpe Wk *RHAM* ME8 116 D2
Thorpewood Av *SYD* SE26 45 J7
Thorsden Wy *NRWD* SE19 * 68 F2
Thrale Wy *RHAM* ME8 116 F1
Thread La *FAV* ME13 151 J4
Three Acres Site *FOLKN* CT19 * 220 C5
Three Corners *BXLYHN* DA7 30 C8
Three Elm La *RTON* TN11 256 B8
TONN TN10 189 L7
Three Gates Rd *HART* DA3 95 H3
Three King's Yd *SWCH* CT13 237 K12
Three Leg Cross Rd *WADH* TN5 310 E7
Three Oak La *STHWK* SE1 25 G1
Three Oaks La *WADH* TN5 308 H2
Threshers Dr
MAID/BEAR ME14 141 L8
Threshers Fld *EDEN* TN8 * 276 B3
Thriffwood *FSTH* SE23 45 K8
Thrift La *BH/WHM* TN16 * 133 K3
The Thrift *RDART* DA2 53 K8
Throwley Cl *ABYW* SE2 29 K2
Throwley Dr *HB* CT6 128 D5
Throwley Rd *FAV* ME13 245 P1
Thrupp Paddock *BRDST* CT10 179 K4
Thrush Cl *WALD* ME5 101 J6
Thrush St *WALW* SE17 24 D4
Thruxted La *RCANTW* CT4 248 C8
Thundersland Rd *HB* CT6 129 J5
Thurbarn Rd *CAT* SE6 70 C2
Thurland Rd *BERM/RHTH* SE16 25 H2
Thurlby Rd *WNWD* SE27 68 B1
Thurlestone Ct
MAID/BEAR ME14 * 12 F1
Thurlestone Rd *WNWD* SE27 44 B8
Thurloe Wk *GRAYS* RM17 34 B2
Thurlow Av *HB* CT6 129 K4
Thurlow Hl *DUL* SE21 44 D6
Thurlow Park Rd *DUL* SE21 44 C7
Thurlow St *WALW* SE17 24 F4
Thurlow Wk *WALW* SE17 24 F4
Thurrock Park Wy *GRAYS* RM17 34 E6
Thursland Rd *SCUP* DA14 73 M2
Thursley Crs *CROY/NA* CR0 105 J2
Thursley Rd *ELTH/MOT* SE9 48 A8
Thurston Dr *STRD* ME2 81 L6
Thurston Pk *WSTB* CT5 126 F4
Thurston Rd *DEPT* SE8 26 C8
Thwaite Cl *ERITH* DA8 30 D5
Thyer Cl *ORP* BR6 90 D7
Thyssel La *RYE* TN31 325 J7
Tibbenham Pl *CAT* SE6 46 C7
Tibbs Court La *STPH/PW* TN12 279 K11
Ticehurst Cl *STMC/STPC* BR5 73 H4
Ticehurst Rd *FSTH* SE23 45 M7
Tichborne Cl *MAIDW* ME16 140 D7
Tickford Cl *ABYW* SE2 29 K1
Tickham La *RSIT* ME9 147 J6
Tickners La *LYDD* TN29 329 N4
Tidenham Gdns *CROY/NA* CR0 86 F6
Tideswell Rd *CROY/NA* CR0 88 B6
The Tideway *ROCH* ME1 100 D5
Tidford Rd *WELL* DA16 29 G8
Tiepigs La *WWKM* BR4 88 F5
Tiger La *HAYES* BR2 71 J8
Tilbrook Rd *BKHTH/KID* SE3 47 K1
Tilbury Cl *PECK* SE15 25 G6
STMC/STPC BR5 73 J6
Tilbury Rd *RHAM* ME8 103 H3
Tilden Cl *RASHW* TN26 301 Q6
Tilden Gill Rd *TENT* TN30 315 P2
Tilden La *STPH/PW* TN12 258 H10
STPH/PW TN12 280 H1
Tilden Rd *HDCN* TN27 261 M11
Tilebarn Cnr *TONN* TN10 195 H1
Tile Farm Rd *ORP* BR6 90 E6
Tile Flds *RMAID* ME17 169 L3
Tile Kiln Hl *CANTW/ST* CT2 153 H8
Tile Kiln La *BXLY* DA5 50 F8
FOLKN CT19 10 A1
Tile Kiln Rd *KEN/WIL* TN24 202 F4
Tile Lodge Rd *HDCN* TN27 263 N6
Tilford Av *CROY/NA* CR0 105 H2
Tilghman Wy *SNOD* ME6 113 J4
Tillard Cl *RCANTW* CT4 268 E2
Till Av *EYN* DA4 94 A3
Tiller Rd *POP/IOD* E14 26 B2
Tillery La *LYDD* TN29 329 L6
Tillingbourne Gn
STMC/STPC BR5 73 H8
Tillingdown Hl *CTHM* CR3 130 A8
Tillingdown La *CTHM* CR3 156 A3
Tillingham Av *RYE* TN31 225 G4
Tillingham La *RYE* TN31 224 A4
Tillmans *BGR/WK* TN15 240 F2
Tilmans Md *EYN* DA4 94 A3
Tilsden La *CRBK* TN17 298 H10
Tilson Cl *CMBW* SE5 24 F6
Tilton Rd *BGR/WK* TN15 240 D2
Tilt Yard Ap *ELTH/MOT* SE9 48 A4
Timber Bank *MEO* DA13 239 M5
Timberbank *WALD* ME5 101 H7
Timber Cl *CHST* BR7 72 B6
Timbercroft La
WOOL/PLUM SE18 28 F5
Timberland Cl *PECK* SE15 * 25 H6
Timber Pond Rd
BERM/RHTH SE16 25 L1
Timbertop Rd *BH/WHM* TN16 132 B4
Timber Tops *WALD* ME5 115 L5
Timms Cl *BMLY* BR1 72 A8
Timothy Cl *BXLYHS* DA6 49 M3
Timperley Cl *DEAL* CT14 * 209 J3
Tina Gdns *BRDST* CT10 179 K7
Tinbridge Oast *FAV* ME13 * 150 B4
Tindal St *BRXN/ST* SW9 24 C7
Tinker Pot La *BGR/WK* TN15 111 H8
Tinkerpot Ri *BGR/WK* TN15 111 H8
Tinkers La *WADH* TN5 310 E6
Tinsley Cl *SNWD* SE25 69 J7
Tintagel Crs *EDUL* SE22 45 G2
Tintagel Gdns *STRD* ME2 18 C4
Tintagel Rd *STMC/STPC* BR5 91 K5
Tintern Rd *MAIDW* ME16 140 D6
Tipton Dr *CROY/NA* CR0 86 F7
Tirrell Rd *CROY/NA* CR0 86 D2
Tisdall Pl *WALW* SE17 24 E3
Titan Rd *GRAYS* RM17 34 B4
Titchfield Rd
MAID/SHEP ME15 168 A7
Tithe Barn La *ASH* TN23 204 A3
Tithepit Shaw La *WARL* CR6 130 A3
Titsey Hl *OXTED* RH8 158 A2
WARL CR6 157 L2
Titsey Rd *OXTED* RH8 158 A5
Tiverton Cl *CROY/NA* CR0 87 G3
Tiverton Dr *ELTH/MOT* SE9 48 D6
Tiverton St *STHWK* SE1 24 D2
Tivoli Brooks *MARG* CT9 14 F7
Tivoli Gdns *WOOL/PLUM* SE18 27 M3
Tivoli Park Av *MARG* CT9 14 D7
Tivoli Rd *MARG* CT9 14 F7
WNWD SE27 68 D2
Tobago St *POP/IOD* E14 26 B1
Tobruk Wy *WALD* ME5 101 G7
Toby Gdns *RTON* TN11 256 B5
Toby Rd *LYDD* TN29 335 M3
Todd Crs *SIT* ME10 120 B1
Toddington Crs *WALD* ME5 114 E4
Toft Av *GRAYS* RM17 34 E3
Toledo Paddock *GILL* ME7 7 M3
Tolgate La *STRD* ME2 19 G4
Tolgate Wy *MAID/BEAR* ME14 140 F2
Tolhurst La *WADH* TN5 310 B8
Tolhurst Rd *STPH/PW* TN12 278 D2
Tollemache Cl *MSTR* CT12 181 J3
Toll Ga *DEAL* CT14 209 H5
Tollgate Cl *WSTB* CT5 126 D5
Tollgate Dr *DUL* SE21 44 F7
Tollgate Ms *BGR/WK* TN15 240 F2
Tollgate Pl *HDCN* TN27 283 M4
Tollgate Rd *RDART* DA2 52 E5
The Tollgate *RBTBR* TN32 323 R12
Toll La *HDCN* TN27 264 D6
Tolsey Md *BGR/WK* TN15 240 F1
Tolsford Cl *FOLKN* CT19 219 L7
RFOLK CT18 218 D2
Tom Cribb Rd
WOOL/PLUM SE18 28 D2
Tom Joyce Cl *SNOD* ME6 113 G6
Tomlin Cl *SNOD* ME6 113 H5
STPH/PW TN12 281 R5
Tomlin Dr *MARG* CT9 178 F6
Tom Smith Cl *GNWCH* SE10 26 F5
Tonbridge By-Pass
RTON TN11 255 N4
TON TN9 277 R1
Tonbridge Chambers
TON TN9 * 194 E5
Tonbridge Rd *BGR/WK* TN15 240 B6
MAIDW ME16 166 C2
RTON TN11 188 A7
RTON TN11 189 L6
RTON TN11 256 A5
RTWE/PEM TN2 197 L6
SEV TN13 162 B5
STPH/PW TN12 256 H7
WBY/YAL ME18 165 H6
WBY/YAL ME18 241 R9
Tonbridge Wy *RYE* TN31 332 D7
Tonford La *CANTW/ST* CT2 171 G6
Tonge Rd *SIT* ME10 120 D5
Tong La *STPH/PW* TN12 296 C2
Tong Rd *STPH/PW* TN12 279 L12
Tongswood Dr *HAWK* TN18 312 G8
Tontine St *FOLK* CT20 11 K5
Tookey Rd *NROM* TN28 331 J8
Tooley St *GVW* DA11 54 E5
STHWK SE1 25 G1
Tootswood Rd *HAYES* BR2 88 F1
Topcliffe Dr *ORP* BR6 90 F7
Top Dartford Rd *SWLY* BR8 75 H3
Topley Dr *HOO/HM* ME3 59 M2
Topley St *ELTH/MOT* SE9 47 K2
Topmast Point *POP/IOD* E14 * 26 B1
Top Pk *BECK* BR3 88 F1
Top Rd *TENT* TN30 327 P2
Torbay Rd *STPH/PW* TN12 257 L9
Torcross Dr *FSTH* SE23 45 K7
Tormore Ms *DEAL* CT14 209 H5
Tormore Pk *DEAL* CT14 209 H5
Tormount Rd
WOOL/PLUM SE18 28 F5
Toronto Cl *DVE/WH* CT16 213 J6
Toronto Rd *GILL* ME7 101 M1
TIL RM18 35 H8
Torrens Rd *BRXS/STRHM* SW2 44 A3
Torrens Wk *GVE* DA12 79 M2
Torrey Dr *BRXN/ST* SW9 24 B8
Torridge Gdns *PECK* SE15 45 K2
Torridge Rd *THHTH* CR7 86 C1
Torridon Rd *CAT* SE6 46 E6
Torrington Cl *WBY/YAL* ME18 241 Q9
Torrington Pl *ASH* TN23 * 2 B9
Torrington Rd *ASH* TN23 2 B9
Torrington Sq *CROY/NA* CR0 * 86 E3
Tor Rd *WELL* DA16 29 K7
Torr Rd *PGE/AN* SE20 69 L4
Torver Wy *ORP* BR6 90 E6
Tothill St *MSTR* CT12 180 F6
Totnes Rd *WELL* DA16 29 J6
Totton Rd *THHTH* CR7 68 B7
Toulmin St *STHWK* SE1 24 D1
Toulon St *CMBW* SE5 24 D6
Tourmaline Dr *SIT* ME10 119 K3
Tournay Cl *ASH* TN23 204 C3
Tourney Cl *HYTHE* CT21 307 L10
Tourney Rd *LYDD* TN29 334 D4
Tourtel Rd *CANT* CT1 5 H2
Toussaint Wk
BERM/RHTH SE16 25 H2
Tovey Sq *GILL* ME7 84 A7
Tovil Cl *PGE/AN* SE20 69 H6
Tovil Gn *MAID/SHEP* ME15 12 C9
Tovil Hl *MAID/SHEP* ME15 166 F4
Tovil Rd *MAID/SHEP* ME15 12 E9
Tower Bridge Rd *STHWK* SE1 24 F2
Tower Cl *GVE* DA12 79 M2
ORP BR6 91 G5
PGE/AN SE20 69 J4
Tower Cft *EYN* DA4 93 M5
Tower Est *LYDD* TN29 321 L7
Tower Gdns *HYTHE* CT21 222 D4
MAID/BEAR ME14 168 C2
Tower Hamlets Rd *DVW* CT17 8 A3
Tower Hamlets St *DVW* CT17 8 A3
Tower Hl *DVW* CT17 8 A4
E/WMAL ME19 241 Q2
WSTB CT5 126 F2
Tower La *MAID/BEAR* ME14 168 B1
Tower Mill Rd *PECK* SE15 24 F6
Tower Park Rd *DART* DA1 51 G3
Tower Rd *BELV* DA17 30 D3
BXLYHN DA7 50 C2
DART DA1 51 K5
ORP BR6 91 G5
WSTB CT5 126 F3
Towers Rd *GRAYS* RM17 34 D4
Tower St *DVW* CT17 8 A4
RYE TN31 225 H3
Towers Vw *KEN/WIL* TN24 202 F4
Towers Wd *EYN* DA4 76 E5
Tower Vw *CROY/NA* CR0 87 M4
E/WMAL ME19 164 C2
Tower Wy *CANT* CT1 * 4 E4
Tower Whf *GVW* DA11 * 54 C2
Town Acres *TON* TN9 194 F1
Towncourt Crs *STMC/STPC* BR5 90 D1
Towncourt La *STMC/STPC* BR5 90 E2
Townfield Cnr *GVE* DA12 55 K6
Towngate Wood Pk
TONN TN10 * 189 G6
Town Hall Pde
BRXS/STRHM SW2 * 44 A2
Town Hl *E/WMAL* ME19 138 D4
RRTW TN3 296 B9
Town Hill Cl *E/WMAL* ME19 138 D4
Townland Cl *HDCN* TN27 300 F4
Townlands Rd *WADH* TN5 309 L5
Town La *RCANTW* CT4 170 D7
Townley Rd *BXLYHS* DA6 50 B2
EDUL SE22 44 F3
Townley St *RAM* CT11 17 H7
WALW SE17 24 E4
Town Rd *HOO/HM* ME3 58 B7
RCANTW CT4 268 E1
Townsend Farm Rd *RDV* CT15 215 G3
Townsend Rd *SNOD* ME6 112 F4
WOOL/PLUM SE18 28 C2
Townsend St *WALW* SE17 24 E3
Townsend Ter *DVW* CT17 * 217 J4
Townshend Cl *SCUP* DA14 73 J3
Townshend Rd *CHST* BR7 72 C2
Town Square Crs *GRH* DA9 53 G5
Town Wk *FOLK* CT20 11 J6
Townwall St *DVE/WH* CT16 8 E5
Towpath Wy *CROY/NA* CR0 87 G2
Towton Rd *WNWD* SE27 44 D7
Toynbec Cl *CHST* BR7 72 C1
Toy's Hl *BH/WHM* TN16 187 K1
The Tracies *RSIT* ME9 118 D3
Tradescant Dr *MEO* DA13 97 J2
Tradewinds *WSTB* CT5 126 C7
Trafalgar Av *PECK* SE15 25 G5
Trafalgar Gv *GNWCH* SE10 26 E5
Trafalgar Ms *RAM* CT11 * 17 H7
Trafalgar Rd *BRCH* CT7 181 J2
DART DA1 51 M7
GNWCH SE10 26 F4
GVW DA11 55 H5
ROCH ME1 113 K1
Trafalgar St *GILL* ME7 7 J4
WALW SE17 24 E4
Trafalgar Wy *CROY/NA* CR0 86 A5
Trafford Rd *THHTH* CR7 86 A1
Tram Rd *RYE* TN31 225 M7
The Tram Rd *FOLK* CT20 11 M5
Tramways *CHAT* ME4 101 K3
Tranquil Ri *ERITH* DA8 30 F4
Tranquil V *BKHTH/KID* SE3 26 F8
Transfesa Rd *STPH/PW* TN12 279 L1
Transformer Av *LYDD* TN29 335 N11
Transmere Rd *STMC/STPC* BR5 90 D2
Transom Sq *POP/IOD* E14 26 C4
Tranton Rd *BERM/RHTH* SE16 25 J2
Trapfield Cl *MAID/BEAR* ME14 168 D1
Trapfield La *MAID/BEAR* ME14 168 D1
Trapham Rd *MAIDW* ME16 12 A3
Travers Gdns *RSIT* ME9 145 G4
Travers Rd *DEAL* CT14 209 H4
Travertine Rd *WALD* ME5 115 J4
Treasury Vw *RCANTE* CT3 251 M1
Trebble Rd *SWCM* DA10 53 M4
Trebilco Cl *RTWE/PEM* TN2 197 G6
Tredegar Rd *RDART* DA2 51 H8
Tredown Rd *SYD* SE26 69 K2
Tredwell Cl *HAYES* BR2 71 L8
Tredwell Rd *WNWD* SE27 68 C1
Treebourne Rd *BH/WHM* TN16 132 B3
Tree La *BGR/WK* TN15 240 B9
Treetops *BGR/WK* TN15 136 F3
GVE DA12 79 J2
TON TN9 194 E6
Treetops Cl *ABYW* SE2 29 M4
Tree View Cl *NRWD* SE19 68 F5
Treewall Gdns *BMLY* BR1 71 J1
Tregony Rd *ORP* BR6 91 G7
Treherne Ct *BRXN/ST* SW9 * 24 C7
Trelawn Crs *WALD* ME5 115 J3
Trelawn Rd *BRXS/STRHM* SW2 44 B3
Trellyn Cl *MAIDW* ME16 166 A3
Treloar Gdns *NRWD* SE19 68 E3
Tremaine Cl *BROCKY* SE4 46 B8
Tremaine Rd *PGE/AN* SE20 69 J6
Trenchard Cl *KEN/WIL* TN24 3 K8
Trenchard St *GNWCH* SE10 26 E4
Trench Rd *TONN* TN10 188 E7
Trenear Cl *ORP* BR6 91 H7
Trenham Dr *WARL* CR6 130 B2
Trenholme Rd *PGE/AN* SE20 69 J4
Trenholme Ter *PGE/AN* SE20 69 J4
Trent *TIL* RM18 36 D3
Trentham Dr *STMC/STPC* BR5 73 H8
Trenton Cl *MAIDW* ME16 140 C6
Trent Rd *BRXS/STRHM* SW2 44 A3
WALD ME5 101 J8
Tresco Cl *BMLY* BR1 70 F3
Tresco Rd *PECK* SE15 45 J2
Tressillian Crs *BROCKY* SE4 46 B1
Tressillian Rd *BROCKY* SE4 46 B1
Trevale Rd *ROCH* ME1 100 C4
Trevarno Ter
MAID/SHEP ME15 * 12 C9
Trevelyan Cl *DART* DA1 52 A2
Trevereux Hl *OXTED* RH8 186 B2
Trevino Dr *WALD* ME5 115 G3
Treviso Rd *FSTH* SE23 45 L7
Trevithick Dr *DART* DA1 52 A2
Trevithick St *DEPT* SE8 26 B5
Trevor Cl *HAYES* BR2 89 G3
Trevor Dr *MAIDW* ME16 140 C8
Trewin Cl *DIT/AY* ME20 139 L3
Trewsbury Rd *SYD* SE26 69 L2
Triangle Est *LBTH* SE11 * 24 A4
The Triangle *BFN/LL* DA15 * 49 H5
Tribune Ct *IOS* ME12 64 C5
Tribune Dr *SIT* ME10 120 A3
Trident Cl *STRD* ME2 82 F6
Trident St *BERM/RHTH* SE16 25 L3
Triggs Rw *RSIT* ME9 * 121 L7
Trigon Rd *VX/NE* SW8 24 A6
Trilby Rd *FSTH* SE23 45 L7
Trilby Wy *WSTB* CT5 126 C7
Trim St *NWCR* SE14 26 A5
Trimworth Rd *FOLKN* CT19 10 B3
Trinity Church Sq *STHWK* SE1 24 D2
Trinity Cl *HAYES* BR2 89 M4
LEW SE13 46 E2
RTWE/PEM TN2 23 L4
Trinity Ct *ELTH/MOT* SE9 48 C4
Trinity Crs *FOLK* CT20 10 F7
Trinity Gdns *BRXN/ST* SW9 * 44 A2
DART DA1 51 L4
FOLK CT20 11 G7
Trinity Gv *GNWCH* SE10 26 D7
Trinity Ms *PGE/AN* SE20 * 69 K5
Trinity Pl *BXLYHS* DA6 50 A2
DEAL CT14 209 H5
RAM CT11 17 L4
Trinity Ri *BRXS/STRHM* SW2 44 C5
Trinity Rd *FOLK* CT20 10 E5
GILL ME7 7 K1
GVE DA12 55 K5
IOS ME12 64 D3
RASHE TN25 202 E5
SIT ME10 120 A2
Trinity Sq *BRDST* CT10 179 J6
MARG CT9 15 G3
Trinity St *STHWK* SE1 24 D1
Trinty Hl *MARG* CT9 15 G3
Trio Pl *STHWK* SE1 24 D1
Tristan Gdns *STH/RUST* TN4 200 D1
Tristan Sq *BKHTH/KID* SE3 46 F1
Tristram Rd *BMLY* BR1 71 G1
Tritton Cl *KEN/WIL* TN24 203 J4
Tritton Flds *KEN/WIL* TN24 203 H4
Tritton Gdns *LYDD* TN29 321 J8
Tritton La *NROM* TN28 331 J7
Tritton Rd *WNWD* SE27 44 E8
Triumph Cl *CDW/CHF* RM16 33 K3
Trivett Cl *GRH* DA9 53 H3
Trojan Wy *CROY/NA* CR0 86 A6
Trolling Down Hl *RDART* DA2 52 C7
Troodos Hl *MAID/BEAR* ME14 141 G5
Troon Cl *BERM/RHTH* SE16 * 25 J4
Trosley Av *GVW* DA11 55 J7
Trosley Rd *BELV* DA17 30 B5
Trossachs Rd *EDUL* SE22 44 F3
Trothy Rd *STHWK* SE1 25 H3
Trottiscliffe Rd *E/WMAL* ME19 239 P10
Trotts La *BH/WHM* TN16 159 H5
Trotwood Cl *WALD* ME5 115 H5
Troubridge Cl *KEN/WIL* TN24 205 K4
Troughton Ms *MARG* CT9 14 D6
Troughton Rd *CHARL* SE7 27 J4
Troutbeck Rd *NWCR* SE14 25 M7
Troy La *EDEN* TN8 192 A1
Troy Rd *NRWD* SE19 68 E3
Troys Md *RMAID* ME17 169 L3
Troy Town *PECK* SE15 45 H1
Troy Town La *RASHE* TN25 289 K4
Trubridge Rd *HOO/HM* ME3 59 L8
Trueman Cl *CANTW/ST* CT2 153 H6
Trundle St *STHWK* SE1 24 D1
Trundleys Rd *DEPT* SE8 25 M5
Trundley's Ter *DEPT* SE8 25 L3
Truro Cl *RHAM* ME8 102 E2
Truro Rd *GVE* DA12 55 L8
RAM CT11 17 L5
Truro Wk *TONN* TN10 189 G8
Truslove Rd *WNWD* SE27 68 B2
Trycewell La *BGR/WK* TN15 240 C3
Tuam Rd *WOOL/PLUM* SE18 28 E5
Tubbenden Cl *ORP* BR6 90 F5
Tubbenden Dr *ORP* BR6 90 E7
Tubbenden La *ORP* BR6 90 E7
Tubbenden La South *ORP* BR6 90 E8
Tubs Hl *SEV* TN13 20 F4
Tubs Hill Pde *SEV* TN13 * 20 F4
Tudeley La *TON* TN9 194 F6
Tudeley Rd *TON* TN9 195 H6
Tudor Av *LYDD* TN29 321 J8
MAID/BEAR ME14 141 J7
Tudor Byway *KEN/WIL* TN24 203 G5
Tudor Cl *BRCH* CT7 176 E5
BRXS/STRHM SW2 * 44 A4
CHST BR7 72 A5
DART DA1 51 J4
GVW DA11 54 F6
SAND/SEL CR2 130 A1
Tudor Ct *CANTW/ST* CT2 * 171 K1
ELTH/MOT SE9 * 47 M2
RTWE/PEM TN2 200 F4
SWLY BR8 92 D3
Tudor Crs *RSEV* TN14 136 B3
Tudor Dr *RSEV* TN14 136 B2
Tudor End *KEN/WIL* TN24 203 G6
Tudor Gdns *WWKM* BR4 88 D6
Tudor Gv *HOO/HM* ME3 83 G1
RHAM ME8 102 F5
Tudor Pde *ELTH/MOT* SE9 * 47 M2
Tudor Pl *NRWD* SE19 * 69 G4
Tudor Rd *BECK* BR3 70 D7
CANT CT1 4 D7
FOLKN CT19 219 L7
KEN/WIL TN24 203 G6
NRWD SE19 69 G4
SNWD SE25 87 J1
Tudor Wy *STMC/STPC* BR5 90 E2
Tudway Rd *BKHTH/KID* SE3 47 K2
Tufa Cl *WALD* ME5 115 J4
Tufnail Rd *DART* DA1 52 A4
Tufton Rd *KEN/WIL* TN24 2 E5
RHAM ME8 103 G4
Tufton St *ASH* TN23 2 B5
MAID/BEAR ME14 13 H4
Tugboat St *THMD* SE28 28 F1
Tugela Rd *CROY/NA* CR0 86 E2
Tugela St *CAT* SE6 46 A7
Tugmutton Cl *ORP* BR6 90 C7
Tulip Cl *CROY/NA* CR0 87 L4
Tulip Tree Cl *TON* TN9 194 D5
Tulse Cl *BECK* BR3 70 D7
Tulse Hl *BRXS/STRHM* SW2 44 C6
Tulsemere Rd *WNWD* SE27 44 D7
Tumblefield Rd *BGR/WK* TN15 238 E6
Tumblers Hl *RMAID* ME17 260 G6
Tummons Gdns *SNWD* SE25 68 F6
Tunbury Av *WALD* ME5 115 G2
Tunbury Av South *WALD* ME5 115 G4
Tunis Ct *CANT* CT1 172 E8
Tunis Rw *BRDST* CT10 179 L8
Tunnel Av *GNWCH* SE10 26 F2
Tunnel Rd *BERM/RHTH* SE16 25 K1
RTW TN1 23 G3
Tunstall Cl *ORP* BR6 90 F7
Tunstall Rd *BRXN/ST* SW9 44 A2
CANTW/ST CT2 172 B5
CROY/NA CR0 86 F4
RSIT ME9 145 K1
Tunstock Wy *BELV* DA17 29 M2
Tupman Cl *ROCH* ME1 19 G9
Tuppy St *WOOL/PLUM* SE18 28 D2
Turgis Cl *RMAID* ME17 260 F1
Turketel Rd *FOLK* CT20 10 D5
Turkey Oak Cl *NRWD* SE19 68 F5
Turks Hall Pl *STRD* ME2 * 98 F8
Turmine Ct *IOS* ME12 65 H8
Turnagain La *CANT* CT1 4 F4
Turnberry Cl
BERM/RHTH SE16 * 25 J4
Turnberry Wy *ORP* BR6 90 E4
Turnbull Cl *RDART* DA2 52 F5
Turnden Gdns *MARG* CT9 179 H3
Turnden Rd *CRBK* TN17 298 D10
Turner Av *CRBK* TN17 298 G10
Turner Cl *CMBW* SE5 24 C7
SIT ME10 120 B2
Turner Ct *CMBW* SE5 * 44 E2
DART DA1 51 K3
Turner Rd *BH/WHM* TN16 106 B6
RDART DA2 53 J8
TONN TN10 189 H8
Turners Av *TENT* TN30 315 N1
Turners Gdns *SEV* TN13 162 B6
Turners Green La *WADH* TN5 309 L3
Turners Green Rd *WADH* TN5 309 L3
Turners Meadow Wy *BECK* BR3 70 A5
Turner's Oak Shaw *HART* DA3 95 M5
Turners Pl *EYN* DA4 * 76 D5
Turner St *HOO/HM* ME3 38 C8
RAM CT11 17 K5
Turners Wy *CROY/NA* CR0 86 B5
Turney Rd *DUL* SE21 44 D5
Turnham Rd *BROCKY* SE4 45 M3
Turnpike Cl *DEPT* SE8 26 A6
HYTHE CT21 222 B3
Turnpike Dr *ORP* BR6 108 B3
Turnpike Hl *HYTHE* CT21 222 B2
Turnpike La *CDW/CHF* RM16 35 L4
Turnpike Link *CROY/NA* CR0 86 F5
Turnstone *HART* DA3 78 B7
Turnstone Cl *RSIT* ME9 227 M9
SAND/SEL CR2 104 D4
Turnstone Rd *WALD* ME5 115 K3
The Turnstones *GVE* DA12 55 L7
Turp Av *CDW/CHF* RM16 34 D1
Turpington Cl *HAYES* BR2 89 M2
Turpington La *HAYES* BR2 89 M1
Turpin La *ERITH* DA8 31 H5
Turquand St *WALW* SE17 24 D3
Tuscan Dr *WALD* ME5 115 K4
Tuscan Rd *WOOL/PLUM* SE18 28 E4
Tuskar St *GNWCH* SE10 26 F4
Tutsham Wy *STPH/PW* TN12 279 J3
Tuxford Rd *STH/RUST* TN4 277 Q12
Tweed *TIL* RM18 36 D3
Tweed Rd *TONN* TN10 188 F8
Tweed Ter *HYTHE* CT21 * 222 B4
Tweedy Rd *BMLY* BR1 71 H5
Twelve Acres *KEN/WIL* TN24 3 H9
Twickenham Cl *CROY/NA* CR0 86 A6
Twigg Cl *ERITH* DA8 30 F6
The Twins *STPH/PW* TN12 * 282 E8
Twisden Rd *E/WMAL* ME19 139 G5
Twisleton Ct *DART* DA1 51 L4
Twiss Av *HYTHE* CT21 222 E3
Twiss Gv *HYTHE* CT21 222 E3
Twiss Rd *HYTHE* CT21 222 E3
Twitton La *RSEV* TN14 135 K2
Twitton Mdw *RSEV* TN14 135 K2
Two Gates Hl *HOO/HM* ME3 58 A8
Twydall Gn *RHAM* ME8 102 C2
Twydall La *RHAM* ME8 102 C3
Twyford Cl *RHAM* ME8 103 H3
Twyford Ct
MAID/BEAR ME14 141 L7
Twyford Rd *RTON* TN11 256 B4
Twyne Cl *CANTW/ST* CT2 173 H3
Tydcombe Rd *WARL* CR6 130 B5
Tydeman Rd
MAID/SHEP ME15 168 A3
Tye La *ORP* BR6 90 D8
Tyers Est *STHWK* SE1 * 24 F1
Tyers Ga *STHWK* SE1 24 F1
Tyers St *LBTH* SE11 24 A4
Tyers Ter *LBTH* SE11 24 A4
Tyeshurst Cl *ABYW* SE2 29 M4
Tyland La *MAID/BEAR* ME14 141 G2
Tyler Cl *CANTW/ST* CT2 172 A6
E/WMAL ME19 139 G5
Tyler Dr *RHAM* ME8 116 F1
Tyler Hill Rd *CANTW/ST* CT2 153 H7
Tylers Cl *GDST* RH9 156 A8
Tylers Green Rd *SWLY* BR8 92 D2
Tyler St *GNWCH* SE10 26 F4
Tyler Wy *WSTB* CT5 127 M2
Tylney Av *NRWD* SE19 69 G2
Tylney Rd *BMLY* BR1 71 L6
Tyndale Pk *HB* CT6 129 J5
Tyndall Rd *WELL* DA16 49 G1
Tyne Cl *WALD* ME5 101 J8
Tynedale Cl *RDART* DA2 52 E6

Tynemouth Rd
WOOL/PLUM SE18 28 F4
Tyne Rd TONN TN10 188 E8
Typhoon Rd E/WMAL ME19 164 A2
Tyron Wy SCUP DA14 72 F1
Tyrrell Av WELL DA16 49 H3
Tyrrell Rd EDUL SE22 45 H2
Tyrrells Hall Cl GRAYS RM17 34 E5
Tyrwhitt Rd LEW SE13 46 B1
Tysoe Ct IOS ME12 65 G8
Tyson Av MARG CT9 177 K4
Tyson Gdns FSTH SE23 * 45 K5
Tyson Rd FOLKN CT19 11 M1
FSTH SE23 45 K5

U

Uckfield La EDEN TN8 193 K8
Uden Rd LYDD TN29 321 N5
Udimore Rd RYE TN31 224 D5
Uffington Ct RCANTE CT3 251 R7
Uffington Rd WNWD SE27 68 B1
Ufford St STHWK SE1 24 B1
Ufton Cl MAID/SHEP ME15 167 M4
Ufton La SIT ME10 119 M6
Ulcombe Gdns CANTW/ST CT2 172 B6
Ulcombe Hl RMAID ME17 261 N4
Ulcombe Rd HDCN TN27 283 L2
RMAID ME17 260 F2
Ulley Rd KEN/WIL TN24 203 G4
Ullswater Cl BMLY BR1 70 F3
Ullswater Gdns RCANTE CT3 251 Q11
Ullswater Rd WNWD SE27 44 C8
Ulstan Cl CTHM CR3 156 F1
Ulster Rd MARG CT9 15 G8
Ulundi Rd BKHTH/KID SE3 26 F5
Ulverscroft Rd EDUL SE22 45 H3
Undercliff FOLK CT20 223 M2
Undercliffe Rd DEAL CT14 211 L4
Undercliff Rd LEW SE13 46 B1
Underdown Av CHAT ME4 101 G4
Underdown La HB CT6 129 G7
Underdown Rd DVW CT17 217 J2
HB CT6 129 G5
Underhill Rd EDUL SE22 45 H3
FOLK CT20 219 J8
Underlyn La STPH/PW TN12 259 J12
Underriver House Rd
RTON TN11 255 R2
Undershaw Rd BMLY BR1 46 F8
Underwood CROY/NA CR0 105 H1
RFOLK CT18 292 G11
Underwood Cl CANT CT1 174 B4
KEN/WIL TN24 203 G5
MAID/SHEP ME15 12 F8
The Underwood ELTH/MOT SE9 48 A7
Undine Rd POP/IOD E14 26 C3
Unicorn Wk GRH DA9 53 G3
Union Crs MARG CT9 15 G4
Union Pk MAID/SHEP ME15 * 260 A1
Union Pl CANT CT1 5 H2
CHAT ME4 6 E6
Union Quay DVW CT17 8 C7
Union Rd CROY/NA CR0 86 D3
DEAL CT14 209 L3
HAYES BR2 89 L1
IOS ME12 65 L6
RAM CT11 17 L2
RCANTW CT4 175 G8
Union Rw MARG CT9 15 G4
Union Sq RTWE/PEM TN2 * 22 E8
Union St CANT CT1 5 H2
CHAT ME4 6 E6
DVW CT17 8 D7
FAV ME13 149 K2
IOS ME12 64 B3
MAID/BEAR ME14 13 G4
RAM CT11 17 K5
ROCH ME1 19 K8
WADH TN5 311 J6
Unity Cl CROY/NA CR0 105 G3
WNWD SE27 68 D2
Unity Pl RAM CT11 17 L4
Unity St IOS ME12 64 E3
SIT ME10 119 M6
Unity Wy WOOL/PLUM SE18 27 L2
University Gdns BXLY DA5 50 A5
University Rd CANTW/ST CT2 171 L2
University Wy DART DA1 51 L1
Unwin Cl DIT/AY ME20 140 B2
PECK SE15 25 H5
Upbury Wy CHAT ME4 6 F6
Upchat Rd HOO/HM ME3 82 F1
Upchurch Wk MARG CT9 179 H3
Updale Rd SCUP DA14 73 G1
Updown Wy RCANTW CT4 248 G8
Upfield CROY/NA CR0 87 J5
Uphill RFOLK CT18 220 C1
Upland Rd BXLYHN DA7 50 A1
CTHM CR3 130 F6
EDUL SE22 45 H3
SAND/SEL CR2 86 E8
Uplands BECK BR3 70 B6
CANTW/ST CT2 172 A5
Uplands Cl SEV TN13 20 D3
STRD ME2 81 L7
Uplands Rd ORP BR6 91 J4
Uplands Wy IOS ME12 64 D8
SEV TN13 20 C2
Uplees Rd FAV ME13 123 G3
Upnor Rd STRD ME2 19 M1
Upnor Wy WALW SE17 24 F4
Upper Abbey Rd BELV DA17 30 A3
Upper Approach Rd
BRDST CT10 183 K2
Upper Austin Lodge Rd
EYN DA4 93 L8
Upper Av MEO DA13 78 F5
Upper Barn Hl
MAID/SHEP ME15 258 D2
Upper Beulah Hl NRWD SE19 68 F5
Upper Brents FAV ME13 123 L8
Upper Bridge St CANT CT1 5 G6
RASHE TN25 266 G11
Upper Britton Pl GILL ME7 7 H4
Upper Brockley Rd BROCKY SE4 26 A8
Upper Bush Rd STRD ME2 99 G3
Upper Chantry La CANT CT1 5 H6
Upper Court Rd CTHM CR3 156 F1
Upper Cumberland Wk
RTW TN1 23 G9
Upper Dane Rd MARG CT9 15 K6
Upper Denmark Rd ASH TN23 2 B9
Upper Dr BH/WHM TN16 132 B4
Upper Dumpton Park Rd
RAM CT11 17 J4
Upper Dunstan Rd
STH/RUST TN4 196 E7
Upper Elmers End Rd
BECK BR3 69 M8
Upper Fant Rd MAIDW ME16 166 D3
Upper Field Rd SIT ME10 120 C4
Upper Free Down HB CT6 129 H7
Upper Gore La SWCH CT13 * 253 M7
Upper Green Rd RTON TN11 240 C12
Upper Grosvenor Rd RTW TN1 22 F3
Upper Gv MARG CT9 15 G4
SNWD SE25 68 F8
Upper Grove Rd BELV DA17 30 A5
Upper Haysden La
STH/RUST TN4 194 A7
Upper Holly Hill Rd BELV DA17 30 C4
Upper Hunton Hl MAID/SHEP
ME15 258 F2
Upper Luton Rd WALD ME5 7 J8
Upper Malthouse Hl
HYTHE CT21 222 C3
Upper Marsh STHWK SE1 24 A2
Upper Ml WBY/YAL ME18 164 E5
Upper Nellington RRTW TN3 200 C1
Upper Park Rd BELV DA17 30 C3
BMLY BR1 71 J5
Upper Profit RRTW TN3 200 B2
Upper Rd DVE/WH CT16 9 J1
MAID/SHEP ME15 13 K7
Upper St Ann's Rd FAV ME13 149 J3
Upper Sheridan Rd BELV DA17 30 B3
Upper Shirley Rd CROY/NA CR0 87 K6
Upper Spring La
BGR/WK TN15 240 A4
Upper Stephens RRTW TN3 200 B2
Upper Stone St
MAID/SHEP ME15 13 H6
Upper Strand St SWCH CT13 237 K12
Upper St DEAL CT14 211 L4
DEAL CT14 272 H2
RMAID ME17 169 G8
RMAID ME17 169 M2
STH/RUST TN4 200 E1
Upperton Rd SCUP DA14 73 G2
Upper Tulse Hl
BRXS/STRHM SW2 44 A5
Upper Vicarage Rd
KEN/WIL TN24 203 G4
Upper Wickham La WELL DA16 29 J8
Upstall St CMBW SE5 24 C7
Upton Cl BXLY DA5 50 A4
FOLKN CT19 10 D1
Upton Quarry RRTW TN3 200 A2
Upton Rd BRDST CT10 179 J8
BXLYHS DA6 49 M2
THHTH CR7 68 E6
WOOL/PLUM SE18 28 D5
Upton Rd South BXLY DA5 50 A4
Uptons HDCN TN27 283 K3
Upwood Rd LEE/GVPK SE12 47 H4
Uridge Crs TONN TN10 194 F1
Uridge Rd TONN TN10 194 F1
Urlwin St CMBW SE5 24 D5
Urlwin Wk BRXN/ST SW9 24 B7
Urquhart Cl WALD ME5 101 H8
Ursuline Dr WGOS CT8 177 G6
Usborne Cl STPH/PW TN12 281 R6
Usborne Ms VX/NE SW8 24 A6
Uvedale Cl CROY/NA CR0 105 J5
Uvedale Crs CROY/NA CR0 105 J5
Uvedale Rd OXTED RH8 157 L7

V

Valance Vw CRBK TN17 * 282 F10
Valan Leas HAYES BR2 70 F7
Vale Av RTW TN1 22 F6
STH/RUST TN4 196 C4
Valebrook Cl FOLK CT20 219 K8
Vale Cl ORP BR6 90 B7
Vale Dr WALD ME5 100 E8
Vale End EDUL SE22 45 G2
Valence Rd ERITH DA8 30 E6
Valenciennes Rd SIT ME10 119 M6
Valentia Pl BRXN/ST SW9 44 B2
Valentine Av BXLY DA5 49 M7
Valentine Cl GILL ME7 102 B4
Valentine Pl STHWK SE1 24 C1
Valentine Rd
MAID/SHEP ME15 167 M6
Valentyne Cl CROY/NA CR0 105 K5
Vale Pl RAM CT11 17 G6
Valerian Cl WALD ME5 114 F1
Vale Ri TON TN9 195 H5
Vale Rd BMLY BR1 72 B6
BRDST CT10 183 J1
DART DA1 51 J6
GVW DA11 54 F6
HAWK TN18 312 C7
MAID/SHEP ME15 259 K1
RAM CT11 16 F6
RDV CT15 210 C2
RTW TN1 22 F6
STH/RUST TN4 196 C4
TON TN9 194 F5
WSTB CT5 126 E5
Vale Sq RAM CT11 17 H6
Valestone Cl HYTHE CT21 223 J1
Vale St WNWD SE27 44 E8
Valeswood Rd BMLY BR1 71 G2
The Vale BRDST CT10 183 K1
CROY/NA CR0 87 L5
Valetta Wy ROCH ME1 19 H9
Vale View Rd DVW CT17 217 J2
RCANTE CT3 251 P12
Valiant Rd WALD ME5 115 K3
Valkyrie Av WSTB CT5 126 C5
The Vallance RSIT ME9 147 H3
Valley Cl DART DA1 51 G4
Valley Dr GVE DA12 79 L1
MAID/SHEP ME15 167 G7
RTON TN11 256 C3
SEV TN13 21 H7
Valleyfield Rd
STRHM/NOR SW16 68 A2
Valley Forge Cl TONN TN10 195 J1
Valley Gdns GRH DA9 53 J4
Valley Gv CHARL SE7 27 K4
Valley La BGR/WK TN15 238 H3
MEO DA13 239 N3
Valley Ri WALD ME5 115 G3
Valley Rd CANT CT1 4 C8
DART DA1 51 G4
DVW CT17 212 F6
ERITH DA8 30 D3
FOLK CT20 223 M1
GILL ME7 101 M1
HART DA3 95 J5
HAYES BR2 70 F6
MARG CT9 182 B1
RCANTW CT4 270 D3
STH/RUST TN4 200 E1
STMC/STPC BR5 73 J5
STRHM/NOR SW16 68 A1
The Valley RMAID ME17 259 J2
Valley Vw BH/WHM TN16 132 B4
GRH DA9 53 J4
RDV CT15 * 272 D5
STH/RUST TN4 196 D3
Valley View Rd ROCH ME1 100 C4
Valley View Ter EYN DA4 * 94 A4
Valley Wk CROY/NA CR0 87 K5
HYTHE CT21 223 J2
Valliers Wood Rd BFN/LL DA15 48 F6
Valmar Rd CMBW SE5 24 D7
Vambery Rd WOOL/PLUM SE18 28 D5
Vanbrugh Flds BKHTH/KID SE3 27 G5
Vanbrugh Hl GNWCH SE10 26 F4
Vanbrugh Pk BKHTH/KID SE3 27 H6
Vanbrugh Park Rd
BKHTH/KID SE3 27 G6
Vanbrugh Park Rd West
BKHTH/KID SE3 27 G6
Vanbrugh Ter BKHTH/KID SE3 27 G7
Vanburgh Cl ORP BR6 90 F4
Vancouver Cl ORP BR6 91 H7
Vancouver Dr RHAM ME8 102 D4
Vancouver Rd FSTH SE23 45 M7
Vandyke Cross ELTH/MOT SE9 47 M3
Vanessa Cl BELV DA17 30 B4
Vanessa Wk GVE DA12 80 A2
Vanessa Wy BXLY DA5 50 E8
Vange Cottage Ms ROCH ME1 * 19 H9
Vange Ms ROCH ME1 * 19 H9
Vanguard Cl CROY/NA CR0 86 C4
THHTH CR7 68 C8
Vanguard St DEPT SE8 26 B7
Vanguard Wy CROY/NA CR0 87 G7
EDEN TN8 186 B4
EDEN TN8 191 M7
EDEN TN8 274 D3
EGRIN RH19 274 E8
OXTED RH8 157 M4
STRD ME2 82 F5
WARL CR6 104 E7
Vanity La RMAID ME17 259 J3
Vanity Rd IOS ME12 230 E4
Vanoc Gdns BMLY BR1 71 H1
Vanquisher Wk GVE DA12 56 A8
Vansittart St NWCR SE14 25 M6
Varcoe Rd BERM/RHTH SE16 25 J4
Varne Pl FOLKN CT19 221 G7
Varne Rd FOLKN CT19 221 G8
Varnes St DIT/AY ME20 114 A7
Vassall Rd BRXN/ST SW9 24 B6
Vauban Est BERM/RHTH SE16 * 25 G2
Vauban St BERM/RHTH SE16 25 G2
Vaughan Av TONN TN10 189 H7
Vaughan Dr SIT ME10 120 A1
Vaughan Rd CMBW SE5 24 D8
WELL DA16 29 G8
Vaughan St BERM/RHTH SE16 26 A1
Vaughan Williams Cl DEPT SE8 26 B6
Vauxhall Av CANT CT1 172 D6
HB CT6 128 B6
Vauxhall Cl GVW DA11 55 G5
Vauxhall Crs CANT CT1 * 172 D6
SNOD ME6 113 G7
Vauxhall Gdns TON TN9 194 F6
Vauxhall Gv VX/NE SW8 24 A5
Vauxhall Industrial Rd
CANT CT1 172 D5
Vauxhall La RTON TN11 195 G7
STH/RUST TN4 196 C2
Vauxhall Pl DART DA1 51 M5
Vauxhall Rd CANTW/ST CT2 172 D5
Vauxhall St LBTH SE11 24 A4
Vauxhall Wk LBTH SE11 24 A4
Vectis Dr SIT ME10 120 A1
Veda Rd LEW SE13 46 B2
Veles Rd SNOD ME6 113 G5
Venetian Rd CMBW SE5 24 D8
Venner Rd SYD SE26 69 K3
Venners Cl BXLYHN DA7 30 F8
Ventnor Cl WALD ME5 101 K5
Ventnor Rd NWCR SE14 25 L6
Venture Cl BXLY DA5 49 M5
LYDD TN29 321 J8
Venus Rd WOOL/PLUM SE18 28 A2
Verbania Wy EGRIN RH19 274 A12
Verdant La BMLY BR1 47 G8
CAT SE6 46 F6
Verdayne Av CROY/NA CR0 87 L4
Verdayne Gdns WARL CR6 130 B2
Verdun Rd WOOL/PLUM SE18 29 H5
Vere Rd BRDST CT10 183 K1
Vereth Rd RAM CT11 17 G7
Vermont Rd NRWD SE19 68 E3
STH/RUST TN4 200 D1
Verney Rd BERM/RHTH SE16 25 J4
Verney Wy BERM/RHTH SE16 25 J4
Vernham Rd WOOL/PLUM SE18 28 D5
Vernon Cl BGR/WK TN15 111 L3
STMC/STPC BR5 73 J7
Vernon Pl CANT CT1 5 G6
DEAL CT14 209 L1
Vernon Rd RTW TN1 196 F7
SWCM DA10 54 A4
Veroan Rd BXLYHN DA7 29 M8
Verona Gdns GVE DA12 79 M1
Versailles Rd PGE/AN SE20 69 H4
Veryan Cl STMC/STPC BR5 73 K8
Vesper Ct HDCN TN27 284 D8
Vesta Rd BROCKY SE4 25 M8
Vestey Ct WGOS CT8 177 H4
Vestris Rd FSTH SE23 45 L7
Vestry Rd CMBW SE5 24 F7
RSEV TN14 136 B5
Vevey St FSTH SE23 45 A7
Vexil Cl PUR RM19 32 E3
Viaduct Cl MSTR CT12 16 F2
Viaduct Ter EYN DA4 * 76 D6
RASHW TN26 * 318 C2
The Viaduct DVW CT17 8 D9
Vian St LEW SE13 46 C1
Via Romana GVE DA12 56 C6
Vibart Gdns BRXS/STRHM SW2 44 A5
Viburnum Cl ASH TN23 204 B1
Vicarage Cl DIT/AY ME20 140 A2
ERITH DA8 30 D5
HOO/HM ME3 61 H2
STRD ME2 99 H8
Vicarage Ct BECK BR3 * 69 M7
Vicarage Crs MARG CT9 * 15 G7
Vicarage Dr BECK BR3 70 B5
GVW DA11 54 D4
Vicarage Gdn MSTR CT12 233 R10
Vicarage Gdns RCANTE CT3 251 R2
Vicarage Gv CMBW SE5 24 E7
Vicarage Hl BH/WHM TN16 159 J4
RCANTW CT4 268 E1
Vicarage La ASH TN23 2 C5
DEAL CT14 209 G4
DEAL CT14 272 H2
FAV ME13 149 H4
FAV ME13 246 H3
GVE DA12 56 B7
HDCN TN27 263 M6
HOO/HM ME3 84 A2
MAID/SHEP ME15 166 C6
RCANTW CT4 291 Q5
RDV CT15 215 G3
RDV CT15 252 C12
RSIT ME9 226 D11
SWCH CT13 * 237 J12
Vicarage Pk WOOL/PLUM SE18 28 D4
Vicarage Pl MARG CT9 14 F6
Vicarage Rd BXLY DA5 50 C6
CROY/NA CR0 86 B6
FOLK CT20 10 B8
GILL ME7 7 H4
IOS ME12 * 65 L6
SIT ME10 119 M3
STH/RUST TN4 196 C3
STRD ME2 19 H2
STRD ME2 98 F8
WBY/YAL ME18 257 R4
WOOL/PLUM SE18 28 D4
Vicarage Sq GRAYS RM17 34 B5
Vicarage St BRDST CT10 179 G8
FAV ME13 149 L1
Vicarage Wy BUR/ETCH TN19 322 F2
Vicars Hl LEW SE13 46 C2
Vicars Oak Rd NRWD SE19 68 F3
Vicary Wy MAIDW ME16 12 A2
Vickers Cl RFOLK CT18 220 B1
Vickers Rd ERITH DA8 30 E4
Victor Av MARG CT9 179 G3
Victoria Av BRDST CT10 179 H5
CDW/CHF RM16 34 D1
HYTHE CT21 222 C3
MARG CT9 15 L7
RDV CT15 215 J3
WGOS CT8 177 J6
Victoria Cl CDW/CHF RM16 34 D1
RMAID ME17 262 B7
WALD ME5 114 E3
Victoria Ct HYTHE CT21 * 222 D4
MAIDW ME16 * 12 D6
Victoria Crs ASH TN23 2 B7
DVE/WH CT16 8 C3
NRWD SE19 68 F3
Victoria Dr E/WMAL ME19 164 A3
EYN DA4 76 E6
HB CT6 128 D4
Victoria Gdns BH/WHM TN16 132 B1
Victoria Gv FOLK CT20 11 J5
HYTHE CT21 223 J3
Victoria Hill Rd SWLY BR8 75 G5
Victoria Ms DEAL CT14 * 209 K3
Victoria Pde RAM CT11 16 E4
RAM CT11 17 M5
Victoria Pk DEAL CT14 * 209 K4
DVE/WH CT16 8 F3
HB CT6 129 G4
Victoria Pl FAV ME13 149 K2
HYTHE CT21 * 222 C1
Victoria Rd ASH TN23 2 B7
BFN/LL DA15 49 G8
BRDST CT10 179 H7
BXLYHS DA6 50 B3
CANT CT1 4 D7
CHAT ME4 7 G9
CHST BR7 72 B2
DART DA1 51 L3
DEAL CT14 209 L4
DEAL CT14 211 K5
EDEN TN8 192 D5
ERITH DA8 30 F5
FOLKN CT19 11 H4
GVW DA11 55 G6
HAYES BR2 89 L1
HYTHE CT21 222 D4
MARG CT9 15 G6
NROM TN28 331 M8
RAM CT11 17 L4
RFOLK CT18 221 J3
RTON TN11 256 C7
RTW TN1 23 G3
SEV TN13 21 H6
SIT ME10 119 L5
STH/RUST TN4 196 B4
WALD ME5 114 F3
Victoria Rd West NROM TN28 331 L8
Victoria Rw CANT CT1 5 H2
Victoria St BELV DA17 30 A4
DIT/AY ME20 114 A7
DVW CT17 213 J8
GILL ME7 7 L7
IOS ME12 64 C4
MAIDW ME16 12 C6
NROM TN28 330 H7
ROCH ME1 19 K8
STRD ME2 19 H3
Victoria Ter IOS ME12 * 66 B8
ROCH ME1 100 B3
Victoria Vls RTW TN1 * 23 H4
Victoria Wy CHARL SE7 27 J4
Victoria Works STMC/STPC BR5 90 E1
Victor Rd PGE/AN SE20 69 L4
Victory Cl CDW/CHF RM16 33 K3
Victory Pk STRD ME2 * 82 F6
Victory Pl NRWD SE19 * 68 F3
WALW SE17 24 D3
Victory Rd RDV CT15 211 G8
Victory St IOS ME12 64 C3
Victory Wy BERM/RHTH SE16 25 M1
GRH DA9 52 D2
Vidgeon Av HOO/HM ME3 59 L7
View Cl BH/WHM TN16 132 B2
Viewfield Rd BFN/LL DA15 49 K6
Viewland Rd WOOL/PLUM SE18 29 G4
Viewlands Av BH/WHM TN16 133 K6
View Rd HOO/HM ME3 58 C6
The View ABYW SE2 29 M4
Vigerons Wy CDW/CHF RM16 35 J3
Vigilant Cl SYD SE26 69 H1
Vigilant Wy GVE DA12 80 A2
Vigo Hl E/WMAL ME19 239 L7
Vigo Rd BGR/WK TN15 238 H6
Viking Cl BRCH CT7 176 A5
STRD ME2 18 D9
Viking Rd GVW DA11 54 D8
Viking Wy BELV DA17 30 D2
BGR/WK TN15 94 F8
Villa Cl GVE DA12 56 C7
Villacourt Rd WOOL/PLUM SE18 29 H6
Village Green Av
BH/WHM TN16 132 D3
Village Green Rd DART DA1 51 H2
Village Green Wy
BH/WHM TN16 132 D3
The Village CHARL SE7 27 K5
Village Wy BECK BR3 70 B8
HNHL SE24 44 E4
RASHW TN26 318 D2
Villa Rd BRXN/ST SW9 44 B1
HOO/HM ME3 81 J2
Villas Rd WOOL/PLUM SE18 28 D3
Villa St WALW SE17 24 E4
Villiers Rd BECK BR3 69 L6
CANT CT1 172 E8
Vincennes Est WNWD SE27 68 E1
Vincent Cl BFN/LL DA15 48 F6
BRDST CT10 182 F2
FOLK CT20 223 M1
HAYES BR2 71 J8
Vincent Gdns IOS ME12 64 D4
Vincent Pl KEN/WIL TN24 203 J7
Vincent Rd CROY/NA CR0 86 F3
DIT/AY ME20 114 D6
MARG CT9 181 M1
SIT ME10 120 D6
WOOL/PLUM SE18 * 28 C3
Vincents Cl BERM/RHTH SE16 25 M1
Vincent Sq BH/WHM TN16 106 B7
Vine Av SEV TN13 21 H4
Vine Cl RAM CT11 183 H3
Vine Court Rd SEV TN13 21 J4
Vinegar Yd STHWK SE1 24 F1
Vine Lands LYDD TN29 334 C3
The Vineries CAT SE6 * 46 B6
GILL ME7 83 M8
Vine Rd ORP BR6 107 L1
Viners Cl SIT ME10 119 M8
Vines La ROCH ME1 19 J7
RTON TN11 255 R4
The Vine SEV TN13 21 J4
Vine Wk STPH/PW TN12 281 R6
Vine Yd STHWK SE1 * 24 D1
Vineyard Cl CAT SE6 46 B6
Vineyard Crs RHAM ME8 103 J4
Vineyard La WADH TN5 310 D7
Viney Bank CROY/NA CR0 104 E3
Viney Rd LEW SE13 46 C1
Viney's Gdns TENT TN30 301 P12
Vining St BRXN/ST SW9 44 B2
Vinson Cl FAV ME13 124 E8
ORP BR6 91 H4
Vinten Cl HB CT6 155 J1
Vinters Pk MAID/BEAR ME14 * 141 L8
Vinters Rd MAID/BEAR ME14 13 K4
Vintners Wy MAID/BEAR ME14 167 M1
Viola Av ABYW SE2 29 J3
Violet Av MSTR CT12 182 F3
Violet Cl DEPT SE8 26 A5
WALD ME5 115 H5
Violet Gdns CROY/NA CR0 86 C8
Violet La CROY/NA CR0 86 C8
Virgil St STHWK SE1 24 A2
Virginia Rd GILL ME7 83 K6
THHTH CR7 68 D5
WSTB CT5 127 H5
The Vista ELTH/MOT SE9 47 M5
Vivian Sq PECK SE15 45 J1
Vixen Cl WALD ME5 101 K7
Vlissingen Dr DEAL CT14 209 K1
Voce Rd WOOL/PLUM SE18 28 E6
Volante Dr SIT ME10 119 M2
Volante Wy GVE DA12 79 M1
Volta Wy CROY/NA CR0 86 A4
Vulcan Cl WALD ME5 101 J6
WSTB CT5 126 D6
Vulcan Rd BROCKY SE4 26 A8
Vulcan Ter BROCKY SE4 26 A8
Vulcan Wy CROY/NA CR0 105 K4
The Vyne BXLYHN DA7 50 C1

W

Wacher Cl CANTW/ST CT2 172 A7
Wadard Ter SWLY BR8 * 93 K1
Wadding St WALW SE17 24 E3
Waddington Dr RFOLK CT18 220 B1
Waddington Wy NRWD SE19 68 D5
Waddon Cl CROY/NA CR0 86 B6
Waddon Court Rd CROY/NA CR0 86 B7
Waddon Marsh Wy
CROY/NA CR0 86 A4
Waddon New Rd CROY/NA CR0 86 C6
Waddon Park Av CROY/NA CR0 86 B7
Waddon Rd CROY/NA CR0 86 B6
Wade Av STMC/STPC BR5 91 L3
Wade House STHWK SE1 * 25 H1
Wades Cl LYDD TN29 320 A12
Wadeville Cl BELV DA17 30 B4
Wadham Pl SIT ME10 120 C7
Wadhurst Cl PGE/AN SE20 69 J6
Wadhurst Rd CROW TN6 308 B6
RRTW TN3 294 C12
WADH TN5 308 E1
Wadlands Rd HOO/HM ME3 38 C8
Waghorn Rd SNOD ME6 113 H5
Waghorn St CHAT ME4 7 G9
PECK SE15 45 H1
Wagner St PECK SE15 25 K6
Wagoners Cl MAID/BEAR ME14 167 M1
Wagon La STPH/PW TN12 257 M12
Wagtail Gdns SAND/SEL CR2 104 C4
Wagtail Wk BECK BR3 88 D1
Wagtail Wy STMC/STPC BR5 73 L8
Waid Cl DART DA1 52 A4
Wain Ct IOS ME12 65 H8
Wainscott Rd STRD ME2 82 E3
Wainscott Wk STRD ME2 82 E2
Wainwright Pl KEN/WIL TN24 2 E9
Waite Davies Rd
LEE/GVPK SE12 47 G5
Waite St PECK SE15 25 G5
Wakefield Gdns NRWD SE19 68 F4
Wakefield Rd GRH DA9 53 K3
Wakefield St GVW DA11 * 55 J4
Wakefield Wy HYTHE CT21 222 C4
Wakehurst Cl RMAID ME17 258 G2
Wakeley Rd RHAM ME8 103 J4
Wakely Cl BH/WHM TN16 132 B4
Wake Rd ROCH ME1 100 D5
Walcheren Cl DEAL CT14 209 K1
Walcorde Av WALW SE17 24 D3
Walcot Sq LBTH SE11 24 B3
Waldeck Gv WNWD SE27 44 C8
Waldeck Rd DART DA1 52 A5
Waldegrave Rd BMLY BR1 89 M1
NRWD SE19 69 G4
Waldegrove CROY/NA CR0 87 G6
Walden Av CHST BR7 72 A1
Walden Cl BELV DA17 30 A4
Walden Gdns THHTH CR7 68 A8
Waldenhurst Rd
STMC/STPC BR5 91 L5
Walden Pde CHST BR7 * 72 A3
Walden Rd CHST BR7 72 A3
Waldens Cl STMC/STPC BR5 91 L3
Waldenshaw Rd FSTH SE23 45 K6
Waldens Rd STMC/STPC BR5 91 M2
The Waldens RMAID ME17 261 M3
Waldershare Av SWCH CT13 207 H2
Waldershare La RDV CT15 273 M11
Waldershare Rd RDV CT15 272 H8
Walderslade Rd CHAT ME4 101 G6
Walderslade Woods
WALD ME5 114 E2
Waldon TIL RM18 36 C3
Waldo Rd BMLY BR1 71 K7
Waldram Crs FSTH SE23 45 K6
Waldram Park Rd FSTH SE23 45 L6
Waldrist Wy ERITHM DA18 30 A1
Waldron Dr MAID/SHEP ME15 167 G7
Waldron Gdns HAYES BR2 70 E7
Waldronhyrst CROY/NA CR0 86 C7
Waldron Rd BRDST CT10 183 L3
The Waldrons CROY/NA CR0 86 D7
OXTED RH8 185 G1
Walerand Rd LEW SE13 26 D8
Wales Cl PECK SE15 25 J6
Walkden Rd CHST BR7 72 B1
Walker Cl DART DA1 51 G1
WOOL/PLUM SE18 28 D3
Walker La BRCH CT7 176 A5
Walkerscroft Md CAT SE6 46 C7
DUL SE21 44 D6
Walkhurst Rd CRBK TN17 313 Q1
Walkley Rd DART DA1 51 J3
The Walk OXTED RH8 184 B3
Wallace Cl RTWE/PEM TN2 201 H5
Wallace Gdns SWCM DA10 53 M4
Wallace Ms FOLKN CT19 220 E6
Wallace Rd GRAYS RM17 34 B3
ROCH ME1 100 F5
Wallace Wy BRDST CT10 183 H1

Wallbridge La RHAM ME8 ....103 L2
Wallbutton Rd BROCKY SE4 ...25 M8
Wall Cl HOO/HM ME5 ......59 L6
Waller Rd CRBK TN17 .....282 D12
Wallers RRTW TN29 ....335 M2
NWCR SE14 ....25 L8
Wallers Rd FAV ME13 .....149 H2
Wallis Av MAID/SHEP ME15 ..167 M8
Wallis Cl RDART DA2 ......51 H8
Wallis Pk CVW DA11 ....54 C3
Wallis Rd KEN/WIL TN24 ....203 J3
Wall Rd KEN/WIL TN24 ......2 L7
The Wall SIT ME10 ....119 M4
Walmer Castle Rd DEAL CT14 ..209 H6
Walmer Cl ORP BR6 ....90 E7
Walmer Ct DEAL CT14 * 209 H8
Walmer Gdns DEAL CT14 ....209 H7
MSTR CT12 ....181 M8
SIT ME10 ....119 J6
Walmer Rd WSTB CT5 ....126 F5
Walmers Av HOO/HM ME3 ....59 M7
Walmer Ter WOOL/PLUM SE18 ..28 D3
Walmer Wy DEAL CT14 .....209 H7
FOLK CT20 ....10 A5
Walmsley Rd BRDST CT10 ...179 J3
Walner Gdns NROM TN28 ....331 J6
Walner La NROM TN28 ......331 J6
Walnut Cl DEPT SE8 ....26 A5
KEN/WIL TN24 ....203 D1
STPH/PW TN12 ....279 K3
WALD ME5 ....101 J2
Walnut Hill Rd MEO DA13 ...78 D7
Walnuts Rd ORP BR6 ....91 H4
Walnut Tree Av DART DA1 ...51 M7
Walnut Tree Cl CHST BR7 ....72 D5
Walnut Tree Ct DIT/AY ME20 ..139 J4
Walnut Tree Dr SIT ME10 ...119 L5
Walnut Tree La CANTW/ST CT2 ..173 J4
MAID/SHEP ME15 ......167 H8
Walnut Tree Ms HYTHE CT21 ..222 E2
Walnut Tree Rd ERITH DA8 ...30 F4
GNWCH SE10 * 26 F4
Walnut Tree Wk WALW SE17 ..24 D3
Walnut Wy RTWE/PEM TN2 ..197 G6
SWLY BR8 ....74 E6
Walpole Av E/WMAL ME19 ...139 C4
GRAYS RM17 ....34 D3
Walpole Rd CROY/NA CRO ...86 C5
HAYES BR2 ....89 L1
MARG CT9 ....15 G3
Walsby Dr SIT ME10 ....119 B1
WALD ME5 ....115 G4
Walsham Rd NWCR SE14 ....25 L8
Walsingham Cl RHAM ME8 ...116 C2
Walsingham Pk CHST BR7 ....72 E6
Walsingham Rd CROY/NA CRO ..105 H5
STMC/STPC BR5 ....73 J5
Walsingham Wk BELV DA17 ...30 B5
Walter Burke Av ROCH ME1 * ..99 M6
Walter's Farm Rd TENT TN9 ..144 F4
Walter's Green Rd RTON TN11 ..276 G10
Walters Rd HOO/HM ME3 ....59 M7
SNWD SE25 ....68 A4
Walters Yd BMLY BR1 * 45 L4
Waltham Cl DART DA1 ......51 H4
KEN/WIL TN24 ....3 K5
MARG CT9 ....179 J3
STMC/STPC BR5 ....91 L4
Waltham Gdns FOLKN CT19 ...11 J1
Walton Gn CROY/NA CRO 105 K6
Walton Manor Cl FOLKN CT19 ..220 E5
Walton Rd FOLKN CT19 .....11 J8
SCUP DA14 ....49 J8
TONN TN10 ....10 B1
Walton's Hall Rd SLH/COR SS17 ..36 B1
The Waltons FOLKN CT19 ....220 D5
Walt Whitman Cl HNHL SE24 * ..44 C2
Walworth Pl WALW SE17 ....24 C4
Walworth Rd WALW SE17 ....24 C4
Walwyn Av BMLY BR1 ....71 L7
Wanden La HDCN TN27 .....262 E12
Wandle Rd CROY/NA CRO 86 D6
Wandle Side CROY/NA CRO ...86 A6
Wanless Rd HNHL SE24 .....44 D1
Wanley Rd CMBW SE5 ......44 E2
Wansbury Wy SWLY BR8 ....93 H1
Wansey St WALW SE17 ......24 C3
Wansgell Cl BMLY BR1 .....71 K6
Wansunt Rd BXLY DA5 ......50 D5
Wantage Rd LEE/GVPK SE12 ..47 G3
Wantsum Cl HB CT6 ....232 A4
Wantsum Wk BRCH CT7 .....233 J4
HB CT6 ....232 B3
RCANTE CT3 ....232 E8
Wantsume Lees SWCH CT13 ..236 H11
Wantsum Wy BRCH CT7 .....233 M7
Warbank Cl CROY/NA CRO ...105 K4
Warbank Crs CROY/NA CRO ...105 K4
Warberry Park Gdns
STH/RUST TN4 * 22 B3
Warblers Cl STRD SW2 * 18 F4
Wardalis Gv NWCR SE14 * ...25 K6
Ward Av GRAYS RM17 ......34 C3
Ward Cl ERITH DA8 ....30 E5
SAND/SEL CR2 ....86 F5
WADH TN5 ....309 K5
Warden Bay Rd IOS ME12 ...230 A2
Warden Cl MAIDW ME16 ....166 A1
Warden House Ms DEAL CT14 ..209 H5
Warden Mill Cl WBY/YAL ME18 ..164 D1
Warden Point Wy WSTB CT5 * ..126 C2
Warden Rd IOS ME12 ......229 P1
ROCH ME1 ....100 D2
Warden Ter WBY/YAL ME18 * ..164 C4
Warden View Gdns IOS ME12 ...230 A4
Wardes WBY/YAL ME18 * 257 Q3
Ward La WARL CR6 ....130 B2
Wardour Cl BRDST CT10 ....183 L1
Wardsbrook Rd WADH TN5 ...310 E10
Wards Hill Rd IOS ME12 ....229 J5
Ward's La WADH TN5 ......309 H6
Wardwell La RSIT ME9 .....226 D11
Warehorne Rd RASHW TN26 ..318 C3
Warepoint Dr THMD SE28 ....28 D7
Ware St MAID/BEAR ME14 ...142 A2
SAND/SEL CR2 ....86 F5
Warham Rd CROY/NA CRO ...86 A8
RSEV TN14 ....136 A2
Waring Cl ORP BR6 ....107 L5
Waring Dr ORP BR6 ....107 L1
Waring Rd SCUP DA14 .....49 K3
Waring St WNWD SE27 .....68 C1
Warland Rd BGR/WK TN15 ..111 L1
WOOL/PLUM SE18 ......28 E6
Warlingham Rd THHTH CR7 ...68 C8

Warmington Rd HNHL SE24 ...44 D4
Warminster Rd SNWD SE25 ...69 H6
Warminster Sq SNWD SE25 ...69 H6
Warmlake Rd RMAID ME17 ...260 C4
Warndon St BERM/RHTH SE16 ..25 K3
Warne Pl BFN/LL DA15 * 49 J4
Warner Rd BMLY BR1 ......71 J4
CMBW SE5 ....24 D7
Warner St CHAT ME4 ......6 D8
Warnett Ct SNOD ME6 * 113 H1
Warnford Gdns
MAID/SHEP ME15 ......167 H5
Warnford Rd ORP BR6 .....91 G8
Warre Av RAM CT11 ....16 B8
Warren Av BMLY BR1 ......71 G5
ORP BR6 ....91 C8
SAND/SEL CR2 ....104 C2
Warren Cl BXLYHS DA6 ....50 B3
FOLKN CT19 ....221 G7
SIT ME10 ....120 C7
Warren Ct BGR/WK TN15 ....21 J4
CHARL SE7 * 27 K4
Warren Dr BRDST CT10 .....179 H8
ORP BR6 ....91 G8
The Warren Dr WGOS CT8 ...177 C6
Warren Gdns ORP BR6 .....91 H8
Warren Hts RASHE TN25 * ...289 M12
Warren La CDW/CHF RM16 ...33 L3
KEN/WIL TN24 ....202 D7
OXTED RH8 ....185 H4
RDV CT15 ....293 R2
RSIT ME9 ....117 K2
WOOL/PLUM SE18 ......28 C2
Warren Pk WARL CR6 ......130 C4
Warren Rd BXLYHS DA6 ....50 B3
CROY/NA CRO 86 F4
DART DA1 ....51 M8
FOLKN CT19 ....221 G7
HAYES BR2 ....89 H5
MEO DA13 ....78 D2
MEO DA13 ....98 D2
NROM TN28 ....331 L7
ORP BR6 ....91 G8
SCUP DA14 ....49 K6
WALD ME5 ....114 E5
The Warrens HART DA3 .....26 B1
Warren St HDCN TN27 * 283 R1
RMAID ME17 ....244 A11
The Warren GVE DA12 .....79 L1
RASHE TN25 ....289 M12
RTON TN11 ....276 H5
WADH TN5 ....310 F9
Warren Vw WGOS CT8 .....177 C6
RASHE TN25 ....202 C7
Warren Wy RDV CT15 ......221 G7
Warren Wood Cl HAYES BR2 ..89 H5
Warren Wood Rd ROCH ME1 ..100 B6
Warrington Rd CROY/NA CRO ..86 C6
STPH/PW TN12 ....279 K3
Warspite Rd WOOL/PLUM SE18 ..27 K1
Wartem Rd DART DA1 ......183 J4
ORP BR6 ....91 H6
Warwick Cl BXLY DA5 .....50 A5
ORP BR6 ....91 H6
Warwick Crs ROCH ME1 ....100 A3
SIT ME10 ....119 K4
Warwick Dr RAM CT11 .....16 D1
Warwick Gdns MEO DA13 ...97 H5
THHTH CR7 * 67 L4
Warwick Pk RTW TN1 ......201 J4
RTWE/PEM TN2 ....201 J4
Warwick Pl GVW DA11 .....54 C3
MAIDW ME16 ....12 C6
Warwick Rd CANT CT1 .....5 M5
DEAL CT14 ....209 L7
KEN/WIL TN24 ....203 H5
MARG CT9 ....15 M4
PGE/AN SE20 ....69 J6
RTW TN1 ....22 F7
SCUP DA14 ....73 J2
THHTH CR7 ....68 B4
WELL DA16 ....49 K1
WSTB CT5 ....126 E3
Warwickshire Pth DEPT SE8 * ..26 A4
Warwick Ter WOOL/PLUM SE18 ..28 E5
Warwick Wy DART DA1 .....51 M7
Washford Farm Rd ASH TN23 ..204 B6
Washington Cl DVE/WH CT16 ..213 H5
Washington La LYDD TN29 ...329 N7
Washneys Rd ORP BR6 .....107 N7
Washpond La WARL CR6 ....131 N4
Washwell La WADH TN5 ....309 H3
Wassall La CRBK TN17 .....314 E10
Wass Dro RCANTE CT3 .....235 C6
Wastdale Rd FSTH SE23 ....45 H1
Watchbell La RYE TN31 ....225 H4
Watchbell St RYE TN31 ....225 H4
Watchester Av RAM CT11 ...16 F9
Watchester La MSTR CT12 ...180 B2
Watchmans Ter WALD ME5 ...101 K3
Watcombe Rd SNWD SE25 ...87 J2
Waterbank Rd CAT SE6 .....46 C8
Waterbrook Av KEN/WIL TN24 ..205 J7
Watercress Dr RSEV TN14 ...136 A5
Watercress La ASH TN23 ...204 B3
Watercroft Rd RSEV TN14 ...108 A4
Waterdale Rd ABYW SE2 ....29 H5
Waterditch La RMAID ME17 ..244 A11
Waterdown Rd STH/RUST TN4 ..200 A4
Waterfall Rd RASHW TN26 ...286 C4
Water Farm RCANTW CT4 ....291 G1
Waterfield Cl BELV DA17 ....30 B2
Waterfield Dr WARL CR6 ....130 A5
Waterfield Gdns SNWD SE25 ..68 F4
Waterfront WTHK RM20 ....33 H2
Watergate St DEPT SE8 ....26 B6
Waterham Rd FAV ME13 ....125 K4
Waterhead Cl ERITH DA8 ....30 D7
Wateringbury Cl
STMC/STPC BR5 ......73 J7
Wateringbury Rd
E/WMAL ME19 ....165 G2
Waterlakes EDEN TN8 ......192 G1
Water La CANT CT1 4
CANTW/ST CT2 ....173 C4
E/WMAL ME19 ....138 D1
EDEN TN8 ....148 B1
FAV ME13 ....148 F5
HAWK TN18 ....312 D2
HDCN TN27 ....282 H5
HDCN TN27 ....284 H5
MAID/BEAR ME14 ......142 H1
MAID/SHEP ME15 ......258 C1
NWCR SE14 ....25 K6
OXTED RH8 ....157 M4
PUR RM19 ....33 H2
RMAID ME17 ....261 N2
RSEV TN14 ....109 L1
Waterloo Crs DVE/WH CT16 ..8 C5
Waterloo Hl IOS ME12 .....65 H1
Waterloo Rd RAM CT11 ....17 G7
TON TN9 ....194 B5
Waterloo Rd CRBK TN17 ...298 D3

FOLK CT20 ....219 L8
GILL ME7 ....7 H7
SIT ME10 ....119 L4
STHWK SE1 ....24 B1
TON TN9 ....194 N5
WSTB CT5 ....126 E3
Waterloo St GVE DA12 .....55 M5
MAID/SHEP ME15 ......15 H7
Waterloo Ter MAID/BEAR ME14 ..13 H1
MEO DA13 ....239 M6
Waterman's La
STPH/PW TN12 ....279 L6
Waterman Sq PGE/AN SE20 ...69 K4
Watermans Wy GRH DA9 ....55 J3
Watermeadow Cl ERITH DA8 ...31 J6
GILL ME7 ....102 A7
Watermead La CAT SE6 .....46 C5
Watermead Rd CAT SE6 .....70 D1
Watermens Sq PGE/AN SE20 * ..69 K4
Water Ms PECK SE15 ......45 K2
Watermill Cl MAIDW ME16 ...140 F2
Watermill La EYN DA4 .....76 C6
Watermint Cl STMC/STPC BR5 ..73 L8
Waters Cottages WADH TN5 ..309 H6
Waters Edge MAID/SHEP ME15 ..12 B6
Watersend Rd DVE/WH CT16 ..212 D4
Waterside DART DA1 ......50 F3
BERM/RHTH SE16 ......274 A12
KEN/WIL TN24 ....3 K7
MAID/BEAR ME14 ......12 E3
Waterside Av BECK BR3 ....88 C1
Waterside Cl BERM/RHTH SE16 ..25 H1
FAV ME13 ....149 L5
Waterside Ct DIT/AY ME20 * ..138 F3
LEW SE13 ....46 E2
STRD ME2 ....73 K6
Waterside Dr WGOS CT8 ....177 J4
Waterside Ga MAIDW ME16 * ..140 E5
Waterside La GILL ME7 ....84 A6
Waterside Ms WBY/YAL ME18 ..164 E5
Waterside Vw IOS ME12 ....230 D1
Water Slippe RTON TN11 ...256 G6
Watersmeet CHAT ME4 .....83 J4
Watersmeet
MAID/SHEP ME15 ......167 H4
Waterson Rd CDW/CHF RM16 ..35 J3
Waters Pl GILL ME7 ......102 B7
Waters Rd CAT SE6 ....46 F8
Waterstone Pl FAV ME13 * ..149 L5
Water St DEAL CT14 ....209 L7
Waterton Av GVE DA12 ....55 M5
Water Tower Hl CROY/NA CRO ..86 E7
Waterworks Cottages
RSEV TN14 ....136 N6
Waterworks La RDV CT15 ...210 C6
Waterworks Rd MAIDW ME16 ..140 C6
Watery La BGR/WK TN15 ....137 J6
RCANTW CT4 ....249 K12
SCUP DA14 ....49 J6
Watkin Rd FOLKN CT19 ....11 H2
Watkins Cl STPH/PW TN12 ...282 H3
Watkins Wy BXLY DA5 .....50 E7
Watling Av WALD ME5 .....7 L9
Watlings Cl CROY/NA CRO ...87 M2
Watling St BXLYHS DA6 ....50 D5
CANT CT1 ....4 F5
DART DA1 ....51 J4
GVE DA12 ....80 C5
GVW DA11 ....79 J2
MEO DA13 ....54 C8
PECK SE15 ....24 B7
STRD ME2 ....18 B3
WALD ME5 ....7 M9
Watson Av SWLY BR8 ......69 M2
Watson Av WALD ME5 .....100 B8
Watson Rd ASH TN23 ......33 H7
Watsons Cl RASHE TN25 ....202 F7
Watsons Hl SIT ME10 .....119 M4
Watson's St DEPT SE8 ....26 C6
Watts' Av ROCH ME1 ......19 J5
Watts Cl SNOD ME6 ......113 J5
WADH TN5 ....309 H5
Watt's Cross Rd RTON TN11 ..255 G8
Watts La CHST BR7 ....72 C5
Watt's Rd STHWK SE1 .....24 E1
Watts St CHAT ME4 ....5 K7
Wat Tyler Rd BKHTH/KID SE3 ..26 E7
Wat Tyler Wy MAID/SHEP ME15 ..13 J3
Wauchope Rd WSTB CT5 ....126 A2

Wavell Dr BFN/LL DA15 ....48 F4
Wavel Pl SYD SE26 ....69 G2
Waveney Av PECK SE15 ....45 J2
Waveney Rd TONN TN10 ....188 B4
Waverley Av IOS ME12 ....229 R1
Waverley Cl HAYES BR2 ...89 L1
RMAID ME17 ....258 B2
WALD ME5 ....115 L3
Waverley Crs
WOOL/PLUM SE18 ......28 E5
Waverley Dr RTWE/PEM TN2 ..197 J3
Waverley Gdns CDW/CHF RM16 ..14 A7
Waverley Rd MARG CT9 ....14 A7
SNWD SE25 ....69 J8
WOOL/PLUM SE18 ......28 D4
Wavertree Rd
BRXS/STRHM SW2 .....44 B1
Wayborough Hl MSTR CT12 ..181 G5
Wayfaring Gn GRAYS RM17 ..34 A4
Wayfield Rd WALD ME5 ....101 G6
Way Hl MSTR CT12 ....181 H6
Waylands SWLY BR8 ......75 G6
Waylands Cl RSEV TN14 ....134 D1
Waylett Pl WNWD SE27 ....44 B8
Wayne Cl BRDST CT10 .....179 H5
ORP BR6 ....91 G6
Waynflete Av CROY/NA CRO ..86 C6
Wayside CROY/NA CRO * 105 G1
TENT TN30 ....301 N11
Wayside Av TENT TN30 ....301 N11
Wayside Dr EDEN TN8 .....192 E2
Wayside Gv CHST BR7 .....72 A1
Wayville Rd DART DA1 .....52 C5
Weald Cl BERM/RHTH SE16 ...25 J4
HAYES BR2 ....89 M5
MAID/SHEP ME15 ......167 K7
MEO DA13 ....97 H5
RSEV TN14 ....255 F4
Weald Ct RTON TN11 ......188 A1
Wealden Av TENT TN30 ....301 N11
Wealden Cl TONN TN10 ....188 C3
Wealden Ct WALD ME5 * ...7 M8
Wealden Forest Pk HB CT6 * ..231 J1
Wealden Wy DIT/AY ME20 ..139 M5
Wealdhurst Pk BRDST CT10 ..162 A6
The Weald CHST BR7 ......72 A6
KEN/WIL TN24 ....204 D1
Weald Vw RBTBR TN32 ....323 R12
STPH/PW TN12 ....279 N8
WADH TN5 ....309 H1
MEO DA13 ....79 J3
MEO DA13 ....239 R1
RRTW TN3 ....277 N11
RTON TN11 ....256 D10
TON TN9 ....194 F4
WBY/YAL ME18 ....241 J7
Weald View Rd TON TN9 ....194 N6
Wealdway BGR/WK TN15 ...241 M3
E/WMAL ME19 ....239 N11
HRTF TN7 ....198 D7
Wear Bay Crs FOLKN CT19 ..221 G8
Wear Bay Rd FOLKN CT19 ..221 J3
Weardale Av RDART DA2 ....52 D7
Weardale Rd LEW SE13 ....46 E3
Wearside Rd LEW SE13 ....46 E5
Weatherall Cl FAV ME13 ...151 J1
Weatherly Cl ROCH ME1 ....19 K9
Weatherly Dr BRDST CT10 ..183 J3
Weavering Ct MAID ME2 ....82 C5
Weavering St
MAID/BEAR ME14 ......142 A8
Weavers La GVW DA11 ....55 H6
STPH/PW TN12 ....282 A5
Weavers La RSEV TN14 ....136 B2
The Weavers HDCN TN27 ...300 F4
Weaver Wk WNWD SE27 ...44 C1
Weavers Wy ASH TN23 ....204 B6
Webb Cl FOLKN CT19 ......220 B6
HOO/HM ME3 ....59 L7
Webber Cl ERITH DA8 .....31 J6
Webber Rw STHWK SE1 ....24 B2
Webb St STHWK SE1 ......24 F3
Webb Rd BKHTH/KID SE3 ...27 G5
Webbs Meadow BGR/WK TN15 ..21 J2
Webb St STHWK SE1 ......24 F2
Webster Rd BERM/RHTH SE16 ..25 H1
RHAM ME8 ....103 G4
Webster Rd RFOLK CT18 ...220 C1
Weddington La RCANTE CT3 ..236 B11
Wedgewood Cl MAIDW ME16 ..140 C8
Wedgewood Dr WALD ME5 ...101 H6
Wedgwood BH/WHM TN16 * ..132 B7
Wedgwood Wy NRWD SE19 ..68 D1
Weeds Wood Rd WALD ME5 ..115 G1
Weekes Ct QBOR ME11 * ...64 B8
Weeks Ct MAIDW ME16 * ...64 B8
Week St MAID/BEAR ME14 ...12 D3
Weeks La HDCN TN27 .....283 P12
Weighall Rd LEE/GVPK SE12 ..47 H2
Weigall Rd LEE/GVPK SE12 ..47 H2
Weighton Rd PGE/AN SE20 ..69 H5
Weir Rd BXLY DA5 ....50 C5
Weird Wd HART DA3 ......78 D2
Welbeck Av BFN/LL DA15 ...49 H6
BMLY BR1 ....71 H1
Welby St CMBW SE5 ......24 D6
Weld Cl STPH/PW TN12 ....282 A5
Welland Cl BFN/LL DA15 ...71 H1
Welland Rd TONN TN10 ....194 E1
Wellands Cl HAYES BR2 ....89 M5
Welland St GNWCH SE10 ...26 D5
Wellbrook Rd ORP BR6 ....90 B7
Well CANTW/ST CT2 ......173 H3
RTON TN11 ....255 N12
STRHM/NOR SW16 .....44 A1
Wellcome Av DART DA1 ....51 M2
Weller Av ROCH ME1 .....100 E8
Weller Pl ORP BR6 * 106 F5
Weller Rd STH/RUST TN4 ...200 D1
Wellers Cl BH/WHM TN16 ..159 H5
Weller St STHWK SE1 .....24 C1
Wellesley Av DEAL CT14 ...209 K7
Wellesley Cl BRDST CT10 ...183 J2
CHARL SE7 * 27 G5
WGOS CT8 ....177 H6
Wellesley Court Rd
CROY/NA CRO 86 E5
Wellesley Gv CROY/NA CRO ..86 E5
Wellesley Rd ASH TN23 ....2 C4
CROY/NA CRO 86 C1
DVE/WH CT16 ....8 D4
IOS ME12 ....64 E4
MARG CT9 ....15 L6
WGOS CT8 ....177 H6
Wellesley Vls KEN/WIL TN24 * ..2 D3
Well Fld HART DA3 ....78 A8
Wellfield Rd FOLK CT20 ....10 C1
Wellfit St HNHL SE24 .....44 C1
Well Hall Pde ELTH/MOT SE9 ..48 A2
Well Hall Rd ELTH/MOT SE9 ..48 A2
Well Hl ORP BR6 ....92 C8
Well Hill La ORP BR6 .....109 G8
Wellhouse Rd BECK BR3 ...70 A8
Wellhurst Cl ORP BR6 ....107 L2
Welling High St WELL DA16 ..49 J1
Wellington Av BFN/LL DA15 ..49 H4
Wellington Cl NWCR SE14 * ..177 H1
WGOS CT8 ....177 H1
Wellington Cottages
HAWK TN18 ....312 C5
Wellington Crs RAM CT11 ..17 L6
Wellington Gdns CHARL SE7 ..27 K4
MARG CT9 * 15 H3
Wellington Gv GNWCH SE10 ..26 E6
Wellingtonia Wy EDEN TN8 ..192 D3
Wellington Ms HYTHE CT21 ..223 H5
Wellington Pde BFN/LL DA15 * ..49 H3
DEAL CT14 ....211 M3
Wellington Pl FOLK CT20 ..223 J2
MAID/BEAR ME14 ......12 E2
Wellington Rd BELV DA17 ...30 A4
BXLY DA5 ....49 L4
CROY/NA CRO 86 B6
DART DA1 ....51 L4
DEAL CT14 ....209 L4
DVE/WH CT16 ....212 A4
FOLK CT20 ....219 L8
GILL ME7 ....7 K6
HAYES BR2 ....71 L1
SIT ME10 ....119 J4
STMC/STPC BR5 ....91 J2
TIL RM18 ....35 H8
WGOS CT8 ....177 H6
Wellington St GVE DA12 ...55 K5
WOOL/PLUM SE18 ......28 E4
WSTB CT5 ....126 E3
Wellington Ter FOLK CT20 * ..223 J2
Wellington Wy E/WMAL ME19 ..164 A2
Welling Wy ELTH/MOT SE9 ..48 A1
Wellis Gdns MARG CT9 ....14 B7
Well La CANTW/ST CT2 ....173 H5
FAV ME13 ....148 B6
RDV CT15 ....215 G3
Wellmeade Dr SEV TN13 ...162 A6
Wellmeadow Rd LEW SE13 ..46 F4
Well Penn Rd HOO/HM ME3 ..58 C1
Well Rd MAID/BEAR ME14 ...13 N2
Wells Av CANTW/ST CT2 ...173 J3
Wells Cl BH/WHM TN16 ....159 H5
NROM TN28 ....331 L7
RTW TN1 ....22 F9
SAND/SEL CR2 ....86 F5
TENT TN30 ....315 M1

Wells Park Rd SYD SE26 ...45 K5
Wells Pl CMBW SE5 ......24 D7
Wells Rd BMLY BR1 ......72 C2
FOLKN CT19 ....10 A2
STRD ME2 ....18 B1
West St E/WMAL ME19 ....138 F7
MAID/SHEP ME15 ......259 K1
Wells Wy CMBW SE5 .....24 E8
FAV ME13 ....125 J8
Well Winch Rd SIT ME10 ..119 L4
Welsdene Rd MARG CT9 ...177 H3
Welsford St STHWK SE1 ...25 H4
Welson Rd FOLK CT20 ....10 C5
Welton Cl TON TN9 ......194 C6
Welton Rd WOOL/PLUM SE18 ..28 F6
Wemmick Cl ROCH ME1 ...100 E6
Wemyss Rd BKHTH/KID SE3 ..27 G8
Wemyss Wy CANT CT1 ....4 M3
Wenderton La RCANTE CT3 ..234 H11
Wendover Cl STRD ME2 ...99 J8
Wendover Rd ELTH/MOT SE9 ..47 L8
HAYES BR2 ....71 J2
Wendover Wy ORP BR6 ...91 L5
WELL DA16 ....49 H3
Werhams La LYDD TN29 ...329 R5
LYDD TN29 ....330 A3
Wensley Cl ELTH/MOT SE9 ..48 A8
Wentland Cl CAT SE6 ....46 E7
Wentland Rd CAT SE6 ....46 E7
Wents Wd MAID/BEAR ME14 ..142 A8
Wentworth Av MARG CT9 ...177 K4
Wentworth Cl CVW DA11 ...79 H2
HAYES BR2 * 89 H5
ORP BR6 ....90 F8
RFOLK CT18 ....291 H11
Wentworth Crs PECK SE15 ..25 H6
Wentworth Dr DART DA1 ...51 H5
HOO/HM ME3 ....58 C5
MSTR CT12 ....102 H1
SIT ME10 ....119 K4
Wentworth Gdns HB CT6 ...128 E2
Wentworth Pl CDW/CHF RM16 ..34 E2
Wentworth Rd CROY/NA CRO ..86 B6
Wenvoe Av BXLYHN DA7 ...30 A6
Wernbrook St WOOL/PLUM SE18 ..28 D5
Wesley Cl SNWD SE25 * ...69 H8
Wesley Cl MAIDW ME16 ...166 A3
STMC/STPC BR5 ....73 K7
WALW SE17 ....24 C3
Wesley Ter RFOLK CT18 * ..291 H11
Wessex Dr ERITH DA8 ....30 F8
Wessex Wk BXLY DA5 * ...50 E7
West Ap STMC/STPC BR5 ..90 F2
Westbere La CANTW/ST CT2 ..173 J3
Westbourne ASH TN23 ....204 B5
Westbourne Dr FSTH SE23 ..45 L6
Westbourne Gdns FOLK CT20 ..10 E7
Westbourne Rd BXLYHN DA7 ..29 L6
CROY/NA CRO 87 G2
SYD SE26 ....69 L3
Westbourne St SIT ME10 ..119 M4
Westbrook MAID/SHEP ME15 ..167 G8
Westbrook Av MARG CT9 ...14 A6
Westbrook Cottages MARG CT9 ..14 B6
Westbrook Dr STMC/STPC BR5 ..91 L4
Westbrook Rd CHAT ME4 ...101 H3
GNWCH SE10 ....26 F5
THHTH CR7 ....68 B2
Westbrooke Crs WELL DA16 ..48 E1
Westbrooke Rd BFN/LL DA15 ..48 E1
WELL DA16 ....49 K1
Westbrook Gdns MARG CT9 ..14 A6
Westbrook La HB CT6 ....128 C6
Westbrook Rd BKHTH/KID SE3 ..27 J7
MARG CT9 ....14 B6
THHTH CR7 ....68 B2
Westbury Crs DVW CT17 ...217 J3
Westbury Rd BMLY BR1 ...71 L1
CROY/NA CRO 86 D1
DVW CT17 ....217 J3
PGE/AN SE20 ....69 J6
WGOS CT8 ....177 J6
Westbury Ter BH/WHM TN16 ..159 H5
West Cliff Av HB CT6 ....128 B2
West Cliff Ct HB CT6 ....128 C6
Westcliff Dr IOS ME12 ...65 L6
Westcliff Gdns FOLK CT20 ..11 H6
HB CT6 ....128 C6
Westcliff Ms MARG CT9 * ..183 J1
West Cliff Prom RAM CT11 ..17 G9
West Cliff Rd BRDST CT10 ..183 K2
RAM CT11 ....17 G7
Westcliff Rd MARG CT9 ...14 A6
Westcliff Terrace Man
RAM CT11 * 16 D8
Westcombe Hl BKHTH/KID SE3 ..27 H5
Westcombe Park Rd
BKHTH/KID SE3 ....26 F5
West Common Rd HAYES BR2 ..89 H5
Westcott Av GVW DA11 ...55 H8
Westcott Cl BMLY BR1 ....71 M1
CROY/NA CRO 105 G3
Westcott Rd WALW SE17 ...24 B5
West Ct MAID/SHEP ME15 ..167 H4
Westcourt La RCANTW CT4 ..271 G1
Westcourt Pde GVE DA12 * ..56 A8
Westcourt St CHAT ME4 ...6 E3
West Crescent Rd GVE DA12 ..55 J4
West Cross TENT TN30 ....315 M2
West Cross Gdns TENT TN30 ..315 M2
West Cross Ms TENT TN30 * ..315 L2
Westdale Rd WOOL/PLUM SE18 ..28 D5
Westdean Av LEE/GVPK SE12 ..47 J2
Westdean Cl DVW CT17 ...212 J7
Westdown Rd CAT SE6 ....46 D6
WALD ME5 ....100 B8
West Dumpton La RAM CT11 ..183 H1
West End BGR/WK TN15 ...136 E3
BH/WHM TN16 ....160 A3
Westerdale Rd GNWCH SE10 ..27 H4
Westergate Rd ABYW SE2 ..29 L6
Westerham Cl CANTW/ST CT2 ..172 B5
MARG CT9 ....179 H4
RHAM ME8 ....102 F3
Westerham Dr BFN/LL DA15 ..49 H4
Westerham Hl BH/WHM TN16 ..133 G8
Westerham Rd BH/WHM TN16 ..159 H5
HAYES BR2 ....89 M7
OXTED RH8 ....157 H7
RSEV TN14 ....160 A1
SEV TN13 ....161 H1
SIT ME10 ....119 K6
Westerhout Cl DEAL CT14 ..209 H5
Westerley Crs SYD SE26 * ..70 A2
Western Av ASH TN23 ....204 D1
CHAT ME4 * 5 H1
HAWK TN18 ....312 C7

HB CT6 128 E5
IOS ME12 64 E6
RCANTW CT4 175 G8
WTHK RM20 * 33 G3
Western Cl DVW CT17 8 A9
Western Cross Cl GRH DA9 53 K4
Western Docks DVW CT17 * 8 C9
Western Esp BRDST CT10 183 L3
HB CT6 128 D4
Western Gdns KEN/WIL TN24 3 G9
Western Link FAV ME13 149 H1
Western Rd BGR/WK TN15 240 E2
BRXN/ST SW9 44 B1
DEAL CT14 209 K3
HAWK TN18 312 C7
MAIDW ME16 166 D2
MARG CT9 178 F5
RTW TN1 23 J1
STH/RUST TN4 196 C4
WADH TN5 309 L3
Western Undercliff RAM CT11 16 C9
Western Wy THMD SE28 28 F1
Westferry Rd POP/IOD E14 26 B1
Westfield CANTW/ST CT2 153 H7
SEV TN13 136 B8
Westfield Cl GVE DA12 79 K3
Westfield La RFOLK CT18 218 E2
Westfield Rd BECK BR3 70 A6
BRCH CT7 176 C6
BXLYHN DA7 50 D1
CROY/NA CR0 86 C5
MARG CT9 177 L5
Westfields HDCN TN27 285 N1
Westfield Sole Rd
MAID/BEAR ME14 115 L5
Westfield St WOOL/PLUM SE18 27 L2
Westfield Ter CRBK TN17 298 C12
Westfield Vls STPH/PW TN12 * 280 C4
Westgate Av BRCH CT7 181 K1
Westgate Bay Av WGOS CT8 177 G4
Westgate Cl CANTW/ST CT2 171 K4
Westgate Court Av
CANTW/ST CT2 4 A3
Westgate Gv CANTW/ST CT2 4 D3
Westgate Hall Rd CANT CT1 * 4 E3
Westgate Rd BECK BR3 70 D5
DART DA1 51 L4
FAV ME13 149 M2
SNWD SE25 69 J8
Westgate Rbt CANTW/ST CT2 4 D3
Westgate Ter WSTB CT5 126 E3
West Gn SIT ME10 227 N12
West Gv GNWCH SE10 26 D7
Westgrove La GNWCH SE10 26 D7
West Hallowes ELTH/MOT SE9 47 L6
Westhall Pk WARL CR6 130 B5
Westhall Rd WARL CR6 130 B4
Westharold SWLY BR8 74 E7
West Heath Cl DART DA1 * 51 G4
West Heath La SEV TN13 162 A6
West Heath Rd BXLYHN DA7 29 L5
DART DA1 51 G4
West Hl DART DA1 51 L4
ORP BR6 106 E6
OXTED RH8 157 J8
West Hill Bank OXTED RH8 157 J8
Westhill Cl GVE DA12 55 J6
West Hill Dr DART DA1 51 K4
West Hill Ri DART DA1 51 L4
West Hill Rd HB CT6 128 D4
West Holme ERITH DA8 30 D7
Westholme ORP BR6 90 F3
Westhorne Av ELTH/MOT SE9 47 L3
Westhurst Dr CHST BR7 72 C2
West Hythe Rd HYTHE CT21 321 M1
West Kent Av GVW DA11 54 D4
Westland Dr HAYES BR2 89 G5
Westlands Av SIT ME10 119 J5
Westlands Rd HB CT6 128 C6
Westlands Wy OXTED RH8 157 J5
Westland Wy RFOLK CT18 220 C2
West La BERM/RHTH SE16 25 J1
HOO/HM ME3 43 H7
IOS ME12 64 B3
SIT ME10 120 B5
West Lawn Gdns FOLK CT20 223 L2
West Lea DEAL CT14 209 K2
Westleigh Dr BMLY BR1 71 M6
Westleigh Rd WGOS CT8 177 G5
Westmarsh Cl
MAID/SHEP ME15 168 A6
Westmarsh Dr MARG CT9 179 H3
Westmarsh Dro RCANTE CT3 235 P5
Westmead DIT/AY ME20 139 K1
Westmeads Rd WSTB CT5 126 F3
West Ml GVW DA11 55 G4
West Mill Rd DIT/AY ME20 139 K1
Westminster Av THHTH CR7 68 C6
Westminster Bridge Rd
STHWK SE1 24 B2
Westminster Rd CANT CT1 172 D5
Westminster Wk MSTR CT12 * 16 F1
Westmoat Cl BECK BR3 70 D4
Westmoors ASH TN23 204 A5
Westmoor St CHARL SE7 27 L3
Westmoreland Av WELL DA16 48 F1
Westmoreland Dr RSIT ME9 226 D10
Westmoreland Pl HAYES BR2 * 71 H7
Westmoreland Rd HAYES BR2 71 H8
WALW SE17 24 E5
Westmoreland Ter
PGE/AN SE20 * 69 J4
Westmore Rd BH/WHM TN16 132 B7
Westmorland Cl
MAID/SHEP ME15 167 M6
Westmorland Gn
MAID/SHEP ME15 167 M6
Westmorland Rd
MAID/SHEP ME15 167 M6
West Motney Wy RHAM ME8 103 H2
Westmount Av CHAT ME4 6 C6
Westmount Rd ELTH/MOT SE9 28 A8
ELTH/MOT SE9 48 A1
West Norman Rd DVE/WH CT16 8 F3
West Oak BECK BR3 70 E5
Weston Av WTHK RM20 33 G4
Weston Gv BMLY BR1 71 G4
Weston Rd BMLY BR1 71 G5
STRD ME2 18 E3
Weston St STHWK SE1 24 E2
Westonville Av MARG CT9 177 L4
Westover Gdns BRDST CT10 179 H6
Westover Rd BRDST CT10 179 H6
Westow Hl NRWD SE19 68 F3
Westow St NRWD SE19 68 F3
West Pde HYTHE CT21 222 C5
West Pk ELTH/MOT SE9 47 M7
West Park Av MARG CT9 179 G4
STH/RUST TN4 196 D4
West Park Rd MAID/SHEP ME15 13 K8
West Parkside GNWCH SE10 26 F1
WARL CR6 130 F1
West Pas IOS ME12 * 64 B3
West Pl LYDD TN29 328 H5
Westree Ct MAIDW ME16 12 D6
Westree Rd MAIDW ME16 12 D6
West Rdg SIT ME10 119 L7
Westrise TON TN9 194 D6
West Rd CRBK TN17 296 G10
CRBK TN17 297 M5
FOLK CT20 223 K1
GILL ME7 83 H6
MSTR CT12 237 K5
West Shaw HART DA3 77 L6
West Side RDV CT15 210 B8
West Sq LBTH SE11 24 C2
West St ASH TN23 2 A5
BGR/WK TN15 238 E10
BMLY BR1 71 H5
BXLYHN DA7 50 A2
CROY/NA CR0 86 D7
DEAL CT14 209 K2
DVW CT17 8 A3
E/WMAL ME19 138 C5
ERITH DA8 30 E3
FAV ME13 149 K1
GILL ME7 7 L2
GRAYS RM17 34 B5
GVW DA11 55 J4
IOS ME12 64 B2
MAID/SHEP ME15 258 E4
NROM TN28 330 H7
QBOR ME11 64 A8
RASHW TN26 286 D2
RMAID ME17 240 D11
RMAID ME17 243 M9
RYE TN31 225 H4
SIT ME10 119 M5
STRD ME2 82 C4
West Street Pl CROY/NA CR0 * 86 D7
West Ter BFN/LL DA15 * 48 F6
FOLK CT20 11 J6
West Thurrock Wy WTHK RM20 33 J4
West Undercliff RYE TN31 224 F4
Westview CHAT ME4 83 J3
West Vw HDCN TN27 * 283 J2
West View Cl HB CT6 128 D7
West View Rd DART DA1 52 A4
SWLY BR8 92 E2
WARL CR6 130 A5
West Wk MAIDW ME16 166 C2
West Wy CROY/NA CR0 87 M5
STMC/STPC BR5 90 E1
WWKM BR4 88 E2
Westway RMAID ME17 258 H2
RTWE/PEM TN2 278 A10
West Way Gdns CROY/NA CR0 87 L5
Westways BH/WHM TN16 159 H4
EDEN TN8 192 D3
Westwell Cl STMC/STPC BR5 91 L4
Westwell Ct TENT TN30 315 L2
Westwell La RASHE TN25 202 B5
RASHE TN25 264 E8
Westwood Av NRWD SE19 68 D5
Westwood Cl BMLY BR1 71 L7
Westwood Hl SYD SE26 69 H2
Westwood La WELL DA16 49 H2
Westwood Pk FSTH SE23 45 J5
Westwood Pl FAV ME13 149 L4
SYD SE26 * 69 H2
Westwood Rd BRDST CT10 182 F1
MAID/SHEP ME15 167 H6
MEO DA13 77 M2
West Wood Rd RSIT ME9 117 J6
Westwood Rd STH/RUST TN4 277 R12
STPH/PW TN12 256 H7
West Woodside BXLY DA5 49 M6
Westwood Wy SEV TN13 20 D1
Wetheral Dr WALD ME5 115 J1
Weybridge Cl WALD ME5 115 K1
Weybridge Ct STHWK SE1 * 25 J4
Weybridge Rd THHTH CR7 68 B8
Weyburn Dr MSTR CT12 16 B1
Wey Cl WALD ME5 101 K8
Weyhill Cl MAID/BEAR ME14 141 K7
Weyman Rd BKHTH/KID SE3 27 K7
Weymouth Cl FOLKN CT19 219 L7
Weymouth Rd FOLKN CT19 219 L7
Weymouth Ter FOLKN CT19 * 219 L6
Wey St RASHW TN26 318 G6
Wharfedale Gdns
STRHM/NOR SW16 68 A8
Wharfedale Rd MARG CT9 15 J6
RDART DA2 52 D6
Wharf La HOO/HM ME3 38 C7
Wharf Rd GILL ME7 * 83 K6
GRAYS RM17 34 A5
GVE DA12 55 M4
MAID/SHEP ME15 12 C8
Wharfside Cl ERITH DA8 31 G4
The Wharf GRH DA9 * 53 J2
Wharncliffe Gdns SNWD SE25 68 F6
Wharncliffe Rd SNWD SE25 68 E6
Wharton Gdns KEN/WIL TN24 3 H8
Wharton Rd BMLY BR1 71 J5
Whateley Rd EDUL SE22 45 G3
PGE/AN SE20 69 L4
Whatman Cl MAID/BEAR ME14 141 K7
Whatman Rd FSTH SE23 45 L5
Whatmer Cl CANTW/ST CT2 173 H3
Wheatcroft Cl SIT ME10 120 C5
Wheatcroft Gv RHAM ME8 103 G6
Wheatear Wy WALD ME5 101 J6
Wheatfield E/WMAL ME19 138 F4
Wheatfield Cl CRBK TN17 298 F8
Wheatfield Dr CRBK TN17 298 F9
Wheatfield Lea CRBK TN17 298 F8
Wheatfields MAID/BEAR ME14 167 L1
WALD ME5 115 L3
Wheatfield Wy CRBK TN17 298 F8
Wheathill Rd PGE/AN SE20 69 J6
Wheatley Cl GRH DA9 53 H3
Wheatley Rd MSTR CT12 182 F4
WSTB CT5 126 F3
Wheatley Terrace Rd
ERITH DA8 31 G5
Wheatsheaf Cl FAV ME13 151 H6
MAID/SHEP ME15 167 J5
Wheat Sheaf Cl POP/IOD E14 26 B3
Wheatsheaf Gdns IOS ME12 64 C4
Wheatsheaf Hl RSEV TN14 108 E3
RSEV TN14 254 B1
Wheatsheaf La RDV CT15 210 C7
Wheatsheaf Wy TONN TN10 189 G7
Wheeler Av OXTED RH8 157 J7
Wheeler Pl HAYES BR2 71 J8
Wheeler's La RMAID ME17 259 K6
The Wheelers RHAM ME8 102 C7
Wheeler St HDCN TN27 283 M4
MAID/BEAR ME14 13 H3
Wheelock Cl ERITH DA8 30 C6
The Wheelwrights
RMAID ME17 * 242 E11
Wheelwrights Wy SWCH CT13 253 N7
Wheler Ct FAV ME13 149 H2
Wheler Rd HDCN TN27 264 B5
Whenman Av BXLY DA5 50 D7
Whetsted Rd STPH/PW TN12 278 G1
Whetstone Rd BKHTH/KID SE3 27 K8
Whidborne Cl DEPT SE8 26 B8
Whiffen's Av CHAT ME4 6 D4
Whiffen's Avenue W CHAT ME4 * 6 D4
Whiffen Wk E/WMAL ME19 139 J4
Whimbrel Cl SIT ME10 120 A1
Whimbrel Gn DIT/AY ME20 139 G3
The Whimbrels CHAT ME4 * 83 J4
Whinchat Rd THMD SE28 28 E2
Whinfell Av RAM CT11 182 C6
Whinfell Wy GVE DA12 80 A1
Whinless Rd DVW CT17 217 H1
Whinyates Rd ELTH/MOT SE9 47 M1
Whippendell Cl STMC/STPC BR5 73 J5
Whippendell Wy
STMC/STPC BR5 73 J5
Whistler Rd TONN TN10 189 H7
Whiston Av RASHW TN26 302 D1
Whitacre Ms LBTH SE11 24 B4
Whitbread Rd BROCKY SE4 45 M2
Whitburn Rd LEW SE13 46 C3
Whitby Cl BH/WHM TN16 132 A5
GRH DA9 53 H3
Whitby Rd FOLK CT20 219 L7
WOOL/PLUM SE18 28 A3
Whitby Ter DVE/WH CT16 * 213 J6
Whitcher Cl NWCR SE14 25 M5
Whitchurch Cl MAIDW ME16 12 C4
Whitcombe Cl WALD ME5 115 K3
White Acre Dr DEAL CT14 211 J1
Whiteacre La RCANTW CT4 268 A9
White Av GVW DA11 55 G8
Whitebeam Av HAYES BR2 90 B3
Whitebeam Cl ASH TN23 202 A7
BGR/WK TN15 136 F3
BRXN/ST SW9 * 24 A6
Whitebeam Dr RMAID ME17 258 G2
White Bear Pas
STH/RUST TN4 * 22 F7
Whitebine Gdns
STPH/PW TN12 257 K7
Whitebread La RYE TN31 325 L5
White Cliffs Country Trail
RDV CT15 210 A3
SWCH CT13 237 Q12
SWCH CT13 253 P7
Whitecliff Wy FOLKN CT19 221 G7
White Cottage Rd TONN TN10 188 F7
Whitecroft SWLY BR8 74 F6
Whitecroft Cl BECK BR3 70 E8
Whitecroft Wy BECK BR3 70 D8
Whitefield Cl STMC/STPC BR5 73 K7
Whitefield Rd STH/RUST TN4 22 E1
Whitefoot La CAT SE6 70 E1
Whitefoot Ter BMLY BR1 47 G8
White Friars SEV TN13 161 M5
Whitefriars SWCH CT13 237 J12
Whitefriars Meadow
SWCH CT13 * 206 B1
Whitefriars St CANT CT1 5 G5
Whitegate Cl STH/RUST TN4 196 C5
Whitegates Av BGR/WK TN15 111 K1
Whitegates La WADH TN5 308 H1
Whitehall LYDD TN29 329 J5
Whitehall Bridge Rd
CANTW/ST CT2 4 C3
Whitehall Cl CANTW/ST CT2 4 D4
Whitehall Ct SIT ME10 * 120 A7
Whitehill Dr RMAID ME17 261 L3
Whitehall Gdns CANTW/ST CT2 4 D4
Whitehall La ERITH DA8 31 G8
GRAYS RM17 34 D5
Whitehall Rd CANTW/ST CT2 4 D4
GRAYS RM17 34 D3
HAYES BR2 89 L1
MAID/BEAR ME14 143 H7
MSTR CT12 16 D2
SIT ME10 119 M7
THHTH CR7 86 B1
Whitehall Wy RASHE TN25 307 J4
White Hart Cl SEV TN13 162 B6
White Hart Pde SEV TN13 * 20 B1
The White Hart Pde SEV TN13 * 20 B1
White Hart Rd ORP BR6 91 H3
WOOL/PLUM SE18 28 F3
White Hart St LBTH SE11 24 B4
White Hart Wd SEV TN13 162 B7
White Hart Yd GVE DA12 * 55 K4
Whitehaven Cl HAYES BR2 71 H8
Whitehead Cl RDART DA2 51 K8
Whiteheads La
MAID/BEAR ME14 168 C1
Whitehill BGR/WK TN15 238 G10
White Hl RASHE TN25 265 R4
RASHE TN25 266 B5
White Hill Cl RCANTW CT4 249 P9
Whitehill La GVE DA12 55 L8
Whitehill Pde GVE DA12 55 K8
White Hill Rd
MAID/BEAR ME14 116 E4
Whitehill Rd DART DA1 51 H3
GVE DA12 55 K7
MEO DA13 77 L4
MEO DA13 97 J6
White Horse Hl CHST BR7 72 B1
RFOLK CT18 220 D2
Whitehorse Hl WALD ME5 7 H8
White Horse La CANT CT1 * 4 F4
MAID/SHEP ME15 168 B7
RCANTW CT4 291 K6
Whitehorse La SNWD SE25 68 F8
Whitehorse Rd CROY/NA CR0 86 D3
White Horse Rd MEO DA13 239 Q4
Whitehouse Cl HOO/HM ME3 83 M1
Whitehouse Crs ROCH ME1 114 B5
Whitehouse Dro RCANTE CT3 236 G6
White House Rd RSEV TN14 161 L8
Whitelake Rd TONN TN10 188 F8
White La BH/WHM TN16 158 A1
Whiteleaves Ri STRD ME2 99 J3
Whiteley Rd NRWD SE19 68 E2
White Lion Ct PECK SE15 * 25 K5
Whitelocks Cl RCANTW CT4 270 C2
White Ldg NRWD SE19 68 C4
White Lodge Cl SEV TN13 21 H3
White Marsh Ct WSTB CT5 * 126 F3
Whitenbrook HYTHE CT21 223 H2
Whiteness Gn BRDST CT10 179 J4
Whiteness Rd BRDST CT10 179 K4
White Oak Cl TON TN9 * 194 E6
White Oak Dr BECK BR3 70 D6
White Oak Gdns BFN/LL DA15 49 G5
White Oak Sq SWLY BR8 * 74 F7
White Post Gdns RCANTE CT3 236 B12
White Post Hl EYN DA4 94 B3
White Post La MEO DA13 79 J8
Whitepost La MEO DA13 239 L3
White Post St PECK SE15 25 K6
White Rd CHAT ME4 101 H4
White Rock Ct MAIDW ME16 12 D6
White Rock Pl MAIDW ME16 12 D6
Whites Cl GRH DA9 53 K4
Whites Grounds STHWK SE1 24 F1
Whites Grounds Est
STHWK SE1 * 24 F1
Whites Hl DEAL CT14 272 H3
White's La HAWK TN18 312 E7
Whites Meadow BMLY BR1 * 72 B8
Whitethorn Gdns CROY/NA CR0 87 J5
Whitewall Rd STRD ME2 19 M3
Whitewall Wy STRD ME2 19 M3
Whiteway Rd QBOR ME11 64 A7
Whitewebbs Wy
STMC/STPC BR5 73 G5
Whitewood Cottages
BH/WHM TN16 132 B6
White Wood Rd SWCH CT13 253 N8
Whitfeld Rd ASH TN23 2 B9
Whitfield Av BRDST CT10 179 H6
DVE/WH CT16 213 J7
Whitfield Ct DVE/WH CT16 213 H3
Whitfield Hl DVE/WH CT16 213 G5
Whitfield Rd BXLYHN DA7 30 A6
GNWCH SE10 26 E7
Whitgift Av SAND/SEL CR2 86 D8
Whitgift St CROY/NA CR0 86 D6
LBTH SE11 24 A3
Whiting Crs FAV ME13 149 H1
Whitmore Rd BECK BR3 70 A7
Whitmore St MAIDW ME16 166 D3
Whitney Wk SCUP DA14 73 M3
Whitstable Cl BECK BR3 70 A5
Whitstable Pl CROY/NA CR0 86 D7
Whitstable Rd CANTW/ST CT2 4 B1
FAV ME13 149 M2
HB CT6 128 B6
Whitstone La BECK BR3 88 C1
Whittell Gdns SYD SE26 45 K8
Whittington Ter RDV CT15 * 271 Q9
Whitworth Rd SNWD SE25 68 F7
WOOL/PLUM SE18 28 B6
Whitworth St GNWCH SE10 26 F4
Whorlton Rd PECK SE15 45 H1
Whybornes Cha IOS ME12 65 K6
Whybourne Crest
RTWE/PEM TN2 23 K9
Whyman Av CHAT ME4 101 H4
Whytecliffs BRDST CT10 183 K3
Wichling Cl CANTW/ST CT2 172 B6
STMC/STPC BR5 91 L4
Wickenden Crs KEN/WIL TN24 3 M8
Wickenden Rd SEV TN13 21 K1
Wicken La HDCN TN27 264 D8
Wickens Meadow
RSEV TN14 * 135 L5
Wickers Oake NRWD SE19 * 69 G1
The Wickets KEN/WIL TN24 * 205 J4
The Wicket CROY/NA CR0 88 B8
Wickham Av CROY/NA CR0 87 M5
RAM CT11 183 K5
Wickham Cha WWKM BR4 88 E3
Wickham Cl RSIT ME9 118 C3
Wickham Ct WWKM BR4 * 88 E7
Wickham Court La
RCANTE CT3 234 C11
Wickham Court Rd WWKM BR4 88 D5
Wickham Crs WWKM BR4 88 D5
Wickham Fld RSEV TN14 * 135 L2
Wickham Gdns BROCKY SE4 46 A1
STH/RUST TN4 196 A8
Wickham La ABYW SE2 29 H5
RCANTE CT3 234 C12
Wickham Rd BECK BR3 70 C7
BROCKY SE4 46 A1
CDW/CHF RM16 35 K1
CROY/NA CR0 87 K5
RCANTE CT3 234 C12
Wickham St LBTH SE11 24 A4
ROCH ME1 100 E2
WELL DA16 28 F8
Wickhams Wy HART DA3 96 A1
Wickham Ter QBOR ME11 * 64 A8
Wickham Wy BECK BR3 70 D8
Wickhurst Rd RSEV TN14 254 H2
Wick La RCANTW CT4 271 J6
Wicks Cl ELTH/MOT SE9 71 L1
Wicksteed Cl BXLY DA5 50 E8
Wickwood St CMBW SE5 24 C8
Widbury RRTW TN3 * 200 A2
Widbury Cl RRTW TN3 200 A2
Widecombe Rd ELTH/MOT SE9 47 M8
Widgeon Rd ERITH DA8 31 J6
STRD ME2 81 L7
Widgeon Wk RFOLK CT18 220 C2
Widmore Lodge Rd BMLY BR1 71 L6
Widmore Rd BMLY BR1 71 K6
Widred Rd DVW CT17 8 A3
Wierton Hl RMAID ME17 259 Q6
Wierton La RMAID ME17 259 R3
Wierton Rd RMAID ME17 259 R5
Wife of Bath Hl
CANTW/ST CT2 171 K5
Wigmore La RDV CT15 272 E4
Wigmore Rd RHAM ME8 102 C8
Wigmore Wd RDV CT15 272 D5
Wigton Pl LBTH SE11 24 B4
Wigwam Paddocks BRCH CT7 176 D5
Wihtred Rd RSIT ME9 120 E7
Wilberforce Rd FOLK CT20 223 M2
RMAID ME17 259 J2
Wilberforce Wy GVE DA12 79 L2
Wilbrough Rd BRCH CT7 176 D6
Wilcox Cl RCANTE CT3 251 N12
Wilde Cl TIL RM18 35 K8
Wildernesse Av BGR/WK TN15 136 E8
Wildernesse Mt SEV TN13 136 C8
Wilderness Gdns RYE TN31 324 H6
Wilderness Hl MARG CT9 15 J4
Wilderness Rd CHST BR7 72 C4
OXTED RH8 157 K8
Wilde Rd ERITH DA8 30 C6
Wildfell Cl MAID/BEAR ME14 115 K5
Wildfell Rd CAT SE6 46 C5
Wild Goose Dr PECK SE15 25 K7
Wildish Rd FAV ME13 149 H1
Wildman Cl RHAM ME8 116 E2
Wild's Rents STHWK SE1 24 F2
Wildwood Cl LEE/GVPK SE12 47 G5
RMAID ME17 261 M3
Wildwood Gld GILL ME7 102 B8
Wiles Av NROM TN28 331 J7
Wilfred Rd RAM CT11 16 F4
Wilfred St GVE DA12 55 J4
Wilgate Green Rd FAV ME13 245 P3
Wilkes Rd BRDST CT10 183 H2
Wilkie Rd BRCH CT7 176 D5
Wilkinson Dr DEAL CT14 209 L6
Wilkinson Gdns NRWD SE19 68 F5
Wilkinson St VX/NE SW8 24 A6
Wilks Av DART DA1 52 A7
Wilks Cl RHAM ME8 103 J3
Wilks Gdns CROY/NA CR0 87 M4
Will Adams Wy RHAM ME8 102 A2
Will Crooks Gdns
ELTH/MOT SE9 47 L2
Willement Rd FAV ME13 149 J2
Willenhall Rd
WOOL/PLUM SE18 28 C4
Willersley Av BFN/LL DA15 49 G6
ORP BR6 90 E6
Willersley Cl BFN/LL DA15 49 G6
Willesborough Ct KEN/WIL TN24 3 M6
Willesborough Rd
KEN/WIL TN24 3 K2
Willesley Gdns CRBK TN17 298 G7
Willett Cl STMC/STPC BR5 90 F2
Willett Rd THHTH CR7 86 B1
Willetts Hl MSTR CT12 180 A6
Willetts La RRTW TN3 198 D1
Willett Wy STMC/STPC BR5 90 E1
William Av FOLKN CT19 10 E2
MARG CT9 178 F5
William Barefoot Dr
ELTH/MOT SE9 48 B7
William Booth Rd PGE/AN SE20 69 H5
William Cl LEW SE13 46 D1
William Ellis Wy
BERM/RHTH SE16 * 25 H2
William Gibbs Ct FAV ME13 * 149 L2
William Hall Ter FAV ME13 * 149 H3
William Judge Cl TENT TN30 315 Q2
William Luck Cl
STPH/PW TN12 256 H7
William Margrie Cl PECK SE15 * 25 H8
William Petty Wy
STMC/STPC BR5 91 K4
William Pitt Av DEAL CT14 209 J3
William Pitt Cl HYTHE CT21 222 E3
William Rigby Dr IOS ME12 64 F6
William Rd ASH TN23 2 A9
STRD ME2 99 K3
Williamson Cl GNWCH SE10 27 G4
Williamson Rd LYDD TN29 335 M4
William St FAV ME13 * 149 L2
GRAYS RM17 34 D5
GVE DA12 55 J5
HB CT6 129 G4
RHAM ME8 103 H3
SIT ME10 119 M6
STH/RUST TN4 22 E1
Willicombe Pk RTWE/PEM TN2 23 M3
Willingdon ASH TN23 204 B6
Willingdon Pl DEAL CT14 209 K7
Willingdon Rd DVE/WH CT16 213 H4
Willington Gn
MAID/SHEP ME15 167 M6
Willington St
MAID/SHEP ME15 167 M7
Willis Ct IOS ME12 65 G8
Willis La RASHW TN26 319 M4
Willis Rd CROY/NA CR0 86 D3
ERITH DA8 30 D3
Willop Wy LYDD TN29 321 L6
Willoughby Av CROY/NA CR0 86 A7
Willoughby Wy CHARL SE7 27 J3
Willow Av BFN/LL DA15 49 H4
BRDST CT10 183 G1
FAV ME13 149 H2
HOO/HM ME3 83 M2
SWLY BR8 75 G8
Willow Bank RBTBR TN32 322 G10
Willowbank Cl LYDD TN29 331 P1
Willowbank Dr HOO/HM ME3 59 M1
Willowbrook Est PECK SE15 * 25 G6
Willowbrook Rd PECK SE15 25 G5
Willowby Gdns RHAM ME8 116 F1
Willow Cl BUR/ETCH TN19 322 B5
BXLY DA5 50 A4
CANTW/ST CT2 172 B6
HAYES BR2 90 A1
HOO/HM ME3 * 41 M4
HYTHE CT21 307 R12
MARG CT9 178 F3
STMC/STPC BR5 91 J2
Willow Ct BRDST CT10 * 179 K8
Willow Crs STPH/PW TN12 278 D2
STPH/PW TN12 282 A4
Willow Dr LYDD TN29 331 N2
RASHW TN26 318 D2
Willow Farm Wy HB CT6 129 K7
Willowfields Cl
WOOL/PLUM SE18 28 F4
Willow Gra HOO/HM ME3 * 59 L8
Willow Gv CHST BR7 72 B3
Willowherb Cl CHAT ME4 83 K4
Willow La STPH/PW TN12 279 N4
WOOL/PLUM SE18 28 A3
Willow Lea TONN TN10 188 F6
Willowmead DIT/AY ME20 138 F3
Willow Ms RBTBR TN32 322 G9
Willow Mt CROY/NA CR0 86 F7
Willow Pk RSEV TN14 135 L3
Willow Ri MAID/SHEP ME15 168 A4
Willow Rd DART DA1 51 K6
DEAL CT14 208 D6
DIT/AY ME20 139 G2
ERITH DA8 31 H7
STRD ME2 18 B6
WSTB CT5 126 D8
Willows Ct CANTW/ST CT2 * 171 K1
Willowside SNOD ME6 113 H4
The Willows BECK BR3 * 70 B5
BGR/WK TN15 * 240 C3
CANTW/ST CT2 * 173 H5
GRAYS RM17 34 E5
HB CT6 * 128 E5
HOO/HM ME3 * 43 J7
RASHW TN26 303 N4
RHAM ME8 102 F3
RSIT ME9 118 C3
SIT ME10 227 N12
WALD ME5 * 115 G4
Willow Ter EYN DA4 * 93 M5
PGE/AN SE20 * 69 J5
Willow Tree Cl HB CT6 129 L4
KEN/WIL TN24 3 K6
Willow Tree Rd RTWE/PEM TN2 22 B9
Willow Tree Wk BMLY BR1 71 J5
Willowtree Wy
STRHM/NOR SW16 68 B5
Willow V CHST BR7 72 B3
Willow Wk DART DA1 * 51 M3
MEO DA13 239 L3
ORP BR6 90 C6
RTWE/PEM TN2 197 H5
STHWK SE1 24 F3
Willow Wy HDCN TN27 301 J6
MAID/SHEP ME15 13 K7
MARG CT9 14 B8
SYD SE26 45 J8
WSTB CT5 127 K5
Willow Waye RDV CT15 272 E6
Willow Wents WBY/YAL ME18 241 Q8
Willow Wood Crs SNWD SE25 86 F2
Willow Wood Rd MEO DA13 239 L3
Willrose Crs ABYW SE2 29 J4
Willshaw St NWCR SE14 26 B7
Willson's Rd RAM CT11 16 F7
Wilman Rd STH/RUST TN4 196 D6
Wilmar Gdns WWKM BR4 88 C4
Wilmar Wy BGR/WK TN15 136 E6
Wilmington Av ORP BR6 91 K5
Wilmington Court Rd
RDART DA2 51 H8
Wilmington Wy RHAM ME8 102 C3
Wilmot Cl PECK SE15 * 25 H6
Wilmot Rd DART DA1 51 J3
Wilmott Pl SWCH CT13 253 N7
Wilmount St WOOL/PLUM SE18 28 C3
Wilson Av DEAL CT14 209 G6
ROCH ME1 100 E4
Wilson Cl KEN/WIL TN24 3 M6
MAID/SHEP ME15 167 M6
RTON TN11 188 B8
SAND/SEL CR2 86 E8
Wilson Gv BERM/RHTH SE16 25 J1
Wilson La EYN DA4 77 G6
Wilson Rd CMBW SE5 24 E7
TONN TN10 189 H8
Wilsons La MAID/SHEP ME15 258 F1
Wilsons Wy MEO DA13 239 L2
Wiltie Gdns FOLKN CT19 11 H4
Wilton Cl DEAL CT14 209 J4
Wilton Dr DIT/AY ME20 139 J5
Wilton Rd ABYW SE2 29 K2
FOLKN CT19 10 E3
MSTR CT12 182 C4

Wilton Ter *SIT* ME10 * 119 J4
Wiltshire Cl *RDART* DA2 ....52 E5
Wiltshire *WALD* ME5 ....K5
Wiltshire Av *BRXN/ST* SW9 ......
ORP BR6 ....91 H3
THHTH CR7 ....68 B7
Wiltshire Wy
MAID/SHEP ME15 ....167 K5
RTWE/PEM TN2 ....197 G6
Wimbart Rd
BRXS/STRHM SW2 *
Wimborne Av *STMC/STPC* BR5 ...73 A5
Wimborne Cl *LEE/GVPK* SE12 .....47 G3
Wimborne Pl *MSTR* CT12 ....16 C2
Wimborne Wy *BECK* BR3 ....69 L7
Wimbourne Dr *RHAM* ME8 ....102 E7
Wimpole Cl *HAYES* BR2 ....71 K8
Winans Wk *BRXN/ST* SW9 ....24 B8
Winch Cl *CRBK* TN17 ....298 G10
Winchcomb Gdns
ELTH/MOT SE9 ....47 M1
Wincheap *CANT* CT1 ....4 C8
Wincheap Rbt *CANT* CT1 ....4 C8
Winchelsea Av *BXLYHN* DA7 ......30 A6
Winchelsea Cl *DVW* CT17 * 217 J2
Winchelsea Rd *DVW* CT17 ....217 J2
RYE TN31 ....225 G4
WALD ME5 ....101 J8
Winchelsea St *DVW* CT17 ....217 J2
Winchelsea Ter *DVW* CT17 ....217 J2
Winchester Cl *HAYES* BR2 ....71 G1
LBTH SE11 * 24 C3
Winchester Crs *GVE* DA12 ....55 J4
Winchester Gdns *CANT* CT1 * 5 G8
Winchester Ms *DEAL* CT14 ....209 H8
Winchester Ov *SEV* TN13 * 27 J7
Winchester Pk *HAYES* BR2 * 71 G7
Winchester Pl
MAID/BEAR ME14 * 13 H2
Winchester Rd *BXLYHN* DA7 ....29 L8
HAWK TN18 ....312 D7
HAYES BR2 ....71 G7
ORP BR6 ....91 K7
TONN TN10 ....195 G1
Winchester Wy *RHAM* ME8 ....103 H5
Winch Rd *RSIT* ME9 * 145 L3
Winch's Garth *STPH/PW* TN2 ......282 A4
Wincliff Rd *TON* TN9 ....194 E5
Wincott Pde *LBTH* SE11 * 24 B3
Wincott St *LBTH* SE11 ....24 B3
Wincrofts Dr *ELTH/MOT* SE9 ......48 D3
Windall Cl *NRWD* SE19 ....69 H5
Windermere *FAV* ME15 ....149 M3
Windermere Av *RAM* CT11 ....16 A5
ORP BR6 ....90 C6
Windermere Cl *DART* DA1 ....51 J6
ORP BR6 ....90 C6
Windermere Dr *RHAM* ME8 ....102 E8
Windermere Gdns
RCANTE CT3 ....251 Q11
Windermere Gv *SIT* ME10 ....119 J4
Windermere Rd *BXLYHN* DA7 ......30 D8
CROY/NA CR0 ....87 G2
WWKM BR4 ....88 F5
Windfield Cl *SYD* SE26 ....69 L1
Windham Av *CROY/NA* CR0 ....105 J4
Wind Hl *HDCN* TN27 ....263 P6
Windhover Wy *GVE* DA12 ....79 M1
Winding Hl *FAV* ME15 ....246 E3
Windlass Rd *DEPT* SE8 ....25 M3
Windley Cl *FSTH* SE23 ....45 K7
Windmill Av *MSTR* CT12 ....182 E2
Windmill Cl *BERM/RHTH* SE16 * ..25 H3
CANT CT1 ....5 L4
KEN/WIL TN24 ....2 L7
LEW SE13 * 26 C4
RCANTW CT4 ....175 H8
STRD ME2 ....82 C4
Windmill Ct *RMAID* ME17 ....259 N4
Windmill Dr *HAYES* BR2 ....89 K7
Windmill Gv *CROY/NA* CR0 ....86 D3
Windmill Hts
MAID/BEAR ME14 * 168 C7
Windmill Hl *BGR/WK* TN15 ....241 K2
RMAID ME17 ....261 M9
STPH/PW TN12 ....
Windmill La East
E/WMAL ME19 ....138 C7
Windmill La West
E/WMAL ME19 ....138 B7
Windmill Pde *RAM* CT11 * 16 F7
Windmill Pk *BGR/WK* TN15 ....241 K2
Windmill Pl *RAM* CT11 * 16 A6
Windmill Quay Rd *IOS* ME12 ......228 G4
Windmill Ri *IOS* ME12 ....65 M7
Windmill Rd *CANT* CT1 ....5 M5
CROY/NA CR0 ....86 D3
GILL ME7 ....7 J7
HB CT6 ....129 H7
RSEV TN14 ....185 K3
SIT ME10 ....162 M4
WSTB CT5 ....126 E6
Windmill Rw *LBTH* SE11 * 24 B4
Windmill St *GVE* DA12 ....55 J5
HYTHE CT21 ....222 C4
RTWE/PEM TN2 ....23 K6
STRD ME2 ....82 C4
Windmill Vw *MSTR* CT9 * 15 J3
Windmill Wk *MSTR* CT12 ....182 E4
STHWK SE1 * 24 B1
Windrose Cl *BERM/RHTH* SE16 ....25 L1
Windrush La *FSTH* SE23 ....45 L8
Windsor Av *CDW/CHF* RM16 ......34 C1
CHAT ME4 ....6 D1
MARG CT9 ....15 L6
Windsor Cl *BRDST* CT10 ....179 H8
CHST BR7 ....72 C2
MAID/BEAR ME14 * 13 K1
WNWD SE27 ....68 D1
Windsor Ct *MARG* CT9 * 15 L7
MARG CT9 * 178 F2
Windsor Dr *DART* DA1 ....51 H4
ORP BR6 ....107 H1
SIT ME10 ....119 J4
Windsor Gdns *HB* CT6 ....128 C6
IOS ME12 ....230 C2
Windsor Gv *WNWD* SE27 ....68 D1
Windsor Ms *CAT* SE6 ....46 D6
NROM TN28 ....331 K5
Windsor Rd *BXLYHS* DA6 ....49 M2
CANT CT1 ....171 M3
GILL ME7 ....7 J4
GVE DA12 ....79 J2
MSTR CT12 ....182 A6
TONN TN10 * 188 C3
Windsor Wk *CMBW* SE5 ....24 E8
Windspoint Dr *PECK* SE15 * 25 H5
Windward Rd *ROCH* ME1 ....100 D4
Windy Rdg *BMLY* BR1 ....71 M5
Windyridge *GILL* ME7 ....101 M4
Winfield La *BGR/WK* TN15 ....240 D7

Winford Ms *ROCH* ME1 ....100 B3
Winfreds Cl *DVW* CT17 ....314 D6
Wingate Rd *FOLKN* CT19 ....220 E6
SCUP DA14 ....K2
Wingfield *GRAYS* RM17 ....34 A4
Wingfield Ms *PECK* SE15 * 45 H1
Wingfield Rd *GVW* DA11 ....55 G3
Wingfield St *PECK* SE15 ....45 H1
Wingham Cl *MAID/SHEP* ME15 ...168 A4
RHAM ME8 ....102 F2
Wingham Rd *RCANTE* CT3 ....251 N1
Wingham Well La *RCANTE* CT3 ....251 N1
Wingmore Rd *HNHL* SE24 ....44 D1
Wing Rd *IOS* ME12 ....230 G4
Wingrove Dr
MAID/BEAR ME14 ....141 M8
STRD ME2 ....19 K3
Wingrove Hl *DVW* CT17 ....212 F7
Wingrove Rd *CAT* SE6 ....46 F7
Winifred Av *MSTR* CT12 ....179 L8
Winifred Rd *DART* DA1 ....51 J3
ERITH DA8 ....30 F4
MAID/SHEP ME15 ....168 A2
Winlaton Rd *BMLY* BR1 ....70 E1
Winn Common Rd
WOOL/PLUM SE18 ....28 F5
Winnipeg Cl *DVE/WH* CT16 ....213 J6
Winnipeg Dr *ORP* BR6 ....107 L1
Winn Rd *LEE/GVPK* SE12 ....47 H6
Winser Rd *CRBK* TN17 ....314 F8
Winsford Rd *CAT* SE6 ....46 A3
Winstanley Crs *RAM* CT11 ....17 G2
Winstanley Rd *IOS* ME12 ....64 D3
Winston Av *E/WMAL* ME19 ....164 C2
Winston Cl *CANT* CT1 ....5 H6
GRH DA9 ....53 G4
Winston Ct *BRCH* CT7 ....176 D5
Winston Dr *STRD* ME2 ....82 B5
Winstone Scott Av *DVW* CT17 ....199 M1
Winston Gdns *HB* CT6 ....129 L5
Winston Rd *STRD* ME2 ....81 L8
Winterage La *RFOLK* CT18 ....292 C10
Winterborne Av *ORP* BR6 ....90 E6
Winterbourne Rd *CAT* SE6 ....46 A6
THHTH CR7 ....68 B8
Winterbrook Rd *HNHL* SE24 ....44 D4
Winter Dr *RFOLK* CT18 ....292 G12
Winterfield La *E/WMAL* ME19 ....138 C7
Wintergreen Cl *CHAT* ME4 ....83 K4
Winterstoke Crs *RAM* CT11 ....183 K5
Winterstoke Rd *CAT* SE6 ....46 A6
Winterstoke Wy *RAM* CT11 ....17 M3
Winton Av *RCANTE* CT3 ....269 P2
Winton Cl *DUL* SE21 ....45 G8
Winton Rd *ORP* BR6 ....90 C7
Winton Wy *STRHM/NOR* SW16 ....68 B2
Wireless Rd *BH/WHM* TN16 ....132 C1
The Wirrals *WALD* ME5 ....115 H1
Wirral Wood Cl *CHST* BR7 ....72 B3
Wiseacre *RRTW* TN3 ....296 B10
Wise's La *BGR/WK* TN15 ....238 D3
Wishart Rd *BKHTH/KID* SE3 ....27 L7
The Wish *RASHW* TN26 ....317 N3
Wish Ward *RYE* TN31 ....225 G4
Wisley Rd *STMC/STPC* BR5 ....73 K4
Wistaria Cl *ORP* BR6 ....90 C5
Wisteria Gdns *SWLY* BR8 ....74 E6
Wisteria Rd *LEW* SE13 ....46 E2
Witches La *SEV* TN13 ....161 H1
Witham Rd *PGE/AN* SE20 ....69 K7
Witham Wy *STRD* ME2 ....18 D4
Withens Ct *STMC/STPC* BR5 * 73 K4
Witherby Cl *SAND/SEL* CR2 ....86 F8
Witherston Wy *ELTH/MOT* SE9 ...48 F3
Witham Rd *RRTW* TN3 ....199 H1
Witley Crs *CROY/NA* CR0 ....105 H1
Witney Pth *FSTH* SE23 * 45 L8
Wittersham Cl *WALD* ME5 ....101 J8
Wittersham La *RYE* TN31 ....327 L9
CRBK TN17 ....326 B1
TENT TN30 ....315 K12
TENT TN30 ....327 L2
Wivenhoe *ASH* TN23 ....204 B8
Wivenhoe Cl *PECK* SE15 ....45 H1
RHAM ME8 ....103 H3
Wiverton Rd *SYD* SE26 ....69 K3
Wodehouse Cl *PECK* SE15 ....25 G7
Wodehouse Rd *DART* DA1 ....52 B2
Wokindon Rd *CDW/CHF* RM16 ....35 J2
Woldham Pl *HAYES* BR2 ....71 J8
Woldham Rd *HAYES* BR2 ....71 J8
Woldingham Av *CTHM* CR3 ....130 A6
Wolds Dr *ORP* BR6 ....90 B7
Wolfe Cl *HAYES* BR2 * 89 H2
Wolfe Cl *CHARL* SE7 ....27 L4
Wolfe Rd *MAIDW* ME16 ....166 C3
Wolfington Rd *WNWD* SE27 ....44 F2
Wolfram Cl *LEW* SE13 ....46 F3
Wolf's Hl *OXTED* RH8 ....185 H1
Wolf's Rd *OXTED* RH8 ....158 A8
Wolfs Wd *OXTED* RH8 ....185 H2
Wollaston Cl *RHAM* ME8 ....116 A2
WALW SE17 * 24 C1
Wollaston Ct *DEAL* CT14 ....209 H8
Wolseley Av *HB* CT6 ....128 C5
Wolseley Pl *KEN/WIL* TN24 * 2 A1
Wolseley Rd *STH/RUST* TN4 ......196 F4
Wolseley St *STHWK* SE1 ....25 G1
Wolsey Cl *ELTH/MOT* SE9 * 48 A4
Wolsey Crs *CROY/NA* CR0 ....105 J4
Wolsey Ms *ORP* BR6 * 91 G7
Wolsley Cl *DART* DA1 ....50 F2
Wolvercote Rd *ABYW* SE2 ....29 L1
Wombwell Gdns *GVW* DA11 ....54 F2
Wood Av *FOLKN* CT19 ....220 A6
Woodbank Rd *BMLY* BR1 ....70 E4
Woodbastwick Rd *SYD* SE26 ......69 L3
Woodberry Dr *SIT* ME10 ....120 C5
Woodberry Gv *BXLY* DA5 ....50 B8
Woodbine Gv *PGE/AN* SE20 ....69 J7
Woodbine Rd *BFN/LL* DA15 ....48 B6
Woodbridge Dr
MAID/SHEP ME15 ....166 A8
Woodbrook Rd *HDCN* TN27 ....264 D6
Woodbrook Rd *ABYW* SE2 ....29 H5
Woodbury Av *EGRIN* RH19 ....274 A12
CROY/NA CR0 ....87 G5
STH/RUST TN4 ....196 E6
Woodbury Gdns *BMLY* BR1 ....47 J8
Woodbury La *TENT* TN30 ....315 M2
Woodbury Park Gdns
STH/RUST TN4 ....23 G1
Woodbury Rd *HAWK* TN18 ....312 F5
WALD ME5 ....114 F4
Woodchurch Cl *BFN/LL* DA15 .....48 B5
WALD ME5 ....101 J8
Woodchurch Crs *RHAM* ME8 ......102 D3

Woodchurch Dr *BMLY* BR1 ....71 L4
Woodchurch Rd *BRCH* CT7 ....181 L5
RASHW TN26 ....303 N5
RASHW TN26 ....317 N5
Wood Cl *BXLY* DA5 ....50 F1
DIT/AY ME20 ....139 M5
Woodclyffe Dr *CHST* BR7 ....72 B6
Woodcock La *CRBK* TN17 ....313 N6
RMAID ME17 ....262 G5
Woodcocks *HDCN* TN27 ....283 L4
Woodcombe Crs *FSTH* SE23 ......45 K6
Woodcote Cl *WSTB* CT5 ....127 L4
Woodcote Av *THHTH* CR7 ....68 A3
Woodcote Dr *ORP* BR6 ....90 E7
Woodcote Pl *WNWD* SE27 * 68 C2
Wood Cottage La *FOLKN* CT19 ....219 L6
Woodcourt *ELTH/MOT* SE9 ....48 D4
Woodcroft Ms *DEPT* SE8 ....25 L5
Woodcut Rd *THHTH* CR7 ....86 C1
Woodcut *MAID/BEAR* ME14 ....141 H5
Woodcutters Av
CDW/CHF RM16 ....34 D1
Wood Dene *PECK* SE15 * 25 J7
Wood Dr *CHST* BR7 ....71 M3
SEV TN13 ....27 D8
Wooden Bridge Ter
WNWD SE27 * 44 E7
Woodend *NRWD* SE19 ....68 D3
Wood End *SWLY* BR8 ....74 A8
Woodfall Dr *DART* DA1 ....51 G2
Woodfarrs *CMBW* SE5 ....44 E2
Woodfield Av *FOLKN* CT19 ....219 L6
WNWD SE19 ....68 D4
Woodfield Rd *TON* TN9 ....194 D3
Woodfields *SEV* TN13 ....161 L6
Woodford Av *MAID/SHEP* ME16 ..166 E1
Woodford Gv *E/WMAL* ME19 ......164 C1
Woodford Rd *MAIDW* ME16 ....166 C1
Woodgate *RCANTW* CT4 ....269 P2
Woodgate Cl *FAV* ME13 ....149 K1
Woodgate La *RSIT* ME9 ....118 C1
Woodgate Wy *TON* TN9 ....195 H5
Woodhall Av *DUL* SE21 ....45 G8
Woodhall Ter *QBOR* ME11 * 64 D8
Woodham Rd *CAT* SE6 ....46 D8
Woodhatch Cl *ORP* BR6 ....90 A1
Woodhayes Rd *WIM/MER* SW19 ..
Wood Hl *CANTW/ST* CT2 ....153 M7
Woodhill *WOOL/PLUM* SE18 ....27 M3
Woodhill Pk *RTWE/PEM* TN2 ......197 M7
Woodhouse Cl *EDUL* SE22 ....45 G8
Woodhurst *WALD* ME5 ....114 E1
Woodhurst Av *STMC/STPC* BR5 ...90 D2
Woodhurst Cl *STRD* ME2 ....18 F7
Woodhurst La *OXTED* RH8 ....184 F1
Woodhurst Pk *OXTED* RH8 ....157 K8
Woodhurst Rd *ABYW* SE2 ....29 H5
Woodknoll Dr *CHST* BR7 ....72 A5
Woodland Av *BRCH* CT7 ....176 D7
Woodland Dr *OXTED* RH8 ....157 J8
E/WMAL ME19 ....138 B5
HART DA3 ....78 D7
NRWD SE19 ....68 F3
STH/RUST TN4 ....196 E6
Woodland Gv *GNWCH* SE10 ....26 F5
Woodland Hl *NRWD* SE19 ....68 F3
Woodland Ri *BGR/WK* TN15 ......162 D1
OXTED RH8 ....157 M12
Woodland Rd *HB* CT6 ....128 C7
NRWD SE19 ....68 F3
RFOLK CT18 ....291 K10
STH/RUST TN4 ....196 E6
THHTH CR7 ....68 A8
Woodlands *CANTW/ST* CT2 ....153 G6
FAV ME15 ....151 K2
MAID/BEAR ME14 * 13 G7
RTWE/PEM TN2 ....278 C10
STPH/PW TN12 ....279 J2
WALD ME5 ....115 H3
Woodlands Av *BFN/LL* DA15 ......47 M8
SNOD ME6 ....86 G5
Woodlands Cl *BMLY* BR1 ....72 A4
CDW/CHF RM16 ....34 F2
MAID/BEAR ME14 * 141 A6
SWLY BR8 ....74 D6
WBY/YAL ME18 ....165 H5
Woodlands Ct
STH/RUST TN4 ....196 D3
Woodlands Dr *HYTHE* CT21 ....223 H1
Woodlands La *GVE* DA12 ....80 E2
Woodlands Pde
DIT/AY ME20 * 139 L5
Woodlands Pk *BXLY* DA5 ....74 E1
Woodlands Park Rd
BKHTH/KID SE3 ....26 F5
Woodlands Ri *SWLY* BR8 ....75 G6
Woodlands Rd *BMLY* BR1 ....71 M4
BXLYHN DA7 ....49 M1
DIT/AY ME20 ....139 K4
GILL ME7 ....102 A3
KEN/WIL TN24 ....2 B4
RCANTE CT3 ....251 M9
SIT ME10 ....120 C6
TON TN9 ....194 D7
Woodlands St *LEW* SE13 ....46 H5
Woodlands Ter *GILL* ME7 * 102 A2
SWLY BR8 * 92 D2
The Woodlands *CMBW* SE5 * 24 C1
LEW SE13 ....46 E6
NRWD SE19 ....68 A1
ORP BR6 ....108 A1
Woodlands Vw *TENT* TN30 ....326 F11
Woodland Wy *ABYW* SE2 ....29 L4
BRDST CT10 ....179 K4
CANTW/ST CT2 ....171 L1
CROY/NA CR0 ....87 H4
E/WMAL ME19 ....138 B5
LYDD TN29 ....321 H5
MAID/BEAR ME14 ....141 J6
STMC/STPC BR5 ....72 D8
SWCH CT13 ....253 P5
WWKM BR4 ....88 D6
Wood La *ASH* TN23 ....204 F8
CRBK TN17 ....300 B10

RDART DA2 ....53 G8
Woodlark Rd *CHAT* ME4 ....83 J4
Woodlea *DIT/AY* ME20 ....138 F3
HART DA3 ....78 D7
KEN/WIL TN24 ....2 D7
Woodlea Dr *HAYES* BR2 ....88 F1
Woodleas *MAID/WK* ME15 ....166 A3
Woodley Rd *ORP* BR6 ....91 K2
Wood Lodge Gdns *BMLY* BR1 .....71 M4
Wood Lodge Gra *SEV* TN13 * 21 J7
Woodman Rd *WSTB* CT5 ....127 L4
Woodmere *ELTH/MOT* SE9 ....48 L5
Woodmere Av *CROY/NA* CR0 ......87 L3
Woodmere Cl *CROY/NA* CR0 * 87 L3
Woodmere Gdns *CROY/NA* CR0 ...87 L3
Woodmere Wy *BECK* BR3 ....88 E1
Woodmount *SWLY* BR8 ....92 E3
Woodnesborough La
SWCH CT13 ....253 N6
Woodnesborough Rd
SWCH CT13 ....253 R1
Woodpecker Dr *RSIT* ME9 ....227 M9
Woodpecker Gld *RHAM* ME8 * 102 G3
HART DA3 ....78 D7
ORP BR6 ....91 H8
RHAM ME8 ....102 D7
Woodpecker Ms *LEW* SE13 ....46 E2
Woodpecker Mt *CROY/NA* CR0 ...104 D3
Woodquest Av *HNHL* SE24 ....44 C3
Wood Ride *STMC/STPC* BR5 ....72 E8
Wood Rd *BH/WHM* TN16 ....132 B4
HYTHE CT21 ....223 H2
Woodrow *WOOL/PLUM* SE18 ......27 M3
Woodrow Cha *HB* CT6 ....129 H8
Woodruff Pl *RHAM* ME8 ....103 L1
Woodrush Pl *CHAT* ME4 ....83 J4
Woodsgate Wy
RTWE/PEM TN2 ....197 L7
Woods Hl *RCANTW* CT4 ....267 P8
Woodside *ASH* TN23 ....204 B8
FAV ME15 * 151 J7
MEO DA13 ....259 L5
ORP BR6 ....91 H8
RHAM ME8 ....102 D7
Woodside Av *CHST* BR7 ....72 D2
SNWD SE25 ....87 G3
Woodside Cl *BXLYHN* DA7 ....50 E2
DVE/WH CT16 ....212 F5
Woodside Court Rd
CROY/NA CR0 ....87 H3
Woodside Crs *SIT* ME10 ....119 J4
Woodside Dr *RDART* DA2 ....74 F1
Woodside Gdns *SWLY* BR8 ....74 F1
Woodside Gn *CROY/NA* CR0 ....87 H2
Woodside Pde *BFN/LL* DA15 * 48 B6
Woodside Pk *SNWD* SE25 ....87 H2
Woodside Rd *BFN/LL* DA15 ....48 B6
BMLY BR1 ....89 M3
BXLYHN DA7 ....50 E2
CANTW/ST CT2 ....173 G2
MAID/SHEP ME15 ....167 K6
RTWE/PEM TN2 ....160 C2
SEV TN13 ....21 H3
SNWD SE25 ....87 J2
TON TN9 ....194 E6
Woodside Wy *CROY/NA* CR0 ......87 K2
Woods Ley *RCANTE* CT3 ....236 A11
Wood's Pl *DVW* CT17 ....213 J7
STHWK SE1 * 24 F2
Wood's Rd *PECK* SE15 ....25 J7
Woodstock Av *BXLY* DA5 ....50 A6
Woodstock Gdns *BECK* BR3 ....70 C5
Woodstock Rd *CROY/NA* CR0 * ...86 D3
DEAL CT14 ....209 K5
SIT ME10 ....119 M8
STRD ME2 ....18 D4
Woodstock Wy
KEN/WIL ME7 ....202 G1
Wood St *GILL* ME7 ....6 F1
GRAYS RM17 ....34 D5
IOS ME12 ....64 D3
RSIT ME9 ....147 G3
RTW TN1 ....23 H4
STRD ME2 ....99 G3
WSTB CT5 ....75 K5
Woodsyre *SYD* SE26 ....68 G6
Wood V *FSTH* SE23 ....45 J6
Woodvale Av *SNWD* SE25 ....69 H5
WSTB CT5 ....127 K5
Wood Vw *GRAYS* RM17 ....34 F3
Wood View Cl *BGR/WK* TN15 .....111 K2
Woodview Cl *ORP* BR6 ....90 D1
SAND/SEL CR2 ....104 C4
Woodview Crs *RTON* TN11 ....188 B4
Woodview Ri *STRD* ME2 ....82 A4
Woodville Cl *CANT* CT1 ....4 C7
LEE/GVPK SE12 ....47 L1
Woodville Gv *WELL* DA16 ....49 H1
Woodville Pl *GVE* DA12 ....55 J5
Woodville Rd *MAID/SHEP* ME15 ..13 H8
MSTR CT12 ....182 A6
THHTH CR7 ....68 A3
Woodville St
WOOL/PLUM SE18 ....27 M3
Woodward Cl *GRAYS* RM17 ....34 C3
Woodwarde Rd *EDUL* SE22 ....44 C3
Woodward Hts *GRAYS* RM17 ......34 C3
Woodward Ter *GRH* DA9 ....52 F4
Wood Wy *ORP* BR6 ....90 B7
Wood Whf *GNWCH* SE10 ....26 C3
Woodyard La *DUL* SE21 ....44 F8
The Woodyard *DEAL* CT14 * 209 L3
Woodyates Rd *LEE/GVPK* SE12 ...47 L6
Woolacombe Rd
BKHTH/KID SE3 ....27 K8
Woolaston Cl
MAID/SHEP ME15 ....167 G4
Woolcomb Cl *RHAM* ME8 ....103 J1
Woolcomber St *DVE/WH* CT16 * ..8 C4
Wooldeys Rd *RHAM* ME8 ....103 G3
Wooler St *WALW* SE17 ....24 F7
Woollett Rd *SIT* ME10 ....119 J4
Woollett Cl *DART* DA1 ....51 H2
Woollett Rd *MAID/SHEP* ME15 ...13 G3
Woolley Cl *STH/RUST* TN4 ....196 C3
Woolley Rd *MAID/SHEP* ME15 ....168 A5
STH/RUST TN4 ....196 C4
Woolmer Dr *KEN/WIL* TN24 ....205 M4
Woolpack Hl *RFOLK* TN25 ....289 L12
Woolreeds Rd *ASH* TN23 ....204 B8
Woolstapers Wy
BERM/RHTH SE16 ....25 H2
Woolwich Church St
CHARL SE7 ....27 L3
Woolwich Cl *WALD* ME5 ....101 H6
Woolwich Common
WOOL/PLUM SE18 ....28 B6
Woolwich Foot Tnl
CAN/RD E16 ....28 B1

Woolwich High St
WOOL/PLUM SE18 ....28 B2
Woolwich Manorway
CAN/RD E16 ....28 C1
Woolwich New Rd
WOOL/PLUM SE18 ....28 B5
Wootton La *RDV* CT15 ....292 H3
Wopsle Cl *ROCH* ME1 ....100 E6
Worbeck Rd *PGE/AN* SE20 ....69 J7
Worcester Av *E/WMAL* ME19 .....164 B5
Worcester Cl *CROY/NA* CR0 ......88 A5
GRH DA9 ....53 J2
IOS ME12 ....65 K7
MEO DA13 ....79 G4
STRD ME2 ....18 B1
Worcester Dr *SIT* ME10 ....119 L3
Worcester La *RCANTW* CT4 ......174 F2
Worcester Rd
MAID/SHEP ME15 ....167 L6
Wordsworth Cl *TIL* RM18 ....35 K8
WALD ME5 ....101 K6
Wordsworth Gdns
RCANTE CT3 ....251 Q11
Wordsworth Rd
MAID/BEAR ME14 ....141 G6
PGE/AN SE20 ....69 L4
STHWK SE1 * 25 G3
WELL DA16 ....28 F7
Wordsworth Wy *DART* DA1 ....52 B2
DIT/AY ME20 ....139 H1
Worgan St *BERM/RHTH* SE16 ....25 L1
LBTH SE11 * 24 A4
Workhouse La
MAID/SHEP ME15 ....258 H1
Workhouse Rd *E/WMAL* ME19 ....239 R9
FAV ME13 ....245 Q8
RMAID ME17 ....260 H5
World's End *RSIT* ME9 ....147 M2
Worlds End La *ORP* BR6 ....107 M2
Worleys Dr *ORP* BR6 ....90 E7
Worlingham Rd *EDUL* SE22 ....45 G2
Wormdale Hl *RSIT* ME9 ....118 C6
Wormdale Rd *RSIT* ME9 ....118 B5
Wormdale Ct
MAID/SHEP ME15 * 167 H4
Worships Hl *SEV* TN13 ....20 A2
Worsley Bridge Rd *CAT* SE6 ......70 A2
Worth Cl *ORP* BR6 ....91 G7
Worthing Cl *WTHK* RM20 ....33 M5
Worthington Dr *DVE/WH* CT16 ...8 C4
Worth La *FOLK* CT20 ....223 H2
Wortley Rd *CROY/NA* CR0 ....86 B3
Wotton Cl *MAID/SHEP* ME15 .....167 M8
Wotton Gn *STMC/STPC* BR5 ......73 L8
Wotton Rd *ASH* TN23 ....204 B8
Wouldham Rd *ROCH* ME1 ....97 K7
WTHK RM20 ....33 M5
Wouldham Ter
Wraightsfield Av *LYDD* TN29 ......321 J7
Wraik Hl *WSTB* CT5 ....152 C1
Wrangleden Cl
MAID/SHEP ME15 ....167 M8
Wrangleden Rd
MAID/SHEP ME15 ....167 M8
Wrangling La *MEO* DA13 ....112 A2
Wrekin Rd *WOOL/PLUM* SE18 ....28 D6
Wren Cl *DIT/AY* ME20 ....139 G4
SAND/SEL CR2 ....104 C4
STMC/STPC BR5 ....73 M4
Wren Ms *LEW* SE13 * 46 F2
Wren Rd *CMBW* SE5 ....24 E7
Wrens Ct *RSIT* ME9 * 145 K1
Wrens Ct *GVW* DA11 ....73 C6
Wrens Cross
MAID/SHEP ME15 * 13 G6
Wrens Rd *RSIT* ME9 ....145 G3
Wrentham Av *HB* CT6 ....128 C3
Wrenthorpe Rd *BMLY* BR1 ....70 F1
Wren Wk *TIL* RM18 ....35 K8
Wren Wy *WALD* ME5 ....101 W3
Wrickelmarsh Rd
BKHTH/KID SE3 ....27 K7
Wrigglesworth St *NWCR* SE14 ...25 L6
Wright Cl *LEW* SE13 ....46 F2
RHAM ME8 ....102 D3
Wrights Rd *SNWD* SE25 ....69 G4
Wright's Wy *IOS* ME12 ....229 M5
Wrotham Hill Rd
BGR/WK TN15 ....238 C7
Wrotham Rd *BGR/WK* TN15 ....240 F1
BRDST CT10 ....183 L1
GVW DA11 ....54 F1
MEO DA13 ....79 K3
WELL DA16 ....29 K7
Wrotham Water La
E/WMAL ME19 ....239 K9
Wrotham Water Rd
E/WMAL ME19 ....239 J9
Wrottesley Rd
WOOL/PLUM SE18 ....28 D5
Wroxton Rd *PECK* SE15 ....25 J8
Wulfere Wy *SNOD* ME6 ....86 G2
Wulfred Wy *BGR/WK* TN15 ....137 Q4
Wyatt Park Rd
BRXS/STRHM SW2 ....44 A7
Wyatt Pl *STRD* ME2 ....18 A4
Wyatt Rd *DART* DA1 ....51 G1
Wyatt St *MAID/BEAR* ME14 ......13 H4
Wybourne Ri *RTWE/PEM* TN2 ....201 J3
Wychbury La *HOO/HM* ME3 ....59 P2
Wych Elm Wy *HYTHE* CT21 ......307 R12
Wycherley Cl *BKHTH/KID* SE3 ....27 G6
Wycherley Crs *DVE/WH* CT16 ....213 J8
Wychwood Av *THHTH* CR7 ....68 C7
Wycliffe Cl *WELL* DA16 ....29 J5
Wycliffe Rw *GVW* DA11 ....55 G6
Wychurst Rd *CROY/NA* CR0 ......87 H3
Wydeville Manor Rd
LEE/GVPK SE12 ....71 J1
Wye Cl *ORP* BR6 ....91 G2
Wye Gdns *MARG* CT9 ....179 J3
Wye Rd *BGR/WK* TN15 ....240 F1
GVE DA12 ....55 L2
RASHE TN25 ....203 J1
TONN TN10 ....188 F3
Wykeham Cl *GVE* DA12 ....227 N2
QBOR ME11 ....
Wykeham Gv *RMAID* ME17 ....169 H6
Wykeham Rd *SIT* ME10 ....120 C5
Wykeham St *STRD* ME2 ....82 C5
Wyke Manor Rd
MAID/BEAR ME14 ....13 G4
Wyke Rd *CHAT* ME4 ....100 F3
Wyles St *GILL* ME7 ....7 J1
Wyles St *FSTH* SE23 ....45 J5
Wylie Rd *HOO/HM* ME3 ....59 M7
Wynan Rd *POP/IOD* E14 ....26 M1
Wyncham Av *BFN/LL* DA15 ....48 F6

Wyncote Wy SAND/SEL CR2 104 C3
Wyncroft Cl BMLY BR1 72 A7
Wyndcliff Rd CHARL SE7 27 J5
Wyndham Av MARG CT9 15 M5
RTON TN11 255 N12
Wyndham Cl ORP BR6 90 D4
RTON TN11 255 N12
Wyndham Est CMBW SE5 24 D6
Wyndham Rd CHAT ME4 100 F3
CMBW SE5 24 D6
DVW CT17 217 J1
Wyndham Wy RASHE TN25 202 C7
The Wynd HDCN TN27 264 C4
Wyndy La RASHE TN25 202 C7
Wyneham Rd HNHL SE24 44 E3
Wynell Rd FSTH SE23 45 L8
Wyness Ct STRD ME2 * 19 G1
Wynford Gv STMC/STPC BR5 73 J7
Wynford Pl BELV DA17 30 B5
Wynford Wy ELTH/MOT SE9 48 A8
Wynne Rd BRXN/ST SW9 24 B8
Wynn Rd WSTB CT5 127 H2
Wynn's Av BFN/LL DA15 49 H3
Wynnstow Pk OXTED RH8 185 G1
Wynton Gdns SNWD SE25 86 F1
Wynyard Ter LBTH SE11 * 24 A4
The Wytchlings RMAID ME17 261 L3
Wytherling Cl
MAID/BEAR ME14 142 A8
Wythes Cl BMLY BR1 72 A6
Wythfield Rd ELTH/MOT SE9 48 A4
Wyvern Cl DART DA1 51 K5
ORP BR6 91 J6
SIT ME10 119 M2
SNOD ME6 113 H6
Wyvern Wy KEN/WIL TN24 3 G3
Wyvill Cl RHAM ME8 102 F8

Y

Yalding Cl STRD ME2 82 C4
Yalding Gv STMC/STPC BR5 73 L8
Yalding Hl WBY/YAL ME18 257 R3
Yalding Rd BERM/RHTH SE16 25 H2
Yantlet Dr STRD ME2 81 K6
Yardhurst Gdns MARG CT9 179 J2
Yardley Cl TON TN9 195 G2
Yardley Park Rd TON TN9 194 F2
The Yard RCANTW CT4 270 E4
Yarnton Wy ABYW SE2 29 K1
Yarrow Cl BRDST CT10 183 K2
Yarrow Ct MAID/BEAR ME14 142 A8
Yarrow Rd WALD ME5 114 F1
Yateley St WOOL/PLUM SE18 27 L2
Yates Cl RYE TN31 332 F7
Yaugher La RSIT ME9 117 J2
Yeates Dr SIT ME10 120 B1
Yeats Cl LEW SE13 * 26 E8
Yelsted La MAID/BEAR ME14 115 L6
RSIT ME9 117 H4
Yelsted Rd RSIT ME9 117 H6
Yeoman Dr GILL ME7 102 A4
Yeoman Gdns KEN/WIL TN24 205 L2
STPH/PW TN12 278 H3
Yeoman La MAID/BEAR ME14 168 C2
Yeoman Pk MAID/SHEP ME15 168 B3
Yeoman's Mdw SEV TN13 20 E8
Yeoman St BERM/RHTH SE16 25 M3
Yeoman Wy MAID/SHEP ME15 168 C3
Yeovil Cl ORP BR6 90 F5
Yester Dr CHST BR7 71 M4
Yester Pk CHST BR7 72 A4
Yester Rd CHST BR7 72 A4
Yevele Cl QBOR ME11 64 B8
Yew Cl ASH TN23 204 B1
Yewdale Cl BMLY BR1 70 F3
Yew Rd HOO/HM ME3 83 M2
The Yews GVE DA12 55 L7
Yew Tree Cl BRDST CT10 183 G1
DEAL CT14 * 209 H5
DIT/AY ME20 139 M4
HART DA3 78 E6
RASHE TN25 307 N5
SEV TN13 161 J1
WALD ME5 115 L4
WELL DA16 29 H7
Yew Tree Gdns BRCH CT7 176 D6
CANTW/ST CT2 * 173 H5
Yew Tree Green Rd
STPH/PW TN12 279 R8
Yew Tree Ms DEAL CT14 209 H6
Yewtree Rd BECK BR3 70 A7
Yew Tree Rd LYDD TN29 331 N2
STH/RUST TN4 196 D5
Yoakes La LYDD TN29 330 B5
Yoakley Sq MARG CT9 15 G8
Yoke Cl STRD ME2 * 19 G1
Yokosuka Wy GILL ME7 84 C8
RHAM ME8 102 B1
Yolande Gdns ELTH/MOT SE9 47 M3
Yopps Gn BGR/WK TN15 240 D8
York & Albany Cl DEAL CT14 209 J8
York Av BFN/LL DA15 48 F7
BRDST CT10 183 K1
GILL ME7 7 H5
WALD ME5 114 F2
York Cl CMBW SE5 * 24 D8
York Gv PECK SE15 25 K7
York Hl STRHM/NOR SW16 44 C8
WALD ME5 7 J9
Yorkland Av WELL DA16 49 G2
York Ms FOLKN CT19 * 219 M6
York Pde TONN TN10 188 F7
York Ri ORP BR6 90 F4
York Rd BH/WHM TN16 132 A5
CANT CT1 4 D7
CROY/NA CR0 86 B3
DART DA1 52 A5
DEAL CT14 209 L6
GVE DA12 55 K8
GVW DA11 54 E5
HB CT6 128 E4
KEN/WIL TN24 203 G6
MAID/SHEP ME15 13 K9
ROCH ME1 100 D2
RTW TN1 22 E4
SAND/SEL CR2 104 C4
STHWK SE1 24 A1
TONN TN10 189 G8
York St BRDST CT10 183 L1
DVE/WH CT16 8 D5
RAM CT11 17 K6
York Street Rbt DVW CT17 8 D6
York Ter BRCH CT7 176 E6
ERITH DA8 30 D7
Young Cl DEAL CT14 209 J3
Young's Pl RDV CT15 216 A4
Ypres Ct CANT CT1 172 E8
Ypres Dr SIT ME10 227 N12

Z

Zambra Wy BGR/WK TN15 136 E6
Zampa Rd BERM/RHTH SE16 25 K4
Zangwill Rd BKHTH/KID SE3 27 L7
Zealand Rd CANT CT1 4 E8
Zelah Rd STMC/STPC BR5 91 J3
Zenoria St EDUL SE22 45 G2
Zermatt Rd THHTH CR7 68 D8
Zetland Av GILL ME7 101 M3
Zillah Gdns RHAM ME8 102 C7
Zion Pl GVW DA11 55 J5
MARG CT9 15 H3
THHTH CR7 68 E8
Zion Rd THHTH CR7 68 E8

Index - featured places

AAIS
DART DA1 51 M5
The Abbey Clinic
BELV DA17 30 A4
Abbey Court School
STRD ME2 18 C1
Abbey Primary School
ABYW SE2 29 K2
Abbey (rems of)
ABYW SE2 29 J5
The Abbey School
FAV ME13 149 K4
Abbey Trading Estate
SYD SE26 69 M2
Abbey Wood School
ABYW SE2 29 H2
ABC Cinema
CAT SE6 46 C6
GVE DA12 55 J4
The Academy at Peckham
PECK SE15 25 G7
Acorn Business Centre
MAIDW ME16 166 D3
Acorn Industrial Park
DART DA1 51 G4
Acorn Trading Centre
WTHK RM20 33 M5
Acumen (Anglo School)
NRWD SE19 68 F5
Adamsrill Primary School
FSTH SE23 45 M8
Addey & Stanhope School
NWCR SE14 26 A7
Addington Business Centre
CROY/NA CR0 105 K4
The Addington Golf Club
CROY/NA CR0 104 E3
Addington High School
CROY/NA CR0 105 K6
Addington Palace Golf Club
CROY/NA CR0 104 D1
Addiscombe CC
CROY/NA CR0 87 H6
Adisham CE Primary School
RCANTE CT3 251 M9
Admiral Hyson Industrial Estate
BERM/RHTH SE16 25 J3
Adult Education Centre
CANT CT1 4 F2
DART DA1 52 A5
GILL ME7 7 K3
MARG CT9 14 F5
POP/IOD E14 26 D2
ROCH ME1 19 L7
TON TN9 194 E4
Agora Shopping Centre
PECK SE15 25 H8
Airport Industrial Estate
BH/WHM TN16 132 C1
Albany Centre & Theatre
DEPT SE8 26 A6
Albany Clinic
BFN/LL DA15 73 H1
Albion J & I School
BERM/RHTH SE16 25 K1
Albion Street Health Centre
BERM/RHTH SE16 25 K1
Alderwood Primary School
ELTH/MOT SE9 48 E4
Aldington Primary School
RASHE TN25 305 R8
Alexander McLeod
Primary School ABYW SE2 29 J4
Alexandra Hospital
WALD ME5 115 G5
Alexandra Infant School
PGE/AN SE20 69 L4
Alexandra Junior School
SYD SE26 69 L3
Alfred Salter Primary School
BERM/RHTH SE16 25 L1
Alleyns School
EDUL SE22 44 F3
Allhallows Primary School
HOO/HM ME3 41 M4
Allington Primary School
MAIDW ME16 140 C6
All Saints CE Junior School
NRWD SE19 68 F5
All Saints CE Primary School
BKHTH/KID SE3 26 F8
CHAT ME4 6 F8
MAID/SHEP ME15 13 G6
All Saints Industrial Estate
MARG CT9 14 E6
All Souls CE Primary School
FOLKN CT19 219 M7
Alma Primary School
BERM/RHTH SE16 25 H3
Alscot Road Industrial Estate
STHWK SE1 25 G3
Amherst School
SEV TN13 20 A2
Anchorage Point
Industrial Estate
CHARL SE7 27 K2
Anchor Bay Industrial Estate
ERITH DA8 31 G6
Anchor Business Park
SIT ME10 120 C3
Anchorians All Weather
Sports Club RHAM ME8 103 G4
Anerley School
PGE/AN SE20 69 H5
Angel Centre
DART DA1 51 M4
Angel Indoor Bowling
TON TN9 194 F4
Angel Leisure Centre
TON TN9 194 F4
Angel Walk Shopping Precinct
TON TN9 194 E4
Angerstein Business Park
GNWCH SE10 27 H3
Anglesea Centre
GVW DA11 55 J4
Angley School
CRBK TN17 298 E8
Anthony Roper Primary School
EYN DA4 93 M5
Apiary Business Park
RMAID ME17 260 E3
Applegarth Primary School
CROY/NA CR0 105 G1
Aquarius Golf Club
PECK SE15 45 K3
Archbishop Michael
Ramsey School
CMBW SE5 24 C6
Archbishop's Palace
MAIDW ME16 12 F6
The Archbishops School
CANTW/ST CT2 171 M2
Archbishop Tenisons CE School
CROY/NA CR0 87 G6
Archbishop Tenison's School
VX/NE SW8 24 A5
Archcliffe Fort
DVW CT17 8 C9
Archers Court School
DVE/WH CT16 213 J4
Arches Leisure Centre
GNWCH SE10 26 E5
Arden Business Park
STRD ME2 82 F6
Arden Junior School
GILL ME7 7 L1
Arden Theatre
FAV ME13 149 K2
Arena Essex
WTHK RM20 33 H1
Argent Business Park
QBOR ME11 227 P3
Argyle Shopping Centre
RAM CT11 17 J6
Arklow Trading Estate
NWCR SE14 25 M5
Arlington Square
Shopping Centre MARG CT9 14 D5
Arnhem Wharf Primary School
POP/IOD E14 26 A2
Arnolds Business Park
STPH/PW TN12 257 K8
Arts Centre
BMLY BR1 71 L5
GVE DA12 55 J4
Art School
BECK BR3 87 M1
Ashburton Community School
CROY/NA CR0 87 J3
Ashburton Primary School
CROY/NA CR0 87 J2
Ashfield Farm
RCANTW CT4 268 H11
Ashford Borough Museum
ASH TN23 2 B5
Ashford Business Park
KEN/WIL TN24 205 K5
Ashford Civic Centre
ASH TN23 2 D6
Ashford College
ASH TN23 2 B5
Ashford Golf Club
RASHE TN25 202 C4
Ashford International Hotel
KEN/WIL TN24 202 E7
Ashford Market
KEN/WIL TN24 205 J5
Ashford School
ASH TN23 2 D4
Ashford South CP School
ASH TN23 204 D3
Ashford Town FC
RASHW TN26 304 C5
Ashgrove Trading Estate
BMLY BR1 70 E3
Ashleigh Commercial Estate
CHARL SE7 27 K3
Ashmead Primary School
DEPT SE8 26 B8
Ashmole Primary School
VX/NE SW8 24 A5
Aspen House School
CMBW SE5 24 C5
Assembly Hall Theatre
RTW TN1 23 G5
Associated Newspapers
BERM/RHTH SE16 25 L2
Astor College for the Arts
DVW CT17 217 J1
The Astor of Hever Community
School MAIDW ME16 166 D2
Astor Theatre
DEAL CT14 209 K3
Athelney Primary School
CAT SE6 46 B8
The Atman Clinic
STH/RUST TN4 196 D7
Austin Lodge Golf Club
EYN DA4 110 D3
Avenue Theatre
SIT ME10 120 A6
Avicenna Medical Centre
E/WMAL ME19 138 F3
Axton Chase School
HART DA3 78 A7
Aycliffe County
Primary School
DVW CT17 217 H5
Aylesford Cemetery
DIT/AY ME20 140 A3
Aylesford Primary School
DIT/AY ME20 139 L4
Aylesford Priory
DIT/AY ME20 139 M3
Aylesford School
DIT/AY ME20 139 L4
Aylesham Cemetery
RCANTW CT4 270 G3
The Aylesham Centre
PECK SE15 25 H7
Aylesham Health Centre
RCANTE CT3 251 P12
Aylesham Industrial Estate
RCANTE CT3 271 K1
Aylesham Primary School
RCANTE CT3 251 P12
Aylwin Secondary School
BERM/RHTH SE16 25 G3
Babington House School
CHST BR7 72 A3
Bad Apple Theatre Company
RTW TN1 23 J3
Balfour Infant School
CHAT ME4 100 F4
Balfour Junior School
CHAT ME4 6 A9
Balfour Medical Centre
GRAYS RM17 34 D3
Balgowan Primary School
BECK BR3 69 M6
Ballard Business Park
STRD ME2 18 D8
Balmoral Clinic
GILL ME7 7 K3
Bannockburn Primary School
WOOL/PLUM SE18 29 G3
Bapchild & Tonge CE
Aided School SIT ME10 120 E6
Barham CE Primary School
RCANTW CT4 270 D4
Barham Crematorium
RCANTW CT4 270 H6
Baring Primary School
LEE/GVPK SE12 47 H5
Baring Road Medical Centre
LEE/GVPK SE12 47 H7
Barkantine Clinic
POP/IOD E14 26 B1
Barming Primary School
MAIDW ME16 166 A3
Barnehurst Primary School
BXLYHN DA7 30 D7
Barnehurst Public Pay &
Play Golf Club BXLYHN DA7 50 E1
Barnes Cray Primary School
DART DA1 51 H2
Barnsole Infant School
GILL ME7 101 M1
Barnsole Junior School
GILL ME7 101 M1
Barrington Primary School
BXLYHN DA7 29 L8
Barrow Grove Junior School
SIT ME10 119 L5
The Barry Clinic
STH/RUST TN4 196 D7
Barton Business Park
CANT CT1 174 E2
Barton Court Grammar School
CANT CT1 5 J5
Barton Junior School
DVE/WH CT16 213 K7
Baston School
HAYES BR2 89 J5
Bata Medical Centre
TIL RM18 36 D3
Bath Factory Estate
HNHL SE24 44 D4
Bayham Abbey
RRTW TN3 295 M7
The Bay Museum
RDV CT15 215 J4
Bbc Radio Kent
CHAT ME4 6 B4
Beacon Hill Industrial Estate
PUR RM19 32 C3
Bean Primary School
RDART DA2 53 K8
Bearsted Golf Club
MAID/BEAR ME14 142 C8
Bearsted Green Business Centre
MAID/BEAR ME14 142 D8
Bearsted Vineyard
MAID/SHEP ME15 168 F3
Beauherne Community School
CANTW/ST CT2 4 A5
Beaver Industrial Estate
ASH TN23 204 E4
Beaverwood School for Girls
CHST BR7 72 F3
Beckenham Business Centre
BECK BR3 69 M3
Beckenham Crematorium
SNWD SE25 69 K7
Beckenham CC
BECK BR3 70 C4
Beckenham Hospital
BECK BR3 70 A6
Beckenham Leisure Centre
BECK BR3 69 M5
Beckenham Place Park
Golf Course BECK BR3 70 C3
Beckenham RFC
BECK BR3 69 M8
Beckenham Town FC
BECK BR3 88 B1
Becket Sports Centre
DART DA1 51 K4
Beckley CE Primary School
RYE TN31 325 P9
Beckmead School
BECK BR3 88 B4
Bedensfield Clinic
SCUP DA14 73 M2
Bedgebury Junior School
CRBK TN17 297 M12
Bedonwell Clinic
ABYW SE2 29 M5
Bedonwell Medical Centre
BELV DA17 30 A4
Bedonwell Primary School
BELV DA17 29 M5
Beechcroft Farm Industrial
Estate BGR/WK TN15 95 L6
Beechings Way Industrial
Centre RHAM ME8 102 C1
Beechwood School Sacred
Heart RTWE/PEM TN2 201 M1
Bellenden Primary School
PECK SE15 45 H1
Bellenden Road Business Centre
PECK SE15 25 G8
Bellenden Road Retail Park
PECK SE15 25 G7
Bellerbys College Mayfield
WADH TN5 308 H5
Bellingham Trading Estate
CAT SE6 46 C8
Bell Shopping Centre
SIT ME10 120 A5
Bell Wood Community Junior
School MAID/SHEP ME15 167 M8
Bell Wood Infant School
MAID/SHEP ME15 167 M8
Belmont
FAV ME13 245 N4
Belmont Farm Business Centre
RASHW TN26 285 R8
Belmont Primary School
BXLYHN DA7 30 B6
Belvedere Link Business Park
BELV DA17 30 D2
Belvedere Primary School
BELV DA17 30 C3
Benedict House Preparatory
School BFN/LL DA15 73 G1
Benenden CE Primary School
CRBK TN17 313 N3
Benenden Hospital
CRBK TN17 300 B10
Benenden School
CRBK TN17 313 M1
Benham Business Park
RASHE TN25 307 L7
Bennett Memorial Diocesan CE
School STH/RUST TN4 196 B7
Bensham Manor School
THHTH CR7 86 D1
Benson Primary School
CROY/NA CR0 87 M6
Bentley Street Industrial Estate
GVE DA12 55 K4
Bermondsey Trading Estate
BERM/RHTH SE16 25 K3
Bessemer Grange J & I School
EDUL SE22 44 F2
Bessemer Park Industrial Estate
BRXN/ST SW9 44 C2
Bethany School
CRBK TN17 280 G12
Bethersden Business Centre
RASHW TN26 302 D4
Bethersden Primary School
RASHW TN26 285 N12
Bethlem Royal Hospital
BECK BR3 88 B3
Beths Grammar School for Boys
BXLY DA5 50 B4
Beulah Infant School
THHTH CR7 68 D6
Bexley College
ERITH DA8 30 D3
Bexley CC
BXLY DA5 50 B6
Bexley Grammar School
WELL DA16 49 J2
Bexleyheath Centre
BXLYHS DA6 49 M2
Bexleyheath Golf Club
BXLYHS DA6 49 M3
Bexleyheath Marriott Hotel
BXLYHS DA6 50 C2
Bexleyheath School
BXLYHN DA7 50 A1
Bexley Hospital
BXLY DA5 50 F7
Bexley RFC
BXLY DA5 50 B5
Bickley Park CC
BMLY BR1 71 M6
Bickley Park Preparatory
School BMLY BR1 71 L7
Bickley Park School
BMLY BR1 71 M6
Bidborough CE Primary School
STH/RUST TN4 277 R6
Biddenden Vinyards &
Cider Works HDCN TN27 300 G8
Biggin Hill Airport
BH/WHM TN16 106 B6
Biggin Hill Business Park
BH/WHM TN16 132 C1
Biggin Hill Primary School
BH/WHM TN16 132 D2
Birchington Primary School
BRCH CT7 176 D7
Birchington & Westgate
Health Clinic
BRCH CT7 176 F5
Birchmere Business Park
THMD SE28 29 G1
Birchwood Park Golf Club
RDART DA2 74 D4
Birchwood Primary School
SWLY BR8 74 E5
Bird College
SCUP DA14 49 H8
Birkbeck Primary School
SCUP DA14 49 J8
Bishop Challoner School
HAYES BR2 70 E6
Bishop Justus CE (Secondary)
School HAYES BR2 89 M3
Bishop Thomas Grant School
STRHM/NOR SW16 68 A2
Bishops Down Primary School
STH/RUST TN4 196 B8
Blackfen School for Girls
BFN/LL DA15 49 J4
Blackheath Bluecoat CE School
BKHTH/KID SE3 27 J6
Blackheath Business Estate
GNWCH SE10 26 D7
The Blackheath Clinic
BKHTH/KID SE3 47 H2
Blackheath High School GDST
BKHTH/KID SE3 27 G8
Blackheath High Senior School
BKHTH/KID SE3 27 H6
Blackheath Hospital
BKHTH/KID SE3 47 G1
Blackheath Preparatory School
BKHTH/KID SE3 27 H7
Blackheath RFC
(The Rectory Field)
BKHTH/KID SE3 27 J6
Blacklands County
Junior School
E/WMAL ME19 139 G6
Black Lion Leisure Centre
GILL ME7 7 H1
Blackshots Leisure Centre
CDW/CHF RM16 34 E1
Blackthorn Medical Centre
MAIDW ME16 166 B2
The Blazing Donkey Country
Hotel & Inn DEAL CT14 253 Q7
Bleak House Dickens Maritime
& Smuggling BRDST CT10 183 M1
Blean CP School
CANTW/ST CT2 171 J1
Blenheim Primary School
ORP BR6 91 L5
Blenheim Shopping Centre
PGE/AN SE20 69 K4
Bleriot Memorial
DVE/WH CT16 9 G2

Bliby Business Centre RASHE TN25 305 J6
Blubery House Cranbrook School CRBK TN17 298 G8
Blue Chalet Industrial Park BGR/WK TN15 111 J1
Bluewater Shopping Centre GRH DA9 53 H5
Bobbing Primary School RSIT ME9 119 J2
The Bob Hope Theatre ELTH/MOT SE9 48 A4
Bodiam Castle (NT) RBTBR TN32 324 A5
Bodiam CE Primary School RBTBR TN32 323 Q5
Bodiam Manor School RBTBR TN32 323 R5
Bonus Pastor School BMLY BR1 70 F1
Borden CE Primary School RSIT ME9 119 G6
Borden Grammar School SIT ME10 119 M6
Borough Cemetery RTWE/PEM TN2 201 K5
Borough Green Primary School BGR/WK TN15 240 F2
Borstal Manor Junior School ROCH ME1 100 A3
Bough Beech Sailing Club EDEN TN8 254 C9
Boughton Golf Club FAV ME13 150 E6
Boughton Monchelsea Primary School RMAID ME17 259 N3
Boughton Under Blean Primary School FAV ME13 151 G6
Bourne Road Industrial Park DART DA1 50 E3
Bower Grove School MAIDW ME16 166 C3
The Bower Mount Clinic MAIDW ME16 12 B5
Bowes Industrial Centre MEO DA13 97 G7
Bowling Alley
BERM/RHTH SE16 25 L2
BXLYHS DA6 50 A2
LEW SE13 46 D1
MAID/BEAR ME14 13 H4
MARG CT9 15 G4
MARG CT9 15 J2
ORP BR6 91 H4
WSTB CT5 126 E2
Bowling Centre
ASH TN23 2 D5
CHAT ME4 6 D5
The Bow Window Inn Hotel RCANTE CT3 251 J1
Boxgrove Primary School ABYW SE2 29 K2
Boxmend Industrial Estate RMAID ME17 260 A2
Boyd Business Centre STRD ME2 19 M3
Brabourne CE Primary School RASHE TN25 289 P9
Bradbourne School RSEV TN14 135 M7
Bradfields School WALD ME5 101 H7
Bradstow School BRDST CT10 183 K2
Brampton Primary School BXLYHN DA7 29 L8
Branbridges Industrial Estate STPH/PW TN12 257 K8
Brands Hatch Motor Racing Circuit HART DA3 94 F7
Brandshatch Place Hotel BGR/WK TN15 95 H7
Brattle Farm Museum STPH/PW TN12 281 Q8
Breaside Preparatory School BMLY BR1 71 K5
Breaside Pre Preparatory School BMLY BR1 71 H4
Bredgar CE Primary School RSIT ME9 145 H4
Bredhurst CE Primary School GILL ME7 116 C4
Bredinghurst School PECK SE15 45 K2
Brenchley & Matfield CE Primary School STPH/PW TN12 279 K9
Brenley Corner FAV ME13 150 D5
Brent Knoll School FSTH SE23 45 L8
The Brent Primary School RDART DA2 52 D5
Brenzett Aeronautical Museum LYDD TN29 329 N2
Brenzett District CE Primary School LYDD TN29 329 M3
Brian Johnston Centre BGR/WK TN15 136 E8
Briary Primary School HB CT6 128 D7
Bricklehurst Manor Preparatory School WADH TN5 309 R10
Brickmakers Industrial Estate SIT ME10 120 C3
Bridge Country Leisure Club WSTB CT5 125 M3
Bridge Industrial Centre MAID/SHEP ME15 12 C8
The Bridge Leisure Centre SYD SE26 70 A2
Bridge & Patrixbourne CE Primary School RCANTW CT4 175 H7
Bridge Place Country Club RCANTW CT4 250 D9
Bridge Road Business Centre ASH TN23 204 C1
Bridge View Industrial Estate
QBOR ME11 227 P3
WTHK RM20 33 H5
Bridgewood Manor Hotel WALD ME5 114 E2
Brigstock Medical Centre THHTH CR7 86 C1
Brindishe Primary School LEE/GVPK SE12 47 G3
The British School DEAL CT14 209 L2
Brit School for Performing Arts SNWD SE25 86 E2
Brittania Business Park DIT/AY ME20 139 M5
Brixton Academy BRXN/ST SW9 44 B1
Brixton College for Further Education BRXS/STRHM SW2 44 A3
Brixton Recreation Centre BRXN/ST SW9 44 B1
Broad Hembury Holiday Park RASHW TN26 304 E4
Broadlands Industrial Estate CANTW/ST CT2 153 G6
Broadmead Primary School CROY/NA CR0 86 E2
Broad Oak Industrial Estate CANTW/ST CT2 172 C6
Broadstairs CC BRDST CT10 183 H3
Broadstairs Health Centre BRDST CT10 183 K1
Broadstairs Youth & Leisure Centre BRDST CT10 179 L8
Broadwater Down Primary School RTWE/PEM TN2 201 G4
Broadway Shopping Centre
BXLYHS DA6 50 B2
MAIDW ME16 12 E5
Broadway Square Shopping Centre BXLYHN DA7 50 B2
Brockhill Country Park HYTHE CT21 222 A1
Brockhill Park School (Lower) HYTHE CT21 222 B2
Brockhill Park School (Upper) HYTHE CT21 222 B1
Brocklebank Industrial Estate GNWCH SE10 27 H3
Brockley Cross Business Centre BROCKY SE4 45 M1
Brockley Primary School BROCKY SE4 46 A3
Brockwell Lido HNHL SE24 44 C4
Broke Hill Golf Club RSEV TN14 108 E3
Bromley Cemetery BMLY BR1 71 G4
Bromley College of Further & Higher Education
BMLY BR1 71 H5
HAYES BR2 89 L2
Bromley County Court BMLY BR1 71 H5
Bromley Court Hotel BMLY BR1 70 F3
Bromley FC HAYES BR2 89 J1
Bromley Golf Club HAYES BR2 89 M3
Bromley High School GDST BMLY BR1 72 B8
Bromley Hospitals NHS Trust ORP BR6 91 G7
Bromley Industrial Centre BMLY BR1 71 L7
Bromley Mall Indoor Market BMLY BR1 71 H6
Bromley Museum ORP BR6 91 J3
Bromley Road Infant School BECK BR3 70 C5
Bromley Road Retail Park CAT SE6 46 C7
Bromley Tennis Centre ORP BR6 90 E6
Brompton Medical Centre GILL ME7 6 E1
Brompton Westbrook Primary School GILL ME7 6 F4
Bromstone CP School BRDST CT10 183 G1
Bronte School GVW DA11 55 H5
Brook Community Primary School RASHE TN25 288 H5
Brooke House School for the Deaf MARG CT9 177 L3
Brookfield Industrial Estate ASH TN23 204 C1
Brookfield Infant School DIT/AY ME20 139 H3
Brookfield Junior School DIT/AY ME20 139 G3
Brook Industrial Park STMC/STPC BR5 73 K8
Brookland CE Primary School LYDD TN29 329 J5
Brooklands Primary School BKHTH/KID SE3 47 H1
Brookmarsh Trading Estate DEPT SE8 26 C6
The Brook Theatre CHAT ME4 6 D4
Broome Park Golf Club RCANTW CT4 270 G8
Broomhill Bank School RRTW TN3 277 R11
Broomhill Lodge Hotel RYE TN31 327 K11
Broomsleigh Business Park CAT SE6 70 A2
Brothwick Wharf DEPT SE8 26 B4
Brunel Engine House BERM/RHTH SE16 25 K1
Brunswick Centre Industrial Estate ASH TN23 204 C1
Brunswick House Clinic MAIDW ME16 12 C3
Brunswick House Primary School MAIDW ME16 12 C3
Brunswick Park Primary School CMBW SE5 24 E6
Bryony School RHAM ME8 102 D6
Bryony School (Upper) RHAM ME8 103 G8
Buckland Hospital DVW CT17 213 H8
Bullers Wood School CHST BR7 72 A5
Burgess Business Park CMBW SE5 24 E6
Burgess Park Tennis Centre CMBW SE5 24 D5
Burnham Trading Estate DART DA1 51 L2
Burnhill Business Centre BECK BR3 70 B5
Burnt Ash Infant School BMLY BR1 71 H2
Burnt Ash School BMLY BR1 71 G2
Burnt Oak Junior School BFN/LL DA15 49 H6
Burrswood Medical Centre RRTW TN3 199 H5
Bursted Wood Primary School BXLYHN DA7 30 C8
Burwood School ORP BR6 91 L5
The Business Academy Bexley ERITHM DA18 29 M1
The Butterfly Centre RDV CT15 292 G6
Butterfly Sports Club ELTH/MOT SE9 48 C4
Byron School GILL ME7 7 K7
Bysing Wood CP School FAV ME13 149 H1
Cage Green Primary School TONN TN10 189 G8
The Caldecott Community Care for Children RASHE TN25 288 H11
Callis Grange Nursery & Infant School BRDST CT10 179 J6
Camber Castle RYE TN31 225 H7
Camber Sands Holiday Park RYE TN31 332 E7
Camberwell Business Centre CMBW SE5 24 E6
Camberwell College of Arts CMBW SE5 24 F7
Camberwell Leisure Centre CMBW SE5 24 E7
Camberwell New Cemetery FSTH SE23 45 L4
Camberwell Trading Estate CMBW SE5 24 C8
Camden Centre RTW TN1 23 G3
Camden House Clinic BKHTH/KID SE3 26 F8
Camelot Primary School PECK SE15 25 J6
Camer Park Country Park MEO DA13 97 K3
Campanile Hotel GRH DA9 52 E1
Camping & Caravanning Club Site FOLKN CT19 221 H6
Canada Water Retail Park BERM/RHTH SE16 25 L2
Canal Industrial Park GVE DA12 55 L4
Cannock House School ORP BR6 92 A8
Cannon Wharf Business Centre DEPT SE8 25 M3
Canterbury Bowling Club CANT CT1 4 F7
Canterbury Cathedral CANT CT1 5 G4
Canterbury Christ Church College
CANT CT1 5 H4
CANTW/ST CT2 4 F3
RCANTE CT3 173 G8
Canterbury Christ Church University College MARG CT9 15 H4
Canterbury City FC & Greyhound Racing (Kingsmead Stadium) CANTW/ST CT2 172 B7
Canterbury City Retail Park CANT CT1 172 E5
Canterbury Environment Centre CANT CT1 4 F4
Canterbury Golf Club CANT CT1 174 F1
Canterbury Health Centre CANT CT1 5 G6
The Canterbury High School CANTW/ST CT2 4 B4
Canterbury Indoor Market CANTW/ST CT2 4 E3
Canterbury Industrial Estate NWCR SE14 25 L5
Canterbury Industrial Park RCANTE CT3 234 B4
Canterbury Pilgrims Hospital CANT CT1 4 E4
Canterbury Road Health Centre MARG CT9 14 B5
Canterbury Road Primary School SIT ME10 120 C6
Canterbury & St Augustines Magistrates Court CANT CT1 5 H4
Canterbury Tales CANT CT1 4 F4
Cantium Retail Park STHWK SE1 25 H5
Capel-le-Ferne Primary School RFOLK CT18 221 K2
Capel Primary School RTON TN11 278 C2
Capital Industrial Estate BELV DA17 30 C3
Capstone Farm Country Park GILL ME7 101 L6
Cardwell Primary School WOOL/PLUM SE18 28 A3
Cartwright & Kelsey Primary School RCANTE CT3 235 R11
Cascades Leisure Centre GVE DA12 80 B1
Casino ROCH ME1 19 L7
Castle CANT CT1 4 E6
Castleacres Industrial Park SIT ME10 120 C3
Castle Bank CRBK TN17 282 A11
Castle Clinic DVE/WH CT16 8 E4
Castlecombe Primary School ELTH/MOT SE9 71 M2
Castle Community School DEAL CT14 209 K5
Castle Hill Primary School CROY/NA CR0 105 H1
Castle Remains RMAID ME17 260 F6
Castle Road Business Precinct SIT ME10 120 C4
Castle Road Industrial Estate SIT ME10 120 C5
Castle View Business Centre ROCH ME1 19 L5
Catford Cricket & Sports Club CAT SE6 46 C6
Catford Cyphers CC CAT SE6 46 A7
Catford Girls School CAT SE6 46 E8
Catford Trading Estate CAT SE6 46 C7
Catford Wanderers Sports Club CAT SE6 70 D1
Cathedral Gateway CANT CT1 4 F4
Cathedral School of St Savior & St Mary Overie STHWK SE1 24 D1
Cator Park School for Girls BECK BR3 69 M4
Cecil Road Primary School GVW DA11 55 G6
The Cedars School ROCH ME1 100 D1
Central Business Park STRD ME2 82 F6
Centrale Shopping Centre CROY/NA CR0 86 D5
Central Hall Theatre & Cinema CHAT ME4 6 D5
Central Park Arena DART DA1 51 M6
Chadwell St Mary Primary School CDW/CHF RM16 35 H3
Chaffinch Business Park BECK BR3 69 L7
Chalklin Business Park RTWE/PEM TN2 197 H5
Challock CP School RASHE TN25 265 N4
Chambers Wharf BERM/RHTH SE16 25 H1
The Channel School FOLKN CT19 220 D6
Channel Tunnel Exhibition Centre (summer only) RFOLK CT18 219 J5
Channel Tunnel Passenger Terminal RFOLK CT18 219 J5
Chantry Primary School GVE DA12 55 K5
Chapter School STRD ME2 81 L6
Charing CE Primary School HDCN TN27 264 B6
Charles Darwin School BH/WHM TN16 132 E1
Charles Dickens Centre & Eastgate House ROCH ME1 19 L7
The Charles Dickens High School BRDST CT10 183 H1
Charles Edward Brook School CMBW SE5 24 C7
Charles Edward Brook Upper School CMBW SE5 24 C7
Charlotte Turner Primary School DEPT SE8 26 B5
Charlton Athletic FC (The Valley) CHARL SE7 27 K4
Charlton CE Primary School DVE/WH CT16 213 K7
Charlton Health & Fitness Centre CHARL SE7 27 K4
Charlton House CHARL SE7 27 L5
Charlton Manor Junior School CHARL SE7 27 L6
Charlton RFC ELTH/MOT SE9 48 C5
Charlton School CHARL SE7 27 M5
Charlton Shopping Centre DVE/WH CT16 8 B3
The Charter School EDUL SE22 44 E3
Chartham CP School RCANTW CT4 248 D8
Chart Hills Golf Club HDCN TN27 283 P11
Chart Sutton Business Estate RMAID ME17 260 C3
Chartwell Business Centre BMLY BR1 71 L7
Chatham Dockyard (World Naval Base) CHAT ME4 83 G6
Chatham Girls Grammar School WALD ME5 7 L9
Chatham Grammar Boys School CHAT ME4 101 G4
Chatham House Grammar School RAM CT11 17 J4
Chatham South School CHAT ME4 100 F5
Chatsworth Infant School BFN/LL DA15 49 H6
Chaucer Business Park
BGR/WK TN15 137 J5
WSTB CT5 127 H4
Chaucer College Canterbury CANTW/ST CT2 171 L2
Chaucer Hospital CANT CT1 174 B5
The Chaucer Hotel CANT CT1 5 G5
Chaucer Technology School CANT CT1 5 M6
Chelsfield Lakes Golf Centre ORP BR6 108 D2
Chelsfield Park Hospital ORP BR6 92 A8
Chelsfield Primary School ORP BR6 91 M8
Chequers Shopping Centre MAID/BEAR ME14 13 G5
Cheriton Primary School FOLK CT20 219 K7
Cherry Garden Pier BERM/RHTH SE16 25 J1
Cherry Garden School BERM/RHTH SE16 25 H3
Cherry Lodge Golf Club BH/WHM TN16 132 F3
Cherry Orchard Primary School CHARL SE7 27 K6
Chestfield CC WSTB CT5 127 J5
Chestfield Medical Centre WSTB CT5 127 L3
Chestfield (Whitstable) Golf Club WSTB CT5 127 L5
Chevening Cross RSEV TN14 134 F6
Chevening Primary School RSEV TN14 135 G8
Cheyne Middle School IOS ME12 64 F3
Chiddingstone Castle EDEN TN8 276 C2
Chiddingstone CE Primary School EDEN TN8 276 D2
Childeric Primary School NWCR SE14 25 M6
Chilham St Marys CE Primary School RCANTW CT4 247 N10
Chilston Park RMAID ME17 262 F4
Chilston Park Hotel RMAID ME17 262 G4
Chilton CP School RAM CT11 16 B7
Chiltonian Industrial Estate LEE/GVPK SE12 47 G4
Chislehurst Caves CHST BR7 72 B5
Chislehurst Cemetery CHST BR7 72 F2
Chislehurst Golf Club CHST BR7 72 C4
Chislehurst Natural Health Centre CHST BR7 72 C3
Chislehurst & Sidcup GRM School BFN/LL DA15 49 J7
Chislet CE Primary School RCANTE CT3 232 D12
Christchurch CE Junior School RAM CT11 16 F7
Christ Church Centre RTW TN1 22 F6
Christ Church CE Primary School
BRXN/ST SW9 24 B7
BRXS/STRHM SW2 44 A6
FOLKN CT19 11 H4
FSTH SE23 45 L7
WOOL/PLUM SE18 28 B7
Christ Church High School ASH TN23 204 C6
Christ Church Primary School ERITH DA8 30 E5
Christian Meeting Hall BECK BR3 70 B5
Christine King 6th Form College LEW SE13 46 E1
Chrysolute Primary School STHWK SE1 24 E2
Chunnel Industrial Estate ASH TN23 2 B7
Church Down Adult School LEE/GVPK SE12 47 H7
Churchfield School WOOL/PLUM SE18 29 G3
Churchfields Primary School BECK BR3 69 L7
Churchill Business Park BH/WHM TN16 159 J4
Churchill CE Primary School BH/WHM TN16 159 H3
Churchill Clinic WALD ME5 101 H6
The Churchill Hotel DVW CT17 8 E6
Churchill House School RAM CT11 17 H8
The Churchill School RFOLK CT18 220 B1
Churchill Theatre HAYES BR2 71 H6
Church Road Business Centre SIT ME10 120 D3
Church Stairs WAP E1W 25 J1
Church Trading Estate ERITH DA8 31 H6
Cinema 3 CANTW/ST CT2 171 M1
Cineworld Cinema BXLYHS DA6 50 C2
City Banking College STHWK SE1 24 E1
City Business Centre BERM/RHTH SE16 25 K1
City Business Park CANT CT1 172 D6
City & Guilds of London-Art School LBTH SE11 24 C4
The City of London Academy
EDUL SE22 45 H3
STHWK SE1 25 H4
City of London Polytechnic Sports Ground ELTH/MOT SE9 47 K7
City Wall ROCH ME1 19 J6
Civic Centre & Bromley Palace BMLY BR1 71 J6
Civic Centre & Woodville Halls GVW DA11 55 J5
Civil Service Sports Ground ELTH/MOT SE9 47 K4
Clanricarde Medical Centre RTW TN1 22 F5
Claredon Hotel BKHTH/KID SE3 27 G8
Clare House E/WMAL ME19 139 G5
Clare House Primary School BECK BR3 70 D6
Claremont Primary School RTW TN1 23 H7
Clarendon House Grammar School RAM CT11 17 H6
Clarendon & Westbury Community Centre DVW CT17 217 J2
Clearways Industrial Estate BGR/WK TN15 111 K2
Cleeve Park School SCUP DA14 49 K8
Cliffe Woods County Primary School HOO/HM ME3 58 D5
Clifton Hotel FOLK CT20 11 G7
Cliftonville Theatre MARG CT9 15 J2
CM Booth Collection of Historic Vehicles CRBK TN17 314 D6
Coalhouse Fort TIL RM18 36 F7
Cobbs Wood Industrial Estate ASH TN23 204 C1
Cobbswood Industrial Estate ASH TN23 204 D1
Cobham Primary School GVE DA12 80 B7
Cobourg Primary School CMBW SE5 25 G4
Cobtree Manor Park Golf Club MAID/BEAR ME14 140 E2
Cobtree Medical Centre RMAID ME17 260 F5
Coldecott School RASHE TN25 306 A2
Coldharbour Industrial Estate CMBW SE5 24 D8
Coldharbour Leisure Centre ELTH/MOT SE9 48 A7
Coldharbour Sports Ground ELTH/MOT SE9 48 B7
Colebrook Industrial Estate RTWE/PEM TN2 197 H4
Colfes Preparatory School LEE/GVPK SE12 47 J4
College Square Shopping Centre MARG CT9 15 G4
Colliers Green CE Primary School CRBK TN17 298 C3
Collingwood Industrial Estate RMAID ME17 260 F3
Coloma Convent Girls School CROY/NA CR0 87 L6
Colyers Lane Medical Centre ERITH DA8 30 E7
Colyers Primary School ERITH DA8 30 E7
Combe Bank Senior School RSEV TN14 160 D1

Comber Grove Primary School CMBW SE5 24 D6
Comelle House Trading Estate DEPT SE8 25 M4
Comfort Inn RAM CT11 17 M4
The Commodore Catamaran Yacht Club IOS ME12 65 G3
Community Arts Centre GNWCH SE10 26 C6
Community Centre (Island History Trust) POP/IOD E14 26 D3
Community College & School GNWCH SE10 26 D6
Community Education Centre & Library RYE TN31 225 H4
Community Support Centre DVW CT17 213 J8
Compass Centre CHAT ME4 83 J5
Complementary Health Centre LEW SE13 46 F4
Concorde Business Park BH/WHM TN16 132 C1
Coney Hill School HAYES BR2 89 G5
Connaught Barracks (MOD) DVE/WH CT16 213 M7
Connections Business Park RSEV TN14 136 A6
Conquest Industrial Estate STRD ME2 18 E7
Consort Clinic PECK SE15 45 J1
Convent Preparatory School GVE DA12 55 K7
Conway Medical Centre WOOL/PLUM SE18 28 E4
Conway Primary School WOOL/PLUM SE18 28 F3
Coopers Lane Primary School LEE/GVPK SE12 47 H7
Coopers Technology College CHST BR7 72 D5
Cooting Road Industrial Estate RCANTE CT3 271 J1
Corinthian Sports Club HART DA3 95 L2
Corn Exchange ROCH ME1 19 K6
Cornwallis School MAID/SHEP ME15 259 L2
Corpus Christi RC Primary School BRXS/STRHM SW2 44 A3
Cossington House Surgery CANT CT1 5 H7
Cottage Industrial Estate DIT/AY ME20 140 C3
The County Hotel CANT CT1 4 F4
County Primary Infant School RHAM ME8 102 F5
County Square Shopping Centre ASH TN23 2 B4
Courtwood Primary School CROY/NA CR0 104 E4
Coward Industrial Estate CDW/CHF RM16 35 J4
Cowgate Cemetery DVW CT17 8 C5
Coxheath Primary School RMAID ME17 258 H2
CPFC Soccer & Sports Centre BRXN/ST SW9 44 A1
Crabble Corn Mill DVW CT17 213 G6
Crampton Primary School WALW SE17 24 C3
Cranbrook CE Primary School CRBK TN17 298 G7
Cranbrook Clinic CRBK TN17 298 G8
Cranbrook RFC CRBK TN17 298 G7
Cranbrook School CRBK TN17 298 G8
Crawford Primary School CMBW SE5 24 D7
Crayfield Industrial Park STMC/STPC BR5 73 K6
Crayfields Business Park STMC/STPC BR5 73 K5
STMC/STPC BR5 91 K1
Crayford Commercial Centre DART DA1 50 F3
Crayford Industrial Estate DART DA1 51 G3
Crayford Leisure Centre & Greyhound Stadium DART DA1 50 F4
Crayford Medical Centre DART DA1 51 G3
Craylands Primary School SWCM DA10 53 L3
Crayside Industrial Estate DART DA1 51 H1
Cray Valley Golf Club STMC/STPC BR5 73 M5
Creek Road Health Centre DEPT SE8 26 B5
Creek Road Industrial Estate DEPT SE8 26 C5
Crest Industrial Estate STPH/PW TN12 280 H3
Crockenhill Primary School SWLY BR8 92 D2
Crockham Hill CE Primary School EDEN TN8 186 D3
Crofton Leisure Centre BROCKY SE4 46 B4
Crofton School BROCKY SE4 46 B4
Crook Log Primary School BXLYHS DA6 49 L2
Crook Log Sports Centre WELL DA16 49 L1
Crossways Academy Sixth Form BROCKY SE4 25 M8
Crowden House Cranbrook School CRBK TN17 298 H8
Crown Court Clinic ROCH ME1 19 L8
Crown Lane Primary School WNWD SE27 68 D1
Crown Woods School ELTH/MOT SE9 48 D3
Croydon Cemetery THHTH CR7 86 A1
Croydon Clocktower Cinema CROY/NA CR0 86 D6
Croydon College CROY/NA CR0 86 E5
Croydon Fairfield Halls Cinema CROY/NA CR0 86 E6
Croydon FC SNWD SE25 87 K1
Croydon High Junior School GDST SAND/SEL CR2 104 A5
Croydon Indoor Bowling Club SAND/SEL CR2 86 D8
Croydon Road Industrial Estate SNWD SE25 69 K8
Croydon Sports Arena SNWD SE25 87 K1
Cryalls Business Estate SIT ME10 119 K5
Crystal Business Centre SWCH CT13 237 L11
Crystal Palace FC (Selhurst Park) SNWD SE25 68 F8
Crystal Palace Museum NRWD SE19 69 G3
Cuaco Sports Ground BECK BR3 70 B3
Cubitt Town Primary School POP/IOD E14 26 D2
Cudham CE Primary School BH/WHM TN16 132 F2
Culverstone Green Primary School MEO DA13 239 K2
Cutty Sark Clipper Ship GNWCH SE10 26 D5
Cuxton Industrial Estate STRD ME2 99 K3
Cygnet Leisure Centre GVW DA11 54 F6
Cypress Infant School SNWD SE25 68 F6
Cypress Junior School SNWD SE25 68 F6
Cyprus College of Art WNWD SE27 68 C1
D2 Trading Estate SIT ME10 120 C3
Daily Telegraph POP/IOD E14 26 B2
Dajen Business Park CHAT ME4 101 K4
Dale Hill Hotel & Golf Club WADH TN5 310 C8
Dalmain Primary School FSTH SE23 45 M6
Dame Janet Community Junior School MSTR CT12 182 E3
Dame Janet Infant School MSTR CT12 182 E3
Dame Sybil Thorndike Health Centre ROCH ME1 100 D1
Damilola Taylor Centre PECK SE15 25 G6
Dane Court Grammar School BRDST CT10 183 G1
Danecourt School (Special School) GILL ME7 102 A3
Dane John Mound & Monument CANT CT1 4 E6
Danley Middle School IOS ME12 64 F6
Danson Primary School WELL DA16 49 J2
Danson Watersports Centre BXLYHS DA6 49 K3
Darenth Primary School RDART DA2 77 G3
Darenth Valley Golf Club RSEV TN14 109 M6
Darent Industrial Park ERITH DA8 31 L4
Darent Valley Hospital RDART DA2 52 E6
Darrick Wood Primary School ORP BR6 90 C7
Darrick Wood School ORP BR6 90 C6
Darrick Wood Sports Centre ORP BR6 90 D6
Darrick Wood Swimming Pool ORP BR6 90 C6
Dartford County Court DART DA1 51 M4
Dartford FC EYN DA4 76 B5
RDART DA2 52 C6
Dartford Golf Club DART DA1 51 J7
Dartford Grammar School for Boys DART DA1 51 K4
Dartford Grammar School for Girls DART DA1 51 K5
Dartford Hospital School HART DA3 78 B7
Dartford Magistrates Court DART DA1 51 L4
Dartford Museum & Library DART DA1 51 M5
Dartford Natural Health Centre DART DA1 51 M5
Dartford Technology College DART DA1 51 K5
Dartford Tunnel WTHK RM20 32 E7
Dartford West Health Centre DART DA1 51 K4
Darwin Leisure Centre BH/WHM TN16 132 E2
David Livingstone Primary School THHTH CR7 68 D5
David Lloyd Health Club MAIDW ME16 12 F6
David Lloyd Tennis Centre SCUP DA14 73 K2
David Salomon's House RRTW TN3 196 A5
Davidson J & I School CROY/NA CR0 87 G3
Davington Primary School FAV ME13 149 J1
Days Inn STHWK SE1 24 B2
Days Lane Primary School BFN/LL DA15 49 G4
Deacon Industrial Estate DIT/AY ME20 140 B3
Deacon Trading Centre STRD ME2 18 F5
Deacon Trading Estate TON TN9 195 G4
Deal Castle DEAL CT14 209 L4
Deal Rowing Club DEAL CT14 209 L2
Deal Squash Racket Club DEAL CT14 209 L1
Deal Town FS & S Club DEAL CT14 209 J5
Deal Victoria & Barnes CC DEAL CT14 209 J7
Deal & Walmer Community Health Clinic DEAL CT14 209 J4
Deangate Ridge Athletics Stadium HOO/HM ME3 59 K5
Deangate Ridge Golf Club HOO/HM ME3 59 K6
Deansfield Primary School ELTH/MOT SE9 48 B1
Deanwood Primary Education Technology School RHAM ME8 116 E1
De Bradelei Wharf Shopping Centre DVW CT17 8 D6
Delce Junior School ROCH ME1 100 D3
Delta Wharf GNWCH SE10 26 E1
Deneholm Primary School CDW/CHF RM16 34 D1
Denture Clinic SWCH CT13 206 B1
Denvale Trade Centre STMC/STPC BR5 91 J1
Deptford Business Centre DEPT SE8 25 L4
Deptford Green School NWCR SE14 26 A6
Deptford Park Business Centre DEPT SE8 25 M4
Deptford Park Primary School DEPT SE8 25 M4
Deptford Trading Estate DEPT SE8 25 M4
Descovery Business Park BERM/RHTH SE16 25 H2
Design Museum STHWK SE1 25 G1
Detling CE Primary School MAID/BEAR ME14 142 B4
De Vere Village Hotel MAIDW ME16 140 F4
Dickens House Museum BRDST CT10 183 L1
Diggerland STRD ME2 18 C9
Diocesan & Payne Smith CE Primary School CANT CT1 5 G3
Discovery School E/WMAL ME19 164 E2
Ditton CE Junior School DIT/AY ME20 139 K4
Ditton Infant School DIT/AY ME20 139 K4
Docklands Medical Centre POP/IOD E14 26 B3
Docklands Sailing Centre POP/IOD E14 26 B2
Docklands Sailing & Watersports Centre POP/IOD E14 26 A2
Dockley Road Industrial Estate BERM/RHTH SE16 25 G2
Dockyard Industrial Estate WOOL/PLUM SE18 27 M2
Doddington Place RSIT ME9 244 D1
Doddington Primary School RSIT ME9 244 C2
Dog Kennel Hill Primary School CMBW SE5 44 F1
Dolphin Sailing Barge Museum SIT ME10 120 B4
Dominican Priory CANT CT1 4 F3
Dominoes Health Centre GRAYS RM17 34 B5
Donnington Manor Hotel SEV TN13 135 J4
Dormansland Primary School LING RH7 274 A4
Dorset Road Industrial Estate IOS ME12 64 B5
Dorset Road Infant School ELTH/MOT SE9 47 M7
Dorton College of Further Education BGR/WK TN15 136 D8
Dorton House School BGR/WK TN15 136 E8
The Dover Business Centre DVW CT17 8 A6
Dover Castle & Secret War Time Tunnels DVE/WH CT16 9 G4
Dover College DVW CT17 8 B4
Dover Cruise Liner Terminal 1 DVW CT17 217 M4
Dover Cruise Liner Terminal 2 DVW CT17 217 M5
Dover Grammar School for Boys DVW CT17 217 H1
Dover Grammar School for Girls DVE/WH CT16 8 B1
Dover Harbour Board Offices DVW CT17 8 E6
Dover Health Centre DVE/WH CT16 8 D3
Dover Leisure Centre DVE/WH CT16 8 F4
Dover Museum DVE/WH CT16 8 D5
Dover Road Primary School GVW DA11 54 F6
Dover Water Sports Centre DVW CT17 8 E6
Downderry Primary School BMLY BR1 70 F1
Downe Primary School ORP BR6 106 F5
Downham Health Centre BMLY BR1 70 F1
Down House-Home of Charles Darwin ORP BR6 106 E6
The Downs CE Primary School DEAL CT14 209 J7
Downsview Infant School KEN/WIL TN24 203 H4
Downsview Primary School NRWD SE19 68 D4
SWLY BR8 75 H7
Downs Way County Primary School OXTED RH8 157 K5
Drapers Mill CP School MARG CT9 15 J8
Dreamland Amusement Park MARG CT9 14 E5
Dreamland Cinema/Bingo MARG CT9 14 E5
The Drop Redoubt DVW CT17 8 C6
Druidstone Park & Art Park CANTW/ST CT2 153 G5
Duke of Clarence Trading Estate IOS ME12 64 B2
Duke of York School RDV CT15 214 A5
Dulverton Primary School BFN/LL DA15 48 E7
Dulwich College DUL SE21 44 F6
Dulwich College Preparatory School DUL SE21 44 F8
Dulwich College Track DUL SE21 44 F7
Dulwich Hamlet FC EDUL SE22 44 F2
Dulwich Hamlet Junior School DUL SE21 44 E4
Dulwich Hospital EDUL SE22 44 F2
Dulwich Leisure Centre EDUL SE22 45 H2
Dulwich Medical Centre EDUL SE22 45 H3
Dulwich Picture Gallery DUL SE21 44 E5
Dulwich Preparatory School CRBK TN17 299 K9
Dulwich & Sydenham Hill Golf Club DUL SE21 45 H7
Dulwich Village CE Infant School DUL SE21 44 F4
Dungeness Power Station LYDD TN29 335 M11
Dungeness Power Stations' Visitor Centre LYDD TN29 335 L10
Dunkerleys Hotel & Restaurant DEAL CT14 209 L3
Dunkirk CP School FAV ME13 151 L6
Dunn Street Farm RASHE TN25 265 K8
Dunraven School & Upper School STRHM/NOR SW16 44 A8
Dunton Green Primary School SEV TN13 135 K6
Duppas Junior School CROY/NA CR0 86 C8
Durand Primary School BRXN/ST SW9 24 A7
Durands Wharf BERM/RHTH SE16 26 A1
Durgates Industrial Estate WADH TN5 309 K4
Dymchurch Martello Tower LYDD TN29 320 H10
Dymchurch Primary School LYDD TN29 320 G9
Eaglesfield School WOOL/PLUM SE18 28 B7
Ealdham Primary School ELTH/MOT SE9 47 K2
East Borough Primary School MAID/BEAR ME14 13 K3
Eastchurch CE Primary School IOS ME12 229 P1
Eastcote Primary School ELTH/MOT SE9 48 E1
East Court School RAM CT11 183 K6
East Farleigh Primary School MAID/SHEP ME15 166 B7
East Greenwich Christ Church CE Primary School GNWCH SE10 26 F3
East Kent Business Centre DVE/WH CT16 8 E6
East Kent Light Railway RDV CT15 272 B6
East Kent Retail Park BRDST CT10 178 E8
Eastling Primary School FAV ME13 244 H4
Eastmead Trading Estate ASH TN23 2 C8
East Peckham Primary School STPH/PW TN12 257 J6
Eastry Medical Surgery SWCH CT13 253 N7
Eastry Primary School SWCH CT13 253 N7
East Stour Primary School KEN/WIL TN24 205 G5
East Thamesmead Business Park ERITHM DA18 30 A1
East Tilbury Junior & Infant Schools TIL RM18 36 D4
Eastwell Manor Hotel RASHE TN25 265 Q9
East Wickham Primary School WELL DA16 29 G7
Ebbsfleet Industrial Estate GVW DA11 54 B3
Ebury Hotel CANT CT1 5 K7
Ecclesbourne Primary School THHTH CR7 86 D1
Edenbridge & District War Memorial Hospital EDEN TN8 192 D6
Edenbridge Golf & Tennis Centre EDEN TN8 192 B3
Edenbridge Leisure Centre EDEN TN8 192 D3
The Edenbridge Medical Centre EDEN TN8 192 D3
Edenbridge Primary School EDEN TN8 192 D4
Eden Business Centre ASH TN23 2 C8
Edenham High School CROY/NA CR0 87 M3
Edgebury Primary School CHST BR7 72 D1
Edmund Waller Primary School NWCR SE14 25 L8
Effra Road Retail Park BRXS/STRHM SW2 44 B3
Egerton CE Primary School HDCN TN27 262 H10
Eglinton Junior School WOOL/PLUM SE18 28 B5
Eglinton Primary School WOOL/PLUM SE18 28 B6
Elaine County Primary School STRD ME2 18 B4
Elbourne Trading Estate BELV DA17 30 C2
Elephant & Castle Shopping Centre LBTH SE11 24 C3
Elfrida Primary School CAT SE6 70 C1
Elham CE Primary School RCANTW CT4 291 Q5
Eliot Bank Primary School FSTH SE23 45 J7
Elizabeth Trading Estate NWCR SE14 25 L5
Ellingham Industrial Centre ASH TN23 204 D6
Ellington High School RAM CT11 16 E4
Ellington School For Girls RAM CT11 16 E4
Elliott Park School IOS ME12 65 J6
Elm Court Industrial Estate GILL ME7 115 M2
Elm Court School WNWD SE27 44 C7
Elmhurst School CROY/NA CR0 86 E7
The Elms Medical Centre HOO/HM ME3 59 L8
Elmwood Primary School CROY/NA CR0 86 C3
Elm Wood Primary School WNWD SE27 44 E8
Eltham Bus Station ELTH/MOT SE9 48 A3
Eltham Cemetery ELTH/MOT SE9 48 D2
Eltham CE Primary School ELTH/MOT SE9 48 A3
Eltham College Junior School ELTH/MOT SE9 47 L6
Eltham College Senior School ELTH/MOT SE9 47 L7
Eltham Crematorium ELTH/MOT SE9 48 E2
Eltham Green School ELTH/MOT SE9 47 L4
Eltham Health Clinic ELTH/MOT SE9 47 M3
Eltham Health & Fitness Centre ELTH/MOT SE9 48 B4
Eltham Hill Tech College ELTH/MOT SE9 47 M4
Eltham Palace (remains) ELTH/MOT SE9 47 M5
Eltham Pools ELTH/MOT SE9 47 M3
Eltham Warren Golf Club ELTH/MOT SE9 48 C3
Empire Cinema SWCH CT13 237 J12
English Martyrs RC Primary School STRD ME2 19 H1
Ennersdale Primary School LEW SE13 46 E3
Enterprise Business Centre DVE/WH CT16 213 H3
Enterprise Business Park POP/IOD E14 26 C1
Enterprise Industrial Estate BERM/RHTH SE16 25 K4
Eric Liddell Sports Centre ELTH/MOT SE9 47 L7
Erith Cemetery ERITH DA8 30 C5
Erith & District Hospital ERITH DA8 30 E5
Erith Health Centre ERITH DA8 30 F5
Erith Library & Museum ERITH DA8 30 F4
Erith Playhouse ERITH DA8 31 G4
Erith School ERITH DA8 30 D6
Erith School Community Sports Centre ERITH DA8 30 D6
Erith Small Business Centre ERITH DA8 31 G5
Erith Sports Centre ERITH DA8 30 F5
Erith Stadium ERITH DA8 30 F5
Etchingham CE Primary School BUR/ETCH TN19 322 C3
Etchinghill Golf Club RFOLK CT18 218 E1
Ethelbert Road Infant School FAV ME13 149 J3
Eureka Leisure Park KEN/WIL TN24 202 F6
The Eurogate Business Park ASH TN23 2 B4
Eurolink Business Centre BRXS/STRHM SW2 44 B2
Eurolink Industrial Centre SIT ME10 120 B4
Eurolink Industrial Estate SIT ME10 120 C4
Europa Trading Estate ERITH DA8 30 E4
WTHK RM20 33 L4
European School of Osteopathy MAID/BEAR ME14 141 K2
Evegate Business Centre RASHE TN25 306 A3
Eveline Lowe Primary School STHWK SE1 25 H4
Eversley Medical Centre THHTH CR7 86 B2
Executive Golf Club at Cranbrook CRBK TN17 299 N9
Express by Holiday Inn CANTW/ST CT2 170 D3
CROY/NA CR0 86 D5
DART DA1 52 C2
GNWCH SE10 27 G2
Eynsford Castle EYN DA4 93 M5
Eynsford CC EYN DA4 93 M5
Eythorne Elvington Primary School RDV CT15 272 D5
Faircharm Trading Estate DEPT SE8 26 C6
Fairchildes Primary School CROY/NA CR0 105 K6
Fairfax Business Centre MAID/SHEP ME15 260 A1
Fairfield Pool & Leisure Centre DART DA1 51 M5
Fairlawn Primary School FSTH SE23 45 K5
Fairview Community Junior School RHAM ME8 102 D8
Fairview Industrial Estate OXTED RH8 157 J8
OXTED RH8 185 H3
Fairview Industrial Park RASHW TN26 318 G2
Fairwood Industrial Park ASH TN23 204 C2
The Falstaff Hotel CANTW/ST CT2 4 E3
The Family Medical Centre WALD ME5 115 K3
Fan Museum GNWCH SE10 26 D6
Farleigh Court Golf Club WARL CR6 104 F6
Farleigh Primary School WARL CR6 130 C3
Farleigh Rovers FC WARL CR6 130 E2
Farleigh Trading Estate MAID/SHEP ME15 12 C9
Farnborough Primary School ORP BR6 90 E8
Farningham Woods (Nature Reserve) SWLY BR8 75 L8
Farrington & Stratford House School CHST BR7 72 E4
Faversham Cottage Hospital FAV ME13 149 K2

Faversham Golf Club FAV ME13 245 P3
Faversham Industrial Estate FAV ME13 150 A2
Faversham Town FC FAV ME13 149 L4
Fawkham CE Primary School HART DA3 95 H4
Fawkham Manor Hospital HART DA3 95 K4
The Fayreness Hotel BRDST CT10 179 K3
Featherby Infant School RHAM ME8 102 B2
Featherby Junior School RHAM ME8 102 B2
Fenstanton J & I School BRXS/STRHM SW2 44 B6
The Ferry Inn IOS ME12 123 K1
Finchcocks CRBK TN17 296 H8
Firepower (Museum of Artillery) WOOL/PLUM SE18 28 C2
Five Bridges LBTH SE11 24 A4
Flackley Ash Hotel RYE TN31 326 D10
Flagship Brewery CHAT ME4 83 G6
Flamsteed House Museum GNWCH SE10 26 E6
Flaxman Sports Centre CMBW SE5 24 D8
Fleetdown J & I School RDART DA2 52 D7
Fleetway Sports Club GVE DA12 55 K6
Fleur de Lis Heritage Centre FAV ME13 149 K2
Fleur de Lys Gallery FOLK CT20 10 A9
Flicks Cinema DEAL CT14 209 L3
Florence Nightingale Museum STHWK SE1 24 A1
Folkestone CC FOLKN CT19 10 E3
Folkestone Invicta FC FOLKN CT19 10 D3
Folkestone Race Course RASHE TN25 307 M7
Folkestone Rowing Club FOLK CT20 223 M2
Folkestone RFC RFOLK CT18 218 F7
The Folkestone School for Girls FOLK CT20 10 B7
Folkestone Sports Centre & Ski Slope FOLKN CT19 10 F2
Folkestone Yacht & Motor Boat Club FOLKN CT19 11 M5
Follys End Christian High School SNWD SE25 86 F2
Fondu Sports Club PUR RM19 32 D3
Fordcombe CE Primary School RRTW TN3 277 J12
Fordgate Business Park BELV DA17 30 D1
The Foreland School BRDST CT10 179 K7
Forestdale Primary School CROY/NA CR0 104 D3
Forest Hill Business Centre FSTH SE23 45 K7
Forest Hill Industrial Estate FSTH SE23 45 K7
Forest Hill School FSTH SE23 45 L8
Forest Hills Pools FSTH SE23 45 K7
Forge Close Clinic HAYES BR2 89 H4
The Former Health Centre CHARL SE7 27 L3
Forster Park Primary School CAT SE6 46 F8
Fort Amherst Heritage Park & Caverns CHAT ME4 6 D3
Fort Luton Museum CHAT ME4 101 H4
Fort Pitt Grammar School ROCH ME1 6 A6
Fossdene Primary School CHARL SE7 27 J4
Fosse Bank New School RTON TN11 188 B6
Fosters Primary School WELL DA16 29 K8
Four Elms Primary School EDEN TN8 187 J8
Foxfield Primary School WOOL/PLUM SE18 28 D4
Fox's Cross WSTB CT5 152 C2
Franklin Industrial Estate PGE/AN SE20 69 K5
The Frank Walters Business Park BRDST CT10 183 G1
Frant CE Primary School RRTW TN3 294 A9
The Freda Gardham Community School RYE TN31 225 J3
Freight Services Centre DVE/WH CT16 9 J4
Fremlin Walk Shopping Centre MAID/BEAR ME14 12 F4
French Hospital ROCH ME1 19 K7
Frewen College RYE TN31 325 K8
Friars School ASH TN23 286 G9
The Friends of Canterbury Cathedral CANT CT1 5 G3
Frittenden CE Primary School CRBK TN17 282 F11
Fulston Manor School SIT ME10 120 A7
Furley Park Primary School ASH TN23 304 F3
Furness School SWLY BR8 75 G3
Furness Swanley FC SWLY BR8 92 E1
Gads Hill School STRD ME2 81 K3
Galley Hill Industrial Estate SWCM DA10 53 M3
Galleywall Primary School BERM/RHTH SE16 25 J3
Gallions Mount Primary School WOOL/PLUM SE18 29 G4
Gaphouse School BRDST CT10 183 K3
Gardener Industrial Estate BECK BR3 69 M2
The Garden of England Crematorium RSIT ME9 227 K12
Garlinge Infant School MARG CT9 14 A9
Garrison Cricket Ground Pavilion GILL ME7 7 G3
Garrison Sports Stadium GILL ME7 7 G1
Gate House Wood Touring Park BGR/WK TN15 239 K12
Gateway Business Centre BECK BR3 69 M3
WOOL/PLUM SE18 28 D2
Gateway Community College North CDW/CHF RM16 35 G1
Gaza Trading Estate RTON TN11 255 L6
Gemini Business Estate NWCR SE14 25 L4
Geoffrey Whitworth Theatre DART DA1 51 H2
George Green School POP/IOD E14 26 D4
The George Hotel CRBK TN17 298 G8
RYE TN31 225 H4
George Spurgen Comm Primary School FOLKN CT19 11 L1
Georges Turles House Clinic CANTW/ST CT2 4 B3
Giffin Business Centre DEPT SE8 26 B6
Gilbert Scott Primary School SAND/SEL CR2 104 D2
The Gillingham College GILL ME7 102 A1
Gillingham FC (Priestfield Stadium) GILL ME7 83 M8
Gillingham Golf Club GILL ME7 101 M3
Gillingham Ice Bowl GILL ME7 102 B4
Gillingham Library & Arts Centre GILL ME7 7 H2
Gillingham Medical Centre GILL ME7 102 A1
The Glade Business Centre WTHK RM20 33 G4
The Glades Shopping Centre BMLY BR1 71 H6
Glebe School WWKM BR4 88 E4
Glencoe Junior School CHAT ME4 6 E9
Globe Industrial Estate GRAYS RM17 34 D5
Globe Works Industrial Estate GRAYS RM17 34 D4
Gloucester Primary School PECK SE15 24 F6
Goacher's Brewery MAID/SHEP ME15 166 F4
Godden Green Clinic BGR/WK TN15 163 G3
Godinton House ASH TN23 286 H5
Godinton Primary School ASH TN23 202 A8
Godinton Way Industrial Estate ASH TN23 2 A5
Goldsmiths College DEPT SE8 26 B5
LEW SE13 46 F2
NWCR SE14 26 A7
Goldsmiths College Sports Ground SCUP DA14 50 A8
Goldsmiths University of London NWCR SE14 26 A7
Goldwyn Community Special School ASH TN23 286 G5
Gonville Primary School THHTH CR7 86 A1
Goodnestone CE Primary School RCANTE CT3 252 B7
Goodnestone Park Gardens RCANTE CT3 252 A8
Goodrich J & I School EDUL SE22 45 H4
Good Shepherd RC Primary School BMLY BR1 71 G1
CROY/NA CR0 105 G2
Goose Green Primary School EDUL SE22 45 G2
Goose Green Trading Estate EDUL SE22 45 H2
Gordonbrock Primary School BROCKY SE4 46 B3
Gordon Primary School ELTH/MOT SE9 48 A2
STRD ME2 18 E2
Gore Court CC SIT ME10 119 J4
Goudhurst & Kilndown CE Primary School CRBK TN17 297 N5
Grace School FOLK CT20 11 K5
Grain Power Station HOO/HM ME3 63 J2
Granby Sports Club ELTH/MOT SE9 71 M2
Grand Shaft (Lower Entrance) DVW CT17 8 C7
Grand Shaft (Upper Entrance) DVW CT17 8 B7
The Grange Medical Centre RAM CT11 17 G7
Grange Moor Hotel MAIDW ME16 12 B7
Grange Park College E/WMAL ME19 138 D3
The Granville School SEV TN13 20 F3
Granville Theatre & Cinema RAM CT11 17 M5
Gravel Hill Primary School BXLYHS DA6 50 C3
Graveney CP School FAV ME13 124 E8
Gravesend County Court GVE DA12 55 J4
Gravesend CC GVW DA11 55 H5
Gravesend Grammar School GVE DA12 55 L5
Gravesend Grammar School for Girls GVW DA11 55 H6
Gravesend Museum GVE DA12 55 J4
Gravesend & Northfleet FC GVW DA11 54 B3
Gravesend & North Kent Hospital GVW DA11 55 H4
Gravesend Rowing Club GVE DA12 55 K4
Gravesend Yacht Club GVE DA12 55 L4
Graves Yard Industrial Estate WELL DA16 29 H8
Grays Athletic FC GRAYS RM17 34 C5
Grays Business Centre GRAYS RM17 34 D2
Grays Convent School GRAYS RM17 34 C3
Grays County Court GRAYS RM17 34 B5
Grays Farm Primary School STMC/STPC BR5 73 J5
Grays Health Centre GRAYS RM17 34 B4
The Grays School GRAYS RM17 34 C2
Great Chart CC ASH TN23 286 H8
Great Chart Primary School ASH TN23 204 A3
Great Comp Garden BGR/WK TN15 241 K3
Great Dixter RYE TN31 324 H6
Great Hall Arcade RTW TN1 22 F6
Great Hollanden Business Centre RTON TN11 255 R3
Greatness Park Cemetery RSEV TN14 136 C7
Greatstone Primary School NROM TN28 331 L11
Greenacre School WALD ME5 101 G8
Greenacres Primary School ELTH/MOT SE9 48 B7
Greenfields School HDCN TN27 301 J7
Greenhithe Health Clinic GRH DA9 53 J3
Greenland Pier BERM/RHTH SE16 26 A2
Green Lane Business Park ELTH/MOT SE9 48 B7
Greenshields Industrial Estate CAN/RD E16 27 H1
Greenslade Primary School WOOL/PLUM SE18 28 E5
Green Street Green Primary School ORP BR6 107 L1
Greenvale Infant School CHAT ME4 101 H3
Greenvale Primary School SAND/SEL CR2 104 C5
Greenvale School FSTH SE23 45 M8
Greenwich Centre Business Park DEPT SE8 26 C6
Greenwich Cinema GNWCH SE10 26 D6
Greenwich College GNWCH SE10 26 D6
Greenwich Community College WOOL/PLUM SE18 28 C3
WOOL/PLUM SE18 28 E5
Greenwich Industrial Estate CHARL SE7 27 J3
GNWCH SE10 26 C6
Greenwich Natural Health Centre GNWCH SE10 26 D6
Greenwich Pier GNWCH SE10 26 D4
Greenwich Theatre & Art Gallery GNWCH SE10 26 E6
Griffen Manor School WOOL/PLUM SE18 28 F7
Grinling Gibbons Primary School DEPT SE8 26 A5
Groombridge Place Gardens & Enchanted Forest RRTW TN3 199 K5
Groombridge St Thomas CE A Primary School RRTW TN3 199 K7
Grosvenor Casino RAM CT11 17 L6
Grosvenor Medical Centre RTW TN1 22 F3
Grove Bowls Club RTW TN1 23 G6
Grove Dairy Farm Business Centre RSIT ME9 119 H3
Grove Ferry Boat Club RCANTE CT3 234 G2
Grove Medical Centre DEPT SE8 25 M3
Grove Park CP School SIT ME10 119 J3
Guardian Industrial Estate STPH/PW TN12 280 H2
Guardian Newspapers POP/IOD E14 26 C1
Guelder Rose Medical Centre STPH/PW TN12 282 A5
Guildhall Museum ROCH ME1 19 K6
Gulbenkian Theatre CANTW/ST CT2 171 L1
Guru Nanak Sports Club GVE DA12 55 K5
Guston CE Primary School DVE/WH CT16 213 M6
Gypsy Moth IV GNWCH SE10 26 D5
Haberdashers Askes Hatcham College NWCR SE14 25 L8
Hadlow College CANT CT1 5 K5
Hadlow College of Agriculture & Horticulture RTON TN11 256 A5
Hadlow School RTON TN11 256 B5
Hailey Road Business Park ERITHM DA18 30 B1
Haimo Primary School ELTH/MOT SE9 47 L3
Haine Hospital MSTR CT12 182 D1
Haine Industrial Estate MSTR CT12 182 C4
Halfway Houses Primary School IOS ME12 64 E7
Halling Primary School STRD ME2 113 J2
Hall Place BXLY DA5 50 D4
Halstead Place School RSEV TN14 108 D6
Halstead Primary School RSEV TN14 108 E6
Halstow Primary School GNWCH SE10 27 G4
Hamilton House Hotel GNWCH SE10 26 E7
Hamilton Road Industrial Estate WNWD SE27 68 E1
Hamlet International Industrial Estate ERITH DA8 30 E4
Hammerwood Park EGRIN RH19 274 H11
Hammonds Corner LYDD TN29 330 F7
Hampton Pier Yacht Club HB CT6 128 C4
Hampton Primary School HB CT6 128 D6
Hampton Road Industrial Park CROY/NA CR0 86 D2
Hamsey Green Infant School WARL CR6 130 A2
Hamsey Green Junior School WARL CR6 130 A2
Ham Street Primary School RASHW TN26 318 C1
Harbinger Primary School POP/IOD E14 26 B3
Harbour School RDV CT15 216 F2
Harcourt CP School FOLKN CT19 219 M6
Harden Road Industrial Estate LYDD TN29 334 E2
Harenc School SCUP DA14 73 K2
Harrietsham CE Primary School RMAID ME17 242 F11
Harris City Technology College NRWD SE19 69 G5
Hartley Primary School HART DA3 95 M1
Hartsdown Leisure Centre MARG CT9 14 C7
Hart Street Business Centre MAIDW ME16 12 E6
Harvey Clinic FOLK CT20 11 H5
The Harvey Grammar School for Boys FOLKN CT19 10 D3
Haseltine Primary School CAT SE6 70 A1
Haslemere Industrial Estate MAID/SHEP ME15 168 A8
Hastings Clinic BRXS/STRHM SW2 44 A3
Hatcham Mews Business Centre NWCR SE14 25 L6
Hawes Down Clinic WWKM BR4 88 E5
Hawes Down Primary School WWKM BR4 88 E4
Hawkhurst CE Primary School HAWK TN18 312 C9
HAWK TN18 312 D7
Hawkhurst Cottage Hospital HAWK TN18 312 A7
Hawkhurst Golf Club HAWK TN18 312 C7
Hawkhurst Squash Club HAWK TN18 312 B7
Hawkinge Crematorium RFOLK CT18 292 E12
Hawkinge Health Centre RFOLK CT18 220 C1
Hawkins Clinic DEAL CT14 209 K3
Hawkwell Business Centre RTWE/PEM TN2 278 C7
Hawley Health Centre MARG CT9 14 F5
Hawthorn Farm Caravan Park RDV CT15 210 C8
Hayesbrook School TON TN9 194 D5
Hayes Grove Priory Hospital HAYES BR2 89 H5
Hayes Primary School HAYES BR2 89 J4
Hayes School HAYES BR2 89 J5
Hayes Tennis Club HAYES BR2 71 J8
Haymerle School PECK SE15 25 H5
Haysden Country Park TON TN9 194 A5
Hazelwood School OXTED RH8 185 H1
Hazlitt Theatre MAID/BEAR ME14 13 G4
Headcorn CC HDCN TN27 283 M3
Headcorn Primary School HDCN TN27 283 K3
Heath Farm School HDCN TN27 263 N6
Heathfield College HAYES BR2 106 B1
Heath House Preparatory School BKHTH/KID SE3 27 G8
Heavers Farm Primary School SNWD SE25 87 G1
Heber Primary School EDUL SE22 45 G4
Hedgend Industrial Estate BRCH CT7 233 N6
Helen Alison School MEO DA13 97 H3
Hempstead House Country Hotel RSIT ME9 120 F7
Hempstead Infant School GILL ME7 102 B8
Hempstead Junior School GILL ME7 116 B1
Hempstead Valley Shopping Centre GILL ME7 116 B1
Henley Business Park STRD ME2 19 M4
Henry Fawcett Primary School LBTH SE11 24 B5
Henwick Primary School ELTH/MOT SE9 47 L1
Henwood Business Centre KEN/WIL TN24 2 F4
Henwood Industrial Estate KEN/WIL TN24 2 F3
The Hereson School RAM CT11 17 L2
Heritage Centre & Town Model RYE TN31 225 G4
Herne Bay FC HB CT6 129 G6
Herne Bay Golf Club HB CT6 129 G7
Herne Bay High School HB CT6 128 E6
Herne Bay Museum Centre HB CT6 129 G4
Herne Bay Primary School HB CT6 129 G5
Herne Bay West Industrial Estate HB CT6 128 D6
Herne CE Junior School HB CT6 129 H8
Herne Hill School HNHL SE24 44 D3
Herne Hill Stadium (Cycle Centre) DUL SE21 44 E4
Herne Infant School HB CT6 155 J1
Hernhill CE Primary School FAV ME13 151 H3
Heronsgate Primary School THMD SE28 28 E2
Herringham Primary School CDW/CHF RM16 35 J2
Hersden Community Primary School RCANTE CT3 155 M8
Hever Castle and Gardens EDEN TN8 193 L6
Hever Castle Golf Club EDEN TN8 193 L4
Hever CE Primary School EDEN TN8 193 L7
Hextable Primary School SWLY BR8 75 G3
Higgs Industrial Estate BRXN/ST SW9 44 C1
Higham Primary School HOO/HM ME3 57 K8
High Elms Country Park ORP BR6 107 H2
High Elms Golf Club ORP BR6 107 H2
Highfield Business Centre CANT CT1 4 C7
Highfield Industrial Estate FOLKN CT19 11 M2
Highfield Infant School HAYES BR2 70 F8
Highfield Junior School HAYES BR2 70 F8
High Firs Primary School SWLY BR8 75 G8
High Halden CE Primary School RASHW TN26 301 R6
High Halstow Primary School HOO/HM ME3 59 L2
Highshore School PECK SE15 25 G7
Highsted Grammar School for Girls SIT ME10 120 A7
The Highway Primary School ORP BR6 91 K8
Highworth Grammar School for Girls KEN/WIL TN24 202 D8
Hildenborough CE Primary School RTON TN11 255 R7
Hilden Grange School RTON TN11 194 E1
Hilden Oaks School TONN TN10 194 E1
Hillborough Business Park HB CT6 232 A5
Hill Mead Infant School BRXN/ST SW9 44 C2
Hillmead Primary School BRXN/ST SW9 44 C2
Hill School BH/WHM TN16 159 G1
Hills Grove Primary School WELL DA16 29 K6
Hillside Industrial Estate FOLK CT20 223 M1
Hillside Primary School STMC/STPC BR5 91 K3
Hilltop Primary School STRD ME2 82 D4
Hillview School for Girls TON TN9 195 G5
Hilly Fields Medical Centre BROCKY SE4 46 B3
Hilton Business Centre ASH TN23 204 E5
Historical Society Museum CHAT ME4 6 C3
The Historic Dockyard Chatham CHAT ME4 83 G5
Hitherfield Primary School STRHM/NOR SW16 44 B7
Hither Green Cemetery CAT SE6 47 G7
Hither Green Primary School LEW SE13 46 E4
HM Prison Belmarsh THMD SE28 28 F2
HM Prison Canterbury CANT CT1 5 J4
HM Prison Elmley IOS ME12 229 N6
HM Prison Maidstone MAID/BEAR ME14 12 F2
HM Prison Rochester ROCH ME1 100 C5
HM Prison Standford Hill IOS ME12 229 L5
HM Prison Swaleside IOS ME12 229 M5
HM Young Offender Institution DVW CT17 217 J3
Hoath CP School RCANTE CT3 155 M4
Hogbarn Caravan Park RMAID ME17 242 H6
Holbeach Primary School CAT SE6 46 B5
Holborn College WOOL/PLUM SE18 27 L3
Holbury Centre ERITH DA8 31 H6
Holiday Inn BGR/WK TN15 239 K12
BXLY DA5 50 C4
KEN/WIL TN24 2 E1
WALD ME5 100 E8
Hollingbourne Primary School RMAID ME17 169 M3
Hollydale Primary School PECK SE15 25 K8
Holmesdale Community School Technology College SNOD ME6 113 H6
Holmewood House School RRTW TN3 200 B3
Holos Clinic SWCH CT13 237 K12
Holtye Golf Club EDEN TN8 275 L10
Holy Cross RC Primary School CAT SE6 46 D6
Holy Family RC Primary School BKHTH/KID SE3 47 J2
The Holy Family RC Primary School RMAID ME17 259 R1
Holy Innocents C Primary School ORP BR6 91 G6
Holy Trinity CE Primary School BRXS/STRHM SW2 44 A5
DART DA1 51 K3
FSTH SE23 45 K7
GVE DA12 55 K5
Holy Trinity College BMLY BR1 71 K5
Holy Trinity Foyer MAID/BEAR ME14 13 H4
Holy Trinity Lamorbey CE Primary School BFN/LL DA15 49 H6

Holy Trinity & St Johns CE Primary School MARC CT9 15 G5
Holywell Primary School RSIT ME9 103 M2
Homefarm Estate DIT/AY ME20 140 A4
Homeopathic Hospital RTW TN1 22 E5
Homewood School TENT TN30 301 N12
Honeycrest Industrial Park STPH/PW TN12 281 R4
Honiton House School MARG CT9 15 K3
Honor Oak Crematorium FSTH SE23 45 L3
Honor Oak Gallery FSTH SE23 45 L4
Honor Oak Health Centre BROCKY SE4 45 M2
Hook Lane Primary School WELL DA16 49 H1
Hoo St Werburgh Primary School HOO/HM ME3 59 L8
The Hope Anchor Hotel RYE TN31 225 G4
Hopewell School ASH TN23 204 B4
Hop Farm & Country Park STPH/PW TN12 257 K9
Horizon Industrial Estate PECK SE15 25 H5
The Horniman Museum & Gardens FSTH SE23 45 J6
Horniman Primary School FSTH SE23 45 J6
Horn Park Primary School LEE/GVPK SE12 47 J5
Horsmonden Primary School STPH/PW TN12 279 R11
Horsted Primary School WALD ME5 100 E8
Horsted Retail Park WALD ME5 100 E7
Horton Kirby CE Primary School EYN DA4 76 D7
Horton Kirby Trading Estate EYN DA4 76 D6
Hospital Barn Farm MAID/SHEP ME15 258 E1
Hotel du Vin & Bistro RTW TN1 23 G5
Hotel Ibis GNWCH SE10 26 D5
WTHK RM20 33 G5
Hothfield Village Primary School RASHW TN26 286 E2
Hoverspeed Terminal DVW CT17 8 E8
Howard Primary School CROY/NA CR0 86 D7
Howard School RHAM ME8 102 E5
Howland Quay BERM/RHTH SE16 25 L2
Howletts Wild Animal Park RCANTW CT4 175 K3
HSBC Sports Club BECK BR3 69 M3
Hugh Christie Technology College TONN TN10 189 G7
Hull Park Sports Club DEAL CT14 209 G3
Hundred of Hoo School HOO/HM ME3 59 K8
Hunton CE Primary School MAID/SHEP ME15 258 C6
Huntsman Sports Club BKHTH/KID SE3 47 H2
Hurst Green School OXTED RH8 185 H2
Hurstmere School BFN/LL DA15 49 J6
Hurst Primary School BXLY DA5 49 L6
Hythe Community Clinic HYTHE CT21 222 D3
Hythe Community School HYTHE CT21 222 C4
Hythe CC HYTHE CT21 222 D3
Hythe Imperial Golf Club HYTHE CT21 222 F3
The Hythe Imperial Hotel HYTHE CT21 222 E4
Hythe Ranges HYTHE CT21 321 R2
Hythe St Leonard CE Junior School HYTHE CT21 222 C3
Hythe & Saltwood Sailing Club HYTHE CT21 222 D4
Hythe Swimming Pool HYTHE CT21 222 E4
Ichthus Primary School CMBW SE5 24 F6
Ide Hill CE Aided Primary School RSEV TN14 187 M1
Iden Croft Herbs STPH/PW TN12 282 B7
Ifield School GVE DA12 79 K2
Ightham Primary School BGR/WK TN15 240 A4
IKEA Store Croydon CROY/NA CR0 86 A4
IKEA Store Lakeside WTHK RM20 33 J4
Ilderton Primary School BERM/RHTH SE16 25 K5
Imperial College at Wye RASHE TN25 266 F11
Imperial Oyster Cinema WSTB CT5 126 D3
Imperial Retail Park GVW DA11 55 H4
Imperial War Museum STHWK SE1 24 B2
Indoor Bowls & Sports Centre CHAT ME4 6 C3
Information Communications & Technology Centre Canterbury College CANT CT1 5 H6
Innkeeper's Lodge BECK BR3 88 B2
MAID/BEAR ME14 12 F2
RCANTW CT4 174 E5
STH/RUST TN4 196 C3
Invicta Grammar School for Girls MAID/BEAR ME14 13 L4
Invicta Primary School BKHTH/KID SE3 27 H5
Invicta Sports Club DART DA1 51 L3
IQRA Independent School BRXN/ST SW9 44 B1
Island Clinic POP/IOD E14 26 D1
Isle of Sheppey Cemetery IOS ME12 64 E6
Istead Rise Primary School MEO DA13 78 F5
Ivydale Primary School BROCKY SE4 45 L2
Iwade Primary School RSIT ME9 227 L9
James Allens Preparatory Girls School EDUL SE22 44 E3
James Dixon Primary School PGE/AN SE20 69 H5
James Wolfe Primary School GNWCH SE10 26 C6
Jempsons Trading Estate RYE TN31 225 G4
Jenner Health Centre FSTH SE23 45 M6
Jessop Primary School HNHL SE24 44 C2
Jewish Community Theatre CMBW SE5 44 E1
John Ball Primary School BKHTH/KID SE3 26 F8
John Dixon Clinic BERM/RHTH SE16 25 J2
John Donne Primary School PECK SE15 25 J7
John Goodhew Medical Centre SIT ME10 227 M12
John Mayne CE Primary School HDCN TN27 300 E4
John Roan Lower School BKHTH/KID SE3 27 G6
John Roan School BKHTH/KID SE3 26 F6
John Ruskin College SAND/SEL CR2 104 D2
John Ruskin Primary School WALW SE17 24 D5
John Stainer Primary School BROCKY SE4 45 M1
John Wilson Business Park WSTB CT5 127 J4
Joseph Conrad's Grave CANTW/ST CT2 4 A2
Joseph Wilson Industrial Estate WSTB CT5 127 G6
Joydens Wood Infant School RDART DA2 74 F1
Joydens Wood Junior School BXLY DA5 74 F1
Joy Lane Autism Unit WSTB CT5 126 D6
Jubilee Corner RMAID ME17 261 M10
Jubilee Country Park HAYES BR2 72 C8
Jubilee Hall CANT CT1 4 C7
Jubilee Primary School BRXS/STRHM SW2 44 B4
The Judd School TON TN9 194 D5
Julians Primary School STRHM/NOR SW16 68 B1
The Julie Rose Stadium KEN/WIL TN24 3 K1
Junior Kings School CANTW/ST CT2 172 F4
Juno Way Industrial Estate NWCR SE14 25 L5
Jury's Inn Hotel CROY/NA CR0 86 D5
Kangley Business Centre SYD SE26 70 A2
Kavanagh Cinema HB CT6 129 G4
Kearsney Abbey DVE/WH CT16 212 E5
Kelsey Park School BECK BR3 70 B7
Kemnal Technology College STMC/STPC BR5 73 J4
Kemsing Primary School BGR/WK TN15 137 G3
Ken Barrington Centre LBTH SE11 24 A5
Kenden Business Park STRD ME2 19 M1
Kender Primary School NWCR SE14 25 K7
Kengate Industrial Estate HYTHE CT21 222 A4
Kennington CE Junior School KEN/WIL TN24 203 G4
Kennington CC KEN/WIL TN24 203 G4
Kensington Avenue Primary School THHTH CR7 68 B5
Kent Battle of Britain Museum RFOLK CT18 220 A1
Kent & Canterbury Hospital CANT CT1 174 B4
Kent College CANTW/ST CT2 171 K2
Kent College J & I School CANTW/ST CT2 171 H4
Kent College School RTWE/PEM TN2 278 A6
Kent County Crematorium HDCN TN27 264 C8
Kent County CC (St Lawrence Ground) CANT CT1 5 J9
Kent County Opthalmic & Aural Hospital MAID/BEAR ME14 13 G3
Kent County Showground MAID/BEAR ME14 142 D3
Kent & East Sussex Railway HAWK TN18 325 Q1
RBTBR TN32 324 A6
RYE TN31 325 J4
Kent & East Sussex Steam Railway TENT TN30 315 J6
Kent Institute of Art & Design ROCH ME1 19 M9
Kent Institute of Art & Design Canterbury College CANT CT1 5 J6
Kent International Airport MSTR CT12 181 L4
Kent Kraft Industrial Estate GVW DA11 54 A2
Kent Oil Refinery HOO/HM ME3 62 E1
Kent Park Industrial Estate PECK SE15 25 J5
Kent Private Clinic SWCH CT13 237 K12
Kent & Sussex Crematorium RTWE/PEM TN2 201 J5
Kent & Sussex Hospital STH/RUST TN4 22 E3
Kestner Industrial Estate GRH DA9 53 H2
Keston CE Primary School HAYES BR2 89 L8
Keynes College CANTW/ST CT2 171 L1
Keyworth Primary School WALW SE17 24 C4
Kidbrooke Park Primary School BKHTH/KID SE3 27 K8
Kidbrooke School BKHTH/KID SE3 27 L8
Kilmorie Primary School FSTH SE23 45 M7
The King Ethelbert School BRCH CT7 176 F6
Kingfisher Community Primary School WALD ME5 101 J6
The Kingfisher Medical Centre DEPT SE8 26 A5
King's College Hospital CMBW SE5 44 D1
Kings College London CMBW SE5 24 E8
Kings College School of Medicine & Dentistry CMBW SE5 24 D8
DUL SE21 44 E4
Kingsdale School DUL SE21 44 F8
Kingsdown Industrial Estate DIT/AY ME20 139 J5
Kingsdown & Ringwould CE Primary School DEAL CT14 211 K4
Kings Farm Infant School GVE DA12 79 K2
GVE DA12 80 B1
Kings Hill Business Park E/WMAL ME19 164 B1
Kings Hill Golf Club E/WMAL ME19 164 C3
Kings Hill Primary School E/WMAL ME19 164 B2
Kingsley Primary School CROY/NA CR0 86 A4
Kingsmead County Primary School CANT CT1 5 G2
Kingsmead Leisure Centre CANTW/ST CT2 5 G1
Kings North CE Primary School ASH TN23 204 E8
Kingsnorth Industrial Estate ASH TN23 204 E5
HOO/HM ME3 60 E7
Kingsnorth Power Station HOO/HM ME3 60 E8
Kings Preparatory School ROCH ME1 19 J8
Kings Road Clinic WALD ME5 101 L4
Kings School ROCH ME1 19 J7
Kings School of English BECK BR3 70 A6
Kings School Recreation Centre CANTW/ST CT2 4 F1
The Kings School CANT CT1 5 G3
Kings Stairs BERM/RHTH SE16 25 J1
Kingstanding Business Park RTON TN11 197 J3
Kingswood Primary School RMAID ME17 261 M3
WNWD SE27 68 E1
Kitchener Barracks CHAT ME4 6 D2
Kit's Coty House DIT/AY ME20 114 D7
Klondyke Industrial Estate QBOR ME11 227 N1
Knights Park Industrial Estate STRD ME2 18 E6
Knights Templar Church (Ruins) DVW CT17 8 A8
Knockhall Community Primary School GRH DA9 53 K3
Knole Park Golf Club BGR/WK TN15 21 L4
Laban Centre DEPT SE8 26 C6
Laddingford Farm Industrial Estate WBY/YAL ME18 257 N9
Lady Boswells CE Primary School BGR/WK TN15 21 K6
Ladycross Business Park EGRIN RH19 274 B6
Lady Joanna Thornhill (End) Primary School RASHE TN25 266 F11
Ladywell Arena LEW SE13 46 C4
Ladywell Cemetery BROCKY SE4 46 A3
Ladywell Leisure Centre LEW SE13 46 D3
Laker Industrial Estate BECK BR3 70 A2
Lakeside Retail Park WTHK RM20 33 H3
Lakeside Shopping Centre WTHK RM20 33 J2
Laleham School MARG CT9 178 E3
Lamberhurst CE Primary School RRTW TN3 296 C7
Lamberhurst Golf Club RRTW TN3 296 C7
Lambeth Education LBTH SE11 24 B5
Lambeth Palace STHWK SE1 24 A2
Lamb House RYE TN31 225 H4
Lamorbey Swimming Centre BFN/LL DA15 49 H7
Langafel CE Primary School HART DA3 78 B7
Langbourne Primary School DUL SE21 44 F8
Langdon Cliffs Visitor Centre & Viewpoint (NT) DVE/WH CT16 9 L2
Langdon Primary School RDV CT15 210 B8
Langley Park Girls School & Sports Centre BECK BR3 88 C1
Langley Park Golf Club BECK BR3 88 E2
Langley Park School for Boys BECK BR3 88 C2
Langton Green CP School RRTW TN3 199 M1
Lansdowne Primary School SIT ME10 120 D6
TIL RM18 35 G8
Lansdowne Road Clinic RTW TN1 23 H4
Lansdowne School BRXN/ST SW9 44 A1
Larkfield Leisure Centre DIT/AY ME20 139 H2
Larkfield Priory Hotel DIT/AY ME20 139 G4
Larkfield Trading Estate DIT/AY ME20 113 J8
Larkin's Brewery EDEN TN8 276 F2
Lashenden (Headcorn) Airfield HDCN TN27 283 P7
Lathe Barn LYDD TN29 321 J4
Launcelot Primary School BMLY BR1 71 H1
Lawn Primary School GVW DA11 54 D4
Lawrence Trading Estate GNWCH SE10 26 F3
GRAYS RM17 34 D3
Leathermarket Gardens STHWK SE1 24 E1
Leathersellers Sports Ground ELTH/MOT SE9 47 K5
Leeds & Broomfield CE Primary School RMAID ME17 169 H6
Leeds Castle RMAID ME17 169 L6
Leeds Castle Golf Club RMAID ME17 169 L5
Lee Manor Primary School LEW SE13 46 F4
Leesons Primary School STMC/STPC BR5 73 H7
The Leigh City Technology College (East Campus) DART DA1 52 C6
The Leigh City Technology College DART DA1 52 B6
The Leigh City Technology College (West Campus) DART DA1 52 B6
Leigh Green Industrial Estate TENT TN30 315 R3
Leigh House Clinic CANTW/ST CT2 4 D2
Leigh Primary School RTON TN11 255 N12
Le Meridien Selsdon Park Hotel & Golf Course SAND/SEL CR2 104 B5
Lesnes Abbey ABYW SE2 29 L3
Lessness Heath Primary School BELV DA17 30 B4
Lewisham Bridge Primary School LEW SE13 46 C1
Lewisham Business Centre NWCR SE14 25 L5
Lewisham Centre LEW SE13 46 D1
Lewisham College DEPT SE8 26 B7
Lewisham Crematorium CAT SE6 47 G7
Lewisham Police Station LEW SE13 46 D2
Leybourne Business Centre E/WMAL ME19 138 F3
Leybourne SS Primary School E/WMAL ME19 138 F3
Leyton Cross DART DA1 51 H7
Liberty Square E/WMAL ME19 164 C2
Lilian Bayliss Technology School LBTH SE11 24 A4
Lime Tree Restaurant & Hotel RMAID ME17 243 L12
Limpsfield CE Infant School OXTED RH8 158 A7
Limpsfield Chart Golf Club OXTED RH8 158 B7
Limpsfield Grange School OXTED RH8 157 M5
Limpsfield Lawn Tennis Club OXTED RH8 157 M6
Linden Grove CP School ASH TN23 204 D5
The Link Secondary School CROY/NA CR0 86 A7
Liongate Clinic STH/RUST TN4 22 F1
Little Acorns School RASHW TN26 301 M8
Littlebourne CE Primary School RCANTE CT3 251 J1
Littlebrook Business Centre DART DA1 52 D1
Little Danson Welfare Clinic WELL DA16 49 H2
Little Hickmotts School STPH/PW TN12 281 N1
Little Satmar Holiday Park RFOLK CT18 221 K2
Littlestone Golf Club NROM TN28 331 M7
Little Switzerland Camping & Caravan Site FOLKN CT19 221 H5
Little Theatre FOLK CT20 223 M2
Little Thurrock Primary School GRAYS RM17 34 E2
Livesey Museum for Children PECK SE15 25 J5
Livingstone Hospital DART DA1 52 A5
Lloyds CHAT ME4 6 C2
Lloyds Register CC DUL SE21 44 E6
Loaland Business Centre STRD ME2 19 M1
Lock Meadow Leisure Complex MAIDW ME16 12 F6
Lock Meadow Market MAIDW ME16 12 F7
Lombard Business Park CROY/NA CR0 86 A3
Lombard Trading Estate CHARL SE7 27 J3
London Arena POP/IOD E14 26 C2
London Beach Hotel & Golf Club TENT TN30 301 M9
The London Golf Club BGR/WK TN15 238 B2
London Guildhall University Sports Ground LEE/GVPK SE12 47 K7
London House School WGOS CT8 177 H4
London International Cruise Terminal TIL RM18 55 H2
London Ladies & Girls FC CAT SE6 70 C2
London Lane Clinic BMLY BR1 71 G4
London Living Theatre SYD SE26 69 L1
London Road Medical Centre THHTH CR7 86 B2
London Road Trading Estate SIT ME10 119 L5
London Transport Bus Depot BXLYHN DA7 50 C1
Longlands Primary School BFN/LL DA15 48 F8
Long Lane AFC BKHTH/KID SE3 27 K8
Long Mead Primary School RTON TN11 188 E8
Longport Police Station RFOLK CT18 219 J6
Loose Infant School MAID/SHEP ME15 167 H8
Loose Junior School MAID/SHEP ME15 167 H7
Lordswood Health Centre WALD ME5 115 K4
Lordswood Industrial Estate WALD ME5 115 K4
Lordswood Leisure Centre WALD ME5 115 K2
Loughborough Primary School CMBW SE5 24 C8
Lovell's Wharf GNWCH SE10 26 E4
Lower Halstow School RSIT ME9 226 C11
Lower Sydenham Industrial Estate CAT SE6 70 A2
Lowfield Medical Centre DART DA1 51 M5
Lucas Vale Primary School DEPT SE8 26 B7
Luddenham Primary School FAV ME13 122 F8
Lullingstone Castle EYN DA4 93 K8
Lullingstone Park Golf Club ORP BR6 92 E7
Lullingstone Roman Villa EYN DA4 93 J6
Lunsford Primary School DIT/AY ME20 139 H3
Luton Infant School CHAT ME4 101 K3
Luton Junior School WALD ME5 101 K3
Luton Medical Centre WALD ME5 101 K4
Lydd-Ashford Airport LYDD TN29 334 H2
Lydd Camp LYDD TN29 334 C4
Lydd County Primary School LYDD TN29 334 D3
Lydden CP School RDV CT15 212 A1
Lydden International Motor Racing Circuit RCANTW CT4 271 L11
Lydd Golf Club LYDD TN29 330 F12
Lydd Town Museum LYDD TN29 334 C3
Lyminge CE Primary School RFOLK CT18 291 M10
Lympne CE Primary School HYTHE CT21 307 M10
Lympne Industrial Estate HYTHE CT21 307 K10
Lyndean Industrial Estate ABYW SE2 29 K2
Lyndhurst Primary School CMBW SE5 24 E8
Lynsted & Norton Primary School RSIT ME9 147 H2
Mace Industrial Estate KEN/WIL TN24 2 D3
Madginford Park Infant School MAID/SHEP ME15 168 A3
Madginford Park Junior School MAID/SHEP ME15 168 B3
Magnet Estate CDW/CHF RM16 33 K4
Mahatma Gandhi Industrial Estate BRXN/ST SW9 44 C1
Maidstone General Hospital MAIDW ME16 166 B1
Maidstone Grammar School MAID/SHEP ME15 13 J8
Maidstone Grammar School for Girls MAIDW ME16 12 D2
Maidstone Industrial Centre MAIDW ME16 12 E3
Maidstone Lawn Tennis Club MAIDW ME16 140 D8
Maidstone Leisure Centre MAID/SHEP ME15 13 L8
Maidstone Museum & Bentlif Art Gallery MAID/BEAR ME14 12 F3
Maison Dieu House DVE/WH CT16 8 C3
Malcolm Primary School PGE/AN SE20 69 K4
Malham Road Industrial Estate FSTH SE23 45 L6
The Malling School E/WMAL ME19 139 G6
Malory School BMLY BR1 71 H1
Malthouse Business Park RYE TN31 326 F11
Manford Industrial Estate ERITH DA8 31 J5
Manor Brook Medical Centre BKHTH/KID SE3 27 J8
Manor Clinic FOLK CT20 11 H6
Manor Hotel GVE DA12 79 L3
Manor Oak Primary School STMC/STPC BR5 91 L1
Manor Park Country Park E/WMAL ME19 138 C7
Manor Way Industrial Estate GRAYS RM17 34 D6
Manston Caravan & Camping Park MSTR CT12 182 A3
Manzoori Clinic SWLY BR8 75 G4
Maple House Independent Montessori THHTH CR7 68 D8
Maple House School THHTH CR7 68 D7
Maplesden Noakes School MAIDW ME16 12 C1
Marden Lodge Primary School CTHM CR3 130 A6
Marden Medical Centre STPH/PW TN12 280 H3
Marden Primary School STPH/PW TN12 280 G4
Margate Business Centre MARG CT9 14 F4
Margate Caves MARG CT9 15 G3
Margate FC MARG CT9 14 D7

Margate Lawn Tennis Club *MARG* CT9 14 E8
Margate Museum *MARG* CT9 14 F3
Marina Office *DVW* CT17 8 D8
Marine Road Clinic *DEAL* CT14 209 L4
Marion Vian Primary School *BECK* BR3 87 L1
Maritime Industrial Estate *CHARL* SE7 27 J3
Maritime Museum *GNWCH* SE10 26 F3
RAM CT11 17 L7
Marlborough CC *DUL* SE21 45 H6
Marlborough House School *HAWK* TN18 312 B7
Marlborough Park School *BFN/LL* DA15 49 H6
Marlborough Road Industrial Estate *DEAL* CT14 209 G7
Marle Place *STPH/PW* TN12 296 D1
Marlowe Arcade Shopping Centre *CANT* CT1 4 F5
Marlowe Business Centre *NWCR* SE14 25 M6
Marlowe Park Medical Centre *STRD* ME2 81 L8
Marlowe Theatre *CANT* CT1 4 F3
Marriott Tudor Park Hotel & Country Club *MAID/BEAR* ME14 168 E2
Martello Industrial Estate *FOLKN* CT19 221 G7
Marvels Lane Primary School *LEE/GVPK* SE12 71 K1
Mary Bax's Stone *DEAL* CT14 207 H4
Mascalls School *STPH/PW* TN12 279 K5
Masonic Library & Museum *CANTW/ST* CT2 4 E4
Matrix Business Centre *DART* DA1 51 M3
The Maudsley Hospital *CMBW* SE5 24 E8
Maundeney Primary School *WALD* ME5 101 H8
May Avenue Industrial Estate *GVW* DA11 55 G6
Maybrook Industrial Estate *CANT* CT1 172 D6
Mayday University Hospital *THHTH* CR7 86 C2
Mayplace Primary School *BXLYHN* DA7 50 E2
Maypole Primary School *BXLY* DA5 50 F7
McArthur Glen Designer Outlet *ASH* TN23 204 F4
Meadowgate School *BROCKY* SE4 45 L1
Meadowside Leisure Centre *BKHTH/KID* SE3 47 K2
The Meadow Special School *STMC/STPC* BR5 73 H4
Meadows School *STH/RUST* TN4 196 C2
Meadow View Industrial Estate *RASHW* TN26 318 F2
Mead Road Infant School *CHST* BR7 72 D3
The Mead School *RTWE/PEM* TN2 22 E9
Medway City Estate *STRD* ME2 6 A1
Medway Civic Centre *STRD* ME2 19 H4
Medway Community College *CHAT* ME4 101 H4
Medway Crematorium *WALD* ME5 114 F4
Medway Heritage Centre *CHAT* ME4 6 C3
Medway Little Theatre *ROCH* ME1 19 L8
Medway Maritime Hospital *GILL* ME7 7 H6
Medway RFC *ROCH* ME1 100 C3
Medway Secure Training Centre *ROCH* ME1 100 C6
Medway Towns Rowing Club *ROCH* ME1 100 B2
Medway Trading Estate *MAIDW* ME16 12 E7
Medway Valley Leisure Park *STRD* ME2 99 M2
Medway Yacht Club *HOO/HM* ME3 83 J2
Melbourne CP School *DVE/WH* CT16 213 K5
Mellish Industrial Estate *WOOL/PLUM* SE18 27 L2
Memorial Hospital *WOOL/PLUM* SE18 28 B8
Meopham CP School *MEO* DA13 97 H3
Meopham Medical Centre *MEO* DA13 97 H5
Meopham School *MEO* DA13 97 H5
Mereworth Community Primary School *WBY/YAL* ME18 241 P9
Meridian Clinic *BRXN/ST* SW9 44 A1
Meridian Locality Mental Health Centre *CHARL* SE7 27 K5
Meridian Primary School *GNWCH* SE10 26 E4
Meridian Sports Club *CHARL* SE7 27 M6
Meridian Trading Estate *CHARL* SE7 27 J3
Merlin Primary School *BMLY* BR1 47 H8
Mermaid Inn Hotel *RYE* TN31 225 G4
Mersham Primary School *RASHE* TN25 305 P2
Merton Court Preparatory School *SCUP* DA14 73 K1
Metro Business Centre *SYD* SE26 70 A3
Metropolitan Police Hayes Sports Club *HAYES* BR2 89 G5
Michael Faraday Primary School *WALW* SE17 24 E4
Middle Park Primary School *ELTH/MOT* SE9 47 L5
Middlesex Hospital Sports Ground *CHST* BR7 73 G2
Midfield Primary School *CHST* BR7 73 H4
Mid Kent Business Park *SNOD* ME6 113 J5
Mid Kent College of FE *CHAT* ME4 100 E7
Mid Kent College of Higher & Further Education *ROCH* ME1 100 E2
Mid Kent Golf Club *GVW* DA11 55 J8
Mid Kent Shopping Centre *MAIDW* ME16 140 D6
Mierscourt Primary School *RHAM* ME8 103 G6
The Mildmay Hotel *DVW* CT17 8 A5
Milehams Industrial Estate *PUR* RM19 32 B2
Milestone School *HART* DA3 96 A4
Mile Town Industrial Park *IOS* ME12 64 B4
Military Barracks *WOOL/PLUM* SE18 28 B4
Millennium Harbour Development *POP/IOD* E14 26 A1
The Millennium Primary School *GNWCH* SE10 27 G2
Millennium Quay *DEPT* SE8 26 C5
Millennium Wharf Development *POP/IOD* E14 26 E2
Mill Hall Business Estate *DIT/AY* ME20 139 L3
Mill Lane Trading Estate *CROY/NA* CR0 86 A6
Millside Industrial Estate *DART* DA1 51 L2
Millwall FC (The New Den) *BERM/RHTH* SE16 25 K4
Milstead & Frinsted CE Primary School *RSIT* ME9 145 M8
Milton Court Primary School *SIT* ME10 119 M3
Milton Road Business Park *GVE* DA12 55 K5
Minnis Bay Sailing Club *BRCH* CT7 233 R2
Minster Abbey *IOS* ME12 65 L6
MSTR CT12 180 F8
Minster Abbey Gatehouse Museum *IOS* ME12 65 L6
Minster CE Primary School *MSTR* CT12 180 E8
Minster College *IOS* ME12 65 G7
Minster in Sheppey Primary School *IOS* ME12 65 K7
Minster & Rayment Rural Life Museum *MSTR* CT12 180 F7
Minster-Thanet Cemetery *MSTR* CT12 180 E5
Minterne Junior School *SIT* ME10 119 L7
Minters Industrial Estate *DEAL* CT14 208 F5
Moatbridge School *ELTH/MOT* SE9 47 L4
Moatlands Golf Club *STPH/PW* TN12 279 K6
Model Village *RAM* CT11 17 H9
Mongeham Primary School *DEAL* CT14 209 G5
Monks Hill Sports Centre *SAND/SEL* CR2 104 C2
Monks Orchard Primary School *CROY/NA* CR0 87 L1
Monson Primary School *NWCR* SE14 25 L6
Montbelle Primary School *ELTH/MOT* SE9 48 C8
Montbelle School *ELTH/MOT* SE9 72 C1
Montgomery Grant Maintained School *RCANTE* CT3 173 K1
Montpellier Business Park *ASH* TN23 204 C2
Moor House School *OXTED* RH8 185 G2
Morden College Homes *BKHTH/KID* SE3 27 H8
Morden Mount Primary School *LEW* SE13 26 C8
Morehall Primary School *FOLKN* CT19 10 B2
More Park RC Primary School *E/WMAL* ME19 138 E5
Moreton Industrial Estate *SWLY* BR8 75 J8
Morley Business Centre *TON* TN9 195 G4
Morley College *STHWK* SE1 24 B2
Mote CC *MAID/SHEP* ME15 13 K7
Mote Park Sailing Club *MAID/SHEP* ME15 167 M2
Motor Museum *RAM* CT11 17 H8
Motorway Industrial Estate *DIT/AY* ME20 140 D3
Mottingham Community Health Clinic *ELTH/MOT* SE9 71 M1
Mottingham Primary School *ELTH/MOT* SE9 48 A8
The Mount Camphill Community School *WADH* TN5 308 G3
Mudchute City Farm *POP/IOD* E14 26 D3
Mulberry Business Centre *BERM/RHTH* SE16 25 L1
Mulgrave Primary School *WOOL/PLUM* SE18 28 B3
Mundella Primary School *FOLKN* CT19 11 J2
Murray Business Centre *STMC/STPC* BR5 73 J7
Murston Infant School *SIT* ME10 120 C5
Murston Junior School *SIT* ME10 120 C4
Museum of Canterbury with Rupert Bear *CANT* CT1 4 E4
Museum of Kent Life *MAIDW* ME16 140 E4
The Museum *CRBK* TN17 298 C8
Music School *MAID/SHEP* ME15 12 F6
TON TN9 194 E5
Myatt Garden Primary School *BROCKY* SE4 26 A8
Myatts Field Clinic *BRXN/ST* SW9 24 C7
Napier Primary School *GILL* ME7 7 L5
Napier Road Secondary School *GILL* ME7 7 M5
National Maritime Museum *GNWCH* SE10 26 E5
National Nature Reserve *RASHW* TN26 318 E1
National Pinetum & Garden *CRBK* TN17 311 L1
National Sports Centre *NRWD* SE19 69 H3
Nature Reserve *CROY/NA* CR0 104 D5
FAV ME13 123 J3
FAV ME13 149 G6
FAV ME13 247 J5
FOLKN CT19 221 H5
HB CT6 155 J4
HDCN TN27 284 H4
HOO/HM ME3 39 M8
IOS ME12 228 H9
IOS ME12 231 J9
LYDD TN29 335 J8
MSTR CT12 233 R9
MSTR CT12 237 M2
RASHE TN25 289 L2
RASHW TN26 286 E1
RCANTW CT4 268 E9
ROCH ME1 113 K4
RYE TN31 225 M8
RYE TN31 326 A11
WADH TN5 310 C5
Natwest Sports Club *BECK* BR3 70 A3
Negus 6th Form Centre *WOOL/PLUM* SE18 28 E5
Neptune Industrial Estate *STRD* ME2 6 B1
Nevill Golf Club *RTWE/PEM* TN2 201 L6
New Addington Pools & Fitness Centre *CROY/NA* CR0 105 H4
New Ash Green Primary School *HART* DA3 96 A5
New Atlas Wharf Development *POP/IOD* E14 26 A2
The New Beacon School *SEV* TN13 161 L5
New Caledonian Wharf *BERM/RHTH* SE16 26 A2
New Century Cinema *SIT* ME10 120 B5
New Cross Sports Arena *NWCR* SE14 25 M6
New Hythe Business Park *DIT/AY* ME20 113 K8
Newington CE Primary School *RSIT* ME9 118 C2
Newington Industrial Estate *RSIT* ME9 118 A3
WALW SE17 24 D3
Newington Infant School *MSTR* CT12 16 C2
Newington Junior Foundation School *MSTR* CT12 16 B3
Newlands Primary School *RAM* CT11 17 J1
New Road Business Estate *DIT/AY* ME20 139 J5
New Road Industrial Estate *IOS* ME12 64 B4
New Road Primary School *CHAT* ME4 6 E7
New Royal Cinema *FAV* ME13 149 L2
The New School at West Heath *SEV* TN13 162 A7
Newstead Wood School for Girls *ORP* BR6 90 E6
New Woodlands School *BMLY* BR1 70 F1
SYD SE26 45 J8
Nightingale Primary School *WOOL/PLUM* SE18 28 C5
Nineacres School *WOOL/PLUM* SE18 28 E4
Nizels Golf & Leisure Club *RTON* TN11 255 M4
The Noble Clinic *STPH/PW* TN12 279 L9
Nonington CE Primary School *RDV* CT15 252 B12
Norbury Complementary Therapy Clinic *STRHM/NOR* SW16 68 A5
Norbury Health Centre *STRHM/NOR* SW16 68 A6
Norbury Manor Secondary Girls School *STRHM/NOR* SW16 68 A5
Norbury Trading Estate *STRHM/NOR* SW16 68 A6
Normandy Primary School *ERITH* DA8 30 E7
Norman Park Athletics Track *HAYES* BR2 89 J2
North Borough Junior School *MAID/BEAR* ME14 141 G6
Northbourne CE Primary School *DEAL* CT14 253 R12
Northbourne Court *DEAL* CT14 208 B4
Northbourne Park Preparatory School *DEAL* CT14 253 P11
Northbrook CE School *LEW* SE13 46 F3
North Clinic *BMLY* BR1 71 H5
North Croydon Medical Centre *THHTH* CR7 86 C2
Northdown CP School *MARG* CT9 178 F4
Northdown Industrial Estate *BRDST* CT10 179 H7
North Downs Business Park *RSEV* TN14 135 H2
North Downs Golf Club *GDST* RH9 156 F3
Northend Primary School *ERITH* DA8 31 G7
North End Trading Estate *ERITH* DA8 30 F6
North Farm Industrial Estate *RTWE/PEM* TN2 197 H4
Northfleet Cemetery *GVW* DA11 54 D6
Northfleet Industrial Estate *GVW* DA11 54 A2
Northfleet School for Girls *GVW* DA11 54 E7
Northfleet Technology College *GVW* DA11 54 E6
North Foreland Golf Club *BRDST* CT10 179 K5
Northgate Clinic *CANT* CT1 5 H2
Northiam CE Primary School *RYE* TN31 325 J8
North Kent Magistrates Court *CHAT* ME4 6 D4
Northpoint Business Estate *STRD* ME2 19 M2
The North School *KEN/WIL* TN24 2 F6
Northumberland Heath Medical Centre *ERITH* DA8 30 E6
Northumberland Heath Primary School *ERITH* DA8 30 C6
North West Kent College *DART* DA1 51 K7
GVE DA12 56 A6
Northwood Primary School *ERITHM* DA18 29 M2
The Norton Knatchbull School *KEN/WIL* TN24 3 G5
Norwood Heights Shopping Centre *NRWD* SE19 68 F3
Norwood School *WNWD* SE27 68 D2
Notre Dame RC Primary School *WOOL/PLUM* SE18 28 C5
Novotel London Waterloo *STHWK* SE1 24 A3
Nugent Industrial Park *STMC/STPC* BR5 73 K8
Nunnery Fields Hospital *CANT* CT1 4 F9
Nuralite Industrial Centre *HOO/HM* ME3 57 H5
Oakfield Preparatory School *DUL* SE21 44 E7
Oakfield Primary School *DART* DA1 51 L7
Oakfield Road Industrial Estate *PGE/AN* SE20 69 J4
Oakland Primary School *BH/WHM* TN16 132 B2
Oaklands Primary School *WALD* ME5 115 G1
Oakley School *RTWE/PEM* TN2 197 K8
TONN TN10 188 E8
Oak Lodge JMI School *WWKM* BR4 88 C3
The Oaks Infant School *SIT* ME10 119 L7
Oak Tree County Primary School *ASH* TN23 204 C3
Oak Trees Community School *MAID/SHEP* ME15 167 L6
Oakwood Hospital *MAIDW* ME16 166 C1
Oakwood Park Grammar School *MAIDW* ME16 166 D2
Oakwood Trading Estate *BRDST* CT10 179 G6
The Oast Golf Club *RSIT* ME9 120 F4
Oasthouse Theatre *RHAM* ME8 103 G5
Oastpark Golf Club *SNOD* ME6 112 F7
Occupational Health Centre *CROY/NA* CR0 86 E6
Odeon Cinema *BECK* BR3 70 B6
CANT CT1 5 G5
ELTH/MOT SE9 47 M2
HAYES BR2 71 H6
MAIDW ME16 12 F6
RTWE/PEM TN2 197 J5
Offham CC *E/WMAL* ME19 241 Q2
Offham Primary School *E/WMAL* ME19 241 Q1
Old Beckenhamian RFC *WWKM* BR4 88 E6
Old Bellgate Wharf Development *POP/IOD* E14 26 A2
Old Bexley Business Park *BXLY* DA5 50 C5
Old Bexley CE Primary School *BXLY* DA5 50 A6
Oldborough Manor Community School *MAID/SHEP* ME15 167 J6
Old Brockleians Sports Ground *ELTH/MOT* SE9 47 K4
Old Bromlians CC *HAYES* BR2 89 J1
Old Cemetery *EDUL* SE22 45 J4
Old Colfeian Sports Club *LEE/GVPK* SE12 47 H3
Old Elthamians Sports Club *CHST* BR7 72 F3
The Old Guild Theatre *GVW* DA11 54 E6
Old Hospital *RCANTW* CT4 291 Q4
Old Jamaica Business Estate *STHWK* SE1 25 G2
Old Judd RFC *TON* TN9 194 E3
Old Lighthouse *LYDD* TN29 335 P11
The Old Museum *RYE* TN31 325 N11
The Old Oast Business Centre *DIT/AY* ME20 140 B3
Old Palace School *CROY/NA* CR0 86 C6
The Old Priory School *RAM* CT11 17 G7
Old Railway Works (Industrial Estate) *KEN/WIL* TN24 2 F9
Old Royal Naval College *GNWCH* SE10 26 E4
Old Royal Observatory Greenwich *GNWCH* SE10 26 E6
Old St James' Church (ruins) *DVE/WH* CT16 8 F4
Old Salehurst School *RBTBR* TN32 322 C8
Old Station Museum *CAN/RD* E16 28 B1
Old Timber Yard Industrial Estate *MSTR* CT12 182 C5
Old Wilsonians Sports Club *WWKM* BR4 88 F4
Oliver Goldsmith Primary School *CMBW* SE5 25 G7
Om Medical Centre *IOS* ME12 64 D3
Orbital Park *KEN/WIL* TN24 205 J5
Orchard Business Centre *MAIDW* ME16 140 D5
RTWE/PEM TN2 197 G5
SYD SE26 70 A2
TON TN9 195 G5
Orchard Industrial Estate *MAID/SHEP* ME15 260 A2
Orchard Medical Centre *RMAID* ME17 258 H3
Orchard Place Business Centre *E/WMAL* ME19 241 M3
Orchard Primary School *SCUP* DA14 73 J2
The Orchard School *CANT* CT1 4 F8
Orchard Shopping Centre *DART* DA1 51 M4
The Orchard Theatre *DART* DA1 51 M4
Orchard Way Primary School *CROY/NA* CR0 87 M3
Orion Business Centre *BERM/RHTH* SE16 25 L4
Orpington College of FE *ORP* BR6 91 H4
The Orpington Halls *ORP* BR6 91 H5
Orpington Mental Health Centre *ORP* BR6 91 G6
Orpington Retail Park *STMC/STPC* BR5 73 K8
Ospringe CE Primary School *FAV* ME13 149 H3
Otford Primary School *RSEV* TN14 135 M2
Our Lady of Grace RC Primary School *CHARL* SE7 27 J5
Our Lady of Hartley RC Primary School *HART* DA3 96 A1
Our Lady of Lourdes RC Primary School *LEW* SE13 46 E1
Our Lady of the Rosary RC School *BFN/LL* DA15 48 F4
Our Lady & St Philip Neri Infant School *FSTH* SE23 45 L8
Our Lady & St Phillip Neri Junior School *SYD* SE26 69 M1
Our Ladys Catholic Primary School *DART* DA1 51 L4
Oval Business Centre *LBTH* SE11 24 A4
Oval House Theatre *LBTH* SE11 24 B5
Oval Primary School *CROY/NA* CR0 86 F4
Owletts (NT) *GVE* DA12 80 A7
Owl House *RRTW* TN3 295 R6
Oxted Health Centre *OXTED* RH8 157 L7
Oxted & Limpsfield Hospital *OXTED* RH8 157 J6
Oxted School *OXTED* RH8 157 L6
Paddock Wood Business Centre *STPH/PW* TN12 279 K2
Paddock Wood Primary School *STPH/PW* TN12 279 K3
Painters Ash Primary School *GVW* DA11 54 E8
Painters Farm Caravan & Camping Site *FAV* ME13 148 E6
Palace Industrial Estate *MAID/SHEP* ME15 260 A1
Palace Wood Junior School *MAIDW* ME16 140 D7
Palmarsh Primary School *HYTHE* CT21 321 Q1
Palm Bay County Primary School *MARG* CT9 179 G2
Palmer's College *GRAYS* RM17 35 G3
The Pantiles Shopping Arcade *RTWE/PEM* TN2 22 E8
Paper Mills *DIT/AY* ME20 139 K2
SIT ME10 227 Q12
Parchmore Medical Centre *THHTH* CR7 68 D7
Parish CE Primary School *BMLY* BR1 71 H4
Parish Church CE Primary School *CROY/NA* CR0 86 C6
Parker Industrial Centre *RDART* DA2 52 D5
Park Farm Industrial Estate *FOLKN* CT19 220 C5
Park Farm Recreation Centre *ASH* TN23 204 D7
Park Farm Retail Park *FOLKN* CT19 220 C5
Park Hall Trading Estate *WNWD* SE27 44 D8
Park Hill Junior School *CROY/NA* CR0 86 E6
Park House RFC *HAYES* BR2 89 K5
Park Mall Shopping Centre *ASH* TN23 2 B4
Park Medical Centre *BERM/RHTH* SE16 25 L3
Park Mews Small Business Centre *HNHL* SE24 44 D4
Park Road Industrial Estate *SWLY* BR8 75 G7
Parkside Business Estate *DEPT* SE8 26 A5
Parkside Community Primary School *CANT* CT1 172 E7
Parkway Primary School *ERITHM* DA18 29 M2
Park Way Primary School *MAID/SHEP* ME15 167 J4
Park Wood Golf Club *BH/WHM* TN16 132 D8
Parkwood Hall School *SWLY* BR8 75 J7
Parkwood Industrial Estate *MAID/SHEP* ME15 260 B1
Parkwood Primary School *RHAM* ME8 102 F8
Pashley Manor & Gardens *BUR/ETCH* TN19 311 J10
Passenger Terminal Building *DVE/WH* CT16 9 J4
Passport Language Schools *BMLY* BR1 71 J5
The Pavilion Leisure Centre *BMLY* BR1 71 H6
The Pavilion Shopping Centre *TON* TN9 194 E4
Paxton Primary School *NRWD* SE19 69 G3
Peall Road Industrial Estate *CROY/NA* CR0 86 A2
Peasmarsh CE Primary School *RYE* TN31 326 E12
Peckham Park Primary School *PECK* SE15 25 H6
Peckham Pulse Healthy Living Centre *PECK* SE15 25 H7
Peckham Rye Primary School *PECK* SE15 45 J1
Pedham Place Industrial Estate *SWLY* BR8 93 H1

The Peel Trading Centre TON TN9 194 F3
Pelham Primary School BXLYHN DA7 50 A1
Pembroke Lodge Museum & Art Gallery BRCH CT7 176 C6
Pembury Hospital RTWE/PEM TN2 197 K5
Pembury Primary School RTWE/PEM TN2 278 A9
Pencester Surgery DVE/WH CT16 8 D4
Pendragon Secondary School BMLY BR1 47 H8
Pennypot Industrial Estate HYTHE CT21 222 A4
Penshurst CE Primary School RTON TN11 276 H5
Penshurst Place & Gardens RTON TN11 277 J5
Pentagon Shopping Centre CHAT ME4 6 D5
Pent Valley Technology College FOLKN CT19 10 A1
Perry Court Rudolf Steiner School RCANTW CT4 248 F10
Perry Hall Primary School ORP BR6 91 G2
Perrymount Primary School FSTH SE23 45 L7
Petham CP School RCANTW CT4 268 F2
Pharos DVE/WH CT16 9 G3
Phoenix Community Primary School KEN/WIL TN24 203 G6
Phoenix Industrial Estate STRD ME2 19 L3
Phoenix Leisure Centre CAT SE6 46 C5
Pickford Lane Medical Centre BXLYHN DA7 29 M7
Pickhurst Infant School HAYES BR2 88 F2
Pickhurst Junior School HAYES BR2 89 G2
Pier Pavilion Sports Centre HB CT6 128 F4
Pier Road Industrial Estate GILL ME7 83 L6
Pilgrims Way CP School CANT CT1 5 L7
Pilgrims Way J & I School PECK SE15 25 K5
Pilton Estate CROY/NA CR0 86 C5
Pine Lodge Touring Park MAID/SHEP ME15 169 G3
The Pines Garden RDV CT15 215 H4
Pioneer Business Park RAM CT11 16 F2
Platt CE Primary School BGR/WK TN15 240 H2
Platt Industrial Estate BGR/WK TN15 240 H1
Plaxtol Primary School BGR/WK TN15 240 D10
Playhouse Theatre WSTB CT5 126 E4
Plaza Cinema OXTED RH8 157 K7
Pluckley CE Primary School HDCN TN27 285 N2
Plumcroft Primary School WOOL/PLUM SE18 28 D5
Plumstead Leisure Centre WOOL/PLUM SE18 29 G4
Plumstead Manor School WOOL/PLUM SE18 28 E4
The Pointer School BKHTH/KID SE3 27 H7
Polo Farm Sports Club RCANTE CT3 175 G1
Portal House School RDV CT15 215 H3
Portland Medical Centre SNWD SE25 87 J1
Port Lympne Wild Animal Park, Mansion & Garden HYTHE CT21 306 H11
Port Richborough Business Park SWCH CT13 237 K5
P&O Stena Line DVW CT17 8 B9
Postley Industrial Centre MAID/SHEP ME15 13 H9
Poulton Business Park DVW CT17 213 G8
Poultwood Public Golf Club RTON TN11 189 J4
Pound Park Nursery School CHARL SE7 27 L4
Poverest Primary School STMC/STPC BR5 91 H1
Powell-Cotton Museum, Quex House & Gardens BRCH CT7 176 E8
The Powell School DVE/WH CT16 213 J5
Power Industrial Estate ERITH DA8 31 G7
Pratts Bottom Primary School ORP BR6 108 B5
Premier Business Park CHAT ME4 101 J4
Premier Cinema PECK SE15 25 H8
Premier Lodge DVE/WH CT16 8 F5
GVE DA12 79 K3
PUR RM19 32 F3
TON TN9 195 G6
WBY/YAL ME18 164 F5
Prendergast School BROCKY SE4 46 B2
Preston Hall Hospital DIT/AY ME20 140 A4
Preston Primary School RCANTE CT3 235 K7
PR for Schools SYD SE26 45 K8
Princes Golf Club SWCH CT13 237 Q10
Princes Park Medical Centre WALD ME5 101 J7
Princess Christian's Hospital RTON TN11 188 B3
The Princess Royal University Hospital ORP BR6 90 B6
Priory Fields School DVW CT17 217 J1
Priory Hill IOS ME12 230 G4
Priory House School CAT SE6 46 C6
Priory Infant School RAM CT11 17 H5
Priory Leisure Centre STMC/STPC BR5 91 K4
Priory School STMC/STPC BR5 91 K4
Priory Shopping Centre DART DA1 51 L4
Priory Special School SNWD SE25 69 G8
The Priory ORP BR6 91 J3
Progress Business Park CROY/NA CR0 86 A5
Pumping Station Museum CHAT ME4 6 D5
Purfleet Industrial Park PUR RM19 32 A1
Purfleet Primary School PUR RM19 32 B3
Pysons Road Industrial Estate BRDST CT10 182 F2
Quarry Hill Infant School GRAYS RM17 34 C4
Quarry Hill Junior School GRAYS RM17 34 C4
Quarry Wood Industrial Estate DIT/AY ME20 139 L3
DIT/AY ME20 139 M6
Quebec House BH/WHM TN16 159 J4
Quebec Industrial Estate BERM/RHTH SE16 25 M1
Queenborough Business Centre QBOR ME11 227 P2
Queenborough First School QBOR ME11 64 C8
Queenborough Yacht Club QBOR ME11 63 M8
Queen Elizabeth Hospital CHARL SE7 28 A5
Queen Elizabeths Grammar School FAV ME13 149 L1
Queen Elizabeth the Queen Mothers Hospital MARG CT9 15 H8
Queen Marys Hospital SCUP DA14 73 H2
Queens Hall & Winter Gardens MARG CT9 15 G2
The Queens House GNWCH SE10 26 E5
Queen's Road Cemetery CROY/NA CR0 86 D2
Queens Road Practice NWCR SE14 25 L7
Queen Victoria Cottage Hospital RTON TN11 194 F7
Queen Victoria Memorial Hospital HB CT6 129 J5
Quex Caravan Park WGOS CT8 177 H7
RAF Manston History Museum MSTR CT12 181 K3
Raglan Primary School HAYES BR2 71 K8
Railton Road Clinic BRXN/ST SW9 44 C3
Railway Street Industrial Estate GILL ME7 7 M2
Rainbow Quay BERM/RHTH SE16 25 M2
Rainham Mark Grammar School RHAM ME8 102 E3
Rainham School for Girls RHAM ME8 102 D5
Rainham Shopping Centre RHAM ME8 103 G4
Ramac Industrial Estate CHARL SE7 27 H4
Ramada Hotel DVE/WH CT16 213 G3
Ramsgate Athletic & FC RAM CT11 16 D6
Ramsgate Boat Club RAM CT11 17 H6
Ramsgate Brewery RAM CT11 17 L6
Ramsgate Holy Trinity Primary School RAM CT11 183 K4
Ramsgate New Port Ferry Terminal RAM CT11 17 H9
The Ramsgate School MSTR CT12 182 D3
Ramsgate Sports Centre RAM CT11 17 G5
Ramsgate Swimming Pool RAM CT11 16 E3
Rangefield Primary School BMLY BR1 70 F2
Range Road Industrial Estate HYTHE CT21 222 B4
Rathfern Primary School CAT SE6 46 A6
Ravensbourne College of Design & Communication CHST BR7 72 B2
The Ravensbourne School HAYES BR2 71 J8
Ravensquay Business Centre STMC/STPC BR5 91 J1
Ravens Wood School HAYES BR2 89 L6
Raynehurst Junior School GVE DA12 56 A8
Reay Primary School BRXN/ST SW9 24 A6
Rectory Business Centre SCUP DA14 73 J1
Rectory Paddock School STMC/STPC BR5 73 K6
Reculver Country Park HB CT6 232 D3
Reculver Primary CE Primary School HB CT6 232 B5
Reculver Towers & Roman Fort HB CT6 232 D2
Red Gates School CROY/NA CR0 86 B8
Redhill Junior School CHST BR7 72 C2
Redriff Primary School BERM/RHTH SE16 25 M1
Regent Fitzroy MARG CT9 179 G4
Regional Sports Centre TIL RM18 35 J8
Regis Business Park IOS ME12 64 B4
Regis Industrial Estate IOS ME12 64 B4
Regis Manor Community Primary School SIT ME10 119 M2
Remains of St Mary's Church HB CT6 232 E2
Research Centre RSIT ME9 145 M4
Research Development & Business Centre CANTW/ST CT2 171 K1
Restoration House ROCH ME1 19 K8
Richborough Business Park SWCH CT13 237 K10
Richborough Castle SWCH CT13 236 H8
Rich Industrial Estate PECK SE15 25 J5
STHWK SE1 24 F2
Richmond First School IOS ME12 64 E4
Richmond Infant School GILL ME7 7 K1
The Ridge Golf Club RMAID ME17 261 J4
Ridge View School TONN TN10 189 G7
Riding School E/WMAL ME19 165 J1
The Ripple School DEAL CT14 210 D1
Ripple Vale School DEAL CT14 210 F1
Ritzy Cinema BRXN/ST SW9 44 B2
River Court School RCANTW CT4 248 E7
River CP School DVW CT17 212 F6
Riverside Business Centre TON TN9 194 E4
Riverside Business Park KEN/WIL TN24 2 E4
Riverside Country Park GILL ME7 84 E8
Riverside Industrial Estate CANT CT1 172 C7
DART DA1 51 M3
HYTHE CT21 307 N12
Riverside Primary School BERM/RHTH SE16 25 H1
RHAM ME8 103 H4
Riverside Retail Park CANT CT1 4 B8
RSEV TN14 136 B5
Riverside School ASH TN23 204 C2
Riverside Swimming Centre ERITH DA8 30 F4
Riverston School LEE/GVPK SE12 47 H3
The River Surgery DVE/WH CT16 212 F5
Riverview Clinic GVE DA12 80 A2
Riverview Primary School GVE DA12 79 M1
Robert Browning Primary School WALW SE17 24 E4
The Robert Napier School GILL ME7 101 M2
Robertsbridge Community College RBTBR TN32 322 E9
Rochester Airport ROCH ME1 100 D6
Rochester Airport Industrial Estate ROCH ME1 100 D7
Rochester Castle ROCH ME1 19 J6
Rochester Cathedral ROCH ME1 19 J7
Rochester & Cobham Park Golf Club GVE DA12 80 E7
Rochester Grammar School for Girls ROCH ME1 100 D3
Rochester Health Centre ROCH ME1 100 E2
Rockliffe Manor Primary School WOOL/PLUM SE18 29 G5
Rockmount Primary School NRWD SE19 68 D3
Rodmersham Primary School RSIT ME9 146 C2
Rodmersham Squash Club RSIT ME9 146 B3
Rolvenden Primary School CRBK TN17 314 D6
Roman Industrial Estate CROY/NA CR0 86 F3
Roman Museum CANT CT1 5 G4
Roman Painted House DVE/WH CT16 8 D5
Romney Hythe & Dymchurch Railway LYDD TN29 320 F11
LYDD TN29 321 K6
LYDD TN29 335 P8
NROM TN28 331 K9
Romney Warren Golf Club NROM TN28 331 M7
Roper House School for the Deaf CANTW/ST CT2 4 D2
Ropery Business Park CHARL SE7 27 K3
Rope Walk Shopping Centre RYE TN31 225 G3
Roseacre Junior School MAID/BEAR ME14 168 B1
Rose Bruford College BFN/LL DA15 49 J6
DEPT SE8 26 C5
Rose & Crown Hotel TON TN9 194 F3
Rose Hill School STH/RUST TN4 22 A1
Rose McAndrew Clinic BRXN/ST SW9 24 A8
Rosemead Preparatory School DUL SE21 44 D7
Rosendale Primary School DUL SE21 44 D5
Rose Street School IOS ME12 64 C3
Rosherville CE Primary School GVW DA11 54 F4
Rotherhithe Civic Centre BERM/RHTH SE16 25 K1
Rotherhithe Primary School BERM/RHTH SE16 25 K3
Rowhill Grange Hotel & Spa RDART DA2 75 H2
Rowhill School RDART DA2 75 K1
Royal Albion Hotel BRDST CT10 183 L1
Royal Arsenal WOOL/PLUM SE18 28 C2
Royal Blackheath Golf Club ELTH/MOT SE9 48 A5
Royal Cinque Ports Golf Club DEAL CT14 207 K8
Royal Cinque Ports Yacht Club DVE/WH CT16 8 E6
Royal Engineers Museum GILL ME7 6 F1
Royal Museum & Art Gallery with Buffs Museum CANT CT1 4 F4
Royal National Theatre CMBW SE5 24 B6
Royal Observatory Greenwich GNWCH SE10 26 E5
Royal Park Primary School SCUP DA14 49 M8
Royal Russell School CROY/NA CR0 104 A1
Royal St Georges Golf Club SWCH CT13 237 N12
Royal School for Deaf Children WGOS CT8 177 H4
The Royal School for Deaf Children MARG CT9 15 H5
Royal Star Arcade MAID/BEAR ME14 12 F4
Royal Temple Yacht Club RAM CT11 17 J7
Royal Terrace Pier GVE DA12 55 K3
Royal Tunbridge Wells Business Park RTWE/PEM TN2 197 G4
Royal Victoria Hospital FOLKN CT19 11 G3
Royal Victoria Place Shopping Centre RTW TN1 23 G3
The Royal Wells Inn STH/RUST TN4 22 E4
Royston Primary School BECK BR3 69 L5
RSPB Reserve GILL ME7 84 E5
IOS ME12 228 A7
LYDD TN29 334 G4
LYDD TN29 335 J6
RTON TN11 197 L1
Rural Heritage Centre RCANTW CT4 291 R3
Rushey Green Primary School CAT SE6 46 C6
Ruskin House School HNHL SE24 44 D3
Russell Hotel MAID/BEAR ME14 141 J6
RTW TN1 22 F4
Rusthall Medical Centre STH/RUST TN4 200 C1
Ruxley Corner Industrial Estate SCUP DA14 73 L3
Ruxley Park Golf Centre STMC/STPC BR5 73 L5
Ryarsh CP School E/WMAL ME19 138 B1
Rye Art Gallery RYE TN31 225 H3
Rye Castle Museum RYE TN31 225 H4
Rye Community Clinic RYE TN31 225 G3
Rye Football & CC RYE TN31 225 H3
Rye Golf Club RYE TN31 332 A6
Rye Harbour Sailing Club RYE TN31 225 M6
Rye Industrial Estate RYE TN31 225 J5
Ryelands Primary School SNWD SE25 87 J1
Rye Lodge Hotel RYE TN31 225 H4
Rye Sports Centre RYE TN31 225 G3
Saatchi Gallery STHWK SE1 24 A1
Sackville School RTON TN11 255 R7
Sacred Heart RC Primary School WADH TN5 309 J4
Sacred Heart RC School CMBW SE5 24 D7
Safari Cinema CROY/NA CR0 86 C4
St Albans Road Infant School DART DA1 52 A4
St Alfege with St Peter CE Primary School GNWCH SE10 26 D5
St Andrews CE School CROY/NA CR0 86 C7
St Andrews Medical Centre STH/RUST TN4 196 D4
St Andrews Primary School BRXN/ST SW9 24 A8
St Andrews School ROCH ME1 19 J8
St Annes RC Primary School LBTH SE11 24 A5
St Anselms RC Primary School DART DA1 52 B3
St Anselms RC School CANT CT1 174 D4
St Anthonys RC Primary School EDUL SE22 45 G4
PGE/AN SE20 69 J5
St Anthonys School MARG CT9 178 F4
St Augustine of Canterbury RC Primary School RHAM ME8 116 E2
St Augustine's Abbey CANT CT1 5 J4
St Augustines Abbey RAM CT11 17 G8
St Augustines Business Park HB CT6 128 A6
St Augustines Catholic Primary School HYTHE CT21 222 F3
St Augustines College WGOS CT8 177 H5
St Augustines Cross MSTR CT12 181 M8
MSTR CT12 237 M1
St Augustine's Golf Club MSTR CT12 181 L8
St Augustines Primary School BELV DA17 30 A2
St Augustines RC Primary School CAT SE6 70 C2
STH/RUST TN4 196 D6
St Barnabas CE Primary School RTW TN1 23 H1
St Bartholomews CE Primary School SYD SE26 69 K1
St Bartholomews Hospital ROCH ME1 6 A5
SWLY BR8 75 G7
St Bartholomews RC Primary School SWLY BR8 74 F7
St Bartholomews School SIT ME10 120 A2
St Barts Hospital Sports Ground CHST BR7 72 E3
St Benedicts School WALD ME5 115 K3
St Botolphs CE Primary School GVW DA11 54 E5
St Catherines RC Girls School BXLYHS DA6 50 C3
St Chads RC Primary School SNWD SE25 86 F1
St Christophers School BECK BR3 70 D6
CANT CT1 5 J8
St Columbas RC Boys School BXLYHS DA6 50 C3
St Crispins CP School WGOS CT8 177 H6
St Cyprians Greek Orthodox Primary School THHTH CR7 68 D6
St Davids College WWKM BR4 88 C3
St Dunstans College CAT SE6 46 A6
St Eanswythes CE Primary School FOLK CT20 11 K6
St Edmunds Catholic School DVE/WH CT16 213 K7
St Edmunds Junior School CANTW/ST CT2 171 K2
St Edmunds RC Primary School POP/IOD E14 26 B3
St Edmunds School CANTW/ST CT2 171 K2
St Edwards RC Primary School IOS ME12 64 C3
St Ethelberts Catholic Primary School RAM CT11 17 K3
St Faiths Adult Education Centre MAID/BEAR ME14 12 F4
St Faiths at Ash School RCANTE CT3 235 R12
St Fidelis Catholic Primary School ERITH DA8 30 D5
St Francesca Cabrini Primary School FSTH SE23 45 K4
St Francis Catholic Primary School MAID/BEAR ME14 13 G3
St Francis RC Primary School PECK SE15 25 H5
St George's Business Centre ASH TN23 204 B1
St Georges Business Park SIT ME10 120 C5
St Georges CE High School BRDST CT10 178 F8
St Georges CE Middle School IOS ME12 65 M7
St Georges Centre GVW DA11 55 J4
St Georges CE Primary School BGR/WK TN15 238 E10
BMLY BR1 71 K6
PECK SE15 24 F6
St Georges CE School GVW DA11 55 H7
St Gregorys Catholic Comprehensive School STH/RUST TN4 196 C6
St Gregory's Cemetery CANT CT1 5 J3
St Gregory's Centre CANT CT1 5 H4
St Gregorys College WGOS CT8 177 H4
St Gregorys RC Primary School MARG CT9 14 F9
St Helens CE Primary School HOO/HM ME3 38 C8
St Helens RC Primary School BRXN/ST SW9 44 B1
St Hilarys School SEV TN13 21 G1
St James CE J & I School BERM/RHTH SE16 25 H2
St James CE Primary School HOO/HM ME3 43 J7
NWCR SE14 25 M7
St James Infant School E/WMAL ME19 139 G5
St James Medical Centre CROY/NA CR0 86 E3
St James RC Primary School HAYES BR2 90 C1
St James's J & I School RTWE/PEM TN2 23 J4
St James the Great RC Primary School PECK SE15 25 G7
THHTH CR7 68 C6
St John Business Centre MARG CT9 15 G6
St John Fisher Catholic School CHAT ME4 6 C9
St John Fisher RC Comprehensive School CHAT ME4 6 A7
St John Fisher RC Primary School ERITHM DA18 29 M2
St Johns Angell Town CE Primary School BRXN/ST SW9 24 C8
St Johns CE Infant School CHAT ME4 6 B7
St John's Cemetery MARG CT9 178 B6
St Johns CE Primary School CROY/NA CR0 87 L6
MAID/BEAR ME14 167 L1
PGE/AN SE20 69 K4
STH/RUST TN4 196 E6
CTHM CR3 156 A4
St Johns Infant School STH/RUST TN4 22 E1
St Johns RC Comprehensive School GVE DA12 55 L6
St Johns RC Primary School BERM/RHTH SE16 25 M1
GVE DA12 55 L6
St Johns & St Clements CE J & I School PECK SE15 45 H1
St John the Baptist CE Primary School CAT SE6 70 D1
St John the Divine CE Primary School CMBW SE5 24 C6
St Josephs Academic RC School BKHTH/KID SE3 46 F1
St Joseph's Annexe ABYW SE2 29 K5
St Josephs Catholic Infant School NRWD SE19 68 D3
St Josephs Catholic Primary School BMLY BR1 71 K4
St Josephs College STRHM/NOR SW16 68 C3
St Josephs RC Junior School CMBW SE5 24 D6
NRWD SE19 68 D3
St Josephs RC Primary School BERM/RHTH SE16 25 K2
DART DA1 50 E2
DEPT SE8 26 B6
GNWCH SE10 26 F4
RCANTE CT3 251 Q12

STHWK SE1 25 H1
St Josephs RC School
GVW DA11 54 E5
St Josephs School
BRDST CT10 179 J8
St Judes CE Primary School
HNHL SE24 44 C4
St Katharines Knockholt CE Primary School
RSEV TN14 134 A3
St Katherines School
SNOD ME6 113 G6
St Lawrence CE Primary School
BGR/WK TN15 163 K2
St Lawrence College
RAM CT11 17 H2
St Lawrence Industrial Estate
RAM CT11 16 D3
St Leonard's Tower (remains)
E/WMAL ME19 138 B7
St Lukes CE Infant School
STH/RUST TN4 196 F6
St Lukes CE Primary School
POP/IOD E14 26 E3
WNWD SE27 68 D2
St Lukes School
THHTH CR7 68 B8
St Margaret Clitherow Primary School *TONN* TN10 188 E7
St Margaret Lee CE Primary School *LEW* SE13 46 F2
St Margarets at Cliffe Primary School *RDV* CT15 215 H3
St Margarets at Troy Town Primary School *ROCH* ME1 19 J9
St Margarets CE Primary School
WOOL/PLUM SE18 28 D5
St Margarets Collier Street CE Primary School
STPH/PW TN12 258 C12
St Margaret's Infant School
RHAM ME8 102 F5
St Margarets Old School
BGR/WK TN15 163 G8
St Marks CE Primary School
DIT/AY ME20 114 A7
HAYES BR2 71 H7
LBTH SE11 24 A5
SNWD SE25 69 H8
STH/RUST TN4 200 E4
St Martin in the Fields High School
BRXS/STRHM SW2 44 C6
St Martins CE Primary School
FOLK CT20 219 J8
St Martins Hospital
CANT CT1 174 E1
St Martins School
DVW CT17 217 H2
St Mary CE Primary School
FOLKN CT19 221 G7
St Mary Magdalene CE Primary School *WOOL/PLUM* SE18 28 A3
St Mary Magdalene Peckham CE Primary School
PECK SE15 25 J8
St Mary Magdalen's Primary School *BROCKY* SE4 45 M2
St Mary of Charity CE Primary School *FAV* ME13 149 L2
St Marys Abbey
E/WMAL ME19 138 D5
St Mary & St Joseph Catholic School *SCUP* DA14 73 G2
St Marys Catholic Primary School
GILL ME7 7 M2
WSTB CT5 127 G3
St Marys CE Junior School
OXTED RH8 157 K6
St Marys CE Primary School
ASH TN23 202 D8
DVE/WH CT16 8 E3
LEW SE13 46 C3
SWLY BR8 74 F8
St Mary's Church
DVE/WH CT16 9 G3
St Mary's High School
CROY/NA CR0 86 D4
St Marys Island CE (Aided) Primary School *CHAT* ME4 83 J3
St Marys Medical Centre
STRD ME2 19 H2
St Marys Primary School
STRD ME2 19 G2
St Marys RC J & I School
CROY/NA CR0 86 E4
St Marys RC Primary School
BECK BR3 70 D4
DEAL CT14 209 G6
ELTH/MOT SE9 48 B3
TIL RM18 35 G8
St Marys Westbrook
FOLK CT20 10 D5
St Matthews CE Infant School
ROCH ME1 100 B3
St Matthews Primary School
STH/RUST TN4 196 E5
St Michaels CE Junior School
MAIDW ME16 12 C7
St Michaels CE Primary School
RYE TN31 327 M11
TENT TN30 301 N10
St Michaels CE Aided Primary School Hall *WELL* DA16 29 K7
St Michaels Primary School
HRTF TN7 198 C8
St Michaels RC Primary School
CHAT ME4 6 C7
St Michaels RC Secondary School *BERM/RHTH* SE16 25 H1
St Michaels Sydenham CE Primary *SYD* SE26 69 M1
St Mildreds Infant School
BRDST CT10 183 J1
St Nicholas at Wade Camping Site *BRCH* CT7 233 M7
St Nicholas at Wade CE Primary School *BRCH* CT7 233 M7
St Nicholas CE Infant School
STRD ME2 18 E3
St Nicholas' Cemetery
ROCH ME1 100 D2
St Nicholas CE Primary School
NROM TN28 330 H6
St Nicholas Court
BRCH CT7 233 L7
St Nicholas School
CHST BR7 72 D4
St Nicholas Special School
CANT CT1 4 F8
St Olaves Grammar School
ORP BR6 91 J6
St Olaves Preparatory School
ELTH/MOT SE9 48 C7
St Patricks RC Primary School
WOOL/PLUM SE18 28 E3
St Paulinus CE Primary School
DART DA1 50 F2
St Pauls CE Infant School
RRTW TN3 200 C1
St Pauls CE Primary School
SWLY BR8 75 J5
WALW SE17 24 C4
St Pauls CE Junior School
STH/RUST TN4 200 C1
St Pauls Cray CE Primary School *STMC/STPC* BR5 73 K7
St Pauls Cray Health Clinic
STMC/STPC BR5 73 H6
St Pauls Infant School
MAID/BEAR ME14 141 H6
St Pauls RC School
WOOL/PLUM SE18 29 H5
St Peter Chanel RC Primary School *SCUP* DA14 73 K2
St Peter & Paul RC Primary School *CHST* BR7 72 F6
St Peters CE Junior School
BRDST CT10 179 J6
St Peters CE Primary School
DIT/AY ME20 140 A2
FOLKN CT19 11 M5
GDST RH9 184 B3
RTWE/PEM TN2 23 J6
WALW SE17 24 E4
St Peters Infant School
ROCH ME1 100 D2
St Peters Methodist Primary School *CANT* CT1 4 E4
St Peters RC Primary School
SIT ME10 119 L6
WOOL/PLUM SE18 28 C4
St Peters School of English
CANT CT1 4 F3
St Philip Howard Catholic Primary School *HB* CT6 128 F4
St Phillips Infant School
SYD SE26 69 J1
St Philomenas RC Primary School *STMC/STPC* BR5 91 K3
St Radigund's Abbey
RDV CT15 216 C1
St Radigunds Community Primary School *DVW* CT17 213 H8
St Richards RC Primary School
DVE/WH CT16 8 D1
St Ronans School
HAWK TN18 312 G7
St Saviours CE Primary School
HNHL SE24 44 D1
St Saviours RC Primary School
LEW SE13 46 D2
St Saviours School
WGOS CT8 177 H5
St Simon of England RC Primary School *ASH* TN23 204 D3
St Simon Stock RC School
MAIDW ME16 166 D1
St Stephens CE Infant School
MAID/SHEP ME15 12 D9
St Stephens CE Primary School
DEPT SE8 26 B8
GDST RH9 184 A7
St Stephens Junior School
CANTW/ST CT2 172 A6
St Stephens Primary School
TON TN9 195 G5
St Stephens RC Primary School
WELL DA16 49 H1
St Teresas RC Primary School
KEN/WIL TN24 202 D7
St Thomas a' Becket RC Primary School
ABYW SE2 29 H2
St Thomas Becket RC Primary School *SNWD* SE25 87 H2
St Thomas' Hall
CANT CT1 5 G4
St Thomas More RC Primary School
BXLYHN DA7 30 A8
ELTH/MOT SE9 47 M1
WALD ME5 115 H1
St Thomas More RC School
ELTH/MOT SE9 48 B4
St Thomas of Canterbury RC Primary School
GRAYS RM17 34 C3
RHAM ME8 102 C3
St Thomas Primary School
SEV TN13 21 G7
St Thomas RC Primary School
CANT CT1 5 H3
St Thomas School
SIT ME10 120 D7
St Thomas the Apostle College
PECK SE15 25 K7
St Ursulas Convent School
GNWCH SE10 26 E6
St Vincents Catholic Primary School *ELTH/MOT* SE9 71 M1
St Werburgh CP Junior School
HOO/HM ME3 59 K8
St Werburgh Medical Centre
HOO/HM ME3 59 M7
St William of Perth RC Primary School *ROCH* ME1 100 C3
St William of York Primary School *FSTH* SE23 45 M6
St Winifreds Catholic Junior School *LEE/GVPK* SE12 47 G4
St Winifreds RC Infant School
LEW SE13 46 F3
Salehurst CE Primary School
RBTBR TN32 322 G10
Salmestone CP School
MARG CT9 14 F8
Salmestone Grange
MARG CT9 14 F9
Saltwood CE Primary School
HYTHE CT21 222 C1
Samphire Hoe Country Park
RDV CT15 216 E6
Samuel Jones Industrial Estate
PECK SE15 24 F6
Sandgate Primary School
FOLK CT20 10 B6
Sandgate Trading Estate
BERM/RHTH SE16 25 J4
Sandhurst CP School
HAWK TN18 313 M12
Sandhurst Primary School
CAT SE6 46 F5
Sandling Primary School
MAID/BEAR ME14 141 J5
Sandown Clinic
DEAL CT14 209 L1
Sandown Primary School
DEAL CT14 209 K2
Sandwich Industrial Estate
SWCH CT13 237 K12
Sandwich Infant School
SWCH CT13 237 J12
Sandwich Junior School
SWCH CT13 206 A2
Sandwich Lawn Tennis Club
SWCH CT13 237 L12
Sandwich Leisure Park
SWCH CT13 236 H12
Sandwich Sailing & Motor Boat Club *SWCH* CT13 253 R2
Sandwich Sports & Leisure Centre *SWCH* CT13 206 A2
Sandwich Technology School
SWCH CT13 206 A2
Saxon Way Primary School
GILL ME7 7 M1
Sayer Clinic
CROY/NA CR0 86 A7
Schooling Licensed Conveyancers *GRAYS* RM17 34 C4
School of Health
RDART DA2 52 C4
Scotney Castle Garden (NT)
RRTW TN3 296 E10
Scotts Park Primary School
BMLY BR1 71 K5
Seabrook CE Primary School
HYTHE CT21 223 J3
Seasalter Sailing Club
WSTB CT5 125 J2
Sea Street Industrial Estate
HB CT6 128 D6
Seaview Caravan Park
HB CT6 127 M1
Sedgehill School
CAT SE6 70 C2
Sedleys CE Primary School
MEO DA13 78 B2
Selhurst High School for Boys
SNWD SE25 86 E2
The Selhurst Medical Centre
SNWD SE25 86 F2
Sellindge Primary School
RASHE TN25 306 H4
Sellindge Sports Club
RASHE TN25 307 J4
Selling CE Primary School
FAV ME13 246 G3
Selsdon Community Centre
SAND/SEL CR2 104 A4
Selsdon High School
SAND/SEL CR2 104 C2
Selsdon Primary School
SAND/SEL CR2 104 B3
Selsted CE Primary School
RDV CT15 292 H3
Senacre Technology College
MAID/SHEP ME15 167 L7
Senacre Wood Primary School
MAID/SHEP ME15 167 M6
SENCO
STRD ME2 99 J3
Sene Valley Golf Club
HYTHE CT21 222 F1
Seven Islands Leisure Centre
BERM/RHTH SE16 25 K2
Seven Mills Primary School
POP/IOD E14 26 B1
Sevenoaks Business Centre
RSEV TN14 136 B7
Sevenoaks CC
SEV TN13 21 J5
Sevenoaks Hospital
SEV TN13 136 B7
Sevenoaks Library, Museum & Art Gallery *BGR/WK* TN15 21 J6
Sevenoaks Primary School
SEV TN13 21 G1
Sevenoaks RFC
BGR/WK TN15 21 K6
Sevenoaks School
BGR/WK TN15 21 K9
Sevenoaks School Track
BGR/WK TN15 21 K9
Sevenoaks Swimming Centre
BGR/WK TN15 21 K6
Sevenoaks Way Industrial Estate
STMC/STPC BR5 73 K7
Shakespeare Business Centre
BRXN/ST SW9 44 C1
Shamel Business Centre
STRD ME2 19 K3
Shatterlocks Infant School
DVE/WH CT16 213 J7
Shawcroft School
STMC/STPC BR5 91 M1
Shears Green Primary School
GVW DA11 55 G8
Shearway Business Park
FOLKN CT19 220 A5
Sheerness Clinic
IOS ME12 64 D4
Sheerness Golf Club
IOS ME12 65 G6
Sheldon Business Centre
STRD ME2 19 M1
Sheldwich CP School
FAV ME13 246 B3
Shell & Dunkirk Memorials
DVW CT17 8 E6
Shenstone School
DART DA1 50 E3
Shepherd Neame Brewery
FAV ME13 149 L1
Shepherds Community School
BROCKY SE4 46 A1
Sheppey College
IOS ME12 64 C2
Sheppey Community Hospital
IOS ME12 65 H8
Sheppey Little Theatre
IOS ME12 64 E3
Sheppey RFC
IOS ME12 65 H6
Sheppey Yacht Club
IOS ME12 64 F3
Shepway Cross
HYTHE CT21 307 M11
Shepway Infant School
MAID/SHEP ME15 167 M5
Shepway Junior School
MAID/SHEP ME15 167 M5
Sheridale Business Centre
STRD ME2 18 E6
Sherington Primary School
CHARL SE7 27 J5
Sherwin Knight Primary School
STRD ME2 18 C7
Sherwood Park Infant School
RTWE/PEM TN2 197 G7
Sherwood Park Primary School
BFN/LL DA15 49 J4
RTWE/PEM TN2 197 G7
Shipbourne Primary School
RTON TN11 240 B12
Shirley Clinic
CROY/NA CR0 87 K4
Shirley High School
CROY/NA CR0 87 L6
Shirley Oaks Hospital
CROY/NA CR0 87 K3
Shirley Park Golf Club
CROY/NA CR0 87 J5
Shirley Wanderers RFC
WWKM BR4 88 D7
Shiva Medical Centre
IOS ME12 65 J7
Sholden CE Primary School
DEAL CT14 208 F4
Shooters Hill Golf Club
WOOL/PLUM SE18 28 D7
Shooters Hill Post 16 Campus
WOOL/PLUM SE18 28 B6
The Shopping Centre
MARG CT9 14 F4
Shoreham County Primary School *RSEV* TN14 109 L5
Shorncliffe Military Cemetery
HYTHE CT21 223 K2
Shorne CE Primary School
GVE DA12 80 F2
Shornecliffe Industrial Estate
FOLK CT20 223 L1
Shorne Wood Country Park
GVE DA12 80 D5
Showcase Bluewater Cinema
GRH DA9 53 G6
Sibertswold Primary School
RDV CT15 271 R9
Sibton Park (School)
RFOLK CT18 291 L9
Sidcup Cemetery
BXLY DA5 49 L7
Sidcup Golf Club
BFN/LL DA15 49 H7
Sidcup Health Centre
SCUP DA14 49 H8
Sidcup Sports Club
SCUP DA14 73 G1
Sidney Cooper Gallery
CANT CT1 4 E3
Silver Screen Cinema
DVE/WH CT16 8 E4
FOLK CT20 11 K6
Simon Langton Grammar School for Boys *CANT* CT1 174 B5
Simon Langton Grammar School for Girls *CANT* CT1 174 C4
Simpsons Industrial Estate
RYE TN31 225 K6
Singleton Medical Centre
ASH TN23 204 A3
Singlewell Primary School
GVE DA12 79 L3
Sir Francis Drake Primary School *DEPT* SE8 25 M4
Sir Joseph Williams Maths School *ROCH* ME1 100 C4
Sir Roger Manwoods School
SWCH CT13 206 B1
The Sir William Nottidge Technology School
WSTB CT5 127 G5
Sissinghurst CE Primary School *CRBK* TN17 299 K5
Site of Greenwich Hospital
GNWCH SE10 27 G4
Sittingbourne Adult Education Centre
SIT ME10 119 K6
Sittingbourne Industrial Park
SIT ME10 119 K4
SIT ME10 120 A4
Sittingbourne & Kemsley Light Railway
SIT ME10 120 C1
Sittingbourne Memorial Hospital *SIT* ME10 120 A6
Sittingbourne & Milton Regis Golf Club *RSIT* ME9 118 C6
Sittingbourne Retail Park
SIT ME10 119 M1
Sittingbourne Sports Centre
SIT ME10 120 B6
Six Bridges Trading Estate
STHWK SE1 25 H4
The Skinners Company School
STH/RUST TN4 196 D7
Skinner Street Primary School
GILL ME7 7 J2
Ski Slope
STMC/STPC BR5 73 L5
Slade Green FC
ERITH DA8 31 J7
Slade Green Primary School
ERITH DA8 31 H6
Slade Primary School
TON TN9 194 E3
Sloane Hospital
BECK BR3 70 E5
Smallhythe Place (NT)
TENT TN30 315 P8
Smarden Business Estate
HDCN TN27 284 A10
Smarden Primary School
HDCN TN27 284 D7
Smeeth CP School
RASHE TN25 289 L12
Smiths Court Hotel
MARG CT9 15 L3
Snodland CE Primary School
SNOD ME6 113 G5
Snodland Clinic
SNOD ME6 113 H5
Solefield School
SEV TN13 162 B5
The Somerfield Hospital
MAIDW ME16 12 B3
South Avenue Infant School
SIT ME10 120 B6
South Aylesford Retail Park
DIT/AY ME20 139 M5
Southborough Cemetery
STH/RUST TN4 196 A3
Southborough Primary School
HAYES BR2 90 B1
South Borough Primary School
MAID/SHEP ME15 13 H9
South Chelsea College
BRXN/ST SW9 44 A2
South Croydon Sports Club
SAND/SEL CR2 86 F8
Southfields School
GVE DA12 79 K2
South Kent College
ASH TN23 2 C6
ASH TN23 204 C5
DVE/WH CT16 8 D3
FOLK CT20 10 F5
South Kent Hospital
FOLK CT20 219 M8
Southlake Primary School
ABYW SE2 29 L1
Southlands School
NROM TN28 331 K7
South Lewisham Health Centre *CAT* SE6 70 D1
South London Gallery
CMBW SE5 24 F7
South London Tamil School
CROY/NA CR0 86 D3
South London Theatre
WNWD SE27 44 D8
South Norwood Country Park
SNWD SE25 69 K8
South Norwood Hill Medical Centre *SNWD* SE25 68 F6
South Norwood Medical Centre
SNWD SE25 68 F8
South Norwood Pools & Fitness Centre
SNWD SE25 87 H1
South Norwood Primary School
SNWD SE25 87 H1
South of England Rare Breeds Centre *RASHW* TN26 303 L12
South Park Hotel
SAND/SEL CR2 86 F7
South Quay Plaza
POP/IOD E14 26 C1
South Rise Primary School
WOOL/PLUM SE18 28 E4
Southwall Industrial Estate
DEAL CT14 209 J2
Southwark College
BERM/RHTH SE16 25 J2
CMBW SE5 24 F6
Southwark Park Primary School *BERM/RHTH* SE16 25 J2
Southwark Park Sports Centre
BERM/RHTH SE16 25 K3
Southwark Sports Ground
DUL SE21 45 G6
The Space Arts Centre Cinema
POP/IOD E14 26 A3
The Spa Hotel
STH/RUST TN4 22 B5
Spa Industrial Park
RTWE/PEM TN2 197 H5
Spa Valley Railway
RRTW TN3 199 M5
Spectrum Business Centre
STRD ME2 82 F5
Spectrum Business Estate
MAID/SHEP ME15 260 A1
Speldhurst CE Primary School
RRTW TN3 277 P10
Spinnens Acre County Junior School *WALD* ME5 115 L4
Splashworld Swimming Centre
WELL DA16 49 L2
Spotlites Theatre Company
CHAT ME4 6 F6
Springfield Christian School
CAT SE6 46 A8
Springfield Industrial Estate
HAWK TN18 312 C6
Spring Grove School
RASHE TN25 203 M1
Spring Park Primary School
CROY/NA CR0 88 B6
Springvale Retail Park
STMC/STPC BR5 73 K7
STMC/STPC BR5 91 L1
Squerryes Court Manor House & Gardens *BH/WHM* TN16 159 H6
Stade Court Hotel
HYTHE CT21 222 D4
Stafford Cross Business Park
CROY/NA CR0 86 A8
Stafford House Tutorial College
CANT CT1 5 K8
Stag Theatre
SEV TN13 21 H7
Stalham Business Centre
QBOR ME11 227 P2
Standard Industrial Estate
CAN/RD E16 27 L1
Stanhope CP School
ASH TN23 204 D6
Stanley Technical High School
SNWD SE25 69 G7
Stansted CE Primary School
BGR/WK TN15 238 E4
Stanton Square Industrial Estate *CAT* SE6 70 A1
Staple Cross MCP Primary School *RBTBR* TN32 323 Q11
Staplehurst Primary School
STPH/PW TN12 281 R6
Starborough Castle
EDEN TN8 192 A8
Steam Tug 'Cervia'
RAM CT11 17 K7
Stella Maris Catholic Primary School *FOLKN* CT19 11 G2
Stelling Minnis CE Primary School *RCANTW* CT4 269 J7
Stewart Fleming Primary School *PGE/AN* SE20 69 K7
Stifford Primary School
GRAYS RM17 33 M4
Stillness Primary School
BROCKY SE4 45 M4
Stocks Green Primary School
RTON TN11 188 B8
Stockwell Park School
BRXN/ST SW9 24 A7
Stockwell Primary School
BRXN/ST SW9 44 A1
Stodmarsh National Nature Reserve *RCANTE* CT3 234 C6
Stoke Community School
HOO/HM ME3 41 K8
Stone Bay School
BRDST CT10 179 L7
Stone Chapel
FAV ME13 148 F2
Stonegate CE Primary School
WADH TN5 310 A12
Stone House Hospital
RDART DA2 52 D4
Stone Lake Retail Park
CHARL SE7 27 K3
Stour Leisure Centre
KEN/WIL TN24 2 D6
Stour Retail Park
CANT CT1 172 E6
Stour Valley Industrial Estate
RCANTW CT4 248 F5
Stowting CE Primary School
RASHE TN25 290 E9
Stpeters CE Infants School
STH/RUST TN4 196 C5
Streatham & Clapham High School (Preparatory)
BRXS/STRHM SW2 44 A6
Streatham & Croydon RFC
THHTH CR7 86 B1
Streatham Wells Primary School
BRXS/STRHM SW2 44 A7
Streete Court School
GDST RH9 156 D8
Strood Cemetery
STRD ME2 18 D6
Strood Retail Park
STRD ME2 19 G4
Strood Swimming Pool
STRD ME2 18 D3

Strood Yacht Club STRD ME2 18 F6
Sturry CE Primary School CANTW/ST CT2 173 H2
Stutfall Castle HYTHE CT21 307 K12
Sudbourne Primary School BRXS/STRHM SW2 44 A3
Summerlands Special School HDCN TN27 264 C9
Sundridge & Brasted CE Primary School RSEV TN14 160 D3
Sundridge Park Golf Club BMLY BR1 71 K3
Sunnyhill Primary School STRHM/NOR SW16 68 A1
Surex Swimming Pools BH/WHM TN16 132 C1
Surrey Docks Farm BERM/RHTH SE16 26 A1
Surrey Docks Health Centre BERM/RHTH SE16 25 M1
Surrey Docks Watersports Centre BERM/RHTH SE16 25 M2
Surrey Quays Leisure Park BERM/RHTH SE16 25 L2
Surrey Quays Shopping Centre BERM/RHTH SE16 25 L2
Surrey Square J & I School WALW SE17 24 E4
Surry CCC (The Oval) LBTH SE11 24 A5
Sussex Road Primary School TON TN9 194 D5
Sutcliffe Park Athletics Track ELTH/MOT SE9 47 J3
Sutton at Hone CE Primary School EYN DA4 76 B4
Sutton Valence Preparatory School RMAID ME17 260 D5
Sutton Valence Primary School RMAID ME17 260 F6
Sutton Valence School RMAID ME17 260 E6
Swadelands Specialist School RMAID ME17 243 K12
Swalecliffe Primary School WSTB CT5 127 J3
The Swan Brewery WBY/YAL ME18 241 M11
Swan Business Park DART DA1 51 L2
Swanley School SWLY BR8 74 E7
Swanscombe Business Centre SWCM DA10 53 M3
Swan Valley Community School SWCM DA10 54 A5
Sweetwoods Park Golf Club EDEN TN8 275 M9
The Sweyne Junior School SWCM DA10 54 A5
Swingate Infant School WALD ME5 115 K4
Sydenham Girls School SYD SE26 45 J8
Sydenham High School Junior Department SYD SE26 69 J1
Sydenham High School (Secondary) SYD SE26 69 J2
Sydenham High School Sports Ground BECK BR3 70 B2
TA Centre DVW CT17 8 A1
Taberner House CROY/NA CR0 86 D6
Tait Road Industrial Estate CROY/NA CR0 86 E3
Tandridge Golf Club OXTED RH8 184 D1
Tannery Trading Estate TON TN9 194 F4
Target Business Centre MAID/SHEP ME15 260 A1
Tatsfield Primary School BH/WHM TN16 132 C7
Tavy Clinic ABYW SE2 29 K1
TCA Leisure Centre TIL RM18 35 H8
Teardrop Industrial Park SWLY BR8 93 K1
Technical Procurement Sports Club RASHE TN25 202 E3
Temple Ewell CE Primary School DVE/WH CT16 212 E4
Temple Hill Primary School DART DA1 52 B3
Temple Mill Primary School STRD ME2 82 C3
Temple of Bacchus CMBW SE5 24 D8
Temple School STRD ME2 82 C4
Tennis Club GILL ME7 101 M2
Tenterden CE Junior School TENT TN30 315 N2
Tenterden Golf Club TENT TN30 301 Q12
Tenterden Infant School TENT TN30 315 M2
Tenterden Leisure Centre TENT TN30 315 N2
Tenterden Vineyard Park TENT TN30 315 P8
Terence Macklin Gallery WSTB CT5 126 E3
Teynham Medical Centre RSIT ME9 121 K7
Teynham Parochial CE Primary School RSIT ME9 121 K7
Thames Barrier CAN/RD E16 27 L1
Thames Barrier Information & Learning Centre WOOL/PLUM SE18 27 L2
Thameside Industrial Estate CAN/RD E16 27 M1
Thameside Primary School GRAYS RM17 34 D5
Thameside Theatre GRAYS RM17 34 B4
Thames Industrial Park TIL RM18 36 D3
Thames View Primary School RHAM ME8 102 E3
Thamesview School GVE DA12 56 A8
Thanet Business Centre MARG CT9 15 H4
Thanet College MARG CT9 14 F4
Thanet Crematorium MARG CT9 178 B6
Thanet Reach Business Park BRDST CT10 182 F1
Thanet Technical College BRDST CT10 183 K2
Thanet Wanderers RUFC BRDST CT10 179 J7
Thanington (Canterbury) School of Music CANTW/ST CT2 171 J7
Theatre Centre BECK BR3 70 C6
Theatre Royal MARG CT9 15 G4
Theodore McLeary Primary School EDUL SE22 45 G2
Thistlebrook Industrial Estate ABYW SE2 29 K2
The Thomas Aveling School ROCH ME1 100 D5
Thomas Francis Academy BRXN/ST SW9 44 C2
Thomas Peacocke Community College RYE TN31 225 G3
Thomas Tallis School BKHTH/KID SE3 47 J1
Thornhills Medical Centre DIT/AY ME20 139 H4
Thornlea Health Centre RDV CT15 271 R8
Thornton Heath Health Centre THHTH CR7 68 D8
Thornton Heath Pools & Fitness Centre THHTH CR7 68 D8
Thorntree Primary School CHARL SE7 27 L4
Thurlow Park School WNWD SE27 44 C7
Thurrock Athletics Stadium CDW/CHF RM16 34 E1
Thurrock & Basildon College CDW/CHF RM16 35 G3
Thurrock Business Centre WTHK RM20 33 G5
Thurston Industrial Estate LEW SE13 46 C1
Ticehurst CE Primary School WADH TN5 310 E9
Tidemill Primary School DEPT SE8 26 B6
Tilbury Fort TIL RM18 55 K2
Tilbury/Gravesend Passenger Ferry TIL RM18 55 J2
Tilbury Manor Infant School TIL RM18 35 J6
Tilbury Manorjunior School TIL RM18 35 J6
Tiller Centre (Swimming Baths) POP/IOD E14 26 B2
Tiller Leisure Centre POP/IOD E14 26 B2
Tilling Green Infant School RYE TN31 224 F4
Timbercroft Primary School WOOL/PLUM SE18 28 F6
Titan Industrial Estate GRAYS RM17 34 B3
Tivoli Industrial Estate MARG CT9 14 E6
Tollgate Primary School CROY/NA CR0 87 K2
Tomas Seth Business Park QBOR ME11 227 P1
Tom Thumb Theatre MARG CT9 15 L3
Tonbridge Castle TON TN9 194 E3
Tonbridge Cemetery TONN TN10 188 F8
Tonbridge FC (Longmead Stadium) RTON TN11 188 E8
Tonbridge Grammar School for Girls TON TN9 194 F6
Tonbridge Market TON TN9 194 E3
Tonbridge Oast Theatre RTON TN11 194 C1
Tonbridge RFC TON TN9 194 E4
Tonbridge School TONN TN10 194 E2
Tonbridge School Athletics Track TONN TN10 194 E2
Tonbridge Swimming Pool TON TN9 194 E3
Tonbridge Town Sailing Club RTON TN11 277 R1
Torridon Primary School CAT SE6 46 E7
Tovil Green Business Park MAID/SHEP ME15 166 F4
Tower Bridge Primary School STHWK SE1 25 G1
Tower Industrial Estate BGR/WK TN15 238 C8
SNWD SE25 69 H8
Tower Retail Park DART DA1 51 G3
The Towers School KEN/WIL TN24 203 G3
Townley Grammar School for Girl BXLYHS DA6 50 A4
Town Medical Centre SEV TN13 21 H7
Toy & Model Museum RRTW TN3 296 D6
Tramshed Theatre WOOL/PLUM SE18 28 C3
Travel Inn
BGR/WK TN15 241 K1
CDW/CHF RM16 33 K2
E/WMAL ME19 138 F2
FOLKN CT19 220 B6
GILL ME7 102 A3
GVW DA11 55 H4
GVW DA11 55 H7
KEN/WIL TN24 205 J6
MAID/BEAR ME14 169 H2
MAIDW ME16 140 C6
MAIDW ME16 140 E4
OXTED RH8 158 D4
PUR RM19 32 A4
RASHE TN25 264 F11
RDV CT15 214 A5
RDV CT15 215 D5
SAND/SEL CR2 87 H8
SIT ME10 119 J3
STHWK SE1 24 A1
WSTB CT5 126 D7
Travelodge
FAV ME13 170 A3
GRH DA9 52 F3
KEN/WIL TN24 202 F6
MSTR CT12 182 D1
WSTB CT5 125 M7
WTHK RM20 33 G2
Treetops Special School GRAYS RM17 34 C3
Trenchwood Medical Centre TONN TN10 188 F8
Trinity Business Centre BERM/RHTH SE16 26 A1
Trinity College Centre PECK SE15 24 F6
Trinity College of Music GNWCH SE10 26 D5
Trinity Hospital GNWCH SE10 26 E4
Trinity School CROY/NA CR0 87 K5
Trinity School Belvedere BELV DA17 30 D3
Trinity Theatre & Arts Centre RTW TN1 22 F4
Trinity Trading Estate SIT ME10 120 A3
Trosley Country Park MEO DA13 239 M6
Trottiscliffe CE Primary School E/WMAL ME19 239 M8
Tudor Court Primary School CDW/CHF RM16 34 A1
Tudor House MARG CT9 15 G3
Tuke School PECK SE15 25 J7
Tunbridge Wells Borderers Sports Club RTWE/PEM TN2 201 H6
Tunbridge Wells Girls Grammar School STH/RUST TN4 196 C7
Tunbridge Wells Golf Club STH/RUST TN4 22 A6
Tunbridge Wells Grammar School STH/RUST TN4 196 D5
Tunbridge Wells High School RTWE/PEM TN2 197 H7
Tunbridge Wells Hockey Club RTWE/PEM TN2 23 H9
Tunbridge Wells Independent Hospital RRTW TN3 199 J2
Tunbridge Wells Museum & Art Gallery RTW TN1 22 F4
Tunbridge Wells Nuffield Hospital RTWE/PEM TN2 23 L5
Tunbridge Wells Sports Centre STH/RUST TN4 196 D6
Tunbury Primary School WALD ME5 115 G4
Tunnel Avenue Trading Estate GNWCH SE10 26 E1
Tunnel Industrial Estate WTHK RM20 33 G3
Tunstall CE Primary School RSIT ME9 145 K1
Turney School DUL SE21 44 D5
Turnham Primary School BROCKY SE4 45 M2
Twenty Twenty Industrial Estate MAIDW ME16 140 D5
Two Chimneys Caravan Park BRCH CT7 177 G8
Twydall Health & Welfare Clinic RHAM ME8 102 C2
Twydall Infant School RHAM ME8 102 C3
Twydall Junior School RHAM ME8 102 C3
The Type Museum BRXN/ST SW9 24 A7
Tyrwhitt Drake Museum of Carriages MAID/SHEP ME15 13 G6
UCI Cinema
WTHK RM20 33 G3
BERM/RHTH SE16 25 L2
UCI Filmworks Cinema GNWCH SE10 27 G3
UGC Cinema STRD ME2 99 M2
Ulcombe CE Primary School RMAID ME17 261 N7
Underling Industrial Estate STPH/PW TN12 259 L11
Unicorn Primary School BECK BR3 88 C1
Union Mill CRBK TN17 298 G9
United Medical & Dental Schools STHWK SE1 24 A2
University Hospital Lewisham LEW SE13 46 C3
University of Greenwich
DART DA1 52 A7
E/WMAL ME19 164 B1
ELTH/MOT SE9 48 E4
GNWCH SE10 26 E4
WOOL/PLUM SE18 28 B2
University of Greenwich at Medway CHAT ME4 83 J5
University of Greenwich (Mansion Site) ELTH/MOT SE9 48 D4
University of Greenwich Sports Ground
ELTH/MOT SE9 47 M2
ELTH/MOT SE9 48 D5
University of Kent at Canterbury CANTW/ST CT2 153 L8
University of Kent Canterbury CANTW/ST CT2 171 L1
University of London NWCR SE14 25 M7
Upbury Arts College GILL ME7 7 G5
Upchurch River Valley Golf Club RHAM ME8 103 L3
Upland Primary School BXLYHN DA7 50 A1
Uplands Community College WADH TN5 309 L5
Upnor Castle STRD ME2 83 G3
Upper Brents Industrial Estate FAV ME13 123 L8
Upton Day Hospital BXLYHS DA6 49 M2
Upton Junior School BRDST CT10 183 J1
Upton Primary School BXLY DA5 49 M3
Upton Road School BXLYHS DA6 49 M3
Ursuline College & St Angela's School WGOS CT8 177 G5
The Vale Medical Centre FSTH SE23 45 M7
Valence School BH/WHM TN16 159 L4
Vale View Community School DVW CT17 217 J2
Valley Park Community School MAID/BEAR ME14 13 M4
Valley Primary School HAYES BR2 71 G6
Valmar Trading Estate CMBW SE5 24 D7
Vauxhall Primary School LBTH SE11 24 A4
Vauxhall Road Industrial Estate CANT CT1 172 D5
Vestry Industrial Estate RSEV TN14 136 A5
VI Components Industrial Park ERITH DA8 30 F4
Victoria Business Centre WELL DA16 29 H8
Victoria Hospital DEAL CT14 209 J4
Victoria Hotel CANTW/ST CT2 4 A3
Victoria Industrial Park DART DA1 51 L3
Victoria Road Primary School ASH TN23 2 A6
Victoria Wharf Industrial Estate DEPT SE8 26 A4
Vigo RFC MEO DA13 239 P4
Vigo Villiage School MEO DA13 239 M5
Viking Ship 'Hugin' MSTR CT12 182 B8
The Vine Medical Centre MAIDW ME16 12 A7
Vintners Park Crematorium MAID/BEAR ME14 141 L7
VIP Trading Estate CHARL SE7 27 K3
Virgo Fidelis Convent Schools NRWD SE19 68 D3
Voyager Business Estate BERM/RHTH SE16 25 H2
VUE Cinema
CROY/NA CR0 86 A5
WTHK RM20 33 H2
Vulcan Business Centre CROY/NA CR0 105 K3
Waddon Clinic CROY/NA CR0 86 B8
Waddon Infant School CROY/NA CR0 86 B8
Wadhurst Business Park WADH TN5 308 G2
Wadhurst CE Primary School WADH TN5 309 L4
Wainscott Primary School STRD ME2 82 E3
Wakeley Junior School RHAM ME8 103 H4
Walderslade Medical Centre WALD ME5 101 H7
Walderslade Primary School WALD ME5 115 H2
Waldo Industrial Estate BMLY BR1 71 K7
The Wallace Centre DEPT SE8 26 C5
Wallett's Court Country House Hotel RDV CT15 214 E3
Walmer Castle & Gardens DEAL CT14 209 L8
Walmer & Kingsdown Golf Club DEAL CT14 211 L5
Walmer Lawn Tennis & Croquet Club DEAL CT14 209 L7
Walnut Leisure Centre ORP BR6 91 H4
Walnuts Shopping Centre ORP BR6 91 H4
Walworth Lower School WALW SE17 24 E4
Walworth Upper School WALW SE17 24 F4
Warden House Primary School DEAL CT14 209 H4
Warders Medical Centre TON TN9 194 F3
Warehouse Theatre CROY/NA CR0 86 E5
Warlingham Park School WARL CR6 130 F2
Warlingham RFC & John Fisher Sports Club WARL CR6 130 A2
Warlingham School WARL CR6 130 A2
Warlingham Sports Club WARL CR6 130 C3
Warmlake Business Estate RMAID ME17 260 F4
Warren Primary School CDW/CHF RM16 33 K2
Warren Retail Park KEN/WIL TN24 202 E7
Warren Road Primary School ORP BR6 91 G7
Warren Wood County Primary School ROCH ME1 100 D5
Warsop Trading Estate EDEN TN8 192 E5
Warwick Leadlay Gallery GNWCH SE10 26 D5
Waterfront Leisure Centre WOOL/PLUM SE18 28 B2
Watergate School
CAT SE6 70 C2
LEW SE13 46 C2
Watermill Museum EDEN TN8 191 L5
Watling Street Surgery CANT CT1 4 E5
Watts Charity Almshouses ROCH ME1 100 D1
Wavelengths Leisure Pool & Library DEPT SE8 26 B6
Waverley Lower Secondary School EDUL SE22 45 J3
Waverley School PECK SE15 45 K3
Wayfield County Primary School WALD ME5 101 H6
Weald Community Primary School RSEV TN14 255 J3
Weald of Kent Golf Club HDCN TN27 260 H12
The Weald of Kent Grammar School TON TN9 195 G6
Weald Sports Centre CRBK TN17 298 F7
Wellesley House School BRDST CT10 183 J2
The Welling Clinic WELL DA16 29 H8
Welling Medical Centre WELL DA16 49 G2
Welling School WELL DA16 29 J7
Welling United FC WELL DA16 49 K1
The Wernher Collection at Ranger's House GNWCH SE10 26 E7
Wesley Sports Centre FAV ME13 149 L3
West Borough CP School MAIDW ME16 166 C2
West Borough Sports Centre MAIDW ME16 166 D2
Westbrooke School WELL DA16 49 L1
Westcourt Primary School GVE DA12 55 M7
Westerham Golf Club BH/WHM TN16 159 L4
Westfield Business Centre STRD ME2 19 J3
Westgate Archway & Museum CANTW/ST CT2 4 E3
Westgate & Birchington Golf Club WGOS CT8 177 G5
Westgate College RNID WGOS CT8 177 H3
Westgate Hall CANTW/ST CT2 4 E3
Westgate Pavilion & Theatre WGOS CT8 177 H3
Westgate Primary School DART DA1 51 L5
West Gate Towers CANT CT1 4 F3
West Hill Primary School DART DA1 51 K4
West India Pier POP/IOD E14 26 A1
West Kent College TON TN9 194 D5
West Kent College of Further Education STH/RUST TN4 196 D6
West Kent Golf Club ORP BR6 106 D6
West Kingsdown Industrial Estate BGR/WK TN15 111 K3
West Kingsdown Medical Centre BGR/WK TN15 111 L3
Westlands School SIT ME10 119 J5
West Lane Trading Estate SIT ME10 120 B4
West Lodge Preparatory School BFN/LL DA15 49 G8
West Malling CE Primary School E/WMAL ME19 138 C5
West Malling Golf Club E/WMAL ME19 239 P11
West Malling Industrial Park E/WMAL ME19 239 R11
Westmeads Community Infant School WSTB CT5 126 E4
Westminster Business Square LBTH SE11 24 A4
Westminster Industrial Estate WOOL/PLUM SE18 27 L2
West Minster Primary School IOS ME12 64 B5
Westmount Centre DVW CT17 8 A5
West Norwood Clinic WNWD SE27 44 D7
West Norwood Crematorium WNWD SE27 44 D8
West Thamesmead Business Park THMD SE28 29 G2
West Thornton Primary School CROY/NA CR0 86 A3
West Thurrock Primary School WTHK RM20 33 H5
West View Hospital TENT TN30 315 K3
West Wickham Swimming Baths WWKM BR4 88 D4
Westwood College WELL DA16 48 E2
Westwood Industrial Estate MARG CT9 178 D7
Westwood Language College for Girls NRWD SE19 68 D4
Westwood Primary School WELL DA16 48 F2
Whaddon House Clinic CMBW SE5 44 F1
Wheelbarrow Park Estate STPH/PW TN12 280 G2
White Cliffs Business Park DVE/WH CT16 213 H2
White Cliffs Experience DVE/WH CT16 8 D5
Whitefriars CANT CT1 4 F5
Whitehall Industrial Estate MSTR CT12 16 E1
Whitehill Infant School GVE DA12 55 K8
Whitehorse Manor Primary School THHTH CR7 68 E8
Whitehouse Surgery DVW CT17 8 A5
The Whitemill Museum SWCH CT13 236 H11
White Oak Primary School SWLY BR8 74 F6
Whitfield CP School DVE/WH CT16 213 H2
Whitfield Surgery DVE/WH CT16 213 H2
Whitgift Almshouses CROY/NA CR0 86 D5
Whitgift School SAND/SEL CR2 86 D8
Whitgift Shopping Centre CROY/NA CR0 86 D5
Whitstable County Junior School WSTB CT5 126 E4
Whitstable Health Centre WSTB CT5 126 F2
Whitstable Museum & Gallery WSTB CT5 126 E4
Whitstable RFC WSTB CT5 127 K3
Whitstable St Alphege CE Primary & Infants School WSTB CT5 126 E4
Whitstable & Seasalter CE Junior School WSTB CT5 126 F3
Whitstable & Seasalter Golf Club WSTB CT5 126 D4

Whitstable & Tankerton
  Hospital *WSTB* CT5 ....127 H3
Whitstable Yacht Club
  WSTB CT5 ....126 E3
Wickhambreaux CE
  Primary School *RCANTE* CT3 ....234 D11
Wickham Court School
  WWKM BR4 ....88 E7
Wickham Theatre
  WWKM BR4 ....88 E6
Widmore Centre
  BMLY BR1 ....71 K6
Wildernesse Golf Club
  BGR/WK TN15 ....136 F8
Wildernesse School
  BGR/WK TN15 ....136 D7
Wildernesse Sports Centre
  BGR/WK TN15 ....136 D7
Wildwood Wildlife Park
  HB CT6 ....154 F5
Willesborough Health Centre
  KEN/WIL TN24 ....205 J4
Willesborough Industrial Park
  KEN/WIL TN24 ....3 M7
Willesborough Primary School
  KEN/WIL TN24 ....3 L8
William Harvey Hospital
  KEN/WIL TN24 ....205 M2
Willow Bank Industrial Estate
  RSIT ME9 ....227 M7
Willow Business Park
  SYD SE26 ....45 K8
Willowfield School
  HNHL SE24 ....44 D2

The Willows Clinic
  CHST BR7 ....72 B3
Wilmington Boys Grammar
  School *RDART* DA2 ....51 J8
Wilmington Grammar School
  for Girls *RDART* DA2 ....51 J7
Wilmington Hall School
  RDART DA2 ....51 H8
Wilmington Primary School
  RDART DA2 ....51 J8
Winchcombe Business Centre
  PECK SE15 ....24 F5
Wincheap Industrial Estate
  CANT CT1 ....4 C7
Wincheap Park & Ride
  CANT CT1 ....4 A8
Wincheap Primary School
  CANT CT1 ....4 D8
Windmill Business Centre
  MEO DA13 ....97 G6
Wingfield Primary School
  BKHTH/KID SE3 ....47 H1
Wingham Bird Park
  RCANTE CT3 ....235 K12
Wingham Business Centre
  RCANTE CT3 ....252 A2
Wingham Industrial Estate
  RCANTE CT3 ....252 A3
Wingham Primary School
  RCANTE CT3 ....251 R2
Winterbourne Infant School
  THHTH CR7 ....68 B8
Wittersham CE Primary School
  TENT TN30 ....326 G3

Woldingham Golf Club
  WARL CR6 ....130 C6
Woldingham School
  GDST RH9 ....156 D3
Wolsey Junior School
  CROY/NA CR0 ....105 J2
Woodbrook School
  BECK BR3 ....70 A5
Woodchurch CE Primary
  School *RASHW* TN26 ....302 H10
Woodfalls Business Centre
  WBY/YAL ME18 ....257 N7
Woodhill Primary School
  CHARL SE7 ....27 M3
Woodlands Health Centre
  STPH/PW TN12 ....279 J2
Woodlands Manor Golf Club
  BGR/WK TN15 ....111 J8
Woodlands Medical Centre
  LEW SE13 ....46 E4
Woodlands Park
  HDCN TN27 ....301 J6
Woodlands Primary School
  GILL ME7 ....102 A1
  TONN TN10 ....189 H7
Woodlands Road Cemetery
  GILL ME7 ....84 A8
Woodlea Primary School
  CTHM CR3 ....130 E8
Woodside Health Centre
  SNWD SE25 ....87 J1
Woodside Infants School
  CROY/NA CR0 ....87 H3

Woodside Primary School
  CDW/CHF RM16 ....35 G2
Woodside School
  BELV DA17 ....30 C3
Wood Wharf Business Park
  POP/IOD E14 ....26 D1
Woolmans Wood Caravan Park
  WALD ME5 ....114 D1
Woolpack Corner
  HDCN TN27 ....300 F6
Woolwich Cemetery
  WOOL/PLUM SE18 ....29 G6
Woolwich County Court
  WOOL/PLUM SE18 ....28 B2
Woolwich Crown Court
  THMD SE28 ....28 F1
World End
  TIL RM18 ....55 J2
Worsley Bridge Junior School
  BECK BR3 ....70 B4
Worth CP School
  DEAL CT14 ....206 C4
Wotton Trading Estate
  ASH TN23 ....204 E5
Wrencote
  CROY/NA CR0 ....86 D6
Wren Industrial Estate
  MAID/SHEP ME15 ....260 A1
Wrotham Heath Golf Club
  BGR/WK TN15 ....241 L2
Wrotham Road Health Clinic
  GVW DA11 ....55 J6

Wrotham Road
  Primary School
  GVW DA11 ....55 J5
Wrotham Secondary School
  BGR/WK TN15 ....238 F12
Wyborne Primary School
  ELTH/MOT SE9 ....48 C6
Wye Business Park
  RASHE TN25 ....266 F10
Wye Crown
  RASHE TN25 ....267 K11
The Wyvern School
  KEN/WIL TN24 ....3 K7
Yalding Organic Gardens
  WBY/YAL ME18 ....257 Q6
Yalding St Peter & St Paul
  WBY/YAL ME18 ....257 R4
Yew Tree Industrial Estate
  DIT/AY ME20 ....139 L3
Yew Tree Park
  RCANTW CT4 ....268 G3
York Road Junior School &
  Language Unit
  DART DA1 ....52 A5
Young England RFC
  VX/NE SW8 ....24 A6
Ypres Tower
  RYE TN31 ....225 H4
Zobel College
  SEV TN13 ....21 H5

Acknowledgements

The Post Office is a registered trademark of Post Office Ltd. in the UK and other countries.

Schools address data provided by Education Direct.

Petrol station information supplied by Johnsons

One-way street data provided by © Tele Atlas N.V. Tele Atlas

Garden centre information provided by

Garden Centre Association   Britains best garden centres

Wyevale Garden Centres

The boundary of the London congestion charging zone supplied by
Transport for London

The statement on the front cover of this atlas is sourced, selected and quoted
from a reader comment and feedback form received in 2004.